T0189115

# Communications in Computer and Information Science     711

*Commenced Publication in 2007*
Founding and Former Series Editors:
Alfredo Cuzzocrea, Xiaoyong Du, Orhun Kara, Ting Liu, Dominik Ślęzak,
and Xiaokang Yang

More information about this series at http://www.springer.com/series/7899

Brajesh Kumar Kaushik · Sudeb Dasgupta
Virendra Singh (Eds.)

# VLSI Design and Test

21st International Symposium, VDAT 2017
Roorkee, India, June 29 – July 2, 2017
Revised Selected Papers

 Springer

*Editors*
Brajesh Kumar Kaushik
Indian Institute of Technology Roorkee
Roorkee
India

Virendra Singh
Indian Institute of Technology Bombay
Mumbai
India

Sudeb Dasgupta
Indian Institute of Technology Roorkee
Roorkee
India

ISSN 1865-0929    ISSN 1865-0937 (electronic)
Communications in Computer and Information Science
ISBN 978-981-10-7469-1    ISBN 978-981-10-7470-7 (eBook)
https://doi.org/10.1007/978-981-10-7470-7

Library of Congress Control Number: 2017961805

Printed on acid-free paper

This Springer imprint is published by Springer Nature
The registered company is Springer Nature Singapore Pte Ltd.
The registered company address is: 152 Beach Road, #21-01/04 Gateway East, Singapore 189721, Singapore

# Preface

VLSI Design and Test (VDAT) is a leading event of the VLSI Society of India. The 21st symposium in this series, the VLSI Design and Test Symposium (VDAT 2017), was held from June 29 to July 2, 2017, at the Indian Institute of Technology Roorkee, India. The objective of the symposium is to bring professional engineers, academics, and researchers from India and abroad to discuss emerging topics of VLSI and related fields on a common platform and to share new ideas, experiences, and knowledge. The chief guest at the event was Dr. V. K. Saraswat, Padma Shri, Padma Bhushan, Member NITI Aayog.

The scientific program consisted of peer-reviewed paper presentations in parallel technical sessions. In addition, keynote lectures, presentations by industry professionals, panel discussions, tutorials, and a poster presentation were conducted during the conference. Research contributions in the following areas were invited for VDAT 2017:

 1. Digital Design
 2. Analog/Mixed Signal
 3. VLSI Testing
 4. Devices and Technology – I
 5. VLSI Architectures
 6. Emerging Technologies and Memory
 7. Devices and Technology – II
 8. System Design
 9. Low Power Design and Test
10. RF Circuits
11. Architecture and CAD
12. Design Verification

This year we received 246 papers from around the world. After a rigorous review process, the Program Committee selected 48 regular papers and 27 short papers for the proceedings (the acceptance rate was 30%). In all, 150 expert reviewers were involved in rating the papers and on an average each paper received at least three independent reviews. The program of the symposium spanned over four days; the main conference program was preceded by a day of tutorial presentations that had six tutorials delivered by eminent researchers and practitioners in the field. The symposium hosted the following tutorials:

1. Gauri Sankar Malla, "Achieving the Best STA Accuracy for Advanced Nodes."
2. N. R. Mohapatra and Mr. Pardeep Kumar, "Computational Lithography for Advanced CMOS Nodes."
3. M. Hasan, "Circuit and System Design Issues for IoT Sensor Node."
4. K. Bhattacharya, "Design of Modern mm-Wave Transmitters and Power Amplifiers in Silicon and FD SoI CMOS."

5. Nishit Gupta and Deepak Jharodia, "Transaction Level Modelling with System C for System Level Design."
6. H. S. Jatana and Ashutosh Yadav, "Advanced Analog Design."

Several invited talks and keynote speeches were delivered by experts from India and abroad enlightening the participants on various aspects of emerging issues in VLSI research. These talks were delivered by Prof. P. Chakrabarti (IIT-BHU), Dr. Devesh Dwivedi (Global Foundaries, Bangalore), Prof. Maryam Shojaei (IIT-Bombay), Dr. Sudarshan Kumar (HSMC), Mr. Subhasish Mukherjee (Cadence), Mr. Sanjay Gupta (Vice President and India Country Manager, NXP), and Prof. Masahiro Fujita (Tokyo University). VDAT 2017 was a focused research event encompassing themes related to various disciplines of VLSI.

We sincerely thank all the officials and sponsors for their support in recognizing the value of this conference. We would like to express our thanks to the keynote speakers and the tutorial speakers for kindly agreeing to deliver their lectures. Thanks to the authors and reviewers of all the papers for their quality research work. We heartily thank every member of the Conference Committee for their unyielding support in making this event a success.

November 2017

Brajesh Kumar Kaushik
Sudeb Dasgupta
Virendra Singh

# Organization

VDAT 2017 was organized by the Department of Electronics and Communication Engineering, Indian Institute of Technology Roorkee, India.

## Patron

| | |
|---|---|
| Ajit Kumar Chaturvedi | IIT Roorkee, India |

## Advisory Committee

| | |
|---|---|
| Jaswinder Ahuja | VLSI Society of India, India |
| Vishwani D Agarwal | Auburn University, USA |
| Manoj Sachdev | University of Waterloo, Canada |
| V. Ramgopal Rao | Indian Institute of Technology Delhi, India |
| Kewal K. Saluja | University of Wisconsin, Madison, USA |
| Kaustav Banerjee | University of California, Santa Barbara, USA |
| Debashish Dutta | R&D Group, Ministry of Electronics & IT, Government of India |

## General Chairs

| | |
|---|---|
| M. Jagadesh Kumar | JNU, India |
| Debashis Ghosh | ECE, IIT Roorkee, India |

## Publicity Chairs

| | |
|---|---|
| Brajesh Kumar Kaushik | IIT Roorkee, India |
| Hafizur Rahaman | IIEST, Shibpur, India |
| A. Panda | NIST, India |

## Organization Chairs

| | |
|---|---|
| Anand Bulusu | IIT Roorkee, India |
| Sanjeev Manhas | IIT Roorkee, India |

## Program Chairs

| | |
|---|---|
| Sudeb Dasgupta | IIT Roorkee, India |
| Virendra Singh | IIT Bombay, India |

## Tutorial Chairs

| | |
|---|---|
| Bishnu Prasad Das | IIT Roorkee, India |
| Arnab Dutta | IIT Roorkee, India |

## Fellowship Chairs

| | |
|---|---|
| N. P. Pathak | IIT Roorkee, India |
| Meenakshi Rawat | IIT Roorkee, India |

## Transport Chairs

| | |
|---|---|
| Rajib Panigrahi | IIT Roorkee, India |
| Pyari Mohan Pradhan | IIT Roorkee, India |

## Website Chairs

| | |
|---|---|
| Brijesh Kumar | IIT Roorkee, India |
| R. Balasubramanian | IIT Roorkee, India |

## Finance Chairs

| | |
|---|---|
| M. V. Kartikeyan | IIT Roorkee, India |
| A. Patnaik | IIT Roorkee, India |
| Brijesh Kumar | IIT Roorkee, India |

## Sponsorship Chairs

| | |
|---|---|
| Sanjeev Manhas | IIT Roorkee, India |
| Bishnu Prasad Das | IIT Roorkee, India |
| Karun Rawat | IIT Roorkee, India |
| Preet Yadav | NXP Semiconductors India Pvt. Ltd., India |
| Gaurav Trivedi | IIT Guwahati, India |

## Accommodations

| | |
|---|---|
| Dharmendra Singh | IIT Roorkee, India |
| Madhav. J. Nigam | IIT Roorkee, India |
| Vinod Pankajakshan | IIT Roorkee, India |

## Publication Chairs

| | |
|---|---|
| Brajesh Kumar Kaushik | IIT Roorkee, India |
| Sudip Roy | IIT Roorkee, India |

# Technical Program Committee

| | |
|---|---|
| Amit Acharyya | IIT Hyderabad, India |
| Pratima Agarwal | IIT Guwahati, India |
| S. R. Ahamed | IIT Guwahati, India |
| Satyadev Ahlawat | IIT Bombay, India |
| Naushad Alam | AMU, Aligarh, India |
| Sk Subidh Ali | IIT Tirupati, India |
| Sankaran Aniruddhan | IIT Madras, India |
| Ansuman Banerjee | Indian Statistical Institute, Kolkata, India |
| Gaurab Banerjee | Indian Institute of Science, Bangalore, India |
| Kunal Banerjee | Intel Labs |
| Swapna Banerjee | IIT Kharagpur, India |
| Lava Bhargava | MNIT Jaipur, India |
| Bhargab B. Bhattacharya | Indian Statistical Institute, Kolkata, India |
| Enakshi Bhattacharya | IIT Madras, India |
| Tarun Kanti Bhattacharyya | IIT Kharagpur, India |
| Santosh Biswas | IIT Guwahati, India |
| D. Boolchandani | NIT Jaipur, India |
| Anand Bulusu | IIT Roorkee, India |
| Indrajit Chakrabarti | IIT Kharagpur, India |
| Parthasarathi Chakrabarti | IIT BHU, India |
| Susanta Chakraborti | IIEST, India |
| Amlan Chakraborty | University of Calcutta, Kolkata, India |
| Rajat Subhra Chakraborty | IIT Kharagpur, India |
| Anjan Chakravorty | IIT Madras, India |
| Rajeevan Chandel | NIT Hamirpur, India |
| David Chang | National Cheng Kung University, Taiwan |
| Abhijit Chatterjee | Georgia Tech, USA |
| Amitabh Chatterjee | IIT Guwahati, India |
| Shouribrata Chatterjee | IIT Delhi, India |
| Anupam Chattopadhyay | Nanyang Technological University, Singapore |
| Santanu Chattopadhyay | IIT Kharagpur, India |
| Yogesh Chauhan | IIT Kanpur, India |
| Shailesh Chouhan | Aalto University, Finland |
| Bijoy Krishna Das | IIT Madras, India |
| Bishnu Das | IIT Roorkee, India |
| Debesh K. Das | Jadavpur University Kolkatta, India |
| Sayantan Das | Verific Design Automation, Kolkata, India |
| Amitava Dasgupta | IIT Madras, India |
| Sudeb Dasgupta | Indian Institute of Technology, Roorkee, India |
| Sujay Deb | IIIT Delhi, India |
| M. Jamal Deen | Academy of Science, Royal Society of Canada |
| Madhav Desai | IIT Bombay, India |
| Soumyajit Dey | IIT Kharagpur, India |
| Arnab Dutta | IIT Roorkee, India |

| | |
|---|---|
| Ramen Dutta | Marvell Technology Group, Switzerland |
| Siddharth Duttagupta | IIT Bombay, India |
| Masahiro Fujita | Tokyo University |
| Manoj Singh Gaur | MNIT Jaipur, India |
| Priyankar Ghosh | IBM India Software Labs, India |
| Santosh Ghosh | Intel Corporation, USA |
| Chandan Giri | IIEST Shibpur, India |
| Neeraj Goel | IIT Ropar, India |
| Prasanta Kumar Guha | IIT Kharagpur, India |
| Mridula Gupta | Delhi University, India |
| Shalabh Gupta | IIT Bombay, India |
| Aritra Hazra | IIT Madras, India |
| Tsung-Yi Ho | National Tsing Hua University, Taiwan |
| Juinn-Dar Huang | National Chiao Tung University, Taiwan |
| Srivatsava Jandhyala | IIIT Hyderabad, India |
| Ram Rakesh Jangir | GJU Hisar, India |
| Satyabrata Jit | IIT BHU, India |
| John Jose | IIT Guwahati, India |
| Veezhinathan Kamakoti | IIT Madras, India |
| Hemangee Kapoor | IIT Guwahati, India |
| Sougata Kar | NIT Rourkela, India |
| Chandan Karfa | IIT Guwahati, India |
| Abhijit Karmakar | CEERI, India |
| Alika Khare | IIT Guwahati, India |
| Abhinav Kranti | IIT Indore, India |
| Subir Kumar | Sarkar Jadavpur University Kolkatta, India |
| Subrat Kumar | Panda Capillary Technologies, Bangalore, India |
| Brajesh Kumar Kaushik | IIT Roorkee, India |
| Santanu Kundu | LSI India Research and Development Pvt. Ltd., India |
| Subhadip Kundu | Synopsys India Pvt. Ltd., Bangalore, India |
| Kusum Lata | LNMIIT Jaipur, India |
| Sushanta Mandal | Centurion University, Odisha, India |
| Sanjeev Manhas | IIT Roorkee, India |
| Jimson Mathew | IIT Patna, India |
| Anzhela Matrosova | Tomsk State University, Russia |
| Bodhisatwa Mazumdar | New York University Abu Dhabi, UAE |
| Usha Mehta | Nirma University, Ahmedabad, India |
| Prabhat Mishra | University of Florida, USA |
| Debasis Mitra | IIEST Shibpur, India |
| Srobona Mitra | Synopsys India Pvt. Ltd., Bangalore, India |
| Nihar Mohapatra | IIT Gandhinagar, India |
| Arijit Mondal | IIT Patna, India |
| Samrat Mondal | IIT Patna, India |
| Shaibal Mukherjee | Indian Institute of Technology (IIT) Indore, India |
| Subhankar Mukherjee | Cadence Design Systems, Noida, India |
| Debdeep Mukhopadhyay | IIT Kharagpur, India |

| | |
|---|---|
| Madhu Mutyam | IIT Madras, India |
| Deleep R. Nair | IIT Madras, India |
| Pradeep Nair | IIT Bombay, India |
| Nagarjuna Nallam | IIT Guwahati, India |
| Ashutosh Nandi | NIT Kurukshetra, India |
| Sukumar Nandi | IIT Guwahati, India |
| Sergei Ostanin | Tomsk State University, Russia |
| Roy Paily | IIT Guwahati, India |
| Ajit Pal | IIT Kharagpur, India |
| Bhaskar Pal | Synopsys India Pvt. Ltd., Bangalore, India |
| Pankaj Pal | NIT Uttarakhand, India |
| Ajit Panda | NIST, India |
| Preeti Ranjan Panda | IIT Delhi, India |
| Soumya Pandit | IRPE, University of Calcutta, Kolkata, India |
| Chetan Parikh | IIIT Bangalore, India |
| Mahesh Patil | IIT Bombay, India |
| Sachin Patkar | IIT Bombay, India |
| Kolin Paul | IIT Delhi, India |
| Sajal Paul | ISM-IIT Dhanbad, India |
| Gayadhar Pradhan | National Institute of Technology, Patna, India |
| Amit Prakash Singh | GGS-IPU, India |
| Hafizur Rahaman | Indian Institute of Engineering Science and Technology (IIEST), Shibpur, India |
| Balwinder Raj | NIT Jalandhar, India |
| Arvind Rajawat | MANIT, Bhopal, India |
| Ashwani Rana | NIT Hamirpur, India |
| Surendra Rathod | SPIT, Mumbai, India |
| Karun Rawat | IIT Roorkee, India |
| Debdutta Ray | IIT Madras, India |
| Subir Roy | IIIT Bangalore, India |
| Sudip Roy | IIT Roorkee, India |
| Debasri Saha | University of Calcutta, India |
| Mounita Saha | Synopsys India Pvt. Ltd., Bangalore, India |
| Vineet Sahula | MNIT Jaipur, India |
| Raj Sarin | NIT Jalandhar, India |
| Arnab Sarkar | IIT Guwahati, India |
| Chandan Kumar Sarkar | Jadavpur University, Kolkatta, India |
| Kewal Sauja | University of Wisconsin Madison, USA |
| Manoj Saxena | Delhi University, India |
| Saurabh Saxena | Indian Institute of Technology Madras, India |
| Indranil Sengupta | IIT Kharagpur, India |
| G. K. Sharma | IIT Madras, India |
| Maryam Shojaei Baghini | IIT Bombay, India |
| Ashok Sihag | BML Munjal University, India |
| Suraj Sindhia | Intel, India |
| Adit Singh | Auburn University, USA |

## Sponsors

Ministry of Electronics and Information Technology, Government of India
VLSI Society of India
CSIR India
HP
Cadence
Springer
IEEE CAS/SSC, Roorkee Chapter
IEEE UP Section
Tektronix
ISRO
REDINGTON
Eigen
FOREVISION

# Contents

**VLSI Testing**

**Emerging Technologies and Memory**

**Devices and Technology – II**

**System Design**

## Design Verification

# Digital Design

# Flexible Composite Galois Field $GF((2^m)^2)$ Multiplier Designs

M. Mohamed Asan Basiri$^{(\boxtimes)}$ and Sandeep K. Shukla

Department of Computer Science and Engineering, Indian Institute of Technology,
Kanpur 208016, India
asanbasiri@gmail.com, sandeeps@cse.iitk.ac.in

**Abstract.** Composite Galois Field $GF((2^m)^n)$ multiplications denote the multiplication with extension field over the ground field $GF(2^m)$, that are used in cryptography and error correcting codes. In this paper, composite versatile and vector $GF((2^m)^2)$ multipliers are proposed. The proposed versatile $GF((2^m)^2)$ multiplier design is used to perform the $GF((2^x)^2)$ multiplication, where $2 \leq x \leq m$. The proposed vector $GF((2^m)^2)$ multiplier design is used to perform $2^k$ numbers of $GF((2^{\frac{m}{2^k}})^2)$ multiplications in parallel, where throughput is comparatively higher than other designs and $k \in \{0, 1, ...(log_2 m)-1)\}$. In both the works, the hardware cost is the trade-off while the flexibility is high. The proposed and existing multipliers are synthesised and compared using 45 nm CMOS technology. The throughputs of the proposed parallel and serial vector $GF((2^8)^2)$ multipliers are 72.7% and 53.62% greater than Karatsuba based multiplier design [11] respectively.

**Keywords:** Cryptography · Galois multiplication
Karatsuba multiplication

## 1 Introduction

The hardware based Galois field multipliers play major role in crypto graphy [1] and error correcting codes. The parameter metrics involved in any hardware design are throughput and hardware cost (area and power dissipation). Here, anyone can be optimized at the cost of others. The papers [2–4] show Reed Solomon code related applications, which require $GF(2^m)$ multipliers for various $m$ values. Vector processing is an important feature in hardware designs, where more number of similar operations can be done in parallel. Homomorphic encryption using matrices is explained in [5], where vector Galois field multiplications are performed using GPU.

### 1.1 Related Works

The following literatures are found in composite Galois field multiplications. The papers [6–9] explain the composite Galois field $GF((2^m)^n)$ multiplication. The

© Springer Nature Singapore Pte Ltd. 2017
B. K. Kaushik et al. (Eds.): VDAT 2017, CCIS 711, pp. 3–14, 2017.
https://doi.org/10.1007/978-981-10-7470-7_1

equations from (1) to (9) show the $GF((2^m)^n)$ multiplication. Here, $A$ and $B$ are the inputs while the output is $Y$. The irreducible polynomials over $GF(2^n)$ and $GF(2^m)$ are $Q$ and $P$ respectively.

$$Y = A.B \ mod \ Q = Y_{n-1}x^{n-1} + Y_{n-2}x^{n-2} + ....Y_0 \tag{1}$$

$$A = (A_{n-1}x^{n-1} + A_{n-2}x^{n-2} + ....A_0), \ A_i \in GF(2^m) \tag{2}$$

$$B = (B_{n-1}x^{n-1} + B_{n-2}x^{n-2} + ....B_0), \ B_i \in GF(2^m) \tag{3}$$

$$Q = (x^n + Q_{n-1}x^{n-1} + ... + Q_1.x + Q_0), \ Q_i \in GF(2^m) \tag{4}$$

$$A_i = (a_{m-1}x^{m-1} + a_{m-2}x^{m-2} + ....a_0), \ a_i \in GF(2) \tag{5}$$

$$B_i = (b_{m-1}x^{m-1} + b_{m-2}x^{m-2} + ....b_0), \ b_i \in GF(2) \tag{6}$$

$$Y = \{\sum_{i=0}^{n-1}\sum_{j=0}^{n-1} X_{ij}.x^{i+j}\}_{x^n \rightarrow (Q_{n-1}x^{n-1}+...+Q_1.x+Q_0)} \tag{7}$$

$$X_{ij} = A_i.B_j \ mod \ P, \ X_{ij} \in GF(2^m); \ 0 \le i,j \le (n-1) \tag{8}$$

$$P = (x^m + p_{m-1}x^{n-1} + ....p_0), \ p_i \in GF(2) \tag{9}$$

The aforementioned equations can be reduced for $GF((2^m)^2)$ as shown in (10) to (14), which requires six $GF(2^m)$ multiplications. Here, $A_1$, $A_0$, $B_1$, $B_0$, $Q_1$, $Q_0 \in GF(2^m)$.

$$Y = Y_1x + Y_0 = (A_1x + A_0).(B_1x + B_0) \tag{10}$$

$$Y = A_1.B_1x^2 + (A_1.B_0 + B_1.A_0)x + A_0.B_0 \tag{11}$$

$$Y = A_1.B_1.(Q_1x + Q_0) + (A_1.B_0 + B_1.A_0)x + A_0.B_0 \tag{12}$$

$$Y_1 = (A_1.B_0 + B_1.A_0 + A_1.B_1.Q_1) \tag{13}$$

$$Y_0 = (A_0.B_0 + A_1.B_1.Q_0) \tag{14}$$

Hybrid field $GF((2^m)^n)$ multiplier is shown in [10] that requires $n$ cycles. Also, the multiplier circuit proposed in [10] is used for $GF(2^n)$ multiplication if $m = 1$. The Karatsuba based $GF((2^m)^2)$ multiplication is shown in [11], where the composite irreducible polynomial is considered as $Q = (x^2 + x + Q_0)$. Hence, the aforementioned equations can be changed into as shown in (15) to (16), which requires four multiplications.

$$L = A_0.B_0; \ H = A_1.B_1; \ K = (A_1 + A_0).(B_1 + B_0) \tag{15}$$

$$Y_1 = K \oplus L; \ Y_0 = (Q_0.H) \oplus L \tag{16}$$

## 1.2   Contribution of This Paper

In this paper, composite versatile and vector $GF((2^m)^2)$ multipliers are proposed. The proposed versatile $GF((2^m)^2)$ multiplier design is used to perform the $GF((2^x)^2)$ multiplication, where $2 \leq x \leq m$. Here, the term versatility is to mention the ability of $GF((2^m)^2)$ multiplier to perform various length multiplications $(GF((2^x)^2)$ multiplications with $2 \leq x \leq m)$, where one multiplication can be done at a time. The proposed vector $GF((2^m)^2)$ multiplier design is used to perform $2^k$ numbers of $GF((2^{\frac{m}{2^k}})^2)$ multiplications in parallel, where $k \in \{0, 1, ... (log_2 m) - 1)\}$. Here, the term vector is to mention the ability of $GF((2^m)^2)$ multiplier to perform multiple multiplications at a time. In both the works, the hardware cost is the trade-off while the flexibility is high. Also, the objective of the proposed vector designs is to improve the throughput. The proposed and existing multipliers are synthesised and compared using 45 nm CMOS technology.

The rest of the paper is organized as follows: Sect. 2 states the proposed versatile and vector $GF((2^m)^2)$ multipliers. Design modelling, implementation, and results are shown in Sect. 3, followed by a conclusion in Sect. 4.

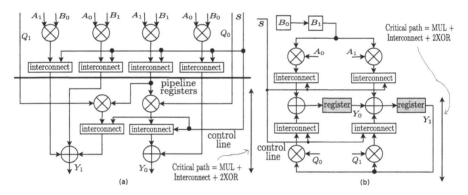

**Fig. 1.** $GF((2^8)^2)$ proposed (a) parallel (b) serial versatile/vector multipliers designs

## 2   Proposed Versatile and Vector $GF((2^m)^2)$ Multipliers

Figure 1(a) and (b) show the $GF((2^8)^2)$ proposed parallel and serial versatile/vector multipliers respectively. According to the Eqs. (13) and (14), the 8-bits inputs are $A_1$, $A_0$, $B_1$, $B_0$, $Q_1$, and $Q_0$. Here, the interconnect circuit is used for versatile and vector compatibility. The control line $s$ is used to perform various vector and versatile multiplications using the proposed architecture, which are shown in Table 2. As shown in Fig. 1(a) and (b), the critical path includes a multiplier, interconnect unit, and two 2-bit XOR gates. The critical path depth of Fig. 1(a) and (b) are shown in Eq. (17). Here, $T(XOR)$, $T(MUL)$, and $T(CON)$ are circuit depth of 2-bit XOR gate, proposed $GF(2^m)$ multiplier, and proposed interconnect circuit respectively. The proposed parallel and serial $GF((2^m)^2)$ multipliers require one and two cycles to produce the output. Table 1 shows the operation of $GF((2^8)^2)$ proposed serial versatile/vector

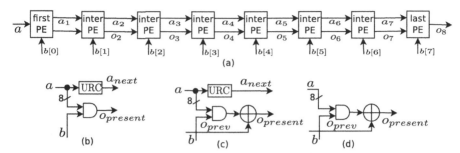

Here, $a$ and $b$ are input ports; $o_2$, $o_3$, $o_4$, $o_5$, $o_6$, $o_7$, and $o_8$ are output ports.

**Fig. 2.** $GF(2^8)$ proposed (a) versatile multiplier with cell architectures (b) first PE, (c) inter PE, and (d) last PE

multipliers. The multipliers used in Fig. 1(a) and (b) follow the algorithm as shown in Algorithm 1. Accordingly, the multiplier architectures are proposed in the Figs. 2 and 3 to perform versatile and vector operations respectively.

---

**Algorithm 1.** Algorithm for $GF(2^m)$ multiplication

---

**Input**: $A(x)$, $B(x)$, and irreducible polynomial $G(x) = x^m + P(x)$, where $A(x)$, $B(x)$, and $P(x)$ are of degree $(m-1)$.
**Output**: $C(x)^m = A(x).B(x) \bmod G(x)$, where the degree of the output is $(m-1)$
1: $C^0(x)=0$ and $A^0(x)=A(x)$
2: **for** $i = 1$ **to** $m$ **do**
3:     $C^i(x) = b_{i-1}.A^{i-1}(x) + C^{i-1}(x)$
4:     $A^i(x) = (A^{i-1}(x) << 1) \bmod G(x)$     //unit reduction step
5: **end for**

---

$$T_{critical} = T(MUL) + T(CON) + 2T(XOR) \qquad (17)$$

$$T(verse, m) = T(first\ PE) + T(last\ PE) + T(inter, verse) \qquad (18)$$

$$T(vector, m) = T(first\ PE) + T(last\ PE) + T(inter, vector) \qquad (19)$$

**Table 1.** Operation of $GF((2^8)^2)$ proposed serial versatile/vector multipliers as shown in Fig. 1(b)

| Cycle | $Y_0$ | $Y_1$ |
|---|---|---|
| 1 | $B_1.A_0$ | $B_1.A_1$ |
| 2 | $B_1.A_1.Q_0+B_0.A_0$ | $B_1.A_0+B_1.A_1.Q_1+B_0.A_1$ |

Algorithm 2 shows the proposed vector $GF((2^x)^2)$ multiplication using $GF((2^m)^2)$ multiplier, where $x = \frac{m}{2^k}$, $k \in \{0, 1, ...(log_2 m)-1)\}$, $2^k$ is the total number of vector operations possible, and $[\pi]$ represents the bits involved in the

**Algorithm 2.** Proposed algorithm for vector $GF((2^x)^2)$ multiplication using $GF((2^m)^2)$ multiplier, where $x = \frac{m}{2^k}$, $k \in \{0, 1, ...(log_2m)\text{-}1)\}$

**Input**: $A_0$, $A_1$, $B_0$, $B_1$, $Q_0$, $Q_1$ with $m$-bits wide
**Output**: $Y_0^c$ and $Y_1^c$ with $m$-bits wide, where $c = 0$ to $(2^k) - 1$.
1: **Parallel for** $c = 0$ to $(2^k) - 1$ **do**
2:    $[\pi] = [((c+1)x - 1), ..., (cx+1), cx]$, where $msb$ and $lsb$ are $((c+1)x - 1)$ and $cx$ respectively.
3:    $Y_1^c[\pi] = ((A_1^c[\pi].B_0^c[\pi]) + (B_1^c[\pi].A_0^c[\pi]) + (A_1^c[\pi].B_1^c[\pi].Q_1[\pi]));$
4:    $Y_0^c[\pi] = ((A_0^c[\pi].B_0^c[\pi]) + (A_1^c[\pi].B_1^c[\pi].Q_0^c[\pi]));$
5: **end for**

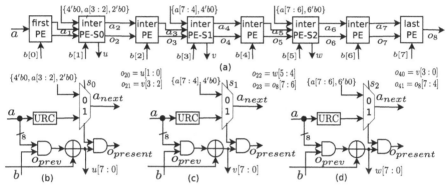

Here, $a$ and $b$ are input ports; $o_{20}$, $o_{21}$, $o_{22}$, $o_{23}$, $o_{40}$, $o_{41}$, and $o_8$ are output ports.

**Fig. 3.** $GF(2^8)$ proposed (a) vector multiplier with cell architectures (b) inter PE-S0, (c) inter PE-S1, and (d) inter PE-S2

each vector operation. In 2-bit vector multiplication using $GF((2^8)^2)$, $[\pi]$ will be $[0, 1]$, $[2, 3]$, $[4, 5]$, and $[6, 7]$, where $0 \leq c \leq 3$. In 4-bit vector multiplication using $GF((2^8)^2)$, $[\pi]$ will be $[0, 1, 2, 3]$ and $[4, 5, 6, 7]$, where $0 \leq c \leq 1$. In 8-bit multiplication using $GF((2^8)^2)$, $[\pi]$ will be $[0, 1, 2, 3, 4, 5, 6, 7]$, where $c = 0$. Figure 2(a) shows the $GF(2^8)$ proposed versatile multiplier, whose first, inter, and last processing elements (PEs) are shown in Fig. 2(b), (c), and (d) respectively. Figure 3(a) shows the $GF(2^8)$ proposed vector multiplier, whose first PE, last PE, inter PE, inter PE-S0, inter PE-S1, and inter PE-S2 are shown in Figs. 2(b), (c), (d) and 3(b), (c), and (d) respectively.

$$T(inter, verse) = (m - 2).T(inter\ PE) \tag{20}$$
$$T(inter, vector) = T(inter) + T(inter\_S) \tag{21}$$
$$T(inter\_S) = (log_2m)(inter\ PE\_S) \tag{22}$$
$$T(inter) = (m - (log_2m) - 2).T(inter\ PE) \tag{23}$$
$$T(first\ PE) = T(URC) \tag{24}$$
$$T(last\ PE) = T(AND) + T(XOR) \tag{25}$$

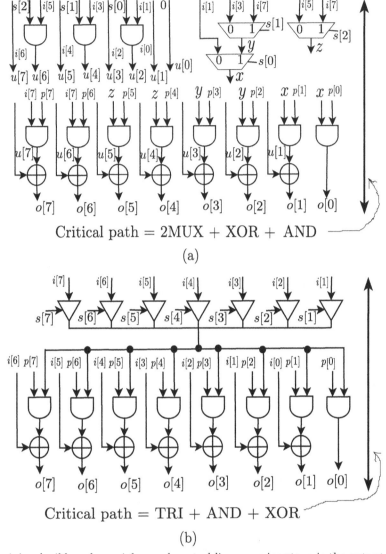

Critical path = 2MUX + XOR + AND

(a)

Critical path = TRI + AND + XOR

(b)

Here, $i$, irreducible polynomial $p$, and control line $s$ are inputs; $o$ is the output port.

**Fig. 4.** Unit reduction circuit (URC) for $GF((2^8)^2)$ proposed (a) vector and (b) versatile multipliers

$$T(inter\ PE) = T(URC) \tag{26}$$

$$T(inter\ PE\_S) = T(URC) + T(MUX) \tag{27}$$

$$T(urc, verse) = T(TRI) + T(AND) + T(XOR) \tag{28}$$

$$T(urc, vector) = T(AND) + T(urc, M) + T(XOR) \tag{29}$$

$$T(urc, M) = ((log_2 m) - 1).T(MUX) \tag{30}$$

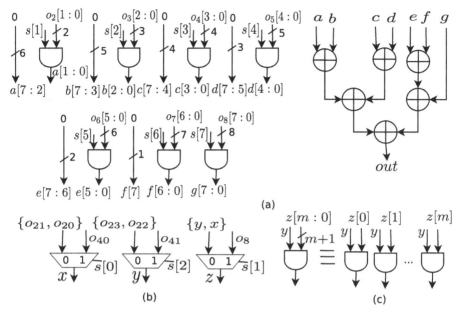

In (a), $o_2$, $o_3$, $o_4$, $o_5$, $o_6$, $o_7$, $o_8$, and control line $s$ are input ports while the output port is $out$; In (b), $o_{20}$, $o_{21}$, $o_{22}$, $o_{23}$, $o_{40}$, $o_{41}$, $o_8$, and control line $s$ are input ports while the output port is $z$.

**Fig. 5.** Interconnect circuit for $GF((2^8)^2)$ proposed (a) versatile, (b) vector multipliers, and (c) AND gate with $(m + 1)$-bit input $z$ and 1-bit input $y$.

The critical path of $GF(2^m)$ proposed multiplier block used in $GF((2^m)^2)$ versatile multiplier is shown in Eq. (18). Here, $T(first\ PE)$, $T(last\ PE)$, and $T(inter\ PE)$ are critical path depth of first, last, and inter PEs used in proposed versatile/vector $GF(2^m)$ multipliers respectively. The critical path of $GF(2^m)$ proposed multiplier block used in $GF((2^m)^2)$ vector multiplier is shown in Eq. (19). Here, $T(inter\_S)$ represents the combined critical path of inter PE-S0, inter PE-S1, and inter PE-S2. Similarly, $T(URC)$, $T(AND)$, $T(XOR)$, and $T(MUX)$ represent the critical path depth of unit reduction circuit (URC), 2-bit AND gate, 2-bit XOR gate, and 2-to-1 multiplexer respectively. The critical path of URC used in proposed versatile $GF(2^m)$ multiplier as shown in Fig. 4(b) includes a tri-state buffer, 2-bit AND gate and 2-bit XOR gate. Similarly, the critical path of URC used in proposed vector $GF(2^m)$ multiplier as shown in Fig. 4(a) includes a two 2-to-1 multiplexers, 2-bit AND gate and 2-bit XOR gate. The critical path depth of URC used in proposed versatile and vector $GF(2^m)$ multiplier multipliers are shown in Eqs. (28) and (29) respectively. Here, $T(TRI)$ represents the critical path of tri-state buffer. Figure 4(a) and (b) represent URC for $GF((2^8)^2)$ proposed vector and versatile multipliers respectively. Figure 5(a) and (b) represent interconnect circuits for $GF((2^8)^2)$ proposed versatile and vector multipliers respectively. The critical paths of interconnect circuits (ICs) for

$GF((2^8)^2)$ proposed versatile and vector multipliers are shown in the Eqs. (31) and (32) respectively. Figure 5(c) represents the AND gate used in Figs. 2, 3 and 5. Here, one bit input $(y)$ is bit wise ANDed with $(m + 1)$-bit input $(z)$ to produce $(m+1)$-bit output. In overall, $GF((2^m)^2)$ proposed versatile/vector parallel and serial multipliers are designed using six and four $GF(2^m)$ multipliers, that are connected to dedicated interconnect circuits (CONs). The $GF(2^m)$ multipliers/CONs are used to perform the required multiplication in versatile and vector $GF((2^m)^2)$ multipliers with respect to the $m$-bit and $log_2 m$-bit control lines $(s)$ respectively.

$$T(CON, verse) = T(AND) + (log_2(m - 1))T(XOR) \tag{31}$$

$$T(CON, vector) = ((log_2 m) - 1))T(MUX) \tag{32}$$

**Table 2.** Proposed composite versatile and vector $GF((2^8)^2)$ multiplications with respect to control line

| Control line $(s[7:0])$ | Versatile multiplication | Control line $(s[2:0])$ | Vector multiplications |
|---|---|---|---|
| 00000010 | one $GF((2^2)^2)$ | 000 | four $GF((2^2)^2)$ |
| 00000100 | one $GF((2^3)^2)$ | 101 | two $GF((2^4)^2)$ |
| 00001000 | one $GF((2^4)^2)$ | 100 | two $GF((2^2)^2)$ and one $GF((2^4)^2)$ |
| 00010000 | one $GF((2^5)^2)$ | 001 | two $GF((2^2)^2)$ and one $GF((2^4)^2)$ |
| 00100000 | one $GF((2^6)^2)$ | 111 | one $GF((2^8)^2)$ |
| 01000000 | one $GF((2^7)^2)$ | others | undefined |
| 10000000 | one $GF((2^8)^2)$ | | |
| others | undefined | | |

## 3   Design Modelling, Implementation, and Results

Table 3 shows a theoretical comparison of various composite Galois field $GF((2^m)^2)$ multiplier designs. Here, the versatility for proposed vector multiplier designs are marginal because these can be used to perform $GF((2^x)^2)$ multiplications, where $x = \frac{m}{2^k}$, $k \in \{0, 1, ...(log_2 m) - 1)\}$. For example, proposed vector $GF((2^8)^2)$ can be used to perform $GF((2^2)^2)$, $GF((2^4)^2)$, and $GF((2^8)^2)$ multiplications only. Here, $GF((3^x)^2)$, $GF((5^x)^2)$, $GF((7^x)^2)$ cannot be performed, whereas in proposed versatile design, these multiplications are possible. Table 4 shows the comparison of critical path delay, frequency, area,

**Table 3.** Theoretical comparison of various composite Galois field $GF((2^m)^2)$ multiplier designs

| $GF((2^m)^2)$ multipliers | $MR$ | $MX$ | $MC$ | $x$ | Critical path depth | Versatility | Parallel multiplications |
|---|---|---|---|---|---|---|---|
| Conventional | 6 | 1 | $N$ | $m$ | $2T(MUL)+$ $2T(XOR)$ | NO | NO |
| Hybrid [10] | 4 | 1 | $2N$ | $m$ | $T(MUL)+$ $2T(XOR)$ | NO | NO |
| Karatsuba based [11] | 4 | 1 | $N$ | $m$ | $2T(MUL)+$ $T(XOR)$ | NO | NO |
| Proposed parallel versatile | 6 | 1 | $N$ | $\in \{2,3,4,...m\}$ | $T(MUL)+$ $T(CON)+$ $2T(XOR)$ | **HIGH** | NO |
| Proposed parallel vector | 6 | $2^k$ | $\lceil \frac{N}{2^k} \rceil$ | $\frac{m}{2^k}; k \in \{0,1, ...(log_2 m)-1\}$ | $T(MUL)+$ $T(CON)+$ $2T(XOR)$ | **MARGINAL** | YES |
| Proposed serial versatile | 4 | 1 | $2N$ | $\in \{2,3,4,...m\}$ | $T(MUL)+$ $T(CON)+$ $2T(XOR)$ | **HIGH** | NO |
| Proposed serial vector | 4 | $2^k$ | $2\lceil \frac{N}{2^k} \rceil$ | $\frac{m}{2^k}; k \in \{0,1,...(log_2 m)-1)\}$ | $T(MUL)+$ $T(CON)$ $+2T(XOR)$ | **MARGINAL** | YES |

$T(XOR)$, $T(MUL)$, and $T(CON)$ are circuit depth of 2-bit XOR gate, proposed/existing $GF(2^m)$ multiplier, and proposed interconnect circuit respectively. $MR$ is the number of $GF(2^m)$ multipliers required. $MX$ is the number of $GF((2^x)^2)$ multiplications in parallel. $MC$ is the number of cycles for $N$ $GF((2^x)^2)$ multiplications. Here, the conventional design follows the Eqs. (13) and (14).

switching power, leakage power, power delay product (PDP), and throughput between various $GF((2^8)^2)$ multiplier designs using 45 nm CMOS library with Cadence Genus and Innovus. Here, the proposed parallel designs require more area than proposed serial designs. On the other hand, the proposed serial designs require more cycles than the proposed parallel designs. Since the hybrid multiplier design [10] requires only one multiplier in the critical path, the delay for [10] is less than others. Also, the proposed designs include one proposed multiplier along with the interconnect circuit in their critical path. Therefore, the delay for proposed designs are greater than [10]. The throughput of the proposed vector designs is much higher than other designs. The throughputs of the proposed parallel and serial vector $GF((2^8)^2)$ multipliers are 72.7% and 53.62% greater than Karatsuba based multiplier design [11] respectively. Similarly, the throughputs of the proposed parallel and serial vector $GF((2^8)^2)$ multipliers are 76.7% and 60.5% greater than hybrid multiplier design [10] respectively. Figures 6 and 7 show the chip layout diagram for proposed parallel versatile and vector $GF((2^8)^2)$ multipliers using 45 nm CMOS technology.

**Table 4.** Performance analysis for various $GF((2^8)^2)$ multiplier designs using 45 nm CMOS technology with Cadence

| $GF((2^8)^2)$ multipliers | Delay (ps) | Frequency (MHz) | # cycles | Total delay (ps) | Throughput (MSamples/s) |
|---|---|---|---|---|---|
| Conventional | 1048.6 | 953.65 | 1 | 1048.6 | $\frac{1}{1048.6ps} = \mathbf{953.74}$ |
| Hybrid [10] | 587.1 | 1703.28 | 2 | 1174.2 | $\frac{1}{1174.2ps} = \mathbf{851.64}$ |
| Karatsuba based [11] | 998.9 | 1001.10 | 1 | 998.9 | $\frac{1}{998.9ps} = \mathbf{1001.1}$ |
| **Proposed parallel versatile** | **997.0** | **1003.01** | 1 | **997.0** | $\frac{1}{997.0ps} = \mathbf{1003.0}$ |
| **Proposed parallel vector** | **1091.2** | **916.42** | 1 | **1091.2** | $\frac{4}{1091.2ps} = \mathbf{3665.6}$ |
| **Proposed serial** | **914.9** | **1093.02** | 2 | **1829.8** | $\frac{1}{1829.8ps} = \mathbf{546.51}$ |
| **Proposed serial vector** | **926.5** | **1079.33** | 2 | **1853.0** | $\frac{4}{1853.0ps} = $ **2158.66** |
| | Total area ($\mu m^2$) | Switching power (nw) | Leakage power (nw) | PDP ($\times 10^3$ fJ) | |
| Conventional | 2337.91 | 201275.78 | 147.32 | 211.21 | |
| Hybrid [10] | 1748.30 | 102620.35 | 110.50 | 60.31 | |
| Karatsuba based [11] | 1606.04 | 140450.31 | 100.72 | 140.39 | |
| **Proposed parallel versatile** | **4122.84** | **95327.17** | **247.80** | **95.28** | |
| **Proposed parallel vector** | **4631.01** | **167543.26** | **264.57** | **183.11** | |
| **Proposed serial versatile** | **2521.20** | **75201.71** | **153.75** | **68.94** | |
| **Proposed serial vector** | **2831.76** | **121057.41** | **163.39** | **112.31** | |

Power delay product (PDP) = (Switching power + Leakage power) × Delay; Total delay = Number of cycles × Delay; The proposed versatile $GF((2^8)^2)$ multiplier can be used to perform $GF((2^y)^2)$ multiplications, where $y \in \{2,3,4,5,6,7,8\}$; The proposed vector $GF((2^8)^2)$ multiplier can be used to perform one $GF((2^8)^2)$ or two $GF((2^4)^2)$ or four $GF((2^2)^2)$ or one $GF((2^4)^2)$ and two $GF((2^2)^2)$ multiplications in parallel. The conventional and existing multipliers [10,11] can be used to perform one $GF((2^8)^2)$ multiplication. Throughput is maximum number of input or output samples per second [12].

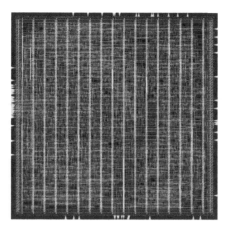

**Fig. 6.** Chip layout diagram for proposed parallel versatile $GF((2^8)^2)$ multiplier with core area as $4535.12\,\mu m^2$, die space around core as 2.5 $\mu m$, and total chip area as $5233.08\ \mu m^2$ using 45 nm technology.

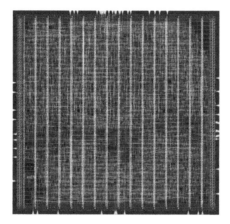

**Fig. 7.** Chip layout diagram for proposed parallel vector $GF((2^8)^2)$ multiplier with core area as $5094.11\ \mu m^2$, die space around core as 2.5 $\mu m$, and total chip area as $5831.84\ \mu m^2$ using 45 nm technology.

## 4  Conclusion

In this paper, composite versatile and vector $GF((2^m)^2)$ multipliers are proposed. The proposed versatile $GF((2^m)^2)$ multiplier design is used to perform the $GF((2^x)^2)$ multiplication, where $2 \leq x \leq m$. The proposed vector $GF((2^m)^2)$ multiplier design is used to perform $2^k$ numbers of $GF((2^{\frac{m}{2^k}})^2)$ multiplications in parallel, where throughput is comparatively higher than other designs and $k \in \{0, 1, ...(log_2 m) - 1)\}$. In both the works, the hardware cost is the trade-off while the flexibility is high. The proposed and existing multipliers are synthesised and compared using 45 nm CMOS technology. The throughputs of the proposed parallel and serial vector $GF((2^8)^2)$ multipliers are 72.7% and 53.62% greater than Karatsuba based multiplier design [11] respectively.

# References

1. Mohamed Asan Basiri, M., Shukla, S.K.: Hardware optimizations for Crypto Implementations. In: IEEE International Symposium on VLSI Design and Test, pp. 1–6, Guwahati (2016)
2. Chang, H.-C., Lin, C.-C., Chang, F.-K., Lee, C.-Y.: A universal VLSI architecture for reedsolomon error-and-erasure decoders. IEEE Trans. Circuits Syst. I Regul. Pap. **56**(9), 1960–1967 (2009)
3. Fu, S.-Z., Lu, B.-X., Pan, Y.-H., Shen, J.-H., Chen, R.-J.: Architecture design of reconfigurable reed solomon error correction codec. In: IEEE International Conference on Advanced Infocomm Technology, Taiwan, pp. 234–235 (2013)
4. Song, M.K., Won, H.S., Kong, M.H.: Architecture for decoding adaptive Reed-Solomon codes with varying block length. In: IEEE International Conference on Consumer Electronics, pp. 298–299 (2002)
5. Wang, W., Chen, Z., Huang, X.: Accelerating leveled fully homomorphic encryption using GPU. In: IEEE International Symposium on Circuits and Systems (ISCAS), Melbourne, pp. 2800–2803 (2014)
6. Abu-Khader, N., Siy, P.: Systolic Galois field exponentiation in a multiple-valued logic technique. Integr. VLSI J. **39**(3), 229–251 (2006)
7. Sunar, B., Savas, E., Koc, C.K.: Constructing composite field representations for efficient conversion. IEEE Trans. Comput. **52**(11), 1391–1398 (2003)
8. Lv, J., Kalla, P., Enescu, F.: Verification of composite Galois field multipliers over $GF((2^m)^n)$ using computer algebra techniques. In: IEEE International High Level Design Validation and Test Workshop (HLDVT), Santa Clara, pp. 136–143 (2011)
9. Su, J., Lu, Z.: Parallel structure of $GF(2^{14})$ and $GF(2^{16})$ multipliers based on composite finite fields. In: IEEE International Conference on ASIC, Beijing, pp. 768–771 (2011)
10. Paar, C., Fleischmann, P., Soria-Rodriguez, P.: Fast arithmetic for public-key algorithms in Galois fields with composite exponents. IEEE Trans. Comput. **48**(10), 1024–1034 (1999)
11. Pontarelli, S., Salsano, A.: On the use of Karatsuba formula to detect errors in $GF((2^n)^2)$ multipliers. IET Circuits Devices Syst. **6**(3), 152–158 (2012)
12. Casseau, E., Le Gal, B.: Design of multi-mode application-specific cores based on high-level synthesis. Integr. VLSI J. **45**, 9–21 (2012)

# Estimating the Maximum Propagation Delay of 4-bit Ripple Carry Adder Using Reduced Input Transitions

Manan Mewada$^{(\boxtimes)}$, Mazad Zaveri, and Anurag Lakhlani

SEAS, Ahmedabad University, Ahmedabad, India
{manan.mewada, mazad.zaveri,
anurag.lakhlani}@ahduni.edu.in

**Abstract.** Adders are invariably present in arithmetic units, and they are needed for implementing the operations: addition/subtraction, multiplication, division, etc. Due to the crucial role of adder in arithmetic unit, it is necessary to satisfactorily characterize the maximum propagation delay of the adder. To characterize 4-bit Ripple Carry Adder (RCA), ideally 261,632 input transitions are required [1], which is a humongous number. In this paper, we have proposed a method to estimate maximum propagation delay of 4-bit RCA, using only 44 input transitions (applied as primary-secondary and subsequently as secondary-primary). We applied our proposed method on 4-bit RCAs designed using seven different Full Adder (FA) circuits and simulated them in LTspice. The results from our proposed method (reduced input transitions) are compared with the results obtained by applying 261,632 input transitions (all possible transitions) to the 4-bit RCA. The simulation results prove that the maximum delay estimated by our proposed method is very close to the exact maximum delay of 4-bit RCA (found by applying ideal 261,632 input transitions), and has maximum 5.99% deviation.

**Keywords:** Ripple Carry Adder · Delay estimation

## 1 Introduction

Almost all processing devices (e.g. microprocessor, DSP processors, etc.) contain arithmetic unit inside them, and adders are the basic building blocks of the arithmetic unit. Apart from addition operation, adders are also used in other operations, such as: subtraction, multiplication, division, etc. The maximum clock frequency of the processing device dependents on the delay of the arithmetic unit; hence, it is necessary to satisfactorily characterize the maximum propagation delay of the adder.

Different input test patterns have been suggested in literature to estimate maximum propagation delay of Full Adder (FA) and Ripple Carry Adder (RCA) [1–4] using reduced input transitions; however, all these input test patterns underestimate the delay of RCA, as compared to the exact maximum propagation delay (found by applying all possible input transitions) of FA and RCA. As suggested in [1], to characterize $n$-bit RCA ideally $2^{(2n+1)}(2^{(2n+1)} - 1)$ input transitions are required, which is a humongous number, when $n$ is large.

© Springer Nature Singapore Pte Ltd. 2017
B. K. Kaushik et al. (Eds.): VDAT 2017, CCIS 711, pp. 15–23, 2017.
https://doi.org/10.1007/978-981-10-7470-7_2

In this paper, we suggest a new method (modified average delay method) to estimate maximum propagation delay of 4-bit RCA, and we have compared our result with the exact maximum propagation delay found by applying all possible input transitions (261,632 input transitions for 4-bit RCA) and maximum propagation delay estimated by input test pattern suggested in [1]. Rest of the paper is organized as follows: Sect. 2 discusses our input test pattern to estimate maximum propagation delay of individual FA of 4-bit RCA. In Sect. 3, we introduce the average delay method to estimate maximum propagation delay of 4-bit RCA. Simulation environment for 4-bit RCA is shown in Sect. 4. Section 5 includes simulation results and comparison. Finally, conclusion is drawn out in Sect. 6.

## 2  Input Test Pattern to Estimate Maximum Propagation Delay of Individual FA of 4-bit RCA

To estimate maximum propagation delay of a FA, we need to provide 44 input transitions [1]. An $n$-bit RCA consists of $n$ FAs. Hence, to estimate maximum propagation delay of each FAs within the RCA, each FA of the RCA should be provided 44 input transitions [1]. All three inputs of $FA_0$ (i.e. the FA in the Least Significant Bit (LSB) position) of 4-bit RCA can be controlled directly, but the input carry ($C_{in}$) of the remaining three FAs of 4-bit RCA cannot be controlled directly. Hence, the $C_{in}$ of all FAs (except the LSB FA) of 4-bit RCA should be controlled indirectly. Figure 1 shows our primary-secondary input test pattern pair which contains 44 input transitions in each (as suggested in [1]). These primary-secondary input test patterns are designed such that individual FA of RCA can be forced to all possible 44 input transitions irrespective of its position in RCA. Primary input test pattern contains required 44 input transitions for individual FA and is also capable of regenerating required $C_{in}$ signal for secondary input test pattern. The secondary input test pattern is not used to characterize FA, but used to regenerate required $C_{in}$ signal for primary input test pattern. In other words, the required $C_{in}$ signal of the primary pattern is automatically generated by the previous secondary pattern, and the required $C_{in}$ signal of the secondary pattern is automatically generated by the previous primary pattern. This alternating behavior of patterns, allows us to indirectly apply all the important input transitions to each alternative FAs of 4-bit RCA.

```
A   |0 0 0 0 0 0 0 1 0 1 0 1 0 1 0 0 0 1 0 1 0 1 0 0 0 1 0 1 0 1 0 1 0 1 1 1 1 1 1 1 1 1 1 0|
B   |0 0 0 1 0 1 0 0 0 0 0 1 0 1 0 1 0 0 0 1 0 1 1 1 1 0 1 1 1 1 1 0 1 1 0 0 0 1 0 1 0 1 1 1 0|
Cin |0 1 0 0 0 1 0 0 0 1 0 0 0 1 1 1 1 1 1 0 1 1 0 1 0 1 0 0 0 1 1 0 1 1 0 1 0 0 0 1 1 1 0 1 0|
```
Primary

```
A   |0 1 0 0 0 0 0 1 0 1 0 0 0 1 1 0 1 1 1 0 1 1 0 0 0 1 0 0 0 1 0 1 0 1 1 1 1 0 1 1 1 1 0 1 0|
B   |0 1 0 1 0 1 0 0 0 0 0 0 0 1 1 1 1 0 1 0 1 1 1 1 1 0 1 0 1 1 1 0 1 1 0 0 0 0 0 1 0 1 0 1 0|
Cin |0 0 0 0 0 1 0 0 0 1 0 1 0 1 0 1 0 1 0 1 0 1 0 1 0 1 0 1 0 1 1 0 1 1 0 1 0 1 0 1 1 1 1 1 0|
```
Secondary

Fig. 1. Primary-secondary input test pattern (44 transitions in each)

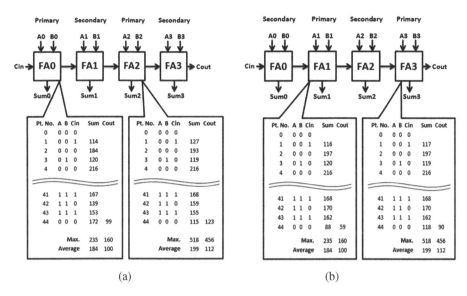

**Fig. 2.** Example for 28T CMOS [5] based 4-bit RCA (a) Primary-secondary arrangement and measured propagation delay (for *Sum* and $C_{out}$ signals) of even numbered FAs (b) Primary-secondary arrangement and measured propagation delay of odd numbered FAs [all delays are in ps]

As shown in Fig. 2(a), to find maximum propagation delay of the even numbered FAs in 4-bit RCA, primary input test pattern should be provided to $FA_0$ (LSB FA) and $FA_2$, and secondary input test pattern should be provided to $FA_1$ and $FA_3$. Figure 2(b) shows the arrangement to find out maximum propagation delay of odd numbered FAs ($FA_1$ and $FA_3$) in 4-bit RCA. *A*, *B* and $C_{in}$ column in dialog boxes of Fig. 2 shows the binary inputs applied to individual FA of 4-bit RCA; and *Sum* and $C_{out}$ column shows delay for each transition (i.e., {000} to {001}, {001} to {000} etc.). Maximum and average delays of individual FA of 4-bit RCA are shown at the bottom of the dialog boxes.

Using primary-secondary input test pattern, delays of individual FA of 4-bit RCA are measured in two steps; first, delays are measured for even numbered FAs ($FA_0$ and $FA_2$) and in second step delays are measured for odd numbered FAs ($FA_1$ and $FA_3$). Simply adding maximum propagation delays of individual FAs of 4-bit RCA does no lead to correct estimation of maximum propagation delay of 4-bit RCA. The reason is that, (based on our simulations/observations) the maximum propagation delays of MSB FAs ($FA_2$ and $FA_3$) are drastically influenced by the glitches generated from LSB FAs ($FA_0$ and $FA_1$), leading to the increase in the maximum propagation delay for MSB FAs. The particular transition(s) that causes the exact maximum propagation delay (among all possible 261,632 input transitions) for 4-bit RCA may not necessarily have glitches due to LSB FAs, and hence, simple addition of maximum propagation delays of individual FAs of 4-bit RCA overestimates the maximum propagation delay of 4-bit RCA. In case of 28T CMOS FA based 4-bit RCA [5], exact maximum carry propagation delay ($C_{in}$ to $C_{out}$) is found to be 615 ps, whereas, the estimated maximum carry propagation delay (by adding maximum delays of individual FAs) is 1192 ps, which is an overestimation.

The primary-secondary input test pattern pair also contains 20 input transitions, which cause the carry to propagate from $C_{in}$ to $C_{out}$ and 12 input transitions which cause the carry to propagate from $C_{in}$ to $Sum_3$. However, these transitions are very few as compared to all possible carry propagation transitions (causing propagation of $C_{in}$ to $C_{out}$, and propagation of $C_{in}$ to $Sum_3$) for the 4-bit RCA. Hence, it may underestimate maximum propagation delay of 4-bit RCA. Maximum carry propagation delay estimated using 20 transitions for 28T CMOS FA based 4-bit RCA is 573 ps, which is an underestimation, as compared to the exact maximum carry propagation delay (615 ps).

## 3  Average Delay Method to Estimate Maximum Propagation Delay of 4-bit RCA

The average delay of FA (found using the arrangement in Fig. 2) captures its behavior (relative to its position) in the RCA. Some FAs are designed with good driving capacity, and hence, average delay of each FA in RCA is nearly same; while other FAs that do not have good driving capacity, have increasing average delay for each successive FA in the RCA. This statement is supported by the simulations carried out on 4-bit RCAs designed using seven different FAs [5–10]. 28T CMOS FA [5] and Chang FA [6] generate $C_{out}$ using inverters and Mariano FA [7] is designed such that the $C_{in}$ cannot be directly connected to $Sum$ or $C_{out}$ for any input condition. Hence, these FAs have good driving capacity, and simulation results (Fig. 3) shows that the average delay of these individual FAs of 4-bit RCA does not drastically change for each successive FA in the RCA. On the other hand, Narasimha FA [8], Bhattacharyya FA [9], TFA FA [10] and TG CMOS FA [10] have compromised driving capacity, when used within RCA. For these FAs, average delay is increasing for each successive FA in the RCA. From our observations, we can conclude that, average delay of FA provides enough information about its behavior within the RCA.

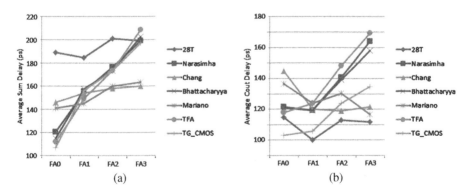

**Fig. 3.** Average *Sum* and $C_{out}$ Delay of 4-bit RCA designed using 7 different FAs

**Table 1.** Calculation steps to estimate maximum propagation delay using average delay method

| | Step 2 | | Step 3 | | Step 4 | | Step 5 | |
|---|---|---|---|---|---|---|---|---|
| | Avg. Sum | Avg. $C_{out}$ | Diff. *Sum* | Diff. $C_{out}$ | Div. *Sum* | Div. $C_{out}$ | Max. *Sum* | Max. $C_{out}$ |
| $FA_0$ | 189 | 115 | 0 | 0 | 0 | 0 | 235 | 157 |
| $FA_1$ | 184 | 100 | (184 −189) = −5 | (100 −115) = −15 | (−5/184) = −0.027 | (−15/100) = −0.15 | (−0.027 * 235) + 235 = 229 | (−0.15 * 157) + 157 = 133 |
| $FA_2$ | 201 | 113 | (201 −189) = 12 | (113 −115) = −2 | (12/201) = 0.06 | (−2/113) = −0.018 | (0.06 * 235) + 235 = 249 | (−0.018 * 157) + 157 = 154 |
| $FA_3$ | 119 | 112 | (199 −189) = 10 | (112 −115) = −3 | (10/119) = 0.05 | (−3/112) = −0.027 | (0.05 * 235) + 235 = 247 | (−0.027 * 157) + 157 = 153 |
| Step 6 | | | Max. Propagation Delay | | | | 157 + 133 + 154 + 247 = 691 ps | 157 + 133 + 154 + 153 = 597 ps |

Following steps are carried out to estimate maximum propagation delay of 4-bit RCA (for both, sum and carry), using the average delay of each FA (as per arrangement in Fig. 2) of 4-bit RCA:

1. Provide primary pattern to each FA of RCA using primary-secondary input test pattern (As discussed in Sect. 2).
2. Find the average of the delays (for both, *Sum* and $C_{out}$) for each individual FA of the RCA (See Fig. 2). (Refer columns 2 and 3 of Table 1; example is for 28T CMOS FA based 4-bit RCA).
3. Take the difference of average delays of $FA_1$, $FA_2$ and $FA_3$ of 4-bit RCA, with average delay of $FA_0$. For $FA_0$, this difference is zero but for $FA_1$, $FA_2$ and $FA_3$, differences could be either negative, positive or zero. (Refer columns 4 and 5 of Table 1).
4. Divide these differences with the average delays of individual FA of RCA (Refer columns 6 and 7 of Table 1). These values corresponding to individual FAs of RCA are used to estimate maximum *Sum* and $C_{out}$ delay for the individual FAs, in the next step (i.e. step 5).
5. Multiply values obtained in step 4 with the maximum *Sum* and $C_{out}$ delays of $FA_0$ (found as per arrangement in Fig. 2), and add it with the maximum *Sum* and $C_{out}$ delays of $FA_0$ (Refer columns 8 and 9 of Table 1). This will provide estimated maximum *Sum* and $C_{out}$ delays for each FA of 4-bit RCA.
6. Finally, add maximum $C_{out}$ delays of $FA_0$, $FA_1$ and $FA_2$ with the maximum *Sum* delay of $FA_3$ to estimate maximum sum delay (propagation delay from $C_{in}$ to $Sum_3$) of 4-bit RCA. Similarly, add maximum $C_{out}$ delays of all FAs to estimate maximum carry delay (propagation delay from $C_{in}$ to $C_{out}$) of 4-bit RCA. (Refer last row of Table 1).

Our proposed average delay method (exemplified by above steps) suppresses the effect of glitches, when estimating the maximum propagation delay of individual FA of the RCA. These maximum propagation delay values of FAs (step 5), can be used to estimate maximum propagation delay of 4-bit RCA (as suggested in step 6). The estimated maximum propagation delays (for sum and carry both) for 4-bit RCA designed using seven different FAs are shown in Table 2. We can clearly see the difference between maximum propagation delay estimated by average delay method and exact maximum propagation delay. Average delay method over estimates maximum propagation delay of sum for most of the cases. This is because, the transition causing the exact maximum propagation delay (for the RCA) may not lead to maximum propagation delay (simultaneously) on all the individual FAs. Hence, it overestimates maximum sum propagation delays of 4-bit RCA in most cases. There same reasoning is true for the maximum carry propagation delay for 4-bit RCA designed using Chang, TFA, TG CMOS and Mariano FAs.

**Table 2.** Delay estimation for 4-bit RCA using average delay method and modified average delay method (All numbers are in ps)

| 4-bit RCA designed using | All input transitions | | Average delay method | | Primary-secondary | | Modified average delay method | |
|---|---|---|---|---|---|---|---|---|
| | Sum | Carry | Sum | Carry | Sum | Carry | Sum | Carry |
| 28T CMOS [5] | 697 | 615 | 691 | 597 | 653 | 573 | (691 + 653)/2 = 672 | (597 + 573)/2 = 585 |
| Chang [6] | 701 | 744 | 861 | 745 | 541 | 709 | (861 + 541)/2 = 701 | (745 + 709)/2 = 727 |
| Mariano [7] | 651 | 654 | 825 | 733 | 555 | 633 | (825 + 555)/2 = 690 | (733 + 633)/2 = 683 |
| Narasimha [8] | 830 | 846 | 841 | 823 | 788 | 791 | (841 + 788)/2 = 815 | (823 + 791)/2 = 807 |
| Bhattacharyya [9] | 936 | 983 | 969 | 935 | 868 | 915 | (969 + 868)/2 = 919 | (935 + 915)/2 = 925 |
| TFA [10] | 971 | 1058 | 1099 | 1071 | 836 | 1040 | (1099 + 836)/2 = 968 | (1071 + 1040)/2 = 1056 |
| TG CMOS [10] | 770 | 751 | 860 | 813 | 674 | 736 | (860 + 674)/2 = 767 | (813 + 736)/2 = 775 |

We observed that the average delay method tends to overestimate the maximum propagation delay; and 20 transitions (for $C_{in}$ to $C_{out}$) and 12 transitions (for $C_{in}$ to $Sum_3$) of primary-secondary input test pattern (discussed in Sect. 2) underestimates the maximum propagation delay. A more correct estimation of maximum sum and carry propagation delays for 4-bit RCA can be obtained by averaging the sum and carry delay values of average delay method and 18 + 12 transitions of primary-secondary input test pattern. We call it the modified average delay method. Simulation results and calculations for modified average delay method are also shown in Table 2.

This modified average delay method is only applicable if the input test pattern is able to force all FAs of RCA to all possible 44 input transitions (i.e., input test pattern shown in Fig. 1) Otherwise it calculates wrong average delay of each FA of RCA and draws us towards the wrong estimation of maximum propagation delay.

## 4 Simulation Environment

4-bit RCAs based on seven different FAs were designed and simulated in LTspice using BSIMv4 22 nm model (level = 54). Maximum frequency of the inputs was 200 MHz. Test bed used for simulation of 4-bit RCA is shown in Fig. 4 [11–15]. Input inverters are used to generate realistic inputs for 4-bit RCA, and the output inverters are used to introduce load at the output of the 4-bit RCA. Numbers in Fig. 4 indicate the gate width in nano meter (nm).

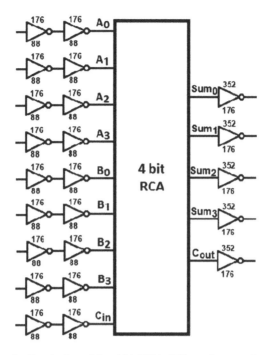

**Fig. 4.** Test bed used for 4-bit RCA (All numbers are in nm)

As discussed in Sect. 1, to characterize $n$-bit RCA ideally $2^{(2n+1)}(2^{(2n+1)}-1)$ input transitions are required. In case of 4-bit RCA, ideally 261,632 input transitions are required. Among these 261,632 input transitions only 24,000 transitions cause carry to propagate throughout the 4-bit RCA (found using analysis done in MATLAB). The Piecewise Linear (PWL) files listing input transitions were also generated using MATLAB. Voltage values/waveforms of all input and output transitions of the 4-bit RCA, from LTspice simulations, were exported, and then analyzed using MATLAB.

## 5  Simulation Results

Table 3 shows the maximum sum and carry propagation delay results for 4-bit RCA designed using seven different FAs. Maximum sum and carry propagation delay results are obtained by applying all possible 261,632 input transitions, average delay method, modified average delay method, and input test pattern suggested in [1]. Table 4 shows the percentage deviation of the delays estimated by average delay method, modified average delay method and input test pattern suggested in [1], as compared to the exact delays obtained after applying all possible 261,632 input transitions.

As shown in Table 4, modified average delay method shows a maximum 5.99% (overestimation) deviation for sum delay for Mariano FA based 4-bit RCA, and maximum 5.9% (underestimation) deviation for carry delay for Bhattacharyya FA based 4-bit RCA. Results obtained for pattern suggested in [1], shows a maximum

22.82% (underestimation) deviation for sum delay for Chang FA based 4-bit RCA, and maximum 6.92% (underestimation) deviation for carry delays for Bhattacharyya FA based 4-bit RCA.

**Table 3.** Maximum propagation delay results (All numbers are in ps)

| 4-bit RCA designed using | All input transitions | | Average delay method | | Modified average delay method | | Pattern suggested in [1] | |
|---|---|---|---|---|---|---|---|---|
| | Sum | Carry | Sum | Carry | Sum | Carry | Sum | Carry |
| 28T CMOS [5] | 697 | 615 | 691 | 597 | 672 | 585 | 653 | 572 |
| Chang [6] | 701 | 744 | 861 | 745 | 701 | 727 | 541 | 709 |
| Mariano [7] | 651 | 654 | 825 | 733 | 690 | 683 | 555 | 633 |
| Narasimha [8] | 830 | 846 | 841 | 823 | 815 | 807 | 789 | 791 |
| Bhattacharyya [9] | 936 | 983 | 969 | 935 | 919 | 925 | 868 | 915 |
| TFA [10] | 971 | 1058 | 1099 | 1071 | 968 | 1056 | 836 | 1040 |
| TG CMOS [10] | 770 | 751 | 860 | 813 | 767 | 775 | 674 | 736 |

**Table 4.** Percentage deviations in estimated delay compared to exact delay

| 4-bit RCA designed using | Average delay method | | Modified average delay method | | Pattern suggested in [1] | |
|---|---|---|---|---|---|---|
| | Sum | Carry | Sum | Carry | Sum | Carry |
| 28T CMOS [5] | −0.86 | −2.93 | −3.59 | −4.88 | −6.31 | −6.99 |
| Chang [6] | 22.82 | 0.13 | 0 | −2.28 | −22.82 | −4.7 |
| Mariano [7] | 26.73 | 12.08 | 5.99 | 4.43 | −14.75 | −3.21 |
| Narasimha [8] | 1.33 | −2.72 | −1.81 | −4.61 | −4.94 | −6.5 |
| Bhattacharyya [9] | 3.53 | −4.88 | −1.82 | −5.9 | −7.26 | −6.92 |
| TFA [10] | 13.18 | 1.23 | −0.31 | −0.19 | −13.9 | −1.7 |
| TG CMOS [10] | 11.69 | 8.26 | −0.39 | 3.2 | −12.47 | −2 |
| | 26.73 | 12.08 | 5.99 | 5.9 | 22.82 | 6.99 |

# 6   Conclusion

Our proposed method provides a satisfactory estimation of maximum propagation delay of 4-bit RCA, using only 44 input transitions (primary-secondary input test pattern), and based on our average delay analysis. Our proposed method requires only 44 input transitions (applied as primary-secondary and subsequently as secondary-primary) to find the maximum propagation delay for 4-bit RCA, as opposed to 261,632 input transitions. This is a significant reduction in the characterization time and effort. Our proposed method shows a maximum 5.99% deviation for sum delay and 5.9% deviation for carry delay, as compared to the exact delays. Our proposed method has satisfactorily worked on RCA based on seven different FA circuits, and hence, our method has the potential to be applied to other FAs not considered in this work.

# References

1. Mewada, M., Zaveri, M.: An input test pattern for characterization of a full-adder and n-bit ripple carry adder. In: 2016 International Conference on Advances in Computing, Communications and Informatics (ICACCI), pp. 250–255. IEEE (2016)
2. Shams, A.M., Bayoumi, M.A.: A framework for fair performance evaluation of 1-bit full adder cells. In: 42nd Midwest Symposium on Circuits and Systems, 1999, vol. 1, pp. 6–9. IEEE (1999)
3. Mewada, M., Zaveri, M.: An improved input test pattern for characterization of full adder circuits. Int. J. Res. Sci. Innov.-IJRSI 3(1), 222–226 (2015)
4. Bushnell, M., Agrawal, V.: Essentials of Electronic Testing for Digital, Memory and Mixed-Signal VLSI Circuits, vol. 17. Springer Science & Business Media, New York (2004) https://doi.org/10.1007/b117406
5. Zimmermann, R., Fichtner, W.: Low-power logic styles: CMOS versus pass-transistor logic. IEEE J. Solid-State Circuits 32(7), 1079–1090 (1997)
6. Chang, C.H.: A review of 0.18-um full adder performances for tree structured arithmetic circuits. IEEE Trans. Very Large Scale Integr. (VLSI) Syst. 13(6), 686–695 (2005)
7. Aguirre-Hernandez, M., Linares-Aranda, M.: CMOS full-adders for energy-efficient arithmetic applications. IEEE Trans. Very Large Scale Integr. VLSI Syst. 19(4), 718–721 (2011)
8. Konijeti, N.R., Ravindra, J.V.R., Yagateela, P.: Power aware and delay efficient hybrid CMOS full-adder for ultra deep submicron technology. In: 2013 European Modelling Symposium (EMS), pp. 697–700. IEEE (2013)
9. Bhattacharyya, P., Kundu, B., Ghosh, S., Kumar, V., Dandapat, A.: Performance analysis of a low-power high-speed hybrid 1-bit full adder circuit. IEEE Trans. Very Large Scale Integr. VLSI Syst. 23(10), 2001–2008 (2015)
10. Shams, A.M., Darwish, T.K., Bayoumi, M.A.: Performance analysis of low-power 1-bit CMOS full adder cells. IEEE Trans. Very Large Scale Integr. VLSI Syst. 10(1), 20–29 (2002)
11. Goel, S., Kumar, A., Bayoumi, M.A.: Design of robust, energy-efficient full adders for deep-submicrometer design using hybrid-CMOS logic style. IEEE Trans. Very Large Scale Integr. VLSI Syst. 14(12), 1309–1321 (2006)
12. Zhang, M., Gu, J., Chang, C.H.: A novel hybrid pass logic with static CMOS output drive full-adder cell. In: Proceedings of the 2003 International Symposium on Circuits and Systems, ISCAS 2003, vol. 5, p. V. IEEE (2003)
13. Aranda, M.L., Báez, R., Diaz, O.G.: Hybrid adders for high-speed arithmetic circuits: a comparison. In: 2010 7th International Conference on Electrical Engineering Computing Science and Automatic Control (CCE), pp. 546–549. IEEE (2010)
14. Yeo, K.S., Roy, K.: Low Voltage, Low Power VLSI Subsystems. McGraw-Hill, Inc., New York (2009)
15. Shubin, V.V.: New high-speed CMOS full adder cell of mirror design style. In: 2010 International Conference and Seminar on Micro/Nanotechnologies and Electron Devices (EDM), pp. 128–131. IEEE (2010)

# VLSI Implementation of Throughput Efficient Distributed Arithmetic Based LMS Adaptive Filter

Mohd. Tasleem Khan$^{(\boxtimes)}$ and Shaik Rafi Ahamed

Indian Institute of Technology Guwahati, Guwahati, India
{tasleem,rafiahamed}@iitg.ernet.in

**Abstract.** A new throughput efficient implementation scheme for least mean square (LMS) adaptive filter using distributed arithmetic (DA) is presented for IEEE 802.11b PHY scenarios. It is based on pre-computing and storing the filter partial products in lookup tables (LUTs). In contrast to fixed coefficients filter, an adaptive filter requires each stored partial product to be updated time-to-time. This paper presents a new strategy for DA based adaptive filter using offset binary coding (OBC) technique. The proposed strategy eliminates two oldest sample and allows possible decomposition of LUT into four sub-LUTs. Hence, the proposed approach provides significant improvement in throughput at the cost of few 2-to-1 multiplexers. Synthesis results have shown that the proposed scheme occupies almost similar area and improves the throughput by several fold. For instance, a 32- tap adaptive filter with the proposed implementation produces nearly 1.8 MSPS (million samples per second) more throughput as compared to the best existing scheme.

**Keywords:** Distributed arithmetic (DA)
Finite impulse response (FIR) filter · Least mean square (LMS)
Look-up table (LUT)

## 1 Introduction

Adaptive filters are widely used in many signal processing applications such as echo and noise cancellation, system identification and modeling, equalization [1]. The necessity of high performance adaptive filters become the major concern in many digital signal processing (DSP) applications. In present scenario, the demand of data rate in the customer end applications is increasing while the computational requirements proportionally going up. Several algorithmic level approaches have suggested that the adaptive filter requires tradeoff in throughput and computational complexities. The basic computational units involved in adaptive filter consists of a finite-impulse-response (FIR) filter and weight updating unit. It comprises of several multiply-and-accumulate (MAC) units depending on its tap-size. Due to simplicity and satisfactory convergence

© Springer Nature Singapore Pte Ltd. 2017
B. K. Kaushik et al. (Eds.): VDAT 2017, CCIS 711, pp. 24–35, 2017.
https://doi.org/10.1007/978-981-10-7470-7_3

of least mean square (LMS) algorithm, it is widely considered to update the filter coefficients [2]. The presence of physical multipliers in MAC based FIR filter, it occupies large chip area and consumes more power. In the recent past, a multiplierless technique known as distributed arithmetic (DA) is widely used for the realization of FIR filter [3]. It is made up of a look-up table (LUT) and a shift-accumulate unit, which is useful for realizing large tap-size filters. In this technique, the partial products are stored in LUT and, the output is produced in fixed number of clock cycles based on the input wordlength. In the case of an adaptive filter, the partial products are required to update time-to-time. However, it is found that the throughput of DA based adaptive filter is limited by LUT size. Several high throughput approaches have been suggested for efficient realization of adaptive filters using DA [4,10]. An extra LUT was used by Allred et al. to update the partial products stored in LUT as demanded by DA [5]. They have shown that the throughput filter is independent of number of filter taps. Later, Guo and DeBrunner [6,7] have proposed a single LUT architecture to perform both filtering and coefficient update operations. They exploited the commutative property of convolution to store the partial products of input samples. A new strategy based on offset-binary-coding (OBC) scheme was proposed by Prakash and Shaik [10] to update the filter partial products. They have shown that the throughput of filter can be increased by maintaining two smaller LUTs. Based on the idea presented in [10], we proposed a new throughput efficient scheme for DA based adaptive filter. It pre-computes and stores OBC combination of filter weights and input samples in two separate LUTs. The proposed approach have developed a new strategy to update the LUT by eliminating two consecutive oldest samples. The rest of the paper is organized as follows. Section 2 presents the pre-requisite of least mean square (LMS) adaptive filter and followed by the concepts of DA. Section 3 presents the proposed architecture and a new LUT updating strategy [10] for IEEE 802.11b PHY scenarios. In Sect. 4, the performance of proposed design with existing schemes are compared in terms of computational complexities and synthesis results. Conclusion is given in Sect. 5.

## 2    Prerequisite of DA Based Adaptive Filter

Figure 1 shows a $N$-tap conventional MAC-based LMS adaptive filter consisting of an FIR filter and weight updating block (WUB). The critical path (as shown by dashed line) of FIR filter determines the speed of overall filter. It is growing linearly with tap-size of filter. Hence, such implementation of LMS adaptive filter cannot be used in high speed scenarios like IEEE 802.11b PHY. The following presents an overview of LMS adaptive filter and fixed coefficient DA based FIR filter.

As shown in Fig. 1, the output $y(n)$ can be written as

$$y(n) = \sum_{m=0}^{N-1} w_m(n)x(n-m) \tag{1}$$

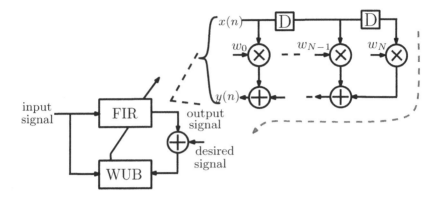

**Fig. 1.** Block diagram of conventional MAC based LMS adaptive filter with critical path shown by dotted line, where 'D' denotes a register.

where $w_m(n)$ represents the filter weights at time instant $n$ with $m \in [0, N-1]$. An error signal $e(n)$ is computed by subtracting the output signal $y(n)$ from the desired signal $d(n)$ as

$$e(n) = d(n) - y(n) \tag{2}$$

Using $e(n)$ as computed in (2), the filter weights are updated, according to

$$w_m(n+1) = w_m(n) + \mu e(n)x(n-m) \tag{3}$$

where $\mu$ is step-size. The above criterion (3) is famous Widrow Hoff least mean square (LMS) algorithm.

Consider a DA based adaptive filter which consists of filtering LUT (F-LUT), weight updating LUT (W-LUT) and shift-accumulate (SA) block as shown in Fig. 2. It process the input sample $x(n)$ and the produces the corresponding output sample $y(n)$. The following mathematics are the pre-requisite for the implementation of fixed coefficient DA based FIR filter.

The input samples $x(n-m)$ are represented in 2's complement, as per

$$x(n-m) = x_{n-m} = -x_{m,B-1} + \sum_{j=1}^{B-1} x_{m,j} 2^{-j} \tag{4}$$

By substituting (4) in (1) and re-arranging, we have

$$y(n) = \sum_{j=0}^{B-1} b_{B-1-j} 2^{-j} \tag{5}$$

where,

$$b_{B-1-j} = \sum_{m=0}^{N-1} w_m x_{m,B-1-j} 2^{-j} \tag{6}$$

$$b_{B-1} = -\sum_{j=0}^{B-1} w_m x_{B-1} \tag{7}$$

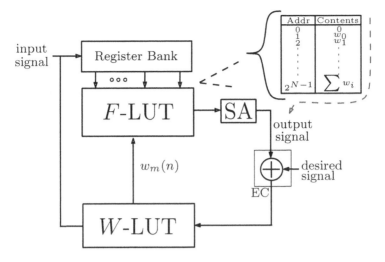

**Fig. 2.** Block diagram of conventional DA based LMS adaptive filter with critical path shown by dotted line, with $w_m$ denotes the filter weights for $m \in [0, N-1]$.

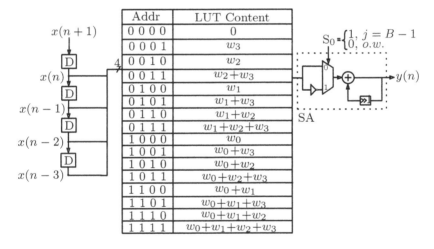

**Fig. 3.** Implementation of a four tap FIR filter using binary DA.

It can be noted from (6) that the terms $b_{B-1-j}$ could take $2^N$ possible combinations since $x_{m,B-1-j} \in [0,1]$. This can be pre-computed and stored in a LUT with the set of address lines $x_{m,B-1-j}$. Those are basically the least significant bits (LSBs) of each register present in the register bank as shown in Fig. 3. The partial products will be accessed from the LUT and then shifted and accumulated for $B$ clock cycles, where $B$ is wordlength of input samples.

It can be noted from Fig. 3 that the combinations stored in LUT grows exponentially with filter tap-size *i.e.*, $2^N$. It can be reduced to half by representing the input samples as $x_{n-m} = (1/2)[x_{n-m} - (-x_{n-m})]$ and commonly known as

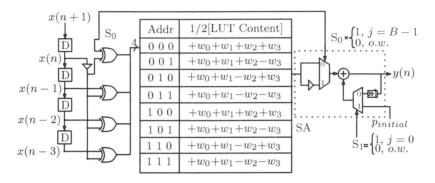

**Fig. 4.** Implementation of a four tap FIR filter using offset binary coding (OBC) DA.

offset binary coding (OBC). Thus, by combining (4) with above representation gives

$$x_{n-m} = \frac{1}{2}[-(x_{m,B-1} - \overline{x}_{m,B-1})$$
$$+ \sum_{j=1}^{B-1} (x_{m,B-1-j} - \overline{x}_{m,B-1-j})2^{-j} - 2^{-(B-1)}] \qquad (8)$$

Let

$$p_{m,B-1-j} = \begin{cases} -(x_{m,B-1} - \overline{w}_{m,B-1}), & \text{if } j = B - 1 \\ x_{m,B-1-j} - \overline{w}_{m,B-1} & \text{otherwise} \end{cases}$$

Therefore,

$$y(n) = \sum_{j=0}^{B-1} (\sum_{m=0}^{N-1} \frac{1}{2} w_m p_{m,B-1-j})2^{-j} + p_{initial}2^{-(B-1)} \qquad (9)$$

Define

$$c_{B-1-j} = \sum_{m=0}^{N-1} \frac{1}{2} w_m p_{m,j} \qquad (10)$$

$$p_{initial} = -\frac{1}{2} \sum_{m=0}^{N-1} w_m \qquad (11)$$

Hence,

$$y(n) = \sum_{j=0}^{B-1} c_{B-1-j}2^{-j} + p_{initial}2^{-(B-1)} \qquad (12)$$

where the term $c_{B-1-j}$ requires half combinations to be stored in LUT for a given set of $w_m$ with $(m = 0, 1, ..., N - 1)$. The other half can be obtained using XOR gates as shown in Fig. 4. In addition, it requires initial term $p_{initial}$ which is to be added during initial cycle of shift-accumulation.

F-LUT

| Address | $1/2$[LUT Contents$(n)$] |
|---|---|
| 0 0 0 | $+w_0(n)+w_1(n)+w_2(n)+w_3(n)$ |
| 0 0 1 | $+w_0(n)+w_1(n)+w_2(n)-w_3(n)$ |
| 0 1 0 | $+w_0(n)+w_1(n)-w_2(n)+w_3(n)$ |
| 0 1 1 | $+w_0(n)+w_1(n)-w_2(n)-w_3(n)$ |
| 1 0 0 | $+w_0(n)-w_1(n)+w_2(n)+w_3(n)$ |
| 1 0 1 | $+w_0(n)-w_1(n)+w_2(n)-w_3(n)$ |
| 1 1 0 | $+w_0(n)-w_1(n)-w_2(n)+w_3(n)$ |
| 1 1 1 | $+w_0(n)-w_1(n)-w_2(n)-w_3(n)$ |

W-LUT

| Address | $1/2$[LUT Contents$(n)$] |
|---|---|
| 0 0 0 | $+x(n-1)+x(n-2)+x(n-3)$ |
| 0 0 1 | $+x(n-1)+x(n-2)-x(n-3)$ |
| 0 1 0 | $+x(n-1)-x(n-2)+x(n-3)$ |
| 0 1 1 | $+x(n-1)-x(n-2)-x(n-3)$ |
| 1 0 0 | $-x(n-1)+x(n-2)+x(n-3)$ |
| 1 0 1 | $-x(n-1)+x(n-2)-x(n-3)$ |
| 1 1 0 | $-x(n-1)-x(n-2)+x(n-3)$ |
| 1 1 1 | $-x(n-1)-x(n-2)-x(n-3)$ |

**Fig. 5.** Contents of W-LUT and F-LUT at time instant $n$ for a four-tap filter.

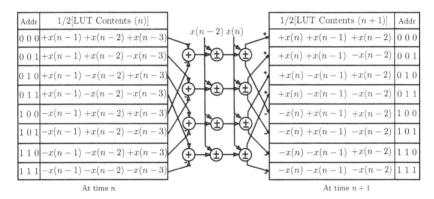

**Fig. 6.** Update scheme of W-LUT from time instant $n$ to $n+1$ for a four-tap filter.

## 3  Proposed Scheme

The block diagram of proposed architecture is similar to shown in Fig. 2. The register bank stores the input samples whose least-significant-bits (LSB) are used address vector for F-LUT. The OBC combinations of input samples and filter weights, respectively, stored the F-LUT and W-LUT. An error signal is calculated as shown in EC block for updating W-LUT contents.

Figure 5 shows the content of F-LUT and W-LUT, respectively, storing the OBC combinations of filter weights and input samples at time instant $n$. It is interesting to note that all the OBC combinations of filter weights are stored in W-LUT whereas F-LUT stores the OBC combinations except recent input sample $x(n)$.

The address index of F-LUT at time $n$ addressed by $a$ can be expressed as

$$F_a(n) = \frac{1}{2}[w_0(n) + \sum_{m=1}^{N-1} w_m(n)(-1)^{q_{N-1-m}^a+1}] \tag{13}$$

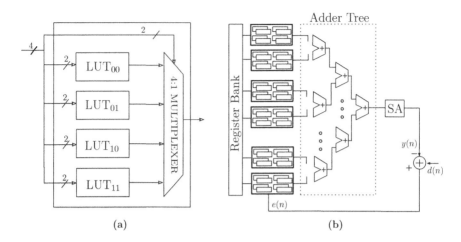

**Fig. 7.** (a) Splitting of a LUT into four sets of smaller LUTs using 4-to-1 multiplexer (b) Splitted LUTs are added using an adder tree.

where, $q_l^a$ is $l$-th bit in the $N$-bit representation $(q_l^a)$ of address $a$. That is,

$$a = \sum_{m=0}^{N-2} q_m^a 2^m \tag{14}$$

In the similar manner, all the addresses of W-LUT consisting of input samples $x(n-m)$ with $m \in [0, N-1]$ and $n$ being a time instant which can be expressed in the form as

$$W_a(n) = \frac{1}{2}[x(n) + \sum_{m=1}^{N-1} x(n-m)(-1)^{q_{N-1-m}^a+1}] \tag{15}$$

where the recent input sample $x(n)$ is not stored in W-LUT. Hence, the contents of $W_a(n)$ at time $n-1$ can now be expressed as

$$W_a(n) = \frac{1}{2}[\sum_{m=1}^{N-1} x(n-m)(-1)^{q_{N-1-m}^a+1}] \tag{16}$$

The contents of W-LUT for a four-tap filter at time instant $n$ are shown to left side of Fig. 6. It can be noted that merely upper half OBC combinations of input samples are stored in W-LUT. In the proposed implementation, the update scheme for W-LUT from time instants $n$ to $n+1$ is explained as follows.

The subtraction of first address location content of W-LUT from its 4-th address location content would generate a term independent of oldest $x(n-3)$ as well as next oldest input sample $x(n-2)$. However, it is observed that by adding next oldest sample $x(n-2)$ again will result in rotation of addresses for the update of coefficients. For example, consider $N = 4$ the subtraction of first and fourth address locations content of W-LUT would result in $1/2[+x(n-1)]$ which is independent of the oldest sample $x(n-3)$ as well as next oldest sample $x(n-2)$. The subtraction and addition of term $1/2[x(n-2)]$ would result in $1/2[x(n-1)$ $-x(n-2)]$ and $1/2[x(n-1)+x(n-2)]$ terms, respectively. Furthermore, the 2's complement version of the above terms that is, $-1/2[x(n-1)-x(n-2)]$ and $-1/2[x(n-1)+x(n-2)]$ are to be stored in same consecutive address locations of $1/2[x(n-1)-x(n-2)]$ and $1/2[x(n-1)+x(n-2)]$ terms. In addition, the most recent sample $x(n)$ is added and subtracted appropriately to update the contents first and fourth address locations, second and fifth so on of W-LUT. In the similar manner, the remaining address locations of W-LUT are updated using sum and difference of term $1/2[\pm x(n) \pm x(n-2)]$. Mathematically, the new entries $W_i(n+1)$ of W-LUT can be obtained from the old addresses

$$W_i(n+1) = \frac{1}{2}[(-1)^{i+4}x(n) + (-1)^i x(n-2)$$
$$(-1)^{i+1}\{W_{4\lfloor\frac{i}{4}\rfloor}(n) - W_{4\lfloor\frac{i}{4}\rfloor+1}(n)\}] \tag{17}$$

When the new input sample $x(n+1)$ arrives, the right-shifted version of it, that is $1/2[x(n+1)]$ is obtained by simply right shifting as shown in Fig. 6. It has to be delayed by one clock cycle, and added or subtracted based on even and odd address locations, respectively. Note that, the term $p_{initial}$ can be stored in a register which is nothing but the additive inverse of F-LUT corresponding to last address location.

1: **loop**
   $y(n) = \sum_{j=0}^{B-1} c_{B-1-j} 2^{-j}$
2:   **for** $a = 0$ to $2^{N-1} - 1$ **do**
   $W_a(n+1) = \frac{1}{2}[(-1)^{a+4}x(n) + (-1)^a x(n-2) + (-1)^{a+1}\{W_{4\lfloor\frac{a}{4}\rfloor}(n) - W_{4\lfloor\frac{a}{4}\rfloor+1}(n)\}$
3:   **end for**
4:   $e(n) \leftarrow d(n) - y(n)$
5:   **for** $a = 0$ to $2^{N-1} - 1$ **do**
   $F_a(n+1) \leftarrow F_a(n) + \mu e(n)\{W_a(n) + x(n)\}$
6:   **end for**
7:   **return** $y(n)$
8:   $n \leftarrow n + 1$
9: **end loop**

**Fig. 8.** Algorithm explaining proposed DA based adaptive filter.

## 3.1 Throughput Enhancement Methods

The throughput of based DA adaptive filter is limited by the access time of LUT. To overcome this problem, the proposed scheme first splits both F-LUT and W-LUT into set of four small LUTs as shown in Fig. 7(a). This will result

**Table 1.** Time and hardware complexities for proposed and existing schemes.

| Design | Throughput | Adders (per cycle) | Registers | SH | Memory |
|---|---|---|---|---|---|
| DA$_0$ [5] | $1/[m_0(T_R + (k - 1).T_M + T_A)]$ | $m.(2^{k-1} + 2^k) + m.B - 1$ | $m.(1 + k) + 2$ | $m$ | $2m.(2^k - 1)$ |
| DA$_1$ [6] | $1/[m_1(T_R + T_A)]$ | $m.(2^{k-1} + k) + m.B - 1$ | $m.(2 + 2k) + 1$ | $m.k$ | $m.(2^k - 1)$ |
| DA$_2$ [6] | $1/[m_1(T_R + T_A + T_M)]$ | $m.(2^{k-1} + k + 1) + m.B + 1$ | $m.(2 + 2k) + 1$ | $m.k$ | $m.2^{k-1}$ |
| DA$_3$ [10] | $1/[m_2(T_R + (k + 1).T_M + 2T_A)]$ | $m.(2^{k/2+1} + 2^{k/2+2} + 2) + m.B + 1$ | $m.(4 + k) + 2$ | $m$ | $m.2^k$ |
| Proposed | $1/[m_3(T_R + (k + 2).T_M + 3T_A)]$ | $m.(2^{k/4+1} + 2^{k/4+2} + 3) + m.B + 1$ | $m.(4 + k) + 2$ | $m$ | $m.2^k$ |

$T_R$ = LUT access time, $T_M$ = 2-to-1 multiplexer delay and $T_A$ = adder delay, $N = m{\times}k$, $m_0 = 2^k + max(B, 2^{k-1}) + \log_2 m$, $m_1 = 2^{k-1} + \log_2 m + W+1$, $m_2 = 2^{k/2} + max(W, 2^{(k/2)-1}) + \log_2 m + 1$, $m_3 = 2^{k/4} + max(W, 2^{(k/4)-1}) + \log_2 m + 1$. In addition, the above listed hardware complexities for proposed design requires $4mk$ 2-to-1 multiplexers whereas DA$_2$ scheme requires $2mk$ 2-to-1 multiplexers. The design [7] is based on delayed LMS (DLMS) and requires register look-up table, hence, the comparison is skipped.

in significant less access time. Moreover, it has been observed that the access time of $F$-LUT and $W$-LUT are still high, especially for large taps. This can be reduced further by splitting a large $N$-tap filter into $m$ small sub filters with of each tap-size $k$ such that $N = m \times k$. Due to this decomposition, an adder tree of depth $\log_2 m$ is required as shown in Fig. 7(b). Mathematically, it can be written as

$$c_{B-1-j} = \frac{1}{2} \sum_{l=0}^{m-1} \sum_{s=l}^{k-1} w_s p_{s,j} \qquad (18)$$

where $0 \leq s \leq l(k - 1)$ and $0 \leq l \leq m$. The algorithm explaining the overall operation of the proposed filter is shown in Fig. 8.

## 4     Results and Discussions

The proposed scheme is validated by simulating in verilog. For the sake of clarity, we considered the schemes in [5] as DA$_0$, and the first and second schemes in [6] are, respectively, referred as DA$_1$ and DA$_2$ and the scheme in [10] is referred as DA$_3$. A large order $N$ filter is splitted into $m$ small filters of order $k$ such that $N = m \times k$.

### 4.1     Time and Hardware Complexities

The throughput of proposed and existing schemes depends on the LUT size. The longest time is required to update LUT in the whole system operation, especially

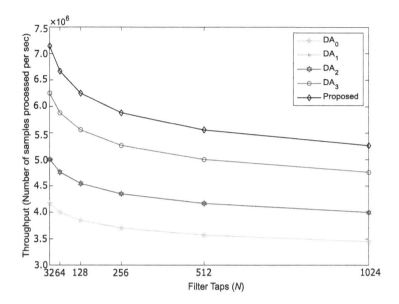

**Fig. 9.** Throughput comparison plot for proposed and existing schemes for various filter taps $(N)$ with $k = 4$.

for large taps. The proposed implementation reduced the update time of W-LUT by carrying out its operation in parallel with SA operation. Thus, it takes the maximum time involved, that is, $max(B, 2^{k/4} - 1)$. While the update time involved in F-LUT would be $2^{k/4}$ clock cycles during which $p_{initial}$ term is also updated. $log_2 m$ clock cycles for adder tree are also required. In addition, a single clock cycle is required to compute the $e(n)$. Therefore, the proposed design would take a total of $max(B, 2^{k/4} - 1) + 2^{k/4} + log_2 m + 1$ clock cycles. As depicted in Fig. 10, the significant improvement in throughput is achieved for proposed design by setting the system clock at $100\,\text{MHz}$ with $k = 4$. It is clear that throughput of proposed filter is outperformed for all the filter tap-size whereas the $DA_0$, $DA_1$, $DA_2$ and $DA_3$ schemes are suffered from the large number of clock cycles. In particular, the throughput values of proposed filter are significantly high for large sub-filter tap size $k$. For example, a 32-tap adaptive filter with the proposed implementation produces nearly 1.8 MSPS (million samples per second) more throughput as compared to $DA_3$ scheme. In Table 1, we have also listed the number of hardware components involved in proposed and existing designs. It has been found that the number of additions involved for updating the LUTs, coefficients, and adding the entries from LUTs are $m.(2^{k/4+1}+2^{k/4+2}+3)+m.B+1$. In addition, the proposed design slightly increased the complexity of 2-to-1 multiplexers. On the other hand, the number of registers and shifters are same as that of $DA_3$ scheme. Whereas $DA_0$, $DA_1$, $DA_2$ and $DA_3$ designs involve significantly more number of additions, as can be seen from their direct exponential relationship with $k$. It is shown that the proposed schemes require less addition cost than $DA_0$, $DA_1$, $DA_2$ and $DA_3$ whereas the proposed second scheme needs slightly more addition operations than our first proposed approach (Fig. 9).

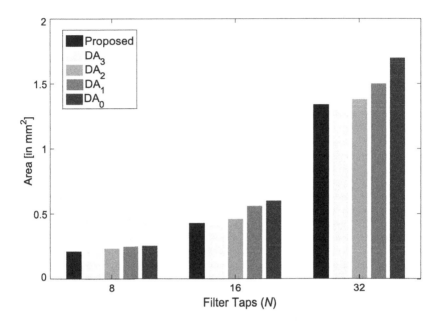

**Fig. 10.** Area comparison of proposed and existing schemes for $N = 8, 16$ and 32.

**Table 2.** Comparison of power (in mW) consumption for sub-filter tap-size $k = 4, 8$ with tap-size $N = 16, 32$ and 64

| Design | Filter taps $(N)$ | | | | | |
|---|---|---|---|---|---|---|
| | 16 | | 32 | | 64 | |
| | $k = 4$ | $k = 8$ | $k = 4$ | $k = 8$ | $k = 4$ | $k = 8$ |
| DA$_0$ [5] | 15.83 | 11.87 | 19.82 | 14.94 | 37.15 | 24.95 |
| DA$_1$ [6] | 14.15 | 8.65 | 17.65 | 11.45 | 32.81 | 17.93 |
| DA$_2$ [6] | 12.56 | 8.54 | 15.88 | 10.43 | 26.77 | 16.88 |
| DA$_3$ [10] | 12.23 | 8.34 | 14.63 | 9.56 | 21.56 | 15.87 |
| Proposed | 12.81 | 9.01 | 15.27 | 11.31 | 22.78 | 16.93 |

## 4.2 Synthesis Results

We have performed the synthesis for both proposed and existing schemes using UMC 180-nm CMOS Technology by Cadence 14.1 RTL Compiler. The area results are shown in Fig. 10 for various filter-taps by taking the wordlengths of input and filter weight as 8-bits. It is clear that the proposed design consumes slightly more area in splitting the LUT using 2-to-1 multiplexers as compared to DA$_3$ scheme. The designs DA$_1$ and DA$_2$ schemes, on the other hand, have low memory requirement but requires more hardware complexity. In addition, DA$_2$ scheme has extra storage registers and adder units for the pre-computations certain terms. In contrast, the proposed scheme exploits OBC combinations for the input samples and filter weights which lowers area as well as power consumption. Table 2 depicts the power consumption of proposed design and various existing schemes as compared to the $DA_0$ scheme. It can be noted that the proposed scheme has almost similar power consumption figures as that of $DA_3$ scheme. Moreover, these values are almost constant for large tap-size filter. For example, a filter with tap-size $N = 32$ and $N = 64$ consumes nearly 15% more power over $DA_3$ scheme.

## 5   Conclusion

In this paper, we have presented a new throughput efficient architecture of DA based LMS adaptive filter for IEEE 802.11b PHY scenarios using OBC scheme. The proposed technique updates the W-LUT by eliminating oldest and next old sample, thereby allowing both the LUTs to be splitted into four smaller LUTs. As a result, the throughput for large sub-filter tap size is significantly improved just at the cost few multiplexers over the similar scheme [10]. The proposed design can be adopted for filters of any order, and is particularly useful for filters with large tap-size and sub filter tap-size.

## References

1. Haykin, S.: Adaptive Filter Theory. Information and System Sciences Series. Prentice-Hall, Upper Saddle River (1996). 07458
2. Haykin, S., Widrow, B.: Least-Mean-Square Adaptive Filters, vol. 31. John Wiley, New York (2003)
3. Croisier, A., Esteban, D., Levilion, M., Riso, V.: Digital filter for PCM encoded signals, US Patent 3,777,130, 4 December 1973
4. Cowan, C., Mavor, J.: New digital adaptive-filter implementation using distributed-arithmetic techniques. In: IEE Proceedings F, Communications, Radar and Signal Processing, vol. 128, no. 4, pp. 225–230 (1981)
5. Allred, D.J., Yoo, H., Krishnan, V., Huang, W., Anderson, D.V.: LMS adaptive filters using distributed arithmetic for high throughput. IEEE Trans. Circuits Syst. I Regul. Papers **52**(7), 1327–1337 (2005)
6. Guo, R., DeBrunner, L.S.: Two high-performance adaptive filter implementation schemes using distributed arithmetic. IEEE Trans. Circuits Syst. II Express Briefs **58**(9), 600–604 (2011)
7. Guo, R., DeBrunner, L.S.: A novel adaptive filter implementation scheme using distributed arithmetic. In: 2011 Conference Record of the Forty Fifth Asilomar Conference on Signals, Systems and Computers (ASILOMAR), pp. 160–164. IEEE (2011)
8. Park, S.Y., Meher, P.K.: Low-power, high-throughput, and low-area adaptive FIR filter based on distributed arithmetic. IEEE Trans. Circuits Syst. II Express Briefs **60**(6), 346–350 (2013)
9. Surya Prakash, M., Shaik, R.A.: High performance architecture for lms based adaptive filter using distributed arithmetic. IPCSIT (2012)
10. Prakash, M.S., Shaik, R.A.: Low-area and high-throughput architecture for an adaptive filter using distributed arithmetic. IEEE Trans. Circuits Syst. II Express Briefs **60**(11), 781–785 (2013)

# Realization of Multiplier Using Delay Efficient Cyclic Redundant Adder

K. Dheepika[1], K. S. Jevasankari[1], Vippin Chandhar[2],
and Binsu J. Kailath[1(✉)]

[1] IIITDM Kancheepuram, Chennai 600127, Tamil Nadu, India
kdheepika7@gmail.com, jevasankari@gmail.com,
bkailath@iiitdm.ac.in
[2] Scientific Games, White Field 560066, Karnataka, India
svippinchandhar@gmail.com

**Abstract.** Digital Adders and Multipliers are the backbone of Digital Signal Processing systems. A novel adder which uses Recursive Doubling technique for carry generation is propounded in this paper. A Multiplier based on Quarter square algorithm is designed and implemented using the proposed Cyclic Redundant Adder on Field Programmable Gate Array. The proposed Cyclic Redundant adder is compared amongst the recent high performance adders like Ling Adder, Carry Shifting Adder with carry increment and Carry Look Ahead Adder. The Cyclic Redundant adder has been observed to be the fastest with the least time delay of 2.719 ns for 64 bit input.

**Keywords:** Recursive doubling · Cyclic Redundant Adder
Carry Shifting Adder · Quarter square algorithm
Field Programmable Gate Array (FPGA)

## 1 Introduction

Adders are one of the most crucial and irreplaceable circuits of any digital system from a multiplier design to a complex filter design for DSP applications. A real time efficient adder architecture has to be optimized for parameters like delay, area and power. There always exists a tradeoff between these parameters for a desired application. In a given system any of these parameters would be critical. Many adder architectures have been proposed, all of which have some disadvantages. Thus, scrutinizing architectures of adders and putting forth their novel models has been much essential for a fast and accurate functioning of the entire system.

Based on the application, different adder architectures have been evolved in the course of time, for its' performance enhancement with any of its parameters as a critical parameter. For less time and area, parallel carry computation is preferred. The following are some adders of those kinds: Carry-Look Ahead adder [3], where the carry is anticipated ahead of time. Ling adder [4], here the carry is predicted in a non-redundant way. It's an advanced version of Carry-Look Ahead adder. Carry Shifting Adder [5], where shifting of carry from $i_{th}$ index to $(i + 1)_{th}$ index based on the algorithm (Vedic) occurs, thereby still reducing the critical parameter time delay. Carry Shifting Adder

B. K. Kaushik et al. (Eds.): VDAT 2017, CCIS 711, pp. 36–47, 2017.
https://doi.org/10.1007/978-981-10-7470-7_4

with increment [1], has been reported as an improved form of Carry Shifting Adder. Here the input operands are divided into halves, so that next level of parallel carry computation is achieved.

The proposed adder architecture, named as Cyclic Redundant Adder (CyRA), also involves simultaneous carry computation. Here recursive doubling of stages namely kill, generate and propagate is performed to get the carry. The input operands and the shifted carry are $XOR_{ed}$ to get the sum.

Implementing proposed adder in an application stands as a proof of the utility of the adder. Multiplication comes first among the choices of application, as it is a preliminary block in most of the systems. Initially, for many years, the main concern was how to improve the technique of binary multiplication beyond the repetitive Add and Shift [11]. Based on Daddas' suggestion on parallel multipliers, the binary multiplication of both Ling [7] and Chen [8] were applicable to a maximum of eight bit numbers and any number larger than 8 bits, had to be decomposed for a parallel formation of the result. Then that was extended to any number of bits without having to decompose the number into segments of eight bits, thus resulting in a substantial saving of hardware by Jayashree [9]. Later, an application of the quarter square multiplication technique used in analog computing was proposed for digital multiplication [10].

This Quarter square multiplier block consists of adder and squarer sub-blocks. In this multiplier, the proposed adder is put in place of the conventional adder units for the performance comparisons. The squarer is also a model of reduced partial products. As a whole, the performance of this multiplier is compared along with traditional Booth and Wallace tree multiplier algorithms. These comparisons are carried out in FPGA platforms namely, Artix-7 and Virtex-5 families. CyRA and its comparisons with other adders are implemented in Artix-7 board, while multiplier with CyRA and its performance comparisons are done with Virtex-5

The overview of various existing adders and their pros and cons are presented in Sect. 2. A brief description of proposed adder (CyRA) is dealt in Sect. 3. Then, Sect. 4 describes the algorithm behind the optimal multiplier blocks and finds a gap of adder application over an efficient multiplier. Section 5 composes of simulation and implementation results, mainly time delay and number of LUT slices as metrics, of proposed adder (CyRA), comparisons among adders and among multipliers. Finally, Sect. 6 concludes the paper.

## 2  Adder Architectures

### 2.1  Carry-Look Ahead Adder

Carry-Look Ahead logic uses the concepts of generating and propagating carries. The speed is improved significantly in Carry-Look Ahead adder by reducing the amount of time required to determine carry bits. By pre-processing the two numbers being added, the carry-look ahead adder anticipates the carry. With Ai and Bi as the two input operands of an adder block,

$$G_i = A_i \cdot B_i \tag{1}$$

$$P_i = A_i \oplus B_i \tag{2}$$

$$S_i = P_i \oplus C_i \tag{3}$$

$$C_{i+1} = G_i + (P_i \cdot C_i) \tag{4}$$

Here, $G_i$, $P_i$ and $S_i$ are the corresponding generate, propagate and sum of an adder stage, given by (1–3). The equation of Carry generation in ahead of time is given by (4), where $C_i$ is the input carry, and $C_{i+1}$ is the output carry. The disadvantage felt with Carry-Look Ahead adder is that the, carry logic block gets very complicated for more than 4-bits. The recursive carry expressions of a 4-bit carry look-ahead block are specified as,

$$C_0 = C_0 \tag{5}$$

$$C_1 = G_0 + C_0 P_0 \tag{6}$$

$$C_2 = G_1 + G_0 P_1 + C_0 P_0 P_1 \tag{7}$$

$$C_3 = G_2 + G_1 P_2 + G_0 P_1 P_2 + C_0 P_0 P_1 P_2 \tag{8}$$

$$C_4 = G_3 + G_2 P_3 + G_1 P_2 P_3 + G_0 P_1 P_2 P_3 + C_0 P_0 P_1 P_2 P_3 \tag{9}$$

## 2.2   Ling Adder

The Ling adder designed using ling's recurrence, is an advancement of Carry Look-Ahead Adder by the utilization of pseudo carry. This approach allows a single local propagate signal to be removed from the critical path and replacement of XOR gate by OR gate thus, results in faster and less expensive architecture.

$$G_i = A_i \cdot B_i \tag{10}$$

$$T_i = A_i + B_i \tag{11}$$

Here, $G_i$ and $T_i$ are the generate and propagate terms of $i_{th}$ bit respectively. By factoring the propagate term ($T_i$) from the carry expression ($C_{i+1}$), a new carry called pseudo carry ($H_i$) is formed and it improves the addition speed of the adder. The pseudo carry ($H_i$) and carry ($C_i$) used in Ling's recurrence is,

$$H_i = G_i + C_i \tag{12}$$

$$C_i = T_i \cdot H_{i-1} \tag{13}$$

Initially, $C_i = C_0$. Here, the complexity of carry computation is reduced at the price of increased complexity in the sum [2].

### 2.3  Carry Shifting Adder Using Multiplexer

Based on parallel computation of carry, there comes another adder called Carry Shifting Adder (CSHA) by using multiplexer.

For 'n' bit inputs A and B, indexing from 0 to (n − 1), the addition is done as follows. The Generate and Propagate terms are found as given in (1) and (2) and carry ($C_{in}$) is concatenated to the position zero of the generate terms. Here the Carry is shifting from its position 'i' to the next position 'i + 1' in the Generate when,

$$P_i \cdot (G_i.Cin) = 1 \tag{14}$$

If (14) is valid, then sum $S_i$ and generate $G_i$ terms are,

$$S_i = 0 \tag{15}$$

$$G_{i+1} = 1 \tag{16}$$

Or else, the sum $S_i$ is given as,

$$S_i = P_i \circ G_i \tag{17}$$

This is iterated till the last stage (n − 1). The calculated $G_n$ is the $C_{out}$. No carries overlap in this approach [5].

### 2.4  Carry Shifting Adder with Increment

The Carry Shifting Adder with Carry Increment Circuit is an improved version [1]. For the input operands A and B of equal length (n), the addition is done as stated for the Carry Shifting Adder after splitting inputs into two equal halves of MSB and LSB i.e., (n/2) length each.

This parallel execution of Carry Shifting Adder results in significant improvement of the speed.

## 3  The Proposed Cyclic Redundant Adder

The proposed Cyclic Redundant Adder is based on the simple principle of a full adder circuit. Generally, the generation of carry part consumes maximum delay. In CyRA, the carry is computed in a parallel manner, which makes the computation of the adder fast by reducing the delay. This adder optimizes the parallel carry computation using the parallel prefix circuit. The technique used in parallel prefix circuit is recursive doubling technique. Here we define three states based on the input operands.

- When A and B are 0, regardless of the state of C, $C_{i+1} = 0$, it is called as kill state.
- When A and B are 1, regardless of the state of C, $C_{i+1} = 1$, it is called as generate state.

- When A and B are not equal, $C_{i+1} = C_i$ and it is called as propagate state.

| A | B | State | |
|---|---|-------|---|
| 0 | 0 | Kill | K |
| 0 | 1 | Propagate | P |
| 1 | 0 | Propagate | P |
| 1 | 1 | Generate | G |

State diagram given in Fig. 1, explains the functioning of the recursive doubling technique. In this technique, if the current state is kill or generate, then the state in the next stage will also be kill or

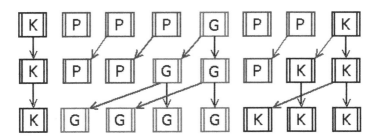

**Fig. 1.** Recursive doubling technique

generate respectively. If the current state is propagate, then the corresponding state in the next stage is given as,

$$\text{Next state} = \text{state of (current cell number} - x),$$

where $x = 2^{n-1}$ and n is the stage number.

The Recursive Doubling has to be done $(r - 1)$ times, (where r is the number of bits), in the worst case when all states are propagate at initial stage. The procedure can be terminated when all the states of the current stage are generate or kill. The worst case recursive doubling is given in Example 1 in Fig. 2.

|  | Example 1 | Example 2 | Example 3 | Example 4 |
|--|-----------|-----------|-----------|-----------|
| a[3:0] | 0 1 0 1 | 1 1 0 1 | 0 1 1 0 | 0 0 1 0 |
| b[3:0] | 1 0 1 0 | 0 0 1 1 | 1 0 1 0 | 1 0 1 0 |
|  | P P P P | P P P G | P P G K | P K G K |
|  | P P P K | P P G G | P G G K | K K G K |
|  | P K K K | G G G G | G G G K | 0 0 1 0 |
|  | K K K K | 1 1 1 1 | 1 1 1 0 |  |
| Carry | 0 0 0 0 |  |  |  |
| Carry | 0 0 0 0 | 1 1 1 1 | 1 1 1 0 | 0 0 1 0 |
| a[3:0] | 0 1 0 1 | 1 1 0 1 | 0 1 1 0 | 0 0 1 0 |
| b[3:0] | 1 0 1 0 | 0 0 1 1 | 1 0 1 0 | 1 0 1 0 |
| Sum | 0 1 1 1 1 | 1 0 0 0 0 | 1 0 0 0 0 | 0 1 1 0 0 |

**Fig. 2.** Example of CyRA

The carry generated from the Recursive Doubling Technique is to be shifted by one bit to left and XOR$_{ed}$ with the two inputs to get the final sum as output. Some examples are explained in the Fig. 2. Here, it is seen that, the proposed adder has log(n) time complexity, where 'n' is the number of corresponding stage.

## 4 Quarter Square Multiplier Using CyRA

The adders discussed in the preceding section are all based on parallel carry computations. It's therefore apparent to look upon on their practical implementation to realize their significance.

The Quarter square algorithm for multiplication [8, 9], results in significant savings in storage requirements. It is based on squares of sum and difference as:

$$(A + B)^2 - (A - B)^2 = 4(A \cdot B) \tag{18}$$

Here, A and B are inputs. From the sum of, squared sum and squared difference, we get $4(A \cdot B)$ as the output as presented in Fig. 3. By shifting the resultant bit stream to the right by 2 bits, the product AB is obtained.

Conventional adder and subtractor blocks, present in the quarter square multiplication algorithm are replaced with the proposed CyRA (Cyclic Redundant Adder) block. For subtractor, the 2's complement of one operand and the actual other operand are taken as input to the adder block.

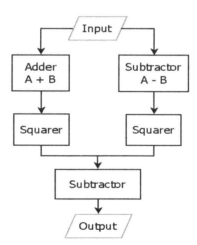

**Fig. 3.** Block diagram of quarter square multiplier

It may be noted that in Fig. 4, the term 10 means a[1].a[0], the term 22 means a[2]. a[2] and so on. The partial products of the squarer block, in the quarter square multiplication algorithm are reduced as in Fig. 4, which in turn decreases the time complexity of the multiplication operation. The partial products are symmetric as the number is squared. When a 1 and 1 is added or 0 and 0 is added, the carry which has to be added to the next state is the same digit which was added 1 or 0. It can be observed from Fig. 4 that when 20 and 02 terms are added, the carry is also 20 and is added to the next state.

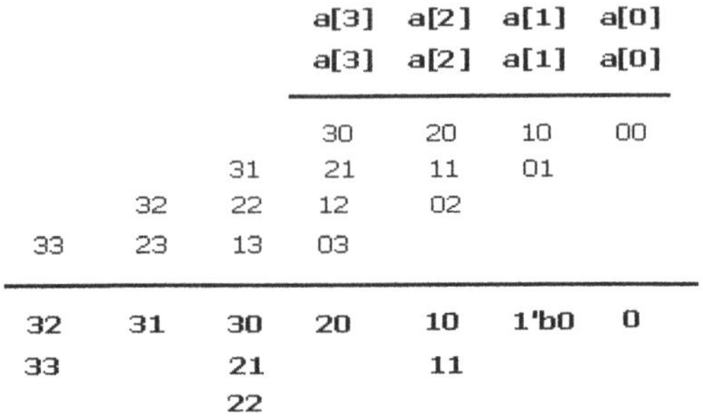

|     |     |     |     | a[3] | a[2] | a[1] | a[0] |
|-----|-----|-----|-----|------|------|------|------|
|     |     |     |     | a[3] | a[2] | a[1] | a[0] |
|     |     |     |     | 30   | 20   | 10   | 00   |
|     |     |     | 31  | 21   | 11   | 01   |      |
|     |     | 32  | 22  | 12   | 02   |      |      |
|     | 33  | 23  | 13  | 03   |      |      |      |
|     | 32  | 31  | 30  | 20   | 10   | 1'b0 | 0    |
|     | 33  |     | 21  |      | 11   |      |      |
|     |     |     | 22  |      |      |      |      |

**Fig. 4.** Reduced partial products of a squarer

## 5 Simulation and Results

The proposed Cyclic Redundant Adder is designed using Verilog Hardware Description Language (HDL). It is modelled in Structural Verilog using multiplexers as well as modelled in Behavioral Verilog upto 64 bits. The Quarter Square Multiplier and Squarer using both the models of CyRA along with Booth and Wallace tree multiplier of 8 bits are implemented using ISE Design Suite 14.7 on Field Programmable Gate Array, Artix7 Family, XC7A100T Device, CSG324 Package, −1 Speed. The results of two models of CyRA are given in Table 1. Logic level, one of the synthesis parameters, which gives the level of combinational logic between two timing end points, is also compared. Lower the logic level, higher the performance of the model. Plot of delay in nanoseconds and area in number of LUTs out of 63400 against the number of bits are presented in Fig. 5.

**Table 1.** Implementation results of CyRA Adder

| No of bits | Structural model | | | Behavioral model | | |
|-----------|-----------|------|---------------|-----------|------|---------------|
|           | Delay (ns) | LUTs | Level of logic | Delay (ns) | LUTs | Level of logic |
| 4         | 2.022     | 7    | 4             | 2.719     | 12   | 5             |
| 8         | 3.724     | 19   | 6             | 2.719     | 24   | 5             |
| 16        | 5.819     | 60   | 9             | 2.719     | 48   | 5             |
| 32        | 7.551     | 181  | 10            | 2.719     | 96   | 5             |
| 64        | 8.676     | 445  | 12            | 2.719     | 192  | 5             |

8-bit Multipliers are implemented using Booth, Wallace and CyRA and the results are given in Table 2. Delay required by each of these multipliers and the area requirement in terms number of LUTs out of 63400 are compared in Figs. 6 and 7. It can be observed that Multiplier based on Quarter Square Algorithm using CyRA has the least delay and uses twice the number of LUTs used in Booth algorithm.

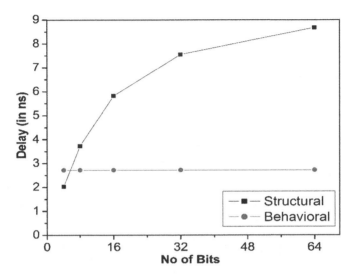

**Fig. 5.** Time delay comparison between CyRA Architectures

**Table 2.** Implementation summary of 8 bit Multipliers

| 8 bit Multipliers | | Delay (ns) | LUTs | Level of logic |
|---|---|---|---|---|
| Booth Multiplier | | 16.249 | 183 | 27 |
| Wallace Tree Multiplier | | 13.645 | 119 | 15 |
| Quarter Square Multiplier | Using Structural (CyRA) | 12.106 | 402 | 25 |
| | Using Behavioral (CyRa) | 11.878 | 340 | 27 |
| Squarer | Using Structural (CyRA) | 9.441 | 149 | 14 |
| | Using Behavioral (CyRa) | 7.937 | 154 | 14 |

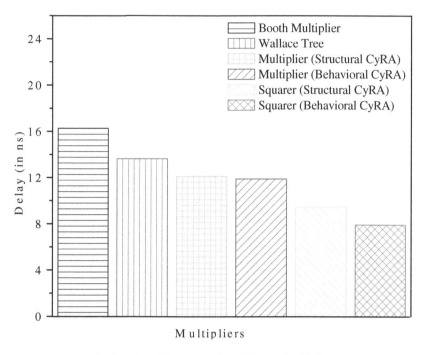

**Fig. 6.** Time delay comparison between Multipliers

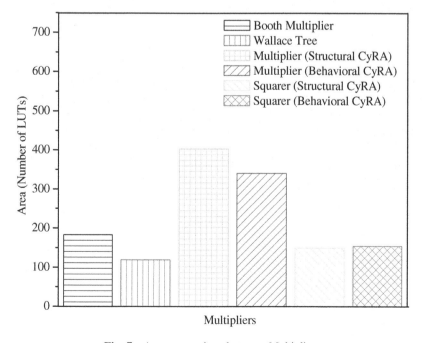

**Fig. 7.** Area comparison between Multipliers

**Table 3.** Synthesis results of CyRA compared with existing Adder Architectures

| Bits | Parameters | CLA | Ling | CSHA | CSHA (Increment) | CyRA (Structural) | CyRA (Behavioral) |
|---|---|---|---|---|---|---|---|
| 16 | Delay (ns) | 7.64 | 8.972 | 7.64 | 6.937 | 6.568 | 2.719 |
| | Area (LUTs) | 16 | 18 | 16 | 26 | 59 | 48 |
| | Level of Logic | 10 | 12 | 10 | 7 | 7 | 5 |
| 32 | Delay (ns) | 11.879 | 11.992 | 11.879 | 10.003 | 7.999 | 2.719 |
| | Area (LUTs) | 32 | 64 | 32 | 49 | 187 | 96 |
| | Level of Logic | 18 | 19 | 18 | 14 | 8 | 5 |
| 64 | Delay (ns) | 20.358 | 18.977 | 20.358 | 14.412 | 8.549 | 2.719 |
| | Area (LUTs) | 64 | 136 | 64 | 103 | 445 | 192 |
| | Level of Logic | 34 | 34 | 34 | 23 | 9 | 5 |

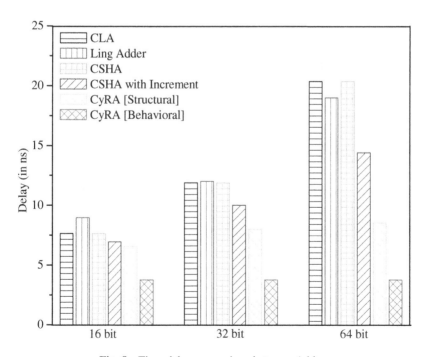

**Fig. 8.** Time delay comparison between Adders

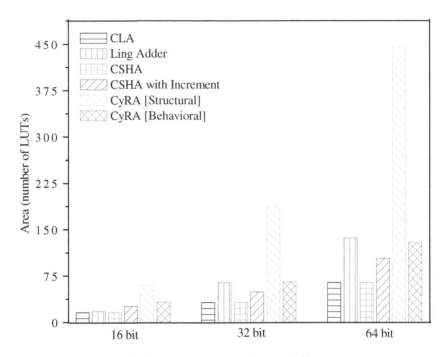

**Fig. 9.** Area comparison between Adders

In Table 3, the synthesis results (on FPGA Virtex5 Family, XC5VLX30 Device, FF324 package, −3 speed), of proposed adder CyRA is compared with existing adders namely, Carry-Look Ahead adder, Ling adder, Carry Shifting adder and Carry Shifting adder with increment [1], with respect to time delay in nanoseconds. The results from comparison of time delay are plotted in Fig. 8 and area in terms of number of LUTs out of 19200 is plotted in Fig. 9, against the number of bits.

## 6   Conclusion

The Behavioral and Structural model of the proposed Cyclic Redundant Adder is designed using Verilog HDL and implemented on FPGA for varying input bits up to 64 bits. The proposed adder's performance is compared with Carry-look ahead adder, Ling adder, Carry shifting adder with increment based on their delay and area. It has been observed that Behavioral CyRA has the least delay and an area similar to that of Ling Adder whereas, Structural CyRA has least area in case of lower input bits. The performance of CyRA increases with increase in number of input bits based on delay because of recursive doubling technique. The proposed adder is found to be the fastest among all the existing adders.

# References

1. Barakat, M., Saad, W., Shokair, M., Elkordy, M.: Implementation of efficient portable low delay adder using FPGA. In: 28th International Conference on Microelectronics ICM (2016)
2. Suganya, R., Meganathan, D.: High performance VLSI adders. In: 3rd International Conference on Signal Processing, Communication and Networking ICSCN (2015)
3. Katz, R.H.: Contemporary Logic Design. Benjamin Publishing Co., CA (1994)
4. Ling, H.: High-speed binary adder. IBM J. Res. Dev. **25**, 156–166 (1981)
5. Saji Antony, M., Sri Ranjani Prasanthi, S., Indu, S., Pandey, R.: Design of high speed Vedic multiplier using multiplexer based adder. In: International Conference on Control Communication & Computing India ICCC (2015)
6. Dadda, L.: Some schemes for parallel multipliers. Alta Freq. **19**, 349–356 (1965)
7. Ling, H.: High speed binary parallel adder. IEEE Trans. Electron. Comput. **EC15**, 799–802 (1966)
8. Chen, T.C.: A binary multiplication scheme based on squaring. IEEE Trans. Comput. **C20**, 678–680 (1971)
9. Jayashree, T., Basu, D.: On binary multiplication using the quarter square algorithm. IEEE Trans. Comput. **C25**, 957–960 (1976)
10. Johnson, E.L.: A digital quarter square multiplier. IEEE Trans. Comput. **C29**, 258–261 (1980)
11. Ling, H.: High-speed computer multiplication using a multiple-bit decoding algorithm. IEEE Trans. Comput. **C19**, 706–709 (1970)

# Fast Architecture of Modular Inversion Using Itoh-Tsujii Algorithm

Pravin Zode[1($\boxtimes$)], R. B. Deshmukh[1], and Abdus Samad[2]

[1] Visvesvaraya National Institute of Technology, Nagpur, India
ppzode@ycce.edu, monal810@yahoo.com
[2] Yeshwantrao Chavan College of Engineering, Nagpur, India
ersamad93@gmail.com

**Abstract.** Modular inversion is a very common primitive used for the cryptographic computations. It is the most computation intensive unit which demands more resources as compared to other primitives. Inside the modular inversion arithmetic circuits, considerable speed up with optimized architecture is required. This paper proposes an optimized parallel architecture for Itoh-Tsujii modular inversion algorithm for the field $GF(2^{256})$ by introducing $2^3$ blocks. The comparative results with conventional architecture show the 30% reduction in LUT requirement with 37% in combinational delay.

**Keywords:** Modular inversion · Galois Field (*GF*) · Fermat's little theorem Euclidean algorithm · Extended Euclidean algorithm

## 1 Introduction

Galois Field arithmetic grabs a substantial growth in recent years due to its applications in numerous cryptographic systems. The mathematics in the Galois Field basically includes three types of function: (i) modular addition (ii) modular multiplication and (iii) modular inversion. Among them, the modular inversion has gathered significant attention as its properties are proven to be useful in the field of cryptography. The Extended Euclidean algorithm and Fermat's little theorem are two most popular methods for large finite field inversion [1]. For extension fields $GF(2^m)$, the Itoh-Tsujii inversion algorithm [2] is the best alternative. It reduces extension field inversion to inversion in binary field for which inversion operation becomes easier. The inversion in binary field is done either using look-up tables or with a series of binary squaring and multiplication operations. The Itoh-Tsujii algorithm is applicable to finite fields $GF(2^m)$ in normal basis representation. However, the original reference deals with composite fields $GF((2^n)^m)$. This paper applies the idea of Itoh-Tsujii algorithm to composite fields $GF((2^n)^m)$ in polynomial basis representation. Although the use of exponentiation operations required in the algorithm make it much complex for general fields in a polynomial basis representation. The exponentiations can be computed with a very low complexity for certain classes of finite fields.

This paper is organized as follows; Sect. 2 discusses brief overview of mathematical background and related work of Itoh-Tsujii Algorithm, equations for Fermat's little algorithm and develops a method for realizing Itoh-Tsujii algorithm. Section 3

© Springer Nature Singapore Pte Ltd. 2017
B. K. Kaushik et al. (Eds.): VDAT 2017, CCIS 711, pp. 48–55, 2017.
https://doi.org/10.1007/978-981-10-7470-7_5

gives an idea about previous works done in this field. Section 4 proposes the modifications in hardware implementation of Itoh-Tsujii algorithm. Experimental results are discussed in Sect. 5 and Sect. 6 concludes the paper.

## 2  Mathematical Background

The extended Euclidean algorithm is a modification of the Euclidean algorithm used to calculate GCD of two numbers. It contains recursive division operations that are not suitable for hardware implementation. Hence, this procedure is mainly used in software that is based on modular inversion. The Fermat's little theorem [1], on the other hand, is mainly based on exponentiation of numbers which are relatively more hardware oriented. This approach is used as a reference to implement modular inversion in hardware architectures. The following subsection describes the mathematics of Fermat's little theorem.

### 2.1  Fermat's Little Theorem Based Inversion in $GF(2^m)$

Let $\alpha$ is an element in a Galois Field $GF(2^m)$. The term $\alpha^{-1} \in GF(2^m)$ can be determined using following expression:

$$\alpha^{-1} = \alpha^{2^m-2} = \alpha^{2(2^{m-1}-1)} = \alpha^{2(1+2+\ldots+2^{m-2})} \tag{1}$$

Now the term $1 + 2 + \ldots + 2^{m-2}$ can be factorized in two ways:

$$\begin{aligned} &a.\, 1 + 2(1+2).\left(1+2^2+2^4+\ldots+2^{m-4}\right) \text{ if } m-1 \text{ is odd} \\ &b.\, (1+2).\left(1+2^2+2^4+\ldots+2^{m-3}\right) \text{ if } m-1 \text{ is even} \end{aligned} \tag{2}$$

### 2.2  Itoh-Tsujii Multiplicative Inversion in $GF(2^m)$

The Itoh-Tsujii algorithm is the modified form of Fermat's little theorem. It evaluates the inversion using a series of recursive multiplications and squarings. Factorization of the expression $1 + 2 + 2^2 + \ldots + 2^{m-2}$ is carried out in such a way that minimum number of additions are required for implementation. For example, if m = 9, then the above expression can be decomposed as $1 + 2 + 2^2 + \ldots + 2^7 = (1+2).(1+2^2).(1+2^4)$. Since, it includes only three additions, it is most useful for hardware implementation. The number of plus signs in the decomposition of the statement $1+2+\ldots+2^{m-2}$ denotes the number of multiplications required to implement the inversion. The job of this algorithm is to reduce the number of multiplication blocks as much as possible. The Itoh-Tsujii algorithm is based on the simple idea shown in (2) [3]. From these two expressions one can easily derive that the number of multiplications sufficient to determine the inverse of an element $\alpha \in GF(2^m)$.

Addition chain can also be used to reduce the number of multiplications [4]. It is a series of successive numbers formulated such that each number can be obtained by addition of two of its precedent numbers. An addition chain with minimum number of elements is generated and inverse can be computed using the expression

$$\alpha^{-1} = [\beta_{m-1}(\alpha)]^2$$

Where $\beta_k = \alpha^{2^k - 1}$

For simplicity, we shall denote $\beta_k(\alpha)$ by $\beta_k$. For the analytical approach, we use the identity

$$\beta_{k+j} = (\beta_k)^{2^j} \beta_j = (\beta_j)^{2^k} \beta_k \tag{3}$$

For an element $\alpha \in GF(2^m)$ the inverse can be calculated as $\alpha^{-1} = [\beta_{255}(\alpha)]^2$ [5]. The term $\beta_{255}(\alpha)$ is obtained using (3) and an addition chain for 255 given by

$$U_{255} = \{1, 2, 3, 6, 12, 15, 30, 60, 120, 240, 255\}$$

## 3   Related Work

Hardware architectures for modular inversion are proposed in [1] for extended Euclidean algorithm and Itoh-Tsujii algorithm, using polynomial as well as Gaussian normal basis. The Itoh-Tsujii algorithm is used to determine the modular inversion for the field $GF(2^m)$. It was first proposed in [2] for the normal basis representation. A lot of work has been done to improve the original algorithm and make it feasible to analyse for different basis representation. In [4], a theoretical model to implement Itoh-Tsujii algorithm on a $k$-input LUT based FPGA is presented. This idea was further reviewed in [5], where a modified Itoh-Tsujii algorithm was proposed for efficient implementations on FPGA platforms. A fast implementation of the algorithm was proposed in [6] which can evaluate the inverse in 10 clock cycles for $GF(2^{233})$ and $GF(2^{409})$ fields. In [7], the Itoh-Tsujii algorithm is generalized for the fields $GF(q^m)$ using polynomial basis representation. In this paper, we propose an optimized parallel architecture of Itoh-Tsujii algorithm for $GF(2^{256})$ on FPGA platform.

## 4   Proposed Work

In this paper, the architecture of Itoh-Tsujii algorithm is modified in order to achieve efficient implementation on FPGA. We assess the analytical complexity of the addition chain shown in Table 1 as follows. The algorithm performs 10 iterations (since $\beta_1(\alpha)$ is $\alpha$ itself) and one field multiplication per iteration. Thus, we conclude that a total of 10 field multiplication calculations are required. This is much better than the Fermat's little theorem implementation which requires 255 multiplications. However, the number of square blocks required is still very high. The Itoh-Tsujii algorithm requires 254 square computation blocks. A hybrid Karatsuba multiplier is used for multiplication operation in binary field. The efficiency of architecture is estimated in terms of maximum

**Table 1.** Inverse of $\alpha \in GF(2^{256})$ using conventional squarer blocks [5]

| S.No. | $\beta_k(\alpha)$ | Expression | $N_s$ |
|---|---|---|---|
| 1 | $\beta_1(\alpha)$ | $\alpha$ | |
| 2 | $\beta_2(\alpha)$ | $\beta_{1+1}(\alpha) = (\beta_1(\alpha))^2 . \beta_1(\alpha)$ | 1 |
| 3 | $\beta_3(\alpha)$ | $\beta_{2+1}(\alpha) = (\beta_2(\alpha))^2 . \beta_1(\alpha)$ | 1 |
| 4 | $\beta_6(\alpha)$ | $\beta_{3+3}(\alpha) = (\beta_3(\alpha))^{2^3} . \beta_3(\alpha)$ | 3 |
| 5 | $\beta_{12}(\alpha)$ | $\beta_{6+6}(\alpha) = (\beta_6(\alpha))^{2^6} . \beta_6(\alpha)$ | 6 |
| 6 | $\beta_{15}(\alpha)$ | $\beta_{12+3}(\alpha) = (\beta_{12}(\alpha))^{2^3} . \beta_3(\alpha)$ | 3 |
| 7 | $\beta_{30}(\alpha)$ | $\beta_{15+15}(\alpha) = (\beta_{15}(\alpha))^{2^{15}} . \beta_{15}(\alpha)$ | 15 |
| 8 | $\beta_{60}(\alpha)$ | $\beta_{30+30}(\alpha) = (\beta_{30}(\alpha))^{2^{30}} . \beta_{30}(\alpha)$ | 30 |
| 9 | $\beta_{120}(\alpha)$ | $\beta_{60+60}(\alpha) = (\beta_{60}(\alpha))^{2^{60}} . \beta_{60}(\alpha)$ | 60 |
| 10 | $\beta_{240}(\alpha)$ | $\beta_{120+120}(\alpha) = (\beta_{120}(\alpha))^{2^{120}} . \beta_{120}(\alpha)$ | 120 |
| 11 | $\beta_{255}(\alpha)$ | $\beta_{240+15}(\alpha) = (\beta_{240}(\alpha))^{2^{15}} . \beta_{15}(\alpha)$ | 15 |
| Total | | | 254 |

combinational delay and power. In case of conventional (parallel) architecture of Itoh-Tsujii algorithm, a large number of cascaded square blocks are used, which degrades the performance of the device. The use of Quad [5] and Octet block improves the speed of modified architecture.

### 4.1 Significance of Quad Circuits

Since the number of squaring operations is as high as 255 for conventional Itoh-Tsujii algorithm over the $GF(2^{256})$, we need to improve the circuit in order to reduce the number of blocks for square operation. The quad circuit can be used to overcome this problem [6]. A quad circuit is a block which performs the operation of raising the input by a power of four instead of squaring operation. In Itoh-Tsujii algorithm, we can use any exponentiation circuit of the form $2^n$. In this paper, the advantages of using $2^2$ circuits on FPGAs for exponentiation in fields with irreducible trinomials are observed. Quad circuits offer the best LUT utilization for an FPGA with four or six input LUTs. The irreducible trinomial for the field is $x^9 + x + 1$. We observe from Table 2 that the quad circuit's LUT requirement significantly reduced by around 25% [5]. This is because the quad circuit utilizes FPGA resources better than the squarer. Moreover, since quad is a single stage combinational circuit, both circuits have the same delay of one LUT. These observations are scalable to larger fields like $GF(2^{233})$ and $GF(2^{193})$ [4].

The limitation of using quad circuits instead of squarers depends on the fields generated by irreducible polynomial. When irreducible pentanomials are used for generating the field instead of irreducible trinomials, the saving of area is almost negligible due to the fact that a quad circuit and two cascaded squarers will have about the same area. Unfortunately there is no irreducible trinomial for $GF(2^{256})$ field. However, the combination of squarer and quad computation blocks, significant improvement in overall area delay product is possible. Based on these observations we propose a hybrid-Itoh-Tsujii algorithm for fields generated by irreducible pentanomials which use quad exponentiation circuits as well as squarer circuits. Table 3 shows the evaluation of $\beta_{255}(\alpha)$ using an improved Itoh-Tsujii algorithm implemented using hybrid approach.

**Table 2.** LUTs required for a squarer and quad circuit for $GF(2^9)$ [5]

| Output bit | Squarer circuit | | Quad circuit | |
|---|---|---|---|---|
| | $b(x)^2$ | #LUTs | $b(x)^4$ | #LUTs |
| 0 | $b_0$ | 0 | $b_0$ | 0 |
| 1 | $b_5$ | 0 | $b_7$ | 0 |
| 2 | $b_1 + b_5$ | 1 | $b_5 + b_7$ | 1 |
| 3 | $b_6$ | 0 | $b_3 + b_7$ | 1 |
| 4 | $b_2 + b_6$ | 1 | $b_1 + b_3 + b_5 + b_7$ | 1 |
| 5 | $b_7$ | 0 | $b_8$ | 0 |
| 6 | $b_3 + b_8$ | 1 | $b_6 + b_8$ | 1 |
| 7 | $b_8$ | 0 | $b_4 + b_8$ | 1 |
| 8 | $b_4 + b_8$ | 1 | $b_2 + b_4 + b_6 + b_8$ | 1 |
| Total LUTs | | 4 | | 6 |

**Table 3.** Inverse of $\alpha \in GF(2^{256})$ using quad blocks [5]

| S.No. | $\beta_k(\alpha)$ | Expression | Ns | Nq |
|---|---|---|---|---|
| 1 | $\beta_1(\alpha)$ | $\alpha$ | | |
| 2 | $\beta_2(\alpha)$ | $\beta_{1+1}(\alpha) = (\beta_1(\alpha))^2 . \beta_1(\alpha)$ | 1 | |
| 3 | $\beta_3(\alpha)$ | $\beta_{2+1}(\alpha) = (\beta_2(\alpha))^2 . \beta_1(\alpha)$ | 1 | |
| 4 | $\beta_6(\alpha)$ | $\beta_{3+3}(\alpha) = \left((\beta_3(\alpha))^4\right)^2 . \beta_3(\alpha)$ | 1 | 1 |
| 5 | $\beta_{12}(\alpha)$ | $\beta_{6+6}(\alpha) = (\beta_6(\alpha))^{4^3} . \beta_6(\alpha)$ | | 3 |
| 6 | $\beta_{15}(\alpha)$ | $\beta_{12+3}(\alpha) = \left((\beta_{12}(\alpha))^4\right)^2 . \beta_3(\alpha)$ | 1 | 1 |
| 7 | $\beta_{30}(\alpha)$ | $\beta_{15+15}(\alpha) = \left((\beta_{15}(\alpha))^{4^7}\right)^2 . \beta_{15}(\alpha)$ | 1 | 7 |
| 8 | $\beta_{60}(\alpha)$ | $\beta_{30+30}(\alpha) = (\beta_{30}(\alpha))^{4^{15}} . \beta_{30}(\alpha)$ | | 15 |
| 9 | $\beta_{120}(\alpha)$ | $\beta_{60+60}(\alpha) = (\beta_{60}(\alpha))^{4^{30}} . \beta_{60}(\alpha)$ | | 30 |
| 10 | $\beta_{240}(\alpha)$ | $\beta_{120+120}(\alpha) = (\beta_{120}(\alpha))^{4^{60}} . \beta_{120}(\alpha)$ | | 60 |
| 11 | $\beta_{255}(\alpha)$ | $\beta_{240+15}(\alpha) = \left((\beta_{240}(\alpha))^{4^7}\right)^2 . \beta_{15}(\alpha)$ | 1 | 7 |
| Total | | | 6 | 124 |

## 4.2   Significance of $2^3$ Circuits

The idea of combining multiple squarer blocks into a single unit is further explored using a $2^3$ circuit. The proposed logic block is a combinational unit, mathematically equivalent to three cascaded squarer blocks. However, combining multiple blocks into a single unit results in efficient LUT utilization and less computation time. Also, 3 completly divides 255, the architecture consists of $2^3$ blocks only, except at the initial stage for precomputation of the term $\alpha^7$ and the final stage of inversion [5]. Table 4 shows the evaluation of $\beta_{255}(\alpha)$ using an optimized Itoh-Tsujii algorithm architecture implemented using $2^3$ blocks. It is observed that the cascade blocks of Quads and Squarer block shown in Table 3 is completely eliminated.

**Table 4.**  Inverse of $\alpha \in GF(2^{256})$ using Octet blocks

| S.No. | $\beta_k(\alpha)$ | Expression | Ns | No |
|---|---|---|---|---|
| 1 | $\beta_1(\alpha)$ | $\alpha$ | | |
| 2 | $\beta_2(\alpha)$ | $\beta_{1+1}(\alpha) = (\beta_1(\alpha))^2 . \beta_1(\alpha)$ | 1 | |
| 3 | $\beta_3(\alpha)$ | $\beta_{2+1}(\alpha) = (\beta_2(\alpha))^2 . \beta_1(\alpha)$ | 1 | |
| 4 | $\beta_6(\alpha)$ | $\beta_{3+3}(\alpha) = (\beta_3(\alpha))^8 . \beta_3(\alpha)$ | | 1 |
| 5 | $\beta_{12}(\alpha)$ | $\beta_{6+6}(\alpha) = (\beta_6(\alpha))^{8^2} . \beta_6(\alpha)$ | | 2 |
| 6 | $\beta_{15}(\alpha)$ | $\beta_{12+3}(\alpha) = (\beta_{12}(\alpha))^8 . \beta_3(\alpha)$ | | 1 |
| 7 | $\beta_{30}(\alpha)$ | $\beta_{15+15}(\alpha) = (\beta_{15}(\alpha))^{8^5} . \beta_{15}(\alpha)$ | | 5 |
| 8 | $\beta_{60}(\alpha)$ | $\beta_{30+30}(\alpha) = (\beta_{30}(\alpha))^{8^{10}} . \beta_{30}(\alpha)$ | | 10 |
| 9 | $\beta_{120}(\alpha)$ | $\beta_{60+60}(\alpha) = (\beta_{60}(\alpha))^{8^{20}} . \beta_{60}(\alpha)$ | | 20 |
| 10 | $\beta_{240}(\alpha)$ | $\beta_{120+120}(\alpha) = (\beta_{120}(\alpha))^{8^{40}} . \beta_{120}(\alpha)$ | | 40 |
| 11 | $\beta_{255}(\alpha)$ | $\beta_{240+15}(\alpha) = (\beta_{240}(\alpha))^{8^5} . \beta_{15}(\alpha)$ | | 5 |
| Total | | | 2 | 84 |

The architecture for Itoh-Tsujii algorithm considering a special class of irreducible polynomial, $m(x) = x^{256} + x^{10} + x^5 + x^2 + 1$ for $GF(2^{256})$ is presented in Fig. 1. It uses field multiplication, field squaring and field Octet operators as its primary building blocks. We also show how this version of the algorithm can be parallelized to improve the efficiency when implemented in hardware platforms.

## 5   Result and Discussions

The comparison of performance of various exponentiation blocks on the binary fields with irreducible polynomials is shown in Table 5. The use of $2^n$ circuit improves the performance of exponentiation. For Virtex-6 and 7, both area and speed of Octet architecture is improved. This is due to higher utilization factor of respective FPGAs. The purpose of optimization of FPGA design is to ensure that the resources of the device are utilized completely. The smallest programmable unit in the FPGA is the

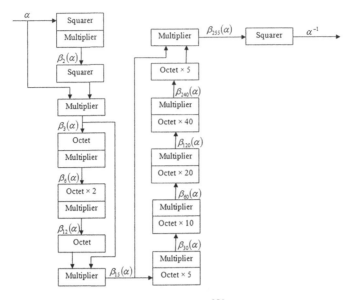

**Fig. 1.** Architecture of ITA for $GF(2^{256})$ using Octet Blocks

lookup table, which generally has four (or six) inputs. The LUTs are used to implement any Boolean logic function of four (or six) variables. When a logic function with less than four (or six) variables is implemented using LUT, the LUT is underutilized. An optimized implementation is obtained when each LUT is utilized up to the maximum extent. The proposed $2^3$ blocks are best-utilized using Virtex-6 and Virtex-7 FPGA platforms.

**Table 5.** Comparison of squarer and quad circuits on xilinx virtex FPGAs

| Field | Squarer circuit | | Quad circuit | | Octet circuit | | Size ratio | | Delay ratio | |
|---|---|---|---|---|---|---|---|---|---|---|
| | $LUT_s$ | Delay $D_s$ (ns) | $LUT_q$ | Delay $D_q$ (ns) | $LUT_o$ | Delay $D_o$ (ns) | $LUT_q/2(LUT_s)$ | $LUT_o/3(LUT_s)$ | $D_q/2(D_s)$ | $D_o/3(D_s)$ |
| $GF(2^{193})$ | 96 | 1.48 | 145 | 1.48 | – | – | 0.75 | – | 0.5 | – |
| $GF(2^{233})$ | 153 | 1.48 | 230 | 1.48 | – | – | 0.75 | – | 0.5 | – |
| $GF(2^{256})$ | 255 | 1.081 | 380 | 1.750 | 536 | 2.069 | 0.74 | 0.70 | 0.80 | 0.63 |

**Table 6.** Comparison with NIST binary fields having irreducible trinomials

| Field | Algorithm | LUTs | Delay (ns) | T (ns) |
|---|---|---|---|---|
| $GF(2^{256})$ | Squarer ITA | 256945 | 342.215 | 342.215 |
| | Squarer + Quad ITA | 240825 | 291.127 | 291.127 |
| | Squarer + Octet ITA | 237709 | 243.599 | 243.599 |

Table 6 compares various parameters of our architectures with generic architectures. These results show that in case of finite fields with irreducible pentanomial, the parameters of the circuit can be improved enough to be compared with finite fields with irreducible trinomials. The results show almost 40% improvement in cumulative delay when octet architecture is used.

## 6 Conclusion

This paper optimizes the parallel Itoh-Tsujii inverse algorithm to implement on FPGA platforms using Squarer, Quad and Octet blocks. Hybrid Itoh-Tsujii algorithm is put forward for the fields generated by irreducible pentanomials. Area-delay product is considerably reduced by using Octet block. The octet block of proposed architecture requires 30% less area and increases the speed of operation by 37%. An FPGA architecture of the Octet Itoh-Tsujii algorithm architecture results in 40% and 20% improved delay as compared with squarer and quad architectures respectively.

## References

1. Trujillo-Olaya, V., Velasco-Medina, J.: Hardware architectures for inversion in GF $(2^m)$ using polynomial and gaussian normal basis. In: ANDESCON IEEE 2010 Conference Publications, pp. 1–5 (2010)
2. Itoh, T., Tsujii, S.: A fast algorithm for computing multiplicative inverses in GF$(2^m)$ using normal bases. Inf. Comput. **78**(3), 171–177 (1988)
3. Dimitrov, V., Järvinen, K.: Another look at inversions over binary fields. In: 2013 IEEE 21st Symposium on Computer Arithmetic, pp. 211–218 (2013)
4. Roy, S.S., Rebeiro, C., Mukhopadhyay, D.: Theoretical modelling of the Itoh-Tsujii inversion algorithm for enhanced performance on k-LUT based FPGAs. In: Proceedings of the Design, Automation & Test in Europe Conference & Exhibition (DATE), Grenoble, France, vol. 1, pp. 1–6, March 2011
5. Rebeiro, C., Roy, S.S., Reddy, D.S., Mukhopadhyay, D.: Revisiting the Itoh-Tsujii inversion algorithm for FPGA platforms. IEEE Trans. Very Large Scale Integr. (VLSI) Syst. **19**(8), 1508–1512 (2011)
6. Parrilla, L., Lloris, A., Castillo, E., et al.: Minimum-clock-cycle Itoh-Tsujii algorithm hardware implementation for cryptography applications over GF$(2^m)$ fields. Electron. Lett. **48**(18), 1126–1128 (2012)
7. Guajardo, J., Paar, C.: Itoh-Tsujii inversion in standard basis and its application in cryptography and codes. Des. Codes Cryptogr. **25**(2), 207–216 (2002)

# Performance Optimized 64b/66b Line Encoding Technique for High Speed SERDES Devices

Jatindeep Singh[✉], Satyajit Mohapatra, and Nihar Ranjan Mohapatra

Department of Electrical Engineering, Indian Institute of Technology,
Gandhinagar 382355, India
jatindeep_singh@btech2012.iitgn.ac.in,
satyajit_mohapatra@iitgn.ac.in

**Abstract.** The 64b/66b technique conventionally is suited for low BER fiber optic channels, but can be extended for higher BER channels by including proper error correcting code and preamble. A modified 64b/66b line encoding technique for the design of high speed SERDES is proposed. Unlike earlier 8b/10b technology, run-length is no more guaranteed but is statistically bound. Generated polynomials are statistically tested in MATLAB prior VHDL implementation. Optimal selection of primitive polynomial limits run length to 11 and provides sub-optimal data security. Proposed 64/66b encoding technique reduces overhead by 15.8% (at 6.3% CRC) with respect to conventional 8b/10b, while is also suited for high BER channels like wireless and free space. A performance optimum between security, run-length, ISI and DC equalization, this scheme finds potential application in space camera electronics, 5G technology and other IOT applications like driverless cars that require to handle large volumes of real time data with sufficient security on high BER wireless channels.

**Keywords:** Serializer-Deserializer (SERDES) · Inter-Symbol Interference (ISI)
Cyclic redundancy check (CRC) · Encoding technique · Bit error rate (BER)

## 1 Introduction

High resolution imagers for remote sensing require processing of multiple video port to typically yield $\geq 12$ bit digitized video data. This is conventionally achieved by parallel data transmission using multiple cables/interface package. However, for future missions parallel data transfer at high speed requires >8000 cables between camera electronics and data handling system. Increase in video ports results in increased harness weight, volume and power. At high data rates, problems associated with EMI/EMC, clock skew and crosstalk become more critical. These introduce design complexity and limit the maximum distance of a parallel link, constraining parallel network to inside-the-box application. It also requires to address jitter and timing margins related issues. This calls for high-speed transmission medium (>1Gbps) within spacecraft subsystems. A possible solution identified is SERDES interface which performs parallel to serial conversion at the transmitting end, transmit the serial stream preferably over differential medium (for better noise margin and signal integrity) and

© Springer Nature Singapore Pte Ltd. 2017
B. K. Kaushik et al. (Eds.): VDAT 2017, CCIS 711, pp. 56–61, 2017.
https://doi.org/10.1007/978-981-10-7470-7_6

finally convert the serial data back to parallel at the receiving end. It results in considerable reduction in interconnects and overcomes issues of crosstalk. These devices use CMOS technology with LVDS interface, for low power and noise immunity. It typically comprises of encoder/decoder, PLL, mux/de-mux and timing-control circuit. SERDES architectures suitable for space application [1] include parallel clock/strobe SERDES and SERDES with encoder/decoder. The second architecture provides advantages of DC balancing, pre-emphasis and clock embedding that are mandatory for very high speed serial data transfer. High-speed SERDES devices must meet requirements of high frequency operation, intensive equalization technique, low power consumption, small area and robustness. When implemented on space qualified ASIC platform, it offers the desired communication reliability and efficiency required in harsh space environments. Off the shelf devices [2] available from few vendors suffer from limitation of poor reduction factor, no clock embedding and non-availability in required operating frequency. Most of them operate in excess of >1Gbps with their patented design. Information regarding internal functional blocks is not available, which is required from reliability point of view. In addition to cost being on higher side, non-availability of space qualified parts might hamper future mission timelines. Line encoding can potentially help improve speed by reducing overheads without necessitating improvement in SERDES devices [3]. Asynchronous mode data transfer is most suited due to non-requirement of high speed clock transmission along with data. However it further adds to the requirement of critical clock and data recovery circuit at receiver that add to requirement of an encoding technique.

Typical 8b/10b SERDES interface achieves speed of 250 Mbps, corresponding to a transmission of 8-bit at 25 MSPS, thereby reducing the interface by a factor of 8. Higher factors can potentially be achieved with 12b/14b and 64b/66b encoding. The 64b/66b scheme originally proposed by Walker [4] provides acceptable transition density with small overhead. With large overheads ($\sim$25%), it is quite challenging to achieve high speed using available space grade electronics. But with the help of 64b/66b encoding data rates up to 10 GbPS can be achieved. The paper is further organized in five sections. Critical design requirements, suitable architectures and analysis of the 64b/66b technique and proposed modification is carried out in Sect. 2. Detailed hardware and software implementation of proposed architecture is discussed. System verification and brief analysis of achieved results, its implications and potential applications are summarized in Sect. 3 followed by concluding remarks.

## 2  System Analysis and Design

Line encoding can potentially help in improving speed by reducing overheads without necessitating improvements in SERDES devices. As overhead requirement of 8b/10b is 25%, it is challenging to achieve 10 GbPS with currently available devices. Space qualified products that could run at just over 10 GbPS, could hardly be pushed to the 12.5 GbPS limit required to support earlier 8b/10b and 12/14b technologies. Therefore a new encoding technique with lesser overhead was looked into. In 8/10b, 8-data bits are logically separated into two separate sub-blocks of 5 and 3. If 8-bit output is considered, all the codes from 0 to 255 will be used, so can't guarantee DC balancing.

So, 2 overhead bits are considered. For 10-bit output, $^{10}C_5 = 252$ cases are perfectly DC balanced and $2 \times {}^{10}C_4 = 420$ cases have disparity of ±2. Similarly 12b/14b encoding is divided into 7b/8b and 5b/6b. There are $2^{12} = 4096$ data characters and 22 control characters. Disparity is bound between ±4 at all levels. The implemented system architecture with 64b/66b encoding scheme is shown in Fig. 1a. It consists of the encoder/decoder, scrambler/descrambler modules, CRC encoding module and the transmitter/receiver sections. At the input of encoder, a preamble specifies whether the data is a pure data or control. Further the use of sync bit reduces the misreading of 64-bit data as pure data or control as in case of error '1' can change to '0'. Word alignment is provided by addition of sync preamble. 0b01 represent data while 0b10 represent mix of data and control characters, or control characters only. Preambles 0b00 and 0b11 are treated as code error and packet is invalidated at the receiving end. Therefore, the presence of preamble bits makes run length in this case deterministically less than 64.

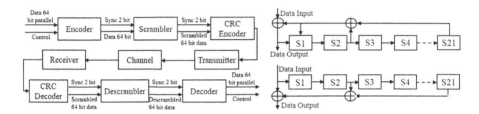

**Fig. 1.** (a) The 64/66b system architecture (b) Multiplicative scrambler descrambler implement

In traditional 8b/10b encoding, a combinational logic acting on this running average between set of eight bits is used to encode the remaining two bits to create a set of 10 bits and guarantee a DC balanced 10 bits output. Unlike earlier technologies, in 64/66b encoding, run-length is no more guaranteed but statistically bound. Instead it uses scrambling polynomial based algorithm is used to force transitions and hence randomize the bits within the packet. Therefore selection of primitive polynomial for scrambling is detrimental to performance of the 64/66b system. Statistical simulations for various primitive polynomial are carried out in Matlab to understand the effect of order of polynomial on run length. It is observed that while both $10^{th}$ and $21^{st}$ order polynomials exhibit minimum run length (10 and 11 respectively), security offered by $21^{st}$ order polynomial is significantly higher ($2^{21}$–0.5 ppm) and sub-optimal. Therefore instead of implementing standard self-synchronous scrambler (i.e. $x^{58} + x^{39} + 1$) which increases computational complexity and has a higher run length, we go for $21^{st}$ order primitive polynomial $x^{21} + x^2 + 1$. This scrambler is very hard (practically impossible) to attack and robust against emulation since the initial state of the scrambler is unknown to malicious user. This result opens up complete set of new applications which require secure high speed transmission over high BER channels like wireless and free space. This scheme finds potential application in space camera electronics, 5G technology and IOT systems like driverless cars that require to handle large volumes of real time data with optimal security on high BER wireless channels. Extended Galois primitive polynomial [5, 6] offers maximum suitability for implementing the 64b/66b encoding technique. Strategic extension of Galois field scrambling polynomial is implemented in the 64/66b encoder. Multiplicative scrambler (Fig. 1b) has been implemented in our design to overcome issues of repetitive pseudo random pattern generation and reset during cases of frame sync lost [7]. For high speed application we have implemented parallel (Fig. 2a) scrambling using the protocol logic. The new 64-bit word in every clock are applied to a 64-bit parallel scrambler. As S-2 ($2^{nd}$ bit of LFSR) is being used in scramble D-3scram-D-32, designing the polynomial $x^{21} + x^2 + 1$ is computationally complex due to several XOR used, thus limiting chances to develop a parallel scrambler. Properties of polynomial in GF(2) enable us to use $x^{21} + x^{19} + 1$ instead of $x^{21} + x^2 + 1$ to gain desired result through parallel implementation.

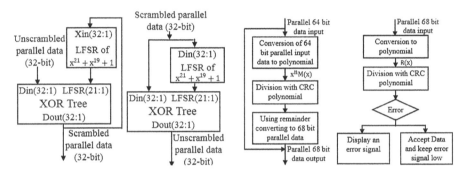

**Fig. 2.** (a) 64 bit parallel scrambler descrambler (b) The CRC encoder decoder implementation

We have implemented CRC using $4^{th}$ order polynomial $x^4 + x^2 + 1$, to keep the overhead low to 9.4% while adding significant error handling capability (Fig. 2b) to the system.

## 3    Results and Discussion

Scrambling polynomials are implemented in MATLAB and Simulink is used for verifying the accuracy of the achieved results. The circuit was coded in VHDL at module and system levels. Thorough system verification similar to [5] was carried on FPGA. An overview of the verification process for cases-I & II is demonstrated in Fig. 3a. The behavioral simulation along with the cyclic redundancy check algorithms implemented in encoder and decoder for $21^{st}$ and $58^{th}$ order scrambler is shown in Fig. 3b.

To decrease the run length further, we propose the use of additional scrambler serially with existing one. The proposed polynomial being $x^{21} + x^{19} + 1$. The output of both scramblers were tested against an input pattern of 10,000 bits. The pattern was intentionally divided into bins of run length 50 to measure ability of scrambler to randomize it. As evident from Fig. 4a, proposed selection of $21^{st}$ order scrambling polynomial limits run length to 11 while providing suboptimal security in contrast to

| [Case-1]: Input Pattern | CRC | Output Pattern (HEX) | CRC:O/P | LED | RST | | |
|---|---|---|---|---|---|---|---|
| EABC1234A542AB42 | 6 | EABC1234A542AB42 | 00(HEX) | HIGH | 0 | | |
| B1298CBEA5121623 | 1 | B1298CBEA5121623 | 00(HEX) | HIGH | 1 | | |
| B1101CFE054A1923 | 0 | B1101CFE054A1923 | 00(HEX) | HIGH | 2 | | |
| C124EF7F45228542 | 7 | C124EF7F45228542 | 00(HEX) | HIGH | 3 | | |
| | | | | | | | |
| [Case-2]: Input Pattern | CRC | Output Pattern (HEX) | CRC:O/P | LED | RST | | |
| F100FAFFAA211531 | 6 | F100FAFFAA211531 | 00(HEX) | HIGH | 0 | | |
| A11C8F4FA512413F | 2 | A11C8F4FA512413F | 00(HEX) | HIGH | 1 | | |
| DAA0231052075440 | 3 | DAA0231052075440 | 00(HEX) | HIGH | 2 | | |
| B1101CFE054A1923 | F | FFFFFFFFFFFFFFFF | 1E(HEX) | LOW | 3 | | |

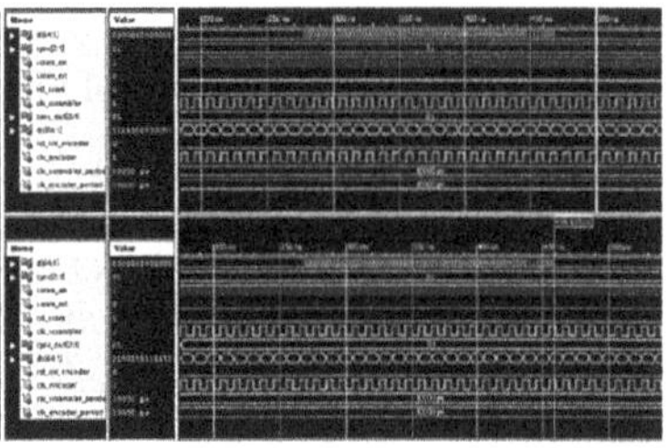

**Fig. 3.** (a) Hardware Verification Vectors (b) Behavioral simulation for scrambler (58,21 order)

conventional 58th order polynomial which could limit run length to 18. Though the 9th order polynomial limits run length to 10, the 21st order polynomial provides significantly higher security ($2^{21}$–0.5 ppm). Therefore the high data security ($2^{21-9}$) is worth trading off for a single bit degradation in run length. A brief comparative overview of implemented 64b/66b technique with existing 8b/10b technique is summarized in Fig. 4b.

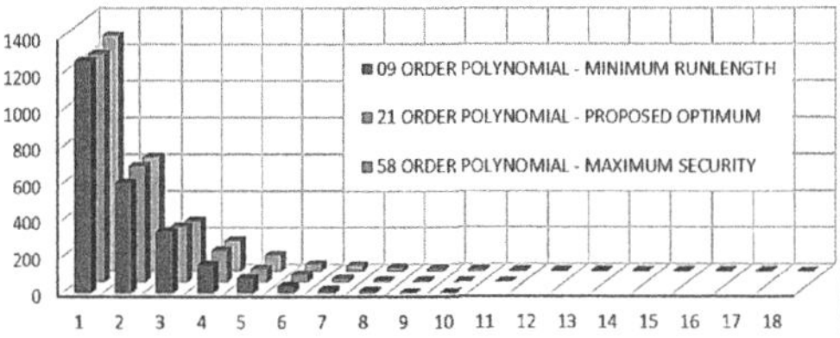

| Encoding | 8B/10B | 64B/66B |
|---|---|---|
| Run length | 05 | Relies on Scrambler Capacity (11@X21) |
| DC Balance | Disparity ±2 | Not Guaranteed |
| Word Sync. | "Comma" K | Synchronization Header |
| Control Char. | K-Characters | Control Codes |
| % Overheads | 25% | 3.175% (9% @ CRC) |
| Implementation Technique | A Look Up Table Type Approach | Scrambling + Non-Scrambled Sync Pattern & Control Type |

■ 09 ORDER POLYNOMIAL - MINIMUM RUNLENGTH
■ 21 ORDER POLYNOMIAL - PROPOSED OPTIMUM
■ 58 ORDER POLYNOMIAL - MAXIMUM SECURITY

**Fig. 4.** (a) Run length plot with order of scrambler (b) Comparative overview of the technique.

The proposed design occupies small portion of the available logic resources, indicating that it can be integrated with other functional blocks of the sub-system. The implemented 64b/66b encoding technique is highly efficient as it requires overhead of only 3.18% and therefore is potentially efficient for transferring large volumes of data in Mega Bytes. Proposed 21st order polynomial limits run length to 11 and provide sub-optimal data security. It opens up set of new applications that require secure high speed data transfer over high BER channels like wireless and free space. A performance optimum between security, run-length and ISI, this scheme finds potential application in satellite imaging, 5G communication and IOT systems like driverless cars that require to handle large volumes of real time data with sufficient security on high BER wireless channels. The output of scrambler is verified against input of pattern of 10,000 bits. The hardware verification of system is complete and successfully demonstrated on Actel ProASIC3 low power spaceflight radiation tolerant FPGA [8].

# References

1. Stauffer, D.R., Mechler, J.T., Sorna, M.A., Dramstad, K., Ogilvie, C.R., Mohammad, A., Rockrohr, J.D.: High Speed Serdes Devices and Applications. Springer, Boston (2009). https://doi.org/10.1007/978-0-387-79834-9
2. Datasheet of the COTS SERDES (Texas Instruments Part No. TLK2711, DS90UR241)
3. Richard, T., Donald, A., Steve, D., et al.: U.S. Patent No. 20,030,217,215, Washington (2003)
4. Walker, R., Dugan, R.: 64b/66b low overhead proposal for seriel links, IEEE 802.3 (2000)
5. Gupta, H.S., et al.: 64b/66b Line Encoding for High Speed Serializers, IEEE VLSID (2017)
6. http://www2.siit.tu.ac.th/prapun/ecs455/ece5610501PolynomialsOverGaloisField.pdf
7. Weldon Jr., E.J.: U.S. Patent No. 4,723,246. Washington, DC US 06/759,491 (1988)
8. Radiation-Tolerant ProASIC3 Low Power Spaceflight Flash FPGA, Datasheet, Rev5 (2012)

# A New Multi-objective Hardware-Software-Partitioning Algorithmic Approach for High Speed Applications

Naman Govil[1], Rahul Shrestha[2(✉)], and Shubhajit Roy Chowdhury[2]

[1] International Institute of Information Technology (IIIT) Hyderabad,
Hyderabad 500032, India
namangov@gmail.com
[2] School of Computing and Electrical Engineering, Indian Institute of Technology
(IIT) Mandi, Mandi 175005, Himachal Pradesh, India
{rahul_shrestha,src}@iitmandi.ac.in

**Abstract.** Designing embedded systems efficiently has always been of significant interest. This has tremendously scaled-up for contemporary applications with their increasing complexity and the need to satisfy multiple conflicting constraints. This paper presents a high-speed Hardware Software Partitioning (HSP) technique for the design of such systems. The Partitioning problem has been modeled as a multi-dimensional optimization problem with the aim of minimizing the area utilization, power dissipation, time of execution and system memory requirement of the implementation. A two-phased algorithm has been proposed which also takes into consideration the communication costs between hardware and software Processing-Engines (PEs) while partitioning. Detailed empirical analysis of the proposed algorithm is presented to ascertain its efficiency, quality and speed.

**Keywords:** Hardware Software Partitioning · Heuristic algorithms

## 1 Introduction

The problem of HSP has proven to be NP-hard [1] and its exact solution can be generated only when the problem size is small. Some of the algorithms for exact solutions developed over the years are based on integer linear programming and dynamic programming. These algorithms tend to be become slower with the increase in problem size and hence renders ineffectiveness in the design.

In order to mitigate this problem, heuristic techniques were utilized to explore the solution space and reach sub-optimal solutions. Some of the recent reported works that incorporate communication costs into partitioning decision are [2–4], however, their results are inadequate because they get significantly slower as the problem size increases. In some papers, the communication cost factor considerations are incomplete, based on assumptions made to decrease the complexity of solutions [5]. Thereby, our work attempts to address these problems by developing a fast and efficient algorithm that incorporates communication costs completely.

© Springer Nature Singapore Pte Ltd. 2017
B. K. Kaushik et al. (Eds.): VDAT 2017, CCIS 711, pp. 62–68, 2017.
https://doi.org/10.1007/978-981-10-7470-7_7

## 2   Multi-objective Optimization of Partitioning

### 2.1   Problem Modeling

We model HSP as a multi-objective optimization problem as explained below. Here, $a_i$: area cost of node $B_i$, $p_i$: power cost of node $B_i$, $e_i$: time of execution cost of node $B_i$, $m_i$: memory cost of node $B_i$. The maximum allowable power, time and memory constraint by $P$, $E$ and $M$, respectively. Summarizing problem $\boldsymbol{P}$ as:

$$\text{Maximize} \left( \sum_{i=1}^{n} a_i \times y_i \right) \mid \sum_{i=1}^{n} e_i \times y_i \leq E$$
$$\cap \sum_{i=1}^{n} p_i \times y_i \leq P \cap \sum_{i=1}^{n} m_i \times y_i \leq M. \tag{1}$$

We assume that all the blocks are initially placed in software and a new term referred as communication profit ($\delta_i$) has been introduced. It is defined as the communication cost saving in moving a block $B_i$ to hardware. Mathematically,

$$\delta_i = comm\_SW(B_i) - comm\_HW(B_i) \tag{2}$$

where $comm\_SW(B_i)$ $\{comm\_HW(Bi)\}$ denotes the communication time of $B_i$ and its neighbors, both $B_{i-1}$ as well as $B_{i+1}$, when $B_i$ is assigned to software (hardware).

## 3   Proposed Solutions

### 3.1   Two-Phased Greedy Heuristic

As discussed earlier, the modeled problem is NP-hard. Therefore, it is not possible to generate the exact (or optimal) solutions in polynomial time with the increase in problem size. Thus, meta-heuristic solutions which can provide sub-optimal solutions are utilized. We call the proposed algorithm **PGMA** (or Phased Greedy Metaheurisitic Algorithm). Next, we present both the phases of the PGMA.

**PGMA - Phase 1.** In order to take communication costs into consideration while partitioning, we introduce a ratio, similar to the profit-to-weight ratio, called Profit[i] or $P[i]$ metric for the $i^{th}$ block, defined as:

$$P[i] = \left( \frac{a[i] + \delta_i}{w_1 \times p_i + w_2 \times e_i + w_3 \times m_i} \right)$$

where $w_1$, $w_2$ and $w_3$ are the weights reflecting the importance. Such weights can be set with respect to the magnitude of importance each cost is to be rendered relative to others. It is to be noted that $w_1 + w_2 + w_3 = 1$. The phase 1 of the solution proposed in this paper is an extension of the HEA algorithm that is presented in [2], where the metric has been constructed by considering all the relevant costs affecting the optimization. This phase is a heuristic process which begins by placing all the blocks in software ($x_i = 0$ for all blocks). Then, the metric $P[i]$ is computed for each block.

Next, the block with maximum $P[i]$ is selected and shifted to hardware if none of the constraints like execution time, power and memory requirement are overshot. Thereafter, the communication costs of neighboring blocks to the block being shifted to hardware are updated. Eventually, all the aforementioned steps are repeated for each block. The pseudo-code corresponding to this proposed algorithm has been presented in Algorithm 1, as shown below:

---

**Algorithm 1 . PGMA - Phase 1**

---

**Inputs**: Cost data for each block $(a_i, p_i, e_i, m_i)$.
**Inputs**: Communication cost data $(c_i^{ss}, c_i^{sh}, c_i^{hs}, c_i^{hh})$.
$C_0$: Total power constraint.
$C_1$: Total execution-time constraint.
$C_2$: Total memory-usage constraint.
$R_k \leftarrow \sum_{i=1}^{n} a_{ik} \times x_i$ for $k = \{1, 2 \ \& \ 3\}$.
**Note**: $R_0$ corresponds to power, $R_1$ corresponds to time & $R_2$ corresponds to memory.

**for** $i = 1$ to $n$ **do**
    $P[i] = (a[i] + \delta_i) / (w_1 \times p_i + w_2 \times e_i + w_3 \times m_i)$;
    $x_i = 0$;
**for** $i = 1$ to $n$ **do**
    Find block with maximum $P[i]$, say $B_j$;
    **if** $R_k + a_{jk} < C_k \ \forall \ k \in \{1, 2, 3\}$ **then**
        $x_i = 1$;
        Update communication costs for $B_{j-1}$ & $B_{j+1}$;
        $R_k = R_k + a_{ij} \ \forall \ k \in \{1, 2, 3\}$;

---

This phase of the algorithm provides an intermediate solution array $X$ (all $x_i's$) which will be used in Phase 2 of PGMA.

**PGMA Phase - 2.** The phase 2 of PGMA is initiated by taking the intermediate solution array (derived from phase 1) and is improved upon to generate better results. For this process, a parameter termed as utility ratio ($UR$) has been defined as follows:

$$UR_i = \left( \frac{a_i}{w_1 \times p_i + w_2 \times e_i + w_3 \times m_i} \right)$$

where $a_i$: area cost of node $B_i$, $p_i$: power cost of node $B_i$, $e_i$: time of execution cost of node $B_i$, $m_i$: memory cost of node $B_i$, and $w_i, w_2, w_3$: weights reflecting importance.

In phase 2, a heuristic repair operator is applied on the non-optimal solution vector from phase 1. This operator consists of two phases: the first part is called DROP phase where each variable (block) is examined in ascending order of utility ratios. Hence, the item being examined is excluded or DROPPED from the solution set if it is infeasible (violating any constraints). On the other side, second part has been referred as ADD phase in which all the items are examined in decreasing order of utility ratios. Here, each item that is not included in the solution for far gets added to the solution set if it does not violate any resource constraints. Therefore, idea behind using the concept of utility ratios is to remove the items with lowest profit per weight ratio and to add items with the highest profit per weight ratio as possible. Finally, the pseudo-code for PGMA phase - 2 has been included in Algorithm 2, as shown below. The solution vector obtained after running this repair operator is the final solution of our work.

---

**Algorithm 2 .** PGMA Phase - 2 (Greedy Repair)

**Inputs**: Intermediate solution vector $X$ sorted by utility ratios.
$X_f$: Final solution vector
$C_1$: Power constraint.
$C_2$: Execution time constraint.
$C_3$: Memory usage constraint.
$R_k \leftarrow \sum_{i=1}^{n} a_{ik} \times x_i$ for $k = \{1, 2 \ \& \ 3\}$.
**Note**: $R_1$ corresponds to power, $R_2$ or corresponds to time, $R_3$ corresponds to memory.

**Note**: $k = 1$ for power factor, $k = 2$ for execution time factor, $k = 3$ for memory usage factor.

$j \leftarrow n$
**DROP Phase**:
**while** $R_k > C_k$ for any $k \in \{1, 2 \ \& \ 3\}$ **do**;
  **if** $x[j] == 1$ **then**
    $x[j] \leftarrow 0$;
    $R_k \leftarrow (R_k - aij) \ \forall \ k \in \{1, 2 \ \& \ 3\}$;
  $j \leftarrow j - 1$;
**ADD Phase**:
**for** $j = 1$ to $n$ **do**
  **if** $x[j] == 0$ and $(R_k + a_{jk}) < C_k \ \forall \ k \in \{1, 2 \ \& \ 3\}$ **then**
    $x[j] \leftarrow 1$;
    $R_k \leftarrow (R_k + aij) \ \forall \ k \in \{1, 2 \ \& \ 3\}$;
$X_f = \{x_0, x_1, x_2 ...... x_n\}$

---

Subsequently, the time complexity analysis of PGMA for both the phases are provided below.

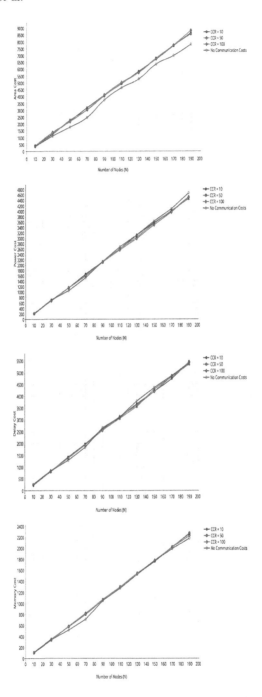

**Fig. 1.** Cost variations with CCR (communication-to-computation ratio)

*Time Complexity*: In phase 1, the communication profits $(\delta_i)$ are calculated in $O(n)$. Subsequently, when the $P[i]$ metrics are calculated, it makes the complexity $O(n^2)$. In phase 2, both ADD and DROP phases run in a $n$-dimensional loop with the worst case of checking for all three constraints. Thereby, this results in the time complexity of $O(3.n)$. Thus, the total time complexity of the algorithm is given by $O(n^2)$.

## 4   Results and Discussion

In this section, a detailed empirical analysis of the proposed algorithm has been carried out. There are no widely accepted benchmarks to compare the performance of different algorithms in HSP, primarily, due to large differences in co-design environments. Thus, the evaluation of algorithms is performed largely based on the experimental results [6,7]. This paper presents an exhaustive empirical analysis to confirm and validate the working of proposed algorithm. The algorithms were implemented in high-level programming language like C and were run on an Intel Core$^{\text{TM}}$ i5-2430M 64-bit, 4 GB RAM host machine. Here, $CCR$ is termed as communication basis (or communication-to-computation ratio) which depicts the relative importance given to communication costs compared to other costs. Smaller values of $CCR$ reflect the coarse granularity (computation intensive) cases, while larger values reflect the fine granularity (communication intensive) cases.

Figure 1 depicts the variation of all four cost parameters with the number of nodes. It shows that there is divergence of each cost when $CCR$ value is increased. In order to compensate for the pseudo-randomness in cost generation, 20 instances are generated and their average is taken as the representative number (cost) for a particular $n$. It can be observed that there is an overall increasing trend in the values of area, power, time of execution and memory requirement as the number of nodes increases. As the effect of communication costs is increased (increased $CCR$) in the reported work [5], the performance of their proposed algorithm degrades. However, here it can be seen that **PGMA** does not loose its effectiveness with the increase in $CCR$.

## 5   Conclusion

In this paper, we solve the problem of HW/SW Partitioning by proposing a high speed algorithm which takes into consideration the communication costs between the hardware and software units. We develop a fast paced partitioning algorithm (with run-time as low as 18 ms for partitioning $n$=1000 blocks) usable at run-time, rather than the traditional design time only use.

# References

1. Arató, P., Mann, Z.Á., Orbán, Á.: Algorithmic aspects of hardware/software partitioning. ACM Trans. Des. Autom. Electron. Syst. (TODAES) **10**(1), 136–156 (2005)
2. Wu, J., Sun, Q., Srikanthan, T.: Algorithmic aspects for multiple-choice hardware/software partitioning. Comput. Oper. Res. **39**(12), 3281–3292 (2012)
3. Li, S.G., Feng, F.J., Hu, H.J., Wang, C., Qi, D.: Hardware/software partitioning algorithm based on genetic algorithm. J. Comput. **9**(6), 1309–1315 (2014)
4. Jiang, Y., Zhang, H., Jiao, X., Song, X., Hung, W.N., Gu, M., Sun, J.: Uncertain model and algorithm for hardware/software partitioning. In: 2012 IEEE Computer Society Annual Symposium on VLSI (ISVLSI), pp. 243–248. IEEE (2012)
5. Wu, J., Srikanthan, T., Chen, G.: Algorithmic aspects of hardware/software partitioning: 1D search algorithms. IEEE Trans. Comput. **59**(4), 532–544 (2010)
6. Wang, G., Gong, W., Kastner, R.: A new approach for task level computational resource bi-partitioning. In: Fifteenth IASTED International Conference on Parallel and Distributed Computing and Systems, vol. 1, pp. 439–444. Citeseer (2003)
7. López-Vallejo, M., López, J.C.: On the hardware-software partitioning problem: system modeling and partitioning techniques. ACM Trans. Des. Autom. Electron. Syst. (TODAES) **8**(3), 269–297 (2003)

# A Framework for Branch Predictor Selection with Aggregation on Multiple Parameters

Moumita Das[1], Ansuman Banerjee[1(✉)], and Bhaskar Sardar[2]

[1] Indian Statistical Institute, Kolkata, India
{moumita.das,ansuman}@isical.ac.in
[2] Jadavpur University, Kolkata, India
bhaskargit@yahoo.co.in

**Abstract.** The performance of a branch predictor is measured not only by the prediction accuracy - parameters like predictor size, energy expenditure, latency of execution play a key role in predictor selection. The task of selecting the best predictor considering all the different parameters, is therefore, a non-trivial one, and is considered one of the foremost challenges. In this paper, we present a framework that systematically addresses this important challenge using the concept of aggregation and unification and makes a predictor selection based on different parameters. We present experimental results of our framework on the Siemens and SPEC 2006 benchmarks.

**Keywords:** Branch prediction · Rank aggregation
Prediction accuracy

## 1 Introduction

Designing efficient dynamic branch predictors that reside inside the processor and are invoked during program execution has always been one of the top priority research tasks in computer architecture. Energy expenditure, number of clock cycles, vary widely across predictors, for the same program. This variability in performance may be due to the fact that these prediction policies are often based on widely different philosophies, have different types and sizes of data structures at run-time, different numbers and slices of the internal registers, alias tables etc. A predictor choice that optimizes all the parameters is therefore, a non-trivial task and the problem of interest in this paper. This motivated us to examine the problem of parameter-driven predictor selection in a multi-objective optimization setting.

In this paper, we propose an aggregation based weighted multi-objective optimization framework that can determine the aggregate rank of predictors in a manner such that individual parameters are well captured. The weights give the user an ability to specify problem specific importance values to the parameters, and our framework can automatically adapt its selection. Traditional approaches to aggregation [6] typically average the impact of individual

© Springer Nature Singapore Pte Ltd. 2017
B. K. Kaushik et al. (Eds.): VDAT 2017, CCIS 711, pp. 69–74, 2017.
https://doi.org/10.1007/978-981-10-7470-7_8

parameters. Considering the fact that the parameters of consideration in our problem context are incomparable and uncorrelated, and therefore, not suitable candidates for averaging-based aggregation, we use the rank aggregation method with the parameters associated with user specific priorities [3].

The framework proposed in this paper may have multiple applications in the branch predictor design context. Our framework can be used to systematically evaluate and compare the performance of a new predictor design with respect to existing ones, considering the different parameters of interest. In the current process, designers typically carry out this benchmarking by examining the performance of the new design individually with respect to the different parameters, along with a comparison with other off-the-shelf predictors. Another important use of our framework can be in the choice of the components to be used in a hybrid predictor design.

## 2   The Predictor Ranking Framework

Our framework takes in the following inputs:

- A set of predictors $\mathcal{P}_1, \mathcal{P}_2, \ldots, \mathcal{P}_n$.
- A set of parameters (accuracy, core energy, latency etc.) $\mathcal{K}_1, \ldots, \mathcal{K}_r$.
- The predictor profiles $\mathcal{R}_1, \mathcal{R}_2, \ldots, \mathcal{R}_n$, where each $\mathcal{R}_i$ corresponds to a predictor $\mathcal{P}_i$ for $i = 1, 2, \ldots, n$. Each $\mathcal{R}_i$ represents a tuple $< \mathcal{K}_1^{(i)}, \mathcal{K}_2^{(i)}, \ldots, \mathcal{K}_r^{(i)} >$ containing the values of the parameters for the predictor $\mathcal{P}_i$.
- For each predictor $\mathcal{P}_i$, each parameter may as well be optionally associated with a weight/priority value $\mathcal{W}_1^{(i)}, \mathcal{W}_2^{(i)}, \ldots, \mathcal{W}_r^{(i)}$.

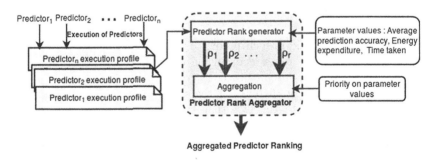

**Fig. 1.** The overall system architecture

Figure 1 shows the overall architecture of our framework. For a given program, the average performance outputs (the values of the parameters of interest) are monitored and stored in a profile database when run with different predictors on a set of designated test inputs. Once the execution profiles are generated through simulation and the parameter values recorded, they are passed on to the aggregation block. We begin by generating the individual parameter based rankings

$\rho_1, \rho_2, \ldots, \rho_r$ of the predictors, where $\rho_i$ corresponds to the rank of the predictor based on the parameter $\mathcal{K}_i$ for $i = 1, 2, \ldots, r$. This is achieved by a sorted ordering of the predictor set based on each parameter. The next step generates an aggregate ranking $\rho_A$ of the predictors considering the individual parameter based rankings $\rho_1, \rho_2, \ldots, \rho_r$ obtained above with the parameters associated with priority values if any. We discuss the two major building blocks of the aggregator below.

## 2.1 Predictor Rank Generator

This block takes as input the parameter values (e.g., prediction accuracy, energy expenditure, latency etc.) of the predictors. The ranking of the predictors with respect to a parameter $\mathcal{K}_i$ is generated by sorting the predictors based on their values of $\mathcal{K}_i$ either in ascending order or in descending order depending on the ordering objective of $\mathcal{K}_i$. The output of this block is a set of ranked lists $\rho_1, \rho_2, \ldots, \rho_r$ for each parameter $\mathcal{K}_1, \mathcal{K}_2, \ldots, \mathcal{K}_r$.

## 2.2 Aggregation

The objective of this piece is to analyze and select the best predictor from the individual parameter based rankings. The number of parameters may be many in number, and hence, generate many ranked lists. To add to this, a predictor may have widely varying rank positions in the different rank lists, thus making the aggregation task even harder. The objective of this stage is to come up with an aggregate ranking considering the individual predictor based rankings. In this work, we propose an Integer Linear Programming (ILP) based optimization formulation to achieve this aggregation, based on Kemeny aggregation [6].

In this Kemeny aggregation method, an aggregate ranked list is generated that minimizes the number of pair-wise disagreements between predictor pairs between the individual rank lists. Intuitively, if a predictor $P_i$ is ranked before a predictor $P_j$ in most of the individual rank lists, the aggregate list should reflect this. For predictors $P_1$ and $P_2$, a binary variable $Z_{P_1 P_2}$ can be defined as:

$$Z_{P_1 P_2} = \begin{cases} 1, & \text{if in the aggregate list, } P_1 \text{ comes before } P_2. \\ 0, & \text{otherwise.} \end{cases}$$

Consider another variable $n_{P_1 P_2}$ which denotes the number of individual parameter rank lists that rank $P_1$ ahead of $P_2$ and $n_{P_2 P_1}$ has a similar interpretation. Such variables are defined for each predictor pair. The objective of aggregation is to come up with an aggregate list that minimizes the number of disagreements with the individual parameter rank lists. This is expressed by the following ILP optimization formulation.

$$\text{Minimize} \sum_{P_1 \neq P_2} n_{P_1 P_2} \times Z_{P_2 P_1}, \text{subject to}$$
$$Z_{P_1 P_2} \in \{0, 1\}, Z_{P_1 P_2} + Z_{P_2 P_1} = 1, and \quad Z_{P_1 P_2} + Z_{P_2 P_3} + Z_{P_3 P_1} \leq 2$$
$$\forall P_1, P_2, P_3 : P_1 \neq P_2, P_1 \neq P_3, P_2 \neq P_3$$

The first constraint states that the $Z_{P_i P_j}$ variables are binary. Constraint 2 expresses for any predictor pair $P_i$, $P_j$, one of them has to be ranked ahead of the other, thus both the binary variables cannot be 0 or 1. The third constraint is the transitivity constraint between predictor triplets. Without this, the aggregate ranking may assign values to the binary variables with a cyclic majority: $P_i$ ahead of $P_j$, $P_j$ ahead of $P_k$, and $P_k$ ahead of $P_i$. The output of the optimization is a value $(0/1)$ for each binary variable $Z_{P_i P_j}$, that leads to the minimum value of the objective, subject to the constraints, and a final aggregate rank list. The top position in the list is the predictor our framework finds to be most suitable, considering all the parameters. In general, predictors in the higher ranks of this list are more suitable candidates than ones in the lower ranks, when all the parameters are considered. Predictor ranking based on weighted Kemeny method can be formulated in the similar way.

# 3    Experimental Results

## 3.1    Experimental Setup

In this paper, we used the Tejas Architectural simulator [9]. For this experiment, we used six single stream dynamic branch predictors - GShare, GAg, GAp, PAp, TAGE and Bimodal. We fixed the storage budget for all these predictors as given in the Championship Branch Prediction competitions (CBP) [1]. We used a maximum storage budget of 32KB and modified the predictor designs present inside the simulator codebase to perform with this constraint. We report our experiments of running Tejas simulations on the Siemens benchmark programs [2] and the SPEC CPU 2006 [4] benchmarks.

## 3.2    Results on Siemens and SPEC 2006 Benchmarks

Table 1 shows the three different rank lists generated by the Predictor Rank Generator component of our framework for six predictors. For every individual predictor, these rank lists were prepared based on three different parameter values - the average prediction accuracy, processor core energy expenditure, and latency/time taken, as discussed in Sect. 2. It is interesting to note that the rank lists are different. The aggregated rank list for each program is generated by the aggregator component based on all the three parameters, both with and without priorities as shown in Table 1. Results show that there is quite a difference between the aggregated lists for each program with and without considering priorities. Therefore, we show both in our results below.

# 4    Related Work

Researchers have extensively explored the role of a branch predictor considering the energy/performance tradeoff for processor design [8]. In [5], researchers

**Table 1.** Aggregated rank lists for Siemens (replace, totinfo) and SPEC 2006 (403.gcc, 400.perlbench)benchmarks

| Benchmark programs | Predictor rank lists | | | Aggregated list | | | |
| --- | --- | --- | --- | --- | --- | --- | --- |
| | Average prediction Acc (%) | Core energy (nanojoule) | Execution time (micro second) | Unweighted method | Weighted methods | | |
| | | | | | Acc:0.5 CoreEn:0.0 Time:0.5 | Acc:1.0 CoreEn:0.0 Time:0.0 | Acc:0.4 CoreEn:0.3 Time:0.3 |
| replace | TAGE | TAGE | GAp | TAGE | TAGE | TAGE | TAGE |
| | Bimodal | GAg | GAg | GAg | GAg | Bimodal | GAg |
| | GAg | GAp | Bimodal | GAp | Bimodal | GAg | GAp |
| | GShare | PAp | PAp | Bimodal | GShare | GShare | Bimodal |
| | GAp | GShare | TAGE | PAp | GAp | GAp | PAp |
| | PAp | Bimodal | GShare | GShare | PAp | PAp | GShare |
| totinfo | TAGE | Bimodal | TAGE | TAGE | TAGE | TAGE | TAGE |
| | GShare | GAp | PAp | Bimodal | GAp | GShare | Bimodal |
| | GAg | GAg | GAp | GAp | PAp | GAg | GAp |
| | Bimodal | GShare | Bimodal | GShare | GAg | Bimodal | GShare |
| | GAp | PAp | GShare | GAg | GAg | GAp | GAg |
| | PAp | TAGE | GAg | PAp | TAGE | PAp | PAp |
| 403.gcc | GShare | GAg | GAg | GAg | GAg | GShare | GAg |
| | GAg | TAGE | TAGE | TAGE | TAGE | GAg | TAGE |
| | GAp | Bimodal | GAp | GAp | GAp | GAp | GAp |
| | TGE | GAp | GShare | GShare | GShare | TAGE | GShare |
| | Bimodal | PAp | Bimodal | Bimodal | Bimodal | Bimodal | Bimodal |
| | PAp | GShare | PAp | PAp | PAp | PAp | PAp |
| 400.perlbench | TAGE | PAp | TAGE | TAGE | TAGE | TAGE | TAGE |
| | Bimodal | GAp | GAp | GAp | Bimodal | Bimodal | GAp |
| | GAp | TAGE | Bimodal | Bimodal | GAp | GAp | Bimodal |
| | GShare | GAg | GShare | GShare | GShare | GShare | GShare |
| | GAg | GShare | GAg | GAg | GAg | GAg | GAg |
| | PAp | Bimodal | PAp | PAp | PAp | PAp | PAp |

showed that a branch predictor design optimized for accuracy can have a negative impact on overall instructions per clock (IPC) when the wire delays or the clock rates increase. The rank aggregation method helps to combine many different rank orderings on the same set of candidates or alternatives to achieve a better ordering [3, 7] that minimizes the disagreements between the individual ones.

# 5  Conclusion

The motivation behind this work was to come up with a systematic exploration framework that can consider multiple performance parameters and find the aggregated rank of every predictor for a program. We believe that our framework can be of great value for evaluating a new prediction policy.

# References

1. The journal of instruction-level parallelism, championship branch prediction. https://www.jilp.org/cbp/
2. Software artifacts repository. http://sir.unl.edu/portal/index.php
3. Ghosh, R., et al.: CoCOA: a framework for comparing aggregate client operations in BPO services. In: SCC, pp. 539–546. IEEE (2016)
4. Henning, J.L.: SPEC CPU2006 benchmark descriptions. ACM SIGARCH Comput. Architect. News **34**(4), 1–17 (2006)
5. Jiménez, D.A., et al.: The impact of delay on the design of branch predictors. In: MICRO, pp. 67–76. ACM (2000)
6. Kemeny, J.G.: Mathematics without numbers. Daedalus **88**(4), 577–591 (1959)
7. Liu, Y.T., et al.: Supervised rank aggregation. In: WWW, pp. 481–490. ACM (2007)
8. Parikh, D., et al.: Power issues related to branch prediction. In: HPCA, pp. 233–244. IEEE (2002)
9. Sarangi, S.R., et al.: Tejas: a java based versatile micro-architectural simulator. In: PATMOS 2015, pp. 47–54. IEEE (2015)

# FPGA Implementation of a Novel Area Efficient FFT Scheme Using Mixed Radix FFT

Thilagavathy R, Susmitha Settivari$^{(\boxtimes)}$, Venkataramani B$^{(\boxtimes)}$,
and Bhaskar M$^{(\boxtimes)}$

Department of ECE, NIT Trichy, Tiruchirappalli, India
thilagavathy_77@yahoo.co.in,
susmitha.settivari@gmail.com,
{bvenki,bhaskar}@nitt.edu

**Abstract.** In the literature, mixed radix FFT scheme has been proposed to facilitate the computation of FFT in parallel using multiple lower radix FFT modules. Alternately, the speed of the FFT can be increased using Radix-2 decimation-in-frequency (DIF) FFT algorithm with Multipath Delay Commutator (R2MDC) architecture. In this paper, a novel FFT scheme which combines the R2MDC architecture with the serial version of mixed radix FFT scheme is proposed. To study the efficacy of this approach, an 8-point FFT is implemented using R2MDC architecture. Using this, 16-point, 32-point and 64-point FFTs are realized with the serial version of mixed radix scheme and also using only R2MDC architecture on Xilinx Virtex-5 FPGA. From the implementation results, it is found that the hardware requirement for the proposed approach reduces by 25%–53% at the cost of speed compared to the other schemes reported in the literature including that using only R2MDC architecture. The proposed scheme is preferred for low sampling rate applications such as biomedical signal processing.

**Keywords:** Composite-Radix FFT · Field Programmable Gate Array (FPGA) Modular FFT · Radix- 2 DIF FFT · Verilog HDL

## 1 Introduction

Discrete Fourier Transform (DFT) [1] is the basis for performing Fourier analysis in many applications such as digital communication, speech/image processing and radar signal processing [2]. The number of arithmetic operations required for computing DFT reduces from $O(N^2)$ to $O(N\log_2 N)$ using the FFT algorithm [3].

FFT can be used to extract different frequencies in the biomedical signal from its time domain representation [4]. For biomedical signals, the sampling rates are of the order of few kilo samples/second. Hence the FFT algorithms which are area efficient but not speed can be employed for them in order to reduce the cost.

Field Programmable Gate Arrays (FPGAs) may be used for the computation of FFT. High throughput and simple synchronization control using multiple data paths can be achieved by different multi-path delay commutator (MDC) architectures proposed in [5]. In view of this, it is adopted in this paper for the FPGA implementation of an

© Springer Nature Singapore Pte Ltd. 2017
B. K. Kaushik et al. (Eds.): VDAT 2017, CCIS 711, pp. 75–80, 2017.
https://doi.org/10.1007/978-981-10-7470-7_9

8-point FFT. A serial implementation scheme for the mixed radix FFT is also proposed in this paper and it is combined with R2MDC architecture to achieve area efficiency.

## 2  Mixed Radix FFT and the Concept of Modularity

Mixed radix FFT algorithm, a variation of Cooley-Tukey algorithm, realizes a DFT of composite size which has more than one factor which may include prime numbers. It can also be implemented using DIT and DIF algorithms. In this paper, mixed radix FFT with DIT algorithm is implemented. In this algorithm, the number of points, N is decomposed into factors such as $N = p_1.p_2.p_3...p_r$.

If $N = p_1.N_1$, where $N_1 = p_2.p_3...p_r$, then the input sequence x(n) can be separated into $p_1$ subsequences of $N_1$ points each. The N point DFT can be written as [6]:

$$X(k) = \sum_{n=0}^{N_1-1} x(np_1)W_N^{np_1k} + ... + \sum_{n=0}^{N_1-1} x(np_1+p_1-1)W_N^{(np_1+p_1-1)k} \tag{1}$$

For example, let N = 32 then $N = p_1 * N_1$ where $p_1 = 4$ and $N_1 = 8$. Using the four subsequences with 8 elements each, $X(k)$ is given by:

$$X(k) = X_1(k) + X_2(k)W_{32}^k + X_3(k)W_{32}^{2k} + X_4(k)W_{32}^{3k} \tag{2}$$

where,

$$X_i(k) = \sum_{n=0}^{7} x(4n+i-1)W_8^{nk}, 1 < i < 4 \tag{3}$$

It is observed from (2) and (3) that 32-point DFT is divided into four small DFTs of 8-point each. Here, the concept of modularity can be used so that a single 8-point FFT block (base module) can be re-used to generate the DFTs of all four subsequences.

As point size increases, the base module is re-used based on number of subsequences ($p_1$) i.e. '$p_1$' times. In this paper, base module is considered as 8-point FFT but any sized FFT can be used to implement large point DFT by modularity.

## 3  Design Methodology of Modular FFT

The block diagram of modular FFT for 32-point DFT is shown in Fig. 1

**FFT-8 block:** The FFT-8 module (base module) forms the heart of the Modular FFT system. It is an 8-point FFT block designed using the R2MDC DIF FFT architecture as mentioned in [5] with the serial input replaced by a ROM providing two inputs in parallel to butterfly stage 1 (BFI) block (2-parallel R2MDC). It is designed to be modular so that it can be reused to find the FFT of larger length by feeding subsequences of length 8, one after the other. The base module has been designed using the pipelined architecture to compensate for the reduction in the speed due to the serial implementation scheme used for the larger FFT block.

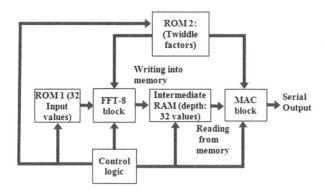

**Fig. 1.** Modular FFT block diagram for 32-point DFT

The output from FFT-8 block comes after four clock cycles due to the R2MDC architecture and thereafter after every clock cycle, the output is obtained. The output is written into RAM accordingly in N/2 clock cycles

**ROM/RAM:** The input samples required for N = 32 point DFT and the precomputed twiddle factors required for FFT-8 and MAC blocks are stored in ROM 1 and ROM 2 respectively. The complex input values are generated using MATLAB. Real part and imaginary part of the input data and the twiddle factors are represented using 16-bit signed binary form.

RAM is used to store intermediate results generated by the FFT-8 block. In this paper, True Dual-port RAM block is used to write and read from the memory in the same clock cycle. Once the DFTs of all four subsequences are calculated and written into RAM, the write enable is deactivated and the read enable is activated so as to fetch data from memory and feed forward to the MAC block.

**Control Logic Unit:** All modules in the block diagram are synchronized with a clock and reset signal which are generated from the Control Logic Unit.

Initially, the counter denoted as write counter is initialized and the input data is read from the ROM 1 as per (3), using the count value as address and fed into FFT-8 block. Simultaneously, the twiddle factors required for the different butterfly stages are read from ROM 2 and fed into FFT-8 block. The address to fetch the twiddle factors are taken from the lower bits of count value.

The output data from FFT-8 block is in bit-reversed order. But the data is written into RAM in the proper order. A second counter called read counter is initialized to generate address to fetch data from RAM and feed into the MAC block. This counter operates when read enable is made high. The twiddle factors required in the MAC block as per (2) are also fetched using the read counter as address.

**MAC Block:** MAC block gets the data from RAM which is multiplied with the twiddle factors and accumulated as per (2) and generates the output.

In this paper, the MAC block is designed using both multiple MAC blocks in parallel and also using a single MAC unit. Either Single MAC or multiple MACs may be chosen based on Area/Speed requirement. In multiple MAC as per (2), three multiply and accumulate units are required to get the final output. The latency is (N/2 + N) clock cycles. But this count doubles as the point size increases and more resources are utilized. For resource minimization, single MAC design is proposed and only one MAC unit is used to obtain the output at the cost of a latency of (N/2 + N * $p_1$) clock cycles.

## 4  FPGA Implementation Results

All the modules in Fig. 1 are coded in Xilinx ISE Design Suite in Verilog HDL, simulated and synthesized using Xilinx Virtex-5 XC5VLX110T-2ff1136 FPGA Device.

The modular FFT implementation is carried out for N = 16, 32 and 64 points using 8-point FFT as base module. Table 1 provides the summary of resource utilization of 16, 32 and 64 points implemented with three different approaches namely full length 2- parallel R2MDC architecture, Modular FFT with multiple MAC and modular FFT

**Table 1.** Resource utilization summary in Virtex-5 FPGA device

| N | FFT Design | Registers | LUTs | IOBs | BRAM | DSP | Latency |
|---|---|---|---|---|---|---|---|
| 8 | 2-parallel R2MDC | 196 | 6,480 | 68 | 8 | 4 | 8 |
| 16 | 2-parallel R2MDC | 454 | 11,854 | 69 | 6 | 8 | 16 |
| | Modular FFT[a] | 782 | 8,019 | 38 | 9 | 8 | 24 |
| | Modular FFT[b] | 783 | 7,802 | 38 | 6 | 8 | 40 |
| 32 | 2-parallel R2MDC | 970 | 14,554 | 70 | 6 | 12 | 32 |
| | Modular FFT[a] | 1,360 | 12,548 | 39 | 11 | 16 | 48 |
| | Modular FFT[b] | 1,300 | 8,866 | 39 | 7 | 8 | 144 |
| 64 | 2-parallel R2MDC | 1,998 | 22,122 | 71 | 8 | 16 | 64 |
| | Modular FFT[a] | 2,516 | 22,474 | 41 | 16 | 32 | 96 |
| | Modular FFT[b] | 2,326 | 10,408 | 40 | 6 | 8 | 544 |

[a]Proposed Modular FFT with multiple MAC
[b]Proposed Modular FFT with single MAC

**Table 2.** Comparison of reduction in resources in Table 1

| N | Architecture | LUTs | IOBs | BRAM | DSP |
|---|---|---|---|---|---|
| 16 | Reduction[a] | 34% | 45% | – | – |
| | Reduction[b] | – | – | 33% | – |
| 32 | Reduction[a] | 39% | 44% | – | 33% |
| | Reduction[b] | 29% | – | 36% | 50% |
| 64 | Reduction[a] | 53% | 44% | 25% | 50% |
| | Reduction[b] | 54% | – | 62.5% | 75% |

[a]Percentage reduction in resources using
Single MAC compared to 2-parallel R2MDC
[b]Percentage reduction in resources using
Single MAC compared to Multiple MAC

with single MAC. It is observed that modular FFT with single MAC design has reduced hardware utilization. The percentage reduction in resources are given in Table 2.

Table 3 gives the comparison results of the proposed designs with that reported in [7]. To compare with [7], the designs are simulated in Virtex-6 FPGA, but Virtex-5 FPGA will suffice because of less resource utilization of proposed architecture. The N-point DFT computation through DIT FFT algorithm requires $(N/2)\log_2 N$ complex multiplications and a complex multiplier requires 4 real multiplications. Hence the number of DSPs in [7] are 128 for 16-point and 320 for 32-point FFT respectively compared to the proposed architecture. It is observed that with the proposed modular FFT architecture, the hardware utilization is very less.

The speed of the modular approach is reduced by a factor $(p_1 + 0.5)$ (the no. of subsequences each of length N1) compared to that of the direct approach using only 2-parallel R2MDC architecture.

**Table 3.** Comparison results of proposed design with earlier work in Virtex-6 FPGA device

| N & data width | FFT Design | Slices (Used (%)) | Fully used LUT-FF pairs (Used (%)) | IOBs (Used (%)) | DSPs (Used (%)) |
|---|---|---|---|---|---|
| 16 | [7] | 2,402 (0%) | 295 (12%) | 51 (4%) | 128 (14%) |
|  | Modular FFT[a] | 781 (0%) | 436 (5%) | 38 (3%) | 8 (1%) |
|  | Modular FFT[b] | 784 (0%) | 439 (5%) | 38 (3%) | 8 (1%) |
| 32 | [7] | 5,620 (1%) | 545 (9%) | 99 (8%) | 320 (37%) |
|  | Modular FFT[a] | 2,763 (1%) | 2,577 (16%) | 71 (5%) | 48 (5%) |
|  | Modular FFT[b] | 532 (1%) | 333 (4%) | 72 (6%) | 24 (2%) |

[a]Proposed Modular FFT with multiple MAC
[b]Proposed Modular FFT with single MAC

## 5 Conclusions

In this paper, a modular approach to build large point DFTs using small point FFTs has been proposed. The proposed modular approach has less hardware complexity and resource utilization than direct FFT implementation. It can also be extended to large points without vast increase in hardware utilization. Depending on the latency requirement, one can choose multiple MAC or single MAC implementation of the proposed modular FFT.

# References

1. Oppenheim, A.V., Schafer, R.W., Buck, J.R.: Discrete-Time Signal Processing, 2nd edn. Prentice-Hall, NJ (1998)
2. Rao, K.R., Kim, D.N., Hwang, J.J.: Fast Fourier Transform: Algorithms and Applications. Signals and Communication Technology. Springer, Dordrecht (2010). https://doi.org/10.1007/978-1-4020-6629-0
3. Zonst, A.E.: Understanding the FFT, A Tutorial on the Algorithm and Software for Laymen. Citrus press
4. Yang, L., Chen, T.W.: A low power 64-point bit-serial FFT engine for implantable biomedical applications. In: Euromicro Conference on Digital System Design (DSD), pp. 383–389, August 2015
5. Ayinala, M., Brown, M., Parhi, K.K.: Pipelined parallel FFT architectures via folding transformation. IEEE Trans. Very Large Scale Integr. (VLSI) Syst. **20**(6), 1068–1081 (2012)
6. Xiao, Y., Zhao, W., Chen, L., Huang, S., Wang, Q.: Fast Quasi-synchronous harmonic algorithm based on weight window function — mixed radix FFT. In: 2016 IEEE International Workshop on Applied Measurements for Power Systems (AMPS), pp. 1–6, September 2016
7. Saenz, S.J., Raygoza, J.J., Becerra, E.C., Cisneros, S.O., Dominguez, J.R.: FPGA design and implementation of radix-2 fast fourier transform algorithm with 16 and 32 points. In: 2015 IEEE International Autumn Meeting on Power Electronics and Computing (ROPEC), pp. 1–6, November 2015

# Analog/Mixed Signal

# Low Voltage, Low Power Transconductor for Low Frequency $G_m$-C Filters

Hanumantha Rao G.$^{(\boxtimes)}$ and Rekha S.

Department of Electronics and Communication Engineering, NITK Surathkal,
Mangalore, India
hanu.vnk@gmail.com, rsbhat_99@yahoo.com

**Abstract.** A low voltage, low power bulk-driven transconductor for low frequency Transconductance-C ($G_m - C$) filters is proposed. The transconductor is designed in UMC 180 nm technology with supply voltage of 0.5 V. The transconductance ($G_m$) is tunable from 12 nS to 100 nS, which is suitable for low frequency $G_m - C$ filters. The power consumption is 120 nW. As an application, a $2^{nd}$ order Butterworth low pass filter (LPF) with cutoff frequency tunable from 110 Hz to 960 Hz is designed.

**Keywords:** Bulk-driven · Low-voltage · Low-power
Low-frequency filters

## 1 Introduction

Continuous time (CT) filters are one of the important building blocks of analog pre-processing in wearable and implantable medical devices such as heart rate detectors, breathing detectors, cardiac-pacemakers, cochlear implants etc. They are used to limit the frequency band and to eliminate the out-of-band noise. As the signals involved in the above mentioned applications are of low frequency, typically 10 mHz to 10 KHz [1], it is mandatory to design such filters with low cutoff frequency. The other major requirements of these filters are low power consumption, low noise and less area as these medical devices are portable and battery operated.

The popular topologies of CT filters are Active-RC and $G_m - C$ structures. To design Active-RC filters with low cutoff frequency, large resistors and capacitors are required, which occupy a large area on the chip. Hence, simple Active-RC filters are not suitable for low frequencies. However, certain circuit techniques have been developed such as current steering [2,3], Pseudo resistor based Active-RC filter [4,5], R-2R ladder network [6,7] based filter etc., for low frequencies. But all these techniques have their own limitations as far as power, area, thermal noise, high sensitivity to changes in bias voltage etc., are concerned. In general, $G_m - C$ filters are preferred over Active-RC filters for low frequencies.

In $G_m - C$ filters, the cutoff frequency is determined by $\frac{G_m}{2\pi C}$. To get low cutoff frequency, either $G_m$ should be low or capacitor should be large. But,

B. K. Kaushik et al. (Eds.): VDAT 2017, CCIS 711, pp. 83–92, 2017.
https://doi.org/10.1007/978-981-10-7470-7_10

large capacitors occupy more area on the chip. By using impedance scaler circuits [8,9] the capacitance value can be increased with less silicon area. But these circuits not only consume extra power but also produce extra noise. Therefore, a transconductor with small $G_m$ is preferred for the realization of low frequency filters. Current division and current cancellation techniques to reduce $G_m$ are reported in [9,10]. These techniques require more power and suffer from offset voltage. Floating-gate transistors [11,12] capacitively attenuate the input voltage and reduce the $G_m$. But, these transistors occupy more silicon area and need extra processing steps.

According to ITRS-2015 (International Technology Road map for Semiconductors), by about the year 2024, the power supply for digital circuits will be at 0.55 V. The main motive for this scaling of supply voltage is to reduce the dynamic power of digital logic circuits. Analog circuits have to work with these low supply voltages as they exist along with digital circuits in a typical System-on-chip (SoC). But the supply voltage scaling in analog circuits, results in the reduction of signal swing, and hence reduces dynamic range. As the threshold voltage ($V_{th}$) of the transistors is scaled at a slower rate than supply voltage, this problem is magnified. Thus, the existing analog circuits should be modified in order to have the same or even better performance under low voltage conditions.

In order to avoid above mentioned problems, bulk-driven transistors [13] can be used, where the signal is applied to the bulk terminal rather than the gate terminal. This reduces the $V_{th}$ of transistor and allows rail-to-rail input voltage swing even under low supply voltages such as 0.5 V. The bulk transconductance is typically 0.2–0.4 times that of gate transconductance, which is the major requirement for the low frequency $G_m - C$ filters. The transconductance can be reduced further by current scaling circuits. Therefore, a low voltage, low power transconductor with low $G_m$ can be realized by using bulk-driven input transistors and current scaling circuits.

This paper proposes the design of fully differential tunable bulk-driven transconductor. As an application a $2^{nd}$ order Butterworth LPF is designed to demonstrate the performance of the transconductor. The rest of the paper is organized as follows. In Sect. 2, design of tunable bulk-driven transconductor is discussed. Section 3 deals with the simulation results. Finally conclusions are drawn in Sect. 4.

## 2    Transconductor Design

### 2.1    Tunable Bulk-Driven Transconductor

A tunable single ended bulk-driven transconductor is shown in Fig. 1, where $V_{in}$ and $V_o$ represent input and output voltages respectively. $V_{in}$ is given to the bulk terminal of the input transistor $M_1$. $I_{in}$ represents the current of transistor $M_1$ and $I_o$ represents the output current. The transistor $M_1$ is biased by a constant current of 10 nA that is mirrored by constant current source $I_{DC}$. $M_2$ mirrors the current $I_{in}$ to $M_3$ through Variable Gain Current Mirror [14] with a current gain K.

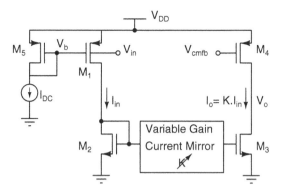

**Fig. 1.** Tunable single ended bulk-driven transconductor

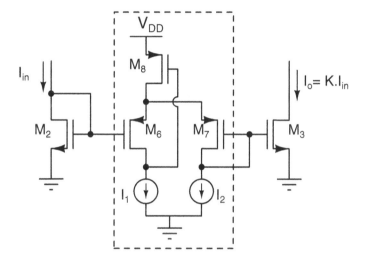

**Fig. 2.** Variable gain current mirror

The Variable Gain Current Mirror circuit is shown in Fig. 2. The currents $I_1$ and $I_2$ are generated from a reference current source (not shown in Figure). $M_2$, $M_3$, $M_6$ and $M_7$ are biased in the weak-inversion region and form trans-linear loop [15]. The relation among the gate-source voltages of $M_2$, $M_3$, $M_6$ and $M_7$ can be expressed as (1).

$$V_{GS2} + V_{SG6} = V_{SG7} + V_{GS3} \qquad (1)$$

For an NMOS transistor operating in weak-inversion region, the drain current can be written as

$$I_{Dn} = A_n e^{B_n (V_{GSn} - V_{tn})} \left(1 - e^{\frac{-V_{DSn}}{V_T}}\right) \qquad (2)$$

where,

$$A_n = \mu_n C_{ox} \frac{W}{L}(m_n - 1)V_T^2$$

$$B_n = \frac{1}{m_n V_T}$$

$V_T = \frac{kT}{q}$, is the volt-equivalent of temperature and $m_n$ is sub-threshold slope factor and its value lies between 1.1 and 1.4. For $V_{DSn} \geq 4V_T$, the current $I_{Dn}$ can be assumed to be independent of $V_{DSn}$ i.e. $(1 - e^{-\frac{V_{DSn}}{V_T}}) \approx 1$. Then (2) can be simplified to (3).

$$I_{Dn} \approx A_n e^{B_n(V_{GSn} - V_{tn})} \tag{3}$$

Similarly, the drain current for a PMOS can be written as (4)

$$I_{Dp} \approx A_p e^{B_p(V_{SGp} - |V_{tp}|)} \tag{4}$$

From the Eqs. (3) and (4), $V_{GSn}$ and $V_{SGp}$ can be derived as (5) and (6) respectively.

$$V_{GSn} = \frac{1}{B_n} \ln(\frac{I_n}{A_n}) + V_{tn} \tag{5}$$

$$V_{SGp} = \frac{1}{B_p} \ln(\frac{I_p}{A_p}) + |V_{tp}| \tag{6}$$

The transistors $M_2$, $M_3$ and $M_6$, $M_7$ in the Fig. 2 are matched. By substituting (5) and (6) in (1), the relation among the currents $I_{in}$, $I_o$, $I_1$ and $I_2$ can be derived as (7)

$$I_o = K.I_{in} \tag{7}$$

where $K = (\frac{I_1}{I_2})^{\frac{m_p}{m_n}}$ is the current gain.

When $I_1 = I_2$, the current gain is 1 as $V_{SG6} = V_{SG7}$, $V_{GS2} = V_{GS3}$. When $I_1 > I_2$, the current gain is $>1$ as $V_{SG6} > V_{SG7}$, $V_{GS2} < V_{GS3}$. When $I_1 < I_2$, the reverse is true and the current gain is $< 1$. Therefore the output current of the transconductor can be scaled by varying the currents $I_1$ or $I_2$, which in turn scales the effective transconductance of the circuit.

## 2.2   Fully Differential Bulk-Driven Transconductor

A fully differential tunable bulk-driven transconductor is shown in Fig. 3. The input transistors $M_1$ and $M_2$ are biased by using a current source of 10 nA (not shown in the Figure). $M_5$-$M_{10}$ and current sources $I_1$, $I_2$ form Variable Gain Current Mirror. All the transistors are operating in weak-inversion region. $C_c$ is used as compensating capacitor to improve the phase margin.

The output differential current, $i_{od}$ is given by (8)

$$i_{od} = K.g_{mb}.v_{id} \tag{8}$$

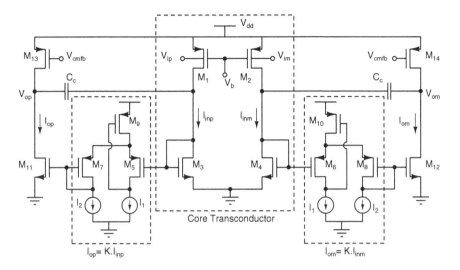

**Fig. 3.** Fully differential bulk-driven transconductor

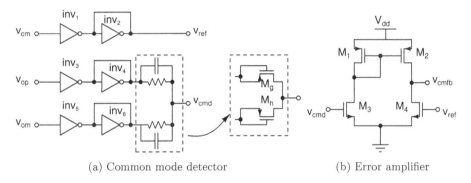

(a) Common mode detector               (b) Error amplifier

**Fig. 4.** CMFB circuit [16]

where $i_{od} = I_{op} - I_{om}$ is the output differential current, $g_{mb}$ is the bulk-driven transconductance of the input transistor $M_1$ or $M_2$ and $v_{id} = V_{ip} - V_{im}$ is the input differential voltage.

The effective transconductance $G_m$ is given by (9)

$$G_m = K.g_{mb} \qquad (9)$$

The voltage gain of the transconductor is given by (10)

$$A_v = K.g_{mb}.(r_{11} \parallel r_{13}) \qquad (10)$$

where $r_{11}$ and $r_{13}$ are small signal output resistances of $M_{11}$ and $M_{13}$ respectively.

The transconductor uses a supply voltage of 0.5 V. The input common mode voltage ($V_{cm}$) is fixed at 0.25 V. Gates of $M_{13}$ and $M_{14}$ are biased with a common mode feedback voltage ($V_{cmfb}$) which sets the output common mode voltage to 0.25 V. A common mode feedback (CMFB) circuit proposed in [16] (Fig. 4) is used in this work. In Fig. 4(a), inverters 3 to 6 along with transistors $M_g$ and $M_h$ form common mode detector. Inverters 3 and 5 sense the output voltages of the transconductor. Inverters 4 and 6 have their outputs shorted to inputs. This arrangement reduces the gain of sensing inverters, thus enhancing the linearity of the sensing inverters and entire CMFB circuit. Transistors $M_g$ and $M_h$ are connected such that they offer high resistance along with a capacitor. This arrangement gives the average ($V_{cmd}$) of the sensed voltages. $V_{cmd}$ is compared with the reference voltage $V_{ref}$ using a simple error amplifier shown in Fig. 4(b). The error amplifier output voltage $V_{cmfb}$ is fed back to the transconductor to set the output common mode to the reference voltage ($V_{cm}$).

## 3   Simulation Results

The transconductor is designed and simulated in UMC 180 nm technology. $G_m$ tuning of the transconductor is done by varying $I_1$ from 2 nA to 18 nA by fixing $I_2$ at 10 nA. This varies the current gain, K and hence $G_m$. The simulated $G_m$ against the input differential voltage for different $I_1$ values is shown in Fig. 5. $G_m$ is tuned from 12 nS to 100 nS by fixing $I_2$ at 10 nA and varying $I_1$ from 2 nA to 18 nA in steps of 4 nA. The values of $I_1$ and $I_2$ can be digitally controlled by using current splitting circuits implemented as in [17]. It is observed that an equal increment in $I_1$, gives almost an equal increment in $G_m$.

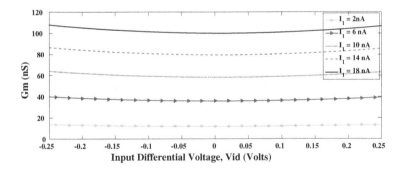

**Fig. 5.** $G_m$ tuning

The magnitude and phase response of the proposed transconductor are shown in Fig. 6. The open loop DC gain is 30.3 dB, unity-gain frequency is 4.6 KHz and the phase margin is 80°. To test the linearity, the transconductor is connected in unity feedback configuration. The total harmonic distortion (THD) is less than −40 dB for an input signal of 1 $V_{pp}$ differential. Table 1 lists the parameters of the proposed transconductor. A performance comparison of the proposed transconductor with other similar works found in the literature is given in Table 2. It can

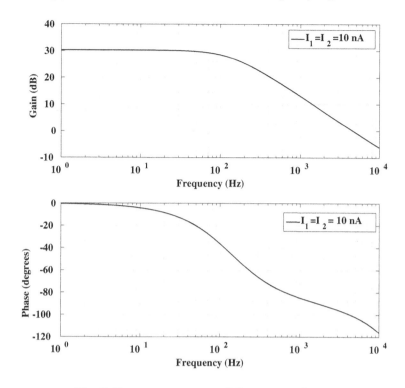

**Fig. 6.** Frequency response of the transconductor

**Table 1.** Parameters of the transconductor

| Parameter | Simulated values |
|---|---|
| Technology ($\mu$m) | 0.18 |
| Supply voltage (volts) | 0.5 |
| Transconductance (nS) | 12–100 |
| DC Gain(dB) | 30.3 |
| UGB (KHz) | 4.6 |
| Phase margin (degrees) | 80 |
| $V_{in-pp}$ for 1% THD (volts) | 1.0 |
| Input referred noise at 100 Hz ($\dfrac{\mu V}{\sqrt{Hz}}$) | 3.6 |
| Input referred noise from 50 Hz–5 KHz ($\mu V$) | 50 |
| Dynamic range (dB) | 77 |
| Power (nW) | 120[a] |

[a] At $I_1 = 18$ nA and $I_2 = 10$ nA, including CMFB

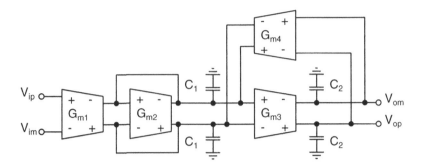

**Fig. 7.** $G_m - C$ biquad

**Table 2.** Comparison of the proposed transconductor with other similar works

| Parameters | [14] | [18] | [12] | [19] | This work |
|---|---|---|---|---|---|
| Technology ($\mu$m) | 0.18 | 0.35 | 0.8 | 1.2 | 0.18 |
| Supply voltage (volts) | 0.8 | 0.8 | 1.5 | 1.35 | 0.5 |
| DC gain (dB) | 72.2 | 61 | - | - | 30.3 |
| $G_m$ (nS) | 300–3000 | 66 n | 0.46–82 | 16.6 | 12–100 |
| UGB (KHz) | 15 with $C_L$=20 pF | 0.195 with $C_L$=25 pF | - | - | 4.6 |
| Phase margin (degrees) | 90 | 81 | - | - | 80 |
| Input referred noise ($\mu V RMS$) | - | 80 | 110 | 17.29 | 50 |
| $V_{in-pp}$ for 1% THD (volts) | 1.6 | 0.1 | 1.2 | 0.24 | 1 |
| Dynamic range (dB) | 75 | 52.9 | 73 | 73.9 | 77 |
| Power ($\mu$W) | 8.3 | 0.040 | $\approx$1 | 1.35 | 0.12 |

be seen that, performance of the proposed transconductor is better in terms of power and $G_m$ tunability. Hence, it can be very efficiently used for low voltage, low frequency filters.

A fully differential $2^{nd}$ order Butterworth LPF, shown in Fig. 7 [20], is designed and simulated to evaluate the performance of the proposed transconductor. The cutoff frequency of the filter is tuned from 110 Hz to 960 Hz as shown in Fig. 8. The filter cutoff frequency can be tuned to the required value by controlling the currents $I_1$ and $I_2$, so that it fits into the desired frequency range of different bio-potentials such as electromyogram (EMG), electroencephalogram (EEG), electrocardiogram (ECG) etc.

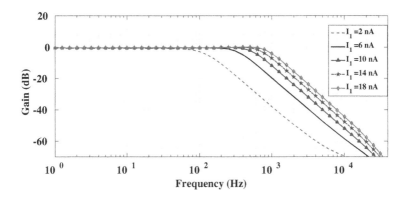

**Fig. 8.** Frequency response of the filter

## 4    Conclusion

A fully differential low voltage, low power bulk-driven transconductor for low frequency $G_m - C$ filters is presented. It offers 30.3 dB DC gain, 4.6 KHz unity gain frequency and 80° phase margin. The transconductor consumes a power of 120 nW with 0.5 V supply. A $2^{nd}$ order Butterwoth LPF with the cutoff frequency tunable from 110 Hz to 960 Hz is designed as an application of the proposed transconductor. By adjusting the currents $I_1$ and $I_2$, the cutoff frequency can be tuned to fit into the desired frequency range of different bio-potentials. Filter response closely matches with ideal $2^{nd}$ order filter response upto an attenuation of 60 dB.

**Acknowledgment.** The authors would like to thank Department of Information Technology, MCIT, Government of India, for the necessary tool support provided to carry out this work under SMDP, VLSI project.

## References

1. Webster, J.: Medical Instrumentation: Application and Design. Wiley, Hoboken (2009)
2. Wong, A., Pun, K.-P., Zhang, Y.-T., Hung, K.: A near-infrared heart rate measurement IC with very low cutoff frequency using current steering technique. IEEE Trans. Circ. Syst. I Regul. Pap. **52**(12), 2642–2647 (2005)
3. Li, H., Zhang, J., Wang, L.: 5 mHz highpass filter with-80 dB total harmonic distortions. IET Electron. Lett. **48**(12), 698–699 (2012)
4. Shiue, M.-T., Yao, K.-W., Gong, C.-S.A.: Tunable high resistance voltage-controlled pseudo-resistor with wide input voltage swing capability. Electron. Lett. **47**(6), 377 (2011)

5. Tajalli, A., Leblebici, Y.: Power and area efficient MOSFET-C filter for very low frequency applications. Analog Integr. Circ. Signal Process. **70**(1), 123–132 (2012)
6. Alzaher, H.A., Tasadduq, N., Mahnashi, Y.: A highly linear fully integrated powerline filter for biopotential acquisition systems. IEEE Trans. Biomed. Circ. Syst. **7**(5), 703–712 (2013)
7. Roy, S.D.: On resistive ladder networks for use in ultra-low frequency active-RC filters. Circ. Syst. Signal Process. **34**(11), 3661–3670 (2015)
8. Silva-Martinez, J., Vazquez-Gonzalez, A.: Impedance scalers for IC active filters. In: Proceedings of IEEE International Symposium on Circuits and Systems 1998, pp. 151–154 (1998)
9. Solis-Bustos, S., Silva-Martnez, J., Maloberti, F., Sinchez-Sinencio, E.: A 60-dB dynamic-range CMOS sixth-order 2.4-Hz low-pass filter for medical applications. IEEE Trans. Circ. Syst. II Analog Digital Signal Process. **47**(12), 1391–1398 (2000)
10. Silva-Martinez, J., Salcedo-Suer, J.: IC voltage to current transducers with very small transconductance. Analog Integr. Circ. Signal Process. **13**(3), 285–293 (1997)
11. Rodriguez-Villegas, E., Yfera, A., Rueda, A.: A 1.25-V micropower Gm-C filter based on FGMOS transistors operating in weak inversion. IEEE J. Solid-State Circ. **39**(1), 100–111 (2004)
12. Mourabit, A.E., Lu, G.N., Pittet, P.: Wide-linear-range subthreshold OTA for low-power, low-voltage, and low-frequency applications. IEEE Trans. Circ. Syst. I Regul. Pap. **52**(8), 1481–1488 (2005)
13. Guzinski, A., Bialko, M.A., Matheau, J.C.: Body driven differential amplifier for application in continuous-time active-C filter. In: Proceedings of ECCD 1987, pp. 315–319 (1998)
14. Yodtean, A., Thanachayanont, A.: Sub 1-V highly-linear low-power class-AB bulk-driven tunable CMOS transconductor. Analog Integr. Circ. Signal Process. **75**(3), 383–397 (2013)
15. Serrano-Gotarredona, T., Linares-Barranco, B., Andreou, A.G.: A general translinear principle for subthreshold MOS transistors. IEEE Trans. Circ. Syst. I Fundam. Theory Appl. **46**(5), 607–616 (1999)
16. Rekha, S., Laxminidhi, T.: Common mode feedback circuits for low voltage fully-differential amplifiers. J. Circ. Syst. Comput. **25**(10), 1650124 (2016)
17. Linares-Barranco, B., Serrano-Gotarredona, T.: On the design and characterization of femtoampere current-mode circuits. IEEE J. Solid-State Circ. **38**(8), 1353–1363 (2003)
18. Cotrim, E.D., de Carvalho Ferreira, L.H.: An ultra-low-power CMOS symmetrical OTA for low-frequency Gm-C applications. Analog Integr. Circ. Signal Process. **71**(2), 275–282 (2012)
19. Veeravalli, A., Sanchez-Sinencio, E., Silva-Martnez, J.: Transconductance amplifier structures with very small transconductances: a comparative design approach. IEEE J. Solid-State Circ. **37**(6), 770–775 (2002)
20. Schaumann, R., Xiao, H., Mac, V.V.: Design of Analog Filters, 2nd edn. Oxford University Press, Inc., New York (2009)

# An Improved Highly Efficient Low Input Voltage Charge Pump Circuit

Naresh Kumar[✉], Raja Hari Gudlavalleti, and Subash Chandra Bose

CSIR-Central Electronics Engineering Research Institute, Pilani, Rajasthan, India
nkjmintu2@gmail.com, {rajahari,subash}@ceeri.res.in

**Abstract.** Conventional charge pump circuit based on dynamic charge transfer switch (CTS) is limited by its efficiency due to the threshold voltage of MOS transistor. This paper proposes an improved dynamic CTS based charge pump circuit by modifying the conventional circuit architecture at the output stage by a PMOS transistor with appropriate control signals. A four-stage dynamic CTS based charge pump circuit with pumping capacitance of 50 pF, clock frequency of 20 MHz and load current of 100 μA is designed and simulated in Cadence environment using UMC 0.18 μm CMOS technology. As compared to conventional architecture, this modification has reduced the voltage loss at the output to 1.3% as compared to 9% for 1 V input and 6% as compared to 20% for 0.3 V input voltage. The core dimension of the layout is 750 μm × 530 μm.

**Keywords:** DC-DC converter · Charge pump · CMOS

## 1 Introduction

Charge pump (CP) circuits are capacitive DC-DC boost converters that provide a DC output voltage higher than the input supply voltage. Capacitive DC-DC converter circuits occupy less silicon area and can be fully integrated on-chip as compared to inductor based DC-DC converters. Recent developments in sub-micron technologies have scaled down the supply voltages. To combat the performance degradation of analog and mixed signal circuits due to reduced supply voltages, multiple supply strategy is implemented. This strategy meets both low power operation and high-performance requirements in an integrated chip (IC). However, CP circuits are also used in other applications for biasing sensors requiring higher voltage than the input supply voltage [1], programming of EEPROM [2, 3], fully-integrated energy harvesting circuits for boosting the voltage obtained from ambient sources [4, 5] etc. The first integrated CP circuit was proposed by Dickson [6]. CP circuit proposed by Dickson is simply a chain of series connected diode and capacitor. Further diodes were replaced with gate-drain connected MOS transistors for on-chip implementation.

Conventional architecture of the Dickson CP with MOS transistors is shown in Fig. 1. As shown in Fig. 1, MD1-MD5 are diode-connected MOS transistors, $V_{in}$ is the input supply voltage to the CP, which also acts as the supply voltage of clock generation circuits (not shown in the figure). Clk1 and Clk2 are fully differential non-overlapping clock signals. When Clk1 is low, node 1 is initially charged to $V_{in} - V_{th}$ (where $V_{th}$ is the

© Springer Nature Singapore Pte Ltd. 2017
B. K. Kaushik et al. (Eds.): VDAT 2017, CCIS 711, pp. 93–102, 2017.
https://doi.org/10.1007/978-981-10-7470-7_11

threshold voltage of NMOS transistor), and when Clk1 is high, node 1 is boosted by an amount $\Delta V$. $\Delta V$ can be expressed as [7]

$$\Delta V = \left( \frac{C}{C+C_s}.V_{in} - \frac{I_L}{\left(C+C_s\right).f} \right) \tag{1}$$

where $V_{Clk} = V_{in}$, $C$ is the pumping capacitance which is equal in size ($C1 = C2 = C3 = C4 = C$), $C_s$ is the parasitic capacitance associated with each pumping node, $f$ is the frequency of clock signals, and $I_L$ is the output load current. As all the transistors and capacitors of the CP are equal in size, so the boosted voltage at each node is equal to the $\Delta V$ (except output node 5). Voltage is boosted at each stage of CP, hence the voltage gain, A$v$ of each stage of the CP is given by the voltage difference between two consecutive nodes of CP which can be expressed as

$$Av = V_N - V_{N-1} \tag{2}$$

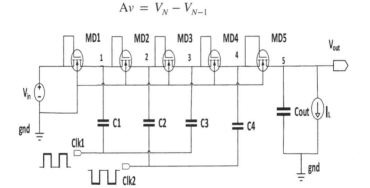

**Fig. 1.** Four stage Dickson charge-pump circuit [5].

Where $V_N$ and $V_{N-1}$ are the consecutive node voltages of the CP. Solving Eq. (2), A$v$ can be written as

$$Av = \left( \frac{C}{C+C_s}.V_{in} - \frac{I_L}{\left(C+C_s\right).f} \right) - V_{th} = \Delta V - V_{th} \tag{3}$$

As shown in Eq. (3) for positive voltage gain, $\Delta V$ should be greater than the threshold voltage of MOS transistor ($V_{th}$). Output voltage ($V_{out}$) of CP is given as

$$V_{out} = V_{in} + N.Av - V_{th} \tag{4}$$

Or one can write Eq. (4) as [8]

$$V_{out} = V_{in} + N.\left( \frac{C}{C+C_s}.V_{in} - \frac{I_L}{\left(C+C_s\right).f} \right) - (N+1)V_{th} \tag{5}$$

As shown in Eq. (5) a voltage drop occurs at each stage of the CP due to the threshold voltage of MOS transistor, it becomes critical in an application where the input supply voltage is low (in the range of threshold voltage of MOS transistor). Hence, the effect of threshold voltage drop at the output voltage of CP is the main drawback of Dickson CP.

To reduce the effect of the threshold voltage of MOS transistor or to increase the pumping gain of the CP, many circuits have been reported [7–9]. Static Charge transfer switch (CTS) based CP is proposed [7, 8], that uses auxiliary MOS switch chain along with diode connected MOS transistor chain of Dickson CP. These auxiliary MOS switches connected with each stage are driven by a higher voltage generated from next stage of the CP to eliminate the effect of the threshold voltage in the main switch chain [7, 8]. If the auxiliary MOS switches can be turned ON and OFF at the designated clock period, they can allow the charge to be pushed only in the forward direction without any voltage drop and Eq. (5) can be written as

$$V_{out} = V_{in} + N.\left( \frac{C}{C + C_s}.V_{in} - \frac{I_L}{(C + C_s).f} \right) - V_{th} \qquad (6)$$

But unfortunately, the auxiliary MOS switch cannot be turned OFF completely in the designated clock period, because the gate voltage of the auxiliary switch during the OFF period of the switch is high enough to keep the switch turned ON [7, 8]. The auxiliary MOS switches are always ON and the charge flow in both forward as well as backwards direction. The flow of charge in the backward direction is called reverse charge sharing. Due to reverse charge sharing effect the voltage fluctuation at each pumping node are different and smaller than the predicted one. As a result, the overall voltage pumping gain of this topology is reduced. To overcome this drawback a dynamic Charge Transfer switch based CP is proposed [7], that provide dynamic control to each charge transfer switch so that it can be turned ON and OFF completely during designated clock period.

Simulated results of dynamic CTS CP match with the theoretical value. But as shown in Eq. (6) pumping gain is limited by the threshold voltage drop at the output stage of the CP, which degrade the output voltage of the CP by the threshold voltage of the MOS transistor, and this voltage drop at the consecutive nodes is increased due to body effect [10].

In both topologies discussed above CTS cannot be used at the output stage of CP because there is no required signal present to control the switch. Various techniques have been proposed to reduce the effect of $V_{th}$ such as bootstrapping the clock signal [7], auxiliary MOS based charge transfer block using floating well [9]. However, these techniques increase the complexity or require additional masks for fabrication which would further increase the cost. This paper proposes an improved dynamic charge transfer switch based charge pump architecture that provides higher pumping efficiency in a standard CMOS process technology.

## 2 Proposed Charge Pump

### 2.1 Circuit Description

Figure 2 shows the schematic diagram of the proposed charge pump circuit based on dynamic CTS with auxiliary PMOS transistor at the output stage. In this schematic, MD1-MD5 (MDs) are diode-connected NMOS transistors, MS1-MS4 (MSs) are charge transfer switches (CTS). MS1-MS4 and MD-MD4 connected in parallel to each other. Pass transistors MN1-MN4 (MNs) and MP1-MP4 (MPs) are used to dynamically control of the CTS, so that MSs can be turned ON and OFF completely to remove reverse charge sharing. Clock signals Clk1 and Clk2 are kept out-of-phase with same amplitude ($V_{in}$) to bootstrap the charge at each node (1–5).

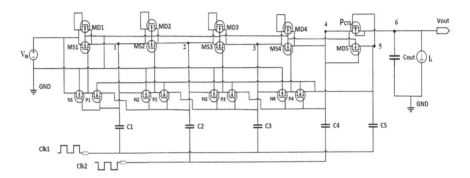

**Fig. 2.** Schematic diagram of four stage proposed charge pump.

### 2.2 Operation of the Circuit

Initially, all the pumping capacitors are at zero potential. Under this condition when the input voltage is applied, the proposed charge pump circuit acts as Dickson charge pump. The MSs acts as diode-connected MOS transistors, this condition is prevails until the voltages at the nodes reaches the threshold voltage of the NMOS transistor.

After establishing voltage greater than the threshold voltage of NMOS at each node, MSs transistors start working as switches and allow the charge to transfer from one node to another without any voltage drop. Under this condition, when Clk1 goes low and Clk2 goes high the diode MD1 turned ON, but the voltage at node 2 is greater than node 1. MP1 conduct and the gate of MS1 is connected to node 2. Therefore, the MS1 switch turns ON and capacitor C1 is charged to the input voltage $V_{in}$. The voltage at node 1 becomes equal to the input voltage $V_{in}$ and therefore MN1 is turned OFF. In the next clock half cycle, Clk1 goes high and Clk2 goes low, MD1 is turned OFF. The voltage at node 2 becomes equal to the voltage at node 1 therefore, MP1 turned OFF. But the voltage at node 1 is greater than $V_{in}$ therefore, MN1 conducts and the gate of MS1 is connected to $V_{in}$ which makes MS1 turn OFF completely. As shown in Fig. 2 gate of PMOS switch which acts as an auxiliary transistor is connected to node 5. Voltage at node 5 is boosted by Clk1 and voltage at node 4 is boosted by Clk2. When Clk2 is high and Clk1 is low then the voltage at node 4 is higher than the node 5. Hence, gate-to-source $|V_{gs}|$ voltage become greater than the threshold voltage of PMOS $|V_{thp}|$ transistor, PMOS transistor conduct and voltage at node 4 is transferred to node 6 without any voltage drop. In the next clock half cycle, when Clk2 is low and Clk1 is high, then the voltage at node 5 is higher than the voltage at node 4. Hence, $|V_{gs}|$ become less than the $|V_{thp}|$ which turn OFF the PMOS transistor and higher voltage of node 4 remain stored in output capacitor. By using this technique, the voltage drop at the output of charge pump is removed as compared to an NMOS transistor at the output state [7]. Hence, output voltage of proposed charge-pump circuit is given as

$$V_{out} = V_{in} + N.\left( \frac{C}{C + C_s}.V_{in} - \frac{I_L}{(C + C_s).f} \right) \tag{7}$$

Or if parasitic effect is neglected then the output voltage $(V_{out})$ can be written as [11]

$$V_{out} = (N + 1)V_{in} - N\frac{I_L}{C.f} \tag{8}$$

As shown in Fig. 2, the output capacitor is charged and discharged periodically which causes a ripple in the output voltage of the CP. Amplitude $(V_R)$ of this ripple is given as [8, 11]

$$V_R = \frac{I_L}{f.C_{out}} \tag{9}$$

Ripple voltage can be reduced either by increasing the frequency of the clock or by using a large output capacitance. Using large capacitor at the output stage increases the time to reach steady state and also increases silicon chip area.

## 3   Simulation Results

Four-stage proposed CP based on dynamic CTS CP circuit with pumping capacitance of 50 pF, clock frequency of 20 MHz is designed and simulated in Cadence environment using UMC 0.18 μm CMOS technology.

### 3.1   Circuit Performance

Figure 3 shows the simulated output voltage of proposed CP circuit with varying load current at different input supply voltages. As load current increases the output voltage of CP decreases linearly as shown in Eq. (7). Figure 4 shows the difference between simulated output voltage and theoretical value (assuming parasitic capacitor $(Cs) = 0$) of the output voltage at varying input supply voltage and constant load current (50 μA). The maximum difference between the simulated and theoretical output voltage of proposed CP circuit is 54 mV at input voltage 0.8 V. This shows that the proposed simple technique is highly efficient. Proposed CP provide output voltage variation less than 10 mV across process corner and less than 8 mV with the temperature change from −40 °C to 100 °C.

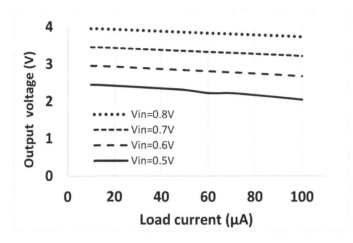

**Fig. 3.** Simulated output voltage of the proposed CP with varying load at different input voltage.

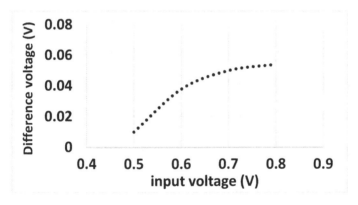

**Fig. 4.** Difference between the theoretical and simulated Output voltage of proposed CP with varying input voltage.

### 3.2 Architecture Comparison

Figures 5 and 6 shows the comparison of simulated output voltage for different CP topologies and percentage loss in the output voltage at different input voltages respectively. For reasonable comparison size and values of all MOS switches, capacitors, clock frequency and load current are kept similar. Figure 5 shows that the output voltage of proposed CP is highest compared to the other topologies. Figure 6 shows that the voltage loss in output voltage is minimum in the proposed CP circuit.

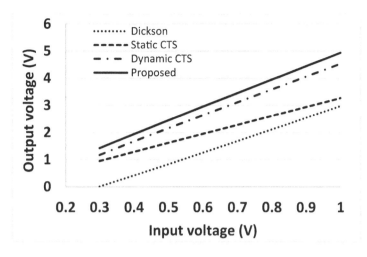

**Fig. 5.** Comparison of different CP topologies with the varying input voltage.

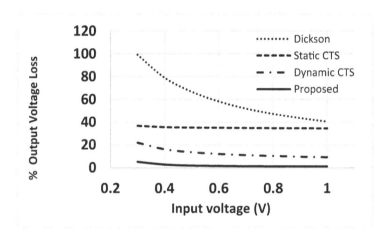

**Fig. 6.** Percentage loss in the output voltage of different CP topologies with the varying input voltage.

As compared to conventional dynamic CTS based architecture, the proposed circuit reduced the voltage loss at the output to 1.3% as compared to 9% for 1 V input and 6% as compared to 20% for 0.3 V input voltage. And reduced the voltage loss from 99% to 6% for 0.3 V input and from 40.5% to 1.3% for 1 V input voltage compared to the Dickson CP.

### 3.3 Post Layout Simulation Results

Figure 7 shows the layout diagram of the proposed CP circuit. The core dimensions of the layout are 750 μm × 530 μm, where 96% of this area is occupied by the capacitors.

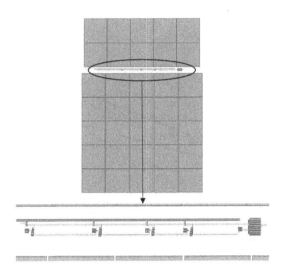

**Fig. 7.** Layout diagram of proposed CP.

Figure 8 shows the voltage difference between pre-layout and post-layout simulation results of CP circuit with varying load currents and the constant input voltage (0.6 V). As shown in Fig. 8 maximum voltage difference between pre-layout and post-layout simulation results is 46 mV at a load current 100 μA. This is basically due to the parasitic resistances and capacitances formed at each node of CP.

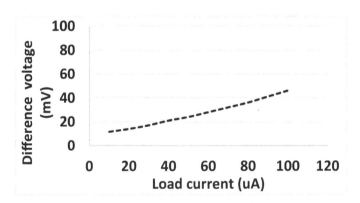

**Fig. 8.** Difference between Pre-layout and Post-layout output voltage of proposed CP with different load current.

Table 1 shows the performance summary of the proposed CP and also, shows the comparison with previous work. By comparing the post-layout simulation results given in the references as shown in Table 1, the technique proposed in this work has higher boosting efficiency at a lower input voltage and can deliver more load current above 0.5 V input voltage. Also, Proposed CP has 4.6 times higher voltage compared to the Dickson CP at 400 mV input which is higher than the architecture proposed by [12] that has 3.12 times higher voltage compare to Dickson CP at 380 mV. The chip is ready for fabrication.

**Table 1.** Performance summary and comparison of charge pumps

| | [2] | [3] | [4] | [9] | [12] | This work |
|---|---|---|---|---|---|---|
| Process | TSMC 0.35 μm | 0.18 μm | TSMC 0.18 μm | UMC 0.18 μm | 65 nm | UMC 0.18 μm |
| Min. input voltage | 3.3 V | 1.8 V | 0.45 V ~ 0.55 V | 500 mV | 290 mV | 300 mV |
| Output voltage | 17.5 V | 5.62 V | 1.26 V | 2 V | 1.285 V @Vin = 0.5 V | 1.42 V @ Vin = 0.3 V |
| Output current | 5–6 μA | – | 310 μA | 50 μA @ Vin = 1.4 V | – | 100 μA @ Vin > 0.5 V |
| Boosting efficiency | 41% | 62% | 84% | 80% | 86% @ Vin = 0.5 V | 94.67% @ Vin = 0.3 V 98% @ Vin > 0.45 V |
| Chip area | – | – | 850 μm × 850 μm | – | 3000 μm² | 750 μm × 530 μm |

# 4 Conclusion

A dynamic CTS based highly efficient CP has been designed. Maximum achievable pumping efficiency is 94.67% for input voltage of 0.3 V and 98% for input voltage greater than 0.45 V. Proposed CP is capable of boosting the input supply voltage as low as 0.3 V and can deliver a load current up to 100 μA for input voltage greater than 0.5 V and 40 μA for input voltage less than 0.5 V.

# References

1. Aaltonen, L., Halonen, K.: Pseudo-continuous-time readout circuit for a 300 °/s capacitive 2-axis micro-gyroscope. IEEE J. Solid-State Circ. **44**(12), 3609–3620 (2009)
2. Yinl, H., Pengl, X., Wangl, J., Weil, Z., Gonf, N.: Analysis and design of CMOS charge pump for EEPROM. In: 12th IEEE International Conference on Solid-State and Integrated Circuit Technology (ICSICT), Guilin, China, pp. 28–31 (2014)
3. Rahman, L.F., Reaz, M.B.I., Ali, M.A.M.: A Low-voltage charge pump circuit for RFID tag EEPROM. In: Fourth International Conference on Emerging Trends in Engineering & Technology, pp. 244–246 (2011)
4. Huang, H.Y., Yen, S.Z., Chen, J.H., Hong, H.C., Cheng, K.H.: Low-voltage indoor energy harvesting using photovoltaic cell. In: 2016 IEEE 19th International Symposium on Design and Diagnostics of Electronic Circuits & Systems (DDECS), Kosice, Slovakia, pp. 1–4 (2016)
5. Zhou, J., Huang, M., Zhang, Y., Zhang, H., and Yoshihara, T.: A novel charge sharing charge pump for energy harvesting application. In: IEEE International SoC Design Conference, Jeju, South Korea, pp. 373–376 (2011)
6. Dickson, J.: On-chip high-voltage generation in NMOS integrated circuits using an improved voltage multiplier technique. IEEE J. Solid-State Circ. **11**(6), 374–378 (1976)
7. Wu, J.T., Chang, K.L.: MOS charge pump for low-voltage operation. IEEE J. Solid-State Circ. **33**(4), 592–597 (1998)
8. Pylarinous, L.: Charge pumps: an overview. In: Proceedings of the IEEE International Symposium on Circuits and Systems, Bangkok Thailand, pp. 1–7 (2003)

9. Shabana, S., Thej, C., Sankar, H., Pandava, R., Dutta, A., Singh, S.G.: Design of highly efficient charge pump for energy harvesting RFID application. In: Asia Pacific Conference on Postgraduate Research in Microelectronic & Electronics, Hyderabad India, pp. 46–50 (2012)

10. Razavi, B.: Design of Analog CMOS Integrated Circuits, International Edn. Tata McGraw-Hill (2001)

11. Palumbo, G., Pappalardo, D.: Charge pump circuits: an overview on design strategies and topologies. IEEE Circ. Syst. Mag. **10**, 31–45 (2010)

12. Mohammadi, B., Rodrigues, J.: Ultra low energy and area efficient charge pump with automatic clock controller in 65 nm CMOS. In: IEEE Asian Solid-State Circuits Conference, Xiamen, Fujjan, China, pp. 1–4 (2015)

# A Calibration Technique for Current Steering DACs - Self Calibration with Capacitor Storage

Pallavi Darji[1]([⊠]) and Chetan Parikh[2]

[1] Electronics and Communication Department, Dharmsinh Desai University,
Nadiad 387 001, India
paldarji@yahoo.co.in
[2] International Institute of Information Technology, Bangalore, India

**Abstract.** High resolution DACs require large transistors to obtain the desired accuracy according to the Pelgrom model [1], which increases the area drastically. To overcome this area accuracy trade off, several calibration techniques were investigated. This paper presents a modified self calibration technique for current-steering (CS) digital-to-analog converters (DACs). In the digital calibration technique calibrating DACs (CALDACs) are connected across each bit, which requires calibration. High resolution CALDAC increases the accuracy at a cost of increment in the area. To overcome this problem, this technique is slightly modified. Instead of using CALDAC of 6 or 8 bits across each bit, here a single CALDAC is used to calibrate each bit, and its equivalent calibrated value in terms of analog voltage is stored across the capacitor (instead of within SRAM memory in digital form), which is connected in the place of CALDAC by using an extra-auxiliary transistor. MOSFET as a switch is used for simultaneous switching and to hold the correct voltage after turning off switches, injection nulling switch type track and hold circuit is used. To demonstrate this technique, a 10-bit binary-weighted CS DAC is implemented in a $0.18\,\mu m$ CMOS process. With worst-case process parameter variations, simulated integral and differential nonlinearities of the calibrated DAC are less than $0.32\,\mathrm{LSB}$.

**Keywords:** Self calibration · Digital-to-analog converter
Binary weighted current steering · Track and hold
Injection nulling switch · Calibrating DAC

## 1 Introduction

A major area of investigation in CS DACs is maintaining high accuracy as measured by differential nonlinearities (DNLs) and integral nonlinearities (INLs) in the presence of transistor parameter variations, which are caused by process variations and temperature. One of the best method to design a small-sized precise CS DAC is by using different calibration techniques.

Various techniques such as self-calibration [2–7], self-trimming, dynamic element matching [5,6], and on-chip calibration [8,9] have been proposed to manage

© Springer Nature Singapore Pte Ltd. 2017
B. K. Kaushik et al. (Eds.): VDAT 2017, CCIS 711, pp. 103–114, 2017.
https://doi.org/10.1007/978-981-10-7470-7_12

a device mismatch without a substantial area increment. The calibration circuit basically includes a measurement circuit, correction circuit, and storage element. There are basically two types of calibration technique, foreground and background. Foreground calibration technique does conversion after completing calibration of each bit, while background calibration does both simultaneously. The foreground digital calibration scheme includes a comparator, successive approximation register (SAR), calibrating DAC (CALDAC), SRAM, and controller circuits. The CALDAC is connected across the main current source transistor, whose current deviates because of process parameter variations. An amount of error current is processed, converted into its corresponding digital form, and stored in SRAM. The high-resolution sigma delta ADC [5] was used to convert the error current into digital bits. The inclusion of this ADC enlarges the die area, slows down the operation, and increases the cost of the chip. To overcome these disadvantages, Researches [10] have proposed to use high speed current comparators instead of the high resolution ADCs and also used the LSB part of the DAC for conversion, which saves area marginally and obtains high resolution. Instead of adjusting the current, the correction voltage can be used to tune substrate bias voltage of the main current source transistor [7].

In the background analog calibration scheme, the difference between reference and actual currents (which deviates because of temperature, aging, and process parameter variation) is stored on the capacitor connected at the gate of auxiliary transistor across the main transistor. The background process eliminates the use of calibrated elements and performs calibration continuously.

In this paper, we have used single CALDAC instead of multiple CALDAC across each bit for calibration of CS DAC and Track and Hold circuit with Injection nulling switch technique is used to hold voltage constant after turning off a switch. To demonstrate this technique, a 10-bit current-steering DAC prototype is implemented in a $0.18\,\mu$m CMOS process. The paper is organized as follows: the calibration technique is described in Sect. 2. The circuit implementation of critical constituent blocks are described in Sect. 3. Simulation results are presented in Sect. 4. The paper is concluded in Sect. 5.

## 2    Calibration Technique-Self-Calibration with Capacitor Storage (SCCS) Technique

The basic circuit diagram of a CS DAC with the proposed digital calibration circuit is shown in Fig. 1. The circuit comprises of a 10-bit CSDAC, a comparator, a successive approximation register (SAR) logic circuit, and an 8-bit CALDAC. In the circuit, the current source $I_{main}$ and the transistor $M_m$, at the left of Fig. 1, belong to the main CS DAC; $I_{main}$ is mirrored to all the binary-weighted current source cells of the DAC. $M_1$ and $M_2$ represent one of these cascoded current sources. The circuit is operated in two phases: (1) Normal operation; and (2) Calibration. In the normal operation, switching transistors $M_{sw}$ and $M_{swb}$ are connected to the load resistor $R_L$ and $R_{LB}$ simultaneously to obtain analog-equivalent output voltage $V_{out}$ and the complement of voltage $V_{out}$.

In the calibration phase, the switching transistors $M_{REF}$ and $M_{CAL}$ are connected to the 'Ref' and 'Cal' node, respectively. The comparator, SAR circuit, and 8-bit CALDAC as well as one pMOS current mirror circuit preceding the comparator ($M_{PC1}$ and $M_{PC2}$) and another after CALDAC ($M_{PL1}$ and $M_{PL2}$) and $M_{NL}$ transistor are common for all bits. The auxiliary transistor Me with capacitor is used as a correction circuit. Switches $S_1$ to $S_{10}$ are used for simultaneous calibration of each bit of a 10-bit CS DAC.

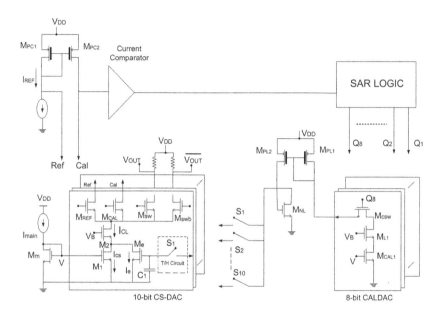

**Fig. 1.** Self-calibration with capacitor storage (SCCS) technique

The following are the steps of the calibration process: It is initiated at the first bit; A dummy cell having current equal to the LSB current of CS DAC is parentally connected at node 'Ref' as $I_{ref}$ (top left side of Fig. 1). This $I_{ref}$ is increased progressively for each bit by connecting calibrated bits at node 'Ref'. The circuit aims to bring current $I_{CL}$ in $M_2$ as close to the reference current $I_{ref}$ as possible. Before calibration, the currents in $M_1$ and $M_2$ are the same, and flow to the output in normal operation mode. Process or temperature variations or ageing cause the current in $M_1$ to change from its ideal value. When the switching transistor $M_{CAL}$ is turned on, this cell is connected at the input of the comparator through node 'Cal'. The comparator compares this current with $I_{ref}$. The output of the comparator is either logic 0 or 1, depending on the current $I_{CL}$. In the first clock cycle, the SAR MSB bit is set at logic 1 and the remaining bits are set at logic 0. Therefore, the current corresponding to the MSB bit in CALDAC flows as $I_e$. Now $I_e + I_{CS} = I_{CL}$ compares with $I_{ref}$. If $I_{CL} > I_{ref}$, the MSB bit resets, and SAR sets the next MSB-1 bit. This process continues until $I_{CL} < I_{ref}$. When $I_{CL} < I_{ref}$, that bit remains set, and the next LSB bit is set. This comparison continues upto 8bits of CALDAC and $I_{CL}$ becomes approximately $I_{ref}$. This approximation depends on the design of CALDAC and the amount of error introduced by mirror circuits in the calibration path. The voltage corresponding to $I_e$ stored across the capacitor and switch corresponding to that bit, is turned off. For calibrating the next bit, the switching transistor $M_{ref}$ of the first cell, which was already calibrated, connects the current cell to node 'Ref', and $M_{CAL}$ of next current cell is connected to node 'Cal'.

# 3    Implementation of SCCS Technique

As shown in Fig. 1, a calibration circuit consists of a current comparator, SAR logic circuit, and CALDAC. In addition, auxiliary transistors are present in a 10-bit CS-DAC cell, with capacitors for each bit. To hold the correct voltage after turning off switches, Track and Hold (TH) circuits are required for each bit.

## 3.1    Current Comparator

Figure 2 illustrates the current comparator having a single input and output and generates a high or low logical output according to the comparison of the analog input current with a reference current. In an ideal comparator with infinite gain, for input currents higher than the reference current, the comparator outputs logical one and for the input currents lower than the reference current, it produces zero at the output.

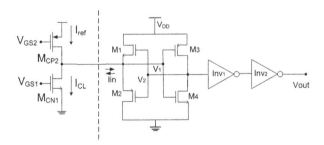

**Fig. 2.** Current comparator circuit

The current comparator proposed by Traff [11] is preceded with PMOS and NMOS transistor as shown in Fig. 3. $I_{in}$ represents the difference between the input and reference currents, and $V_2$ represents the compared result, which can be amplified by following CMOS inverting stages to output a rail-to-rail signal. This current comparator uses a source-follower ($M_1$ and $M_2$) at the input stage and a CMOS inverter ($M_3$ and $M_4$) as a positive feedback. This type of current comparator [12,13] is found more suitable as compared to current mirror type current comparator because of its lower input resistance and shorter response time.

In Fig. 2, when $I_{ref} < I_{CL}$. current flows in transistor $M_{CP2}$ and $M_{CN1}$ is corresponding to $I_{ref}$, and that operates transistor $M_{CN1}$ in triode region. Hence, $V_1$ is reduced and $V_2$ increased. Full high logic voltage at $V_{out}$ is produced by two inverters, and that is required to keep MSB in CALDAC ON and SAR logic turns on next MSB-1 bit.

When $I_{ref} > I_{CL}$. current flows in transistor $M_{CP2}$ and $M_{CN1}$ is corresponding to $I_{CL}$, and that operates transistor $M_{CN1}$ in saturation region. Hence, $V_1$ is increased and $V_2$ is decreased. Again full rail low logic voltage at $V_{out}$ is produced by inverters which turns off that MSB-1 bit of CALDAC. The difference between $I_{ref}$ and $I_{CL}$ should be greater than $0.05\,\mu AA$ in order to change logic level at $V_{out}$.

## 3.2    SAR Analog to Digital Converter

Basic function of SAR ADC is to convert analog input signal successively into its equivalent binary code. It is appropriate choice due to its low power operations. In this study, SAR ADC was used to convert an amount of error current into a digital code. In other words, 1-bit is determined in each clock cycle by using binary search algorithm.

Figure 3 illustrates the SAR ADC block diagram of the circuit presented in [14]. This circuit includes a ring counter and a code register.

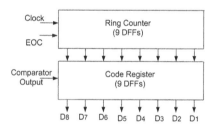

**Fig. 3.** SAR block diagram

For each conversion, in clock cycle 0, the end-of-conversion (EOC) signal was high and all the flip-flop outputs $D_8$ to $D_1$ were reset to zero; the EOC signal is low for the remaining cycles. At the rising edge of the clock, this flip-flop loads the result from the comparator. In the first clock cycle, the most significant flip-flop is set to one, which corresponds to MSB $D_8$ of a digital word of the DAC. Since comparator output is presented as a input of the code register, if it is '1', then $D_8$ remains set else it resets and at same time $D_7$ sets to '1'. Again comparator output is checked by code register and $d_7$ bit is either set or resest. This process is repeated up-to LSB $D_1$. At the end of each conversion, the EOC signal sets. This type of SAR logic converts each sample in 8-clock cycles.

## 3.3  Calibrating DAC

Circuit diagram of 8 bit Calibrating DAC (CALDAC) is shown in Fig. 1 at the bottom right side. It is designed on basis of the required maximum error current required for calibration. According to the Pelgrom model [1], this error current is calculated for a 10-bit CS DAC and it is approximately $15\,\mu$A. Widths of the current source transistors are selected on the basis of the current requirement and length $L = 1\,\mu$m to reduce the channel length modulation effect. Larger length and cascode transistors improve accuracy of CALDAC.

## 3.4  Track and Hold Circuit

Figure 4 shows basic TH circuit [15]. When a MOS transistor $M_1$ is turned on, voltage across capacitor $V_{out}$ will be same as $V_{IN}$. Now, when switch is turned off, the voltage stored across capacitor is getting change due to two reasons: charge injection effect and clock feedthrough. When $M_1$ is switched off, the channel disappears. The charges, by which the channel was formed, moved out of the transistor and some were "injected" on $C_S$, causing a change of stored voltage. This effect is called charge injection (CI) [16]. Through the parasitic capacitance $C_P$ between the gate and either of the terminal, the abrupt transition change in the clocking voltages causes a sudden flow of charge toward $C_S$. This effect is called clock feed-through (CKFT) [15,16]. Hence even though calibration circuit performs accurate calibration, error is observed and nonlinearity would not be improved.

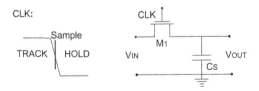

**Fig. 4.** Track and Hold Circuit

Because this voltage is used for further processing in the system, the system accuracy is destroyed. To overcome this problem, various error minimization techniques have been published like dummy switch [15,17], transmission gate [15], bottom plate sampling [18] and injection-nulling switch (INS) [19]. INS technique is used because of its best performance among all.

Figure 5 shows the injection-nulling switching (INS) technique in which one more set of transistor and capacitor is used with a simple TH circuit. In this technique the error voltage is reduced by the simultaneous turning on and off of transistors $M_1$ and $M_n$. The operation of the INS technique is explained with respect to four phases ($\tau 1, \tau 2, \tau 3, \tau 4,$). The clocks used for both transistors are also shown on the right of Fig. 9. During phase $\tau 1$, when $M_1$ and $M_N$ are both turned on, $C_S$ and $C_N$ are charged to $V_{IN}$ and $V_{OUT} = V_{IN}$. During phase $\tau2$, transistor $M_N$ is turned OFF and injects some charges onto the capacitor $C_N$ while the voltage on $C_S$ is remained unaffected. Furthermore, turning off $M_1$

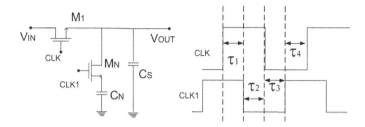

**Fig. 5.** Track and Hold Circuit: Injection Nulling Switch

during phase $\tau3$ injects some charges onto $C_S$. These charges will introduce an error at the output voltage. Therefore, output voltage is given by

$$V_{OUT\tau3} = V_{OUT\tau1} - V_{E1} \qquad (1)$$

During phase $\tau4$ (the nulling phase), turning on $M_N$ absorbs some charges from both the capacitors $C_N$ and $C_S$ to form a channel underneath of its gate. Hence, charges injected by $M_1$ are absorbed by $M_N$, which results in obtaining the desired voltage across $C_S$, as shown in following equation.

$$V_{OUT\tau4} = V_{OUT\tau1} - V_{E1} + V_{E2} \qquad (2)$$

Output voltage is approximately equal to the input voltage, provided that the transistors $M_1$ and $M_N$ are of the appropriate size to generate $V_{E1} = V_{E2}$.

## 4   Simulation Results

Circuit simulations were performed in LTspice-IV [20]. A standard 180-nm CMOS process was used. SPICE model parameters for the BSIM3 model were obtained from the MOSIS site [21].

### 4.1   Track and Hold Circuit

The TH circuit is used for each bit. The size of transistors, as a switch, is selected as minimum as possible: For the 180-nm CMOS technology, it is $W/L = 0.3/0.2$. TH circuits with all four different error minimization techniques are simulated for $V_{in} = 0.6$ V with clock fall time of 0.1 ns, and the results are tabulated in Table 1. The table shows reduction error voltage $V_E$ in each TH circuits. INS provides effective minimization of the stored voltage after switching off compared with other techniques, and therefore TH with the INS technique is used in this study. Such TH circuits with INS are required across each cell.

**Table 1.** Comparison of TH circuit Techniques

| Technique | Theoretical $V_E$ | Simulated $V_E$ |
| --- | --- | --- |
| Dummy Switch | $-9\,\text{mV}$ | $-7.8\,\text{mV}$ |
| Transmission Gate | $-1.3\,\text{mV}$ | $-2\,\text{mV}$ |
| Bottom Plate Sampling | $-3.3\,\text{mV}$ | $-3\,\text{mV}$ |
| Injection Nulling Switch | $130\,\mu\text{V}$ | $165\,\mu\text{V}$ |

## 4.2   10-Bit CS DAC

A prototype 10-bit CS DAC was realized by using a fingering technique [12]. Large size transistors are realized in form of parallel connected small (unit) transistors. This pattern reduces layout related error (gradient, random) and to make layout compact. As shown in Fig. 6 intrinsic CS DAC (ideal) and fingering CS DAC having maximum INL is around 5 LSB. It is presented due to Channel length modulation effect. Parameter variations (mismatch, ageing and temperature) are introduced per bit causes $INL_{max}$ around 17 LSB. Here, 3% variation in width and 5% variation in threshold voltage are incorporated on main Current source transistors.

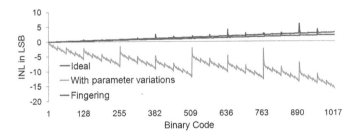

**Fig. 6.** INL plot for 10-bit Current Steering DAC

## 4.3   Calibration of Single Bit

To avoid propagation of LSBs error into MSBs, calibration was initiated from the first bit itself, which also gives flexibility in selection of transistor sizes. Figure 7 shows the functionally of the SAR logic circuit during calibration of the 1st bit with $2.5\,\mu\text{A}$ current, with its calibration. Because of the parameter mismatch, ageing and temperature effects, this current was reduced to $1.93\,\mu\text{A}$. In this study, this current was reduced by decreasing the width of the current source transistor $M_{SC}$. Initially SAR sets the MSB $Q_8$ of CALDAC to logic 1 and progressed upto LSB $Q_1$. Those bits remained set or reset according to the signal received from the comparator output. If the comparator output is logic 0, then the bit reset, and if its output is logic 1, the bit remained set (Fig. 7).

Figure 7(b) shows how $1.93\,\mu\text{A}$ is calibrated to $2.44\,\mu\text{A}$. V(cmpi) indicates the output of the comparator and Id(Mcs1) indicates the erroneous current, which is $1.93\,\mu\text{A}$. The lower part of Fig. 7 depicts how the comparator output changes from 1 to 0 or vice versa to correct this current upto the reference current Id(62x) of $2.5\,\mu\text{A}$. After calibration, the amount of error remaining is $0.06\,\mu\text{A}$.

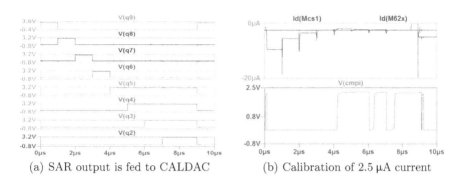

(a) SAR output is fed to CALDAC          (b) Calibration of $2.5\,\mu\text{A}$ current

**Fig. 7.** Calibration of single bit

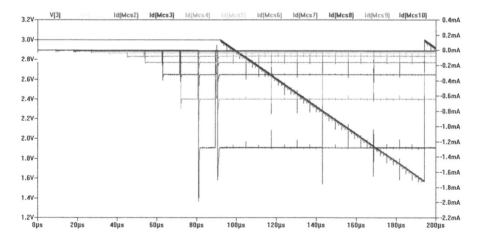

**Fig. 8.** Calibration of each bit and analog equivalent output voltage

## 4.4   Measurement of Nonlinearity

Each bit was calibrated and the nonlinearity was measured for the digital input pattern from 0000000000 to 1111111111. Figure 8 shows foreground calibration for $100\,\mu\text{S}$, and conversion takes place in next $100\,\mu\text{S}$. The amount of glitches are higher for higher order bits because of larger size of transistors present in the binary-weighted CS DAC. Figure 9 shows DNL and INL before calibration, and Fig. 10 shows DNL and INL after calibration of CS DAC, respectively. This digital calibration technique reduces DNL from 10 to 0.25 LSB and INL from 17 to 0.32 LSB.

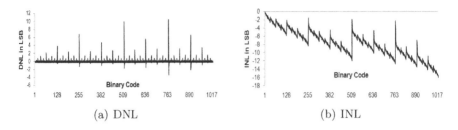

(a) DNL                                    (b) INL

**Fig. 9.** Before calibration

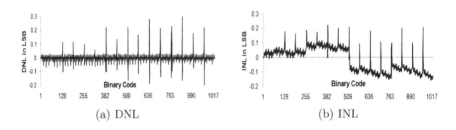

(a) DNL                                    (b) INL

**Fig. 10.** After calibration

## 5    Conclusion

The 10-bit CS-DAC was digitally calibrated from the 1st bit, and the obtained DNL and INL are found less than 0.32 LSB at 10 MHz with power dissipation of 4.3 mW. In this technique, we used a single CALDAC to calibrate each bit. Therefore, multiple CALDACs were replaced with a single transistor and a capacitor, and a TH circuit with INS was used per bit to maintain accuracy. To compare area requirement, the area occupied by the 8-bit CALDAC was assumed to be X $\mu m^2$. According to the Ikeda et al. technique [10], for calibrating a 10-bit CS DAC, 10X $\mu m^2$ CALDAC is required. As this type of calibration is dynamic in nature, it requires periodical calibration because of current leakage in MOS switches; hence, temperature and aging effects are also nullified.

## 6    Future Scope

Because periodical refreshment is required to compensate for the leakage charge through switching MOSFET, use of a refresher circuit has become necessary in such types of calibration schemes. Wong et al. [22] proposed a leakage cancellation technique for the switched-capacitor track and hold circuit in which the leakage charge is compensated by using the exact replica of the TH circuit across the main TH circuit. This technique yields approximately 96% improvement in the voltage drift. Therefore, inclusion of this technique with the TH circuit greatly reduces the refresh time.

# References

1. Kinget, P.R.: Device mismatch and tradeoffs in the design of analog circuits. IEEE J. Solid-State Circ. **40**(6), 1212–1224 (2005)
2. Bechthum, E., Radulov, G., van Roermund, A.: A novel temperature and disturbance insensitive DAC calibration method. In: IEEE International Symposium on Circuits and Systems (ISCAS) (2011)
3. Cong, Y., Randall, L.G.: TA 1.5 V 14 b 100 MS/s self-calibrated DAC International Solid-State Circuits Conference, (ISSCC) (2003)
4. Tiilikainen, M.P.: 14-bit 1.8V 20-mW 1 mm$^2$ CMOS DAC. IEEE J. Solid-State Circ. **36**(7), 1144–1147 (2001)
5. Dongmei, Z., Dongbing, F., Jiangang, S., Kaicheng, L.: Digital static calibration technology used for 16-bit DAC. In: 8th International Conference on ASIC, pp. 1081–1084 (2009)
6. Tsai, J.H., Chen, Y., Lai, Y., Shen, M., Huang, P.: A 14-bit 200MS/s current-steering DAC achieving over 82 dB SFDR with digitally-assisted calibration and dynamic matching techniques. In: International Symposium on VLSI DAT (2012)
7. Chi, J., Chu, S., Tsai, T.: A 1.8 V 12-bit 250-MS/s 25-mW self-calibrated DAC. In: Proceedings of the ESSCIRC, pp. 222–225 (2010)
8. Maunu, J., Pankaala, M., Marku, J., Poikonen, J., Laiho, M., Paasio, A.: Current source calibration by combination selection of minimum sized devices. In: International Symposium on Circuits and Systems, ISCAS (2006)
9. Virtanen, K., Maunu, J., Poikonen, J., Paasio, A.: A 12-bit current-steering DAC with calibration by combination selection. In: International Symposium on Circuits and Systems, ISCAS, pp. 1469–1472 (2007)
10. Ikeda, Y., Frey, M., Matsuzawa, A.: A 14-bit 100 MS/s digitally calibrated binary-weighted current-steering CMOS DAC without calibration ADC. In: IEEE Asian Solid-State Circuits Conference, pp. 356–359 (2007)
11. Traff, H.: Novel approach to high speed CMOS current comparators. Electron. Lett. **28**(3), 310–311 (1992)
12. Wayne, K.: Current-mode CMOS multiple-valued logic circuits. IEEE J. Solid-State Circ. **29**(2), 95–107 (1994)
13. Freitas, D., Wayne, K.: CMOS current comparator circuit. Electron. Lett. **19**(17), 695–697 (1983)
14. Anderson, T.: Optimum control logic for successive approximation analog-to-digital converters. Deep Space Netw. Progr. Rep. **13**, 168–176 (1972)
15. Behzad, R.: Design of Analog CMOS Integrated Circuits. Tata McGraw Hill, New Delhi (reprint), original (New York) (2002)
16. Dai, L., Harjani, R.: CMOS switched-Op-amp-based sample-and-hold circuit. IEEE J. Solid-State Circ. **35**(1), 109–113 (2000)
17. John, D., Martin, K.: Analog integrated circuit design. Wiley, New York (2008)
18. Baptista, A.J.G.: Novel techniques for the design and practical realization of switched-capacitor circuits in deep-submicron CMOS technologies. Thesis report (2009)

19. Lee, W., Chan, P.: An injection-nulling switch for switched-capacitor circuit applications. IEEE Trans. Instrum. Meas. **54**(6), 2416–2426 (2005)
20. Engelhardt, M.: LTSpice/SwitcherCAD IV. Linear Technology Corporation (2011)
21. Christine, T.: MOSIS-A gateway to silicon. IEEE Circ. Devices Mag. **4**(2), 22–23 (1988)
22. Wong, L., Hossain, S., Andrew, T., Jorgen, E., Dominic, H., Hans, N.: A very low-power CMOS mixed-signal IC for implantable pacemaker applications. IEEE J. Solid-State Circ. **39**(12), 2446–2456 (2004)

# Characterization and Compensation Circuitry for Piezo-Resistive Pressure Sensor to Accommodate Temperature Induced Variation

M. Santosh, Anjli Bansal[(✉)], Jitendra Mishra, K. C. Behra, and S. C. Bose

CSIR-Central Electronics Engineering Research Institute, Pilani, India
santosh.manabala@gmail.com, anjlibansal92@gmail.com,
jmishra92@gmail.com, kanhucharan@yahoo.com, bose.ceeri@gmail.com

**Abstract.** The paper presents a simple circuit for piezo-resistive pressure sensors which compensates the temperature dependency of sensors. The output of piezo-resistive sensors generally, decreases with the increase in temperature when subjected to constant voltage excitation. To control the change with temperature, a varying excitation method is used. The proposed technique utilizes current steering DACs and a digital controller to compensate the variations. The technique is experimentally verified at hardware level where the digital control circuit is implemented on FPGA and tested with ASICs comprising of interface circuit. For the purpose of compensation, temperature is sensed using the same sensor. The temperature resolved is less than 1 °C for a range of 10 °C to 70 °C with zero pressure correction technique. The test results for implementation show that the sensitivity and offset shift is compensated by a factor of 10 and 44 respectively. The complete fabricated chip, consisting of interface circuit and algorithm occupies 10 mm² area.

**Keywords:** Piezo-resistive · Voltage excitation · Current steering DACs · FPGA Sensitivity · Offset

## 1 Introduction

MEMS (Micro Electro Mechanical Systems) pressure sensors are used to measure ambient/differential pressure electronically, used in many applications like avionics, automobiles, biomedical industries etc. Both avionics (Micro Air Vehicle) and automobile applications measure altitude by a barometric pressure sensor. Different applications demand suitable pressure transduction principal i.e. piezo-resistive, capacitive or piezo-electric sensing mechanism [1]. Piezo-resistive sensor has gained wide acceptance due to ease of fabrication, scalability and linear output. The sensor consists of four piezo-resistors arranged in the wheat-stone bridge configuration. The resistance of resistors varies with the application of pressure and ideally, should remain constant with temperature variation. But in reality, the resistances also change with temperature. The temperature effect on sensor's sensitivity leads to nonlinear differential output. Apart from thermal impact, fabrication errors result into a

© Springer Nature Singapore Pte Ltd. 2017
B. K. Kaushik et al. (Eds.): VDAT 2017, CCIS 711, pp. 115–126, 2017.
https://doi.org/10.1007/978-981-10-7470-7_13

mismatch of bridge resistors. Such mismatch generates a non-zero output offset even at zero applied pressure. The generated differential output offset also varies with temperature [1]. In order to remove the zero pressure offset error and nonlinearities of sensor, several compensation circuits and algorithms are reported in literature [2–5].

Two side-by-side bridge sensors are used [2–4], one for pressure and the other for temperature measurement. In the previous techniques, offset is compensated with the help of nullifying resistor internal to sensor and the sensitivity drift is compensated by changing voltage bias of pressure sensing bridge. For such techniques, fabrication process related to two bridges and an extra internal resistor becomes complicated.

In order to reduce process complexity and hardware requirement, pressure and temperature are measured simultaneously by a single bridge [6] or an additional temperature sensor embedded on sensor [7]. A single bridge based sensing requires a complex signal conditioning circuit with multiple feed-back loops i.e. comprising of variable gain differential amplifier, tunable current generator, ADC, DAC, PROM and control logic. Addition of an on-chip temperature sensor leverages the signal conditioning circuit complexity [7]. The major limitation with the second approach comprises of collecting huge amount of sensor specific characterized data and multiple high resolution DAC's for controlling variable gain amplifier.

Another technique uses a microprocessor for the temperature compensation of bridge type piezo-resistive pressure sensor. The microprocessor controls the reference voltage applied to the dual slope integrator included in the analogue to digital converter used for signal conditioning [8]. Although, microcontroller based solutions have gained wide acceptance and provided solutions with reasonable power but occupied large footprint on the developed board. Applications such as avionics require a minimum geometry and weight budget conditioning circuit, which are difficult to achieve from microcontroller based solutions (rather a control unit assisted by a look-up table based solution) [9]. Such devices are co-fabricated with sensor and mixed-signal circuits to achieve required weight and power budget at the expense of higher fabrication cost especially designed for batch fabricated MEMS sensors under controlled conditions.

In all the techniques described in literature, both offset and gain related digital compensation values are pre-stored in memory for temperature compensation, leading to complicated characterization process. Gain and offset values control is achieved by inserting variable gain amplifier and tunable current source in conjunction with an external temperature sensor. Proposed work eliminates the requirement of external temperature sensor. Instead, the modified bridge senses the pressure as well as temperature simultaneously. The output offset is compensated with the help of DAC thus, eliminating the need of tunable current regulator [2]. Also, an extra digital circuit for offset compensation [2, 6] is eliminated as the same digital circuit meant for sensitivity compensation also used for offset compensation as well. Thus, the proposed technique is less hardware extensive with a simpler compensation algorithm as compared to previously reported work. The technique implementation is carried out using an in-house piezo-resistive pressure sensor (designed and fabricated in-house) working up to 30 Bar (with sensitivity 1.2 mV/bar for full bridge bias voltage of 3.3 V) for a temperature range of 10 °C to 70 °C. The sensitivity and offset drift with respect to room temperature is −11.7% and −21% respectively (for amplified output of sensor).

## 2 Sensor Characterization

The fabricated sensor implemented by four resistors in bridge configuration, vary in opposite direction with the application of pressure [1]. Figure 1 shows the SEM image of fabricated sensor.

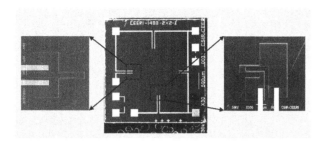

**Fig. 1.** SEM image of fabricated pressure sensor showing the implemented resistors

In order to bias the sensor, superior current biasing scheme [7] is implemented in the proposed work. In contrast to reported work [7], the fabricated sensor does not have two independent on-chip temperature sensors. In the current implementation, the bridge resistors sense both temperature and applied pressure.

Figure 2 shows the electrical equivalent of sensor connection. Resistors R1 and R2, do not match perfectly with each other due to fabrication error. The mismatches in resistors are compensated in current implementation by un-equal bias current sources i.e. I1 and I2 are different. The sensor resistors R1 and R2 are much more sensitive to temperature than pressure when characterized individually. Thus, the voltage drop across R1 is used to measure the temperature and differential output across R1 and R2 is used to measure the output variation with pressure.

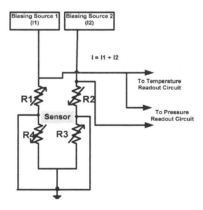

**Fig. 2.** Sensor in wheat-stone bridge configuration

Figure 3 represents the differential output of sensor with variation of pressure. Biasing current to the resistors is kept fixed where I1 is 0.2 mA and I2 is 0.224 mA. The temperature is 40 °C which is assumed to be the reference temperature for the purpose of compensation. Figure 4 shows the shift in the average sensitivity and offset relative to reference temperature under same bias condition.

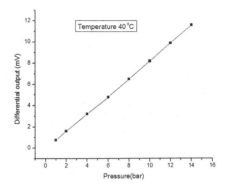

**Fig. 3.** Output response of sensor with pressure at reference temperature (with unequal bias current)

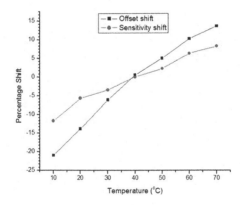

**Fig. 4.** Percentage shift in the offset and sensitivity with temperature

## 3    Proposed Architecture

In the proposed technique, full bridge MEMS sensor is configured as half bridge by connecting the two output terminals and the bias point to ground as shown in Fig. 5. The other two terminals, meant for externally tunable resistor (zero pressure output offset compensation resistor), are connected with tunable current sources used to bias the half bridge.

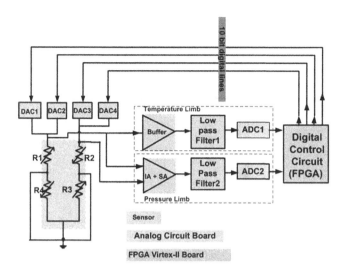

**Fig. 5.** Architecture for temperature calibration in pressure sensor

10-Bit current steering DACs are used as current sources in order to bias the bridge. DAC1, DAC3 are coarse and DAC2, DAC4 are fine resolution current sources for compensation of the sensor related errors. Two readout circuitries are used to measure temperature and pressure respectively.

Temperature readout circuit consists of a buffer along with filter and ADC. Pressure readout circuit consists of an instrumentation amplifier along with second inverting gain amplifier providing sufficient gain at output, low-pass filter and ADC. A 10-bit SAR ADC is used for data conversion [10].

The converted digital data is fed to digital control circuit implemented using Vertex-II pro FPGA board. The sensor compensation control algorithm is implemented on FPGA board (connected through expansion header pins J1–J4) using VHDL language. The readout circuit (shown in Fig. 5) consists of all analog modules assembled on a single PCB board. The system clock is 1 kHz which is generated from an arbitrary wave form generator. Figure 6 shows the complete implementation of analog modules PCB connected with FPGA board through various input output pins (expansion header pins J1–J4) available on FPGA.

**Fig. 6.** Complete setup for compensation of sensor output

# 4   ASIC Implementation

The targeted application requires considerable reduction in weight and volume of implemented architecture shown in Fig. 5. The volume reduction is achieved by integrating all the analog sub-modules and control algorithm on a single chip using AMS 0.35 μm CMOS technology. The analog sub-modules are DAC, ADC, IA (Instrumentation Amplifier), Buffer, Inverting gain amplifier and digital control circuit (DCC) implementing the algorithm.

A traditional 10-bit segmented current steering DAC is designed with a tunable reference current source from 10 nA to 1 mA [11]. Two different reference currents act as coarse and fine DAC. The implemented ADC samples the input directly on the DAC and comparison is achieved by cascaded inverters [10]. A buffer is required to drive the high capacitive input (approximately 10 pF) of ADC. The sensor output is amplified by an IA based on three op-amps based approach [12]. The mismatch of on-chip resistors is minimized by a common-centroid layout approach, which has direct impact on CMRR of IA. A second inverting amplifier is also cascaded with IA to control the cumulative gain of amplifying stages, offset and thermal noise generated from sensor. Both IA and second amplifier is designed using high gain folded-cascode buffered output amplifier.

The analog block is separated by a double guard ring from digital block. The resistor variations with process and temperature are controlled by sizing the dimension and adapting suitable resistor design strategy [13]. A grounded signal shield isolates the substrate injection noise getting merged with analog signal. Table 1 shows the detailed testing results of fabricated chip. The active-RC analog filters are implemented off-chip on fabricated PCB (basically area constraint) [12]. Figure 7 shows the block level implementation using the designed ASIC and other components. An external memory is interfaced with ASIC (the fabrication technology node does not support on chip memory) to store the compensation co-efficient.

**Table 1.** Measurement data result

| Sub-blocks | Operating conditions | Measurement results | Make & type |
|---|---|---|---|
| DAC | Supply voltage: 3.3 V | Resolution: 10 Bit<br>**DNL: −0.7/0.3<br>**INL: −1.4/1.9<br>Output Range: 10 nA–1 mA<br>SNR: 57 dB for 10 Hz input<br>@ 16 kHz sampling rate<br>Conversion speed: 100 KSPS<br>ENOB: 8.1 | Make: in-house designed &<br>fabricated at Euro practice<br>Technology: 0.35 um,<br>3.3 V, triple metal, double<br>poly<br>Type: Current Steering |
| Sensor | Bias voltage: 3.3 V | Sensitivity: 1.2 mV/Bar<br>Burst pressure: 40 Bar<br>Maximum applied pressure:<br>15 Bar | Make: In-house designed &<br>fabricated<br>Type: piezo-resistive |
| IA | Supply voltage: 3.3 V | ICMR: 0.3 V to 2.5 V<br>Gain: 1–45 V/V<br>CMRR:60 dB @ 1 kHz<br>Output offset: 6 mV<br>OCMR: 150 mV to 2.5 V<br>Output Transient Noise:<br>700 μV at full gain | In-house designed &<br>fabricated at Euro practice<br>Technology: 0.35 um,<br>3.3 V, triple metal, double<br>poly<br>Type: three op-Amps based<br>architecture |
| Filter | Supply voltage: 3.3 V | ICMR: 0.3 V-2.5 V<br>3-dB cutoff<br>frequency < 20 Hz<br>Pass band gain: 1 V/V<br>Order: 2nd | Make: same as IA<br>Type: sallen-key<br>architecture |
| ADC | Supply voltage: 3.3 V | Resolution: 10 Bit<br>**DNL: 0.3/−0.6<br>**INL: 1.2/−3.0 | Make: same as IA<br>Type: Successive<br>approximation architecture |
| | Reference voltage:<br>2.5 V | Input Range: 0–2.5 V<br>SNR: 56 dB for 10 Hz input<br>@ 16 kHz sampling rate<br>Conversion speed: 200 KSPS<br>ENOB: 7.9 | |

**DNL & INL are respectively calculated in the ADC input voltage operating range of 0–2.5 V.

The die photo of chip designed with all the on chip analog modules i.e. four DACs, two ADCs, IA, amplifier and also, digital compensation circuit is shown in Fig. 8. The size of die is 10 mm$^2$.

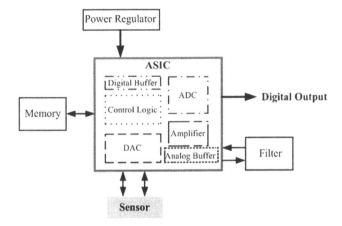

**Fig. 7.** Block level implementation of ASIC designed for sensor

**Fig. 8.** Die photo of fabricated chip (ASIC) with analog and digital module

## 5    Test Analysis

The output of sensor (in mV) varies with temperature i.e. offset and sensitivity both varies.

In order to satisfy the input range of ADC and to detect the pressure variation efficiently (i.e. to increase sensitivity), raw output is further amplified with a system gain of 80 V/V. The amplified output of sensor at different temperatures is shown in Fig. 9 (uncompensated data). Temperature is varied by 10 °C in range of 10 °C to 70 °C. Figure 10 presents the output of sensor at same temperatures after compensation with pressure variation.

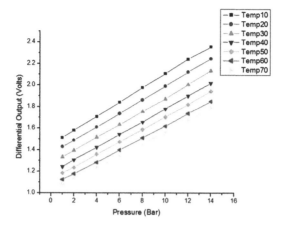

**Fig. 9.** Readout circuit output

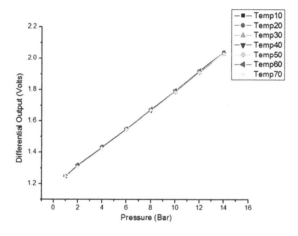

**Fig. 10.** Output of sensor after compensation

The percentage sensitivity and offset variation is calculated with respect to reference temperature for amplified sensor output. Sensitivity shift is reduced by a factor of 10 and offset shift is reduced by a factor of 44. The respective plots are shown in Figs. 11 and 12 for uncompensated and compensated data.

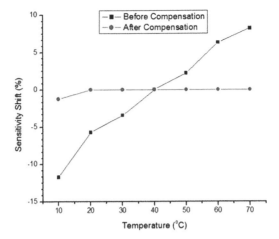

**Fig. 11.** Percentage variation in sensitivity with temperature

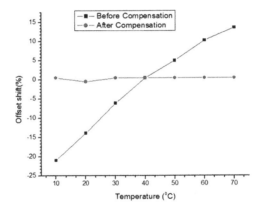

**Fig. 12.** Percentage variation in offset with temperature

# 6   Comparison

Table 2 represents the comparison of present work with the previous works [3, 5, 14].

**Table 2.**   Comparison of performance

| Parameters | Present work | [5] | [14] | [3] |
|---|---|---|---|---|
| Technology | 0.35 μm CMOS | 3 μm CMOS | – | 2 μm CMOS |
| Supply | 3.3 V | ±5 V | – | 5 V |
| Temperature sensor | Not required | PTAT Element | Not used | Required |
| Ref. Temperature1 | 40 °C | 25 °C | 26 °C | 25 °C |
| Offset after compensation | ±0.48% | ±3.5% (increases after sensitivity compensation) | 1.6% (relative error after compensation with reduction factor of 10) | 2–4% |
| Sensitivity after compensation | −1.248% (Worst Case) | ±0.5% | | |
| Temperature compensation range | 10 °C to 70 °C | −30 °C to +100 °C | −40 °C to 70 °C | −40 °C to 120 °C |
| Chip area (mm$^2$) | 10 | – | – | 34 |

# 7   Conclusion

Current steering DAC's are used to compensate sensor offset and non-linearity (sensitivity variation). The temperature compensation algorithm compensates thermal drift through the DAC without an additional temperature sensor. The implemented algorithm does not require a detailed characterization of sensor. The characterization in the present technique is much simpler than methods reported in literature where a larger lookup table needs to be stored. In this technique, the same values stored for temperature are used to compensate the temperature effect. A total error of 40% is reduced. The hardware requirement and multiple feed-back loops are redundant in the proposed approach. The Compensation is achieved for a temperature range of 10 °C to 70 °C (suitable for MAV application).

**Acknowledgement.**   MEMS Group of CSIR-CEERI fabricated the pressure sensor. The designing of sensor was carried out by S. Santosh Kumar and Dr. B. D. Pant. The chip fabrication cost supported by DiT, India.

# References

1. Senturia, S.D.: Microsystem Design, 1st edn. Springer, New York (2004). https://doi.org/10.1007/b117574
2. Krechmery, et al.: Pressure transducer with integral digital temperature compensation. In: U.S. Patent 4 765 188 (1988)

3. Machul, O., Hammerschmidt, D., Brockherde, W., Hosticka, B.J., Obermeier, E., Krause, P.: A smart pressure transducer with on-chip readout, calibration and nonlinear temperature compensation based on spline-functions. In: ISSCC, San Francisco (Cal.), pp. 198–199 (1997)
4. Philip, C.J., et al.: Signal conditioner for MEMS based Piezoresitive sensor. In: Vth ICIIS, India (2010)
5. Gakkestad, J., Ohlckers, P., Halbo, L.: Effects of process variations in a CMOS circuit for temperature compensation of piezoresistive pressure sensors. Sens. Actuators **A48**, 63–71 (1995)
6. Keller, H.W., et al.: Method for temperature compensation and measuring circuit therefore. In: U.S. Patent 4 715 003A (1987)
7. Peng, K.H., Uang, C.M., Chang, Y.M.: The temperature compensation of the Silicon Piezo-Resistive Pressure Sensor using the Half-Bridge Technique. In: Proceedings of SPIE, vol. 5343, pp. 292–301 (2004)
8. Herman, J., et al.: Microprocessor controlled sensor signal conditioning circuit. In: U.S. Patent 5 764 541 (1998)
9. BMP085 Datasheet
10. Behera, K.C., Santosh, M., Bose, S.C.: A low-power 12-bit SAR ADC for remote pressure measurement. Analog Integr. Circs. Sig. Process. **86**, 99 (2016). https://doi.org/10.1007/s10470-015-0656-2
11. Bosch, A.V., Borremans, M.A.F., Steyaert, M.S.J., Sansen, W.: A 10-bit 1-GSample/s Nyquist current-steering CMOS D/A converter. In: IEEE JSSC, vol. 36 (2001)
12. Arney, R.P., Webster, J.G.: Analog Signal Processing. Wiley, USA (1999)
13. Drennan, P.G.: Integrated circuit device mismatch modelling and characterization for analog circuit design. Ph. D. Thesis. Arizona State University (1999)
14. Reverter, F., et al.: Novel and low-cost temperature compensation technique for piezo-resistive pressure sensor. In: XIX IMEKO World Congress, Portugal, pp. 2084–2087 (2009)

# FEM Based Device Simulator for High Voltage Devices

Ashok Ray[1](✉), Gaurav Kumar[1](✉), Sushanta Bordoloi[1,3],
Dheeraj Kumar Sinha[1], Pratima Agarwal[2], and Gaurav Trivedi[1]

[1] Department of Electronics and Electrical Engineering,
Indian Institute of Technology Guwahati, Guwahati 781039, Assam, India
{ashok.ray,gkumar2012,d.sinha,trivedi}@iitg.ernet.in
[2] Department of Physics, Indian Institute of Technology Guwahati,
Guwahati 781039, Assam, India
pratima@iitg.ernet.in
[3] Department of Electronics and Communication Engineering,
National Institute of Technology Mizoram, Aizawl 796012, Mizoram, India
b.sushanta@iitg.ernet.in

**Abstract.** TCAD simulation of electronic device has always been the basic approach to understand solid state electronics and to frame roadmap for the evolution of future technology. Design of devices on these materials require better understanding of the physical insights to the internals of the device structure. In such a scenario, TCAD tool can help to visualize internal dynamics of carriers and fields in the device structure, thus helping to improve them further. Device structures are evolving continuously leading to an increase in complexity of computation of simulation. There is an increasing challenge to these simulators to improvise compact device models, whereby generating precise results. The responsibility of TCAD designers is ever increasing to develop improved solvers featuring better predictive capabilities. In this work, an effort has been made to compare the performance of an FEM based proposed simulator with conventional available device simulator. A simple *pn* junction diode is designed in both the simulators and a comparison of different electrical properties has been done by incorporating similar models and exactly same material parameters.

**Keywords:** Silicon carbide · High voltage device
Finite element method · Drift-diffusion · TCAD simulation

## 1 Introduction

Electronics design and technology is advancing fast, so there is a need as well as compulsion to keep up with the developments. Ability to quickly design and test devices based on emerging materials is the need of the hour in post CMOS era. The responsibility to quickly design such devices, not only lies on the designer but is also the onus of a smart device simulator. TCAD plays a vital role for

© Springer Nature Singapore Pte Ltd. 2017
B. K. Kaushik et al. (Eds.): VDAT 2017, CCIS 711, pp. 127–135, 2017.
https://doi.org/10.1007/978-981-10-7470-7_14

pushing the advancements in research and development of semiconductor devices by optimizing the existing technology. It helps to evolve better device geometries by incorporating ever evolving device models. Different types of device structures and geometries can be implemented in a TCAD simulator, which further, with the help of various semiconductor models (such as; Drift-Diffusion, Hydrodynamics, Boltzmann (Monte Carlo), Quantum Corrected Boltzmann, Non-equilibrium Greens Function [1]) can help us to predict approximate device characteristics. Power electronics sector is expanding fast and silicon based devices are not able to meet the ever growing power density and operational temperature due to their low breakdown electric field and thermal conductivity. There is lot of research happening on futuristic high power semiconductor materials, among them Silicon Carbide (SiC) and Galium Nitride (GaN) are popular [2–6].

Many device physics models are incorporated in a simulator. These models are a set of mathematical equations which mimic the device physics. Any general device model is in the form of a partial differential equations (PDEs), which first needs to be converted to a numerically solvable problem with the help of various discretization schemes. Numerous PDEs with suitable boundary conditions are solved on a specific device geometry to simulate different transport models of a semiconductor device. The computation complexity of such a problem increases if the device structure is complicated, which also leads to various convergence issues. For regular and simple structure these PDEs can be analytically solved, but one has to resort to numerical methods if the structure is complicated. Among the various discretization techniques available, finite difference method (FDM), finite element method (FEM) are the popular ones. A FDM is faster as well as is less computational intensive for simpler one dimensional (1D) structures but it tends to perform poor when the structure complexity increases. In this work, we have used FEM to discretize several PDEs and proposed a simulator for high power devices [7,8]. We have implemented a SiC junction diode using our simulator. To validate the performance of the proposed simulator, we have compared our results with a conventional and popular TCAD tool *Sentaurus*. Rest of the paper is organized as follows: Sect. 2 describes the Silicon Carbide material. Section 3 explains the working principle of the proposed simulator along with the involved device equations. Section 4 describes the implementation details and results. Section 5 concludes the paper.

## 2    Silicon Carbide Material System

Silicon Carbide (SiC) was first synthesized by Berzelius in the year 1824 [9]. It is a wide band-gap (WBG) semiconductor having a high saturation drift velocity along with good thermal conductivity. Because of the wide band-gap, it can sustain high electric field before breaking down. It has been in use to design high power devices which generally work at elevated voltage and temperatures. High temperature sensors have also been designed using SiC [10]. Due to their wide band-gap, they are inherently radiation hardened and hence can also be used for space applications. A silicon carbide unit cell evolves by the stacking of silicon and carbon bi-layers. Various polytypes can be created by stacking silicon and carbon bi-layers in different ways. There are more than 250 polytypes [11] that are available in SiC family. All the polytypes can be divided on the basis of crystallographic arrangement as cubic (C), hexagonal (H) and rombohedral (R). Few polytypes of SiC are 3C (cubic, three layers stacked in the sequence of *ABCABC...*), 2H (wurtzite, layers stacked as *ABAB..*), 4H (hexagonal, layers stacked as *ABCBABCB...*) and 6H (hexagonal, layers stacked as *ABCACBABCACB...*). Among the polytypes, 4H-SiC and 6H-SiC are popular owing to their better electronic properties [12]. Figure 1(a) shows the stacking sequence for 4H and 6H SiC. Stacking of the silicon and carbon bi-layers are similar in 2H and 3C, where *AB* and *ABCA* layers are required respectively. In this paper the simulation has been setup on 4H-SiC. A comparison of different material properties of 4H and 6H SiC is presented in Table 1.

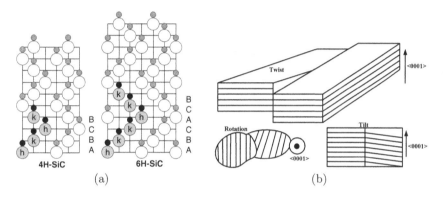

**Fig. 1.** (a) Stacking sequence indicating bond composition and location in 4H and 6H silicon carbide [13]; (b) Common defects in silicon carbide [14].

The doping in SiC can be done either during epitaxy or by ion implantation. Nitrogen and phosphorus are *n*-type dopants, for *p*-type, aluminium and boron are used. Dopant diffusion in silicon carbide is very low, hence the activation needs to done at elevated temperature above 1400 °C [15]. Annealing at such high temperatures tend to degrade the surface morphology of silicon carbide. Dopants in SiC are selected based on lowest ionization energy. In 4H-SiC the *n*-type dopant, nitrogen has an activation energy of 45 meV as compared to phosphorus whose value is 80 meV. Similarly, the activation energies for *p*-type dopants (in 4H-SiC) are 200 meV and 300 meV for aluminium and boron respectively [16]. In SiC as mentioned earlier, the stacking creates different polytpes. Because of such a stacking, cubic and hexagonal bonds are formed. Such a bonding creates cubic($k$) and hexagonal($h$) sites [13]. Same type of dopant occupying $h$ and $k$ sites will have different ionization energies. Ionization energies at $h$ and $k$ sites is shown in Table 1. There are different numbers of hexagonal and cubic bonds in 4H and 6H SiCs. Equal number of cubic and hexagonal bonds are available in 4H variant where as there are two-third cubic and one-third hexagonal bonds in 6H type. This creates a sharing rule of dopants between $h$ and $k$ sites. A dopant is distributed equally in 4H between hexagonal and cubic bonds, the distribution in 6H being two-thirds at cubic site and one-third at hexagonal sites. Such a dopant sharing at two sites creates a situation called incomplete ionization. Silicon carbide wafers can be grown either by sublimation growth or chemical vapor deposition. Molecular beam epitaxy can also be used for the growth of the same. When a wafer is grown, it is important to maintain the same polytype throughout the wafer but instability in growth mechanism may occur and in the same wafer there may be different polytypes. This defect arises in SiC wafer due to change in the crystal stacking sequence during the growth phase. This is called polytype instability. Another defect that can be found on a typical SiC wafer is the micropipes. This defect arises due to high strain energy along the core of a dislocation, which leads to sublimation and a void is created which is hollow. Micropipe defect is of major concern as this would limit the current handling capacity of SiC device to few amperes [17]. Low angle grain boundaries (LAGBs) is another kind of defect. This defect is predominant with large diameter wafers. Dislocations can also occur in a SiC wafer during growth, which are also a type of defect. These dislocations are dangerous as they tend to migrate when subsequent layers are grown using epitaxy [18]. Common defects in silicon carbide are shown in Fig. 1(b).

**Table 1.** Material properties comparison of semiconductors [13,16].

| Property | 4H-SiC | 6H-SiC |
|---|---|---|
| Bandgap (eV) | 3.3 | 3.0 |
| Relative dielectric constant | 9.7 | 9.7 |
| Breakdown field | $\parallel$c-ax:3.0 | $\parallel$c-ax:3.0 |
| (MV/cm) at $N_D = 10^{17}$ cm$^{-3}$ | – | $\perp$c-ax:>1 |
| Thermal conductivity (W/cmK) | 3–5 | 3–5 |
| Intrinsic carr. conc. (cm$^{-3}$) @300 K | $\approx 10^{-7}$ | $\approx 10^{-5}$ |
| Electron mobility | $\parallel$c-ax:800 | $\parallel$c-ax:60 |
| @$N_D = 10^{16}$ cm$^{-3}$ (cm$^2$/Vs) | $\perp$c-ax:800 | $\perp$c-ax:400 |
| Saturated electron velocity ($10^7$ cm/s) | 2 | 2 |
| Donor shallowest ionization energy (meV) | N:45 & P:80 | N:85 & P:80 |
| Acceptor shallowest ionization energy (meV) | Al:200 & B:300 | Al:200 & B:300 |
| INCOMPLETE IONIZATION (N doped) (meV): | | |
| $h$–site | 50 ±5 | 80 ±5 |
| $k_1$ site | 90±5 | 140 ±5 |
| $k_2$ site | – | 145±5 |

where, $\parallel$ is the parallel and $\perp$ is the perpendicular direction to $c - axis$.

# 3    Simulator Working Principle and Incorporation of Device Equations

Various transport models can be used to simulate semiconductor devices based on their geometric dimensions. Electrical properties of a device having dimensions of the order of $\mu$m can be accurately simulated using Drift-Diffusion (DD) model. We have also incorporated DD model in proposed simulator to perform simulations of a SiC based $pn$ junction diode. Any simulator extracts the device characteristics by solving a set of five basic semiconductor equations from DD model, they are as follows

1. **Poisson's equation**

$$\epsilon_s \bigtriangledown \cdot E = -\epsilon_s \bigtriangledown^2 \psi = q(p - n + N_d - N_a), \tag{1}$$

2. **Drift diffusion equations**

$$J_n = qn\mu_n \bigtriangledown \psi + qD_n \bigtriangledown n, \tag{2}$$

$$J_p = qp\mu_p \bigtriangledown \psi - qD_p \bigtriangledown p, \tag{3}$$

3. **Continuity equations**

$$\frac{\partial n}{\partial t} = \frac{1}{q} \bigtriangledown \cdot J_n + (G_n - R_n), \tag{4}$$

$$\frac{\partial p}{\partial t} = -\frac{1}{q} \bigtriangledown \cdot J_p + (G_n - R_n) \tag{5}$$

where $\psi$ is potential, $J_n$ and $J_p$ stands for electron and hole drift/diffusion component $\mu$ is mobility, $D$ is diffusion coefficient, $G$ and $R$ are the net generation and recombination rates respectively, $n$ & $p$ specifies the electron and hole density in conduction and valance band respectively, $q$ is electronic charge, $J$ is current density, $\epsilon_s$ is dielectric permittivity of the semiconductor material and $t$ represents time.

There is a systematic approach to incorporate the models, boundary conditions, material parameters and meshing mechanism. The steps involved in the simulation of a semiconductor device is indicated in Fig. 2. The specified structure is meshed wherein nodes are formed (intersection points of meshes). The PDEs are linearized over the meshed domain and then they are solved over the region. As the simulator reads the structure which has already been meshed, a first hand estimation of the charge is done by just solving the Poisson's equation. After this initial guess, all the above mentioned equations are solved self-consistently using various numerical techniques such as, Newton-Raphson, Gauss Seidel, etc. The solution from these numerical techniques will give approximate results for electrical properties of the device. The solution provided by Poisson's equation is potential, where as continuity equation calculates the current using potential profile given by Poisson's equation. All these PDEs along with PDEs from different models of carrier generation-recombination are incorporate in the proposed simulator and solved using FEM discretization methodology. Implementation details, device geometry and its physical properties are described in next section.

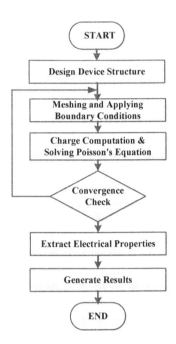

**Fig. 2.** Simulation flow of a typical device simulator [17].

## 4    Implementation Details and Results

The proposed simulator incorporated Drift-Diffusion model to simulate SiC based devices. The fundamental devices equations for drift-diffusion has been discretized using finite element method. To carry out the discretization process, whole geometry (domain) of a device is divided into large number of small elements (finite elements) using linear shape (or basis) functions [19,20]. The solution of the equation is then evaluated over these finite small elements to compute the global solution. This process converts an infinite dimension problem to a finite dimension problem. Now, this finite dimensional problem can be represented in form of matrix and solution in computed using any direct or iterative solver. The basis function can be taken as any geometrically simple element, such as triangle, rectangular, tetrahedrons, cubes, hexahedrons etc. The necessary condition for these basis function is that, it depend linearly on $x, y, z$ coordinates, and is defined in a way that it has a value of "1" for node $j$ (with coordinates as $\mathbf{p_j} = \{x_j, y_j, z_j\}^T$) and has "0" value for all other nodes.

In this work, 4H-SiC has been used to design a *pn* junction diode. Uniform doping has been used to form the junction in device. The doping levels were fixed to 1e16 cm$^{-3}$ for both $n$ and $p$ type dopants. The dimension of the structure used is 30 μm × 5 μm. The meshing on the structure was fixed globally at a value of 0.9375 μm × 0.625 μm. The mobility has been assumed to be constant. Shockley-Read-Hall model dependent on doping and temperature has been used

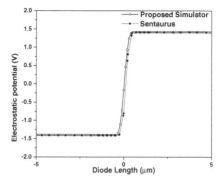

**Fig. 3.** Comparison of potential variation across the junction.

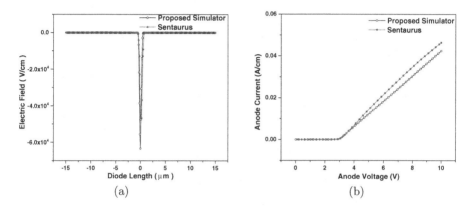

**Fig. 4.** (a) Comparison of electric field variation across the diode; (b) Comparison of forward biased anode current.

for carrier generation-recombination. The contacts to the diode was set to ohmic. The physical parameters that were used in the simulation are: a band gap of 4H-SiC was fixed at 3.3 eV, relative dielectric constant was set at a value of 10.32, electron and hole mobilities were fixed at 950 and 113 $(cm^2/Vs)$ respectively as per suggestion in [13].

Forward bias simulations were performed on the device structure to calculate its electrical properties and they were compared with TCAD Sentaurus results. The forward bias characteristics obtained were in agreement with the observed value in literature [21]. To validate the results of proposed simulator, similar models and material parameters were incorporated in both the simulators. Figure 3 shows a comparison of calculated potential in the device with Sentaurus. The graph has been plotted in the vicinity of junction ($\pm 5$ μm) to show the observable difference between results of two simulators. However the length of the diode is 30 μm ($\pm 15$ μm). Electric field comparison has been shown in Fig. 4(a). A variation between the two profiles is observed at the junction which may be attributed to the different step size used in the calculation. Figure 4(b) presents the comparison of forward biased anode current for a SiC (4H) based $pn$ junction diode. A close match in the cut-in voltage as well as forward conduction current is observed. Presented results validates the effectiveness of the proposed simulator.

## 5  Conclusion

To suffice the need of efficient devices in the rapid growing power electronics industry, better device designs need to emerge whereby enhancing the device performance and efficiency. TCAD simulations helps to get quicker device designs and fabrication. This will promote better devices to get marketed quickly, so that they can be incorporated in the evolving circuit designs. Available commercial simulators are very costly and so not in the reach of every researcher. In this paper, we have presented a high-voltage device simulator. To improve the accuracy of the simulations, we have used FEM to implement different PDEs of a device simulator. Results for a SiC based high power $pn$ junction diode has been presented and compared with Sentaurus. A close match between the results have been observed, which validated the proposed simulator.

## References

1. Pourfath, M., Sverdlov, V., Selberherr, S.: Transport modeling for nanoscale semiconductor devices. In: 2010 10th IEEE International Conference on Solid-State and Integrated Circuit Technology (ICSICT), pp. 1737–1740 (2010)
2. Whitaker, B., Barkley, A., Cole, Z., Passmore, B., Martin, D., McNutt, T.R., Lostetter, A.B., Lee, J.S., Shiozaki, K.: A high-density, high-efficiency, isolated onboard vehicle battery charger utilizing silicon carbide power devices. IEEE Trans. Power Electron. **29**(5), 2606 (2014)
3. Mao, S., Wu, T., Lu, X., Popovic, J., Ferreira, J.A.: Three-phase active front-end rectifier efficiency improvement with silicon carbide power semiconductor devices. In: 2016 IEEE Energy Conversion Congress and Exposition (ECCE), pp. 1–8. IEEE (2016)
4. Wang, Z., Shi, X., Tolbert, L.M., Wang, F.F., Liang, Z., Costinett, D., Blalock, B.J.: A high temperature silicon carbide MOSFET power module with integrated silicon-on-insulator-based gate drive. IEEE Trans. Power Electron. **30**(3), 1432 (2015)
5. Peng, K., Eskandari, S., Santi, E.: Characterization and modeling of a gallium nitride power HEMT. IEEE Trans. Ind. Appl. **52**(6), 4965 (2016)
6. Baliga, B.J.: Gallium nitride devices for power electronic applications. Semicond. Sci. Technol. **28**(7), 074011 (2013)
7. Kumar, G., Singh, M., Bulusu, A., Trivedi, G.: A parallel device simulator based on finite element method. In: 2015 International Conference on Computational Science and Computational Intelligence (CSCI), pp. 30–35 (2015)
8. Kumar, G., Singh, M., Ray, A., Trivedi, G.: An FEM based framework to simulate semiconductor devices using streamline upwind Petrov-Galerkin stabilization technique. In: 2017 27th International Conference Radioelektronika (RADIOELEKTRONIKA), pp. 1–5 (2017)

9. Kimoto, T., Cooper, J.A.: Fundamentals of Silicon Carbide Technology: Growth, Characterization, Devices and Applications. Wiley, Hoboken (2014)
10. Rao, S., Pangallo, G., Corte, F.G.D.: Highly Linear Temperature Sensor Based on 4H-Silicon Carbide p-i-n Diodes. IEEE Electron Device Lett. **36**(11), 1205 (2015)
11. Daulton, T., Bernatowicz, T., Lewis, R., Messenger, S., Stadermann, F., Amari, S.: Polytype distribution of circumstellar silicon carbide: microstructural characterization by transmission electron microscopy. Geochim. Cosmochim. Acta **67**(24), 4743 (2003)
12. Codreanu, C., Avram, M., Carbunescu, E., Iliescu, E.: Comparison of 3C-SiC, 6H-SiC and 4H-SiC MESFETs performances. Mater. Sci. Semiconductor Process. **3**(12), 137 (2000)
13. Sentaurus Device User Guide, Version L-2016.03, March 2016
14. Shur, M., Rumyantsev, S.L., Levinshten, M.E.: SiC Materials and Devices, vol. 1. World Scientific, Singapore (2006)
15. Sundaresan, S.G., Rao, M.V., Tian, Y., Schreifels, J.A., Wood, M.C., Jones, K.A., Davydov, A.V.: Comparison of solid-state microwave annealing with conventional furnace annealing of ion-implanted SiC. J. Electron. Mater. **36**(4), 324 (2007)
16. Chen, W.-K.: The VLSI Handbook. CRC Press, Boca Raton (2016)
17. Neudeck, P.G., Powell, J.A.: Performance limiting micropipe defects in silicon carbide wafers. IEEE Electron Device Lett. **15**(2), 63 (1994)
18. Shur, M.: SiC Materials and Devices. Selected Topics in Electronics and Systems. World Scientific, Singapore (2007)
19. Oden, J.T.: An Introduction to the finite element method with applications to nonlinear problems. SIAM Rev. **31**(3), 512 (1989)
20. Mohamed, N., Sujod, M.: Finite elements in semiconductor devices. In: International Conference on Information Management and Engineering, pp. 108–110 (2009)
21. Elasser, A., Kheraluwala, M.H., Ghezzo, M., Steigerwald, R.L., Evers, N.A., Kretchmer, J., Chow, T.P.: A comparative evaluation of new silicon carbide diodes and state-of-the-art silicon diodes for power electronic applications. IEEE Trans. Ind. Appl. **39**(4), 915 (2003)

# Synapse Circuits Implementation and Analysis in 180 nm MOSFET and CNFET Technology

Sushma Srivastava[1(✉)] and S. S. Rathod[2]

[1] Faculty of Technology, Pacific Academy of Higher
Education and Research University, Udaipur, India
sushsri2012@gmail.com
[2] Electronics Engineering Department, Sardar Patel Institute of Technology,
Mumbai, India

**Abstract.** Neuromorphic hardware circuits and systems emulate the operational and organizational principles of biological networks. The basic components building up these large-scale networks are the neurons and the synapses. The synapses serve as interconnections between the neurons for computation and transfer of information in real as well as artificial neural systems. Synapses in the neuronal networks can be static with a constant gain or dynamic with modification in the synaptic strength during computation. In short term dynamical plastic synapses, the synaptic strength changes in the time scale of milliseconds to minutes and the change is reversible. The short term dynamic synapses can be both depressing, when synaptic strength decreases, or facilitating when it increases. In this paper, we have worked on a static synapse and a short term dynamical depressing synapse circuit already reported in literature. We have ported these circuits to 180 nm MOSFET technology and CNFET technology and studied their response in terms of their functionality, the average power consumption and area occupancy. The simulations in this work have been carried out using HSPICE software.

**Keywords:** Neuromorphic · CNFET · Synapse · Synaptic plasticity

## 1 Introduction

Neuromorphic Engineering is a branch of electronics that deals with the implementation of hardware circuits and systems based upon the functional and organizational principles of biological nervous system. The Silicon Neuron and Synapse circuits are the basic building blocks of these systems. The analog VLSI implementation of these circuits with transistors working in sub threshold regime results into area and power efficient synapse circuits. The pioneering work in this field was done by Carver Mead at Caltec in mid 1980s [1]. Synapses are the communication links between the neurons in the biological networks as well as the hardware VLSI based neural networks. In the process of signal transfer, synapse converts the input spike voltage pulses from presynaptic neuron to an output current which is injected in the membrane of the postsynaptic neuron.

© Springer Nature Singapore Pte Ltd. 2017
B. K. Kaushik et al. (Eds.): VDAT 2017, CCIS 711, pp. 136–143, 2017.
https://doi.org/10.1007/978-981-10-7470-7_15

The synapses can be static with a constant gain or dynamic with changed efficacy for a short time during signal transmission. The static synapses can be excitatory or inhibitory. The excitatory synapse source current into the postsynaptic membrane capacitor leading to its depolarization where as the inhibitory synapse sinks current from the postsynaptic membrane capacitor leading to its hyperpolarization. The short term dynamic synapse on the other hand induces temporary modifications in the neural circuitry and has a short time scale on the order of milliseconds to seconds. These changes in the synaptic efficacy basically reflect the presynaptic activity [2]. The short term dynamic synapses of two types have been observed which have opposite effects on the synaptic efficiency. They are known as short term depression and short term facilitation. The short term dynamic synaptic efficiencies return to their base line level with discontinuation of the presynaptic activity. Further, the response of the dynamic synapse depends upon the frequency of the presynaptic spikes [3]. They take a recovery time of few hundreds of milliseconds before attaining the maximum amplitude.

One of the main requirements for synaptic circuits in large scale VLSI neural networks is compactness. The implementation of MOSFET based synaptic circuit at improved technology node provide advantage of less area and power but is a challenging task. It would be appropriate to port these circuits to novel device technologies like Carbon Nanotube Field Effect Transistors (CNFET) technology, which offer advantages over MOSFET technologies in terms of area and power consumption, to facilitate implementation of denser and low power efficient large-scale networks.

## 2  Synapse Circuits

We have studied and analyzed the synapse circuits of excitatory synapse with constant weight proposed by Indiveri [4] and the short term dynamic synapse circuit model of synaptic depression proposed by Liu [5] in this work.

### 2.1  Excitatory Synapse Circuit with Constant Weight

The static excitatory synapse circuit, characterised by a constant weight, implemented in this work has been proposed by Indiveri [4]. The circuit diagram is shown in Fig. 1. It consists of four transistors and a capacitor. The input pulse from the prsynaptic neuron Vs is applied to the gate terminal of transistor M1 which acts as a switch. The weight of the synaptic strength, Vw, is applied to the gate of transistor M2. The voltage Ve applied to the source terminal of transistor M3 is used to set the time constant of the synapse.

The capacitor C1 charges towards Ve through the diode connected transistor M3. On arrival of an input spike pulse the transistor M1 switches on and C1 dischages via M1 and M2 at a rate set by voltage Vw. The capacitor voltage drives transistor M4 and the current flowing through it increases

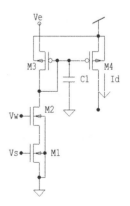

**Fig. 1.** Exciatory synapse circuit [4]

exponentially with the decreasing capacitor voltage. In between the spikes as the transistor M1 is in off state, the capacitor charges towards Ve leading to a decrease in current Id which increses again when another spike appears and the process continues until it reaches a mean steady state value.

## 2.2  Short Term Dynamic Plastic Synapses

The short term dynamic synapses are reversible and can be depressing or facilitating, or combination of both. We have worked on a depressing synapse in this work. The depressing synapse circuit considered here is proposed by Liu [5] and is shown in Fig. 2.

The presynaptic input pulse Vpre is given to the gate terminal of transistor M3. The transistor M3 acts as switch and switches on in presence of an input spike pulse. This allows the discharge current Ir to flow through transistors M2 and M3 and the rate of discharge is controlled by the discharge voltage Vd applied to the gate of transistor M2. Therefore, the quantity of charge removed and hence the rate of discharge of capacitor C1 depends upon Ir and which further depends upon the voltage Vd.

In between the spikes the transistor M3 remains in off state and capacitor C1 charges towards Va via diode connected transistor M1. Thus, the voltage at node Vx and hence the synaptic strength is determined by Va. The voltage at node Vx is the input voltage given to the gate of the transistor M5.

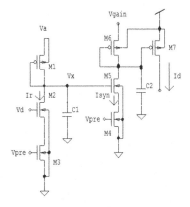

**Fig. 2.** Short    term    depressing Synapse circuit [5]

In an event of spike pulse generation, transistor M4 too switches on resulting into a presynaptic current Isyn, flowing through transistors M5 and M4, which varies exponentially with the voltage Vx. The synaptic current Isyn is converted to an equivalent current with some gain and a time constant through a current mirror formed by the transistors M6, M7 and capacitor C2 by adjusting the voltage Vgain.

## 3   Circuit Simulation and Result Discussion

The synapse circuit models for excitatory synapse with constant weight proposed by Indiveri [4] and the short term dynamic synapse circuit model of synaptic depression proposed by Liu [5] have been studied for their output response and its dependence on various circuit parameters in this work.

These circuits are simulated in 180 nm MOSFET technology and verified for their output response and its dependence upon varying circuit parameters. The same circuits are then ported to CNFET technology with adjusted parameter values and a similar study is done to verify the feasibility of using this technology for implementation of these circuits. The CNFET technology of HSPICE software is based on the CNFET model proposed by Deng [6, 7]. The CNFETs in this work are considered to be containing a single walled semiconducting CNT between the source and drain with chirality of (19, 0). The diameters of CNTs with chirality of (19, 0) is 1.48 nm and has a threshold voltage of 0.29 V [8]. The variable parameter values are fixed below the threshold voltage of the devices in both the MOSFET based as well as CNFET based circuits to ensure subthreshold operation.

### 3.1 Excitatory Synapse Circuit Simulation and Result Analysis

The excitatory synapse circuit of Fig. 1 has been simulated using 180 nm MOFET technology with a supply voltage of 1.8 V and CNFET technology with a supply voltage of 0.9 V. A sequence of pulses at a constant rate, at a frequency of 50 Hz, is applied as the pre-synaptic input Vs to the synapse circuit in Fig. 1. The effect of change in the values of Ve with a constant synaptic weight Vw (Fig. 3(a) in 180 nm MOSFET technology and Fig. 3(b) in CNFET technology) as well as the response of the output with constant Ve and changing synaptic weight by change in the value of Vw is observed (Fig. 4(a) in 180 nm MOSFET technology and Fig. 4(b) in CNFET technology).

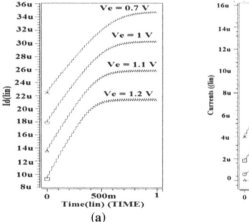

(a)                                    (b)

**Fig. 3.** (a) Excitatory synapse output current for different values of Ve with 50 Hz input spike and Vw = 0.35 V (180 nm MOSFET technology) (b) Excitatory synapse output current for different values of Ve with 50 Hz input spike and Vw = 0.25 V (CNFET technology)

The simulation outputs observed in Fig. 3(a) and (b) show that increase in the value of Ve modifies the gain as well as the time constant of the output current Id in 180 nm MOSFET technology and the CNFET technology respectively.

In Fig. 4(a) and (b) it is observed that the gain of the circuit increases with the increasing value of Vw. Figure 5(a) and (b) show the response of the excitatory synapse circuit to the spike input Vs of increasing rate but fixed values of Ve and Vw in180 nm MOSFET technology and the CNFET technology respectively. It is observed that the circuit integrates the input spikes till the output current Id reaches a steady state value. The rate of integration increases with the increased frequency of the input spikes Vs resulting into a higher steady state value for higher input frequency as observed in Fig. 5(a) and (b).

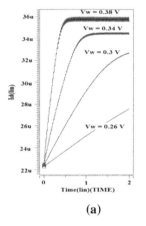
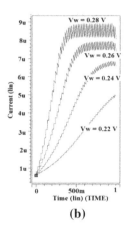

(a)                                    (b)

**Fig. 4.** (a) Excitatory synapse output current for different values of Vw with 50 Hz input spike and Ve = 0.9 V (180 nm MOSFET technology) (b) Excitatory synapse output current for different values of Vw with 50 Hz input spike and Ve = 0.45 V (CNFET technology)

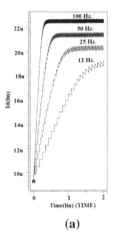
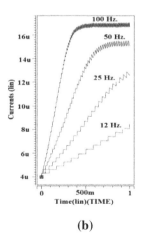

(a)                                    (b)

**Fig. 5.** (a) Excitatory synapse output current for different frequencies of input spike with Ve = 1.2 V and Vw = 0.35 V (180 nm MOSFET technology) (b) Excitatory synapse output current for different frequencies of input spike with Ve = 0.35 V and Vw = 0.25 V (CNFET technology)

## 3.2    Short Term Dynamic Depressing Synapse Circuit Simulation and Result Analysis

The depressing synapse circuit of Fig. 2 is simulated in 180 nm MOSFET technology and CNFET technology with the adjusted parameter values ensuring sub threshold operation of the circuit.

The steady state value of Vx and its dynamics depends upon the potential Vd as shown in Fig. 6(a) and (b) for 180 nm MOSFET technology and CNFET technology respectively. A comparison of the average power consumption of the excitatory synapse and the short-term depressing synapse circuits simulated with the input spike trains of 50 Hz frequency in 180 nm MOSFET technology and CNFET technology in Table 1 show that the average power consumption in CNFET based depressing synapse circuits is an order of magnitude lower than that in 180 nm MOSFET implementation.

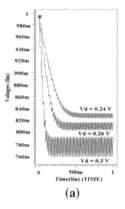
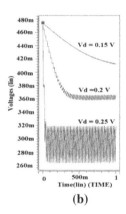

(a)                                      (b)

**Fig. 6.** (a) Short term depressing synapse: Potential at Vx for different values of Vd, input voltage spikes of 50 Hz, Vgain = 0.5 V and Va = 1 V (180 nm MOSFET technology) (b) Short term depressing synapse: Potential at Vx for different values of Vd, input voltage spikes of 50 Hz, Vgain = 0.5 V and Va = 0.5 V (CNFET technology)

**Table 1.** Average power consumption with 50 Hz. Spike input

| Implementation technology | Average power consumption (W) | |
|---|---|---|
| | 180 nm MOSFET technology | CNFET technology |
| Excitatory synapse circuit | $4.2557 \times 10^{-05}$ | $1.1761 \times 10^{-06}$ |
| Short term depressing synapse circuit | $9.9240E \times 10^{-05}$ | $8.9803 \times 10^{-06}$ |

## 4  Conclusion

We have studied the response of the static and short-term dynamic excitatory synapse circuits in this work. In this process, we have ported a static excitatory synapse circuit and a short term dynamic depressing synapse circuit reported in literature to 180 nm MOSFET technology and verified its output characteristics and its dependence on variable parameters. The circuit simulation outputs verify the functionality of the circuits.

We have also explored the possibility of implementation of the static excitatory circuit and a short term dynamic depressing synapse circuit in CNFET technology which would benefit the circuits and hence the complex hardware neural networks in terms of area, power and integration density. The CNFET circuits operate at a supply voltage of 0.9 V thus offering the advantage of low power consumption as observed in Table 1. The average power consumption in CNFET based depressing synapse circuits is an order of magnitude lower than that in 180 nm MOSFET implementation. Further, the area occupied by these circuits will be smaller as compared to the same circuit implementation at an advanced technological node using the conventional MOSFETs. These circuits can be integrated with the integrate and fire neuron circuits implemented in 180 nm MOSFET [9] and CNFET technologies resulting into compact and low power hardware neural networks. Further, the possibility of implementation of neuromorphic circuit components in CNFET technology of proper functionality with smaller power consumption and lower area can be advantageous and can be explored in realization of complex real time neuromorphic systems with large number of synapses integrated to the neurons on a single chip.

## References

1. Mead, C.: Analog VLSI and Neural Systems. Addison-Wesley Longman Publishing Co., Inc., Boston (1989)
2. Liu, S.C., Delbruck, T., Indiveri, G., Whatley, A., Douglas, R.: Event-Based Neuromorphic Systems. Wiley, New York (2015). ISBN 978-0-470-01849-1
3. Thomson, A., Deuchars, J.: Temporal and spatial properties of local circuits in neocortex. Trends Neurosci. **17**, 119–126 (1994)
4. Indiveri, G.: Computation in neuromorphic analog VLSI systems. In: Neural Nets WIRN Vietri-01-Proceedings of the 12th Italian Workshop on Neural Nets, Vietrisul Mare, Salerno, Italy, 17–19 May 2001, pp. 3–20 (2001). https://doi.org/10.1007/978-1-4471-0219-9_1, ISSN 1431-6854
5. Liu, S.C.: Analog VLSI circuits for short-term dynamic synapses. EURASIP J. Appl. Signal Process. **2003**(7), 620–628 (2003). https://doi.org/10.1155/S1110865703302094. ISSN 1110-8657
6. Deng, J., Wong, H.-S.P.: A compact SPICE model for carbon- nanotube field effect transistors including nonidealities and its application — Part I: model of the intrinsic channel region. IEEE Trans. Electron Devices **54**(12), 3186–3194 (2007). https://doi.org/10.1109/TED.2007.909030

7. Deng, J., Wong, H.-S.P.: A compact SPICE model for carbon- nanotube field effect transistors including nonidealities and its application — Part II: full device model and circuit performance benchmarking. IEEE Trans. Electron Devices **54**(12), 3195–3205 (2007). https://doi.org/10.1109/TED.2007.909043
8. Sinha, S.K., Chaudhury, S.: Comparative study of leakage power in CNTFET over MOSFET device. J. Semiconductors **35**(11), 114002 (2014). http://iopscience.iop.org/article/10.1088/1674-4926/35/11/114002/pdf. ISSN: 1674-4926
9. Srivastava, S., Rathod, S.S.: Silicon neuron-analog CMOS VLSI implementation and analysis at 180 nm. In: Third International Conference on Devices, Circuits and Systems (ICDCS 2016), Karunya University, Coimbatore, India, pp. 28–32. IEEE Conference Publications, March 2016. https://doi.org/10.1109/ICDCSyst.2016.7570617

# A 10 MHz, 73 ppm/°C, 84 µW PVT Compensated Ring Oscillator

Vivek Tyagi$^{1(\boxtimes)}$, M. S. Hashmi$^1$, Ganesh Raj$^2$, and Vikas Rana$^2$

$^1$ Indraprastha Institute of Information Technology, New Delhi, India
{vivek15118,mshashmi}@iiitd.ac.in
$^2$ STMicroelectronics, Greater Noida, India
ganeshraj277@gmail.com, vikas18feb@gmail.com

**Abstract.** A 10 MHz, 84 µW PVT compensated ring oscillator is presented in 0.11 µm BCD9S (Bipolar CMOS DMOS) technology. The proposed ring oscillator is inherently temperature compensated and produces a frequency deviation of ±0.7% in typical corner, ±2.25% in slow corner and ±0.75% in fast corner around 10 MHz across −40 °C to 150 °C at a regulated supply of 1.8 V. The proposed oscillator exhibits less sensitivity to PVT variations and requires less area when compared to the state-of-the-art oscillators.

**Keywords:** PVT compensation · BCD · PTAT · CTAT · Automotive

## 1 Introduction

High accuracy CMOS based frequency reference is required for clock generation in data converter circuits in applications such as biomedical, embedded memories, digital controller etc. It has been reported that a non-MEMS based frequency reference exhibits significant advantage over the traditional MEMS based counterpart in terms of power as well as area [1]. However, such non-MEMS based designs suffer from significant frequency deviations across different process corners, voltage variations, and temperature ranges. In recent years, PVT compensated oscillators, which requires temperature and process compensation bias circuits, have been proposed [1–5]. These designs, although very effective, consume significant power and chip area [3, 4]. In this paper, for the first time, design scheme of ring oscillator, exhibiting inherent immunity to temperature and voltage variations and improved tolerance to process variations, is presented. These features make this proposed design a potential candidate for embedded memories. Furthermore, the validation of this design has been carried out in BCD technology to demonstrate its usefulness for smart power applications such as electro-medical, automotive, and aerospace considering the suitability of BCD technology in these applications [6].

There are many approaches available in literature for PVT compensation strategies and few recent approaches are listed below. A 7 MHz ring oscillator utilizing additional on-chip compensation circuit, buffer, and comparators resulting in significantly large area and power consumption is reported in [1]. An alternative architecture to synthesize 1 MHz reference uses a fixed current to charge MIM capacitors, and latch at output to

© Springer Nature Singapore Pte Ltd. 2017
B. K. Kaushik et al. (Eds.): VDAT 2017, CCIS 711, pp. 144–152, 2017.
https://doi.org/10.1007/978-981-10-7470-7_16

store the value [2] but it achieves less frequency deviation at the cost of higher power consumption. A current controlled relaxation oscillator controlled by a current that is proportional to the electron mobility is presented in [3]. It consumes very low power but is able to generate a reference of only 150 kHz. Another design which employs feedback loop to compensate temperature variations generates 10 MHz reference but is not suitable for applications such as automotive owing to its operation limited to 100 °C [4]. A slight improvement to this technique to synthesize 30 MHz was reported in [5] but again the temperature was limited to 100 °C.

This work reports a novel strategy for process, voltage, and temperature (PVT) compensation in the ring oscillator for generation of stable frequency reference. The proposed oscillator exhibits less sensitivity to PVT variations when compared to the state-of-the-art oscillators. A 10 MHz PVT compensated oscillator is designed and simulated in 110 nm BCD9S (Bipolar CMOS DMOS) process technology. Simulation results show the maximum frequency deviation of ±2.25% for −40 °C to 150 °C across all process corners and a maximum power consumption of 84 μW from 1.8 V supply.

## 2 Ring Oscillator Architecture

Figure 1 shows the architecture of proposed ring oscillator. First two inverter stages comprising of transistors M0–M3 are current starved stages and remaining three stages consisting of transistors M4–M9 are biased at supply voltage. The PMOS transistor M18 is used as a capacitor after first stage and is biased either in the inversion or in the accumulation region to get maximum value of gate capacitance. In this design, most of the loop delay (almost 99.9%) comes from the first stage itself and it arises due to charging of large gate capacitance present at 'CAP' node. The charging current $\left(I_{cap}\right)$ of capacitor can be written as:

$$I_{cap} = I_{bias} \frac{\left(\dfrac{W}{L}\right)_{11}}{\left(\dfrac{W}{L}\right)_{10}} \tag{1}$$

Where $I_{bias}$ represents the reference current, which is assumed to be constant across PVT variations and W/L denotes the aspect ratio of the respective transistors. Subsequently, the charging time $\left(T_{charging}\right)$ of gate capacitor (C) can be expressed as:

$$T_{charging} = \frac{CV_{cap}}{I_{cap}} \tag{2}$$

$$\text{Where, } V_{cap} = V_{GSM3} \tag{3}$$

The second stage of ring oscillator is also current starved hence fixed current is used to charge the output node of second stage which consists of small parasitic gate capacitance of M4 and M5.

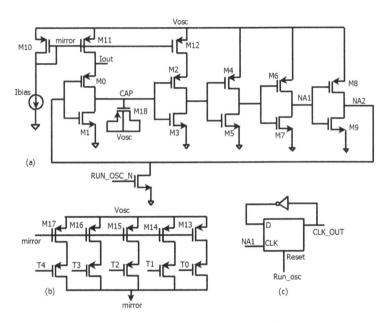

**Fig. 1.** (a) Schematic diagram of proposed PVT compensated ring oscillator. (b) Trimming bits transistors T0–T4 used to vary the width of diode connected transistor M10. (c) D flip-flop is used to generate the clock having 50% duty cycle

For the sake of simplicity, it is assumed that the transistors M11 and M12 are equal sized matched transistors, hence equal current flows through them, therefore voltage developed across capacitor $(V_{GSM3})$ can be written as:

$$V_{GSM3} = V_{THM3} + \sqrt{\frac{2I_{cap}}{\mu_n C_{ox}\left(\dfrac{W}{L}\right)_3}} \tag{4}$$

### 2.1 Principle of Temperature Compensation

In Eq. (2), the capacitor (C) and current $(I_{cap})$ are independent of temperature variations but $V_{cap}$ is a temperature dependent term. However, the dependence of $V_{cap}$ or $V_{GSM3}$ on temperature is apparent in (4).

$$\frac{V_{GSM3}}{dT} = \frac{V_{THM3}}{dT} + \frac{d}{dT}\left(\sqrt{\frac{2I_{cap}}{\mu_n C_{ox}\left(\dfrac{W}{L}\right)_3}}\right) \tag{5}$$

The first term in above equation represents threshold voltage dependence and second term represents overdrive voltage dependence on temperature. The threshold voltage exhibits negative temperature coefficient and its value is process dependent and can't be controlled by the designer. However, positive temperature coefficient of overdrive voltage can be altered by varying the aspect ratio of transistor M3. The dependence of $V_{GSM3}$ on temperature can be nullified if negative temperature coefficient of threshold voltage is equal to the positive temperature coefficient of overdrive voltage of M3.

## 2.2 Principle of Process Compensation

The significant loop delay arises due the first stage, hence it can be written as:

$$T_{delay} \approx T_{1st\ stage} \tag{6}$$

This delay arises in first stage is due to charging of capacitor which acts as a load after first stage. This can be written as:

$$T_{1st\ stage} = \frac{CV_{cap}}{I_{cap}} \tag{7}$$

The frequency of operation is considered as inverse of $T_{1st\ stage}$ and it can be written as:

$$f_{osc} = \frac{1}{T_{delay}} = \frac{I_{cap}}{CV_{cap}} \tag{8}$$

In Eq. (8), capacitor (C) is gate capacitor of M18 and $V_{cap}$ is the maximum voltage developed across capacitor during charging. The oscillation frequency is significantly impacted by process parameter variations, since oscillation frequency is inversely proportional to process dependent terms such as capacitance and voltage developed across capacitor during charging $(V_{cap})$. In order to obtain the desired oscillation frequency of operation, $I_{cap}$ can also be varied in different process corners.

In Fig. 1, T0–T4 represents trimming bits transistors, which act as switches for M13–M17 transistors. These switches are used to control the effective width of transistor M10. From Eq. (1) it can be inferred that the increase in width of transistor M10 will decrease the capacitor charging current $(I_{cap})$.

# 3   Simulation Results

A 10 MHz oscillator is designed in BCD9S 110 nm STMicroelectronics process technology to validate the effectiveness of the proposed PVT compensation strategy. The design is simulated for five process corners MAX, MIN, TYP, MAX_MIN (NFPS) and MIN_MAX (NSPF) across −40 °C to 150 °C operating temperature. All the simulations are performed on post-layout generated netlist. Figure 2(a) represents the layout view of proposed PVT compensated ring oscillator. It is evident from Fig. 2(b), that the aspect ratio of M3 decides the stability and accuracy of $V_{GSM3}$ across temperature. The frequency of oscillation remains temperature compensated across process variations as shown in Fig. 3. Due to the process variations, the maximum frequency deviation of ±18% is obtained. The temperature compensation behavior is observed because size of the transistor M3 is compensating the $V_{cap}$ variations across process.

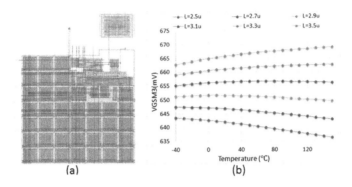

(a)                                    (b)

**Fig. 2.** (a) Layout of proposed PVT compensated Ring Oscillator (b) Variation of $V_{GSM3}$ across temperature range of −40 °C to 150 °C

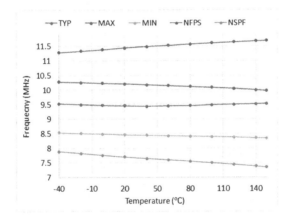

**Fig. 3.** Variation of frequency across different process corners from −40 °C to 150 °C without using trimming bits

### 3.1 Monte Carlo Simulation Results

Monte-Carlo simulations are also performed in statistical process corner at −40 °C, 27 °C and 150 °C for better estimation of the impact of process variations and random mismatch variations on oscillator's frequency. The parameters obtained from Monte-Carlo simulations are shown in Fig. 4 and tabulated in Table 1.

**Table 1.** Various parameters obtained from Monte Carlo Simulations

| Temperature | −40 °C | 27 °C | 150 °C |
|---|---|---|---|
| Mean (μ) (MHz) | 10.01496 | 10.1323 | 9.84257 |
| Standard Deviation (σ) (MHz) | 0.13061 | 0.1598 | 0.10277 |
| Coefficient of variation (%) | 1.30 | 1.58 | 1.04 |
| μ ± 3 σ Range (MHz) | 9.55–10.45 | 9.56–10.66 | 9.49–10.22 |

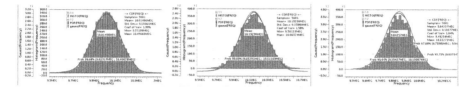

**Fig. 4.** Monte Carlo simulation results for Temperature = −40 °C (b) Temperature = 27 °C (c) Temperature = 150 °C

## 3.2 Frequency Variations Due to Supply Voltage and Reference Current

The frequency of oscillator do not exhibits significant dependence on supply voltage variations and it can be seen in Fig. 5(a). For ±10% variation in supply voltage of 1.8 V, the frequency variation of ±3.1% is obtained. The accuracy of reference current significantly impacts the accuracy of oscillation frequency and it is also validated in simulation result. Figure 5(b) represents that, for ±4% variation in reference current, ±3.75% variation in oscillator's frequency is observed.

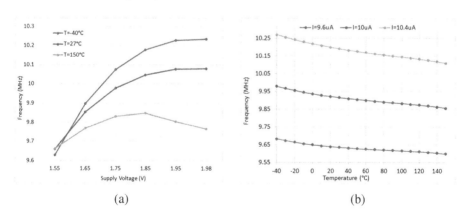

(a)                                        (b)

**Fig. 5.** (a) Variation of frequency across supply voltage (1.8 V ± 10%) variations (b) Variation of frequency across reference current (10 μA ± 4%) variations

### 3.3   Frequency Variation Across Different Process Corners

Figure 6(a) represents that in different process corners, correct oscillation frequency can be obtained by selecting proper value of trimming code. The trimming bits are used to modulate the charging current of capacitor according to the process corner and try to correct the oscillation frequency as shown in Fig. 6(b). For TYP, MIN, MAX, NFPS and NSPF process corners, the frequency deviation of $\pm 0.7\%$, $\pm 2.25\%$, $\pm 0.75\%$, $\pm 0.45\%$ and $\pm 1\%$ is achieved. It is also important to study the transient behavior of internal nodes of ring oscillator. It can be observed from Fig. 7, that the 'CAP' node charges up to 695 mV by constant current in charging phase and discharges instantly to ground in discharge phase. The final clock output observed after D flip-flop having rail-to-rail swing and 50% duty cycle exhibits frequency very close to 10 MHz.

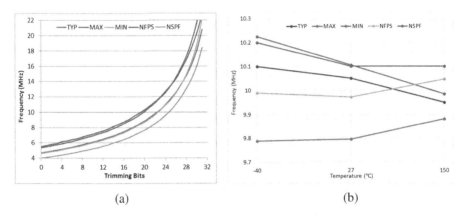

(a)                                          (b)

**Fig. 6.**  (a) Variation of frequency across different trimming bits combination (b) Variation of frequency across −40 °C to 150 °C for different process corners using different trimming codes

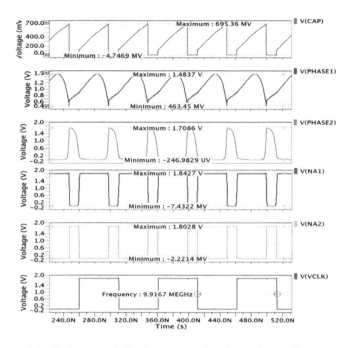

**Fig. 7.** Transient behavior of internal nodes of ring oscillator

**Table 2.** Comparison of the proposed frequency reference with state-of-the-art designs

| Work | Process (nm) | Frequency (MHz) | Frequency variation (%) | Area in mm² | TC (ppm/°C) | Power (μW) |
|---|---|---|---|---|---|---|
| [1], exp | CMOS 250 | 7 | ±0.84 @ −40 °C to 125 °C | 1.6 | 315 | 1500 |
| [2], exp | CMOS 130 | 1 | ±0.5 @25 °C to 180 °C | 0.0072 | 108 | 428 |
| [3], exp | CMOS 65 | 0.15 | ±0.5 @ −55 °C to 125 °C | 0.2 | 300 | 51 |
| [4], exp | CMOS 350 | 30 | ±0.7 @ −20 °C to 100 °C | 0.22 | 180 | 180 |
| [5], sim | CMOS 28 | 30 | ±0.285@ −20 °C to −100 °C | – | 34 | 252 |
| This work, sim | BCD9S 110 | 10 | ±0.7 @ −40 °C to −150 °C | 0.0027 | 73 | 84 |

exp: Experimental Result, sim: Simulated Result

Furthermore, it is also imperative to note here that the presented design in this work is based around simplified circuit architecture and this essentially leads to smaller area and lower power consumption. It has been validated in the simulation framework. Finally, the Table 2 provides the comparison of this work with various state-of-the-art designs. It is apparent that the design of frequency reference reported in this work shows significantly improved performance in terms of power saving and area and extremely good insensitivity to process, voltage, and temperature variations.

## 4    Conclusions

A novel strategy of PVT compensation is presented which shows less sensitivity than state-of-the-art designs. Simulation result shows that the frequency of oscillator exhibits sensitivity of less than $\pm 2.25\%$ across process and temperature variations, temperature coefficient of 73 ppm/°C and consumes a maximum power of 84 μW at 150 °C in MAX process corner. These features make this design very exciting for smart power applications.

## References

1. Sundaresan, K., Allen, P., Ayazi, F.: Process and temperature compensation in a 7-MHz CMOS clock oscillator. IEEE J. Solid-State Circuits **41**(2), 433–442 (2006)
2. Sadeghi, N., Bakhtiar, A.S., Mirabbasi, S.: A 0.007 mm$^2$ 108-ppm/1-MHz relaxation oscillator for high-temperature applications up to 180 in 0.13 μm CMOS. IEEE Trans. Circuits Syst. I, Reg. Papers **60**(7), 16921701 (2013)
3. Sebastiano, F., Nauta, B., et al.: A 65-nm CMOS temperature compensated mobility-based frequency reference for wireless sensor networks. In: Proceedings of ESSCIRCs, pp. 102–105, September 2010
4. Ueno, K., Asai, T., Amemiya, Y.: A 30 MHz, 90-ppm/°C fully integrated clock reference generator with frequency-locked loop. In: IEEE 35th ESSCIRC, Athens, Greece, pp. 392–395, September 2009
5. Lahiri, A., Tiwari, A.: A 140 μA 34 ppm/°C 30 MHz clock oscillator in 28 nm CMOS bulk process. In: IEEE 26th International Conference on VLSI Design (VLSID), Pune, India, pp. 173–178, January 2013
6. Baliga, B.J.: An overview of smart power technology. IEEE Trans. Electron Devices **38**(7), 1568–1575 (1991)

# VLSI Testing

# Deterministic Shift Power Reduction in Test Compression

Kanad Basu[1]([✉]), Rishi Kumar[1], Santosh Kulkarni[1,2], and Rohit Kapur[2]

[1] Synopsys India Pvt. Ltd., Bangalore, India
{`kanad.basu,rishi.kumar,Santosh.Kulkarni`}@synopsys.com
[2] Synopsys Inc., Mountain View, CA, USA

**Abstract.** Over the years semiconductor design complexities have increased to multi million gates. With increase in design sizes, power consumption saving has become a key challenge. The power consumption in test modes is found to be higher, as all the logic blocks are used simultaneously. Some techniques to save test mode power during shift and capture cycles are already in use. But the existing techniques are not deterministic and does not provide user control mechanism. This paper proposes a mechanism called Shift Power Chain ($SPC$) to deterministically control and reduce shift power in test compression mode. Our mechanism provides significant reduction in peak and average shift power. We present the experimental results on large scale industrial designs as well as $ISCAS$'89 and *Opencore* benchmarks.

## 1 Introduction

Power dissipation during shift and capture cycles in scan based testing is known to be significantly higher than circuit operation in normal functional mode [1]. The two major drawbacks of this are as follows:

- Higher power leads to higher temperature and hence thermal effects which may compromise with the structural reliability of the design.
- High power may result in corruption of test data which severely affects the quality of service and results in yield loss.

To overcome these challenges, various power reduction schemes have been proposed by different researchers. These schemes can be classified into mainly four categories: (i) DFT schemes (ii) Test scheduling schemes (iii) Automatic Test Pattern Generation (ATPG) schemes and (iv) X-filling schemes. DFT based schemes modify the circuit under test by using hardware solutions to reduce switching activity of the circuit. Test scheduling algorithms will determine the test patterns to be applied to particular scan chains in the design at different cycles depending on the state of the scan chain. ATPG methods generate test patterns to minimize switching activity and hence reduce power. X-filling techniques fill up the don't cares in the patterns in smart ways so as to cause minimal switching. Among these, DFT based schemes are generally found to be

B. K. Kaushik et al. (Eds.): VDAT 2017, CCIS 711, pp. 155–167, 2017.
https://doi.org/10.1007/978-981-10-7470-7_17

more effective in reducing power compared to the others. On the other hand, X-filling techniques are most compatible with existing design flows and do not require any hardware overhead.

Similar to traditional scan based testing, shift and capture power are high in test compression techniques. In this paper, we propose a novel deterministic shift power reduction technique. Our proposed method is a combination of DFT based and X-filling methods. Experiments on large industrial circuits and standard benchmarks ($ISCAS$ and $Opencores$) have shown promising results for our method.

The rest of the paper is organized as follows. Section 2 describes the related work. Section 3 provides some background on bounded adjacent fill based X-filling for minimizing power. Section 4 presents our proposed approach. Experimental results are shown in Sect. 5. Finally, Sect. 6 concludes the paper.

## 2    Related Work

As mentioned before, power dissipation during shift and capture cycles in test modes is much higher than functional mode. Various architecture based and software based techniques for power reduction were mentioned in Sect. 1. The $DFT$ based power reduction methods modify the circuit to enable lower switching activity during shift and capture cycles. These include dynamic partitioning of scan chains [3], mutually exclusive scan segment activation [4], maintaining test times of pre-adapted test architectures [5] and pattern-directed circuit virtual partitioning [6].

X-filling techniques are some of the most popular methods to reduce power during scan based testing. The ATPG patterns generated usually have lots of don't care bits or $X$s. X-filling algorithms intelligently fill up these $X$s so that the overall switching activity of the circuit is reduced. These methods are flexible in the sense that the interference is minimal from both $DFT$ and $ATPG$ point of view. There is no circuit modification necessary and ATPG algorithms also need not be changed.

Our proposed approach uses an X-filling technique bounded adjacent fill [7] along with an external dedicated chain, $SPC$, to deterministically reduce shift power. We set a peak shift power budget and generate patterns which abide by this budget. Details of our method are presented in Sect. 4.

## 3    Background

As described before, the proposed approach is a combination of DFT based and X-filling methods. We have used bounded adjacent fill algorithm developed by Chandra et al. [7] as X-filling technique. It would be useful to give some background on bounded adjacent X-filling technique. Power dissipation in a circuit is directly proportional to the amount of switching activity of the circuit. [8] has shown that the switching activity in the scan chains is closely related to that of the circuit under test. Therefore, any method which reduces toggles in the scan chains can affect the power dissipation during testing. This is true for both shift and capture modes.

Shift power reduction can be performed by rearranging the distribution of specified bits in the input test patterns. Capture power reduction, on the other hand, is much more difficult, because the functional mode input vectors are much more strongly correlated than the input test vectors. Most *ATPG* X-filling techniques focus on reducing the shift power. The popular X-filling techniques are: *Fill* − 0, *Fill* − 1, *Adjacent Fill* and *Random Fill*. *Fill* − 0 and *Fill* − 1 algorithms fill all the don't cares with 0s and 1s respectively. *Random Fill* algorithms, on the other hand, fill the don't cares randomly with 0s and 1s. *Adjacent Fill* algorithms generally look at the last most specified bit and replicate it.

The performance of *Adjacent Fill* algorithms for capture power reduction is not satisfactory. [7] observed that scan out data is well correlated with scan in data. Also, it was seen that if the scan in data is biased towards filling the scan cells with 0s, post-capture data is similar, which results in less toggles. These observations inspired the authors to develop a new algorithm known as *Bounded Adjacent Fill*. In *Bounded Adjacent Fill*, some specified bits in the patterns at pre-determined intervals are fixed to zero. After that, regular *Adjacent Fill* is applied. This results in lower capture power. An illustrative example taken from [7] is shown in Fig. 1. As can be seen, for the example input test vector, the number of toggles for capture power is 6 in case of *Adjacent Fill*, but is only 4 for *Bounded Adjacent Fill*.

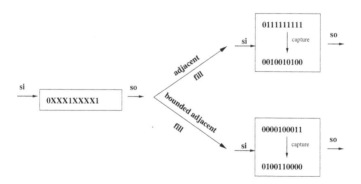

**Fig. 1.** Comparison of Adjacent Fill and Bounded Adjacent Fill

## 4    Shift Power Chain

In this section, we will present our proposed *DFT* Architecture. The section is divided into 2 parts. In Sect. 4.1, we describe the *DFT* architecture and in Sect. 4.2, the test generation algorithm is proposed.

## 4.1   SPC Aware DFT Architecture

Shift Power Control chain is a dedicated external chain for shift-power control mechanism in test compression. The Power control chain is actually a register of scan cells. Each of the scan cell either enables or disables group of scan chains. The enabled group of chains would be allowed to toggle during $SHIFT$. And the disabled group of chains would remain constant throughout $SHIFT$. Figure 2 shows the $SPC$ chain in Test Compression architecture. The Constant Fill Logic is basically array of $AND$ logic placed between the scan chains and decompressor. Test patterns are $AND$'ed with $SPC$ register bits and then propagated to scan chains. The constant fill logic fills the scan chains with 0 depending on the particular value in the register of the shift power control chain. Each register bit of the $SPC$ chain are allocated for one or more scan chains. When a particular scan chain needs to be turned off, the corresponding register bit forces the constant value through it.

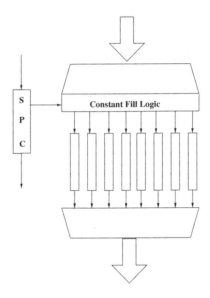

**Fig. 2.** Shift Power Control chain in Test Compression architecture

A Shift Power Control chain is an N bit register made up of control cells. Structure of a control cell is shown in Fig. 3. A control cell consists of two stages: shift stage and update stage. The shift stage is a scan flop that shifts every bit, so changes during the shift stage for every $SHIFT$. Update stage is a latch controlled by a Scan Enable, and updated only during Capture stage and held constant during $SHIFT$.

The shift power control chain mechanism along with control logic is shown in Fig. 4. A group of scan chains are connected to a $SPC$ register. In this example, Group 1 consists of chains 1, 2, 3 and 4. Like wise Group 2, 3 and 4 are

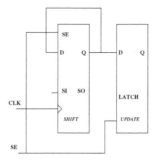

**Fig. 3.** Structure of SPC control cells

group of chains. Group 4 is controlled by Reg 1 bit of $SPC$ register. Whenever the particular group of chains need to be shut off, a 0 bit is forced from the corresponding $SPC$ register. The intended group of scan chains are filled with constant 0 via the $AND$ gate and toggling activity is avoided in them.

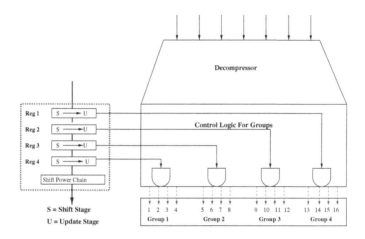

**Fig. 4.** Shift power control mechanism

The shift power chain is extra register logic. In general, $SPC$ length can be equal to the total chain count in test compression. As each $SPC$ bit would control a chain, this gives maximum controllability of chains. But it should not exceed shift length of patterns. Hence, $SPC$ length is set using the formula; Shift power chain length

$$S = min\{M, N\} \tag{1}$$

where $M$ denotes maximum shift length and $N$ denotes total number of internal chains. The maximum chain ratio per $SPC$ bit leads to deterministic shift power budget. Maximum Chain ratio per SPC bit $(CR)$ is defined as:

$$CR \simeq \frac{N}{S} \tag{2}$$

The shift power peak budget $MiB$ is computed as a ratio of $CR$ and $N$, represented as percentage.

$$MiB = \frac{CR}{N} \times 100\% \tag{3}$$

The calculated $MiB$ is the minimum shift power any pattern generated on that particular design will have. To allow $ATPG$ some band-width, we provide $SPC$ Budget which is greater than the $MiB$ calculated for the design.

Although the disabled group of chains would still shift, but they shift constant values to the chains. The toggle activity would be limited to the enabled chains. This limits the per pattern bit transitions to enabled chains during $SHIFT$, thus reducing the $SHIFT$-power. The targeted power budget should be greater than the calculated $MiB$.

### 4.2  SPC Aware ATPG Algorithm

Figure 5 represents the flowchart for our SPC aware test generation algorithm. We assume the fault-list of the circuit to be tested is available. From the faultlist, we choose a particular fault as primary fault. We generate tests for this fault and notice the changelist ($CL$). By changelist, we mean the number of flops that have toggled due to the test. Since the number of flops toggled directly correlate to the power dissipated, this step is used to generate tests while keeping a check on the shift power. A budget on the maximum allowable shift power is available via user input as a percentage of scan cells which can toggle. This is translated to a budget on the number of flops that are allowed to toggle. If the changelist obtained from the test generated due to the primary fault exceeds the budget, the primary fault is discarded (note, it is not thrown away but kept away separately for later analysis). A new primary fault is chosen and this step continues until one is obtained whose changelist fits the allowed budget.

Now, we record the $SPC$ registers with chains required for toggled flops. To explain this step, we use Fig. 4. For example, if, after test generation for primary fault, the flops that toggled are in chains 3, 10 and 12. Since chain 3 corresponds to Register 4 in the $SPC$ chain, it should be held at 1. The other chains 10 and 12 correspond to Register 2, which should also be kept constant at 1. Therefore the two registers 2 and 4 should be recorded as 1 in this case.

Once the primary fault is selected and the shift registers are recorded, we proceed to find secondary faults. From the remaining fault list, another fault is chosen as secondary fault. As with primary fault, test is generated and changelist is obtained. This changelist is called Additional Changelist ($ACL$). The sum of $CL$ and $ACL$ is then computed to find whether it fits our budget. If the sum is higher than the budget, the secondary fault is discarded and a counter $NumFails$ is incremented. If the value of $NumFails$ exceeds a predetermined abort limit, the secondary fault searching is stopped. On the other hand, if the sum of the two changelists fits the budget, the new test is merged with the one generated for the primary fault. The corresponding SPC registers are also recorded. Please note that there will never be any conflict in $SPC$ registers for different faults. This is because the only requirement that a SPC register must satisfy is whether it is on. The off condition is flexible. As an example, consider the previous primary fault which is setting 1 in Registers 1 and 3 in the $SPC$. If a new secondary fault requires any of these two registers to be 1, it will not be bothered since they are already 1. If the fault requires Register 0 or 2 to be 1, they can be set to 1 easily, since they didn't affect the primary fault pattern. Thus, 0 on a particular register in SPC will not be a strong requirement and hence, can be easily overwritten. The new changelist is a combination of $CL$ and $ACL$. On the other hand, any test for a secondary fault which attempts to reset an already set $SPC$ register will be discarded for the current test pattern.

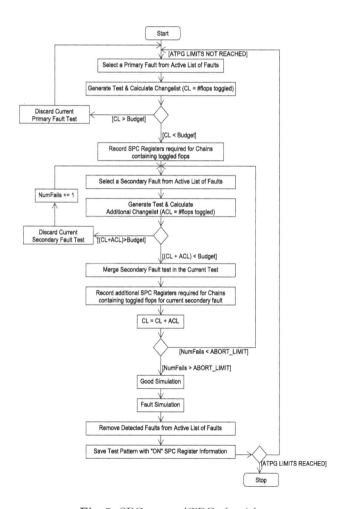

**Fig. 5.** SPC aware ATPG algorithm

Selection of secondary faults will continue until the $NumFails$ counter reaches abort limit. This $ATPG$ algorithm makes use of bounded adjacent fill (described in Sect. 3) to fill in the don't care bits left after selection of primary and secondary faults to take care of both shift and capture power. This is followed by a good simulation and a fault simulation. Faults which are already detected are removed from the fault list. The test patterns with $SPC$ register information are recorded. The whole step is then restarted with a primary fault identification unless a predetermined $ATPG$ limit is reached.

## 5    Experiments

### 5.1    Experimental Setup

We have applied our approach on the state of the art test compression engine $zScan$ [2]. Large industrial benchmarks with flip-flops ranging from 6866 to 1182470 have been used for our experiments. For confidentiality purpose, we can't reveal the names of the designs. However, to give an idea of the design sizes, we use Table 1. Other than these, we have also performed experiments on popular $ISCAS$'89 and $opencore$ benchmarks.

**Table 1.** Number of flip-flops for experimental circuits

| Circuit | D1 | D2 | D3 | D4 | D5 | D6 | D7 | D8 | D9 |
|---|---|---|---|---|---|---|---|---|---|
| Flip-flop count | 6866 | 86594 | 120561 | 134813 | 157204 | 232453 | 235134 | 261263 | 1182470 |

### 5.2    Results

**Experiments on Industrial Circuits.** We would like to first describe our experimental results on the industrial circuits described in Table 1. In Fig. 6, comparisons of peak and average shift power are presented for the 9 designs using both the regular approach (without $SPC$) and our proposed approach (with $SPC$). Although the Peak Shift Power Budget obtained using Eq. (3) in Sect. 4.1, we choose the peak $SPC$ budget for a design such that it is the ceiling value of the average shift power obtained from the runs without $SPC$. The budget is shown as a dotted line in Fig. 6. The dark blue and black columns represent the peak shift power without and with $SPC$ respectively, while the grey and the green columns represent the corresponding values for average shift power. As can be seen, for both peak and average shift power, our proposed approach provides significant savings. The maximum peak power savings obtained is 53.68%, while the maximum average power savings obtained is 22.41%, both for $D5$. For all the circuits, we see that the $SPC$ budget line traces the average shift power obtained from runs without $SPC$.

We would now like to see how much the coverage and pattern count numbers get affected because of $SPC$ compared to the regular approach, without $SPC$.

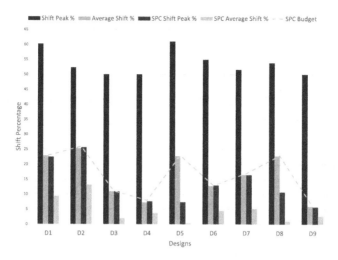

**Fig. 6.** Comparison of shift powers for experimental circuits (Color figure online)

**Table 2.** Comparison of coverage and pattern count with $SPC$ on industrial circuits

| Design | Without SPC | | With SPC | |
|--------|-------------|--|----------|--|
| | Coverage(in %) | Pattern count | Coverage(in %) | Pattern count |
| D1 | 94.82 | 1942 | 91.87 | 4218 |
| D2 | 92.67 | 4476 | 92.56 | 5227 |
| D3 | 99.74 | 2985 | 99.69 | 4097 |
| D4 | 91.03 | 7091 | 90.96 | 7643 |
| D5 | 97.99 | 23773 | 94.6 | 19636 |
| D6 | 84.37 | 17996 | 83.69 | 7958 |
| D7 | 95.22 | 24309 | 93.35 | 21412 |
| D8 | 91.05 | 20347 | 89.48 | 10922 |
| D9 | 98.03 | 22783 | 97.26 | 11466 |

The comparison is shown in Table 2. The maximum coverage hit is 3.39% for D5. However, it must be mentioned that this comes with a benefit of a decrease of almost 10000 patterns and as we have seen in Fig. 6, 53.68% power savings. The pattern counts are seen to decrease mostly. For some cases, like D1, the pattern counts increase by 2276. The largest reduction in pattern count is 11317, obtained for D9.

**Experiments on ISCAS'89 Benchmarks.** We would like to perform the same set of experiments on $ISCAS$'89 benchmark circuits. The comparison of power numbers are shown in Fig. 7. As before, the peak shift power budget is shown using a dotted line. However, unlike Fig. 6, in this case we choose the *SPC* budget for a design such that it is equal to the average values of peak shift and capture shift power obtained from the runs without *SPC*. Similar to Fig. 6, our proposed approach is seen to provide significant power savings compared to existing methods. The maximum peak power saving is 22.63% for *s9234* and the maximum average power savings is 21.23%, for the largest circuit, *s35932*.

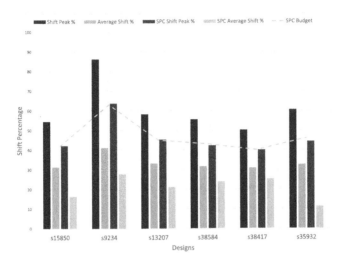

**Fig. 7.** Comparison of shift powers for *ISCAS*'89 benchmarks

The coverage and pattern count numbers are presented in Table 3. The maximum coverage hit is 2.83%, obtained for *s15850*. However, the corresponding average shift power savings for this circuit is 14.94%. Except for the largest benchmark *s35932*, all the benchmarks had a pattern count reduction compared to the one without *SPC*.

**Table 3.** Comparison of coverage and pattern count with *SPC* on *ISCAS*'89 benchmarks

| Design | Without SPC | | With SPC | |
|--------|-------------|---------------|---------------|---------------|
| | Coverage(in %) | Pattern count | Coverage(in %) | Pattern count |
| s15850 | 94.72 | 63 | 91.89 | 57 |
| s9234 | 96.74 | 92 | 95.53 | 88 |
| s13207 | 98.42 | 81 | 96.32 | 70 |
| s38584 | 99.78 | 142 | 98.21 | 137 |
| s38417 | 99.77 | 161 | 98.62 | 149 |
| s35932 | 99.8 | 32 | 99.07 | 33 |

**Experiments on Opencore Benchmarks.** We have chosen 6 *opencore* benchmarks for our experiments; CPU 8080 Processor(*cpu*8080), Navre Processor (*navre*), Next 80186 processor (*next*186), Next Z80 Processor (*nextz*80), PIC16C5x microcomputer emulator (*p16c5x*) and MIPS 32 Standalone Processor (*mips*32). The shift power numbers are shown in Fig. 8. The shift power budget, shown by a dotted line, is calculated in the same way as for *ISCAS* benchmarks in Fig. 7. In all cases, we see significant peak and average power savings. The maximum peak power savings is 28.37%, obtained for *next*186, while the maximum average power savings is 18.66%, obtained for *cpu*8080.

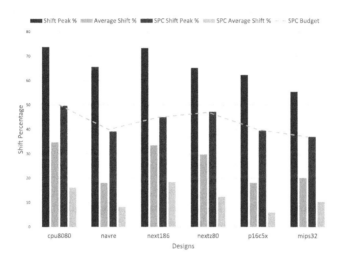

**Fig. 8.** Comparison of shift powers for *opencore* benchmarks

**Table 4.** Comparison of coverage and pattern count with *SPC* on *Opencore* benchmarks

| Design | Without SPC | | With SPC | |
|---|---|---|---|---|
| | Coverage(in %) | Pattern count | Coverage(in %) | Pattern count |
| cpu8080 | 97.63 | 453 | 96.3 | 438 |
| navre | 99 | 420 | 97.82 | 414 |
| next186 | 98.1 | 586 | 97.3 | 574 |
| nextz80 | 98.44 | 416 | 97.15 | 396 |
| p16c5x | 78.89 | 237 | 73.53 | 211 |
| mips32 | 99.82 | 575 | 99.47 | 568 |

The interesting aspect of the *opencore* benchmarks is that the pattern count is never inflated for any of the 6 benchmarks. The pattern count numbers are shown in Table 4. The coverage hit, shown in the same table is also very less, the

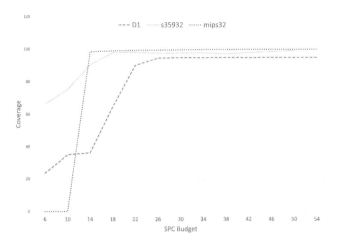

**Fig. 9.** Variation of coverage with peak shift power budget

maximum being 5.36% for $p16c5x$. It should be remembered that for the same benchmark, we obtain 22.89% peak power savings.

**Variation of Coverage and Pattern Count with Shift Power Budget.** In this experiment, we would like to see how the coverage and pattern count vary with peak shift power budget. We have used 3 circuits for this purpose – Design D1 from Sect. 5.1, $s35932$ from the $ISCAS$'89 benchmarks and $mips32$ from *opencores*. The results are presented in Figs. 9 and 10 for coverage and log of power count (to the base 10) respectively. A logarithamic graph has been used for Fig. 10 for scaling.

The peak shift power budget is varied linearly in steps of 4% from 6% to 54% and the corresponding coverage and pattern count are noticed. Coverage variation for $D1$ and $s35932$ are seen to be kind of similar. The coverage increases initially and then becomes constant at $SPC$ budget of 22% and 26% respectively. For $mips32$, SPC peak values of 6% and 10% were smaller than the minimum $SPC$ Budget and hence patterns could not be generated for those values of SPC peak values. Therefore, those values are absent in Fig. 10 and 0 in Fig. 9. There is a steep rise in coverage when $SPC$ Budget is varied from 10% to 14%, after which, it remains constant.

The pattern count variation for $D1$ and $s35932$ is seen to follow a similar trend initially. The pattern counts increase to improve the coverage till $SPC$ Budget of 22% and 26% respectively for the two circuits (It should be noted that at similar values the coverage stabilized for them). After that, with increase in $SPC$ budget, pattern count is seen to decrease since $ATPG$ has more controllability with increase in budget. For $mips32$, it is seen that the pattern count is stable when we vary the budget from 14%.

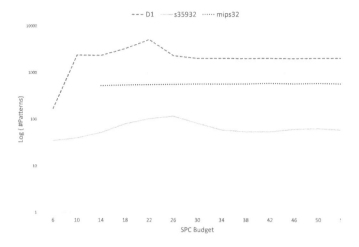

**Fig. 10.** Variation of pattern count with peak shift power budget

# 6   Conclusion

Power dissipation of a circuit during shift and capture modes of testing exceed that of functional mode. In this paper, we have presented a deterministic DFT-based approach to reduce shift power dissipation with minimal impact on coverage. Experimental results on large industrial benchmarks as well as *ISCAS* and *opencore* benchmarks show significant reduction in shift power using the proposed methodology.

# References

1. Girard, P.: Survey of low-power testing of VLSI circuits. IEEE Des. Test Comput. **19**(3), 82–92 (2002)
2. Chandra, A., Kulkarni, S., Chebiyam, S., Kapur, R.: Designing efficient combinational compression architecture for testing industrial circuits. In: VDAT, pp. 1–6 (2015)
3. Almukhaizim, S., Sinanoglu, O.: Peak power reduction through dynamic partitioning of scan chains. In: ITC (2008)
4. Rosinger, P., Al-Hashmi, B., Nicolici, N.: Scan architecture with mutually exclusive scan segment activation for shift and capture power reduction. IEEE TCAD **23**(7), 1142–1153 (2004)
5. Whetsel, L.: Adapting scan architectures for low power operation. In: ITC, pp. 863–872 (2000)
6. Xu, Q., Hu, D., Xiang, D.: Pattern-directed circuit virtual partitioning for test power reduction. In: ITC (2007)
7. Chandra, A., Kapur, R.: Bounded adjacent fill for low capture power scan testing. In: VTS, pp. 131–138 (2008)
8. Sankaralingam, R., et al.: Static compaction techniques to control scan vector power dissipation. In: VTS, pp. 35–40 (2000)

# Pseudo-BIST: A Novel Technique for SAR-ADC Testing

Yatharth Gupta[1(✉)], Sujay Deb[1(✉)], Vikrant Singh[2], V. N. Srinivasan[2],
Manish Sharma[2], and Sabyasachi Das[2]

[1] Department of Electronics and Communication Engineering,
Indraprastha Institute of Information Technology, New Delhi, India
{yatharth15119,sdeb}@iiitd.ac.in
[2] STMicroelectronics, Greater Noida, U.P., India
{vikrant.singh,vn.srinivasan,manish.sharma-dlh,
sabyasachi.das}@st.com

**Abstract.** This paper presents an improved approach for testing and measuring the different parameters of an Analog to Digital Converter (ADC). The proposed methodology Pseudo-BIST is a combination of ATE (Automatic Test Equipment) and BIST (Built-In Self-Test). Pseudo-BIST provides a novel multi-processing technique where data conversion and calculation of static parameters takes place at the same instant. The proposed method has been applied to a SAR-ADC with test time reduction of more than 76% for a single site SAR-ADC and 93% reduction in time for 8 site ADCs. Pseudo-BIST also achieves a 50–70% reduction in area overhead as compared to BIST consisting of a high precision DAC.

**Keywords:** BIST · ATE · ADC · DAC · Static parameters

## 1 Introduction

There has been a significant amount of development in the field of Design for Testability (DFT) and Testing of any Systems-On-Chip (SOC) reducing cost and test time [2]. But still there is scope for better measures for validation of different SOC which can further improve test time and cost. Different DFT techniques have been devised for mixed signal designs [5–8] such as testing the whole output on Automatic Test Equipment (ATE) as described further in this section later using histogram based ramp method or as histogram testing using sine waves [3], Built-In Self-Test (BIST) [4], transient response analysis and supply current monitoring. Reducing different parameters like test time can be achieved using less amount of test vectors in ATE or for N-bit ADC we can use M lower bits for testing where M < N as there is more switching in lower bits as compared to higher bits. But using less number of test vectors or lower bits of code results in less test coverage which is a side effect while achieving less test time. While in BIST [4], an internal DAC is used which itself needs to be very accurate and consumes a lot of extra area.

Data converters are a crucial part in the modern electronics industry. They act like a bridge between two different worlds of analog and digital. Data Converters broadly

© Springer Nature Singapore Pte Ltd. 2017
B. K. Kaushik et al. (Eds.): VDAT 2017, CCIS 711, pp. 168–178, 2017.
https://doi.org/10.1007/978-981-10-7470-7_18

classified as Analog to Digital Converters (ADC) and Digital to Analog Converters (DAC) are the basic mixed signal designs. ADCs are of different types, classified on basis of their conversion rates and resolution. Flash, Successive Approximation Register (SAR), Sigma-Delta, Pipelined, etc. are some of the types of ADC. Different ADCs are used for different purposes like Flash and pipelined are used for high speed while Sigma-Delta and SAR used for high resolution. SAR-ADC occupies a significant amount of market of ADCs as they can be used in importable devices, biomedical instruments and many other important applications.

SAR-ADC consists of a Track and Hold, a Comparator, a DAC, and SAR Logic as shown in Fig. 1. The SAR Logic is used for generation of each bit of the digital code depending on the output of the comparator. The SAR Logic is explained in the flow shown in Fig. 2. In the flowchart, N is the number of bits of SAR-ADC.

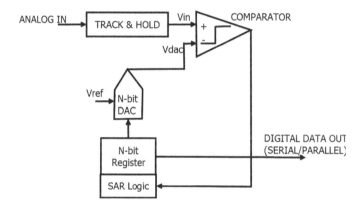

**Fig. 1.** SAR ADC architecture

The basic testing methodology for a SAR-ADC is Histogram based Linearity testing. The testing mechanism usually followed is shown in Fig. 3. A ramp, which is more accurate than the ADC under test, is provided on ADC's analog input through an analog source at the tester along with $V_{ref}$. Each step of the ramp is converted by ADC under test and the resulting conversion gives digital codes which are sent to tester and stored. Considering a 12-bit ADC, input ramp will start a few codes below "zero" and will end a few codes above "$V_{ref}$", to explore all possible input values of the ADC, even in case of Offset and Full-scale Error.

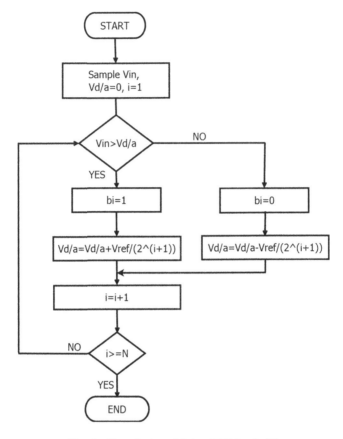

**Fig. 2.** Flowchart explaining SAR Logic [1]

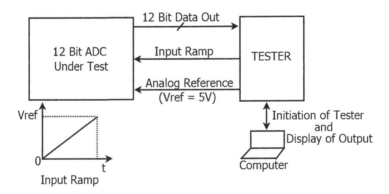

**Fig. 3.** Current testing architecture

But there are certain issues when it is implemented on an ATE while measuring different static parameters like Offset Error, Gain Error, Total Unadjusted Error (TUE), Differential Non-Linearity (DNL), and Integral Non-Linearity (INL). Major Disadvantages of testing ADC on tester is that the time required for data conversion and calculation of these parameters is very high. It is so because first the whole ramp is provided and then ADC converts each level of ramp and stores the data. After whole ramp is converted then only the calculation are done, so due to serial processing it is a very time consuming process.

In this paper, a Pseudo-BIST is proposed which will be testing the SAR-ADC for different parameters and reducing a significant amount of test time. In the next section, we will be focusing on testing strategy using Pseudo-BIST for SAR-ADC. Results and Conclusion will be discussed in further sections.

## 2    Proposed Methodology

Pseudo-BIST is a proposed testing methodology which is a combination of both ATE and BIST. The BIST part of Pseudo-BIST is a hardware generated through RTL described in Verilog. The architecture of Pseudo-BIST is shown in Fig. 4. Pseudo-BIST is used to test a 12-bit SAR-ADC. 10 samples (hits) are taken for each of the $2^{12} = 4096$ codes. Each code is equivalent to 1 LSB which is Vref/4096. In this Pseudo-BIST parallel processing of data and storing data is done in the batch of 25 codes which is equivalent to $25 \times 10 = 250$ hits. 25 codes are processed at a time to compensate the effects of noise. The BIST consists of a 50 3-bit registers array which will be storing the number of hits occurred for each code. At a given instant it calculates the parameters for first 25 codes and stores the next 25 codes in parallel fashion. The whole methodology is described below.

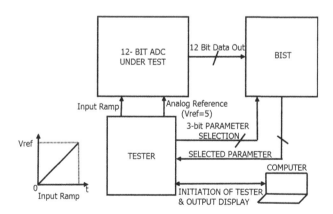

**Fig. 4.** Pseudo-BIST architecture

There are three major parts of Pseudo-BIST:

1. ATE providing the Ramp signal 10 codes below "zero" voltage and 10 codes above "Vref".
2. BIST doing all the calculations of different parameters and storing the values in the registers.
3. ATE capturing the different values of parameters.

The 10 codes below 0 level will be stored to code 0 and 10 codes above Vref will be stored to code 4095 only. This is so as these extra 10 codes are for noise compensation at offset and Full-Scale stage. So, the hits for code 0 and 4095 will be 110 instead of 10 as 10 hits of their own with 10 * 10 hits of rest 10 codes.

There are three modes of functionality in the Pseudo-BIST:

1. Full-Scale Error Measurement Mode
2. Offset Error Measurement Mode
3. Other Parameter Calculation Mode

The working of Pseudo-BIST is depicted in the flowchart shown in Fig. 5 along with the error measurement described in further subsections.

## 2.1    Full Scale Error Measurement Mode

Full-Scale Error is the difference between the ideal full-scale point and actual full-scale point. In this mode, ramp is provided for 25 codes below from $V_{ref}$ to 10 codes above $V_{ref}$. In the first 350 clock cycle hits corresponding to each code are stored. For each hit the ADC starts converting the ramp. At the End of Conversion (EOC) the counter value corresponding to code out of the 25 codes is incremented in their corresponding counter e.g. code 4070's hit counts will be stored in counter 1 and code 4090's hit counts will be stored in counter 20 and so on. Full-Scale Error is the difference between the ideal full-scale point and actual full-scale point. In this mode, ramp is provided for 25 codes below from $V_{ref}$ to 10 codes above $V_{ref}$. In the first 350 clock cycle hits corresponding to each code are stored. For each hit the ADC starts converting the ramp. At the End of Conversion (EOC) the counter value corresponding to code out of the 25 codes is incremented in their corresponding counter e.g. code 4070's hit counts will be stored in counter 1 and code 4090's hit counts will be stored in counter 20 and so on.

$$FSE = (Observed\ Hits\ for\ code\ 4095 - Ideal\ Hits)/Ideal\ Hits \qquad (1)$$

Since computing division internally inside the BIST will lead to extra hardware and time. This division will lead to a fractional part and storing that inside a register will require extra bits. To reduce this extra hardware and extra time in computation, the Full-Scale Error that is presented as result to tester is:

$$FSE_{P.B.} = Observed\ Hits\ for\ code\ 4095 - Ideal\ Hits \qquad (2)$$

Ideal Hits is equal to 110 and Observed Hits is the actual content of Full-Scale Counter register i.e. counter corresponding to code 4095 counting the number of hits

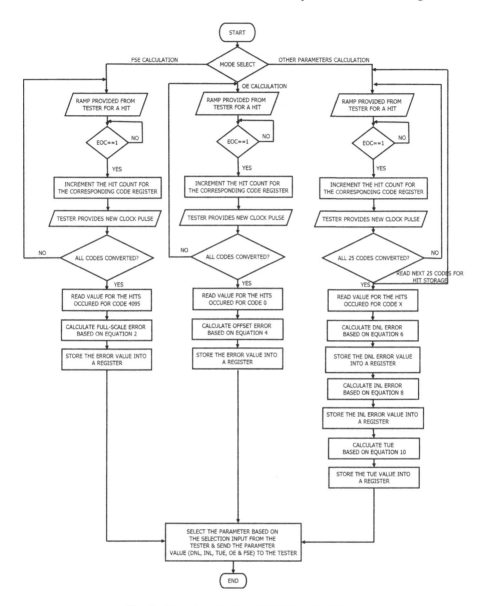

**Fig. 5.** Flowchart for Pseudo-BIST methodology

having a maximum value of 110. This Full-Scale Error value will be a multiple of 110. The Full-Scale Error value is stored in register for transferring it out to Tester. The Full-Scale Error is calculated in the beginning as we need it for the calculation of TUE for each code as described in Subsect. 2.3.

## 2.2 Offset Error Calculation Phase

Offset Error is the difference between the actual offset and ideal offset point which is 0.5 LSB. For the Offset Error Measurement Phase, ramp is provided from 10 codes below 0 voltage level to 25 codes above 0 level. Each of the 350 steps of ramp are converted and at each of EOC the counter value corresponding to the code obtained will get incremented to the corresponding counter as explained in Subsect. 2.1. $0^{th}$ counter which will be having 110 hits instead of 10 hits will be checked for Offset Error. Per Histogram Method the Offset Error (OE) is computed as mentioned in Eq. 3.

$$OE = (Ideal\,Hits - Observed\,Hits\,for\,code\,0)/Ideal\,Hits \tag{3}$$

To reduce the extra hardware and extra time in computation of division, the Offset Error that is presented as result to tester is:

$$OE_{P.B.} = Ideal\,Hits - Observed\,Hits\,for\,code\,0 \tag{4}$$

Ideal Hits is equal to 110 and Observed Hits is the actual content of Offset Counter register i.e. counter corresponding to code 0 counting the number of hits having a maximum value of 110. This Offset Error value will be a multiple of 110. The Offset Error value is stored in register for transferring it out to Tester.

## 2.3 Other Parameters Calculation Mode

Ramp is provided from code 0 to code 4095 in continuation with each code having 10 hits. In first 250 clock cycles the code hits for each of the 25 codes is stored in their respective counter registers. Then in next 250 cycles processing on these 25 codes is done while storing the next 25 codes parallel on the remaining 25 counter registers out of 50. After 500 clock cycles, all the counters are filled with the value of number of hits for code 0–49. Then the first 25 counter values are cleared and then the next 25 codes are written and so on.

For each hit the ADC converts the ramp. At the End of Conversion (EOC) the counter value corresponding to code out of the 25 codes is incremented in their corresponding counter. Once the values are updated then the Pseudo-BIST calculates different parameters which are described below.

**Differential Non-linearity.** Differential Non-Linearity is defined as the difference between the actual step size and the ideal step size which is equal to 1 LSB. In Histogram Methodology, DNL for a code X is calculated as given by Eq. 5.

$$DNL(X) = (Observed\,Hits\,for\,code\,X - Ideal\,Hits)/Ideal\,Hits \tag{5}$$

DNL value achieved from the above stated Eq. 5 will be a fractional value. There will be the same problem as in offset and full-scale error so a modified formula is used as given by Eq. 6 to reduce the calculation time and storage registers size.

$$DNL_{P.B.}(X) = Observed\,Hits\,for\,code\,X - Ideal\,Hits \tag{6}$$

The Ideal Hits in Eqs. 5 and 6 is equal to 10. The observed hits for code X mentioned in Eqs. 5 and 6 is the hits achieved when the ramp is converted to a digital code by the ADC.

**Integral Non-linearity.** Integral Non-Linearity is the deviation of the values on the actual transfer function from straight line which is the best fit line. In Histogram Methodology, Integral Non-Linearity (INL) for a code X is calculated as described by Eq. 7.

$$INL(X) = INL(X - 1) + DNL(X) \tag{7}$$

This INL value is the summation of all the DNLs from code 0 to code X. The DNL used in Eq. 7 is the DNL described by Eq. 5. Since the DNL described by Eq. 5 has fractional part so the INL being summation of all DNLs it will be having it too. The modified equation which is used for Pseudo-BIST is stated in Eq. 8.

$$INL_{P.B.}(X) = INL_{P.B.}(X - 1) + DNL_{P.B.}(X) \tag{8}$$

$INL_{P.B.}$ will also be a multiple of 10 because the $DNL_{P.B.}$ is multiple of Ideal Hits i.e. 10.

**Total Unadjusted Error.** Total Unadjusted Error (TUE) is defined as the maximum deviation between the actual and the ideal transfer curves. It is a combination of all the other parameters including DNL, INL, Offset and Full-Scale Error. It is calculated as in Eq. 9 for Histogram based linear testing.

$$TUE(X) = \text{Offset Error} + (\text{Full-Scale Error} - \text{Offset Error}) * X / 4095 + INL(X) \tag{9}$$

Calculation of TUE is a complex one with TUE dependent on all other parameters calculated till now. So it will lead to a lot of fractional part along with the division with 4095 so to avoid it TUEP.B. described in Eq. 10 is used.

$$TUE_{P.B.}(X) = OE_{P.B.} * 4095 + (FSE_{P.B.} - OE_{P.B.}) * X + INL_{P.B.}(X) * 4095 \tag{10}$$

$TUE_{P.B.}$ is now a multiple of 4095 * 10 i.e. 40950. It was verified that multiplying with 4095 is less hardware and time consuming than multiplying with 4095. $TUE_{P.B.}$ is the maximum error between the ideal and obtained voltage level so the value at each step is compared to last step value and if $TUE_{P.B.}$ is maximum at suppose code Z then the $TUE_{P.B.}$ is not calculated for the codes after code Z. This process of $TUE_{P.B.max}$ is also applied to the calculation of $TUE_{max}$.

After the calculation of the different parameters everything is stored in their respective registers. Then for the verification the tester sends a 3-bit selection signal for selecting the different parameters to be seen on the tester.

# 3   Results

Pseudo-BIST, a combination of ATE and BIST was used in this methodology. It was used to test a 12-bit ADC. Analog reference voltage for the ADC is 5 V. So, at first the setup is created. Ramp was given from the tester for the BIST to calculate all the parameters. At every step of ramp BIST waits for EOC and as soon as conversion is over. The hit is stored into a counter and this procedure goes on until all codes are converted. Then the BIST calculates the different errors as described in the methodology in Sect. 2. Table 1 shows the selection matrix for the different errors calculated by the Pseudo-BIST.

**Table 1.** Output parameters selection

| S. No. | Parameter select | Parameter sent to tester |
|---|---|---|
| 1. | 000 | FSE |
| 2. | 001 | OE |
| 3. | 010 | DNL |
| 4. | 011 | INL |
| 5. | 100 | TUE |
| 6. | 101 | No output |
| 7. | 110 | No output |
| 8. | 111 | No output |

DNL, INL and few other important parameters measured are mentioned in Table 2 below.

**Table 2.** Output parameters value

| Parameter name | Max. measured value | Min. measured value |
|---|---|---|
| OE | 0.8 | −1.2 |
| DNL | 0.7 | −0.6 |
| INL | 0.9 | −1.6 |
| TUE | 1.8 | −1.3 |

All the parameters mentioned in the table above are in LSB. For example Max. DNL is 0.7 LSB.

The test time and area parameters for Pseudo-BIST are discussed in the subsections below.

### 3.1    Test Time Reduction

There is a drastic reduction in test time using this methodology as there are multiple things happening at a time. In the FSE calculation phase, the main time reduction comes in terms of the calculation being done in the BIST itself not on ATE as one of the main delay components is sending each ADC code onto ATE. Same is the case with OE calculation phase. The main reduction in time happens in the DNL/INL/TUE calculation phase since in a clock period there are 50 codes that are being used. As lower 25 codes are used for calculation of parameters and the higher 25 codes being generated from ramp and their hits are stored into the counters. Table 3 describes the total time required for testing a single site ADCs as well as multiple site ADCs using only ATE histogram based test and the Pseudo-BIST.

**Table 3.** Test time comparison for ADC

| Number of sites | Only ATE | Pseudo-BIST |
|---|---|---|
| 1 | Z s | 0.237Z s |
| 8 | Y s | 0.069Y s |

Let the time for testing a single site of ADC at ATE takes Z s, then Pseudo-BIST only takes nearly 24% of time compared to ATE. Similarly for 8 sites ADC at ATE takes Y s time, then Pseudo-BIST takes around only 7% of time compared to the ATE. From the above table it is observed that using multi-processing in Pseudo-BIST drastically reduced the test time. It was so because the time for data-processing was reduced as there was less data transfer from hardware to the ATE along with the parallel processing of storing codes and the calculation.

### 3.2 Hardware Increase Compared to Normal BIST

As in BIST testing ramp is generated from the high precision DAC. There are 2 main challenges in the DAC based BIST as it takes extra area and very high precision DAC is very costly. The BIST of Pseudo-BIST includes only the calculation unit along with around 170 flip flops for storing data (number of hits and different parameters). So, using Pseudo-BIST the area is drastically reduced by approximately 60–70% as DAC is not being used and number of storage units are reduced too compared to a normal ADC-BIST.

## 4   Conclusion

This paper described a better approach to test an ADC which is Pseudo-BIST. It includes the best part of both an ATE and a BIST. As ATE is very time consuming but easy to work on, on the other hand BIST being less time consuming but takes a lot of extra hardware. So, this paper includes both the features less time along with the onus of less area compared to BIST. The time for a single site is reduced by 76% and for 8 sites it is further reduced to 93%. While using Pseudo-BIST we will be having 10–20% extra area for BIST compared to ATE but in comparison to BIST we will be having a 50–70% reduction in the area. As this process includes ATE, BIST along with parallelism so this idea can be used to test other designs like DACs, other ADCs, etc. drastically reducing the test time and hardware.

**Acknowledgements.** The authors would like to thank the DFT Team in Automotive and Discrete Group at ST Microelectronics, India for providing tools, technologies and for providing technical support throughout the work.

# References

1. John, D., Martin, K.: Analog Integrated Circuits. Wiley, New York (1997)
2. Poehl, F., et al.: Production test challenges for highly integrated mobile phone SoCs. In: Proceedings of IEEE European Test Symposium, pp. 17–22 (2010)
3. Blair, J.: Histogram measurement of ADC nonlinearities using sine waves. IEEE Trans. Instr. Meas **43**(3), 373–383 (1994)
4. Zagursky, V., Gertners, A.: Testing technique for embedded ADC. In: IEEE Asia-Pacific Conference on Circuits and Systems, Microelectronics and Integrating Systems, APCCAS 1998, Proceedings (Cat. No. 98EX242), Chiangmai, pp. 775–778 (1998)
5. Goyal, S., et al.: Test time reduction of successive approximation register A/D converter by selective code measurement. In: IEEE International Conference on Test, Austin, TX, pp. 8, 225 (2005)
6. Stratigopoulos, H.G., Barragan, M.J., Mir, S., Le Gall, H., Bhargava, N., Bal, A., Evaluation of low-cost mixed-signal test techniques for circuits with long simulation times. In: 2015 IEEE International Test Conference (ITC), Anaheim, CA, pp. 1–7 (2015)
7. Huang, X.L., et al.: A self-testing and calibration method for embedded successive approximation register ADC. In: 16th Asia and South Pacific Design Automation Conference (ASP-DAC 2011), Yokohama, pp. 713–718 (2011)
8. Carbone, P., Petri, D.: Noise sensitivity of ADC histogram test. IEEE Trans. Instr. Meas **47**(3), 1001–1004 (1998)

# SFG Based Fault Simulation of Linear Analog Circuits Using Fault Classification and Sensitivity Analysis

Rahul Bhattacharya$^{(\boxtimes)}$ ⓘ, S. H. M. Ragamai, and Subindu Kumar

Department of Electronics Engineering, Indian Institute of Technology
(Indian School of Mines), Dhanbad, India
rahulece83@gmail.com, hansaragamai@gmail.com,
subindukumar@hotmail.com

**Abstract.** This paper presents a new approach for simulating single analog faults in linear analog circuits modeled in MATLAB/Simulink environment. The proposed approach consists of namely, modeling fault free, and faulty analog circuits in MATLAB/Simulink environment using signal flow graph, simulating both models applying an input test stimulus and identifying the presence of faults by comparing the maximum error voltage measured at the output with a predefined threshold. The parametric faults are modeled in terms of component tolerances. Apart from this, catastrophic faults are also considered in terms of short and open faults. The proposed approach initially identifies the type of fault to be simulated. Based on fault type, it builds the signal flow graph (SFG) of the faulty circuit. We have also shown that parametric faults are sensitive to frequency of the input test sinusoid. Our proposed approach exploits 'PSpice® Advanced Sensitivity Analysis' which identifies less sensitive parametric faults at a given frequency of input sinusoid. The effectiveness of the proposed method is verified by fault modeling and fault simulation of a biquadratic and leapfrog filter circuit. The proposed fault simulation method provides a speedup over the traditional circuit simulator like PSPICE.

**Keywords:** Analog fault simulation · Sensitivity Analysis · Parametric faults
Catastrophic faults · Signal flow graph

## 1 Introduction

Although nearly 80% of the electronic circuits in the electronic equipment are digital, around 80% of faults occurs mainly in the analog parts [1]. In recent years analog circuit test cost is often found to be as much as 50% of the total test cost [2]. So test methods are needed which can reduce the cost and time. Fault simulation is an integral part of electronic circuits testing. While fault simulation methods for digital circuits [3] have achieved a good degree of success, research in the areas of analog circuit fault simulation has not achieved the same height. The lack of suitable analog fault models is the prime reason for such hindrance. Moreover, long simulation time is the most common complaint about designing analog circuitry and simulating faults adds even more simulation time. There are several approaches of analog circuits fault simulation

© Springer Nature Singapore Pte Ltd. 2017
B. K. Kaushik et al. (Eds.): VDAT 2017, CCIS 711, pp. 179–190, 2017.
https://doi.org/10.1007/978-981-10-7470-7_19

reported by authors in various literature in the field of analog circuit testing. In this context, FSPICE [4], SABER [5] and iMACSIM [6] suffer from prohibitively long simulation time. DRAFTS [7] is a discretized serial fault simulator developed in C/C++ platform for analog circuits. Variyam and Chatterjee [8] discussed a fast fault simulator called FLYER which can simulate both soft and hard faults as long as the fault effects can be depicted by linearized circuit representations. Stephen Sunter [9] discussed several key challenges of analog fault simulation and potential solutions for reducing simulation time. Recently, Mentor Graphics analog fault simulator Tessent® DefectSim™ [9] can reduce total fault simulation time by many orders of magnitude compared to some of the previous approaches while compromising simulation accuracy. Yelten et al. [10] proposed a methodology that identifies impactful parametric faults in large analog modules embedded in industrial mixed-signal systems with a constrained simulation budget. This is achieved by introducing an iterative search leveraging parameters' sensitivity information. In contrast, our proposed approach focuses on fault simulation of SFG-based behavioral models of linear analog circuits and leverages 'PSpice® Advanced Sensitivity Analysis' to identify suitable test frequency which can detect the parametric variation. Moreover, our approach is restricted to linear analog circuits only. Sunter [11] pointed out several inconsistencies between intuition and theory/practice in selecting random defects for a conventional analog defect simulator. Although it is more practical to consider the relative likelihood (RL) of each potential defect, all defects are assumed equally likely in this work, for simplification. To date, most of the fault simulation algorithms discussed in the literature so far are built in high-level languages (e.g., C, C++, System C etc.). But MATLAB-Simulink [12, 13] environment has not been explored to that extent. This paper identifies that due to numerous advantages e.g. command line/graphical user interface, customizable block libraries, solvers, capability of interfacing with other CAD tools and portability to VHDL-AMS modeling platform [14], MATLAB-Simulink [15] environment can be exploited for high level modeling and fault simulation of linear analog circuits.

In this paper we present a MATLAB-Simulink based fault simulation framework for linear analog circuits represented using signal flow graph [16]. In this work we make use of hierarchical fault models [17] for catastrophic as well as parametric faults for passive components only. Unlike other fault simulators, catastrophic faults are classified to find an equivalence with parametric faults such that faulty SFG of analog circuits for simulating parametric faults can also be re-used for simulating a class of catastrophic faults. This simplifies proposed fault simulation framework. The proposed approach exploits 'PSpice® Advanced Sensitivity Analysis' [18, 19] to identify components which are negligibly less sensitive at a given frequency of input test sinusoid.

The paper is organized as follows. Section 2 discusses the modeling of fault-free linear analog circuit, namely, biquadratic and leapfrog filter through building of their signal flow graph (SFG) and implementing them in MATLAB-Simulink [13] platform. Section 3 summarizes how analog fault models can be built and faulty SFGs can be implemented in MATLAB-Simulink. In Sect. 4, we discuss how 'Advanced Sensitivity Analysis' can be useful to shorten the parametric fault list and select the frequency of input test sinusoid judiciously. The proposed fault simulation flow along with fault simulation results to validate the approach are presented in Sect. 5 with the help of some circuit examples. Finally, the paper is concluded in Sect. 6.

## 2  Modeling Analog Circuit in MATLAB-Simulink

Any linear analog circuit can be represented using signal flow graph (SFG) [16]. An SFG can be represented in terms of Adders/Subtractors, Gain and Integrator blocks in MATLAB-Simulink. To demonstrate the approach, we have considered the modeling of a biquadratic and leapfrog filter [7, 14, 16] shown in Figs. 1 and 2 respectively.

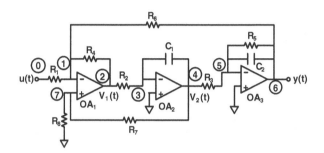

**Fig. 1.** Biquadratic filter.

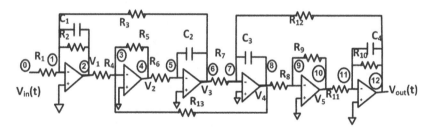

**Fig. 2.** Leapfrog filter.

### 2.1  Building SFG of Linear Analog Circuit

Any linear analog circuit's dynamics can be represented by a set of linear differential nodal equations. The linear differential nodal equations at nodes 1, 2, 3 in Fig. 1 can be given by Eqs. (1), (2) and (3). The SFG of biquadratic filter corresponding to Eqs. (1), (2) and (3) is shown in Fig. 3.

$$V_1(s) = -\frac{R_4}{R_1}u(s) - \frac{R_4}{R_6}y(s) + \frac{R_8}{R_7+R_8}\left(1+\frac{R_4(R_1+R_6)}{R_1R_6}\right)V_2(s) \qquad (1)$$

$$V_2(s) = -\frac{1}{sR_2C_1} V_1(s) \tag{2}$$

$$y(s) = -\frac{\frac{1}{sR_3C_2}}{1 + \frac{1}{sR_5C_2}} V_2(s) \tag{3}$$

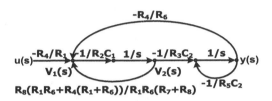

**Fig. 3.** SFG of fault free biquadratic filter.

Similarly SFG of leapfrog filter can be represented as shown in Fig. 4.

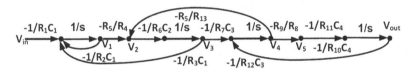

**Fig. 4.** SFG of fault free leapfrog filter.

## 2.2   Modeling and Simulation of SFG in MATLAB-Simulink

Once the SFG of a linear analog circuit is derived, its Simulink [13] model can be implemented by a system of interconnected Adders/Subtractors, Gain and Integrators. The Simulink model of biquadratic filter is shown in Fig. 5. Simulation can be carried out for any given sinusoidal input u(t). Ode45 (Dormand-Prince) [20] is chosen as an ordinary differential equation solver for simulation of Simulink model. The sampling rate can be chosen judiciously to satisfy Nyquist criteria and achieve higher accuracy. The test input for biquadratic filter is 200 mV p-p sinusoid with a frequency of 500 Hz. So, $u(t) = 0.1\sin(2\pi * 500t)$. The nominal values of components of biquadratic filter are chosen as follows.

$R_1 = R_2 = R_3 = R_4 = R_5 = R_6 = R_7 = R_8 = 10\,\text{k}\Omega$, and $C_1 = C_2 = 0.01\,\mu\text{F}$.

The nominal values of components of leapfrog filter are chosen as follows.

$R_1 = R_2 = R_3 = R_4 = R_5 = R_6 = R_7 = R_8 = R_9 = R_{10} = R_{11} = R_{12} = R_{13} = 10\ \text{k}\Omega$,
$C_1 = C_4 = 0.01\text{nF}$ and $C_2 = C_3 = 0.02\ \text{nF}$

The response of PSPICE and Simulink are shown in Fig. 6. Simulation results show that performance of biquadratic filter matches well with that of SPICE simulation.

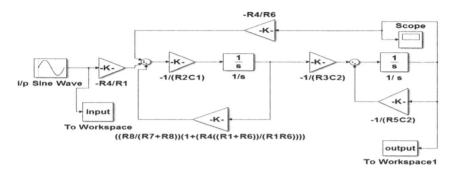

**Fig. 5.** Simulink model of signal flow graph of the biquadratic filter.

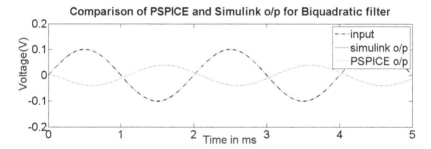

**Fig. 6.** Response of fault free biquadratic filter to sinusoidal input $u(t) = 0.1\sin(2\pi * 500t)$.

## 3    Building Fault Models

Fault model is the abstract representation of a real defect in a circuit or system which captures its functionalities and behavior. Analog circuits have no simple fault model. The accepted analog fault models [16] are catastrophic faults and parametric faults. The parametric faults are component variations which can cause the behavior of the fault-free device to deviate significantly from nominal values. Catastrophic faults manifest themselves as a sudden and large deviation in a component value resulting in shorted and open circuits. It may be noted that only single faults are considered for demonstration and the faults modeled are limited to faults in passive components only. In the subsequent subsections, the fault modeling is illustrated with the help of a case study of biquadratic filter. The same approach can be applicable to model faults in any other linear analog circuits e.g. leapfrog filter etc. without any loss of generality.

### 3.1   Modeling Parametric Faults

Parametric faults are modeled by varying nominal values of circuit components from their nominal values. Single parametric faults are considered i.e. nominal value of one component is deviated up to upper and lower limiting values at a time such that the output voltage falls outside the acceptable range when the circuit component crosses these limits.

In this work, parametric faults are modeled by varying nominal values of components of biquadratic filter by ±50% as shown in Table 2. For example, due to parametric fault in resistor $R_5$, its nominal resistance may change from 10 kΩ to either 5 kΩ or 15 kΩ. So, in Simulink model of Fig. 5, the constant values of 'Gain' blocks corresponding to only $R_5$ are changed accordingly while the structure of SFG in Fig. 3 remains unchanged.

### 3.2   Modeling Catastrophic Faults

The catastrophic faults generally we come across in analog circuits are short and open faults. Short faults can be modeled by placing a significantly very large capacitor or small resistor between two nodes while open faults can be modeled by suddenly changing resistance of a resistor or capacitance of a capacitor to a significantly very large or small value respectively. Catastrophic short faults are categorized into three groups for simplicity.

**Group I.** The catastrophic faults which does not change the structure or topology of original SFG. This may occur under the following cases.

(a)  *A resistive short fault between two nodes i and j where i and j are already connected through a resistor.*
(b)  *A capacitive short fault between two nodes i and j where i and j are already connected through a capacitor.*
(c)  *An open fault which can be modeled by changing resistance or capacitance of a resistor or capacitor to a considerably large or small value respectively.*

To model short fault under group-I, an equivalent capacitor or resistor can be placed between i and j and effectively it can be considered as a parametric fault. For open fault, component value changes from nominal to very large or small one and effectively it can be considered as a parametric fault too.

**Group II.** The catastrophic faults which causes change of original SFG without introducing any extra state. This may occur under the following cases.

(a)  *A resistive short fault across a capacitor.*
(b)  *A resistive short fault across two unconnected nodes.*

Suppose there is a resistive short $R_f$ of 10Ω between the output node 4 of op-amp $OA_2$ and its negative terminal 3 in the biquadratic filter. Such faults can be modeled by rebuilding the faulty SFG as shown in Fig. 7(a) and introducing extra 'Gain' blocks in Simulink model as shown in Fig. 8(a).

**Group III.** The catastrophic faults which causes change in the original fault-free SFG with extra states. This may occur under the following cases.

(a) *A capacitive short fault across a resistor.*
(b) *A capacitive short fault across two unconnected nodes.*

Suppose there is a capacitive short fault $C_f$ of 10 nF between output node 2 of op-amp $OA_1$ and its negative terminal 1 in the biquadratic filter. Due to the occurrence of large parasitics or coupling capacitances, ac malfunction occurs and gives rise to additional faulty states. Such faults can be modeled by rebuilding the faulty SFG as shown in Fig. 7(b) and introducing extra 'Gain' and 'Integrator (1/s)' blocks in Simulink model as shown in Fig. 8(b).

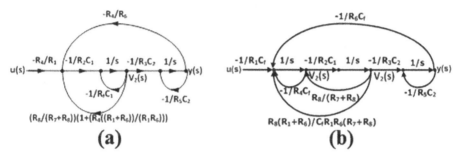

**Fig. 7.** SFG of faulty biquadratic filter (a) Resistive short $R_f$ (b) capacitive short $C_f$.

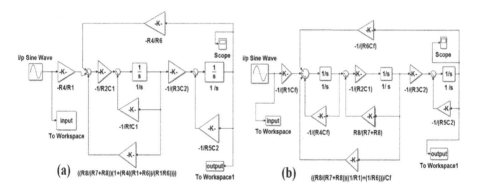

**Fig. 8.** Simulink model of biquadratic filter under (a) resistive short fault $R_f$ (b) capacitive short $C_f$.

## 4   Advanced Sensitivity Analysis

The circuit sensitivity [21, 22] is a function of input test frequency. Sensitivity analysis simplifies the problem of parametric fault simulation in two ways. Firstly, given a set of input test frequencies, 'Advanced Sensitivity Analysis' can be carried out for each frequency and the least sensitive components whose sensitivity is less than 50 (in linear scale) can be identified before fault simulation. If the number of such components with lesser sensitivity falls below 10% of the total components, that test frequency can be rejected as shown in Fig. 9. Thus, sensitivity analysis helps to judiciously select a suitable set of test frequencies which can detect maximum number of parametric faults while reducing overall fault simulation time. Secondly, if any component is found to be least sensitive against almost all test frequencies, that component can be eliminated from the list of parametric faults as shown in Fig. 9.

To demonstrate the usefulness of 'Advanced Sensitivity Analysis', two test frequencies 1 kHz and 3.75 kHz are randomly chosen for fault simulation of biquadratic filter. Table 1 shows the relative sensitivities of passive components of the biquad filter on a linear scale using Advanced Sensitivity Analysis [18, 19] at test frequency 1 kHz and 3.75 kHz respectively. The relative sensitivities are measured for each component having a tolerance of 50% and taking maximum and minimum values of the outputs as the measurements. The relative sensitivities of $R_7$ and $R_8$ are less than 50 at frequencies 1 kHz and 3.75 kHz. So, we can eliminate the less sensitive components from the fault list of parametric faults.

**Table 1.** Results of advanced sensitivity analysis of biquadratic filter at frequency of 1 kHz and 3.75 kHz.

| Component | Nominal value | @Min[a] | @Max[b] | Relative sensitivity (linear scale) @ 1 kHz | Relative sensitivity (linear scale) @ 3.75 kHz |
|---|---|---|---|---|---|
| $R_1$ | 10 kΩ | 15 kΩ | 5 kΩ | −256.0672μ (95) | −112.2593μ (82) |
| $R_2$ | 10 kΩ | 15 kΩ | 5 kΩ | −14.3431μ (5) | −99.8125μ (73) |
| $R_3$ | 10 kΩ | 15 kΩ | 5 kΩ | −229.6856μ (85) | −130.3426μ (95) |
| $R_4$ | 10 kΩ | 5 kΩ | 15 kΩ | 82.3461μ (30) | 130.5576μ (96) |
| $R_5$ | 10 kΩ | 5 kΩ | 15 kΩ | 211.3712μ (79) | 26.1070μ (19) |
| $R_6$ | 10 kΩ | 5 kΩ | 15 kΩ | 182.3249μ (68) | 5.4207μ (3) |
| $R_7$ | 10 kΩ | 5 kΩ | 15 kΩ | 119.6646μ (44) | 24.8114μ (18) |
| $R_8$ | 10 kΩ | 15 kΩ | 5 kΩ | −109.9554μ (41) | −26.2065μ (19) |
| $C_1$ | 0.01 μF | 15 nF | 7.5 nF | −11.1531μ (4) | −96.6011μ (71) |
| $C_2$ | 0.01 μF | 15 nF | 7.5 nF | −40.2723μ (15) | −113.0600μ (83) |

[a] Parameter value used to calculate the worst-case minimum measurement.
[b] Parameter value used to calculate the worst-case maximum measurement.

## 5   Fault Simulation Results

Once the fault list is prepared after fault modeling and sensitivity analysis for parametric faults, the faults are injected serially one by one, faulty Simulink models developed in Sect. 3 are simulated by applying test sinusoid of different frequencies (randomly chosen) and 200 mV p-p amplitude. The error voltage is measured at each sampling instant by taking the absolute difference between fault-free and faulty response. A threshold of 0.01 V is used to detect parametric faults. The flow chart for simulating faults is shown in Fig. 9.

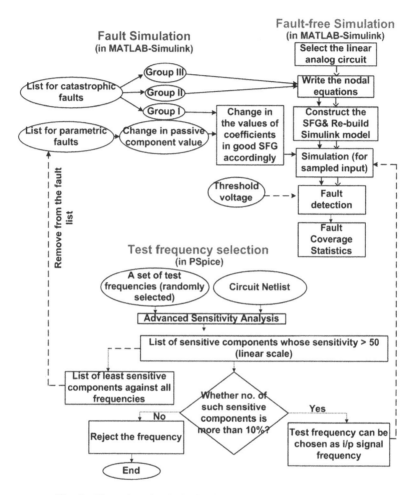

**Fig. 9.** Flow chart for fault simulation of linear analog circuits.

## 5.1   Fault Simulation of Biquadratic Filter

The fault simulation results of Biquadratic filter are given in Table 2 at various frequencies. Some of the faults (parametric and catastrophic faults) are less sensitive at the frequencies of Test Set 1 and they are highly sensitive at the frequencies of test set 2. At 1 kHz the relative sensitivity of $C_1$ is negligibly less as shown in Table 1 and so is not observable in Table 2, while at 3.75 kHz, the relative sensitivity of $C_1$ is substantially high as shown in Table 1 and $C_1$ parametric fault is detected at 3.75 kHz. The fault coverage for Test Set 1 and Test Set 2 are found to be 55.26% and 87.50% respectively as shown in Table 2. It is also found that average fault simulation time per fault presented in Table 2 is 0.32 s using our proposed MATLAB-Simulink based simulator while it is 1.43 s using PSPICE simulator and 0.15 s using the approach in [7].

## 5.2  Fault Simulation of Leapfrog Filter

In case of leapfrog filter shown in Fig. 2, nearly 80% fault coverage can be achieved using similar flow of fault simulation. It is also observed that average fault simulation time per fault in case of leapfrog filter is 0.35 s using our proposed flow while it is 0.6 s using PSPICE simulator and 0.23 s using the approach in [7].

**Table 2.**  Fault simulation results of biquadratic filter.

| Description of fault | | | | | | | | |
|---|---|---|---|---|---|---|---|---|
| Parametric fault | | | Test set 1 | | | Test set 2 | | |
| Component | Nominal value | Faulty value | Frequency (HZ) | Max.error voltage (V) | Detect | Frequency (HZ) | Max.error voltage (V) | Detect |
| $R_1$ | 10 kΩ | 15 kΩ | 100 | 0.0114 | Y | 4.37e+01 | 0.0114 | Y |
| $R_1$ | 10 kΩ | 5 kΩ | 100 | 0.0266 | Y | 3.85e+00 | 0.0267 | Y |
| $R_2$ | 10 kΩ | 15 kΩ | 1000 | 0.0053 | N | 2.34e+03 | 0.0080 | N |
| $R_2$ | 10 kΩ | 5 KΩ | 1000 | 0.0054 | N | 3.75e+03 | 0.0103 | Y |
| $R_3$ | 10 kΩ | 15 kΩ | 1000 | 0.0103 | Y | 1.56e+03 | 0.0106 | Y |
| $R_3$ | 10 kΩ | 5 kΩ | 1000 | 0.0210 | Y | 2.16e+03 | 0.0261 | Y |
| $R_4$ | 10 kΩ | 15 kΩ | 1000 | 0.0050 | N | 2.83e+03 | 0.0079 | N |
| $R_4$ | 10 kΩ | 5 kΩ | 1000 | 0.0108 | Y | 1.99e+03 | 0.0132 | Y |
| $R_5$ | 10 kΩ | 15 KΩ | 1000 | 0.0098 | N | 1.18e+03 | 0.0096 | N |
| $R_5$ | 10 kΩ | 5 kΩ | 1000 | 0.0147 | Y | 1.06e+03 | 0.0146 | Y |
| $R_6$ | 10 kΩ | 15 kΩ | 100 | 0.0100 | Y | 4.37e+01 | 0.0100 | Y |
| $R_6$ | 10 kΩ | 5 kΩ | 100 | 0.0150 | Y | 4.37e+01 | 0.0150 | Y |
| $C_1$ | 0.0 1μF | 0.02 μF | 1000 | 0.0101 | Y | 2.47e+03 | 0.0132 | Y |
| $C_1$ | 0.0 1μF | 0.005 μF | 1000 | 0.0054 | N | 3.75e+03 | 0.0103 | Y |
| $C_2$ | 0.0 1μF | 0.02 μF | 1000 | 0.0128 | Y | 2.47e+03 | 0.0143 | Y |
| $C_2$ | 0.0 1μF | 0.005 μF | 1000 | 0.0076 | N | 3.75e+03 | 0.0131 | Y |
| Short fault | | | Test set 1 | | | Test set 2 | | |
| Short type | Shorted nodes-(group) | Short value | Frequency (HZ) | Max.error voltage (V) | Detect | Frequency (HZ) | Max.error voltage (V) | Detect |
| Resistive | 1, 2-(Group I) | 10 Ω | 100 | 0.0398 | Y | 7.33e+02 | 0.0389 | Y |
| Resistive | 1, 2-(Group I) | 1 kΩ | 1000 | 0.0316 | Y | 2.83e+03 | 0.0215 | Y |
| Resistive | 3, 4-(Group II) | 10 Ω | 500 | 0.0395 | Y | 1.20e+03 | 0.0370 | Y |
| Resistive | 3, 4-(Group II) | 1 kΩ | 1000 | 0.0312 | Y | 3.23e+03 | 0.0192 | Y |
| Resistive | 5, 6-(Group I) | 10 Ω | 100 | 0.0399 | Y | 9.23e+02 | 0.0383 | Y |
| Resistive | 5, 6-(Group I) | 1 kΩ | 1000 | 0.0329 | Y | 3.83e+03 | 0.0176 | Y |

*(continued)*

**Table 2.** (*continued*)

| Description of fault | | | | | | | | | |
|---|---|---|---|---|---|---|---|---|---|
| Capacitive | 1, 2-(Group III) | 10 nF | 100 | 0.0011 | N | 2.34e+03 | 0.0354 | Y | |
| Capacitive | 1, 2-(Group III) | 0.1 μF | 100 | 0.0063 | N | 3.06e+03 | 0.0264 | Y | |
| Capacitive | 3, 4-(Group I) | 10 nF | 100 | 0.0011 | N | 3.02e+00 | 3.27e-5 | N | |
| Capacitive | 3, 4-(Group I) | 0.1 μF | 100 | 0.0093 | N | 1.20e+ 03 | 0.0374 | Y | |
| Capacitive | 5, 6-(Group I) | 10 nF | 100 | 0.0015 | N | 13.06e+02 | 0.0147 | Y | |
| Capacitive | 5, 6-(Group I) | 0.1 μF | 100 | 0.0127 | Y | 2.60e + 03 | 0.0305 | Y | |
| Open fault | | | Test set 1 | | | Test set 2 | | | |
| Component | Node-(group) | Open value | Frequency (HZ) | Max.error voltage (V) | Detect | Frequency (HZ) | Max.error voltage (V) | Detect | |
| $R_6$ | 6-(Group I) | 1 MΩ | 1000 | 0.0439 | Y | 1500 | 0.0344 | Y | |
| $R_7$ | 7-(Group I) | 1 MΩ | 1000 | 0.0730 | Y | 1160 | 0.0753 | Y | |
| $R_8$ | 7-(Group I) | 1 MΩ | 1000 | 0.0153 | Y | 2600 | 0.0109 | Y | |
| $C_2$ | 6-(Group I) | 1 pF | 900 | 0.0136 | Y | 4660 | 0.0293 | Y | |
| Fault Coverage | | | 55.26% | | | 87.50% | | | |

# 6  Conclusion

The fault simulation approach presented in this paper, considers single analog faults targeting passive components only. This method can be extended to Op-amp faults if they can be modeled at behavioral or transfer function level. The accuracy of fault simulation can be increased further by approximating integral operators using higher order numerical approximation. Choice of threshold voltage to detect faults is one of the key parameters in our proposed fault simulation approach. Lesser the threshold voltage, higher is the chance of fault detection. But if it is comparable with noise voltage, fault-free circuit may be interpreted as faulty one. It may be noted that our proposed approach is restricted to linear analog circuits only. 'PSpice® Advanced Sensitivity Analysis' included in this work helps to judiciously select the frequency of test sinusoid such that fault coverage can be increased.

# References

1. Binu, D., Kariyappa, B.S.: A survey on fault diagnosis of analog circuits: Taxonomy and state of the art. Int. J. Electron. Commun. (AEU) **73**, 68–83 (2017). Elsevier
2. Sindia, S.: High sensitivity signatures for test and diagnosis of analog, mixed-signal and radio-frequency circuits. Doctoral dissertation (2013)
3. Molnar, L., Gontean, A.: Fault simulation methodes. In: Proceedings of the 12th IEEE International Symposium on Electronics and telecommunications (ISETC), pp. 194–197 (2016)

4. Renovell, M., Camborn, G., Auvergne, D.: FSPICE: a tool for fault modeling in MOS circuits. Integr. VLSI J. **3**, 245–255 (1985)
5. Getreu, I.: Behavioral modeling of analog blocks using the SABER simulator. In: Proceedings of the MWCAS, pp. 977–980 (1989)
6. Singh, J., Saleh, R.: iMACSIM: a program for multi-level analog circuit simulation. In: Proceedings of the ICCAD, pp. 16–19 (1991)
7. Nagi, N., Chatterjee, A., Abraham, J.A.: Fault simulation of linear analog circuits. J. Electron. Testing **4**, 345–360 (1993). https://doi.org/10.1007/BF01239077
8. Variyam, P.N., Chatterjee, A.: FLYER: fast fault simulation of linear analog circuits using pomnomial waveform and perturbed state representation. In: Proceedings of the 10th IEEE International Conference on VLSI Design, pp. 408–412, January 1997
9. Sunter, S.: Analog fault simulation challenges and solutions. MENTOR GRAPHICS White Paper. https://www.mentor.com/products/silicon-yield/resources/
10. Yelten, M.B., Natarajan, S., Xue, B., Goteti, P.: Scalable and efficient analog parametric fault identification. In: 2013 IEEE/ACM International Conference on Computer-Aided Design (ICCAD), San Jose, CA, pp. 387–392 (2013)
11. Sunter, S.: Experiences with an industrial analog fault simulator and engineering intuition. In: 2015 IEEE 20th International Mixed-Signals Testing Workshop (IMSTW), Paris, pp. 1–5 (2015)
12. Modeling and Simulation - MATLAB & Simulink – MathWorks. https://www.mathworks.com/discovery/modeling-and-simulation.html
13. The Mathworks. Simulink User Guide, 2013b edn. (2013)
14. Umer Farooq, M., Xia, L., Azmadi Hussin, F., Saeed Malik, A.: High level fault modeling and fault propagation in analog circuits using NLARX automated model generation technique. In: Proceedings of the 4th IEEE International Conference on Intelligent and Advanced Systems (ICIAS), pp. 846–850 (2012)
15. Bhattacharya, R., Kumar, S., Biswas, S.: Resource optimization for emulation of behavioral models of mixed signal circuits on FPGA: A case study of DC-DC buck converter. Int. J. Circuit Theory Appl. **45**, 1701–1741 (2017). Wiley https://doi.org/10.1002/cta.2323
16. Ramadoss, R., Bushnell, M.L.: Test generation for mixed signal devices using signal flow graph. J. Electron. Testing: Theory Appl. **14**(3), 189–205 (1999)
17. Nagi, N., Abraham, J.A.: Hierarchical fault modeling for linear analog circuits. J. Analog Integr. Circuits Signal Process. **10**, 89 (1996). https://doi.org/10.1007/BF00713981
18. Fitzpatrick, D.: Analog Design and Simulation using OrCAD Capture and PSpice. Elsevier, Amsterdam (2012)
19. PSPICE Advanced analysis user's guide. www.ee.bgu.ac.il/∼spice/Additional/pspaugca.pdf
20. Ashino, R., Nagase, M., Vaillancourt, R.: Behind and beyond the MATLAB ODE suite. Int. J. Comput. Math. Appl. **40**, 491–512 (2000)
21. Rosenblum, A.L., Ghausi, M.S.: Multiparameter sensitivity in active RC networks. IEEE Trans. Circuit Theory **18**, 592–599 (1971)
22. Mandache, L., Iordache, M., Dumitriu, L.: Sensitivity and tolerance analysis in analog circuits using symbolic methods. In: Proceedings of the 10th IEEE International Conference on Development and Application Systems, Suceava, Romania, pp. 230–235, 27–29 May 2010

# A Cost Effective Technique for Diagnosis of Scan Chain Faults

Satyadev Ahlawat[1], Darshit Vaghani[1], Jaynarayan Tudu[2(✉)], and Ashok Suhag[3]

[1] Computer Architecture and Dependable Systems Labaratory, Department of Electrical Engineering, Indian Institute of Technology Bombay, Mumbai, India
{satyadev,vaghani}@iitb.ac.in
[2] Department of Computer Science and Automation, Indian Institute of Science, Bengaluru, India
jayttudu@csa.iisc.ernet.in
[3] School of Engineering and Technology, BML Munjal University, Gurgaon, India
ashok.suhag@bml.edu.in

**Abstract.** Scan based diagnosis plays a critical role in failure mode analysis for yield improvement. However, as the logic circuitry associated with scan chains constitute a significant fraction of a chip's total area the scan chain itself can be subject to defects. In some cases, it has been observed that scan chain failures may account up to 50% of total chip failures. Hence, scan chain testing and diagnosis have become very crucial in recent years. This paper proposes a hardware-assisted low complexity and area efficient scan chain diagnosis technique. The proposed technique is simple to implement and provides maximum diagnostic resolution for *stuck-at* faults. The proposed technique can be further extended to diagnose scan chain's timing faults.

**Keywords:** Scan design · Scan chain fault · Fault diagnosis

## 1 Introduction

Almost every complex circuit today employ scan-based Design-for Testability ($DFT$) architecture to enhance testability and diagnostic capabilities. The effectiveness of these techniques rely upon the proper functioning of the scan design i.e., the scan chain itself is fault free. However, it has been reported in the literature that the chip area consumed by the scan path along with the scan control signals may range from 15% to 30%. Furthermore, it has been observed that 10% to 30% of the total defects may cause the scan chain to fail [1]. A faulty scan chain hinders the chip failure mode analysis process for yield enhancement. The presence of a fault in scan chains can be easily detected by performing a simple flush test, however, identifying the exact location of the fault in the scan chain is a tedious task. Several techniques have been proposed in the literature for diagnosing scan chain faults. These techniques can be broadly classified into three main categories: 1. simulation-based [2–4], 2. tester-based [5–7], and 3. hardware-assisted [8–12]. The simulation-based techniques make use of the failure logs of

© Springer Nature Singapore Pte Ltd. 2017
B. K. Kaushik et al. (Eds.): VDAT 2017, CCIS 711, pp. 191–204, 2017.
https://doi.org/10.1007/978-981-10-7470-7_20

scan tests from the tester and use inject-and-evaluate approach to identify the defective scan cell [2]. Unfortunately, due to limited failing buffer size capacity of the tester, not all the failing pattern/cycles data can be recorded. The limited availability of failing log data from the tester may result in false identification or reduced diagnostic resolution. The simulation based techniques do not have any hardware overhead, however, the diagnostic resolution is comparatively poor compared to hardware-assisted diagnosis techniques. Also, the simulation-based techniques are very complex and time consuming.

In tester-based approach, a physical failure analysis (*PFA*) device is used in conjunction with the tester. While the scan patterns are shifted in through the scan chain by the tester, *PFA* is used to observe and analyze the defective response of the scan cells at different physical locations. In one such approach [5], E-beam is used to detect the toggles in a scan chain while a stream of alternating 0's and 1's are shifted in the scan chain by the tester. The toggles disappear at the location of the *stuck-at* fault. The tester based techniques can accurately locate the defect site when probable physical defect location is very small, however, the diagnosis time and associated *PFA* cost is prohibitively high.

A good review of simulation-based and tester-based diagnosis techniques is provided in a recent paper by Huang et al. [1]. These techniques do not use any extra circuitry for diagnosis of scan chain faults and hence no area overhead. However, these techniques have some serious drawbacks like poor diagnostic resolution, long diagnosis time, and prohibitively high instrumentation cost. The hardware-assisted techniques, on the other hand, have a much better diagnostic resolution as compared to simulation-based and tester-based techniques. These techniques often use custom scan cell design or add extra circuitry in the scan path to facilitate scan chain fault diagnosis. The extra circuitry added to the scan design is used either to *set/reset* every scan cell in the scan chain or flip its content.

S. Edirisooriya and G. Edirisooriya [8] insert a two-input *XOR* gate between the scan cells. The XOR gate is used as an inverter to invert the content of a scan cell before shifting it into the next scan cell. By inserting a XOR gate between every pair of scan cells a maximum resolution of 1 can be achieved. In another hardware-based technique, the authors [9] use partner scan chains to diagnose scan chain faults. These partner scan chains are connected with each other through extra routing wires such that during diagnostic mode, the content of bad scan chain can be observed by the good partner scan chain. Narayanan and Das [10] use extra circuitry to *set/reset* the scan out port of the scan cell for effective diagnosis of scan chain faults. In another such approach [11], Wu uses custom scan cells with *set/reset* capability to locate the exact position of a fault in the scan chain. The technique in [11] is capable of diagnosing both *stuck-at* and *hold-time* faults. However, there is a trade-off between diagnostic resolution and hardware overhead. In a recent work [12], Dounavi et al. use a modified scan architecture that uses charging/discharging of a global diagnosis-line to locate the faulty scan cell. This technique has a high diagnostic resolution, however, the static power consumption is very high because of a direct path formation between power supply node and the ground node.

In spite of having much better diagnostic resolution compared to simulation and tester based techniques, most of the hardware-based techniques are unacceptable in practical designs. The hardware-based techniques have some practical issues like power consumption due to extra circuitry during functional mode, testing of extra circuitry, and area overhead. These issues has been outlined in a recent work [13] which also proposes a solution. However the technique in [13] considers only stuck-at faults. In this paper, we propose a new hardware-based scan chain diagnosis technique. In this technique, a custom scan cell design is used to achieve *set/reset* capability for enhancing the diagnostic capability. The proposed technique can be used to diagnose both stuck-at and timing faults in the scan chain. The major advantages of the proposed technique are as follows:

1. The proposed scan cell design eliminates the need for separate *set* and *reset* control signal for diagnosis and has minimum area overhead compared to the existing hardware-assisted diagnosing techniques.
2. The proposed diagnosis technique has the maximum diagnostic resolution (to be precise, 1) for *stuck-at* faults and hence can locate the exact position of the faulty scan cell.
3. The proposed technique can be extended to diagnose hold time faults at the cost of slightly diminished diagnostic resolution.
4. The new scan cell has little performance overhead compared to conventional scan cell design.

The remainder of the paper is organized as follows: Sect. 2 describes the fault type identification procedure. Section 3 elaborates on the implementation of the proposed scan cell. Further, this section describes diagnosis of stuck-at scan chain faults. Section 4 explains the extension of the proposed technique to diagnose hold time faults in a scan chain. Section 5 compares the merits of the proposed technique with the existing hardware-based techniques. This section also discusses the post layout timing simulation results. The paper is concluded in Sect. 6.

## 2    Preliminaries and Fault Type Identification

In scan inserted circuits, the scan chain is used to load/unload the test stimuli/ response for test and diagnosis purpose. However, the presence of defects in the scan circuitry may cause the scan chain to fail and invalidate the test and diagnosis process. Many factors contribute to the presence of defects in a scan chain. Some of these factors, such as faulty fabrication line, technology process variation effects, resistive short or open interconnect, may manifest in a number of ways. The presence of a short or open interconnect at the scan cell's input/output ports can result either as a *stuck-at-0* or a *stuck-at-1* fault. A faulty scan cell with a stuck-at-0 (1) fault will change all the bits shifting through it to 0 (1). As a result, the shifted out sequence will consist all $0's$ (1) no matter what sequence is shifted in.

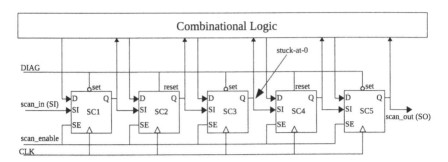

**Fig. 1.** Example Scan chain with a single $sa0$ fault

Hold time fault is another commonly observed scan chain fault. The hold time violation is generally caused by clock skew, which could be a result of process variation or improper clock tree design. There are three types of scan chain hold time faults which have been observed in practice [11]. In a type-I hold time fault, a scan cell captures faulty value only in case its scan input $SI$ has a rising transition i.e., 0 to 1 transition. The type-I fault is caused by the faster rise time of the $Q$ of the preceding scan cell that feeds the faulty scan cell with clock skew. The clock skew at the faulty scan cell is large enough that the rising transition of the preceding scan cell from the present cycle overwrites the valid data at the $SI$ input before it gets captured in the faulty cell. However, for falling transition the clock skew is small enough such that before the arrival of the falling transition at scan input the valid data gets captured. Similarly, in a type-II fault, the faulty scan cell fails only if its $SI$ input has a falling transition i.e., 1 to 0 transition. In case of type-III fault, the faulty scan cell has a large enough clock skew such that it fails for both rising and falling transitions at the $SI$ input.

The impact of hold time faults on scan chain is different than stuck-at faults. A hold time fault allows a proper shifting of sequences consisting all $0's$ or all $1's$. However, if a transition exists in the sequence the faulty scan cell acts as a shadow copy of its preceding scan cell. As a result, the faulty scan cell captures the same value as its preceding scan cell. This makes the bit following the problematic transition appears one cycle earlier than expected at the scan out port of the scan chain. In another word, the scan chain appears effectively one bit shorter because of a hold time violation. For example, in the case of a good scan chain, the input sequence 0001011100 will be observed as it is on the scan out port $SO$. However, in case of a type-I, type-II, and type-III hold time faults the shifted out response will be 0001111100, 0000001100, and 0000101110 respectively.

The scan chain failure detection and fault type identification are relatively very simple tasks, however, finding the location of the faulty scan cell (i.e., scan chain diagnosis) is a very tedious process. In this work, extra circuitry is added to the conventional scan cell which can be used to *set/reset* the scan cell during scan/diagnose mode.

## 2.1  Fault Type Identification

The scan chain failure detection and fault type can be identified by applying a simple flush test. To explain fault type identification and scan chain diagnosis process, an example scan chain of length five is shown in Fig. 1. To identify the *stuck-at* fault a flush test comprising a sequence of all $0's$ or all $1's$ can be used. To identify a *stuck-at-1* fault a stream of $0's$ can be shifted in by applying the clock five times. After five clock cycle, if a 1 appears at the *scan_out* port then there is a *stuck-at-1* fault. In case a 0 appears at the $(SO)$ port after five clock cycles then that means the scan chain is free from *stuck-at-1* faults. Similarly, a sequence of $1's$ can be used to verify the scan chain for *stuck-at-0* faults. Once the type of fault is identified the scan chain diagnosis techniques are used to identify the exact location of the faulty scan cell.

To identify a hold time fault in a scan chain the input sequences as proposed in [11] can be used. These sequences can identify the presence as well as the type of hold time faults. The sequences for the hold type faults are as follows: (A) Sequence 1: 1111100000 (B) Sequence 2: 0000011111 (C) Sequence 3: 0000010000 (D) Sequence 4: 1111101111

By observing the responses of all the above four sequences the type of hold time fault can be identified. The presence of extra $1's$ in the response of sequence 1 with no extra $0's$ in the response of sequence 2 indicates a type-I fault. The number of extra $1's$ in the observed response gives the number of faults present in the scan chain. Similarly, the presence of extra $0's$ in the response of sequence 2 with no extra $1's$ in the response of sequence 1 indicates a type-II fault. Again, the number of extra $0's$ in the observed response gives the number of faults present. If there is one-bit shift in the observed responses for both sequence 3 and sequence 4 then there is a type-III fault. The number of extra shifts in the response gives the number of faults present in the scan chain.

**Table 1.** Scan chain state in different diagnosis phases

| scan cell states | | | | | | |
|---|---|---|---|---|---|---|
| cycle no. ↓ | $SC1$ | $SC2$ | $SC3$ | $SC4$ | $SC5$ | phase ↓ |
| initialization | $X$ | $X$ | $X$ | $X$ | $X$ | |
| $clk - i_1$ | 1 | $X$ | $X$ | $X$ | $X$ | |
| $clk - i_2$ | 1 | 1 | $X$ | $X$ | $X$ | |
| $clk - i_3$ | 1 | 1 | 0 | $X$ | $X$ | |
| $clk - i_4$ | 1 | 1 | 0 | 0 | $X$ | |
| $clk - i_5$ | 1 | 1 | 0 | 0 | 0 | ← detection |
| cell *set* | 1 | 1 | 0 | 1 | 1 | |
| $clk - d_1$ | 1 | 1 | 0 | 0 | 1 | |
| $clk - d_2$ | 1 | 1 | 0 | 0 | 0 | ← diagnosed |

# 3    Fault Diagnosis Using Proposed Scan Cell

Consider a *stuck-at-0* fault at the output port ($Q$) of $3^{rd}$ scan cell ($SC3$) in the example scan chain shown in Fig. 1. As explained in the previous subsection, a *stuck-at-0* fault can be identified by simply shifting a stream of $1's$ through the scan chain. The steps involved in fault diagnosis process and the values of all the scan cells during fault identification and diagnosis procedure are listed in Table 1.

The initial values in all the scan cells are represented by $X's$ as the values in the scan cells are not known when the scan chain is switched from functional mode to test or shift mode. The cycle-wise values of the scan cells during the shift operation can also be seen from Table 1. The fifth cycle $clk - i_5$ in the table represents the fault identification cycle. Let us assume that all the scan cells in the scan chain have *set* capability and all the cells can be *set* to 1 together by using a global control signal. After the detection of a *stuck-at-0* fault in the fifth clock cycle, the control signal can be asserted to *set* all the scan cells to 1. During the *set* operation, the clock either needs to be kept inactive or at a constant logic high/low level depending upon the requirement of the *set/reset* circuitry. Once the cells are *set* to 1, the scan chain contents are shifted out by applying the scan clock. At the first clock cycle, a 1 will be observed at the $SO$ port. However, on the second clock cycle, a 0 will be observed due to the *stuck-at-0* fault that exists at the output port of the third scan cell $SC_3$. The second scan/diagnose cycle $clk - d_2$ shown in Table 1 represents the cycle in which the fault is diagnosed. Observation of a faulty 0 value after two clock cycles locates the position of the faulty scan cell (i.e., $SC_3$ in the example scan chain).

Similarly, the scan chain can be diagnosed for *stuck-at-1* fault by following the same sequence of steps. Instead of a sequence of all $1's$, a sequence of all $0's$ needs to be used to identify a *stuck-at-1* fault. Also, all the scan cells must have *reset* capability. The number of clock cycles after which the faulty value is observed at the $SO$ port tells the location or index of the faulty scan cell. In order to diagnose a scan chain for both *stuck-at-0* as well as *stuck-at-1* faults, all the scan cells must have both *set* and *reset* capability. However, to integrate both set and reset capability in the scan cell most of the existing hardware-assisted scan chain diagnosis techniques use two separate global control signals. The control signal routing and associated circuitry make the area overhead prohibitively high to implement these techniques in practical designs for diagnosis purpose. In this paper, we propose a very low-cost scan cell design that has both *set* and *reset* capability and uses only a single global control signal.

## 3.1    Proposed Scan Cell

The schematic design of the proposed scan cell is shown in Fig. 2. As it can be observed from the schematic design, in the proposed scan cell the feedback path inverter is replaced by a *NAND* gate in both master and slave latch. The inputs of *NAND* gate $n_1$ are driven by inverter $i_1$ and diagnosis control line called *DIAG*. Similarly, inputs of *NAND* gate $n_2$ are driven by inverter $i_2$ and *DIAG*.

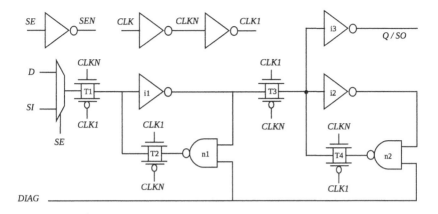

**Fig. 2.** Proposed scan cell design with *set/reset* circuitry

The logical operation performed by $NAND$ gate is represented by $c = \overline{a.b}$. So, if one of the $NAND$ gate input is permanently tied to logic 1 value, it imitates as a logical inverter. Therefore, during the functional mode and the test mode, $DIAG$ is permanently kept at a logic high level and the proposed scan cell operates as a regular scan cell. In diagnostic mode of operation, $DIAG$ line will set or reset the scan cell depending upon whether the clock signal $CLK$ is at the positive logic level or negative logic level. It should be noted that the *set/reset* operation can not be performed during the functional mode of operation.

***Set* operation.** The *set* operation of the proposed scan cell is explained in Fig. 3. To set the scan cell, a negative pulse of width $t_{set}$ at $DIAG$ line is applied when the scan clock $CLK$ is high (1). When the $CLK$ changes from low (0) to high (1), transmission gate $T1$ gets disabled and isolates the master latch from the scan input $SI$. Now as soon as $DIAG$ is pulled low (0), the output of $NAND$

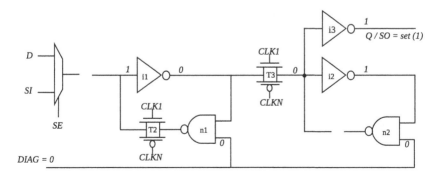

**Fig. 3.** *Set* operation in proposed scan cell

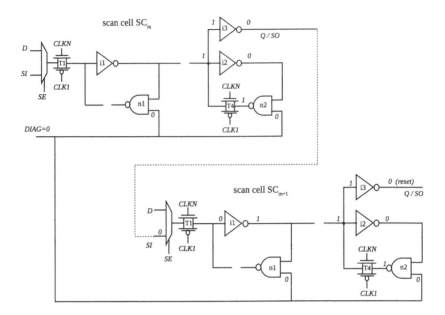

**Fig. 4.** *Reset* operation in proposed scan cell

gate $n_1$ is forced to logic 1. Also, a high value at $CLK$ enables the transmission gates $T2$ and $T3$. This allows the $NAND$ to drive inverter $i_1$ and force its output to logic 0. This, in turn, forces the outputs of inverter $i_2$ and $i_3$ to logic 1. This sets the *scan-out* port $SO$ of the scan cell to 1. Note that transmission gate $T4$ remains disabled as long as $CLK$ is 1, the output of slave latch's $NAND$ gate $n_2$ remains disconnected.

The timing requirement for the *set* operation is shown in Fig. 5. It should be noted that the $DIAG$ signal must be pulled to 0 only after the clock $CLK$ gets 0 to 1. The $DIAG$ must be pulled back to 1 before the clock $CLK$ gets to 0. Thus, the minimum pulse width time for which the $DIAG$ signal needs to be pulled down for proper set operation must satisfy the condition $t_{set} < 0.5*t_{CLK}$. The $t_{set}$ is decided by the feedback path delay of the master latch. This timing requirement is easily satisfiable as the scan clock is generally supplied by the tester. Also, in the test mode, the scan clock frequency is kept low due to the power constraint. In case $t_{set}$ is higher than half of the scan clock period the clock can be kept inactive at a logic high (1) level until the scan cell is properly *set*. Once the scan cell is *set*, the $CLK$ can be again activated to shift out the scan chain values for diagnosis. So, there is no impact of the *set* operation timing requirement on the scan shift clock frequency. The *set* operation can be used to diagnose the scan chain *stuck-at-0* faults.

**Reset operation.** The *reset* operation of the proposed scan cell is shown in Fig. 4. Application of a low pulse of width $t_{reset}$ on the $DIAG$ line while the $CLK$ is low (0) will *reset* the scan cell. Figure 4 shows two successive scan cells with index number $SC_m$ and $SC_{m+1}$ of a scan chain. When the $CLK$ gets 1 to 0, transmission gate $T1$ and $T4$ gets enabled. Also, a low (0) $CLK$ signal disables the transmission gate $T3$ and isolates the slave latch from the master latch.

The *reset* operation is performed by using slave latch's $NAND$ gate $n_2$ while the clock $CLK$ is low (0). While $CLK$ is 0, pulling down the $DIAG$ signal to 0 will force the output of the $NAND$ gate $n_2$ to 1. This, in turn forces, the output of inverter $i_3$ ($i_2$) to 0 and *reset* the output port $SO$. However, as the $CLK$ turns from 0 to 1, the value stored in the master latch gets transferred to the slave latch. This may overwrite the *reset* value of the scan out port $SO$. To ensure that the $SO$ port of the scan cell remains *reset*, the clock period must be such that the $SO$ port *reset* (0) value gets enough time to propagate through the scan path and get latched into master latch of the succeeding scan cell, while the $CLK$ is 0. For example, while the $CLK$ is low (0), the *reset* (0) value at the $SO$ port of $SC_m$ cell must get enough time to propagate to master latch of the succeeding cell $SC_{m+1}$ and get latched into it. Similarly, at the same time master latch of scan cell $SC_m$ will latch the *reset* value (0) coming from its preceding scan cell $SC_{m-1}$. This will ensure that when $CLK$ turns high, the scan cells remain *reset*.

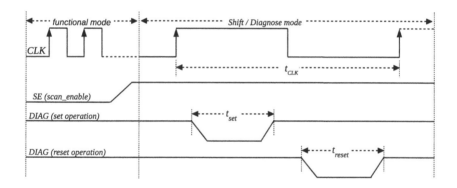

**Fig. 5.** Timing requirement for *set/reset* operation

It should be noted that since the first scan cell in the scan chain gets its value from the primary input pin *scan_input*, the value at the primary input pin must supply a 0 during the *reset* cycle. Note that transmission gate $T2$ remains disabled as long as $CLK$ is 0, the output of slave latch's $NAND$ gate $n_1$ remains disconnected. The timing requirement for the *reset* operation is shown in Fig. 5. The minimum pulse width $t_{reset}$ required to *reset* the scan cell is decided by the feedback path delay of the slave latch. The minimum pulse width $t_{set}$ and $t_{reset}$ will be equal for both *set* and *reset* operations. The other timing constraints for *reset* operation comes from the propagation time taken by the *reset* value of a scan cell to get latched into the master latch of succeeding scan cell. However, to avoid any performance penalty on the scan shift frequency the clock can be kept inactive at a constant 0 level during the *reset* operation. Once the scan cells are properly *reset*, scan clock can be applied to scan out the scan chain states for diagnosis. By using the *reset* capability, the scan chain can be diagnosed for *stuck-at-1* faults.

The proposed scan cell is capable of diagnosing *stuck-at* faults, however, it can not be used to diagnose hold time faults. To diagnose both *stuck-at* and hold time faults we propose a revised version of the proposed scan cell. The revised version of the proposed scan cell is more area efficient, however, it has a slightly diminished diagnostic resolution. The hold time fault diagnosis technique is explained in detail in the next section.

**Table 2.** Hold time fault diagnosis

| Type-I fault diagnosis | | | | | | |
|---|---|---|---|---|---|---|
| cycle no. ↓ | $SC1$ | $SC2$ | $SC3$ | $SC4$ | $SC5$ | phase ↓ |
| initialization | $X$ | $X$ | $X$ | $X$ | $X$ | |
| $clk - d_1$ | 1 | 0 | 1 | 0 | 1 | cell *set-reset* |
| $clk - d_2$ | 0 | 1 | 1 | 1 | 0 | |
| $clk - d_3$ | 1 | 0 | 1 | 1 | 1 | |
| $clk - d_4$ | 0 | 1 | 1 | 1 | 1 | ← *diagnosed* |
| Type-II fault diagnosis | | | | | | |
| initialization | $X$ | $X$ | $X$ | $X$ | $X$ | |
| $clk - d_1$ | 1 | 0 | 1 | 0 | 1 | cell *set-reset* |
| $clk - d_2$ | 0 | 1 | 0 | 1 | 0 | |
| $clk - d_3$ | 1 | 0 | 0 | 0 | 1 | |
| $clk - d_4$ | 0 | 1 | 0 | 0 | 0 | |
| $clk - d_5$ | 1 | 0 | 0 | 0 | 0 | ← *diagnosed* |
| Type-III fault diagnosis | | | | | | |
| initialization | $X$ | $X$ | $X$ | $X$ | $X$ | |
| $clk - d_1$ | 1 | 0 | 1 | 0 | 1 | cell *set-reset* |
| $clk - d_2$ | 0 | 1 | 1 | 1 | 0 | |
| $clk - d_3$ | 1 | 0 | 0 | 1 | 1 | |
| $clk - d_4$ | 1 | 1 | 1 | 0 | 1 | ← *diagnosed* |

## 4   Hold Time Fault Diagnosis

The presence and type of hold time fault can be identified by using the procedure as explained in subsection II-A. Once the fault type is identified the exact location of the fault needs to be found out. To locate the fault in the scan chain, a sequence of alternative 1 and 0 bits can be used. Assume that the scan chain shown in Fig. 1 has scan cells at odd index number with set capability and scan cells at even index number with reset capability. Thus by using the *DIAG* signal the scan cells $SC_1$, $SC_3$, $SC_5$ can be set and scan cells $SC_2$, $SC_4$ can be reset simultaneously. Further, assume that the scan cell $SC_3$ has a type-I hold time fault at its $SI$ input and the output of scan cell $SC_5$ is directly driving the *scan-out* port of the scan chain.

The steps involved in diagnosing the type-I fault are listed in upper part of Table 2. The scan chain is initialized with unknown values in all the scan cells. In the first diagnose cycle $d_1$, all the odd cells get *set* while all the even cells get *reset*. As scan cell $SC_5$ gets *set*, a 1 value is observed at *scan-out* port during the first diagnose cycle $d_1$. In the second clock $d_2$, a fast rising transition occurs at the $Q$ output of $SC_2$ (i.e., $SI$ input of $SC_3$). Due to the type-I fault, the faulty scan cell $SC_3$ behave as a shadow of scan cell $SC_2$ and captures the same value. However, all the other scan cells capture the right values and 0 is observed in the second diagnosis cycle $d_2$. In the third cycle $d_3$, since there is a falling transition at the $SI$ input of $SC_3$ the fault remains inactive. All the scan cells shift the correct values in cycle $d_3$ and 1 is observed. In the fourth cycle $d_4$ the scan cell again captures the wrong value due a fast rising transition at its $SI$ input. Because of the faulty value captured during the second cycle, 1 is observed at the *scan-out* in the fourth cycle $d_4$.

Observation of the faulty value in fourth diagnose cycle $d_4$ locates the position of the type-1 fault i.e., between third and fourth scan cell from the output side. Hence the type-I faults can be diagnosed with a maximum diagnostic resolution of 1 (precise diagnosis). However, assuming a type-II fault at the same location and following the diagnosis steps listed in middle part of Table 2, the error is observed at the fifth clock cycle $d_5$. Therefore, the probable fault location is either between $SC_3$ and $SC_2$ or $SC_2$ and $SC_1$. Hence, the diagnostic resolution for type-II faults is 2. Similarly, type-III faults can also be diagnosed using the similar steps which are listed in lower part of Table 2. The diagnostic resolution for type-III faults is also 1. A similar procedure can be used to diagnose the stuck-at fault. The steps involved in diagnosing a *stuck-at-0* and *stuck-at-1* fault at the output of scan cell $SC_3$ are listed in Table 3. Note that in the case of *stuck-at-1* fault the diagnostic resolution is 2 as the diagnostic value at the fault site is same as the fault value. The overall diagnostic resolution for the proposed scheme is $1 - 2$.

The proposed scan cell shown in Fig. 2 is further modified for diagnosing hold time faults. To diagnose the hold time violation faults we propose a revised version of the proposed scan cell implementation. The schematic diagram of the variant of the proposed scan cell is shown in Fig. 6. As it can be observed from the schematic diagram, instead of an inverter in the feedback path the master latch has a *NOR* gate. It should be noted that to set the cell in positive clock cycle the $\overline{DIAG}$ signal must be pulled high (1). This can be done by using the inverted value of the $DIAG$ signal. Note that the cell can only be reset, however, to diagnose hold time faults some cells need to be reset and other cells need to be set. To achieve set capability instead of using a NOR gate in the master latch's feedback path if a NAND gate is used the cell will have set capability. By using two separate scan cells one with set feature and another with reset feature and connecting them in an alternative fashion in a scan chain both stuck-at and hold time faults can be diagnosed.

**Table 3.** Stuck-at fault diagnosis

| stuck-at-0 fault diagnosis | | | | | | |
|---|---|---|---|---|---|---|
| cycle no. ↓ | $SC1$ | $SC2$ | $SC3$ | $SC4$ | $SC5$ | phase ↓ |
| initialization | $X$ | $X$ | $X$ | $X$ | $X$ | |
| $clk - d_1$ | 1 | 0 | 0 | 0 | 1 | cell *set-reset* |
| $clk - d_2$ | 0 | 1 | 0 | 0 | 0 | |
| $clk - d_3$ | 1 | 0 | 0 | 0 | 0 | ← *diagnosed* |
| stuck-at-1 fault diagnosis | | | | | | |
| initialization | $X$ | $X$ | $X$ | $X$ | $X$ | |
| $clk - d_1$ | 1 | 0 | 1 | 0 | 1 | cell *set-reset* |
| $clk - d_2$ | 0 | 1 | 1 | 1 | 0 | |
| $clk - d_3$ | 1 | 0 | 1 | 1 | 1 | |
| $clk - d_4$ | 0 | 1 | 1 | 1 | 1 | ← *diagnosed* |

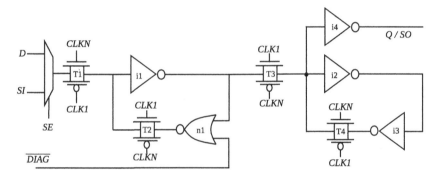

**Fig. 6.** Revised version of proposed scan cell with *reset*

## 5    Experimental Results

The post layout timing simulation of the proposed scan cell design has been
carried out using *UMCs* 65 nm technology at operating voltage of 1.2 V. The
post layout timing simulation results are listed in Table 5. The propagation delay
$t_{pd}$ of the proposed scan cell with both set and reset features degrades by 10 ps.
Whereas the propagation delay of proposed scan cell design with only reset
feature degrade by 19 ps as compared to the conventional scan cell. This can
be minimized by placing the *NOR* based scan cell with reset capability only in
the non-critical functional paths. The scan design implementation in [8, 11] loads
the output node of each scan cell with the parasitic capacitance of *XOR* gate or
multiplexer respectively.

In terms of area overhead, the proposed scan cell is highly efficient compared to the existing hardware-based diagnosis techniques. The proposed design

**Table 4.** Comparison with existing diagnosis techniques

| Parameters of comparison | | | | |
|---|---|---|---|---|
| Diagnosis Technique ↓ | *transistor count* | *control signal(s)* | *maximum resolution* | *fault type(s)* |
| Edirisooriya and Edirisooriya [8] | 16 | 1 | 1 | *sa* |
| Schafer et al. [9] | $6-8$ | 1 | 1 | *sa* |
| Narayanan and Das [10] | 12 | $1-2$ | $1-2$ | *sa* |
| Wu [11] | $6-8$ | $1-2$ | 1 | *sa, hold* |
| Dounavi and Tsiatouhas [12] | 4 | 2 | 1 | *sa* |
| Proposed design 1 | 4 | 1 | 1 | *sa* |
| Proposed design 2 | 2 | 1 | $1-2$ | *sa, hold* |

**Table 5.** Post layout timing simulation results at 500 MHz

| Proposed scan cell with both set and reset feature | | |
|---|---|---|
| Mode ↓ Parameter → | $t_{cq} + t_{setup} = t_{pd}$ | *Time gain* |
| Functional/Test mode | 401 ps + 354 ps = 755 ps | −10 ps |
| Proposed scan cell with only set feature | | |
| Functional/Test mode | 401 ps + 353 ps = 754 ps | −9 ps |
| Proposed scan cell with only reset feature | | |
| Functional/Test mode | 400 ps + 369 ps = 769 ps | −24 ps |
| Conventional scan cell | | |
| Functional/Test mode | 397 ps + 348 ps = 745 ps | − |

uses only four extra transistors compared to conventional scan cell. Note that the revised design of the proposed scan cell uses only two extra transistors per scan cell. Comparison of the existing and the proposed scan chain diagnostic techniques in terms of transistor count, number of control signals, maximum diagnostic resolution, and type of faults diagnosed is done in Table 4. It can be observed that the proposed technique uses least numbers of extra transistors. The number of extra transistors used in [8–11] is 3 times to 8 times higher. The technique in [12] uses four extra transistors and a global diagnose line. The static power consumption during the test mode in [12], is prohibitively high because of a direct path formation between power supply node and the ground node. Furthermore, it can only diagnose *stuck-at* faults.

The proposed technique uses only one global diagnose control signal for both the proposed approaches. The proposed technique also offers the maximum diagnostic resolution for both *stuck-at-0* and *stuck-at-1* faults. By extending the proposed scan cell design both hold time and *stuck-at* faults can be diagnosed. The technique by Wu [11] can diagnose both stuck-at and hold time faults, however, it uses 3 to 4 times extra transistors compared to the proposed technique. In terms of area overhead, the revised design of the proposed scan cell is highly efficient. The proposed scan cell design does not have any special timing and test requirements and complies with the existing industrial design and test flow.

# 6  Conclusion

In this paper, we have proposed a hardware assisted scan chain fault diagnosis technique. The proposed technique is very simple to implement and is capable of diagnosing both *stuck-at* and timing faults in scan chains. The proposed technique has the maximum diagnostic resolution for *stuck-at* faults and hence can locate the exact position of the faulty scan cell. Furthermore, the proposed technique is capable of diagnosing hold time faults with slightly diminished diagnostic resolution In addition to that, the proposed design incurs insignificant area overhead and has minimal performance overhead.

# References

1. Huang, Y., Guo, R., Cheng, W.T., Li, J.C.M.: Survey of scan chain diagnosis. IEEE Des. Test Comput. **25**(3), 240–248 (2008)
2. Guo, R., Venkataraman, S.: An algorithmic technique for diagnosis of faulty scan chains. IEEE Trans. Comput. Aided Des. Integr. Circuits Syst. (TCAD) **25**(9), 1861–1868 (2006)
3. Kundu, S.: On diagnosis of faults in a scan-chain. In: The 11th Annual IEEE VLSI Test Symposium on Digest of Papers, (VTS), pp. 303–308, April 1993
4. Stanley, K.: High-accuracy flush-and-scan software diagnostic. IEEE Des. Test Comput. **18**(6), 56–62 (2001)
5. De, K., Gunda, A.: Failure analysis for full-scan circuits. In: Proceedings of IEEE International Test Conference (ITC), pp. 636–645, October 1995
6. Song, P., Stellari, F., Xia, T., Weger, A.J.: A novel scan chain diagnostics technique based on light emission from leakage current. In: Proceedings of International Test Conference (ITC), pp. 140–147, October 2004
7. Stellari, F., Song, P., Xia, T., Weger, A.J.: Broken scan chain diagnostics based on time-integrated and time-dependent emission measurements. In: 30th International Symposium for Testing and Failure Analysis (ISTFA), pp. 52–57 (2004)
8. Edirisooriya, S., Edirisooriya, G.: Diagnosis of scan path failures. In: Proceedings of the 13th IEEE VLSI Test Symposium (VTS), pp. 250–255, April 1995
9. Schafer, J.L., Policastri, F.A., McNulty, R.J.: Partner srls for improved shift register diagnostics. In: Digest of Papers, 10th Anniversary of IEEE VLSI Test Symposium (VTS), pp. 198–201, April 1992
10. Narayanan, S., Das, A.: An efficient scheme to diagnose scan chains. In: Proceedings of International Test Conference (ITC), pp. 704–713, November 1997
11. Wu, Y.: Diagnosis of scan chain failures. In: Proceedings of IEEE International Symposium on Defect and Fault Tolerance in VLSI Systems (Cat. No.98EX223), pp. 217–222, November 1998
12. Dounavi, H.M., Tsiatouhas, Y.: Stuck-at fault diagnosis in scan chains. In: Proceedings of the 9th IEEE International Conference on Design Technology of Integrated Systems in Nanoscale Era (DTIS), pp. 1–6, May 2014
13. Ahlawat, S., Vaghani, D., Gulve, R., Singh, V.: A Low Cost Technique for Scan Chain Diagnosis. In: Proceedings of the 50th IEEE International Symposium on Circuits and Systems (ISCAS), 28–31 May 2017

# Multi-mode Toggle Random Access Scan to Minimize Test Application Time

Anshu Goel[✉] and Rohini Gulve[✉]

Computer Architecture and Dependable Systems Lab,
Indian Institute of Technology Bombay, Mumbai 400076, India
{anshug,rohini.gulve}@ee.iitb.ac.in

**Abstract.** Random Access Scan (RAS) as a design-for-test technique gained importance recently with the ability to update each flip-flop independently. Thus, with this ability, the test application time reduces drastically in comparison to the traditional Serial Scan technique. In this paper, we have proposed a Multi-Mode Toggle RAS architecture that reduces the test application time using the T-Flip-Flop based cell design. More importantly, the proposed RAS architecture gives the ability to update multiple flip-flops together thereby leading to a reduction in test application time. In the proposed RAS architecture, there are two modes of operation in case of test mode. In direct test mode, multiple flip-flops will be toggled together, however, in the decoder test mode only one flip-flop will be toggled at a time. An algorithm for the placement of scan flip-flops is also proposed for optimal performance in the proposed architecture. Experimental results show an average of 56% reduction in test data volume as compared to the traditional RAS architecture. Also, on an average, a speedup of 2.7x in test application time is achieved.

**Keywords:** Toggle scan flip-flop · Direct mode · Scan cell placement

## 1 Introduction

The manufacturing test is crucial for VLSI circuits. It is one of the major factors in total chip cost. With increasing design complexity, test cost factor increases taking up more than 30% of the design cost [7]. Test cost mainly depends on Automatic Test Equipment (ATE) utilization, in terms of test application time and test data volume stored on equipment. Thus, researchers concentrate on minimization of above-mentioned factors. Design for Testability (DFT) which minimizes the test cost is always active research area. Scan based DFT techniques dominate in the industry as a prominent technique. This is adopted widely due to better controllability and observability provided at internal memory elements. In traditional serial scan chain, all flip-flops are stitched in the form of a shift register with test control scan-in and scan-out pins. For a modern design with the increase in the number of flip-flops, the length of the single scan chain increases. This has caused an increase in loading and unloading time of scan register. For

© Springer Nature Singapore Pte Ltd. 2017
B. K. Kaushik et al. (Eds.): VDAT 2017, CCIS 711, pp. 205–216, 2017.
https://doi.org/10.1007/978-981-10-7470-7_21

updating even a few number of flip-flops entire scan chain has to be loaded through shift operation. This is the main reason for increased test application time. Many different approaches have been proposed in the literature towards minimizing the undesirable issues of the single scan chain. One of them is, Partial Scan approach proposed by Agrawal et al. [3] where the authors were able to reduce test application time with a trade-off between the ease of testing and test cost. Another approach is the multiple scan chain DFT technique, which addresses the issues of test application time and test data volume in the serial scan. The ease of accessing flip-flops in the design leads to the application of possible test inputs which may not be exercised in normal operation of the design. Non-functional state excitation induces power issues during testing in scan-based DFT.

Random Access Scan (RAS) is an alternate solution to the limitations of serial scan which was first proposed by Ando [4] in 1980. RAS architecture is able to provide a solution for all the three issues namely test application time, test data volume and test power simultaneously. Flip-flops in the design can be accessed as memory elements through scan architecture by selecting each flip-flop individually using address decoder as shown in Fig. 1. Baik et al. [6] in 2004, reported up to 99% and 60% reduction in power consumption and test data volume, respectively. The speedup of 3x in test application time has been observed. Later, Baik et al. [5] proposed an improved version of RAS Progressive Random Access Scan (PRAS) having a SRAM like grid structure for reading and writing of scan flip-flops. PRAS showed appreciable improvement in test application time, test data volume and test power as compared to traditional serial scan design techniques.

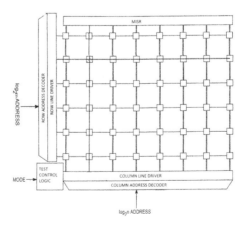

**Fig. 1.** Random Access Scan architecture

Besides PRAS design, there have been many variants of RAS proposed by the research community. A toggle (T flip-flop) was based architecture proposed by Mudlapur et al. in 2005 [9]. This eliminates the need of scan-enable and scan-in pins completely, thus reducing the routing overhead. Yao et al. [11] proposed a complete Built-in Self-test (BIST) based on the Word-Oriented RAS architecture (WOR-BIST). The results showed that it has less area overhead as compared to traditional Serial Scan design, however, it provides very poor fault coverage. Hu et al. [8] proposed a Localized Random Access Scan where scan flip-flops are divided into groups based on the layout information. They have introduced a new scan flip-flop that reduces the need for a global signal. However, this doesn't reduce test application time. Raghavendra et al. [1] proposed another variant of RAS technique named Serial Input Random Access Scan (SIRAS) where loading of address bits takes place serially using Address Shift Register (ASR). Along with this, they have proposed another architecture called Variable Word Length Random Access Scan (VWLRAS) that uses 3 additional pins in the column decoder to select multiple scan flip-flops together, thus able to achieve 2–3 times speed up in test application time as compared to conventional RAS.

The basic research work in the area of testability of VLSI circuits focus on minimization of test time and test power dissipation. As random access scan-based DFT technique updates only one flip-flop in each cycle, it provides lowest bound on power during test load compared to serial shifting. This bound is much lower than the possible power consumption of the circuit in normal mode. The basic motivation of this work is to utilize the margin between the lowest bound and operational limit to improve on the other factors such as test length and test data volume. In this work, we propose a Multi-mode Random Access Scan architecture with toggle flip-flop as scan element. The proposed design operates in two modes namely direct mode and decoder mode. In direct mode, multiple flip-flops are updated together, while in decoder mode only one flip-flop is updated at a time. In addition to this, an algorithm for deciding scan flip-flops position in RAS array is also discussed. The read operation is done after the response capture using the Multiple Input Shift Register (MISR) as used in [2, 5, 8–10].

The remaining paper is organized in the following way. Section 2.1 briefly describes the functioning operation of the T-flip-flop scan cell which is used in the proposed RAS architecture. The proposed architecture with its operation is described in Sect. 2. Section 3 describes the algorithm for scan cell ordering. Hardware implementation and simulation results are discussed in Sects. 4 and 5, respectively. Finally, Sect. 6 concludes the work.

## 2    Proposed RAS Architecture

In this paper, a new Random Access Scan architecture is proposed which operates in two modes during testing. The first test mode is the decoder mode where each scan flip-flop is accessed individually using the output of the row and column address decoder. The second test mode is the direct mode where multiple scan cells are addressed using the same address. Thus, as illustrated in Fig. 2, where the two decoders become transparent so that the address pins take direct control of the rows and columns drivers for updating multiple scan flip-flops together.

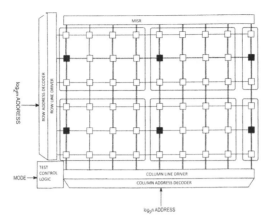

**Fig. 2.** Direct Test mode

In the direct test mode, the row and column address pins are latched to multiple rows and columns of the RAS structure, respectively. Through this kind of arrangement, the entire RAS grid structure is accessed as a small block which is formed proportionate to the row and column address pins. In direct test mode, each row/column address pin directly controls many row/column lines. As the number of row/column lines are less as compared to the row/column lines required to be addressed, thus there is a repetition of the same address row/column address pins after all the available rows/columns address pins are addressed.

For example, a total of 7 address pins i.e. 3 pins for row address and 4 pins for column address are required for addressing the whole RAS grid of $6 \times 9$ structure as shown in Fig. 2. So, 6 row lines will be driven with these 3 row address lines. Therefore, the 1st and 4th line will be driven by same row address pin. Similarly, would be the case for the column pins for driving the column lines. Thus, with these address pins, a block of $3 \times 4$ of RAS scan flip-flops from the address pins directly. Correspondingly, the whole RAS structure is divided into blocks of $3 \times 4$ until no more blocks can be formed. The remaining scan flip-flops form blocks with either the same column size or row size. Therefore, four blocks of $3 \times 4$ size and two blocks of $3 \times 1$ size are formed from the whole $6 \times 9$ RAS structure as shown in Fig. 2. By using this direct test mode optimally, the test application time will reduce considerably as compared to previous related work.

## 2.1   T-Flip-Flop Based Scan Cell

While, in conventional RAS, a scan flip-flop requires a scan-in signal, a scan-enable signal and a decoder signal for each scan flip-flop. However, the T-flip-flop proposed in Mudlapur et al. [9] eliminates the need of scan-in and scan-enable signals. The basic operational modes of this T flip-flop are Functional mode, and Test mode. During the functional mode of operation, the row and column lines are '0's leading to disabling of the decoder. Thus, AND gate output for each scan cell is '0' latching the combinational data to the master at the clock pulse and the slave is latched subsequently (Fig. 3).

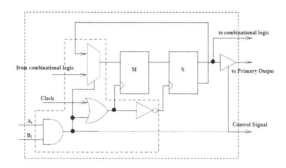

**Fig. 3.** T-Flip-Flop based scan design [9]

While in the test mode, after stopping the clock, the row and column decoders select a flip-flop. The inverted output from the slave is latched to the master, thus toggling the value of the scan flip-flop.

## 2.2    Working

Since the T flip-flop used in the proposed architecture doesn't have reset capability, so in order to clear all the flip-flops, a built-in circuit is used that would first read the contents of flip-flops and then clear them. If the flip-flop's state is '0' then the flip-flop is not toggled and if the flip-flop's state is '1' then the flip-flop is toggled. Thus, through this process, all the scan flip-flops are initially cleared. After resetting all the scan flip-flops, each toggle vector generated by combining the expected responses of the previously applied test vector with the desired test vector is applied. Here, a toggle vector scan cell value will be '1' if the expected response of the previous vector and the test vector to be loaded next have different values while the toggle vector will be '0' if both will have same values. A toggle vector set is shown in Table 1.

**Table 1.** Toggle vector set

| Test vectors | Expected responses | Toggle vectors |
|---|---|---|
| V1:001111 | R1:101101 | T1:001111 |
| V2:110001 | R2:110110 | T2:011100 |
| V3:111010 | R3:000101 | T3:001100 |
| V4:101101 | R4:010111 | T4:101000 |

A toggle vector is applied in two phases. Firstly, the direct test mode followed by the decoder test mode. An effective address is computed for grouping all possible combinations of the scan flip-flops that are likely to toggle using a same direct mode address. Since grouping is required to be computed once only thus, the execution the direct test mode is carried out once. After the execution of the direct test mode, the decoder test mode addresses the remaining scan flip-flops, individually. Thus, the major task is the computation of the address for the direct test mode.

## 2.3  Direct Test Mode Address Computation

In order to compute an effective direct mode address such that all the possible combinations are covered, there is a need to obtain a combined block from the whole RAS structure. Grouping of various scan flip-flops from different blocks is carried out according to the priorities assigned. The priority of $0 > 1 > X$ is considered for grouping, where 0 represents that the scan flip-flop is not required to toggle, 1 represents that the scan flip-flop must be toggle and X represents that it doesn't matter whether that scan flip-flop gets toggled or not. For example, we have design whose toggle vectors require a total of 54 scan flip-flops as shown in Fig. 4.

| 0 | X | X | X | X | 0 | X | 0 |
|---|---|---|---|---|---|---|---|
| X | 0 | 1 | 1 | 1 | 1 | 1 | 1 |
| X | 0 | X | X | X | X | X | X |
| X | X | 0 | 0 | 0 | 0 | 1 | 0 |
| 0 | 0 | 1 | X | 0 | 1 | X | 1 | X |
| X | X | 0 | X | 0 | X | X | X |

| 0 | 0 | 0 | 0 |
|---|---|---|---|
| 0 | 0 | 1 | 1 |
| 0 | 0 | 0 | X |

**Fig. 4.** Toggle vector                    **Fig. 5.** Combined block

After grouping together all the possible combinations of scan flip-flops, the combined block is obtained as described earlier. With the help of this combined block, the address for the direct mode is computed. The direct mode address is computed through the process of elimination of the 0's from the combined block formed leaving behind only 1's and X's. Thus, using the elimination method, we first eliminate the highest priority 0s from the combined block by addressing either the corresponding row or the corresponding column address with 0s. This process is repeated iteratively until only the 1 s and Xs are only left to be addressed. For a scan flip-flop that has to be toggled, both the row and column are required to be high. Hence, the remaining 1 s in the combined block are addressed by setting both the corresponding row and column to 1.

This whole process is explained in the form of an algorithm along with takes a toggle vector as its input and gives the address for the direct test mode. The proposed algorithm is as follows.

1. Computing the number of 0's and 1's in all the rows and columns in the obtained combined block.
2. Each row (column) represents a weighted pair of the number of '0's and the number of '1's.
3. From all the weight-pair, the row (column) pair having the maximum difference between the weight of '0's and '1's is made '0' is deleted and the weight-pair are updated for other rows (columns).
4. Steps 2–3 are iteratively carried out till the remaining weight-pairs have no weight for '0'.
5. The corresponding row and column are made 1 for a non-zero '1' weight.

For each iteration, the repeated values of rows and columns i.e Rs and Cs have been calculated from the updated combined block RAS as in Fig. 5

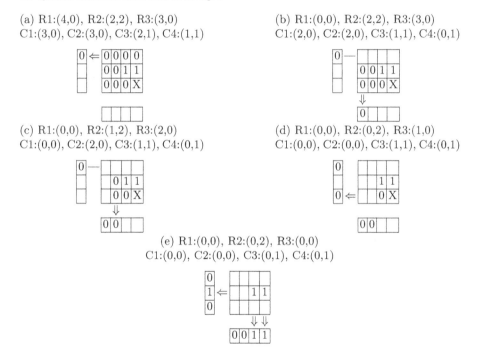

(a) R1:(4,0), R2:(2,2), R3:(3,0)
C1:(3,0), C2:(3,0), C3:(2,1), C4:(1,1)

(b) R1:(0,0), R2:(2,2), R3:(3,0)
C1:(2,0), C2:(2,0), C3:(1,1), C4:(0,1)

(c) R1:(0,0), R2:(1,2), R3:(2,0)
C1:(0,0), C2:(2,0), C3:(1,1), C4:(0,1)

(d) R1:(0,0), R2:(0,2), R3:(1,0)
C1:(0,0), C2:(0,0), C3:(1,1), C4:(0,1)

(e) R1:(0,0), R2:(0,2), R3:(0,0)
C1:(0,0), C2:(0,0), C3:(0,1), C4:(0,1)

**Fig. 6.** Iteration of the Proposed Algorithm to generated Direct Test Mode address

The example above illustrates the working of the proposed algorithm. By referring Fig. 4, the combined block is computed as shown Fig. 5. The weighted-pairs are calculated for each of the three rows and four columns and the whole process of computing address step-by-step is illustrated in Fig. 6. Through the address computed for direct test mode, eight scan flip-flops toggle together. Thus, reducing the test application time.

# 3   Scan Cell Re-ordering

In order to achieve the maximum advantage from the direct test mode, a specific ordering of scan flip-flops is required such that the scan flip-flops are placed at positions where maximum grouping can be achieved during address computation for direct test mode. Thus, for a toggle vector set, there is a need for identification of those scan flip-flops that toggle together for the maximum instances and can be placed at desired position in the RAS structure. For solving the above-stated problem, a graph-theoretic formulation is proposed as follows.

**Table 2.** Toggle vectors and Original scan cell order

| Toggle vectors | SF1 | SF2 | SF3 | SF4 | SF5 | SF6 |
|---|---|---|---|---|---|---|
| Toggle Vector 1 | 0 | 0 | 1 | 1 | 1 | 0 |
| Toggle Vector 2 | 0 | 1 | 1 | 1 | 0 | 0 |
| Toggle Vector 3 | 0 | 0 | 1 | 1 | 0 | 1 |
| Toggle Vector 4 | 1 | 0 | 1 | 0 | 0 | 0 |

## 3.1   Graph Formulation

A toggle vector set for DUT is be represented as in Table 2. This information can be formulated in the form of a graph. The graph will represent scan cells, possible groupings, and the amount of toggling. The procedure for graph formulation is as follows:-

- Each scan cell is represented as a node in the graph.
- The grouping between any two possible scan cell is represented by an undirected edge between respective nodes.
- The amount of toggling of the two scan cells together is represented by the weight of the edge between respective nodes of the scan cells.

Computation of the amount of toggling: Each scan cells for a given toggle vector test set toggles. The number of times a pair of scan cells toggle together i.e. the number of times the two scan cells are 1 together gives the amount of toggling. As the toggling is same irrespective of the direction of the order of scan cell, the constructed graph would be an undirected graph. Table 2 shows the toggle vectors that are generated in Table 1 and the original order. The rows represent different toggle vectors and columns represent the scan cells. An undirected weighted graph is constructed as in Fig. 7. The constructed graph is a complete graph as all the nodes scan cells are linked with each other.

The RAS grid structure requires the placement of the maximum toggling scan cell flip-flops in positions suitable for grouping. In the above mentioned example, the two nodes SF3 and SF4 are most compatible and should be placed at positions 2,5 for grouping. The position of placing these compatible nodes are such that at the time of grouping they can be grouped together. Thus, scan cell is ordered as SF1-SF3-SF2-SF5-SF4-SF6 as shown in Table 3.

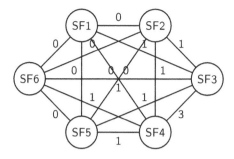

**Fig. 7.** A complete weighted graph

**Table 3.** Ordered Scan cell

| Toggle vectors | SF1 | SF3 | SF2 | SF5 | SF4 | SF6 |
|---|---|---|---|---|---|---|
| Toggle vector 1 | 0 | 1 | 0 | 1 | 1 | 1 |
| Toggle vector 2 | 0 | 1 | 1 | 0 | 1 | 0 |
| Toggle vector 3 | 0 | 1 | 0 | 0 | 1 | 0 |
| Toggle vector 4 | 1 | 1 | 0 | 0 | 0 | 0 |

# 4    Hardware Implementation

In conventional RAS architecture, for reducing the area overhead due to test circuitry, there is a row and a column decoder, each of $\sqrt{n}$ bits instead of 'n' bits. In order to achieve optimal performance, the row and column decoder should be built in such way that an $m \times n$ number of scan flip-flops can be addressed as stated in [9] row decoder decodes m lines and column decoder decodes n lines. Therefore, the number of address shift register (ASR) required would be of $\log_2 m + \log_2 n$ depth.

In the proposed MMRAS architecture, besides these decoders, there is a requirement of an additional $2 \times 1$ multiplexer for each row and column line of the RAS structure. The selection line of the multiplexer is controlled by the test control unit that decides the operating test mode. The T-flip-flop based scan design eliminates the need for Scan-Enable and Scan-In signals which is being routed to every flip-flop. In the proposed RAS architecture, there is a requirement of one extra signal to the multiplexers that simplifies the complex implementation of this RAS architecture as described in Fig. 8. Here, the black shaded scan flip-flops are those that have same select lines during direct mode and will be grouped together.

## 4.1    Test Data Volume Analysis

We derive an expression for the test data volume for the proposed architecture. To write the address shift register, a total number of $\log_2 m + \log_2 n$ data bits are

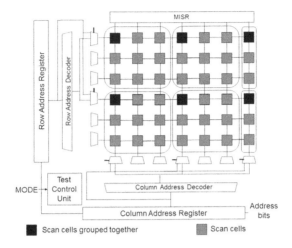

**Fig. 8.** Multi Mode Toggle RAS architecture

required. Then in direct test mode, a maximum of $w_i$ writes would be required for the toggle vector. Hence, the estimated test data volume for the proposed design (TDM) will be given by.

$$TDM = (\log_2 m + \log_2 n + 1) \times \sum_{n=1}^{T} w_i + T \times PI \qquad (1)$$

where T is the total number of toggle vectors applied. Similarly, the test data volume for conventional RAS (TDC) is.

$$TDC = (\log_2 M + 1) \times \sum_{n=1}^{T} d_i + T \times PI \qquad (2)$$

where $d_i$ is the number of scan flip-flops that are required to be written for an actual test vector.

## 5  Experimental Results

The proposed architecture was modeled and tested on ISCAS89 benchmark circuits. The test application time and test data volume has been calculated and is shown in Table 4. While comparing the various architectures i.e. Conventional RAS and Multi-Mode Toggle RAS, the number of test pins are kept same. The fully specified test patterns generated using TetraMax ATPG tool from Synopsys are used. Further, C/C++ is used for all the toggle vector computation and the algorithm application for scan cell ordering.

The test response read mechanism is same while comparing both the architectures. The reason for this argument lies in the fact that the read mechanism

**Table 4.** Comparison of test application time, speed up, test data volume and reduction in test data volume

| Circuit | # FF | # Patt. | Test application time | | | Test data volume | | |
|---|---|---|---|---|---|---|---|---|
| | | | PRAS | MMTRAS | Speed up | PRAS | MMTRAS | red(%) |
| s27 | 3 | 7 | 60 | 27 | 2.22 | 88 | 55 | 37.5 |
| s298 | 14 | 29 | 1330 | 335 | 3.97 | 1417 | 422 | 70.22% |
| s344 | 15 | 18 | 955 | 295 | 3.24 | 1117 | 457 | 59.09% |
| s349 | 15 | 20 | 1050 | 325 | 3.23 | 1230 | 505 | 58.94% |
| s382 | 21 | 37 | 2376 | 846 | 2.81 | 2487 | 957 | 61.52% |
| s386 | 6 | 70 | 1676 | 568 | 2.95 | 2166 | 1058 | 51.15% |
| s400 | 21 | 37 | 2334 | 864 | 2.7 | 2445 | 975 | 60.12% |
| s420 | 16 | 75 | 4010 | 38 | 105.53 | 5360 | 1385 | 74.16% |
| s444 | 21 | 36 | 2826 | 1092 | 2.59 | 2934 | 1200 | 59.1% |
| s510 | 6 | 60 | 1424 | 244 | 5.84 | 2564 | 1384 | 46.02% |
| s526 | 21 | 60 | 5118 | 1632 | 3.14 | 5298 | 1812 | 65.8% |
| s526a | 21 | 59 | 5052 | 1674 | 3.02 | 5229 | 1851 | 64.6% |
| s641 | 19 | 44 | 3018 | 1020 | 2.96 | 4558 | 2560 | 43.84% |
| s713 | 19 | 36 | 2826 | 978 | 2.89 | 4086 | 2238 | 45.23% |
| s820 | 5 | 112 | 2232 | 688 | 3.24 | 4248 | 2704 | 36.35% |
| s820a | 5 | 112 | 2232 | 688 | 3.24 | 4248 | 2704 | 36.35% |
| s832 | 5 | 110 | 2192 | 640 | 3.43 | 4172 | 2620 | 37.2% |
| s838 | 32 | 151 | 17112 | 30 | 570.4 | 22246 | 5164 | 76.79% |
| s953 | 29 | 116 | 4644 | 1284 | 3.62 | 6500 | 3140 | 51.69% |
| s1238 | 18 | 156 | 13818 | 5928 | 2.33 | 16002 | 8112 | 49.31% |
| s1423 | 74 | 44 | 13616 | 6056 | 2.25 | 14364 | 6804 | 52.63% |
| s1488 | 6 | 116 | 2780 | 1208 | 2.3 | 3128 | 1556 | 50.26% |
| s5378 | 179 | 126 | 202986 | 103572 | 1.96 | 207396 | 107982 | 47.93% |
| s13207 | 716 | 171 | 1346796 | 586003 | 2.3 | 1357398 | 596605 | 56.05% |
| s15850 | 534 | 144 | 845856 | 364694 | 2.32 | 856944 | 375782 | 56.15% |
| s35932 | 1728 | 21 | 281064 | 146052 | 1.92 | 281799 | 146787 | 47.91% |
| s38417 | 1636 | 368 | 620184 | 192540 | 3.22 | 630488 | 202844 | 67.83% |

is kept same for the proposed architecture and all the responses will be shifted out through the MISR as is the case for conventional RAS architecture. Hence, we have considered only the write test data volume. From the results, it can be observed that in the designs s838 and s420, there is exceptionally less test application time. This is due to the fact that in these design the amount of toggling is very less for the application of test patterns. While on the other hand in conventional RAS, these test patterns are required to be loaded even if the value of the scan flip-flop is not changing. The reduction in Test Data Volume is from 36% as observed in s820 to 77% in s838 design. Hence, both these factors will lead to a reduction in the test cost.

## 6   Conclusion

In conclusion, a Multi-Mode Toggle RAS architecture has been proposed to improve the test application time. The technique developed takes the best of both architectures i.e. Progressive RAS (PRAS) and Variable Word Length RAS (VWLRAS). Various advantages of RAS over other DFT techniques are also discussed. The main advantage of RAS being the reduction in test application time by 60%, which itself is unique.

The proposed toggle RAS architecture require the two major techniques. The direct mode address computation is the major task to be accomplished. But before this, scan cell reordering is the necessary step that would lead to improvement in test time considerably. The experimental results on benchmark circuits show that using the proposed architecture we get an average speed up in the range of 1.9x to 570x and test data volume reduction from 36% to 77%.

## References

1. Adiga, R., Arpit, G., Singh, V., Saluja, K.K., Fujiwara, H., Singh, A.D.: On minimization of test application time for RAS. In: 2010 23rd International Conference on VLSI Design, pp. 393–398. IEEE (2010)
2. Adiga, R., Arpit, G., Singh, V., Saluja, K.K., Singh, A.D.: Modified T-Flip-Flop based scan cell for RAS. In: 15th IEEE European Test Symposium, pp. 113–118. IEEE (2010)
3. Agrawal, V.D., Cheng, K.T., Johnson, D.D., Lin, T.S.: Designing circuits with partial scan. IEEE Design Test Comput. 5(2), 8–15 (1988)
4. Ando, H.: Testing VLSI with random access scan. In: Digest of the Computer Society International Conference(COMPCON), pp. 50–52 (1980)
5. Baik, D.H., Saluja, K.K.: Progressive random access scan: a simultaneous solution to test power, test data volume and test time. In: IEEE International Conference on Test, 10 pp. IEEE (2005)
6. Baik, D.H., Saluja, K.K., Kajihara, S.: Random access scan: a solution to test power, test data volume and test time. In: 17th International Conference on VLSI Design, Proceedings, pp. 883–888. IEEE (2004)
7. Bushnell, M.L., Agrawal, V.D.: Essentials of Electronic Testing for Digital, Memory and Mixed-Signal VLSI Circuits. Kluwer Academic Publishers, Boston (2000)
8. Hu, Y., Fu, X., Fan, X., Fujiwara, H.: Localized random access scan: towards low area and routing overhead. In: Proceedings of the 2008 Asia and South Pacific Design Automation Conference, pp. 565–570. IEEE Computer Society Press (2008)
9. Mudlapur, A.S., Agrawal, V.D., Singh, A.D.: A novel random access scan flip-flop design. In: Proceedings of 9th VLSI Design and Test Symposium, vol. 226 (2005)
10. Mudlapur, A.S., Agrawal, V.D., Singh, A.D.: A random access scans architecture to reduce hardware overhead. In: IEEE International Conference on Test, 9 pp. IEEE (2005)
11. Yao, C., Saluja, K.K., Sinkar, A.A.: WOR-BIST: a complete test solution for designs meeting power, area and performance requirements. In: 2009 22nd International Conference on VLSI Design, pp. 479–484. IEEE (2009)

# Performance Analysis of Disability Based Fault Tolerance Techniques for Permanent Faults in Chip Multiprocessors

Avishek Choudhury[1(✉)] and Biplab K. Sikdar[2]

[1] New Alipore College, Kolkata 700053, India
avishek.nac.cs@gmail.com
[2] IIEST Shibpur, Howrah 711103, India
biplab@cs.iiests.ac.in

**Abstract.** Dynamic Voltage and Frequency Scaling (DVFS) for reducing power dissipation in Multicore Chips causes cell failure in Cache Memory. Various fault tolerance techniques have been introduced and the analysis of their impacts becomes necessary. Keeping the lowest overhead of Disabling techniques in mind, this work attempts to analyse its performance in Multicore Chips. The parameter Expected Miss Ratio for Multicore ($EMR_{MC}$) as a function of Probability of Cell Failure ($P_{fail}$) is proposed and evaluated. Simulation on Singlecore and Multicore system configuration is done separately to compare the results. It is observed that the Expected Miss Ratio is hardly affected below the lower bound of $P_{fail}$ i.e. 1e-5 where $EMR_{MC}$ remains lower than Expected Miss Ratio for Singlecore($EMR_{SC}$) with a static difference. Above the lower bound, both $EMR_{SC}$ and $EMR_{MC}$ starts increasing and for $P_{fail}$ higher than 1e-3 i.e. the upper bound, $EMR_{MC}$ often converges with $EMR_{SC}$. Within these bounds, $EMR_{MC}$ remains up to 19.3% lower than the $EMR_{SC}$.

**Keywords:** Chip multiprocessor · Permanent fault · Fault tolerance
Expected Miss Ratio · Multicore

## 1 Introduction

The increased processing demand influenced the introduction of Chip Multiprocessors (CMPs). However, with a large number of cores on a single die, the power consumption in CMPs increases exponentially [1]. DVFS came into role to achieve the processing demand in lower power supply. But, unfortunately it shows an inverse relationship with reliability [2].

The cache is susceptible to failure in lower Voltage and limits the threshold i.e. $VDD_{MIN}$ of a processor [3]. Various techniques for fault tolerance in cache have been introduced [4–11] which comes with significant overhead. So the analysis of their impacts becomes necessary. One of the basic fault tolerance techniques is the disability based technique in which faulty portions of a cache is disabled. Due to its simplicity and low overhead, it is often preferred if expected fault rate is low.

© Springer Nature Singapore Pte Ltd. 2017
B. K. Kaushik et al. (Eds.): VDAT 2017, CCIS 711, pp. 217–224, 2017.
https://doi.org/10.1007/978-981-10-7470-7_22

This influenced us to analyse the performance of Block Disabling in Multicore Chips with distributed Last Level Cache (LLC). A study on the impact of Block Disability based Fault Tolerance Technique for a Single Bank cache has been reported in [12]. But no study was done on the effectiveness of Fault Tolerance Techniques in Multicore Chips with distributed cache banks.

In this work, we have proposed the parameter Expected Miss Ratio in MultiCore ($EMR_{MC}$) as the function of Probability of Failure ($P_{fail}$). The parameter is analysed by implementing block disabling in Chip Multiprocessors. It is observed that the Expected Miss Ratio is hardly affected below the lower bound of $P_{fail}$ i.e. 1e-5 where $EMR_{MC}$ remains lower than $EMR_{SC}$ with a static difference. For higher $P_{fail}$ as 1e-3, both $EMR_{SC}$ and $EMR_{MC}$ increases and $EMR_{MC}$ often converges with $EMR_{SC}$. All the Simulations are carried out in the Multi2Sim 5.0 simulation framework with benchmark programs included in the SPLASH-2 and PARSEC 3.0 benchmarks suites.

## 2   Baseline Architecture

This work concentrates on the Tiled-CMP architecture that provides a scalable solution for Chip Multiprocessor designs. A tile-based CMP architecture which is comprised of a number of identical tiles connected via a switched direct network as shown in Fig. 1.

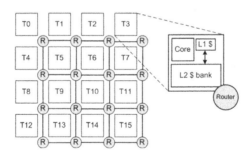

**Fig. 1.** Tiled CMP architecture

## 3   The Analytical Model

This model for uncorrelated faults in Chip Multiprocessors determines different parameters that describe the behaviour of the cache in presence of uncorrelated faults with permanent cell failure probability $P_{fail}$. The $EMR_{MC}$ (Expected Miss Ratio in Multi Core) is calculated for a given processor.

### 3.1   Probability of Block Failure and Its Distribution

If the cache has C cores, each of N banks with S Sets per Bank and B Blocks per Set where number of bits is k per block and probability of cell failure is $P_{fail}$, then the probability of block failure is:

$$P_{bf} = [1 - (1 - P_{fail})^k] \tag{1}$$

where k is the number of bits per block.

Probability Distribution of $i$ Block failures considering all possible cases:

$$P_{bf}(i) = \binom{B}{i} P_{bf}^i (1 - P_{bf})^{(B-i)} \tag{2}$$

where $i$ is the number of faulty blocks per set.

As we are considering set associative mapping, the number of faulty blocks in a set affects the Miss Rate but their locations are irrelevant as a page can be mapped into any block in the set.

### 3.2   Expected Miss Ratio in Multicore ($EMR_{MC}$)

For assessing the impact of block disabling in Multicore, we have incrementally disabled blocks in all core simultaneously and analysed the impact. Expected Miss in Multicore can be defined as

$$
\begin{aligned}
EM_{MC} &= \sum_{i=0}^{B} E_{Miss}^i \\
&= \sum_{i=0}^{B} M_i \cdot P_{bf}^i
\end{aligned}
\tag{3}
$$

where $EM_{MC}$ is the Expected Miss of the whole cache, $E_{Miss}^i$ is the number of miss for $i$ blocks disabled in all cores. $M_i$ is the number of miss for $i$ faulty disabled blocks in all cores and $P_{bf}^i$ probability of $i$ blocks become faulty. $M_i$ can further be defined as

$$
M_i = \begin{cases} \sum_{j=0}^{C-1} m_j & \text{if } i = 0 \\ \sum_{j=0}^{C-1} \sum_{k=0}^{i-1} A_{jk} + \sum_{j=0}^{C-1} m_j & \text{if } i \neq 0 \end{cases}
\tag{4}
$$

where $m_j$ is the miss for all healthy way in $j^{th}$ core, $A_{jk}$ is the number of access to $k^{th}$ way of $j^{th}$ core.

Finally EMR is calculated as

$$EMR_{MC} = EM_{MC}/A \tag{5}$$

where A is the number of access to all Cores.

# 4    Methodology

For finding the parameters in Multicore, we have extended the methodology used in [12] for analysing Disabling technique in Single Cache bank to our Multicore distributed cache bank environment.

## 4.1    Miss Calculation

The Expected Miss in Multicore is calculated as follows:

  (i) Initially a two dimensional matrix is populated with the number of access for each way in every set for all cores.
 (ii) The accesses to each way are then added to get the accesses for each way for all sets in every core.
(iii) The entries are added cumulatively to get the misses when blocks are disabled cumulatively.
(iv) Now these entries are added to the miss to get the number of miss if that way is disabled.
 (v) Now these misses are per core are added together to find the overall miss due to block failure.

## 4.2    EMR Calculation

To compute Expected Miss Ratio (EMR) of Eq. 3,

  (i) We intersect these misses with their Probability Distribution obtained from Eq. 2.
 (ii) These Expected Misses are added to get the overall Expected Miss of the system using Eqs. 3 and 4.
(iii) The overall Expected Miss is divided by the number of access for whole system (A) and to get the EMR for whole system using Eq. 5.

# 5    Evaluation

The evaluation of Block Disabling in Multicore architecture is done using the Multi2Sim 5.0 simulation framework for CPU-GPU heterogeneous computing with benchmark programs included in the SPLASH-2 and PARSEC 3.0 benchmark suites. Simulation results for mainly fft program is given here for lookup.

## 5.1    System Configuration

We have configured Multi2sim with 8 cores of x86 model of frequency 1k. Each of these cores is associated with a dedicated L1 cache and a shared L2 cache. Each of the 8 L1 cache has 4 sets & 256 ways having block size 64. It uses LRU replacement technique and cache writeback policy. The underlying cache coherence protocol used is NMOESI. Data latency kept as 2 units.

The L2 cache is shared among the 8 cores & connected with 8 L1 caches. Each L2 has 4 ways & 256 ways & each block of size 64. It also uses the LRU replacement technique & writeback policy. The main memory is also having blocks of same size having data access latency is of 200 units.

## 5.2 Results

To evaluate the performance of disabling technique for fault tolerance in multicore, we simulate the technique separately on single core as well as multicore architecture. In both the cases, we compare the performances by varying the $P_{fail}$. Accordingly, we also calculate the $P_{bf}$. As we assume 256 ways in L2, we need to consider 257 possible cases starting from 0 faulty ways among 256 to 256 faulty ways among 256 ways.

With a certain $P_{fail}$ say 0.00001, $P_{bf}$ becomes 0.000639798.

### Calculation of EMR in Single Core

- Given the probability distribution of faulty blocks in Table 1 and block disabling in singlecore, we get the number of misses as in the Table 1.

**Table 1.** Calculation of expected miss in Single Core

| No of faulty ways | $P_{bf}^i$ | $M_i$ | $E_{miss}^i$ |
|---|---|---|---|
| 0 | 0.84888 | 2214 | 1879.41 |
| 1 | 0.13913 | 2226 | 309.69 |
| 2 | 0.01136 | 2238 | 25.42 |
| 3 | 0.00062 | 2250 | 1.39 |
| 4 | 2E-05 | 2262 | 0.00 |
| : | : | : | : |
| 256 | 0 | 4461 | 0.00 |

Table 1 shows how Expected Miss can be calculated for Single core chip. The first column contains the number of faulty blocks. The second column contains probability of $i$ block failure as distributed and obtained from Table 1. The third column contains misses that occurred in the simulation in the environment we set up. The last column contains the intersection of the previous two columns as the Expected Miss for $i$ faulty blocks in our simulation.

- Using Eqs. 3 and 4, we get the overall Expected Miss i.e. 2215.965461 in this case and the Expected Miss Rate for all Cores as 0.496741865.

## Calculation of EMR in Multi Core

- With the same $P_{fail}$ say 0.00001 where $P_{bf}$ becomes 0.000639798, the Probability Distribution becomes same as in Disabling method in Single Core Architecture.
- The corresponding number of misses is given in the Table 2.

**Table 2.** Calculation of expected miss in Multicore

| No of faulty ways | $P_{bf}^i$ | $M_i$ | $E_{miss}^i$ |
|---|---|---|---|
| 0 | 0.84888 | 2043 | 1734.26 |
| 1 | 0.13913 | 2072 | 288.27 |
| 2 | 0.01136 | 2096 | 23.80 |
| 3 | 0.00062 | 2121 | 1.31 |
| 4 | 2E-05 | 2149 | 0.05 |
| : | : | : | : |
| 256 | 0 | 4461 | 0.00 |

Table 2 shows how expected miss in Multicore can be calculated. The first column contains number of faulty blocks and second column contains its distribution. The third column contains number of miss occurred in the same simulation in multicore. The last column contains the product of the two previous columns as Expected Miss in multicore for $i$ block failures.

- Using Eqs. 3 and 4, Expected Miss for $i$ faulty ways is calculated as 2047.687278 and the Expected Miss Rate is 0.486155574.

### 5.3    Analysis

**Analysis of Expected Miss Ratio.** Next we show the EMRs obtained by varying $P_{fail}$ in the following Table 3.

**Table 3.** Comparison of EMR

| Pfail | EMRsc | EMRmc | Performance gain % |
|---|---|---|---|
| 0.000001 | 0.4963 | 0.4581 | 7.71 |
| 0.000005 | 0.4965 | 0.4585 | 7.66 |
| : | : | : | : |
| 0.001 | 0.539 | 0.5357 | 0.62 |

Table 3 shows the comparison of Expected Miss Ratio in Singlecore vs Multicore. The first column contains the Probability of Call failure. The second and third column contains Expected Miss Ratio for Singlecore and Multicore respectively. The last column contains the gain in Expected Miss Ratio in Multicore over Singlecore.

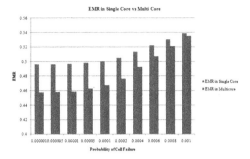

**Fig. 2.** EMR in single core vs multi core

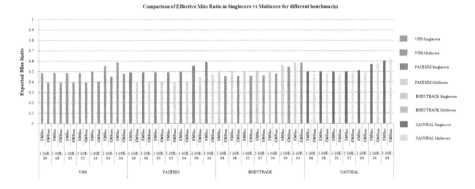

**Fig. 3.** Expected Miss Ratio in Singe core vs Multicore for different benchmarks

From the data in Table 3, we get the graph of EMR for Probability of Failures in Fig. 2.

Figure 2 shows the comparison between Expected Miss Ratios in Single Core vs Multicore. The x-axis contains Probability of Cell failure and the y-axis contains the Expected Miss Ratio.

- From Fig. 2, it is observed that the lower bound of $P_{fail}$ i.e. 1e-5 below which the Expected Miss Ratio is hardly affected and $EMR_{MC}$ remains lower than $EMR_{SC}$ with a static difference.
- Also it is observed that beyond the lower bound, both the $EMR_{SC}$ and $EMR_{MC}$ increases and for $P_{fail}$ higher than 1e-3, $EMR_{MC}$ converges with $EMR_{SC}$.

Figure 3 shows the Expected Miss Ratio for Single core and Multicore for different benchmark programs of PARSEC 3.0 benchmark suite. The x-axis contains different probability of cell failures and the y-axis contains the Expected Miss Ratio.

From Fig. 3, it can be stated that the EMR in Multicore block disabling stays lower than the EMR in Single Core Block disabling up to 19.3%.

# 6    Conclusion

This work evaluates the performance of Block disabling in Multicore chips with distributed cache banks and compares it with the performance of block disabling in Singlecore. For the performance evaluation, a parameter $EMR_{MC}$ i.e. the function of probability of cell failure $P_{fail}$, is proposed and calculated for different values of $P_{fail}$.

It pairs to the fact that EMR in Multicore stays lower than the EMR in Single Core for Block disabling based fault tolerant cache. For $P_{fail}$ lower than 1e-5, $EMR_{MC}$ remains lower than $EMR_{SC}$ with a static difference. Beyond this both $EMR_{SC}$ and $EMR_{MC}$ starts increasing. For $P_{fail}$ higher than 1e-3 i.e. the upper bound, $EMR_{MC}$ often converges with $EMR_{SC}$. Within theses bounds, $EMR_{MC}$ remains up to 19.3% lower than the $EMR_{SC}$.

# References

1. Skotnicki, T., Hutchby, J., King, T.-J., Wong, H.-S., Boeuf, F.: The end of CMOS scaling: toward the introduction of new materials and structural changes to improve MOSFET performance. IEEE Circuits and Devices Mag. 21(1), 16–26 (2005)
2. Banaiyanmofrad, A., Homayoun, H., Dutt, N.: Using a flexible fault-tolerant cache to improve reliability for ultra low voltage operation. ACM Trans. Embed. Comput. Syst. 14(2), 32:1–32:24 (2015)
3. Ghasemi, H.R., et al.: Low-voltage on-chip cache architecture using heterogeneous cell sizes for multi-core processors. In: IEEE International Symposium on High-Performance Computer Architecture, pp. 38–49, February 2011
4. Ozdemir, S., et al.: Yield-aware cache architectures. In: Proceedings of International Symposium on Microarchitecture (2006)
5. Pour, F., Hill, M.D.: Performance implications of tolerating cache faults. Trans. Comput. 42(3), 257–267 (1993)
6. Sohi, G.: Cache memory organization to enhance the yield of high-performance VLSI processors. Trans. Comput. 38(4), 484–492 (1989)
7. Ansari, A., et al.: Enabling ultra low voltage system operation by tolerating on-chip cache failures. In: Proceedings of International Symposium on Low Power Electronics and Design (2009)
8. Vergos, H.T., Nikolos, D.: Performance recovery in direct-mapped faulty caches via the use of a very smallfully associative spare cache. In: Proceedings of International Computer Performance and Dependability Symposium (1995)
9. Ladas, N., Sazeides, Y., Desmet, V.: Performance-effective operation below Vccmin. In: Proceedings of International Symposium on Performance Analysis of Systems & Software (2010)
10. BanaiyanMofrad, A., et al.: REMEDIATE: a scalable fault-tolerant architecture for low-power NUCA cache in tiled CMPs. In: Proceedings of IGCC (2013)
11. Chaiken, D., Fields, C., Kurihara, K., Agarwal, A.: Directory-based cache coherence in large-scale multiprocessors. Trans. Comput. 23(6), 49–58 (1990)
12. Sanchez, D., Sazeides, Y., Cebrian, J.M., Garcia, J.M., Arago J.L.: Modeling the impact of permanent faults in caches. ACM Trans. Archit. Code Optim. 10(4) (2013). Article 29

# Devices and Technology – I

# Low-Power Sequential Circuit Design Using Work-Function Engineered FinFETs

Ashish Soni[(✉)], Abhijit Umap, and Nihar R. Mohapatra

Indian Institute of Technology Gandhinagar, Ahmedabad, India
{ashish.soni,abhijit.umap,nihar}@iitgn.ac.in

**Abstract.** Sequential circuits like pulsed latches and semi-dynamic flip-flops are extensively used in state-of-the-art high performance microprocessors. In this paper, we proposed a novel approach of exploiting the metal gate workfunction to reduce the power consumption and area of the pulsed latches and semi-dynamic flip-flops made using FinFETs. Compared to the design using standard shorted gate FinFETs, the proposed pulsed latch reduces the dynamic and leakage power by 37% and 42% respectively. Similarly, the proposed semi-dynamic flip-flop shows a reduction of 24% and 32% respectively in dynamic and leakage power consumption compared to the standard design. The proposed circuits also show significant improvement in static noise margin and reduction in area.

**Keywords:** FinFETs · Pulsed latch (PL)
Semidynamic flip-flop (SDFF) · Workfunction engineering (WFE)
Shorted gate FinFET (SG-FinFET)

## 1 Introduction

FinFETs or multi-Gate MOS transistors had been adopted for 22 nm and below CMOS technology nodes to sustain technology scaling [1]. The FinFETs have a thin silicon fin surrounded by metal gates on either sides of the fin. The two gates are electrically coupled providing a stronger gate control over the channel. The stronger gate control improves the sub-threshold swing [2] and reduces the sub-threshold leakage current. The reduced leakage with higher drive current, increased intrinsic gain, increased voltage gain without degradation of noise or linearity [3] make FinFETs an attractive choice for digital and analog circuit design. Further, the FinFETs provide more flexibility in circuit designing as they can be used in shorted-gate (SG) or in independent-gate (IG) mode. In IG mode, the back gate bias is used to tune the threshold voltage ($V_T$) of the devices, thereby controlling the leakage current. The IG-FinFETs have been successfully used to reduce the power consumption of the circuits [4]. However, there are few challenges that have come along with the advantages of FinFET technology. One of them is the width quantization [1], which is a major technology disrupter for the FinFET based circuit design. For circuits like latches and flip-flops, proper

© Springer Nature Singapore Pte Ltd. 2017
B. K. Kaushik et al. (Eds.): VDAT 2017, CCIS 711, pp. 227–238, 2017.
https://doi.org/10.1007/978-981-10-7470-7_23

sizing of the transistors is needed to ensure correct functionality, which is very difficult to achieve in circuit design using FinFETs. This limitation sometimes increases the overall size of the FinFET based circuits compared to their planar counterpart.

The pulsed latches [6] and semidyamic flip-flops [7] are extensively used in state-of-the-art microprocessors. It is reported in [6] that about 95% of the latching mechanism in a microprocessor is done using pulsed latches. The semidynamic flip-flops are one of the fastest families of flip-flops. They are primarily used in pipelines of high-performance microprocessors [8]. Hence, it is absolutely necessary to improve these circuits in terms of area, delay, power consumption and noise immunity. In this paper, we explore the performance of pulsed latches and semi-dynamic flip-flops using novel workfunction engineered Fin-FETs. It is shown that the workfunction engineered FinFETs can be easily and cost-effectively (without any additional mask and process steps) integrated to the standard FinFET process flow. By smartly using these workfunction engineered FinFETs with standard SG FinFETs, the overall power consumption and area of pulsed latches and semi-dynamic flip-flops can be strongly reduced while maintaining the same propagation delay. The paper is organized as follows. The standard and workfunction engineered FinFETs are described in Sect. 2. The design of a pulsed latch and a semidynamic flip-flop using workfunction engineered FinFETs are described in Sects. 3 and 4 respectively. The new latches and flip-flops are compared to a standard design (using SG FinFETs) for different process corners under parametric fluctuations. Finally, the conclusions are presented in Sect. 5.

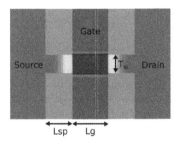

**Fig. 1.** The schematic showing the 2-D cross section of the FinFET used in this work

## 2    Workfunction Engineering and FinFETs

The Sentaurus TCAD platform [11] is used in this work to design and simulate the standard SG and workfunction engineered FinFETs. Figure 1 shows the 2-D cross section of a FinFET. The Table 1 lists the technological parameters of the same. The fin thickness ($T_{si}$) is chosen to be very less compared to the gate length ($L_g$) to have better electrostatics and reduced short channel effects. The channel is chosen to be intrinsic (doping: $10^{16} cm^{-3}$, Resistivity: $1.5 \Omega - cm$) to mitigate the effects of random dopant fluctuations (RDF). The source and drain are heavily doped. The doping of the source/drain extension region gradually reduces with a Gaussian profile from edge of source/drain towards the undoped channel region. The model parameters are appropriately tuned to match the simulation data with the experimental data published in literature [5]. For device simulation, the hydrodynamic model is used to account for the temperature effects. Several advanced mobility models are used to simulate the transport of carriers in silicon channel accurately. The density gradient quantum potential model is activated to capture the quantum confinement effect of carriers. The band to band tunneling model is also used.

**Table 1.** FinFET technology parameters

| Parameters | Abbreviations | Values |
|---|---|---|
| Gate length | $L_g$ | 20 nm |
| Fin thickness | $T_{si}$ | 10 nm |
| Fin height | H | 40 nm |
| Spacer thickness | $L_{sp}$ | 16 nm |
| Oxide thickness | EOT | 1 nm |
| Channel doping | $N_{CH}$ | $1 * 10^{16} \, cm^{-3}$ |
| Source/Drain doping | $N_{SD}$ | $1 * 10^{20} \, cm^{-3}$ |
| Supply voltage | VDD | 0.9 V |

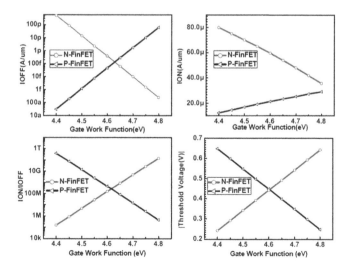

**Fig. 2.** Plot for $I_{ON}, I_{OFF}, I_{ON}/I_{OFF}$ and $V_T$ Vs workfunction

The $I_{ON}$, $I_{OFF}$ of the device can be very well controlled by tuning $V_T$. Further, the pulsed latch requires precise control of $V_T$ to match other devices in the circuit for better performance. Figure 2 shows $V_T$, $I_{ON}$, $I_{OFF}$, and $I_{ON}/I_{OFF}$ as a function of gate workfunction. As shown the $V_T$ and other device parameter are linearly dependent on gate metal workfunction. This method of tuning the device parameter with metal workfunction is referred as workfunction engineering.

In this work, the metals with workfunctions of 4.4 ev and 4.8 ev are used as the gate for standard (STD) SG nFinFET and pFinFET whereas the metals with workfunctions of 4.8 ev and 4.4 ev are used as gate for the workfunction engineered (WFE) nFinFET and pFinFET. In WFE FinFETs, the nFinFET has the p-metal workfunction (4.8 ev) and pFinFET has the n-metal workfunction (4.4 ev). The other technological parameters of the WFE-FinFET is same as standard one. Figure 3 schematically depicts the process flow to fabricate the gate stack of STD- as well as WFE-FinFETs. As shown the WFE-FinFETs could be easily integrated without any additional mask and process steps. The DC parameters of STD- as well as WFE-FinFETS are listed in Table 2. The $V_T$ of WFE-FinFETs are 400 mv higher than that of STD-FinFETs. $\approx 10^4$X improvement in $I_{ON}/I_{OFF}$ is also recorded.

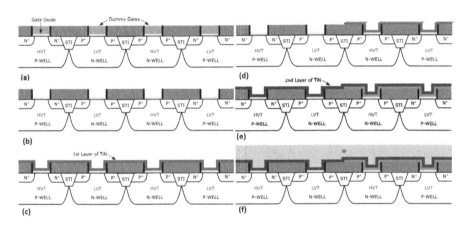

**Fig. 3.** The process flow for integrating the STD and WFE FinFETs on the same chip. The schematic diagram of the gate stack, (a) after complete front-end processing. (b) after the removal of the dummy gate. (c) after deposition of Metal-1 layer (Workfunction-4.4 eV). (d) after removal of the Metal-1 layer from STD nFinFET and WFE pFinFET. (e) after deposition of Metal-2 layer (Workfunction-4.8 eV). (f) Tungsten fill and CMP

## 3    The Pulsed Latch

A latch can capture data during a very short period of clock waveform where the latch is sensitive. If the pulse clock waveform triggers a latch, it will start behaving as edge triggered flip-flops because the rising and falling edges of the

**Table 2.** DC Characteristics of STD-FinFET and WFE- FinFETs

| Parameters | STD-NFinFET | WFE-NFinFET | STD-PFinFET | WFE-PFinFET |
|---|---|---|---|---|
| $I_{ON}(\mu A/\mu m)$ | 1290 | 500 | 805 | 247 |
| $I_{OFF}(nA/\mu m)$ | 34.4 | 0.004 | 7.33 | 0.002 |
| $I_{ON}/I_{OFF}$ | $3.76 * 10^4$ | $1.25 * 10^8$ | $1.1 * 10^5$ | $1.24 * 10^8$ |
| $V_T(mv)$ | 240 | 640 | -248 | -648 |
| $DIBL(mV/V)$ | 48.18 | 49.04 | 43.70 | 43.87 |
| $SS(mV/decade)$ | 72.66 | 72.69 | 70.8 | 70.8 |

short duration pulse are almost identical in terms of timing [10]. The Setup and hold time can be expressed with respect to the rising and falling edge of the pulse clock respectively. Hence we can say that the pulsed latch is very similar to the edge-triggered flip-flop in view of the timing model.

The pulsed latch requires pulse generators that generate a very short duration pulse with the given clock signal and the pulse width is chosen such that it facilitates the transition. Figure 4 shows the implementation of pulsed brute-force latch with STD-FinFETs (PL-STD). The number of fins used for each transistor is shown in brackets. The PL-STD composed of two blocks: the brute-force latch and the pulse generator circuit. The inverters I1, I2, I3 and transmission gate T1 constitute the brute-force latch. The chain of inverters DI1 DI5, NAND gate (DNAND composed of P1, P2, N1 and N2) and inverters (INV1, INV2) represent the pulse generator circuit. The clock signal and its delayed inverted version generate a pulse required for operation of the brute-force latch. Note that for correct operation of the pulsed latch, the pulse width generated by the pulse generator should be wide enough for the latch to change its output during the transparent phase. At the same time, the pulse width should not be more since it will increase the hold time. Further, the input stage of latch (inverter I1 with transmission gate T1) should be strong enough (compared to the feedback inverter I3) to change its output during transparent phase. As mentioned earlier, the correct functionality of the pulsed latch will depend on the duration of the transmission phase which depends on the dimensions of transistors used in DI1 to DI5. Note that the propagation delay of the inverters designed with modern technologies is very small. So a large number of inverters are required to have a wide pulse at the transmission gate T1. The large number of inverters increases the area as well as dynamic and leakage power consumption of the circuit. In this work, we have used WFE-FinFETs to design these inverters (DIn). The WFE-FinFETs have 400 mV higher $V_T$ and 60–70% lower $I_{ON}$ compared to the STD-FinFETs. Therefore the delay of a single inverter (minimum size) is higher than that designed with the STD-FinFETs. At this point, some readers may claim that the delay of inverters designed using STD-FinFETs can be increased by reducing the width of transistors. But, the minimum width of a FinFET is fixed $(2H + T_{si})$ and the width could only be increased or decreased in multiples of $(2H + T_{si})$. So, modulating the delay through width variation is not a very flexible option in FinFET based circuits. Figure 5 shows the implementation of pulsed latch with STD-FinFETs and WFE-FinFETs (PL-WFE). In this new design, the inverters in the delay chain are designed using WFE-FinFETs. The I3 is also implemented using WFE-FinFET to make it weaker compared to I1 and T1. Table 3 summarizes different pulsed latch configurations implemented using STD-FinFETs and WFE-FinFETs. All the transistors which are not specified in the table are STD-FinFETs. The above mentioned configurations are characterized for CLOCK-to-Q propagation delay, power consumption, static noise margin, and setup($T_{su}$)/hold time($T_h$). A capacitive load($C_L$) of 0.5fF is connected at the output node. The simulation is done for a clock frequency of 2.5 GHz at 105 °C. The pulsed latches are characterized for all four corners i.e., Fast-Fast(FF), Fast-Slow(FS), Slow-Fast(SF), Slow-Slow(SS) and a worst case situation, referred to as worst-case (WC) corner. The WC corner is the condition when transistors of the delay inverters are fast, latch driver I1 and T1 are slow and feedback inverter I3 is fast. For corner analysis, ±10 variations are considered in gate length ($L_g$), oxide thickness (EOT) and fin thickness ($T_{si}$) and ±50 meV variation in gate metal workfunction. Because of large simulation time required for Monte-Carlo simulations to be carried out in order to perform corner simulations, we have employed a different strategy. We have considered the corners as follow: the transistor with -10 gate length, -10 oxide thickness, +10 fin width and -50 mV $V_T$ compared to the reference transistor (Table 1) is considered as fast corner while the transistor with +10 gate length, +10 oxide thickness, -10 fin width and +50 mV $V_T$ compared to the reference transistor is considered to be the slow corner. Figures 6 and 7 shows the dynamic and leakage power consumption respectively for different configurations of pulsed latches (mentioned in Table 3). The WFE-FinFET based pulsed latches show lower dynamic power consumption because of lesser number of inverters (lower activity factor). The PL-WFE3 configuration consumes 37% less dynamic power compared to the PL-STD. For calculation of leakage power, the CLOCK is gated low and all four possible combinations of input D and output Q are considered. The leakage power consumption of pulsed latches based on WFE-FinFETs is significantly less compared to that based on STD-FinFETs because of the reduced leakage current of WFE FinFETs (higher $V_T$, refer Table 2). The configuration PL-WFE3 has least leakage power consumption (42% lower than PL-STD) since it has highest number of WFE FinFETs. Figure 8 shows the CLOCK-to-Q propagation delay for different configuration of pulsed latches. The propagation delay is calculated as time difference between the instances when the active edge of both CLOCK and Q reaches 50% of supply voltage. The propagation delay, specified in this work is the average of high-to-low and low-to-high propagation delay of output Q. As shown, the WFE-FinFET pulsed latches show 8.5% reduction in delay because of the weaker I3.

Table 4 summarizes the setup time ($T_{su}$), hold time ($T_h$) and sequencing overhead ($T_{su} + T_h$) for different configuration of pulsed latches. $T_{su}$ is the D changing to CLOCK duration which results in 1% more delay than the minimum

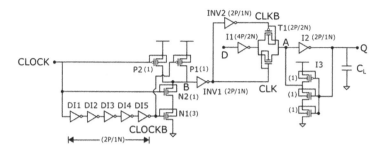

**Fig. 4.** Schematic showing the implementation of a Pulsed Latch (PL-STD) using STD-FinFETs

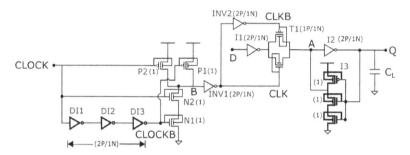

**Fig. 5.** Schematic showing the implementation of a Pulsed Latch using STD-FinFETs and WFE-FinFETs. The WFE-FinFETs are smartly used to reduce the power consumption and reduce area. The BOLD part shows the changes done between two designs.

**Table 3.** Configurations of WFE-FinFET Pulsed Latches analyzed in this work

| Configuration | DI1 | DI2 | DI3 | I3 |
|---|---|---|---|---|
| PL-WFE1 | WFE | STD | STD | WFE |
| PL-WFE2 | WFE | STD | WFE | WFE |
| PL-WFE3 | WFE | WFE | WFE | WFE |
| PL-WFE4 | STD | WFE | WFE | WFE |

**Table 4.** Setup time, hold time and sequencing overhead of the FinFET based Pulsed Latches

| Configurations | $T_{su}(ps)$ | $T_h(ps)$ | $T_{su} + T_h(ps)$ |
|---|---|---|---|
| PL-STD | 10.7 | -4.4 | 6.3 |
| PL-WFE1 | 9.6 | -3 | 6.6 |
| PL-WFE2 | 9.1 | -3.3 | 5.8 |
| PL-WFE3 | 9.95 | -3.6 | 6.35 |
| PL-WFE4 | 9.5 | -2.95 | 6.55 |

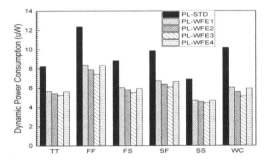

**Fig. 6.** The dynamic power consumption of the FinFET based pulsed latches simulated for different configurations and process corners

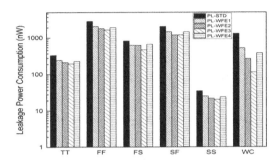

**Fig. 7.** The leakage power consumption of the FinFET based pulsed latches simulated for different configurations and process corners

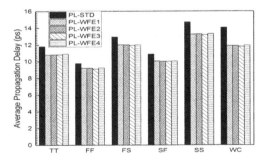

**Fig. 8.** The propagation delay of the FinFET based pulsed latches simulated for different configurations and process corners

input to output delay ($T_{DQ-min}$). The $T_h$ is calculated as the CLOCK to D changing duration which results in negligible glitch at the output node. The weak I3 in case of WFE-FinFET pulsed latches, results in accurately capturing data even if data comes more close to CLOCK. This helps in reduction of $T_{su}$ and $T_h$ for WFE-FinFET based pulsed latches. The weak I3 also helps in improving the static noise margin (SNM) of the FinFET based pulsed latches upto 32% as shown in Fig. 9.

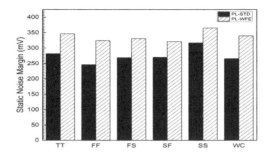

**Fig. 9.** The static noise margin (SNM) of FinFET based pulsed latches simulated for different process corners

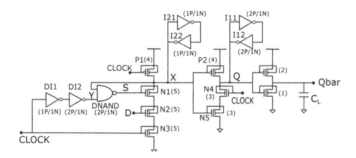

**Fig. 10.** Schematic showing the Implementation of semi-dynamic flip-flop (SDFF-STD) using standard SG FinFETs

## 4   The Semidynamic Flip-Flop

Figure 10 shows a semi-dynamic flip-flop (SDFF) implemented with the STD-FinFETs (SDFF-STD). The number of fins used for each transistor is shown in brackets. The SDFF operates in two phases, (a) pre-charge phase and (b) evaluation phase [4]. The pre-charge phase begins with the falling edge of CLOCK. During pre-charge phase, the internal node X is pulled high, the node S is kept high, the input D is cutoff from Q and the static latch (I11-I12) holds the data. The evaluation phase begins with rising edge of the CLOCK. The node X will be discharged or will remain high depending on D thus passing input D to output Q. For correct operation of the SDFF, the node S should not become low before the node X changes its state (1→0) completely. This is ensured by correct design of DI1, DI2 and DNAND (to provide sufficient delay for the clock to allow node X discharge properly). Figure 11 shows the implementation of SDFF

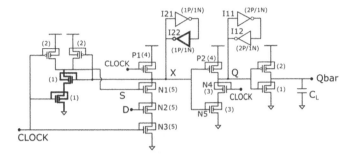

**Fig. 11.** Schematic showing the Implementation of semi-dynamic flip-flop (SDFF-WFE) using WFE FinFETs. The BOLD part shows the changes done between two designs

using WFE-FinFETs and STD-FinFETs. The fall time of node S is increased by implementing the pull down stack of DNAND using WFE-FinFETs (400mV higher $V_T$). The increased delay of this modified pull down stack ensures correct functionality of SDFF. The inverters DI1-DI2 are also no longer required in this case thereby saving area as well as power. Note that in the SDFF, the inverter I22 opposes the transistor stack N1, N2, N3 to discharge node X while D = 1 and S = 1. In the new design, the I22 is made weaker by replacing the transistors there with the WFE-FinFETs.

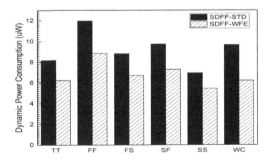

**Fig. 12.** The dynamic power consumption of the FinFET based pulsed latches simulated for different configurations and process corners

Figures 12 and 13 shows the dynamic and leakage power consumption of both the flops. The SDFF-WFE is characterized for all four corners (FF, FS, SF and SS) along with the WC corner as mentioned in Sect. 3. As shown the SDFF-WFE consumes upto 24% less dynamic power, upto 32% less leakage power because of the elimination of DI1, DI2 and presence of WFE-FinFETs in the pull-down stack of DNAND. Figure 14 shows average CLOCK-to-$Q_{bar}$ propagation delays for both the flops. The propagation delay of SDFF-WFE is slightly less compared to SDFF-STD because of the reduced contention at

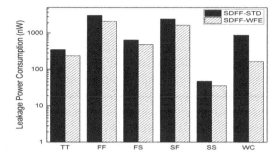

**Fig. 13.** The leakage power consumption of the FinFET based pulsed latches simulated for different configurations and process corners

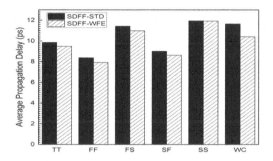

**Fig. 14.** The propagation delay of the FinFET based semi-dynamic flip-flops for different process corners

node X when it is discharging. The $T_{su}$, $T_h$ and sequencing overhead for both the flops is shown in Table 5. The $T_{su}$ is calculated as D changing to CLOCK duration which results in a minimum D to $Q_{bar}$ delay ($T_{DQbar-min}$). The $T_h$ is the time taken for CLOCK to D transition, which results in CLOCK to $Q_{bar}$ ($T_{CQbar}$) delay equal to CLOCK to $Q_{bar}$ duration at minimum D to $Q_{bar}$ delay ($T_{DQbar-min}$). Both the $T_{su}$ and $T_h$ of SDFF-WFE are improved compared to that of SDFF-STD. The area of SDFF-WFE will be lower (not estimated in this work) because of the elimination of inverters DI1 and DI2.

**Table 5.** Setup time, hold time and sequencing overhead of the FinFET based semi-dynamic flip flops

| Configurations | $T_{su}(ps)$ | $T_h(ps)$ | $T_{su} + T_h(ps)$ |
|---|---|---|---|
| SDFF-STD | 10.7 | -4.4 | 6.3 |
| SDFF-WFE | 9.6 | -3 | 6.6 |

# 5    Conclusions

To summarize, it was shown that the WFE-FinFETs can be easily and cost-effectively (without any additional mask and process steps) integrated to the STD-FinFET process flow. The new pulsed latches and semi-dynamic flip-flops were designed by smartly using the WFE-FinFETs with the STD-FinFETs. The correct functionality of both the sequential circuits was ensured by meeting various timing constraints. The robustness of these circuits under process variation was studied by performing corner analysis. The PL-WFE3 (pulsed latch configuration with all delay inverters made up of WFE-FinFETs) have shown 37% reduction in dynamic power consumption and 42% reduction in the leakage power consumption compared to the PL-STD. Similarly, the semi-dynamic flip-flops designed using WFE-FinFETs have shown 24% and 32% reduction in dynamic and leakage power consumption. The proposed circuits also exhibited improved noise margin at the same sequencing head. Therefore, to conclude, the work function engineered FinFETs could be smartly used with the STD-FinFETs to realize low power and compact sequential circuits.

# References

1. Colinge, J.-P. (ed.): FinFETs and other Multi-gate Transistors. Springer, New York (2008)
2. Hisamoto, D., et al.: FinFET a self-aligned double gate MOSFET scalable to 20 nm. IEEE Trans. Electron Devices **47**(12), 2320–2325 (2000)
3. Stojanovic, V., Oklobdzija, V.G.: Comparative analysis of master-slave latches and flip-flops for high-performance and low-power systems. IEEE J. Solid-State Circuits **34**(4), 536–548 (1999)
4. Muttreja, A., Agarwal, N., Jha, N.K.: CMOS logic design with independent-gate FinFETs. In: 2007 25th International Conference on Computer Design, ICCD 2007. IEEE (2007)
5. Hu, C.: 3D FinFET and other sub-22nm transistors. In: 2012 19th IEEE International Symposium on the Physical and Failure Analysis of Integrated Circuits (IPFA). IEEE (2012)
6. Naffziger, S.D., et al.: The implementation of the Itanium 2 microprocessor. IEEE J. Solid-State Circuits **37**(11), 1448–1460 (2002)
7. Klass, F.: Semi-dynamic and dynamic flip-flops with embedded logic. In: 1998 Symposium on VLSI Circuits, Digest of Technical Papers, pp. 108–109. IEEE (1998)
8. Klass, F., et al.: A new family of semi-dynamic and dynamic flip-flops with embedded logic for high-performance processors. IEEE J. Solid-State Circuits **34**(5), 712–716 (1999)
9. Shin, Y., Paik, S.: Pulsed-latch circuits: a new dimension in ASIC design. IEEE Des. Test Comput. **28**(6), 50–57 (2011)
10. Yang, B.-D.: Low-power and area-efficient shift register using pulsed latches. IEEE Trans. Circuits Syst. I Regul. Pap. **62**(6), 1564–1571 (2015)
11. Sentaurus Device User Guide: Synopsis Inc. Mountain View, CA, USA (2012)

# Vertical Nanowire FET Based Standard Cell Design Employing Verilog-A Compact Model for Higher Performance

Satish Maheshwaram[1(✉)], Om Prakash[2], Mohit Sharma[3], Anand Bulusu[2], and Sanjeev Manhas[2]

[1] Marri Laxman Reddy Institute of Technology and Management, Hyderabad, India
satishm@mlritm.ac.in
[2] Indian Institute of Technology Roorkee, Roorkee 247667, India
[3] Xilinx Hyderabad, Hyderabad, India

**Abstract.** In sub 10 nm technology node, vertical silicon nanowire (VNW) FET device has become a promising substitute due to its better gate controllability, short channel immunity, high $I_{ON}/I_{OFF}$ ratio and CMOS compatibility. This paper presents, a standard cell library using physics based Verilog-A compact model for 10 nm vertical SiNW FET device. A unified compact model included all the nanoscale effects (e.g. short channel effects, mobility degradation, velocity saturations etc.) as well as the parasitic capacitance and resistance model, which are highly dominant in lower technology nodes. The compact model is well matched with TCAD simulation data at 10 nm VNW FET device level. The cell library builds comprises of INVERTER, NAND, NOR and Ex-OR gate cells. Further, we compared the 10 nm VNW FET based standard cell performance to 45 nm bulk CMOS based standard cell library. It is found that the VNWFET based cells library design have an advantage of delay by ~4X and power consumption by ~14X against the 45 nm CMOS technology.

**Keywords:** Cell library · Parasitic capacitance and parasitic resistance model Verilog-A compact model and vertical nanowire FET

## 1 Introduction

Continuous miniaturization of the conventional bulk CMOS technology in sub-22 nm regime faces several severe challenges, such as short channel effects (SCEs), poor gate controllability, rising exponential dependence leakage current, and process variations during fabrication. Therefore, new device materials and architecture are needed to continue the performance gain. Hence, the novel 2D, 3D devices such as silicon-on-insulator MOSFET (SOI), double gate FinFETs [1], Tri-gate FinFET, lateral and vertical nanowire field effect transistor (NW FET) [2] are the most promising candidates compared to the traditional planar CMOS technology. Out of all these future devices, nanowire FET with vertical nanowire structure or Vertical NW FET is the most potential candidate due to the better gate controllability, short channel impurity, CMOS compatibility and occupying lowest silicon area [3, 4]. Furthermore, the VNW FET based circuit

© Springer Nature Singapore Pte Ltd. 2017
B. K. Kaushik et al. (Eds.): VDAT 2017, CCIS 711, pp. 239–248, 2017.
https://doi.org/10.1007/978-981-10-7470-7_24

design and performance analysis become quite attractive for better performance low area design.

For a VNW FET based circuit design, a time efficient physics based Verilog-A compact model is needed because TCAD device/circuit simulation is enormously time taking (which takes more than 1 day for circuit simulation). The proposed Verilog-A model for VNW FET included all the short channel effects, velocity saturation, quantum confinement effect (due to narrow diameter of VNW FET) and mobility degradation [1]. Further we have also included the parasitic capacitance and resistance, which are highly dominating at nano-scale devices. In this paper, we have shown the calibration of Verilog-A compact model with TCAD data at device level. With the calibrated model card, the cell library has been designed. The standard cell library comprises of basic gates such as INVERTER, NAND, NOR and EX-OR gate. We investigated the sizing, propagation delay and power characterization of VNWFET based basic gates. The cell library is demonstrated for the wide range of input rise/fall time (5 ps to 25 ps) and output load (FO3 and FO4). In addition, the delay and power consumption of VNWFET based cell design is compared against the 45 nm CMOS technology.

## 2   Core Model Description and Validation

A compact Verilog-A model has been employed for VNWFET based circuit simulation. The VNWFET core model included all the short channel effect such as DIBL and $V_{th}$ roll off. Apart from that, other secondary effects such as velocity saturation, mobility degradation and quantum confinement models are accurately included. All these model equations are well demonstrated in our previous work [2]. More importantly, parasitic resistance and capacitance model which are highly dominant at nano scale dimensions are incorporated accurately. Figure 1 shows the VNWFET 2D device structure indicating parasitic resistance and capacitance. Since, VNWFET is an asymmetric device and characterized as a source bottom-drain top (Fig. 1) and drain bottom-source top. Accordingly parasitics are also different in two different VNW FET device structure and the models are presented in previous work [3]. Figs. 2 and 3 shows the excellent agreement of $I_d$-$V_g$ and $I_d$-$V_d$ characteristics between model and TCAD for both n, p VNWFET. The dimensions of n VNWFET are $L_G$ = 15 nm, R = 5 nm, $t_{ox}$ = 2 nm, S/$D_{ext}$ = 10 nm and p VNWFET are $L_G$ = 15 nm, R = 7.5 nm, $t_{ox}$ = 2 nm, S/$D_{ext}$ = 10 nm. The calibration or agreement of the characteristic has been done by slightly modifying the parameters such as work-function of gate metal for $V_{th}$ matching. Further, velocity saturation and mobility degradation model parameters in compact model are tuned to match the curve in transition region and $I_{ON}$ respectively. To account for the asymmetric architecture of VNWFET, we have calibrated the $I_d$-$V_g$ characteristic for source bottom and source top structure of n, p VNWFET as shown in Fig. 4. Thus, the parasitic resistance and capacitance models incorporated into the compact model can also predict the behavior due to asymmetric structure.

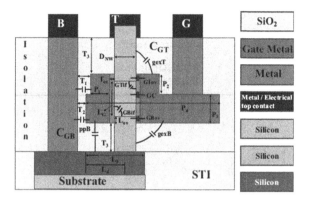

**Fig. 1.** Shows the VNWFET 2D cross section geometry with Parasitic capacitances and resistances [3]

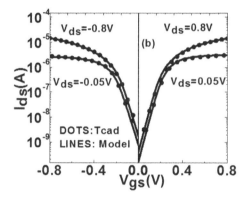

**Fig. 2.** $I_d$-$V_g$ characteristic comparison between model and TCAD of n, p VNW FET

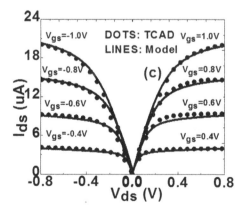

**Fig. 3.** $I_d$-$V_d$ characteristic comparison between model and TCAD of n, p VNW FET

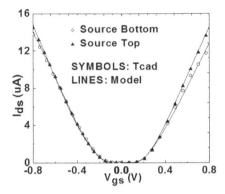

**Fig. 4.** $I_d$-$V_g$ characteristic comparison between model and TCAD of n, p VNW FET with source top and bottom configurations

# 3   Standard Cell Library

The standard cell library accurately and efficiently captures the behavior of a set of high quality timing and model parameters. The cell library is extensively utilized in many circuit design tools for various applications, such as logic synthesis, static time analysis (STA), high level design language simulation, power analysis [4, 5]. In this section, we concisely explain the important steps for formation of a 10 nm VNW FET based standard cell library.

## 3.1   Inverter Gate Sizing

Unlike MOSFET and FinFET, the drive strength depends upon the width and height of the transistor respectively. Whereas, due to the cylindrical structure of VNWFET, the drive strength mainly depends upon the diameter and number of wires in parallel. Therefore, the diameter as a parameter has been considered in our study for modulating the drive strength of transistor. The inverter requires equal drive strength of pull up and pulls down transistor for equal rise and fall delay of output. For equal drive strength of inverter shown in Fig. 5(a), the radius of p, n VNW FET is taken as 7.5 nm and 5 nm respectively. In Fig. 5(b) it can be seen that the inverter VTC obtained from compact model matches very well with TCAD results. To design a multiple drive strength logic cells such as INV 2X, INV 3X, INV 4X, INV 8X extra transistors in parallel to the existing INV1X transistors were added for equal rise-fall delay. The HSPICE simulation using Verilog-A model with parameters model card have been used to investigate the rise and fall delay of inverter.

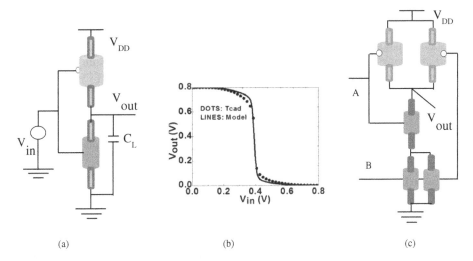

(a)                              (b)                              (c)

**Fig. 5.** (a) Illustrate the 10 nm VNWFET based inverter 1X (b) Inverter VTC obtained from compact model and TCAD (c) shows the schematic of 10 nm VNWFET based NAND gate

## 3.2  Sizing of Other Combinational Circuits NAND/NOR

The sizing approaches of combinational circuits such as NAND, NOR and EX-OR is different from the inverter sizing due to the stacking effect in NAND/NOR. The staking effect comes into effect for NAND, NOR in pull-up (p VNW FET in series) and pull down (n VNW FET in series) transistor respectively. Due to that, the drive strength of stacked transistor is less than the transistor connected in parallel (pull up, pull down of NAND and NOR respectively). The staking effect for VNWFET based combinational circuit has been solved by adding an extra wire to any of the staked transistor. We have verified this staking effect using HSPICE simulation. Figure 5 (c) shows the schematic of VNWFET SiNW FET based NAND gate, where the pull down transistor have an extra wire to the staked transistor connected to the ground to get equal rise and fall delay. In the same way, we can also use extra transistor in the pull-up of NOR gate to solve stacking problem. However, for multiple drive strength logic cells design such as NAND2X, NOR2X, EX-OR2X etc., extra transistor in parallel to the existing NAND1X transistor were used for equal rise and fall delay.

## 3.3  Timing Parameter

Timing parameters is important factor that decides the speed and slew rate of the logic cell, it also include timing parameter constrain such as setup time and hold time in sequential cell. In order to consider a timing parameter, we have calculated the propagation delay from input to output of circuits and transition time that output takes while output changes according to input transition. Propagation delay is accounted as the time interval when the input signal crosses 50% of the power supply ($V_{dd}$) to the time when output crosses 50% of the power supply ($V_{dd}$) [6]. In order to compute the above indicated parameters, we assume single input switching method which states that only one input will makes a transition at a time and keeping the other input at constant supply voltage. As such propagation delay, transition times are measured for every input, keeping other input as a constant. 2D-LUTs are generated for propagation delay while varying the input transition time and output load. The Table 1 show 2D LUTs for INVERTER and NAND gate delay for various (5 ps to 25 ps) of input slew and Fan-out (FO4 and FO3).

**Table 1.** 2D LUT for INVERTER and NAND gate delay

| Rise/Fall Time | FO$_4$ Load Delay (ps) | | FO$_3$ Load Delay (ps) | |
|---|---|---|---|---|
| | INVERTER | NAND | INVERTER | NAND |
| 5 ps | 9.4 | 11.70 | 7.46 | 9.37 |
| 9 ps | 9.9 | 12.25 | 8.0 | 9.90 |
| 13 ps | 10.7 | 12.81 | 8.78 | 10.53 |
| 17 ps | 11.4 | 13.64 | 9.45 | 11.16 |
| 21 ps | 11.9 | 14.12 | 9.95 | 11.70 |
| 25 ps | 12.09 | 14.56 | 10.13 | 12.33 |

### 3.4  Input Capacitance

We adopt the input current integration method to calculate the input capacitance of any circuits. We integrated the input current at any particular circuit over the transition time at which input switches, divided by the power supply voltage difference over time. The input capacitance of INV1X, NAND1X or INV2X, NAND2X will not be same, as with increasing number of wires parasitic also increase.

### 3.5  Power Consumption/Dissipation Analysis

To precisely estimate the total power dissipation during the circuit operation. We have considered all power dissipation components which comprises of, switching power, leakage power and short circuit power dissipation. Switching power dissipations arises when there is charging or discharging of load node capacitance with input signal probability. Short circuit power dissipation arises when both the pull up and pull down transistor of the inverter are simultaneously ON, which leads to a direct current path from $V_{dd}$ to ground. In order to measure leakage power, the average current flowing from $V_{dd}$ to ground when the input and the output signal do not transit is multiplied with the $V_{dd}$. 2D-LUTs are generated for power consumption while varying the input transition time and output load. The Table 2 shows 2D LUTs for INVERTER and NAND gate power consumption for various (5 ps to 25 ps) of input slew and Fan-out (FO4 and FO3).

**Table 2.** 2D LUT for INVERTER and NAND gate power consumption

| Rise/Fall Time | FO$_3$ Load Power (µW) | | FO$_4$ Load Power (µW) | |
|---|---|---|---|---|
| | INVERTER | NAND | INVERTER | NAND |
| 5 ps | 0.7816 | 0.5376 | 0.920 | 0.710 |
| 9 ps | 0.7824 | 0.6097 | 0.930 | 0.723 |
| 13 ps | 0.7844 | 0.6107 | 0.935 | 0.730 |
| 17 ps | 0.7869 | 0.6116 | 0.938 | 0.736 |
| 21 ps | 0.7890 | 0.6145 | 0.947 | 0.743 |
| 25 ps | 0.7924 | 0.6172 | 0.960 | 0.754 |

## 4   Simulation Results

In this section, we show the delay and power efficient 10 nm VNWFET CMOS standard cell library and comparisons with the 45 nm predictive technology model (PTM) bulk CMOS based cell design [7]. The standard cell library comprise of basic gates such as INVERTER, NAND, NOR and EX-OR gate analysis for various input transition (5 ps to 25 ps) and output load capacitances of FO3, FO4. Figure 6(a-b) show the propagation delay (($t_{phl}$ + $t_{plh}$)/2) and power consumption/dissipation in line with the analysis carried out in [8] for VNWFET INV1X with fanout FO3 and FO4 load. Further, for multiple drive strength such as INV2X, INV3X, INV4X the number of wires in pull up and pull down transistor increases by twice and thrice respectively. Figure 6(a-b) shows the significant increase in the delay of inverter with input slew, whereas power consumption become almost constant. One can observe that the delay of VNW FET inverter improved by ~3X time and power consumption having huge advantage ~12X compared to 45 nm CMOS technology due to smaller gate capacitance, superior gate controlability and short channel immunity.

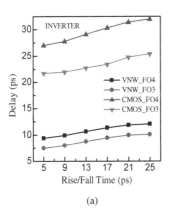

(a)

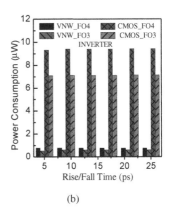

(b)

**Fig. 6.** Shows the delay, power consumption comparison between 10 nm VNWEFT and bulk CMOS based INVERTER gate at various input transition and fan-out FO3, FO4

Figures 7 and 8(a-b) shows the propagation delay and average power consumption of NAND and NOR gate for various input transition and output fan-out load. The VNWFET NAND gate has a delay advantage of ~4X and power consumption ~14X when compared to 45 nm CMOS technology. VNWFET NOR gate have a delay advantage of ~4.5X and power consumption ~14X against the 45 nm bulk CMOS technology. Further, we have compared the delay and power consumption of VNWFET EX-OR gate as shown in Fig. 9. The VNWFET EX-OR gate have an advantage of propagation delay ~3.8X and propagation delay of ~14X against the 45 nm bulk CMOS technology. The comparision of delay, power consumption result shows the advantage of selecting VNWFET over bulk CMOS logic gate for high speed and low power efficient application.

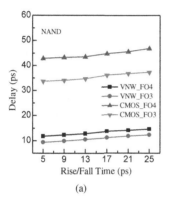
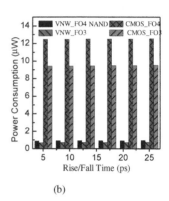

(a)                                          (b)

**Fig. 7.**  Shows the comparison of delay, power consumption between 10 nm VNWEFT and 45 nm bulk CMOS based NAND 1X gate at various input transition and fan-out FO3, FO4

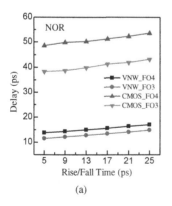
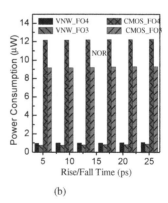

(a)                                          (b)

**Fig. 8.**  Shows the comparisons of delay, power consumption between 10 nm VNWEFT and 45 nm bulk CMOS based NOR gate 1X gate at various input transition and fan-out FO3, FO4

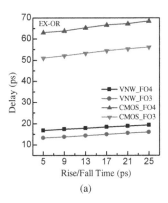
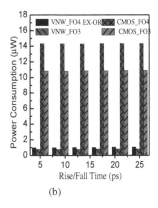

(a)                                          (b)

**Fig. 9.** Shows the delay, power consumption comparison between VNWEFT and CMOS based EX-OR gate for different input slew and load capacitance

# 5    Conclusions

In summary, this paper presents a precise physics based Verilog-A compact model calibration for 10 nm vertical silicon nanowire field effect transistor (VNWFET). The compact model accurately included all the short channel effects, velocity saturation, mobility degradation and quantum confinement effect model. The model also integrated the parasitics, which are highly dominant in nano-scale devices. Thereafter, with the TCAD calibrated model card at device level, we have developed VNW FET based standard cell library. The cell library includes the basic gates such as INVERTER, NAND, NOR and EX-OR gate. The delay and power consumption for various input transition and output load for basic logic gates have been investigated. It is found that the VNWFET cells have an advantage of delay ~4X and power consumption ~14X compared to 45 nm CMOS technology. Therefore, VNWFET based circuit analysis is highly preferable for high speed and low power applications. Further for future works, ISCAS benchmark circuits can be designed using the developed VNWFET based standard cell library.

**Acknowledgements.** We Dr. Satish Maheshwaram and Mr. Mohit Sharma, would like to thank our co-author Mr. Om Prakash and our supervisors Dr. Anand Bulusu, Dr. Sanjeev Manhas who have redone the work (after our graduation) on standard cell library delay and power analysis at Indian Institute of Technology Roorkee to make this a better research work.

# References

1. Goel, E., Kumar, S., Singh, K., Singh, B., Kumar, M., Jit, S.: 2-D analytical modeling of threshold voltage for graded-channel dual-material double-gate MOSFETs. IEEE Trans. Electron Devices **63**(3), 966–973 (2016)

2. Sharma, M., Maheshwaram, S., Prakash, O., Bulusu, A., Saxena, A.K., Manhas, S.K.: Compact model for vertical silicon nanowire based device simulation and circuit design. In: ISOCC, pp. 107–108 (2015)
3. Maheshwaram, S., Manhas, S.K., Kaushal, G., Anand, B., Singh, N.: Vertical nanowire CMOS parasitic modeling and its performance analysis. IEEE Trans. Electron Devices **60**(9), 2943–2950 (2013)
4. Xie, Q., Lin, X., Wang, Y., Dousti, M.J., Shafaei, A., Ghasemi-Gol, M., Pedram, M.: 5 nm FinFET standard cell library optimization and circuit synthesis in near-and super-threshold voltage regimes. In: Proceedings of the IEEE Computer Society Annual Symposium on VLSI, ISVLSI, pp. 424–429 (2014)
5. Xie, Q., Lin, X., Wang, Y., Chen, S., Dousti, M.J., Pedram, M.: Performance comparisons between 7-nm FinFET and conventional bulk CMOS standard cell libraries. IEEE Trans. Circuits Syst. II Express Briefs **62**(8), 761–765 (2015)
6. Prakash, O., Sharma, M., Bulusu, A.: Lateral silicon nanowire based standard cell design for higher performance. In: APCCAS, vol. 2, pp. 135–138 (2016)
7. 16 nm PTM-MG. http://ptm.asu.edu/
8. Cui, T., Xie, Q., Wang, Y., Nazarian, S., Pedram, M.: 7 nm FinFET standard cell layout characterization and power density prediction in near- and super-threshold voltage regimes. In: 2014 International Green Computing Conference IGCC (2015)

# Analysis of Electrolyte-Insulator-Semiconductor Tunnel Field-Effect Transistor as pH Sensor

Ajay Singh[1], Rakhi Narang[2], Manoj Saxena[3], and Mridula Gupta[1(✉)]

[1] Semiconductor Devices Research Laboratory, Department of Electronic Science,
University of Delhi, South Campus, New Delhi 110021, India
ajay.does@gmail.com, mridula@south.du.ac.in
[2] Department of Electronics, Sri Venkateswara College, University of Delhi, New Delhi, India
rakhinarang@gmail.com
[3] Department of Electronics, Deen Dayal Upadhyaya College,
University of Delhi, New Delhi, India
saxena_manoj77@yahoo.co.in

**Abstract.** In this paper, an analysis of Silicon on Insulator (SOI) Electrolyte Insulator Semiconductor (EIS) Tunnel Field Effect Transistor (TFET) has been investigated for pH sensing application using 3-D device simulator "Sentaurus". The electrolyte region has been considered an intrinsic semiconductor material in which the electron and hole charges represent the mobile ions in the aqueous solution. The dielectric constant, energy bandgap and electron affinity of electrolyte region are 78, 1.5 eV and 1.32 eV respectively. The effect of pH has been examined on the device electrostatics such as, surface potential, threshold voltage and drain current. The pH response is defined as the amount of threshold voltage shift when the pH (in the injected solution) is varied from lower to higher values.

**Keywords:** EISFET · TCAD · SOI tunnel FET · pH sensor · Surface potential Drain current

## 1 Introduction

In the bioscience area pH value plays a vital role for developing rapid, portable, and high-sensitivity pH sensors for very small amount of fluids. The pH value of blood is considered as the best pointer of human health [1]. The pH value is also important in the investigation of life science and in numerous biochemical reactions [1–8]. Small change in pH value drastically affects the activity of cells [2], cellular organelles [3], enzymes [4] and proteins [3–6]. In environmental [7] and food industry [8] related applications, pH sensing also contributes a vital role. Therefore, accurate and fast examination of pH values is one of the most vital tasks in various fields of study.

From starting, different electrochemical and non-electrochemical methods have been used for measuring the pH value. In this regard, solid-state devices have shown great promise in achieving unprecedented speed, sensitivity, and portability in chemical sensing. Field-effect transistor based device is used as pH-sensor for the measurement

© Springer Nature Singapore Pte Ltd. 2017
B. K. Kaushik et al. (Eds.): VDAT 2017, CCIS 711, pp. 249–258, 2017.
https://doi.org/10.1007/978-981-10-7470-7_25

of $H^+$ ions concentration in aqueous solution [9, 10] i.e., ion sensitive field effect transistor. FET device is commonly used in the sensing area due to low cost, low noise, low power consumption, small in size and easily interfaced with the electronic circuit. First FET based sensor, i.e., ISFET, was reported in 1970 by Bergveld [9]. Furtherance to this he reported in 1972 [11], measurement of ionic and effluxes around a nerve. In ISFET, he demonstrated that the metal gate of conventional MOSFET is absent and the gate oxide material is exposed to an electrolyte. The device conduction is controlled by the ion activity in the electrolyte and hence this device functions as an ion sensitive transducer. Signal generation at the interface between the gate oxide material and the electrolyte varies with the specific ion activity in the electrolyte causing a shift in threshold voltage and hence the drain current of the device.

Currently, research interest has been focused upon overcoming the challenges associated with conventional MOSFET in terms of stability and disturbance resistibility [12]. In addition, it has the limitation of poor sub-threshold slope (SS) at room temperature [13–16] and also suffers from theoretical limit of the maximum achievable sensitivity and the detection time is large [17].

In this paper, the tunnel FET is used as pH sensor wherein the conduction mechanism is controlled by band to band tunneling [18, 19]. Tunnel FET is one of the promising alternatives to overcome the limitation and retaining all other advantages associated with conventional MOSFET for sensing application [20–23].

In the present work, we have demonstrated n-type Silicon on insulator tunnel EIS-TFET based pH-sensor through simulation technique by using commercial device simulator, sentaurus [24]. The simulation method deals with a simulation domain that includes both semiconductor and electrolyte regions. The electrolyte solution is considered as the type of the semiconductor material in which the hole and electron charges represent the mobile ions in the solution [25, 26]. The modulation of drain current in SOI Tunnel EIS-TFET based pH sensor is due to change in the ionic concentration of the electrolyte and hence, hydrogen ions ($H^+$ ions) and hydroxyl ions ($OH^-$ ions) of the solution. Therefore, various pH sensor characteristics can be evaluated using this simulation technique, such as the pH sensitivity as well as the drain current fluctuation.

## 2  Device Architecture

Figure 1 shows the device architecture of SOI Tunnel EIS-TFET which has been simulated in the present work. The device channel thickness is 20 nm and gate oxide thickness is 2 nm which acts as adhesion layer. The channel length of the device is about 500 nm, source and drain extension length is 200 nm. The thickness of electrolyte region is 100 nm. Source region is doped by p-type impurity material is about $1 \times 10^{19}$ cm$^{-3}$ and drain region is doped by n-type impurity material is about $1 \times 10^{18}$ cm$^{-3}$. The thickness of buried oxide layer is 145 nm.

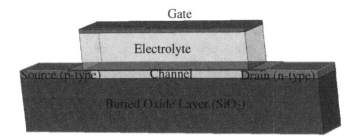

**Fig. 1.** Schematic of SOI Tunnel EISFET.

## 3   Simulation of Electrolyte

In this paper, electrolyte is defined as an intrinsic semiconductor material by considering the dielectric constant to be 78, 1.5 eV energy bandgap and 1.32 eV electron affinity of water. The charge distribution in actual electrolyte is represented by the Poisson–Boltzmann (PB) equation [27]. In this work, we have assumed a 1:1 electrolyte (e.g. H$^+$–Cl$^-$) and the original form of the PB equation can be written as below:

$$\frac{\partial^2 \psi}{\partial x^2} = -\frac{q}{\varepsilon_w} \left[ C_0^{H^+} e^{\left(-\frac{q\psi}{kT}\right)} - C_0^{Cl^-} e^{\left(\frac{q\psi}{kT}\right)} \right] \tag{1}$$

Where, $C_0^{H^+}$ and $C_0^{Cl^-}$ represent H$^+$ and Cl$^-$ ion concentrations at the electrically neutral condition. The semiconductor equation expects the Fermi-Dirac distribution of hole and electron is very close to the PB equation. The semiconductor equation for an intrinsic material can be rearranged as follows:

$$\frac{\partial^2 \psi}{\partial x^2} = -\frac{q}{\varepsilon_{si}} \left[ p_0 \frac{1 + e^{\left(\frac{E_i - E_v}{kT}\right)}}{1 + e^{\left(\frac{E_i - E_v}{kT}\right)} e^{\left(\frac{q\psi}{kT}\right)}} - n_0 \frac{1 + e^{\left(\frac{E_c - E_i}{kT}\right)}}{1 + e^{\left(\frac{E_c - E_i}{kT}\right)} e^{\left(-\frac{q\psi}{kT}\right)}} \right] \tag{2}$$

Where, $p_0$ and $n_0$ denote the hole and electron concentrations in the equilibrium condition respectively.

The charge distribution in the electrolyte is represented by the PB equation which describes the charge density distribution. Charge concentration depends on the concentration of specific ions in the solution. Figure 2 gives a representation of the position of positive and negative charges in electrolyte at pH 7 (i.e., with the same concentration of H+ and OH− ions) and null voltage. If the positive and negative charges are non-uniformly distributed then the potential is not constant in the electrolyte region. The positive charges are attracted toward the silicon dioxide side and the negative charges toward the reference electrode side at thermodynamic equilibrium.

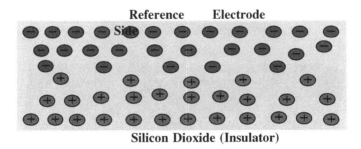

**Silicon Dioxide (Insulator)**

**Fig. 2.** Schematic representation of charge position at equilibrium ($V_g = 0$).

The ionic charge concentration in the electrolyte which is given as:

$$C_i = N_V = N_C = N_A C_0 \tag{3}$$

Where $N_A$ is Avogadro's number (1/mol) and $C_0$ the ion molar concentration ($M = 1000$ mol/m$^3$) in the bulk of the solution and $C_i$ is the ionic charge concentration in the electrolyte which is equal to the density of state of intrinsic semiconductor material. From the above Eq. (3), pH can be calculated as given below:

$$pH = -\log \left( \frac{C_i \times 10^3}{N_A} \right) \tag{4}$$

The above relationship between pH value and the density of state of intrinsic semiconductor material is shows in the Fig. 3.

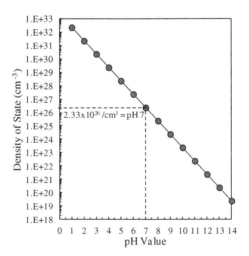

**Fig. 3.** Variation of density of state of intrinsic semiconductor with respect to pH Value.

The concentration of $H^+$ ions, in pure water is $10^{-7}$ mol/L and the number of molecules per mole is $6.022 \times 10^{23}$ (Avogadro's number), the concentration of $H^+$ is around $6.022 \times 10^{13}$/cm$^3$. $OH^-$ concentration in the pure water is the same as $H^+$. The mass action law states that $[OH^-]$ $[H^+]$ in pure water is $3\text{-}4 \times 10^{26}$/cm$^3$ at room temperature, and the number is preserved if the impurity molecules are added to change either $[H^+]$ or $[OH^-]$. Mass action law of water is similar to the mass action law followed in semiconductor where n-p product correspond to $[OH^-]$ $[H^+]$; n-p in silicon is $2.2 \times 10^{20}$/cm$^3$ at room temperature.

If $[H^+]$ is larger (smaller) than $[OH^-]$, the solution is called an acid (base). The concentration of electrons and holes are denoted by number/cm$^3$ whereas the ion concentration in an electrolyte is expressed by mol/L. For conversion of mol/L to number/cm$^3$ is simply to multiply $6.022 \times 10^{20}$/cm$^3$/ (mol/L).

The comparison of electrolyte region with the experimental data has already done in our previous work [28].

## 4    Results and Discussion

In this section, we have discussed the impact of pH value on the device characteristics such as surface potential electric field, energy band gap, threshold voltage and drain current.

Figure 4 shows the variation of surface potential for different pH value injected in electrolyte. As the pH value increases by changing the density of state of given electrolyte material intrinsic silicon the surface potential of the channel region decreases. It is known that the electrolyte works as the gate in EIS-TFET therefore, when the density of state $N_v$ which means $[H^+]$ carrier ions decreases at the interface of adhesion layer ($SiO_2$) and electrolyte region the channel is back towards from the strong inversion to weak inversion. Due to this surface potential of channel region decreases when pH increases.

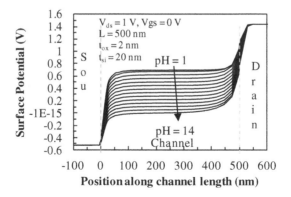

**Fig. 4.** Surface potential variation along channel position of SOI tunnel EISFET for different pH value.

Figure 5 shows the impact of pH value on the electric field of SOI EIS-TFET. At the source side junction of SOI tunnel EIS-TFET, pH value of electrolyte region increases by decreasing the density of state $N_v$ the peak of electric field decreases whereas it increase at the drain end of the channel region of SOI tunnel EISFET at $V_{ds}$ is 1 V and $V_{gs}$ is 1 V.

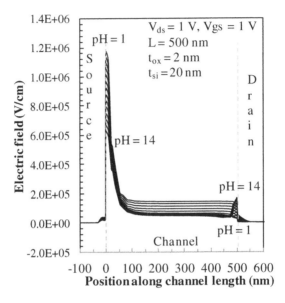

**Fig. 5.** Electric Field variation along channel position of SOI tunnel EISFET for different pH value.

Figure 6 shows the impact of pH value on energy band gap of SOI tunnel EISFET at $V_{ds}$ is 1 V and $V_{gs}$ is 1 V. As the pH value of electrolyte region increases then the conduction and valence bands of channel region shift upward in comparison of valence band of source region of SOI tunnel EISFET. The barrier width increases with pH value and the electron transport from valence band of source region to conduction band of channel region decreases. Therefore, the current conduction in SOI tunnel EISFET is reduced.

The effect of pH values on the drain current of SOI Tunnel EISFET is depicted in Fig. 7. If the pH of electrolyte decreases from pH of water then the on-current of device increases whereas when the pH value is more than the pH of water the on-current decreases. In other words, as electrolyte become "acidic" the barrier width of device decreases and on-current increases whereas as the electrolyte become more "base" the barrier width of device increases and the on-current decreases.

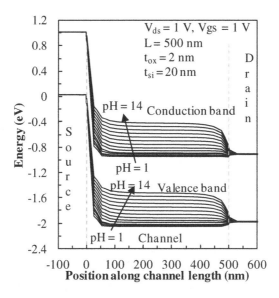

**Fig. 6.** Energy variation along channel position of SOT tunnel EISFET for different pH value.

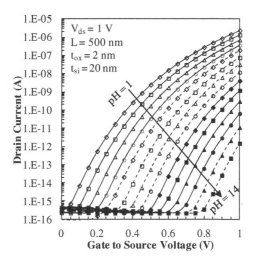

**Fig. 7.** Drain current variation of SOI tunnel FET for different pH value.

Figure 8 shows the variation of ratio of on-current and off-current when the pH value of electrolyte is changed. If pH value decreases from pH value of water means the electrolyte become acidic the ratio of on-current and off-current increases but it decreases when pH value increases from pH value of water means electrolyte becomes base.

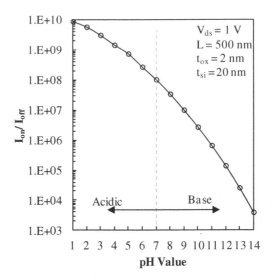

**Fig. 8.** $I_{on}/I_{off}$ ratio variation of SOI tunnel FET for different pH value.

Figure 9 shows the impact of pH variation on the threshold voltage of the device. When the electrolyte becomes acidic by decreasing the pH value of electrolyte, i.e. pH value of electrolyte lesser that that of water, then the threshold voltage decreases whereas it increase when electrolyte becomes base by increasing the pH value than that of pH value of water.

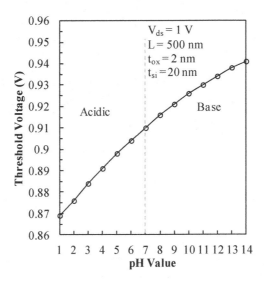

**Fig. 9.** Threshold voltage variation of SOI tunnel FET for different pH value.

# 5 Conclusion

In this report, SOI tunnel Field Effect Transistor has been investigated as a pH sensor. The effect of pH value has been analyzed on surface potential, electric field, energy band, drain current and threshold voltage of the device. The electrolyte has been considered as the intrinsic semiconductor material with dielectric constant 78, energy band is 1.5 eV and electron affinity is 1.32 eV of water. The results have been simulated with device simulation tool Sentaurus.

# References

1. Cheng, Y., Xiong, P., Yun, C.S., Strouse, G., Zheng, J., Yang, R., et al.: Mechanism and optimization of pH sensing using SnO2 nanobelt field effect transistors. Nano Lett. **8**, 4179–4184 (2008)
2. Li, X.J., Schick, M.: Theory of tunable pH-sensitive vesicles of anionic and cationic lipids or anionic and neutral lipids. Biophys. J. **80**, 1703–1711 (2001)
3. Nakamura, N., Tanaka, S., Teko, Y., Mitsui, K., Kanazawa, H.: Four Na +/H + exchanger isoforms are distributed to Golgi and post-Golgi compartments and are involved in organelle pH regulation. J. Biol. Chem. **280**, 1561–1572 (2005)
4. Chen, Y., Wang, X., Hong, M., Erramilli, S., Mohanty, P.: Surface-modified silicon nano-channel for urea sensing. Sens. Actuators B Chem. **133**, 593–598 (2008)
5. Kummer, U., Zobeley, J., Brasen, J.C., Fahmy, R., Kindzelskii, A.L., Petty, A.R., et al.: Elevated glucose concentrations promote receptor-independent activation of adherent human neutrophils: an experimental and computational approach. Biophys. J. **92**, 2597–2607 (2007)
6. Yang, A.S., Honig, B.: On the pH dependence of protein stability. J. Mol. Biol. **231**, 459–474 (1993)
7. Frost, R., Griffin, R.: Effect of pH on adsorption of arsenic and selenium from landfill leachate by clay minerals. Soil Sci. Soc. Am. J. **41**, 53–57 (1977)
8. Royce, P.N.: A discussion of recent developments in fermentation monitoring and control from a practical perspective. Critical Rev. Biotechnol. **13**, 117–149 (1993)
9. Bergveld, P.: Development of an ion-sensitive solid-state device for neurophysiological measurements. IEEE Trans. Biomed. Eng. **17**(1), 70–71 (1970)
10. Martinoia, S., Massobrio, G., Lorenzelli, L.: Modeling ISFET microsensor and ISFET-based microsystems: a review. Sens. Actuators B: Chem. **105**, 14–27 (2005)
11. Bergveld, P.: Development, operation, and application of the ion-sensitive field-effect transistor as a tool for electrophysiology. IEEE Trans. Biomed. Eng. **19**(5), 342–351 (1972)
12. Im, Y., Lee, C., Vasquez, R.P., Bangar, M.A., Myung, N.V., Menke, E.J., Penner, R.M., Yun, M.: Investigation of a single Pd nanowire for use as a hydrogen sensor. Small **2**(3), 356–358 (2006)
13. Ionescu, A.M., Riel, H.: Tunnel field-effect transistors as energy-efficient electronic switches. Nature **479**(7373), 329–337 (2011)
14. Seabaughand, A.C., Zhang, A.C.: Low-voltage tunnel transistors for beyond CMOS logic. Proc. IEEE **98**(12), 2095–2110 (2010)
15. Goel, E., et al.: 2-D analytical modeling of threshold voltage for graded-channel dual-material double-gate MOSFETs. IEEE Trans. Electron Devices **63**, 966–973 (2016)
16. Rawat, G., et al.: Analytical modeling of threshold voltage of ion-implanted Strained-Si-on-Insulator (SSOI) MOSFETs. J. Nanoelectron. Optoelectron. **9**(3), 442–448 (2014)

17. Sarkar, D., Banerjee, K.: Proposal for tunnel-field-effect-transistor as ultra-sensitive and label-free biosensors. Appl. Phys. Lett. **100**(14), 143108 (2012)
18. Sarkar, D., Banerjee, K.: Metallic-nanoparticle assisted enhanced band-to-band tunneling current. Applied Physics Letters 99(13), 133116 (2011)
19. Sarkar, D., Krall, M., Banerjee, K.: Electron-hole duality during band-to-band tunneling process in graphene-nanoribbon tunnel-field-effect-transistors. Appl. Phys. Lett. **97**(26), 263109 (2010)
20. Narang, R., Sasidhar Reddy, K.V., Saxena, M., Gupta, R.S., Gupta, M.: A dielectric-modulated tunnel-FET-based biosensor for label-free detection: analytical modeling study and sensitivity analysis. IEEE Trans. Electron Devices **59**(10), 2809–2817 (2012)
21. Narang, R., Saxena, M., Gupta, M.: Comparative analysis of dielectric-modulated FET and TFET-based biosensor. IEEE Trans. Nanotechnol. **14**(3), 427–435 (2015)
22. Singh, A., Narang, R., Saxena, M., Gupta, M.: Ambipolar behaviour of Tunnel Field Effect Transistor (TFET) as an advantage for biosensing applications. In: Jain, V.K., Verma, A. (eds.) Physics of Semiconductor Devices. ESE, pp. 171–174. Springer, Cham (2014). https://doi.org/10.1007/978-3-319-03002-9_43
23. Kumar, S., et al.: A compact 2D analytical model for electrical characteristics of double-gate tunnel field-effect transistors with a SiO2/High-k stacked gate-oxide structure. IEEE Trans. Electron Devices **63**(8), 3291–3299 (2016)
24. TCAD: Sentaurus Device User Manual, Synopsys, CA (2013)
25. Chung, I.Y., Jang, H., Lee, J., Moon, H., Seo, S.M., Kim, D.H.: Simulation study on discrete charge effects of SiNW biosensors according to bound target position using a 3D TCAD simulator. Nanotechnology **23**, 065202 (2012)
26. Pittino, F., Palestri, P., Scarbolo, P., Esseni, D., Selmi, L.: Models for the use of commercial TCAD in the analysis of silicon-based integrated biosensors. Solid-State Electron. **98**, 63–69 (2014)
27. Grahame, D.C.: The electrical double layer and the theory of electrocapillarity. Chem. Rev. **41**(3), 441–501 (1947)
28. Singh, A., Narang, R., Saxena, M., Gupta, M.: Analytical model of pH sensing characteristics of junctionless silicon on insulator ISFET. IEEE Trans. Electron Devices **64**(4), 1742–1750 (2017)

# Exploiting Characteristics of Steep Slope Tunnel Transistors Towards Energy Efficient and Reliable Buffer Designs for IoT SoCs

Japa Aditya[1(✉)], Vallabhaneni Harshita[2], and Ramesh Vaddi[1]

[1] Nano Scale Integrated Circuits and Systems for Self-Powered IoT Laboratory, DSPM International Institute of Information Technology, Naya Raipur 493661, Chattishgarh, India
{aditya,ramesh}@iiitnr.edu.in
[2] Electronics and Communication Engineering, Vignan's Institute of Information Technology, Visakhapatnam, India
vharshita92@gmail.com

**Abstract.** Energy efficient buffer circuits enable high speed and reliable information transfer among sub-systems of System on Chip (SoC). A novel buffer circuit design exploiting the steep slope characteristics of tunnel FETs (TFET) has been proposed and benchmarked with 20 nm Si FinFET technology. The analysis is performed considering the parameters such as iso-area, iso-energy, iso-speed and noise margins for energy efficiency and reliability. It is clearly evident that TFET buffers exhibit improved speed of operation and high energy efficiency over FinFET buffers for scaled supply voltages, demonstrating suitability for applications such as Internet of things (IoT) SoCs. To further exemplify the buffer circuit performance, TFET/FinFET pass transistor based full adder carry circuit is implemented whose output load is driven by TFET/FinFET buffer. Unlike FinFET buffer circuits, TFET buffers prove to be reliable and energy efficient in driving larger loads despite the area overhead caused due to the unidirectional current conduction of TFETs.

**Keywords:** Buffer circuits · Energy efficiency · FinFET · Full adder · IoT
Reliability · Tunnel FETs

## 1 Introduction

Internet of things (IoT) enable more devices for better connected world and this requires designing sensor node SoCs with high energy efficiency and reliability. Buffer circuits are important components in interfacing subsystems of SoC and also for driving large loads with high speed. With CMOS technology scaling, designing energy efficient and reliable buffer circuits for SoCs is an increasing challenge. Emerging alternative and steep slope device architectures like tunnel FETs have attracted wide attention for energy efficient system designs due to their lower standby leakage, sub 60 mV/dec subthreshold swing and high $I_{on}/I_{off}$ ratio [1–5]. The important TFET design challenges like ambipolarity, enhanced miller effect, and unidirectional current conduction are addressed by several device and circuit level optimization techniques [6–8, 18, 19]. It is evident from recent works that

© Springer Nature Singapore Pte Ltd. 2017
B. K. Kaushik et al. (Eds.): VDAT 2017, CCIS 711, pp. 259–269, 2017.
https://doi.org/10.1007/978-981-10-7470-7_26

TFET circuits demonstrate high computational speed and energy efficiency [9–12, 16, 17] with CMOS scaling. TFET devices are also found to be promising candidates for power conversion circuits in various energy harvesting applications [13, 14]. TFET based buffer circuits which can be efficiently used for interfacing subsystems of SoC are not much explored to the best of our knowledge. This paper demonstrate the efficiency of TFET devices in designing buffer circuits and show the reliability of TFET buffer circuits in full adder design. Rest of the paper is organized as follows. Section 2 presents the TFET device structure, characteristics, and models used for circuit design. In Sect. 3, TFET based energy efficient buffer circuit designs are presented and analyzed by comparing with the base line FinFET designs. Finally, conclusions are offered in Sect. 4.

## 2   TFET Device Structure, Characteristics and Models

In this work, look up table (*LUT*) based double gate hetero junction TFET and Si FinFET *Verilog-A* models [13–15] at 20 nm have been explored for circuit simulations in *Cadence Virtuoso* environment. Structure of TFET and FinFET devices used are shown in Fig. 1.

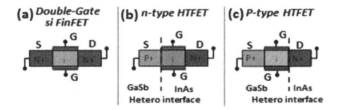

**Fig. 1.** Device schematics of double-gate (a) Si FinFET (b) n-HTFET and (c) pHTFET with gate-length of 20 nm [10].

Figure 2(a) and (b) present the TFET and FinFET $I_D$-$V_G$ characteristics (both linear and log scale) demonstrating high on-current (~7x improvement at $V_{DD} = 0.3$ V) and lower subthreshold swing (30 mV/dec) compared to the base line FinFET.

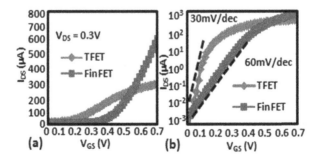

**Fig. 2.** $I_{DS}$-$V_{GS}$ characteristics comparison of double- gate HTFET with double gate Si FinFET (a) linear scale (b) log scale.

# 3  Energy Efficiency and Reliability Analysis of TFET Based Buffer Circuits

## 3.1  TFET Based Buffer Designs and Benchmarking with Si FinFETs

Buffer is a circuit designed by cascading even number of inverter stages. In this section, a static complementary TFET inverter based 2, 4 and 6-stage buffers are designed as shown in Fig. 3.

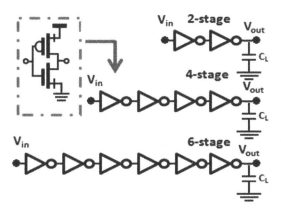

**Fig. 3.** Complementary TFET inverter based 2, 4 and 6-stage buffer design.

An aspect ratio of 2 is followed to achieve energy efficiency and symmetrical $t_{pHL}$ and $t_{pLH}$ (Fig. 4) values for the inverter [18] at which the switching threshold value is observed to be close to half of $V_{DD}$. The transient characteristics (Fig. 5) of TFET 6-stage buffer with varying load prove that the output is an exact replica of the input with

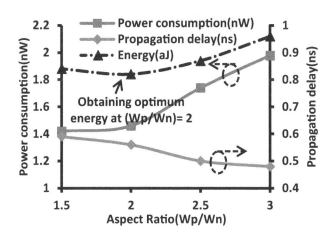

**Fig. 4.** Energy consumption of static CTFET reference inverter with varying transistor aspect ratio at $V_{DD} = 0.2$ V [18].

small propagation delay. Further analysis has been carried out considering identical area, speed, energy and noise margins of both TFET and FinFET buffer circuits by varying load capacitance from 1 fF to 1 pF.

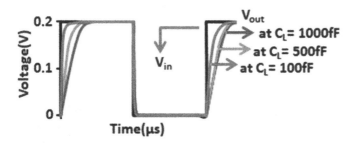

**Fig. 5.** Transient characteristics of TFET 6-stage buffer with varying load capacitance ($C_L$).

### 3.2    TFET vs FinFET Buffer Circuits for Iso-area (Identical Transistor Sizes)

From Figs. 6 and 7 it is observed that, the propagation delay and energy of 2, 6-stage FinFET buffers driving 100fF load capacitance, at a supply voltage of 0.2 V are approximately 15x larger than that of TFET buffers due to the high Ion/Ioff ratio of TFET devices. And FinFET buffers have failed to drive larger loads (more than 100fF) at supply voltage of 0.2, as shown in Fig. 7.

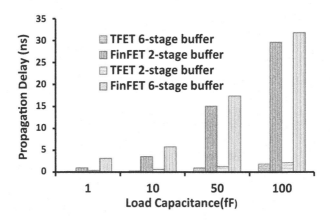

**Fig. 6.** 2, 6-stage TFET and FinFET buffer: Propagation Delay Vs Load Capacitance at 0.2 V supply voltage.

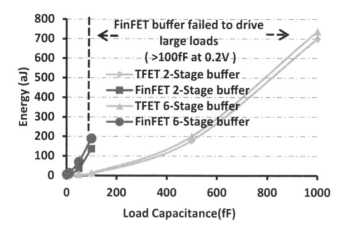

**Fig. 7.** 2, 6 stage TFET and FinFET buffer: Energy consumption vs Loadcapacitance at 0.2 Vsupply voltage.

### 3.3 TFET vs FinFET Buffer Circuits for Iso-energy

Potential of TFET and FinFET buffers in driving large loads are examined by for iso-energy conditions. TFET buffers consuming same energy as FinFET buffers are capable of driving larger loads as evident from Fig. 8. The energy consumed by TFET 2-stage buffer at $C_L = 100fF$ and FinFET 2-stage buffer at $C_L = 10fF$ are approximately equal (13aJ). This proves that TFET buffers can drive 10x larger loads with same energy compared to that of FinFET buffers.

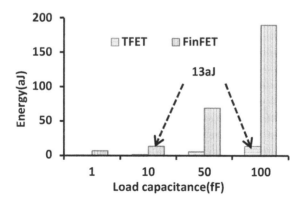

**Fig. 8.** 2 stage TFET and FinFET buffer: Energy consumption Vs Load capacitance at 0.2 V supply voltage.

### 3.4  TFET vs FinFET Buffer Circuits for Iso-speed

At a supply voltage of 0.4 V, 2-stage TFET buffer with $C_L$ = 50fF operates at the same speed as a 2-stage FinFET buffer with $C_L$ = 10fF as can be seen in Fig. 9. For a supply voltage of 0.4 V, TFET buffers can drive ~5x larger loads than FinFET buffers with same speed. Also TFET buffers are observed to be capable of driving 50x larger loads than FinFET buffers with same speed at a supply voltage of 0.2 V. The steep slope characteristics of TFET device lead to large driving capability of TFET buffers s.

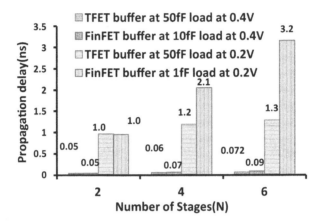

**Fig. 9.** TFET and FinFET buffer: Propagation delay Vs number of stages for 0.2V and 0.4 V supply voltages.

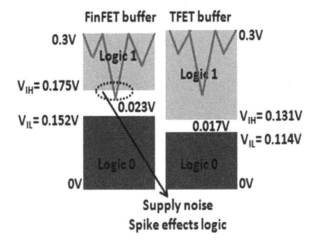

**Fig. 10.**  2-stage TFET and FinFET buffer: Noise margin at supply voltage of 0.3 V.

## 3.5 Noise Margin Analysis

Noise margins ($NM_L$, $NM_H$) of TFET and FinFET buffers are calculated at different supply voltages and analysis has been performed at 0.3 V. From Fig. 10, the high level noise margin ($NM_H$) for TFET buffer is very large than that of FinFET buffer. This reveals the fact that TFET buffers are highly capable of nullifying power supply noise effect and signal loss, thereby making the buffer design highly reliable. Also the intermediate range ($V_{IH}$-$V_{IL}$) for TFET buffer is less than that of FinFET buffer. This means that TFET buffer can switch between logic levels with much ease.

Table 1 summarizes the performance comparison of 2-stage TFET and FinFET buffers driving 100fF load capacitance. At a supply voltage of 0.2 V, 2-stage TFET buffer achieves 16x higher speed and energy efficiency compared to FinFET buffers. A 2-stage buffer is reliable with large high level noise margin ($NM_H$) compared to FinFET buffers for supply voltages in the range of 0.2 to 0.4 V.

**Table 1.** Proposed 2- stage TFET and FinFET buffer performance comparison.

| 2-stage buffer at a Load capacitance, $C_L = 100fF$ | | | | |
|---|---|---|---|---|
| Parameter | | Supply voltage, $V_{DD} = 0.2$ V | | Supply voltage, $V_{DD} = 0.4$ V | |
| | | TFET | FinFET | TFET | FinFET |
| Propagation Delay(ns) | | 1.82 | 29.56 | 0.087 | 0.375 |
| Power(nW) | | 5.13 | 5.23 | 20.77 | 21.17 |
| Energy(aJ) | | 8.47 | 137 | 1.64 | 7.035 |
| Noise margin (V) | $NM_L$ | 0.078 | 0.104 | 0.168 | 0.201 |
| | $NM_H$ | 0.106 | 0.074 | 0.214 | 0.175 |

## 3.6 TFET/FinFET Buffers Driving Output of Full-Adder Carry Circuit

Figure 11 shows a full adder carry circuit which consists of nTFET based pass transistor AND/OR gates, a TFET based multiplexer and a 2-stage buffer. The outputs of AND/OR logic ($Y_1$ and $Y_2$) are combined by a $2 \times 1$ multiplexer (which is conditioned by $C_{in}$) to yield carry output of full adder. To restore the logic swing lost due to pass transistor AND/OR gates, a TFET based 2-stage buffer is introduced at the output stage. Since TFETs are unidirectional devices, circuit current flows only from drain to source in case of nTFET and from source to drain in case of pTFET. Due to the unidirectional current conduction, TFET based AND/OR logic uses an additional transistor each, compared to FinFET design. To illustrate the functionality of the TFET pass transistor AND logic consider inputs A is at logic 0 and B is at logic 1, transistor $T_1$ switches ON (but doesn't allow current due to unidirectional current conduction), $T_2$ switches OFF and $T_3$ switches ON. Consequently output of the AND gate discharges through $T_3$ and becomes logic 0.

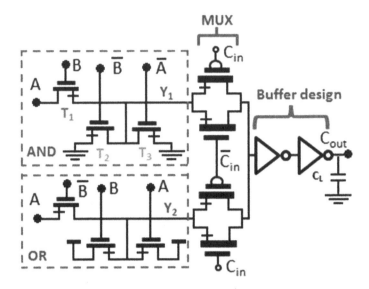

**Fig. 11.** TFET Pass transistor AND/OR based full adder carry at supply voltage of 0.3 V.

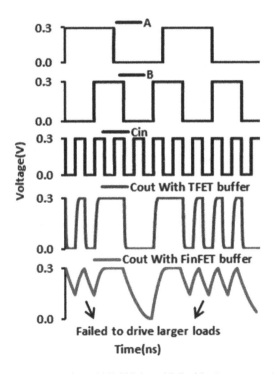

**Fig. 12.** TFET/FinFET Pass transistor AND/OR based full adder (carry output) transient response at a load capacitance of 2 pF.

Figure 12 shows the transient response of full adder carry output with TFET/FinFET buffers. FinFET buffer is unable to reproduce the output at a high load capacitance of 2 pF due at lower supply voltages. Inspite of additional area overhead caused by the unidirectional current conduction (in implementation of pass transistor AND/OR [19]), the TFET based full adder design has reported high energy efficiency in driving the large loads (from Fig. 13). It can also be further observed that FinFET design [20] has failed to drive larger loads at such low operating voltages.

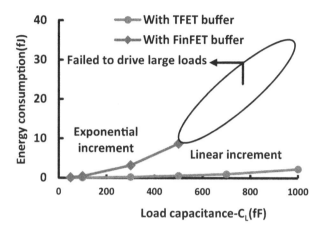

**Fig. 13.** Fulladder carry with TFET and FinFET buffer: Energy consumption Vs Load capacitance at 0.3 V.

# 4  Conclusion

This work explores the characteristics of steep slope tunnel transistors in designing energy efficient buffer circuits. The iso-area, iso-energy, iso-speed and noise margin analysis for 2, 4, and 6-stage TFET and FinFET buffers demonstrate that TFET buffers are reliable and energy efficient in driving larger loads as compared to FinFET buffers. At a supply voltage of 0.2 V, 2-stage TFET buffer achieves 16x higher speed and energy efficiency compared to FinFET buffers. The application of 2-stage TFET buffer circuit further in a pass transistor logic based full adder carry circuit demonstrates that TFET buffer increase the output swing leading to full swing thereby enhancing its reliability and efficiency.

**Acknowledgement.** The authors would like to thank the funding support from Department of Science and Technology (DST) SERC young scientist grant NO: SBFTP/ETA-0101/2014.

# References

1. Cristoloveanu, S., Wan, J., Zaslavsky, A.: A review of sharp-switching devices for ultra-low power applications. IEEE J. Electron Devices Soc. **4**(5), 215–226 (2016)
2. Pandey, R., Mookerjea, S., Datta, S.: Opportunities and challenges of tunnel FETs. IEEE Trans. Circuits Syst.-I **63**(12), 2128–2138 (2016)
3. Morris, D.H., Vaidyanathan, K., Avci, U.E., Liu, H., Karnik, T., Young, I.A.: Enabling high-performance heterogeneous TFET/CMOS logic with novel circuits using TFET unidirectionality and low-$V_{DD}$ operation In: IEEE Symposium on VLSI Technology, pp. 1–2, June 2016
4. Nunez, J., Avedillo, M.: Comparative analysis of projected tunnel and CMOS transistors for different logic application areas. IEEE Trans. Electron Devices **63**(12), 5012–5020 (2016)
5. Kaushal, G., Subramanyam, K., Rao, S.N., Vidya, G., Ramya, R., Shaik, S., Vaddi, R.: Design and performance benchmarking of steep-slope tunnel transistors for low voltage digital and analog circuits enabling self-powered SoCs In: IEEE International Conference on SoC Design (ISOCC), pp. 32–33, November 2014
6. Choi, W.Y.: Miller effect suppression of tunnel field-effect transistors (TFETs) using capacitor neutralization. IET Electron. Lett. **52**(8), 659–661 (2016)
7. Abdi, D., Kumar, M.J.: Controlling ambipolar current in tunneling FETs using overlapping gate-on-drain. IEEE J. Electron Devices Soc. **2**(6), 187–190 (2014)
8. Sahay, S., Kumar, M.J.: Controlling the drain side tunneling width to reduce ambipolar current in tunnel FETs using hetero dielectric BOX. IEEE Trans. Electron Devices **62**(11), 3882–3886 (2015)
9. Pal, A., Sachid, A., Gossner, H., Rao, V.R.: Insights into the design and optimization of tunnel-FET devices and circuits. IEEE Trans. Electron Devices **58**(4), 1045–1053 (2011)
10. Subramanyam, K., Shaik, S., Vaddi, R.: Tunnel FET based low voltage static vs dynamic logic families for energy efficiency. In: IEEE International Symposium on VLSI Design and Test, pp. 1–2, August 2014
11. Shaik, S., Krishna, K.S.R., Vaddi, R.: Circuit and architectural co-design for reliable adder cells with steep slope tunnel transistors for energy efficient computing. In IEEE International Conference on VLSI Design and Embedded Systems (VLSID), pp. 306–311, January 2016
12. Cavalheiro, D., Moll, F., Valtchev, S.: Insights into tunnel FET-based charge pumps and rectifiers for energy harvesting applications. IEEE Trans. Very-Large Scale Integr. (VLSI) Syst. **25**(3), 988–997 (2017)
13. Sedighi, B., HU, X.S., Liu, H., Nahas, J., Niemier, M.: Analog circuit design using tunnel-FETs. IEEE Trans. Circuits Syst. I Regul. Pap. **62**(1), 39–48 (2015)
14. Liu, H., Vaddi, R., Narayanan, V., Datta, S.: Power rectifier using tunneling field effect transistor, U.S. Patent, 12 July 2016
15. Penn State University: Verilog-A Models for Heterojunction Tunnel FETs. http://www.ndcl.ee.psu.edu/downloads.asp
16. Vallabhaneni, H., Japa, A., Shaik, S., Krishna, K.S.R., Vaddi R.: Designing energy efficient logic gates with hetero junction tunnel FETs at 20 nm. In: IEEE Transaction on Electron Devices sponsored Device, Circuit, System Conference, India, pp. 1–5 (2014)
17. Liu, H., Li, X., Vaddi, R., Ma, K., Datta, S., Narayanan, V.: Tunnel FET RF rectifier design for energy harvesting applications. IEEE J. Emerg. Sel. Top. Circuits Syst. **4**(4), 400–411 (2014)
18. Japa, A., Vallabhaneni, H., Vaddi, R.: Reliability enhancement of a steep slope tunnel transistor based ring oscillator designs with circuit interaction. IET Circuits Devices Syst. **10**(6), 522–527 (2016)

19. Kim, S.H., Jacobson, Z., Patel, P., Hu, C., Liu, T.-J.K.: Tunnel FET based pass-transistor logic for ultra-low power applications. In: 2011 IEEE Device Research Conference (DRC), pp. 133–134, June 2011
20. Rabaey, J.M., Chandrakasan, A., Nikolic, B.: Digital Integrated Circuits: A Design Perspective, 2nd edn. Prentice Hall, Upper Saddle River (2002)

# An Efficient VLSI Architecture for PRESENT Block Cipher and Its FPGA Implementation

Jai Gopal Pandey[1(✉)], Tarun Goel[2], and Abhijit Karmakar[1]

[1] CSIR - Central Electronics Engineering Research Institute, Pilani, India
{jai,abhijit}@ceeri.res.in
[2] Academy of Scientific and Innovative Research (AcSIR),
CSIR-CEERI Campus, New Delhi, India

**Abstract.** Lightweight cryptography plays an essential role for emerging authentication-based pervasive computing applications in resource-constrained environments. In this paper, we have proposed resource-efficient and high-performance VLSI architectures for PRESENT block cipher algorithm for the two key lengths 80-bit and 128-bit, namely PRESET-80 and PRESENT-128. The FPGA implementations of these architectures have been done on LUT-6 technology based Xilinx Virtex-5 XC5VFX70T-1-FF1136 FPGA device. These architectures have a latency of 33 clock cycles, run at a maximum clock frequency of 306.84 MHz and provide throughput of 595.08 Mbps. They have been compared with the two different established architectures. It has been observed that the PRESENT-80 architecture consumes 20.3% lesser FPGA slices and there is a gain of 25.4% in throughput. Similarly, the PRESENT-128 architecture requires 20.7% lesser FPGA slices alongwith a reduction in the latency by 27.7% and an overall increase of throughput by 69.1%.

**Keywords:** Lightweight cryptography · PRESENT · Block cipher
VLSI architectures · FPGAs

## 1 Introduction

The modern-day cyber physical systems (CPS) and the internet of things (IoT) infrastructures heavily rely on extensive deployment of tiny computing devices for sensing, computing, controlling and communication purposes [1, 2]. The scope of these devices is widespread; ranging from consumer items to virtually anything. These devices form a pervasive computing infrastructure with an intelligent ecosystem. Uninterrupted system availability, minimal power consumption, an adequate level of data security, resource-efficient hardware architectures, low cost and quick time-to-market are the essential desirables of this ecosystem. Insatiable demands on the system design metrics make the system development task more complex and challenging.

In emerging applications such as smart cities, smart grid, digital locker, connected cars, etc., secure communication is utmost essential. It requires a mechanism, which ensures that unauthorized persons or machines cannot access the communicated information. For securing electronic data communication, cryptography plays an essential role. It

© Springer Nature Singapore Pte Ltd. 2017
B. K. Kaushik et al. (Eds.): VDAT 2017, CCIS 711, pp. 270–278, 2017.
https://doi.org/10.1007/978-981-10-7470-7_27

is a technique which ensures secrecy and the authenticity of electronic data transfer in any insecure channel. In cryptography, the encryption operation is used to convert data into a secure form, known as ciphertext.

The cryptographic process is used for authentication in many emerging applications such as in bank cards, wireless telephones, pay-TV, etc. It is also used for making the access control in many systems such as car locks, lifts, electronic gadgets and many more [3]. In these omnipresent smart devices, there is always a need of high-performance implementation of lightweight cryptographic algorithms for ensuring security in resource constrained environment. Hardware-based security solutions with symmetric key cryptography algorithms are ideally suited to meet the IoT security challenges for the very low area and energy requirements [2]. Thus, resource-constrained hardware architectures of lightweight ciphers are very essential. In a survey of [3], it is emphasized that efficient implementation of the ciphers are closely dependent on the selection of appropriate architectures as they result in low implementation complexity and high performance in actual realization. In the context of lightweight cryptography, ISO/IEC 29192-2 has standardized symmetric block cipher algorithm PRESENT in the year 2012 [4]. It provides adequate security goals alongwith hardware-oriented performance attributes which makes it a prominent choice for developing lightweight cryptographic applications [5]. Some of the related work is described below.

## 1.1 Related Work

The architectural exploration for the PRESENT block cipher with serial, iterative and parallel variants is given in [6]. Further, an investigation of the architectural design space exploration using Spartan-III FPGA can be found in [7]. An FPGA implementation of PRESENT cipher is reported in [8] that uses 117 slices of the Xilinx Spartan-3 XC3S50 FPGA device. Here, a throughput of 28.46 Mbps has been obtained at the maximum frequency of 114 MHz. Two different RAM-based implementations of PRESENT cipher are provided in [9]. Here, the first design occupies 83 slices and the second design consumes 85 slices of Xilinx Spartan XC3S50 device. These realizations produce a throughput of 6.03 Kbps and 5.13 Kbps at 100 kHz system clock respectively. A 8-bit datapath based implementation is provided in [10]. The design consumes 62 slices of the Xilinx Virtex-5 XC5VLX50 device and provides latency of 295 clock cycles with a throughput of 51.32 Mbps at the maximum frequency of 236.574 MHz. One of the implementations using 64-bit datapath, which utilizes 74 slices of the Xilinx Spartan-6 XC6SLX16-3CSG324C FPGA device is provided in [11]. Here, at a maximum clock frequency of 221.63 MHz and with 33 clock latency, a throughput of 221.63 Mbps is obtained. Similar to this a 64-bit datapath based architecture has been synthesized on 87 slices of the Xilinx Virtex-5 XC5VLX50 FPGA device in [12]. Here latency of 47 clocks, maximum clock frequency 221.64 MHz and a throughput of 341.64 Mbps have been reported. In the following section, we provide contributions of this paper.

## 1.2 Our Contributions

In this paper, we propose an efficient VLSI architecture for the PRESENT block cipher. Based on the key length of 80-bit and 128-bit, we provide two different variants of the architecture. These architectures are represented as *Proposed_80* and *Proposed_128* respectively. In both the architectures, the required S-box($S$) is realized by an area-optimized combinational logic datapath. These architectures are synthesized on Xilinx Virtex-5 XC5VFX70T-1-FF1136 FPGA device. The first architecture (with 80-bit key) utilizes 0.51% FPGA slices and the second architecture (with 128-bit key) uses 0.62% of FPGA slices. Here, both the architectures have a latency of 33 clock cycles, runs at a maximum clock frequency of 306.84 MHz and provides throughput of 595.08 Mbps.

Further, the proposed architectures are compared with the established architectures of [11, 12] with 6-input look-up table (LUT-6) technology based FPGAs [13]. Here, the standard platform and the devices with the same device family alongwith the same speed grades are considered for comparisons. For this purpose, the architectures are synthesized on two different FPGA devices of LUT-6 based technology. These devices are Xilinx Spartan-6 XC6SLX16-3CSG324C [11] and Virtex-5 XC5VLX50 [12] FPGAs. By experimental results, it is found that in comparison to the architecture of [11], the *Proposed_80* consumes 20.3% lesser FPGA slices and there is a gain of 25.4% in throughput. Similarly, in comparison to 128-bit key architecture [12], it requires 20.7% lesser FPGA slices and reduction in the latency by 27.7% thus, an overall increase of throughput by 69.1% is observed.

Rest of this paper is organized as follows: in Sect. 2, an overview of the PRESENT algorithm is given. Section 3 describes the proposed architecture for the PRESENT cipher. Section 4 provides experimental results and comparisons with the established architectures. Finally, conclusions are drawn in Sect. 5.

## 2 The PRESENT Algorithm

The PRESENT algorithm operates on the block size of 64-bit. It supports two key lengths of 80-bit and 128-bit. The algorithm is based on the SP-network and consists of 31 rounds [5]. Each of the 31 round consists of an XOR operation, which is required to introduce a round key $K_i$ for $0 \leq i \leq 31$ in which $K_{31}$ is used for the post-whitening operation. In addition to that, there is a linear bitwise permutation layer and a non-linear substitution layer based operation. The non-linear layer uses a single 4-bit S-box which is applied 16-times in parallel in each round. The algorithm requires mainly four functions, which are: Key Scheduling, AddRoundKey, *sboxlayer* and *p-layer* [5].

## 3 An Architecture for PRESENT Block Cipher

The proposed architecture for the PRESENT block cipher is shown in Fig. 1. To save area and compute-time we have considered the iterative type of architecture. Here, 64-bit datapath is chosen that provides optimal trade-off in terms of area, power and latency. The three main components of the architecture are: encryption engine, key scheduling and a controller. The key scheduling block takes 80-bit or 128-bit input key and generates thirty one round keys for the thirty one individual rounds of the cipher.

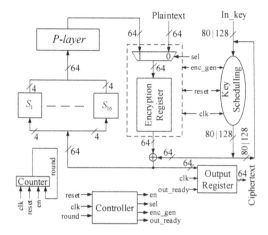

**Fig. 1.** Proposed architecture for the PRESENT cipher.

### 3.1 Datapath of PRESENT Architecture

The architecture shown in the Fig. 1 consists of a 64-bit *Encryption Register*, which is used to store the internal states of encryption operation. A 64-bit state register is used to store the internal state alongwith an 80-bit register (*Proposed_80*) or 128-bit key register (*Proposed_128*) for storing the intermediate round key. In addition to that one 64-bit and another 80-bit (or 128-bit) multiplexers are used to switch the data between load phase and round computation phase. The datapath contains *sboxlayer* (16 S-boxes) and one S-box (*Proposed_80*) or two S-boxes (*Proposed_128*) for key scheduling. Alongwith this, one 64-bit XOR gate, 5-bit XOR gate and a 5-bit up-counter are also used. Here, the S-box(S) is realized by an area-optimized combinational logic circuit.

In the proposed architecture the inputs and outputs are registered. For this, 64-bit register is used to get the ciphertext at the output. By this, the output gets synchronized with the last round. The latency can further be reduced by one more clock cycle if we do not want the output to be registered. However, the register is added to reduce the control logic and for synchronization of output with the last round. After completion of all the rounds, registered output is available after thirty three clock cycles. The main advantage of this architecture is that there is a reduction in the latency alongwith efficient utilization of hardware resources.

Plaintext is loaded in the first clock cycle, in the next clock cycle multiplexer switches the data and then for next 31 cycles all intermediate states are computed. Data is available at the *Encryption Register* and is mixed with intermediate round key. Further, the mixed state is passed to *sboxlayer* for state processing, which provides 64-bit data concurrently to *p-layer* and subsequently, it is passed to the *Encryption Register* through the multiplexer. In the last clock cycle, ciphertext is available at output register. Thus, here, a total of $1 + 31 + 1 = 33$ clock cycles are required to encrypt a single block of 64-bit plaintext.

## 3.2   Architecture for the Key Scheduling Process

Key processing unit works on-the-fly with each round. A 64-bit register stores the round key, the first leftmost 64-bit of the key register is XORed with the intermediate state. At the first clock, the input key is loaded into the key register as shown in Fig. 2.

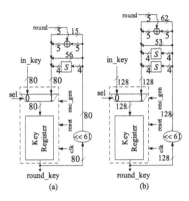

**Fig. 2.** The key-scheduling process in the PRESENT cipher (a) with 80-bit input key (b) with 128-bit input key.

## 3.3   Controller for Encryption Operation

A controller shown in Fig. 3, generates four control signals which are *en*, *enc_gen*, *sel* and *out_ready*. In state $S_0$ the counter is enabled through *en* signal and the inputs are loaded when *sel* = '0'. In state $S_1$ the multiplexers are switched as *sel* gets logic '1'. The *enc_gen* signal is used to start the intermediate operations by enabling the encryption and key registers. The state remains in $S_1$ until counter value reaches 31. Then, the state is switched to state $S_2$ where the counter is disabled through *en* = '0' and *out_ready* signal becomes logic '1'. In the next cycle, ciphertext is available through output register.

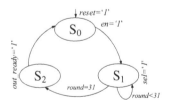

**Fig. 3.** FSM for the PRESENT cipher.

# 4 Experimental Results and Discussions

The proposed architectures are implemented in the VHDL language, and synthesized using Xilinx Design Suite 14.7 for the Virtex-5 XC5VFX70T-1-FF1136 FPGA device on Xilinx ML-507 platform. The device utilization is given in Table 1. Here, the architecture *Proposed_80* utilizes 0.51% FPGA slices and the architecture *Proposed_128* utilizes 0.62% of FPGA slices. The IOBs utilization in the *Proposed_80* architecture is 32.81% and in *Proposed_128* architecture it is 40.31%. Here, both the architectures have the latency of 33 clock cycles, runs at a maximum clock frequency of 306.84 MHz, consumes 23.75 mW power and provide throughput of 595.08 Mbps.

**Table 1.** Device utilization summary for Xilinx Virtex-5 XC5VFX70T-1-FF1136 FPGA.

| Elements | Available resources | Resource utilization *Proposed_80* | Resource utilization *Proposed_128* |
|---|---|---|---|
| Slice LUTs | 44800 | 218 | 266 |
| Slice registers | 44800 | 215 | 263 |
| Total slices | 11200 | 57 | 69 |
| Bonded IOBs | 640 | 210 | 258 |
| Latency | – | 33 | 33 |
| Max.freq. (MHz) | – | 306.84 | 306.84 |
| Throughput (Mbps) | – | 595.08 | 595.08 |

Performance of the design is evaluated in terms of latency, maximum frequency and *throughput* = (max. *freq.* × *total no. of bits*)/ *latency*. To compare the work with the implementation of [11, 12] which uses LUT-6 technology based FPGAs, the design is synthesized for two different Xilinx devices namely, Spartan-6 XC6SLX16-3CSG324C [11] and Virtex-5 XC5VLX50 [12].

Architectural comparisons between *Proposed_80* and [11] is given in Table 2. In comparison to [11], the proposed architecture requires 20.3% lower FPGA slices. Alongwith the efficient utilization of the device resources, the performance of the architecture has also improved. In comparison to [11], the proposed architecture is able to work on an increased maximum frequency by 25.4%, and thus, there is a gain in the throughput by 25.4%.

**Table 2.** Comparison of resource utilization between proposed architecture and architecture [11] on Xilinx Spartan-6 XC6SLX16-3CSG324C FPGA device.

| Elements | Available resources | Architecture (PRE) [11] | *Proposed_80* |
|---|---|---|---|
| Slice LUTs | 9112 | 229 | 221 |
| Slice registers | 18224 | 136 | 224 |
| Total slices | 2278 | 74 | 59 |
| Latency | – | 33 | 33 |
| Max. freq. (MHz) | – | 221.63 | 278.00 |
| Throughput (Mbps) | – | 429.83 | 539.15 |

In the second implementation, in line with [12], we have used 128-bit key size. The synthesis results of the implementations are shown in Table 3. As evident from the table, the proposed architecture requires 20.7% lesser FPGA slices in comparison to the architecture of [12]. Alongwith LUT-FF pair utilization by 96%, we also get improvements in the performance. In the proposed architecture the latency has also reduced by 27.7% and there is an increase of 22.3% in the maximum frequency. The decrease in latency and increase in the maximum frequency result in an overall increase of 69.1% in the throughput which is a significant improvement.

**Table 3.** Comparison of resource utilization between proposed architecture and architecture [12] on Xilinx Virtex-5 XC5VLX50 FPGA device.

| Elements | Available resources | Architecture (iterative) [12] | *Proposed_128* |
|---|---|---|---|
| Slice LUTs | 28800 | 285 | 271 |
| Slice registers | 28800 | 200 | 263 |
| Total slices | 7200 | 87 | 69 |
| Latency | – | 47 | 34 |
| Max. freq. (MHz) | – | 250.89 | 306.84 |
| Throughput (Mbps) | – | 341.64 | 577.58 |

The Virtex-5 XC5VLX50 device as considered in [12] offers 220 I/O pins. For the purpose of comparison with [12], the 128-bit key is brought into the datapath using two clock cycles, thus, incurring an increased latency of 1 clock. As per the iterative architecture of [12], 8-bit input is supplied to 64-bit datapath at a time, thus requiring a total of 16 clock cycles to bring the 128-bit key. Apart from this, it requires 8 more clock cycles for providing 64-bit ciphertext output. In comparison, the proposed architecture completes the processing from plaintext to ciphertext in 34 clock cycles. The design has also been compared with some other popular implementations using LUT-6 technology across different FPGA devices. The 64-bit implementations of PRESENT that are considered for comparison are: iterative architecture [10] denoted as *Iterative:Tay*; basic implementation (PRE) [11], denoted as *PRE:Nino*; the area-optimized design of [11] as *PRE_O1:Nino*; the serial implementation of [12] as *Serial:Hanely*; and the iterative realization of [12] as *Iterative:Hanely*.

A comparison of latency vs. number of slices consumed is shown in Fig. 4. In comparison to the latest implementation of *PRE:Nino* [11], a reduction in slice count is observed. Also, there is a reduction in both the latency and number of used slices with respect to *Iterative:Hanely* [12]. The implementation of *Iterative:Tay* uses slightly less slices in comparison to the *Proposed_128* however, there is an increase in the latency which can be observed in the Fig. 4.

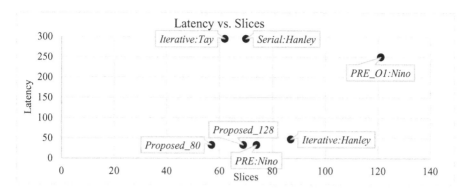

**Fig. 4.** Comparison of latency vs. consumed slices for different PRESENT implementations using LUT-6 based FPGA devices.

## 5 Conclusion

In this paper, we have presented two efficient VLSI architectures for the PRESENT block cipher with key sizes of 80-bit and 128-bit. The proposed architectures efficiently utilize the FPGA slices for providing data security under the resource-constrained environment. The design has been modeled in VHDL language and the architectures have been synthesized in the Xilinx Virtex-5 XC5VFX70T-1-FF1136 FPGA device. The presented architectures consume only 57 and 69 FPGA slices respectively. In comparison to other existing implementations, the proposed architectures show improvement in terms of hardware resources and provide high throughput, which makes them amenable for utilizing in lightweight cryptography applications.

## References

1. Lee, E.A., Seshia, S.A.: Introduction to Embedded Systems – A Cyber-Physical Systems Approach, 1st edn. (2011). http://LeeSeshia.org
2. Xu, T., Wendt, J.B., Potkonjak, M.: Security of IoT systems: design challenges and opportunities. In: IEEE/ACM International Conference on Computer Aided Design, pp. 417–423. IEEE, San Jose, 03 November 2014
3. Eisenbarth, T., Kumar, S., Paar, C., Poschmann, A., Uhsadel, L.: A survey of lightweight-cryptography implementations. IEEE Des. Test Comput. **24**(6), 522–533 (2007)
4. ISO/IEC 29192-2: Information tech.-Security techniques-Part 2:Block ciphers (2012)
5. Bogdanov, A., Knudsen, L.R., Leander, G., Paar, C., Poschmann, A., Robshaw, M.J.B., Seurin, Y., Vikkelsoe, C.: PRESENT: an ultra-lightweight block cipher. In: Paillier, P., Verbauwhede, I. (eds.) CHES 2007. LNCS, vol. 4727, pp. 450–466. Springer, Heidelberg (2007). https://doi.org/10.1007/978-3-540-74735-2_31
6. Rolfes, C., Poschmann, A., Leander, G., Paar, C.: Ultra-lightweight implementations for smart devices – security for 1000 gate equivalents. In: Grimaud, G., Standaert, F.-X. (eds.) CARDIS 2008. LNCS, vol. 5189, pp. 89–103. Springer, Heidelberg (2008). https://doi.org/10.1007/978-3-540-85893-5_7

7. Sbeiti, M., Michael, S., Poschmann, A., Paar, C.: Design space exploration of present implementations for FPGAS. In: 5th Southern Conference on Programmable Logic (SPL), pp. 141–145. IEEE, Sao Carlos, 1–3 April 2009
8. Yalla, P., Kaps, J.P.: Lightweight cryptography for FPGAs. In: International Conference on Reconfigurable Computing and FPGAs (ReConFig 2009), pp. 225–230. IEEE, Cancun, 09 December 2009
9. Kavun, E.B., Yalcin, T.: RAM-based ultra-lightweight FPGA implementation of PRESENT. In: International Conference on Reconfigurable Computing and FPGAs (ReConFig 2011), pp. 280–285. IEEE, Cancum, 30 November–2 December 2011
10. Tay, J.J., Wong, M.L.D., Wong, M.M., Zhang, C., Hijazin, I.: Compact FPGA implementation of PRESENT with Boolean S-Box. In: 6th Asia Symposium on Quality Electronic Design (ASQED), pp. 144–148. IEEE, Kula Lumpur, 04 August 2015
11. Lara-Nino, C.A., Morales-Sandoval, M., Diaz-Perez, A.: Novel FPGA-based low-cost hardware architecture for the PRESENT block cipher. In: 2016 Euromicro Conference Digital System Design (DSD), pp. 646–650. IEEE, Limassol, 31 August 2016
12. Hanley, N., O'Neill, M.: Hardware comparison of the ISO/IEC 29192-2 block ciphers. In: IEEE Computer Society Annual Symposium on VLSI (ISVLSI), pp. 57–62. IEEE, Amherst, 19–21 August 2012
13. Cosoroaba, A., Rivoallon, F.: Achieving higher system performance with the Virtex-5 family of FPGAs, Xilinx WP245, vol. 1 (2006)

# Investigation of TCADs Models for Characterization of Sub 16 nm $In_{0.53}Ga_{0.47}As$ FinFET

J. Pathak$^{(\boxtimes)}$ and A. Darji

Electronics Department, SVNIT, Surat, India
jaypathak050@gmail.com

**Abstract.** At sub 16 nm $In_{0.53}Ga_{0.47}As$ FinFET technology node the fabrication of device is quite complex in many sense. The study of such devices is only possible through TCAD simulations. To understand the behavior of such device the TCAD tool has to incorporate various simulation models related to physics of semiconductor and device geometry. In this paper, we have calibrated 50 nm $In_{0.53}Ga_{0.47}As$ FinFET using various simulation models with experimental results and then same models are used to characterize $I_d - V_g$ and $I_d - V_d$ characteristics and along with the short channel parameters for the sub 16 nm $In_{0.53}Ga_{0.47}As$ FinFET. The analysis is done on two types of devices i.e. Raised S/D with nitride spacers and without nitride spacers. Subthreshold slope SS (mV/dec) and DIBL (mV/V) for raised S/D $In_{0.53}Ga_{0.47}As$ FinFET with spacers is measured as 65.48 and 38.4 respectively, while without spacers it is 84.45 and 44.

**Keywords:** FinFET · TCAD · $In_{0.53}Ga_{0.47}As$ FinFET

## 1 Introduction

The recent era of technology in microelectronics industries are moving from bulk planar FET to FinFET. The continuous scaling beyond 32 nm technology node faces challenges for high-speed applications when we use silicon as material such as low electron mobility. The solution for such problem is III-V semiconductor compound materials, having high injection velocity and electron mobility [1] and 10 times larger than that of silicon devices. The III-V semiconductor material is also facing challenges when it is combined with oxides in FinFET structures.

The sub 16 nm technology node for $In_{0.53}Ga_{0.47}As$ based FinFET is governed by several effects which directly affects the performance. At sub 16 nm node the mobility, energy bandgap, effective mass, metal workfunction, doping etc., have major impact on the operation of the device. The effects have to be incorporated with proper and accurate models at simulation level so as to achieve the perfect characteristics when we go for fabrication of the device. The major contribution of the proposed work is to achieve the better model for sub 16 nm technology

© Springer Nature Singapore Pte Ltd. 2017
B. K. Kaushik et al. (Eds.): VDAT 2017, CCIS 711, pp. 279–286, 2017.
https://doi.org/10.1007/978-981-10-7470-7_28

node by calibrating the fabricated or experimental FinFET device on Technology Computer Aided Desgin (TCAD) tool and then try to extract desired characteristics. This approach provides the accurate parameters like energy bandgap of material, the mobility of carriers, velocity saturation of carriers etc. Hence by extracting the parameters, we can simulate new devices. This method helps us to validate our simulation results for the fabrication of a device with better accuracy. Here in this paper, we have gone through a process of simulating a device using various models for the characterization of sub 16 nm technology node for $In_{0.53}Ga_{0.47}As$ based FinFET. The outline of the paper is as follows: Sect. 2 is about device description of $In_{0.53}Ga_{0.47}As$ based FinFET, Sect. 3 is about simulation models used in TCAD to simulate the device, while in the last section the results obtained for sub 16 nm technology node for $In_{0.53}Ga_{0.47}As$ based FinFET are discussed.

## 2    Device Description

An n-channel $In_{0.53}Ga_{0.47}As$ device structure is taken as reference [2]. CMOS-compatible structural work and cross section schematic of the self-aligned $In_{0.53}Ga_{0.47}As$ FinFET are presented in Fig. 1(a) and (b), respectively. The $In_{0.53}Ga_{0.47}As$ is doped with $5 \times 10^{17}\,cm^{-3}$ concentration of Silicon. The buried oxide thickness is 37 nm and $HfO_2$ is used as oxide with capacitance equivalent thickness of 1.5 nm. The source/drain region doping level with Sn is $6 \times 10^{19}\,cm^{-3}$ and other parameters dimension like height and width of the fin is 15 and 17 nm, respectively. The Table 1 provides other parameters and dimensions information

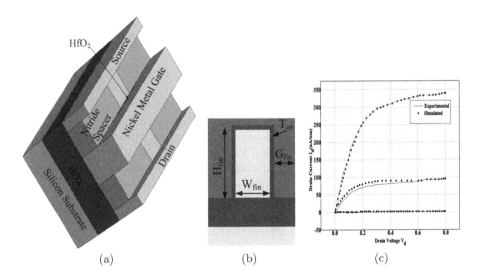

(a)                              (b)                              (c)

**Fig. 1.** InGaAs FinFET structure (a) 3-D view (b) Cross section view along A-A' (c) calibrated for output characteristics at $L_g = 50\,nm$ for $In_{0.53}Ga_{0.47}As$ FinFET.

**Table 1.** Parameters for In$_{0.53}$Ga$_{0.47}$As FinFET [2,6]

| Parameters | Symbol | Value | |
|---|---|---|---|
| | | ITRS parameters | Experimental data |
| Gate length | $L_g$ | 14 nm | 50 nm |
| Gate oxide thickness | $T_{ox}$ | 2.78 nm | 4.56 nm |
| Dielectric constant | $\epsilon_{ox}$ | 22 | 22 |
| Fin doping | $N_{ch}$ | $10^{19}$ cm$^{-3}$ | $5 \times 10^{17}$ cm$^{-3}$ |
| Fin height | $H_{fin}$ | 21.25 nm | 17 nm |
| Fin width | $W_{fin}$ | 8.5 nm | 15 nm |
| S/D doping | $N_d$ | $5 \times 10^{20}$ cm$^{-3}$ | $6 \times 10^{19}$ cm$^{-3}$ |
| Gate extension | $G_{fin}$ | 50 nm | 50 nm |
| Extended fin length | $L_{ext}$ | 20 nm | 12 nm |

of the device. The two different In$_{0.53}$Ga$_{0.47}$As FinFETs i.e. raised S/D with spacers and other is raised S/D without spacers are compared for analysis of the simulation models. These structures have been chosen because they have high *on* current as compared to conventional FinFET [3–5]. The description for 14 nm In$_{0.53}$Ga$_{0.47}$As FinFET are decided by International Technology Roadmap for Semiconductors (ITRS) [6]. The nitride spacer is introduced across the uncovered fins of the raised source/drain device. The body is doped with beryllium of concentration $1 \times 10^{17}$ cm$^{-3}$, while S/D is doped with silicon of concentration $5 \times 10^{19}$ cm$^{-3}$. The doping in body and S/D region is uniformly done throughout the device. The gate of the device is of nickel as it has low contact resistivity. The 3-D TCAD Synopsys tool is used to implement the device.

# 3   Device Calibration

The physics provides the proper description of the device characteristics and properties. The performance of FinFET device is depended on various models for getting accurate simulation results in TCADs. The accuracy of the model is defined when it is properly calibrated with experimental device. Here, the various physics models are used to calibrate the experimental 50 nm In$_{0.53}$Ga$_{0.47}$As FinFET [2]. Considering sub 16 nm technology node In$_{0.53}$Ga$_{0.47}$As FinFET, which has reached to quantum level so it incorporates various phenomenon like scattering effect, surface roughness effects, nonparabolicity nature etc. These physics models are to be introduced apart from basic FinFET device models for successful simulation of 14 nm gate length In$_{0.53}$Ga$_{0.47}$As FinFET. In$_{0.53}$Ga$_{0.47}$As FinFET with 50 nm gate length is calibrated for output characteristics with the help of following simulation models and it is shown in Fig. 1(c).

The carrier's mobility implies the device performance. The *on* current of In$_{0.53}$Ga$_{0.47}$As FinFET is affected by carrier mobility. The Lombardi mobility model is used to consider the mobility degradation caused due to surface roughness scattering and acoustic the scattering at channel/oxide interface [7]. In highly doped semiconductors, scattering of the carriers by charged impurity ions leads to degradation of the carrier mobility during operation of a device. The doping dependence model considers such effects in the carriers. For sub 16 nm devices, the carrier drift velocity is no longer proportional to the high electric field instead it saturates to a finite speed i.e. $v_{sat}$. The Canali model incorporates the high field saturation effect in the device.

The transport of majority charge carriers specially in presence of the electric field created by the voltage applied between the contacts, is so strong that the statistical distribution of particles (charge carriers) strongly deviates from the statistics applicable in equilibrium. The carriers distribution in device, due to electrostatic potential, electron affinity, band gap, effective mass and gradient of concentration are taken into consideration using Drift-Diffusion model (DD).

The process of generation and recombination exchange carriers between the conduction band and the valence band is very important in device physics, in particular, for sub 16 nm technology node devices. The generations and recombination process includes the appearance and vanishing of electrons and holes at the same locations. The Band-band tunneling, Shockley Read-Hall (SRH) and Trap assisted models are used in understanding the characterization.

The features of current sub 16 nm $In_{0.53}Ga_{0.47}As$ FinFET (oxide thickness, channel width) are of quantum- mechanical length scales. Therefore, the wave nature of electrons and holes can no longer be neglected. Hence, the Density-Gradient model (DG) is used to encounter the Quantization effect in the device. The width of fin is less than 10 nm in $In_{0.53}Ga_{0.47}As$ FinFET which directly affect the fitting factor in carrier transport models. The layer thickness below 10 nm in InGaAs materials has extra attention in multivalley band structure. The $L$ and $X$ valleys electron occupancy is crucial at high gate voltages in InGaAs material. The quantization parameter in transport model has to be optimized for proper carrier distribution in multi valleys.

In InGaAs material the band structure exhibit non-parabolic behavior at various valleys. InGaAs material reflects the nonparabolic nature which affects the effective mass of the material and carrier density in the device. The carrier distributions in different valleys affect the drain current in FinFET. The effect of nonparabolicity at sub 16 nm node is crucial in the performance of a device. The both quantization effects and nonparabolicity are essential when the device dimensions move to sub 16 nm $In_{0.53}Ga_{0.47}As$ FinFET devices.

The other models or statistics like Boltzmann statistics are used which governs the electron and hole densities. The Fermi-Dirac model is used for distribution of electrons carriers in channel region. The parameters like mobility, velocity saturation are extracted from the 50 nm channel length using above mentioned models to validate the experimental and simulation results [2]. The mobility of $3400\,cm^2/V.s$ and velocity saturation is around $5 \times 10^5$ cm/s have been observed. Apart from the *on* current models analysis the leakage current estimation is done using the BTBT tunneling. The parameters like subthreshold swing (SS) of

90 mV/dec and drain-induced barrier lowering (DIBL) of 60 mV/V is also achieved through calibration in TCAD which closely match with the experimental results of [2].

## 4   Results and Discussions

The transfer characteristics of sub 16 nm for the two different In$_{0.53}$Ga$_{0.47}$As FinFETs i.e. raised S/D with spacers and other is raised S/D without spacers are carried out using 3D TCAD SDEVICE Synopsys tool [8]. The *on* current calibration is done by introducing the mobility models, carrier transport model, quantum mechanical effects etc. The characterization of a device is also carried out in presence of surface scattering, interface roughness, an analytic nonparabolicity model for energy dispersion in valleys. The crystallographic orientation of the channel is considered (1, 0, 0). The effects of transverse optical phonon mode and coulomb scattering on the high-k gate oxide are also included. Finally, Fermi-Dirac statistics is considered in the simulation due to the high level of doping in their S/D region. The In$_{0.53}$Ga$_{0.47}$As-FinFET devices have significant effects of *off* currents. The *off*-current of 100 nA/μm is fixed to achieve other parameters of the devices. In short channel devices, the source-drain potential has a strong effect on the band bending over a channel region of the device. Hence, the threshold voltages and the subthreshold currents of short channel devices vary with the drain bias. The extraction of the threshold voltage for the device is done with the help of the transconductance method [9]. The threshold voltage is extracted using the assumption of ideal case where $I_d$ = 0 for $V_g < V_t$. With these assumptions $d^2 I_d / dV_g^2$ becomes infinity exactly at $V_g = V_t$. The assumption of $d^2 I_d / dV_g^2 = \infty$ is quiet impractical in real device so at $V_g = V_t$ the value of $d^2 I_d / dV_g^2$ becomes maximum. The Drain Induced Barrier Lowering (DIBL) and Subthreshold Swing (SS) is calculated using Eqs. 1 and 2. The $I_d - V_g$ and $I_d - V_d$ characteristics for 14 nm In$_{0.53}$Ga$_{0.47}$As FinFETs raised S/D without spacers and with spacers are shown in Figs. 2(a),(b) and Figs. 3(a),(b). The short channel parameters have been extracted from these characteristics and listed in Table 2. Parameters such $V_t$ and $I_{on}$ extracted from the characteristics follow the trend of ITRS roadmap [6] shows the accuracy of simulation model used for 14 nm gate length.

$$DIBL = \frac{\delta V_t}{\delta V_d} \tag{1}$$

$$SS = \frac{dV_g}{d(log_{10} I_{ds})} \tag{2}$$

The short channel effects in 14 nm In$_{0.53}$Ga$_{0.47}$As FinFETs with raised S/D structure in presence of spacers are improved as compared to simple raised S/D structure. The improvement can be understood by analyzing the electric field line in the channel. The Fig. 4 provides the condition of electric field lines in both devices and it is observed that the field lines in presence of spacers are high

**Table 2.** Short channel parameters.

|  | Raised source/drain | Raised source/drain with spacers |
|---|---|---|
| $I_{on}(uA/um)$ | 64.3 | 120.1 |
| $V_t$ | 0.18 | 0.2 |
| DIBL | 44 | 38.4 |
| SS | 84.45 | 65.48 |

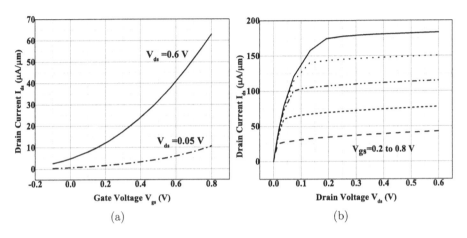

**Fig. 2.** Electrical characteristics for non spacer raised S/D device

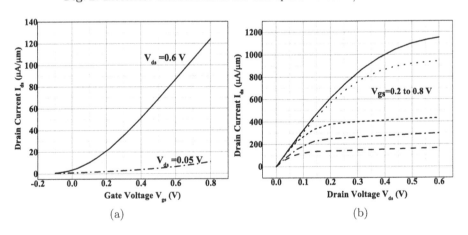

**Fig. 3.** Electrical characteristics for raised S/D structure with spacer.

at $V_g = V_{dd}$ which suggests that it has better control in on state as compared to non-spacers structures. The electric field lines in presence of spacers are more concentrated and higher compared to non-spacers structure. The fringing electric field lines at $V_g = V_{dd}$ provides extra control to the channel. The improvement

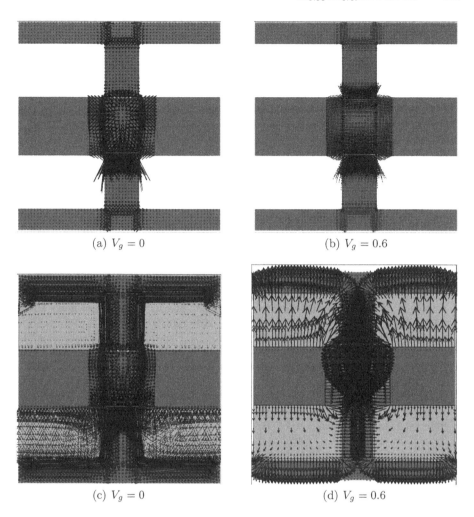

(a) $V_g = 0$                          (b) $V_g = 0.6$

(c) $V_g = 0$                          (d) $V_g = 0.6$

**Fig. 4.** Electric Field contour plot across the channel (a), (b) are for non spacer raised S/D device (c), (d) are raised S/D structure with spacer at $V_g = 0$ and $V_g = 0.6$

in the fringing field leads to higher electron concentration in channel region which indirectly increases the *on* current. The fringing electric field in device is originating from gate through spacer and terminating in the lightly doped channel and results in the change in potential and electron concentration. The large electric field results in severe band bending in the conduction band of the channel material and results into higher electron concentration across a channel. The spacers thus improves additional fringing field which bends the conduction band edge and results in increasing the electron concentration and potential across the channel. The improvement in the potential and electron concentration thus improves short channel effects like SS, DIBL, and $I_{on}$, which is evident from Table 2.

## 5    Conclusions

The $In_{0.53}Ga_{0.47}As$ FinFET at 14 nm node is simulated in TCAD by considering simulation models. The device characterization using these models provides better understanding regarding the behavior of device under various bias conditions. These simulation models have impact on accuracy of the characterization results. The simulation results show that the $In_{0.53}Ga_{0.47}As$ FinFET with 50 nm channel length closely follows the experimental results. The same simulation environment is used for characterization of sub 16 nm $In_{0.53}Ga_{0.47}As$ FinFET with and without spacers. The raised S/D $In_{0.53}Ga_{0.47}As$ FinFET with spacers has shown low short channel effects because of good control of gate on channel through fringing electric field between gate to S/D region. The improvement of 12.74% in DIBL and 22.45% in SS has been observed as compared to the conventional raised S/D $In_{0.53}$ $Ga_{0.47}As$ FinFET without spacers.

## References

1. Kalna, K., Seoane, N.: Benchmarking of scaled InGaAs implant-free nano MOS-FETs. IEEE Trans. Electron Devices **55**(9), 2297 (2008)
2. Djara, V., Deshpande, V., Sousa, M., Caimi, D., Czornomaz, L., Fompeyrine, J.: CMOS-compatible replacement metal gate InGaAs-OI FinFET with ION= 156 μA/μm at VDD=0.5 V and IOFF=100 nA/μm. IEEE Electron Device Lett. **37**(2), 169 (2016)
3. Sachid, A.B., Francis, R., Baghini, M.S., Sharma, D.K., Bach, K.H., Mahnkopf, R., Rao, V.R.: Sub-20 nm gate length FinFET design: can high-k spacers make a difference? In: Proceedings IEEE IEDM, pp. 1–4. IEEE (2008)
4. Tewari, S., Biswas, A., Mallik, A.: Impact of a spacer layer on the analog performance of asymmetric InP/InGaAs nMOSFETs. IEEE Trans. Electron Devices **63**(6), 2313 (2016)
5. Koley, K., Dutta, A., Syamal, B., Saha, S.K., Sarkar, C.K.: Subthreshold analog/RF performance enhancement of underlap DG FETs with high-k spacer for low power applications. IEEE Trans. Electron Devices **60**(1), 63 (2013)
6. ITRS. International Technology Roadmap for Semiconductors. http://www.itrs.net/Links/2009ITRS/Home2013.htm/ (2013)
7. Lombardi, C., Manzini, S., Saporito, A., Vanzi, M.: A physically based mobility model for numerical simulation of nonplanar devices. IEEE Trans. Comput. Aided Design Integr. Circuits Syst. **7**(11), 1164 (1988)
8. Synopsys Inc, Mountain View, CA 2016 (2016)
9. Ortiz-Conde, A., García-Sánchez, F.J., Muci, J., Barrios, A.T., Liou, J.J., Ho, C.S.: Revisiting MOSFET threshold voltage extraction methods. Microelectron. Reliab. **53**(1), 90 (2013)

# Hausdorff Distance Driven L-Shape Matching Based Layout Decomposition for E-Beam Lithography

Arindam Sinharay[(✉)], Pranab Roy, and Hafizur Rahaman

Indian Institute of Engineering Science and Technology, Shibpur, India
arindam.sinharay@gmail.com,
ronmarine14@yahoo.co.in, rahaman_h@yahoo.co.in

**Abstract.** Layout decomposition is a basic step in mask data preparation in e-beam lithography (EBL) writing. For larger throughput in EBL, L-shape-writing technique has recently been developed. It is termed as L-shape fracturing, similar in line with rectangular fracturing. However, implementation of this new technique may yield very thin/narrow features called slivers. For better manufacturability, it is preferable to minimize the overall sliver length. In this paper we propose a novel scheme based on Hausdorff distance metrics for L-shape fracturing with inherent sliver minimization. The proposed scheme starts with finding the concave corner vertices of input layout, and attempts to find a balanced partition of this set of concave corner points of the given layout. Subsequently, Hausdorff distance-based layout fracturing is performed. Experimental results demonstrate efficacy of our proposed algorithm.

**Keywords:** Layout decomposition · L-shape fracturing
Sliver minimization mechanism · Hausdorff distance metrics
E-Beam lithography

## 1 Introduction

E-Beam Lithography (EBL) [2] is widely adopted in the mask manufacturing. It has significant effects on the critical dimension (CD) and accuracy of printed image on wafer. As EBL is capable to generate accurate patterns, it is used in sub-22 nm technology nodes [3], and is well adopted in Double-patterning and Multiple-patterning lithography (DPL/MPL) [4–6] technology. To solve the above issues in manufacturing, a number of researchers proposed different optimization techniques [7–9]. VSB shots are generated for conventional EBL [12] when rectangular fracturing is considered. For faster writing, it is preferable to develop novel fracturing algorithms to generate L-shape in fractured layout. Theoretically, 50% of time and cost optimization in EBL writing can be achieved by adopting L-Shape fracturing technique. Layout fracturing problem is different from well-studied orthogonal polygon decomposition problem [1] in a geometrical computation domain. Each VSB shot should be greater than a pre-defined and fixed threshold value, $\delta$. A shot of width $< \delta$, causes sliver generation. Optimization of sliver [9] length is an important objective in layout fracturing. Several

B. K. Kaushik et al. (Eds.): VDAT 2017, CCIS 711, pp. 287–295, 2017.
https://doi.org/10.1007/978-981-10-7470-7_29

studies are made on rectangular fracturing [10–12, 14] techniques. In the work of [13] heuristic functions are considered for L-shape based decomposition directed towards horizontal decomposition only [13]. However, this may result in inefficient sliver optimization. Integer Linear Programming (ILP) based problem formulation is proposed by Kahng et al [10]. Matching based speed up technique for cost and time optimization are discussed in [9, 10]. Heuristic function driven rectangular shape manufacturing and sliver optimization is proposed by Ma et al [12]. The L-shape fracturing is comparatively a new approach in VSB technology. [15] Presents L-shape fracturing for circuit component partitioning. We incorporate the related concepts in L-shape fracturing for VSB writing. This paper considers L-shape fracturing problem in EBL domain for VSB writing. This geometric fracturing problem is applied to orthogonal polygons. A novel fixed point data clustering method is developed and applied with multiple objectives. At first, the concave corner points are partitioned in two groups with almost equal number of concave corner points. The next step is to choose partition with possible minimum number of computations required. A Hausdorff distance-based orthogonal polygon fracturing is then applied recursively to create L-shape and R-shape (rectangular) features.

The rest of the paper is organized as follows. Basic definitions of Haudorff Distance Metric and Hausdorff Distance Metric Matched L-shaped polygon are given respectively in Sects. 2 and 3. Haudorff distance based matching technique is elaborated in Sect. 4. Sections 5 and 6 respectively discuss the experimental results and the conclusion.

## 2 Haudorff Distance Metric

The Hausdorff distance is very natural distance measure for comparing shapes and patterns. In application domains like pattern recognition, shape matching etc. often, these types of measures are culminated with some numerical value indicating similarities and dissimilarities. Therefore, these geometric shapes are compact subset of $\mathbb{R}^2$. Directly referring Hausdorff distance from H. Alt et al [3], two compact geometric objects, P and Q are considered. The Haudorff distance of P and Q is measured for each point on one object, compared with the closest point on the other and then maximizing over all these values. More formally, the Hausdorff distance between P and Q is defined as

$$\hat{\delta}(P,Q) = max\left(\hat{\delta}(P,Q),\hat{\delta}(Q,P)\right),$$

Where $\hat{\delta}(P, Q) = max_{x\in P} \, min_{y\in Q}\|x, y\|$ = Euclidian distance between $(x,y)$ where $x\epsilon P$ and $y\epsilon Q$.

Throughout this paper, the underlying matric $\|x,y\|$ is considered as Euclidian metric, but many of the considerations presentenced in this paper are valid for other commonly used matrices, as well. As $\hat{\delta}(P,Q)$ is a measure of similarity between P and Q, the directed Hausdorff distance is interesting by itself. In present context, the R-shape tile and L-shape tile are to be matched with input orthogonal polygon (all these are convex polygons by definition (2)). The first result [20] was found in computing

Hausdorff distance between two convex polygons in $\mathbb{R}^2$. In [19] concerning matching of shapes under certain allowable matric value minimizing the Hausdorff distance or simplifying shapes within a certain tolerance with respect to the Hausdorff distance can be found. We propose a technique to compute the Hausdorff distance between the corner points of the polygon. We consider the concave corners of the polygon.

**Problem 1:-** (***Calculating Hausdorff distance between two clusters of fixed concave corner point data***). *Given two clusters A and B, having sets of fixed concave corner points {$a_1, a_2, ..., a_i$} and {$b_1, b_2, ....b_j$} with either i = j or |i-j| = 1. We have to find the maximum of all minimum distances between the sets A and B.*

**Problem 2:-** (***L-shape based layout decomposition***). *Given an input layout in the form of an orthogonal polygon, our objective is to fracture or decompose the orthogonal layout polygon into a set of L-shapes and/or R-shapes to minimize number of shots. The fracturing should be initiated from a Hausdorff distant concave corner vertex. The sliver length of fractured shots should be minimum.*

## 3   Hausdorff Distance Metric Matched L-Shaped Polygon

We know that an L-shape orthogonal polygon has – one concave point and five convex points. Clearly, this concave vertex point has two neighboring convex vertices. We name them according to the clockwise orientation as Left-Convex-Corner point (LCCP) which is the predecessor of concave vertex and the successor vertex as Right-Convex-Corner point (RCCP). We again notice that as the problem space deals with only orthogonal polygon, any concave vertex with its two neighboring convex vertices form a right-angled triangle. That means, each edge joining concave vertex and convex vertex incident 90° externally and 270° internally. Now, the triangle formed with these three points make a right angled triangle where edge connecting two convex vertices forms the hypotenuse of the triangle. Therefore, we can create a super scribed circle of this right angle triangle considering hypotenuse as the diameter. Let us denote it by d. With similar logic, we compute the super scribed circle with other three convex vertices and name the diameter as D.

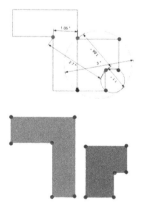

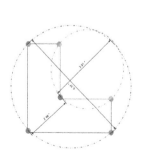

**Fig. 1.** Two super scribed circles touch internally

**Fig. 2.** Difference of two diameters & orthogonal polygon fracturing

*Observation 1:* The circum-circle with diameter d touches internally the circum-circle with diameter D (Fig. (1)).

*Observation 2:* Hausdorff distance point of the concave vertex of L-shaped polygon is just the opposite convex vertex. We name it $d_h(A,B)$.

*Observation 3:* Difference between 'D' and 'd' is equal to $d_h(A,B)$ (Fig. (2)).

**Lemma:** If A and B are two sets of points of concave vertices and convex vertices respectively then, $d_h(A,B) = D-d$; Where D = diameter of outer circle, d = diameter of inner circle.

We have classified the L-shape orthogonal polygons in two ways

- *Balanced L-shape*
- *Imbalanced L-shape*:-Imbalanced property can be further classified in terms of Height of L-shape.
  - **Height-Fatty L-Shape** (HFLS); **Breadth-Fatty L-Shape** (BFLS).

We have tested our Observation (1), (2), (3) in all possible types of L-shapes. All these observations have been tested true for all possible L-shapes.

We summaries' the properties of pattern L-shapes.

**Property 1:**   *It has one concave point and five convex points.*

**Property 2:**   $d_h(A,B) = D-d$.

Depending upon these two properties of L-shape orthogonal polygon, we propose the following theorem.

**Theorem 1:** If for a given orthogonal (Layout) polygon, P, there is an arbitrary concave vertex $v_{cc}$. Let $v_j$ be the Hausdorff distant concave vertex of $v_{cc}$ and the Hausdorff distance is marked by $d_h$. Then we can find a point on the perimeter of P which is cut by the circle having distant D computed as $D = d + d_h$, where d is distance of hypotenuse of right angle triangle with the points $v_{cc}$, LCCP of $v_{cc}$ and RCCP of $v_{cc}$.

# 4   Process of Layout Decomposition

Now we are going to implement our newly derived theorem in an orthogonal layout.

**STEP 1:** Let the given layout be $L_p$. It has 16 vertices. The number of concave vertex = 6. This layout fracturing procedure does not possess any reservation about the starting point. Here, in the test layout polygon, we have taken $V_{16}$ as the concave vertex imitation. We have taken the decision by considering the concave vertex having least value in their x-coordinate (Fig. (3)).

**STEP 2:** In this step, we have found out the immediate to convex vertices of $V_{16}$ (concave vertex under present consideration). $V_1$ is the LCC and $V_{15}$ is RCC. Again, we see that $V_{14}$ is a convex vertex and it is RCC of $V_{15}$.

**STEP 3:** HDD algorithm (no- x) returns $V_{13}$ as the answer to the query of the algorithm. Now, according to the proposed Theorem – (1), we have a new vertex point, $V_{17}$ as the left side neighbor of $V_1$. Therefore, the first decomposition of $L_p$

has been completed. After executing this step, we got two orthogonal layouts $L_{P1}$ and $L_{P2}$ as shown in Fig. 6.

We see that $L_{P1}$ is an orthogonal fractured layout having one concave vertex as $V_{16}$ and five convex vertices are $V_{15}$, $V_{14}$, $V_{13}$, $V_{15}$ and $V_1$. Therefore, it is an L-shape orthogonal polygon. On the other hand, $L_{P1}$ has 4 concave vertices. Therefore, $L_{P1}$ is not an L-shape polygon. Next, we call our proposed set of algorithm on $L_{P2}$. It has been shown in Fig. 7. After four successive calls, the given initial layout $L_P$ is decomposed into four individual polygons. Among them, three polygons are L-shapes and one is R-shape, as shown in Fig. 8.

The overall procedure can be formulated as HDD based-

- Corner point finding ().
- Corner point classification ().
- Finding point of initiation ().
- HDD point as the point of initiation ().
- Layout Decomposition ().

### 4.1   Process of Corner Point Finding and Classification

An orthogonal polygon is considered as an input data i.e. $L_p$. The purpose of finding the corner points are

(a) The set of corner points defines the layout polygon completely.
(b) From the any two neighboring corner points, an edge of the polygon can be computed.
(c) The classification of corner points (discussion is provided below (Fig. (4))) has to be initiated on set of corner points.

Let there be n number of corner points. Therefore, 2n numbers of data (one for x-coordinate and one for y-coordinate) have been taken in a form of circular Queue data structure. For examining the characteristic of $i^{th}$ corner point, we fetch out the duplet data of $(i+1)^{th}$ point and $(i-1)^{th}$ point. We have noticed that for $i^{th}$ point to be a concave point, one of the following four conditions to be satisfied.

$$
\begin{array}{ll}
\text{(i)} & \left(x^+ y^0 \wedge x^0 y^+\right) \\
\text{(ii)} & \left(x^- y^0 \wedge x^0 y^-\right) \\
\text{(iii)} & \left(x^0 y^+ \wedge x^- y^0\right) \\
\text{(iv)} & \left(x^0 y^+ \wedge x^+ y^0\right)
\end{array}
\left.\begin{array}{l} \\ \\ \\ \\ \end{array}\right\}
\text{Where}
\left[\begin{array}{ll}
+ & \text{indicates in increasein value} \\
- & \text{indicates decrease in value} \\
0 & \text{indicates no change in value} \\
\wedge & \text{indicates both conditions to be satisfied}
\end{array}\right.
$$

In the Fig. 5, Arrows indicates the directions of x and y coordinates to and from the considered point. Shadow in the above figure signifies the outer regions of the layout polygon (Fig. 4). We place a pointer to each concave point (coordinates of each point) and store them in an array of pointers. The first group of corner points are those who subtend $90^0$ angle internally. They are called convex corner points (as defined in Definition N). The second group corner points are observed to have subtended $270^0$ internal angle. They are termed as concave corner points.

To compute the convex corner point, we consider the clockwise reading direction (the other direction can as well be considered). We have observed that basic former cases may be happened as shown in the Fig. (4).

We can summaries the above continued form cases algebraically as below:

(a)  $x^o y^+ \wedge x^+ y^o$, b) $x^o y^- \wedge x^- y^o$, c) $x^+ y^o \wedge x^o y^-$, d) $x^- y^o \wedge x^o y^+$

Here $x^+$ (or $y^+$) indicates increase in x (or y) value.

Similarly, $x^-$ (or $y^-$) indicates decrease in x (or y) value and $x^o$ (or $y^o$) indicates no change in x (or y) value.

## 4.2    To Find the Point of Initiation of Layout Fracturing Process

Our algorithmic layout decomposition method intends to decompose the $L_p$ into maximum number of L-shape and R-shape, combined leading to an optimality so that sliver can be minimized as well as shot count can be minimized. B. Yu [16] has shown that the decomposition is preferred from a concave point.

Because, by [15], we have got to know that total number of corner point $t_C$, total number of concave corner point $C_c$ is defined by the following relation

$$t_C = 2C_c + 4$$

From this equation, we can summarize the following:

(a)  R-shape has no concave corner points with total 4 corner points.
(b)  L-shape has 1 concave corner points with total 6 corner points.
(c)  On L-shape must have two convex corner points on both sides as neighboring corner points.

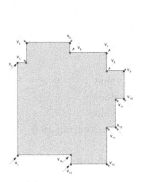

**Fig. 3.** Orthogonal layout polygon

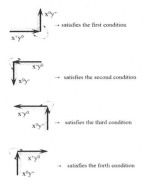

**Fig. 4.** Different types of concave corners

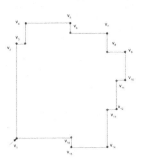

**Fig. 5.** Convex and concave corner points of layout polygon outline

Convex and Concave Corner Points of Layout Polygon outline.

With these observations and our derived property on L-shape (discussed in Sect. (3)), we have pointed out the following as the precondition of initiation of layout fracturing:

1. We shall start decomposition, considering at least any of concave corner points.
2. For L-shape decomposition, a concave corner points should have two consecutive convex corner points as the both side as neighbor points.
3. We can perform $H_{cut}$ or $V_{cut}$ from the HDD concave corner point, provided the cut not producing sliver.
4. We have started our search for such concave corner point having least x-coordinate followed by least y-coordinate.

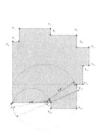 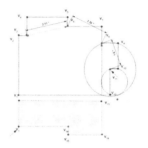 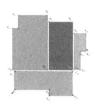

**Fig. 6.** Initiation of layout fracture technique

**Fig. 7.** Layout after first iteration

**Fig. 8.** Final fractured form of layout

In the Fig. (6), $v_{16}$ has been considered as the point of initiation of layout decomposition process. We define this point of initiation of cut as the HDD point of initiation. In the Fig. (6), $v_{13}$ is the above defined point.

### 4.3    Layout Fracturing Process

By Theorem (1), an arbitrary concave vertex $v_{cc}$ has been found out. $v_{16}$ is that concave vertex. Then the Hausdorff distant concave vertex from $v_{16}$ has been computed. In the current testing layout polygon, $v_{13}$ is the Hausdorff Distant point. Then a new point of intersection of outer circle with the edge $(v_1, v_2)$ has been found out. Let this new point be named as $v_{17}$. Joining $(v_{13}, v_{17})$ we segregate the input layout $L_p$. An L-shape tile containing the corner points $(v_1, v_{17}, v_{13}, v_{14}, v_{15}, v_{16})$ has been formed and the resulting rest of the vertices along with newly induced $v_{17}$ forms $L'_{p1}$. As we know, an L-shape tile contains six corner points, no further decomposition is needed on the polygon formed by $(v_1, v_{17}, v_{13}, v_{14}, v_{15}, v_{16})$ set of vertices. Therefore, in the recursive call, only $L'_{p1}$ will be processed. Successive decomposition has finally resolved by returning three L-shape tiles and one R-shape tiles as optimum result. Hence our proposed method successfully decomposed the input polygon into $L_{p1}$, $L_{p2,}$ $L_{p3}$ (all L-shape tiles) and $L_{p4}$ as rectangular tile.

## 5 Experimental Results

Experiments for the proposed Hausdorff Distance Driven L-shape fracturing algorithm are performed using MATLAB 2014a computational geometry toolbox. The experiments are carried out on Intel core I3-2330 M processor machine on Windows 2007 operating system with 8 GB DDR3 RAM. ISCAS 85&89 benchmarks are scaled down to 28 nm logic nodes followed by accurate lithographic simulation performed to Metal 1 layers. Table 1 summarizes the results of experiments for the proposed algorithms. The approaches in [13] have been carried over in present experimental environment and the results are compared with the newly developed algorithm under consideration. All fracturing methods are evaluated based on sliver length with respect to the threshold distance as 5 nm. For each benchmark, the numbers of shots and slivers are noted for the proposed method and the method described in [13]. It is interesting to note that for all the benchmarks considered, our proposed method performs better than [13], and are better than the results reported in [16] for most of the benchmarks. Moreover, CPU time requirements in our cases are quite reasonably small.

**Table 1.** Results and comparison

| Circuits | Polygon | [13] | | [16] | | HDD algorithm | |
|----------|---------|------|-------------|------|-------------|---------------|-------------|
| | | Shot# | Sliver (μm) | Shot# | Sliver (μm) | Shot# | Sliver (μm) |
| **C432** | **1109** | 6898 | 48.3 | 4214 | 7.4 | **3858** | **5.76** |
| **C499** | **2216** | 13397 | 96 | 8112 | 11.8 | **7550** | **11.14** |
| **C1355** | **3262** | 23283 | 185.2 | 13936 | 24.8 | **13559** | **20.22** |
| **C2670** | **7933** | 56619 | 525.4 | 34102 | 114.8 | **31361** | **67.55** |
| **C7552** | **21253** | 151643 | 1334.6 | 91157 | 290.7 | **89755** | **144.84** |
| **S1488** | **4611** | 37126 | 303.7 | 22099 | 31.6 | **21251** | **38.59** |
| **S38417** | **67696** | 454307 | 4040.2 | 275054 | 729 | **259514** | **505.69** |
| **S35932** | **26267** | 163956 | 1470.4 | 100629 | 284 | **83361** | **199.81** |
| **S38584** | **168319** | 1096363 | 10045.2 | 666906 | 1801.7 | **632787** | **1206.37** |

## 6 Conclusion

In this paper, we proposed an algorithm for EBL with the new Hausdorff Distance Driven L-shape based Layout fracturing for sliver minimization. This is a new approach for integrating Hausdorff distance metric. It has shown best metric for sliver minimization as evident from experimental results. This approach claims to be the first algorithmic endeavour with the Hausdorff metric in EBL L-shape decomposition with sliver minimization. To the best of our knowledge, the researchers of [16] first introduced the concept of L-shape layout decomposition. To find out a new way of L-shape fracturing, we have developed a parallel and independent method. Proposed method has the same computational complexity as of [16].

# References

1. O'Rourke, J.: Orthogonal polygon. In: Art Gallery Theorems and Algorithms, pp. 31–80. Oxford University Press (1987). Chapter 2
2. Pain, L., Jurdit, M., Todeschini, J., Manakli, S., Icard, B., Minghetti, B., Bervin, G., Beverina, A., Leverd, F., Broekaart, M., Gouraud, P., Jonghe, V.D., Brun, P., Denorme, S., Boeuf, F., Wang, V., Henry, D.: Electron beam direct write lithography flexibility for ASIC manufacturing: an opportunity for cost reduction. In: SPIE, vol. 5751 (2005)
3. Arisawa, Y., Aoyama, H., Uno, T., Tanaka, T.: EUV flare correction for the half-pitch 22 nm node. In: SPIE, vol. 7636 (2010)
4. Kahng, A.B., Park, C.-H., Xu, X., Yao, H.: Layout decomposition for double patterning lithography. In: IEEE/ACM International Conference on Computer-Aided Design (ICCAD), pp. 465–472 (2008)
5. Yu, B., Yuan, K., Zhang, B., Ding, D., Pan, D.Z.: Layout decomposition for triple patterning lithography. In: IEEE/ACM International Conference on Computer-Aided Design (ICCAD), pp. 1–8 (2011)
6. Jiang, S., Ma, X., Zakhor, A.: A recursive cost-based approach to fracturing. In: Proceedings of SPIE, vol. 7973 (2011)
7. Sahouria, E., Bowhill, A.: Generalization of shot definition for variable shaped e-beam machines for write time reduction. In: Proceedings of SPIE, vol. 7823 (2010)
8. Elayat, A., Lin, T., Sahouria, E., Schulze, S.F.: Assessment and comparison of different approaches for mask write time reduction. In: SPIE, vol. 8166 (2011)
9. Yuan, K., Yu, B., Pan, D.Z.: E-Beam lithography stencil planning and optimization with overlapped characters. IEEE Trans. Comput.-Aided Des. (TCAD/ICS) **31**(2), 167–179 (2012)
10. Kahng, A.B., Xu, X., Zelikovsky, A.: Yield-and cost-driven fracturing for variable shaped-beam mask writing. In: Proceedings of SPIE, vol. 5567 (2004)
11. Kahng, A.B., Xu, X., Zelikovsky, A.: Fast yield-driven fracture for variable shaped-beam mask writing. In: Proceedings of SPIE, vol. 6283 (2006)
12. Dillon, B., Norris, T.: Case study: the impact of VSB fracturing. In: Proceedings of SPIE, vol. 7028 (2008)
13. Ma, X., Jiang, S., Zakhor, A.: A cost-driven fracture heuristics to minimize sliver length. In: SPIE, vol. 7973 (2011)
14. Rourke, J.O., Tewari, G.: The structure of optimal partitions of orthogonal polygons into fat rectangles. In: 14th Canadian Conference on Computational Geometry - CCCG02, vol. 28 (1), pp. 49–71, May 2004
15. Lopez, M.A., Mehta, D.P.: Efficient decomposition of polygons into L-shapes with application to VLSI layouts. ACM Trans. Des. Autom. Electron. Syst. (TODAES) **1**(3), 371–395 (1996)
16. Yu, B., Gao, J.-R., Pan, D.Z.: L-Shape based layout fracturing for E-Beam lithography. In: 2013 18th Asia and South Pacific Design Automation Conference (ASP-DAC), Yokohama, pp. 249–254 (2013)

# VLSI Architectures

# Energy-Efficient VLSI Architecture & Implementation of Bi-modal Multi-banked Register-File Organization

Sumanth Gudaparthi[1] and Rahul Shrestha[2(✉)]

[1] Center for VLSI and Embedded System Technologies,
International Institute of Information Technology (IIIT) Hyderabad,
Hyderabad 500032, India
sumanth.gudaparthi@gmail.com
[2] School of Computing and Electrical Engineering,
Indian Institute of Technology (IIT) Mandi,
Mandi 175005, Himachal Pradesh, India
rahul_shrestha@iitmandi.ac.in
https://faculty.iitmandi.ac.in/~rahul_shrestha/

**Abstract.** For the execution of high-end applications of present-day scenario, processor consumes profound energy and its significant fraction is due to intensive register-file access in the processor architecture. Such fraction of energy required by the processor defers to reduce with the advancement of semiconductor technology and thereby, it is essential to design energy-efficient register-file architecture for the contemporary scenario. This paper presents new register-file architecture called the bi-modal multi-banked register-file organization to capture short term reused and short lived operands to alleviate load on register file to read and write. Additionally, instruction decode stage of the processor architecture is restructured to capture the reused and short lived register operands. On incorporating these new features, we have conceived a processor architecture that has been synthesized and post-layout simulated in 180 nm complementary metal-oxide semiconductor (CMOS) technology node. It consumes 35 mW of total power at 200 MHz of clock frequency. The bi-modal multi-banked register-file organization stores a fraction of data bandwidth, which is local to the functional units, resulting in the reduction of cost for supplying data to the execute stage. Subsequently, the proposed architecture is made to execute MiBench benchmark kernels and it showed up to 55% improvement in energy saving over an embedded reduced instruction-set computer (RISC) processor architecture.

**Keywords:** Register files · Computer architecture
Embedded processor · Energy conservation
CMOS and very-large scale-integration (VLSI) design

© Springer Nature Singapore Pte Ltd. 2017
B. K. Kaushik et al. (Eds.): VDAT 2017, CCIS 711, pp. 299–312, 2017.
https://doi.org/10.1007/978-981-10-7470-7_30

# 1    Introduction

Reduction of energy consumption in the processor design for recent applications has become necessary for extending the battery life. Scaling down of CMOS process accommodates numerous transistors on a single chip and hence enhances the performance of processor from area, power and speed perspectives. Albeit, shorter interconnects are required for chip design and this scales up the resistance as well as capacitance per unit length [1]. Register files, being dominated by interconnects, consume significant fraction of energy in the processor system-on-chip (SoC). Various techniques have been proposed to reduce the energy consumption of the register file [2]. Tabkhi et al. [3] introduces an application-guided function-level register file power-gating (AFReP) approach to efficiently manage and reduce the register-file static-power consumption. Transport triggered architecture that uses software to control the data movement claims to reduce the unnecessary usage of register file. Speculative avoidance of register allocations to transient-values reported in [4] is a set of micro-architectural extensions that predict transient values those are not required to reconstruct the precise state following the branch miss-predictions. Tseng and Asanovic [5] evaluated seven techniques to reduce the energy dissipation for accessing the processor register file at the cost of total area and delay overhead. Gonzlez et al. [6] exploited the concept of partial value locality and suggested a new integer-register file organization which lowers the energy consumption of register file. Multiple levels of bypassing on register files have been employed to enhance the performance and reduce the power consumption (increased energy saving) [7]. Register file cache (RFC) is one of such mechanisms implemented to reduce the number of reads/writes from/to the register file using smaller register-file caches. Many different forms of RFC mechanisms have been reported since the advent of this concept [8]. Balfour et al. [9] suggested a hierarchical register organization that uses software to capture short-term reuse and locality in inexpensive registers. On the other side, the amount of energy consumed to access the register file reduces with the deduction in its size. Thereby, we have proposed a bimodal multi-banked register-file organization to reduce the energy consumed by the register file. The primary idea of this work is to store the short lived registers in a smaller register file to decline the access of main register file resulting in the depreciation of total energy consumed. Most of the replacement mechanisms to update the small register file use the register operands from the previous instructions to predict future register operands. Though due to locality, there is good possibility of the register operand being repeated in future and this leads to additional energy consumption. Such miss-predictions can be avoided by using a decode queue and our novel replacement policy.

# 2    Proposed Architectures and Algorithms

This section presents the proposed techniques and VLSI architecture of processor. Specifically, new hardware modules and replacement policies incorporated in the suggested processor architecture are discussed in this section.

## 2.1   DRF and Decode Queue Modules

The DRF is a small four-entry register-bank placed along with the architect register file (referred as MRF in this paper) in the decode stage of pipeline, as shown in Fig. 1. DRFs store the data of register operands which might be utilized by future instructions. This has been achieved by capturing short term reused registers and short lived registers using the proposed replacement algorithm. As discussed earlier, the amount of energy consumed for accessing data from smaller register files is significantly low. Thereby, if the majority of register file access is performed through DRF then the energy consumption due to register file access can be profoundly reduced. If the register reads and writes of the future instructions are known priory then such technique of storing values from MRF in DRF will reduce the MRF access and thus consume lesser energy for register file access. The DRF controller module sends the select signals to multiplexers which decide whether to route the data from MRF or DRF to the functional unit, as shown in Fig. 1. On the other side, a decode queue of size $N_{st}$ has been incorporated in the decode stage of pipeline. Read and write addresses of the instructions after being decoded are place in this decode queue module. It is to be noted that the decode queue is a simple first-in first-out (FIFO) queue,

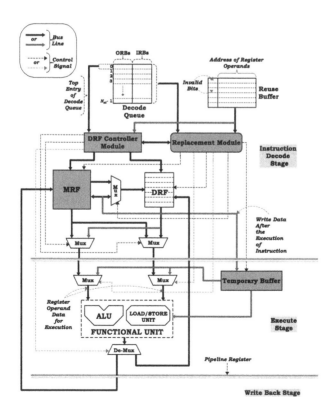

**Fig. 1.** Block diagram of the proposed processor architecture.

as shown in the Fig. 1. Each entry of such queue is divided into two blocks viz. input register block (IRB) and output register block (ORB). The read and write addresses of the instructions are stored in IRB and ORB respectively. In the suggested processor architecture, entire data in the decode queue is visible to replacement module. This makes the register addresses of the future $N_{st}-1$ instructions visible to the replacement module, enabling processor to avoid any possible miss-predictions. Each instruction after being decoded, waits until its respective register addresses reach the top of decode queue. This waiting time is necessary to predict the future register accesses. As the size of the decode queue is very small, the affect on instruction per cycle due to decode queue is negligible.

## 2.2   Reuse Buffer

Reuse buffer module has been included in the decode stage of the processor architecture, as shown in Fig. 1. It contains the addresses of register operands in MRF whose data is stored in DRF. Once the content of DRF is updated with new value then the reuse buffer is subsequently updated with the relevant register address. It is to be noted that the average energy consumed for accessing the data from the reuse buffer is 0.25 pJ. The register addresses of each instruction are individually as well as periodically compared with the values stored in reuse buffer with the aid of replacement algorithm. Subsequently, control signals are accordingly generated for every instruction, whether to update or retain the contents of DRF (and reuse buffer). Each location in the reuse buffer is associated with an additional bit which is termed as invalid bits. A set of invalid bit indicates that the data of register operand pointed by specific buffer is dead and is no more valid. A register operand is said to be dead when a write operation is performed on it and the data in this operand gets updated to a new value. Additionally, the invalid bit is set when the duplication of data occurs. For example, the same register operand can be pointed by two registers in the DRF and this leads to reduced accuracy in the reuse prediction. Thereby, an invalid check module has been implemented which checks for such adverse circumstances and sets or resets the invalid bits, as shown in Fig. 1.

## 2.3   DRF Controller Module

In the suggested processor architecture, the DRF controller module has been incorporated in the instruction decode stage. This controller module decides to whether read the data of the register reads from MRF or DRF. Every single time the register addresses of a new instruction enters the top of decode queue, DRF controller checks for the availability of those register operands in the reuse buffer. If a match is detected between the top entry of IRB and the reuse buffer entry, then the data is read from DRF at the matched location. On the other hand, if a match is detected between the top entry of ORB and the reuse buffer entry then the respective matched reuse buffer location is invalidated immediately, indicating that it is a dead register.

We proposed a method that takes into account the update signal from the replacement module and the register addresses from the top entry of the decode queue to decide whether to read the data from DRF or MRF. Such mechanism is illustrated in Algorithm 1. In this algorithm, if the *Update* signal is asserted by replacement module then the register reads instruction in the decode stage (i.e., the top entry of IRB) and is compared with the values in reuse buffer for equality. If a mismatch is noticed for any of the register addresses at the top entry of IRB then the DRF controller reads the data of that specific register operand from the MRF. The DRF controller later updates the DRF and reuse buffer with the register operands data and address. Conversely, if a mismatch is detected when the *Update* signal is not asserted then the mismatched register operand is read from MRF but the controller does not update the DRF (and reuse buffer) with the data (and address) of the register operand. Eventually, if no mismatch is detected irrespective of *Update* signal then it means that the data of register operands is already present in DRF. Thereby, the read operation for such operand is performed through DRF and this alleviates the total energy consumed. The control select signals are generated accordingly for the multiplexers in the execute stage which decides whether to take the data from MRF or DRF. Subsequently, the final values of data, either from DRF or MRF, is transferred to the execute stage for execution of instructions. Thereafter, the results are written back to either MRF or DRF, as per the signals asserted by the replacement module.

---

**Algorithm 1.** Proposed Algorithm

---

1: **if** (*Update*) **then**
2:  **if** (*Top most entry of IRB* ≠ *atleast one entry of reuse buffer*) **then**
3:    *Read the data of the unmatched operand from MRF;*
4:    *Update DRF (& reuse buffer) with the data (& address) of unmatched operand from the MRF;*
5:  **else**
6:    *Read the data from DRF;*
7:  **end if**
8: **else**
9:  **if** (*Top most entry of IRB* ≠ *atleast one entry of reuse buffer*) **then**
10:   *Read the data of unmatched operand from MRF;*
11:   *Do not update DRF (& reuse buffer);*
12:  **else**
13:   *Read the data from DRF;*
14:  **end if**
15: **end if**

---

### 2.4   Replacement Module

The DRF (and reuse buffer) is updated every time a new register operand is highly reused or short lived than any of the register operands represented by the reuse buffer. Such decisions for DRF updating are determined based on following three factors:

1. When a short lived register file is detected.
2. When a live register is actively used in future $N_{st}$ number of instructions.
3. Atleast one entry of reuse buffer does not match with any entry in IRB and viceversa.

A register is defined as short lived, if its life time $\leq N_{st}$. In order to detect the short lived registers, all the register operands till future $N_{st}$ instructions should be visible to the replacement module. Therefore, the size of decode queue must be equal to $N_{st}$. To detect short lived registers, the top most entry of the ORB (location 0) is compared with the remaining ORB entries (location 1 to $N_{st}$-1) of the decode queue. If equality is detected at any of the remaining ORBs then it's a short lived register and a short lived signal ($sl$) is set. On setting $sl$, the computed data of the respective matched register-operand is stored only in DRF, and not in MRF, by the replacement module. Since these are short lived registers, storing the value in MRF is redundant and any operations on this short lived register during its life time is carried through DRF. Thereby, reducing the power consumption because it subsides the total writes to MRF. Consider the following assembly code:

- $I_1$: *addu* \$3, \$2, \$1;
- $I_2$: *addu* \$5, \$4, \$3;
- $I_3$: *subu* \$3, \$7, \$8;

Here, \$3 is a short lived register with a life time between the instructions $I_1$ and $I_3$. In such situation, writing the value of \$3 in MRF after the execution of $I_1$ would consume more energy. Instead, if the value of \$3 is stored in DRF, the energy consumption would significantly reduce due to smaller size of DRF. The read operation on \$3 by the consecutive instruction $I_2$ is performed through DRF by the replacement module; thereby, reducing the read energy. This module generates finite state machine based control signal for de-multiplexer which has been incorporated in the execute stage of the proposed processor architecture, as shown in Fig. 1, to redirect the result of ALU to DRF rather than to write back stage. Moreover, when $I_3$ issues a write operation on \$3, the value present in DRF can be invalidated and the final value is written back to the MRF. Such mechanism would reduce the energy consumption, as one register read and one register write has been carried out from DRF instead of MRF in the above code.

   In other case, some of the registers may not be short lived but can be actively accessed during its life time. Continuous operation of such registers from MRF is not energy efficient. Thereby, this work divides these actively reused registers in two categories:

1. The registers those are actively used for a period of $N_{st}$, from the time a new data is allocated to the register. In this case, the top most entry of the ORB (location 0) is compared with the later IRB entries (location 1 to $N_{st}$-1). If equality is detected then the active-reuse immediate signal ($ari$) is set.
2. The registers those are live for more than $N_{st}$ time period but are active in the future $N_{st}$ number of instructions. The top most entry of the IRB (location 0)

is compared with the remaining IRB entries (location 1 to $N_{st}$-1). If equality is detected, the active reuse distant signal ($ard$) is set.

When $ari$ is set, the computed data of the respective matched register operand is stored both in DRF and MRF by the replacement module. When ($ard$) is set, the first read of the respective matched register operand is read from the MRF and is stored in DRF. We notice that if either of $ari$ and $ard$ is set then the data of respective register operand is present in both DRF and MRF for some given time frame. Thereby, when a future instruction uses the same register operand, it is read from DRF until this module is updated with a new value. However, a peculiar condition can occur, as shown in the following code block of FFT benchmark:

- $I_1$: $lw$ \$2, 60(\$f$_p$);
- $I_2$: $slt$ \$2, \$2, 16384;

In the above code, it can be observed that the register \$2 is a short lived instruction, as the write addresses of instructions $I_1$ and $I_2$ are same. When register operands of $I_1$ reaches the top of decode queue, $sl$ is set leading to data of \$2 being stored in DRF (say in some location X) and not in MRF. As discussed earlier, energy consumed is reduced by avoiding the write operation in MRF and accessing the data directly from DRF. However, when the register operands of the next instruction $I_2$ reaches the top of decode queue, the DRF controller module detects a match between its read operand (\$2) and a value in reuse buffer at location X. Thereby, DRF controller module tries to read \$2 from location X of DRF. Simultaneously, the top most entry of the ORB (\$2) matches with the value in the reuse buffer at location X indicating that it is a dead value. Thus, the invalid bit is set for location X of reuse buffer. Assuming that both of these happen at the same time, the data at location X is read and invalidated simultaneously. However, this might lead to unpredictable results. This complexity aggravates with increase in the intensity of such instructions. One way to mitigate this issue is to invalidate location X of the reuse buffer and directly read the data from the MRF. We compare the top most entry of the ORB with its consecutive entries of ORB and IRB values. If such a case is noticed then the operation is directly stored in MRF instead. However, if there are many such instruction in a specific program then writing and reading from the MRF is again a waste of energy. Such code block can be seen in most of the benchmarks and the following is a small block of code from FFT benchmark.

- $I_1$: $lw$ \$3, 64(\$f$_p$);
- $I_2$: $lw$ \$2, 44(\$f$_p$);
- $I_3$: $slt$ \$2, \$3, \$2;
- $I_4$: $andi$ \$2, \$2, 0×00ff;

**Proposed Solution.** To avoid aforementioned peril, this paper presents energy efficient mechanism to the register file organization, as shown in Fig. 2. This

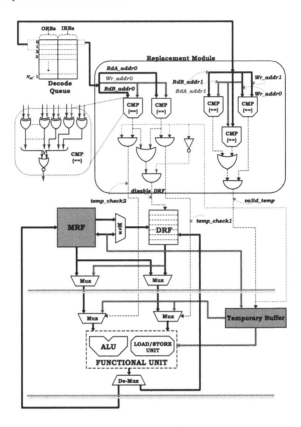

**Fig. 2.** Additional hardware in instruction decode and execute stages of the suggested processor to overcome the hazard caused by overlap of DRF invalidate and DRF read.

mechanism uses a temporary register which is parallel to the pipeline register between decode and execute stages acting as a bypass register. When the top most entry of ORB matches with its consecutive entries of ORB and IRB values, a signal *valid_temp* is set. Subsequently, this control signal is used as select and enable signals for de-multiplexer and temporary buffer, respectively, in the execute stage, as shown in Fig. 2. Similarly, the de-multiplexer controlled by *valid_temp* signal decides whether to write back the data to MRF or store it in temporary buffer such that the next consecutive instruction is capable of reading the data from this buffer rather than from the DRF. On the other hand, the top most entries of ORB and IRB are compared. Subsequently, signals are set for each IRB entry which matches with any entry of ORB at the top row of decode queue. For convenience, we assume that there are two values in IRB (*RdA_addr* and *RdB_addr*) and one value in ORB (*Wr_addr*) for each entry of decode queue. The signal *temp_check1* is set when *valid_temp* is set and *RdA_addr* matches with *Wr_addr*, and *temp_check2* is set when *valid_temp* is set and *RdB_addr* matches with *Wr_addr*. These signals are used as select lines for the multiplexers those are situated prior to the functional unit. Such multiplexers route the data either from the multiplexed output of DRF or temporary buffer and this mechanism has been illustrated in Algorithm 2.

---

**Algorithm 2.** *Proposed Algorithm*

---

```
 1: if (valid_temp) then
 2:    if (Write address (Wr_addr) == Read address A (RdA_addr)) then
 3:       temp_check1 = 1;
 4:    else
 5:       temp_check1 = 0;
 6:    end if
 7:    if (Write address (Wr_addr)== Read address B (RdB_addr)) then
 8:       temp_check2 = 1;
 9:    else
10:       temp_check2 = 0
11:    end if
12: else
13:    Read from DRF or MRF
14: end if
```

---

**Additional Hazards.** As discussed earlier, if the top most entry of ORB matches with any of the values in reuse buffer then the invalid bit is set for that specific location of the reuse buffer. Assuming that value of register operand $2 is present in DRF, consider the following code:

- $I_1$: *addu* $7, $8, $9;
- $I_2$: *subu* $2, $2, $6;

When the register addresses of $I_2$ reach the top of decode queue, invalid bit is set at a location of reuse buffer which points $2. However, the DRF controller module sends a signal to read the value of $2 from DRF. This gives rise to one new hazard where, even the write address for $I_1$ is not pointed to $2 and the *valid_temp* signal is set low. In such case, the DRF is disabled using *disable_DRF* signal and the read operation on $2 takes place from MRF in $I_2$, thereby, mitigating such hazard. As the $2 data present in DRF is not short lived, its copy will be available at MRF. On the other side, if *valid_temp* signal is low and any of the top entries of ORB and IRB match then the *disable_DRF* signal disables DRF and reads the data from MRF. The key advantage of such proposed mechanism is that the data is read from DRF or temporary buffer to reduce the load on MRF. Thereby, improving the energy efficiency of the processor.

Additionally, there is a possibility that only one location of DRF is ready to be updated; however, the replacement module detects a short lived register and an actively reuse register simultaneously. Then the priority is rendered to short lived register and the location of DRF is updated with the short lived register. During this time, the actively reused register reads the register operand from MRF. At some particular time frame, there may not be short lived register or an actively reused live register in the decode queue. However, there can be a specific register operand in DRF which is not used by any of the next $N_{st}$ number of instructions. In this case, the unmatched DRF register is updated with the earliest new register operand in the IRB. Consider the following assembly code.

- $I_1$: *addu* $8, $2, $1;
- $I_2$: *addu* $5, $4, $3;
- $I_3$: *subu* $3, $7, $6;

Assuming that the value of $N_{st} = 3$ and when the registers of $I_1$ reach the top of decode queue, the DRF contains the data of the register operands $1, $3, $4 and $9. It is noticed that the register address of $9 does not match with any of the register operand addresses in IRB. We do not as well have a short lived or actively reused register in the IRB. Thereby, the location of DRF containing the value of $9 is replaced with the most recent register operand and in this case with $2.

As the value of $N_{st}$ increases, register operands of some more future instructions can be accommodated in the decode queue. This makes more instructions visible to the replacement module. In the proposed architecture, $N_{st}$ is set to three which makes only the future two instructions visible to the replacement module. Using $N_{st} = 3$ gives us the minimum amount of energy saved using the bi-modal register file organization. The energy saving can be further increased using greater values of $N_{st}$. The value of $N_{st}$ should not be very large so as to complicate the replacement module logic or allowing decode queue consume more energy.

## 3    Experimental Results and Comparisons

### 3.1    VLSI Implementation

Motivation behind this implementation is to determine accurate energy consumption of the proposed architecture which is built over an in-order pipeline processor. It has been coded using Verilog hardware-descriptive language and then simulated using reliable test bench for the functional verification. Subsequently, this code has been gate-level synthesized, with the realistic design constraints, using standard cell libraries of UMC 180 nm-CMOS process. On performing static timing analysis on the gate-level netlist of this architecture, it could operate with a maximum clock frequency of 200 MHz. Physical back-end design of this architecture is carried out by instantiating the gate-level netlist using library exchange format (LEF) file of 180 nm CMOS process. Such cells are placed over the floor-planned core area, which is surrounded by power and ground rails for providing voltage supply and ground, respectively, for all the CMOS cells. Thereafter, such placed cells are clock tree synthesized, signal and power routed to complete the chip layout, whose post-layout simulations and STA are subsequently performed to ensure the design is reliable and free from timing-violations respectively. Final chip-layout of the proposed processor architecture is shown in Fig. 3(a). Finally, the post-layout simulated values of important design parameters of our processor architecture are listed in Table 1.

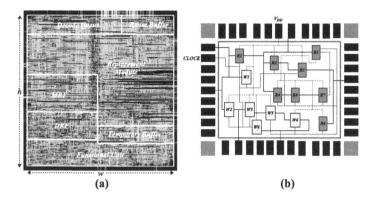

**Fig. 3.** (a) Chip layout of the proposed processor architecture in 180 nm-CMOS process with the dimension of $h = 461.22$ μm and $w = 458.25$ μm; (b) Schematic of chip core for the processor including routed standard/mcaro cells activated during write and read operations. $R1$-$R7$ and $W1$-$W6$ indicate the sets of cells activated for read and write operations respectively.

**Table 1.** Post-layout simulated results of the proposed processor architecture.

| Design parameters | Obtained values |
|---|---|
| Technology (nm) | 180 |
| Supply voltage (V) | 1.8 |
| Area (mm$^2$) | 0.21 |
| Register file Size (bits) | $32 \times 32$ |
| Max. clock frequency (MHz) | 200 |
| Standard cell count | 7011 |
| Dynamic power (mW) | 33.79 |
| Leakage power (nW) | 831.52 |

## 3.2  Energy Calculation, Results and Comparisons

Parasitic extraction of the final chip layout has been carried out to generate standard-parasitic exchange-format (SPEF) file, which is an IEEE standard for quantifying the parasitic data such as wire resistances and capacitances of the entire layout. These capacitance values from SPEF file are used for computing the energy consumed by the proposed architecture. In this work, energy consumed by processor for read and write operations are separately determined. To accomplish such process, standard and macro cells activated during the read and write operations are identified, as shown in Fig. 3(b). It represents the schematic of chip core area that includes activated cells for read and writes. Capacitances of all these paths, separately for read and write operations, are determined from the SPEF file. Each of these capacitances across the standard cells includes the sum of interconnect capacitance of the wire, load and input capacitances of the cells. If $i$ and $j$ represents source and destination cells then $C_{ij}$ represents total capacitance between them. Thereby, gross energy consumed due to write or read operation can be computed as

$$E_{r/w} = 1/2 \times \sum_{\delta:i,j} C_{ij} \times V_{DD}^2 \tag{1}$$

where $V_{DD}$ represents supply voltage, which is 1.8 V for 180 nm-CMOS process, and $\delta$ represents all write or read operations. Thereby, Table 2 shows the energy consumed per read and write operation of the proposed processor with 32-bit register file and different entry sizes of 32 and 4 bits. It can be observed that the write operation consumes 51.7% and 44% more energy than read operations in both 32 × 32-bit and 4 × 32-bit register files respectively. This is because the conventional multi-ported memory cell for register file typically uses two bit lines per write port and one bit line per read port, as well as one word line per every port to control the connection of the cell to the bit lines of the corresponding port. Thus, there are $N_{read} + N_{write}$ word lines for every row in the array, and $N_{read} + 2 \times N_{write}$ bit lines. Thus, the write operation consumes more energy than the read operations.

**Table 2.** Energy consumption of different sized register files

| Register file size | Energy per Read | Energy per Write |
|---|---|---|
| 32 × 32-bit (2R + W) | 6.31 pJ | 13.06 pJ |
| 4 × 32-bit (2R + 2W) | 1.6 pJ | 2.86 pJ |

**Results and Comparisons.** This paper compares average energy consumed by the suggested processor with bimodal multi-banked register-file organization and replacement module against the conventional processor with in-order scheduling pipeline. Subsequently, the evaluation of benefits provided by the combination of bimodal register file and temporary buffer will be discussed in this section (Fig. 4).

Table 3 shows the instruction count and the energy consumed by conventional register file and the bimodal multi-banked register file with temporary buffer for the MiBench benchmark kernels. It can be seen that the register file organization presented in this work achieved a maximum energy saving of 54.79% for *CRC32* benchmark and minimum energy saving of 43.85% for *stringsearch* benchmark, as shown in Table 3. Additionally, it shows the percentage of energy saved using the bi-modal multi-banked register file organization and the percentage of total amount of energy that the temporary buffer accounts for in the total energy saving. Thereby, it can be observed that the temporary buffer is more effective in *dijkstra* and *ADPCM* benchmarks with 14.3% and 6.44% respectively.

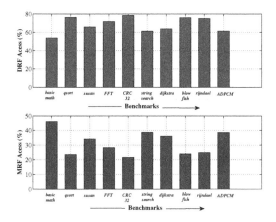

**Fig. 4.** The percentages of total register reads carried out on MRF and DRF of the proposed processor architecture, while running the standard benchmarks, without the use of temporary buffer.

**Table 3.** Comparison of energy consumed by the proposed and conventional processor architectures when implemented using 180 nm CMOS technology node and running various standard benchmark kernels.

| Benchmarks | Inst. Count | Energy[‡] (nJ) | Energy[✠] (nJ) | Energy Sav.[§] | Temp. Buff. Share[£] |
|---|---|---|---|---|---|
| basicmath | 180302852 | 3393932.73 | 1848223.45 | 45.6 % | 2.1 % |
| qsort | 7348 | 113.97 | 52.61 | 53.84 % | 1.3 % |
| susan | 27342 | 498.4 | 254.52 | 48.93 % | 2.56 % |
| FFT | 10611 | 174.85 | 84.7 | 51.55 % | 1.73 % |
| CRC32 | 6325 | 95.31 | 43.1 | 54.79 % | 1.07 % |
| stringsearch | 300710 | 5205.67 | 2922.9 | 43.85 % | 2 % |
| dijkstra | 6963898 | 130768.53 | 61171.07 | 53.22 % | 14.43 % |
| blowfish | 7674 | 120.73 | 55.93 | 53.67% | 1.37 % |
| rijndael | 7864 | 124.78 | 58.36 | 53.22 % | 1.49 % |
| ADPCM | 33236056 | 272724.79 | 149524.87 | 45.17 % | 6.44 % |

‡ : Reference register file organization.
✠ : Bi-modal multi-banked register file organization with $N_{st} = 3$.
§ : Percentage of energy saved by the proposed processor, based on bi-modal multi-banked register-file organization, in comparison with the reference register-file organization based processor.
£ : Percentage of temporary buffers share in the total amount of energy saved by the proposed processor.

# 4    Conclusion

This paper presented new register-file architecture to address contemporary issue of energy consumption required to run embedded applications. We incorporated the replacement module and DRF controller to capture the reused and short-lived operands in the register file. Subsequently, we implemented a bi-modal multi-banked register-file organization to store the captured operands, eventually, reducing the load of reading and writing on the main register file. Thereafter, VLSI design of the proposed register-file organization on processor architecture was carried out using 180 nm CMOS process and the energy consumption has been precisely calculated. Consequently, the register file organization is designed by modifying the architectural simulator where the benchmark kernels were made to run on the reference and the proposed architectures. Comparatively, the proposed register-file organization consumed 55% lesser energy and this can be further improved with bigger $N_{st}$. However, this architecture consumes more area due to the additional hardware modules. Nevertheless, this drawback can be mitigated to some extent by scaling down the CMOS process.

# References

1. Hennessy, J.L., Patterson, D.A.: Computer Architecture. A Quantitative Approach, 5th edn. Morgan Kaufmann Publishers Inc., San Francisco (2011)
2. Ayala, J.L., Lopez-Vallejo, M., Veidenbaum, A., Lopez, C.A.: Energy aware register file implementation through instruction predecode. In: IEEE International Conference on Application-Specific Systems, Architectures, and Processors, pp. 86–96 (2003)
3. Tabkhi, H., Schirner, G.: Application-guided power gating reducing register file static power. IEEE Trans. Very Large Scale Integr. (VLSI) Syst. **22**, 2513–2526 (2014)
4. Balkan, D., Sharkey, J., Ponomarev, D., Ghose, K.: Predicting and exploiting transient values for reducing register file pressure and energy consumption. IEEE Trans. Comput. **57**, 82–95 (2008)
5. Tseng, J.H., Asanovic, K.: Energy-efficient register access. In: 13th Symposium on Integrated Circuits and Systems Design, pp. 377–382 (2000)
6. Gonzalez, R., Cristal, A., Ortega, D., Veidenbaum, A., Valero, M.: A content aware integer register file organization. In: 31st Annual International Symposium on Computer Architecture, pp. 314–324 (2004)
7. Zeng, H., Binghamton, N.Y., Ghose, K.: Register file caching for energy efficiency. In: Proceedings of the 2006 International Symposium on Low Power Electronics and Design, pp. 244–249 (2006)
8. Yung, R., Wilhelm, N.C.: Caching processor general registers. In: IEEE International Conference on Computer Design: VLSI in Computers and Processors (1995)
9. Balfour, J., Harting, R.C., Dally, W.J.: Operand registers and explicit operand forwarding. IEEE Comput. Archit. Lett. **8**, 60–63 (2009)

# Performance-Enhanced $d^2$-LBDR for 2D Mesh Network-on-Chip

Anugrah Jain[✉], Vijay Laxmi, Meenakshi Tripathi, Manoj Singh Gaur, and Rimpy Bishnoi

Malaviya National Institute of Technology, Jaipur, India
anugrahjain4u@gmail.com, rimpybishnoi@gmail.com,
{vlaxmi,mtripathi.cse,gaurms}@mnit.ac.in

**Abstract.** Growing demand for high-performance computing is necessitating faster on-chip communication. Network-on-Chip (NoC) with networking theory and methods for faster on-chip communication has emerged as a potential option. Due to transistor scaling down to submicron technologies, NoC also suffers from permanent or transient failures. Logic Based Distributed Routing (LBDR) has been proposed as a flexible fault tolerant routing implementation framework for Mesh-Based NoCs with link and router faults. The routing logic overhead remains invariant to the size of the topology making it scalable. LBDR is restricted to provide only minimal paths and can not support all failures. $d^2$-LBDR was developed to support non-minimal paths and thus would handle all single and double link permanent failures. Though, $d^2$-LBDR successfully covers all single and double link permanent failures but still restricts the available number of fault-free paths. In this paper, we present how this limitation on the available number of fault-free paths affects NoC performance. Based on our analysis, we present a new selection logic which enhances $d^2$-LBDR to explore all available fault-free paths. Our proposed solution having a marginal overhead in area and power provides higher performance (7% improvement in average flit latency and 4% improvement in average network throughput when subject to two link faults in a 64-Node NoC).

**Keywords:** Network-on-Chip · Fault tolerance · Logic based routing

## 1 Introduction

In the previous years, NoC has emerged as a scalable and reliable communication alternative for many-core architectures like Chip Multiprocessors (CMP) and Multiprocessor System-on-Chip (MPSoCs). Several NoC ingredients including topology, routing, switching and network interfaces gained particular attention from the researchers [1]. Literature proposed variety of NoC topologies including mesh, torus, fat tree, and butterfly. Figure 1 shows a $4 \times 4$ mesh-based NoC. Aggressive technology scaling improves transistor density and speed but

© Springer Nature Singapore Pte Ltd. 2017
B. K. Kaushik et al. (Eds.): VDAT 2017, CCIS 711, pp. 313–323, 2017.
https://doi.org/10.1007/978-981-10-7470-7_31

increases the probability of fault occurrence during manufacturing and owing to aging. Wear-out and variability increases as the Silicon features approach the atomic scale. Future designs will consist of 10 % of defective components due to manufacturing, wear-out and variation [2]. We need to explore solutions to create reliable systems from unreliable components.

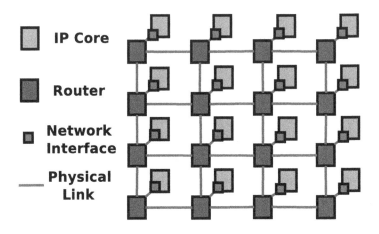

**Fig. 1.** 4 × 4 mesh-based Network-on-Chip

NoC will play a vital role in future communication-centric many-core designs. A faulty NoC element may shut down the communication between system components. The interconnect architecture must be able to tolerate failures. Due to the availability of multiple redundant paths between the nodes, NoC allows us to circumvent the failed components. In consequences, several fault tolerant routing approaches have been developed. They are topology independent and can be applied to any network topology resulting from the failures.

Segment-Based (SR) routing is one of the well-known topology agnostic approach that provides high performance without using virtual channels [3]. Figure 2(a) shows a 4 × 4 mesh-based NoC realizing SR routing. In general, bi-directional routing restrictions are applied in a zig-zag manner to avoid deadlocks. Another popular topology agnostic approach, known as Up*/Down* routing, is based on a directed acyclic graph (DAG) constructed from the network topology of NoC, where each node represents a router (with their associated IP), and each edge accounts for a physical channel in the network [4]. A 4 × 4 mesh-based NoC with Up*/Down* routing is depicted in Fig. 2(b). Up*/Down* routing assigns direction to all the operational links in the network. Movement of a packet in the link direction shows an upward move and movement of a packet opposite to the link direction shows a downward move. A packet in its lifespan can take one or more upward moves followed by one or more downward moves. A packet after taking a downward move can not take an upward move to avoid deadlocks to occur in the network.

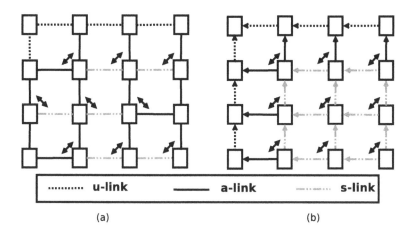

**Fig. 2.** $4 \times 4$ mesh-based NoC with (a) SR (b) Up*/Down* routing

Routing can be implemented in two ways either by using routing tables or by using combinational logic elements. Literature demonstrated non-scalability of the table-based approach and proposed a flexible and scalable distributed routing implementation approach, known as LBDR (logic based distributed routing) [5]. LBDR is a fault tolerant approach but supports only minimal paths and can support only a few failures. Several extensions for the LBDR have been proposed to support non-minimal paths in the network [6]. $d^2$-LBDR is the most recent with best fault coverage. It supports non-minimal paths and covers all single and two link permanent failures that can occur in the network [7]. Section 2 gives an overview of LBDR and $d^2$-LBDR. We then present our analysis of $d^2$-LBDR in Sect. 3 followed by our proposed selection logic in Sect. 4. We evaluate our proposal in Sect. 5. The paper concludes with Sect. 6.

## 2 Background

LBDR is based on the concept of routing restrictions which is an alternative way to implement a deadlock-free routing algorithm in the network. Routing algorithm prohibits few turns, and such turns are represented by routing restrictions. LBDR stores topology and routing information into few bits. Routing bits show possible routing turns that a packet can take in the next hop router, whereas connectivity bits show neighbors connected to the current router. Due to the support of only minimal paths, LBDR does not allow a packet to circumvent all failures [5].

Solutions have been proposed to support non-minimal paths in LBDR. A module named FORKS which replicates some messages has been used. The module requires virtual cut-through switching and a complex router arbiter [6]. In spite of this, some failure combinations need a non-trivial dynamic reconfiguration procedure to avoid deadlocks [8].

$d^2$-LBDR proposed as a solution to restore the use of wormhole switching, keeping router architecture simple, while achieving the same fault coverage as the best LBDR version. Without requiring any complex dynamic reconfiguration procedure, it supports all single and double link permanent failures [7]. $d^2$-LBDR also proposed a classification of 1-link failures that may be present in a 2D Mesh NoC realizing SR routing. And it can be used for other routing algorithms such as Up*/Down*. Figure 2 shows classification of 1-link failures that may be present in a $4 \times 4$ mesh network when using SR routing and Up*/Down* routing. $d^2$-LBDR analysis on the types of 1-link failures is discussed as follows:

- Unrestricted link ($u$-link): Routers connecting the link contains no bi-directional routing restriction.
- Anti-symmetric link ($a$-link): One of the two routers connecting the link contains one bi-directional routing restriction or each router connecting the link contains one bi-directional routing restriction but in opposing direction.
- Symmetric link ($s$-link): Both routers connected to the link must contain one bi-directional routing restriction in the same direction.

LBDR can support failures on $u$-links or $a$-links. To deal with such failures, the only thing which is required is the removal of routing restriction located in the same segment of the failed link. And it can easily be removed because cycle in the segment is broken by the faulty link itself [7]. To handle more complex $s$-link failures, $d^2$-LBDR used mask logic. With mask logic, it successfully covers all 1-link failure cases without moving routing restrictions between the segments. A deroute strategy (which is the combination of a global deroute, a clockwise deroute, and an anti-clockwise deroute) was used in $d^2$-LBDR to support all 2-link failures that may occur in the network. We present an overview of $d^2$-LBDR approach as follows:

- *Routing Logic:* $d^2$-LBDR used four connectivity bits ($C_n$, $C_s$, $C_e$ and $C_w$) and twelve routing bits ($R_{nn}$, $R_{ne}$, $R_{nw}$, $R_{ss}$, $R_{se}$, $R_{sw}$, $R_{ee}$, $R_{en}$, $R_{es}$, $R_{ww}$, $R_{wn}$ and $R_{ws}$) for encapsulation of topology and routing information. $C_n$ with value one shows a router is connected to its North neighbor. $R_{ne}$ with value one indicates whether packets routed through the North output port can later at the next hop take the East output port.
- *Mask Logic:* Sometimes failures can create a situation where the routing algorithm provides two paths, but one of them will no longer be available. $d^2$-LBDR uses mask logic to handle this situation. Mask logic uses mask bits, one ($M_{xy}$) per routing bit $R_{xy}$ and two distance bits ($DF_x$, $DF_y$) for keeping distance between current router and the faulty location. $R_{xy}$ bit for the incoming packet can be evaluated (possibly masked) when both $R_{xy}$ and the associated mask bit ($M_{xy}$) are set to one, and the destination router falls under failed area. $d^2$-LBDR mask logic and a working example for 2D mesh network with one $s$-link failure are depicted in Fig. 3. Distance bits encapsulate fault location. Initially (for a fault-free case), these bits are set to the maximum distance in $X$ and $Y$ dimensions, respectively. A network with failures needs to update their distance bits at the affected routers. Only a larger

distance in either $X$ or $Y$ dimensions needs to be updated. At node S of a network containing one link failure as shown in Fig. 3(b), $DF_x$ needs to be set to value 2 and $M_{se}$ and associated $R_{se}$ should be set to value 1 to enable the mask logic. With such setting, South-to-East turn ($R_{se}$) at node S will be forbidden for destination set $D_1$ and allowed for destination $D_0$. In this way, $d^2$-LBDR prevents a situation where no path either minimal or non-minimal is available for the incoming packet [7]. Our analysis will discuss this in more detail.

– *Deroute Strategy:* Mechanisms needs a non-minimal path to circumvent faulty location, and deroute strategy provides this support. The deroute strategy of $d^2$-LBDR composed of clockwise, anti-clockwise and global deroute mechanisms. Clockwise deroute provides an output port located in 90° clockwise direction of the desired output port in which a packet wants to go whereas anti-clockwise does the opposite. For example in Fig. 3(b), the clockwise deroute strategy will provide North output port to a packet that wants to go from node D1 to node D0 whereas anti-clockwise deroute will provide North output port to a packet that wants to go to from node D0 to node D1. Global deroute mechanism of $d^2$-LBDR provides output port based on values set in the deroute registers ($dr_0$ and $dr_1$) [7].

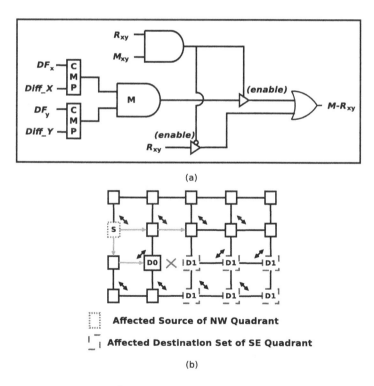

(a)

(b)

Fig. 3. (a) $d^2$-LBDR mask logic and (b) an example

With using masking and deroute strategy, $d^2$-LBDR successfully covers all single and double link permanent failures, but it limits the available number of fault-free paths. In next section, we present our analysis of how limiting the available number of fault-free paths affects NoC performance.

## 3  Our Analysis

$d^2$-LBDR mask logic plays a vital role in deciding which route should be forbidden or which route should be allowed by the routing logic for an incoming packet. With the use of mask logic and deroute strategy, $d^2$-LBDR completes its job successfully. But there are some cases of more than one $s$-link failures in which it limits the available number of fault-free paths. Figure 4 represents two of them. Figure 4(a) shows a $5 \times 5$ mesh network which is using SR routing and contains two $s$-link failures, one failure is in the North-East quadrant, and another failure is in the South-East quadrant of the router node $S$ in the network. $D_1$ and $D_2$ are the two affected destination sets from the node $S$. Ideally, at $S$, $DF_x$ must be set to value 3 to cover the affected destination set $D_1$, and same $DF_x$ needs to be set to value 2 to cover the affected destination set $D_2$. But $d^2$-LBDR mask logic uses only one distance register and can store only one value. $DF_x$ of router $S$ needs to be set to value 2 to cover both $s$-link failures successfully but restricts the available number of fault-free paths. At node $S$, for all packets which are going for North-East quadrant and whose destination is two hops away in x-dimension, will be sent to the East output port, irrespective of an available fault-free path via the North output port.

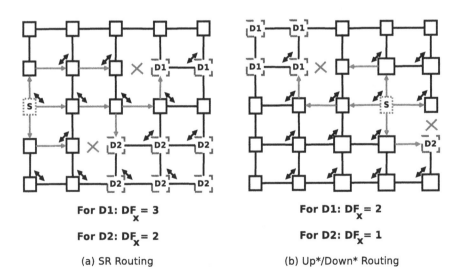

For D1: $DF_x = 3$

For D2: $DF_x = 2$

(a) SR Routing

For D1: $DF_x = 2$

For D2: $DF_x = 1$

(b) Up*/Down* Routing

**Fig. 4.** Counter example of $d^2$-LBDR with two $S$-link failures in a network realizing (a) SR routing and (b) Up*/Down* routing

A similar situation for the same sized mesh network when using Up*/Down* routing is depicted in Fig. 4(b). Ideally, at node $S$ in Fig. 4(b), $DF_x$ must be set to value 2 to cover the affected destination set $D_1$ whereas, $DF_x$ should be set to value 1 to cover the affected destination set $D_2$. But $d^2$-LBDR mask logic finally set $DF_x$ to value 1 to support the given situation of two $s$-link failures. And thus limiting the available number of fault-free paths and affecting NoC performance. The probability of occurring such situations in a 2D mesh network increases when we go from SR routing to Up*/Down* routing as it solely depends on the total number of $s$-links occur in the network. In general, SR routing with its zig-zag routing restrictions has total $(N-1).(N-2)$ number of $s$-links whereas Up*/Down* routing has total $2.(N-1).(N-2)$ number of $s$-links in a given $N \times N$ mesh network, where $N$ represents the dimension of the mesh. Based on our analysis we are presenting a new selection logic for masking strategy of $d^2$-LBDR in the following section.

# 4   Proposed Selection Logic

As discussed in the previous section, multiple $s$-link failures in the relatively different quadrants may generate different masking requirements and can limit the available number of fault-free paths. Our proposed strategy encapsulates faulty locations in corresponding distance bit register sets whereas $d^2$-LBDR minimizes it to only one set $(DF_x, DF_y)$ and thus limiting the available number of fault-free paths. We are using four distance bit register sets, one for each quadrant (i.e. $(DF_x^{ne}, DF_y^{ne})$, $(DF_x^{nw}, DF_y^{nw})$, $(DF_x^{sw}, DF_y^{sw})$ and $(DF_x^{se}, DF_y^{se})$). Our proposed selection logic with four distance bit register sets enables $d^2$-LBDR mask logic to explore all fault-free paths available in the network. Our proposed new selection logic, workflow, and its truth table are depicted in Fig. 5. The truth table illustrates working of the selection logic. Our selection logic is made up of two $4 \times 1$ multiplexers and few logic gates. The output of our selection logic will feed into mask logic for $d^2$-LBDR as shown in Fig. 5(b).

$$\Delta DF_x = Max(DF_x^{ne}, DF_x^{nw}, DF_x^{sw}, DF_x^{se}) - Min(DF_x^{ne}, DF_x^{nw}, DF_x^{sw}, DF_x^{se}) \tag{1}$$

$$\Delta DF_y = Max(DF_y^{ne}, DF_y^{nw}, DF_y^{sw}, DF_y^{se}) - Min(DF_y^{ne}, DF_y^{nw}, DF_y^{sw}, DF_y^{se}) \tag{2}$$

The improvement in path diversity or the maximum difference between masking requirements can be calculated using Eqs. (1) and (2), where maximum and minimum do not include their highest possible value (i.e. maximum distance in the respective dimension and a value zero). Our proposed selection logic enables $d^2$-LBDR to use remained path diversity and is evaluated in Sect. 5. Our following working example will explain how our proposed selection logic enables masking of $d^2$-LBDR to explore all fault-free paths available in the network.

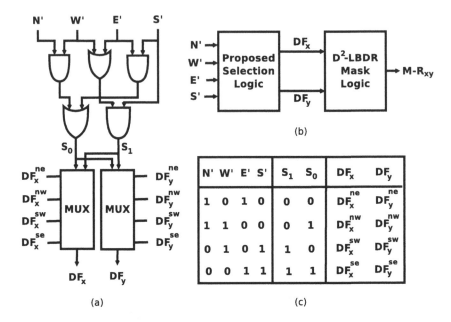

**Fig. 5.** (a) Proposed selection logic, (b) workflow, and its (c) truth table

## 4.1 Working Example

We first use the network realizing SR routing as discussed in the previous section and shown in Fig. 4(a). At node S, for each packet that wants to go in North-East quadrant, our selection logic outputs $S_0$ and $S_1$ to low and performs the selection of appropriate distance bit registers set $(DF_x^{ne}, DF_y^{ne})$. Distance bit $DF_x^{ne}$ when set to value 3, enables masking of the corresponding routing bit (i.e. $R_{ne}$) only when the destination of the packet is at least three hops away in x-dimension. Earlier, it was set to value 2 and limiting the fault-free path of hop one. Here, we can say that the improved path diversity with the proposed selection logic is equal to one hop which is same as $\Delta DF_x$, computed from Eq. 1. Now, we use the network which is realizing Up*/Down* as shown in Fig. 4(b). For packets that want to go in the North-West quadrant, our selection logic outputs $S_0$ to high and $S_1$ to low, performing the selection of the appropriate distance bit register set $(DF_x^{nw}, DF_y^{nw})$. The value set to 2 for $DF_x^{nw}$ now masks corresponding routing bit (i.e. $R_{nw}$) only when the destination of the packet is at least two hops away from the current node S in x-dimension. Similarly, we can handle cases for remaining quadrants. For NoC with no failures, mask bits are set to zero and distance bit register sets (all $DF_x$'s and $DF_y$'s) are set to the maximum distance along $X$ and $Y$ dimensions, respectively. In the presence of at least one s-link failure, both mask bits, and corresponding distance bit register sets are modified only at affected routers. Changes are done at offline and out of concern for this paper.

# 5   Results

This section presents the performance evaluation of selection logic for $d^2$-LBDR in 2D Mesh NoCs. We have used two topology agnostic routing approaches (SR and Up*/Down*) for evaluation purpose.

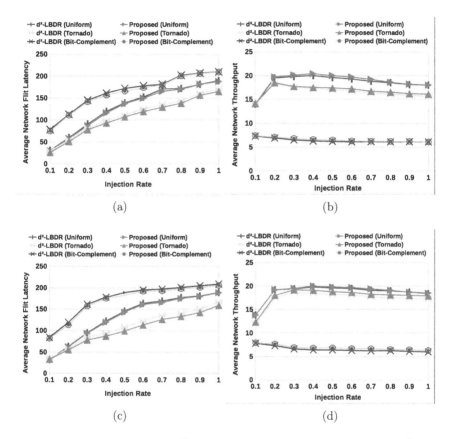

**Fig. 6.** Performance evaluation of $d^2$-LBDR and proposed selection logic with $d^2$-LBDR on $8 \times 8$ mesh-based NoC when using (a), (b) SR and (c), (d) Up*/Down* routing

## 5.1   Performance Evaluation

We have used a cycle accurate interconnection network simulator, named as GARNET [9] and performed our experiment on the representative set of two $s$-link permanent failures requiring distinct masking in distinct quadrants of the NoC router. Average performance results for $8 \times 8$ mesh topology under different synthetic traffic profiles (i.e. uniform random, tornado and bit-complement) are as shown in Fig. 6. Presented results are average over eight simulation runs. Each run is for a different pair of $s$-link failures. The evaluation shows $d^2$-LBDR with modified mask logic performs 7% better in terms of average network flit latency cycles and 4% better in terms of average network throughput for networks realizing SR routing and Up*/Down* routing. The gained performance is directly related to $\Delta DF_x$ and $\Delta DF_y$ calculated using Eqs. (1) and (2). Therefore, it can be stated that the proposed solution will perform much better for large sized mesh-based NoCs.

## 5.2 Area and Power Overhead

We have implemented $d^2$-LBDR and proposed selection logic with $d^2$-LBDR in Verilog HDL. Both approaches were synthesized using Synopsys Design Vision (32 nm target library). Area and power overhead analysis of both approaches are presented in Table 1. Due to LBDR is a scalable approach, area and power overhead of the proposed logic would remain constant throughout the various network sizes.

**Table 1.** Area and power overhead analysis

| Approach | Area ($\mu m^2$) | Power ($\mu w$) |
|---|---|---|
| $d^2$-LBDR | 583 | 19 |
| Proposed | 745 | 23 |

## 6 Conclusion

We have proposed a new selection logic that enables $d^2$-LBDR mask logic to explore all available fault-free paths in case of failures. Our proposed selection logic selects appropriate values for mask logic so that the routing logic will forbid no fault-free path. With marginal area and power overhead, our solution provides significant improvement (7% in average flit latency and 4% in average network throughput) for $8 \times 8$ mesh-based NoC. The improvement thus achieved is directly related to $\Delta DF_x$ and $\Delta DF_y$. Hence, our solution would be more beneficial for large-sized mesh networks. Future work shall include ways for handling single or double link transient faults using one of the non-trivial dynamic reconfiguration procedures.

## References

1. Dally, W., Towles, B.: Principles and Practices of Interconnection Networks. Morgan Kaufmann Publishers Inc., San Francisco (2003)
2. Fick, D., DeOrio, A., Hu, J., Bertacco, V., Blaauw, D., Sylvester, D.: Vicis: a reliable network for unreliable silicon. In: Proceedings of the 46th Annual Design Automation Conference, pp. 812–817. ACM (2009)

3. Mejia, A., Flich, J., Duato, J., Reinemo, S.-A., Skeie, T.: Segment-based routing: an efficient fault-tolerant routing algorithm for meshes and tori. In: Proceedings of the 20th International Conference on Parallel and Distributed Processing, IPDPS 2006, Washington, DC, USA, pp. 105–105. IEEE Computer Society (2006)
4. Schroeder, M.D., Birrell, A.D., Burrows, M., Murray, H., Needham, R.M., Rodeheffer, T.L., Satterthwaite, E.H., Thacker, C.P.: Autonet: a high-speed, self-configuring local area network using point-to-point links. IEEE J. Sel. A. Commun. **9**(8), 1318–1335 (2006)
5. Flich, J., Duato, J.: Logic-based distributed routing for NoCs. IEEE Comput. Archit. Lett. **7**(1), 13–16 (2008)
6. Rodrigo, S., Flich, J., Roca, A., Medardoni, S., Bertozzi, D., Camacho, J., Silla, F., Duato, J.: Cost-efficient on-chip routing implementations for CMP and MPSoC systems. IEEE Trans. Comput. Aided Des. Integr. Circuits Syst. **30**(4), 534–547 (2011)
7. Bishnoi, R., Laxmi, V., Gaur, M.S., Flich, J.: $d^2$-LBDR: distance-driven routing to handle permanent failures in 2D mesh NoCs. In: Proceedings of the 2015 Design, Automation & Test in Europe Conference & Exhibition, pp. 800–805. EDA Consortium (2015)
8. Ghiribaldi, A., Ludovici, D., Triviño, F., Strano, A., Flich, J., Sánchez, J.L., Alfaro, F., Favalli, M., Bertozzi, D.: A complete self-testing and self-configuring NoC infrastructure for cost-effective MPSoCs. ACM Trans. Embed. Comput. Syst. (TECS) **12**(4), 106 (2013)
9. Agarwal, N., Peh, L.-S, Jha, N.K.: Garnet: a detailed interconnect model inside a full-system simulation framework (2008)

# ACAM: Application Aware Adaptive Cache Management for Shared LLC

Sujit Kr Mahto[✉] and Newton[✉]

Computer Architecture and Dependable Systems Lab.
Department of Electrical Engineering, Indian Institute of Technology Bombay,
Mumbai 400076, India
{sujitkumar,newton}@ee.iitb.ac.in

**Abstract.** Modern Chip Multiprocessors (CMPs) are typically multi-core systems with shared last level cache (LLC). Effective utilization of the shared cache resource can be a challenge when the demands of competing applications conflict with each other. At times, in order to accommodate new data required by one application, the other application's useful data may get evicted. Such negative interference results into increase in memory miss and degrades system's performance. Hence, a technique is required which optimally manages the LLC even in the presence of such conflicting demands.

Various LLC management techniques have been proposed to efficiently manage shared caches. The state-of-the-art replacement policies like Static Re-reference Interval Prediction (SRRIP) and Application Aware Behavior Re-reference Interval Prediction (ABRip) evict a cache block based on their re-usability in the near future. SRRIP makes the replacement decisions per block basis whereas ABRip also considers the cache behavior of an application to minimize conflicting data demands. Hence, ABRip outperforms SRRIP for workload mixes where one application is cache friendly, and the other one is streaming. However, ABRip does not perform well when the workload mix is Cache friendly-Cache friendly. We propose Application Aware Adaptive Cache Management policy that adapts to both types of workload mixes. The proposed replacement policy reduces LLC misses per kilo instruction *(mpki)* up to 22.74% and 12.7% compared to SRRIP and ABRip respectively on a CMP system running SPEC CPU2006 workloads. Our policy effectively utilizes the shared LLC and outperforms both SRRIP and ABRip with performance gains of up to 10.12% and 9.36% respectively.

**Keywords:** LLC Replacement Policy · Least Recently Used
Set Dueling

## 1 Introduction

The performance gap between the memory and microprocessor has been widening for last 4 decades as memory speeds have increased slowly compared to that

© Springer Nature Singapore Pte Ltd. 2017
B. K. Kaushik et al. (Eds.): VDAT 2017, CCIS 711, pp. 324–336, 2017.
https://doi.org/10.1007/978-981-10-7470-7_32

of the CPU speed [1]. Generally, two or three levels of cache hierarchy are used to bridge this gap. In a multicore system, L1 and L2 are generally used as a private cache, and L3 is used as shared LLC for better resource utilization. As the access latency between LLC and main memory is typically high (100–400 cycles), effective management of LLC is critical to system's performance. One of the approaches to effectively manage the LLC is to optimize its replacement policy. As memory request to shared LLC comes from applications with different memory characteristics, the cache access pattern is highly diverse. Memory request from one application interferes with the other application hence increases conflict misses at LLC.

For shared LLC, the optimal replacement policy should allocate more cache resources to the application that shows more data reuse. In a multicore processor, conventionally Least Recently Used (LRU) is used to manage shared caches. However, LRU policy allocates cache resources to an application on the basis of its cache access rate. It does not consider if the application shows temporal locality and hence gives more ways to an application having high cache access rate [5,9]. However, it is not necessary that an application having higher cache access rate also shows more temporal locality and system benefits from such logical cache partitioning.

Several ideas have been proposed in the literature [5–7,9] to efficiently manage LLC. Recently proposed replacement policies like SRRIP [6] and ABRip [7] associates counters to each cache block to track its position in the LRU recency stack and use them to predict whether the cache block will get re-referenced in next few cache accesses or not. On a cache block replacement, both policies evict those cache blocks which are predicted to get re-referenced in far future. ABRip, apart from the block level counters, also associates counter at each core level to differentiate between the cache reuse behavior of applications running on the multicore system. These core level counters help ABRip in classifying the application as cache friendly (Cf) or non-cache friendly (Str). As ABRip also considers application's past cache reuse behavior while deciding about the block's re-reference interval, it performs well compared to SRRIP when the workload mix is Cf-Str. Non-cache friendly application includes the application with data reuse, but working data sets larger than the cache size (*Thrashing application*) and applications which do not show any data-reuse (*Streaming application*). This classification helps in giving (or associating) more ways (or cache size) to a Cf workload when Cf-Str workload mix is running on the cores. However, ABRip fails to adapt when workload mix is Cf-Cf as shown in [7] because, for such workload mixes, ABRip does unfair cache partitioning thus favoring one of the application at the disadvantage of other.

The cache access pattern to LLC is inherently highly diverse in nature. The workload mixes running on the cores can be of Cf-Cf, Cf-Str, or Str-Str type. As mentioned in the previous paragraph, different policies are efficient for different combination of workloads, e.g., SRRIP performs better for Cf-Cf workload mixes whereas ABRip outperforms SRRIP for Cf-Str type of workload combinations. Hence, a cache replacement policy should be adaptive to different types of cache access pattern and various combination of workloads. Techniques like Set Dueling Monitor (SDM) [5] and Auxiliary Tag Directory (ATD) [9] have been earlier used to dynamically choose the best policy among competing replacement policies.

In this paper, we propose Application Aware Adaptive Cache Management (ACAM) for shared LLC. We dynamically switch between two different eviction policies, i.e., taking eviction decision by differentiating application behavior (ABRip) or by considering cache data re-usability only (SRRIP), to make replacement policy adaptive to the different type of cache access pattern and different combination of workloads running on the cores. We use techniques like SDM and ATD to learn the type of cache access pattern so that we can make best possible eviction decision. We evaluate the proposed policy on a set of SPEC CPU2006 workloads running on dual core systems sharing 4MB of LLC.

The rest of the paper is organized as follows. Section 2 explains the background of our work. Our proposal is discussed in Sect. 3. Section 4 provides details about the experimental methodology adopted. Experimental results are discussed in Sect. 5. Related work is discussed in Sect. 6, and in Sect. 7 we conclude the paper.

## 2   Background

The commonly used LRU replacement policy inserts a block at Most Recently Used (MRU) position, i.e., at the top of recency stack and evicts the block from LRU position, i.e., from the bottom of the recency stack. It performs well for smaller caches such as L1 and L2 which significantly utilize the temporal and spatial locality present in the application. However, for LLC, it performs poorly because most of the blocks inserted to LLC never get re-referenced due to filtering of the temporal locality by smaller cache as observed by several studies [8]. To mitigate this problem, recently proposed replacement policies like LRU Insertion Policy (LIP) [8] and SRRIP [6] insert new block at LRU and closer to LRU position respectively. Only if the block gets hit, it is promoted to MRU position predicting that the cache block is useful and will get re-referenced again in near future.

To study the efficacy of LRU replacement policy on shared caches, we performed experiments to understand the cache reuse behavior under LRU policy for various SPEC CPU2006 benchmark applications. In our experiment, we studied impact on *mpki* of the applications due to variation in the associativity of LLC keeping number of sets and cache block size constant. Figure 1 shows that as associativity increases, *mpki* of *bzip* and *gcc* benchmark reduces indicating their cache reuse behaviour. Whereas *mpki* of *milc* and *libquantum* benchmark remains almost constant which shows their streaming cache access behavior. Based on this observation, we categorize *bzip* and *gcc* as Cf workloads and *libquantum* and *milc* as Str workloads. LRU replacement policy does not perform well for shared caches as it allocates cache resources based on the rate of demand and does not consider whether an application has temporal locality or not. We observed that *mpki* of *bzip* is 5.27 while running mixes (*bzip-libquantum*) on dual core system implementing LRU replacement policy in LLC. From Fig. 1, we inferred that *mpki* of *bzip* is 5.27 when it is given 4 out of 8 ways, i.e., allocating half of the cache resources to application *bzip* and the another half to *libquantum*. However, allocating half of the cache resource to *libquantum* does not give performance benefit as it shows streaming cache access behavior with zero reuse. Other replacement policies like Thread-Aware Dynamic Insertion Policy (TADIP) [5], SRRIP manage LLC more efficiently in such cases compared to the LRU policy.

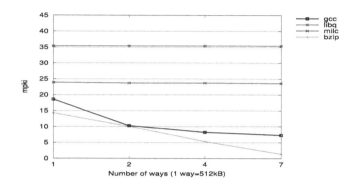

**Fig. 1.** Memory characteristic of few SPEC CPU2006 benchmarks

SRRIP manages shared caches well as it promotes only re-referenced cache blocks to MRU position, hence filtering out streaming blocks from the blocks having spatial or temporal locality. However, it under-performs compared to ABRip when the workload mix consists of a Str application with high cache access rate and a cache-friendly application with low cache access rate. In such a scenario, before the cache-friendly application's blocks get re-referenced and promoted to MRU, they are replaced by blocks of the high access rate Str application. ABRip uses N more *k-bit* saturating counters per set to differentiate the behavior of applications running on N cores. The value of this counter is used as core level RRPV ($Cr$). It defines a value of the counter associated with each cache block as block level RRPV ($Br$). If cache block from any application gets a hit, then its $Cr$ is promoted to 0. This helps in factorizing the behavior of an application. It defines Application Behavior aware RRPV ($ABr$) as a linear combination of $Br$ and $Cr$.

$$ABr = Br + \alpha * Cr \qquad (1)$$

Higher value of $\alpha$ gives more weightage to $Cr$ than $Br$. ABRip ($\alpha = 0$) will work same as SRRIP. It evicts cache block which is having $ABr$ value, that is calculated by Eq. (1), greater than or equal to $ABr_{max}$ value. $ABr_{max}$ is defined as $Br_{max}$ plus $\alpha$ times $Cr_{max}$. As cache block of Cf application will re-referenced more than that of Str application, $ABr$ of Str application's block will reach its maximum value faster compare to Cf application's block which helps in preserving Cf application's block longer in LLC.

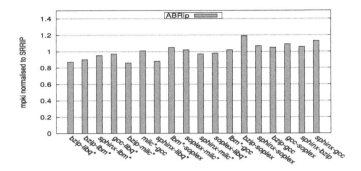

**Fig. 2.** *mpki* Comparison: Benchmarks with (*) are non-cache friendly application and rest are cache-friendly application

To understand the effectiveness of ABRip and SRRIP on Cf-Str and Cf-Cf workload-mixes, we studied each policies' LLC misses. Figure 2 shows the *mpki* comparison of ABRip ($\alpha = 3$) normalized to SRRIP. The X-axis represents the combination of SPEC CPU2006 benchmarks mentioned in Table 2a. On X-axis, first 12 combinations of benchmarks are the combination of Cf-Str workloads whereas following six combinations of benchmarks are the combination of Cf-Cf workloads. *mpki* of ABRip is higher for Cf-Cf workloads compared to SRRIP because ABRip gives higher priority to an application whose cache blocks get first hit by promoting its $Cr$ value to 0 until $Cr$ value of other application also gets promoted to 0. It protects blocks with $Cr = 0$ from early eviction. However, in Cf-Cf workloads, both applications have temporal locality. So, it hurts the performance of Cf-Cf workloads, whereas, by the same mechanism of protecting blocks with $Cr = 0$, it performs better for Cf-Str workloads. We illustrate such scenario in Fig. 3 for replacement policies ABRip ($\alpha = 2$) and ABRip ($\alpha = 0$) in shared LLC. In policy ABRip ($\alpha = 0$), we give zero weight to $Cr$ and take a decision based on the value of $Br$ only. It works similarly as SRRIP. Here, we consider two applications X and O are running on two cores. The mixed cache access pattern as seen by LLC is ($O_1$, $X_1$, $X_2$, $O_1$, $X_1$, $X_2$, $O_3$, $X_1$). Both applications show temporal locality. We assume that the cache blocks ($O_1$, $O_2$, $O_3$, $X_2$) are initially present in the cache. Request for block $O_1$ come, and it is a cache hit resulting in the update of the $Cr$ value of application O to 0. Then, request for block $X_1$ comes and gets a miss. In both policies, block $X_2$ gets evicted. Then, request for block $X_2$ comes and gets miss again. Despite that block $O_2$ has higher $Br$ value and has stayed longer in cache than block $X_1$, block $X_1$ get evicted in policy ABRip ($\alpha = 2$) because $Cr$ value of application X is higher than that of application O. Whereas in policy ABRip ($\alpha = 0$), block $O_2$ get evicted because it does not consider the $Cr$ value of application and make a decision considering $Br$ value only. In policy ABRip ($\alpha = 2$), $Cr$ value of application O is protecting their other blocks from getting evicted and give less number of way to application X. It hurts the performance of application X. Here, we get six hits in ABRip ($\alpha = 0$) whereas in ABRip ($\alpha = 2$) we get only three hits which are shown by blue shaded box in the Fig. 3. Hence, our study identifies and has illustrated the reason for poor performance of ABRip in case of Cf-Cf workload mixes. In our next section, we describe the advanced and adaptive version of ABRip which efficiently manages LLC for all combination of workload-mixes.

| ABRip with $\alpha=2$ | | | | | | Access Pattern | ABRip with $\alpha=0$ | | | | | |
|---|---|---|---|---|---|---|---|---|---|---|---|---|
| Core-RRPV | | Data Blocks | | | | | Core-RRPV | | Data Blocks | | | |
| 0-0 | X-3 | $O_1$-0 | $O_2$-2 | $O_3$-1 | $X_2$-2 | $O_1$ | 0-0 | X-3 | $O_1$-0 | $O_2$-2 | $O_3$-1 | $X_2$-2 |
| 0-0 | X-3 | $O_1$-1 | $O_2$-3 | $O_3$-2 | $X_1$-2 | $X_1$ | 0-0 | X-3 | $O_1$-1 | $O_2$-3 | $O_3$-2 | $X_1$-2 |
| 0-0 | X-3 | $O_1$-2 | $O_2$-4 | $O_3$-3 | $X_2$-2 | $X_2$ | 0-0 | X-3 | $O_1$-2 | $X_2$-2 | $O_3$-2 | $X_1$-2 |
| 0-0 | X-3 | $O_1$-0 | $O_2$-4 | $O_3$-3 | $X_2$-2 | $O_1$ | 0-0 | X-3 | $O_1$-0 | $X_2$-2 | $O_3$-2 | $X_1$-2 |
| 0-0 | X-3 | $O_1$-1 | $O_2$-5 | $O_3$-4 | $X_1$-2 | $X_1$ | 0-0 | X-0 | $O_1$-1 | $X_2$-2 | $O_3$-3 | $X_1$-0 |
| 0-0 | X-3 | $O_1$-2 | $O_2$-6 | $O_3$-5 | $X_2$-2 | $X_2$ | 0-0 | X-0 | $O_1$-1 | $X_2$-0 | $O_3$-3 | $X_1$-0 |
| 0-0 | X-3 | $O_1$-2 | $O_2$-6 | $O_3$-0 | $X_2$-2 | $O_3$ | 0-0 | X-0 | $O_1$-1 | $X_2$-0 | $O_3$-0 | $X_1$-0 |
| 0-0 | X-3 | $O_1$-3 | $O_2$-7 | $O_3$-1 | $X_1$-2 | $X_1$ | 0-0 | X-0 | $O_1$-1 | $X_2$-0 | $O_3$-0 | $X_1$-0 |

**Fig. 3.** Access pattern Example: Here, $Br_{max} = 3$, $Cr_{max} = 3$, $ABr_{max}$ for $\alpha = 2$ is 9 and for $\alpha = 0$ is 3. Blue shaded box represents re-referenced block. (Color figure online)

# 3 Proposed Methodology

## 3.1 Advanced ABRip

Advanced ABRip (a-ABRip) is an advanced version of ABRip with modifications in its insertion policy. In ABRip, new blocks are inserted at $Br$ equal to $(Br_{max}-1)$ whereas, in a-ABRip, new blocks are inserted at $(ABr_{max}-1)$. For most of the time when Cf-Str combinations of workload is running on the cores, the $Cr$ value of Str application is equal to $Cr_{max}$ and that of Cf application is equal to 0. So, the $ABr$ value of newly inserted block of Str application will be equal to $(ABr_{max}- + \alpha * Cr_{max})$, i.e., LRU position. Whereas for Cf application, it is inserted with $ABr$ value equal to $(ABr_{max}- 1)$ as its $Cr = 0$, i.e., closer to LRU position. This helps in reducing interference from Str application further and reduces $mpki$ more for Cf-Str combination of workloads. In SRRIP, it has been shown that inserting blocks closer to LRU position works better compared to other insertion positions. Eviction and promotion policy of a-ABRip is same as that of ABRip.

## 3.2 Application Aware Adaptive Cache Management (ACAM)

As shown in Fig. 2, for some workload-mixes ABRip has fewer cache misses compared to SRRIP and for other workload-mixes ABRip has more misses. So, different eviction policies perform better for the different combination of workloads. Hence, the replacement policy should be adaptive by dynamically choosing the best performing policy.

The characteristics of a workload-mix, whether it is Cf-Cf or Cf-Str, running on a multicore system can be understood by its mixed cache access pattern as seen by the shared LLC. If the cache access pattern shows that both the applications have temporal locality, then eviction decisions can be taken based on data re-usability, i.e., SRRIP policy. However, if it shows that one of the application has temporal locality while the other application has streaming cache access behavior and causes interference to the first application, then eviction decisions can be taken by differentiating application's behavior, i.e., a-ABRip policy. To make our replacement policy adaptive to different combination of workloads and different type of cache access patterns, we use SDM [5] and ATD [9] to dynamically switch the replacement policy between a-ABRip ($\alpha = 3$) and SRRIP, based on the types of cache access pattern.

**SDM.** SDM estimates the miss or miss rate of given policy by dedicating few sets to each policy. We use two SDMs on Main Tag Directory (MTD), one for a-ABRip ($\alpha = 3$) and other for SRRIP. After a fixed number of cache accesses (i.e., *phase*), we compare the miss rate of both SDMs and choose the winner policy for remaining sets. Here, we consider 90,000 cache accesses for each *phase*. The winner policy is then implemented on the remaining sets. The winner policy in each *phase* can be different and is chosen dynamically based on the type of its cache access pattern. After every *phase*, we reset the counter values. We use 32 sets for each SDM. In previous work [5,8,10], the authors have compared cache miss of SDMs for comparison. However, in our experiments, we observed that sometimes the number of cache access to one SDM is very high compared to that of other SDM for the same *phase*. So, there is more chance that cache miss of SDM which gets high cache access will be more than that of the other SDM which gets low cache access. For fair comparison, we compare the cache miss rate of SDMs instead of cache miss. To make comparisons more accurately, we have also used ATD where both SDMs see the same cache access pattern as the same sets are dedicated to both competing replacement policies.

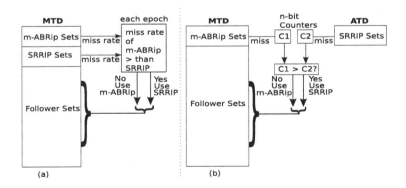

**Fig. 4.** ACAM Implementations: (a) ACAM-SDM (b) ACAM-ATD

**ATD.** Here we use one SDM on MTD for a-ABRip policy and we create ATD for SRRIP policy to be used as other SDM. ATD and MTD have the same associativity. We create ATD of those 32 sets that are dedicated to a-ABRip policy in the first SDM on MTD so that both SDMs will see same cache accesses and it will be a fairer comparison. We use saturating counters to count the number of misses of both SDMs. After every *phase*, we compare the counters to decide the winner policy. We implement the winner policy on remaining sets of MTD. On completion of each *phase*, we reset the counter value. Figure 4 shows the implementation of ACAM using SDM and ATD.

## 4    Experimental Methodology

### 4.1    Simulation Infrastructure

To evaluate our proposed policy ACAM, we used Sniper [2] multicore x86 simulator. Three level of memory hierarchy was used where L1 and L2 were used as private cache and L3 as shared cache. Table 1 shows the parameter values of baseline processor architecture used. Our cache hierarchy is roughly comparable to the Intel Core i7 [4]. Architecture parameters of the simulated system used here is same as the one used in recent work on shared cache [7].

**Table 1.** Architecture parameter of simulated system

| L1-D Cache | 32 KB, 4-Way, LRU, Private, 4-cycles |
|---|---|
| L1-I Cache | 32 KB, 4-Way, LRU, Private, 4-cycles |
| L2 Cache | 256 KB, 8-Way, LRU, Private, 8-cycles |
| L3 Cache | 4 MB, 8-way, Shared, 30-cycles |
| Main memory latency | 175 Cycles |
| Baseline Processor | x86 Nehalem microarchitecture, 2.67 GHz, 4-wide fetch, 128-entry ROB |

### 4.2    Workloads Combination

On a dual core CMP having shared LCC, we evaluate ACAM replacement policy on 18 different combinations of SPEC CPU2006 benchmarks [3] shown in Table 2a. Out of 18 combinations, 12 are Cf-Str workload combinations, and 6 are Cf-Cf workload combinations. We do not evaluate our policy on Str-Str workload combinations because they do not show any changes in performance irrespective of different replacement policies. We also evaluate our policy on 13 different combinations of SPEC CPU2006 benchmarks shown in Table 2b on 4-core CMPs to understand the scalability of our architecture. We implemented SRRIP with maximum block level RRPV = 15 (i.e., m = 4 bits counter used) and ABRip ($\alpha = 3$) and $ABr_{max} = 60$ (i.e., 6 bit counter used at the block level and 4 bit counter used at core level) and evaluate its performance to compare with that of ACAM replacement policy.

**Table 2.** Combination of workloads under evaluation

(a) DualCore

| Workloads Combination | Type | Workloads Combination | Type |
|---|---|---|---|
| bzip-libq | Cf-Str | sphinx-milc | Cf-Str |
| bzip-lbm | Cf-Str | soplex-libq | Cf-Str |
| sphinx-lbm | Cf-Str | lbm-gcc | Str-Cf |
| gcc-libq | Cf-Str | sphinx-gcc | Cf-Cf |
| bzip-milc | Cf-Str | bzip-soplex | Cf-Cf |
| milc-gcc | Str-Cf | sphinx-soplex | Cf-Cf |
| sphinx-libq | Cf-Str | bzip-gcc | Cf-Cf |
| lbm-soplex | Str-Cf | gcc-soplex | Cf-Cf |
| soplex-milc | Cf-Str | sphinx-bzip | Cf-Cf |

(b) QuadCore

| Mix Name | Workloads Combination | Type |
|---|---|---|
| MIX_01 | bzip-gcc-milc-libq | Cf-Cf-Str-Str |
| MIX_02 | bzip-gcc-lbm-milc | Cf-Cf-Str-Str |
| MIX_03 | bzip-sphinx-milc-libq | Cf-Cf-Str-Str |
| MIX_04 | bzip-sphinx-libq-lbm | Cf-Cf-Str-Str |
| MIX_05 | bzip-lbm-milc-libq | Cf-Str-Str-Str |
| MIX_06 | gcc-lbm-milc-libq | Cf-Str-Str-Str |
| MIX_07 | soplex-lbm-milc-libq | Cf-Str-Str-Str |
| MIX_08 | sphinx-lbm-milc-libq | Cf-Str-Str-Str |
| MIX_09 | bzip-gcc-soplex-libq | Cf-Cf-Cf-Str |
| MIX_10 | bzip-gcc-soplex-milc | Cf-Cf-Cf-Str |
| MIX_11 | bzip-gcc-sphinx-libq | Cf-Cf-Cf-Str |
| MIX_12 | bzip-gcc-sphinx-lbm | Cf-Cf-Cf-Str |
| MIX_13 | bzip-gcc-soplex-sphinx | Cf-Cf-Cf-Cf |

# 5   Results and Discussion

## 5.1   Performance Improvement

Figure 5 shows the performance comparison of ABRip, a-ABRip and ACAM using SDM and ATD over baseline SRRIP. a-ABRip improves the performance for most combination of Cf-Str workloads over ABRip by inserting Str application block at LRU position and Cf application block at closer to LRU position. However for Cf-Cf combination of workloads, SRRIP outperforms both policies, i.e., a-ABRip and ABRip. On an average for Cf-Str combination of workloads, a-ABRip outperforms ABRip by 1.22%.

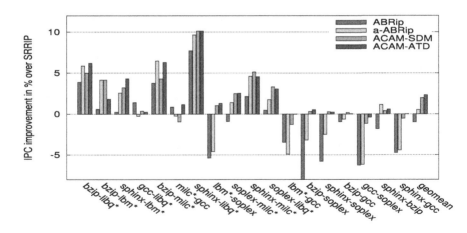

**Fig. 5.** Performance Comparison: Benchmarks with (*) are non-cache friendly application and rest are cache-friendly application

Using SDM, ACAM outperforms SRRIP and ABRip for most combination of workloads by being adaptive to cache access pattern. It gives maximum performance benefit of 10.12% over SRRIP for workload combination *sphinx-libquantum*. However for some combination of workloads such as *milc-gcc*, *lbm-gcc*, *gcc-soplex* and *sphinx-gcc*, it fails to adapt and lose performance compare to SRRIP. On average, it gives performance improvement of 1.97% and 2.99% over SRRIP and ABRip respectively.

Using ATD, ACAM outperforms SRRIP and ABRip for all combination of workloads except *gcc-soplex* where it loses performance by 0.4% compare to SRRIP. It gives performance gain up to 10.12% for workloads *sphinx-libquantum* compared to SRRIP and 9.36% for workloads *bzip-soplex* over ABRip. On average, it gives performance improvement of 2.32% and 3.33% over SRRIP and ABRip respectively.

Figure 6 shows the performance comparison of ACAM-ATD and ABRip over baseline SRRIP for multi-programmed workloads on 4-core CMPs. The X-axis represents different workload combinations shown in Table 2b. ABRip gives maximum performance benefit of 11.95% for Mix-5. On an average, ABRip gives performance benefit of 6.38% over SRRIP. On top of ABRip, ACAM-ATD gives performance benefit of 4.68% on average. It gains performance by more than 10% compared to SRRIP for 10 out of 13 workload mixes. It gives maximum performance benefit of 19.22% over SRRIP for Mix-2. It outperforms SRRIP policy in all workload mixes and gives performance improvement of 11.35% on average which verifies that our approach is scalable to a large number of cores.

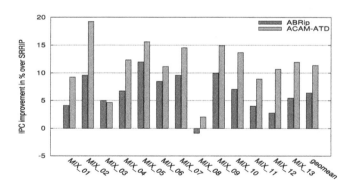

**Fig. 6.** IPC comparison of multi-programmed workloads: Combination shown in Table 2b

## 5.2 *mpki* Comparison

Figure 7 shows the *mpki* comparison of ABRip and ACAM-ATD over baseline SRRIP on a dual core CMPs. ACAM using ATD reduces *mpki* up to 22.53% over SRRIP for workloads *bzip-milc*. For Cf-Cf workload mixes, ABRip increases *mpki* by 9.94% over SRRIP. By choosing the best policy based on cache access

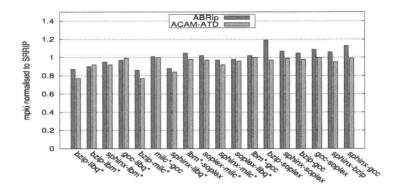

**Fig. 7.** *mpki* Comparison: Benchmarks with (*) are non-cache friendly application and rest are cache-friendly application

pattern, ACAM-ATD decreases *mpki* by 1.7% for Cf-Cf workload mixes and by 8.28% for Cf-Str workload mixes on an average over SRRIP.

### 5.3   Hardware Overhead

In order to implement ABRip over SRRIP, additional hardware required is 20 bits per set, i.e., 0.5% on top of SRRIP. a-ABRip does not require extra hardware on top of ABRip. In ACAM using SDM, additional hardware required on top of ABRip is 4 11-bits saturating counters and logic circuit is required to monitor and compare the miss rate to decide the winner policy. Hence hardware overhead to implement ACAM using SDM is very low on top of ABRip. In order to implement ACAM using ATD, hardware required to create ATD contributes to major portion of total hardware overhead over ABRip. Assuming 40 bit physical address space, total hardware require to create ATD is 1.16 KB. In addition to this, 2 11-bits saturating counters and logic circuit is required to compare the cache misses to decide the winner policy. Total hardware overhead to implement ACAM using ATD is 0.026% on top of ABRip.

## 6   Related Work

The replacement policy of LLC impacts system's performance considerably. Hence, many researchers from academia and industry have significantly contributed with their research work to the improvement in replacement policy managing LLCs. In this section, we summarize prior literature that is relevant to improving LLC's performance.

Jaleel et al. [5] proposed a policy for shared LLC which tried to reduce the interference from non-cache friendly application by inserting its most of cache block at LRU position using Bimodal Insertion Policy (BIP). Using SDM, they implemented BIP policy for non-cache friendly application and LRU policy for cache friendly application. However, LRU policy failed to manage cache blocks efficiently at private LLC even for cache friendly application [6].

Qureshi and Patt [9] logically partitioned the LLC dynamically. They used Utility Monitor (UMON) circuit to track the utility of LLC for each application. Based on each application cache's utility, they partitioned the *ways* in cache-sets among the applications sharing the LLC. They implemented two UMON circuits for dual core CMPs. Auxiliary tag directory (ATD) and counter for UMON circuit were used to study the cache's utility. However, they also used LRU as underlying replacement policy which is not efficient in managing *dead* blocks in LLC.

Wu et al. [10] observed the performance of DRRIP [6] LLC replacement policy in the presence of L2 cache prefetcher. They found that the cache blocks brought into LLC due to the prefetch requests pollute the cache. They tried to reduce such interferences by changing the insertion and promotion policy of prefetched cache blocks. Prefetched cache blocks brought in LLC were inserted at LRU position and were not promoted to MRU even on cache hit.

## 7    Conclusion

In this paper, we first proposed a-ABRip which helps further in reducing interference to Cf application from Str application when compared to ABRip for Cf-Str combination of workloads. However for Cf-Cf combination of workloads, SRRIP outperforms a-ABRip. To make replacement policy adaptive to different types of cache access pattern and different combination of workloads, we proposed a policy ACAM that switches between a-ABRip ($\alpha = 3$) and SRRIP based on type of cache access pattern. To learn the cache access pattern and decide which eviction policy is better for the next phase of program, we used SDM and ATD. We compared our policy with ABRip and SRRIP for SPEC CPU2006 benchmark. We found our policy ACAM-SDM outperforms ABRip and SRRIP by 2.97% and 1.96% respectively. ACAM-ATD outperforms SRRIP and ABRip by 2.32% and 3.33% respectively on average on 2-core CMPs. On 4-core CMPs, ACAM using ATD outperforms SRRIP and ABRip by 11.35% and 4.68% respectively on average.

## References

1. Borkar, S., Chien, A.A.: The future of microprocessors. Commun. ACM **54**(5), 67–77 (2011)
2. Carlson, T.E., Heirman, W., Eeckhout, L.: Sniper: Exploring the level of abstraction for scalable and accurate parallel multi-core simulation. In: Proceedings of 2011 International Conference for High Performance Computing, Networking, Storage and Analysis, p. 52. ACM (2011)
3. Henning, J.L.: SPEC CPU2006 benchmark descriptions. ACM SIGARCH Comput. Archit. News **34**(4), 1–17 (2006)
4. Intel: Intel Core i7 Processor. http://www.intel.com/products/processor/corei7/specifications.htm

5. Jaleel, A., Hasenplaugh, W., Qureshi, M., Sebot, J., Steely Jr., S., Emer, J.: Adaptive insertion policies for managing shared caches. In: Proceedings of the 17th International Conference on Parallel Architectures and Compilation Techniques, pp. 208–219. ACM (2008)
6. Jaleel, A., Theobald, K.B., Steely Jr., S.C., Emer, J.: High performance cache replacement using re-reference interval prediction (RRIP). In: ACM SIGARCH Computer Architecture News, vol. 38, pp. 60–71. ACM (2010)
7. Lathigara, P., Balachandran, S., Singh, V.: Application behavior aware re-reference interval prediction for shared LLC. In: Proceedings of the 33rd IEEE International Conference on Computer Design (ICCD), pp. 172–179. IEEE (2015)
8. Qureshi, M.K., Jaleel, A., Patt, Y.N., Steely Jr., S.C., Emer, J.: Adaptive insertion policies for high performance caching. In: ACM SIGARCH Computer Architecture News, vol. 35, pp. 381–391. ACM (2007)
9. Qureshi, M.K., Patt, Y.N.: Utility-based cache partitioning: A low-overhead, high-performance, runtime mechanism to partition shared caches. In: Proceedings of the 39th Annual IEEE/ACM International Symposium on Microarchitecture, IEEE Computer Society (2006) 423–432
10. Wu, C.J., Jaleel, A., Martonosi, M., Steely Jr., S.C., Emer, J.: Pacman: Prefetch-aware cache management for high performance caching. In: Proceedings of the 44th Annual IEEE/ACM International Symposium on Microarchitecture, pp. 442–453. ACM (2011)

# Adaptive Packet Throttling Technique for Congestion Management in Mesh NoCs

N. S. Aswathy[1(✉)], R. S. Reshma Raj[1], Abhijit Das[2], John Jose[2(✉)], and V. R. Josna[1]

[1] Goverment Engineering College Bartonhill, Trivandrum, Kerala, India
nsaswathy1993@gmail.com, reshmaraj26@gmail.com, josna.chandu@gmail.com
[2] Indian Institute of Technology Guwahati, Guwahati, Assam, India
{abhijit.das,johnjose}@iitg.ernet.in

**Abstract.** Network on Chip is an emerging communication framework for multi-core systems. Due to increasing number of cores and complex workloads, congestion management techniques in NoC are gaining more research focus. Packet throttling is one of a cost effective technique for congestion management. It delays the packet injection into the network, thereby regulating traffic in network and hence provide ease of packet movement generated by other critical applications. Finding point of throttling and rate of throttling are two major design issues that can impact the performance and stability of any throttling algorithm. Existing state of the art throttling techniques use local throttling decision coordinated by a single central controller. We overcome the issues related with this by partitioning the network into number of subnetworks, each with a zonal controller. Our experiment results in $8 \times 8$ 2D mesh with real traffic workloads consisting of SPEC 2006 CPU benchmarks shows an average packet latency reduction of 6.2% than the state of the art packet throttling techniques.

**Keywords:** Network congestion · Packet throttling

## 1 Introduction and Related Work

Design and scalability issues associated with increasing core counts on Chip Multi-Processors (CMPs) is a prominent research domain in computer architecture over the last decade. Communication among cores in these CMPs housing processors, caches and memory controllers is an important task that requires deeper exploration for better performance and throughput. Thus designing a scalable interconnect is critical for future energy efficient CMP designs.

Network-on-Chip (NoC), is a scalable, packet switched and distributed interconnect framework that offer much lower latency and higher bandwidth than their traditional bus based counter parts. In a tiled CMP each processing core encloses superscalar processor, a private L1 cache and slice of shared L2 cache distributed all over the CMP. Each of these processing core is connected to a

© Springer Nature Singapore Pte Ltd. 2017
B. K. Kaushik et al. (Eds.): VDAT 2017, CCIS 711, pp. 337–344, 2017.
https://doi.org/10.1007/978-981-10-7470-7_33

switching device called a router. Inter core communication is needed in the event of an L1 cache miss because the L2 look up happen at a core different from the source core due to the SNuCA based L2 cache block mapping. They use packet based communication where the packet contains control information like source address, destination address, L2 bank address etc. A source core creates a packet when an L1 miss occurs and it is injected into the local router. Input buffers and handshaking signals between routers facilitate flow control for packet movement between source and destination routers. Wormhole switching [1] is used in NoCs, where each of these packets are divided into smaller flow control units called flits. These packets traverse through the network to the destination core by following the routing algorithm implemented in the router.

As more and more packets compete for shared resources like routers and links, the overall system throughput degrades drastically. This network congestion, if not dealt properly can eventually bring the entire system down. Source throttling is an efficient congestion-control approach for improving system performance. Cores injecting large traffic and crowding the network are throttled temporarily from packet injection.

Source throttling in wormhole networks are studied even before NoC became a popular alternative to traditional bus and crossbar interconnects [1,2]. Global-knowledge-based and self tuned source throttling technique in multiprocessor networks [2] gracefully adapts to the dynamic congestion pattern. Fairness via source throttling (FST) [3], proposes to measure the unfairness in shared memory system. Then based on a threshold, traffic from cores that cause unfairness in the system are throttled down. ACT (Adaptive Cluster Throttling) [4], explore the possibility of making application clusters based on traffic traits and then throttling these clusters alternatively. Nychis et al. [5] propose a low complexity and high performance source throttling technique with application-level awareness for reducing network congestion. Heterogeneous Adaptive Throttling (HAT) [6] which is the first throttling technique combining both application aware and network load aware allows network-sensitive applications to make fast progress by throttling network-intensive applications.

## 2   Motivation

Source throttling is introduced in NoC for tackling with heavy traffics from data intensive applications. The effort is to mitigate congestion by identifying network intensive cores and then selectively throttling packet injections from those cores to reduce congestion in the system. As the congestion goes down, the system performance improves and throttling is disabled.

Since heterogenous applications inject diverse traffic into the network, a source throttling technique must be application aware for deciding on whom to throttle. Blindly throttling applications only based on their traffic pattern might lead to under or over utilization of network resources. A source throttling technique must also be network aware for knowing the throttling rate. Moreover the hardware that implements throttling should be simple. Available techniques in literature are either application oblivious [2], network load unaware [5] or sub-optimal [3,4,6].

In this paper we identify the limitations of HAT [6] and suggest few modifications so as to improve its performance. HAT uses local throttling decisions taken by the respective core. In HAT each application is classified by a central controller either network intensive or network non-intensive applications based on the number of packets it is inject into the network at regular time period. Cores which inject packets greater than a threshold are classified as network intensive and others fall under the group of network non-intensive. All the network intensive applications are throttled in the subsequent time period. The problem with this method is that it may lead to either over throttling or under throttling. Over throttling happens when every core injects packets which is higher than a threshold value set by the central controller leading to throttling of all the cores. Under throttling occurs when most of the cores inject very less packets while few injects packets just higher than the threshold. Even though there is no much congestion in the network, the cores which generate misses above threshold are throttled. Both over throttling and under throttling happen because each core is unaware about what is the injection pattern in other cores. We identify around 7 number of over throttling cases and 8 number of under throttling cases on an average upon implementing HAT using the five SPEC 2006 CPU benchmark mix (Refer Table 1 for workloads).

Another problem with HAT is the single central controller. After receiving packet count updates from each core, the central controller finds out the rate of throttling. But for large networks, having a single central controller is a big bottleneck as it is not a scalable proposal. The single central controller can cause high round trip delay. Let $t$ be the transmission time for the request to the central controller and $d$ be the processing delay at the central controller. The core need to wait $2t + d$ time to receive the response (round trip time). Since there is a single central controller situated at the center of the mesh, both $d$ and $t$ also can be high. Because of the slow response from the central controller, the system stabilization time also increases. Our experimental implemetation of HAT shows that in an $8 \times 8$ mesh, the round trip delay of control packets that carry crucial throttling parameters from a core to the central controller can be around 40-45 cycles. We also find that the central controller can become a hotspot at regular intervals due to flooding of control packets from various other cores.

Exploring further on the above mentioned limitations of HAT, we propose an improved application and network load aware, adaptive source throttling technique with a distributed zonal controller logic that implements differential throttling. Evaluation and comparison studies of our approach with the existing proposals are found in our favour with improved system performance.

## 3   Proposed Method

In our approach, a 2D mesh with an $8 \times 8$ organization is considered. The whole network is logically partitioned into four $4 \times 4$ subnetworks. Instead of using

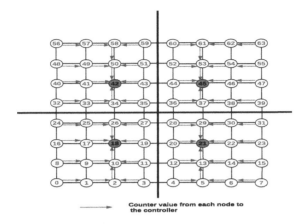

**Fig. 1.** Sending counter values from all nodes to the zonal controllers

a single central controller like in HAT [6], we use four zonal controllers, one for each of the four partitions as shown in Fig. 1. The four zonal controllers (shown in dark colours) eliminate the single central controller bottleneck. The zonal controllers are selected in such a way that it should have at least two-hop neighbour in each of the four directions. This is to ensure that the zonal controller is approximately in the center of the respective partition, so that, the controller can legitimately control all the cores within that partition. We use a 5-bit counter per core to record the cache misses generated by the core.

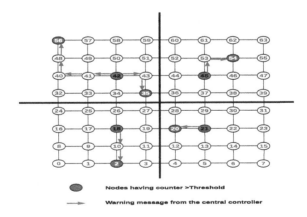

**Fig. 2.** Zonal controller sending warning messages

The whole time period is sequentially divided into a series of three phases: (a) measurement phase-M, (b) processing phase-P and (c) throttling phase-T. During the measurement phase, the counter is incremented for each of the miss generated by the respective core. At the beginning of the processing phase, the miss statistics from each of the cores in the partition is send to the zonal controller as shown in Fig. 1. The zonal controller receives information from each of the core in its partition. For example, all nodes in partition 1 send control packets at the end of measurement phase to node 18. Node 18 will process these information received and determines the throttling parameters. A threshold is set by the zonal controller and warning messages are send back to the respective cores which hold a counter value greater than the threshold as shown in Fig. 2. For example in partition 3 (top left partition) the zonal controller 42 identifies 35 and 56 as the nodes whose cache miss count value during the measurement phase is greater than the threshold. So warning messages are send to 35 and 56 during the processing phase to initiate throttling. Unlike in HAT, here the zonal controller determines which core to be throttled instead of the local core. Hence this approach avoids the problems associated with local throttling decision. During the throttling phase, packets generated from the cores having counter value greater than threshold will be throttled at a pre-determined rate. If throttling rate is 2/3, two packets will be throttled out of the three packets generated. Likewise, if throttling rate is 1/3, one packet will be throttled out of the three packets generated by the core. The counter is updated for each measurement phase based on the number of misses generated by the core during the time window. This ensures that the same core is not throttled every time.

Here we use a time window of 128 cycles for the measurement phase, i.e., for every 128 cycles the counter is updated. For the processing phase we use 32 cycles, i.e., with in this 32 cycles the counter statistics is send to the respective zonal controllers from the cores and the zonal controllers will send the warning message to the cores having counter statistics greater than the threshold of 15. After that for a 128 cycle, the cores which receive the warning message are throttled as per throttling rate mentioned.

Throttling is not blocking packets, it is temporarily delaying packets injected into the network. The throttled packets tries to inject into the network during subsequent cycles. Here we provide 2 cycle delay for each of the throttled packets i.e., after the packet is throttled the core will try to inject the throttled packet after 2 cycles. If a new packet is generated in the core during the same cycle it will be queued in the core just after the throttled packets. Preference will be given to already throttled packets than newly generated packets waiting for injection into the router. This makes sure that none of the throttled packets will be delayed for a longer time duration.

## 4   Experimental Analysis

### 4.1   Simulation Setup

We use Booksim2.0 [7], the cycle accurate NoC simulator for modelling $8 \times 8$ CMP with 2D topology. Booksim supports NoC traffic from real traffic traces in addition to the synthetic traffic patterns. We use the network traces generated by a 64 core CMP (modelled via GEM5 architectural simulator) upon running 64 instances of different SPEC 2006 CPU benchmark applications.

In GEM5 [8], we run one instance of a SPEC 2006 CPU benchmark application on each of the core. Based on the misses per kilo instructions (MPKI) each SPEC application is grouped into Low MPKI (less than 5), Medium MPKI (between 5 and 25) and High MPKI(greater than 25). In our experiment we consider *calculix, gobmk, gromacs, h264ref* under Low MPKI, *bwaves, bzip2, gamess, gcc* under Medium MPKI and *hmmer.nph3, lbm, mcf, leslie3d* under High MPKI. We construct 5 workload mixes based on the proportion of network injection intensity of these applications as given in Table 1. To understand the distribution of benchmarks in workloads, consider workload 3 (WL3). Out of 64 cores, 16 cores run *bwaves* benchmark, 16 cores run *bzip2* benchmark, 16 cores run *gamess* benchmark and the remaining 16 cores run *gcc* benchmark. Similarly other workloads can also be described.

The network trace generated by the above multicore workload is given to Booksim for modelling the NoC events and statistics are collected. Each of the NoC router port is associated with 8 VCs. We use the dimension order routing algorithm. All cache miss requests are single flit packets and cache miss replies are 4-flit packets.

## 4.2 Results and Discussions

If a core is identified as to be throttled for a single throttling phase, then it is called one instance of throttling. Similarly if a core is identified as to be throttled for $m$ consecutive throttling phases and another core is to be throttled for $n$ consecutive throttling phases then altogether it is considered as $(m+n)$ instances of throttling.

**Table 1.** Workload Constitution

| Workload# | SPEC 2006 Benchmarks | | | |
|---|---|---|---|---|
| WL1 | calculix(16) | gobmk(16) | gromacs(16) | h264ref(16) |
| WL2 | calculix(16) | gobmk(16) | gamess(16) | gcc(16) |
| WL3 | bwaves(16) | bzip2(16) | gamess(16) | gcc(16) |
| WL4 | bwaves(16) | bzip2(16) | hmmer.nph3(16) | lbm(16) |
| WL5 | hmmer.nph3(16) | lbm(16) | mcf(16) | leslie3d(16) |

Here, different workload mixes results in different number of throttling instances. From the result analysis, we have identified that a higher MPKI workload leads into a larger number of throttled instances while a lower MPKI workload results in a smaller number of throttled instances. For low MPKI workload(WL1) we have identified 22 throttling instances and for workload WL2 113 instances are identified. The medium MPKI workload WL3 results 495 throttling

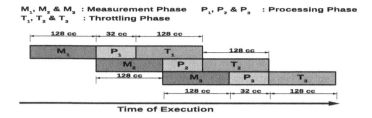

**Fig. 3.** Various phases in the application execution

instances and for the workload WL4 998 throttling instances are identified. The largest number of instances are identified for higher MPKI wokload WL5 which is around 1271.

Figure 3 illustrates how the proposed system behaves in the different phases of execution. Let $M_1, M_2, M_3, ...$ be the different measurement phases, $P_1, P_2, P_3, ...$ be the different processing phases and $T_1, T_2, T_3, ...$ be the different throttling phases of the entire time frame in the application's execution. Consider $M_i$, $P_i$ and $T_i$. During $M_i$ the counter value for each of the core is incremented for every cache miss request from that core. These statistics is send to the respective zonal controllers at the beginning of $P_i$. The zonal controllers will send the warning message to the cores with number of packets greater than the threshold during $P_i$. The cores which receive warning messages are throttled during $T_i$. After the completion of the first measurement phase $M_1$, the next phase of measurement $M_2$ starts the execution in parallel with the processing phase $P_1$. Similarly, a third measurement phase $M_3$ is initiated at the beginning of processing phase $P_2$. This series continues throughout the execution of program in a pipelined manner.

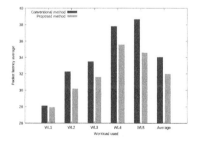

**Fig. 4.** Overall packet latency

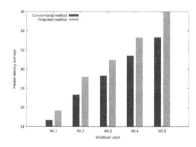

**Fig. 5.** Throttled packet latency

Figure 4 shows the overall packet latency obtained from both conventional method and proposed technique. We can see from the figure that using the proposed method the overall latency of the system is reduced considerably. The control overhead induced by throttling is not affecting the overall packet latency of the network. Figure 5 plots the packet latency of the throttled packets. By packet throttling we are delaying the packet injection. Hence the overall packet latency of throttled packets will be high. Delaying the packets from the congestion causing cores helps the unthrottling cores to inject packets into a least congested network and hence can reach the destination with minimal latency. Thus the average packet latency of the entire network can be reduced.

## 5   Conclusion

Congestion in NoC is a challenging issue to be solved with cost effective techniques. Packet throttling is one kind of such technique, which suppress packet injection into the network from the core causing congestion. We proposed a cost effective packet throttling technique which properly manages the point of throttling and the rate of throttling. Multiple zonal controllers in our technique help to overcome over-throttling and under-throttling issues of the existing throttling techniques. Unthrottled packets get more benefit by throttling of heavy injection cores. Results showed that the number of throttling instances increases with the increase in number of misses. Also, the overall packet latency of the system is decreased by throttling the congestion causing cores.

## References

1. Baydal, E., et al.: A congestion control mechanism for wormhole networks. In: Ninth Euromicro Workshop on Parallel and Distributed Processing. IEEE, pp. 19–26 (2001)
2. Thottethodi, M., et al.: Self-tuned congestion control for multiprocessor networks. In: The Seventh International Symposium on High-Performance Computer Architecture, HPCA, pp. 107–118. IEEE (2001)
3. Ebrahimi, E., et al.: Fairness via source throttling: a configurable and high-performance fairness substrate for multi-core memory systems. ACM SIGPLAN Not. **45**(3), 335–346 (2010). ACM
4. Ausavarungnirun, R., et al.: Adaptive cluster throttling: improving high-load performance in bufferless on-chip networks. Computer Architecture Lab (CALCM), Carnegie Mellon University, SAFARI Technical Report TR-2011-006 (2011)
5. Nychis, G.P., et al.: On-chip networks from a networking perspective: congestion and scalability in many-core interconnects. ACM SIGCOMM Comput. Commun. Rev. **42**(4), 407–418 (2012)
6. Chang, K.K.-W., et al.: HAT: heterogeneous adaptive throttling for on-chip networks. In: IEEE 24th International Symposium on Computer Architecture and High Performance Computing (SBAC-PAD), pp. 9–18. IEEE (2012)
7. Jiang, N., et al.: A detailed and flexible cycle-accurate network-on-chip simulator. In: 2013 IEEE International Symposium on Performance Analysis of Systems and Software (ISPASS), pp. 86–96. IEEE (2013)
8. Binkert, N., et al.: The gem5 simulator. ACM SIGARCH Comput. Architect. News **39**(2), 1–7 (2011)

# Defeating HaTCh: Building Malicious IP Cores

Anshu Bhardwaj[(✉)] and Subir Kumar Roy

International Institute of Information Technology, Bangalore, India
Anshu.aggrawal@iiitb.org, subir@iiitb.ac.in

**Abstract.** Possibility of Hardware Trojans (HT) being present in SOCs designed by integrating hundreds of third party IP (3PIP) cores provided by different vendors is well documented. Our focus in this paper is to highlight the vulnerability of such SOCs to HTs. We achieve this by demonstrating a novel approach to the design of a simple and extremely small footprint HT. We present a detailed discussion to demonstrate that HaTCh, one of the latest and best HT detection technique, will fail to detect our Trojan. The paper concludes by highlighting the vulnerabilities of SOCs designed with 3PIP cores and need for trusted IP cores.

**Keywords:** Hardware Trojan · Malicious IPs · Security
Traffic flow confidentiality · High assurance system

## 1 Introduction

Time and again concerns are being raised with respect to security of FPGA designs especially in sensitive cryptographic applications. FPGA viruses can configure the FPGA to short-circuit [3] or a backdoor in military-grade FPGA device can access or modify sensitive information [4]. Such kind of malicious modifications, called "Hardware Trojans" (HTs) are defined as unspecified functions in hardware. HTs are inserted to disable, or to destroy a system at a future time, or to leak secret keys covertly.

Due to the complexity of most of the IP cores, it is not possible to exhaustively verify them for complete set of combinational and sequential inputs. Also HTs are typically designed to remain inactive during normal functional verification/testing. HT Detection techniques UCI [5], VeriTrust [6], FANCI [7] rely on these attributes of a HT. In Defeating UCI [8] and DeTrust [9], authors have designed HTs that could not be detected by the above approaches. However, the two main drawbacks of the above three approaches are due to their assumption of a shallow temporal depth for the triggering events and their limited ability to detect circuits listed in a small constant set of publicly known HT benchmarks such as TrustHub [11]. Their HT detection ability on publicly unknown HTs [14] is not clear. Very recently Haider et al. [12] proposed a new algorithm called HaTCh (Hardware Trojan Catcher) which can detect any Trojan from a class of deterministic HTs called $H_D$, with negligible small false negative rate and controllable false positive rate. To examine the possibility of successfully inserting a HT in an IP block that could evade detection by HaTCh, we give the design of a low overhead HT that leaks secret encryption keys used in the Advanced Encryption Standard (AES) [18]. Our Trojan implementation is an improvement on the similar Trojans reported in the

© Springer Nature Singapore Pte Ltd. 2017
B. K. Kaushik et al. (Eds.): VDAT 2017, CCIS 711, pp. 345–353, 2017.
https://doi.org/10.1007/978-981-10-7470-7_34

literature [7–11]. We have carried out analysis and demonstrated that these HTs will be detected during the cryptanalysis phase. The design improvement that we propose here will enable the HT to evade detection during functional testing, cryptanalysis, formal verification based approach and the HaTCh algorithm.

The paper is organized into five sections. Section 1 is on introduction. Section 2 gives a brief on HT design and different detection techniques as reported in the literature and possible security violations. In Sect. 3, we describe the design of the proposed HT, its vulnerability analysis and the improvements required with reasoning and measures built to prevent its detection during functional verification, as well as, during cryptanalysis. Section 4 describes different HT detection techniques. For each detection technique we explain rigorously why these schemes will fail to detect our proposed HT. We lay emphasis on our analysis of the vulnerability of the HaTCh algorithm vis-à-vis the proposed HT design as we believe that this is the best reported HT detection algorithm in the literature. This paper ends with conclusion in Sect. 5.

## 2   Motivation and Attack Model

Innovative HT design and detection is a very active area of research, a good glimpse of which can be found in [1, 2, 15]. HT detection using side channel analysis, activation techniques, UCI or malicious trigger circuits have been reported. However, every time any researcher comes up with a new Trojan design, it is countered with an improved detection mechanism and vice-versa, much like an arms race.

### 2.1   Potential Security Violations

Security specialists (for example, Anderson in [16]) have found it useful to place potential security violations in three different categories:

(1) *Unauthorized information release:* An unauthorized person is able to read information stored within a computer. This *extends to traffic analysis* in which the patterns of information usage are observed to infer the information content.
(2) *Unauthorized information modification:* An unauthorized person is able to make changes in stored information– this constitutes a form of sabotage.
(3) *Unauthorized denial of use:* An intruder can prevent an authorized user from referring to or modifying information.

### 2.2   Traffic Flow Confidentiality (TFC)

Whereas, traditional communication security relies on encryption algorithms to protect sensitive information flowing over a network, extensive research has shown that the statistical pattern of traffic generated in any communication has been successfully used to gather information contents or successfully decipher passwords transmitted over encrypted sessions. Security measures called TFC are devised to hide the traffic pattern and is defined as a security protocol in the IPSEC security architecture [17].

# 3   Simple Low Overhead Trojan Design and Implementation

### 3.1   IP Core Specifications and Trojan Idea

The IP core considered in this paper is designed for the following requirements,

(1) *Advanced Encryption Standard (AES) 128-bit encryption engine [18]*
(2) *Pseudo-Random bit Sequence Generator (PRSG)*
(3) *Multiplexer to select between cipher output and PRSG output*
(4) *Automatic transmission of PRSG output whenever there is no cipher output, to enable obfuscation of user traffic in order to provide traffic flow confidentiality*

It may be noted that although the transmission of continuous random pattern on a link would increase the bandwidth and power; for dedicated military networks, these stringent security measures are acceptable for select high profile links [21].

### 3.2   IP Core Design with Embedded Trojan

The AES IP is an open source design [13], as per the standard AES specifications, in Electronic Code Book mode and the user can write their own secret keys. HT is inserted inside this IP Core to leak secret encryption key, as shown in Fig. 1. The proposed Trojan is of always ON type, as the attack model assumes that adversary cannot control inputs and hence cannot trigger HT. The key bits are randomized before transmission by the Trojan, so to a benign observer the flow of output bit patterns appears random, much like the cipher text and/or the PRSG bits, however an eavesdropper with prior knowledge of the proposed Trojan design can extract the encryption key bits.

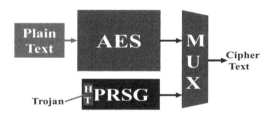

**Fig. 1.**   IP Core with embedded Trojan design

In the HT designs proposed in [11, 15] a 64-bit long pattern is used to spread each key bit. However, when these designs are subjected to cryptanalysis, as per mandatory FIPS 140-2 standard [19], frequent transmission of any particular pattern will be easily detected leading to detection of suspicious behaviour and thereby, detection of the Trojan.

### 3.3   Analysis and Improvement in Trojan to Prevent Detection

As explained above, statistical analysis will easily detect frequent repetition of a 64-bit pattern in a random stream. Slow transmission of key bits, one bit every $2^{64}$ bits, matching the random occurrence probability, means that one bit is leaked every 2.3 Exabytes, making key extraction impractical. Moreover, UCI, FANCI, VeriTrust, etc. will detect the trigger logic or the malicious payload consisting of, for example, registers storing the spreading bit patterns, as suspicious unused logic.

Our proposed HT design is capable of transmitting and receiving key bits clandestinely, over the same output pin without requiring any fixed known bit pattern to spread the key bits. Therefore leakage of key bits will not be detected during functional as well as statistical testing. Further, as the Trojan trigger is not based on occurrence of any rare event; there are no unused circuits/logic to be tagged as malicious.

The proposed Trojan design employs self-synchronizing scramblers [20] also called multiplicative scramblers, used widely in communication systems. The polynomial equation for our PRSG is: $x^{128} + x^{80} + x^{18} + x^{17} + x^{16} + x^{15} + x^{14} + x^{13} + x^{12} + x^{11} + x^{10} + x^9 + x^8 + x^7 + x^6 + x^5 + x^4 + x^3 + x^2 + x^1 + 1$. At the transmitter, key bit is xored with the feedback bit of LFSR, based on the key bit being '1' or '0' the PRSG output will be inverted or not. In the key extractor, a LFSR with same structure as PRSG is running, Fig. 2 below.

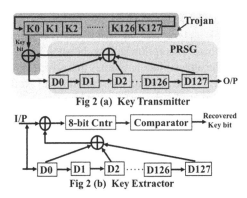

Fig. 2. Malicious transmission of key bits and extraction

The feedback bit of this LFSR is compared (xored) with the incoming data, output of IP block, for the length of the shift register (128). If the key bit is '0' then the PRSG output at the transmitter and feedback bit of key extractor will be same and hence the output of this XOR gate will be '0' throughout and the 8-bit counter value will remain at '0', after 128 clock cycles; while, if key bit is a '1' then since the PRSG output at the transmitter is inverted, XOR gate output at the key extractor side will be '1' and the 8-bit counter value will be 128 at the end of 128 clock cycles. To cater for the channel errors, the comparator compares the counter value with 3 or 125 instead of '0' and '128'. The comparator can be set to any other values like 5 or 123, as well, without impacting design results. Whenever user data is present at the input of the IP core it sends out the encrypted output of the AES block through the output Mux gate. The output of the comparator in the malicious receiver will then be some value close to 64, as there is 50% chance of a mismatch between the feedback bit of extractor and the cipher data bits, which is deemed to be unrelated to key bits. With this approach all the 128 key bits are correctly recovered in the malicious receiver by the adversary.

The salient point of this scheme is that the adversary must only know the feedback polynomial of the PRSG and not the seed value in the PRSGs. Since, the output of transmitter PRSG is used as input of the receiver PRSG, the two PRSGs will fall in step after maximum of 256 bits (i.e. twice the length of PRSG), irrespective of the initial seed value. The feedback polynomial is known to adversary as its part of specifications of IP Core. Further, the length of LFSR for PRSG is carefully chosen to be 128, same as AES block size to enable re-use of counters by the HT and keys are written simultaneously into AES module and the shift register of HT during the same write cycle and using the same write signal, requiring no additional logic. The malicious receiver logic can be implemented independently to extract secret keys by eavesdropping the traffic over the link and need not be the part of actual IP core.

The proposed HT design in Verilog and its insertion in the IP core was successfully implemented in EP3C80F780I7 ALTERA Cyclone III FPGA using Quartus II software (Ver 13.0.1), with the key bits correctly extracted by Trojan operating at a nominal clock frequency of 80 MHz. This Trojan requires addition of a 128-bit shift register and a 2-input XOR gate only, in the golden design. As can be seen in Table 1 below, the small foot-print of the HT ($<< 1\%$ resource overhead) have negligible impact on power consumption, thereby rendering it difficult to detect using side channel and resource overhead analysis based Trojan detection mechanisms.

**Table 1.** Resource and power comparison

| Resource | With Trojan | Without Trojan |
|---|---|---|
| Logic elements | 12,878/81,264 | 12,744/81,264 |
| Dedicated logic registers | 5149/81,264 | 5019/81264 |
| Total pins | 31/430 | 31/430 |
| Memory bits | 628,800/2,810,880 | 628,800/2,810,880 |
| Total power | 118.85 mW | 117.75 mW |
| I/O power | 17.72 mW | 17.71 mW |

# 4   Verifying Trust

## 4.1   Functional Verification

Our benchmark test cases generate matching encrypted data blocks at the outputs of both the AES modules (with and without HT) to confirm that our Trojan does not affect any of the normal existing functional outputs directly. Also 100 millions bits of outputs from the two IP cores, (golden and Trojan infected) are collected in 1000 files each of size 1 Lakh bits and subjected to FIPS140-2 tests for a significance factor of 0.05, Table 2, confirming our claim that an IP core with this HT will pass statistical tests.

**Table 2.** Statistical test results

| Test | With Trojan | Without Trojan |
|------|-------------|----------------|
| Monobit | 905 | 906 |
| Serial | 923 | 923 |
| Poker | 928 | 911 |
| Runs | 919 | 941 |
| AutoCorrelation (d = 1, 8, 16) | 944, 958, 946 | 951, 956, 942 |

## 4.2  Detection Evasion for UCI, VeriTrust and DeTrust

Hicks et al. [5] first addressed the problem of identifying HTs by formulating it as an unused circuit identification problem. Their UCI technique detects a large number of benchmark HT designs from Trust-Hub suite. Gates with low activation probability and that are not driven by functional inputs are marked as suspicious by FANCI [7] and VeriTrust [10], respectively. Sturton et al. [8] and DeTrust [9] subsequently proposed design of HTs that would evade detection by UCI, FANCI and VeriTrust.

From the functional and the behavioural description of our proposed HT design it is clear that since our HT is always active and is driven by functional inputs, all the above three approaches will fail to detect it.

## 4.3  Formal Verification

Another drawback of the above three HT detection approaches is their assumption of a shallow temporal depth for the triggering events which activate HT. Rajendran et al. [10] have used formal methods to detect long temporal depth triggers and unauthorized information leakage by 3PIPs upon violation of a pre-defined set of security properties. The properties defined by them check if either the encryption key bits or any Boolean function on them are directly mapped to (or their values are directly observable on) any of the output bits of the IP core. In our HT design none of the key bits are directly mapped to any of the output port bits. Moreover, each key bit can be seen to be functionally mapped to a 128-bit vector by the PRSG block, with the mapping function being sequential in behaviour. This would render it extremely difficult to code a formal property to infer that the payload constitutes information leakage as the temporal depths over which the encryption key leakage takes place will be over several millions of clock cycles which would be huge for any SAT based bounded model checking tool to verify.

## 4.4  HaTCh

Haider et al. in their paper [12] have proposed a rigorous algorithm HaTCh (Hardware Trojan Catcher) which according to their claim detects any HT from a huge class of deterministic HTs ($H_D$) which is orders of magnitude larger than the small subclass (e.g. TrustHub), considered in the current literature. They have also discussed its superiority compared to existing techniques like FANCI, VeriTrust, Formal Methods etc. and proven its success on a number of Trojans from Trust hub as well as the Trojans referred in DeTrust. The HaTCh algorithm has two steps:

1. The first step is learning phase: In this phase, a set of k input test vectors are applied to the *Core* being checked for presence of HTs. All the input states (wires) that are reached by *Core* during test are white listed and the rest of the states (wires) are considered to be part of the blacklist. At the end of the learning the final blacklist is obtained. In addition, any malicious behavior during this phase is flagged by HaTCh as Trojan Detected and execution is immediately terminated.
2. In the next step called the tagging phase, *Core* is transformed to $Core_{Protected}$ by adding a set of extra logic for each entry in the blacklist; these extra logic circuits propagate a '1' to an observable output in case any of their corresponding blacklist wires are activated.

The approach proposed in HaTCh considers only the set of HTs that maliciously deliver their payload over the I/O channels violating the functional specs of the *Core*.

## 4.5   Defeating HaTCh

As per the first step of HaTCh algorithm, a set of $k$ inputs are applied to the IP Core and its functional I/Os are verified against the expected output. As none of the blocks in the AES module are modified, for every valid plain text input to the AES module corresponding correct cipher output is generated. Next, as a part of the learning phase HaTCh starts the process of blacklisting any unused logic. From Fig. 2(a), it can be seen that the HT is essentially a 128-bit circular shift register and an XOR gate. The PRSG length is chosen to be 128-bit to match the block length of AES. The 8-bit counter free runs; whenever the counter rolls over, in absence of cipher text, it shifts the key register by one-bit position. The new key bit is scrambled by PRSG and this data is transmitted during the idle phase. Logic used to detect presence or absence of cipher text is essential for switching between cipher text and PRSG; however, it is part of the IP core's specifications. Similarly, the 8-bit counter is needed to serially shift out the 128-bit cipher block from the AES module, and therefore, is part of the IP core specs.

At the first application of user plain text input, the AES engine will execute to generate cipher data and shift it out; concurrently the PRSG is operational. It will be changing one of the input of the XOR gate (the other input is fed with a new encryption key bit) resulting in its output also changing randomly, and therefore, this Xor gate will not be flagged as unused logic. As soon as the cipher data is shifted out the, circular shift register having the encryption keys will shift by one-bit position causing each of the registers and wires to change their state; therefore, these will never be blacklisted during the learning phase. Thus, none of the circuit elements in the proposed HT design will be blacklisted by HaTCh algorithm, enabling it to evade detection by HaTCh.

# 5 Conclusion

In this paper, an innovative hardware Trojan design for leakage of cryptographic keys is demonstrated. Insertion of such hardware Trojans are not just limited to cryptographic IP cores alone; this is because in almost all digital communication systems (DCS), toggling patterns called whitening patterns are inserted in the transmitted data to enable clock recovery by Phase Locked Loop (PLL) circuits. The proposed small footprint Trojan can be inserted in modems, set-top boxes, EVMs, ATM machines, etc. to leak protected information stored in them. Verification for detecting security vulnerabilities requires looking for undocumented functionality, which is similar to searching for a needle in a hay-stack. The only remedy for protection from HTs is to restrict IP-cores usage and strictly procure them from known and trusted sources or vendors. Sometimes this may not be practical, therefore it is critical to investigate HTs in IP cores and develop mitigation techniques not only for security sensitive applications like defence and finance, but also for overall critical infrastructure.

# References

1. Tehranipoor, M., Koushanfar, F.: A survey of hardware trojan taxonomy and detection. IEEE Des. Test Comput. **27**(1), 10–25 (2010)
2. King, S., et al.: Designing and implementing malicious hardware. In: Proceedings of the 1st USENIX Workshop Large-Scale Exploits and Emergent Threats (LEET 2008), pp. 1–8. Usenix Assoc. (2008)
3. Hadžić, I., Udani, S., Smith, J.M.: FPGA viruses. In: Lysaght, P., Irvine, J., Hartenstein, R. (eds.) FPL 1999. LNCS, vol. 1673, pp. 291–300. Springer, Heidelberg (1999). https://doi.org/10.1007/978-3-540-48302-1_30
4. Skorobogatov, S., Woods, C.: Breakthrough silicon scanning discovers backdoor in military chip. In: Prouff, E., Schaumont, P. (eds.) CHES 2012. LNCS, vol. 7428, pp. 23–40. Springer, Heidelberg (2012). https://doi.org/10.1007/978-3-642-33027-8_2
5. Hicks, M., et al.: Overcoming an untrusted computing base: detecting and removing malicious hardware automatically. In: Proceedings of the IEEE Symposium on Security and Privacy, pp. 159–172 (2010)
6. Zhang, J., et al.: VeriTrust: verification for hardware trust. IEEE Trans. Comput.-Aided Des. Integr. Circuits Syst. **34**(7), 1148–1161 (2015)
7. Waksman, A., et al.: FANCI: identification of stealthy malicious logic using boolean functional analysis. In: ACM Conference on Computer and Communications Security, pp. 697–708 (2013)
8. Sturton, C., Hicks, M., Wagner, D., King, S.T.: Defeating UCI: building stealthy and malicious hardware. In: IEEE Symposium on Security and Privacy, SP 2011, pp. 64–77 (2011)
9. Zhang, J., Yuan, F., Xu, Q.: DeTrust: defeating hardware trust verification with stealthy implicitly-triggered Hardware Trojans. In: ACM Conference on Computer and Communications Security, pp. 153–166 (2014)
10. Rajendran, J., Dhandayuthapanyy, A., Vedulaz, V., Karriy, R.: Formal security verification of third party intellectual property cores for information leakage. In: 29th International Conference on VLSI Design and 15th International Conference on Embedded Systems (2016)
11. Tehranipoor, M., Karri, R., Koushanfar, F., Potkonjak, M.: Trusthub, http://trust-hub.org

12. Haider, S.K., Jin, C.. Ahmad, M., Shila, D., Khan, O., van Dijk, M.: Advancing the state-of-the-art in hardware trojans detection. IEEE Trans. Dependable Secure Comput. PP(99), 1 (2016). https://doi.org/10.1109/TDSC.2017.2654352
13. https://opencores.org/project,tiny_aes
14. Haider, S.K., Jin, C., van Dijk, M.: Advancing the State-of-the-Art in Hardware Trojans Design, arXiv:1605.08413
15. Jin, Y., Makris, Y.: Hardware Trojans in wireless cryptographic ICs. IEEE Des. Test Comput. **27**(1), 26–35 (2010)
16. Saltzer, J., Schroeder, M.: The protection of information in computer systems. Proc. IEEE **63**(9), 1278 (1975)
17. Kiraly, C., et al.: Traffic flow confidentiality in IPsec: protocol and implementation. In: Third IFIP/FIDIS Summer School. The Future of Identity in the Information Society (2007)
18. [AES], http://csrc.nist.gov/publications/fips/fips197/fips197.pdf
19. csrc.nist.gov/publications/fips/fips140-2/fips1402.pdf
20. http://www.ece.ubc.ca/~edc/3525.jan2014/lectures/lec13.pdf
21. Schutz, R.: Protected Core Networking – Concepts & Challenges (2010), www.dtic.mil/get-tr-doc/pdf?AD=ADA584052

# Low Cost Circuit Level Implementation
# of PRESENT-80 S-BOX

S. Shanthi Rekha and P. Saravanan[(⊠)]

Department of ECE, PSG College of Technology, Coimbatore, India
shanthirekhapsg@gmail.com, dpsaravanan@gmail.com

**Abstract.** PRESENT-80 algorithm is based on Substitution-Permutation Network (SPN) with a data-size of 64-bits and key-size of 80-bits. While the permutation operation can be performed by simple wiring, Substitution operation (S-box) is the only non-linear component consuming maximum resources. The existing works in literature concentrate on the algorithmic implementation of PRESENT. This work is the first of its kind to explore the circuit level implementation of PRESENT algorithm by identifying an optimized architecture for the S-box. This is achieved by realizing the PRESENT S-box using static CMOS logic styles in 180 nm technology. Comparison results of two different architectures of PRESENT S-box using the static CMOS logic styles is tabulated.

**Keywords:** Lightweight ciphers · PRESENT-80 Substitution Box
Static CMOS logic styles · Circuit level implementation
Low cost implementation

## 1 Introduction

IoT, WSN, Smart cards and RFID applications are growing in fast pace with tight security and privacy requirements. Cryptographic algorithms are incorporated into these devices in order to provide the required information security. The general class of cryptographic algorithms are not suitable for these applications because of the stringent area and power requirements. Several lightweight ciphers have been proposed to be adaptable to these environments namely PRESENT, CLEFIA, KATAN etc. Among these PRESENT and CLEFIA are the two ISO/IEC 29192-2 approved lightweight cryptographic ciphers. PRESENT has less hardware complexity compared to CLEFIA and there are various works in literature for the optimized algorithmic implementations of PRESENT. However the circuit level optimization techniques for the algorithm remains unexplored.

PRESENT algorithm was proposed by Bogdanov et al. in 2007 [1], following which authors of [2] have proposed three different architectures for PRESENT algorithm namely (i) A round-based architecture for low cost active smart devices with a 64-bit data-path (ii)A Parallel architecture for high end active smart devices with loop unrolling to achieve highest throughput with a penalty in area (iii) A Serialized approach with a 4-bit data-path for low cost passive smart devices targeting lowest area, as low as 1000 Gate Equivalents (GE). Similarly in [3], iterative and serialized architecture of

© Springer Nature Singapore Pte Ltd. 2017
B. K. Kaushik et al. (Eds.): VDAT 2017, CCIS 711, pp. 354–362, 2017.
https://doi.org/10.1007/978-981-10-7470-7_35

PRESENT are implemented on Virtex FPGA and the results reveal that iterative architecture has a 5x increase in throughput/slice factor compared to the serialized one.

Focusing PRESENT S-box optimization, the proposal in [4] is to choose the S-box for each iteration dynamically out of 16-different S-boxes from various algorithms by xor-ing the key bits to form a 4-bit selection bit. The authors in [5] have proposed a RAM-based S-box in contrast to traditional LUT based design and the proposed design occupies only 83 slices with a throughput of 5.13 kbps at 100 MHz clock on Xilinx device. The idea of expressing PRESENT S-box using Boolean equations is proposed in [6]. Reference [7] has implemented the same with 26 AND gates and 17 OR gates to compute the 4-bit output. Since there is more flexibility in optimizing the Boolean based design compared to RAM based, this paper is based on the Boolean based design for circuit level implementation of PRESENT-80 algorithm.

This work describes circuit level implementation of PRESENT-80 algorithm by incorporating the static logic styles namely Complementary Metal Oxide Semiconductor (CMOS), Pseudo-NMOS, Differential Cascode Voltage Switch Logic (DCVSL), Pass transistor Logic (PTL) and Complementary PTL (CPL) with level restoration logic for two different architectures namely Boolean or Direct implementation and Multiplexer (MUX) based implementation.

The paper is organized as follows. Section 2 describes the proposed work and Sect. 3 gives a detailed discussion on the results obtained followed by Conclusion and Future Work in Sect. 4.

## 2 Static CMOS Logic Styles

Static CMOS circuits offer several advantages namely low sensitivity to noise, good performance and low power consumption with no static power dissipation. Dynamic approach relies on temporary storage of signal values on the capacitance of high-impedance circuit nodes and has the advantage of increased speed. However due to the increased sensitivity to noise, the dynamic circuits are prone to failure [8]. Hence we have considered only Static approach for the PRESENT S-box design. The various logic styles under Static CMOS design are described briefly with its advantages and disadvantages.

### 2.1 Complementary CMOS

Circuits designed using Complementary CMOS logic style consist of a pull up network (PUN) made up of PMOS transistors which connect the output node to VDD to produce a '1' output and pull down network (PDN) made up of NMOS transistors which drives the output node to ground to produce a '0' output, as shown in Fig. 1(a). The primary advantage of such circuits is they have a very less static power dissipation since the PUN and PDN operation is mutually exclusive. However for an N-input gate, 2 N transistors are required thereby resulting in a larger implementation area.

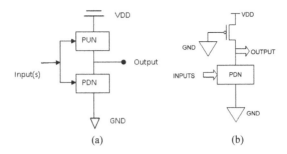

**Fig. 1.** Basic architecture of (a) Complementary CMOS (b) Pseudo NMOS

## 2.2 Pseudo NMOS

Pseudo NMOS logic style comes under the Ratioed logic design where the entire PUN is replaced with a single PMOS load which pulls up the output node to '1' value and the logic function is implemented by the PDN as shown in Fig. 1(b). Thereby the number of transistors required is reduced from 2 N to 'N + 1' for an N-input gate. However since the PMOS load is always ON, static power dissipation is very high, limiting its usage. Though it requires careful sizing of the PMOS load with respect to the NMOS transistors to achieve the desired functionality, due to its reduction in the transistor count, this logic style can be used in large fan-in circuits.

## 2.3 DCVSL

DCVSL logic style combines two concepts namely differential logic and positive feedback. Differential logic requires complementary inputs and produces complementary outputs and positive feedback assures to turn off the load device when not needed. The sizing of the load is still required in DCVSL as in Pseudo NMOS logic style. But the static power dissipation is reduced compared to Pseudo NMOS style. DCVSL AND/NAND and XOR/XNOR gates are shown in Fig. 2.

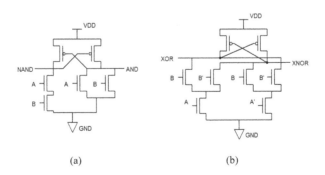

**Fig. 2.** (a) DCVSL AND/NAND (b) DCVSL XOR/XNOR gates

### 2.4 PTL and CPL

A very attractive logic style next to Complementary CMOS is PTL where the primary inputs are allowed to drive both the gate and source-drain terminals.

The logic is implemented using only NMOS transistors and hence it has the minimum requirement of transistor count, thereby reducing the capacitance.

However since NMOS transistors produce a weak '1', a level restorer network is required at the output node. For high performance design, Differential PTL or commonly known as CPL is used which produces complementary outputs and the design is very modular. CPL is the most optimized implementation for AND/NAND and XOR/XNOR gate designs, shown in Fig. 3 and PTL is the best logic style for MUX, shown in Fig. 4. A Level Restoring Circuit is employed at the output node to obtain the full rail voltage swing for both PTL and CPL.

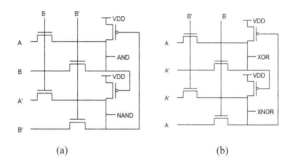

(a)                              (b)

**Fig. 3.** (a) CPL AND/NAND (b) CPL XOR/XNOR gates with level restoration

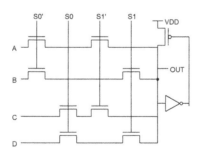

**Fig. 4.** PTL 4:1 MUX with level restoration

## 3 Proposed Work

The Boolean realization of algorithmic implementation of PRESENT S-box has achieved reasonably good area and performance metrics. The S-box is expressed using minimized logic equations of 4 output variables each with 4 input variables as shown in (1), (2), (3) and (4). This conventional method namely the direct form of evaluation is implemented using Complementary CMOS. In order to reduce the number of transistors and further simplify the implementation using only PDN, an alternative logic style namely Pseudo NMOS is considered and the performance comparison results are tabulated in Table 1.

**Table 1.** Performance comparison of PRESENT S-Box direct implementation

| Design | Transistor count | Power | Delay | PDP |
|---|---|---|---|---|
| CMOS | 128 | 0.52 μW | 0.7 μs | 36.68e–12 |
| Pseudo-NMOS | 72 | 234 μW | 100 μs | 23.4e–9 |

$$f0 = a\,b'c + a\,b'd + a'c'd' + a'b\,c + a'c\,d \qquad (1)$$

$$f1 = a\,b\,c' + b'c\,d' + a'b\,c\,d + a'b'c' + b'c'd \qquad (2)$$

$$f2 = a'b'c + a\,b\,d + a'c\,d' + a\,b'c' + a\,b'd' \qquad (3)$$

$$f3 = a'b'd + a'c\,d + a\,b'd' + a\,c\,d' + a\,b\,c'd + a'b\,c'd' \qquad (4)$$

The static logic style namely PTL and its variant CPL is proved to be simple and use less number of transistors than CMOS. However implementing complex Boolean equations using CPL is too cumbersome. Our work has proposed a MUX based implementation for the PRESENT S-box as shown in Fig. 5. A 4-bit 4 × 1 MUX based architecture is designed and its input equations are further simplified to use minimum number of min-terms. The MUX based architecture for implementing a cryptographic Boolean function is derived based on the generalized architecture proposed in [9]. CPL is the best proven technique to implement gates with complementary outputs using least number of transistors and PTL is the optimized logic style for MUX implementation.

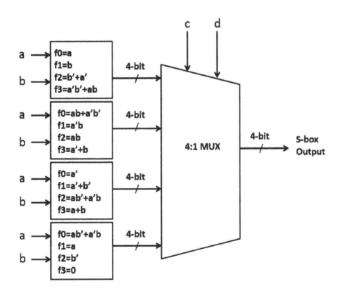

**Fig. 5.** 4:1 MUX based architecture for PRESENT S-box

Hence the complete design is incorporated using CPL and PTL with level restoration. The level restoration logic employed in this design uses a CMOS inverter cascaded with a PMOS load to obtain full voltage swing on the outputs for PTL and two PMOS pull up devices for CPL.

DCVSL, another variant of Pseudo NMOS logic style has less static power dissipation by incorporating a positive feedback logic in the PUN to turn off the load device when not needed. As shown in (5), (6), (7) and (8) the input logic to the 4:1 MUX requires XOR-XNOR gates and AND-NAND gates. Hence these gates are constructed using DCVSL and CPL styles and their performance is compared in Tables 2 and 3.

**Table 2.** Performance comparison of AND/NAND gate implementation

| Design | Transistor count | Power | Delay | PDP |
|--------|------------------|-------|-------|-----|
| CPL | 6 | 0.013 µW | 20 µs | 0.26e–12 |
| DCVSL | 6 | 0.24 µW | 20 µs | 4.7e–12 |

**Table 3.** Performance comparison of XOR/XNOR gate implementation

| Design | Transistor count | Power | Delay | PDP |
|--------|------------------|-------|-------|-----|
| CPL | 6 | 0.27 µW | 10 µs | 27e–13 |
| DCVSL | 8 | 0.44 µW | 10 µs | 44e–13 |

Since our objective is to construct an optimized PRESENT S-box, we have implemented two different circuits for the MUX based architecture: (i) Only using CPL and (ii) A hybrid logic style which uses DCVSL to realize the input logic of the MUX and CPL to realize the MUX itself. The results are tabulated in Table 4.

**Table 4.** Performance comparison of PRESENT S-Box Mux-based implementation

| Design | Transistor count | Power | Delay | PDP |
|--------|------------------|-------|-------|-----|
| CPL | 65 | 0.5 mW | 0.7 µs | 35e–9 |
| DCVSL-CPL | 67 | 0.6 mW | 0.7 µs | 42e–9 |

$$\text{Input 0: } f0 = a; \; f1 = b; \; f2 = b' + a'; \; f3 = a'b' + ab; \tag{5}$$

$$\text{Input 1: } f0 = ab + a'b'; \; f1 = a'b; \; f2 = ab; \; f3 = a' + b; \tag{6}$$

$$\text{Input 2: } f0 = a'; \; f1 = b' + a'; \; f2 = ab' + a'b; \; f3 = a + b; \tag{7}$$

$$\text{Input 3: } f0 = ab' + a'b; \; f1 = a; \; f2 = b'; \; f3 = 0; \tag{8}$$

## 4    Results and Discussions

All the circuits are simulated using CMOS 180 nm technology. The results of conventional implementation of S-box using Boolean logic in Complementary CMOS and

Pseudo NMOS logic styles in Table 1 reveals that Pseudo NMOS logic style shows 44% savings in transistor count. However since the load device is always ON, there is a tremendous increase in average power consumption. When the load size is twice that of NMOS, the power consumption is about 516 µW and when the load device is sized same as NMOS, the average power consumption reduces to 234 µW. The power delay product (PDP) value suggests that CMOS is the best logic style for the Boolean implementation of S-box since the PDP for Complementary CMOS logic style is less by three orders of magnitude compared to Pseudo-NMOS logic style. Pseudo NMOS logic style can be considered when area is the most important factor.

The comparison of DCVSL and CPL for AND-NAND logic functions in Table 2 shows that both the logic styles require same number of transistors but the CPL has about one order of magnitude decreased average power consumption because DCVSL has a power dissipation problem due to cross-over currents i.e. there is a period of time when both the load device and PDN are ON simultaneously creating a short circuit path. Comparison of XOR-XNOR logic implementation using CPL and DCVSL styles shown in Table 3 reveal that the power consumption of CPL decreases one-fold compared to DCVSL, the latter requiring 2 more transistors than CPL.

The results of PRESENT S-box constructed using CPL and DCVSL-CPL hybrid logic is shown in Table 4. CPL shows a 3% savings in number of transistors and 16% savings in PDP. Hence CPL is concluded to be the best logic for MUX-based low-cost implementation of PRESENT S-box.

The existing work described in [10] has implemented an iterative architecture with routing logic for PRESENT encryption using CMOS. Among the three different architectures described for PRESENT in [2], we choose the round based architecture to compare our design because it has reported the best area-power-speed tradeoff for smart card applications. Our 64-bit data-path CPL based MUX architecture implementation will require 4147 transistors reporting a three-fold decrease in area compared to [10] and 39% less transistor count compared to [2]. The Complementary CMOS based Boolean architecture implementation will require 5672 transistors reporting a two-fold decrease in area compared to [10] and 16% less transistor count compared to [2] as shown in Table 5. Compared to Complementary CMOS based Boolean architecture, CPL based MUX architecture shows 26% savings in area.

**Table 5.** Area improvement of PRESENT algorithm with the modified S-box

| Reference | Architecture | Transistor count |
|---|---|---|
| Existing [10] | Iterative 4-bit data-path | 12094 |
| Existing [2][a] | Round based 64-bit data-path | 6820 |
| Complementary CMOS – Boolean [Our work] | Round based 64-bit data-path | 5672 |
| CPL- MUX based [Our work] | Round based 64-bit data-path | 4147 |

[a] Area is reported in terms of Gate Equivalent (GE) in [2]. For comparison, the actual transistor count is obtained by multiplying the GE value with 4 (One GE is equivalent to the area which is required by the two−input NAND gate with the lowest driving strength of the corresponding technology).

# 5    Conclusion and Future Work

Lightweight ciphers are most suitable for resource-constrained devices. PRESENT and CLEFIA are two ISO/IEC 29192-2 approved lightweight ciphers, with PRESENT algorithm being less complex in hardware than CLEFIA. There are various algorithmic optimization works existing in literature to optimize PRESENT implementation on FPGA devices. Our work is the first one to implement circuit level architecture for PRESENT S-box. The direct or Boolean realization and MUX-based architecture is implemented using static CMOS design styles and the results are tabulated. For the direct implementation, Complementary CMOS is preferable since the PDP is less by three-orders of magnitude compared to Pseudo NMOS logic style though there is a 77% increase in area. For the MUX based implementation, CPL logic is best suited since it achieves about 3% savings in area and 16% savings in PDP. Also compared to the existing CMOS PRESENT implementation, our proposed implementations have reported relatively lesser transistor count.

Having obtained an area optimized PRESENT architecture, there is much scope for incorporating security along with the other performance metrics namely power and speed. The future work will aim to incorporate side channel security into the light-weight cipher PRESENT by implementing circuit level countermeasures to thwart the differential and leakage power analysis attacks.

**Acknowledgement.** This work has been done from the Grant Received from Visvesvaraya PhD Scheme for Electronics and IT. This work is also supported by SMDP-C2SD project sponsored by DeitY, Government of India.

# References

1. Bogdanov, A., et al.: PRESENT: an ultra-lightweight block cipher. In: International Workshop on Cryptographic Hardware and Embedded Systems, Vienna, Austria, pp. 450–466 (2007)
2. Rolfes, C., Poschmann, A., Leander, G., Paar, C.: Ultra-lightweight implementations for smart devices–security for 1000 gate equivalents. In: International Conference on Smart Card Research and Advanced Applications, London, UK, pp. 89–103 (2008)
3. Hanley, N., O'Neill, M.: Hardware comparison of the ISO/IEC 29192-2 block ciphers. In: IEEE Computer Society Annual Symposium on VLSI, MA, USA, pp. 57–62 (2012)
4. AlDabbagh, M., et al.: Improving PRESENT lightweight algorithm. In: IEEE Advanced Computer Science Applications and Technologies, Malaysia, pp. 254–258 (2013)
5. Kavun, E.B., Yalcin, T.: RAM-based ultra-lightweight FPGA implementation of PRESENT. In: IEEE, Reconfigurable Computing and FPGAs (ReConFig), Mexico, pp. 280–285 (2011)
6. Sbeiti, M., Silbermann, M., Poschmann, A., Paar, C.: Design space exploration of present implementations for FPGAs. In: 5th Southern Conference on Programmable Logic, SPL, Brazil , pp. 141–145 (2009)
7. Tay, J.J., et al.: Compact FPGA implementation of PRESENT with boolean S-Box. In: 6th Asia Symposium on Quality Electronic Design, Malaysia, pp. 144–148 (2015)
8. Rabaey, J.M., Chandrakasan, A.P., Nikolic, B.: Digital Integrated Circuits, vol. 2. Prentice Hall, Englewood Cliffs (2002)

9. Mukhopadhyay, D., Chowdhury, D.R.: A parallel efficient architecture for large cryptographically robust n × k (k > n/2) mappings. IEEE Trans. Comput. **60**(3), 375–385 (2011)
10. Bellizia, D., Scotti, G., Trifiletti, A.: Implementation of the PRESENT-80 block cipher and analysis of its vulnerability to side channel attacks exploiting static power. In: Mixed Design of Integrated Circuits and Systems, Poland, pp. 211–216 (2016)

# Emerging Technologies and Memory

# Modeling and Analysis of Transient Heat for 3D IC

Subhajit Chatterjee[1](✉), Surajit Kr. Roy[2], Chandan Giri[2], and Hafizur Rahaman[1]

[1] School of VLSI Technology, IIEST Shibpur,
Howrah 711103, West Bengal, India
subhajit20@gmail.com, hafizur@vlsi.iiests.ac.in
[2] Department of Information Technology,
IIEST Shibpur, Howrah 711103, West Bengal, India
suraroy@gmail.com, chandangiri@gmail.com

**Abstract.** Three dimensionally integrated circuit (3D IC) is a promising technology in semiconductor industry. 3D IC provides several benefits over the conventional 2D IC. However, thermal issues are major concern due to high power density. So, thermal management is a challenging task for 3D IC. This paper presents a new thermal model for calculating the temperature of a 3D IC accurately. The model is simulated for 3D ICs to study the effects of various parameters like the thermal conductivities of the interface sub-layers, heat sink, power dissipation etc. on temperature of the IC. It is also observed how these parameters affect the transient thermal behavior of the IC.

**Keywords:** 3D IC · 3D IC thermal model · 3D IC transient heat analysis
3D IC heat equation · 3D IC testing

## 1 Introduction

3D IC has been the topic of academic discussions and publications for quite a while now, and consequently need little introduction. Modern day semiconductor technology is squeezing in more and more transistors into a silicon die, for designing high performance ICs. However, today's IC technology feature size has reached as low as 14 nm, and scaling down the transistor size further is costly and technologically challenging. 3D IC is considered to overcome this bottleneck of technology scaling. A 3D IC is formed by stacking multiple dies vertically, and the dies are interconnected by vertical interconnectors known as Through Silicon Vias (TSVs) [1, 2]. A 3D IC has several advantages like enhanced performance, reduced power consumption, smaller footprint and higher on-chip data bandwidth [2–5]. In spite of these advantages, 3D IC faces some challenges. Thermal management is a major challenge in 3D IC [6–8].

With several dies placed over one another, power density is bound to increase in a 3D IC, giving rise to higher operating temperatures. Also, vertical heat dissipation path in 3D IC is longer than 2D IC. Temperature of a die increases with its location being farther away from the heat sink. Hence, the chip can be damaged permanently due to excessive temperature gradient. So, fast and easy-to-use approaches are needed to

© Springer Nature Singapore Pte Ltd. 2017
B. K. Kaushik et al. (Eds.): VDAT 2017, CCIS 711, pp. 365–375, 2017.
https://doi.org/10.1007/978-981-10-7470-7_36

estimate the temperature distribution of the dies. To mitigate this problem, a thermal analysis of the design is of crucial importance. However, existing thermal models applicable to 2D ICs cannot be applied directly to 3D ICs. Completely different models are required to estimate the temperature of a 3D IC.

Several models exist [5, 9, 10] that estimate the steady state temperature of a 3D IC. However, transient analysis has certain advantages over steady state analysis. Steady state analysis gives the temperatures of the IC when it has reached the steady state. But, the peak temperature that significantly affect the reliability of the circuit, may not occur at the steady state at all. It is a possibility that the peak temperature may occur before the circuit reaches steady state, but reduces as steadiness is reached. Steady state analysis only presents the peak temperature at a single point in time i.e. the steady state, whereas, transient analysis provides the temperature of the IC over time. Thus, thermal models estimate the spatial and temporal thermal profile of a 3D IC. This work proposes a new thermal model for transient analysis based on the heat flow equation in one dimension.

The rest of the paper is organized as follows. In Sect. 2, we investigate the related works present on thermal analysis of 3D IC. Section 3 presents the model that we propose. Section 4 discusses the results observed after simulating various 3D IC structures and finally we conclude and summarize this work in Sect. 5.

## 2   Related Works

Accurate thermal models can help to pinpoint ways to help reduce the peak temperature of a 3D IC. Thermal models for 2D ICs cannot be directly applied to 3D ICs due to the design complexity of 3D ICs. Several analytical and numerical methods are proposed for 3D ICs using conventional heat sinks. There exists some work that proposes to optimize this problem by changing the placement of via for better heat dissipation in 3D ICs [9]. Ayala et al. [5] presented a novel approach to estimate the temperature of a 3D IC by dividing the chip into small cells. However, with modern day deep sub-micron fabrication technology, the number of elements in such models can be huge in order to get more accurate results, leading to longer simulation times. Jain et al. [9] presented a simple thermal model in which the 3D IC stack is divided into horizontal sub-layers to perform steady state thermal analysis. Kleiner et al. [10] proposed a simple one dimensional heat flow model in a 3-die 3D IC. This work considers Finite Element Model (FEM) simulations for investigating the effect of interconnects on temperature distribution in a chip. Authors in [11] have proposed a Joule-heating formula for calculating the temperature gradient of the chip. Skadron et al. [12] have presented a temperature simulator based on thermal resistance model. These works consider steady state analysis to estimate the temperature of the chip. [13–15] present the effect of thermal through silicon via (TTSV), as well as micro-channel cooling on 3D IC. There has also been some works on cooling mechanisms by tweaking the scheduling [16, 17].

The proposed model is based on heat sink. In this work, we apply the idea of segmenting the stack into sub-layers but run transient heat analysis on it, to investigate the thermal behavior of a 3D IC. We take the simplicity of sub-layer wise mathematical segmentation of a 3D IC and then do transient analysis on it, using the heat flow equation in one dimension.

## 3 Proposed Model

We consider a 3D IC composed of multiple vertically stacked dies. At any time, a single or multiple die can be activated. Thermal analysis in 3D IC is complicated due to the several heat sources and thermal resistance of the bonding materials. The proposed model is based on transient analysis. It is assumed that the heat sink is located above the upper-most die and package is placed below the bottom-most die. If a die is active, power is dissipated in the form of heat energy. Our objective is to accurately estimate the temperature of each die within the IC. Figure 1 shows, if a die is active, how the dissipated power flows in form of heat energy.

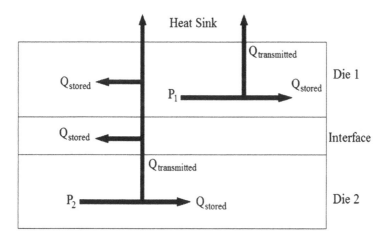

**Fig. 1.** Shows the different heat components when multiple dies are active.

The heat generated by power dissipation i.e. $P_1$ and $P_2$, is either stored in the die i.e. $Q_{stored}$, which increases its own temperature, or is conducted to the surrounding i.e. $Q_{transmitted}$. As the temperature of the dies increases, the values of $Q_{stored}$ and $Q_{transmitted}$ changes, which gives rise to the transient thermal behavior of the IC. If a die is active, heat is generated, and flows in lateral and vertical direction, but, the thickness of the die is very small. So, it is assumed that horizontal heat flow is negligible. The temperature profile due to this flow of heat can expressed by the one-dimensional heat flow equation,

$$\frac{\partial^2 T}{\partial z^2} + \frac{\hat{P}}{K} = \frac{1}{\alpha} \cdot \frac{\partial T}{\partial t} \tag{1}$$

Where $T$ is temperature, $\partial z$ is a very small vertical distance, $t$ is time, $\hat{P}$ is the power generated/dissipated per unit volume, $\alpha$ is thermal diffusivity of the material and is given by the formula:

$$\alpha = \frac{K}{\rho C_p} \qquad (2)$$

Here, $K$ is the thermal conductivity of the material, $\rho$ is the density of the material and $C_p$ is the specific heat capacity of the material under constant pressure. Since the variables of Eq. (1) is not continuous over the whole IC, we convert it to a difference equation,

$$-\frac{1}{A}\frac{\hat{Q}_{z+\Delta z} - \hat{Q}_z}{\Delta z} + \hat{P} = \rho C_p \frac{T_{t+\Delta t} - T_t}{\Delta t} \qquad (3)$$

Where,

$$\frac{\partial}{\partial z}\left(-kA\frac{\partial T}{\partial z}\right) = \frac{\partial \hat{Q}}{\partial z} = \lim_{\Delta z \to 0} \frac{\hat{Q}_{z+\Delta z} - \hat{Q}_z}{\Delta z}$$

But, for better accuracy, we divide the whole stack into very thin sub-layers, such that each sub-layer has a vertical cross-sectional area $A$, and thickness $\Delta z$. So, Eq. (1) is converted to,

$$P_{layer}\Delta t = \lim_{\Delta z \to 0} \hat{Q}_{z+\Delta z}\Delta t - \hat{Q}_z\Delta t + mC_p(T_{t+\Delta t} - T_t) \qquad (4)$$

Where, $P_{layer} = \hat{P}A\Delta z$, is the power dissipated within any given sub-layer of the 3D IC, $m = \rho A\Delta z$ is the mass of the given sub-layer, $\rho$ is the density, and $\hat{Q}$, is the heat flow per unit time at different distances from the heat sink. Figure 2 shows the heat flow at different distances from the heat sink.

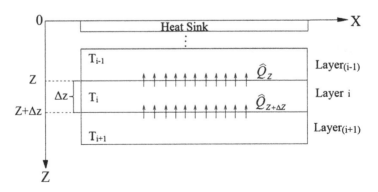

**Fig. 2.** Shows the heat flow at different location within a 3D IC.

Let there be N sub-layers, if the IC stack is divided into very thin sub-layers of thickness $\Delta z$, then, the relation of $\hat{Q}_{z+\Delta z}$ and $\hat{Q}_z$ with temperature of different sub-layers, is given by Eqs. (5) and (6).

$$\hat{Q}_{z+\Delta z} = \frac{K_i^+ \cdot A \cdot (T(i, t+\Delta t) - T(i+1, t+\Delta t))}{\Delta z} \tag{5}$$

Where, $K_{i+}$, is the effective thermal conductivity between sub-layer $i$ and $i+1$, and is given by,

$$K_i^+ = \frac{2K_i \cdot K_{i+1}}{K_i + K_{i+1}}$$

and $T(i, t)$, is $T_i$, at time $t$, and $T(i+1, t+\Delta t)$, is $T_{i+1}$, at time $t+\Delta t$, and so on, and $K_i$ is the thermal conductivity of sub-layer $i$. Also,

$$\hat{Q}_z = \frac{K_i^- \cdot A \cdot (T(i-1, t+\Delta t) - T(i, t+\Delta t))}{\Delta z} \tag{6}$$

Where, $K_{i-}$, is the effective thermal conductivity between sub-layer $i$ and $i-1$, and is given by,

$$K_i^- = \frac{2K_i \cdot K_{i-1}}{K_i + K_{i-1}}$$

Substituting Eqs. (5) and (6) we can write Eq. (4) as,

$$P_i \Delta t - Q(i, t) = G1(i)\Delta T_i + G2(i)\Delta T_{i+1} + G3(i)\Delta T_{i-1} \tag{7}$$

Where,

$$Q(i, t) = \frac{K_i^+ A \Delta t}{\Delta z}[T(i, t) - T(i+1, t)] + \frac{K_i^- A \Delta t}{\Delta z}[T(i, t) - T(i-1, t)],$$

$$G1(i) = \left[\frac{(K_i^+ + K_i^-)A \cdot \Delta t}{\Delta z} + m(i)C_p(i)\right],$$

$$G2(i) = -\left(\frac{K_i^+ A \Delta t}{\Delta z}\right),$$

And,

$$G3(i) = -\left(\frac{K_i^- A \Delta t}{\Delta z}\right),$$

And, $m(i)$ is the mass and $C_p(i)$ is the specific heat capacity of sub-layer $i$, $P_i = P_{layer}$, for sub-layer $i$ and $\Delta T_i = T(i, t + \Delta t) - T(i, t)$, i.e. the change in temperature of sub-layer $i$, over time $\Delta t$.

Equation (7) is the general equation, applied to all the sub-layers in the IC stack, to get their temperature at any time $t$. When a sub-layer is active, $P_i$ is equal to the power dissipation of that sub-layer. But, when the sub-layer is inactive, it is equal to zero. However, two boundary conditions are applied to sub-layer 1 and sub-layer N which modifies the temperature equation of these sub-layers. For sub-layer 1,

$$P_1 \Delta t - Q(1, t) = G1(1) \Delta T_1 + G2(1) \Delta T_2 \tag{8}$$

And, for sub-layer N,

$$P_N \Delta t - \frac{K_N^- A[T(N,t) - T(N-1,t)] \cdot \Delta t}{\Delta z}$$
$$= G3(N) \Delta T_{N-1} + \left[ \frac{K_N^- A \cdot \Delta t}{\Delta z} + m(N) C_p(N) \right] \Delta T_N \tag{9}$$

It is assumed that $T(i, 0) = T_0$ and so, $Q(i, 0) = 0$, where, $T_0$, is the temperature of the heat sink, and is assumed to be constant. $\Delta T_i$, for all the sub-layers is calculated from Eqs. (7), (8) and (9) and added to $T(i, t)$, to get $T(i, t + \Delta t)$. The values of $T(i, t + \Delta t)$, are then used to calculate $Q(i, t + 2\Delta t)$, and the process repeats to find $T(i, t + 2\Delta t)$.

## 4  Results

This section presents the experimental results based on the proposed model. Simulation results are obtained for two different ICs having number of dies 2 and 3 respectively. The die closer to the heat sink is numbered as die 1 and the one away from the heat sink is numbered as die 2. Thickness of the silicon dies is taken to be 300 µm and the interface is taken to be 10 µm thick. The thermal conductivity of silicon is taken to be 148 W/mK and that of the interface is taken to be 0.1 W/mK. The specific heat capacity of silicon is taken to be 710 J/Kg-K and the density is taken as 2329 kg/m3. Thermal conductivity of the heat sink is assumed to be 0.05 W/mK. The package end of the stack is considered to be adiabatic in nature. We simulate the steady state temperature of 3D IC by taking different power consumption for each die. Figure 3 shows this 3D IC structure with 2 dies and their respective parameters.

Consider a 3D IC with two dies, separated by a bonding interface. Our simulation divides a die into several logical sub-layers. The thickness of each such sub-layer is equal to the maximum vertical distance over which the material remains the same at any point of the 3D IC stack. In this case, that thickness is equal to 10 µm which is the thickness of the inter die bond material. So, the heat sink will be followed by 30 logical sub-layers of silicon of 10 µm thickness representing die 1. After that, there exists the interface sub-layer of same thickness and followed by another 30 sub-layers of silicon, equally thick, representing die 2.

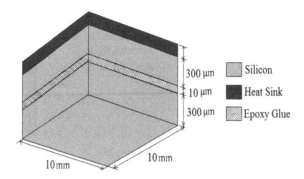

**Fig. 3.** Shows the 3D IC structure taken to verify and simulate the thermal model.

**Table 1.** Shows temperature of the dies for the 3D IC.

| Power dissipation (P1, P2) in W | Temperature (T1, T2) in K | Temperature [9] (T1, T2) in K |
|---|---|---|
| 10, 10 | 309.86, 317.81 | 309.7, 316.8 |
| 2, 18 | 309.86, 325.97 | 308.3, 323.7 |
| 3, 30 | 323.31, 351.26 | N/A |
| 3, 25 | 318.2, 341.03 | N/A |
| 25, 3 | 318.38, 319.96 | N/A |

Table 1 compares the estimated temperature of the proposed model with [9]. P1, P2 are the power dissipation and T1, T2 are the temperature of die 1 and die 2 respectively.

In Table 1, Column 2 and 3, represent the temperature obtained through the proposed model and those reported in [9] respectively. The results show that the temperature of die 1 does not reduce even though its power dissipation is reduced. Because the lower die not only dissipates its own heat but also, the heat conducted from the dies below it. So, die 1 always dissipates the total power dissipated in the whole chip. In general, temperature of a die depends on its own power dissipation as well as the power dissipated in all the dies below it in the stack.

In the next scenario, we include a third die below die 2, of similar dimension and characteristics, separated by a similar interface sub-layer. We try different combination of dies being active simultaneously, with 10 W of power each. Table 2 summarizes the peak temperatures observed for different dies with various combinations of dies being active simultaneously.

The thermal conductivity of the interface sub-layer is taken to be 0.1 W/mK in the above simulation. To investigate its effect, the 3D IC in the last scenario is used with all the 3 die active with 10 W each. It is simulated against varying values of thermal conductivity ($K_{int}$) of the interface material and the peak temperature of each die is observed, as shown in the Fig. 5.

**Table 2.** Lists the peak temperatures of all the dies when different dies being active.

| Active die (10 W each) | Peak temperature in different die in K | | |
|---|---|---|---|
| | Die 1 | Die 2 | Die 3 |
| 1 | 299.17 | 299.17 | 299.17 |
| 2 | 297.28 | 302.24 | 302.24 |
| 3 | 297.19 | 302.05 | 309.68 |
| 1, 2 | 308.38 | 314.26 | 314.26 |
| 1, 3 | 307.37 | 312.23 | 319.86 |
| 2, 3 | 307.42 | 322.56 | 330.19 |
| 1, 2, 3 | 317.64 | 332.78 | 340.41 |

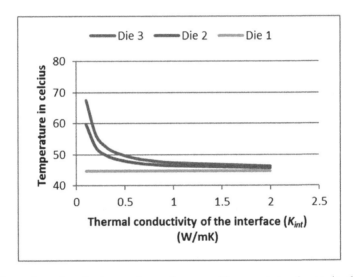

**Fig. 5.** Shows how the die temperatures changes with respect to change in the thermal conductivity of the bonding layer.

From Fig. 5, we see that with little increase in $K_{int}$ at first, the peak temperatures of die 2 and die 3 approaches the peak temperature of die 1 significantly. But, this rate of reduction in peak temperature reduces as $K_{int}$ is increased more.

Thermal resistance of the heat sink also plays a major role in determining the peak temperatures of different dies. Figure 6, shows the variation of the temperatures of the three dies with the effective thermal conductivity of the sink. From the Figs. 5 and 6, it is seen that both the thermal conductivities of the interface bond sub-layer material and the heat sink have a significant effect in reducing the die temperatures at first, but, the rate of reduction decreases to almost no effect with large changes in the thermal conductivities. While the increase in $K_{int}$, brings the temperatures of the higher dies

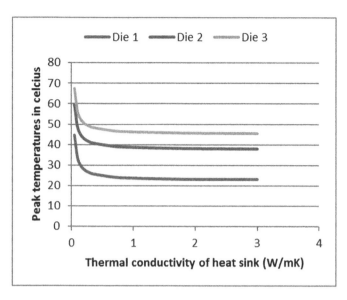

**Fig. 6.** Shows the variation in temperatures of different dies with respect to change in thermal conductivity of the heat sink.

closer to the temperature of the die 1 i.e. which is closest to the sink, the change in the thermal resistance of the heat sink brings down the temperatures of every die in the stack closer to the temperature of the heat sink.

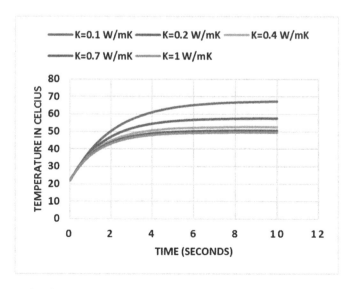

**Fig. 7.** Shows the change in temperature of die 3 with time and different values of heat sink thermal conductivity.

The time required to reach the steady state temperature also depends on $K_{int}$. Figure 7, shows the change in temperature of die 3 with respect to time for various values of $K_{int}$. It is observed that, as $K_{int}$ increases, the steady state temperature decreases. The increase in temperature is exponential in nature and the time required to reach the steady state decreases with increase in $K_{int}$.

# 5    Conclusion

3D IC technology has a huge prospect in near future. This work investigates the temperature of different dies for 3D IC. We have done transient heat analysis with the help of the heat equation in one dimension. Transient analysis inherently has the benefit of providing the varying thermal profile of the 3D IC with respect to time. Several 3D ICs were analyzed using our model. Experimental results show that the proposed model can estimate die temperature of 3D IC accurately. Different parameters of the ICs like power dissipation, thermal conductivities of the interface layers and the heat sink were varied to observe their effect on the temperature. Increase in the thermal diffusivity of the interface layers also reduces the temperature of the dies that are farther away from the heat sink.

# References

1. Topol, A.W., et al.: Three-dimensional integrated circuits. IBM J. Res. Dev. **50**, 494–506 (2006)
2. Banerjee, K., Souri, S.J., Kapur, P., Saraswat, K.C.: 3-D ICs: a novel chip design for improving deep-submicrometer interconnect performance and systems-on-chip integration. Proc. IEEE **89**(5), 602–633 (2001)
3. List, S., Webb, C., Kim, S.: 3D wafer stacking technology. In: Proceedings of Advanced Metallization Conference, pp. 29–36 (2002)
4. Patti, R.S.: Three-dimensional integrated circuits and the future of system-on-chip designs. Proc. IEEE **94**(6), 1214–1224 (2006)
5. Ayala, J.L., Sridhar, A., Cuesta, D.: Thermal modeling and analysis of 3D multi-processor chips. Integr. VLSI J. **43**, 327–341 (2010)
6. Deng, Y., Maly, W.P.: Interconnect characteristics of 2.5-D system integration scheme. In: Proceedings of International Symposium on Physical Design, pp. 171–175 (2001)
7. Deng, Y.S., Maly, W.: 2.5D system integration: a design driven system implementation schema. In: Proceedings of Asia and South Pacific Design Automation Conference, pp. 450–455 (2004)
8. Nelson, D.W., et al.: A 3D interconnect methodology applied to iA32-class architectures for performance improvement through RC mitigation. In: Proceedings of the International VLSI Multilevel Interconnection Conference, pp. 453–464 (2004)
9. Jain, A., Jones, R.E., Chatterjee, R., Pozder, S., Huang, Z.: Thermal modeling and design of 3D integrated circuits. In: Intersociety Conference on Thermal and Thermo-Mechanical Phenomena in Electronic Systems, Orlando, pp. 1139–1145 (2008)
10. Kleiner, M.B., Kuhn, S.A., Ramm, P., Weber, W.: Thermal analysis of vertically integrated circuits. In: IEDM Technical Digest, pp. 487–490 (1995)

11. Im, S., Banerjee, K.: Full chip thermal analysis of planer (2-D) and vertically integrated (3-D) high performance ICs. In: Electron Devices Meeting IEDM Technical Digest. International, pp. 727–730 (2000)

12. Skadron, K., Stan, M.R., Huang, W., Velusamy, S., Sankaranarayanan, K., Tarjan, D.: Temperature-aware microarchitecture. In: International Symposium on Computer Architecture, pp. 2–13 (2003)

13. Qian, H., Liang, H., Chang, C., Zhang, W., Yu, H.: Thermal simulator of 3D-IC with modeling of anisotropic TSV conductance and microchannel entrance effects. In: Asia and South Pacific Design Automation Conference, pp. 485–490 (2013)

14. Cong, J., Zhang, Y.: Thermal via planning for 3-D ICs. In: Proceedings of IEEE/ACM International Conference on Computer Aided Design, pp. 745–752 (2005)

15. Goplen, B., Sapatnekar, S.: Thermal via placement in 3D ICs. In: Proceedings of International Symposium on Physical Design, pp. 167–174 (2005)

16. Aghaee, N., Peng, Z., Eles, P.: Temperature-gradient based test scheduling for 3D stacked ICs. In: IEEE International Conference on Electronics, Circuits, and Systems (ICECS), pp. 405–408 (2013)

17. Xiang, D., Liu, G., Chakrabarty, K., Fujiwara, H.: Thermal-aware test scheduling for NOC-based 3D integrated circuits. In: IFIP/IEEE International Conference on Very Large Scale Integration (VLSI-SoC), pp. 96–101 (2013)

# Memory Efficient Fractal-SPIHT Based Hybrid Image Encoder

Mamata Panigrahy[1](✉), Nirmal Chandra Behera[3], B. Vandana[1],
Indrajit Chakrabarti[2], and Anindya Sundar Dhar[2]

[1] School of Electronics Engineering, KIIT University, Bhubaneswar, India
mamata.panigrahy@gmail.com, vandana.rao20@gmail.com
[2] Department of Electronics and Electrical Communication Engineering,
IIT Kharagpur, Kharagpur, India
{indrajit,asd}@ece.iitkgp.ernet.in
[3] Kolkata Port Trust, Kolkata, India
nirmal.etc@gmail.com

**Abstract.** Hardware implementation of hybrid coder based on fractal and SPIHT image compression technique is presented in this paper. Time complexity of fractal image encoder is improved and the desired image quality at varying bit rates is achieved as a result of this hybridization. LL subband of the wavelet transformed image is used for the fractal encoding activity and other sub-bands are operated with the SPIHT encoder. In this work both the image compression techniques are analyzed and performance of this technique is tested over different test images. This architecture operates at real time and can encode a $256 \times 256$ image within 7 ms.

**Keywords:** Fractal image compression · SPIHT
Iterated function system · DWT · FPGA

## 1 Introduction

Fractal image compression (FIC) technique is based on the principle of iterated function system. To improve compression, this coding approach extracts the self-similarity present within the image and replaces larger regions with smaller similar image sub-blocks. Large amount of similarity present in natural images occupies huge memory space. Thus representing the self similarity via referencing not only saves much storage space but also enhances the efficiency of FIC technique. This method attains a high compression ratio and achieves improved quality reconstructed image. However, extraction of these similar parts through recursive search operation increases the time complexity of the fractal image encoder.

In full search approach, each $N \times N$ range block is compared to all $2N \times 2N$ sized domain block that increases the time complexity to $O[N^4]$. To reduce this computational complexity, classification techniques segment the domain pool into several groups considering different spatial and statistical property of the

© Springer Nature Singapore Pte Ltd. 2017
B. K. Kaushik et al. (Eds.): VDAT 2017, CCIS 711, pp. 376–387, 2017.
https://doi.org/10.1007/978-981-10-7470-7_37

image. Searching a matched block in a small sized domain pool belonging to particular class, reduces the overall encoding time. Jacquin [1] partitioned the image into three type of blocks (*i.e.* flat, edge or texture) based on edge properties. Similarly, taking block mean and variance into consideration, Fisher [2] classified the domain pool into 72 classes. Chen et al. [3] improved compression speed by reducing redundant computations in error calculation and discarding ineffective image blocks by one norm of normalized block measure. Limiting the searching space to the neighboring area, Furao and Hasegawa [4] and Monro and Woolley [5] achieved appreciable speed up in encoding time. Besides several algorithmic modifications done by Tong and Pi [6], Lai et al. [7] and others, different hardware approaches have also been attempted by the researchers [8–11] that partially solves the compression time complexity of the pure fractal encoder.

Researchers also tried to achieve compression at a fast rate without visible blocking artifacts in the reconstructed image. To gain advantage of the transform coders, several researchers [12–14] investigated the relationship and feasibility of fractal encoding in wavelet domain. Fractal coders efficiently represent the straight edges and constant gradient regions that the transform coders fail to encode. Discrete wavelet transform (DWT) facilitates multiresolution analysis of a signal and yields better visual quality at high compression. Additionally, excellent features like energy compaction, localization of sub bands in time, space and frequency makes it suitable for DWT to be associated with fractal image coding. According to Davis [13], coefficients of higher resolution can be predicted from lower resolution coefficients. The sub-sampling, scaling and isometry operations carried out in fractal encoding can be related to the wavelet transform for shifting coefficients to higher resolution, modify them at each scale and to obtain a gain factor respectively. Shapiro's embedded zerotree wavelet (EZW) [15] and Said and Pearlman's set partitioning in hierarchical tree (SPIHT) algorithms [16] based on wavelet transform produces embedded bit stream and provides several excellent features over pure transform and fractal coders. These properties include improved image quality with fast compression and decompression, progressive bit stream created for desired bit rate. Most importantly this scheme can be used for both lossy and lossless coding purpose. The present work thus motivates to implement hardware design for a fractal-SPIHT hybrid encoder.

This hybrid architecture completes the encoding of a $256 \times 256$ image in nearly 7 ms. This enables one to use the structure for real time applications.

The outline of remaining part of the paper is as follows: Sect. 2 includes hybrid fractal image compression method. Section 3 involves proposed VLSI architecture for hybrid fractal encoder. In Sect. 4 simulation results are included and Sect. 5 presents conclusions.

## 2  Hybrid Fractal Image Compression Method

The basic block diagram of hybrid SPIHT Fractal encoder is shown in Fig. 1. Wavelet transform decomposes the original image into four sub-bands namely

LL, LH, HL, HH. At each decomposition level, resolution reduces by half. Applying the DWT recursively to the approximation sub-band (*i.e.* LL band), a wavelet subtree is formed. The coefficients corresponding to the coarse-scale comprises of four children having same spatial orientation. Each decomposition results the next finer level. Therefore, a wavelet subtree comprises of coefficient of the roots along with descendants in other three orientation. As the approximation (LL) sub-band contains most of the energy, it is favorable for fractal image compression. So, quad tree based FIC (QTFIC) technique is only applied to the approximation sub-band of the finest wavelet decomposition level. The detailed information carried by the LH, HL and HH sub-band are processed with modified SPIHT algorithm. This ensures a near lossless compression that improves the visual quality of the reconstructed image.

## 2.1  Quad Tree Based Fractal Image Compression

Real world images are not uniform and they possess varying complexity at different parts of the image. In block based coding techniques like FIC, complex areas can easily be captured by small block size where as smooth parts may be coded with large block size. This work adopts adaptive sized quadtree partitioning to obtain range and domain blocks. Architecture for the fractal-SPIHT hybrid coder is as shown in Fig. 1.

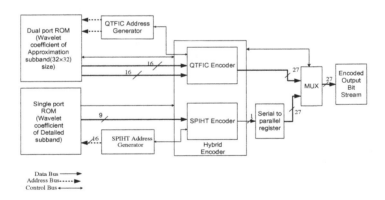

**Fig. 1.** Proposed Fractal-SPIHT hybrid encoder

The QTFIC algorithm comprises of four main steps namely, image partitioning, block mapping, error computation and finally storing the quantized affine parameters. Image is partitioned into variable sized range and domain blocks depending on the threshold value. As domain block size is four times larger than the range block, $2 \times 2$ pixels are averaged to obtain each contracted domain pixel. This geometric transformation equalizes the geometrical size of the range and domain block before mapping. Affine transformation as given in Eq. 1 is applied on the contracted domain block ($D$) to map its intensity with the range block. Scaling coefficient $s_i$ controls the contrast and range average $r_{avg}$ shifts the brightness of the domain block towards the range block. Equation 1 represents the intensity transformation.

$$\tau(D) = s_i(D - d_{avg}I) + r_{avg}I \qquad (1)$$

Additionally, to increase the matching probability, isometric transform can be applied on this geometric and intensity transformed domain block. If the dissimilarity between a range-domain pair is more than the threshold value, this domain block is discarded. If no matched domain block is found in any level after all possible successive search-match operation, then switch to the next quadtree level. Every increment in QT level reduces size of the range block by two in each dimension. Error computation is performed by LSE or SAD measure. Finally, parameters like matched domain index, scaling and translational parameter with the level information is stored in fractal codebook and transmitted to the decoder. To speed up this process, the tolerance limit is also relaxed by twice at each incremented QT level. Further speed up of QTFIC is achieved by its hardware implementation.

## 2.2 Set Partitioning in Hierarchical Tree Scheme

SPIHT algorithm ensures transmission of the coefficients progressively after ordering them by their magnitude. The process can work for the desired bit rate and can be stopped in-between without incurring much distortion. This is because the most significant bit of any coefficient carries its maximum weight and as transmitted first sends most of the information. Progressive transmission initially finds the required number of iterations from the largest coefficient. Then in sorting pass, the coefficients are ordered according to their magnitude and information about number of significant bits in this pass along with their sign bit is sent to the output. Refinement pass operation outputs the $n^{th}$ most significant bit of the coefficients that are transmitted during previous sorting pass operation. Repeating the procedure for all the $n$ iterations, all the coefficients are transmitted. From the magnitude comparison results, the decoder can duplicate the execution path of the encoder and retrieve the ordering information.

$$S_n(\tau) = 1, \quad \max_{i,j \in \tau}\{|c_{i,j}|\} \geq 2^n$$
$$0, \quad otherwise \qquad (2)$$

Sorting algorithm segregates the significant and insignificant coefficients according to Eq. 2 and set partitioning rule forms the subsets containing insignificant elements and subset with single significant element. In the wavelet subtree spatial similarity is found across different sub-bands. The coefficients present at the highest level of the pyramidal structure are the root nodes and each node has either no offsprings or four offsprings (i.e. a $2 \times 2$ adjacent coefficients) at the same spatial orientation in the next level. Accordingly, four set of coordinates are formed that contain (i) offsprings of node $(i, j)$, (ii) Descendants of node

$(i, j)$ (iii) spatial orientation tree roots and (iv) descendants without offsprings. The offsprings are present at location $(2i, 2j)$, $(2i, 2j+1)$, $(2i+1, 2j)$, and $(2i+1, 2j+1)$.

Initial partition is made between the set of root nodes $(i, j)$ belonging to the spatial tree and its descendants. For any coordinate $(i, j)$ if $D(i, j)$ is significant, then this is again partitioned into a set$(L(i, j))$ along with four single element set belonging to offspring set(O). If $L(i, j)$ is found significant, this is segmented into four sets $D(k, l)$ with $(k,l)$ belong to the set of offsprings. As this coding algorithm repeatedly tests to obtain the order of significance, three order lists are formed to store them. These are named as list of insignificant pixels set (LIS), list of insignificant pixel (LIP) and list of significant pixel (LSP). These lists keep track of the coordinate $(i, j)$ that either represent the set $D(i, j)$ or $L(i, j)$ in LIS or a single pixel in LIP or LSP. In this coding if the LIS entry is $D(i, j)$, this is represented by *Type-A* and for the $L(i, j)$ entry it is denoted as *Type-B*.

Sorting pass operation tests the insignificant coefficients of LIP and shifts the significant ones to the LSP set. Similarly, during the significance testing of the coefficients in LIS, the significant set is removed from the LIS entry and partitioned. The resulting subset with more than one elements are inserted back into LIS and the single-coordinate sets are included either with LSP or LIP according to their significance. Accordingly, LSP contains the coordinates of coefficients that pass through refinement pass.

In the hybrid fractal-SPIHT arrangement as the approximation subband is coded with fractal encoder [17], LIP is initialized with an empty set without altering the LSP and LIS sets. In this process the threshold for SPIHT coder is computed by excluding the LL subband coefficients.

# 3   VLSI Architecture for Hybrid Fractal Encoder

The proposed design encodes the approximation subband with QTFIC technique while detailed subbands are coded with modified SPIHT encoder. Both the encoders operate nearly in a concurrent manner. For the desired bit rate, if the bit budget for fractal encoder is known, the remaining bits can be assigned for the SPIHT encoder.

## 3.1   Architecture design for QTFIC

Architecture for the QTFIC is as shown in Fig. 2. Three level Haar wavelet is computed for a $256 \times 256$ test image and $32 \times 32$ coefficients of the approximation subband are saved in a block memory with 512 locations. Each location contains two coefficients of the DWT transformed image. Thus, a 16 bit data bus is connected with the two port memory to supply four coefficients in each cycle.

Two level quadtree structure is formed with range block size $4 \times 4$ and $2 \times 2$. Therefore, the domain blocks are of size $8 \times 8$ and $4 \times 4$ respectively. After fetching the pixels from memory, they are stored in range and domain register banks each containing 16 registers of 8bits. Domain register bank pixels are obtained

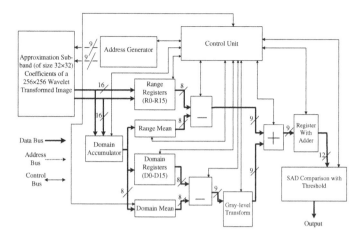

**Fig. 2.** Proposed architecture for QTFIC encoder

after averaging each $2 \times 2$ non-overlapping pixels. The pixel fetching operation obeys the MORTON scan sequence. To save overall memory, the domain block is also fetched from the same initial location from which range block is fetched. Domain block fetching requires 17 clock cycles after which the affine transform is applied on the same. Intensity transformation as shown in Eq. 1 is performed through the scaling parameter and the range mean value. Range and domain block mean computation process is performed in parallel while fetching the pixel values. Scaling the domain pixels by two bit obtains reduction in intensity value by one fourth, one half and three fourth. Adding the range mean with scaled domain pixels shifts its luminance towards the range block. Error measurement between the transformed domain block and range block is performed by sum of absolute difference (SAD). Number of pipeline stages are added to improve the computation performance. Finally a comparison module checks whether the error is within the threshold value. For distortion larger than the threshold, next domain block is searched and matched. Level is incremented if none of the Level-0 block satisfies the threshold criterion. A level-0 and level-1 operation consumes 24 and 12 clock cycles respectively for completing the pixel fetching, affine transform and error computation operation. Finally, for each range block, index of the matched domain block, scaling coefficient and range mean values are stored in the fractal codebook.

## 3.2   Architecture for SPIHT Encoder

The proposed architecture is designed for the modified SPIHT encoder as in [17] and is shown in Fig. 3. This architecture contains address translation unit, memory to store the outputs and modules to carry out sorting pass and refinement pass operation. The address translation module reorder the wavelet transformed image in 1-D array as in [18]. This linear indexing put the offsprings in four consecutive locations and grand children in next 16 locations to easily fetch inter-subband coefficients without additional hardware requirement [19]. Here, instead of representing any coefficient by their coordinate i.e. $(C_{n-1}, ..., C_0, R_{n-1}..., R_0)$, bits are reordered to $(C_{n-1}, R_{n-1}, ..., ...C_1, R_1, C_0, R_0)$. Only incrementing action provides the offsprings and descendants. Two memory modules are required to store the result after the sorting pass and refinement pass operation. RAM1 is a $64\,\mathrm{k} \times 2$ bit memory that stores information of significant and insignificant pixels i.e. the content of the LSP and LIP subsets. If its MSB content is '1', it represents a significant coefficient in LSP and a '0' at LSB denotes an insignificant coefficient. Similarly, RAM2 is a $16k \times 2$ memory used to store the LIS content. A zero content in RAM2 at any of its memory location indicates absence of descendant for the corresponding coefficient or node not attended yet for encoding. The process continues sequentially i.e. sorting pass begins after the refinement pass and in sorting pass LIS pass operation starts after completion of LIP pass.

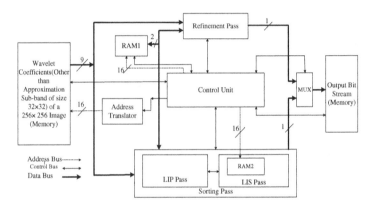

**Fig. 3.** Proposed architecture for SPIHT encoder

**Refinement Pass.** Architecture for the refinement pass operation is as shown in Fig. 4. The refinement pass operation begins after completion of the sorting pass operation indicated by a high $RPI_{busy}$ signal. RAM1 stores a '1' in the MSB or LSB representing the significant or insignificant pixels in the LSP and LIP list respectively. The counter increments each time to access a new significant coefficient indexed by LSP. 'Maxlsp' register stores the maximum address of LSP. Its content is modified after each execution step of refinement pass. This phase outputs the $n^{th}$ most significant bit (MSB) of those coefficients for which $c_i \geq 2^n$ through a 8:1 multiplexer. Here, $c_i$ represents $i^{th}$ wavelet coefficient fetched from the coefficient memory and $n$ represents the number of bits required to represent the maximum valued wavelet coefficient without including the approximation subband given by

$$n = \lfloor (log_2 \max_i \{|c_i|\}) \rfloor, \quad N1 < i \leq N2. \tag{3}$$

where N1, N2 are the last address of the coefficient at LL subband and DWT image respectively.

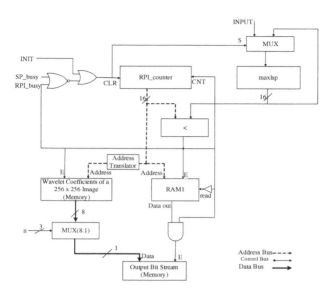

**Fig. 4.** Proposed architecture for refinement pass operation

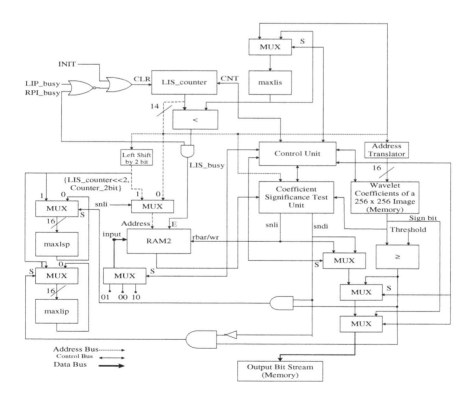

**Fig. 5.** Proposed architecture for LIS pass operation

**Sorting Pass.** LIP pass and LIS pass operations are performed sequentially during the sorting pass operation. The architecture for LIP pass is nearly similar to the refinement pass operation. In LIP pass, coefficients are tested for their significance by comparing with the threshold value. Threshold is computed by finding $2^n$ that requires few AND gates. For the $i^{th}$ significant coefficient, both the MSB and sign bit is sent to output and writes back '10' in $i^{th}$ location of RAM1. Otherwise, it outputs only MSB of the coefficient. Here 'maxlip' stores the maximal address of all nodes in the LIP list.

Architecture for the LIS pass operation is given in Fig. 5. This design includes the address generation mechanism, MaxLIP/ MaxLIS update module along with the significance testing unit. RAM2 is used in LIS pass to store '01', '10' and '00' for type A, B and C operation. Here, two signals namely $sn_{di}$ and $sn_{Li}$ are used to represent significant descendant set with and without off-springs respectively. A 14 bit counter is used for addressing all the descendants. Content of 'maxlsp', 'maxlip' and 'maxlis' registers get updated during this phase. In LIS pass, if $i^{th}$ coefficient of Type-A and its descendant set is significant (*i.e.* $sn_{di}=1$), the sign bit and the MSB bit of its direct descendants is sent to the output. If this coefficient have grand descendants, it is now labeled as Type-B. Content of the $i^{th}$ location in RAM2 changes to '10'. Again, this new set if found significant, $sn_{li}$ becomes high. The content of $i^{th}$ location of RAM2 changes to '00' and the 4i to 4i + 3 locations are changed to '01'.

## 4   Performance Evaluation

Test images of size $256 \times 256$ with different complexity are used for evaluating the performance of the proposed design. A three level Haar wavelet is applied on the test image and the DWT coefficients are stored in the memory. DWT coefficient computation operation is a preprocessing step for the proposed design.

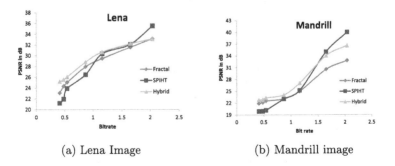

(a) Lena Image                    (b) Mandrill image

**Fig. 6.** PSNR vs bit rate comparison

Variation of image quality and compression time with bit rate (from Matlab simulation) is summarized in this section for pure QTFIC and SPIHT techniques along with their hybrid structure. From Fig. 6 it is found that the fractal coding scheme performs well at low bit rate and SPIHT coding works better at high bit rates. However, at low bit rates (*i.e.* bit rate $< 1$), hybrid technique dominates over pure fractal and SPIHT method. This design achieves nearly 4 dB and 3 dB quality improvement over SPIHT coding for medium complex Lena and high complex Mandrill image respectively. This indicates when higher image quality at high compression ratio is the user demand, one can switch to hybrid fractal-SPIHT technique instead of choosing their pure form. At low bit rates, even the fractal method dominates over the SPIHT technique when image quality is considered.

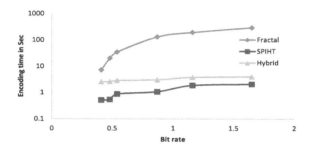

**Fig. 7.** Encoding time comparison for QTFIC, SPIHT and Hybrid technique

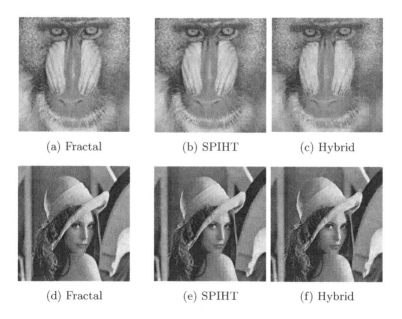

(a) Fractal              (b) SPIHT              (c) Hybrid

(d) Fractal              (e) SPIHT              (f) Hybrid

**Fig. 8.** Image quality comparison for Mandrill and Lena image

However, the PSNR in QTFIC is achieved at the expense of encoding time. Figure 7 depicts the comparison of time spent for encoding the test image Lena at different bit rates for different compression techniques. Exact coding time computation in the hardware design is a difficult task. However, as in hybrid technique fractal coding is used for only $32 \times 32$ pixels, overall encoding time is much less than the QTFIC and slightly more than the pure SPIHT technique. Figure 8 presents the visual image quality of Lena and Mandrill image when encoded at 1.16 and 1.05 bit rates respectively.

**Table 1.** Hardware utilization summary

| Logic utilization | Utilized | Available | % of Utilization |
|---|---|---|---|
| Slice Reg. | 190 | 28800 | 1 |
| Slice LUTs | 380 | 28800 | 1 |
| Slices | 147 | 7200 | 2 |
| Slice LUT-FF pair | 427 | 28800 | 1 |
| Block RAM/FIFO | 5 | 60 | 8 |

Hardware architecture for the hybrid encoder have been coded with verilog HDL and implemented on Virtex-5 xc5vfx30t FPGA. The device utilization summary is given in Table 1. The proposed architecture utilizes 1% of slice registers, 1% of slice LUTs, 13% bonded IOBs, 8% of Block RAM. SPIHT and quadtree partitioning based fractal image encoder encoders operate at maximum clock frequency of 162 MHz and 138 MHz when run independently. However, the hybrid design can operate at maximum frequency of 140 MHz. This hybrid design requires nearly 7 ms time is to complete encoding of a $256 \times 256$ image when operated at maximum frequency.

## 5  Conclusion

In this paper, a fractal-SPIHT hybrid architecture is presented. This design operates at a maximum clock frequency of 140 MHz. Architecture for both SPIHT and quadtree partitioning based fractal image encoder are described in detail and performance of the hybrid design is compared to their pure form. The hybrid encoder overcomes the timing overhead of pure QTFIC coder. The visual quality of the reconstructed image is improved at low bit rates. This approach not only provides good image quality at high compression but also facilitates user to stop at any bit rate without much distortion.

# References

1. Jacquin, A.E.: Fractal image coding: a review. Proc. IEEE **81**(10), 1451–1465 (1993)
2. Fisher, Y.: Fractal Image Compression: Theory and Application. Springer, New York (1994)
3. Chen, H.N., Chung, K.L., Hung, J.E.: Novel fractal image encoding algorithm using normalized one-norm and kick-out condition. Image Vis. Comput. **28**(3), 518–525 (2010)
4. Furao, S., Hasegawa, O.: A fast no search fractal image coding method. Sig. Process. Image Commun. **19**(5), 393–404 (2004)
5. Monro, D.M., Woolley, S.J.: Fractal image compression without searching. In: 1994 IEEE International Conference on Acoustics, Speech, and Signal Processing, ICASSP 1994, p. V-557. IEEE (1994)
6. Tong, C.S., Pi, M.: Fast fractal image encoding based on adaptive search. IEEE Trans. Image Process. **10**(9), 1269–1277 (2001)
7. Lai, C.M., Lam, K.M., Siu, W.C.: A fast fractal image coding based on kick-out and zero contrast conditions. IEEE Trans. Image Process. **12**(11), 1398–1403 (2003)
8. Panigrahy, M., Chakrabarti, I., Dhar, A.S.: Low-delay parallel architecture for fractal image compression. Circ. Syst. Sig. Process. **35**(3), 897–917 (2015)
9. Jackson, D.J., Ren, H., Wu, X., Ricks, K.G.: A hardware architecture for real-time image compression using a searchless fractal image coding method. J. Real-Time Image Proc. **1**(3), 225–237 (2007)
10. Panigrahy, M., Chakrabarti, I., Dhar, A.: VLSI design of fast fractal image encoder. In: 18th International Symposium on VLSI Design and Test, pp. 1–2. IEEE, July 2014
11. Samavi, S., Habibi, M., Shirani, S., Rowshanbin, N.: Real time fractal image coder based on characteristic vector matching. Image Vis. Comput. **28**(11), 1557–1568 (2010)
12. Rinaldo, R., Calvagno, G.: Image coding by block prediction of multiresolution subimages. IEEE Trans. Image Process. **4**(7), 909–920 (1995)
13. Davis, G.M.: A wavelet-based analysis of fractal image compression. IEEE Trans. Image Process. **7**(2), 141–154 (1998)
14. Li, J., Kuo, C.: Image compression with a hybrid wavelet-fractal coder. IEEE Trans. Image Process. **8**(6), 868–874 (1999)
15. Shapiro, J.: Embedded image coding using zerotrees of wavelet coefficients. IEEE Trans. Signal Process. **41**(12), 3445–3462 (1993)
16. Said, A., Pearlman, W.: A new, fast, and efficient image codec based on set partitioning in hierarchical trees. IEEE Trans. Circuits Syst. Video Technol. **6**(3), 243–250 (1996)
17. Iano, Y., da Silva, F.S., Cruz, A.L.: A fast and efficient hybrid fractal-wavelet image coder. IEEE Trans. Image Process. **15**(1), 98–105 (2006)
18. Huang, W., Alvin, W., Kho, Y.H.: VLSI implementation of a modified efficient SPIHT encoder. IEICE Trans. Fundam. Electron. Commun. Comput. Sci. **89**(12), 3613–3622 (2006)
19. Wheeler, F.W., Pearlman, W.A.: SPIHT image compression without lists. In: Proceedings of the IEEE International Conference on Acoustics, Speech, and Signal Processing, ICASSP 2000, vol. 04, pp. 2047–2050 (2000)

# Metal-Oxide Nanostructures Designed by Glancing Angle Deposition Technique and Its Applications on Sensors and Optoelectronic Devices: A Review

Divya Singh[✉]

National Institute of Technology, Imphal, Manipur, India
divs0508singh@gmail.com

**Abstract.** Glancing angle deposited (GLAD) metal-oxide nanostructure films are promising materials for sensors and optoelectronic devices application due to the easy fabrication process, structural dependent properties and a large surface to volume ratio. This paper focuses on the literature reviews of metal-oxide nanostructures deposited by GLAD using all the possible deposition techniques such as thermal/electron-beam evaporation, sputtering magnetron, and pulsed laser deposition. The principle behind the formation of nanostructure through GLAD has also been discussed in details. The detailed analysis of the devices and their principle based on GLAD deposited metal-oxide nanostructures for different optoelectronic and sensor devices are also presented. This literature review will be helpful to understand and explore more on the growth of metal-oxide nanostructures using glancing angle deposition technique for futuristic sensors and optoelectronic device applications.

**Keywords:** Metal-oxide · Sputtering · Sensors · GLAD · PVD

## 1 Introduction

Metal-Oxide Nanostructures have grabbed so many researchers' interest due to their outstanding chemical, electrical, and optical properties as these nanostructures are providing tremendous possibilities for exploring new physical phenomena. Novel physical properties of 1-D Metal-Oxide Nanostructures have made them ubiquitous in science & technology and have now been widely used in many areas such as transparent electronics [1], piezoelectric transducers [2], nanoparticulate catalysts, machinable ceramics, sensors [3], electro-optical and electrochromic devices [4]. From the past studies, different techniques have been found such as chemical vapor deposition [5–8], dc-magnetron sputtering [9], laser deposition [10], sol-gel process [11], electrochemical deposition [12], vapor-liquid-solid (VLS) [13], while among them Glancing Angle Deposition (GLAD) [14, 15] technique is considered as the simplest technique for the growth of vertically aligned nanowires as there is no need of higher temperature or catalysts to proceed process. GLAD technique came as the extended form of Oblique Angle Deposition (OAD) [16] just in order to better control the orientation as well as the structure of nanocolumn arrays. The Experimental-setup got a change in rotating the

© Springer Nature Singapore Pte Ltd. 2017
B. K. Kaushik et al. (Eds.): VDAT 2017, CCIS 711, pp. 388–397, 2017.
https://doi.org/10.1007/978-981-10-7470-7_38

substrate while deposition, substrate rotation alters the apparent location of the vapor source from the perspective of the growing columns. Nanostructures through this technique give a large surface to volume ratios and aspect ratios (length/diameter), such as to increase the porosity nature of the film in order to rise the applications.

This review focuses the past and recent researches on the synthesis of metal-oxide nanostructures through GLAD technique. As the GLAD technique improves the performance of sensors and optoelectronic devices by increasing their sensitivity, selectivity and response time.

## 2   Fundamentals of OAD and GLAD

The term OAD [17] refers the setup where the vapor flux of the source material arrives at the substrate surface at the oblique angle. For the very first time, OAD emerged in 1860, but the reason behind the formation of nanocolumn arrays came in 1950 when Konig and Helwig recognized the important role of atomic scale shadowing [18] also called self-shadowing. OAD and GLAD are the physical vapor deposition technique where deposition lies on atomic shadowing effect i.e. the incident vapor atom arrives at an angle $\alpha$ as shown in Fig. 1 is intercepted by the growing nanocolumns and once the nucleates form it gives shadow in the other part of the substrate due to which no growth occurs in the shadowed part. Further, the vapor flux restricts to give nanocolumn by depositing on the previous nucleates. Thus for the controlling orientations of these nanocolumns, substrate rotation is given and named GLAD technique, a combination of oblique angle and substrate rotation. GLAD also gives a number of structures such as helical, zig-zag and spiral by rotating the substrate in both polar and azimuthal directions, and varying the angle of inclination too. Also, it can be investigated through simulations preferably Monte Carlo method [19]. The substrate position is controlled

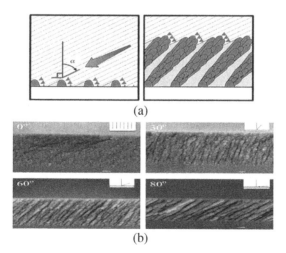

(a)

(b)

**Fig. 1.** (a) Conceptual view of the GLAD process, the incident vapor atoms and growing nanocolumns [14], and (b) SEM cross-section view of Si Films fabricated at different angles [15].

by use of two stepper motors [20] where the first controls rotation about an axis perpendicular to the substrate and the second motor controls rotation about an axis parallel to the substrate surface and perpendicular to the deposition plane. Since the degree of shadowing strongly depends on the angle of incidence [21] so, as the angle of incidence increases, porosity increases.

Jensen *et al.* developed a new GLAD growth method [22] for the high level of control over the porosity of thin film, this method involves regular sweeping of the substrate from side to side about a central axis defining the direction of straight column segments instead of keeping substrate static for each straight column segments which were in traditional GLAD. A schematic illustration of this new method is called as PhiSweep shown in Fig. 2.

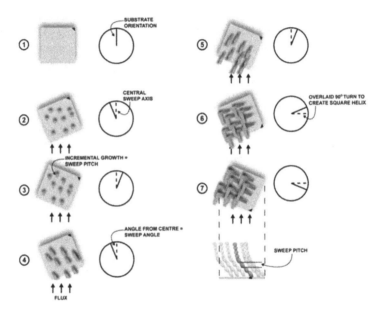

**Fig. 2.** Schematic of Phi-Sweep method for decoupling the directions of incident flux and column growth in GLAD [22].

Robbie and Brett studied on sculptured thin films through GLAD technique [23] also the new method for evolving columnar microstructure into dense capping layer which provides encapsulation and protection for the delicate films. Here they formed capping film by decreasing the flux angle exponentially ($\Theta \propto [1 - A.e^{B.t}]$) with time produced good and dense capping layer with less chance of cracking of the film.

## 3    Designing Metal-Oxide Nanostructures and Their Applications

GLAD metal-oxide nanostructures are finely controllable on their morphological structures by giving the larger surface to volume ratio and the Debye length ($\lambda_D$) comparable to their lateral dimensions, making them applicable for the most commercial sensors and optoelectronic devices. As, sensing mechanism relies on the change in conductivity and band bending due to trapping of electrons by adsorbed molecules [24] and for the optoelectronic devices the main reasons that are the larger surface to volume ratio and comparable Debye length. Steele *et al.* analyzed capacitive humidity sensors [25, 26] by coating counter sunk interdigitated electrode (IDE) substrate with GLAD films.

Since, GLAD is a physical vapor deposition techniques so it is eminently suitable for use with all the directional deposition sources such as thermal/electron-beam evaporation, magnetron sputtering and pulsed laser deposition where electron-beam evaporation and magnetron sputtering are the most commonly used techniques.

## 3.1  Sputtering Deposition

Sputtering deposition relies on plasma (usually noble gases) which are accelerated by an electric field, such as to knock the material from a target a few atoms at a time. This deposition is useful for easily sputtering of the material having the higher melting point also for compounds or mixtures where different components tend to evaporate at different rates [27]. Radio Frequency (RF) sputtering plays an important role in producing highly insulating oxide films.

Liang and Liu reported that self-assembled Zn or ZnO could be fabricated only by oblique-angle RF magnetron sputter on rotating Si substrate by keeping sputtering gas as argon and hydrogen [28]. Due to its higher uniformity and more controls made its usefulness in optoelectronic devices. Deniz *et al.* synthesized nanostructured tungsten (in a pure Ar) and tungsten trioxide films (in an $Ar/O_2$) by pulsed dc magnetron sputtering and employed post-deposition annealing at $500°C$ which yields an amorphous $WO_3$ into polycrystalline form [29]. Annealing gives $WO_3$ nanorods into a highly nanoporous network which makes them applicable for gas sensing.

Wonchoosuk *et al.* reported $NO_2$ gas sensor through carbon doped $WO_3$ nanorods using radio frequency magnetron sputtering where the doping resulted in a reduction in activation energy also detection of $NO_2$ at relatively low operating temperature with high gas response compared to other methods were possible [30]. Figure 3 (a) dynamic resistance response proved the increase in charge carrier concentration in carbon doped nanorods by indicating a lower magnitude of resistance. While Fig. 3 (b) shows the 2 times higher gas response at 5 ppm concentration of $NO_2$ in the case of carbon doping. Horprathum *et al.* reported an ultrasensitive $H_2$ sensor through dc magnetron sputtering platinum (Pt) decorated $WO_3$ nanorods [31]. Gas sensing mechanism has been analyzed with the help of the change in resistance on the exposure of $H_2$ gas. $H_2$ sensing performances were enhanced in platinum decorated nanorods, also depends on the time of deposition i.e. better sensing performance on more time of deposition of Pt but this remains up till 10 ss afterward it deteriorated. The resistance change of more than 5 order magnitude at 1000-3000 ppm $H_2$ concentration at 10 sec of Pt decoration. Oros *et al.* synthesized $SnO_2$ nanorod structure with different $O_2$ flow rate from 12 to 48 sccm as an ethanol sensor and where on increasing flow rate of oxygen not only structure transforms from amorphous to crystalline but also the sensitivity increased [32].

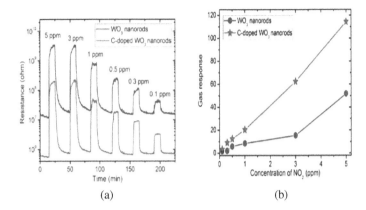

(a)                           (b)

**Fig. 3.** Responses of carbon doped and undoped $WO_3$ nanorods gas sensor (a) Dynamic resistance response, and (b) Gas responses at different concentration of $NO_2$ [30].

### 3.2    Pulsed Laser Deposition

Pulsed laser deposition (PLD) works by an ablation process. It is a variant of the sputtering deposition technique in which laser beam is used for sputtering. Target materials get knocked out through the focused laser beam in the vapor form which makes the deposition onto the substrate. A better control can be achieved in PLD on the deposition parameters such as substrate temperature, partial pressures of gases [33].

Hattori *et al.* fabricated ZnO nanoboxes and nanowires by the combination of a top-down nanoimprint lithography technique and a bottom-up pulsed laser deposition (PLD) technique [34]. This combination gave c-axis oriented ZnO polycrystalline 3D nanoboxes and nanobelts which indicated their application to nanoscale optoelectronic devices because of exhibiting an intense cathodoluminescence (CL) peak at 380 nm at room temperature. Salim *et al.* reported successful growth of cauliflower-like bismuth oxide structure using glancing angle reactive pulsed laser deposition [35], using 9 ns, 1.06 μm Q-switched Nd-YAG laser which resulted in a reduction in particle size and increment in reverse current and built-in potential on increasing tile angles. Marcu *et al.* used high repetition rate laser in an 'eclipse' experimental setup using pulsed laser ablation/vapor-liquid-solid technique [36] for fabricating ZnO nanowire on Au patterned and non-patterned areas and concluded that by increasing the number of laser pulses per train, nanowire length initially increased and further saturated. Also, the analysis is done to compare the center of the shadowed zone and the side zone.

### 3.3    Thermal/Electron-Beam Evaporation

Thermal/electron-beam evaporation gives deposition onto the substrate by heating the source material under high vacuum atmosphere [37]. Chakrabartty *et al.* reported the synthesis of $TiO_2$ nanoparticles arrays on $SiO_x$ thin films using GLAD technique through e-beam evaporator [38]. $SiO_x$ thin films had been deposited on the Si substrate under the base pressure of $2 \times 10^{-5}$ and as like the $TiO_2$ had also been deposited upon the thin film by keeping the substrate holder at a distance of 24 cm from the source material. From the analysis, it had been concluded that the device can be used as sensitive UV-A detector as the blue shift had been observed from PL analysis. Tsoi *et al.* studied $TiO_2$, $SiO_2$, and $Al_2O_3$ GLAD films had been deposited through e-beam evaporation of slanted posts, vertical posts and helical columnar structure [39]. The chemical tunability had been investigated using solution-based and vapor-phase surface functionalization methodologies and concluded that both film structure and surface chemistry influence surface hydrophobicity. As the GLAD films increase porosity, therefore, they are in demand for the sensors. Jeon *et al.* synthesized $SnO_2$ nanobamboos decorated with Au nanoparticles, as the deposition of nanoparticles on the side- wall is not possible through GLAD technique, therefore, the process goes for the deposition of nanoparticles after every 100 nm nanobamboos [40]. And this $SnO_2$ nanobamboos proved to be subjected to the long-term sensitization operation without degradation. Yoo *et al.* found highly sensitive $H_2S$ sensor through e-beam evaporation GLAD synthesized $SnO_2$ nanocolumns decorated with Au and Ag nanoparticles [41]. The gas sensitivities ($S = R_{gas}/R_{air}$) measured and found that it is maximum in the case of Au-catalyzed $SnO_2$ nanocolumns of .009 at 5 ppm of $H_2S$ at 300 °C in comparison of Ag-catalyzed and bare $SnO_2$ nanocolumns.

Mondal *et al.* fabricated two type of detector $SiO_x$ nanowires, and $SiO_x$ thin films and proved nearly six-fold enhancement in photoresponsivity as compared with the thin film [42] as shown in Fig. 4. Ngangbam *et al.* reported a photodetector fabricated with $TiO_2$ nanowire clusters (NWCs) decorated with Ag nanoparticles (NPs) and found from the PL analysis that 2.5 times more intense light came from the $TiO_2$ NWCs without Ag NPs due to large surface to volume ratio while in photoresponsivity, NWCs with Ag NPs showed enhanced photosensitivity [43]. Shuang *et al.* fabricated N-doped $TiO_2$ (TiN) nanorod arrays (NRAs) on F-doped $SnO_2$ and quartz substrates and analyzed that TiN NRAs enhanced photocatalysts property by coupling with the semiconductors and also with the noble metals [44]. Li *et al.* proved that photocatalytic increases on increasing surface area, by fabricating $TiO_2$ GLAD films at a different substrate angles, which gave the best result on $\alpha = 75°$ [45].

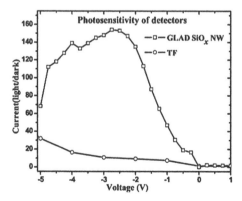

**Fig. 4.** Photosensitivity of the $SiO_x$ TF and $SiO_x$ NWs based devices under white light illumination [42].

Solar (or photovoltaic) cells are the device which absorbs photons from sunlight and excites electrons to higher band leaving behind holes [46]. Solar cells are easily obtainable from GLAD metal oxide nanostructures because they provide high surface area and good electron transport as nanowires provide a direct path to the substrate for fast charge transport. Garcia *et al.* analyzed the already proven, tilting the nanocolumns improves the light entrapment efficiency and thereafter fabricated Dye-sensitized cells from $TiO_2$ zigzag GLAD thin films at the deposition angle of $60°$, $70°$, $80°$, and $85°$ [47]. Figure 5 shows the power conversion efficiency after 1 h immersion in dye (($Bu_4N)_2Ru(debpyH)_2(NCS)$) solution of thin film where after 2 h of dye immersion, best solar performance has been found.

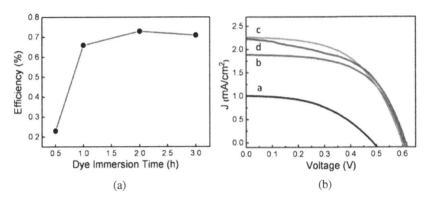

**Fig. 5.** (a) Efficiency vs dye immersion time, and (b) I–V curves at different dye immersion time (a) 30 min, (b) 1 h, (c) 3 h, and (d) 4 h [47]

Leem *et al.* found highly transparent indium tin oxide GLAD films and their performance of a-Si:H/μc-Si:H tandem thin film solar cells and proved that the conversion efficiency of $0°$ ITO/$80°$ ITO increased in comparison to $0°$ ITO/$0°$ ITO [48].

## 4  Conclusion

In summary, this work provides a comprehensive review of the past and recent researches of glancing angle deposited metal-oxide nanostructures through all the possible evaporation approaches. The basic of oblique angle deposition and glancing angle deposition had also been discussed in detail. GLAD deposited metal-oxide nanostructures have a larger surface to volume ratio which makes it favorable for the sensors such as gas, chemical, temperature, and humidity sensors from the discussed review papers. And also it is applicable for the highly sensitive photodetector device. Moreover, GLAD based metal-oxide nanostructures are used in photovoltaic cells due to its photocatalytic properties. Therefore, metal-oxide nanostructures deposited by GLAD technique are promising for next generation sensors and optoelectronic device applications.

**Acknowledgment.** This work was supported by Department of Electronics & Communication Engineering, National Institute of Technology Manipur.

# References

1. Sun, B., Sirringhaus, H.: Solution-processed zinc oxide field-effect transistors based on self-assembly of colloidal nanorods. Nano Lett. **5**, 2408–2413 (2005)
2. Chauhan, I., Aggrawal, S., Chandravati, Mohanty, P.: Metal oxide nanostructures incorporated/immobilized paper matrices and their applications: a review, pp. 1–18. The Royal Society of Chemistry (2015)
3. Xia, Y.N., Yang, P.D., Sun, Y.G., Wu, Y.Y., Mayers, B., Gates, B., Yin, Y.D., Kim, F., Yan, H.Q.: One-dimensional nanostructures: synthesis, characterization, and applications. Adv. Mater. **15**, 353–389 (2003)
4. Lu, J.G., Chang, P., Fan, Z.: Quasi-one-dimensional metal oxide materials-Synthesis, properties, and applications. Mater. Sci. Eng., R **52**, 49–91 (2006)
5. Mathur, S., Singh, A.P., Muller, R., Leuning, T.: Metal-organic chemical vapor deposition of metal oxide films and nanostructures. Ceram. Sci. Technol. **3**, 291–336 (2012)
6. Cheng, G., Stern, E., Guthrie, S., Reed, M.A., Klie, R., Hao, Y., Meng, G., Zhang, L.: Indium oxide nanostructures. Appl. Phys. A **83**, 233–240 (2006)
7. Chang, P.C., Fan, Z., Wang, D., Tseng, W.Y., Chiou, W.A., Hong, J., Lu, J.G.: ZnO nanowires synthesized by vapor trapping CVD method. Chem. Mater. **16**, 5133–5137 (2004)
8. Thabethe, B.S., Malgas, G.F., Motaung, D.E., Malwela, T., Arendse, C.J.: Self-catalytic growth of tin oxide nanowires by chemical vapor deposition process. J. Nanomaterials **2013**, 1–7 (2013)
9. Kiriakidis, G., Dovinos, D., Suchea, M.: Sensing using nanostructured metal oxide thin films. In: Proceedings of SPIE – The International Society for Optical Engineering, vol. 6370, pp. 1–12 (2006)
10. Huotari, J., Lappalainen, J., Puustinen, J., Baur, T., Alepee, C., Haapalainen, T., Komulainen, S., Pylvanainen, J., Spetz, A.L.: Pulsed laser deposition of metal oxide nanoparticles, agglomerates, and nanotrees for chemical sensors. Eurosensors **120**, 1158–1161 (2015)
11. Sui, R., Charpentier, P.: Synthesis of metal oxide nanostructures by direct sol-gel chemistry in supercritical fluids. Chem. Rev. **112**, 3057–3082 (2012)
12. Tong, Y.X., Li, G.R.: Electrodeposition of metal oxide nanostructures: growth and properties. Am. Sci. Publ. **5**, 1–33 (2010)
13. Yu, H.K., Lee, J.L.: Growth mechanisms of metal-oxide nanowires synthesized by electron beam evaporation: a self-catalytic vapor-liquid-solid process. Sci. Rep. **4**, 1–8 (2014)
14. Hawkeye, M.M., Taschuk, M.T., Brett, M.J.: Introduction: glancing angle deposition technology. In: Glancing Angle Deposition of Thin Films: Engineering the Nanoscale, pp. 1–30 (2014)
15. Zhao, Y.P., Ye, D.X., Wang, G.C., Lu, T.M.: Designing nanostructures by glancing angle deposition. In: Proceedings of SPIE, vol. 5219, pp. 59–73 (2003)
16. Krause, K.M., Taschuk, M.T., Harris, K.D., Rider, D.A., Wakefield, N.G., Sit, J.C., Buriak, J.M., Thommes, M., Brett, M.J.: Surface area characterization of obliquely deposited metal oxide nanostructured thin films. Langmuir **26**, 4368–4376 (2009)
17. Barranco, A., Borras, A., Gonzalez-Elipe, A.R., Palmero, A.: Perspectives on oblique angle deposition of thin films: From fundamentals to devices. Prog. Mater Sci. **76**, 59–153 (2016)

18. Hawkeye, M.M., Brett, M.J.: Glancing angle deposition: fabrication, properties, and applications of micro- and nanostructured thin films. J. Vac. Sci. Technol., A **25**, 1317–1335 (2007)

19. Patzig, C., Karabacak, T., Fuhrmann, B., Rauschenbach, B.: Glancing angle sputter deposited nanostructures on rotating substrates: experiments and simulations. J. Appl. Phys. **104**, 1–9 (2008)

20. Robbie, K., Sit, J.C., Brett, M.J.: Advanced techniques for glancing angle deposition. J. Vac. Sci. Technol., B **16**, 1115–1122 (1998)

21. van Kranenburg, H., Lodder, C.: Tailoring growth and local composition by oblique-incidence deposition: a review and new experimental data. Mater. Sci. Eng. **11**, 295–354 (1994)

22. Jensen, M.O., Brett, M.J.: Porosity engineering in glancing angle deposition thin films. Appl. Phys. A **80**, 763–768 (2005)

23. Robbie, K., Brett, M.J.: Sculptured thin films and glancing angle deposition: growth mechanics and applications. J. Vac. Sci. Technol., A **15**, 1460–1465 (1997)

24. Sun, Y.F., Liu, S.B., Meng, F.L., Liu, J.Y., Jin, Z., Kong, L.T., Liu, J.H.: Metal oxide nanostructures and their gas sensing properties: a review. Sensors **12**, 2610–2631 (2012)

25. Steele, J.J., Taschuk, M.T., Brett, M.J.: Response time of nanostructured relative humidity sensors. Sens. Actuators B Chem. **140**, 610–615 (2009)

26. Steele, J.J., Taschuk, M.T., Brett, M.J.: Nanostructured metal oxide thin films for humidity sensors. IEEE Sens. J. **8**(8), 1422–1429 (2008)

27. Setti, G.O., Jesus, D.P.D., Joanni, E.: Self-catalyzed carbon plasma-assisted growth of tin-doped indium oxide nanostructures by the sputtering method. Mater. Res. Express **3**, 1–7 (2016)

28. Liang, Y.H., Liu, C.P.: Self-assembled Zn/ZnO dots on silicon by RF magnetron sputter. Microprocesses and Nanotechnology, pp. 158–159 (2008)

29. Deniz, D., Frankel, D.J., Lad, R.J.: Nanostructured tungsten and tungsten trioxide films prepared by glancing angle deposition. Thin Solid Films **518**, 4095–4099 (2009)

30. Wongchoosuk, C., Wisitsoraat, A., Horprathum, M., Tuantranont, A.: Carbon doped tungsten oxide nanorods $NO_2$ sensor prepared by glancing angle RF sputtering. Sens. Actuators B Chem. **181**, 388–394 (2013)

31. Horprathum, M., Srichaiyaperk, T., Samransuksamer, B., Wisitsoraat, A., Eiamchai, P., Limwichean, S., et al.: Ultrasensitive hydrogen sensor based on Pt-decorated $WO_3$ NanorodsPrepared by Glancing-Angle dc magnetron sputtering. ACS Appl. Mater. Interfaces. **6**, 22051–22060 (2014)

32. Oros, C., Wisitsoraat, A., Horprathum, M.: Fabrication and ethanol sensing characterization of tin oxide nanorods prepared by glancing angle deposition technique. Appl. Phys. Mater. Appl. II **675**, 163–166 (2016)

33. Srinivasarao, K., Rajnikanth, B., Paduangarao, K., Mukhopadhyay, P.K.: Physical investigations on pulsed laser deposited nanocrystalline ZnO thin films. Appl. Phys. A **108**(1), 247–254 (2012)

34. Hattori, A.N., Ono, A., Tanaka, H.: Position-, size-, and shape-controlled highly crystalline ZnO nanostructures. Nanotechnology **22**, 1–5 (2011)

35. Salim, E.T., Wazny, M.S.A., Fakhry, M.A.: Glancing angle reactive pulsed laser deposition (GRPLD) for $Bi_2O_3$/Si heterostructure. Mod. Phys. Lett. B **27**(16), 1–27 (2013)

36. Marcu, A., Stokker, F., Zamani, R.R., Lunga, C.P.: Glancing angle deposition in a pulsed laser ablation/vapor-liquid-solid grow system. Appl. Surf. Sci. **327**, 262–267 (2014)

37. Krishna, M.G., Muralidhar, G.K., Rao, K.N., Rao, G.M., Mohan, S.: A novel electron beam evaporation technique for the deposition of superconducting thin films. Phys. C **175**, 623–626 (1991)
38. Chakrabartty, S., Mondal, A., Sarkar, M.B., Choudhuri, B., Saha, A.K., Bhattacharya, A.: $TiO_2$ nanoparticles arrays ultraviolet-a detector with au schottky contact. IEEE Photonics Technol. Lett. **26**(11), 1065–1068 (2014)
39. Tsoi, S., Fok, E., Sit, J.C., Veinot, J.G.C.: Surface functionalization of porous nanostructured metal oxide thin films fabricated by glancing angle deposition. Chem. Mater. **18**, 5260–5266 (2006)
40. Jeon, J.M., Shim, Y.S., Han, S.D., Kim, D.H., Kim, Y.H., Kang, C.Y., Kim, J.S., Kim, M., Jang, H.W.: Vertically ordered $SnO_2$ nanobamboos for substantially improved detection of volatile reducing gases. The Royal Society of Chemistry pp. 1–8 (2013)
41. Yoo, K.S., Han, S.D., Moon, H.G., Yoon, S.J., Kang, C.Y.: Highly sensitive $H_2S$ sensor based on the metal-catalyzed $SnO_2$ nanocolumns fabricated by glancing angle deposition. Sensors **15**, 15468–15477 (2015)
42. Mondal, A., Singh, N.K., Chinnamuthu, P., Dhar, J.C., Bhattacharyya, A., Choudhury, S.: Enlarged photodetection using $SiO_x$ nanowire arrays. IEEE Photonics Technol. Lett. **24**(22), 2020–2023 (2012)
43. Ngangbam, C., Shougaijam, B., Mondal, A.: Dispersed Ag nanoparticles on $TiO_2$ nanowire clusters for photodetection. TENCON-IEEE, pp. 1–4 (2014)
44. Shuang, S., Xie, Z., Zhang, Z.: Enhanced visible light photocatalytic performance by nanostructured semiconductors with glancing angle deposition method. INTECH, pp. 163–184 (2016)
45. Li, Z., Zhu, Y., Zhu, Q., Ni, J., Zhang, Z.: Photocatalytic properties of $TiO_2$ thin films obtained by glancing angle deposition. Appl. Surf. Sci. **258**, 2766–2770 (2012)
46. Srivastava, G.P., Bhatnagar, P.K., Dhariwal, S.R.: Theory of metal-oxide-semiconductor solar cells. Solid State Electron. **22**(6), 581–587 (1979)
47. Garcia, L.G., Valls, I.G., Cantu, M.L., Barranco, A., Ellipe, A.R.G.: Aligned $TiO_2$ nanocolumnar layers prepared by PVD-GLAD for transparent dye sensitized solar cells. Energy Environ. Sci. **4**, 3426–3435 (2011)
48. Leem, J.W., Yu, J.S.: Glancing angle deposited ITO films for efficiency enhancement of a-Si:H/μc-Si: H tandem thin film solar cells. Opt. Express **19**(S3), A258–A268 (2011)

# Low Write Energy STT-MRAM Cell Using 2T- Hybrid Tunnel FETs Exploiting the Steep Slope and Ambipolar Characteristics

Y. Sudha Vani[1(✉)], N. Usha Rani[1], and Ramesh Vaddi[2]

[1] Department of Electronics and Communication Engineering, V.F.S.T.R University,
Vadlamudi, Guntur 522213, Andhra Pradesh, India
vani.yamani@gmail.com, usharani.nsai@gmail.com
[2] Nano Scale Integrated Circuits and Systems for Self-Powered IoT Laboratory,
DSPM International Institute of Information Technology,
Naya Raipur 493661, Chattishgarh, India
ramesh@iiitnr.edu.in

**Abstract.** Spin Transfer Torque Magnetic Random Access memory (STT-MRAM) is found to be one of the best candidates among all emerging non-volatile memories. High write energy is a bottleneck for CMOS based 1T and 2T STT-MRAM cells with scaling. To reduce the write energy of an STT-MRAM cell, a novel 2T Hybrid (Hetero-junction and Homo-junction) Tunnel Field Effect Transistor (TFET) based STT-MRAM cell has been proposed in this paper. The proposed 2T Hybrid TFET based STT-MRAM cell has less write energy and switching time due to TFET's combined steep-slope and ambipolar characteristics in comparison to 1T/2T-FinFET, 1T/2T Hetero-junction TFET, 1T/2T homo-junction TFET based STT-MRAM cells.

**Keywords:** Ambipolar currents · FinFET · Low write energy · Memory
STT-MRAM · Tunnel FET

## 1 Introduction

STT-MRAM (Spin Transfer Torque Magnetic Random Access Memory) technology has been found to be the best future non-volatile memory technology in recent times. However, STT-MRAM cells suffer from asymmetric switching time and high write energy due to low ON current of CMOS access transistors [1, 2]. STT-MRAM cells require high current for a change in polarization to store the data. FinFETs have been introduced as access transistor in STT-MRAM cell designs [3–5] due to their high $I_{ON}/I_{OFF}$ ratios. In order to further overcome the high write energy issue, researchers proposed different techniques such as NBL (Negative bit line) assist technique [6], 2T-1R dual source line bitcell technique for reducing the excessive and unwanted MTJ current [7], minimized leakage current through no power line in 2T-1MTJ cell [8] and using asymmetric doping at the source/drain (S/D) terminals diminishes the write current without affecting write ability [9]. Steep slope devices such as Tunnel FETs (TFETs) offer low leakage current and high driving capability compared to FinFETs, at scaled voltages below 0.5 V. In the prior

© Springer Nature Singapore Pte Ltd. 2017
B. K. Kaushik et al. (Eds.): VDAT 2017, CCIS 711, pp. 398–405, 2017.
https://doi.org/10.1007/978-981-10-7470-7_39

work, negative differential resistance devices [10] such as Tunnel diodes(TD) or Tunnel field effect transistors have been used to assist the STT-MRAM write and read operations, without change in underlying memory architecture.

In the proposed design, some of the limitations of TFETs such as ambipolar current (OFF current) is used as an advantage in hybrid (Hetero Jn + Homo Jn) TFET structure for MTJ cell. A memory cell with PMA-MTJ (perpendicular magnetic anisotropy-magnetic tunnel junction), FinFET/TFET access transistors and their metrics are analyzed for metrics like switching time and energy consumption of cell, etc., are analyzed. To overcome the drawbacks of 2T/1MTJ with FinFETs, a hybrid (Hetero + Homo) junction TFET structure for MTJ cell is proposed to reduce the switching time and energy.

The rest of the paper as follows. Section 2 provides the device structure and characteristics of FinFET, TFET and PMA-MTJ devices. Section 3 presents the proposed memory cell operation with TFET-MTJ and analyze the comparative results. Section 4 provides the conclusion.

## 2   Devices Structure and Parameters

### 2.1   TFET

In this work, two variants of Tunnel field effect transistors, i.e., 20 nm double-gate InAs homo junction (Homo-junction) TFET and GaSb-InAs near-broken gap hetero junction (hetero junction) TFET (Fig. 1b) are explored [13]. In homo-junction TFET (Fig. 1a), the source and drain terminals are doped with same material i.e. (InAs), in hetero junction TFET (Fig. 1b), source and drain terminals are doped with different materials. TFET is a reverse-biased, gated p-i-n tunnel diode, with asymmetrical source/drain doping. The on-state is enabled by the gate-controlled band-to-band tunneling at the source-channel junction, and a sub-60 mV/decade steep-slope can be achieved in TFET with desired $I_{on}/I_{off}$ over a low-$V_{DD}$ range. The TFET device parameters used for device simulations in generating LUT based *Verilog-A* models for HTFETs [21].

(a)                              (b)

**Fig. 1.**   (a) InAs Homo junction Tunnel FET [12] (b) GaSb-InAs Hetero junction Tunnel FET [11]

The LUT based *Verilog-A* models [11–13] are considered and their symbols (Fig. 2a, b) are plugged into *Cadence Virtuoso* platform for circuit designs. Figure 2c presents the performance comparison of Homo and Hetero junction TFETs, considered for circuit design. Homo junction TFET produces around 3.5 times larger ambipolar currents than the hetero junction TFET (Fig. 2c).

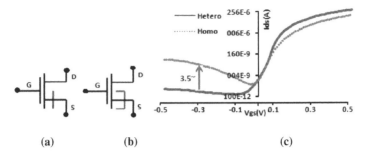

(a)          (b)                              (c)

**Fig. 2.** Symbols of (a) Homo junction TFET (b) Hetero junction TFET (c) $I_{ds}$-$V_{gs}$ characteristics of homo and hetero junction TFETs at $V_{DS} = 0.5$ V

## 2.2 FinFET

FinFET devices provide advantages with scaling in terms of high speed, low operating voltage, [14, 15]. Look-up-table (LUT) based *Verilog-A* models developed from TCAD Sentaurus device simulations are utilized in this work [22].

## 2.3 MTJ Device

Various compact STT-MTJ models have been reported in the recent times [16–18]. In [19], a compact model of CoFeB/MgO PMA-MTJ (perpendicular magnetic anisotropy-magnetic tunnel junction) is used and is considered in this work. This model provides best TMR (tunnel magneto resistance) ratio and switching performance by using time-dependent dielectric breakdown (TDDB) mechanism in oxide barrier. The TMR is defined as the ratio of high and low resistances $R_{AP}$ and $R_P$ respectively. The ratio typically ranges between 50% to 200%, where $R_{AP}$ is the electrical resistance in anti-parallel state and $R_P$ is the resistance in the parallel state.

$$TMR = \frac{R_{AP} - R_P}{R_P} \tag{1}$$

When there is a wide gap between low resistance and high resistance, the sense amplifier provides faster read sensing latency. The resistance of MTJ changes between two states when switching currents($I_P \rightarrow$ AP, $I_{AP} \rightarrow$ P) are greater than critical current ($I_{c0}$) as shown in Fig. 3.

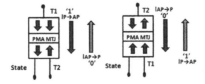

**Fig. 3.** MTJ consisting of three layers with current switching directions.

# 3   Proposed TFET- MTJ Cell Operation

## 3.1   Cell Operation

The basic cell design consists one access transistor and one MTJ(1T/1MTJ), where MTJ stores one bit value internally. MTJ consists of two ferromagnetic layers, pinned layer (PL) and free layer (FL) with oxide barrier. The magnetization directions of two ferromagnetic layer are parallel (P) and anti-parallel (AP) with low resistance (logic 0) and high resistance (logic 1) respectively.

Spin polarized current flows through MTJ, and changes the directions of free layer (FL) that represents the parallel (P) and anti-parallel (AP) conditions, which is greater than the critical current ($I_{c0}$) of MTJ. For changing spin polarization current, sufficient BL, SL voltages have to be given (Fig. 4a) through write scheme [20].

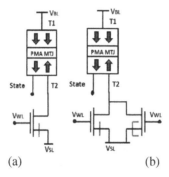

(a)                                    (b)

**Fig. 4.**  (a) Basic cell 1T/1MTJ with homo Jn TFET (b) proposed 2T hybrid memory cell structure

If write current is high, the switching times of P → AP and AP → P directions can be decreased. The pinned layer of MTJ is connected to bit line (BL). In this connection, when negative current ($I_{AP → P}$) is established at T1 terminal, a low resistance is obtained and then the state changes from AP → P. When positive current ($I_{P → AP}$) is established at T1 terminal, a high resistance is obtained and the state is changed from P → AP.

The switching current of $I_{AP → P}$ and $I_{P → AP}$ occurs with large difference due to voltage difference of BL and SL. In $I_{P → AP}$ state, the BL is connected to positive voltage and SL is almost connected to 0 V. In $I_{AP → P}$, the BL is connected to negative voltage and SL is connected to 0 V. This connection does not drive sufficient voltage to MTJ through access transistor. So, the transistor width can be changed and that leads to an increase in area. For avoiding area overhead, a sufficient voltage at SL terminal is applied.

## 3.2   MTJ with Hybrid Access Transistors

The proposed hybrid memory bit cell consists of one hetero Jn TFET, one homo Jn TFET and one MTJ as shown Fig. 4b. The sizing of homo and hetero junction TFETs are taken as W/L = 1 μm/0.02 μm respectively.

At $V_{WL}$ = 0.5 V, $V_{SL}$ = 0 V condition, transistor switches ON ($V_{gs}$ (Hetero Jn TFET) > 0) which produces large amount of current required that reduces the switching time from P → AP. But when word line ($V_{WL}$) and source line ($V_{SL}$) become 0.5 V and 0.8 V respectively due to lower ambipolar current in hetero Jn TFET, MTJ changes its state from AP to P, with high switching time compared to homo Jn TFET (Table 1). This problem can be addressed by using proposed hybrid Access transistor, made using the parallel combination of homo, hetero junction transistors as shown in Fig. 4(b).

**Table 1.** Comparisons of 1T-1MTJ memory cell with different access transistors at WL = 0.5 V

| Parameters | FinFET | | Hetero TFET | | Homo TFET | |
|---|---|---|---|---|---|---|
| | $AP \rightarrow P$ | $P \rightarrow AP$ | $AP \rightarrow P$ | $P \rightarrow AP$ | $AP \rightarrow P$ | $P \rightarrow AP$ |
| BL (V) | −0.5 | 0.5 | −0.5 | 0.5 | −0.5 | 0.5 |
| SL (V) | 0.8 | 0 | 0.8 | 0 | 0.8 | 0 |
| Write current (μA) | 95.5 | 103.2 | 70.3 | 87.7 | 113 | 75.7 |
| Switching ime (nS) | 7.7 | 5.7 | 10 | 7.3 | 5 | 10 |
| Write power (μW) | 47.8 | 51.6 | 35.2 | 43.9 | 56.3 | 37.9 |
| Write energy (fJ) | 368.1 | 294 | 352 | 320.4 | 281.5 | 379 |
| TMR (%) | 108 | | 102 | | 100 | |
| Avg. write energy (fJ) | 331 | | 336.2 | | 330 | |

At $V_{dd}$ = 0.5 V, The FinFET ON current is higher than TFET. So, P → AP state change has taken low write energy compared to TFETs. At negative $V_{gs}$, FinFET provides less OFF current, compared with TFETs. Due to ambipolar conduction of homo junction TFET produced a high OFF curren shown in Fig. 2c. As a result, AP → P state change in hybrid cell achieves low write energy compared to the FinFET and hetero junction TFET ones (Table 2). This is not a possible case in 1T-hetero Jn TEFT/homo Jn TFET/FinFET. As a result, the proposed hybrid cell achieves average low write energy and symmetric switching time compared to 2T FinFET/TFET cells.

**Table 2.** Comparisons of 2T-1MTJ memory cell with different access transistors at WL = 0.5 V

| Parameters | FinFET | | Hetero TFET | | Homo TFET | | Hybrid (Hetero + Homo) TFET | |
|---|---|---|---|---|---|---|---|---|
| | $AP \rightarrow P$ | $P \rightarrow AP$ | $AP \rightarrow P$ | $P \rightarrow AP$ | $AP \rightarrow P$ | $P \rightarrow AP$ | $AP \rightarrow P$ | $P \rightarrow AP$ |
| Write current (μA) | 104 | 112.8 | 76.6 | 101 | 119 | 84.3 | 113 | 108 |
| Switching time (nS) | 6.2 | 4.4 | 9 | 5.6 | 4.3 | 7.6 | 4.5 | 4.8 |
| Write power (μW) | 52 | 56.4 | 38.3 | 50.5 | 59.5 | 42.2 | 56.5 | 54 |
| Write energy (fJ) | 322.4 | 248.2 | 344.7 | 282.8 | 255.9 | 333.4 | 254.25 | 259.2 |
| TMR (%) | 115 | | 108 | | 119 | | 142 | |
| Avg. write energy (fJ) | 285.3 | | 313.7 | | 294.6 | | 256.7 | |

### 3.3   Performance Comparision of Proposed Memory Cell Design

Transient characteristics of STT-MRAM cell with different access transistors at a supply voltage of 0.5 V are shown in Fig. 5. It can be observed that in comparison to FinFET and homo Jn/hetero Jn TFET, proposed hybrid cell achieves high speed switching in the order of 2.

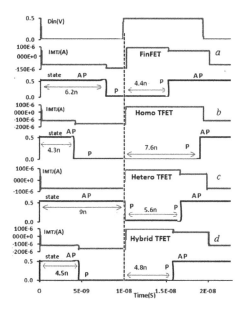

**Fig. 5.** Transient responses of PMA-MTJ with different access transistors (a) FinFET (b) Homo junction TFET (c) Hetero junction TFET (d) Hybrid TFET

Tables 1 and 2 summarize the performance comparison of 1T-1MTJ and 2T-MTJ memory cells with FinFET and TFETs. In Table 2, observe that the proposed hybrid cell shows comparatively symmetric and high speed switching of 4.5 ns, 4.8 ns (AP → P, P → AP respectively). Hybrid cell achieves ~21%, 28% and 18% lower energy consumption when compared to FinFET, hetero Jn TFET, homo Jn TFET cells respectively. The proposed cell can achieve faster read latency due to the high TMR ratio reported compared to other access transistors.

# 4   Conclusion

This work propose and demonstrate a high speed and low write energy STT-MRAM cell design, using hybrid TFET access transistors by achieving high TMR. The proposed cell reduces the switching time and write energy through hetero junction TFET, at ON condition and homo junction TFET at OFF condition. The hybrid cell uses ambipolarity (OFF) current of homo Jn TFET which enhances the switching behavior of STT-MRAM and results in high speed writing capability with symmetric switching behaviour. The proposed hybrid cell shows comparatively symmetric and high speed switching of 4.5 ns, 4.8 ns (AP → P, P → AP respectively). Hybrid cell achieves ~21%, 28% and 18% lower energy consumption when compared to FinFET, hetero Jn TFET, homo Jn TFET cells respectively.

**Acknowledgment.** The authors thank the funding support from Department of Science and Technology (DST) SERC young scientist grant no. SBFTP/ETA-0101/2014.

# References

1. Wolf, S.A., Lu, J., Stan, M.R., Chen, E., Treger, D.M.: The promise of nano magnetics and spintronics for future logic and universal memory. Proc. IEEE **98**(12), 2155–2168 (2010)
2. Kang, W., Zhang, L., Klein, J.O., Zhang, Y., Ravelosona, D., Zhao, W.: Reconfigurable codesign of STT-MRAM under process variations in deeply scaled technology. IEEE Trans. Electron Devices **62**(6), 1769–1777 (2015)
3. Shafaei, A., Wang, Y., Pedram, M.: Low write-energy STT-MRAMs using FinFET-based access transistors. In: 32nd IEEE International Conference on Computer Design (ICCD), pp. 374–379. IEEE, Seoul (2014)
4. Bhattacharya, A., Pal, S., Islam, A.: Implementation of FinFET based STT-MRAM bitcell. In: 2014 International Conference on Advanced Communication Control and Computing Technologies (ICACCCT), pp. 435–439. IEEE, Ramanathapuram (2014)
5. Xu, C., Zheng, Y., Niu, D., Zhu, X., Kang, S.H., Xie, Y.: Impact of write pulse and process variation on 22 nm FinFET-based STT-RAM design: a device-architecture co-optimization approach. IEEE Trans. Multi-Scale Comput. Syst. **1**(4), 195–206 (2015)
6. Farkhani, H., Peiravi, A., Moradi, F.: Low-energy write operation for 1T-1MTJ STT-RAM bitcells with negative bitline technique. IEEE Trans. Very Large Scale Integr. (VLSI) Syst. **24**(4), 1593–1597 (2016)
7. Kim, Y., Gupta, S.K., Park, S.P., Panagopoulos, G., Roy, K.: Write-optimized reliable design of STT MRAM. In: Proceedings of the 2012 ACM/IEEE International Symposium on Low Power Electronics and Design, pp. 3–8. ACM, Redondo Beach (2012)
8. Suzuki, D., Hanyu, T.: Nonvolatile field-programmable gate array using 2-transistor–1-MTJ-cell-based multi-context array for power and area efficient dynamically reconfigurable logic. Jap. J. Appl. Phys. **54**(4S) (2015). 04DE01
9. Choday, S.H., Gupta, S.K., Roy, K.: Write-optimized STT-MRAM bit-cells using asymmetrically doped transistors. IEEE Electron Device Lett. **35**(11), 1100–1102 (2014)
10. Wang, S., Pan, A., Chui, C.O., Gupta, P.: Tunneling negative differential resistance-assisted STT-RAM for efficient read and write operations. IEEE Trans. Electron Devices **64**(1), 121–129 (2017)
11. Liu, H., Cotter, M., Datta, S., Narayanan, V.: Technology assessment of Si and III-V FinFETs and III-V tunnel FETs from soft error rate perspective. In: 2012 IEEE International Electron Devices Meeting (IEDM), pp. 25.5.1–25.5.4. IEEE San Francisco (2012)
12. Japa, A., Vallabhaneni, H., Vaddi, R.: Reliability enhancement of a steep slope tunnel transistor based ring oscillator designs with circuit interaction. IET Circ. Devices Syst. **10**(6), 522–527 (2016)
13. Penn State University: Verilog-A Models for Heterojunction Tunnel FETs. http://www.ndcl.ee.psu.edu/downloads.asp
14. Lin, X., Wang, Y., Pedram, M.: Stack sizing analysis and optimization for FinFET logic cells and circuits operating in the sub/near-threshold regime. In: 15th International Symposium on Quality Electronic Design (ISQED), pp. 341–348. IEEE, Santa Clara (2014)
15. Vallabhaneni, H., Japa, A., Shaik, S., Krishna, K.S.R., Vaddi, R.: Designing energy efficient logic gates with Hetero junction Tunnel fets at 20 nm. In: 2nd International Conference on Devices, Circuits and Systems (ICDCS), pp. 1–5. IEEE, Coimbatore (2014)

16. Fang, B., Zhang, X., Zhang, B.S., Zeng, Z., Cai, J.W.: Tunnel magnetoresistance in thermally robust Mo/CoFeB/MgO tunnel junction with perpendicular magnetic anisotropy. AIP Adv. **5**(6), 067116 (2015)

17. Chun, K.C., Zhao, H., Harms, J.D., Kim, T.H., Wang, J.P., Kim, C.H.: A scaling roadmap and performance evaluation of in-plane and perpendicular MTJ based STT-MRAMs for high-density cache memory. IEEE J. Solid-State Circuits **48**(2), 598–610 (2013)

18. Zhang, Y., Zhao, W., Lakys, Y., Klein, J.O., Kim, J.V., Ravelosona, D., Chappert, C.: Compact modeling of perpendicular-anisotropy CoFeB/MgO magnetic tunnel junctions. IEEE Trans. Electron Devices **59**(3), 819–826 (2012)

19. Wang, Y., Cai, H., de Barros Naviner, L.A., Zhang, Y., Zhao, X., Deng, E., Klein, J.O., Zhao, W.: Compact model of dielectric breakdown in spin-transfer torque magnetic tunnel junction. IEEE Trans. Electron Devices **63**(4), 1762–1767 (2016)

20. Yang, J., Wang, P., Zhang, Y., Cheng, Y., Zhao, W., Chen, Y., Li, H.H.: Radiation-induced soft error analysis of STT-MRAM: a device to circuit approach. IEEE Trans. Comput. Aided Des. Integr. Circuits Syst. **35**(3), 380–393 (2016)

21. Synopsis: TCAD Sentaurus Device Manual (2010)

22. Cadence (R) Virtuoso Spectre Circuit Simulator (2009)

# Enhancing Retention Voltage for SRAM

Ankit Rehani$^{(\boxtimes)}$, Sujay Deb, and Suprateek Shukla

ECE, IIIT-Delhi, New Delhi, India
{ankit16085,sdeb,suprateek16115}@iiitd.ac.in

**Abstract.** In modern integrated chips, most of the power consumption comes from the memory blocks. These memory blocks require high rail voltages due to limited noise margins. Hence, the aim of this work is to design an assist circuitry which allows reduction in the retention voltage and consequently reduces the power consumption of memory. We initially designed a stable SRAM cell in 65 nm CMOS technology along with read and write assist circuits. These assist circuits enabled reduction of operating voltages. Transient Voltage Collapse Write Assist (TVC-WA) improves the *writability* of the SRAM cell by reducing write latency by 44% and Worldline Under Drive Read Assist (WLUD-RA) allows improvement in read stability. Both the circuits allow reduction in the supply voltage of SRAM, thereby reducing its power dissipation.

**Keywords:** SRAM · TVC-WA · WLUD-RA · SNM · Read margin Writability

## 1 Introduction

SRAMs use memory cell with internal feedback that retains its value if power is applied. SRAM is widely used in cache applications [1]. Ensuring SRAM cell stability is an important concern. However, a strong trade-off is seen between maintaining cell stability and reducing power consumption with reduced operating voltages. The existing approaches for reducing SRAM power primarily deals with varying transistor threshold values. But the drawback of high $V_t$ is latency penalty and channel leakage increases on lowering $V_t$. There is a need to explore other methods which could provide promising improvements in stability of bit cell. Negative-bitline write assist proposed in [2,3] has shown good results for heavily strained PMOS channel devices having dominant write margin distributions. Dynamic source voltage ($V_{SS}$) boosting proposed in [4] requires larger current hence larger series connected devices, increasing area and power consumption.

This paper comprises of five sections. General design considerations for 6T SRAM cell are discussed in Sect. 2, where read-write operations as well as the constraints on cell stability like the read margin, the write margin and the static noise margin are discussed. The proposed retention voltage enhancing circuits are

© Springer Nature Singapore Pte Ltd. 2017
B. K. Kaushik et al. (Eds.): VDAT 2017, CCIS 711, pp. 406–413, 2017.
https://doi.org/10.1007/978-981-10-7470-7_40

discussed in Sect. 3, where the design and functioning of TVC-WA and WLUD-RA circuits are explained. Simulation results for the SRAM cell with these retention voltage enhancement circuits are presented in Sect. 4, which is followed by conclusion in Sect. 5.

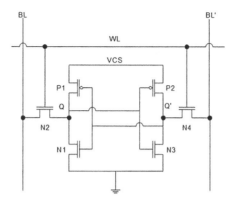

**Fig. 1.** Schematic of 6T SRAM cell

# 2  Design Consideration for 6T SRAM Cell

Standard 6-transistor (6T) SRAM cell is shown in Fig. 1. The 6 T cell achieves its compactness at the expense of more complex peripheral circuitry for reading and writing the cells. This is a good trade-off in large RAM arrays where memory cells dominate overall area. SRAM has smaller cell size, which offers shorter wires and hence, lower dynamic power consumption. To write new data, the desired data and its complement are driven onto the bit-lines BL and BL' and the *WordLine* is raised, overpowering the cross-coupled inverters. However, to read the data stored in cell or present state, the two bitlines BL and BL' are pre-charged high and are left to float. When the *WordLine* is raised, either BL or BL' is pulled down depending on the present state.

The fundamental challenge in designing SRAM is minimizing its size while ensuring the read stability and *writability*. To ensure read stability, the cross-coupled inverters present in SRAM cell should be designed such that they are not affected during a read operation, yet should be weak so that they can be overpowered during a write operation [1].

## 2.1  Cell Stability

To ensure both read stability and *writability*, the transistors must satisfy ratio constraints. In Fig. 1, the NMOS pulldown transistors N1 and N3 forming the cross-coupled inverters, must be strongest. The access transistors N2 and N4 must be of intermediate strength and the PMOS pullup transistors P1 and P2 must be weak [1]. This can be seen by analyzing the read and write operations.

The read margin, and the write margin quantify the cell's read stability and *writability*. They are determined by static noise margin (SNM), when operated in different modes. The SRAM cell has one stable state during write operation and two stable states during read and hold operations. During hold or read operation, SNM quantifies how much noise at the input of the cross-coupled inverters can be tolerated till a stable state is flipped. While during write operation, it quantifies the noise that would cause second stable state in SRAM. Hold margin and read margin increases with increase in Vdd and $V_t$. Read margin can be improved in following cases: (1) when the strength of pulldown transistors N1/N3, is higher compared to strength of access transistors N2/N4, (2) when WordLine "WL" voltage is reduced below Vdd. Similarly, write margin can be improved in the following cases: (1) when the strength of access transistors N2/N4 is increased, (2) when the strength of pullup transistors is reduced, and (3) when the Word-Line "WL" voltage is increased. Hence, a trade-off is seen between read stability and *writability* of the 6T SRAM cell [5]. Since power depends on Vdd, and so does NM, this limits the reduction in Vdd. We can reduce Vdd by improving *writability* and read stability of the SRAM cell. This can be done by introducing assist circuitry. To improve readability, WL bias voltage needs to be reduced; hence we make WLUD-RA. Additionally, to improve *writability*, the strength of nMOS is increased or alternatively charging capability of pMOS is reduced by TVC-WA which reduces *VCS* while performing write operation. However, as WLUD-RA will remain active during both read and write operations and as WL biasing is reduced, some *writability* is compromised to improve read stability.

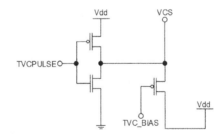

**Fig. 2.** Schematic of transient voltage collapse write assist circuit

# 3    Proposed Retention Voltage Enhancing Circuits

## 3.1    Transient Voltage Collapse Write Assist Circuit

Schematic for TVC-WA circuitry is shown in Fig. 2. During write operations, *VCS* is lowered below data-retention voltage temporarily. This reduces write operation's sensitivity to PMOS pullup transistors P1/P2's $V_t$ variations without affecting read stability, by eradicating the passgate (N2/N4) to pullup (P1/P2) transistors contention. The pulse width of *TVCPULSE* should be such that, when $VCS_{MIN}$ is modulated by controlling *TVC_BIAS* of the clamping circuit, it weakens the P1/P2 devices such that the unselected cell may fail in retaining cell state.

### 3.2    Worldline Under-Drive Read Assist Circuit

Schematic for WLUD-RA is shown in Fig. 3. It adjusts the gate overdrive of access transistors (N2/N4). Control signal determines whether a cell is selected. When control signal is supplied, *WordLine* gets grounded as the nMOS M0 is short-circuited and pMOS M1 is in cutoff. However, when control signal is removed nMOS M0 operates in cutoff and pMOS M1 is in saturation hence short-circuited. Thus, control of *WordLine* is shifted over to the under-drive circuitry. The under-drive circuitry is controlled by *WLBias*. *WLBias* is chosen such that, *WordLine* voltage is reduced but does not get completely pulled down. This occurs due to pullup pMOS M8 to pulldown pMOS M5 contention. Hence, enabling read operation at lower *WordLine* voltage.

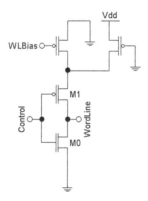

**Fig. 3.** Schematic of wordline under-drive read assist circuit

## 4    Simulation Results

### 4.1    Read-Write Operations

To evaluate our design, at first, we did transient analysis for 6T SRAM cell with conventional read/write test circuit. For read operation without WLUD-RA, read latency of 795.479 ps was observed for a single SRAM cell. Similarly, for write operation without TVC-WA a write latency of 253.6 ps was observed for a single SRAM cell. However, with WLUD-RA an increased read latency of 959.4 ps was observed as shown in Fig. 4 with WordLine voltage reduced

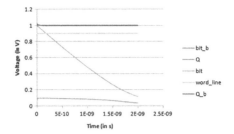

**Fig. 4.** Read '0' operation of 6T SRAM cell using WLUD-RA

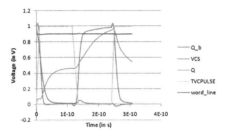

**Fig. 5.** Write '1' operation of 6T SRAM cell using TVC-WA

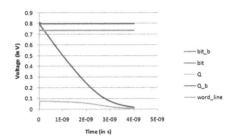

**Fig. 6.** Read '0' operation of 6T SRAM cell using WLUD-RA

to 900.2 mV, while write latency was reduced to 137.38 ps as shown in Fig. 5. Further, the performance of circuit was observed at 120 °C/FF process with reduced operating voltage of 800 mV and the simulation results for read and write operations are shown in Figs. 6 and 7, respectively. At pulse width of 120 ps of TVCPULSE, circuit performs as desired for 120 °C/FF process, with slight increase in read/write latencies. However, when the pulse width of TVCPULSE is increased to 10.5 ns for a 140 °C/FF process, the unselected cell changed its state.

## 4.2   Noise Margins

For checking the cell's stability, test circuits were implemented and Butterfly diagrams as shown in Fig. 8, were plotted. The length of the largest square that

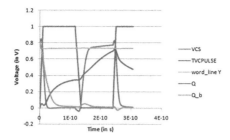

**Fig. 7.** Write '1' operation of 6T SRAM cell using TVC-WA

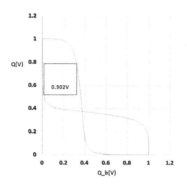

**Fig. 8.** Hold static noise margin of 302 mV is observed

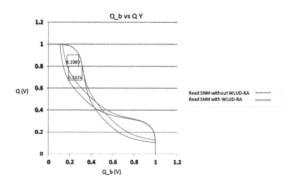

**Fig. 9.** Read SNM of 106 mV without WLUD-RA and 162 mV with WLUD-RA is observed

can be inscribed between the two curves determines the static noise margin [1]. Without using assist circuits, hold static noise margin was observed to be 302 mV as shown in Fig. 8. A read SNM of 106 mV is observed without WLUD-RA and with reduced *WordLine* voltage due to use of WLUD-RA, the read SNM increased to 162.201 mV as shown in Fig. 9. However, for a reduced rail voltage of 800 mV and a *WordLine* voltage of 734 mV, a read margin of 112 mV as shown in Fig. 10. We have shown through simulation results presented in Figs. 6 and 7 that with the help of assist circuits, SRAM cell can operate at 800 mV supply voltage in worst case conditions of 120° C/FF process. Read SNM for different configurations is shown in Table 1. The proposed enhancing circuits show same performance for more than 1-bit memory system.

**Table 1.** Static Noise Margin

| S. No. | 6T SRAM circuit setup | | | Read static noise margin (mV) |
|---|---|---|---|---|
| | Setup | Rail voltage (V) | WordLine voltage (V) | |
| 1 | Without WLUD-RA | 1 | 1 | 106 |
| 2 | With WLUD-RA | 1 | 0.9 | 162.201 |
| | | 0.8 | 0.734 | 112 |

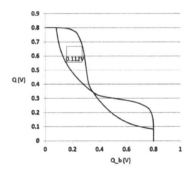

**Fig. 10.** Read SNM of 112 mV is observed with WLUD-RA for Vdd at 800 mV and *WordLine* voltage at 734 mV

## 5 Conclusion

In this paper, we have presented implementation of assist circuits for enhancing retention voltage for SRAM. We have implemented a 6T SRAM cell and improved its read-write operations and stability using a transient voltage collapse write assist and *WordLine* under-drive read assist circuits in 65 nm CMOS technology. With these assist circuits, we were able to successfully do read and write operations on a 6T SRAM cell at 800 mV operating voltage. Improvement is seen in read static noise margin, which is increased to 162.201 mV with WLUD-RA for 1 V operating voltage and 900 mV *WordLine* voltage, whereas it is 112 mV for 800 mV operating voltage with 734 mV *WordLine* voltage compared to 106 mV without WLUD-RA. Thus, read stability of the cell is increased and we are able to operate SRAM cells at lower supply voltage without compromising with Noise Margin.

# References

1. Weste, N.H., Harris, D.M.: CMOS VLSI Design: A Circuits and Systems Perspective. Pearson Education India, Delhi (2005)
2. Pilo, H., Arsovski, I., Batson, K., Braceras, G., Gabric, J., Houle, R., Lamphier, S., Radens, C., Seferagic, A.: A 64MB SRAM in 32nm high-k metal-gate SOI technology with 0.7V operation enabled by stability, write-ability and read-ability enhancements. IEEE J. Solid State Circ. **47**(1), 97–106 (2012)
3. Fujimura, Y., Hirabayashi, O., Sasaki, T., Suzuki, A., Kawasumi, A., Takeyama, Y., Kushida, K., Fukano, G., Katayama, A., Niki, Y., et al.: A configurable SRAM with constant-negative-level write buffer for low-voltage operation with 0.149 $\mu m^2$ cell in 32nm high-k metal-gate CMOS. In: 2010 IEEE International on Solid-State Circuits Conference Digest of Technical Papers (ISSCC), pp. 348–349. IEEE (2010)
4. Bhavnagarwala, A.J., Kosonocky, S., Radens, C., Chan, Y., Stawiasz, K., Srinivasan, U., Kowalczyk, S.P., Ziegler, M.M.: A sub-600-mV, fluctuation tolerant 65-nm CMOS SRAM array with dynamic cell biasing. IEEE J. Solid State Circ. **43**(4), 946–955 (2008)
5. Qiu, H., Takeuchi, K., Mizutani, T., Yamamoto, Y., Makiyama, H., Yamashita, T., Oda, H., Kamohara, S., Sugii, N., Saraya, T., et al.: Statistical write stability characterization in SRAM cells at low supply voltage. IEEE Trans. Electr. Devices **63**(11), 4302–4308 (2016)

# Comparison of SRAM Cell Layout Topologies to Estimate Improvement in SER Robustness in 28FDSOI and 40 nm Technologies

Anand Ilakal[1]([✉]) and Anuj Grover[2][ID]

[1] Manipal Institute of Technology, Manipal, India
anandilkal@gmail.com
[2] ST Microelectronics, Greater Noida, India
anuj.grover@gmail.com

**Abstract.** The impact of high energy particles in digital memory elements becomes important as technology scales down. The memory elements hold high density latches to store data and these latches are susceptible to disturbs due to particle strikes. The alpha particles, neutrons from cosmic rays may cause Single Event Upset (SEU) in memory cells. In this paper, we propose a method to estimate and compare SER robustness of different layout topologies of SRAM cell. We demonstrate that the radiation hardened layout topologies offer much better Soft Error Rate (SER) robustness compared to conventional layout of the 6-T SRAM cell in 28FDSOI and 40 nm technology. The analysis is done using ELDO simulator for a wide range of Linear Energy Transfer (LET) profiles of particle strikes.

**Keywords:** High energy particles · Single-Event-Upset (SEU)
Radiation hardened layout topology

## 1 Introduction

Transient fails on circuits and systems can interrupt electronics operation or crash the systems. Transient errors are largely caused due to high energy radioactive impurities like alpha particles, neutrons and cosmic rays strike semiconductor substrate and lose their energy by ionizing the medium through which they pass, leaving behind a wake of electron-hole pairs. Electron-hole pair generation in the event of a high-energy particle strike is represented in Fig. 1(a). The charge collection of these high-energy particles when they strike off may cause flipping the data in latches and SRAM cells. Technology scaling has led to reduced critical charge and therefore increased radiation sensitivity in memories [1]. A comparison of heavy ion-induced SEU in different technologies like 28 nm, 40 nm and 65 nm dual and triple-well SRAMs over wide range particle Linear Energy Transfer (LET) profiles is done in [2]. In [3], a methodology for the statistical analysis of memory radiation test data, with the aim of identifying trends in the single-event upset (SEU) distribution is proposed. In [4], it is demonstrated that

© Springer Nature Singapore Pte Ltd. 2017
B. K. Kaushik et al. (Eds.): VDAT 2017, CCIS 711, pp. 414–420, 2017.
https://doi.org/10.1007/978-981-10-7470-7_41

the structure of the circuit and its supply voltage in standby mode play a vital role in determining the soft error susceptibility.

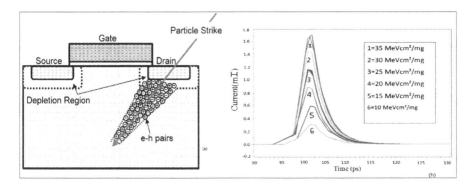

**Fig. 1.** (a) Block diagram of SEU. (b) Current waveform for wide range of LET profiles

In this paper, a method to estimate and compare the SER robustness of different layout topologies of SRAM cell is proposed. Section 2 discusses the modeling of the current sources for different LET profiles and how the modeled current source is used to inject disturbance in the two layout topologies. Section 3 briefly discusses about experimental setup used in this work. Results and conclusion are discussed in the later sections.

## 2   Methodology

### 2.1   Modeling the Current Source

A current source is modelled using the samples of LET profiles of 35 MeV.cm$^2$/mg & 15 MeV.cm$^2$/mg obtained from the testing of 28 nm FDSOI test chips and a generalized equation is derived. Current pulse that results from a particles strikes is traditionally described as a double exponential function [5].

$$I(t) = Ae^{\dfrac{(t-\tau)}{\alpha}} \tag{1}$$

Where A is amplitude ($\mu$A), $\tau$ is time constant for establishing electron-hole pairs and $\alpha$ is decay rate. Current waveforms for a range of LET profiles is shown in Fig. 1(b).

### 2.2   Injecting Modeled Current Source at Different Sensitive Nodes

Consider a test-case for latch (two back-to-back connected inverters) Fig. 2(a). OFF transistors N2 and P1 are susceptible to lead to errors due to particle strikes. When a particle strikes at N2, the device turns ON temporarily and sinks current resulting in a

416    A. Ilakal and A. Grover

noise dip at the output. Similarly, a particle strike at P1 injects current and a voltage
bump appears at node I. This can also lead to loss of data.

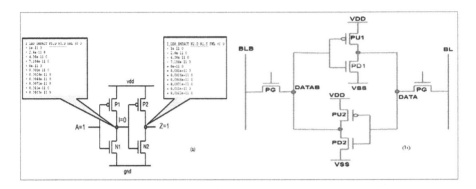

**Fig. 2.** (a) Injecting current source at different nodes of Latch. (b) Schematic diagram of
conventional 6-T SRAM cell.

In the experimental setup, the sensitive nodes are identified and current is injected
on them. The schematic diagram of conventional 6-T SRAM is shown in Fig. 2(b). Stick
diagram of conventional 6T layout is shown in Fig. 3(a) and the updated schematic with
modeled equivalent capacitance and resistance due to metal rails, contacts and vias in
the cell is shown in Fig. 3(b). Figure 4(a) shows stick diagram of a robust multi-finger
latch layout topology where the NMOS devices are laid out in two fingers that are also
spaced apart physically. Figure 4(b) represents its corresponding schematic diagram.

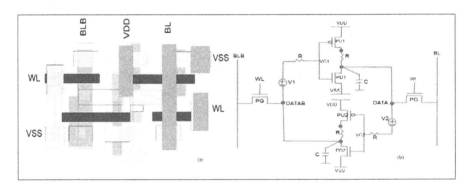

**Fig. 3.**  (a) Stick diagram of conventional 6-T SRAM cell. (b) Schematic diagram of conventional
6-T SRAM cell with metals modelled as resistors and capacitors.

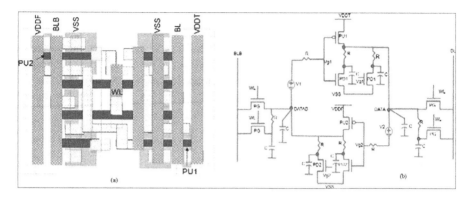

**Fig. 4.** (a) Stick diagram of proposed multi-finger layout topology. (b) Schematic diagram of proposed SRAM cell with metals modelled as resistors and capacitors.

## 3   Experimental Setup

The stability of SRAM circuits depends on the static noise margin (SNM). SNM of a memory cell is characterized by applying noise source voltages at the storage nodes. The SNM represents the largest DC voltage perturbation that can be tolerated without a state flip when the cell is being accessed. Noise sources V1 and V2 are of same magnitude with opposite polarities are connected as shown in Figs. 3(b) and 4(b).

The capacitance of the internal nodes as extracted from the layout can be multiplied with SNM to estimate critical charge of a latch.

To arrive at a 'real' comparison of the two layout topologies, we decided to find the dynamic noise margin (DNM) of the cell for a given word line (WL) pulse width. To obtain the read DNM, the bit line (BL) and bit-bar line (BLB) are connected to supply voltage (VDD) (modeled as two fully charged line capacitances). Initially, the node 'DATA' stores high value (VDD) and node 'DATAB' stores low value (GND). The staircase noise voltages V1 and V2 are swept from −2.0 V to +0.5 V in the presence of the particle strike current pulse.

## 4   Results

In this work, we have simulated the above experiment for LET profiles varying from 10 to 35 MeV.cm$^2$/mg. Degradation of DNM (and therefore critical charge) is estimated for a range of voltages and temperatures. For 28 nm FDSOI technology, the experiment is performed for the supply voltage varying from VDD = 0.5 V to VDD = 1.0 V at 25 °C and 125 °C temperatures. For 40 nm technology, experiment is performed for the supply voltage varying from VDD = 0.7 to VDD = 1.2 V. The experiment is also performed at different process corners. DNM is measured for both the layout topologies. The normalized DNM values are plotted.

As the LET induced current increases, DNM degrades as more charge will collect at higher energy profile. Figure 5(a) and (b) shows the variation of DNM of both the topologies w.r.t different LET energy profiles at VDD = 1 V and 125°C temperature for FS (fast NMOS-slow PMOS) corner in 28 nm FDSOI and 40 nm technologies respectively. DNM improves 1.06X to 36X as energy of particle increases. Moreover, we can see that the conventional layout topology fails at higher energy profile (above 30 MeV.cm²/mg) whereas the robust topology is still robust (Fig. 5(a)).

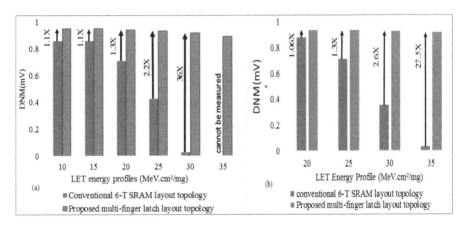

**Fig. 5.** (a) Impact of LET profiles on DNM of both the topologies in 28 nm FDSOI technology. (b) Impact of LET profiles on DNM in 40 nm technology.

Similarly, for 40 nm technology, proposed multi-finger layout topology shows 1.06X to 27.5X gain in DNM for different LET energy profile than that of the conventional layout topology (Fig. 5(b)).

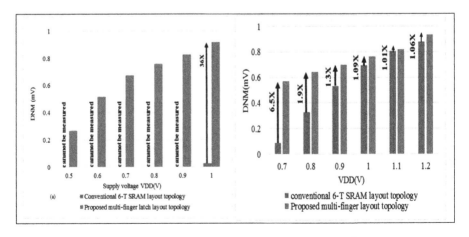

**Fig. 6.** (a) Impact of Supply voltage (VDD) on DNM for 30 MeV.cm²/mg in 28 nm FDSOI technology. (b) Impact of Supply voltage (VDD) on DNM 20 MeV.cm²/mg in 40 nm technology.

As the supply voltage decreases the value of DNM (and critical charge) also decreases. Figure 6(a) shows the effect of VDD on DNM of both layout topologies for 30 MeV.cm$^2$/mg LET profile at 125°C for the FS corner in 28FDSOI technology. Figure 6(b) shows the effect of VDD on DNM for 20 MeV.cm$^2$/mg LET profile at temperature 125°C for the FS corner in 40 nm technology. Supply ranges is 0.7 V to 1.2 V. We observe that the conventional layout topology fails at lower VDD for high energy profiles, whereas the hardened layout topology is still robust.

Figure 7 shows the sensitivity to process corners like FS (Fast-NMOS and Slow-PMOS), FF, SS and SF in 28FDSOI technology. It is plotted for LET energy profile of 30 MeV.cm$^2$/mg, at VDD = 1.0 V and temperature T = 125°C. Proposed rad-hard layout topology shows 36X more gain in DNM for FS corner (worst corner for SNM) than that of the conventional 6-T SRAM layout topology.

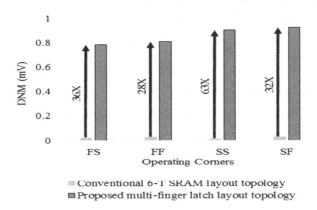

**Fig. 7.** Sensitivity of both the topologies to process corners (for LET energy profile = 30 MeV.cm$^2$/mg, VDD = 1.0 V, T = 125°C) in 28FDSOI technology

One can conclude that the radiation hardened multi-finger layout topology offers more immunity towards noise because of its layout structure.

## 5    Conclusion

In this work, we have proposed a method to estimate and compare SER robustness of different layout topologies of SRAM cells. The current sources corresponding to a wide range of LET strikes was modeled and injected at different sensitive nodes of SRAM cell and its impact on noise margin was observed.

The experiments were performed on two different layout topologies of SRAM cells in 28 nm FDSOI and 40 nm technologies. Further the experiments were carried out for different supply voltages (0.5–1.0 V for 28 nm FDSOI and 0.7–1.2 V for 40 nm) and two temperature 25°C and 125°C at different process corners (FF, FS, SS and SF).

We find that the layout topology where latch is split into multiple fingers that are also spaced apart, is more robust for particles of varying energy across a range of voltages and temperatures.

## References

1. Heijmen, T., et al.: 2004 IEEE IRPS. Proceedings, pp. 675–676 (2004)
2. Chatterjee, I., et al.: IEEE Trans. Nuclear Sci. **61**(6), December 2014
3. Bosser, A., et al.: Rad and Its Effects on Components and Systems (RADECS) (2015)
4. Dong, W., et al.: IEEE/ACM ICCAD Proceedings, pp. 378–385 (2008)
5. Messenger, G.C.: IEEE Trans. Nuclear Sci. **NS-29**(6), December 1982

# Improving the Design of Nearest Neighbor Quantum Circuits in 2D Space

Neha Chaudhuri[✉], Chandan Bandyopadhyay, and Hafizur Rahaman

Indian Institute of Engineering Science and Technology Shibpur,
Howrah 711103, India
neha1731992@gmail.com, chandanb.iiest@gmail.com,
rahaman.h@gmail.com

**Abstract.** Existing quantum circuits restrict qubit interactions to their neighboring qubits which has led to communication overhead. Recent papers have, thus, developed several optimization methods with respect to this constraint. However, most of the works have limited their synthesis methods to 1D quantum architecture and there exist only a few works for multidimensional quantum circuits yet.

Thus, we have focused on qubit-to-qubit interactions over 2D grid to make efficient representations of quantum circuits. Not only we are designing 2D circuit, but also have developed a strategy to make such circuits NN (Nearest Neighbor) based one. Here, we have shown two ways to make a quantum circuit NN compliant in 2D plane. The first approach is a naïve one but the second technique that relied on qubit-to-qubit interactions make efficient representations by minimizing the usage of SWAP gates. We have tested several benchmarks over our developed strategy and also have compared the obtained results with recent developments.

**Keywords:** Quantum synthesis · Nearest-neighbor architecture
Multidimensional quantum circuits · Quantum cost

## 1 Preliminaries

### 1.1 Introduction

Quantum computing [1] is governed by the rules of quantum physics and works on qubits which utilize the phenomena of superposition and entanglement to solve practically unsolvable problems such as factorization (using Shor's algorithm) or database search (using Grover's iteration) much faster, unlike with conventional technologies. These developments in speed of computation led to the increasing interest of researchers to consider logic synthesis of the corresponding quantum circuits.

As a result, several methods came up for the synthesis of quantum circuits. When physical implementations of quantum circuits were attempted, it led to the discovery of several technological constraints. Among them, the limited interaction distance between gate qubits is one of the most common ones and it enforces that computations must be performed between adjacent, i.e. nearest neighbor qubits. Motivated by these promising solutions and a relatively unexplored research area on multi-dimensional

© Springer Nature Singapore Pte Ltd. 2017
B. K. Kaushik et al. (Eds.): VDAT 2017, CCIS 711, pp. 421–426, 2017.
https://doi.org/10.1007/978-981-10-7470-7_42

quantum architecture, we have focused on the synthesis of 2D quantum circuits maintaining NN compliance.

## 1.2   Background

Here we are defining related terms associated with our design model and their descriptions.

*Nearest Neighbor Cost (NNC):* is the distance between gate qubits of two-qubit gates. NNC of a gate is obtained by $NNC_G = |c - t| - 1$, where $c$ is the control line and $t$ is target line of the gate.

*2D Quantum Circuit:* 2D Quantum circuits are represented by a grid structured planar graph $(V, E)$ where a node $v \in V$ represents a qubit and an undirected edge $(u,v) \in E$ represents interaction between qubits $u$ and $v$, where $\{u,v\} \in V$. Each node has a degree of up to four. 2D quantum circuits may have several configurations which depend on the chosen grid structures (see Fig. 1).

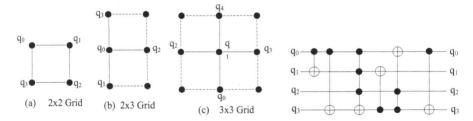

**Fig. 1.** Possible grid configurations for qubit positions in 2D

**Fig. 2(a).** Initial 1D circuit taken as an example

## 2   Proposed Technique

Here we are analyzing the effect of 2-D representation in designing NN compliant quantum circuits. Not only we have shown the different designs in 2-D space, but also have improved the designs so that it requires lesser number of SWAP gates in forming NN compliant circuits.

First, we have stated about a very simple and naïve approach to represent a quantum circuit in 2-D space and then have embedded SWAP gates into the circuit to make it LNN based one. Though this approach takes lesser number of SWAP gates than 1-D based approaches in forming LNN circuits, but there remain scopes to further improve it. Aiming to make the design more efficient, we have come-up with a strategy where we place the gates in a 2-D grid in which qubits are positioned in appropriate places based on some weighted metric calculated by us. This change benefits the design while making it NN compliant one as it takes lesser number of SWAP gates.

For better understanding, in-spite of providing algorithms, here we are explaining both the approaches with examples.

## 2.1 Design 1: A Naive Design Technique for Building NNC Free Quantum Circuit in 2D Space

*Example 1.* Consider the circuit of Fig. 2(a) as an input circuit and we will make it NN compliant one using our technique.

In very first step, transform the input circuit of Fig. 2(a) into a quantum circuit in 1D space. The obtained circuit is given in Fig. 2(b). Now convert the 1D circuit into 2D space by selecting a grid configuration. The resultant circuit is depicted in Fig. 2(c) but this circuit is not NN compliant one. So, find a gate whose NN cost is more than zero then place successive SWAP gates in between control and target line to make the gate NNC free. The final circuit is obtained in Fig. 2(d).

Now, instead of applying the stated procedure if we opted for very basic approach for NN based circuit design strategy over the circuit of Fig. 2(b) to make it LNN compatible one in 1D plane then it would require a total 30 SWAP gates.

On the contrary, when we apply the same in 2D circuit, the numbers of SWAP gates required is 14. Thus, 2D implementation shows an improvement of over 50% even before optimization has been applied.

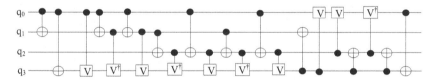

**Fig. 2(b).** Decomposition of given circuit into elementary gates using

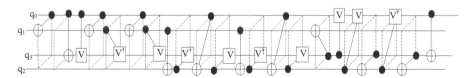

**Fig. 2(c).** Mapping of 1D decomposed circuit into 2D with QC = 22 and NNC = 7

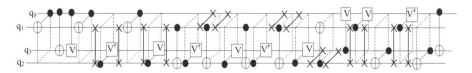

**Fig. 2(d).** 2D quantum circuit with nearest neighbor compliant with QC = 64, SWAP cost = 14 and NNC = 0

In-spite of simply projecting quantum gates over 2-D grid, if some intelligent qubit placement policy can be adhered accompanied with a suitable grid configuration then the improvements in NNC based representation in 2-D space may be gained further. Aim to achieve that, here, we are introducing a qubit placement technique that effectively makes the circuit LNN one by inserting lesser number of SWAP gates in the 2-D design.

## 2.2    Design 2: Incorporation of Qubit Placement Strategy to Obtain Cost Efficient 2D NN Compliant Quantum Circuit

*Example 2.* Like as the first step in previous technique, here also in the first step we transform an input reversible circuit to its equivalent quantum circuit. Let's consider the circuit of Fig. 3(a) is the input circuit and its equivalent quantum circuit in 1D space is obtained in Fig. 3(b).

Computation of connection matrix for the quantum circuit in Fig. 3(b) results in the matrix given in Fig. 3(c). This matrix can be utilized to arrange qubit pairs according to the decreasing values of their corresponding entries. The list obtained for the corresponding matrix is:

$$(a, b) = (b, d) = (c, d) > (a.c) = (b, c) > (b, b) > (a, d) = (a, a) = (c, c) = (d, d)$$

Hence, the decision regarding qubit placement would rely upon the fact that the qubit pairs (a,b), (b,d) and (c,d), with the highest number of gate connectivities between them, need to be given preference while placing adjacent qubits. As a result, the qubit placement which best optimizes the given circuit will be as given in Fig. 3(d).

Now, scan the 1D circuit from left to right and place all the quantum gates in 2D grid to form a 2D quantum circuit. The 2D quantum circuit obtained after this step, from the circuit in Fig. 3(b), and according to qubit placement in Fig. 3(d), has been shown in Fig. 3(e).

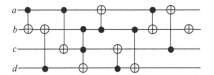

**Fig. 3(a).** Initial 1D circuit taken as an example

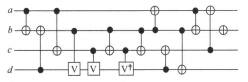

**Fig. 3(b).** Equivalent quantum circuit of Fig. 5(a)

|   | a | b | c | d |
|---|---|---|---|---|
| a | 0 | 3 | 2 | 0 |
| b | 3 | 1 | 2 | 3 |
| c | 2 | 2 | 0 | 3 |
| d | 0 | 3 | 3 | 0 |

**Fig. 3(c).** Computed weight Matrix

**Fig. 3(d).** Resultant qubit placement in 2D plane

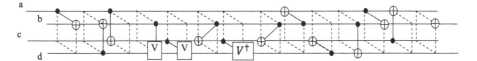

**Fig. 3(e).** Obtained 2D circuit after placing gates over selected grid

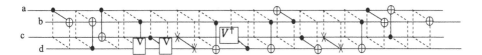

**Fig. 3(f).** Resultant 2D circuit after optimization

Even after optimized qubit placement in 2D plane, we might observe that a few gates in the circuit might still have non-zero NNC. To ensure completely nearest neighbor compliant 2D quantum circuit, we finally need to suggest a localized scheme for optimized insertion of SWAP gates.

So, in the next step we apply SWAP gates before each gate in order to make the communicating qubits adjacent. Now consider the 2D quantum circuit given in Fig. 3(e). Gates $g_6$ and $g_8$ operate on non-adjacent qubits. Thus, localized scheme needs to be applied before $g_6$. We find the qubit order before $g_6$ to be *abdc*. On applying a SWAP gate before $g_6$, the new reordered qubit lines appear as *abcd*. Qubit pair *(b,c)* now has adjacent qubits and hence $g_6$ can be applied. Gates $g_7$ and $g_8$ require *(c,d)* and *(b,c)* pairs of adjacent qubits, respectively. Thus, the existing order of qubit lines can be utilized. For the next upcoming gates, another SWAP gate is applied to bring back the original order of qubit lines, i.e. *abdc*. The resultant 2D quantum circuit with overall zero nearest neighbor cost is finally obtained in Fig. 3(f).

## 3  Experimental Results and Concluding Remarks

The proposed synthesis flow for designing improved LNN circuits has been implemented in C++ on top of RevKit-1.2.1 [3] and also has successfully tested with benchmark functions [4]. Obtained results have been produced in Table 1 and have compared with a recently published work reported in [2, 5].

In this work, we have shown a new synthesis flow for LNN quantum circuits, in which the transformation model converts a given 1D circuit into its 2D representation.

Table 1. Comparison on SWAP cost for NN 2D quantum circuits

| Benchmarks | | | Result from Method1 [2] | | Result from Method2 [2] | | Best results in 1D [5] | Our result | |
|---|---|---|---|---|---|---|---|---|---|
| Name | $n$ | GC | Grid size | No. of SWAP | Grid size | No. of SWAP | No. of SWAP | Grid size | No. of SWAP |
| rd32-v0_67 | 4 | 2 | $2 \times 3$ | 3 | $2 \times 3$ | 2 | 2 | $2 \times 3$ | 2 |
| decod24-v3_46 | 4 | 9 | $3 \times 2$ | 3 | $3 \times 2$ | 3 | 3 | $2 \times 2$ | 3 |
| aj-e11_168 | 4 | 13 | $2 \times 3$ | 24 | $2 \times 3$ | 24 | 36 | $2 \times 3$ | 11 |
| 4_49_17 | 4 | 12 | $2 \times 2$ | 15 | $2 \times 2$ | 13 | 12 | $2 \times 2$ | 8 |
| 4gt10-v1_81 | 5 | 6 | $3 \times 2$ | 16 | $3 \times 2$ | 16 | 20 | $3 \times 2$ | 14 |
| 4gt12-v1_89 | 5 | 5 | $3 \times 2$ | 21 | $3 \times 2$ | 19 | 35 | $3 \times 2$ | 20 |
| 4gt13-v1_93 | 5 | 4 | $3 \times 3$ | 2 | $3 \times 3$ | 2 | 6 | $3 \times 3$ | 2 |
| 4gt4-v0_80 | 5 | 5 | $2 \times 3$ | 17 | $2 \times 3$ | 17 | 34 | $3 \times 2$ | 12 |
| 4gt5_75 | 5 | 5 | $2 \times 4$ | 9 | $3 \times 3$ | 8 | 12 | $3 \times 2$ | 11 |
| 4mod5-v1_23 | 5 | 8 | $2 \times 3$ | 11 | $2 \times 3$ | 11 | 9 | $2 \times 3$ | 9 |
| 4mod7-v0_95 | 5 | 6 | $3 \times 3$ | 13 | $3 \times 3$ | 13 | 21 | $2 \times 3$ | 10 |
| mod8-10_177 | 5 | 14 | $3 \times 3$ | 45 | $2 \times 3$ | 48 | 72 | $2 \times 3$ | 36 |
| hwb5_55 | 5 | 24 | $2 \times 3$ | 48 | $3 \times 2$ | 45 | 63 | $2 \times 3$ | 39 |

# References

1. Nielsen, M., Chuang, I.: Quantum Computation and Quantum Information. Cambridge University Press, Cambridge (2000)
2. Shafaei, A., Saeedi, M., Pedram, M.: Qubit placement to minimize the communication overhead in circuits mapped to 2D quantum architectures. In: ASP-DAC, pp. 495–500 (2014)
3. Soeken, M., Frehse, S., Wille, R., Drechsler, R.: RevKit: a toolkit for reversible circuit design. In: Proceedings of the ISMVL (2008)
4. Wille, R., Grosse, D., Teuber, L., Dueck, G.W., Drechsler, R.: RevLib: an online resources for reversible functions and reversible circuits. In: 38th ISMVL, vol. 24, pp. 220–225, May 2008
5. Shafaei, A., Saeedi, M., Pedram, M.: Optimization of quantum circuits for interaction distance in linear nearest neighbor architectures. In: Design Automation Conference (2013)

# Devices and Technology – II

# Delay and Frequency Investigations in Coupled MLGNR Interconnects

Manish Joshi$^{(\boxtimes)}$, Koduri Teja, Ashish Singh, and Rohit Dhiman

Electronics and Communication Engineering Department,
National Institute of Technology, Hamirpur 177005, HP, India
jmanish.2l@gmail.com, tejal8chowdary@gmail.com,
ashishtu07@gmail.com, rohitdhiman.nitham@gmail.com

**Abstract.** Multilayer Graphene Nano-ribbons (MLGNRs) have been considered as a potential solution to replace conventional Cu for next-generation on-chip interconnects. In this paper, analytical models of transfer gain and crosstalk are derived for coupled three-line MLGNR interconnects using ABCD modeling approach. For this purpose, an equivalent single conductor model of GNRs has been considered. Our proposed model takes into account the impact of mutual inductive and capacitive coupling among the adjacent interconnects. Using the proposed model, the bandwidth of MLGNRs has been determined. It is found that GNR interconnects exhibit higher bandwidth, lesser delay and power as compared to Copper counterparts. The impact of input switching, transition time and interconnect length on crosstalk delay has also been investigated. The proposed analytical results agree well with SPICE simulations.

**Keywords:** ABCD parameters · Crosstalk delay
Equivalent single conductor model · MLGNRs · Transfer gain

## 1 Introduction

Scaling of device dimensions down to nanometer range has resulted in achieving higher switching speeds for nanoelectronics circuits and systems. However, with the downscaling of technology, while local interconnect capacitance reduces, the global interconnect capacitance increases which significantly degrades the performance of system. Currently, Copper (Cu) is the most commonly used interconnect material for on-chip and chip to chip applications. However, increased resistivity of Cu due to surface roughness, grain boundary scattering at scaled interconnect dimensions and demand for higher current density have motivated researchers to explore solutions for interconnect and nano-material devices in future very large scale integration circuits.

During the last few years, breakthrough in the fabrication of (GNRs) has gained the attention of scientific community in its potential for future electronic applications. Graphene exhibits excellent thermal conductivity (3080–5300 $Wm^{-1}K^{-1}$), amazing current-handling capability (upto $10^8$ $Acm^{-2}$), long carrier mean-free path (1 μm at room temperature) to ensure quasi-ballistic transport and reduced electromigration. Such extraordinary properties potentially allow Graphene to replace Cu for future on-chip and chip-chip interconnect applications [1]. Previously, Nasiri et al. [2] have

© Springer Nature Singapore Pte Ltd. 2017
B. K. Kaushik et al. (Eds.): VDAT 2017, CCIS 711, pp. 429–440, 2017.
https://doi.org/10.1007/978-981-10-7470-7_43

presented transmission line based model for GNRs and derived the Nyquist stability criterion and relative stability for MLGNRs. The transmission characteristics of side and top contact MLGNRs are rigorously investigated in [3]. Nishad and Sharma [4] have suggested dielectric insertion to improve MLGNR interconnect performance. Using the equivalent single conductor (ESC) model, delay, power and bandwidth analysis of Cu and MLGNR interconnects has been investigated in [5]. Reina et al. [6] adopted a numerical modal decomposition procedure to characterize crosstalk in GNRs, in which the modal quantities were calculated with a full-wave method. Zhao and Yin [7] and Cui et al. [8] numerically investigated the crosstalk induced delay and noise waveform for coupled MLGNR interconnects. However, these studies are based on numerical methods and there has been a little effort on the analytical modeling of coupled MLGNR interconnects for crosstalk analysis.

In this paper, crosstalk in three-line coupled MLGNRs interconnect system driven and terminated by CMOS drivers has been analyzed using ABCD modeling approach. Analytical expressions characterizing transfer gain and crosstalk induced delay have been derived. The rest of paper is organized as follows: In Sect. 2, methodology to extract equivalent circuit impedance parameters of MLGNRs is described. In Sect. 3, analytical expressions of transfer gain and crosstalk delay using ABCD matrix for coupled three-line interconnects have been derived. In Sect. 4, analytical results are compared with SPICE simulations. Finally, conclusions are drawn in Sect. 5.

## 2    Modeling of MLGNR Interconnects

The cross-sectional view of MLGNR interconnect is shown in Fig. 1, where $W$ is wire width, $H$ is wire height and $T_{ox}$ is the dielectric thickness. The spacing between each graphene layer is denoted by $\delta$ (=0.34 nm) and is the Van-der Waals gap.

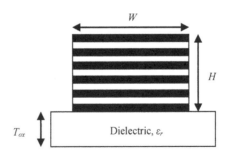

**Fig. 1.**  Schematic of MLGNR interconnect on substrate.

The MLGNR interconnect performance is analyzed by means of an ESC model. The total resistance of MLGNRs is the series combination of lumped contact resistance $R_C$ and distributed resistance $R_S$. The lumped resistance is due to quantum resistance $R_Q$ and imperfect contact resistance between metal and graphene $R_m$ which is equally divided between the two terminals of interconnects.

$$R_C = \frac{R_Q + R_m}{n_{lay}N_{ch}} \tag{1}$$

$$R_Q = \left(\frac{h/2e^2}{N_{ch}N}\right) = \frac{12.94}{N_{ch}N} \text{ k}\Omega \tag{2}$$

where $h$ is the Plank's constant and $e$ is the electronic charge, $N_{ch}$ is the number of conducting channels in each layer. The number of layers ($N$) of MLGNR interconnects can be determined using the relationship [9] as

$$N = \left(1 + Integer\left(\frac{H}{\delta}\right)\right) \tag{3}$$

The distributed scattering resistance is due to the static impurity scattering, defects, line edge roughness scattering, acoustic phonon scattering and primarily depends on the effective mean-free path, $\lambda_{eff}$ which is of the order of μm. The distributed resistance only appears when interconnect length ($l_{GNR}$) is larger than $\lambda_{eff}$. The total equivalent resistance of MLGNR interconnects is given by

$$R_{GNR} = \frac{R_Q l_{GNR}}{n_{lay}N_{ch}\lambda_{eff}} \tag{4}$$

The total inductance of MLGNRs is the series combination of kinetic and magnetic inductances and is expressed as

$$L = L_K + L_M \tag{5}$$

where $L_K$ and $L_M$ are the kinetic and magnetic inductances and are given by (6) and (7) respectively.

$$L_K = \frac{h/4e^2 v_f}{N_{ch}N} \tag{6}$$

$$L_M = \frac{\mu_0 T_{ox}}{W} \tag{7}$$

Usually the value of $L_M$ is very small and is in the range of pH, so $L \approx L_K$. Here $v_f$ is Fermi velocity and is $8 \times 10^5$ m/s for GNRs. The kinetic inductance, $L_K$ represents the kinetic energy of an electron while $L_M$ represents the stored energy of charge carriers in the presence of magnetic field. The equivalent inductance per unit length is given by

$$L_S = \frac{L_K}{n_{lay}} + L_M = \frac{\pi h_r}{W e^2 E_f n_{lay}} + \frac{\mu_0 T_{ox}}{W} \tag{8}$$

In Eq. (8), $E_f$ is Fermi energy, $\mu_o$ is permeability of free space and $h_r$ is reduced Planck constant. The capacitance per unit length depends on quantum capacitance ($C_Q$) and electrostatic capacitances ($C_E$) which are expressed as

$$C_Q = NN_{ch} \frac{4e^2}{hv_f} = NN_{ch} \times 193.18 \ \frac{aF}{\mu m} \tag{9}$$

$$C_E = \frac{\varepsilon_0 \varepsilon_r W}{h} \tag{10}$$

Herein, $\varepsilon_r \approx 1.9$ is the relative permittivity of the medium between the first layer of MLGNR and the ground plane and $\varepsilon_0 = 8.85$ aF/$\mu$m. The equivalent capacitance per unit length is given as follows

$$C = \left( (C_Q)^{-1} + (C_E)^{-1} \right)^{-1} \tag{11}$$

# 3    Transfer Gain and Crosstalk Delay

In this section, the signal propagation characteristics of three-line coupled MLGNR interconnect is analyzed using ABCD model. The coupled distributed interconnect model each driven by non-linear CMOS inverters is shown in Fig. 2. The MLGNR

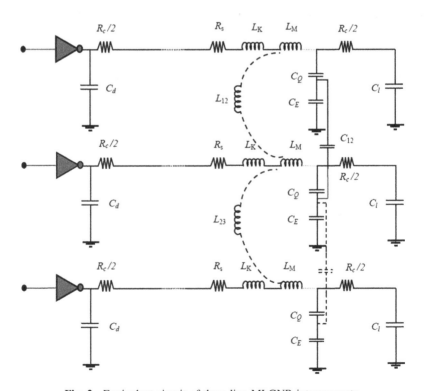

**Fig. 2.** Equivalent circuit of three-line MLGNR interconnects.

interconnect are represented using ESC model. Each line is divided into $n$ infinite small segments, each of length $\Delta x = l_{GNR}/n$ and each segment is represented by an ABCD block. Two cases of switching are considered here i.e. in-phase and out-of-phase.

Using the Kirchhoff equations, the input-output relationship of the first part segment of each line can be written as

$$V_{1i} = V_{1o} + aI_{1i} + N_{L_{12}}I_{2i} + N_{L_{13}}I_{3i}$$
$$I_{1i} = I_{1o} + bV_{1o} + N_{C_{12}}(V_{1o} - V_{2o}) + N_{C_{13}}(V_{1o} - V_{3o})$$
(12)

$$V_{2i} = V_{2o} + aI_{2i} + N_{L_{12}}I_{1i} + N_{L_{23}}I_{3i}$$
$$I_{2i} = I_{2o} + bV_{2o} + N_{C_{12}}(V_{2o} - V_{1o}) + N_{C_{23}}(V_{2o} - V_{3o})$$
(13)

$$V_{3i} = V_{3o} + aI_{3i} + N_{L_{13}}I_{1i} + N_{L_{23}}I_{2i}$$
$$I_{3i} = I_{3o} + bV_{3o} + N_{C_{13}}(V_{3o} - V_{1o}) + N_{C_{23}}(V_{3o} - V_{2o})$$
(14)

Here, $a = (r + sl)\Delta x$, $b = sc\Delta x$, $N_{C12} = sC_{m12}\Delta x$, $N_{C13} = sC_{m13}\Delta x$, $N_{C23} = sC_{m23}\Delta x$, $N_{L12} = sL_{m12}\Delta x$, $N_{L13} = sL_{m13}\Delta x$, $N_{L23} = sL_{m23}\Delta x$ and $s$ is the Laplace variable. $V_{1i}$ is the input voltage of the line 1, $I_{1i}$ is the input current of the line 1. $V_{1o}$ is the output voltage of the line 1, $I_{1o}$ is the output current of the line 1. The subscript in the voltage and current signals shows the line number and input/output. Rearranging the above equations, the $6 \times 6$ ABCD matrix is given by

$$
\begin{bmatrix} V_{1i} \\ V_{2i} \\ V_{3i} \\ I_{1i} \\ I_{2i} \\ I_{3i} \end{bmatrix} = \begin{bmatrix} 1+aN_{11}-N_{L_{12}}N_{C_{12}}-N_{L_{13}}N_{C_{13}} & N_{L_{12}}N_{22}-aN_{C_{12}}-N_{C_{23}}N_{L_{13}} & N_{L_{13}}N_{33}-aN_{C_{13}}-N_{C_{23}}N_{L_{12}} & a & N_{L_{12}} & N_{L_{13}} \\ N_{L_{12}}N_{11}-aN_{C_{12}}-N_{C_{13}}N_{L_{23}} & 1+aN_{22}-N_{L_{12}}N_{C_{12}}-N_{L_{23}}N_{C_{23}} & N_{L_{23}}N_{33}-aN_{C_{23}}-N_{C_{13}}N_{L_{12}} & N_{L_{12}} & a & N_{L_{23}} \\ N_{L_{13}}N_{11}-aN_{C_{13}}-N_{C_{12}}N_{L_{23}} & N_{L_{23}}N_{22}-aN_{C_{23}}-N_{C_{12}}N_{L_{13}} & 1+aN_{33}-N_{L_{13}}N_{C_{13}}-N_{L_{23}}N_{C_{23}} & N_{L_{13}} & N_{L_{23}} & a \\ N_{11} & -N_{C_{12}} & -N_{C_{13}} & 1 & 0 & 0 \\ -N_{C_{12}} & N_{22} & -N_{C_{23}} & 0 & 1 & 0 \\ -N_{C_{13}} & -N_{C_{23}} & N_{33} & 0 & 0 & 1 \end{bmatrix} \begin{bmatrix} V_{1o} \\ V_{2o} \\ V_{3o} \\ I_{1o} \\ I_{2o} \\ I_{3o} \end{bmatrix}
$$
(15)

The new constants $N_{11}$, $N_{22}$, $N_{33}$ in (15) are defined as

$$N_{11} = b + N_{C_{12}} + N_{C_{13}}, \quad N_{22} = b + N_{C_{12}} + N_{C_{23}}, \quad N_{33} = b + N_{C_{13}} + N_{C_{23}}.$$

### 3.1  Case I: Out-of-Phase Switching

In three-line coupled interconnect system, an out-of-phase transition is defined when the middle line transits in opposite direction compared to the adjacent lines. In this case, substituting $V_2 = k_1V_1$ and $V_3 = k_2V_1$ where $k_1 = -1$, $k_2 = 1$, the proposed $6 \times 6$ matrix in (15) for the first line is simplified to

$$
P_1 = \begin{bmatrix} 1+b(a-N_{L_{12}}+N_{L_{13}})+2N_{C_{12}}(1-N_{L_{12}})-2N_{C_{23}}(N_{L_{12}}-N_{L_{13}}) & a-N_{L_{12}}+N_{L_{13}} \\ b+2N_{C_{12}} & 0 \end{bmatrix}
$$
(16)

## 3.2    Case II: In-phase Switching

For in-phase switching, the each line transits in the same direction. Substituting $V_2 = k_1 V_1$ and $V_3 = k_2 V_1$ where $k_1$ and $k_2$ are the switching factors and for in-phase switching case, $k_1 = k_2 = 1$. The proposed $6 \times 6$ matrix can be further simplified and the ABCD parameter matrix of first line is given by

$$P_1 = \begin{bmatrix} 1 + b(a + N_{L_{12}} + N_{L_{13}}) & a + N_{L_{12}} + N_{L_{13}} \\ b & 0 \end{bmatrix} \tag{17}$$

Following the procedure described above, the reduced matrix for other lines can be derived in a similar fashion. Comparing the ABCD matrix of three line interconnect system with that of single line as presented in [10], the equivalent resistance $R_e$, inductance $L_e$ and capacitance $C_e$ of the decoupled interconnect line are given by

$$\begin{aligned} R_e &= R_1 \\ L_e &= L_1 + k_1 L_{m12} + k_2 L_{m13} \\ C_e &= C_1 + (1 - k_1) C_{m12} + (1 - k_2) c_{m13} \end{aligned} \tag{18}$$

In a linear cascaded two-port network, the overall ABCD matrix can be written as product of ABCD matrices of the individual systems. The input/output voltage and currents of each interconnect excluding the driver and load can be written as

$$\begin{bmatrix} V_{1i} \\ I_{1i} \end{bmatrix} = \begin{bmatrix} 1 + b(a + N_{L_{12}} + N_{L_{13}}) & (a + N_{L_{12}} + N_{L_{13}}) \\ b & 1 \end{bmatrix}^n \begin{bmatrix} V_{1o} \\ I_{1o} \end{bmatrix} \tag{19}$$

$$\begin{bmatrix} V_{2i} \\ I_{2i} \end{bmatrix} = \begin{bmatrix} 1 + b(a + N_{L_{12}} + N_{L_{23}}) & (a + N_{L_{12}} + N_{L_{23}}) \\ b & 1 \end{bmatrix}^n \begin{bmatrix} V_{2o} \\ I_{2o} \end{bmatrix} \tag{20}$$

$$\begin{bmatrix} V_{3i} \\ I_{3i} \end{bmatrix} = \begin{bmatrix} 1 + b(a + N_{L13} + N_{L23}) & (a + N_{L13} + N_{L23}) \\ b & 1 \end{bmatrix}^n \begin{bmatrix} V_{3o} \\ I_{3o} \end{bmatrix} \tag{21}$$

Using the methodology described in [11, 12] for a single interconnect, the $n^{th}$ power of matrix $P$ of the decoupled interconnect can be computed as

$$\lim_{n \to \infty} P^n = \begin{bmatrix} \cosh(\theta l_{GNR}) & Z_0 \sinh(\theta l_{GNR}) \\ \frac{1}{Z_0} \sinh(\theta l_{GNR}) & \cos h(\theta l_{GNR}) \end{bmatrix} \tag{22}$$

In the above equation, $Z_0$ and $\theta$ represent characteristic impedance and propagation constant of the decoupled interconnect lines, respectively and are given as

$$Z_0 = \sqrt{\frac{a + N_{L_{12}} + N_{L_{23}}}{b}} = \sqrt{\frac{R_S + s(L_S + L_{m_{12}} + L_{m_{23}})}{b}} \tag{23}$$

$$\theta = \frac{\sqrt{(a+N_{L_{12}}+N_{L_{23}})b}}{\Delta x} = \frac{\sqrt{[R_S+s(L_S+L_{m_{12}}+L_{m_{23}})]b}}{(l_{GNR}/n)} \tag{24}$$

Considering the effect of driver and lumped GNR elements, the proposed ABCD matrix of victim interconnect line can be described by

$$\begin{bmatrix} A & B \\ C & D \end{bmatrix} = \begin{bmatrix} 1+sR_dC_d & R_d \\ sC_d & 1 \end{bmatrix} \begin{bmatrix} 1 & R_c/2 \\ 0 & 1 \end{bmatrix}$$
$$\times \begin{bmatrix} \cosh(\theta l_{GNR}) & Z_0\sinh(\theta l_{GNR}) \\ \frac{1}{Z_0}\sinh(\theta l_{GNR}) & \cosh(\theta l_{GNR}) \end{bmatrix} \begin{bmatrix} 1 & R_c/2 \\ 0 & 1 \end{bmatrix} \tag{25}$$

Further simplification of RHS in Eq. (25) results in a $2 \times 2$ matrix and thus is dimensionally correct. Deriving the relation between input and output voltage for capacitive load $(C_l)$, the voltage gain and crosstalk delay $(\tau_{50\%})$ of victim interconnect can be expressed as [13]

$$Gain = \frac{V_{10}}{V_{1i}} = \frac{1}{A+sC_lB} \tag{26}$$

$$\tau_{50\%} = \left(1.48\xi + e^{-2.9\xi^{1.35}}\right)\sqrt{L_e l_{GNR}(C_e l_{GNR} + C_S)} \tag{27}$$

Here $\xi$ is the damping factor and can be found using [10] for coupled interconnect system.

## 4    Results and Discussion

In this section, the proposed model (Eqs. (26) and (27)) is validated against the SPICE and the effect of various parameters on the propagation characteristics of coupled MLGNR interconnects in 32 nm technology node is investigated, both in the time and frequency domain. The various dimensional parameters are in accordance with the International Technology Roadmap of Semiconductors (ITRS) [14]. Since CNTFTEs suffer from process variability in deep submicron, therefore CMOS inverters have been considered as drivers in this paper. The equivalent output resistance and output capacitance of receiver-driver are denoted by Rdr and Cdr, respectively.

Considering lines *1* and *3* as aggressors and line *2* as victim, the variation of output voltages along the victim line is shown in Figs. 3(a)–(b) during in-phase and out-of-phase switching modes. The near-end voltage is the output of driver while far-end voltage is obtained across the load capacitance.

It can be seen that the near-end and far-end voltages differ in their waveform shapes. This is due to the fact that interconnect parasitics vary along the wire length. Near-end voltage saturates earlier than far-end voltage since it experiences relatively less time constant which in turn depends on the line parasitics.

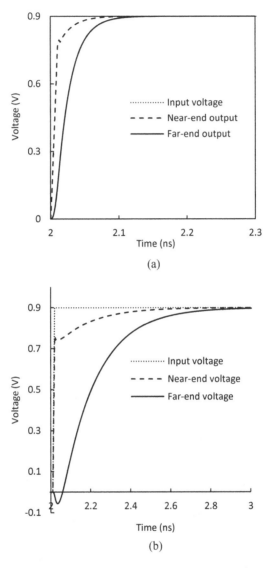

**Fig. 3.** Transient response on victim line 2 during (a) in-phase, and (b) out-of-phase crosstalk analysis.

The transfer function as derived in (25) is used to analyze the frequency response that primarily depends on the GNR equivalent interconnect impedance parasitics and are presented in Table 1. The transfer gain of the proposed analytical model during in-phase and out-of phase switching of the victim net is shown in Fig. 4. The obtained analytical results are in good agreement with SPICE. It can be observed that cut-off frequencies exhibited by MLGNR during in-phase and out-of-phase are 0.8 GHz and 6.31 GHz, respectively. In comparison, Cu exhibits lower cut-off frequency to GNR,

**Table 1.** Interconnect parameters from ITRS.

| Technology node: 32 nm | Global interconnect |
|---|---|
| Width $W$ (nm) | 48 |
| Height $H$ (nm) | 144 |
| Dielectric thickness $T_{ox}$ (nm) | 86.4 |
| Mean free path (μm) | 1.04 |
| Interlayer distance δ (μm) | 0.34 |
| Wire spacing $S$ (nm) | 86.4 |
| Permittivity of free space $\varepsilon_0$ (F/m) | $8.854 \times 10^{-12}$ |
| Permeability of free space $\mu_o$ | $4\pi \times 10^{-7}$ |
| Contact Resistance $R_C$ (Ω) | 1.4366 |
| Interconnect length $l_{GNR}$ (mm) | 1 |
| *Interconnect parasitics* | |
| $R_S$ (kΩ/μm) | 2.54 |
| $L_S$ (μH/μm) | 3.09 |
| $C_S$ (pF/μm) | 4.92 |

indicating thereby that GNRs are more suitable to be used as on-chip interconnects for high-frequency applications.

To test the robustness of proposed analytical model, the crosstalk-induced delay is evaluated at different transition times and is shown in Fig. 5. The delay increases with transition time since the charging and discharging of node capacitances gets limited. For in-phase and out-of-phase switching, the crosstalk delay agrees well with the SPICE results. The percentage error in the estimation of delay does not exceed 10%.

It is found that for all the cases of input transition time, the proposed model matches accurately with the simulation results. It is also observed that crosstalk delay during out-of-phase mode is more compared to in-phase switching. For example, crosstalk induced delays during out-of-phase switching are 58.20 ps and 62.24 ps at transition times of 30 ps and 90 ps, respectively, while the crosstalk delays during in-phase mode are 17.26 ps and 20.73 ps at the same transition times. This fact can be realized by the effect of Miller capacitance when interconnect switch opposite. Consequently, for victim line 2, out-of-phase switching is the worst-case delay.

To further validate the efficacy of the proposed model, the crosstalk-induced delay is compared against the interconnect length and is shown in Fig. 6. It can be seen from Fig. 6 that delay increases with interconnect length. For instance, the crosstalk delays are 23 ps and 168.4 ps at 300 μm and 1000 μm length, respectively. This is due to the fact that interconnect impedance parasitics are linearly proportional to wire length.

The power dissipated by MLGNRs is 6.44 μW and 34.26 μW during in-phase and out-phase switching, respectively. However, the power dissipated by Cu happens to be 11.81 μW and 152.94 μW which is about 83% and 346% higher than GNR during

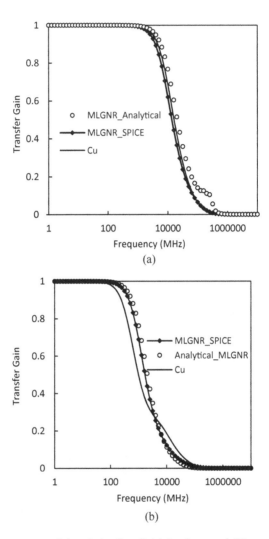

**Fig. 4.** Frequency response of the victim line 2 (a) in-phase and (b) out-of-phase switching modes.

these switching modes. Thus, it can be concluded that GNRs can be effectively used for high-frequency low-power on-chip and chip-chip next-generation interconnect applications.

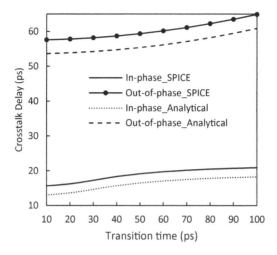

**Fig. 5.** Variation of Crosstalk induced delay as a function of transition time.

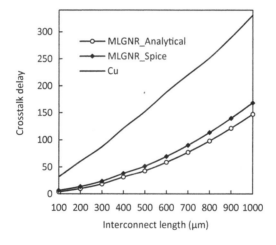

**Fig. 6.** Crosstalk induced delay as a function of interconnect length.

## 5  Conclusions

A distributed three-line interconnect model of MLGNR interconnects is considered. Both capacitive and inductive coupling are considered. Closed-form expressions of transfer gain and crosstalk induced delay have been provided. The frequency response suggests that MLGNRs have higher bandwidth compared to Copper interconnects. In addition, GNRs also dissipate less power, making it a potential candidate for low power and high frequency applications. Crosstalk-induced delay is analyzed in coupled three interconnect lines under in-phase and out-of-phase switching modes. It is observed that delay under out-of-phase is higher than in-phase delay. The impact of transition time on delay is also investigated and it is found that delay increases with transition time. The results of the present investigations shall be beneficial for the design, analysis and optimization of electrical performance of MLGNR interconnects for next generation integrated circuits.

**Acknowledgement.** The authors sincerely acknowledge with gratitude the technical and financial support received from the Science and Engineering Research Board, Department of Science and Technology (SERB-DST), GoI, through Start-Up Grant for Young Scientists (Ref. No.: YSS/2015/001122/ES).

# References

1. Kumar, V., Rakheja, S., Naeemi, A.: Performance and energy-per-bit modeling of multilayer graphene nanoribbon conductors. IEEE Trans. Electron Devices **59**(10), 2753–2761 (2012)
2. Nasiri, S.H., Farshi, M.K.M., Faez, R.: Stability analysis in graphene nano-ribbon interconnects. IEEE Electron Device Lett. **31**(12), 1458–1460 (2010)
3. Zhao, W.S., Yin, W.Y.: Comparative study on multilayer graphene nanoribbon (MLGNR) interconnects. IEEE Trans. Electromagn. Compat. **56**(3), 638–645 (2014)
4. Nishad, A.K., Sharma, R.: Performance improvement in SC-MLGNRs interconnects using interlayer dielectric insertion. IEEE Trans. Emerg. Top. Comput. **3**(4), 470–482 (2015)
5. Wang, W., Liu, P.G., Qin, Y.J.: An unconditional stable 1D-FDTD method for modeling transmission lines based on precise split-step scheme. Prog. in Electromagn. Res. **135**, 245–260 (2013)
6. Reina, A., Jia, X., Ho, J., Nezich, D., Son, H., Bulovic, V., Dresslhaus, M., Kong, J.: Large area, few layer graphene films on arbitrary substrates by chemical vapor deposition. Nano Lett. **9**(1), 30–35 (2009)
7. Zhao, W.S., Yin, W.Y.: Comparative study on multilayer graphene nanoribbon (MLGNR) interconnects. IEEE Trans. Electromagn. Compat. **56**(3), 638–645 (2014)
8. Cui, J.P., Zhao, W.S., Yin, W.Y., Hu, J.: Signal transmission analysis of multilayer graphene nano-ribbon (MLGNR) interconnects. IEEE Trans. Electromagn. Compat. **54**(1), 126–132 (2012)
9. Kumar, V., Rakheja, S., Naeemi, A.: Performance and energy-per-bit modeling of multilayer graphene nanoribbon conductors. IEEE Trans. Electron Devices **59**(10), 2753–2761 (2012)
10. Qian, L., Xia, Y., Shi, G.: Study of crosstalk effect on the propagation of coupled MLGNR interconnects. IEEE Trans. Nanotechnol. **15**(5), 810–819 (2016)
11. Lu, Q.J., Zhu, Z.M., Yang, Y.T., Ding, R.X.: Electrical modeling and characterization of shield differential through silicon vias. IEEE Trans. Electron Devices **62**(5), 1544–1552 (2015)
12. Palit, A.K., Hasan, S., Duganapalli, K.K., Anheier, A.: Distributed RLC transient model of coupled interconnects in DSM chips for crosstalk noise simulation. In: 2nd Electronics System-Integration Technology Conference, pp. 1165–1170. IEEE, Greenwich (2008)
13. Amore, M.D., Sarto, M.S., Tamburrano, A.: Fast transient analysis of next-generation interconnects based on carbon nanotubes. IEEE Trans. Electromagn. Compat. **52**(2), 496–503 (2010)
14. ITRS Homepage. http://www.itrs.net/reports.html. Accessed 03 Apr 2017

# LISOCHIN: An NBTI Degradation Monitoring Sensor for Reliable CMOS Circuits

Ambika Prasad Shah$^{(\boxtimes)}$, Nandakishor Yadav,
and Santosh Kumar Vishvakarma

Nanoscale Devices, VLSI Circuit and System Design Lab,
Electrical Engineering Department, Indian Institute of Technology,
Indore 453552, M.P., India
ambika_shah@rediffmail.com, nkyadav.vlsi@gmail.com,
skvishvakarma@iiti.ac.in

**Abstract.** Reliability and variability issues are the biggest design challenges facing nanoscale high-speed applications. Negative bias temperature instability (NBTI) is the major reliability issues with the scaled devices. Effect of NBTI increases with the time and it increases the threshold voltage of PMOS. This paper presents an NBTI degradation sensor which monitors the change in standby leakage current ($I_{ddq}$) of the test circuit under the stress conditions. The performance of proposed sensor is linear and highly sensitive. Due to high sensitivity, the proposed sensor is best suited for compensation of temporal degradation during measurement. The sensitivity of the proposed sensor further increase at elevated temperature ($125\,^{\circ}$C) compares to room temperature ($27\,^{\circ}$C). The proposed sensor has the improvement in sensitivity of 20.12% and 74.82% as compared to CM based sensor at room temperature and elevated temperature respectively. The transimpedance of the proposed sensor is linear and the linearity is unaffected by the voltage and temperature variations. The proposed sensor is 25% smaller and has faster response compared to CM based sensor. The proposed sensor is also unaffected by the supply voltage variations.

**Keywords:** NBTI · Threshold voltage degradation · Process variation
Reliability · NBTI sensor

## 1 Introduction

With the aggressive scaling of CMOS technology, variability and reliability issues of transistor become dominating part of integrated circuit's performance and lifetime. Device scaling reduces the oxide thickness by ∼30% in each next technology generation [1]. Industrial data unveil that the reliability, especially bias temperature instability (BTI) becomes a major concern if the oxide thickness reduces to less than 2 nm [2]. BTI is a time dependent and causes due to dangling bond defects at $Si/SiO_2$ interface that allows trapping of charges even at small energy into $Si/SiO_2$ interface which increases the threshold voltage and affects the both NMOS and PMOS devices [3]. Negative bias temperature instability

© Springer Nature Singapore Pte Ltd. 2017
B. K. Kaushik et al. (Eds.): VDAT 2017, CCIS 711, pp. 441–451, 2017.
https://doi.org/10.1007/978-981-10-7470-7_44

(NBTI) and positive bias temperature instability (PBTI) are observed in both PMOS and NMOS. However, the effect of NBTI in PMOS is more sizable and is the dominant limiting factor of a device's/circuit lifetime compare to all other components (NBTI in NMOS, PBTI in NMOS and PBTI in PMOS), hence, only NBTI in PMOS is usually considered [4,5]. NBTI leads to significant shifts in the threshold voltage of PMOS over time which creates uncertainty in device/circuit behavior and decreases the device/circuit lifetime. Because of this progressive degradation, it is difficult to ensure the reliability of integrated circuit over their lifetime [6].

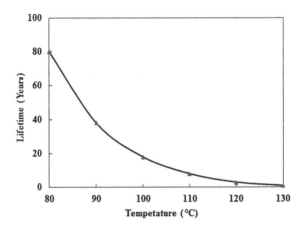

**Fig. 1.** Inverter lifetime degradation due to NBTI under temperature variation [7].

NBTI is prominent in PMOS devices along the entire channel when a negative gate to source voltage is applied or device is operating in accumulation mode (i.e., $V_{gs} < 0$ is called stress state). The threshold voltage ($V_{th}$) of PMOS increases due to NBTI and this shift becomes worst as the technology scales down. $V_{th}$ shift increases by approximately 4% for each new technology generation. Tables 1 and 2 shows the effect of NBTI on threshold voltage shift and drain current ($I_D$) degradation at three different operating temperatures (25 °C, 75 °C, and 125 °C) with stress time of $10^5$ s at technology nodes 90 nm, 65 nm and 45 nm respectively [8,9]. From the Tables 1 and 2, we can observe that the effect of NBTI includes:

- The threshold voltage of PMOS transistor increases.
- Degradation in drain current.
- Speed degradation.

These effects further increase exponentially with the rise in temperature. For example, Fig. 1 shows that the lifetime of an inverter is degraded due to NBTI by 2.2× for every 10 °C increase in temperature [7].

**Table 1.** Threshold voltage shift of PMOS transistor due to NBTI @ stress time of $10^5$ [8,9]

| Technology node | Operating temperature (°C) | | |
|---|---|---|---|
| | 25 °C | 75 °C | 125 °C |
| 90 nm | 17.68 mV | 21.43 mV | 23.96 mV |
| 65 nm | 18.22 mV | 23.12 mV | 25.74 mV |
| 45 nm | 20.68 mV | 25.02 mV | 29.81 mV |

**Table 2.** Drain current degradation of PMOS transistor due to NBTI @ stress time of $10^5$ s [8,9]

| Technology node | Operating temperature (°C) | | |
|---|---|---|---|
| | 25 °C | 75 °C | 125 °C |
| 90 nm | 3.42% | 4.82% | 5.22% |
| 65 nm | 4.83% | 6.20% | 6.86% |
| 45 nm | 5.03% | 7.50% | 7.86% |

The change in threshold voltage under DC stress (i.e. gate terminal of PMOS is grounded) follows a power law model with respect to aging and is given by [10]:

$$\Delta|V_{th_{DC}}| = K_{DC} \times t^n \tag{1}$$

where time constant $n = 0.16$ is assumed for molecular hydrogen diffusion, $t$ is the aging time in seconds and $K_{DC}$ is a technology dependent parameter and it is the function of temperature, supply voltage, device dimensions and interface trap density.

In the real circuit operation, the effective ON time of the PMOS depends on the operating frequency and the gate input probability. The PMOS transistor experiences a recovery process during OFF time when gate terminal of PMOS is connected to supply voltage. Hence, AC stress is the scaled version of DC stress and is given by [10]:

$$\Delta|V_{th_{AC}}| \approx \alpha \times \Delta|V_{th_{DC}}| = \alpha \times K_{DC} \times t^{0.16} \tag{2}$$

Where $\alpha$ is a prefactor depending on the operating frequency and the gate input probability. It is also reported that the lifetime of PMOS under AC stress is ∼4× longer than DC stress.

The general block diagram of NBTI sensing and compensation circuit is shown in Fig. 2(a). It has two sections: primary circuit and secondary circuits. The primary circuit is the circuit under test which is affected by NBTI degradation. The secondary circuit consists of sensor circuit, decision circuit, and bias generator circuit. Degradation is sensed by sensor circuit and the amount of degradation is decided by decision circuit. If the primary circuit is unaffected

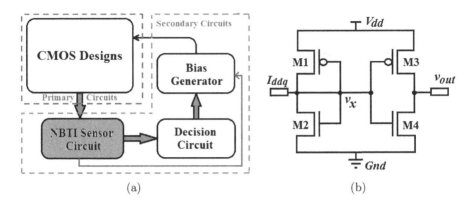

**Fig. 2.** (a) General block diagram of NBTI sensing and compensation circuit (b) Proposed NBTI sensor (LISOCHIN) circuit.

by NBTI, the output of decision circuit will be low, otherwise, it will give some output according to the amount of degradation. Finally, a voltage is generated by a bias generator which is based on the amount of degradation and applied to body/back gate terminal of PMOS to compensate the amount of degradation. The secondary circuits are unaffected by NBTI because they are active during the recovery phase only for short duration.

The organization of the paper is as follows. Section 2 describes the previous work related to NBTI sensing techniques. Section 3 describes the circuit operation of the proposed NBTI sensor. Section 4 explains the simulation results and discussion followed by the conclusion in Sect. 5.

## 2    Related Work

Many researchers have proposed several circuit level techniques to mitigate the process and temporal variations. To remove NBTI degradation in any circuit, we need to first measure the amount of degradation. In most of the literature, NBTI measurement was made by first stress the device and then measure the different device parameter before and after the stress. For measurement purposes, the parameter can be threshold voltage, drain current, transconductance, delay, interface trap density or other device parameters [5]. To measure these parameters, we need to have a respective sensor circuit which senses the change due to NBTI degradation.

Several works have been done for sensing of NBTI degradation. In [11] trip point sensing based compensation technique is used. Trip point voltage decreases with increase in NBTI stress and back gate voltage $(V_B)$ of PMOS. This sensing technique is less sensitive of $V_B$ and has partial linear performance characteristics. In [4] NBTI and HCI sensors have been proposed which is dedicated to the dynamic reliability management (DRM). These two sensors are used to measure the threshold voltage of the stressed device and convert it into the delay. These sensors are less sensitive to temperature, but require a large area and large power consumption. Mostafa et al. [12,13] has proposed an PMOS transistor $|V_{th}|$ sensing circuit. The sizing of PMOS of the sensor is same as the PMOS of the test circuit and NMOS in the sensor has the native threshold voltage. This native threshold voltage is typically around 0V [14]. This sensor works only if the size of all PMOS in test circuit is same and equal to the size of PMOS of the sensor. A standby leakage current ($I_{ddq}$) based NBTI sensing method for SRAM cell is used [15,16]. In this paper, authors have used $I_{ddq}$ to monitor and characterize the temporal degradations. The main drawback of this sensor is that, it required addition bias generator ($V_b$) to ensure the active load in $I_{ddq}$ sensor to work in the sub-threshold region. To do this, asymmetric sizing of transistors is required. The performance of this sensor is nonlinear and is less sensitive to input. In [17], a modified current mirror based approach is proposed. In this sensing technique, power supply current is mirrored and converted into a voltage. This sensing technique is comparatively more stable than $I_{ddq}$ sensor [15], but response time is slow because of power gating scheme is used to operate the sensor.

In this paper, we have proposed a new sensor structure to measure the change in performance of the circuit because of NBTI degradation. The small size of the sensor makes it easy to use in standard cell design with minimum power and area overhead. In this paper, we observe the $V_{th}$ shift due to NBTI and correlate the amount of voltage shift by sensing the $I_{ddq}$. The performance of the sensor is linear and has a high degree of sensitivity to changes in $I_{ddq}$. Better the linearity of the sensor has less probability of error in sensing of leakage current due to threshold voltage shift. For better compensation of threshold voltage shift, the sensor must be highly sensitive, so that it can sense, even a small amount of variation in threshold voltage. The sensor must be unaffected by PVT and temporal variations so that compensation accuracy can be increased.

# 3    Proposed NBTI Sensor

Figure 2(b) shows the proposed LInear and Sensitive On-CHIp NBTI (LISOCHIN) sensor circuit. M1 and M2 are self-drain biased and they are acting as resistors and in combination voltage divider. The output of this voltage divider depends on standby leakage current $I_{ddq}$ which is flowing through the circuit under test (Primary circuits which are affected by NBTI degradation). To enhance the output of voltage divider a push pull amplifier (M3 and M4) is used. The proposed sensor gives the negative change in the output $v_{out}$ with positive change in the $I_{ddq}$ means the slope of the sensor is negative hence the proposed sensor shows the negative resistance behavior. To make positive slope (positive shift in the output with a positive shift in the input), an extra inverter needs to be added at the output side.

The approximate transfer function (transimpedance) of the proposed sensor using small-signal modeling by considering $(g_{m1} + g_{m2}) \times (R_{ds1} \parallel R_{ds2}) \gg 1$ is given by:

$$R = \frac{v_{out}}{I_{ddq}}\bigg|_{I_{out}=0} \approx \frac{-(g_{m3} + g_{m4}) \times (R_{ds3} \parallel R_{ds4})}{(g_{m1} + g_{m2})} \tag{3}$$

As M1 and M2 are identical to M3 and M4 respectively, then $(g_{m1} + g_{m2}) \approx (g_{m3} + g_{m4})$ hence the approximate transimpedance of the sensor will be

$$R \approx -(R_{ds3} \parallel R_{ds4}) \tag{4}$$

Equation 4 shows the negative transimpedance of proposed sensor. To make output directly proportional to the input current, an extra driver inverter needs to be added at the output ($v_{out}$). Transimpedance of the sensor depends on $R_{ds3}$ & $R_{ds4}$ and change in these two resistances are equal and opposite to each other. $R_{ds3}$ & $R_{ds4}$ also depend on the input current $I_{ddq}$ and operating temperature. Hence, transimpedance of the sensor is constant in the input range 0 nA to 100 nA as shown in Fig. 3.

To enhance the output of sensor an additional driver inverter at the output ($v_{out}$) side has been added. If the two transistors of driver inverter (Not shown in the figure) are $M5$ (PMOS) and $M6$ (NMOS) with the same sizing as $M3$ and $M4$ respectively then the final transfer function will become

$$R = \frac{V_{out}}{I_{ddq}}\bigg|_{I_{out}=0} \approx \frac{(R_{ds3} \parallel R_{ds4}) \times (g_{m5} + g_{m6})}{(g_{ds5} + g_{ds6})} \tag{5}$$

Or

$$R \approx (R_{ds3} \parallel R_{ds4}) \times (R_{ds5} \parallel R_{ds6}) \times (g_{m5} + g_{m6}) \tag{6}$$

Here, $V_{out}$ and $v_{out}$ are the output of the sensor with and without driver inverter respectively. From Eq. 6, an additional inverter at the output side further increases the transimpedance by the factor $(R_{ds5} \parallel R_{ds6}) \times (g_{m5} + g_{m6})$. This factor increase the slope of the transfer function means the sensitivity of sensor will increases.

After considering driver inverter, the transfer function of the sensor also depends on $(g_{m5} + g_{m6})$. The slope of transfer function further increases with an increase in the temperature because of $g_{m5}$ and $g_{m6}$ are the function of temperature and they increase with the temperature increases. We have utilized this phenomenon to enhance the output swing and in result, sensitivity increases at the elevated temperature as shown in Fig. 4.

## 4   Simulation Results and Discussion

In this section, we present the simulation results of proposed NBTI sensor and key points to observe from the results. All the simulation has been performed using UMC 65 nm CMOS technology and also considering extra driver inverter at the output side of the proposed sensor. This driver inverter enhances the output swing or slope of the transfer characteristics. As we can observe from Table 2, the leakage current of any circuit under stress changes and these changes are measured using NBTI sensor. The input current range of 0 nA to 100 nA is

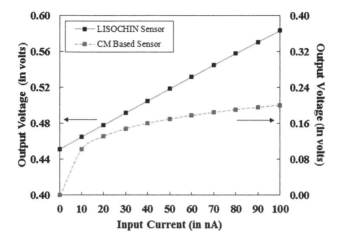

**Fig. 3.** Transfer characteristics of LISOCHIN and CM based sensors at 27 °C

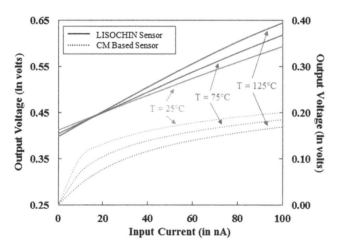

**Fig. 4.** Effect of temperature variation on sensor circuits

considered for the simulation of sensors because the range of leakage current at 65 nm technology is around few nA [18,19]. For the comparison of proposed LISOCHIN sensor, current mirror based sensor (CM based sensor) [15,16] has been considered for validation of results. Effect of voltage and temperature variations is also simulated for both the sensors.

Figure 3 shows the transfer characteristics of LISOCHIN sensor and CM Based sensor. From Fig. 3, it is observed that the proposed LISOCHIN sensor has linear characteristics, whereas CM based sensor has nonlinear performance. The proposed sensor is more sensitive to change in NBTI degradation of test circuit and the sensitivity $(S)$ of LISOCHIN sensor is 1.32 mV/nA compared to 1.098 mV/nA of CM based sensor for the input range of 10 nA to 100 nA at room temperature (27 °C). Table 3 shows the performance comparison of different NBTI sensor circuits.

Effect of temperature variation on LISOCHIN and CM based sensor is shown in Fig. 4. The result shows that the slope of proposed sensor increases with the temperature. As the effect of NBTI occurs at the elevated temperature means the proposed sensor is more sensitive to NBTI degradation of the test circuit at elevated temperature. It is also observed that, the linearity of the transfer function or transimpedance of LISOCHIN sensor is unaffected by temperature variation. The result also shows that the output voltage of CM based sensor decreases with temperature increases means the sensitivity of CM based sensor decreases at elevated temperature. Sensitivity of LISOCHIN sensor is 2.43 mV/nA compare to 1.39 mV/nA of CM based sensor for the input range of 10 nA to 100 nA at elevated temperature (125 °C).

Table 3. Performance comparison of different NBTI sensors

| References | Sensing technique | Sensing quantity | Output quantity | Linearity | Slope |
|---|---|---|---|---|---|
| [15, 16] | CM based | $I_{ddq}$ | Voltage | Non-linear | +ve |
| [11] | Trip-point | $V_{th}$ & $V_B$ | Voltage | Partial linear | −ve |
| [17] | Current | $I_{ddq}$ | Voltage | Linear | −ve |
| [4] | On-chip | $V_{th}$ | Delay | Linear | −ve |
| [12, 13] | $V_{th}$ sensor | $V_{th}$ | Voltage | Linear | +ve |
| Proposed | LISOCHIN | $I_{ddq}$ | Voltage | Linear | −ve/+ve |

Table 4. Effect of supply voltage variation on output voltage and response time @ $I_{ddq} = 10 \ nA$

| Supply voltage (volts) | Output voltage (volts) | | Response time (ns) | |
|---|---|---|---|---|
| | CM based sensor | Proposed sensor | CM based sensor | Proposed sensor |
| 0.90 | 0.1 | 0.43 | 0.63 | 0.62 |
| 0.95 | 0.1 | 0.45 | 0.70 | 0.62 |
| 1.00 | 0.1 | 0.46 | 0.80 | 0.62 |
| 1.05 | 0.1 | 0.48 | 1.07 | 0.62 |
| 1.10 | 0.1 | 0.50 | 1.07 | 0.62 |

Proposed sensor has 20.12% and 74.82% improvement in sensitivity as compared to CM based sensor at 27 °C and 125 °C respectively. The percentage improvement of sensitivity can be calculated as:

$$\%Improvement = \frac{S_{Proposed} - S_{CM\ Based}}{S_{CM\ Based}} \times 100$$

As the slope of transimpedance depends on $g_{m5} + g_{m6}$ and $g_{m5}$ & $g_{m6}$ are the function of temperature, hence slopes further increases with increase in temperature.

We have taken $\pm10\%$ of supply voltage variation for the simulation of both the sensors. Table 4 shows the effect of supply voltage variation, and observe that the LISOCHIN sensor has increased output voltage as compared to CM based sensor for both 10 nA input current. As shown in Table 4 and Fig. 5, the response time of the proposed sensor is less as compared to CM based sensor. It is also observed that the response time of LISOCHIN sensor is unaffected by supply voltage variation, whereas the response time of CM based sensor increases with the increase in supply voltage.

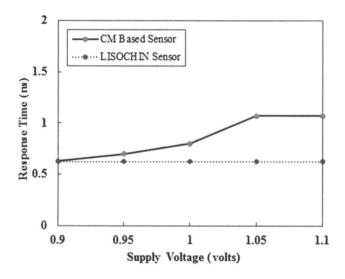

**Fig. 5.** Effect of supply voltage variation on response time

## 5   Conclusion

In this paper, a novel NBTI degradation monitoring sensor circuit is presented. The performance of the proposed LISOCHIN sensor is linear and has a large output swing or high sensitivity. The effect of voltage and temperature variation is also evaluated for both LISOCHIN and CM based sensors and it is found that the proposed sensor is less affected by voltage and temperature variations as compared to CM based sensor. The response time of the proposed sensor is unaffected by the $\pm10\%$ supply variation, whereas response time of CM based sensor increases with an increase in the supply voltage.

The sensitivity of the proposed LISOCHIN sensor is 20.12% more as compared to CM based sensor at room temperature (27 °C) whereas the improvement in sensitivity increases with temperature and has 74.82% more sensitive to NBTI degradation sensing as compared to CM based sensor at the elevated temperature (125 °C).

As the effect of voltage and temperature variation in proposed sensor is less, the performance is linear, more sensitive to NBTI degradation and has a high voltage swing, this sensor is most suited for the applications where the variation of external conditions are more and also affected by PVT variations. The proposed circuit can also be used in IoT nodes, which are installed at the remote locations and has large variations in environmental conditions.

**Acknowledgement.** The authors would like to thank the University Grant Commission (UGC) New Delhi, Government of India for providing financial support and CSIR, Government of India with research project grant no. 22/0651/14/ EMR-II, for simulation software.

# References

1. Borkar, S., et al.: Microarchitecture and design challenges for gigascale integration. MICRO **37**, 3 (2004)
2. Cho, M., Lee, J.D., Aoulaiche, M., Kaczer, B., Roussel, P., Kauerauf, T., Degraeve, R., Franco, J., Ragnarsson, L.Å., Groeseneken, G.: Insight into N/PBTI mechanisms in sub-1-nm-EOT devices. IEEE Trans. Electron Devices **59**(8), 2042–2048 (2012)
3. Panagopoulos, G.D., Roy, K.: A three-dimensional physical model for $V_{th}$ variations considering the combined effect of NBTI and RDF. IEEE Trans. Electron Devices **58**(8), 2337–2346 (2011)
4. Wang, Y., Enachescu, M., Cotofana, S.D., Fang, L.: Variation tolerant on-chip degradation sensors for dynamic reliability management systems. Microelectron. Reliab. **52**(9), 1787–1791 (2012)
5. Schroder, D.K.: Negative bias temperature instability: what do we understand? Microelectron. Reliab. **47**(6), 841–852 (2007)
6. Singh, P., Karl, E., Blaauw, D., Sylvester, D.: Compact degradation sensors for monitoring NBTI and oxide degradation. IEEE Trans. Very Large Scale Integr. VLSI Syst. **20**(9), 1645–1655 (2012)
7. Habchi, R., Salame, C., Khoury, A., Mialhe, P.: Temperature dependence of a silicon power device switching parameters. Appl. Phys. Lett. **88**(15), 153503 (2006)
8. Khan, S., Hamdioui, S.: Temperature impact on NBTI modeling in the framework of technology scaling. In: Proceeding 2nd HiPEAC Workshop on Design for Reliability, Pisa, Italy (2010)
9. Khan, S., Hamdioui, S.: Temperature dependence of NBTI induced delay. In: 16th IEEE International On-Line Testing Symposium (IOLTS), pp. 15–20 (2010)
10. Kim, K.K., Wang, W., Choi, K.: On-chip aging sensor circuits for reliable nanometer MOSFET digital circuits. IEEE Trans. Circuits Syst. II Express Briefs **57**(10), 798–802 (2010)

11. Yadav, N., Jain, S., Pattanaik, M., Sharma, G.: NBTI aware IG-FinFET based SRAM design using adaptable trip-point sensing technique. In: IEEE/ACM International Symposium on Nanoscale Architectures (NANOARCH), pp. 122–128 (2014)
12. Mostafa, H., Anis, M., Elmasry, M.: Adaptive body bias for reducing the impacts of NBTI and process variations on 6T SRAM cells. IEEE Trans. Circuits Syst. I Regul. Pap. **58**(12), 2859–2871 (2011)
13. Mostafa, H., Anis, M., Elmasry, M.: NBTI and process variations compensation circuits using adaptive body bias. IEEE Trans. Semicond. Manuf. **25**(3), 460–467 (2012)
14. Chen, S.L., Ker, M.D.: A new schmitt trigger circuit in a 0.13-/spl mu/m 1/2.5-V CMOS process to receive 3.3-V input signals. IEEE Trans. Circuits Syst. II Express Briefs **52**(7), 361–365 (2005)
15. Kang, K., Alam, M.A., Roy, K.: Characterization of NBTI induced temporal performance degradation in nano-scale SRAM array using $I_{ddq}$. In: IEEE International Test Conference, ITC 2007, pp. 1–10 (2007)
16. Wang, Y., Cotofana, S.D., Fang, L.: Statistical reliability analysis of NBTI impact on FinFET SRAMs and mitigation technique using independent-gate devices. In: IEEE/ACM International Symposium on Nanoscale Architectures (NANOARCH), pp. 109–115 (2012)
17. Wang, Y., Cotofana, S.D., Fang, L.: Analysis of the impact of spatial and temporal variations on the stability of SRAM arrays and the mitigation technique using independent-gate devices. J. Parallel Distrib. Comput. **74**(6), 2521–2529 (2014)
18. Traversi, G., Gaioni, L., Ratti, L., Manghisoni, M., Re, V.: Perspectives of 65 nm CMOS technologies for high performance front-end electronics. In: 21st International Workshop on Vertex Detectors, 026 (2012)
19. Kim, N.S., Austin, T., Baauw, D., Mudge, T., Flautner, K., Hu, J.S., Irwin, M.J., Kandemir, M., Narayanan, V.: Leakage current: Moore's law meets static power. computer **36**(12), 68–75 (2003)

# Performance Analysis of OLED with Hole Block Layer and Impact of Multiple Hole Block Layer

Shubham Negi[1(✉)], Poornima Mittal[1], and Brijesh Kumar[2]

[1] Department of Electronics and Communication Engineering, Graphic Era University,
Dehradun 248002, India
shubhamnegi0192@gmail.com, poornima2822@ieee.org
[2] Department of Electronics and Communication Engineering, Madan Mohan Malaviya
University of Technology, Gorakhpur, UP, India
bkece@mmmut.ac.in

**Abstract.** The organic electronics has become one of the most essential field of research arena due to mechanical flexibility and low temperature fabrication. The organic devices and circuits are improving day by day in their performance and reliability. Organic light emitting diode (OLED) is one of the upcoming fields in this regards. Here, we are trying to improve performance of OLED by adding hole block layers to it. Further impact of number of hole block layers added to device is analyzed. It is observed that adding hole block layers improve device performance to a certain extent and if more and more hole block layers are added, device performance will start to degrade. The organic material based devices & circuits are identified as thrust area by the International Technology Road Map for Semiconductor (ITRS). OLED is considerably better candidate used in large area electronic displays.

**Keywords:** Organic semiconductor material (OSC)
Organic light emitting diode (OLED) · Hole block layer (HBL)
Organic electronics

## 1 Introduction

Light emitting diodes containing organic materials as active layer constitutes the OLED (Organic Light Emitting Diode) [1]. Organic material based devices and their circuits, specially OLED has advantage of having superior color quality and contrast, with a wide variety of colors together which gives excellent picture quality and mechanical flexibility [1–9]. These devices are highly efficient in performance having a small drive current and low power consumption. It is also accompanied by fast electronic response time and a wide viewing angle [10, 11]. Further, flexible OLED device fabrication is possible [1, 2, 5]. Moreover, being organic in nature these are light, thin, flat, compact, robust devices [1, 2] that can be fabricated economically.

OLED possess these above mentioned advantages, and thus are analyzed invariably to enhance their performance. Researchers continuously focused on developing materials which can show enhanced performance and improve luminescence of OLED

© Springer Nature Singapore Pte Ltd. 2017
B. K. Kaushik et al. (Eds.): VDAT 2017, CCIS 711, pp. 452–462, 2017.
https://doi.org/10.1007/978-981-10-7470-7_45

devices. Further focus in early development stages was towards development of RGB OLEDs so that these devices can be incorporated to make display devices [12]. OLED based displays and televisions that are being manufactured now days is direct outcome of these extensive researches. Further other devices based on OLEDs are also being analyzed [13].

Further enhancement in performance of OLED was possible by considering its structure. More layers of OSC were added to the structure of OLED which would directly contribute to enhanced luminescence by increasing charge injection and recombination in device. In this work focus lies in these layers as to how they can help in improving the performance of OLED. Hole Block Layers (HBL) and their effect on OLED performance are analyzed in this work. Along with it what is an optimal number of HBLs that could be used effectively is also analyzed. Does adding on layers each time will improve performance of OLED?

This paper is divided into five sections which includes this introduction. In Sect. 2 a brief discussion is given about different types of layers that can be added in an OLED structure to improve its performance. It is followed by Sect. 3 which gives simulation setup for the work given in this paper. Section 4 discusses results of this work and concluding remarks are given in Sect. 5.

## 2   Different Layers Used in OLED

OLED incorporates different layers to enhance its performance. These can improve charge injection and recombination into OLED and enhance its luminescence. Layers that are added to improve device performance include hole transport layer (HTL), electron transport layer (ETL), hole block layer (HBL) and electron block layer (EBL) to name a few [14]. These layers are required to enhance performance of OLED because organic semiconductor materials are known to favor transport of only a particular type of charge carrier through them [1]. Further mobility of charge carrier is low [1, 2], due to which above mentioned layers are required to enhance and control carrier movement through the OLED.

A good luminescence characteristic is primary for any OLED. Foremost requirement for this is a good charge injection into emission layer (EML). HTL and ETL are employed for this purpose. Work function of anode is matched closely to HOMO (Highest Occupied Molecular Orbital) of hole injection layer (HIL) which reduces the injection barrier for holes which are then transported to EML. Similarly on cathode side, its work function is matched with LUMO (Lowest Unoccupied Molecular Orbital) of electro injection layer (EIL). This helps to easily inject electrons due to reduced barrier height. Further ETL helps in movement of electrons to EML layer.

Hitherto, purpose of bringing the charge carriers to EML is fulfilled by these layers. Now electrons and holes can recombine and give out energy in form of light. But there is a need to confine these charge carriers in EML layer as they have a tendency to move to opposite electrodes. Hole block layers (HBL) and electron block layers (EBL) are used for this purpose [14]. Purpose of these layers is to provide a high barrier for flow of respective charge carriers through them. This affirms most of charge carriers will be restricted to EML layer and will help in recombination.

Figure 1 shows energy band diagram of OLED with HTL, HIL and HBL and EIL. Here m-MTDATA acts as HIL and NPB as HTL. Alq₃ acts as EIL and in combination with QAD it acts as EML. BPhen and BAlq acts as HBL [14]. If we look closely at the energy bands, it can be noticed that cathode's work function is matched close to EIL layer Alq₃. This helps in injection of electrons. Further BAlq and BPhen layers also have a low LUMO level which helps in transportation of electrons to EML layer by providing a staircase formation. At anode side m-MTDATA has HUMO level matched close to work function of ITO, the anode. Thus it helps in injection of holes and acts as a HIL layer. NPB layer has HOMO level close to m-MTDATA and helps in movement of holes and it is working as HTL.

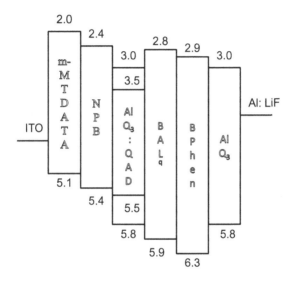

**Fig. 1.** Energy band diagram of OLED.

Until here, all the focus is on injection of charge carriers. But if a closer look is taken at HOMO levels at cathode end and LUMO levels at anode end, it is noticed that BAlq and BPhen layers have a high HUMO level and thus they provide a barrier for movement of holes. Similarly at anode side, NPB and m-MTDATA have high LUMO level which will restrict electron movement. Thus these layers act as HBL and EBL respectively. It is clear from above discussion that these layers can help in improving performance of device. But every time a layer is added it increases a fabrication step. Further it also increases device dimensions as each layer is having a finite thickness. So with improvement in performance it also increases a device dimension which is unwanted.

Hence here we analyze that does adding a layer every time will help improve performance. Here we compare five OLED devices Device A, Device B, Device C, Device D and Device E. Device A is simply a multilayered OLED, and then from Device B to Device E HBLs are added, one at a time, and then performance in compared. It is to be noted here that device dimension is increasing form Device A to Device B, but thereon as number of HBL are increasing, thickness of each HBL layer is decreased. In this manner we are able to maintain same dimension of overall device.

## 3  Simulation Setup

Device A is a simple multilayered OLED, which consists of basic HIL, HTL and EIL layers along with EML layer and two cathodes. The structure of device consists of Al-LiF bilayer cathode, followed by $Alq_3$ as electron injection layer. Then there is EML layer of combination of QAD and $ALq_3$. NPB and m-MTDATA are two layers after EML which works as HTL and HIL layers respectively.

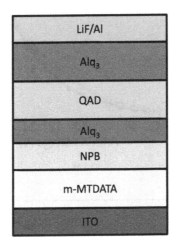

**Fig. 2.** Structure of Device A: multilayered OLED.

**Table 1.** Dimensions of all devices, Device A–Device E (All dimensions are in nm).

| Sr. No. | Layer name | Device A | Device B | Device C | Device D | Device E |
|---------|-----------|----------|----------|----------|----------|----------|
| 1 | Al | 50 | 50 | 50 | 50 | 50 |
| 2 | LiF | 1 | 1 | 1 | 1 | 1 |
| 3 | $Alq_3$ | 60 | 44 | 44 | 44 | 44 |
| 4 | BPhen | – | – | 8 | 6 | 4 |
| 5 | BAlq | – | 16 | 8 | 6 | 4 |
| 6 | TPBi | – | – | – | 6 | 4 |
| 7 | CBP | – | – | – | – | 4 |
| 8 | $Alq_3$ | – | 10 | 10 | 10 | 10 |
| 9 | QAD | 0.1 | 0.1 | 0.1 | 0.1 | 0.1 |
| 10 | $Alq_3$ | 5 | 5 | 5 | 5 | 5 |
| 11 | NPB | 10 | 10 | 10 | 10 | 10 |
| 12 | m-MTDATA | 45 | 45 | 45 | 45 | 45 |
| 13 | ITO | 50 | 50 | 50 | 50 | 50 |

Finally there is ITO anode. Structure of Device A [14] is shown in Fig. 2. Dimension of device is given in Table 1. This device is our reference device that has been taken from a fabricated work [14] by Yang et al. To start our work, we have analyzed Device A in TCAD simulator [15–17], that is industrial standard tool for simulation of organic devices. The result of simulation is matched with fabricated work (hereafter referred to as experimental data). The both results are compared as shown in Fig. 3(a) and (b) and data is summarized in Table 2.

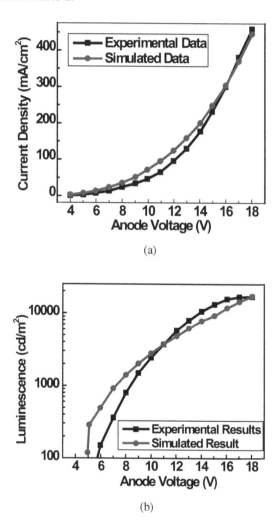

(a)

(b)

**Fig. 3.** A comparison of simulated and experimental results, (a) Comparison of experimental and simulated current density v/s anode voltage, (b) Comparison of experimental and simulated luminescence v/s anode voltage.

**Table 2.** Comparison of simulated and experimental results

| Sr. No. | Parameter name | Experimental results | Simulated results |
|---------|---------------|---------------------|-------------------|
| 1 | Maximum current density ($mA/cm^2$) | 459.862 | 445.791 |
| 2 | Max. Luminescence ($cd/m^2$) | 16916.5 | 17190.1 |

Thereafter, step by step hole block layers were added to device. First in Device B a single hole block layer was added, wherein, thickness of Alq3 layer was decreased and 16 nm of HBL BAlq was added. Thus overall device dimension was same. Device structure was as follow: Al-LiF/Alq$_3$/BAlq/Alq$_3$/QAD/Alq$_3$/NPB/m-MTDATA/ ITO. Structure of this OLED is shown in Fig. 4(a). Device dimension are specified in Table 1.

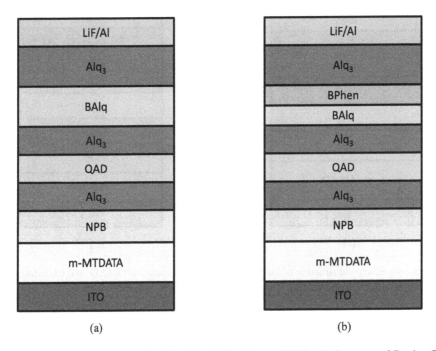

(a)                                          (b)

**Fig. 4.** (a) Structure of Device B: Single hole block layer OLED, (b) Structure of Device C: Double hole block layer OLED.

Subsequently, in Device C another HBL BPhen was added with BAlq but this time the dimension of HBL was split into two, thus each HBL was 8 nm in thickness. This resulted in overall same dimension of device having two HBLs. This structure consists of layers as: Al-LiF/Alq$_3$/BAlq/BPhen/Alq$_3$/QAD/Alq$_3$/NPB/m-MTDATA/ITO. This structure is shown in Fig. 4(b). Dimension of device is given in Table 1. After this triple hole block layer OLED was simulated in which there were three hole block layers and it was Device D. Here each HBL thickness was 6 nm each thus overall device dimension increased by just 2 nm. Structure of this OLED is as: LiF-Al/Alq$_3$/BPhen/BAlq/ TPBi/Alq$_3$/QAD/Alq$_3$/NPB/m-MTDATA/ITO. Again the overall device dimension was same as thickness of each HBL has been decreased. Dimension of this device is again given in Table 1. Its schematic is shown in Fig. 5(a). Finally Device E was simulated with four HBLs. In this device thickness of each block layer was 4 nm. Structure of this device was: LiF-Al/Alq$_3$/BPhen/BAlq/TPBi/CPB/Alq$_3$/QAD/Alq$_3$/NPB/m-MTDATA/ ITO. Table 1 enlists the dimension of this device. Schematic structure of device is shown in Fig. 5(b).

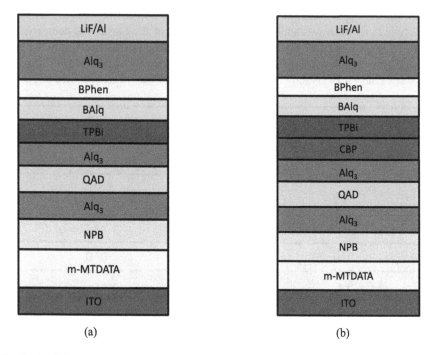

(a)                                    (b)

**Fig. 5.** (a) Schematic structure of Device D: Triple hole block layer OELD, and (b) Schematic structure of OLED with four block layers: Device E.

## 4    Simulation Results

In this section we are comparing the simulation results for all five devices that have analyzed using simulation tools. Comparative plots for luminescence and current density characteristics of these devices are shown in Fig. 6. Both of these plots are against anode voltage. Figure 6(a) shows comparative plot for current density and anode voltage for all five devices. Similarly in Fig. 6(b) there is a comparative plot for Luminescence and anode voltage.

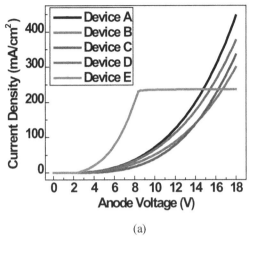

(a)

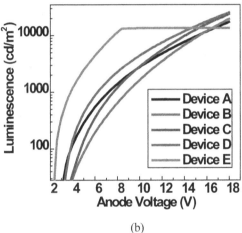

(b)

**Fig. 6.** Comparative plots for simulated devices (a) Comparative plot for current density v/s anode voltage and (b) Comparative plot for luminescence and anode voltage.

It can be seen from graphs that current density is maximum for Device A. Thereafter current density is very small for Device B which goes on increasing to Device D. Thereafter Device E shows saturation in current characteristics at a much lower value of current. Similarly in case of luminescence for devices, it was observed that Device A has least luminescence and it increases to and till Device D. Thereafter there is fall in luminescence in Device E which again saturates. Thus it is implied that from triple block layer to tetra block layer there is a decrease in performance of device.

After looking at device structures we tried to reason why this is happening. We could think of two reasons for this. One is that as there are so many layers at cathode side but each layer is thinner compared to layers in previous devices. So holes could gain enough energy to punch through these layers and escape emission layer. Second reason could be decrease in carrier concentration injection from cathode because of so many interfaces at different layers. So an insight into the device structure was taken with help of Silvaco Atlas simulator to search for actual reason for this response. In our simulated device structure cut line analysis was made and concentration of holes and electrons were analyzed near emission layer for all five devices. A comparative plot for this is shown in Fig. 7, Fig. 7(a) shows plot for maximum hole concentration in simulated devices and Fig. 7(b) shows plot for electron concentration for the same.

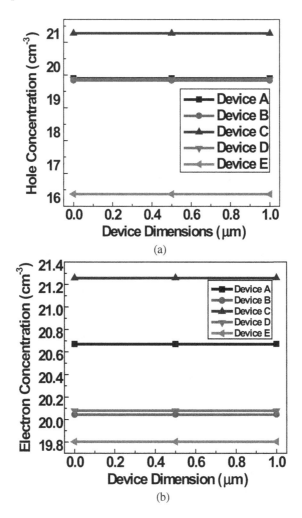

(a)

(b)

**Fig. 7.**    (a) Comparison of hole concentration in simulated devices and (b) Comparison of electron concentration in simulated devices.

Figure 7(a) show that Device B has almost same hole concentration in and near emission layer when compared to Device A. So hole block layer was not effectively able to block holes. But double hole block layer OLED Device C has a high hole concentration and it shows that HBLs were able to block holes quite effectively. And then there is a fall in hole concentration in Device D and Device E. Device D has again same hole concentration as Device A. The reason for this could be decreasing dimensions of HBL because in device E hole concentration is very low. Another reason could be decrease in charge injection at anode as well.

A similar trend was observed in electron concentration. Device B and D are having electron concentration below device A. Device C is having maximum concentration. And Device E is having the least concentration. Now a question arises that if electron and hole concentration are less in Device D how come its luminescence is higher. The only reason for this we could think of was the stair case path given to electrons for injection. In this way they could have more energy stored in them at time of recombination. But a further analysis is required for this theory. As of now we can conclude that increasing hole block layers every time will not always increase device performance. Further there are an optimal number of layers that is feasible to give improved performance. A triple HBL gives the best performance in terms of luminescence for our devices.

# 5 Conclusion

This paper demonstrated the impact of additional hole block layers (HBLs) on the OLED performance. The analysis of five devices is presented, each device is having one more HBL than previous device and furthermore, results are compared. It observed that increasing HBL tends to increase device hole concentration to a certain extent but as the number of these layers keep-on increasing concentration of carriers decrease and performance also begins to degrade. Triple HBL showed good performance even though electron concentration in it is smaller as compared to previous devices. The tetra block layer is implemented and found that electron concentration is far less and thus its performance is worst. Therefore, it concluded that HBLs can be used to improve performance of OLED but only to a certain extent and further increase in number of HBL does not always increase the device performance.

# References

1. Kumar, B., Kaushik, B.K., Negi, Y.S.: Organic thin film transistors: structures, models, materials, fabrication, and applications: a review. Polymer Rev. **54**(1), 33–111 (2014)
2. Kumar, B., Kaushik, B.K., Negi, Y.: S: Perspectives and challenges for organic thin film transistors: materials, devices, processes and applications. J. Mater. Sci. Mater. Electron. **25**(1), 1–30 (2014)
3. Negi, S., Mittal, P., Rawat, S.: Performance analysis of active matrix organic display using vertical channel organic thin film transistor. In: International Conference on Emerging Trends in Communication Technologies (ETCT), Dehradun, India. IEEE (2016)
4. Dodabalapur, A.: Organic Light Emitting Diodes. Solid State Commun. **102**(2–3), 259–267 (1997)
5. Kumar, B., Kaushik, B.K., Negi, Y.S.: Design and analysis of noise margin, write ability and read stability of organic and hybrid 6-T SRAM. Microelectron. Reliab. **54**(12), 2801–2812 (2014)

6. Negi, S., Mittal, P., Kumar, B.: Performance analysis of double block layer OLED and variation in ratio of double block layer. In: 2nd International Conference on Intelligent Communication, Control and Devices (ICICCD 2017), Dehradun, India (2017)
7. Mittal, P., Kumar, B., Kaushik, B.K., Negi, Y.S., Singh, R.K.: Channel length variation effect on performance parameters of organic field effect transistors. Microelectron. J. **43**(12), 985–994 (2012)
8. Kumar, B., Kaushik, B.K., Negi, Y.S., Goswami, V.: Single and dual gate OTFTs based robust organic digital design. Microelectron. Reliab. **54**(1), 100–109 (2014)
9. Malliaras, G.G., Shen, Y., Dunlap, D.H., Murata, H., Kafafi, Z.H.: Non-dispersive electron transport in Alq$_3$. Appl. Phys. Lett. **79**(16), 2582–2584 (2001)
10. Adachi, C., Baldo, M.A., Thompson, M.E., Forrest, S.R.: Nearly 100% internal phosphorescence efficiency in an organic light emitting device. J. Appl. Phys. **90**(10), 5048–5051 (2001)
11. Robinson, M.R., Wang, S., Bazan, G.C., Cao, Y.: Electroluminescence from well-defined tetrahedral oligophenylenevinylene tetramers. Adv. Mater. **12**(22), 1701–1704 (2000)
12. Chan, L., Yeh, H., Chen, C.: Blue light emitting devices based on molecular glass materials of tetraphenylsilane compounds. Adv. Mater. **13**(21), 1637–1641 (2001)
13. Liu, R., Cai, Y., Park, J.M., Ho, K.M., Shinar, J., et al.: Organic Light-Emitting Diode sensing platform: challenges and solutions. Adv. Func. Mater. **21**(24), 4744–4753 (2011)
14. Yang, H., Yi, Z., Jingying, H., Shiyong, L.: Organic light-emitting devices with double-block layer. Microelectron. J. **37**(11), 1271–1275 (2006)
15. ATLAS User's Manual Device Simulation Software. Silvaco International Ltd., Santa Clara, USA (2016)
16. Kumar, B., Kaushik, B.K., Negi, Y.S.: Modeling of top and bottom contact structure organic field effect transistors. J. Vac. Sci. Technol. B Microelectron. Nanometer Struct. **31**(1), 012401-1–012401-7 (2013)
17. Kaushik, B.K., Kumar, B., Prajapati, S., Mittal, P.: Organic Thin-Film Transistor Applications: Materials to Circuits. CRC Press/Taylor and Francis, UK (2016)

# Improved Gate Modulation in Tunnel Field Effect Transistors with Non-rectangular Tapered Y-Gate Geometry

Rakhi Narang[1], Mridula Gupta[2], and Manoj Saxena[3(✉)]

[1] Sri Venkateswara College, University of Delhi, New Delhi 110021, India
rakhinarang@gmail.com
[2] Department of Electronic Science, University of Delhi,
South Campus, New Delhi 110021, India
mridula@south.du.ac.in
[3] Deen Dayal Upadhyaya College, University of Delhi,
Sector-3, Dwarka, New Delhi 110078, India
msaxena@ieee.org

**Abstract.** In this work, a novel approach has been investigated to overcome one of the major issue faced by Tunnel FETs i.e. its low drive current or On-current. The approach employed in the present work makes use of a non-rectangular tapered gate electrode geometry which helps in concentrating the electric field lines emanating from gate electrode towards the source/channel tunneling junction which results in enhancement in the band-to-band tunneling current.

**Keywords:** Tunnel FET · Fringing-field · Simulation · Tapered
Gate modulation · On-current

## 1 Introduction

Tunnel FET is the emerging research device (ERD) considered to be a bright contender for the energy efficient ultra-fast switching applications owing to their steep sub-threshold behavior which can enable threshold voltage and power supply scaling [1, 2]. But there are still some challenges to be conquered before TFET can replace the mature and mainstream CMOS technology [3]. The most prominent drawbacks of TFET which requires immediate attention are the low on-state current and high Miller capacitance.

Earlier reports have shown that the fringing field effect from high-k gate oxide (when deposited only over the channel region as in the case of self-aligned process) improves the performance of n-TFET and deteriorates the performance of a p-TFET [4, 5]. Moreover, the impact of using spacers has also been proposed to improve the performance due to the strengthening of gate to source field close to the tunneling junction [6]. In conventional planar MOSFET/TFET architectures the gate electrode which usually lies above the complete channel region (except underlap structures) controls the current conduction. The electric field from gate electrode is

© Springer Nature Singapore Pte Ltd. 2017
B. K. Kaushik et al. (Eds.): VDAT 2017, CCIS 711, pp. 463–473, 2017.
https://doi.org/10.1007/978-981-10-7470-7_46

perpendicular to the channel region and this field also influences the source/drain region through fringing field lines. For MOSFET operation the gate controllability is required uniformly all along the channel region, particularly at the centre of the channel region which results in lowering of the potential barrier and carrier transfer from source to channel. However, in case of TFET, the tunneling width at the source/ channel junction needs to be modified with the help of gate bias to control the current conduction. The conventional Silicon p-i-n TFET structure suffers from the impediment of lower on-state current because of wide tunneling barrier width and large bandgap [7, 8]. The current can be enhanced by improving the gate modulation at the tunneling junction. In order to do so, Line TFET [9] has been reported which helps in increasing the tunneling area and hence improved tunneling current, but a large gate capacitance. Apart from Line TFETs, the previous studies have reported alternative device designs such as III–V material based TFET, low band-gap material based TFETs, tunnel source/pocket doped TFET and gate all around nanowire type structure for improved gate control [10]. However, in this work, we propose a gate electrode engineered architecture having tapered gate sidewall; which is employed to enhance the gate control at the tunneling junction which results in improved electric field and hence enhanced tunneling. Few patents and experimental demonstrations have also shown the advantage of forming tapered gate electrode [11, 12]. The inversely tapered gate has reportedly been able to overcome the problem of high gate resistance which arises when gate length is scaled [13]. Similar kind of approach has also been extensively used in HEMTs in the form of T-gate and Y-gate to reduce the gate length and also for reducing the gate to source capacitance. The Y-gate process steps using an i-line stepper has been reported in literature for fabricating AlGaN/GaN and InAlN/GaN HEMTs [14, 15]. The process flow of the PNPN n-MOSFET fabrication is described in [16].

## 2   Simulation Methodology

The device under study is an n-type p-n-i-n SOI-TFET with gate length of 100 nm, channel length of 95 nm and 5 nm pocket width, spacer extensions of 50 nm over source and drain as shown in Fig. 1(a) and (b). The details about the device parameters are summarized in Table 1.

Moreover, the junctions are assumed to be abrupt [17]. The device is created in structure and mesh editor Dev-Edit and the characterizations are done using device simulation software Atlas [18]. The following physics based models have been invoked while simulation: Shockley-Read-Hall Recombination model, concentration and field dependent mobility model, trap assisted tunneling model, non-local band-to-band tunneling model with default parameters. In order to ensure fair comparison, the device structures for both MOSFET and TFET (Fig. 1) considered in this study are similar in terms of physical geometry, gate electrode geometry; the major difference among these devices is the dissimilar source and drain doping type for TFET as opposed to similarly doped source and drain for MOSFET (Fig. 1(c)) and a heavily doped pocket between source and channel in case of TFET. Moreover, the off current levels for both MOSFET and TFET are optimized to have a similar value by tuning the gate electrode work-function. The on-current levels cannot be made similar as it will require an impractical gate electrode work-function value for TFET to reach on-current levels similar to that of MOSFET.

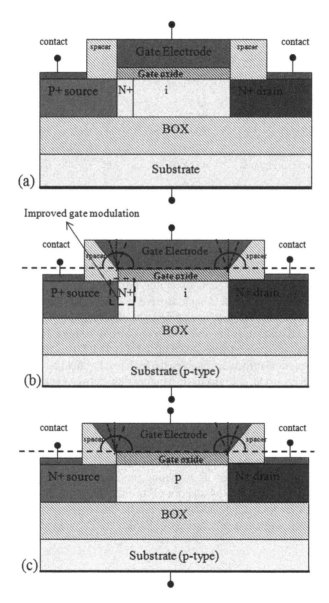

**Fig. 1.** (a) Conventional p-n-p-n TFET (b) Y-gate n-TFET with tapered gate electrode (c) Y-gate n-MOSFET

**Table 1.** Device parameters used in the study

| Parameter | TFET | MOSFET |
|---|---|---|
| Spacer dielectric | $SiO_2$ | $SiO_2$ |
| Gate thickness | 30 nm | 30 nm |
| Source doping | $10^{20}/cm^3$ | $10^{20}/cm^3$ |
| Drain doping | $10^{20}/cm^3$ | $10^{20}/cm^3$ |
| Channel doping | Intrinsic | $10^{15}/cm^3$ |
| Pocket doping | $2 \times 10^{19}/cm^3$ | – |
| Substrate doping | $10^{16}/cm^3$ | $10^{16}/cm^3$ |
| Gate oxide thickness ($HfO_2$) | 5 nm | 5 nm |
| Channel thickness | 25 nm | 25 nm |
| Channel length | 95 nm | 100 nm |
| Pocket thickness | 5 nm | – |
| BOX thickness | 40 nm | 40 nm |
| Tapering angle w.r.t. horizontal channel | 45°, 60°, 90° and 135° | 45°, 60°, 90° and 135° |

## 3    Results and Discussion

The tapered gate electrode sidewall results in the concentration of fringing field lines near the source/channel and drain/channel junctions, which results in enhancement of the electric field influencing the channel region (Fig. 2 (a)–(d)).

As the gate electrode sidewall is made tapered instead of the conventional perpendicular geometry (i.e. 90° with respect to channel), the electric field will start building up in the sharp corner and influences the underneath channel by fringing field effect. The field is strongest for the 45° tapered gate side wall p-n-i-n TFET structure due to following factors; the fringing field effect arising from the high level of field build-up near the sharp corner of the gate electrode, gate electrode fringing field between gate electrode edge and source/drain surface as well as due to the reverse biased heavily doped source pocket junction as evident through electric field contour plot in Fig. 2(a)–(d). The surface potential at the junction is more steeper and the tunneling barrier width is reduced when the angle becomes lower than 90° as depicted through Fig. 3(a) and (b). The enhanced electric field leads to improvement in drive current and reduction of threshold voltage of Silicon p-n-i-n TFET because of its tunneling junction governed current conduction phenomena as evident from Figs. 4 and 5(a). Since the impact of changing the tapering angle is negligible on the surface potential in the channel region and the energy bands, there is hardly any change in drain current of MOSFET (Figs. 4 and 5(c)).

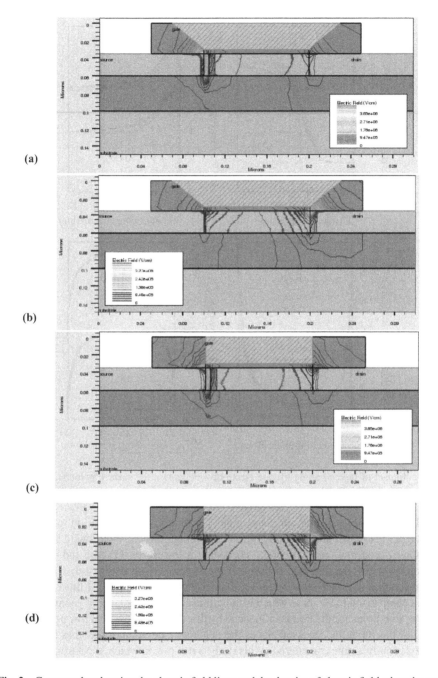

**Fig. 2.** Contour plot showing the electric field lines and the density of electric field when the gate electrode is rectangular (90°) and when it is tapered (45°) (a), (b) TFET, (c) & (d) MOSFET. Vgs = 0.1 V, Vds = 1 V

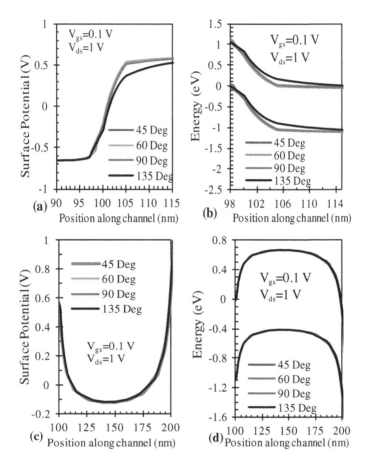

**Fig. 3.** Impact of tapered angle of gate electrode sidewall on the surface potential and energy bands of (a), (b) TFET and (c), (d) MOSFET.

The impact of gate angle on the average sub-threshold swing and on to off current ratio ($I_{on}/I_{off}$) is shown in inset of Fig. 4(a). The average sub-threshold swing is calculated over three decades of current change. The swing is lowest for 90° case and the $I_{on}/I_{off}$ is maximum for 60° (because the off current is low in comparison to 45° case). However, the on state current ($I_{on}$) increases nearly 2.5 times for the 45° case and 2.1 times for the 60° case in comparison to 90° case which is the prime advantage of tapered geometry TFET.

The ambipolar conduction is influenced by this tapered sidewall at low negative gate voltages, but the influence weakens as the negative gate voltage becomes high. Since the device architecture considered in this study is p-n-p-n, in which, the n+ doped pocket between the p+ source and lightly p-doped channel region helps in reducing the tunnel barrier width, improving the lateral electric field at the tunneling junction and results in improvement of on state current. Since the tunneling barrier width is quite low and the electric field is very high, the influence of fringing field effect is more prominent at the highly doped reverse biased p+-n+ tunneling junction for positive gate voltages as also

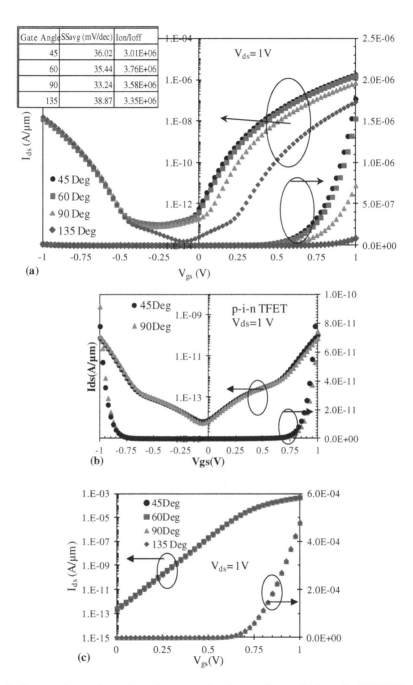

**Fig. 4.** Impact of gate electrode angle on transfer characteristics of (a) p-n-i-n TFET (b) p-i-n TFET and (c) MOSFET and. Inset of (a) shows average sub-threshold swing and $I_{on}/I_{off}$ ratio at various gate angles.

evident from Fig. 4(a). Whereas at drain/channel junction (although drain doping concentration is equal and opposite of source doping) the barrier width is quite high because of the reverse biased applied to the drain region, the impact of fringing field effect is negligibly low and thus ambipolar current does not change much with the change in gate angle. This is the reason that the influence of tapered Y-gate electrode is quite weak on a p-i-n architecture as compared to p-n-p-n as shown in Fig. 4(b). Moreover, p-i-n TFET exhibits an almost symmetric behaviour for positive and negative gate voltage as the source and drain are symmetrically and oppositely doped.

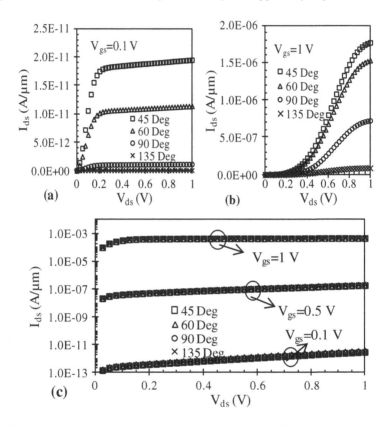

**Fig. 5.** Drain current characteristics of (a), (b) TFET and (c) MOSFET and the impact of tapered gate electrode angle.

An important aspect which influences the digital performance of TFET based circuits is the Miller effect which is quite prominent in TFET due to asymmetric distribution of total gate capacitance among gate-source and gate-drain capacitance. The Miller effect influences the input capacitance (i.e. in case of an amplifier the input capacitance is the product of feedback capacitance and the gain of the amplifier). The feedback capacitance in case of MOSFET/TFET is $C_{gd}$ which is the dominant part of the total gate capacitance $C_{gg}$ in TFETs. The high $C_{gd}$ value of load TFET of an inverter circuit results in high overshoot voltage during transient analysis [8] and thus hampers the circuit performance.

The gate electrode sidewall tapering may result in variation in the capacitance components due to the fringing field effect and thus an analysis of the capacitance voltage characteristics of MOSFET and TFET has also been carried out.

The C-V characteristics of TFET shows that $C_{gd}$ comprises the major portion of total gate capacitance $C_{gg}$ and $C_{gs}$ forms a negligibly small portion of $C_{gg}$ in both linear and saturation regions (Fig. 6(a)). Whereas in case of MOSFET, gate capacitance is equally partitioned between $C_{gs}$ and $C_{gd}$ in the linear region, but $C_{gs}$ dominates in the saturation region (Fig. 6(b)). However, the tapering introduces a negligibly small change in the capacitance components of both TFET and MOSFET as can be observed through Fig. 6 because of low-k dielectric spacer ($SiO_2$). With the usage of a high-k spacer the fringing field increases the total gate capacitance as shown in Fig. 7 which is actually not required from the power dissipation point of the view. Therefore, it is better to use high-k dielectric for gate oxide and a low-k for spacer layer.

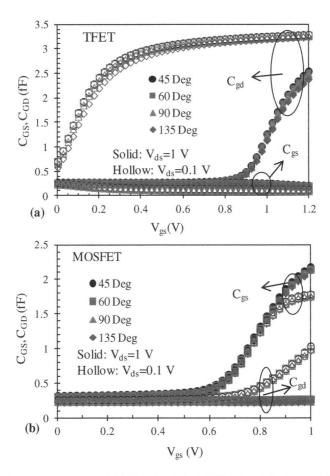

**Fig. 6.** Capacitance components of (a) TFET and (b) MOSFET and the impact of tapered gate electrode angle

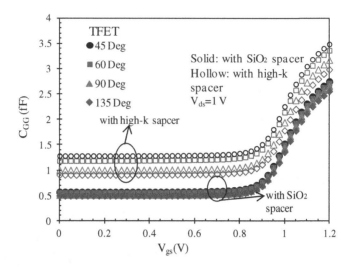

**Fig. 7.** C-V characteristics of Y-gate TFET and MOSFET and the impact of tapered gate electrode angle along with the spacer dielectric constant.

# 4   Conclusion

Thus, in conclusion this work presents an alternative method of using tapered gate electrode geometry to improve the problem of low drain current faced by Silicon tunnel FETs which can prove to be beneficial for fabricating TFETs having high drive current with the matured and widely used Silicon Technology. Although the scaling of Tunnel FETs does not pose challenges in terms of short channel deteriorating effects till the physical gate/channel length is more than 4 times the natural scaling length, but the tapered gate electrode can further curtail the impact of the high gate resistance while scaling the device.

**Acknowledgment.** Authors would like to thank Council of Scientific & Industrial Research (CSIR), India (File No. 22(0724)/17/EMR-II)

# References

1. Seabaugh, A.C., Zhang, Q.: Low-voltage tunnel transistors for beyond CMOS logic. Proc. IEEE **98**, 2095–2110 (2010)
2. Lu, H., Seabaugh, A.: Tunnel field-effect transistors: state-of-the-art. IEEE J. Electron Dev. Soc. **2**(4), 44–49 (2014)
3. Avci, U.E., Morris, D.H., Young, I.A.: Tunnel field-effect transistors: prospects and challenges. IEEE J. Electron Dev. Soc. **3**(3), 88–95 (2015)
4. Virani, H.G., Adari, R.B.R., Kottantharayil, A.: Dual-spacer device architecture for the improvement of performance of silicon n-channel tunnel FETs. IEEE Trans. Electron Dev. **57**, 2410–2417 (2010)

5. Lee, G., Jang, J.-S., Choi, W.Y.: Dual-dielectric-constant spacer hetero-gate-dielectric tunneling field-effect transistors. Semicond. Sci. Technol. **28**, 052001 (2013)
6. Schlosser, M., Bhuwalka, K.K., Sauter, M., Zilbauer, T., Sulima, T., Eisele, I.: Fringing-induced drain current improvement in the tunnel field-effect transistor with high-k gate dielectrics. IEEE Trans. Electron Dev. **56**, 100–108 (2009)
7. Ionescu, A.M., Riel, H.: Tunnel field-effect transistors as energy-efficient electronic switches. Nature **479**(7373), 329–337 (2011)
8. Biswas, A.: Tunnel field effect transistors: from steep-slope electronic switches to energy efficient logic applications. Ph.D. dissertation, École Polytechnique Fédérale De Lausanne (2015)
9. Biswas, A., Alper, C., Michielis, L.D., Ionescu, A.M.: New tunnel-FET architecture with enhanced I ON and improved Miller Effect for energy efficient switching. In: Proceedings of 70th Annual Device Research Conference (DRC), Pennsylvania, USA, pp. 131–132 (2012)
10. Datta, S., Liu, H., Narayanan, V.: Tunnel FET technology: a reliability perspective. Microelectron. Reliab. **54**, 861–874 (2014)
11. Chang, C.P., Pai, C.S., Vuong, T.H.H.: MOSFET with tapered gate and method of manufacturing it. European Patent, EP1091414 A2 (2001)
12. Oh, H.S., Cha, S.J.: Field effect transistors having tapered gate electrodes for providing high breakdown voltage capability and methods of forming same. US Patent, US6046474 A (2000)
13. Kuroi, T., Itoh, Y., Horita, K., Shiozawa, K.: Semiconductor device including inversely tapered gate electrode and manufacturing method thereof. US Patent, US6661066 B2 (2003)
14. Ichikawa, H., Makabe, I., Kouchi, T., Nakata, K., Inoue, K.: InAlN/GaN HEMTs with over 100-GHz fT using an improved Y-gate process by an i-line stepper. In: Proceedings of International Conference on Compound Semiconductor Manufacturing Technology, Arizona, USA, pp. 225–228 (2015)
15. Ichikawa, H., Mizue, C., Makabe, I., Tateno, Y., Nakata, K., Inoue, K.: AlGaN/GaN HEMTs versus InAlN/GaN HEMTs fabricated by 150-nm Y-gate process. In: Proceedings of Asia Pacific Microwave Conference (APMC), Japan, pp. 780–782 (2014)
16. Nagavarapu, V., Jhaveri, R., Woo, J.C.S.: The tunnel source (PNPN) n-MOSFET: a novel high performance transistor. IEEE Trans. Electron Devices **55**(4), 103–1019 (2008)
17. Han, G., Yee, Y.S., Guo, P., Yang, Y., Fan, L., Zhan, C., Yeo, Y.-C.: Enhancement of TFET performance using dopant profile-steepening implant and source dopant concentration engineering at tunneling junction. In: Proceedings of Silicon Nanoelectronics Workshop, pp. 1–2 (2010)
18. Atlas User's Manual, "Device simulation software," SILVACO International Inc., 5.16.3.R

# A 36 nW Power Management Unit for Solar Energy Harvesters Using 0.18 μm CMOS

Purvi Patel$^{(\boxtimes)}$, Biswajit Mishra$^{(\boxtimes)}$, and Dipankar Nagchoudhuri

VLSI and Embedded Systems Research Group, DA-IICT, Gandhinagar 382007, India
{201521008,biswajit_mishra,dipankar_nagchoudhuri}@daiict.ac.in

**Abstract.** This work presents the design of ultra low power (ULP) management unit to be used in conjunction with tiny solar cells or energy harvesters providing very low power for wireless sensor node (WSN) applications for energy autonomy. The power management unit (PMU) is implemented using 0.18 μm CMOS in subthreshold region of MOSFET for reduced power consumption with increased efficiency. It regulates the output voltage at 0.95 V and 0.968 V when the input voltages are 0.98 V and 1.33 V, respectively and achieves maximum 72.3% efficiency. The proposed PMU consumes 36 nW and 56 nW of power, at input voltages of 0.98 V and 1.33 V, respectively, thereby making it suitable for ultra low voltage, low power applications.

**Keywords:** Nanowatt PMU · ULP · Energy harvesting
0.18 μm CMOS

## 1 Introduction

Emerging ULP applications require energy harvesters for complete energy autonomy [1], where battery replacement is cumbersome. Energy harvesting from solar, thermal, piezo, electromagnetic, RF and several other techniques exist that convert micro harvested energy to useful electrical energy [2]. Out of these, solar energy harvesting is widely adopted as it is abundantly available and is affordable with an acceptable power output, that is ideal for ULP applications. Furthermore, with several of these tiny cells together, it is possible to meet the energy budget of the ULP systems. However, it is difficult to power up the system directly from these energy harvesters and often require to undergo level conversions using low dropout (LDO) regulation circuits. Hence, power management is necessary to regulate the harvested energy or voltage in PMU circuits to get a stable power supply [3].

In many battery powered systems, lower input voltages are exploited using novel circuits [4]. This offers opportunity for ULP applications powered by energy harvesters. This is because the voltage output of many DC harvesters such as solar cells have a variable voltage output between 0.3 V to 0.5 V. This variable voltage can further be regulated in the range of sub 1 V with the help of charge pump [3,5–7] and LDOs for the standard electronic circuits to operate [3–7].

© Springer Nature Singapore Pte Ltd. 2017
B. K. Kaushik et al. (Eds.): VDAT 2017, CCIS 711, pp. 474–486, 2017.
https://doi.org/10.1007/978-981-10-7470-7_47

To achieve higher efficiency of these ULP circuits, it is typically designed using switched capacitor or charge pump circuits and then regulating the output voltage using very low power LDOs [5–7]. There have been numerous efforts in designing very low voltage and low power PMUs for ULP systems [4–7].

In this paper, we propose an energy harvesting PMU for solar harvesters. The proposed design of the PMU is carried out with the primary goal of low power dissipation in the PMU circuit itself along with higher efficiency. We have used a combination of low voltage subthreshold circuits and standard CMOS circuits to achieve the same. The design achieves an improvement in terms of performance, power and efficiency when compared to similar work in the literature.

This paper is organized as follows: In Sect. 2, the architecture of the proposed system is discussed. In Sect. 3, the design considerations of the PMU is discussed. Section 4 discusses various blocks of the PMU. In Sect. 5, simulation results are discussed. In Sect. 6, the conclusion and future work is discussed.

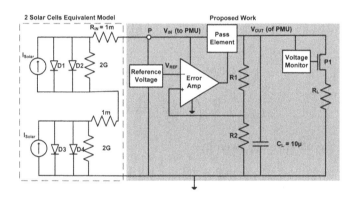

**Fig. 1.** Block diagram of the proposed work

## 2    Proposed Architecture

The proposed PMU shown in Fig. 1, consists of a voltage regulator and a voltage monitor with resistors and capacitors. The voltage regulator circuit comprises of a reference voltage block, an error amplifier, a pass element, and a resistor divider block. Regulating resistors R1 and R2 provide variable resistance and continuously adjust the voltage divider network in order to maintain constant voltage at the output ($V_{OUT}$). The output voltage, across the load capacitor $C_L$ is given by:

$$V_{OUT} = V_{REF} \left[ 1 + \left( \frac{R1}{R2} \right) \right] \tag{1}$$

The error amplifier compares the reference voltage $V_{REF}$, with the sampled voltage from the resistor divider to control the current flowing through the pass element, which further regulates the output voltage ($V_{OUT}$).

The voltage monitor checks whether sufficient output voltage for the load circuit is available using a comparator circuit. The comparator circuit checks as soon as the regulator output voltage decreases below an acceptable pre-defined lower threshold voltage kept at $0.6V_{OUT}$ in our discussion, where the voltage monitor disconnects the load resistor $R_L$ from the supply voltage via the switch P1. It is to be noted that the value of output capacitor $C_L$ should be of reasonable value (typically few μF) to respond to the amplifier for ULP operation [8].

## 3    Design Considerations

The proposed PMU has all the blocks operated in subthreshold region, except the pass element. Following conditions are therefore necessary for designing the sub-circuits: $|V_{TH}| > |V_{GS}|$ and $|V_{DS}| \geq 100\,\mathrm{mV}$

The drain current [9] in the subthreshold region for NMOS and PMOS is calculated as:

$$I_D = I_0 \frac{W}{L} \left(1 - e^{\frac{|V_{GS}|-|V_{TH}|}{\eta V_T}}\right) \left(1 - e^{\frac{-|V_{DS}|}{\eta V_T}}\right) \tag{2}$$

considering $\left(1 - e^{\frac{-|V_{DS}|}{\eta V_T}}\right) \equiv 1$, the drain current becomes,

$$I_D = I_0 \frac{W}{L} \left(1 - e^{\frac{|V_{GS}|-|V_{TH}|}{\eta V_T}}\right) \tag{3}$$

where, $I_0$ is the off current, given by:

$$I_0 = 2 \times \mu C_{ox} \times \eta \times V_T{}^2 \tag{4}$$

where, $\frac{W}{L}$ is the aspect ratio of the transistor. $|V_{GS}|$ and $|V_{DS}|$ are gate to source and drain to source voltage respectively. $|V_{TH}|$ is the threshold voltage of the MOSFET and $V_T$ is the thermal voltage. Subthreshold slope parameter $\eta$ is typically in the range $1 < \eta < 2$ [9], μ is the mobility of the carriers of the MOS devices and $C_{ox}$ is the gate oxide capacitance.

The transconductance and the output resistance of the MOSFET in the subthreshold region is given by:

$$g_m = \frac{I_D}{\eta V_T}; \qquad R_{out} = \frac{\eta V_T}{\lambda I_D} \tag{5}$$

where, $\lambda$ is the channel length modulation parameter.

As shown in Fig. 4, the error amplifier compares the reference voltage with the sampled voltage [10]. The amplifier is designed with a gain parameter $A_V$;

$$A_V = g_{meq} \times R_{out} \tag{6}$$

where, $g_{meq}$ is the overall transconductance and $R_{out}$ is the equivalent output resistance of the amplifier,

$$g_{meq} = g_{m1} \times g_{m3} \tag{7}$$

$$R_{out} = (R_{o1} \parallel R_{o2}) \times R_{o3} \times R_{o4} \times R_{o5} \qquad (8)$$

where, $g_{m1}$ and $g_{m3}$ are the transconductances of the M1 and M3 transistors and $R_{o1}$, $R_{o2}$, $R_{o3}$, $R_{o4}$ and $R_{o5}$ are the output resistances of the transistors M1, M2, M3, M4 and M5 of the error amplifier respectively as shown in Fig. 4.

Further to this, Table 1 consists of the model parameters that are considered for the transistor dimensions to be used in the design of the sub-circuits.

**Table 1.** Model parameters

| Parameter | PMOS | NMOS |
|---|---|---|
| Threshold voltage, $V_{th}(V)$ | $-0.518$ | $0.4616$ |
| Technology parameter, $k = \mu C_{ox}(A/V^2)$ | $0.0625\,\mathrm{m}$ | $0.316\,\mathrm{m}$ |
| Subthreshold slop factor, $\eta$ | $1.6$ | $1.4$ |
| Channel length modulation parameter, $\lambda(V^{-1})$ | $-0.95$ | $0.92$ |

Firstly, a proportional to absolute temperature (PTAT) current reference of 1 nA using drain current Eq. (3) and off current Eq. (4) is designed. With the help of this current reference, reference voltage and voltage divider circuits are designed. With the same current reference, bias voltage circuit for the error amplifier is designed. The bias voltages and current values are used for the sizing of the transistors within the amplifier. This error amplifier is further used as a comparator for the voltage monitor block discussed in the following section.

## 4    Sub Blocks of PMU

### 4.1    PTAT Current Reference

In current source the variation of the current output is proportional to the absolute temperature and the threshold voltage of a PMOS transistor is complementary to the absolute temperature (CTAT). Therefore, in the current reference for compensating these two effects, a PTAT current reference is designed [8]. The PTAT is used in the regulator, voltage reference and the error amplifier. As shown in Fig. 2a, the PTAT consists of M1 to M10 transistors, operating in the subthreshold region. A small PTAT voltage $V_R$ across the source of M2 is given as:

$$V_R = V_T ln \left( \frac{N_2}{N_1} \right) \qquad (9)$$

where, $\frac{N_2}{N_1}$ is the $\frac{W}{L}$ ratio of transistors M2 and M1 respectively. The voltage $V_R$, in Fig. 2a generates a PTAT current through the resistor R, which is used as a bias current for the reference voltage and the error amplifier, where,

$$I_{PTAT} = \frac{V_T}{R} ln \left( \frac{N_2}{N_1} \right) \qquad (10)$$

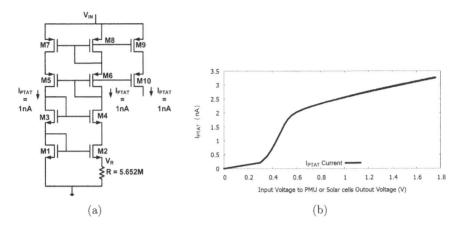

(a)                                                    (b)

**Fig. 2.** (a) PTAT Current Reference Block Diagram (b) PTAT Reference Current (nA)
vs. Input Voltage (V) of the PMU

To find out the response of the PTAT circuit, the PTAT current versus solar cells
output voltage is plotted in Fig. 2b. This is because the current reference circuit
is to be used in conjunction with the solar cells. As can be seen in Fig. 2b, the
PTAT current reference generates 2.56 nA current at $V_{IN} = 0.98$ V and 2.9 nA
at $V_{IN} = 1.33$ V, this input voltage $(V_{IN})$ to the PMU is same as the output
voltage generated from the solar cells. A slight change in the PTAT current from
2.56 nA to 2.9 nA, is observed with an increase in input voltage of the PMU from
0.98 V to 1.33 V.

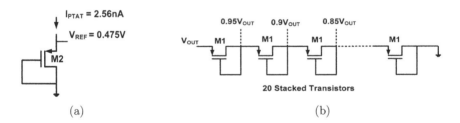

(a)                                                    (b)

**Fig. 3.** (a) Reference Voltage Block used for Error Amplifier (b) Reference Voltages
Generation for Voltage Monitor

## 4.2    Reference Voltage

As shown in Fig. 3a, the reference voltage $V_{REF}$, is generated using the 1 nA PTAT
current reference circuit and the MOS diode. The $V_{REF}$ is designed in such a way
that it produces constant voltage equal to half of the regulator output voltage. As
the reference voltage circuit generates 0.475 V voltage, the designed PMU regulates the output voltage to be at 0.95 V at an input voltage $V_{IN} = 0.98$ V from the
solar cells. The current consumption of the reference voltage circuit is 2.56 nA.

Reference voltages for the voltage monitor are designed with the help of stacked transistors [4] as shown in Fig. 3b. A total of 20 sized transistors are used to divide a voltage equivalent to 50 mV at each stage. From the 20 different voltages that are generated, $0.8V_{OUT}$ and $0.6V_{OUT}$ are used at the comparator output. This further helps in voltage monitor to generate Start and Stop conditions. Current consumption of the designed stacked transistors circuit is found to be 9 pA.

### 4.3  Error Amplifier

A two-stage operational amplifier is shown in Fig. 4. The cascoded gain stage helps in achieving high open loop voltage gain [8]. The error amplifier compares the reference voltage $V_{REF}$ with the sampled voltage from the resistive divider comprising of R1 and R2 (see Fig. 1). The error amplifier also ensures that current passing through the pass element is inversely proportional to the output voltage. To obtain ULP operation, this amplifier is designed in the subthreshold region, where the current consumption of the error amplifier is very low and found to be 11.8 nA at $V_{IN} = 0.98$ V. The frequency response of the amplifier is shown in Fig. 5 with 46.39 dB gain and unity gain bandwidth (UGB) at 206 kHz.

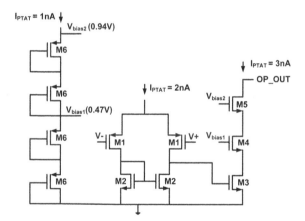

**Fig. 4.** Two stage operational amplifier with cascoded gain stage

The biasing circuit for $V_{bias1}$ and $V_{bias2}$ shown in Fig. 4, is designed with the help of four diode connected MOS transistors and the 1 nA PTAT current reference. The bias voltages $V_{bias1}$ and $V_{bias2}$ are 0.47 V and 0.94 V, respectively at the input voltage ($V_{IN}$) of 0.98 V. By modifying the resistor R in the PTAT current reference (see Fig. 2a), different $I_{PTAT}$ currents can be obtained. In our case, this resistor R is set to be 2.77 MΩ and 1.84 MΩ to obtain 2 nA and 3 nA PTAT currents, respectively.

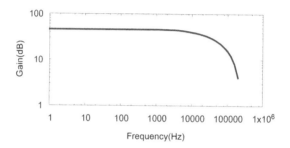

**Fig. 5.** Frequency response of the error amplifier

## 4.4  Pass Element and Voltage Divider

The pass element shown in Fig. 6a, is used to allow the excess input current to the load from the input source. It consists of two PMOS in series, where the M1 and M2 are biased with the output voltage of the error amplifier (OP_OUT) and $V_{bias1}$, respectively. Pass element controls the current delivered to the output capacitor. For a proper operation of the PMU, the pass element is designed in the strong inversion region [11]. To accommodate the deliverable current requirement ($\sim 1\,\text{mA}$), the dimension of the pass element is kept at $\frac{600\,\mu m}{180\,nm}$. The voltage divider or the resistive divider circuit shown in Fig. 6b at the output of the regulator is used to compare the output voltage $V_{OUT}$ with the reference voltage $V_{REF}$. In order to divide the voltage equally across R1 and R2, values of R1 and R2 should be equal, ensuring that $V_{REF}$ is half the value of the $V_{OUT}$. The resistors are diode connected MOSFETs. As shown in Fig. 7, reference voltage generates 0.475 V voltage at $V_{IN} = 0.98$ V using $I_{PTAT} = 2.56\,\text{nA}$. It is also shown that the proposed PMU regulates $V_{OUT} = 0.99$ V, for $V_{IN} = 1.76$ V in no load condition. The variation in $V_{REF}$ when $V_{IN}$ changes is shown in Fig. 7, where a 30 mV slope is observed at $V_{REF}$ when $V_{IN}$ changes by 780 mV (from 0.98 V to 1.76 V).

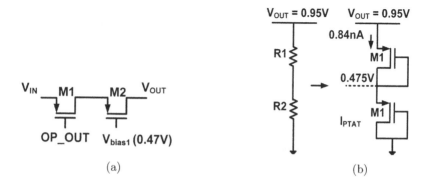

**Fig. 6.** (a) Pass Element for the Error Amplifier (b) Voltage Divider

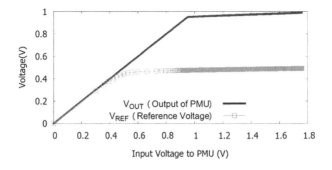

**Fig. 7.** Reference and Output Voltage of the PMU

## 4.5 Voltage Monitor

As shown in Fig. 8a, the voltage monitor [4] consists of two comparators and a DFF (D flip-flop) with an active low reset. The output voltage is regulated with DFF providing the Start/Stop signal for enabling or disabling the PMOS switch P1. It starts to generate the start signal at 0.76 V ($= 0.8 \times 0.95$ V) and the stop signal at 0.57 V ($= 0.6 \times 0.95$ V) as shown in Fig. 8b. The upper and lower threshold voltages for voltage monitor are fixed at $0.8V_{OUT}$ ($\sim 0.8$ V) and $0.6V_{OUT}$ ($\sim 0.6$ V). The values can be altered depending on the application. As soon as the regulator output voltage reaches the upper threshold voltage 0.8 V, voltage monitor connects the load (say an WSN) to the $V_{OUT}$ via the switch P1. It disconnects the load resistor $R_L$ from the output of the regulator as soon as the regulator output voltage decreases below the lower threshold voltage of 0.6 V. This ensures that sufficient energy is available for the WSN for reliable operation.

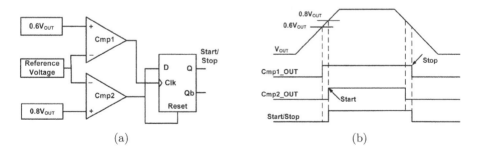

**Fig. 8.** Voltage Monitor (a) Block Diagram of Voltage Monitor (b) Ideal Response of Voltage Monitor

As can be seen in Fig. 8a, the output of first comparator Cmp1, is driven by lower threshold voltage and is connected to the clock terminal of DFF. The

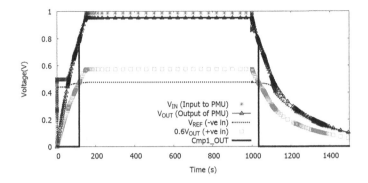

**Fig. 9.** Comparator output

output of second comparator Cmp2, is driven by upper threshold voltage, and is connected to the D input and the active low reset input. The ideal response of the voltage monitor is shown in Fig. 8b. During the operation of the voltage monitor, output of Cmp1 goes to logic high, when the regulator output voltage goes higher than 0.8 V (Start enabled). The output of Cmp2 will be logic low when the regulator output voltage becomes less than 0.6 V (Start disabled or Stop enabled). Approximately, 22 nA of current is consumed by the voltage monitor circuit. Out of which, 11 nA is consumed in each comparator and 10.16 pA is consumed in the DFF.

The transient behavior of the Cmp1 is shown in Fig. 9. As can be seen, when the positive terminal of the Cmp1, is at a higher voltage than 0.475 V ($V_{REF}$), the output Cmp1_$OUT$ is at logic high.

## 5    Simulation Results and Discussion

The schematic simulations were carried out for different sub-blocks of the PMU, using 0.18 μm CMOS physical models. The output capacitor is chosen as 10 μF, a sufficient value for ULP WSN applications.

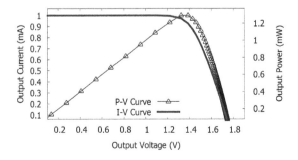

**Fig. 10.** I-V, P-V curves of the two series connected solar cells

In the simulation, input voltage for the PMU is generated by two series connected solar cells [12]. The I-V and P-V characteristics of the solar cells are shown in Fig. 10, where the solar cells equivalent model is characterized by short circuit current $I_{SC} = 1\,mA$ and the open circuit voltage $V_{OC} = 1.76\,V$. These solar cells can deliver upto 1.29 mW of maximum power to the PMU.

Two different conditions: one for low and the other for high input power are considered and discussed in the following sub-section. It is done to show the lower and higher boundaries of the PMU operation.

## 5.1   Analysis for Lower Value of Input Power

Various voltages are used for comparison in the voltage monitor is shown in Fig. 11. With $I_{Solar} = 70\,nA$, $V_{IN} = 0.98\,V$ and the $V_{OUT} = 0.95\,V$ is observed. Therefore, $0.8V_{OUT}$ is equivalent to 0.76 V and $0.6V_{OUT}$ is equivalent to 0.57 V, is fed to the comparator block with that Start and Stop signals enabled correctly. We observed that out of the total current passing through the circuit, 32 nA current is delivered to the $R_L$ and the rest 38 nA is consumed by the PMU. The complete transient response of the voltage monitor is shown in Fig. 12.

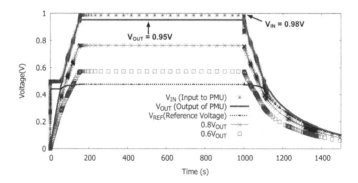

**Fig. 11.** Voltages used for comparison at lower input current

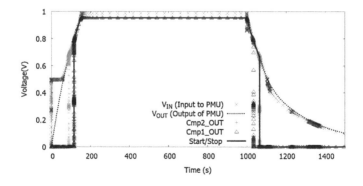

**Fig. 12.** Response of voltage monitor block

## 5.2    Analysis for Higher Value of Input Power

For a higher current, the simulation is carried out and is shown in Fig. 13. Input voltage $V_{IN} = 1.33$ V and $V_{OUT} = 0.968$ V are obtained at the input current, $I_{Solar} \sim 1$ mA. Out of which 42 nA is consumed by the PMU the rest is deliver to $R_L$. Figure 14 presents the maximum linear regulator efficiency and regulator output voltage variation with the load current. As can be seen, the proposed PMU has a maximum efficiency of 72.3%. The PMU can also work with the higher load currents to a maximum of 1 mA. The output voltage is seen to be slightly decreased at a higher load current as shown in Fig. 14.

The current and power consumption of individual block of the PMU for both input voltages at 0.98 V and 1.33 V are shown in Table 2. The proposed PMU consumes 36 nW and 56 nW at $V_{IN} = 0.98$ V and $V_{IN} = 1.33$ V, respectively. Furthermore, Table 3 compares the proposed PMU with the current work discussed in literature. From the Table 3, it can be concluded that proposed PMU has comparable power consumption and efficiency with respect to the mentioned work [4,5,7,13].

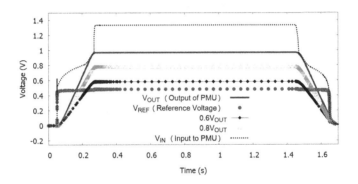

**Fig. 13.** Voltages used for comparison at higher input current

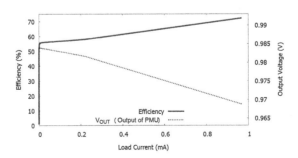

**Fig. 14.** Load analysis and PMU efficiency

**Table 2.** Power and Current consumption

| Block | Sub-block | Current (A) (@ 0.98 V) | Power (W) (@ 0.98 V) | Current (A) (@ 1.33 V) | Power (W) (@ 1.33 V) |
|---|---|---|---|---|---|
| Regulator | Error amplifier | 11.8n | 11.2n | 14.7n | 20n |
| | Reference voltage | 2.56n | 2.43n | 2.9n | 4n |
| | Voltage divider | 0.84n | 0.8n | 0.97n | 1.3n |
| | Pass element | 1.5p | 1.43p | 2p | 2.7p |
| Voltage | Two comparators | 21.8n | 20.7n | 22.15n | 29.5n |
| Monitor | DFF | 10.16p | 9.65p | 10.32p | 13.7p |
| @PMU | - | 38n[*] | 36n | 42n[*] | 56n |

[*] 1 nA current is consumed by insulation resistor kept in parallel with load capacitor to reduce leakage current through capacitor. Hence total current consumption and power consumption of the proposed PMU becomes 38 nA and 36 nW @0.98 V, and 42 nA and 56 nW @1.33 V, respectively.

**Table 3.** Performance comparison to reference works

| Parameter | Proposed work | [4] | [5] | [7] | [13][*] |
|---|---|---|---|---|---|
| Process | 0.18 μm | 0.18 μm | 0.13 μm | 0.18 μm | 65 nm |
| Output voltage regulation (V) | 0.95 | 1.8 | 1.4 | 1.0 | - |
| Load current (mA) | 1.0 | 25 | 0.005 | 0.6–1.1 | - |
| Max efficiency (%) | 72.3 | - | 58 | 70 | - |
| Power dissipation (nW) | 36 | 655 | 1400 | - | 50 |

[*] [13] is for Voltage Monitor Block only.

# 6    Conclusion

The proposed work presents the design of an ULP capacitive solar PMU. The proposed PMU is focused mainly on low power circuit blocks working at sub-threshold voltages. Hence, all blocks of the PMU, except the pass element are designed in subthreshold region. At the input voltage of 0.98 V, the PMU regulates the output voltage to 0.95 V with 36nW of power consumption. For the input voltage of 1.33 V, it regulates the output voltage to 0.968 V with 56 nW power consumption and a maximum efficiency of 72.3%. The minimum voltage at which the PMU starts to operate is at 0.55 V and regulating the output at 0.98 V. Lower power consumption and better efficiency makes the PMU viable for various applications where low voltage, low power operations are required.

# References

1. Botteron, C., Briand, D., Mishra, B., Tasselli, G., Janphuang, P., Haug, F.J., Skrivervik, A., Lockhart, R., Robert, C., de Rooij, N.F., Farine, P.A.: A low-cost UWB sensor node powered by a piezoelectric harvester or solar cells. Sens. Actuators, A **239**, 127–136 (2016)

2. Bandyopadhyay, S., Chandrakasan, A.P.: Platform architecture for solar, thermal, and vibration energy combining with MPPT and single inductor. IEEE J. Solid-State Circuits **47**(9), 2199–2215 (2012)

3. Doms, I., Merken, P., Hoof, C.V., Mertens, R.P.: Capacitive power management circuit for micropower thermoelectric generators with a 1.4 μA controller. IEEE J. Solid-State Circuits **44**(10), 2824–2833 (2009)

4. Mishra, B., Botteron, C., Tasselli, G., Robert, C., Farine, P.A.: A sub-μA power management circuit in 0.18μm CMOS for energy harvesters. In: Design, Automation and Test in Europe Conference and Exhibition (DATE), pp. 1197–1202. IEEE (2013)

5. Shih, Y.C., Otis, B.P.: An inductorless DC-DC converter for energy harvesting with a 1.2 μW bandgap-referenced output controller. IEEE Trans. Circuits Syst. II Express Briefs **58**(12), 832–836 (2011)

6. Kasodniya, S.K., Mishra, B., Desai, N.M.: Ultra low power capacitive power management unit in 0.18μm CMOS. In: 2016 International Conference on VLSI Systems, Architectures, Technology and Applications (VLSI-SATA), pp. 1–5. IEEE (2016)

7. Mondal, S., Paily, R.: An Efficient On-Chip Switched-Capacitor-Based Power Converter for a Microscale Energy Transducer. IEEE Transactions on Circuits and Systems II: Express Briefs, vol. **63**(3), 254–258 (2016)

8. Oporta, H.I.: An Ultra Low Power Frequency Reference for Timekeeping Applications, Master's Thesis, Oregon State University (2008)

9. Calhoun, B.H., Wang, A., Chandrakasan, A.: Modeling and sizing for minimum energy operation in subthreshold circuits. IEEE J. Solid-State Circuits **40**(9), 1778–1786 (2005)

10. Magnelli, L., Amoroso, F.A., Crupi, F., Cappuccino, G., Iannaccone, G.: Design of a 75-nW, 0.5-V subthreshold complementary metal-oxide-semiconductor operational amplifier. Int. J. Circuit Theory Appl. **42**(9), 967–977 (2014)

11. Allen, P.E., Holberg, D.R.: CMOS Analog Circuit Design. Oxford University Press, Oxford (2002)

12. Bonkoungou, D., Koalaga, Z., Njomo, D.: Modelling and simulation of photovoltaic module considering single-diode equivalent circuit model in MATLAB. Int. J. Emerg. Technol. Adv. Eng. **3**(3), 493–502 (2013)

13. Savanth, A., Weddell, A., Myers, J., Flynn, D., Al Hashimi, B.M.: A 50nW voltage monitor scheme for minimum energy sensor systems. In: 2017 30th International Conference on VLSI Design and 2017 16th International Conference on Embedded Systems (VLSID), pp. 81–86 (2017)

# A 10T Subthreshold SRAM Cell with Minimal Bitline Switching for Ultra-Low Power Applications

Swaati[✉] and Bishnu Prasad Das

Department of Electronics and Communication Engineering, IIT Roorkee, Roorkee, India
rajpoot.swaati@gmail.com, bpdasfec@iitr.ac.in

**Abstract.** High noise margins and low power dissipation are the major attributes of the SRAM cells used in ultra-low power applications. This paper proposes a 10T Static Random-Access memory (SRAM) with data aware dynamic feedback control and disturb free read which enhances the noise margins in the sub-threshold region. Exploiting the dynamic threshold MOS transistors (DTMOS) technique reduces the read access time of the proposed memory cell. As this cell offers single ended write operation with the bitlines kept at logic HIGH which leads to large saving in dynamic power due to charging/discharging operation on bitlines. Therefore, proposed SRAM reduces the activity factor of discharging the bitlines for each write pattern. The simulation has been carried out in 65 nm technology node to show the comparison among the existing techniques and proposed cell. The proposed memory cell has write static noise margin (WSNM) of 1.7x and 1.48x compared to iso-area 6T and Schmitt Trigger based (ST2) SRAM cells respectively at supply voltage of 300 mV. Read operation is data controlled which improves the read margin. Dynamic threshold technique increases read current for faster read operation. Read SNM is 2x, 1.16x and 1.4x of iso-area 6T, differential data aware 9T and Schmitt trigger SRAM (ST2) respectively. These features enable the cell for ultralow power applications.

**Keywords:** Activity factor · Dynamic power · SRAM · Subthreshold
Write margin

## 1 Introduction

Memory occupies major portion of chip area. It is anticipated that the memory area will increase further in future version of mobile electronic devices, high-end processor and microcontrollers. In order to increase the battery life of mobile devices, low power memory design is essential. Operating the memory in the sub-threshold region of the transistor can lead to significant reduction of power consumption due to the reduction of dynamic power, gate leakage and standby current of the design. Hence, sub-threshold memory is one of the viable option to achieve low power dissipation. Quadratic reduction in dynamic power and linear reduction in leakage power with respect to supply voltage can be achieved in subthreshold memory cell [1]. As reported in [2], 60% of the dynamic power in memory is due to the charging and discharging of the bitlines during

© Springer Nature Singapore Pte Ltd. 2017
B. K. Kaushik et al. (Eds.): VDAT 2017, CCIS 711, pp. 487–495, 2017.
https://doi.org/10.1007/978-981-10-7470-7_48

write operation. Reducing this dynamic power consumption will significantly improve the battery life of mobile devices.

In the subthreshold region, the data stability of memory cell is severely affected due to (1) the reduction in on-current to off-current ratio ($Ion/Ioff$), (2) local threshold voltage variation and (3) reduction in supply voltage [3]. The traditional 6T Static Random-Access Memory (SRAM) cannot behave properly under such stringent constraints. Several read and write assist techniques have been proposed to improve read and write stability of 6T SRAM which include virtual-ground (CVSS) bias [4, 5], differential CVSS [6], boosted [7] or reduced wordline voltage [7], dual supply scheme [8, 7], and write back schemes [4]. Even with these techniques, the $V_{min}$ (minimum operating voltage) of 6T SRAM lies in the range of 0.45 V to 0.7 V.

Several architectures have been proposed in recent years that aim to increase the write and read stability by increasing number of transistors used by making one or more design modifications. Breaking the feedback between the inverters during write/read stage increase write/read stability as in 7T [9] and 7T [10] cells. However, the stability depends on the transistor that controls the feedback loop. Due to the impact of process variation, feedback may fail to work which leads to marginal benefit in cell stability. 8T [11] isolates storage nodes from the bitlines by inserting buffer between bitlines and storage nodes which improves read stability. However, the write margin remains low and read access delay is increased. The half select stability failure is one of the major issues of that work.

Several techniques to save dynamic write power have been proposed that includes reducing the voltage swing of bitlines and capacitance [12, 13]. In [13], extra logic circuitry in row decoder and DC-to-DC converters are used to precharge and discharge the bitlines which leads to increase in area, reduction in speed and noise margins. Reducing the capacitance of bitlines and wordlines and datalines leads to saving in dynamic write power of the SRAM cell.

In this paper, a new 10T subthreshold SRAM cell is proposed that provides high noise margins and reduced dynamic power dissipation without extra logic circuitry. The major contributions of the paper are as follows:

- The proposed 10T cell reduces the activity factor of SRAM cell to almost '0' during write operation by keeping both the bitlines at logic high value for write operations. The data to be written is managed by *WBL* and *WBLB* control signals.
- Read operation is disturb free by isolating storage nodes from bitlines. DTMOS (Dynamic threshold MOS) technique [14] in read operation reduces threshold voltage for faster read operation.
- As the read and write access transistors are different. They can be sized efficiently to improve the read and write SNMs.
- Leakage current is reduced due to stacking of pull down transistors in read and hold state. Symmetric structure offers symmetric layout and lower mismatch.
- Half select issue arising due to *BL* and *BLB* is reduced.

# 2 Proposed 10T SRAM Cell Design

To achieve higher noise margins and minimum dynamic power consumption, a 10T SRAM cell is designed as shown in Fig. 1. The transistors *M7*, *M8*, *M9* and *M10* have been added to the conventional 6T cell. The transistor *M11* is common to all the SRAM cells in a row. The transistors *M1–M5–M7* and *M2–M6–M8* form two cross coupled inverter pairs. The transistors *M3*, *M4* and *M9*, *M10* act as access transistors for the write and read operations respectively. The symmetric layout structure is drawn to reduce the impact of local process variations. The structure uses the *LE* and *RE* signals to control the transistors *M7* and *M8* which breaks the feedback between inverters using dynamic feedback control. It increases the write margin. *RWL* and *WBL*, *WBLB* signals control the read and write operations respectively. The write operation in the cell exploits write assist dynamic feedback control technique. Even there are two bit-lines, the write operation is functionally single ended. The bit-lines are kept at high value during both write '*0*' and write '*1*' operations. *M9* and *M10* work as switches, only one of them is on during one write operation transferring data to adjacent node and other node value is changed due to inverting operation of another inverter attached to that node. Since bit-line values are never changed and write operation is controlled by switches according to the data to be written power consumed in switching bitlines is fully saved. Read operation is differential and controlled by data stored. Hence read is disturb free leading to higher read margin equivalent to hold margin. The status of the control signals is shown in Table 1.

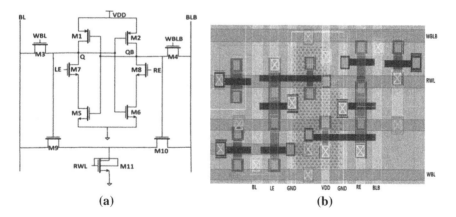

(a)                    (b)

**Fig. 1.** (a) Proposed 10T SRAM Cell (*M11* is common to all the SRAM cells in a row) (b) Layout of Proposed design

**Table 1.** Truth table for proposed design

|        | RWL | BL | LE | RE | BLB | WBL | WBLB |
|--------|-----|----|----|----|-----|-----|------|
| Write 1 | 0 | 1 | 0 | 1 | 1 | 1 | 0 |
| Write 0 | 0 | 1 | 1 | 0 | 1 | 0 | 1 |
| Read | 1 | 1 | 1 | 1 | 1 | 0 | 0 |
| Hold | 0 | 1 | 1 | 1 | 1 | 0 | 0 |

## 2.1  Write Operation

Unlike the conventional SRAM cells, both the bit-lines *BL* and *BLB* are kept high during write operation. In contrast to general writing pattern of SRAM, where data to be written is controlled by values on *BL* and *BLB*, it is controlled by control signals *WBL* and *WBLB* in this proposed SRAM cell. The write operation in the proposed SRAM cell is single ended that is one access transistor is used to write desired value and other one is *OFF*.

For writing '*1*' to the SRAM cell, *RWL* is made logic low which switches off *M11*. *BL* and *BLB* are kept logic high. *WBL* is kept at logic high which makes *M3 ON*. *WBLB* is kept at logic low which turns *M4* off such that write operation becomes single ended. To make the feedback loop cutoff to help in write operation, Data Aware Dynamic Feedback Control write assist technique is employed. For write '*1*', *M7* is turned off and *M8* is turned ON using *LE* = 0 V and *RE* = $V_{DD}$. Since *M7* is turned OFF, feedback loop of the cross-coupled inverter pair is cut-off. There is no pull down path connecting node *Q* to ground to help it maintain its value. It is now directly connected to *BL* through *M3*. Thus, *BL* generates a high voltage bump at node *Q*, which leads to change its value to '*1*' with significant increase in write margin. With *Q* changing its value, the inverter (*M2*–*M8*–*M6*) connected directly at *Q* changes the value at *QB* to '0'. As *M1* source is connected to $V_{DD}$, pull up speed at *Q* is high in this case as compared to conventional CVDD write assist technique. Write '*1*' to the cell is shown in Fig. 2(a). Similarly, the procedure of writing '0' is shown in Fig. 2(b).

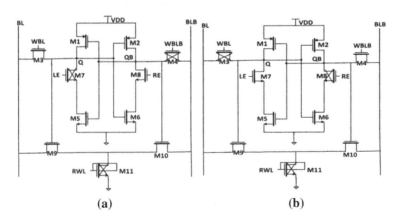

(a)                                  (b)

**Fig. 2.** (a) Write 1 operation (b) Write 0 operation

## 2.2    Read Operation

Read operation is performed by precharging *BL* and *BLB* and turning control signals *RWL* to logic high and *WBLB*, *WBL* to logic low. During the read operation *M7* and *M8* are *ON* by activating the *RE* and *LE* signals, leading to strong cross coupled inverter. The storage nodes *Q* and *QB* are isolated from bitlines completely which leads to disturb-free read operation. This decoupling action helps in increasing the SNM as disturbance does not reach storage nodes *Q* and *QB* as shown in Fig. 3. Body terminal of *M11* is connected to *RWL* making threshold voltage of *M11* dynamic. When *RWL* is activated for read operation it decreases the threshold voltage and discharges the bitline quickly, making read operation faster than all the compared cells with a greater margin. Due to differential signals, design of sense amplifier is simple. As the read and write access transistors are different, the sizing of the access transistors can be performed to improve the read and write margins separately. Read margin is equivalent to hold margin.

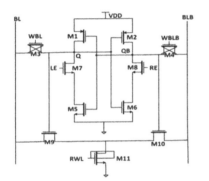

**Fig. 3.** Read operation          **Fig. 4.** Hold operation

## 2.3    Hold Operation

The transistors *M7* and *M8* are *ON* during hold mode. Both *WBL*, *WBLB* and *RWL* are switched *OFF* and two cross-coupled inverters form a strong feedback loop. The hold margin of proposed cell is slightly less compared to hold margin of 6T SRAM cell due to the stacking effect of pull-down NMOS transistors. On the other hand, due to stacking of transistors in pull down, leakage current is reduced in hold state (Fig. 4).

## 2.4    Half- Selected Cell Issue

When a write '0' ('1') operation is performed on a SRAM cell, the voltage at storage node *QB* (*Q*) for row half selected cells will increase because there will be charge transfer from bitline *BLB* (*BL*). In the proposed SRAM cell, the storage node *Q* (*QB*) does not have driving path to bitline *BL* as *M3* (*M4*) is turned *OFF*. Therefore, in the proposed design there are less chances of change in the value stored in the cell as compared to conventional techniques.

# 3  Simulation Results and Discussion

In this section, all the post layout simulation results are presented to confirm the functionality of proposed design. The simulations are done using 65 nm industrial technology node. The operating supply voltage and temperature for the simulations are 0.3 V and 27 °C respectively. To show effectiveness of proposed design, it is compared with 6T iso-area (6T upsized to match the layout area of proposed 10T), 9T [15], 10T [17] and ST2 [16]. Iso-area 6T is 3x upsized of its minimum required W/L ratios for 65 nm technology node. Area occupied by the layout of the proposed design is 3.216 $\mu m^2$ as shown in Fig. 1(b).

## 3.1  Write Ability

The WL voltage is used to assess write ability. In this case, the WL voltage is swept from zero to $V_{DD}$ to find the minimum voltage at which the bit cell is written ($Q$ and $QB$ flip) and is called wordline write margin(WVWL). If the value of WVWL is less, then it is easier to write on the bit cell. The write failure criteria is defined as WVWL $\geq V_{DD}$. Write failure occurs at $V_{DD}$, hence margin is given by $V_{DD}$-WVWL and is denoted as WVWL write margin. Write ability is also assessed using Write Static Noise Margin (WSNM) calculated using butterfly curve.

In iso-area 6T and ST2, there is fight between access and pull down transistor. But in proposed 10T, during write 1 operation, we turn off $M7$ that breaks the feedback loop and no direct path is now for $Q$ node to ground. There is no fight between access and pull down transistor. There is undisturbed charging of $Q$ node through $WBL$. The write margin is slightly lower than 9T and 10T as write operation is single ended. In 9T, write operation is differential. It is a small tradeoff for dynamic write power saved in write operation of proposed 10T. WSNM of proposed 10T is 1.71x and 1.44x as compared with that of iso-area 6T and ST2 and 0.93x as compared to 9T and 10T.

## 3.2  Read Static Noise Margin

RSNM is defined as the maximum amount of voltage noise that a cell can tolerate in read configuration without flipping of $Q$ and $QB$. RSNM is calculated by finding the largest square which fits inside the VTCs (butterfly curves). Read noise margin are equivalent to hold noise margin as read is decoupled and disturb free as noise does not reach internal storage nodes. In 9T and 10T, the internal nodes are float during read operation and data retention time is a factor to be considered but in proposed 10T read path bypasses the storage nodes $Q$ and $QB$ isolating them from bitlines completely during read operation. RSNM of proposed 10T is 2x better than 6T as here no voltage divider is formed between access and pull-down transistor.

### 3.3 Write and Read Access Time

$T_{WA}$ (write access time) is measured as the time required for writing '0' to the storage node $Q$. It is difference of the time when WBLB is *HIGH* and the time when $Q$ falls to 10% of its initial high value (i.e., 90% change). Similarly, $T_{WA}$ for writing '1' to $Q$ is calculated as the difference of the time when WBL is turned *ON* and the time when $Q$ rises to 90% of its initial low value. This ensures correct write operation. Being single ended, it requires more write time for storage nodes compared to all the compared cells as all other cells follow differential write operation.

**Table 2.** Comparison with different structures at 300 mV

|  | 6T (iso-area) | 9T | 10T | ST2 | PROPOSED 10T |
|---|---|---|---|---|---|
| WVWL (mV) | 95 | 248.9 | 249.1 | 147 | 235 |
| WSNM (mV) | 127 | 230 | 230.5 | 145 | 216 |
| RSNM (mV) | 47 | 83 | 87 | 69 | 97 |
| Write access time (ns) | 5.4 | 9 | 9 | 8.89 | 18 |
| Read access time (ns) | 7.4 | 21 | 12.3 | 9.5 | 11 |
| Read current (nA) | 6.38 | 7.05 | 7.7 | 6.9 | 9.7 |
| Write power (nW) | 1.5 | 1.64 | 1.659 | 2.043 | 1.639 |
| Read power (nW) | 1.527 | 1.545 | 1.549 | 1.962 | 1.635 |
| Write method | Differential | Differential | Differential | Differential | Single |
| Read method | Differential | Single | Differential | Differential | Differential |

$T_{RA}$ (read access time or read delay) is measured as the difference of the time when *RWL* (*WL*) is turned *ON* and the time when one of the bitlines is discharged by 50 mV from its initial high value [16]. The 50-mV difference in voltage between the bitlines is sufficient to be spotted by a sense amplifier, thereby avoiding incorrect read operation of the data stored. The read access time for different configurations is shown in Table 2. The read access time of proposed 10T cell is less than 10T cell. Its read current is high compared to 10T cell as result of reduced threshold voltage due to use of DTMOS technique. It is less than 9T cell as it uses single ended read.

## 4    Conclusion

A 10T SRAM cell is proposed to improve read and write stability for subthreshold operation. This 10T cell employs a data-aware-feedback-cutting scheme to enlarge the write margin and the read-disturb free scheme with DTMOS technique. This proposed design is an ultra-low voltage SRAM cell. Its WSNM is 1.7x of the write margin of iso-area 6T cell. The WVWL margin of proposed 10T is higher than 10T, 6T (iso-area) and ST2. Write operation is functionally single ended and write control signals are data aware. As BL and *BLB* are always high, hence activity factor of switching the bitlines during write operation is minimal which reduces dynamic power dissipation during write operation. Design of write driver is also simple as same data is sent on both lines. RSNM is highest among all the cells under consideration. Read SNM is almost equal to hold SNM. Read access time is better than compared 9T and 10T. Due to different access transistors for read and write operation, there sizing can be done efficiently for higher margins. Proposed 10T SRAM cell in hold state has smaller leakage current due to stacking of pull down transistors. Hence the proposed cell has high read and write stability and can be operated at ultra-low voltage of 200–300 mV. The advantage of reduced dynamic power consumption enables it to be used in portable battery operated System-on-Chip (SoC) designs.

# References

1. Rabaey, J.M., Chandrakasan, A., Nikolic, B.: Digital Integrated Circuits: A Design Perspective, 2nd edn. Prentice-Hall, New Delhi (2005)
2. Karandikar, A., Parhi, K.K.: Low power SRAM design using hierarchical divided bit-line approach. In: Proceedings of International Conference Computer Design, pp. 82–88 (1998)
3. Zhai, B., Hanson, S., Blaauw, D., Sylvester, D.: A variation-tolerant sub-200 mV 6-T subthreshold SRAM. IEEE J. Solid-State Circuits of 43(10), 2338–2348 (2008)
4. Pilo, H., Barwin, J., Braceras, G., Browning, C., Burns, S., Gabric, J., Lamphier, S., Miller, M., Roberts, A., Towler, F.: An SRAM design in 65 nm and 45 nm technology nodes featuring read and write-assist circuits to expand operating voltage. In: Symposium on VLSI Circuits, Digest of Technical Papers, pp. 15–16, June 2006
5. Bhavnagarwala, A., Kosonocky, S., Radens, C., Stawiasz, K., Mann, R., Ye, Q., Chin, K.: Fluctuation limits and scaling opportunities for CMOS SRAM cells. In: International Electron Devices Meeting (IEDM) Digest, pp. 659–662, December 2005
6. Suzuki, T., Yamauchi, H., Yamagami, Y., Satomi, K., Akamatsu, H.: A stable 2-port SRAM cell design against simultaneously read/write-disturbed accesses. IEEE J. Solid-State Circuits 43(9), 2109–2119 (2008)
7. Hirabayashi, O., Kawasumi, A., Suzuki, A., Takeyama, Y., Kushida, K., Sasaki, T., Katayama, A., Fukano, G., Fujimura, Y., Nakazato, T., Shizuki, Y., Kushiyama, N., Yabe, T.: A process-variation-tolerant dual-power-supply SRAM with 0.179 m cell in 40 nm CMOS using level-programmable wordline driver. In: IEEE Int. Solid-State Circuits Conference (ISSCC) Digest of Technical Papers, pp. 458–459, February 2009
8. Zhang, K., Bhattacharya, U., Chen, Z., Hamzaoglu, F., Murray, D., Vallepalli, N., Wang, Y., Zheng, B., Bohr, M.: A 3-GHz 70-Mb SRAM in 65-nm CMOS technology with integrated column-based dynamic power supply. IEEE J. Solid-State Circuits 41(1), 146–151 (2006)
9. Bai, N., Wu, X., Yang, J., Shi, L.: A robust high density 7T SRAM bitcell for subthreshold applications. Chin. J. Electron. 20(2), 243–246 (2011)
10. Singh, J., Mathew, J., Pradhan, D.K., Mohanty, S.P.: A subthreshold single ended I/O SRAM cell design for nanometer CMOS technologies. In: 2008 IEEE International SOC Conference, 17–20 September 2008
11. Chang, M.-F., Wu, J.-J., Chen, K.-T., Chen, Y.-C., Chen, Y.-H., Lee, R., Liao, H.-J., Yamauchi, H.: A differential data-aware power-supplied (D-AP) 8T SRAM cell with expanded write/read stabilities for lower VDDmin applications. IEEE J. Solid-State Circuits 45(6), 1234–1245 (2010)
12. Yoshimoto, M.: A 64 kb CMOS RAM with divided word line structure. In: Technical Digest IEEE International Solid-State Circuits Conference, pp. 58–59 (1983)

13. Yang, B., Kim, L.: A low-power SRAM using hierarchical bit line and local sense amplifiers. IEEE J. Solid-State Circuits **40**(6), 1366–1376 (2005)
14. Hwang, M.-E., Roy, K.: A 135 mV 0.13-μW process tolerant 6T subthreshold DTMOS SRAM in 90 nm technology. In: Proceedings IEEE Custom Integrated Circuits Conference, September 2008, pp. 419–422 (2008)
15. Chang, M.F., Chang, S.W., Chou, P.W., Wu, W.C.: A 130 mV SRAM with expanded write and read margins for subthreshold applications. IEEE J. Solid-State Circuits **46**(2), 520–529 (2011)
16. Kulkarni, J.P., Roy, K.: Ultralow-voltage process-variation-tolerant Schmitt-trigger-based SRAM design. IEEE Trans. Very Large Scale Integr. (VLSI) Syst. **20**(2), 319–332 (2012)
17. Hassanzadeh, S., Zamani, M., Hajsadeghi, K.: A 32 kb 90 nm 10T-cell sub-threshold SRAM with improved read and write SNM. In: Proceedings of 21st Iranian Conference Electrical Engineering (ICEE), May 2013, pp. 1–5 (2013)

# Variability Investigation of Double Gate JunctionLess (DG-JL) Transistor for Circuit Design Perspective

Vandana Kumari[1], Manoj Saxena[2(✉)], and Mridula Gupta[3]

[1] Department of Electronics, Maharaja Agrasen College, University of Delhi, New Delhi, India
[2] Department of Electronics, Deen Dayal Upadhyaya College, University of Delhi, New Delhi, India
saxena_manoj77@yahoo.co.in
[3] Department of Electronic Science, University of Delhi, South Campus, New Delhi, India

**Abstract.** Present work investigates the variability in the circuit performance of Double Gate JunctionLess (DG-JL) architecture due to variation in device parameters such as operating temperature (T), doping of the channel ($N_{ch}$) and the variation in the doping profile (like Gaussian). We have also evaluated the impact of interface charges on the performance of DG-JL based CMOS inverter. Conventional CMOS inverter and amplifier circuit are used to demonstrate the performance of the DG-JL architecture. The parameters which are evaluated in this work are transfer characteristics, noise margin, propagation delay, inverter current and amplifier gain. Apart from this, influence of gate oxide permittivity on the transfer characteristics of CMOS inverter has been investigated. Presented results show that, the variation in the doping profile (i.e. from uniform to Gaussian) has lesser impact on the device performance. However, the change in peak doping concentration, operating temperature and influence of interface charges leads to significant change in inverter characteristics in terms of both noise margin and propagation delay.

**Keywords:** Circuits · JunctionLess · Gaussian doping · ATLAS

## 1 Introduction

Recently Double Gate-JunctionLess (DG-JL) has emerged as an alternative candidate for low voltage circuit applications [1]. Other than simple fabrication technique, device also shows immense potential in suppressing various short channel effects. The suitability of DG-JL transistor for circuit applications has been explored by various research groups in past [2, 3]. The preliminary study related to the influence of non-uniform doping profile (i.e. exponentially decreases from surface to bottom of the channel) on the digital performance of DG-JL transistor is also reported by Singh *et al.* in 2017 [4] in which the impact of straggle on the transfer characteristics of CMOS inverter has been examined. However the issues related to the variability in the device parameter (such as temperature and doping (which may occurs during some fabrication steps like ion-implantation [5])) on the circuit performance (such as CMOS inverter, Common source amplifier and three phase ring oscillator) has not been addressed yet in literature

© Springer Nature Singapore Pte Ltd. 2017
B. K. Kaushik et al. (Eds.): VDAT 2017, CCIS 711, pp. 496–503, 2017.
https://doi.org/10.1007/978-981-10-7470-7_49

which has been illustrated in this work. Beside this, at shorter channel length, drain side region becomes more susceptible to degradation due to hot carrier induced interface charges because of strong electric field [6, 7] near the drain side. Thus, the variability in the doping profile (i.e. non-uniform) and the influence of hot carrier induce charges near the drain side of $SiO_2/Si$ interface on the amplifier circuit gain has been examined using extensive device simulation using ATLAS 2D [8] software. Two dimensional view of the uniformly (having interface charges near the drain side) and Gaussian doped DG-JL are shown in Fig. 1(a) and (b). In order to validate the simulation, models available for DG-JL transistor in already published work has been invoked [9]. For designing CMOS circuits, PMOS and NMOS architectures are optimized to have same threshold voltage by changing the metal gate work-function.

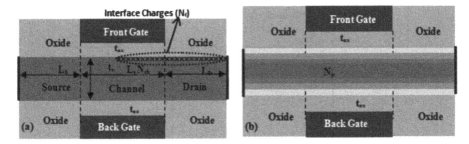

**Fig. 1.** Schematic cross sectional view of Double Gate JunctionLess (DG-JL) Transistor (a) Uniformly doped; $N_{ch}$ is the channel doping and (b) Gaussian doped showing the fixed interface charges near the drain side. L is the channel length taken as 32 nm, $t_{ox}$ is the oxide thickness (1.5 nm), $N_p$ is the peak doping concentration ($10^{19} cm^{-3}$) in Gaussian doped DG-JL Transistor and $t_{ch}$ is the channel thickness (10 nm).

## 2    Inverter Performance

It can be seen from the Fig. 2(a) that, the ON and OFF state of DG-JLT based inverter deteriorates with the enhancement in temperature. Voltage Transfer Characteristic VTC has also be used to study the noise immunity of the circuit in terms of noise margin. The associated current of CMOS inverter as shown in Fig. 2(a) (mainly leakage current) also increases with the enhancement in temperature (55.6% @ 300 K to 400 K) and subsequently showing higher dynamic power dissipation. The deterioration in inverter DC performance i.e. noise margin and leakage current is mainly because of the higher leakage current and sub-threshold slope of the DG-JL transistor with increase in temperature due to the reduction in carrier mobility (because of higher scattering at higher temperature). Results plotted in Fig. 2(b) and (c) prove that the degradation due to hot carrier induced damages leads to deterioration in the inverter switching response. Also the usage of high-k gate dielectric reflects better inverter performance compared to $SiO_2$ (due to reduction in Effective Oxide Thickness EOT which improves the gate control over the carriers) and the degradation in inverter response (due to interface charges) is more prominent in case of high k gate dielectric. The noise immunity of the circuit also deteriorates with interface charges and the change is more significant for high-k (i.e. 12% and 16% for $SiO_2$ and $HfO_2$ gate dielectrics respectively). However the usage of high-k gate dielectric improves the noise immunity of the device (~8%).

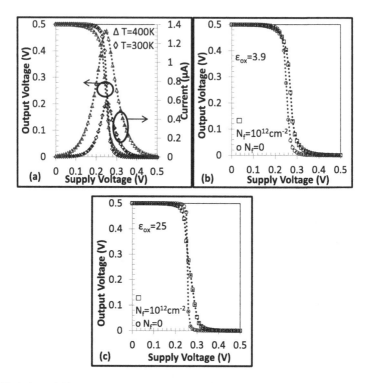

**Fig. 2.** Variation of (a) output voltage and current and (b) output voltage for different interface charges for $SiO_2$ as gate oxide and (c) $HfO_2$ as gate oxide of CMOS inverter with input voltage for uniformly doped DG-JL transistor: L = 32 nm, $L_s$ = $L_d$ = 10 nm, $t_{ch}$ = 10 nm and $N_{ch}$ = $1 \times 10^{19} cm^{-3}$.

The gradual increase in the slope of the characteristics (or deterioration in the ON to OFF switching) is observed in case of uniformly doped DG-JL compared to Gaussian doped DG-JL as shown in Fig. 3(a) because of the inferior sub-threshold slope in case of uniform doping. Also, the shifting of the position of the peak doping conc. from center to surface of the channel improves the VTC. The enhancement in $L_s$ and $L_d$ also leads to the slightly improved switching characteristics of the inverter. Figure 3(b) illustrates that as the straggle value increases, the inverter performance degrades i.e. poor VTC and hence lower noise margin. From the Fig. 3(b), it can be inferred that as the peak doping conc. of Gaussian doping decreases, VTC deteriorates further leading to degradation in the noise immunity of the device due to the lower noise margin NM. Inset of Fig. 3(b) compares the noise margin of CMOS inverter at different channel lengths of Gaussian doped DG-JL. An increase in NM is observed with increase in the channel length and this change is higher in high noise margin ($NM_H$). This improvement in NM is due to the better OFF to ON transition at higher channel length.

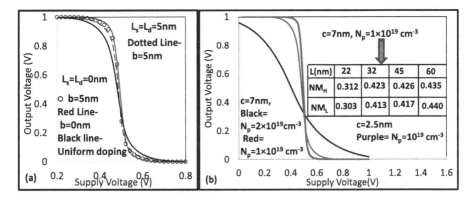

**Fig. 3.** VTC of a CMOS inverter based on (a) Gaussian doped DG-JL transistor at L = 32 nm for different position of peak doping concentration and length of source drain lengths. (b) for different peak doping variation and inset shows Noise margin for Gaussian doped DG-JL having peak at center and $L_s = L_d = 0$ nm. (Color figure online)

Figure 4 illustrates the transient response of CMOS inverter for analyzing the switching behavior of the device in terms of propagation delay. Rise and the fall time of the transient response deteriorates with the enhancement in operating temperature leading to enhancement in the delay of the circuit due to the reduction in drain current after zero crossover point. Compared to voltage transfer characteristics, the transient response of the CMOS inverter improves under the influence of interface fixed charges due to the significantly enhanced drive current leading to reduction in the propagation delay of the device from 34 ps to 10 ps. Figure 4(b) shows that the enhancement in load capacitance leads to the higher propagation delay due to the higher charging and

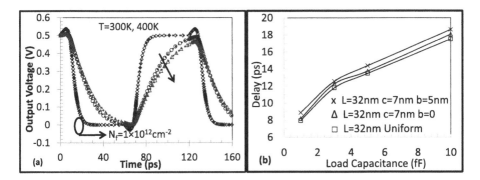

**Fig. 4.** Variation of transient output of DG-JL based CMOS inverter with time at different operating temperatures and interface charges; L = 32 nm, $L_s = L_d = 10$ nm and $N_{ch} = 1 \times 10^{19}$cm$^{-3}$ (b) Variation of propagation delay with load capacitance of a CMOS inverter circuit; $N_p = 1 \times 10^{19}$cm$^{-3}$ and b is the position of the peak doping concentration.

discharging time. Also, the variation in the doping profile from uniform to Gaussian degrades the switching behavior of the device in terms of higher propagation delay. Improvement in the propagation delay can be observed when the doping is maximum at the upper surface and minimum at the bottom.

## 3 Amplifier Performance

Input and output voltage of uniformly doped DG-JL transistor based Common Source (CS) amplifier are plotted in Fig. 5 for different temperature and hot carrier induced charges. Deteriorates in $V_{out}$ of CS amplifier (25% @ 300 K to 400 K) is observed from Fig. 5 with increase in temperature leading to reduction in gain of the circuit mainly because of the lower trans-conductance at higher temperature (when the device is bias above the zero-crossover point). Also the presence of interface charges leads to the higher circuit gain due to the reduction in the drive current of the device.

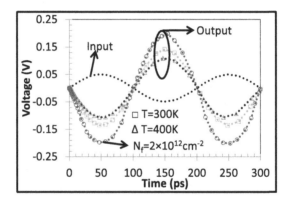

**Fig. 5.** Uniformly doped DG-JL transistor based amplifier voltage with time for different temperature and interface charges; $L = 32$ nm, $L_s = L_d = 10$ nm, and $N_{ch} = 1 \times 10^{19} cm^{-3}$.

Figure 6 shows the influence of straggle angle (i.e. c) on the response of Gaussian doped DG-JL based CS amplifier. With increase in straggle angle (i.e. c), the gain of the amplifier reduces due to the reduction in the overall decay in the doping profile from peak conc. This is because of the reduction in the drain current and hence trans-conductance thereby resulting in the inferior amplifier gain. Thus by proper optimizing the device parameters of Gaussian doped DG-JL transistor, significant enhancement in the device gain can be achieved.

Figure 7 compares output response of uniformly doped DG-JL transistor for different channel doping concentration. Since the enhancement in doping concentrations leads to the lower drive current (due to random dopant fluctuations) of the device and hence eventually leading to lower output voltage and device gain i.e. 72% @ $9 \times 10^{18} cm^{-3}$ to $1 \times 10^{19} cm^{-3}$. By comparing Figs. 6 and 7, it can be observed that without reducing the channel doping, significant improvement in device gain can be achieved by changing the straggle value of the device.

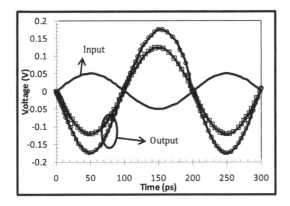

**Fig. 6.** Amplifier output voltage with time for different value of strangle angle □□ c = 2.5 nm, ○○ c = 7 nm; L = 32 nm, $L_s = L_d = 0$ nm, $N_{ch} = 1 \times 10^{19} cm^{-3}$ $t_{ch} = 10$ nm.

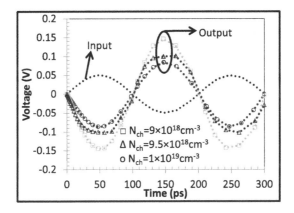

**Fig. 7.** Uniformly doped DG-JL transistor based amplifier voltage (input and output) with time for different channel doping concentration of uniformly doped DG-JL transistor. L = 32 nm, $L_s = L_d = 10$ nm, $N_{ch} = 1 \times 10^{19} cm^{-3}$ $t_{ch} = 10$ nm.

Figure 8(a) and (b) shows the behavior of trans-conductance ($g_m$) and drain conductance ($g_d$) with $V_{gs}$ and $V_{ds}$ respectively. $g_m$ and $g_d$ of the device deteriorates by using uniform doping inside the channel region compared to Gaussian doping. Also, the reduction in $g_m$ is observed by using higher source/drain length ($L_s$ and $L_d$) due to the higher effective channel length. However the drain-conductance of the device improves with the source drain extension (because the applied drain bias is screened near the drain side due to extended drain region). Thus the $g_m/g_d$ of uniformly doped DG-JL is lower than the Gaussian doped device which can further be increased by increasing the source/drain extension region.

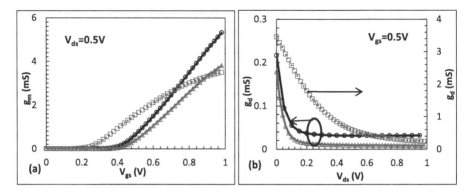

**Fig. 8.** Variation of (a) $g_m$ and (b) $g_d$ with applied voltage; □□: Uniform doped DG-JL ($L_s = L_d = 5$ nm), ΔΔ: Gaussian doped DG-JL ($L_s = L_d = 5$ nm) and ○○ Gaussian doped DG-JL ($L_s = L_d = 0$ nm).

## 4   Three Phase Ring Oscillator

Three phase ring oscillator circuit has been used for investigation in this section and respective delay of the circuit depends on the number of the stage of the oscillator [10]. Figure 9 illustrates the output response of three phase ring oscillator. It can be inferred from the results that source/drain extended device based ring oscillator shows more phase delay in the output response and propagation delay (18%). Delay in the output response also increase with increase in load capacitor (from 0.6 ps @ $C_L = 1$ fF to 2 ps @$C_L = 10$ fF) but the change in the delay is not much significant with the change in the doping profile from Gaussian to uniform at lower load capacitance i.e. $C_L = 1$ fF. The power dissipation of the circuit also reduces with the enhancement in $L_s$ and $L_d$ from 0 nm (231 μW) to 5 nm (134 μW).

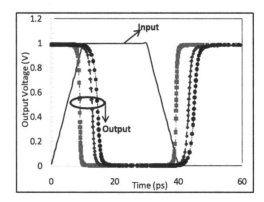

**Fig. 9.** Transient Response of Ring Oscillator at different source/drain extensions and load capacitor; ■; $C_L = 1$ fF and $L_s = L_d = 0$ nm, ◆ $C_L = 10$ fF and $L_s = L_d = 0$ nm and ● $C_L = 10$ fF and $L_s = L_d = 5$ nm.

# 5 Conclusion

Effect of variability in the essential device design parameters (such as variation in doping concentration from uniform to Gaussian and temperature during fabrication) and hot carrier induced damages on circuit performance of CMOS inverter, common source amplifier and Ring Oscillator has been analyzed. Parameters evaluated in the work are noise margin, propagation delay amplifier gain and leakage current etc. The effect of source/drain extension on the circuit performance has been analyzed. Results proved that the noise immunity of the circuit also deteriorates due to the interface defects and the deterioration is lesser for $HfO_2$ gate dielectric. The incorporation in source/drain extension length leads to higher phase delay in the output response and propagation delay (18%). However the calculated power dissipation suppresses with the inclusion of source/drain extension from 231 $\mu$W ($L_s = L_d = 0$ nm) to 134 $\mu$W ($L_s = L_d = 5$ nm). The change in the operating temperature also leads to deteriorates in output voltage of CS amplifier (25% @ 300 K to 400 K) when the device is biased above zero temperature coefficient (at which drain current reduces with increase in temperature).

# References

1. Colinge, J.P., et al.: Nanowire transistors without junctions. Nature Nanotechnol. **5**(3), 225–229 (2010)
2. Choi, S.J., et al.: Nonvolatile memory by all-around-gate junctionless transistor composed of silicon nanowireon bulk substrate. IEEE Electron Device Lett. **32**(5), 602–604 (2011)
3. Han, M.H., et al.: Device and circuit performance estimation of junctionless bulk FinFETs. IEEE Trans. Electron Devices **60**(6), 1807–1813 (2013)
4. Singh, B., et al.: Analytical modeling of sub-threshold characteristics of ion-implanted symmetric double gate junctionless field effect transistor. Mater. Sci. Semicond. Process. **58**, 82–88 (2017)
5. Dubey, S., et al.: A two-dimensional model for the potential distribution and threshold voltage of short-channel double gate metal oxide semiconductor field-effect transistors with a vertical Gaussian-like doping profile. J. Appl. Phys. **108**(3), 034518, 7 (2010)
6. Djeffal, F., et al.: Analytical analysis of nanoscale multiple gate MOSFETs including effects of hot-carrier induced interface charges. Microelectron. Reliab. **49**, 377–381 (2009)
7. Yu, Y.S., et al.: Analytical threshold voltage model including effective conducting path effect (ECPE) for surrounding-gate MOSFETs SGMOSFETs) with localised charges. IEEE Trans. Electron. Dev. **57**, 3176–3180 (2010)
8. ATLAS: 3-D Device Simulator, SILVACO International, Version 5.14.0.R (2010)
9. Kumari, V., et al.: Modeling and simulation of double gate junctionless transistor considering fringing field effects. Solid-State Electron. **107**, 20–29 (2015)
10. Weste, N.H.E., et al.: CMOS VLSI Design: A Circuits and Systems Perspective. Dorling Kindersley Publishing, Noida (2006)

# System Design

# A High Speed KECCAK Coprocessor for Partitioned NSP Architecture on FPGA Platform

Rourab Paul$^{(\boxtimes)}$ and Sandeep Kumar Shukla

Department of Computer Science and Engineering,
Indian Institute of Technology, Kanpur, India
rourab@iitk.ac.in, sandeeps@cse.iitk.ac.in

**Abstract.** The messages in the latest security protocols such as IPSec, TLS and SSL must be handled by high-speed crypto systems. Current computationally extensive cryptographic implementations on different platforms such as software, Application Specific Integrated Circuit (ASIC) and Field Programmable Gate Array (FPGA) without adequate optimization achieve lesser throughput than should be possible. In the paper we consider a cryptographic hashing algorithm KECCAK and its implementations. To achieve better throughput, the proposed implementations of KECCAK explores FPGA design spaces. In this paper three different architectures for KECCAK coprocessor are implemented in Artix-7 (XC7A100T, CSG324) FPGA platform. The Processing Element (PE) handles all communication interfaces, data paths and control signals hazards of Network Security Processor (NSP). A partitioned area in the system ensures that the processor data path is completely isolated from secret key memory. The memory to KECCAK core communication is done by Direct Memory Access Controller (DMA). The performances of the implemented KECCAK are better in terms of throughput and resource usage than the existing work reported in the literature.

**Keywords:** KECCAK · NSP · DMA · TLS/SSL · FPGA
High speed

## 1 Introduction

Hash functions are used for data integrity and authentication purposes. As there are various vulnerabilities in widely-used MD-5, SHA-1 and SHA-2 hash algorithms, the US NIST had initiated the SHA-3 contest in order to select a suitable replacement. In 2009, KECCAK was selected as the winner of the contest and in august 2015, NIST announced that KECCAK became a new hashing standard. In the coming few years, it is expected that KECCAK will become mandatory cryptographic hash algorithm for all mainstream and future network security protocols along with existing standards such as TLS, SSL, SET, IPSec, and PKI. The tremendous growth of high-speed communication technology demands high throughput crypto hardware. Hence, many initiatives are taken to optimize the throughput of KECCAK crypto core.

© Springer Nature Singapore Pte Ltd. 2017
B. K. Kaushik et al. (Eds.): VDAT 2017, CCIS 711, pp. 507–518, 2017.
https://doi.org/10.1007/978-981-10-7470-7_50

Article [1] proposed a KECCAK hardware in Virtex-5 FPGA device which includes the usage of DSP blocks to minimize the consumption of traditional user logic such as look-up tables (LUTs). Authors claimed that incorporating Xilinx DSP48E block in their pipelined design increased the timing performance of the design but the result shows that they achieved only 5.71 Gbps throughput. The DSP blocks have many functions such as SIMD based multiply-accumulator, multiply-adder, and a one- or n-step counter etc., which makes the DSP48E more expensive than normal LUT based Slices. Hence, the achievement of few Gbps throughput with expensive DSP configured AND, XOR, MOD, NOT operation in KECCAK algorithm cannot be a good solution.

The Virtex-5 and Virtex-6 FPGA-based KECCAK hardware in article [2] consumed 88 clock cycle for one KECCAK round. The total 24 rounds required $88 \times 24 = 2112$ clock cycles. The 5 sequential functions of KECCAK rounds such as $\theta$, $\rho$, $\pi$, $\chi$ and $\iota$ are very primitive in nature, nevertheless this implementation folded each function and split their logic load into several clock cycles which increase total latency unnecessarily.

Articles [3] and [4] are the 1 clock 1 round folded KECCAK architectures where $\theta$, $\rho$, $\pi$, $\chi$ and $\iota$ functions are placed into a single clock cycle. Article [4] incorporated a 3 stages pipeline concept based on multi-message hashing hardware where new input arrives at every clock cycle. In the $1^{st}$ pipeline stage $\theta$ is computed. The $\rho$ and $\pi$ step are implemented in the $2^{nd}$ stage. The final stage combines $\chi$ and $\iota$ steps. At each clock cycle, the result of the cyclic shift operation is stored in a register.

Articles [5] and [6] stated KECCAK might be an alternative of AES for some specific applications. Article [5] implemented KECCAK in Virtex-4 FPGA for securing Precision Time Protocol (PTP) standardized by IEC 61850 family for substation communication network applications. They unroll KECCAK by different unrolling factor and attempted to show without compromising with security and latency, KECCAK may become a substitute of AES-128 for HMAC type applications. Article [6] implemented different cipher mode KECCAK in Virtex-7 FPGA Board and showed it is more efficient in terms of resource throughput than AES.

Article [7] explored the KECCAK implementation in different FPGAs of Xilinx and Altera. They achieved 8.023 Gbps maximum throughput for KECCAK-256 in Kintex 7 Xilinx board. They claimed loop unrolled technique cannot increase KECCAK throughput, but we find that the loop unrolled factor by two can double the throughput of normally folded KECCAK architecture.

Article [8] implemented hardware/software co-design based KECCAK for HMAC and PRNG security functions in ZYNQ SoC FPGA platform where the capacity parameter of KECCAK is configurable.

Articles [9] and [10] implemented all candidates of SHA-3 finalist in Xilinx and Altera FPGA platform and tried to find out the most efficient SHA-3 in terms of slices and throughput. [9] claimed only three candidates, KECCAK, Luffa, and CubeHash, have the better throughput to area ratio than the current standard SHA-256. Of the three algorithms, Keccak and Luffa have achieved very high throughputs, while CubeHash outperformed other candidates in terms of minimal resource usage. Article [10] achieved only 0.843 Gbps throughput which implies very less throughput/slice ratio of their architecture.

Article [11] is a very light weight FPGA implementation using only Shift Register and Lookup Tables. The implementation consumed very fewer silicon spaces but compromises with very less throughput.

Article [12] implemented fastest KECCAK in FPGA. They changed the number of pipeline stages and studied various circuit issues of FPGA hardware. The presented implementations in three Virtex FPGA families performed better with respect to throughput by 250% than previous publications.

The contribution of the paper is stated below

- We implemented 3 architectures of KECCAK in FPGA platform such as (i) Folded (FL), (ii) Loop Unrolled Folded (LU2) and (iii) Pipelined Loop unrolled Folded (PPL2-LU2) architecture. To the best of our knowledge, the PPL2-LU2 achieved the highest throughput in existing literature.
- We propose three partitions in NSP architecture such as a processor area, a crypto area and a confidential area. The KECCAK is implemented as a coprocessor placed in the crypto area and the master secret keys are stored in a different confidential portion of the FPGA to prevent all software related attacks from processor area.
- We propose a complete hardware flow of security protocols where crypto applications are implemented as a coprocessor. The parallel execution of master Processing Element (PE) and coprocessor along with DMA make the system more efficient in NSP environment.

The organization of the paper is as follows. In Sect. 2, a details discussion about three KECCAK architecture is presented concerning the parallelism issues of the design. The system architecture and system flow are stated in Sects. 3 and 4, respectively. Implementation of our design and analysis of its results are briefed in Sect. 5. The paper is concluded in Sect. 6.

## 2    KECCAK Architecture

The implemented KECCAK[r, c, d] has bit rate $r = 1088$, capacity $c = 512$ and data word size $d = 64$ [13] which iterates 24 rounds to produce 256 bits digest. For each round one *Round Count* $RC_i$ is generated to address a *Round Constant* $RCon_i$. For each round five consecutive functions such as $\theta$, $\rho$, $\pi$, $\chi$ and $\iota$ modify a value $RI_i$ which comes from 1600 bit state register $SR_i$. The $RC_i$ starts from 0 and ends in 23. It is to be noted that the detail algorithmic description of KECCAK is avoided intentionally due to hard page restriction. In our proposal KECCAK architecture is implemented in 3 different approaches, (i) Folded (FL), (ii) Loop Unrolled Folded (LU2) and (iii) Pipelined Loop unrolled Folded (PPL2-LU2) architecture. The FL, LU2 and PPL2-LU2 iterate 24 rounds in 24, 12 and 6 clocks respectively. The hardware architectures of KECCAK is described in next two sections.

## 2.1   Hardware Components

The KECCAK mainly has three hardware component named as *Round Constant ROM*, *Round Map Block* and *Count Generator*.

**Count Generator.** The *Count Generator* generates round counts $RC_i$ from 0 to 23 for Round Constant ROM block. In the folded architecture the $RC_i$ of *Count Generator* is incremented by one in rising edge of each clock. 24 clocks are required for 24 iterations. In the loop unrolled architecture two round counts $RC_i$ and $RC_{i+1}$ count from 0 to 23 for 24 KECCAK rounds in 12 clocks cycles. In the Pipe-lined Loop unrolled architecture two LU2 *Count Generators* is used to generate 4 $RC_i$s. One *Count Generator* counts 0 to 11, while other one counts 12 to 23 using 6 clocks cycles. Hence, parallel counts of $RC_i$ and $RC_{i+1}$ in 2 LU2 *Count Generator* complete 24 iterations in 6 clocks.

**Round Constant ROM.** The round *Round Constant ROM* intakes *round value* $RC_i$ and produces a 64 bit *Round Constant* $RCon_i$. The mapping between $RC_i$ and $RCon_i$ is based on computational look up table as stated in KECCAK data sheet [13]. One $RC_i$ of the folded architecture can address only one $RCon_i$ in one clock cycle, whereas two *round counts* $RC_i$ and $RC_{i+1}$ of the Loop Unrolled architecture can address two *Round constants* $RCon_i$ and $RCon_{i+1}$ in a single clock. In the Pipe lined architecture, four *Round constants* $RCon_i$, $RCon_{i+1}$, $RCon_{i+12}$ and $RCon_{i+13}$ can be addressed by four *round counts* $RC_i$, $RC_{i+1}$, $RC_{i+12}$ and $RC_{i+13}$ in a single clock.

**Round Map Block.** The *Round Map Block* executes 5 sequential functions $\theta$, $\rho$, $\pi$, $\chi$ and $\iota$. The 32 bit width DMA master port $S\_AXIS\_TDATA$ sends 34 *data word* into 1600 bit width *State Register* $SR_i$. In each round the $SR_i$ is updated by 5 consecutive operations $\theta$, $\rho$, $\pi$, $\chi$ and $\iota$. After 24 rounds the 256 bit hash value is derived from $SR_{i+23}$. In the folded architecture only one $RO_i$ can be calculated from $Ri_i$ in single clock whereas for the LU2 architecture two *Round Outs* $RO_i$ and $RO_{i+1}$ can be generated from initial *Round In* $RI_{i-1}$. In the Pipelined architecture two *Round Map Block*s are used to generate four *Round Outs* $RO_i$, $RO_{i+1}$, $RO_{i+12}$ and $RO_{i+13}$.

## 2.2   Architectures

In these proposal 3 hardware architectures are proposed for KECCAK hash algorithm.

**Folded Architecture.** The Folded KECCAK is a straight forward design where logic load of one round is placed in a single clock of *Round Map Block*. At a rising edge of clock *Count Generator* block generates a new $RC_i$ to address a $RCon_i$ from *Round Constant ROM*. The updated $RCon_i$ and a $RI_i$ register derived from state register $SR_i$ generates $\iota_i$ followed by four consecutive processes $\theta$, $\rho$, $\pi$, $\chi$. The output port of *Round Map Block* $RO_i$ is shorted with $\iota_i$ which updates state register from $SR_i$ to $SR_{i+1}$. The Eq. 1 derives $RO_i$ from $RI_i$.

$$RO_i = Round\ Map\ Block[RI_i, RCon_i] \tag{1}$$

The internal functions of *Round Map Block* are $\theta$, $\rho$, $\pi$, $\chi$ and $\iota$ which are calculated by Eqs. 2 and 3.

$$\iota in_i = \iota_i(\pi_i(\rho_i(\theta_i(RI_i)))) \tag{2}$$

$$RO_i = \iota_i(\iota in_i, RCon_i) \tag{3}$$

Folded architecture requires 24 clock cycles to iterate 24 rounds. The data words in *Round State Register* $SR_i$ is collected from DMA slave port $S\_AXIS\_TDATA$. The hardware architecture of folded design is shown in Fig. 1.

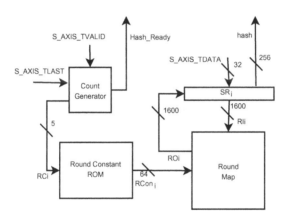

**Fig. 1.** Folded architecture of KECCAK

**Loop Unrolled Architecture (LU2).** In the Loop Unrolled architecture two loops are unrolled to calculate $SR_{i+1}$ directly from $SR_{i-1}$. In the previous architecture, one $RC_i$ was needed to address one $RCon_i$, whereas in Loop Unrolled approach two $RC_i$s are required to address a pair of $RCon_i$s. These two $RC_i$s are incremented by two in each clock. In $1^{st}$ clock $RC_i$ and $RC_{i+1}$ are initialized by 0 and 1 respectively. In $2^{nd}$ clock $RC_i$ becomes 2 and $RC_{i+1}$ becomes 3, and so on at a $12^{th}$ clock they both reach to 22 and 23. Hence, for the $i^{th}$ loop $RC_{i+1}$ can be derived from $RC_{i-1}$ using Eqs. 4 and 5.

$$RC_i = RC_{i-1} + 1 \tag{4}$$

$$RC_{i+1} = RC_{i-1} + 2 \tag{5}$$

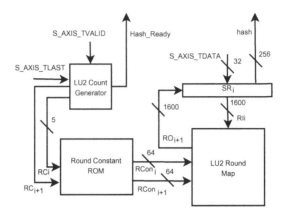

**Fig. 2.** LU2 architecture of KECCAK

As shown in Fig. 2, the $RCon_i$ and $RCon_{i+1}$ are addressed by $RC_i$ and $RC_{i+1}$ respectively are used in *Round Map Block* to compute $RO_{i+1}$ directly from $RI_i$ which is stated in Eq. 6.

$$RO_{i+1} = Round\ Map\ Block[RI_i, RCon_i, RCon_{i+1}] \qquad (6)$$

Inside *Round Map Block* $\rho_i$, $\chi_i$ and $RO_i$ are calculated using Eqs. 2 and 3. The $RO_{i+1}$ is generated using Eqs. 7 and 8

$$\iota in_{i+1} = \iota_{i+1}(\pi_{i+1}(\rho_{i+1}(\theta_i(RI_{i+1})))) \qquad (7)$$

$$RO_{i+1} = \iota_{i+1}(\chi_{i+1}, RCon_{i+1}) \qquad (8)$$

Here it may to be noted that in Loop unrolled architecture we double the logic load of each clock to reduce the required number of clock from 24 to 12, which increases the critical path of the architecture.

**Pipelined Loop Unrolled Architecture (PPL2-LU2).** The LU2 architecture stated in the previous section can be adopted in pipeline design. In this PPL2-LU2 architecture 2 pipeline stages are used to compute 24 KECCAK rounds. In the $1^{st}$ pipeline stage one LU2 *Round Map Block* executes $0^{th}$ round to $11^{th}$ round in 6 clock cycles and in $2^{nd}$ pipeline stages another LU2 *Round Map Block* executes $12^{th}$ round to $23^{rd}$ round in the next 6 clock cycles.

$1^{st}$ **Pipeline Stage:** At the $1^{st}$ clock of the $1^{st}$ Pipeline stage $RC_i$ and $RC_{i+1}$ are initialized by 0 and 1 respectively. After passing the $1^{st}$ 6 clocks in *Count Generator* $RC_i$ and $RC_{i+1}$ reach to 10 and 11, respectively and LU2 *Round Map Block* − 1 transforms the state of register $SR − 1$ from $SR_{i-1}$ to $SR_{i+11}$. Then $SR − 1$ sends his state $SR_{i+11}$ to $SR − 2$.

$2^{nd}$ **Pipeline Stage:** For the next 6 clocks 2 operations are executed parallely. In the $7^{th}$ clock of $1^{st}$ operation *Count Generator* re-initializes $RC_i$ and $RC_{i+1}$

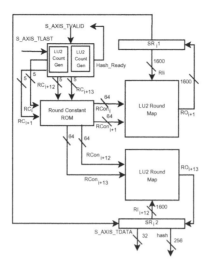

**Fig. 3.** PPL2-LU2 architecture of KECCAK

to 0 and 1 respectively and starts same counting sequence as stated above. The LU2 *Round Map Block* $-1$ grabs a new data word in $SR-1$ and execute pipeline stage-1.

At the $7^{th}$ clock of $2^{nd}$ operation $RC_{i+12}$ and $RC_{i+13}$ start their count from 12 and 13 respectively. By increasing 1 in both $RC_{i+12}$ and $RC_{i+13}$ counts in each clock cycle they reach to 22 and 23 at $12^{th}$ clock. The state register $SR-2$ in LU2 *Round Map Block* $-2$ simultaneously changes state from $SR_{i+11}$ to $SR_{i+23}$ and produces a 256 bit has value at the $23^{rd}$ clock. The PPL2-LU2 design allows a first block at output after 12 clock cycles and it can process a new input block in every six clock cycles. The pictorial presentation of (PPL2-LU2 is shown in Fig. 3.

## 3   System Architecture

The processors offer flexibility, but it weakens the implementation level security of crypto algorithms. In order to avoid side-channel attacks [14], the secret keys must be manipulated regularly using a key management protocol. When a processor accesses and manipulates confidential secret keys, the keys comes in processor registers or in the cache memory, which exposed confidential data for software attacks. We propose an NSP architecture which is partitioned [15] in 3 different areas such as a processor area, a crypto area and a confidential area as shown in Fig. 4. The processor area consists PE, local memory, bus, bus interconnect, DMA, bus streamer between DMA and coprocessor, Data Path Controller (DPC) to set data path connections of coprocessors and other memories. The crypto area consists a Random Number Generator (RNG), Encryption Block, SHA-3 Block and a shared memory shared between PE and coprocessor

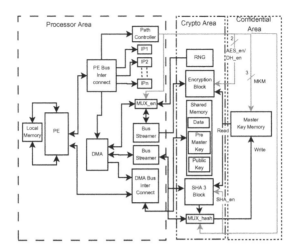

**Fig. 4.** Partition architecture

to store data (plain text, cipher text and hash value), public key and pre-master key. The confidential memory only consists the master key memory.

## 4    System Flow

Let us assume that for an instant, we have a combination of RSA Key Exchange, AES encryption and SHA-3 hash algorithm. A typical security protocol uses several steps for key exchange, encryption and hashing processes.

1. Alice generates a random number named as *client hello* (32 bytes).
2. Alice sends *client hello* to Bob.
3. Bob sends his certificate, public Key and a random number named *server hello* (32 bytes).
4. Alice generates another random number from $RNG$ block placed in the crypto area.
5. Alice encrypts the random number using Bob's public key using RSA algorithm mounted in encryption block of the crypto area. The encrypted random number named *pre master key* is sent to Bob.
6. Bob receives *pre master key*. The KECCAK HMAC algorithm in the crypto area generates a master key (48 bytes) using *pre master key*, *client hello* and *server hello*. Four master keys are generated in this process, such as *client_write_MAC_key*, *server_write_MAC_key*, *client_write_key* and *server_write_key*. Here the MAC keys are for the authentication and integrity, write keys are for the symmetric encryption. Two more keys *client_write_IV* and *server_write_IV* are only generated for implicit *nonce* in Authenticated Encryption with Associated Data (AEAD) cipher.

The four master keys are stored in the four consecutive addresses of *Master Key Memory* (MKM). The MKM is an isolated memory space placed inside the confidential area of NSP. The PE has an access in the address line of MKM but the proposed partitions ensure that no physical data line is established between the processor area and the confidential area, which enforces a prevention from all processor related attacks. DPC is a custom IP connected as slave component of PE through AXI bus. The PE has an access into 8-bit slave register of DPC named as $DPC\_SREG(7:0)$. The least three significant bit of $DPC\_SREG(2:0)$ are connected with Master Key Memory (MKM). The MKM(2) is 1 for memory writing operation and 0 for memory reading operation. MKM(1:0) decides the address of four keys such as 00 for *client_write_MAC_key*, 01 for *client_write_key*, 10 for *server_write_MAC_key*, and 11 for *server_write_key*. $DPC\_SREG(3)$, $DPC\_SREG(4)$ and $DPC\_SREG(5)$ are connected to the enable line of RSA block, SHA block and AES block respectively. $DPC\_SREG(6)$ connected with the selecting input of $MUX\_hash$ to decide whether the hash value will be stored into master key memory for *master key gen process* or into shared memory for *Hash* process. The $DPC\_SREG(7)$ is connected with the selecting input of $MUX\_en$ to decide whether data input of encryption block comes from RNG block for *pre masterkey gen process* or from shared memory for *encryption* process. In Table 1 the DMA addresses and the value of $DPC\_SREG(7:0)$ are shown for 4 different operations such as *Pre master key Generation*, *Master Key Generation*, *Encryption* and *Hash*.

Table 1. DMA addresses & control signals

| Proc name | DMA TxAddr | DMA RxAddr | $MUX\_en$ | $MUX\_hash$ | $RSA\_en$ | $SHA\_en$ | $AES\_en$ | MKM $w\bar{r}{:}ad(1{:}0)$ |
|---|---|---|---|---|---|---|---|---|
| Pre master key gen | × | Pre master | 1 | 0 | 1 | 0 | 0 | × × × |
| Master key gen | Pre master | × | × | 1 | 1 | 0 | 0 | 1 0 0 |
| (*cl_wr_mac_key*, | Pre master | × | × | 1 | 1 | 0 | 0 | 1 0 1 |
| *ser_wr_mac_key*, | Pre master | × | × | 1 | 1 | 0 | 0 | 1 1 0 |
| *cl_wr_key* *ser_write_key*) | Pre master | × | × | 1 | 1 | 0 | 0 | 1 1 1 |
| Encryption | Plain text | Cipher text | 0 | 0 | 0 | 0 | 1 | 0 0 0 |
| Hash | Plain text | Hash text | 0 | 0 | 1 | 0 | 0 | 0 1 0 |

## 5 Implementation and Results

The proposed KECCEAK architectures are implemented in Artix-7 (XC7A100T, CSG324) FPGA platform using Vivado 2015.2 design Suite. The folded architecture achieves 16.49 Gbps throughput which becomes almost double for LU2 architecture. The Folded and LU2 KECCAK achieves better throughput than [1–11,13]. Table 2 shows, the two stages pipeline adopted in PP2-LU2 architecture achieved better throughput than fastest KECCAK till date proposed in

**Table 2.** Comparison table

| Name | Throughput Gbps | Platform | # clock | Clock MHz | # Slices |
|---|---|---|---|---|---|
| Proposed Folded | 16.492 | Artix 7 | 24 | 390.53 | 4188 |
| Proposed LU2 | 19.99 | Artix 7 | 12 | 234.97 | 7139 |
| Proposed PPL2LU2 | 39.98 | Artix 7 | 6 | 234.97 | 8459 |
| [1] | 5.70 | Virtex 5 | 25 | 258 | 2573 |
| DSP V1 [1] | 1.16 | Virtex 5 | 25 | 58 | 3176 |
| DSP V2 [1] | 0.43 | Virtex 5 | 384 | 334 | 3009 |
| Pipelined [1] | 3.12 | Virtex 5 | 49 | 306 | 2326 |
| Sync [1] | 5.56 | Virtex 5 | 25 | 278 | 2517 |
| [13] | 0.07 | Virtex 5 | 5160 | 265 | 444 |
| [2] | 0.08 | Virtex 6 | 2112 | 285 | 188 |
| [3] | 10.25 | Virtex 6 | 24 | 231 | 1043 |
| [4] | 6.07 | Virtex 4 | 25 | 143 | 2024 |
| [5] | 10.54 | Virtex 5 | 20 | 242.77 | 482 |
| [7] 512 | 2.473 | Spartan 3 | 33 | 95.45 | 3362 |
| [7] 512 | 4.795 | Virtex 4 | 33 | 185.05 | 3622 |
| [7] 512 | 3.550 | Virtex 5 | 33 | 137.01 | 1647 |
| [7] 512 | 6.522 | Virtex 6 | 33 | 251.70 | 1181 |
| [7] 512 | 8.023 | Kintex 7 | 33 | 309.69 | 1416 |
| [6] | 9.370 | Virtex 7 | - | 206.70 | 2495 |
| [6] | 0.125 | Virtex 7 | - | 152.23 | 264 |
| [8] DCC | 1.636 | Zed Board | - | 110.74 | 2891 |
| [8] DCCL | 0.25 | Zed Board | - | 104 | 2923 |
| [3] | 13.67 | Virtex 6 | 24 | 301.57 | 915 |
| [3] | 12.49 | Virtex 5 | 24 | 275.56 | 133 |
| [9] | 11.84 | Virtex 6 | - | - | 1165 |
| [9] | 12.77 | Virtex 5 | - | - | 1395 |
| [10] | 0.843 | Virtex 6 | - | 159 | 393 |
| [11] | 0.152 | Virtex 5 | - | 248 | 134 |
| [12] | 27.07 | Virtex 4 | 6 | 282 | 12870 |
| [12] | 34.272 | Virtex 5 | 6 | 357 | 4632 |
| [12] | 37.632 | Virtex 6 | 6 | 392 | 4117 |

article [12]. The timing diagram for KECCAK core is shown in Fig. 5 where DMA sends 34 word through $S\_AXIS\_TDATA$ keeping the $S\_AXIS\_TVALID$ high for 34 clock. The $S\_AXIS\_TLAST$ indicates $34^{th}$ word and starts KECCAK core. The Folded KECCAK takes 24 clock cycles and produces 256 bit hash data which passed to DMA while master port $M\_AXIS\_TVALID$ keeps high. As shown in Fig. 5, the whole computation process are divided into 3 finite states. Memory reading by DMA takes 34 clocks, hashing process takes 24 clock cycles and memory writing takes 8 clock cycles. The timing diagram of LU2 and PP2-LU2 is selfsame with Fig. 5, except the hashing time. LU2 and PP2-LU2 consume 12 and 6 clock cycles respectively. The power consumption of Folded, LU2 and PPL2-LU2 architecture are 166.959 w, 701.979 w and 1754.825 w respectively.

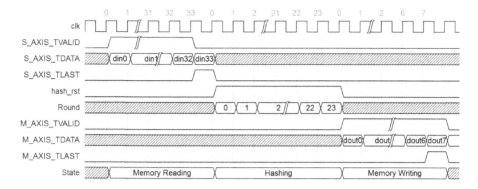

**Fig. 5.** Timing diagram of folded KECCAK architecture

# 6 Conclusions

This paper proposes 3 high-speed architectures for KECCAK hash algorithm. The loop unrolled and pipelined approaches create a major acceleration in PPL2-LU2 architecture. The high-speed KECCAK finds applications mainly in NSP based platform. The security protocol running in proposed partitioned NSP uses KECCAK for hashing and master Key generation purposes. The isolated key memory prevents leakage of key information. DMA provides a smart data transfer between main memory to crypto coprocessor keeping the processor free for control signal generation, data interface hazards, and data path setup tasks.

# References

1. Provelengios, G., Kitsos, P., Sklavos, N., Koulamas, C.: FPGA-based design approaches of keccak hash function. In: 2012 15th Euromicro Conference on Digital System Design, pp. 648–653, September 2012
2. Kerckhof, S., Durvaux, F., Veyrat-Charvillon, N., Regazzoni, F., de Dormale, G.M., Standaert, F.-X.: Compact FPGA implementations of the five SHA-3 finalists. In: Prouff, E. (ed.) CARDIS 2011. LNCS, vol. 7079, pp. 217–233. Springer, Heidelberg (2011). https://doi.org/10.1007/978-3-642-27257-8_14
3. Latif, K., Rao, M.M., Mahboob, A., Aziz, A.: Novel arithmetic architecture for high performance implementation of SHA-3 finalist keccak on FPGA platforms. In: Choy, O.C.S., Cheung, R.C.C., Athanas, P., Sano, K. (eds.) ARC 2012. LNCS, vol. 7199, pp. 372–378. Springer, Heidelberg (2012). https://doi.org/10.1007/978-3-642-28365-9_34
4. Akin, A., Aysu, A., Ulusel, O.C., Savaş, E.: Efficient hardware implementations of high throughput sha-3 candidates keccak, luffa and blue midnight wish for single-and multi-message hashing. In: Proceedings of the 3rd International Conference on Security of Information and Networks, SIN 2010, pp. 168–177. ACM, New York (2010)
5. Moreira, N., Astarloa, A., Kretzschmar, U., Lázaro, J., Molina, E.: Securing IEEE 1588 messages with message authentication codes based on the keccak cryptographic algorithm implemented in FPGAs. In: 2014 IEEE 23rd International Symposium on Industrial Electronics (ISIE), pp. 1899–1904, June 2014

6. Yalla, P., Homsirikamol, E., Kaps, J.P.: Comparison of multi-purpose cores of keccak and AES. In: 2015 Design, Automation Test in Europe Conference Exhibition (DATE), pp. 585–588, March 2015

7. Honda, T., Guntur, H., Satoh, A.: FPGA implementation of new standard hash function keccak. In: 2014 IEEE 3rd Global Conference on Consumer Electronics (GCCE), pp. 275–279, October 2014

8. Ahmed, K.E., Farag, M.M.: Hardware/software co-design of a dynamically configurable sha-3 system-on-chip (soc). In: 2015 IEEE International Conference on Electronics, Circuits, and Systems (ICECS), pp. 617–620, December 2015

9. Gaj, K., Homsirikamol, E., Rogawski, M., Shahid, R., Sharif, M.U.: Comprehensive evaluation of high-speed and medium-speed implementations of five SHA-3 finalists using xilinx and altera FPGAs. IACR Cryptology ePrint Archive 2012, p. 368 (2012)

10. Jungk, B., Apfelbeck, J.: Area-efficient FPGA implementations of the sha-3 finalists. In: 2011 International Conference on Reconfigurable Computing and FPGAs, pp. 235–241, November 2011

11. Winderickx, J., Daemen, J., Mentens, N.: Exploring the use of shift register lookup tables for keccak implementations on xilinx FPGAs. In: 2016 26th International Conference on Field Programmable Logic and Applications (FPL), pp. 1–4, August 2016

12. Michail, H.E., Ioannou, L., Voyiatzis, A.G.: Pipelined sha-3 implementations on FPGA: architecture and performance analysis. In: Proceedings of the Second Workshop on Cryptography and Security in Computing Systems, CS2 2015, pp. 13:13–13:18. ACM, New York (2015)

13. Peeters, M., Bertoni, G., Daemen, J., Van Assche, G.: Keccak sponge function family main document, April 2009. http://keccak.noekeon.org

14. Standaert, F.-X., van Oldeneel tot Oldenzeel, L., Samyde, D., Quisquater, J.-J.: Power analysis of FPGAs: how practical is the attack? In: Y. K. Cheung, P., Constantinides, G.A. (eds.) FPL 2003. LNCS, vol. 2778, pp. 701–710. Springer, Heidelberg (2003). https://doi.org/10.1007/978-3-540-45234-8_68

15. Gaspar, L., Fischer, V., Bossuet, L., Fouquet, R.: Secure extension of FPGA general purpose processors for symmetric key cryptography with partial reconfiguration capabilities. ACM Trans. Reconfigurable Technol. Syst. 5(3), 16:1–16:13 (2012)

# New Energy Efficient Reconfigurable FIR Filter Architecture and Its VLSI Implementation

Naushad Ali$^{(\boxtimes)}$ and Bharat Garg

ABV - Indian Institute of Information Technology and Management Gwalior,
Gwalior 474015, Madhya Pradesh, India
naushad.iiitmg@gmail.com, bharat.iiitm@gmail.com

**Abstract.** High performance and energy efficient reconfigurable FIR filter is the imperative requirement in the modern wireless communication applications. The transposed form block FIR filter based on distributed arithmetic proves to best suit the requirements of such application. Therefore, this paper presents a new energy efficient, multiplier-less transposed form block FIR filter architecture for reconfigurable applications using distributed arithmetic based approach. The proposed architecture provides improved area-delay product (ADP) and reconfigurability by employing efficient coefficient storage unit and multiplication using add-and-shift logic, respectively. The synthesis results at FPGA level show that the proposed architecture exhibits 13.15% and 13.33% reduced energy per sample for the filter length 64 with a block size of 4 and 8 samples respectively, over the existing design. Further, ASIC level results for filter length 64 and block size 8 shows 20.91% reduction in ADP and 32.86% reduction in the area over the existing architecture.

**Keywords:** Energy efficiency · Reconfigurable design · FIR filter

## 1 Introduction

The energy efficiency and high performance are the paramount concern for the modern portable/wearable devices due to exhibiting compute intensive multimedia applications. The performance of these devices significantly depends on the different signal processing units embedded in these devices. Among the various signal processing unit, the Finite Impulse Response (FIR) filter is the most commonly used due to its absolute stability and linear phase. Various applications such as speech and image processing, speaker equalization, echo cancellation and many high-speed digital communication applications including Software Defined Radio (SDR) [4] requires FIR filter as dominant processing unit. Since, the applications like SDR, where a channelizer consists of a bank of FIR filters, selects narrow band signals from a wide-band signal and supports multiple wireless communication standards, a channelizer requires a reconfigurable FIR filter of higher order and sharp cutoff frequency. It also requires high sampling rate to meet the high-frequency specifications. As the number of arithmetic operations increases with the order of the filter, the area and power also increase. Since the FIR filter

© Springer Nature Singapore Pte Ltd. 2017
B. K. Kaushik et al. (Eds.): VDAT 2017, CCIS 711, pp. 519–532, 2017.
https://doi.org/10.1007/978-981-10-7470-7_51

algorithm does not contain any redundant computation, it becomes harder to develop a reconfigurable filter of a large order with constrained resources. Thus, a low power high-performance reconfigurable FIR (Re-FIR) filter is the critical requirement.

Low-power, high-operating frequency, and reconfigurability are the three mutually conflicting design features of FIR filter which makes its design challenging. Many design attempts have been made to address these three issues in a single efficient filter architecture. To reduce implementation the complexity, a computation sharing method is presented [12]. Further, a reconfigurable canonical signed digit based filter architecture [3] and a double-base number system based architecture [2] are also proposed to reduce the number of digits in the coefficients. Since these designs exhibit a significant reconfiguration overhead, they do not give an area delay efficient architecture. A programmable shift method and a constant shift method is presented to develop a Re-FIR architecture of high order filters [6]. A Distributed Arithmetic (DA) based technique [14] with block processing provides high throughput and increased regularity which results in cost-effective and area-time efficient architecture. Though the DA based technique [11] tries to address above limitations, a large number of multipliers and inefficient use of LUTs limits the performance of the filter. In this paper, we propose a multiplier-less DA-based transposed form block FIR filter. The major contributions of the paper are as follows:

- A distributed-arithmetic based approach is analyzed for block processing in transpose form structures to achieve high and scalable throughput FIR filter architecture.
- A new energy efficient reconfigurable FIR filter architecture is proposed.
- The proposed architecture is implemented on FPGA to evaluate hardware effectiveness. Further, ASIC level comparative analysis is also presented.
- The proposed architecture shows 8% and 15% reduced area-delay product and energy per sample respectively over the existing for the filter length of 64 with a block size of 8 samples.

Rest of this paper is organized as follows: Sect. 2 presents the related work on FIR filter architectures followed by basic concepts of transpose form structure, block processing and analysis of the transpose form block FIR filter equations. Section 3 presents the proposed multiplier less transpose form block FIR filter. Section 4 presents the simulation result and analysis to evaluate the efficacy of the proposed filter over the existing. Finally, the conclusion of the paper is given in Sect. 5.

## 2    Related Work

Significant design efforts have been given to reduce the computational complexity and to achieve reconfigurability for a large order of FIR filters either by reducing the number of arithmetic operations or by eliminating the need of multipliers. To reduce the implementation complexity, Park et al. [12] presented a computation sharing vector scaling method by exploiting the Computation Sharing Multiplier (CSHM). In this approach, large constant multiplications are segmented into smaller multipliers and pre-computed. These precomputed values are shared among different select units to compute large multiplication. Although the technique reduces the implementation complexity of the lower order filter, the approach becomes ineffective at the higher order.

Several multiplier-less architectures have been proposed based on Common Sub-Expression Elimination (CSE) and shift-add methods [5,7]. Mahesh et al. [7] present a Constant Shift Method (CSM) and Programmable Shift Method (PSM) using Binary Common Subexpression Elimination (BCSE) method. In the CSM, coefficients are partitioned into fixed coefficient groups to implement constant shifters effectively. Although this technique provides high performance, it consumes more area and power and can be used only for implementing fixed coefficient FIR filter. On the other hand, the PSM uses pre-analysis block to remove the coefficient's redundancy employing BCSE algorithm. Due to the large area and power requirement of the programmable processors which provide reconfigurability, the PSM technique becomes inefficient. Further, both PSM and CSM based architecture exhibit a significant number of multiplexers that increases their implementation cost.

Apart from the computation sharing and subexpression elimination approaches, various attempts are also made to decrease the computational complexity of FIR by reducing the number of digits participating in computations. Canonic Sign Digit (CSD) Reconfigurable FIR (R-FIR) [3] uses a digit based technique, where the number of ones in coefficients is reduced to half by converting the 2's complement coefficients into the CSD representation. In CSD representation, no two consecutive numbers are non-zero. The process of encoding coefficient into CSD requires a large area, making this approach inefficient for large orders. Another digit based technique for FIR filter uses a double-base number system (DBNS) to reduce the number of bits in 2's complement coefficients and inputs by converting them into double base number digits [2]. Since DBNS requires reverse and forward data converters to encode the 2's complement numbers into double base digits and additional arithmetic logic, the area overhead become significantly large.

All the above-mentioned design techniques exhibit significant area overhead when employed to design higher-order/reconfigurable FIR filters. New Multiple Constant Multiplication (MCM) and Distributed Arithmetic (DA) approaches [8,9] have been proposed to achieve high performance and low power filtering. In MCM, the multiplication of one variable (input sample) is performed with several constants (filter coefficients) and the intermediate results are shared to minimize the overall computational complexity of the filter. To further improve the efficiency of the MCM based methods, the CSD representation of coefficients and sharing them across the entire network of adders and shifters is used [10]. As the number of coefficients increases, the MCM method becomes more efficient. However, this method is well suited for large order filters; it can be used to realize only fixed coefficient filters. On the other hand, in DA, the arithmetic operations processed in parallel to reduce the number of multiplications and additions. It uses Look Up Tables (LUTs) to store filter constants, and Multiply-Accumulate (MAC) blocks to compute the final filter output. The DA-based method is popular for its high throughput and area-delay efficiency.

In addition to the filter architectures mentioned above, a low complexity high performance transposed form based FIR filter architecture is also proposed in [13]. Since the realization of FIR filters can be done in the direct form and transpose form structures, the direct form does realize the filter equation directly so it is prone to parameter variations and is not inherently pipelined. Whereas, the transpose forms are preferred because they are pipelined inherently and provides high operating frequency to avail higher rate of sampling. Furthermore, the block processing of FIR filters is preferred over the sample by sample based processing as it provides high and scalable throughput with improved area-delay product efficiency for higher order designs [1]. To take the computational advantage of transpose form and block processing together, Mohanty et al. [11] presented a transpose form block reconfigurable FIR filter [TBR-FIR]. This filter provides improved area-delay product and high sampling rate over the existing designs. Since the complexity of LUTs is excluded in the computation of area and performance, it performs inefficiently while considering the overhead of the reconfiguration. Further, the architecture is multiplier based and therefore, provides poor performance for high order filters. Thus, a DA-based multiplier-less transpose form block FIR filter is required to provide high energy and area-delay product efficiency.

The following subsection presents transposed-form FIR filter to achieve low complexity realization followed by the principle of block processing. Finally, the mathematical analysis of transposed form FIR filter is presented with a DA-based approach.

### 2.1   Transpose Form FIR Filter

The output of $N^{th}$ order FIR filter is a weighted linear combination of (N−1) past input samples with a present input. It is given by Eq. 1.

$$y(n) = \sum_{i=0}^{N-1} h(i)x(n-i) \tag{1}$$

where, $x(n)$ is the input sample, $h(i)$ is the filter coefficient and $N$ is the order of the filter. The Z-domain expression of the transpose form filter is given by:

$$Y(z) = \sum_{i=0}^{N-1} h(i)z^{-i}X(z) \tag{2}$$

This equation can be rearranged to compute recursively as by the Eq. 3.

$$Y(z) = [z^{-1} \ldots (z^{-1}(z^{-1}h(N-1) + h(N-2)) + h(N-3)) \\ \cdots + h(1)) + h(0)]X(z) \tag{3}$$

The recursive relation of Eq. 3 shows that the transpose form provides inherent pipelining which reduces the computational complexity and supports high operating frequency. This paper exploits the inherent pipelining of the transposed form filter to improve the performance of the filter.

## 2.2   Block Processing in FIR Filter

The input to the FIR filters can be given either in the sample by sample form or in the form of blocks. The block by block processing of the input sample provides a high throughput rate and reduces the computation complexity through the efficient block processing algorithm [1]. It also gives the flexibility to process the computations in parallel machines. In this approach, the coefficients H are portioned in the form of blocks while input is linear. On the other hand, separating the inputs X into the block and keeping the coefficients linear provides block processing of input [11]. For the $k^{th}$ block, the filter equation in Z-transform form can be given by Eq. 4.

$$Y_k(z) = \sum_{i=0}^{k} H_{(k-i)} X_i(z) z^{-i} \tag{4}$$

The block processing along with transposed form can be utilized to achieve high performance and scalable throughput. By utilizing block processing for transpose form structure with the block size of 2 samples, the data flow graph for the Eq. 3 with $N = 6$ having two consecutive input samples $x(n)$ and $x(n-1)$ as a block is shown in Fig. 1.

This paper considers block processing of input to achieve high and scalable throughput by dividing the computation in different small product generators that work in parallel. The next subsection presents the mathematical analysis of

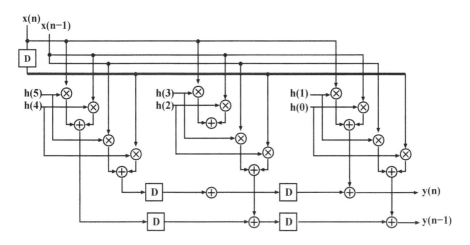

**Fig. 1.** Transpose form block realization with block size = 2.

transpose form block FIR filter equation to derive reconfigurable energy efficient filter architectures.

## 2.3    Analysis of Transpose Form Block FIR Filter Equation

The mathematical expression of the filter with block processing of input is given by 5.

$$y_k = \sum_{i=0}^{N-1} \mathbf{x}_k^i \cdot h(i). \tag{5}$$

In this expression, the filter takes L number of inputs as one block and generates L number of output samples in every cycle. The block of input $X_k$ can be represented as

$$\mathbf{X}_k = \begin{bmatrix} \mathbf{x}_k^0 & \mathbf{x}_k^1 & \cdots \mathbf{x}_k^{N-1} \end{bmatrix} \tag{6}$$

where $\mathbf{x}_k^i$ are input samples and $h(i)$ are filter coefficients. Each $(i+1)^{th}$ element of $X_k$ is given by

$$\mathbf{x}_k^i = \begin{bmatrix} x(kL-i)\, x(kL-i-1) \cdots x(kL-i-L+1) \end{bmatrix}^T. \tag{7}$$

The block size $L$ must be taken such that the N becomes an integer multiple of L, i.e. $N = ML$, where M is the total number of blocks. Further, the index $i$ is also divided as $i = l + ml$ where, $0 \le l \le L-1$ and $0 \le m \le M-1$. By keeping the value of $i = l + ml$ in Eq. 7, we get $\mathbf{x}_k^{(1+\mathbf{mL})} = \mathbf{x}_{k-m}^l$ and Eq. 5 becomes

$$y_k = \sum_{l=0}^{L-1} \sum_{m=0}^{M-1} x_{k-m}^l h(l+mL) \tag{8}$$

where,

$$\mathbf{X}_k = \begin{bmatrix} \mathbf{x}_k^0 & \mathbf{x}_k^1 & \cdots & \mathbf{x}_k^{L-1} & \mathbf{x}_{k-1}^0 & \mathbf{x}_{k-1}^1 & \cdots \mathbf{x}_{k-1}^{L-1} & \cdots \mathbf{x}_{k-M+1}^0 & \mathbf{x}_{k-M+1}^1 & \cdots & \mathbf{x}_{k-M+1}^{L-1} \end{bmatrix}$$

The $X_k$ can be divided in small sub matrices such as $S_k^0 = \{\mathbf{x}_k^0 \quad \mathbf{x}_k^1 \quad \mathbf{x}_k^2 \cdots \mathbf{x}_k^{L-1}\}$ to $S_k^{M-1} = \{\mathbf{x}_{k-M+1}^0 \quad \mathbf{x}_{k-M+1}^1 \quad \mathbf{x}_{k-M+1}^2 \cdots \mathbf{x}_{k-M+1}^{L-1}\}$. Since $S_k^m$ is symmetric, $S_k^m = S_{k-m}^0$ i.e. $S_k^m$ for $0 \le m \le M-1$ are delayed versions of $S_k^0$. Thus, by using $S_k^0$ only, we can derive the rest of the elements. Similarly, $h(l+mL)$ can be decomposed as $C_m = \begin{bmatrix} h(mL) & h(mL+1) \cdots h(mL+L-1) \end{bmatrix}$. So Eq. 8 finally becomes

$$y_k = \sum_{m=0}^{M-1} S_{k-m}^0 C_m \tag{9}$$

If, $S_{k-m}^0 C_m = r_k^m$, then

$$y_k = \sum_{m=0}^{M-1} r_k^m \tag{10}$$

This represents that the output of the filter is obtained by adding the partial products of block processed input $S^0_{k-m}$ and coefficients matrix $C_m$. The above derived low complexity, DA-based transposed form block FIR filter equation Eq. 10 is used in this paper to propose the area efficient reconfigurable FIR filter architecture.

# 3   Proposed Energy Efficient Reconfigurable FIR (EER-FIR) Filter

The proposed reconfigurable FIR filter architecture as shown in Fig. 2 is based on Eq. 10. It provides transpose form block based FIR filter operation with low implementation complexity. The proposed filter computes the output by summing the partial products $(r^m_k)$. To effectively reduce the implementation area of the filter, the partial products are generated using area efficient Shift-ADD Unit (SAU). Furthermore, to improve the performance, the coefficients of the filters are stored in the ROM based LUTs.

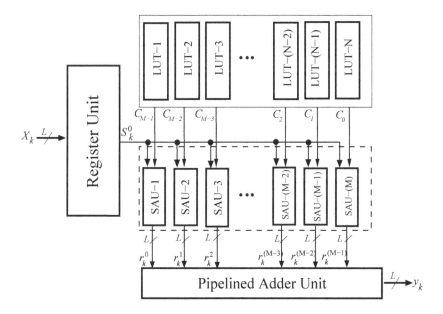

**Fig. 2.** Proposed reconfigurable FIR filter architecture.

The detailed description of proposed EER-FIR filter is given in following subsections.

## 3.1   Register Unit

The register unit is used to process the input sample in the form of blocks and is similar to the one used in [11]. This unit receives $L$ number of input samples every cycle and produces $L$ rows of $S_k^0$, where $L$ is the block size. It uses $(L-1)$ delay registers to produce the delayed version of the input sample. For the block size of $L = 4$, $k^{th}$ block takes four input sample $x(kL), x(kL-1), x(kL-2), x(kL-3)$ and generates four rows of $S_k^0$ ($\mathbf{x}_k^0, x_k^1 x_k^2$, and $\mathbf{x_k^3}$). Thus, the block formulation of input samples is done by register unit which provides scalable throughput and high performance.

### 3.2   Storage Unit

To achieve the reconfigurability, all the coefficients of different filters are stored in this unit. The implementation of the design using LUT requires less memory due to its distributive nature whereas the Block RAM (BRAM) requires large memory. Further, the access time required in LUTs is also smaller compared to the BRAMs. Therefore, we have considered LUTs to implement the proposed design. The storage unit is divided in N-LUTs to improve the accessing time. To implement $P$ number of filters, the depth of each LUT is taken as $P$ words. It shares a common address of $\mathbf{w} = \mathbf{log_2 P}$ bits to access the filter coefficients from the LUT. Further, the filter coefficients are stored such that the coefficients of the specific filter are obtained in single clock cycle using a particular address. For example, if 64 coefficients of 8 different filters are stored at 8 different positions then each LUT is connected to 3-bit address line to select one of the eight filters. For address $w = 000$, all the coefficients belonging to this address are accessed. Thus, this unit provides reconfigurability by selecting a specific type of filter from various filters available in the LUTs (Fig. 3).

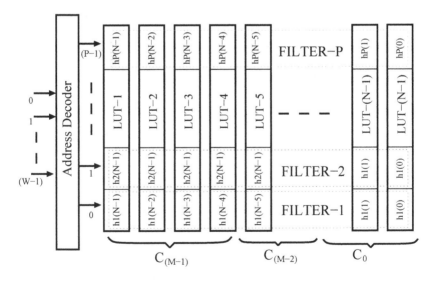

**Fig. 3.** Storage unit architecture for reconfigurable FIR with block size (L) = 4.

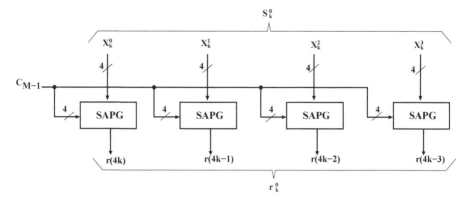

**Fig. 4.** Internal architecture of the SAU-1 with L = 4.

### 3.3  Shift and Add Unit (SAU)

The implementation complexity of FIR filter is further reduced by Shift and Add Unit. This unit generates the partial results $r_k^m$ of the filter by the vector product of input block $S_k^0$ and filter coefficients $C_m$. Each SAU consists of $M$ Shift and Add Product Generator (SAPG). For block size $L = 4$, the internal architecture of SAU-1 is shown in Fig. 4.

The $(m+1)^{th}$ SAU receives $L$ rows of $S_k^0$ and a coefficient vectors $\mathbf{C}_{(M-m-1)}$ and produces $m^{th}$ partial product $r_k^m$ of the filter. As shown in Fig. 4, for the vector product of four rows of each column $(\mathbf{x}_k^0, \mathbf{x}_k^1 \mathbf{x}_k^2, \mathbf{x}_k^3)$ of $S_k^0$ with coefficient vector $C_{M-1}$, it uses four SAPGs. The $(l+1)^{th}$ SAPG receives the $L$ rows of $\mathbf{x}_k^l$ and the coefficient vector $C_m$ and generates a partial products $r(kL - l)$, for $0 \leq l \leq (L-1)$. For instance, the first SAPG as shown in Fig. 4 receives input variables $x(4k), x(4k - 1), x(4k - 2), x(4k - 3)$ and multiply with coefficients $h(4m), h(4m + 1), h(4m + 2), h(4m + 3)$. To achieve this multiplication, SAPG utilizes shift and add algorithm of multiplication instead of a conventional multiplier. Since shift and add multiplier consumes very less power and area as compared to conventional multipliers, it helps to reduce the overall area of FIR filter significantly.

### 3.4  Pipelined Adder Unit

The pipelined adder unit is used to add the partial filter results generated by SAUs. It receives $M$ partial filter results $r_k^m$ from $M$ SAU units in every cycle. These partial products are added using ripple carry adders, connected in the pipelined manner such that $r_k^0$ is delayed by $(M-1)$ unit whereas $r_k^{M-1}$ gets no delay. Thus, this unit generates a block of $L$ filter output for every $L$ samples received by register unit.

The efficiency of proposed design, discussed in next section shows that the complete design architecture obtained by above method provides high performance and low implementation area than all the existing designs.

# 4   Result Analysis

The efficacy of the proposed filter is evaluated and compared to the existing architectures at FPGA and ASIC levels. The following subsections first present the comparative analysis on FPGA level followed by the ASIC level.

## 4.1   FPGA Result Analysis

To evaluate the efficacy of the proposed filter architecture at FPGA level, the proposed and existing filter designs are implemented in Verilog with different block sizes and filter lengths. We have considered the filter lengths of 16, 32, and 64 with block sizes of 4 and 8 samples. Further, each input sample and filter coefficient are of 8-bits and produces the output of 22-bits. The filter coefficients of eight different filters are stored in LUT-ROM to achieve reconfigurability. The designs are implemented on Virtex VC-707 evaluation FPGA board using Xilinx's Vivado 16.2. The Virtex-7 family is based on a 28 nm design and is reported to deliver a two-fold system performance improvement at 50% lower power compared to previous generation Virtex-6 devices. We have also implemented the transpose form block based reconfigurable FIR filter architecture [11], with similar constraints to have an apple-to-apple comparison. The post synthesis results are summarized in Table 1.

It can be observed from the synthesis results that the proposed architecture requires significantly reduced number of LUTs and FFs over the TBR-FIR [11] in all designs of different filter length and block sizes. Further, the value of the gate count decreases more significantly when block size and filter length increases making it more area efficient for large block size and filter length. The gate counts of the filter of different lengths with the block size of 8 samples are shown in Fig. 5.

It is observable from the Fig. 5 that the gate counts decreases significantly when filter length increases for a fixed block size. The power metric of the proposed filter is significantly smaller over the existing. Although the proposed

**Table 1.** FPGA synthesis results for proposed and existing architecture

| | Filter | | #LUTs | #FFs | #Gate (K) | Power (mW) | Delay (ns) | EPS (nJ) |
|---|---|---|---|---|---|---|---|---|
| Block size = 4 | N = 16 | TBR | 3336 | 272 | 18.50 | 370 | 5.12 | 0.47 |
| | | Prop | 1778 | 239 | 6.96 | 350 | 5.51 | 0.49 |
| | N = 32 | TBR | 6594 | 656 | 41.04 | 440 | 5.14 | 0.56 |
| | | Prop | 2291 | 567 | 13.03 | 380 | 5.61 | 0.53 |
| | N = 64 | TBR | 13401 | 1617 | 91.85 | 570 | 5.37 | 076 |
| | | Prop | 4837 | 1143 | 29.61 | 450 | 5.82 | 0.66 |
| Block size = 8 | N = 16 | TBR | 8417 | 306 | 36.88 | 540 | 5.39 | 0.38 |
| | | Prop | 6663 | 288 | 13.57 | 490 | 5.59 | 0.33 |
| | N = 32 | TBR | 13089 | 672 | 80.68 | 600 | 5.96 | 0.44 |
| | | Prop | 5926 | 507 | 26.98 | 530 | 6.30 | 0.42 |
| | N = 64 | TBR | 24468 | 1246 | 142.52 | 800 | 6.14 | 0.60 |
| | | Prop | 8687 | 1168 | 52.87 | 650 | 6.37 | 0.52 |

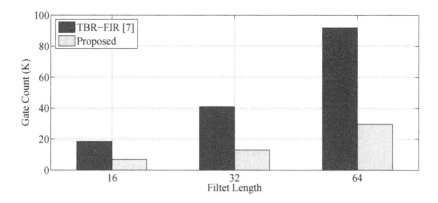

**Fig. 5.** Comparison of gate counts for varying N and L = 8.

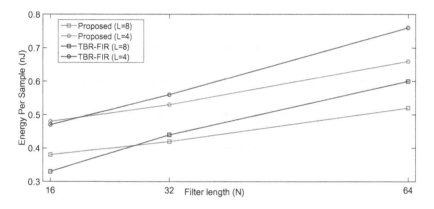

**Fig. 6.** Comparison of energy per sample for varying filter length and block size.

design exhibits slightly increased delay, the power delay product (PDP) of the proposed design is significantly smaller over the existing. The energy per sample (EPS) as shown in the Table is obtained by PDP divided by the block size. The EPS for varying filter length and block size of the proposed filter over the existing exhibits smaller value as shown in Fig. 6. The proposed filter shows 4.2% increased energy for $N = 16$ and $L = 4$ whereas it reduces significantly to more than 13% at $N = 64$ and $L = 8$. Thus, the proposed filter architecture is highly energy efficient for higher order filter designs.

### 4.2 ASIC Result Analysis

The proposed and existing [11] designs are synthesized using Cadence RC-compiler with TSMC-180 nm CMOS technology for the block size 4 and 8 with filter length 16, 32 and 64. The design metrics obtained are summarized in Table 2.

**Table 2.** ASIC synthesis results of existing and proposed architecture

|  | Filter |  | Power (mW) | Delay (ns) | EPS (nJ) |
|---|---|---|---|---|---|
| Block size = 4 | N = 16 | TBR | 443.6 | 22.69 | 9.64 |
|  |  | Prop | 289.1 | 14.25 | 12.81 |
|  | N = 32 | TBR | 921.2 | 58.94 | 60.59 |
|  |  | Prop | 564.6 | 60.59 | 14.85 |
|  | N = 64 | TBR | 1994.1 | 136.76 | 12.59 |
|  |  | Prop | 1227.5 | 98.75 | 14.80 |
| Block size = 8 | N = 16 | TBR | 843.9 | 40.19 | 9.97 |
|  |  | Prop | 555.8 | 17.05 | 12.29 |
|  | N = 32 | TBR | 1768.6 | 111.50 | 11.27 |
|  |  | Prop | 1123.5 | 52.86 | 14.12 |
|  | N = 64 | TBR | 3219.5 | 138.18 | 12.58 |
|  |  | Prop | 2161.4 | 95.02 | 14.82 |

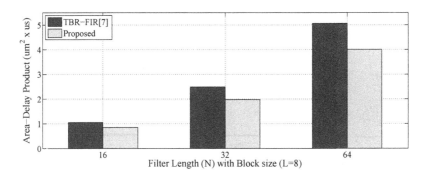

**Fig. 7.** Area-Delay product of proposed and existing filters.

Table 2 shows that the area of proposed design is smaller than the existing architecture for different block sizes and filter lengths. The reduction in area for the block size of 8 with filter length 64 and 16 is 32.86% and 34.13% respectively. Similarly, for the block size of 4 samples and the filter length of 64 and 16, the reduction in area is 38.44% and 33.30% respectively.

Although the delay increases due to shift-add approach, the area-delay product (ADP) per sample is significantly smaller over the existing design as shown in Fig. 7. Similarly, the EPS for different filter length with block size (L) of eight is plotted as shown in Fig. 8 which reflect that the proposed architecture exhibits smaller energy consumption over the existing filter architecture. The synthesis results on the FPGA and ASIC are different due to the difference in technology

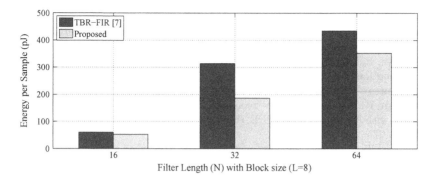

**Fig. 8.** Energy per sample comparison for varying filter length.

nodes, for example, the Vertex-7 is designed with 28 nm technology whereas in ASIC results are evaluated with 180 nm PDK. However, the proposed design provides significantly improved metrics over the existing filter architectures in both the design technologies.

## 5 Conclusion

In this paper, an energy efficient reconfigurable FIR filter architecture is proposed. The energy-efficiency and high performance are achieved by using (1) DA-based approach (2) Transpose form structure for block processing of the input samples and, (3) Multiplier-less architecture. The design are implemented and synthesized on FPGA. The synthesis results at FPGA level show that the proposed architecture exhibits 13.15% and 13.33% reduced energy per sample for the filter length 64 with a block size of 4 and 8 samples respectively, over the existing design. Further, ASIC level results for filter length 64 and block size 8 shows 20.91% reduction in ADP and 32.86% reduction in the area over the existing architecture.

## References

1. Burrus, C.: Block realization of digital filters. IEEE Trans. Audio Electroacoust. **20**(4), 230–235 (1972)
2. Chen, J., Chang, C.H., Feng, F., Ding, W., Ding, J.: Novel design algorithm for low complexity programmable FIR filters based on extended double base number system. IEEE Trans. Circuits Syst. I Regul. Pap. **62**(1), 224–233 (2015)
3. Chen, K.H., Chiueh, T.D.: A low-power digit-based reconfigurable FIR filter. IEEE Trans. Circuits Syst. II Express Briefs **53**(8), 617–621 (2006)
4. Hentschel, T., Fettweis, G.: Software radio receivers. In: Swarts, F., van Rooyen, P., Oppermann, I., Lötter, M.P. (eds.) CDMA Techniques for Third Generation Mobile Systems. The Springer International Series in Engineering and Computer Science, vol. 487, pp. 257–283. Springer, Boston (1999). https://doi.org/10.1007/978-1-4615-5103-4_10

5. Mahesh, R., Vinod, A.P.: Reconfigurable low complexity FIR filters for software radio receivers. In: 2006 IEEE 17th International Symposium on Personal, Indoor and Mobile Radio Communications, pp. 1–5. IEEE (2006)
6. Mahesh, R., Vinod, A.P.: A new common subexpression elimination algorithm for realizing low-complexity higher order digital filters. IEEE Trans. Comput. Aided Des. Integr. Circuits Syst. **27**(2), 217–229 (2008)
7. Mahesh, R., Vinod, A.P.: New reconfigurable architectures for implementing FIR filters with low complexity. IEEE Trans. Comput. Aided Des. Integr. Circuits Syst. **29**(2), 275–288 (2010)
8. Meher, P.K.: Hardware-efficient systolization of DA-based calculation of finite digital convolution. IEEE Trans. Circuits Syst. II Express Briefs **53**(8), 707–711 (2006)
9. Meher, P.K.: New approach to look-up-table design and memory-based realization of FIR digital filter. IEEE Trans. Circuits Syst. I Regul. Pap. **57**(3), 592–603 (2010)
10. Meher, P.K., Pan, Y.: MCM-based implementation of block FIR filters for high-speed and low-power applications. In: 2011 IEEE/IFIP 19th International Conference on VLSI and System-on-Chip (VLSI-SoC), pp. 118–121. IEEE (2011)
11. Mohanty, B.K., Meher, P.K.: A high-performance FIR filter architecture for fixed and reconfigurable applications. IEEE Trans. Very Large Scale Integr. VLSI Syst. **24**(2), 444–452 (2016)
12. Park, J., Jeong, W., Mahmoodi-Meimand, H., Wang, Y., Choo, H., Roy, K.: Computation sharing programmable FIR filter for low-power and high-performance applications. IEEE J. Solid-State Circuits **39**(2), 348–357 (2004)
13. Park, S.Y., Meher, P.K.: Efficient FPGA and ASIC realizations of a DA-based reconfigurable FIR digital filter. IEEE Trans. Circuits Syst. II Express Briefs **61**(7), 511–515 (2014)
14. White, S.A.: Applications of distributed arithmetic to digital signal processing: a tutorial review. IEEE ASSP Mag. **6**(3), 4–19 (1989)

# FPGA-Based Smart Camera System for Real-Time Automated Video Surveillance

Sanjay Singh$^{(\boxtimes)}$, Sumeet Saurav, Ravi Saini,
Atanendu S. Mandal, and Santanu Chaudhury

CSIR-Central Electronics Engineering Research Institute (CSIR-CEERI),
Pilani 333031, Rajasthan, India
sanjay@ceeri.res.in

**Abstract.** Automated video surveillance is a rapidly evolving area and has been gaining importance in the research community in recent years due to its capabilities of performing more efficient and effective surveillance by employing smart cameras. In this article, we present the design and implementation of an FPGA-based smart camera system for automated video surveillance. The complete system is prototyped on Xilinx ML510 FPGA platform and meets the real-time requirements of video surveillance applications while aiming at FPGA resource reduction. The implemented smart camera system is capable of automatically performing real-time motion detection, real-time video history generation, real-time focused region extraction, real-time filtering of frames of interest, and real-time object tracking of identified target with automatic purposive camera movement. The system is designed to work in real-time for live color video streams of standard PAL ($720 \times 576$) resolution, which is the most commonly used video resolution for current generation surveillance systems. The implemented smart camera system is also capable of processing HD resolution video streams in real-time.

**Keywords:** Smart camera system · Automated video surveillance system
FPGA implementation

## 1 Introduction

The last decade saw an explosion of video surveillance activities in most cities and countries. Today, these systems are ubiquitous and can be found at airports, railway and bus terminals, banks and ATMs, departmental stores, offices, etc. In order for these systems to be effective, the cost and difficulty of deployment must be reduced. Continuous monitoring of multiple video streams by a human operator and manual browsing of thousands of video frames for crime scene and forensic analysis are neither reliable nor scalable [1]. This has generated enormous interest in research activities related to automation of these systems among the researchers of integrated systems and computer vision communities. The advantage of automated video surveillance systems over conventional closed-circuit television (CCTV) based surveillance systems lies in the fact that these are self-contained systems capable of performing automatic analysis of a scene by using smart cameras without intervention of human operators [2]. The

© Springer Nature Singapore Pte Ltd. 2017
B. K. Kaushik et al. (Eds.): VDAT 2017, CCIS 711, pp. 533–544, 2017.
https://doi.org/10.1007/978-981-10-7470-7_52

employed smart cameras can intelligently detect relevant motion in a live video stream, decide what to store for further processing, what to communicate, and what to track. The smart cameras not only potentially cut the cost of human resources observing the output of the cameras but also reduce errors caused due to manual operation. However, crucial to these systems are the real-time requirements.

To meet the hard real-time requirements of smart camera systems, very different technologies and design methodologies have been used in literature. These range from use of General Purpose Processors (GPPs) or special purpose Digital Signal Processors (DSPs) or Graphics Processing Units (GPUs) to Application Specific Integrated Circuits (ASICs) or Applications Specific Instruction Set Processors (ASIPs) or even programmable logic devices like Field Programmable Gate Arrays (FPGAs).

Due to rapid advancements in fabrication technology (adoption of finer chip geometries down to 28 nm and higher levels of integrations), there has been stunning growth in the size, functionality, and performance of field programmable gate arrays (FPGAs) in recent years. The size and speed of current generation FPGAs are comparable to ASICs (though ASICs are typically faster, low power, and occupy less area as compared to FPGAs, given the same manufacturing technology). On the other hand, FPGAs limit the extensive design work required for ASICs, shorten the development cycle (results in reduced cost), and admit the possibility of performing algorithmic changes in later stages of system development as well. Furthermore, FPGA structure is able to exploit spatial and temporal parallelism inherent in image processing, computer vision, and pattern recognition applications. Even if one is following the ASIC development route, the functional verification on an FPGA before manufacturing an ASIC is always advised since many errors can be detected and corrected that way by running the FPGA emulation of the ASIC over extended periods and data sets.

With expanding resolutions and evolving algorithms of a smart camera system, there is a need for high performance while keeping the architecture flexible to allow quick and easy upgradability. FPGAs provide real-time performance that is hard to achieve with GPPs/DSPs, limit the extensive design work, time, and cost required for ASICs, and provide the possibility of performing algorithmic changes in later stages of system development. These features make FPGAs a suitable choice for implementing/prototyping smart camera systems.

Developing a complete FPGA-based smart camera system has many open unresolved design and research challenges such as designing efficient hardware architectures and memory controllers, implementing camera and display device interfaces for real-time video capturing and viewing, automatically controlling camera pan-tilt-zoom features in real-time, and so on. These challenges can be handled at different abstraction levels and by various techniques. In this paper, to be able to solve these issues, different area/memory efficient real-time hardware accelerators and input/output interfaces are designed, implemented, and integrated into a complete working system prototype. The overall goal of this paper is to present the complete designed and implemented FPGA-based smart camera system prototype which can cater to various real world surveillance applications like real-time motion detection, video history generation, focused region extraction, and object tracking with automatic purposive camera pan-tilt capabilities. The paper describes the implemented smart camera system level architecture, its functionality, synthesis results, and visual results.

## 2    Developed Smart Camera System

For developing the FPGA-based smart camera system, we have used the Xilinx ML510 (Virtex-5 FX130T) FPGA development platform. As there is no input video interface available with this board for connecting the video input, therefore, we have developed a custom video camera interface by designing the interfaces PCB for connecting the Digilent VDEC1 video decoder board with Xilinx ML510 (Virtex-5 FX130T) FPGA development platform through high speed input/output ports available with this FPGA platform. The reason for selecting this particular FPGA board and details of the physical camera interface design are out of the scope of this article and their details are available in [3]. The smart camera system described in this article is designed and implemented to meet the following requirements and functionalities:

- Video resolution $\geq$ Standard PAL (720 $\times$ 576) Size
- Frame rate $\geq$ 50 fps
- Real-time capturing of live video stream and result display
- Real-time motion detection
- Real-time focused region extraction
- Real-time filtering of frames of interest based on motion detection only in focused regions
- Real-time object tracking for detected targets
- Real-time object history generation
- Real-time automatic purposive camera movement (pan-tilt) to follow target object
- Standalone operation mode
- All proposed, designed, and implemented architectural modules deliver real-time performance and at the same time are area and memory efficient (implemented with limited resources on a single FPGA development platform).

A complete system level architecture of the functional decomposition of a smart camera system addressed, designed, and implemented in this article is depicted in Fig. 1. Starting at the input, the camera feeds the system with a real-time video stream (a sequence of images) of a scene through *Camera Interface* module which extracts the image pixel data from the incoming video stream. After receiving the pixel data from the *Camera Interface* module, the *Motion Detection* module detects the relevant motion in the incoming video stream. Parallelly, focused regions in the incoming video stream are extracted by the *Focused Region Extraction* module. The outputs of these two modules are given to the *Motion Detection in Focused Regions* module for finding motion in only focused areas in a scene. The output of this block can be used to generate the alarm signal for security personnel in case any relevant motion is detected in restricted areas. The output of *Motion Detection in Focused Regions* module is also used for automatic detection of a moving target in the incoming live video stream, and, the detected moving target is then tracked by *Object Tracking* module in subsequent frames. The moving target object for *Object Tracking* module can be selected either manually by moving the camera on the target object or automatically based on the output from *Motion Detection in Focused Regions* module. While in automatic moving target detection and tracking mode, the implemented system starts detecting motion in focused regions at power-on.

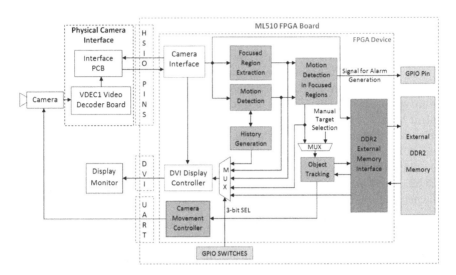

**Fig. 1.** Complete system level architecture of designed and implemented smart camera system.

The size of relevant motion detection region varies, depending on the size of moving object present in the scene. However, the implemented *Object Tracking* module is designed to track a target of maximum 100 × 100 pixel size. For this region, a control logic has been implemented to select the upper most part of size 100 × 100 pixels of moving object. After selecting the upper most part of size 100 × 100 pixels of the moving object, it draws the rectangle on selected region and passes the co-ordinate information to the *Object Tracking* module. In subsequent frames, the *Object Tracking* module tracks the detected 100 × 100 pixel size moving target with purposive camera movement to follow the tracked target object.

As object tracking requires information from multiple video frames, the frame-wise pixel data output by the Camera Interface module is stored in *External DDR2 Memory* through *DDR2 External Memory Interface* controller. *Object Tracking* module also accesses the stored frames/video pixel data through this interface. The output of the *Object Tracking* module is written back to *External DDR2 Memory*. The *Object Tracking* module extracts and updates certain useful parameters internally, such as co-ordinates of new location of tracked object in the current frame. These parameters are used by the *Camera Movement Controller* and the *Object Tracking* module itself in the next frame. Based on the values of new co-ordinates of the tracked object in current frame, the *Camera Movement Controller* generates the necessary commands for purposive camera movement (pan-tilt) in required directions so that it may follow the tracked object. PTZ (Pan-Tilt-Zoom) *Camera* is used to cover a large field of view and follow the tracked object. The output of *Motion Detection* module is further modified by *History Generation* module to generate the history of moving objects in a video stream. The outputs of *Motion Detection* and *Motion Detection in Focused Regions* blocks also enable the filtering of frames of interest based on relevant motion in the video scene which in turn reduces further communication and processing overheads.

The output of every individual module is connected to a *Display Monitor* through a multiplexer (*MUX*) and a *DVI Display Controller*. At any point of time, the output of any module can be viewed on the monitor by appropriately setting the multiplexer control lines. The displayed results are not just images but objects at higher levels of abstraction (e.g. extracted regions of interest, tracked object, filtered frames of interest, history of moving objects, etc.). At the heart of the system are five different efficient hardware units designed for executing intelligent algorithms.

The implemented prototype smart camera system is capable of automatically performing real-time motion detection, real-time video history generation, real-time focused region extraction, real-time motion detection only in focused regions (filtering of frames of interest), real-time object tracking of a manually selected target with automatic purposive camera movement, and real-time automatic moving target detection and tracking with purposive camera movement. Output of any of the five processing modules can be displayed by selecting the output of the associated module for display and sending it to *DVI Display Controller*. This output selection is done by a multiplexer (*MUX*). The output of a particular block can be selected for display based on the value of the 3-bit control signal to the multiplexer. The control signal is provided using *GPIO* (General Purpose Input Output) switches available on the Xilinx ML510 (Virtex-5 FX130T) FPGA development platform.

For developing this complete FPGA based smart camera system, we have designed and implemented four input/output interfaces [3], namely – *Camera Interface, DDR2 External Memory Interface, Camera Movement Controller*, and *DVI Display Controller* and five dedicated VLSI/hardware architectures, namely – *Motion Detection* [4–6], *Focused Region Extraction* [7], *History Generation* [8], *Motion Detection in Focused Regions*, and *Object Tracking* [9, 10]. For details related to the design and implementation of these individual blocks, refer to [3–10].

# 3 Synthesis Results

A top level design module was created which invoked all the five hardware architectures and all the four input/output interfaces. A User Constraint File (UCF) was created to map the input/output ports of the design on the actual pins of the FPGA. All the above mentioned modules of the implemented smart camera system were coded in VHDL and simulated using ModelSim. This top level design was synthesized using Xilinx ISE (Version 12.1) tool chain. The resulting configuration (.bit) file was stored in the Flash Memory to enable automatic configuration of the FPGA at power-on. A standalone complete prototype of real-time smart camera system is built and is shown in Fig. 2. The components of this system are Xilinx ML510 (Virtex-5 FX130T) FPGA platform, Sony EVI D-70P Camera, and display monitor.

FPGA resources utilized by the complete smart camera prototype system are given in Table 1. Maximum operating frequency of the complete integrated system is 125.8 MHz, and, maximum possible frame rate for PAL (720 × 576) size color video is 244 fps. Synthesis results reveal that the complete implemented prototype smart camera system utilized approximately 66% FPGA slices and 73% Block RAMs (on-chip memory) on Xilinx ML510 (Virtex-5 FX130T) FPGA development platform.

**Fig. 2.** Complete system hardware setup.

**Table 1.** FPGA resources utilized by implemented smart camera system.

| Resources | Resources utilized | Total available resources | Percentage of utilization |
|---|---|---|---|
| Slice Registers | 28838 | 81920 | 35.20% |
| Slice LUTs | 39916 | 81920 | 48.72% |
| Route-thrus | 9729 | 163840 | 5.93% |
| Occupied Slices | 13588 | 20840 | 65.20% |
| BRAMS 36 K | 216 | 298 | 72.48% |
| Memory (Kb) | 7776 | 10728 | 72.48% |
| DSP Slices | 3 | 320 | 0.94% |
| IOs | 292 | 840 | 34.76% |
| DCMs | 2 | 12 | 16.67% |

This is because, the implemented hardware accelerators were designed to meet the real-time requirements of video surveillance applications while aiming at FPGA resource reduction. Thus, there is further scope of implementing a few addition features of a smart camera system on the same FPGA development platform.

The implemented smart camera system works in real-time for a standard PAL (720 × 576) resolution live color video stream. All architectures of the implemented smart camera system are adaptable and scalable for other video resolutions also. The system is also capable of processing HD resolution videos in real-time. The seven configuration (.bit) files – one each corresponding to motion detection, history generation, focused region extraction, motion detection in focused regions (filtering of frames of interest), object tracking with purposive camera movement for manually selected target, automatic moving target detection and tracking with purposive camera movement, and complete integrated system are stored in the Compact Flash memory. With the help of three configuration switches available on the Xilinx ML510 (Virtex-5 FX130T) FPGA development platform, the desired configuration (.bit) file can be downloaded onto the FPGA at power-on and the system can be used for that purpose.

# 4 Visual Results and Discussions

The implemented prototype smart camera system can cater to various real world video surveillance applications such as motion detection, focused region extraction, video history generation, and automatic moving target detection and tracking with purposive camera movement. Its real-time test results for these applications are presented in this section. The prototyped system is tested for live colored video streams directly coming from the camera at 25 fps (frames per second) frame rate. The color video resolution is of standard PAL (720 × 576) size.

## 4.1 Motion Detection

The implemented smart camera system for motion detection was tested for different real-world scenarios (both indoor and outdoor), which are broadly classified into two categories *i.e.*, static background situations and pseudo-stationary background situations. Figure 3 shows examples of real-world situation of static background scenario captured by the camera. In Fig. 3, the background is static and the moving objects are present in the scene. Motion detected by our implementation in different frames is shown just below the respective images. It can be clearly seen that only moving objects have been detected by the implemented motion detection system. Figure 4 shows the scenario of pseudo-stationary background with moving foreground objects. In this case, there are moving leaves of the trees in the background. Despite these pseudo-stationary movements in background, only moving objects in the foreground have detected and the movements of leaves of trees in the background (irrelevant motion) have been eliminated. Results of the tests show that the implemented smart camera system is robust enough to detect only the relevant motion in a live video scene and eliminates the continuous unwanted movements in the background itself. All the color frames are

**Fig. 3.** Moving objects in video scene and corresponding motion detected outputs for static background scenarios.

**Fig. 4.** Moving objects in video scene and corresponding motion detected outputs for pseudo-stationary background scenarios.

of PAL (720 × 576) size and are extracted from live video streams (at 25 fps) produced by the implemented system.

## 4.2    Focused Region Extraction

Three different possible situations are considered for testing focused region extraction feature of the implemented smart camera system (Fig. 5). The first row shows the input frames. The extracted focused edge pixels results are shown just below the respective input frame. Figure 5(a) shows the situation where complete scene (both faces are focused) is in focus. The extracted focused edge pixels are shown just below the input frame in Fig. 5(a). The situation of completely out of focus scene is shown in Fig. 5(b). In this case the resulting image (shown just below the input frame in Fig. 5(b)) is blank as no focused edge pixel exists in input image. An example of focused (metallic device) and non-focused (face) objects in same scene is considered in Fig. 5(c). In this case, in the output image (shown just below the input frame in Fig. 5(c)), only focused edge pixels (metallic device) are extracted. The implementation yields good results and works in real-time. All the color frames are of PAL (720 × 576) size and are extracted from live video streams (at 25 fps) produced by the implemented system.

(a)                    (b)                    (c)

**Fig. 5.** Non-focused and focused objects present in the scenes and only focused pixels are extracted.

## 4.3    Video History Generation

Results of video history generation are shown in Fig. 6. Figure 6(a) shows the original extracted video frames from two different live video sequences. Corresponding results produced by the implemented motion detection system for each frame are shown in Fig. 6(b). These results show only the motion blocks in each frame. The results produced by implemented video history generation system for the two video sequences are shown in Fig. 6(c). For each input video sequences, video history frame is generated for 60 frames. The output video history frame for each video sequence shows more meaningful information about the scene and details about the moving object and the trajectory of the moving object. As a single output video history frame is generated for 60 input video frames, the output video frame rate is also reduced, thereby reducing the further communication and processing overheads.

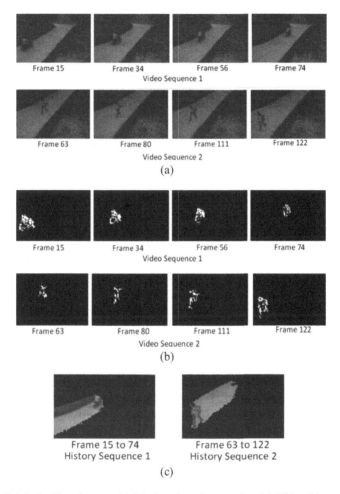

**Fig. 6.** (a) Original video frames; (b) Motion detection results; (c) Video history generation results

## 4.4    Object Detection and Object Tracking

Results of automatic moving target detection and tracking for live video sequences are shown in Fig. 7. All images corresponding to two video sequences are extracted from live output results produced by the implemented smart camera system. In both the video sequences there exists no moving object in the first image. In the second image of both the video sequences, the moving object enters into the scene and system for motion detection in focused regions detects the moving object (results of motion detection in focused regions are not shown as motion detection system is working internally and results are displayed for tracking only). The moving object/person size in both the video sequences is larger than $100 \times 100$ pixel size and the object tracking system implemented is designed to track a target of maximum $100 \times 100$ pixel size.

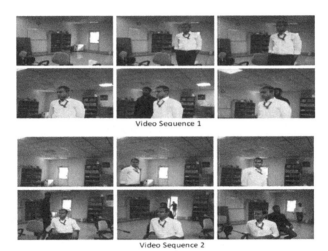

Fig. 7. Automatic moving target detection and tracking with purposive camera movement. (Color figure online)

Therefore, the upper $100 \times 100$ pixel size part (i.e. person's face in this case) of the moving object is selected and red color rectangle is drawn by the implemented control logic. This is shown in the third image of each video sequence. In the remaining three images of each video sequence, the selected $100 \times 100$ pixel size target (person's face in this case) is tracked despite the presence of other moving objects/persons in the video scene. The background also changes due to purposive camera movement to follow the tracked target and to keep the tracked target in the middle of the frame.

### 4.5    Filtering of Frames of Interest

The results of filtering of the frames of interest based on motion detection only in focused regions are shown in Fig. 8. Figure 8(a) shows four different images extracted from different live video streams. Corresponding results produced by focused region extraction system for each image are shown in Fig. 8(b). In Fig. 8(a), Image 1 and Image 3 are focused images and Image 2 and Image 4 are defocused/blurred images. Therefore, results produced by the implemented focused region extraction system for Image 2 and Image 4 are black images, as in both the images there are no focused regions. The results produced by the focused region extraction system for Image 1 and Image 3 show the extracted focused edge regions. Motion detection results for the four images are shown in Fig. 8(c). Moving objects are present in all the four images. Therefore, results produced by the implemented motion detection system show the motion blocks for all the four images, irrespective of the fact that they are focused images or defocused images. The module for motion detection in focused regions detects motion in focused regions only and filters the frames accordingly (i.e. filters the frames which show the motion in focused regions only). Frames filtered by the implemented motion detection in focused regions system are shown in Fig. 8(d). Output frames are filtered for Image 1 and Image 3 as these are focused images.

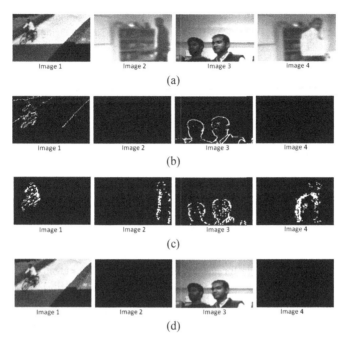

**Fig. 8.** (a) Original video frames; (b) Focused region extraction results; (c) Motion detection results; (d) Filtered frames of interest based on motion detection only in focused regions.

For defocused Image 2 and Image 4, the output frames are not filtered and therefore, the results show black images.

## 5    Conclusions

In this article, we have described the system level architecture, functionality, synthesis results, and visual results of complete smart camera system developed on Xilinx ML510 (Virtex-5 FX130T) FPGA Board. The implemented system is capable of automatically performing real-time motion detection, real-time video history generation, real-time focused region extraction, real-time filtering of frames of interest based on motion detection only in focused regions, real-time object tracking of manually selected target with automatic purposive camera movement, and real-time automatic moving target detection and tracking with purposive camera movement. The system is designed to work in real-time for live color video streams of standard PAL (720 × 576) resolution, which is the most commonly used video resolution for current generation surveillance systems. The system is capable of processing HD resolution video streams in real-time and adaptable to different video resolutions. The developed standalone prototype smart camera system can be effectively used for surveillance applications.

**Acknowledgements.** This work was carried out under a project supported by Department of Electronics & Information Technology (DeitY)/Ministry of Communications and Information Technology (MCIT), Govt. of India.

# References

1. Kandhalu, A., Rowe, A., Rajkumar, R., Huang, C., Yeh, C.C.: Real-time video surveillance over IEEE 802.11 mesh network. In: Proceedings: 15th IEEE Real-Time and Embedded Technology and Applications Symposium, pp. 205–214 (2009)
2. Jiang, H., Ardo, H., Owall, V.: A hardware architecture for real-time video segmentation utilizing memory reduction techniques. IEEE Trans. Circ. Syst. Video Technol. **19**(2), 226–236 (2009)
3. Singh, S., Saurav, S., Shekhar, C., Vohra, A.: Prototyping an automated video surveillance system using FPGAs. Int. J. Image Graph. Sig. Process. (IJIGSP) **8**(8), 37–46 (2016). MECS Press
4. Singh, S., Dunga, S.M., Saini, R., Mandal, A.S., Shekhar, C., Vohra, A., Chaudhary, S.: Hardware accelerator design for change detection in smart camera. In: SPIE Proceedings: International Conference on Graphics and Image Processing (ICGIP 2010), Cairo, Egypt, vol. 8285, Article ID 82852T, pp. 1–5, 1–2 October 2011
5. Singh, S., Mandal, A.S., Shekhar, C., Vohra, A.: Real-time implementation of change detection for automated video surveillance system. ISRN Electronics **2013**, 1–5 (2013). Article ID 691930, Hindawi, USA
6. Singh, S., Shekhar, C., Vohra, A.: FPGA-based real-time motion detection for automated video surveillance systems. Electronics **5**(1), 1–18 (2016). MDPI, Switzerland
7. Singh, S., Saurav, S., Saini, R., Saini, A.K., Shekhar, C., Vohra, A.: Automatic real-time extraction of focused regions in a live video stream using edge width information. In: IEEE Proceedings: 18th International Symposium on VLSI Design and Test (VDAT-2014), PSG College of Technology, Coimbatore, India, 16–18 July 2014, pp. 1–2 (2014)
8. Singh, S., Dunga, S.M., Mandal, A.S., Shekhar, C., Chaudhary, S.: FPGA based embedded implementation of video summary generation scheme in smart camera systems. Adv. Mater. Res. **403–408**, 516–521 (2011). Trans Tech Publications, Switzerland
9. Singh, S., Dunga, S.M., Saini, R., Mandal, A.S., Shekhar, C., Vohra, A.: Hardware accelerator design for tracking in smart camera. In: SPIE Proceedings: International Conference on Graphics and Image Processing (ICGIP 2010), Cairo, Egypt, vol. 8285, Article ID 82852S, pp. 1–5, 1–2 October 2011
10. Singh, S., Saini, R., Saurav, S., Saini, A.K.: Real-time object tracking with active PTZ camera using hardware acceleration approach. Int. J. Image Graph. Signal Process. (IJIGSP) **9**(2), 55–62 (2017). MECS Press

# Effectiveness of High Permittivity Spacer for Underlap Regions of Wavy-Junctionless FinFET at 22 nm Node and Scaling Short Channel Effects

B. Vandana[1](✉), J. K. Das[1], S. K. Mohapatra[1], and B. K. Kaushik[2]

[1] School of Electronics Engineering, KIIT University, Bhubaneshwar, India
{vandana.rao02029, s.k.mohapatra}@ieee.org,
jkdasfet@kiit.ac.in
[2] Department of Electronics and Communication Engineering, Indian Institute
of Technology-Roorkee, Roorkee, India
bkk23fec@iitr.ac.in

**Abstract.** In this work, an attempt has been made to investigate the performance of a new device, Wavy Junctionless FinFET at 22 nm node using low to high permittivity spacer for underlap regions. An alternative $V_{TH}$ extraction method has been demonstrated, which signifies the importance of cannel length at the nanoscale regime. The device layer Silicon film possesses uniform doping profile, where the current is controlled by channel doping and the mobility of charge carriers which account the bulk conduction instead of surface conduction. Due to the scalability of device dimensions, underlap regions are preferred to differentiate the control and the location of dopant atoms along the conduction region and hence this enhances the device performances. The simulation results enlighten the effectiveness of high permittivity of spacer region through performance evaluation. The simulated results exhibit an *SS* of 64 mV/decade, *DIBL* of 26 mV/V and $I_{ON}/I_{OFF}$ ratio of $10^7$.

**Keywords:** Wavy-JL FinFET · Nanowire · Silicon on insulator (SOI)
FinFET · High-κ spacer · Short channel parameters · $V_{TH}$ extraction method

## 1 Introduction

The phenomenal improvement in the scaling of metal-oxide–semiconductor field-effect transistor (MOSFET) is depicted by Moore, which gives the doubling of transistor [1, 2] for every two years. Therefore the era has reached to the attention of atomic structure level. At nano-scale regime, the influence of the short channel (SC) parameters affects the device performances and are described in [3–5]. To verify the limitations of scaling facts, International Technology Roadmap for Semiconductors (ITRS) [6] provided a road map to identify the various perspectives of physical architectural representation and also to the applications governed by the nano-scale regime.

With the tremendous improvement in architectural representation, various multi-gate MOSFETs are innovated and are the most promising approaches to scale

© Springer Nature Singapore Pte Ltd. 2017
B. K. Kaushik et al. (Eds.): VDAT 2017, CCIS 711, pp. 545–556, 2017.
https://doi.org/10.1007/978-981-10-7470-7_53

SCEs and thereby increases gate control over channel charges [7–9]. FinFETs [10–12], have much-improved channel characteristics, and these devices avoid shallow trench isolation effect as well as excellent controllability of gate electrode surrounding the erected silicon body of Si Fin [13, 14].

The inversion mode transistor requires (IMT) ultra-sharp PN junctions, the fabrication is carried out in extremely precise thermal and doping conditions else a part of impurities are diffused into the channel. To overcome the diffusion related problems, an alternative approach is studied through the development of Junctionless Nanowire Transistor (JNT) [15]. In JNT devices the fabrication process required no doping gradients. Several studies show advantages comparing IMT, and JNT [16–19] are discussed. FinFETs suffers effectively inactive spacing between the Fin, to eliminate this an ultrathin body devices are placed in unused regions between the Fins. Due to body thickness below 5 nm the silicon etch does not extend down to the buried oxide which acts as horizontal and vertical channels and named as inverted "T" channel FET [20, 21] these devices are excellent in scaling SCEs. This work merges these three topologies by introducing a Wavy-JLFinFET and identified the optimization of spacer using low to high-κ materials.

At nanoscale regime, the various literature supports high-κ materials and are preferable for spacer and gate oxide to improve the $I_D$, which is required to achieve nearly ideal characteristics for SC parameters. Short channel devices with underlap regions usually suffers from high series resistance ($R_{SD}$) which degrades $I_{ON}$ and introducing the high-κ spacer, will enhance the gate-fringe-field [22] and hence performance improves. Scaling down the device requires a continued reduction of the gate dielectric to few atomic layer thickness. This constraint arises with two considerations; one is to reduce SCEs and other is to increase or maintain the induced charge in the channel as $V_{DD}$ decreases [23]. However, this effect causes a direct tunneling current, through the gate dielectric grows exponentially with decreasing physical thickness of the gate dielectric [24]. It is likely that tunneling currents arising from silicon dioxides ($SiO_2$) at a thickness less than 0.8 nm which cannot be tolerated, even for high-performance systems [25].

Extensive simulations have been carried out to study the impact of high-κ and low-κ dielectrics with respective to the JL inverted "T" FinFET. In this study, various dielectric materials are taken into account to observe the influence of high-κ and the device performance is optimized. The key factors affecting the device performance and the physics behind it are also discussed [26]. An optimized performances analysis of SCEs has been made using $I_{ON}/I_{OFF}$ ratio, DIBL, SS, etc. and a new $V_{TH}$ extraction method is introduced to effectively enhance the process integration $V_{TH}$ characteristics, an experimental analysis is performed and reported in [27]. In this context dielectric materials $SiO_2$, $Si_3N_4$, $HfO_2$ are taken into account for the parametric analysis of spacer. Organization of the paper consists of introduction the Sect. 2, represents the simulating the prefabricated model of Wavy FinFET with all details of process parameter considered for the device. The simulation framework with the models activated during simulation through TCAD parameters required for the device simulation. Section 3 provides the physical insight of SCEs and the impact of high-κ dielectric spacer materials for the device performance analysis that are carried out through the simulator. Finally, the conclusion is drawn.

# 2  Architectural Representation of Wavy-JL FinFET and Simulation Framework

A schematic view of 3D Wavy-JL FinFET is illustrated in Fig. 1(a). The architecture of inversion mode transistor (IMT) has a P-type channel, doping $N_A = 10^{16}$ cm$^{-3}$ and source/drain regions are doped heavily N-Type $N_D = 10^{19}$ cm$^{-3}$. The proposed device merges three different topologies (a) wavy topology comprises 2D fully depleted (FD) ultra-thin bodies (UTBs) and 3D FinFET. (b) The junctionless topology consists of heavy doping profile $N_D = 10^{19}$ cm$^{-3}$ (across S/D/channel) and no doping concentration gradients across the device layer. (c) Silicon on insulator (SOI) topology [28] are used. As the paper explores FinFET architecture, various dielectric materials are considered to optimize the analysis of spacer. The Table 1 replicates the parameters used to concrete the Wavy-JL FinFET estimated for device simulation [29–31].

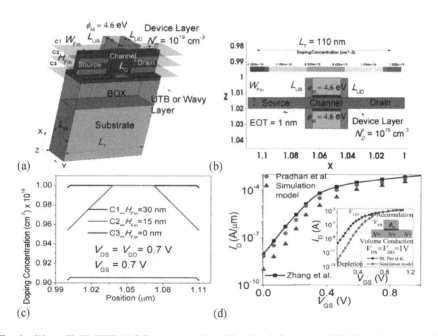

**Fig. 1.** Wavy-JL FinFET (a) 3-D representation. The Metal, Spacer, and Oxide regions are made transparent. (b) A 2D image of doping profile. (c) Position as a function of doping concentration with 3 different cut lines for $H_{Fin}$ values (d) Results of simulation model calibration with the models of Zhang *et al.*, Pradhan *et al.*, [21, 32]. The inset figure views the simulation models are calibrated with conventional JL FinFET with the volume conduction given in [33].

The fixed effective oxide thickness (EOT = 1 nm) reduces the gate control and increases the drain field coupling to channel surface potential. The gate metal work-function $\phi_M = 4.6$ eV is used, and the difference in $\phi_M - \phi_S$ allows the channel to conduct with a shift in $V_{TH}$ at $V_{FB}$. The change in $V_{TH}$ depends on the $N_D$, nanowire thickness $t_{Si}$ and EOT [34]. Figure 1(b) replicates the 2D representation of Wavy-JL

**Table 1.** Essential device parameters considered for the simulation framework

| Parameters | 3D Wavy-JL FinFET |
|---|---|
| Donor doping ($N_D$) | $10^{19}$ cm$^{-3}$ (Source/Drain/Channel) |
| EOT of gate dielectric ($T_{OX}$) | 1 nm |
| Gate work-function ($\phi_M$) | 4.6 eV |
| Drain Supply Voltage ($V_{DD}$) | 0.05 V, 0.7 V |
| Energy gap ($E_G$) | 1.1 eV |
| $L_G$ (nm) | 20 nm |
| Fin width ($W_{Fin}/L_G$) | 0.5 |
| Fin Height ($H_{Fin}/L_G$) | 1.70 |
| UTB | 5 nm |
| Total device length ($L_T$) | 110 nm |
| Total device width ($L_W$) | 32 nm |
| BOX thickness | 35 nm |
| Under-lap Source and Drain ($L_{US}$ and $L_{UD}$) | 5 nm |

FinFET with doping concentration profile, to identify the levels of doping concentration across device layer, 3 different cut lines at C1 = 100%, C2 = 50%, and C3 = 0% are taken. Accordingly, the position as a function of doping concentration graph is plotted shown from Fig. 1(c) at $V_{GS} = V_{DS} = 0.7$ V. Therefore, as the percentage of $H_{Fin}$ decreases the doping concentration ($10^{19}$ to $0.90 \times 10^{18}$ cm$^{-3}$) slightly reduces. This action occurs due to the high doping concentration, as the same voltage is applied to the gate and drain terminals the electron charge carriers are accumulated at the top level of the $H_{Fin}$ and gradually tends to take the shape of Gaussian doping.

The simulations are carried out using sentaurus TCAD [35] simulator. Phillips Unified Mobility Model is used with Lombardi model to account for high-κ induced carrier mobility degradation is considered [36]. For a deeper understanding of the quantum confinement effect, the thickness of Fin and UTB determine the density gradient based quantization models are used. The $\phi_M$ values are taken into account and tuned to achieve the desired $V_{TH}$ value. Hence a suitable empirical parameter $\beta$ is selected to calibrate the drift-diffusion transport model. Inversion Accumulation layer Mobility model includes doping and transverse field dependency which in turn accounts a Coulomb impurity scattering being used. To account the longitudinal and vertical electron field an effective intrinsic density, OldSlotboom band gap narrowing model [37], written as Shockley-Read-Hall mechanism for generation and recombination [38], and quantum mechanical effects are included. The device physical properties are discretized onto a non-uniform mesh of nodes and simulated with appropriate parameterization models [39]. The models activated in our simulation work was validated by simulating the device of Zhang et al., Pradhan et al. [21, 32]. Our proposed device is analyzed by using the same models as per the result is shown in Fig. 1(d). The inset figure represents the models that are held to calibrate Wavy-JL FinFET with the experimental data of conventional JL FinFET of Paz et al. [33]. Therefore the models used for the calibration are in good agreement, which duly enhances the device drivability and the scales down the OFF state leakage currents. The volume conduction takes part above $V_{TH}$, and separates accumulation by $V_{FB}$ are also included and reported in [40].

## 3  Exploring the Impact of High-κ Spacer

The challenges associated with the creation of the ultra-steep doping profiles in FinFET during process integration can be resolved using JLT devices. To observe the device performance, high-κ gate sidewall spacer of 5 nm width are introduced with three dielectric materials ($SiO_2$ = 3.9, $Si_3N_4$ = 7.6, $HfO_2$ = 20). The potential requirement of the high-κ spacer is that $I_{OFF}$ depletes the channel beyond the gate edges towards the source and drain side without affecting the $I_{ON}$. With these considerations JLT, devices have better E-field i.e. below flat band condition for sub-threshold logic applications [41]. The impact of spacer along with the SCEs is discussed in this paper at the nanoscale regime. Further, the small channel parameters required to consider at scaled gate length are $I_{ON}$, $I_{OFF}$, SS, and DIBL is discussed along with this first order derivative ($g_m$) and its generation factor (TGF) is also discussed.

JLT is a gated resistor. Usually, it is an ON device, due to the work function difference between the gate and the Si nanowire the bands are flat and shift in $V_{FB}$ makes the $V_{TH}$ positive. During this flat band condition, the device acts as a resistor and the $I_D$ is expressed by (1) Where $q$ is electron charge, $\mu$ is the mobility, $N_D$ is the doping concentration, $T_{Si}$ is the thickness of the Si nanowire, $W_{Si}$ is the width of the Si nanowire, $L$ is the gate length, and $V_{DD}$ is the supply voltage. Usually, with applied positive $V_{GS}$ the amount of $I_D$ delivered across the drain which is responsible for the conduction at the channel is represented as $I_{ON}$. Whereas the $I_{OFF}$ is evaluated as the amount of $I_D$ with applied zero $V_{GS}$. In OFF condition ($V_{GS}$ = 0 V) the Si nanowire is fully depleted, and below flat-band, the substrate is neutral which is expressed in (2). Where $K$ is the Boltzmann's constant, $T$ is the temperature in Kelvin, $\eta$ is the body factor, and SS is subthreshold slope [42].

$$I_D \approx q\mu N_D \frac{T_{Si} W_{Si}}{L} V_{DD} \tag{1}$$

$$I_{OFF} = 100 \frac{W_{Si}}{L} e^{-qV_{TH}/\eta KT} = 100 \frac{W_{Si}}{L} 10^{-V_{TH}/SS} \tag{2}$$

$$SS = \left[ \frac{\partial \log_{10}(I_D)}{\partial V_{GS}} \right]^{-1} \tag{3}$$

$$DIBL = \frac{\Delta V_{TH}}{\Delta V_{DS}} = \frac{V_{TH1} - V_{TH2}}{V_{DS2} - V_{DS1}} \tag{4}$$

To calculate *SS*, the $I_D$ is plotted in the logarithmic scale against $V_{GS}$. The theoretical value for classical transistor (long channel devices) is 60 mV/decade at room temperature. The supply voltage $V_{DD}$ should be > 0.6 V, if $V_{DD}$ is below 0.6 V, the *SS* is no longer sufficient to induce high on/off current ratio [43]. An Impact ionization is used in SOI MOSFETs to obtain sub-threshold slopes below $k_T/q$ ln10 = 60 mV/decade at room temperature. The mathematical representation of *SS* is shown in (3). At nanoscale regime, the source/drain potential has a substantial consequence over the band bending at a significant portion of the device. Therefore, the $V_{TH}$ and the sub-threshold current of short-channel devices vary with the $V_D$. This effect is referred to as *DIBL* and can be calculated by (4). Found to be *DIBL* < 50 mV. *DIBL* is a short channel parameter that gives the difference in $V_{TH}$ and extracted at $V_{DS1}$ = 50 mV and $V_{DS2}$ = 0.7 V and normalized by this difference of $\Delta V_{DS}$ [44].

To observe the impact of spacer on the device we considered different dielectric materials as M1 = $SiO_2$, M2 = $Si_3N_4$, and M3 = $HfO_2$ and analysis is performed by fixing one of the material at one side and alternatively changing the material on another side. With this observation, a short channel parameter like $I_{ON}$, $I_{OFF}$, *DIBL*, and *SS* is shown in Figs. 2 and 3. Figure 2 represents the change in $L_{UD}$ materials with fixed $L_{US}$ material, and vice versa is also performed and shown in Fig. 3.

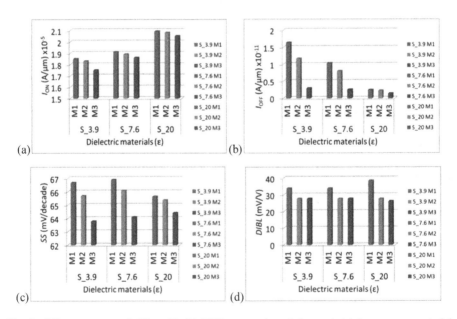

**Fig. 2.** SC parameters of Wavy-JL FinFET are evaluated by maintaining spacer material constant for $L_{US}$ and other three variations at $L_{UD}$, (a) $I_{ON}$, (b) $I_{OFF}$, (c) *SS* and (d) *DIBL*

With the significance of the simulated data the parameters like $I_{ON}$, $I_{OFF}$, *SS* and *DIBL* are evaluated, and the improvement of these parameters are observed with a

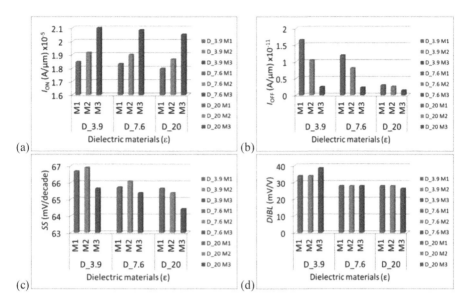

**Fig. 3.** SC parameters of Wavy-JL FinFET are evaluated by maintaining spacer material constant for $L_{UD}$ and other three variations at $L_{US}$, (a) $I_{ON}$, (b) $I_{OFF}$, (c) $SS$ and (d) $DIBL$

particular combination of dielectric materials and is shown with a bar graph representation. The improvement of $I_{ON}$ is found with spacer material $L_{UD}$ as M1 and $L_{US}$ as M3 is shown in Fig. 2(a) and $I_{OFF}$ with the same material M3 both sides is shown in Fig. 2(b). The combination of $L_{UD}$ as M3 and $L_{US}$ as M1shows, a significant improvement in $SS$ which is almost found near to the ideal value in Fig. 2(c) and the $DIBL$, is identified with the same spacer material of M3 shown in Fig. 2(d).

Accordingly, an analysis is performed by changing $L_{US}$ dielectric material with a fixed $L_{UD}$ material. An improvement in $I_{ON}$ is found with the combination of $L_{UD}$ = M1 and $L_{US}$ = M3 and $I_{OFF}$ with same material M3 shown in Fig. 3(a) and (b). With these structures, $SS$ and $DIBL$ show a vast improvement with M3 material for a spacer which is near to ideal values shown in Fig. 3(c) and (d). Underlap FinFET structures are capable of achieving ideal SCEs, especially at smaller $L_G$. These structures are however induced high series resistance along the channel regions, which degrades the $I_{ON}$. To improve this, the high-κ spacer is introduced, which thereby reduces the gate fringe capacitance. The impact of low-κ to high-κ materials on underlap regions are individually represented and shown in Fig. 4. The output characteristics are shown in Fig. 4(a) and the inset figure shows the transfer characteristics and are plotted in linear and logarithmic scale with different dielectric materials. The underlap regions using high-κ material shows a significant improvement at $I_{ON}$ and $I_{OFF}$ in Fig. 4(b) with 10.81% and 91.63%, along with this ON-OFF ratio is found to be $10^7$ from Fig. 4(c) with an improvement of 92.43%. $SS$ and $DIBL$ are evaluated from (3) and (4) accordingly 3.5% and 29.40% of growth are shown in Fig. 4(d).

The conduction mechanism of JLT is possibly obtained between $V_{TH}$ and $V_{FB}$, due to $V_{TH}$ bulk conduction and accumulation is separated by $V_{FB}$ [45]. The combination of

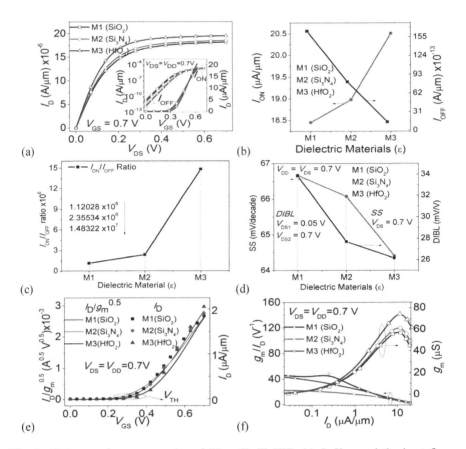

**Fig. 4.** Various performance metrics of Wavy-JL FinFET, (a) $I_D$-$V_{DS}$, and the inset figure represents $I_D$-$V_{GS}$ (b) $I_{ON}$ and $I_{OFF}$, (c) ON-OFF ratio, (d) $SS$ and $DIBL$, (e) $V_{TH}$ extraction method using higher order derivative ($I_D/g_m^{0.5}$) and $I_D$-$V_{GS}$, (f) $TGF$ and $g_m$-$V_{GS}$

$g_m$ and constant current method inherently resolves the prefabrication $V_{TH}$ analytical approaches. This representation is evaluated with the maximum $g_m$ and the $I_D$ method [40, 46]. In this context a new method to extract $V_{TH}$ is adopted in our simulation work reported by Tomaszewski et al. in [27, 47, 48] expression is given as $I_D/g_m^{0.5}$ which is used to evaluate $V_{TH}$ shown in Fig. 4(e). The source/drain voltage drop and the mobility degradation which affecting the E-field are the two reasons that usually effect $V_{TH}$ extraction at decananometer channel length [49]. It is found that the $V_{TH}$ extracted from the constant current method is exactly equal to the $I_D/g_m^{0.5}$ $V_{TH}$ method.

The JL transistor shows lower $g_m$ at room temperature because of the reduced carrier mobility as compared with the IM devices. The mobility is an important parameter for evaluating $g_m$, accordingly from the drift equation the current that flows through the device layer has a high impact on the movement, E-Field, and $N_D$ [19]. Hence $g_m$ as a function of $I_D$ is plotted and shown in Fig. 4(f). The $g_m$ is directly proportional to the difference in charges across S/D edges.

The approximation is prominent that the difference enhances the charge concentration at S/D ends through the spacer dielectric at gate edges [50]. JL devices operate at the partial depletion regime or without formation of accumulation layer. $TGF$ represents the efficiency of converting the $I_D$ in $g_m$ which interprets the conduction level in JL. The high $g_m$ will further enhance the $TGF$ which is the requirement for the realization of circuits operating at low supply voltage for JL FinFET $TGF$ as a function of $I_D$ is plotted and shown in Fig. 4(f). From the graph, it is clear that JLT device with a high-$\kappa$ spacer is less sensitivity to the derivative parameters. From the overall simulation analysis, the spacer as high-$\kappa$ dielectric materials provides a significant improvement in short channel parameters, which thereby enhances the device performance and makes the device more scalable at 22 nm node.

Along with the short channel parameters, the paper also discusses the important output performance metrics such as power dissipation (PD), delay, energy, inductance, and energy-delay product (EDP) etc. in Table 2. The low dissipated power is observed for M3 (HfO$_2$) material as compared with other two dielectric materials (M1 and M2), this improvement is due to the high $I_{OFF}$. The parameters energy, inductance, and EDP are calculated and observe that values increases with the high permittivity dielectric materials.

**Table 2.** Various performance comparison of Wavy-JL FinFET

| Dielectric Materials | PD ($I_{OFF}$ * $V_{DD}$) (pW) | Delay ($CV/I$) (ps) | Energy ($CV^2$) (J) $\times$ $10^{-17}$ | Inductance, $L_{SD}$ (H) (Delay/$g_{ds}$) $\times$ $10^{-8}$ | EDP (JS) $\times$ $10^{-29}$ |
|---|---|---|---|---|---|
| M1 | 11.52 | 1.49 | 1.92 | 1.26 | 2.87 |
| M2 | 5.64 | 1.81 | 2.40 | 1.60 | 4.36 |
| M3 | 0.97 | 2.58 | 3.71 | 1.92 | 9.61 |

# 4   Conclusion

The novel hybrid architecture of MOSFET is incorporated with various topologies like FD-SOI (UTB), no junction doping gradients (JN) and Fin based structure using high-$\kappa$ dielectric spacer materials at 22 nm technology node. This work demonstrates the importance of high-$\kappa$ materials and its impact on spacer are briefly examined. With this high-$\kappa$ spacer, a comparative analysis of different short channel parameters is performed. The various short channel parameters obtained are $SS$ = 64 mV/decade, $DIBL$ = 29 mV/V, $I_{ON}/I_{OFF}$ ratio = $10^7$, $I_{ON}$ and $I_{OFF}$ with 10.81% and 91.63%. The values show a low sensitivity of device characteristics to underlap variations and are very near to ideal values. An alternative $V_{TH}$ extraction method which is equal to the values obtained with the constant current method. The use of a high-$\kappa$ spacer in FinFET architecture is the best candidate for suppressing SCEs and improves device performances.

# References

1. Progress in digital integrated electronics. In: 1975 International Electron Devices Meeting, pp. 11–13 (1975)
2. Dennard, R.H., Gaensslen, F.H., Rideout, V.L., Bassous, E., LeBlanc, A.R.: Design of ion-implanted MOSFET's with very small physical dimensions. IEEE J. Solid-State Circuits 9, 256–268 (1974)
3. Roy, K., Mukhopadhyay, S., Mahmoodi-Meimand, H.: Leakage current mechanisms and leakage reduction techniques in deep-submicrometer CMOS circuits. Proc. IEEE 91, 305–327 (2003)
4. Roll, G.: Leakage Current and Defect Characterization of Short Channel MOSFETs. Logos Verlag Berlin GmbH (2012)
5. Taur, T., Ning, T.H.: Fundamentals of Modern VLSI Devices. Cambridge University Press, New York (1998)
6. The International Technology Roadmap for Semiconductors (2015)
7. Van Dal, M.J.H., Collaert, N., Doornbos, G., Vellianitis, G., Curatola, G., Pawlak, B.J., Duffy, R., Jonville, C., Degroote, B., Altamirano, E., et al.: Highly manufacturable FinFETs with sub-10 nm fin width and high aspect ratio fabricated with immersion lithography. In: 2007 IEEE Symposium on VLSI Technology, pp. 110–111 (2007)
8. Goel, E., Kumar, S., Singh, B., Singh, K., Jit, S.: Two-dimensional model for subthreshold current and subthreshold swing of graded-channel dual-material double-gate (GCDMDG) MOSFETs. Superlattices Microstruct. 106, 147–155 (2017)
9. Rawat, G., Kumar, S., Goel, E., Kumar, M., Dubey, S., Jit, S.: Analytical modeling of subthreshold current and subthreshold swing of Gaussian-doped strained-Si-on-insulator MOSFETs. J. Semicond. 35, 84001 (2014)
10. Subramanian, V., Parvais, B., Borremans, J., Mercha, A., Linten, D., Wambacq, P., Loo, J., Dehan, M., Gustin, C., Collaert, N., et al.: Planar bulk MOSFETs versus FinFETs: an analog/RF perspective. IEEE Trans. Electron Devices 53, 3071–3079 (2006)
11. Sun, X., Lu, Q., Moroz, V., Takeuchi, H., Gebara, G., Wetzel, J., Ikeda, S., Shin, C., Liu, T.-J.K.: Tri-gate bulk MOSFET design for CMOS scaling to the end of the roadmap. IEEE Electron Device Lett. 29, 491–493 (2008)
12. Skotnicki, T., Hutchby, J.A., King, T.-J., Wong, H.-S., Boeuf, F.: The end of CMOS scaling: toward the introduction of new materials and structural changes to improve MOSFET performance. IEEE Circuits Devices Mag. 21, 16–26 (2005)
13. Li, Y., Hwang, C.-H.: Effect of fin angle on electrical characteristics of nanoscale round-top-gate bulk FinFETs. IEEE Trans. Electron Devices 54, 3426–3429 (2007)
14. El-Mamouni, F., Zhang, E.X., Ball, D.R., Sierawski, B., King, M.P., Schrimpf, R.D., Reed, R.A., Alles, M.L., Fleetwood, D.M., Linten, D.: others: Heavy-ion-induced current transients in bulk and SOI FinFETs. IEEE Trans. Nucl. Sci. 59, 2674–2681 (2012)
15. Colinge, J.-P., Lee, C.-W., Afzalian, A., Akhavan, N.D., Yan, R., Ferain, I., Razavi, P., O'Neill, B., Blake, A., White, M., Kelleher, A.-M., McCarthy, B., Murphy, R.: Nanowire transistors without junctions. Nat. Nanotechnol. 5, 225–229 (2010)
16. Lee, C.-W., Afzalian, A., Akhavan, N.D., Yan, R., Ferain, I., Colinge, J.-P.: Junctionless multigate field-effect transistor. Appl. Phys. Lett. 94, 53511 (2009)
17. Colinge, J.-P., Lee, C.-W., Ferain, I., Akhavan, N.D., Yan, R., Razavi, P., Yu, R., Nazarov, A.N., Doria, R.T.: Reduced electric field in junctionless transistors. Appl. Phys. Lett. 96, 73510 (2010)

18. Colinge, J.-P., Ferain, I., Kranti, A., Lee, C.-W., Akhavan, N.D., Razavi, P., Yan, R., Yu, R.: Junctionless nanowire transistor: complementary metal-oxide-semiconductor without junctions. Sci. Adv. Mater. **3**, 477–482 (2011)
19. Doria, R.T., Pavanello, M.A., Trevisoli, R.D., de Souza, M., Lee, C.-W., Ferain, I., Akhavan, N.D., Yan, R., Razavi, P., Yu, R., et al.: Junctionless multiple-gate transistors for analog applications. IEEE Trans. Electron Devices **58**, 2511–2519 (2011)
20. Mathew, L., Sadd, M., Kalpat, S., Zavala, M., Stephens, T., Mora, R., Bagchi, S., Parker, C., Vasek, J., Sing, D.: Inverted T channel FET (ITFET)-Fabrication and characteristics of vertical-horizontal, thin body, multi-gate, multi-orientation devices, ITFET SRAM bit-cell operation. A novel technology for 45 nm and beyond CMOS. In: Technical Digest IEEE International Electron Devices Meeting, IEDM, pp. 713–716 (2005)
21. Zhang, W., Fossum, J.G., Mathew, L.: The ITFET: a novel FinFET-based hybrid device. IEEE Trans. Electron Devices **53**, 2335–2343 (2006)
22. Fossum, J.G., Wang, L.-Q., Yang, J.-W., Kim, S.-H., Trivedi, V.P.: Pragmatic design of nanoscale multi-gate CMOS. In: International Electron Devices Meeting, pp. 613–616 (2004)
23. Wong, H.-S.: Beyond the conventional transistor. IBM J. Res. Dev. **46**, 133–168 (2002)
24. Lo, S.-H., Buchanan, D.A., Taur, Y., Wang, W.: Quantum-mechanical modeling of electron tunneling current from the inversion layer of ultra-thin-oxide nMOSFET's. IEEE Electron Device Lett. **18**, 209–211 (1997)
25. Frank, D.J., Dennard, R.H., Nowak, E., Solomon, P.M., Taur, Y., Wong, H.-S.P.: Device scaling limits of Si MOSFETs and their application dependencies. Proc. IEEE **89**, 259–288 (2001)
26. Cheng, B., Cao, M., Rao, R., Inani, A., Voorde, P.V., Greene, W.M., Stork, J.M.C., Yu, Z., Zeitzoff, P.M., Woo, J.C.S.: The impact of high-K gate dielectrics and metal gate electrodes on sub-100 nm MOSFETs. IEEE Trans. Electron Devices. **46**, 1537–1544 (1999)
27. Tomaszewski, D., Głuszko, G., Łukasiak, L., Kucharski, K., Malesińska, J.: Elimination of the channel current effect on the characterization of MOSFET threshold voltage using junction capacitance measurements. Solid State Electron. **128**, 92–101 (2017)
28. Han, M.-H., Chang, C.-Y., Chen, H.-B., Wu, J.-J., Cheng, Y.-C., Wu, Y.-C.: Performance comparison between bulk and SOI junctionless transistors. IEEE Electron Device Lett. **34**, 169–171 (2013)
29. Colinge, J.P.: The SOI MOSFET: From single gate to multigate. In: Colinge, J.P. (ed.) FinFETs and Other Multi-Gate Transistors, pp. 1–48. Springer, Boston (2008). https://doi.org/10.1007/978-0-387-71752-4_1
30. Ho, B., Sun, X., Shin, C., Liu, T.-J.K.: Design optimization of multigate bulk MOSFETs. IEEE Trans. Electron Devices **60**, 28–33 (2013)
31. Sun, X., Moroz, V., Damrongplasit, N., Shin, C., Liu, T.-J.K.: Variation study of the planar ground-plane bulk MOSFET, SOI FinFET, and trigate bulk MOSFET designs. IEEE Trans. Electron Devices **58**, 3294–3299 (2011)
32. Pradhan, K.P., Sahu, P.K., Rajput, P., Pallempati, M.: Exploration of symmetric high-k spacer (SHS) hybrid FinFET for high performance application. Superlattices Microstruct. **90**, 191–197 (2016)
33. Paz, B.C., Pavanello, M.A., Cassé, M., Barraud, S., Reimbold, G., Faynot, O., Avila-Herrera, F., Cerdeira, A.: From double to triple gate: modeling junctionless nanowire transistors. In: 2015 Joint International EUROSOI Workshop and International Conference on Ultimate Integration on Silicon (EUROSOI-ULIS), pp. 5–8 (2015)
34. Kranti, A., Yan, R., Lee, C.W., Ferain, I., Yu, R., Akhavan, N.D., Razavi, P., Colinge, J.P.: Junctionless nanowire transistor (JNT): properties and design guidelines. In: Proceedings of ESSDERC, pp. 357–360 (2010)

35. Sentaurus TCAD User's Manual. In: Synopsys Sentaurus Device. Synopsys (2012). http://www.synopsys.com/

36. Klaassen, D.B.M.: A unified mobility model for device simulation-I. Model equations and concentration dependence. Solid State Electron. **35**, 953–959 (1992)

37. Del Alamo, J., Swirhun, S., Swanson, R.M.: Simultaneous measurement of hole lifetime, hole mobility and bandgap narrowing in heavily doped n-type silicon. In: 1985 International Electron Devices Meeting, pp. 290–293 (1985)

38. Shockley, W., Read Jr., W.T.: Statistics of the recombinations of holes and electrons. Phys. Rev. **87**, 835 (1952)

39. Saha, S.: MOSFET test structures for two-dimensional device simulation. Solid State Electron. **38**, 69–73 (1995)

40. Jeon, D.-Y., Park, S.J., Mouis, M., Berthomé, M., Barraud, S., Kim, G.-T., Ghibaudo, G.: Revisited parameter extraction methodology for electrical characterization of junctionless transistors. Solid State Electron. **90**, 86–93 (2013)

41. Saini, G., Choudhary, S.: Improving the subthreshold performance of junctionless transistor using spacer engineering. Microelectronics J. **59**, 55–58 (2017)

42. Sahu, P.K., Mohapatra, S.K., Pradhan, K.P.: Zero temperature-coefficient bias point over wide range of temperatures for single-and double-gate UTB-SOI n-MOSFETs with trapped charges. Mater. Sci. Semicond. Process. **31**, 175–183 (2015)

43. Lee, C.-W., Nazarov, A.N., Ferain, I., Akhavan, N.D., Yan, R., Razavi, P., Yu, R., Doria, R. T., Colinge, J.-P.: Low subthreshold slope in junctionless multigate transistors. Appl. Phys. Lett. **96**, 102106 (2010)

44. Trevisoli, R., Doria, R.T., de Souza, M., Pavanello, M.A.: Substrate bias influence on the operation of junctionless nanowire transistors. IEEE Trans. Electron Devices **61**, 1575–1582 (2014)

45. Rios, R., Cappellani, A., Armstrong, M., Budrevich, A., Gomez, H., Pai, R., Rahhal-Orabi, N., Kuhn, K.: Comparison of junctionless and conventional trigate transistors with $Lg$ down to 26 nm. IEEE Electron Device Lett. **32**, 1170–1172 (2011)

46. Schroder, D.K.: Semiconductor Material and Device Characterization. Wiley, Hoboken (2006)

47. Ghibaudo, G.: New method for the extraction of MOSFET parameters. Electron. Lett. **24**, 543–545 (1988)

48. Flandre, D., Kilchytska, V., Rudenko, T.: $gm/Id$ Method for threshold voltage extraction applicable in advanced MOSFETs with nonlinear behavior above threshold. IEEE Electron Device Lett. **31**, 930–932 (2010)

49. Rudenko, T., Barraud, S., Georgiev, Y.M., Lysenko, V., Nazarov, A.: Electrical characterization and parameter extraction of junctionless nanowire transistors. J. Nano Res. **39**, 17–33 (2016)

50. Koley, K., Dutta, A., Syamal, B., Saha, S.K., Sarkar, C.K.: Subthreshold analog/RF performance enhancement of underlap DG FETs with high-k spacer for low power applications. IEEE Trans. Electron Devices **60**, 63–69 (2013)

# Design and Implementation of Ternary Content Addressable Memory (TCAM) Based Hierarchical Motion Estimation for Video Processing

Puja Ghosh and P. Rangababu[✉]

Department of Electronics and Communication Engineering,
National Institute of Technology Meghalaya, Bijini complex, Laitumkurah,
Shillong 793003, India
puja.ghosh93@gmail.com, p.rangababu@gmail.com

**Abstract.** In this paper, block based Hierarchical Motion Estimation (ME) using Ternary Content Addressable Memory (TCAM) is proposed. Conventional works estimate motion using nearest neighbourhood search where the computation of search locations has high complexity. The novelty of the proposed work is to accelerate the estimation process using mixed parallel and pipeline processing with TCAM. This technique searches the pixel variations between current and different reference blocks of a frame simultaneously by checking complete match case as well as partial match case. If matching is found in the same location of block space then there is no motion and if matching is found in different location of block space other than the existing location then it is considered that motion has occurred. Further, if motion occurs in more than one location then the best match is found by Sum of Absolute difference (SAD) between the blocks of pixels of size $8 \times 8$. Motion vectors are computed for complete as well as partial match of $8 \times 8$ block within two $16 \times 16$ blocks. A TCAM engine is designed to store the pixels of the reference frame. Afterwards a search operation is performed using a current block of size $16 \times 16$ with two reference blocks of size $16 \times 16$ or one $32 \times 16$. The number of clock cycles consumed for this operation is 382. It is observed that the consumption of hardware resources is 33%. The complete architecture is designed in verilog and it is implemented in FPGA Virtex-7 and ASIC.

**Keywords:** Ternary Content Addressable Memory (TCAM)
Block Matching Algorithm (BMA) · Sum of Absolute Difference (SAD)
Field Programmable Gate Array (FPGA)
Application Specific Integrated Circuit (ASIC)

## 1 Introduction

The H.264/H.265 is an advanced video coding standard. It shares a number of similar characteristics with other popular compression formats such as MPEG-2

© Springer Nature Singapore Pte Ltd. 2017
B. K. Kaushik et al. (Eds.): VDAT 2017, CCIS 711, pp. 557–569, 2017.
https://doi.org/10.1007/978-981-10-7470-7_54

Video, MPEG-4 Visual, H.263, etc. It is based upon a (Encoder/Decoder) model where block based Motion Estimation (ME) is utilized. The source data is transformed by the encoder into a compressed form occupying a reduced number of bits. There are three main functional units of a video encoder: a prediction model, a spatial model and an entropy encoder. The prediction model eliminates redundancy by creating a prediction of the current video frame. The residual frame is given as input to the spatial model which minimizes spatial redundancy. Vectors and coefficients which occur frequently are represented by the entropy encoder by short binary codes. Video coding has enormous importance in broadcast, Internet, consumer electronics, mobile and security industries [19]. The latest standard H.265 compresses the video into a smaller space, than the preceding standards, so that a compressed video clip takes up less transmission bandwidth and less storage space. The applications of video processing in motion estimation are mobile streaming, video conferencing and video broadcasting etc.

ME using block based algorithm is one of the condemnatory task in today's video compression standards such as H.26x, MPEG-1, -2 and -4. It is a crucial part in video encoding process. Recent years have witnessed various approaches of ME algorithms for video encoding based on best nearest neighborhood search [13,18]. Several algorithms viz., fast search, exhaustive search, diamond search and hexagonal search are popular [6,7]. Motion estimation extricates information about motion from the video sequence and the motion is typically represented utilizing a motion vector (x, y). The displacement of a pixel or a pixel block from the current location due to the occurrence of motion is designated by the motion vector. This provides information about temporal redundancy reduction. Video encoder uses this information for finding the block that best matches in the reference frame to calculate low energy residue and to produce frames which are temporally interpolated. So computing ME within less amount of time is the motivation of present work.

Now-a-days Field Programmable Gate Arrays (FPGAs) are known for acceleration of computing, rapid adaptations to new developments, increased flexibility and appropriate performance. Accelerating the algorithms of application using pipeline and parallel processing approaches and further implementing these onto FPGA is the popular computing procedure. Ternary Content Addressable Memorys (TCAMs) which are popular in pattern matching algorithms have been used in the proposed work for network search engines [16]. Further, the proposed work designs hierarchical ME using mixed parallel and pipeline approaches. It is intended to speed up the computation of ME by faster searching and implementing the design on FPGA. This approach estimates motion of a 2 × 2 block to 16 × 16 block within a 32 × 16 block of a video frame. From this any large size of block based motion estimation can be performed. This technique can reduce the computational complexity of motion estimation over conventional techniques.

The remainder of the paper is arranged as follows. Section 2 describes Related works. Section 3 presents the Motion Estimation. Section 4 describes proposed TCAM based Hierarchical Motion Estimation. Section 5 shows the Results and Discussion followed by conclusion and future work.

# 2   Related Works

In the literature, there exist several designs of block based motion estimation for H.264 and HEVC video standards. Aggarwal *et al.* [1] has proposed TCAM based motion estimation for H.264. The method comprises of storing the reference frame blocks in the memory and concatenating the samples from the prediction block whose least significant bits are replaced by don't cares. This is the motivation for present work. Biswas *et al.* [2] has developed VLSI architecture for enhanced three step search hardware for fast motion estimation. For increasing the speed, the novel addressing mechanism is used and it also reduces the area requirements. The results show a critical path delay of 4.8 ns while the area comes out to be 2.9 K gate count. Byun *et al.* [3] has developed a design for an integer motion estimator of high-efficiency video coding (HEVC). The new structures of a sum of absolute difference (SAD) summation block and of a memory read controller are proposed. There is a reduction in the internal memory read time due to the use of new memory read controller. The recursive quad-tree coding unit structure and the asymmetric motion partitioning mode are supported by the new SAD summation block structure. Chang *et al.* [10] has proposed an efficient design for motion estimation which has joint algorithm and architecture optimization. In this work to reduce the number of search points by 90.5%, the most probable search directions are selected through a statistical analysis.

Khemiri *et al.* [12] has designed a fast configuration for motion estimation (ME) to reduce the computational time of the new high efficiency video coding (HEVC). The Coded Block Flag (CBF), the Early Coding Unit (CU), the Fast Method (CFM) termination (ECU) and the Early Skip Detection (ESD) modes are used in this configuration. The complexity is reduced in average, by 56.75% with a small bit-rate and PSNR degradation. Chi *et al.* [13] has proposed a new cross diamond search algorithm for fast motion estimation which significantly reduces the search space. Medhat *et al.* [15] has presented a highly parallel motion estimation architecture for HEVC. There are 16 processing units in the developed architecture which operate in parallel to calculate the sum of absolute difference. Block sizes from $4 \times 4$ to $64 \times 64$ are processed by the proposed unit. Rohan *et al.* [17] has discussed VLSI design for adaptive rood pattern search (ARPS) of fast motion estimation. It avoids systolic arrays and uses pattern generation methodology with interleaved memory organization for high throughput. Results show, synthesis frequency of 112 MHz, and a gate count of 47.15 K. Rhee *et al.* [18] has proposed a fast mode algorithm with a trade-off between coding gain which results from flexible block partition and high computational complexity.

# 3   Motion Estimation

Motion Estimation (ME) detects the motion of objects in a video sequence and tries to acquire vectors indicating the estimated motion. For each block of MxN block of samples in the current frame to detect a similar block of MxN-sample region in the reference frame, it needs a comparison of the MxN block in the current frame with some or all of the possible MxN blocks in a search area and detecting the region where best match is obtained. Often search area is a region centered on the current block position. Subtracting the candidate region of the reference frame from the current MxN block of current frame, so that the candidate region that minimizes the residual energy is chosen as the best match. It is utilized in applications viz., motion compensated de-interlacing, video stabilization, motion tracking etc. [5]. There are different algorithms for motion estimation out of which three main algorithms are described as (i) Pixel-recursive algorithm (PRA), (ii) phase plane correlation technique and (iii) block-matching algorithm (BMA).

In PRAs, there is iterative refining of ME for individual pixels. Gradient method is applied in pixel recursive algorithms. PRAs are difficult to realize in hardware due to their high computational complexity and less regularity [21]. In phase plane algorithms, motion vectors are detected by utilizing the correlation between current frame and reference frame [8]. Accurate motion vectors are estimated in BMAs on the basis of best matching rectangular pixel block of current frame from the reference frame. The current frame is separated into pixel blocks and motion estimation is accomplished independently for each pixel block. Further, pixel block is identified from the reference frame within the search region. The boundary for the motion vectors is defined by the search region and the number of blocks to evaluate is also limited by the search region. The block that best matches the current block, results the displacement by means of Motion Vector (MV). It incorporates a pair (x, y) of horizontal and vertical displacement values.

Due of their regularity and simplicity, BMAs are more worthy for hardware realization. But it takes 90% of encoding time in most of the implementations [21]. The major challenge of this technique is to find the best match within the search range and extension in number of evaluated candidates needs more computational power. To reduce the computational power various other fast BMAs are proposed which minimize the number of evaluated candidates and endeavour to maintain good block matching accuracy. The varieties of BMAs are briefed in next subsections.

### 3.1  Full Search Block Matching

Every possible pixel block in the search region is evaluated in the full search algorithm. It generates the best block matching motion vector. This type of BMA can give least possible residue for video compression. But this technique requires larger computational power because large amount of candidates are evaluated in full search block matching [20].

### 3.2  Fast Search Block Matching

The basic criteria for fast search algorithm is to reduce the number of candidate evaluations for searching. Different search algorithms such as Three step search

(TSS), Hexagonal search etc., are available more details of this can be found [9,14]. These algorithms differ in a manner how they choose the candidate for searching. Although, in terms of the quality the full search algorithm is the best, but these fast search algorithms are computationally less intensive than full search algorithm. There is a trade off between the quality of the prediction image and the computational complexity of the algorithm.

## 4 Proposed Hierarchical TCAM Based Motion Estimation

Content-addressable memories (CAMs) are useful for search-intensive applications. These are hardware search engines which work faster than algorithmic search approaches. The basic operation of CAM is to compare the input data against the stored data in parallel. Address of the matched data is given as output.

$$bit\_match[i] \; = \; !wcare[i] \; | \; !(wdata[i] \oplus look - up\_data[i]) \tag{1}$$

In a TCAM cell, EXOR operation is performed between the $wdata$ and the $look$-$up\_$ $data$ as shown in (1) to find the bitmatch. If $wdata$ and $look$-$up\_$ $data$ are same then depending on $wcare$, bit match will be $1$ otherwise it is $0$. The location of $2 \times 2$ block which matches will be indicated by the bit match.

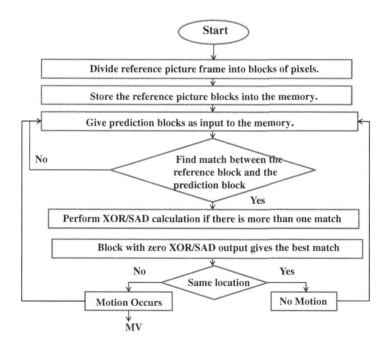

**Fig. 1.** Flow chart of TCAM based motion estimation

CAMs are classified into two types: Binary CAM (BiCAM) and Ternary CAM. In case of BiCAM, *wcare* is high and in case of TCAM, *wcare* is low. The proposed work explores the application of CAM to the ME. Current frame and the reference frame are likely to contain many similarities in video coding. Due to the displacement of the object within the frame there are differences between the frames. The predicting frame is divided into blocks P, referred as the prediction blocks. The error blocks are added to the reference block R, yielding the prediction block. The prediction error is zero when prediction block P is similar to the reference block R. The objective of the proposed design is to find the candidate block that best matches the reference block using CAM technique.

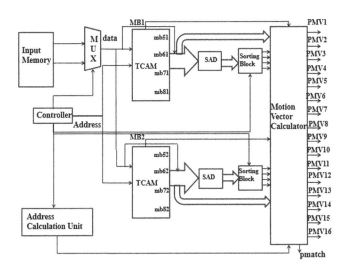

**Fig. 2.** Complete operation for full match

The proposed work starts with the division of the reference frame and current frame into block of pixels 16 × 16 as shown in Fig. 1. In the work, TCAM is designed in a hierarchical manner. Each 16 × 16 block is composed of four 8 × 8 blocks. Further each 8×8 block is composed of four 4×4 blocks which are further composed of four 2×2 blocks. The hierarchical approach is useful to find motion of various block levels such as 2 × 2, 4×4 and 8 × 8. This approach eliminates the requirement of large CAM with high bit length and word length. The two blocks of 16 × 16 are written into the TCAM as *wdata* by the selection mux which is controlled by the state controller for storing the reference blocks of pixels. The blocks of pixels are stored as 16 × 16 blocks (Macroblock). For storing one Macroblock, sixteen 4 × 4 blocks are needed. One 4 × 4 block contains 128 bits. After storing the reference data, current block of pixels 8 × 8 is given as *look-up_ data* input which is selected by the mux logic. After receiving the *look-up_ data*, TCAM engine performs search operation of *look-up_ data* with reference data as shown in Fig. 2. Figure 3 provides the conceptual matching conditions

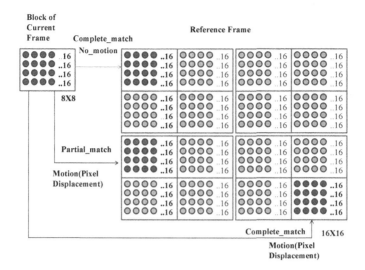

**Fig. 3.** Conceptual diagram of TCAM based motion estimation

of TCAM. Three kinds of matching conditions are observed while matching the current data with the reference data. (i) full match of block of pixels in same location (no motion case) (ii) full match of block of pixels in different location (motion case) (iii) partial match of pixels (motion case).

The internal block diagram of TCAM is shown in Fig. 4. The output signal *MB* will indicate out of the four 8 × 8 blocks in which block match occurs. The output signal *match blocks* will indicate inside each 8 × 8 block which 4 × 4 block matches. In the TCAM, if don't care input is used, output will be asserted as logic *1* even if partial or complete match is found. For these cases, Sum of Absolute Difference (SAD) calculation needs to be performed as shown in Fig. 1 and Fig. 2. For SAD calculation, the difference of each pixel of current block with the corresponding pixel of the reference block is calculated and these differences are summed up and stored into a register. Finally, a linear sorting module is used to find the matched block of pixels, the resultant block of pixels is the minimum difference block. If don't care input is not used then it results the full match as output. In the full match case, SAD calculation is not involved as illustrated in Fig. 2. The output signal *MB* and *match blocks* will indicate the complete match block. Finally after finding the block of complete match and partial match, motion vectors are calculated. Figure 5 shows the method of calculating the motion vectors. All the current blocks of pixels are selected by the controller. For a particular current block, depending on the minimum SAD output, the best match block is selected out of the other reference blocks. After the reference data selection, motion vectors are calculated by subtracting the location of matched data i.e. the location of the data with minimum SAD value from the location of the current data. Finally the motion vectors are obtained for

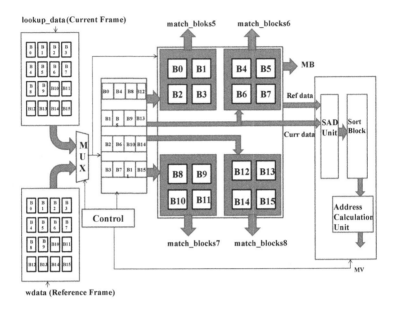

**Fig. 4.** Internal block diagram

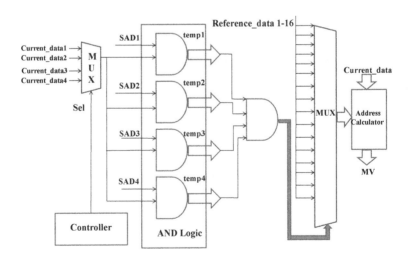

**Fig. 5.** Motion vector calculator

both the full match and partial match cases. Figure 7 shows the EXOR operation
between the *wdata* and the *look-up* data in a TCAM cell.

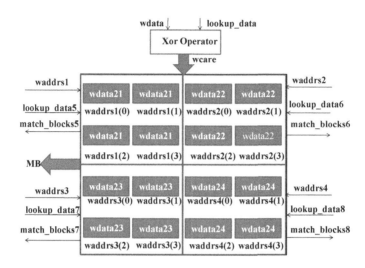

**Fig. 6.** Illustration of searching in one 16 × 16 block of TCAM

As referred to Fig. 6, reference blocks of pixels are stored in the two 16 × 16
TCAM blocks as wdata from the memory in 32 clock cycles. *wdata21*, *wdata22*,
*wdata23* and *wdata24* are the reference datas stored from the memory to the
TCAM. Current blocks of pixels of size 8 × 8 are processed as *look-up* data5,
*look-up* data6, *look-up* data7 and *look-up* data8 in a pipelined manner for
search operation to the TCAMs. Then search operation is performed in a parallel
manner. *wcare* is generated by EXOR operation between the current data and
the reference data for different partial match cases. If all the bits of *wcare* are
*1* then CAM will act as a binary CAM. In this case more number of search
operations are performed. This is useful for the case of full match. If some bits of
*wcare* are *0* then CAM will act as a TCAM which is useful for partial match case.
As shown in Fig. 2, the outputs *MB1* and *MB2* will indicate in the two 16 × 16
TCAM blocks respectively which 8 × 8 block matches. In case of the first 16 × 16
TCAM block, output signal *mb51* will indicate in the first 8 × 8 block which
4 × 4 matches. Similarly *mb61*, *mb71* and *mb81* will indicate in the second, third
and fourth 8 × 8 blocks respectively which 4 × 4 block matches. Both the signals
*mb* and *MB*, require 1 clock cycle, therefore in total two clock cycles are needed
to get the blocks where matches are found. SAD output with minimum value
will indicate where best match is found. Finally the motion vector is calculated
for both full match case and partial match case. Bit requirement and number of
address locations required in a 2 × 2 block and 16 × 16 block is shown in Table 1.

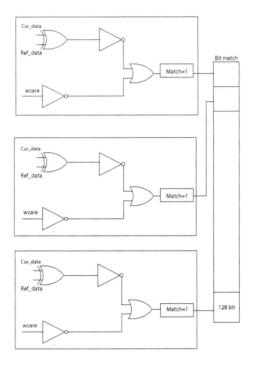

Fig. 7. Bit operation in a TCAM cell

Table 1. Bit requirement in CAM of various sizes

| CAM requirement | $2 \times 2$ | $16 \times 16$ |
|---|---|---|
| Number of address locations | 4 | 256 |
| Data width (in bits) | 32 | 2048 |

# 5    Result and Discussion

TCAM cell is the basic block to estimate the motion. Motion is estimated for two $16 \times 16$ TCAM blocks by using the *MB1* and *MB2* as outputs and also within each $16 \times 16$ block using *match blocks* as outputs. When some bits of *wcare* are considered as don't care, data which completely matches is distinguished from the data which partially matches using SAD calculation. SAD calculation is not needed if none of the bits of *wcare* considered as don't care. Motion of $8 \times 8$ within two blocks of $16 \times 16$ is estimated by calculating the motion vectors. Execution time of the algorithm is accelerated by using the mixed parallel and pipeline approach. In this proposed work, the design is implemented in Virtex-7 VC707. Each sorting block requires 1 clock cycle. The number of clock cycle utilized in implementing SAD block of size $4 \times 4$ is 1. The details of synthesis result of the proposed design has been shown in the Table 2. It can be seen that

**Table 2.** Resource consumption of proposed hierarchical motion estimation

| Modules | Slice registers (607200) | Slice LUTs (303600) | DSP48E (2800) | Max. Frequency (MHz) |
|---------|--------------------------|---------------------|---------------|----------------------|
| ME      | 46625                    | 101534              | 32            | 147.63               |
| Sorting | -                        | 5362                | -             | -                    |
| SAD     | 155                      | 358                 | 1             | 300.98               |

the utilization of Slice registers is 7% whereas the utilization of Slice LUTs is 33% and the proposed design uses 1% of DSP48Es. The presented hardware searches $16 \times 16$ block in $32 \times 16$ block with 382 clock cycles. For searching $16 \times 16$ block in $32 \times 32$ block 764 clock cycles are required. In the design [11] the maximum operating frequency is 130 MHz. The comparison table of the proposed work with the existing works is shown in Table 3. The total number of clock cycle required to estimate the motion of a $16 \times 16$ block within $32 \times 32$ block is 410 with a maximum frequency of 112 MHz in design [2] and the design in [23] requires 1100 clock cycles with a maximum frequency of 354 MHz. Even in designs [4, 22], the number of clock cycles is 4208 and 1240 respectively and the maximum frequency is 50 MHz whereas the proposed design requires 764 clock cycles with a maximum frequency of 147.63 MHz to estimate the motion of a $16 \times 16$ block within $32 \times 32$ block. The reduced number of clock cycle with high operating frequency is due to the mixed parallel and pipeline architecture. The proposed work is implemented in ASIC 90 nm. Results show same number of clock cycles as in FPGA and gate count of 1021 K in the form of NAND $2 \times 1$ including on chip memory and logic.

**Table 3.** Comparison of proposed design with existing designs

| Architecture | Clock cycles | Gate count (K) + Memory (Kbits) | Hardware platform | Max. Frequency (MHz) |
|--------------|--------------|----------------------------------|-------------------|----------------------|
| Chao et al. [22] | 4208 | 9 + 28 | MIPS Processor | 50 |
| Xi et al. [23] | 1240 | 47.3 + 12.992 | ASIC | 50 |
| Rohan et al. [10] | 410 | 47.15 | ASIC | 112 |
| Yao et al. [21] | 1100 | 70 + 24 | ASIC | 354 |
| Proposed Design (ASIC) | 764 | 1021 | ASIC | 100 |
| Proposed Design (FPGA) | 764 | - | FPGA | 147.63 |

# 6    Conclusion and Future Work

An efficient TCAM based motion estimation architecture with reduced processing clock cycle is implemented. Computation of motion vectors using TCAM is the novelty of the proposed work. Search operation is performed in parallel within two $16 \times 16$ macro blocks. The number of clock cycles needed to estimate the motion of four $8 \times 8$ blocks within the block of size $32 \times 32$ is less. The design works with high operating frequency and thus it has low computational complexity. The future work involves increasing the number of search points by using more number of TCAMs and optimization of the hardware in ASIC platform.

# References

1. Aggarwal, G., Khare, R.: Tertiary content addressable memory based motion estimator, 18 January 2011, US Patent 7,873,107
2. Biswas, B., Mukherjee, R., Chakrabarti, I.: Efficient architecture of adaptive rood pattern search technique for fast motion estimation. Microprocess. Microsyst. **39**(3), 200–209 (2015)
3. Byun, J., Jung, Y., Kim, J.: Design of integer motion estimator of HEVC for asymmetric motion-partitioning mode and 4K-UHD. Electron. Lett. **49**(18), 1142–1143 (2013)
4. Chao, W.M., Hsu, C.W., Chang, Y.C., Chen, L.G.: A novel hybrid motion estimator supporting diamond search and fast full search. In: Proceedings of IEEE International Symposium on Circuits and Systems (ISCAS). vol. 2, p. II. IEEE (2002)
5. Chen, Y.R., Tai, S.C.: True motion-compensated de-interlacing algorithm. IEEE Trans. Circuits Syst. Video Technol. **19**(10), 1489–1498 (2009)
6. Cheung, C.H., Po, L.M.: A novel cross-diamond search algorithm for fast block motion estimation. IEEE Trans. Circuits Syst. Video Technol. **12**(12), 1168–1177 (2002)
7. Correa, G., Assuncao, P., Agostini, L., da Silva Cruz, L.A.: Performance and computational complexity assessment of high-efficiency video encoders. IEEE Trans. Circuits Syst. Video Technol. **22**(12), 1899–1909 (2012)
8. Erturk, S., Dennis, T.: Image sequence stabilisation based on DFT filtering. IEEE Proceedings-vision, Image And Signal Processing **147**(2), 95–102 (2000)
9. Huang, Y.W., Chen, C.Y., Tsai, C.H., Shen, C.F., Chen, L.G.: Survey on block matching motion estimation algorithms and architectures with new results. Journal of VLSI Signal Processing Systems **42**(3), 297–320 (2006)
10. Jou, S.Y., Chang, S.J., Chang, T.S.: Fast motion estimation algorithm and design for real time qfhd high efficiency video coding. IEEE Trans. Circuits Syst. Video Technol. **25**(9), 1533–1544 (2015)
11. Kao, C.Y., Lin, Y.L.: A memory-efficient and highly parallel architecture for variable block size integer motion estimation in H. 264/AVC. IEEE Trans. Very Large Scale Integr. VLSI Syst. **18**(6), 866–874 (2010)
12. Khemiri, R., Bahri, N., Belghith, F., Sayadi, F.E., Atri, M., Masmoudi, N.: Fast motion estimation for HEVC video coding. In: Proceedings of International Conference on Image Processing, Applications and Systems (IPAS). pp. 1–4. IEEE (2016)
13. Lam, C.W., Po, L.M., Cheung, C.H.: A novel kite-cross-diamond search algorithm for fast block matching motion estimation. In: Proceedings of International Symposium on Circuits and Systems(ISCAS). vol. 3, pp. III-729. IEEE (2004)
14. Li, R., Zeng, B., Liou, M.L.: A new three-step search algorithm for block motion estimation. IEEE Trans. Circuits Syst. Video Technol. **4**(4), 438–442 (1994)

15. Medhat, A., Shalaby, A., Sayed, M.S.: High-throughput hardware implementation for motion estimation in HEVC encoder. In: Proceedings of IEEE 58th International Midwest Symposium on Circuits and Systems (MWSCAS). pp. 1–4. IEEE (2015)
16. Meiners, C.R., Patel, J., Norige, E., Liu, A.X., Torng, E.: Fast regular expression matching using small TCAM. IEEE/ACM Transactions on Networking (TON) **22**(1), 94–109 (2014)
17. Mukherjee, R., Biswas, B., Chakrabarti, I., Dutta, P.K., Ray, A.K.: Efficient VLSI design of adaptive rood pattern search algorithm for motion estimation of high definition videos. Microprocess. Microsyst. **45**, 105–114 (2016)
18. Rhee, C.E., Lee, K., Kim, T.S., Lee, H.J.: A survey of fast mode decision algorithms for inter-prediction and their applications to high efficiency video coding. IEEE Trans. Consum. Electron. **58**(4) (2012)
19. Richardson, I.E.: The H. 264 advanced video compression standard. John Wiley & Sons (2011)
20. Roma, N., Sousa, L.: Efficient and configurable full-search block-matching processors. IEEE Trans. Circuits Syst. Video Technol. **12**(12), 1160–1167 (2002)
21. Wiegand, T., Sullivan, G.J., Bjontegaard, G., Luthra, A.: Overview of the H.264/AVC video coding standard. IEEE Trans. Circuits Syst. Video Technol. **13**(7), 560–576 (2003)
22. Xi, Y.L., Hao, C.Y., Fan, Y.Y., Hu, H.Q.: A fast block-matching algorithm based on adaptive search area and its VLSI architecture for H.264/AVC. Sig. Process. Image Commun. **21**(8), 626–646 (2006)
23. Yao, S., Guo, H.J., Yu, L., Zhang, K.: A hardware implementation for full-search motion estimation of AVS with search center prediction. IEEE Trans. Consum. Electron. **52**(4) (2006)

# A Custom Designed RISC-V ISA Compatible Processor for SoC

Kavya Sharat$^{(\boxtimes)}$, Sumeet Bandishte, Kuruvilla Varghese,
and Amrutur Bharadwaj

Indian Institute of Science (IISc), Bangalore, India
kavya.sharat@gmail.com, sumeet.bandishte30@gmail.com,
edkuru@dese.iisc.ernet.in, amrutur@ece.iisc.ernet.in

**Abstract.** RISC-V is an open Instruction Set Architecture (ISA) released by Berkeley Architecture Group from the University of California, at Berkeley (UCB) in 2010. This paper presents the architecture, design and complete implementation of a 32-bit customisable processor system containing a mix of features as listed below. The 32-bit processor based on RISC-V ISA, is capable of handling atomic operations in addition to all integer operations supported by the ISA. The design has a priority-based nested interrupt controller, giving the user an added flexibility to program the priority levels of interrupts. In addition, there is a debug unit which provides internal visibility during program execution. An error detection and correction interface to memories, makes the design resilient to radiation induced bit-flips. The on-chip communication interface follows the standard Wishbone specification. The design has been implemented on Xilinx Virtex-7 XC7VX48T FPGA and achieves a peak frequency of 80 MHz, with the processor stand-alone operating at 190 MHz. On a 65 nm technology node, the design operates at a frequency of 170 MHz, while the processor stand-alone, a maximum frequency of 220 MHz. The design occupies a footprint of $1.027\,\text{mm}^2$ with 32-KB on-chip memory.

**Keywords:** Processor · Pipeline · Cache · Interrupt controller
Error handling · Debug unit

## 1 Introduction

Processors are found in a plethora of applications from embedded computers in toys to industrial control systems. Most of them have proprietary ISAs which makes customisation difficult and expensive. A custom designed system based on an open ISA is beneficial for fast and variety of development.

### 1.1 RISC-V

RISC-V is an open-source ISA released by Berkeley Architecture Group from the University of California at Berkeley(UCB) in 2010 [1]. Its aim is to accelerate research and development in the field of computer architecture.

© Springer Nature Singapore Pte Ltd. 2017
B. K. Kaushik et al. (Eds.): VDAT 2017, CCIS 711, pp. 570–577, 2017.
https://doi.org/10.1007/978-981-10-7470-7_55

## 1.2 Related Works

System-on-Chip development in the field of RISC-V started with the release of "Rocket Chip" [7]. It is tethered to an ARM core and requires intervention from the core to emulate DRAM and peripherals.

In [5], the designers have released a soft core in chisel [4], called 'ZSCALE', following the RISC-V RV32IM extension. The 'VSCALE' [6] is the Verilog version of 'ZSCALE'. mRISC-V, a RISC-V based micro controller, is described in [8]. Since, none of these implementations till date have a combination cache, atomic instruction support, configurable nested interrupt handling capability, error handling feature, it was decided to build the entire system from scratch. Many more implementations of RISC-V like PULPino [9], lowRISC [10] have been come up lately.

# 2 Processor System Design

Our system has a 32-bit processor following RV32IMA extensions of RISC-V, Instruction and Data Cache, Wishbone bus interconnect, configurable peripherals, interrupt controller and a Debug Unit.

## 2.1 Processor

The processor is a 5-stage, in-order execution machine. The 5 stages are fetch (F), decode (D), execute (E), memory (M) and write-back (W). The stages and their functionality is similar to that in conventional pipeline, with a few additions. There is an *amo* block is for atomic instructions. Also, the execute stage has a multiplier and divider module.

## 2.2 Cache

The cache architecture is chosen to be 2-way set-associative, since it serves as a balance between increase in miss-rate in case of direct mapped cache and increase in hit-time in case of fully associative cache. The Data and Instruction Cache are of size 16KB each, with 32-byte block size. Write-back policy is used to avoid the cost of writing to memory every time change is made to a cache block.

*Data Cache:* The Data Cache (D-Cache) holds the data section of the program serving load/store requests from the processor. Figure 1 shows the top level view of the data cache.

The command sequencer is the interface to the processor pipeline. It handles requests arriving at both the ports- in D and M stages. It prevents simultaneous read and write to the same cache line. It infers contention from the addresses and gives priority to the M stage request since it is chronologically older.

There are two port control units (PCUs) each handling the request of an access port. After arbitration (if required), the ports control units perform the

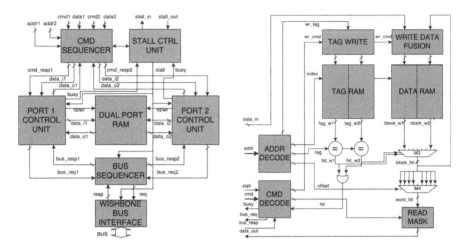

**Fig. 1.** Data Cache organisation          **Fig. 2.** Port Control Unit + RAM

read/write to the Data and Tag RAMs. Figure 2 illustrates a port control logic along with the Data and Tag RAMs for a 2-way set associative configuration.

The address decode extracts index, offset and tag from a 32-bit address. Index addresses the RAMs, tag is used to check for a match and offset is used to extract the word from the cache line. Multiplexer M3 selects between the 2 ways based on the tag check. M4 selects a word (32-bit) from a cache block. When reading data smaller than a word length (32-bit), Read Mask logic extracts data from a word and performs sign extension.

*Instruction Cache:* The Instruction Cache (I-cache) stores the instructions of the program. Figure 3 shows the block schematic of the I-cache.

The instruction cache takes in requests from only the Fetch (F) stage. Hence does not require a command sequencer to handle contentions. Also, a single port RAM suffices for the I-cache. The *cmd* signal input to the I-cache is *rd* (read) as the I-cache is read only. The rest of the blocks and working is as explained in the D-Cache section.

### 2.3 Interrupt Handling

The system currently supports nested interrupts from upto 32 sources. There is a provision to add more interrupts, if required. These interrupts can be dynamically assigned to any of the 4 priority levels.

The handling of interrupts is done by 2 units:

1. Interrupt controller, which is a Wishbone compatible peripheral
2. Interrupt interface towards the processor side.

The interrupt controller receives interrupts from peripherals and sorts them according to priority. It then updates its registers and signals the CPU by

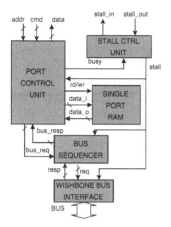

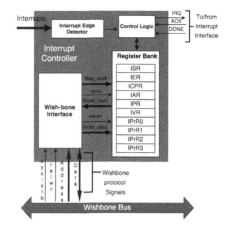

**Fig. 3.** Instruction Cache organisation    **Fig. 4.** Handshake between Interrupt Controller and Interrupt interface

sending an *IRQ* request. The interrupt interface towards the processor side saves the current state of the program onto the stack and then sends an *ACK* signal acknowledging the interrupt controller. The processor vectors to a common interrupt handler and the interrupt service routine queries the interrupt controller, by reading its register bank to determine the source of the interrupt.

The encounter of *ERET* instruction, as specified by RISC-V ISA marks the end of the interrupt service routine [11]. The interrupt interface restores the current state of the program from the stack. A *DONE* signal is sent from the RISC-V core. The interrupt controller updates its registers with this signal.

**Interrupt Controller.** Figure 4 shows the interrupt controller, its internal structure and its interface signals.

*Interrupt edge detector:* This detects a rising edge on any of the interrupt lines, and asserts a trigger on the Control Logic.

*Register bank:* The interrupt controller has a set of memory mapped registers: Interrupt Enable Register (IER), Interrupt Pending Register (IPR), Interrupt Active Register (IAR), Interrupt Current Priority Register (ICPR), Interrupt Status Register (ISR), Interrupt Priority Registers (IPrR0-3) and Interrupt Vector Register (IVR)

*Control Logic:* On a trigger from the Interrupt Edge Detector, the control logic block reads the Interrupt Enable Register (IER) and sends an *IRQ* request, only if the interrupt is enabled. The control logic also updates the Current priority register (ICPR), Status register (ISR), Active (IAR) and Pending registers (IPR). When a second interrupt occurs while an interrupt is in progress, the control logic reads the Register Bank (ICPR and IPrR0-3) to decide whether it has to pre-empt if it is of higher priority level or be kept pending if it is of lower priority level. On the receipt of a *DONE* signal, it updates its registers by clearing the corresponding pending and active bits (IPR and IAR).

*Wishbone Interface:* The interrupt controller has a wishbone interface allowing access to specific registers in its Register Bank. Configuring the priority levels of interrupts by writing to IPrR0-3 and enabling/disabling interrupts by writing to IER is done through the bus interface.

**Interrupt Interface:** The interrupt interface towards the processor side saves the state of the program by injecting a set of stored instructions. When an *IRQ* request signal is received, these instructions are injected to the decode stage. Similarly, an *ERET* signal, triggers injection of instructions to restore the program state.

### 2.4 Debug Unit

The on-chip Debug Unit assists in debugging software running on the processor providing the following capabilities: halt, resume, single step, reset the system, reading register and memory contents. The communication with the host is done with a two-wire cable following the UART (Universal Asynchronous Receiver/Transmitter) protocol. As shown in Fig. 5, the debug unit has 2 submodules: Debug Support Unit (DSU) and Debug Handle Unit (DHU).

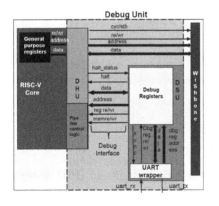
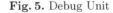
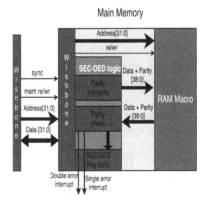

**Fig. 5.** Debug Unit                **Fig. 6.** Error correction interface

**Debug Support Unit (DSU).** The DSU sends commands to the Debug Handle Unit based on the commands received from the user. The DSU has a set of debug registers, controlling program flow. They are not memory mapped and user-programmed through UART. The DSU also has a UART wrapper controlling the transmission and reception of data, adhering to the UART protocol.

**Debug Handle Unit (DHU).** The DHU interfaces to the processor core. It communicates with the DSU through the debug interface as shown in Fig. 5. The DHU provides access the general purpose register and memory contents for read/write operations while debugging. Through the Pipeline Control Logic block, it controls data flow through the pipeline stages.

### 2.5 Error Handling

There is probability of soft errors in memories, due to interference from alpha-particle or cosmic rays, which disrupt program execution. Hence, memories are made fault-redundant using Error Correction Codes (ECCs). The error correction code used in our implementation is Single Error Correction Double Error Detection (SEC-DED) [13].

Figure 6 shows the main memory with error handling interface. Our 32-bit processor, requires 6 bits for single error correction and 1 additional bit for double error detection. The wishbone interface receives synchronisation, memory read/write, address and data signals from the core through the wishbone bus and accordingly asserts signals to the RAM macro. During a memory write operation, the Parity Compute block computes the 7 parity bits, and they are interspersed between the data bits and written to memory [13]. During a memory read, the Parity Check block re-computes the parity bits and compares it with the stored parity bits. Mismatch indicates an error raising single and double error interrupts as shown in Fig. 6. The SEC-DED register bank has memory-mapped Address Register and Correct Data Register which records the erroneous memory address and the corrected data respectively. Single-bit errors in memory are corrected by writing the corrected data to memory in the interrupt service routine. Double-bit errors terminate the program.

## 3 ASIC Implementation

The processor system is implemented on a 65 nm UMC technology node. The design is synthesized using Cadence RTL Compiler into a gate-level netlist. The RAM macro blocks for the instruction and data cache have been generated using the Standard Memory Compiler, Memaker 201201.1.1, provided by Faraday Technology Corporation. Cadence Conformal LEC tool is used to check the equivalence of the golden RTL and the synthesized netlist. In the backend design, we use Cadence Encounter to do the power distribution, floorplanning, placement, clock tree synthesis, design routing and obtain the GDSII file.

## 4 Results

### 4.1 FPGA Implementation

Design and implementation is done in Xilinx Vivado 2015.4 with Virtex-7 FPGA (XC7VX485T) as target. Table 1 shows the resource utilisation after Place and Route. RAM 36/18 refers to SRAM of si ze 36/18 Kilo bits.

**Table 1.** Resource utilisation

| Module | Look-Up tables | Reg | RAM 36 | RAM 18 |
|---|---|---|---|---|
| Top | 14462 | 6927 | 90 | 2 |
| Processor | 4208 | 840 | 0 | 0 |
| D-Cache | 6327 | 3310 | 18 | 0 |
| I-Cache | 807 | 923 | 8 | 2 |
| Interrupt controller | 819 | 354 | 0 | 0 |
| Bus controller | 311 | 156 | 0 | 0 |
| Debug | 356 | 229 | 0 | 0 |

**Table 2.** Comparison of our processor system with Vscale implementation on FPGA

| Parameter | VScale | Our processor | SoC |
|---|---|---|---|
| Look-Up tables | 2500 | 4208 | 14462 |
| Reg | 1006 | 840 | 6927 |
| Max Freq (MHz) | 131 | 190 | 121(no-RMW) 80(RMW) |

The data cache is shown to have the highest resource utilisation due to hardware support for RMW operations. Table 2 shows a comparison of our processor system with Vscale processor from UCB [6] in Xilinx Vivado 2015.4 Design Suite with Virtex-7 FPGA target.

Our processor system offers a frequency speedup of about 1.4x compared to the VScale processor. The full SoC achieves a maximum frequency of 121 MHz without RMW support and 80 MHz with RMW support.

## 4.2   ASIC Implementation

Table 3 shows the results of our design synthesized with 65 nm UMC process technology, as compared with some of the commercial implementations. Though pipelined with five stages, our processor occupies lesser area. However, the overall system area is higher due to the 32KB on-chip RAM, for the instruction cache

**Table 3.** Comparison of ASIC implementation of our processor system with commercial implementations

| Parameter | Shakti F-class [15] | MicroRISC-V [14] | Our System |
|---|---|---|---|
| Architecture | 5-stage | 3-stage | 5-stage |
| Process | 55 nm | 130 nm | 65 nm |
| Area (mm$^2$) | 0.27 | 0.12 (Processor) 0.35 (SoC+RAM) | 0.0497 (Processor) 0.0794 (SoC), 1.027 (SoC+RAM) |
| RAM (on-chip) | Not available | 4 KB | 32 KB |
| Max freq (MHz) | 416 | 100 | 220 (Processor), 170 (SoC) |
| Instance cnt | 25176 | Not available | 24907 |

and data cache. Process, voltage and temperature conditions for corner cases include: *Best case corner* - fast, 1.32 V, $-40°$ C; *Worst case corner* - slow, 1.08 V, $125°$ C

# 5   Conclusion

This paper presents the design and implementation of a RISC-V ISA compatible processor system. The scope of extensions in the design include adding virtual memory support, floating point instruction support and multiple execution modes. Power saving techniques in ASIC flow could be explored.

# References

1. RISC-V, The Free and Open RISC Instruction Set Architecture. RISC-V Foundation (2016). https://riscv.org. Accessed 14 Jun 2016
2. Waterman, A., Lee, Y., Patterson, D.A., Asanovic, K.: The RISC-V instruction set manual, volume i: base user-level ISA. EECS Department, UC Berkeley, Technical report UCB/EECS-2011-62 (2011)
3. Hennessy, J.L., Patterson, D.A.: Computer Architecture: A Quantitative Approach. Elsevier (2011)
4. Chisel. The Regents of the University of California (2015). https://chisel.eecs. berkeley.edu. Accessed 14 Jun 2016
5. Magyar, A., Lee, Y., Ou, A.: Z-Scale: Tiny 32-bit RISC-V Systems with Updates to the Rocket Chip generator. The International House, Berkeley (2015)
6. Verilog version of Z-scale, vscale (2016). https://github.com/ucb-bar/vscale. Accessed 14 Jun 2016
7. Schmidt, C.: "RISC-V" Rocket Chip "Tutorial". UC Berkeley (2015)
8. Duran, L.R.C., et al.: A 32-bit RISC-V AXI4-lite bus-based Microcontroller with 10-bit SAR ADC. In: VII Latin American Symposium on Circuits and Systems (LASCAS) (2016)
9. PULPino. http://www.pulp-platform.org. Accessed 25 May 2017
10. https://en.wikipedia.org/wiki/LowRISC. Accessed 25 May 2017
11. Waterman, A., Lee, Y., et al.: The RISC-V Instruction Set Manual, Volume II: Privileged Architecture. CS Division, EECS Department, University of California, Berkeley (2015)
12. Girard, O.: OpenCores openMSP430, Revision 1.13, 19 May 2015
13. Error Detection and Correction: Supplement to Logic and Computer Design Fundamentals. Pearson Education (2004)
14. Duran, C., Rueda, L., Castillo, G., et al.: A 32-bit 100 MHz RISC-V Microcontroller with 10-bit SAR ADC in 130 nm CMOS GP. In: Third RISC-V Workshop Proceedings (2016)
15. Gupta, S., Gala, N., et al.: SHAKTI-F: a fault tolerant microprocessor architecture. In: IEEE 24th Asian Test Symposium (2015)

# Low Power Design and Test

# An Efficient Timing and Clock Tree Aware Placement Flow with Multibit Flip-Flops for Power Reduction

Jasmine Kaur Gulati[1(✉)], Bhanu Prakash[2], and Sumit Darak[1]

[1] Indraprastha Institute of Information Technology, Delhi, India
{jasmine1481,sumit}@iiitd.ac.in
[2] STMicroelectronics Private Ltd., Greater Noida, Uttar Pradesh, India
shswbp1234@hotmail.com

**Abstract.** Multibit flip-flops (MBFFs) approach have been discussed with significant interest in the literature as the promising way to minimize the power consumption of the clock network in the modern System on Chip (SoC) designs. However, in real designs with complex architectures, MBFFs approach without the full awareness of placement and clock tree information may adversely affect the design attributes. This includes heavy congestion post clock tree synthesis (CTS), long wirelengths leading to higher voltage drop and timing violations. This paper introduces a novel placement methodology, integrated with existing electronic design automation (EDA) flow and tools, for MBFF generation with prerequisite knowledge of clock tree architecture. In addition, an algorithm for minimizing the clock insertion delay (CID) of the design is proposed. The algorithm reduces the CID by identifying the clock tree nets and the clock tree sinks which violate the CID at the early CTS stage. The proposed methodology is validated on two different designs which are complex and target real applications. The proposed methodology leads to 50.46% and 37.7% reduction in flip-flop power consumption for design I and II, respectively. Furthermore, the core density has improved by 12.8% and 9.8% for design I and II, respectively. An average reduction of 9.2% in the CID validates the superiority of the proposed algorithm over existing algorithm.

**Keywords:** Clock tree synthesis · Congestion · Multibit flip-flops
Placement · System-on-chip

## 1 Introduction

In a system-on-chip (SoC), clock distribution network synchronizes the flow of data signals across the data paths. Design of such networks is a challenge that has grown up with technology scaling which in turn affects the system's performance and reliability. The typical synchronous design is becoming more complicated as more functionality (pertaining to the user-required additional features) is being integrated onto the SoC [1]. Coupled with the integration of multi-vendor

© Springer Nature Singapore Pte Ltd. 2017
B. K. Kaushik et al. (Eds.): VDAT 2017, CCIS 711, pp. 581–593, 2017.
https://doi.org/10.1007/978-981-10-7470-7_56

designs with complex clock structures, has made clock tree balancing even more complex. Advanced nodes exhibit wire delay variation, temperature inversion, crosstalk penalty on signal and clock paths, extra pessimism to model on-chip variation, voltage drop profiles etc. With limited power budgets, clock power consumption is a key problem area in the modern VLSI designs, as it influences the correctness, area, speed, and reliability of the synthesized system [2].

Several design methodologies such as clock gating [3,4], power gating [5], buffer sizing [6], and multi-bit flip-flops (MBFFs) [7,8] have been introduced to minimize the power consumption of the clock network. MBFFs proved to be the promising solution for low-power designs. This is because, application of MBFFs results in reduced clock sinks during clock tree synthesis (CTS), which in turn leads to the reduction in parameters such as chip area, power consumption, clock latency, network delay, improved routing resource utilization etc. Figure 1(a) shows an example of a simple clock tree network with 1-bit flip-flops (FFs) and Fig. 1(b) is the clock tree in (a) with 2-bit FFs and hence, fewer number of sinks.

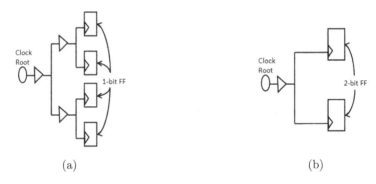

(a)                                        (b)

**Fig. 1.** (a) Clock tree with 1-bit FFs (b) Clock tree in (a) with 2-bit FFs and hence, fewer number of sinks

MBFFs have been introduced at different stages of the design flow i.e. during physical synthesis [9], pre-placement and post-placement [10]. However, it is may not be desirable to introduce MBFFs without floorplan and placement information as it may degrade the timing and congestion budgets. The practical industrial flow infers to MBFFs at the synthesis stage with the knowledge of floorplan. This methodology benefits the designer as it minimizes the congestion and timing violations in the backend flow. For more accurate timing analysis, recent works [11,12] apply MBFFs during the backend flow after the placement stage. However, due to the fixed combination logic cells in the design after their placement, the number of mergeable FFs are fewer. Also, as the size of MBFF increases, it may lead to difficulty in placement legalization and hence congestion in the design.

In the recent work [13], placement optimization with clock tree aware MBFF generation has been introduced to minimize the power consumption and latency of the clock network. The merging of 1-bit FFs is performed according to the clock tree topology. Through the placement iterations, the FFs are progressively merged by referring to the original clock tree topology. Although, this approach offers power reduction without degrading the performance of the design; it has some limitations which include:

- A real design can have millions of instances due to its complex functionality. If the merging of the FFs is improper, then the complete design may suffer from congestion and timing violations. As the number of FFs increases, the need for full scenario exploration coupled with fast turn-around time is a must.
- As the designs today are vast and complex, the single chip is broken down into a hierarchy of modules. The timing budgets are created for the whole design, which permits the engineers to use hierarchical design methodology and work on their modules for the timing closure. The merging algorithm has to follow the hierarchical approach to target the FFs at the same hierarchy level.
- With multi-level clock gating widely used in the design for dynamic power reduction, the grouping of FFs should avoid merging of gated and non-gated FFs to maintain correct functionality of the design.
- Further, SoC designers use benchmark CAD tools for the physical design flow which aims at the minimization of the cost function, PPA (power, performance, and area). The integration of the MBFF merging algorithm with these benchmark tools is must, especially when the technology is advancing to the nanometer range.

To achieve proper and reliable flop merging, it is important to consider all the above-mentioned points and to make the MBFF approach feasible for real designs.

In this paper, we present an efficient placement methodology which not only minimizes clock power but also reduces the clock insertion delay (CID). This methodology is clock tree aware as MBFF generation is done during placement with CTS view present which results in the reduction of FF power consumption and clock wire-length (WL). It has been integrated in combination with the EDA tool, Cadence Innovus. The experiment has been performed on two different designs and the results show that the proposed placement methodology leads to reduced FF power consumption by 50.46% and 37.7% respectively due to the reduction in the number of clock tree sinks without degrading the performance of the design in terms of timing. The core density improves by 12.8% and 9.8% for design I and II, respectively. In addition, applying FF merging algorithm progressively with placement iterations avoids congestion and timing violations. Furthermore, the average CID of the design reduces by 9.2% after the proposed CID reduction algorithm.

This paper is organized as follows. Section 2 explains the proposed placement methodology with the corresponding FF merging and CID reduction algorithms. Experimental results are reported in Sect. 3. Section 4 concludes the paper.

# 2  Proposed Placement Methodology

The proposed methodology offers additional feature to the EDA tools to integrate MBFFs during placement legalization with the knowledge of clock tree structure of the design. The methodology is placement and clock tree aware as presented in Fig. 2 and consists of the following stages:

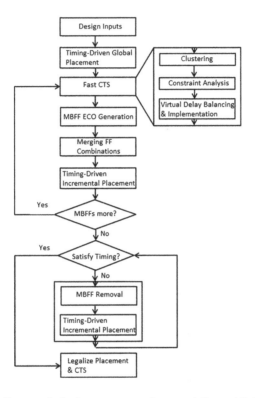

**Fig. 2.** Proposed clock tree aware placement flow with MBFFs

## 2.1  Timing-Driven Global Placement

In the first stage, the timing-aware global placement is performed with the design netlist, MBFF library, floorplan and timing constraints as inputs. Placement is done in the timing-driven mode so that the timing violations can be tested at an early stage. Tool efficiently fulfills the objective of minimized WL and placement density during the placement of logic cells.

## 2.2  Fast CTS

After the cells are placed and the timing is satisfied, CTS is performed. In order to ensure that it does not incur huge runtime, it is done without trial routing. The clock tree is built after clustering and delay balancing. The synthesized clock tree is built to meet the design-rule constraints (DRC) such as maximum capacitance, maximum transition and maximum fanout. The complete clock architecture is ready at this stage and is passed as an input to the next stage to find the merge-able FFs in the clock tree. In the Fig. 3(a), the clock tree generated after CTS as an example is shown and its corresponding levels are shown in Fig. 3(b). The levels determine the depth of the clock tree and the clock latency. The level of the clock tree sink will be further used in the FF merging algorithm.

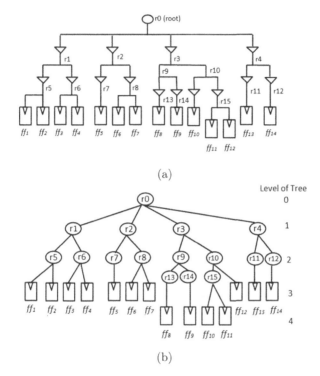

**Fig. 3.** (a) Clock tree structure (b) Corresponding tree with levels

## 2.3   MBFF Engineering Change Order (ECO) Generation

To merge the FFs of a particular clock tree, merge-able conditions are defined. These conditions ensure that the design complexity is taken care of during FF merging. Each clock tree is then checked for its capacity to merge the FFs into MBFFs. A look-up table is created for the candidate merge-able FFs. The merge-able conditions between two FFs $f_i$ and $f_j$, where i and j denote the index of FFs, are derived to ensure the correct and efficient replacement of FFs to MBFFs. These are:

(1) The merging of FFs far from each other affects the placement efficiency and hence, it is desirable to merge FFs placed near to each other. The distance, in terms of coordinates, between $f_i$ and $f_j$ should be less than a maximum set value.

$$dist(f_i, f_j) \leq dist_{max} \qquad (1)$$

In the Eq. 1, $dist_{max}$ is determined from the chip dimensions and the position of FFs after the analysis of clock tree structure.

(2) The two FFs are mergeable if the difference between their respective levels, level(fi, fj), from the root is equal or less than a constant, $k$. In order to preserve the latency of the clock tree, FFs with close tree levels are considered to be merge-able.

$$|level(f_i) - level(f_j)| \leq k \qquad (2)$$

In this paper, the value of the constant $k$ is set to be 1, to ensure maximum merging for best FF power consumption.

(3) The candidate FFs, $f_i$, and $f_j$ should be in the same hierarchy level, $H_i$ and have same pin configurations. As the clock architecture of modern SoC design is hierarchical, this checkpoint is compulsory to ensure the correct merging of FFs.

(4) Either both or none of the candidate FFs should be gated in the same level of clock gating. The designs undertaken consist of multiple levels of clock gating. This condition is of utmost importance because it is difficult to infer during placement if the resultant MBFF should be gated or not in the current level. This decision is critical since it tends to affect the logical functionality of the module.

The Algorithm 1 depicts the proposed approach for FF merging. At first, a particular clock tree is selected and all its sinks are included in the database. On these sinks, the conditions for merging are applied, given by Eqs. 1 and 2. To save the memory and to prevent extra run-time, distance is given the first priority. Inside the circular area, of radius, $dist_{max}$, around $f_i$, all the clock tree sinks are taken for further analysis of merge-able conditions and are added to a list, *mergeflops*. Rest all clock tree sinks are eliminated for merging with $f_i$. With the elimination, the analysis of the other merge-able conditions is broken down into a smaller number of sinks. The other conditions are applied on the *mergeflops*. If more than one FF satisfies all the merge-able conditions, a look-up table is generated and the candidates are added to it. The weight function is given by Eq. 3 is applied on the candidates of the look-up table to find the best match for merging such that the resultant signal net WL, clock latency, and the power consumption is minimum during MBFF generation.

$$w_{f_{ij}} \propto dist(f_i, f_j) \qquad (3)$$

---

**Algorithm 1.** FF Merging

---

1: *clock_trees* ← *get_clock_trees*()
2: **for** *tree* in *clock_trees* **do**
3:    **for** *sink* in *clock_tree_sinks* **do**
4:       *sink_pos* ← *calculate_position*()
5:       *level*(*sink*) ← *level_clock_tree*()
6:       *candidate_merge_list* ← *sinks in that region*
7:       **for** *candidate* in *candidate_merge_list* **do**
8:          *level*(*candidate*) ← *level_clock_tree*()
9:          **if** ($|level(f_i) - level(f_j)| \leq k$) **then**
10:             **if** *hierarchy* && *clock gating* **then**
11:                *mergeflops* ← *candidate*
12:             **end if**
13:          **end if**
14:       **end for**
15:       **for** *mergeableflops* in *mergeflops* **do**
16:          *weight_sink* ← *weight*(*mergeableflops*)
17:       **end for**
18:       *best_to_merge* ← *min*(*weight_sink*)
19:    **end for**
20: **end for**

---

Similarly, the algorithm is repeated for all the sinks of the clock tree. The same algorithm is replicated on other clock trees as well. After performing the merging algorithm, the optimum solution for all FFs is obtained in the combination table. On the basis of the results, the merging of FFs to MBFFs is performed and the netlist with MBFFs is generated.

Figure 4(a) shows the initial stage clock tree before FF merging with the merging conditions applied to the candidate FFs. Figure 4(b) displays the clock tree generated with MBFFs after the application of proposed FF merging algorithm.

## 2.4    Timing-Driven Incremental Placement

After the netlist consisting of MBFFs is generated, incremental placement is done to find the legal location of the MBFF. As the size of MBFF is larger than the single bit flip-flop, congestion and timing constraints can be violated hence timing-driven incremental placement is performed. To ensure that the placement is legalizable and the timing constraints are met, timing-driven incremental placement refines the locations of combinational cells, sequential logic cells, and the newly generated MBFFs. The iterations in placement continue until no more MBFFs can be generated in the clock routing tree. The clock tree is built after every MBFF formation as it lowers the risk in skew due to the movement of FFs during iterative placement.

In case, the timing results obtained from the incremental placement are worse than those in the initial placement stage after the MBFF generation, the MBFFs are iteratively disassembled to single-bit FFs. Once the timing slacks are

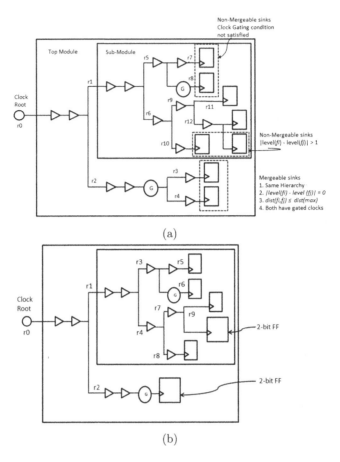

**Fig. 4.** (a) Clock Tree with 1-bit FFs (b) Corresponding clock tree generated with 2-bit FFs after the application of FF merging algorithm

improved, legalized placement with MBFFs is obtained after placement legalization. Further, CTS is performed with MBFFs and the clock routing tree is obtained. At the end, the entire physical design with MBFFs is accomplished up to route stage.

## 3    CID Reduction Algorithm

Another key metric of clock network is CID reduction which acts as a panacea for all. Minimizing CID will result in shorter clock network, less impact on crosstalk, less impact of process variation, and reduction in hold penalties. In order to achieve better performance in terms of insertion delay of the clock tree structure, a novel way to reduce CID of the clocks is discovered by using intuitive and step by step approach. The algorithm works on the following principles:

### 3.1    Identification of the Dominant Clock

The clock termed as the dominant clock is the one with either or all of the characteristics, which are, the one with maximum frequency or the one with maximum number of sinks spread in the clock tree structure or the one with the major timing critical path. After the analysis of clock tree and its balancing requirements, dominant clock is identified.

### 3.2    Extraction of the Outliers of the Dominant Clock

The clock tree sinks which constrain the balancing requirements during CTS and worsens the CID are considered as outliers in this paper. In Fig. 5(a), the insertion delay of FF1–FF4 is less than that of macro blocks and in Fig. 5(b), the insertion delay of entire block is maximum after CTS. In Fig. 5, it can be seen that to balance the CID of FFs with the hard macro (memory), the CID of the FFs needs to be increased. Thus, the hard macro are the outliers which are violating the CID.

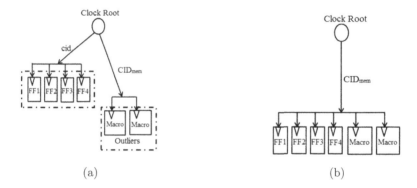

(a)                                                                    (b)

**Fig. 5.** (a) Before CTS balancing cid < CID of FF1–FF4 (b) After CTS balancing

### 3.3    What-If Analysis of the Floorplan

The analysis of the placement pin and the macro placement changes on the sinks with maximum CID is performed. This is done to avoid the timing violations due to the timing paths from the outlier sinks. In the later stage, the chip is divided into four quadrants and the outliers present in each quadrant are extracted and grouped separately. This process is the filtration process wherein, firstly a database of outliers is maintained and later on the basis of their positions and the architecture of clock tree, skew groups are created.

On the basis of the above principles, the algorithm for CID reduction is framed as shown in the Fig. 6. After the timing driven placement, the next step is clock tree prototyping using clustering. The approach is, therefore, to find the outliers for the dominant clock that are increasing the insertion delay and group them for further analysis. Once the outliers groups are determined, the outliers are grouped

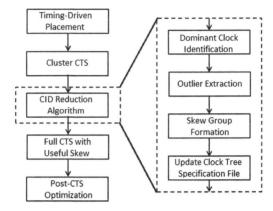

**Fig. 6.** CID Reduction Algorithm

in separate skew groups based on their location on the chip. In this way, parent clock skew group's insertion delay targets are unblocked. With the help of a handful of outliers, each and every clock tree sink is satisfied with the ease of its timing targets. The initially generated clock specification file is modified automatically with the added skew groups and CTS is performed. To fix the timing violations that may occur due to outlier sinks to other sinks, useful skew with CTS is used. This is the generic method through which we are able to unblock parent clock skew group's insertion delay targets. The CTS is followed by the post-CTS optimization to further improve the setup and hold violating paths.

## 4    Experimental Results

The proposed algorithm has been implemented on Red Hat Enterprise Linux v5.9 operating system using Cadence Innovus 15.2. Table 1 illustrates the specifications of the simulation setup and Table 2 shows the design specifications on which the tests are performed. The designs undertaken are complex with security logic embedded in them and target real time applications with considerable amount of power consumption.

**Table 1.** Setup for experiment

| Operating system | Red Hat Enterprise Linux Server release 6.7 (Santiago) |
|---|---|
| Number of processing cores | 14 |
| Vendor ID | Intel(R) Xeon(R) CPU E5-2697 |
| Processor speed (GHz) | 2.6 |
| Tool | Cadence Innovus(TM) v15.20-p005_1 |
| Scripting language | TCL |

**Table 2.** Specifications of design at 28 nm technology node

|  | Design I | Design II |
|---|---|---|
| Total standard cell number | 186920 | 990416 |
| Total hard macros | 18 | 33 |
| Total chip area | $0.65\,\text{mm}^2$ | $2.07\,\text{mm}^2$ |

## 4.1  Comparison of Conventional and Proposed Placement Flow

Table 3 shows the results of the comparative analysis of various attributes performed on the two designs. Due to the applied merging algorithm, the number of clock tree sinks decreases in both designs by 1.5%. The number of merge-able FFs for a design depends on its complexity, logic, and size. As the undertaken designs are that of secured IP and complex, the merge-ability is limited. According to the Table 3, core density improves by 9.8% and clock power reduces by 11.8% for design I. Due to the fewer clock tree sinks, reduction in clock inverters and clock nets, the core density improves. For design II, core utilization increases by 12.8% and clock power optimize by 9%.

**Table 3.** Comparison between the Non-MBFF flow and the proposed MBFF flow for Design I and Design II

|  | Design I | | Design II | |
|---|---|---|---|---|
|  | Baseline flow | Proposed flow | Baseline flow | Proposed flow |
| # of 1-bit FFs | 135623 | 72682 | 23586 | 17333 |
| # of 2-bit FFs | 0 | 1714 | 0 | 3125 |
| # of clock tree sinks | 135623 | 133548 | 23586 | 20458 |
| TNS (ns) | −0.278 | −0.183 | −1007.2 | −566.438 |
| Core density (%) | 71.415 | 78.402 | 73.314 | 82.702 |
| Total WL (m) | 26.22 | 26.23 | 4.2 | 4.1 |
| Clock power (mW) | 37.56 | 33.21 | 7.45 | 6.78 |

Table 4 depicts the analysis of power consumption by the two approaches and it is observed that reduction in power is by 50.46% and 37.7% respectively for two designs. The results for total negative slack (TNS) achieved is also bearable and does not degrade the performance of the designs.

Consequently, the proposed timing and clock tree aware placement flow with MBFF generation leads to improved performance of the designs in terms of chip power by 44%, core density by 11.3% and clock power by 10.4%. Also, the corresponding FF merging algorithm proves effective by considering the real-time design scenarios.

**Table 4.** Comparison of power consumption of the designs

| Power (mW) | Design I | | Design II | |
|---|---|---|---|---|
| | Baseline flow | Proposed flow | Baseline flow | Proposed flow |
| Internal | 130.11 | 119.2 | 31.53 | 26.62 |
| Switching | 342.13 | 114.88 | 54.475 | 31.23 |
| Leakage | 0.024 | 0.023 | 0.0126 | 0.0114 |
| Total | 472.27 | 234.108 | 86.0165 | 57.88 |

## 4.2    Comparison of Proposed CID Reduction Algorithm with Traditional Approach of CTS

According to Table 5, the results of the CID reduction algorithm, average CID cuts by 19.5%. It can be attributed to the outlier group which was excluded from the dominant clock group. It translates effectively into less CID of parent clock and all associated benefits such as controlled clock tree structure and reduced WL. Thus, with a handful of outliers, we are able to improve the rest of clock tree sinks in terms of CID. For the entire design after applying the proposed algorithm, the average CID reduces by 9.2%.

**Table 5.** Experimental results for dominant clock by CID reduction algorithm

| Dominant Clock attributes | Base algorithm | Proposed CID algorithm |
|---|---|---|
| Minimum CID (ns) | 0.954 | 0.740 |
| Maximum CID (ns) | 1.116 | 0.902 |
| Average CID (ns) | 1.078 | 0.868 |
| # of Inverters | 1125 | 1078 |
| WL after CTS (um) | 201323.3 | 198488.836 |

## 5    Conclusion

This paper presented an effective timing and clock tree aware placement flow with MBFF generation and the corresponding algorithm for FF merging. It is focused on the analysis of real-time designs and tackles all complex scenarios efficiently. Experimental results for the presented placement flow show the reduction in power without the degradation in the design performance. In the end, the algorithm for the optimization of CID is also presented which results in reduced average insertion delay of the design. Moreover, the placement flow is integrated with the industry EDA tool.

# References

1. Lorincz, B.H., Cao, Y., Li, X., Mai, K., Pileggi, L.T., Rutenbar, R.A., Shepard, K.L.: Digital circuit design challenges and opportunities in the era of nanoscale CMOS. Proc. IEEE **96**(2), 343–365 (2008)
2. Roy, S., Mattheakis, P.M., Masse-Navette, L., Pan, D.Z.: Evolving challenges and techniques for nanometer SoC clock network synthesis. In: 12th IEEE International Conference on Solid-State and Integrated Circuit Technology (ICSICT), pp. 1–4, October 2014
3. Teng, S.K., Soin, N.: Low power clock gates optimization for clock tree distribution. In: 11th International Symposium on Quality Electronic Design (ISQED), pp. 488–492, March 2010
4. Dev, M.P., Baghel, D., Pandey, B., Pattanaik, M., Shukla, A.: Clock gated low power sequential circuit design. In: IEEE Conference on Information Communication Technologies (ICT), pp. 440–444, April 2013
5. Chen, S.Y., Lin, R.B., Tung, H.H., Lin, K.W.: Power gating design for standard-cell-like structured ASICs. In: Design, Automation Test in Europe Conference Exhibition (DATE), pp. 514–519, March 2010
6. Dai, W.M., Xi, J.G.: Buffer insertion and sizing under process variations for low power clock distribution. In: 32nd Conference on Design Automation (DAC), pp. 491–496 (1995)
7. Lin, M.P.H., Hsu, C.C., Chang, Y.T.: Recent research in clock power saving with multi-bit flip-flops. In: IEEE 54th International Midwest Symposium on Circuits and Systems (MWSCAS), pp. 1–4, August 2011
8. Shyu, Y.T., Lin, J.M., Huang, C.P., Lin, C.W., Lin, Y.Z., Chang, S.J.: Effective and efficient approach for power reduction by using multi-bit flip-flops. IEEE Trans. Very Large Scale Integr. (VLSI) Syst. **21**(4), 624–635 (2013)
9. Santos, C., Reis, R., Godoi, G., Barros, M., Duarte, F.: Multi-bit flip-flop usage impact on physical synthesis. In: 25th Symposium on Integrated Circuits and Systems Design (SBCCI), pp. 1–6, August 2012
10. Lin, M.P.H., Hsu, C.C., Chang, Y.T.: Post-placement power optimization with multi-bit flip-flops. IEEE Trans. Comput. Aided Des. Integr. Circuits Syst. **30**(12), 1870–1882 (2011)
11. Lin, M.P.H., Hsu, C.C., Chang, Y.T.: Design and allocation of loosely coupled multi-bit flip-flops for power reduction in post-placement optimization. In: 21st Asia and South Pacific Design Automation Conference (ASP-DAC), pp. 268–273, January 2016
12. Chen, W., Yan, J.T.: Routability-driven flip-flop merging process for clock power reduction. In: IEEE International Conference on Computer Design (ICCD), pp. 203–208, October 2010
13. Lin, M.P.H., Hsu, C.C., Chen, Y.C.: Clock-tree aware multibit flip-flop generation during placement for power optimization. IEEE Trans. Comput. Aided Des. of Integr. Circuits Syst. **34**(2), 280–292 (2015)

# Primitive Instantiation Based Fault Localization Circuitry for High Performance FPGA Designs

Ayan Palchaudhuri[✉] and Anindya Sundar Dhar

Department of Electronics and Electrical Communication Engineering,
Indian Institute of Technology Kharagpur, Kharagpur 721302, West Bengal, India
{ayanpc,asd}@ece.iitkgp.ernet.in

**Abstract.** The ever increasing demand to push the envelope for achieving superlative metrics of VLSI circuit performance along with denser logic packing and miniaturization of device dimensions, has rendered FPGAs to be more vulnerable to reliability hazards. This has led to reducing of the reliability and lifetime of VLSI chips. In this paper, we have proposed certain circuit techniques which comes along with the original design, to detect the presence of faulty FPGA logic slices, without significant compromise in performance. Primitive instantiation and constrained placement based approach was adopted for the circuit realizations to facilitate tracing of the exact faulty location, so that the faulty zones may be conveniently bypassed for fault-free circuit operation.

**Keywords:** Carry chain · Look-Up Table · Fault localization · FPGA Primitive instantiation

## 1 Introduction

Downsizing of technology nodes and increased logic proliferation within a single chip without appreciable augmentation in chip size has intensified the complexity in the photolithographic process. The chip is thus more susceptible to structural defects, transistor aging, Bias Temperature Instability (BTI), electromigration, dielectric breakdown and hot carrier injection [1,2]. Subsequently, error detection techniques, fault localization and fault tolerance mechanisms are being adopted for FPGA based designs [3,4]. Fast error detection techniques tailored for Xilinx FPGAs has been carried out at the cost of hardware overhead and performance penalty [5]. Ascertaining the presence of any erroneous output through a scan based technique was studied in [6,7]. Self checking logic for on-line fault detection in FPGAs has been studied in [8].

Fault localization circuitry should ideally not deteriorate the performance of the original FPGA based designs, and its topology depends upon the implementation details and the nature of mapping of the original circuit on the FPGA. High performance FPGA implementations have been demonstrated using target FPGA specific *primitive instantiation* [6,9] coupled with placement directives. Along with erroneous output detection, faulty FPGA logic slices may ideally be

© Springer Nature Singapore Pte Ltd. 2017
B. K. Kaushik et al. (Eds.): VDAT 2017, CCIS 711, pp. 594–606, 2017.
https://doi.org/10.1007/978-981-10-7470-7_57

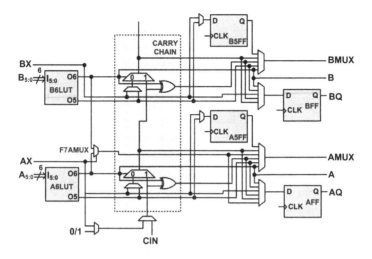

Fig. 1. A partial FPGA slice architecture for Virtex-7 platform.

traced by following a primitive instantiation and constrained placement based approach. Often in the original design, the configured FPGA primitives lie underutilized. This leaves a scope for packing more logic into them with more inputs without incurring any hardware overhead. In this paper, we have mapped the fault localization circuitry on commonly used datapath and controlpath circuits. The methodologies adopted include appropriate routing of "monitor" signals, C-testability, self-dual duplication, and self-checking logic, as deemed amenable and as decided by the nature of the original circuit mapping. Our main contributions are as follows:

- We have studied the feasibility of implementing the above fault localization techniques on arithmetic cores for FPGAs such as counters, adders, comparators, universal shift registers and cellular automata based circuits.
- Implementation results demonstrate that there is only a negligible or tolerable speed penalty, with area overhead only for on-line fault detection techniques, on inserting the most pertinent fault localization circuitry.
- The art of primitive instantiation and issuing placement directives guarantee high speed, area compaction, as well as eases out the task to trace any faulty sites if any, where the original circuit has been mapped.

The organization of the paper is as follows. Section 2 elaborates on the fault localization schemes. In Sect. 3, the implementation results are discussed and elaborated. We conclude in Sect. 4.

# 2   Proposed Architectures

Each slice of Xilinx Virtex-7 FPGA contains four 6-input Look-Up Tables (LUTs), eight FFs, three wide function multiplexers, and a carry chain for fast

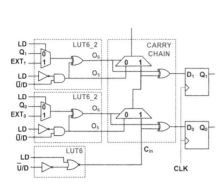

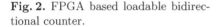

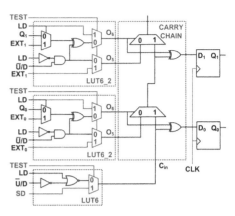

**Fig. 2.** FPGA based loadable bidirectional counter.

**Fig. 3.** FPGA based counter equipped with fault localization capability (Color figure online).

carry propagation [10]. The LUTs primarily realize combinational logic, and in conjunction with the carry chain may realize slightly more complex functions [10]. Each FF has dedicated "set/reset" and "clock enable" pins. A partial slice architecture for Virtex-7 FPGAs from Xilinx is shown in Fig. 1.

Next, we discuss the Xilinx FPGA fabric aware architectures for common datapath and controlpath circuits with the most suitable fault localization circuitry so as to incur minimal speed deterioration and hardware overhead.

## 2.1    Appropriate Routing of Monitor Signals

"Monitor" signals may be defined as logic signals which may be made to propagate along the different circuits contours of an FPGA based implementation to detect any errors or existing functional failures. We illustrate this technique on a loadable, bidirectional counter.

**Loadable Bidirectional Resettable Counter.** The counter comprises of an incrementer/decrementer logic with a feedback loop and a Parallel-Input Parallel-Output register as shown in Fig. 2. Each LUT either loads external data $EXT$ to the FFs, or the previous state to the incrementer/decrementer unit, and computes $O6_i = (\overline{LD} \cdot Q_i + LD \cdot EXT_i) \oplus (\overline{LD} \cdot \overline{U}/D)$, and $O5_i = \overline{LD} \cdot \overline{U}/D$. Here, $LD$ is the control input for external load, $EXT$ is the externally loadable input, $\overline{U}/D$ controls up or down counting, and $Q$ is the counter state. The initial carry input is $C_{in} = \overline{LD + \overline{U}/D}$. The inputs for an up-counter and down-counter are $D_i = Q_i \oplus (Q_{i-1}Q_{i-2}...Q_1Q_0)$ if $i \geq 1$, and $D_i = \overline{Q_i} \oplus (Q_{i-1} + Q_{i-2} + ... + Q_1 + Q_0)$ if $i \geq 1$ respectively. From Fig. 2, it is evident that four LUT inputs are required to realize the design. The un-utilized input is made to drive the $TEST$ mode signal. Since *normal* and *test* modes are

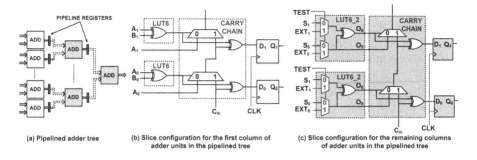

(a) Pipelined adder tree

(b) Slice configuration for the first column of adder units in the pipelined tree

(c) Slice configuration for the remaining columns of adder units in the pipelined tree

**Fig. 4.** FPGA based pipelined adder tree and its corresponding architecture facilitating C-testability.

non-overlapping operations, the $EXT$ and $LD$ pins drives suitable data signals in *test* mode. The select line of the carry chain multiplexer is driven by the $LD$ pin to reliably propagate the $EXT$ vector or the serial data input $SD$ along the contours of the carry chain for fault monitoring. The intermediate carry chain outputs from the multiplexers may be tapped out to facilitate fine-grained fault localization over a smaller region. Thus, the fault localization circuitry modifies the LUT functionality as $O6_i = TEST \cdot LD + \overline{TEST} \cdot ((\overline{LD} \cdot Q_i + LD \cdot EXT_i) \oplus (\overline{LD} \cdot \overline{U}/D))$, and $O5_i = TEST \cdot EXT_i + \overline{TEST} \cdot (\overline{LD} \cdot \overline{U}/D)$. Here, $C_{in} = TEST \cdot SD + \overline{TEST} \cdot (LD + \overline{U}/D)$. The corresponding architecture is depicted in Fig. 3 and does not consume additional hardware compared to the original architecture of Fig. 2. The additional circuitry inserted to achieve fault localization as depicted in Fig. 3 has been shown in red.

## 2.2  C-Testability

Iterative logic arrays (ILA) which may be pseudo-exhaustively tested with only a few test patterns that is independent of the number of ILA cells [11] are called C-testable ILAs, for example, a ripple carry adder (RCA). Consider a 1-bit full adder (FA) with the inputs addend $A$, augend $B$ and carry-in $C_{in}$, and the sum and carry-out as $S$ and $C_{out}$ respectively. For $\{A, B, C_{in}\} = \{0, 0, 0\}$ or $\{0, 1, 0\}$ or $\{1, 0, 0\}$ or $\{0, 1, 1\}$ or $\{1, 0, 1\}$ or $\{1, 1, 1\}$, $C_{out} = C_{in}$. However, for $\{A, B, C_{in}\} = \{1, 1, 0\}$ or $\{0, 0, 1\}$, $C_{out} = \overline{C_{in}}$. The test vectors corresponding to these two set of entries may be applied to every alternate 1-bit FA cells of an RCA during testing.

**Pipelined Adder Tree.** Fig. 4(a) shows a pipelined adder tree, where each of the ADD blocks are 24-bit adders with a total of five stages of addition. C-testable ILAs do not require any additional circuitry to achieve our goal of fault localization, but however necessitates the controllability of inputs for every ADD block of the ILA. Thus, the first column of ADD blocks accepting primary inputs is a normal adder, where each LUT computes the XOR operation of an addend and augend bit to calculate the propagate bit $P_i$. The sum bit is computed as $S_i = P_i \oplus C_{i-1} = A_i \oplus B_i \oplus C_{i-1}$. The carry bit is computed as $C_i = G_i + P_i C_{i-1} = \overline{P_i} A_i + P_i C_{i-1}$, where $G_i = A_i B_i$ is the generate bit. The partial slice configuration for the first stage of adders is shown in Fig. 4(b). Here, each LUT has only two of its inputs utilized. In subsequent addition stages, external inputs are introduced via multiplexers for pseudo-exhaustive testing. Here each LUT computes $O6_j = TEST \cdot EXT_i + \overline{TEST} \cdot S_i$ and $O5_j = TEST \cdot EXT_{i-1} + \overline{TEST} \cdot S_{i-1}$. The partial slice configuration for subsequent stages of addition barring the first stage is shown in Fig. 4(c).

## 2.3   Self Dual Duplication

Any Boolean function $g(X)$ is said to be *self-dual* [12] if $g(X) = \overline{g}(\overline{X})$. A second Boolean function $h(X)$ may be considered such that $h(X) = g(X) \oplus \delta(X)$. Then $\delta(X)$ is defined as a *self-dual complement* (SDC) of $g(X)$, provided that $h(X)$ is self-dual. $\delta(X)$ is chosen such that $\delta(X) = x_i(g(X) \oplus \overline{g}(\overline{X}))$ (for any $i$; $1 \le i \le m$), resulting in $h(X) = \overline{h}(\overline{X})$. Under this circumstance, $h(X)$ will alternate for alternating inputs in a non-erroneous system. We illustrate this paradigm for two FPGA fabric aware comparator architectures, namely a combined LUT and carry chain based comparator architecture, and a completely LUT based pipelined comparator having a tree topology.

**Carry Chain Fabric Based Comparator Design.** The carry chain based comparator shown in Fig. 5(a) comprises of a less-than (LT) and a greater-than (GT) comparator. Their outputs are NOR-ed to realize an equality comparator. Each LUT realizing the LT comparator performs equality and less-than check $e_i$ and $l_i$ respectively using its dual outputs on 2-bit input sub-words, where $e_i = (A_{2i} \odot B_{2i}) \cdot (A_{2i+1} \odot B_{2i+1})$ and $l_i = (\overline{A_{2i+1}} \cdot B_{2i+1}) + ((A_{2i+1} \odot B_{2i+1}) \cdot (\overline{A_{2i}} \cdot B_{2i}))$. The carry chain computes the final result as $L_i = \overline{e_i} l_i + e_i L_{i-1}$, where $L_0 = 0$. Similarly, the GT comparator performs equality and greater-than check $e_i$ and $g_i$ respectively. Here, $g_i = (A_{2i+1} \cdot \overline{B_{2i+1}}) + ((A_{2i+1} \odot B_{2i+1}) \cdot (A_{2i} \cdot \overline{B_{2i}}))$. The carry chain computes the final result as $G_i = \overline{e_i} g_i + e_i G_{i-1}$, where $G_0 = 0$. The self-dual complement for the equality comparison functions $e_i$ for a pair of 2-bit sub-words within each LUT may be any bit out of the input sub-words. For the GT ($g_i$) or LT ($l_i$) functions comparing 2-bit sub-words within each LUT, the self dual complement for either of them may be calculated as $\delta_i = A_i B_i (A_{i-1} \odot B_{i-1})$. During the *test* mode, the original function and its SDC outputs are EX-ORed and made available at the dual outputs which should ideally alternate when inputs are inverted. The comparator with built-in fault localization circuitry is shown in Fig. 5(b).

**A Tree Architecture Based Comparator Design.** A combinational comparator following tree topology was proposed in [13]. This circuit is amenable to LUT mapping as well as a pipelined implementation [14]. Here, each processing block accepts two 2-bit sub-words $A_{i:i-1}$ and $B_{i:i-1}$ and outputs "00"

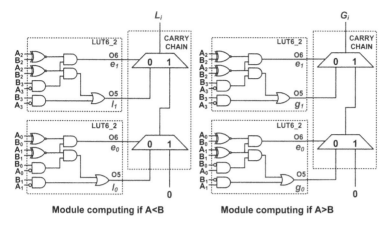

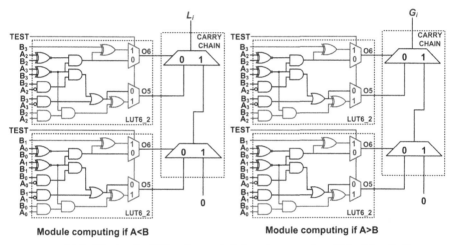

**Fig. 5.** Carry chain based FPGA comparator design and its equivalent circuit with built-in fault localization capability.

if $A_{i:i-1} = B_{i:i-1} = $ "00", "01" if $A_{i:i-1} < B_{i:i-1}$, "10" if $A_{i:i-1} > B_{i:i-1}$, and "11" if $A_{i:i-1} = B_{i:i-1} \neq$ "00". The FPGA based comparator design and the truth table (TT) for each block is shown in Fig. 6(a). For the first row, $O6 = A_i \cdot (B_i \cdot B_{i-1} \cdot \overline{A_{i-1}}) + A_i \cdot \overline{B_i}$, and $O5 = (\overline{A_{i-1}} + B_{i-1}) \cdot B_i + (B_i + B_{i-1}) \cdot \overline{A_i}$. The same pattern is followed for subsequent rows. However, if the TT is examined carefully, and the entry corresponding to $\{A_i, A_{i-1}, B_i, B_{i-1}\} = \{0, 1, 0, 1\}$ is made to output "00" instead of "11", it may be seen that on alternating the primary inputs, the outputs on every LUT in the design will be inverted, and there is no requirement to implement the self dual duplication logic explicitly. The LUTs (processing blocks) now compute $O6 = A_i(A_{i-1} + \overline{B_i}) + \overline{B_{i-1}}(A_i + A_{i-1}\overline{B_i})$ and $O5 = B_i(B_{i-1} + \overline{A_{i-1}}) + \overline{A_i}(B_i + B_{i-1}\overline{A_{i-1}})$.

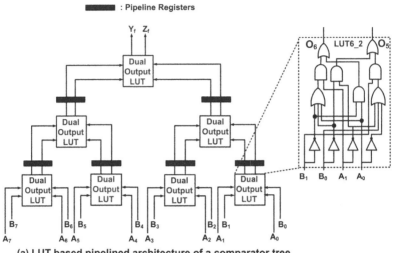

(a) LUT based pipelined architecture of a comparator tree

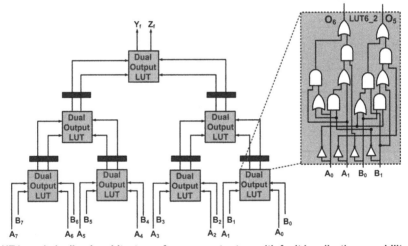

(b) LUT based pipelined architecture of a comparator tree with fault localization capability

**Fig. 6.** Fabric aware architectures for a FPGA based comparator following a tree topology and a similar tree based comparator circuit facilitating fault localization.

## 2.4   Self Checking Logic

The two-rail checker (TRC) is a common self checking logic used in on-line VLSI testing. It accepts two complementary words and outputs complementary bits in the error free condition. Consider two 2-bit words $(a_0, a_1)$ and $(b_0, b_1)$ (where $a_0 = \overline{b_0}$ and $a_1 = \overline{b_1}$) as inputs to a checker, which outputs $c_1$ and $c_2$ where $c_1 = a_0 a_1 + b_0 b_1 = a_0 \odot a_1$ and $c_2 = a_0 b_1 + a_1 b_0 = a_0 \oplus a_1$ are always complementary to each other. This methodology has been studied for two

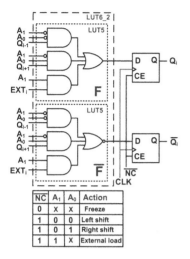

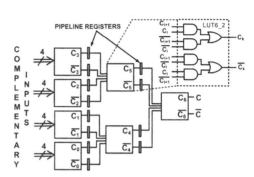

**Fig. 7.** FPGA based universal shift register generating complementary outputs and its function table.

**Fig. 8.** Pipelined two rail checker architecture using LUTs.

circuits: universal shift registers and pseudorandom number generator circuits using 1-D cellular automata logic.

**Universal Shift Register.** Universal Shift Register (USR) is a Finite State Machine (FSM) attributed with bidirectional shifting and parallel load capabilities along with freeze operation. The corresponding architecture and its function table is shown in Fig. 7. Here, both the original and their complementary outputs are individually computed by the two 5-input LUTs embedded within a single 6-input LUT. The complementary registered outputs may be checked for any errors. In order to substantially reduce the I/O pin count, we feed the complementary outputs as inputs to a totally self checking checker (TSC). The entire TSC checker is composed of 2-bit TSC sub-checkers as its building blocks. Each 2-bit TSC sub-checker is implemented using a dual output LUT. The dual outputs of each TSC sub-checker are registered for pipelining the entire architecture. Modern FPGAs come with a hardware support of eight FFs in every slice, which has been used to our advantage to support pipelining. The pipelined two rail checker architecture is shown in Fig. 8.

**One-Dimensional Linear CA Corresponding to Minimal Weight Primitive Polynomials Using Rule-90 and Rule-150.** Maximal length, 1-D linear CA circuits constructed using minimal weight primitive polynomials are attractive from the point of view of VLSI implementation for their regular and cascadable structure, with neighborhood interconnections amongst every CA cell. They find applications in pseudo-random pattern generation [15]. Every

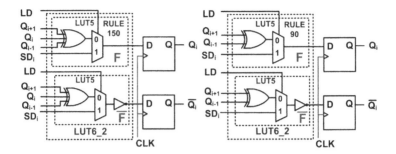

Fig. 9. FPGA based 1-D CA using a combination of Rule-90 and Rule-150.

CA cell is composed of a D-FF and a combinational logic which computes the next state of the CA following a certain *rule*. The combination of rule 90: $Q_i(t+1) = Q_{i-1}(t) \oplus Q_{i+1}(t)$ and rule 150: $Q_i(t+1) = Q_{i-1}(t) \oplus Q_i(t) \oplus Q_{i+1}(t)$ are primarily used to generate maximal length CAs governed by polynomials listed in [16]. The CA architecture shown in Fig. 9 may be initialized with a "seed" value $SD$ on asserting control input $LD$, which plays a key role in determining the quality of pseudorandomness of CA outputs, or allows the CA to come out of any infinite loop such as the "graveyard" state, e.g., the all-zero output state in a XOR-based linear CA. The LUTs realizing the combinational logic compute complementary outputs through its dual output which are fed as inputs to the pipelined TSC checker.

## 3   Results and Discussions

Xilinx Virtex-7 FPGA, device family XC7VX330T, package FFG1157, speed grade -2 was chosen as the target platform. The implementation results obtained from Xilinx ISE 14.7, have been compared with the original circuit and the circuit coupled with fault localization logic. There is no previously reported implementation results on these architectures which abides by a similar philosophy.

In Table 1, the counter circuit has been compared with its equivalent circuit supporting fault localization, having no hardware overhead compared to the original architecture. Thus, each of our proposed $n$-bit ordinary and testable counter occupy ($\lceil \frac{n}{4} \rceil + 1$) slices, ($n + 1$) LUTs and $n$ FFs. Table 2 depicts the FPGA implementation results of the pipelined adder tree and its corresponding architecture that facilitates C-testability, where the speed for both the architectures is pretty close. Similar conclusions for the implementation results shown in Table 3 for a combined LUT and carry chain based comparator and in Table 4 for a tree topology based pipelined comparator solely using LUTs and FFs may be drawn, where the equivalent circuits equipped with fault localization capabilities do not consume additional hardware, and thereby does not suffer from speed deterioration. The $n$-bit carry chain based comparator occupies ($n + 1$) LUTs and ($\lceil \frac{n}{4} \rceil + 1$) slices, whereas, the tree based pipelined comparator occupies ($n - 1$) LUTs.

**Table 1.** Implementation results for the loadable, bidirectional counter

| Operand width | Design style | #FF | #LUT | #Slice | Freq (MHz) |
|---|---|---|---|---|---|
| 32 | Ordinary architecture | 32 | 33 | 9 | 763.36 |
|  | **Testable architecture** | **32** | **33** | **9** | **763.36** |
| 48 | Ordinary architecture | 48 | 49 | 13 | 656.17 |
|  | **Testable architecture** | **48** | **49** | **13** | **656.17** |
| 64 | Ordinary architecture | 64 | 65 | 17 | 575.04 |
|  | **Testable architecture** | **64** | **65** | **17** | **575.04** |
| 96 | Ordinary architecture | 96 | 97 | 25 | 460.62 |
|  | **Testable architecture** | **96** | **97** | **25** | **460.62** |

**Table 2.** Implementation results for pipelined adder tree

| Design style | #FF | #LUT | #Slice | Freq (MHz) |
|---|---|---|---|---|
| Ordinary architecture | 720 | 744 | 186 | 629.72 |
| **C-Testable architecture** | **720** | **744** | **186** | **608.64** |

**Table 3.** Implementation results for the LUT and carry chain based comparator

| Operand width | Design style | #LUT | #Slice | Freq (MHz)* |
|---|---|---|---|---|
| 32 | Ordinary architecture | 33 | 9 | 900.90 |
|  | **Testable architecture** | **33** | **9** | **900.90** |
| 48 | Ordinary architecture | 49 | 13 | 819.67 |
|  | **Testable architecture** | **49** | **13** | **819.67** |
| 64 | Ordinary architecture | 65 | 17 | 751.88 |
|  | **Testable architecture** | **65** | **17** | **751.88** |
| 96 | Ordinary architecture | 97 | 25 | 645.16 |
|  | **Testable architecture** | **97** | **25** | **645.16** |

*The frequency was obtained by inserting registers at the input and output ports.

Tables 5 and 6 report the implementation results for USR and CA based circuits using two-rail pair checker. As most of the circuit inputs in USR and CA are feedback signals owing to their sequential logic, techniques such as self dual duplication or C-testability based fault localization does not hold valid here. Figures 7 and 9 depicts the computation of the complemented outputs via the dual LUT output ports for the USR and CA circuits. This implementation was compared with the same circuit but inclusive of the TSC checker. Implementation results reveal a small amount of speed deterioration owing to the associated

Table 4. Implementation results for the pipelined tree based comparator

| Operand width | Design style | #FF | #LUT | #Slice | Freq (MHz) |
|---|---|---|---|---|---|
| 32 | Ordinary architecture | 60 | 31 | 13 | 1262.63 |
| | **Testable architecture** | **60** | **31** | **13** | **1262.63** |
| 48 | Ordinary architecture | 94 | 47 | 20 | 1175.09 |
| | **Testable architecture** | **94** | **47** | **20** | **1175.09** |
| 64 | Ordinary architecture | 124 | 63 | 25 | 1173.71 |
| | **Testable architecture** | **124** | **63** | **25** | **1173.71** |
| 96 | Ordinary architecture | 190 | 95 | 37 | 1119.82 |
| | **Testable architecture** | **190** | **95** | **37** | **1119.82** |

Table 5. Implementation results for the universal shift register

| Operand width | Design style | #FF | #LUT | #Slice | Freq (MHz) |
|---|---|---|---|---|---|
| 32 | Exclusive of TSC checker | 64 | 32 | 9 | 1333.33 |
| | **Inclusive of TSC Checker** | **124** | **63** | **17** | **1135.07** |
| 48 | Exclusive of TSC checker | 96 | 48 | 12 | 1333.33 |
| | **Inclusive of TSC Checker** | **190** | **96** | **25** | **1079.91** |
| 64 | Exclusive of TSC checker | 128 | 64 | 16 | 1333.33 |
| | **Inclusive of TSC Checker** | **252** | **127** | **32** | **1108.65** |
| 96 | Exclusive of TSC checker | 192 | 96 | 24 | 1333.33 |
| | **Inclusive of TSC Checker** | **382** | **192** | **50** | **1057.08** |

Table 6. Implementation results for 1-D maximal length CA corresponding to minimal weight primitive polynomial

| Polynomial | Design style | #FF | #LUT | #Slice | Freq (MHz) |
|---|---|---|---|---|---|
| 32,28,27,1,0 | Exclusive of TSC checker | 64 | 32 | 8 | 1333.33 |
| | **Inclusive of TSC shecker** | **124** | **63** | **17** | **1122.33** |
| 48,28,27,1,0 | Exclusive of TSC checker | 96 | 48 | 12 | 1333.33 |
| | **Inclusive of TSC checker** | **190** | **96** | **26** | **1135.07** |
| 64,4,3,1,0 | Exclusive of TSC checker | 128 | 64 | 16 | 1333.33 |
| | **Inclusive of TSC checker** | **252** | **127** | **33** | **1052.63** |
| 96,49,47,2,0 | Exclusive of TSC checker | 192 | 96 | 24 | 1333.33 |
| | **Inclusive of TSC checker** | **382** | **192** | **53** | **1033.06** |

routing delays incurred during realization of the tree based TSC checker, but achieves remarkable savings on the output pin count typically serving as error flag outputs corresponding to each LUT. Nevertheless, a speed of over 1000 MHz in the circuit implementation results depicted in Tables 4, 5 and 6 was attainable, as the critical path comprises of a single LUT. The hardware overhead owing to the TSC circuitry only depends upon the number of complementary output pairs of bits driving its inputs.

Any erroneous output obtained may be attributed to some fault owing to hard or soft errors, or other reliability issues, and the faulty slice coordinates on which the logic has been mapped may be traced as the placement coordinates of the circuit is known apriori. Such faulty locations should essentially be bypassed through appropriate mapping constraints.

## 4 Conclusion

Primitive instantiation based high speed datapath and controlpath circuits with built-in fault localization circuitry has been presented. The most well suited fault localization circuitry depends on the nature of FPGA implementation of the ordinary design and the percentage of under-utilization of the configured logic elements. Such circuits are expected to retain their individual performance characteristics, when used as a part of a larger system design. Absolute placement of the primitives in the configured FPGA designs onto designated slice coordinates facilitate easier detection of faulty slices.

## References

1. Rao, P.M.B., Amouri, A., Kiamehr, S., Tahoori, M.B.: Altering LUT configuration for wear-out mitigation of FPGA-Mapped designs. In: 23rd International Conference on Field Programmable Logic and Applications (FPL), pp. 1–8 (2013)
2. Modi, H., Athanas, P.: In-system testing of Xilinx 7-series FPGAs: part 1-logic. In: IEEE International Conference for Military Communications (MILCOM), pp. 477–482 (2015)
3. Basha, B.C., Pillement, S., Piestrak, S.J.: Fault-aware configurable logic block for reliable reconfigurable FPGAs. In: IEEE International Symposium on Circuits and Systems (ISCAS), pp. 2732–2735 (2015)
4. Kyriakoulakos, K., Pnevmatikatos, D.: A novel SRAM-based FPGA architecture for efficient TMR fault tolerance support. In: 19th International Conference on Field Programmable Logic and Applications (FPL), pp. 193–198 (2009)
5. Nazar, G.L., Carro, L.: Fast error detection through efficient use of hardwired resources in FPGAs. In: 17th IEEE European Test Symposium (ETS), pp. 1–6 (2012)
6. Palchaudhuri, A., Dhar, A.S.: Efficient implementation of scan register insertion on integer arithmetic cores for FPGAs. In: 29th International Conference on VLSI Design, pp. 433–438 (2016)
7. Palchaudhuri, A., Amresh, A.A., Dhar, A.S.: Efficient automated implementation of testable cellular automata based pseudorandom generator circuits on FPGAs. J. Cell. Automata **12**(3–4), 217–247 (2017)

606    A. Palchaudhuri and A. S. Dhar

8. Lala, P.K., Burress, A.L.: Self-checking logic design for FPGA implementation. IEEE Trans. Instrum. Meas. **52**(5), 1391–1398 (2003)
9. Ehliar, A.: Optimizing Xilinx designs through primitive instantiation. In: Proceedings of the 7th FPGA world Conference, FPGA world 2010, pp. 20–27. ACM, New York (2010)
10. Xilinx Inc.: 7 Series FPGAs Configurable Logic Block User Guide UG474 (v1.8) (2016). https://www.xilinx.com/support/documentation/user_guides/ug474_7Series_CLB.pdf. Accessed 27 Sept 2016
11. Abramovici, A., Breuer, M.A., Friedman, A.D.: Digital Systems Testing and Testable Design. Wiley, Hoboken (1994)
12. Saposhnikov, V.V., Saposhnikov, V.V., Dmitriev, A., Goessel, M.: Self-dual duplication for error detection. In: Seventh Asian Test Symposium (ATS), pp. 296–300 (1998)
13. Guild, H.H.: Fast versatile binary comparator array. Electron. Lett. **7**(9), 225–226 (1971)
14. Palchaudhuri, A., Dhar, A.S.: High performance bit-sliced pipelined comparator tree for FPGAs. In: 20th International Symposium on VLSI Design and Test (VDAT) (2016)
15. Chaudhuri, P.P., Chowdhury, D.R., Nandi, S., Chattopadhyay, S.: Additive Cellular Automata Theory and its Application, vol. 1. IEEE Computer Society Press, Los Alamito (1997)
16. Cattell, K., Muzio, J.: Technical Report: Tables of linear cellular automata for minimal weight primitive polynomials of degrees up to 300. Issue: 163. University of Victoria (B.C.), Department of Computer Science (1991)

# On Generation of Delay Test with Capture Power Safety

Rohini Gulve[(✉)] and Nihar Hage

Computer Architecture and Dependable Systems Lab, Electrical Engineering,
Indian Institute of Technology Bombay, Mumbai, India
{rohini.gulve,niharhage}@iitb.ac.in

**Abstract.** Manufacturing test application without violation of circuit power budget is one of the primary concern for test engineers today. Excessive power demand often triggers false failures hence reduces the yield. Most of the automatic test pattern generation (ATPG) algorithms and test set modification methods have been proposed to minimize power requirement during the test. However, power reduction achieved is not enough as functional power budget of the circuit is usually much smaller than the high activity producing test patterns. This paper proposes an optimization problem formulation which targets test generation of transition delay faults without exceeding operative power limit. An optimization problem is constructed, and tests have been generated for slow-to-rise and slow-to-fall transition delay faults. The proposed method is capable of producing both Launch-On-Capture and Launch-On-Shift delay vectors. A pseudo SAT-based solver can be exercised to solve the formulated optimization problem. As the problem is optimized to maximize the number of faults detected under functional and power constraints of the circuit, this helps in generating the compact test set. Experiments are conducted on ISCAS89 benchmark circuits support the effectiveness of the proposed technique.

**Keywords:** Delay fault · Testing · ATPG · Low power · Optimization SAT

## 1 Introduction

Delay faults testing is necessary to grade the performance of circuit under test (CUT). Two vector (V1; V2) delay test is done by launching the transition at fault site and propagating it to an observation point. A slow-to-rise (slow-to-fall) fault is tested by sensitizing logic 0 (1) to logic 1 (0) transition at fault site. In almost all the modern circuits, scan-based design for testability (DFT) is implemented to deliver the test and observe the response.

Scan enables the access of internal nets of the circuit. It provides control on states which may or may not reachable through normal functional' operation of the design. However, some test applied through the non-functional state can

© Springer Nature Singapore Pte Ltd. 2017
B. K. Kaushik et al. (Eds.): VDAT 2017, CCIS 711, pp. 607–618, 2017.
https://doi.org/10.1007/978-981-10-7470-7_58

stimulate excessive of activity or transitions. The excessive number of transitions demands more power from power supply than actual power budget of the CUT. Due to the incapability of providing required need of power during test application lead to latching of wrong values in FFs. These errors indicate failure of test and existence of delay faults which may not be present in normal operation. To avoid false failures and resulting yield loss, it is important to keep power dissipation under the practical power limits, $P_F$, during the test.

The power consumption of test applied to scan-based DFT can be categorized as shift power and capture power. Excessive power demand during loading (shift-in) and unloading (shift-out) of test response is referred as excess shift power problem. More switching during shift operation can latch wrong value in the flip-flop (FF) due to the incapability of power source to supply required demand. However, many scan FF designs are proposed to restrict transitions only in the scan chain by gating the input signals of denominational logic. This avoids redundant computation/ activity in the logic block through scan FF output gating. The other severe concern is power consumption during actual test application, i.e. during capture. Application of vector $V_2$ after vector $V_1$ triggers the transition propagation in circuit logic, and then erroneous values can be latched in FFs. The response of vector $V_2$ has to be captured in a single cycle, at a speed of the functional clock. Thus excess capture power reduction through structural modifications is not favorable. However, this problem can be dealt through post processing of generated test vector or by generating power aware vector itself. This work contributes to the generation of capture power safe delay test patterns.

Traditional fault models to illustrate the delay fault behavior are path-based (distributed delay over propagation path) delay fault model or transition based (lumped delay at a gate) delay model. The total number of paths (sequence of gates from primary input/FF to primary output/FF) present in circuits are enormous, and this figure explodes with growing number of FFs as well as design complexity. On the other hand, transition delay fault is gross delay model. The model assumes delay effect is active at an output of the particular gate. Thus number of fault sites are proportional to number of gates in CUT. We have used transition delay fault model to formulate ATPG in this work. Delay test vectors can be applied through either Launch-On-Shift (LOS) and Launch-On-Capture (LOC). The second vector $V_2$ is one bit shifted version of the vector $V_1$ in LOS, and in the case of LOC, later vector is the functional response of former.

To avoid response capture malfunctioning, researchers aim to minimize the capture power as low as possible. One of the favorite post-processing technique to achieve the objective is to take advantage of dont care or X bits available in test patterns [6,9,11]. Filling or assigning an appropriate value (0/1) to X-bit does not degrade the test quality. However, a proper value can block the undesirable transition propagation through logic by controlling the OFF path inputs. The primary challenge in post-processing approach for reducing the capture power is that it can not guarantee that power values will remain within the functional power limit, $P_F$. If the minimum power consumption during the test after processing still surpasses the threshold limit, then the particular pattern has to be removed from the test set. Due to the removal of power unsafe patterns, all unique faults detected by removed patterns will have no test in set thus new test will be generated targeting these faults. Motivated by above problem of capture safe delay test generation, this work contributes to the formulation of ATPG setup in form of an optimization problem. Functional power limit, $P_F$ is provided as an input by the user which will be devised as one of the constraints in ATPG formulation. This procedure generates the test set for transition delay faults with power safety.

The problem can be solved using optimization-SAT (i.e. pseudoSAT) or zero-one linear programming (ZOLP) based optimization solvers. Pseudo-SAT problem accepts the constraints of problems in form of SAT clauses. To utilize ZOLP for solving the problem all the constraints should be expressed in linear inequalities. Work by Gulve and Singh [6] mentions boolean expression modeling in terms of ZOLP equations. Pseudo SAT-based optimization techniques have gained a lot of attention [2,3,10]. We will explain the procedure considering Pseudo-SAT as underline solvers.

Rest of the paper is organized as follows: some of the recent advancements in the field of power-aware test set generation under functional limits are reported in Sect. 2. Sections 3 and 4 explains the various constraints required for proposed optimization formulation to generate delay test. Optimization function definition of the problem which represents the active fault list of ATPG is elaborated in Sect. 5. Finally, Sect. 6 reports the experimental results after implementation of the proposal. Conclusion and future work possible to extend this work is given in Sect. 7.

## 2   Related Work

Many proposals are described in the literature by researchers where attempts have been made to restrict the maximum capture power under a threshold. Weighted switching activity (WSA) is used as a metric for power demand from applied input vector pair. WSA is defined as the summation of the number of switching operation at a net, weighted by a number of fan-outs of a particular net. Li et al. [7] proposes an approach to make test set safe with respect to power. The main steps followed are, firstly remove power risky patterns from the set. The unique faults detected by dangerous patterns will have no test in set thus fault list will be updated with additional undetected faults. In the second step, power safe patterns available in the set are refined by assigning appropriate values to $X$ bits. $X$ filling is done such that resultant vector pair will not violate the threshold limit and also detect some of the faults from updated faults list. After refinement process of all the non-risky patterns if still, fault list is not empty then the new ATPG patterns are generated. Fault update, pattern refinement, and ATPG steps are repeated till fault list is empty. This approach requires the multiple number of ATPG runs which consumes a lot of time. Unlike above method, some of other methods are available which generate the test which is power safe by construction.

Devanathan *et al.* [1] have developed an ATPG engine based on well known PODEM (Path Oriented DEcision Making) algorithm. Power-aware decision making is incorporated during backtracking and selection of propagation D-frontier. This work segregates the safe and risky patterns if any of the global transition activity or regional activity limits are violated. The regions are defined as a group of nets connected to the similar VDD-GND grid on the actual layout. This requires modification in well-developed algorithms in EDA tools which imposes the practical limit on the approach.

Other recent approaches which formulate an optimization problem in terms of pseudo-SAT are [5,8]. Similar to the [1], Eggersgluss and Drechsler remove the power risky patterns based on regional power limit violation. However, new patterns are generated through a SAT-based ATPG approach [4]. The optimization function is defined as the minimization of region WSA under pseudo SAT clauses of gate functionality as constraints. Every time ATPG problem is solved by the solver, an analysis has to be done to guarantee no violation of power limit and only safe solutions are added into the test set otherwise discarded. Sauer *et al.* [8] focus on test generation utilizing pseudo SAT technique and able to keep WSA under desired upper limit during test generation. However, this approach is path based. As already known, the number of paths in the circuit is large and intelligent techniques are required to select preparation paths.

Key features presented this paper are,

- An optimization problem formulation is given for transition delay test generation. The functional power limits are not violated during test generation. This formulation can be extended to include region based power limits as well along with the limit on total circuit switching.
- This formulation targets maximization of total number of faults detection under described constraints. Thus generated test set is compact and small in terms of size.
- Fault simulation is not required after each ATPG run. Information about all the faults detected by generated solution is can be observed by monitoring the fault detection variables values in solution. Proposed formulation can provide all the possibly detected fault by test pair generated.

ATPG set up is eventually formulated as an optimization problem. Proposed problem formulation can be solved using pseudo-SAT solvers. Any optimization problem is defined to either maximize or minimize the optimization function, subject to constraints provided on variables of the problem. SAT clauses are included to impose constraints on the symbolic variables in pseudo-SAT problem.

Optimization function, $F_{opt}$ is defined as the list of active faults. More detailed description about $F_{opt}$ is elaborated in Sect. 6. The second part of the formulation is constraint definitions under which function is subjected to maximize. There are three types of constraints added in optimization problem, (1) to describe the behavior of circuit functionality, (2) fault detection constraints, and (3) power safety constraints. By solving the optimization problem described above, we are generate the two vector transition delay fault test for all the active faults in fault list. All the constraints will be explained in terms of boolean equations which can always be expressed in SAT clauses.

## 2.1    Functional Constraints

In this section, circuit description/functional constraints are described. As delay test consists of two vectors $(V_1, V_2)$, the behavior of circuit under application of two vectors is modeled in two-time frames (TFs). Flip-flops of the circuits are accessible through scan chains. Scan allows loading the vector $V_1$ through scan input pin in time frame one and unloading of response after test application can be done by scan chain unloading. Due to controllability provided by scan DFT, inputs and outputs of state elements (FFs) present in the circuit are considered as primary outputs and primary inputs respectively, these are denoted by PPO and PPI as shown in Fig. 1.

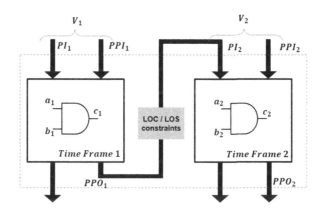

**Fig. 1.** Two vector symbolic description of CUT

The signal value of each net in the different time frame is represented with a unique symbolic variable. Output net of each gate in the circuit is described as a function of input nets of a gate. For example, the input-output relation of an AND gate of time frame one, as shown in Fig. 1, is given as $c_1 = a_1.b_1$ and for time frame 2, it is described with different variable as $c_2 = a_2.b_2$. SAT clauses of above relations i.e., $(a_1 + \overline{c_1})(b_1 + \overline{c_1})(\overline{a_1} + \overline{b_1} + c_1)$ and $(a_2 + \overline{c_2})(b_2 + \overline{c_2})(\overline{a_2} + \overline{b_2} + c_2)$ are added as constraints to optimization problem.

Apart from input-output relations of gates, state elements (FFs) behaviors over two frames are incorporated through LOC or LOS constraints. If LOC scheme is devised then pseudo-primary outputs of time frame one are assigned to pseudo primary inputs of frame 2, i.e., $PPI_2 = PPO_1$. However in case of LOS scheme, $PPI_2$ are defined as one-bit shift from $PPO_1$ (Fig. 1).

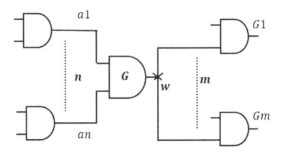

**Fig. 2.** Fault site of CUT

# 3   Fault Detection Constraints

Along with circuit behavior modeling through functional constraints, fault detection constraints have to be defined for each fault site. Delay fault can be activated by forcing a logic transition at the fault site. This transition must be propagated to output in order to successfully test the fault. This section describes formulation required to model an activation of fault and conditions to propagate it to the output points. All the below-defined equations will be added to optimization problem as constraints. We consider output net $(w)$ of each gate as fault site here onward and two faults per site.

## 3.1   Fault Sensitization

Slow-to-rise and slow-to-fall are the two types of delay faults possible at each fault site. To activate these faults, a rising transition (logic 0 in TF1 to logic 1 in TF2) and a falling transition (logic 1 in TF1 to logic 0 in TF2) should be forced at $w$. Transition condition can be described through a XOR operation of two distinguish symbolic variables representing signal values in different time frames. For example, transition at site, $w_T$ is equivalent to XOR of $w_1$ and $w_2$. More preciously rising transition $(w_{RT})$ and falling transition $(w_{FT})$ is given as per Eqs. 2 and 3 respectively. Three additional variables, $w_T$, $w_{RT}$ and $w_{FT}$ are defined at every fault site to model sensitization constraint.

$$w_T = w_1 \otimes w_2 \tag{1}$$

$$w_{RT} = (w_T) \wedge (w_2) \tag{2}$$

$$w_{FT} = (w_T) \wedge (w_1) \tag{3}$$

Condition under which variable $w_{RT}$ $(w_{FT})$ is set to value 1 represent slow-to-rise (slow-to-fall) fault at site w is sensitized.

## 3.2  Fault Propagation

Sensitized fault effect or transition of fault site has to be propagated to at-least one of the primary or pseudo-primary outputs to observe. Consider effect of sensitized fault is implicated at site $x$ in form of transition. Transition or fault effect at any net $x$ can be propagated to next level in the circuit if, (a) output of gates, whose one of the input is $x$, experience a transition and (b) this particular transition is propagated to next level of gates.

Consider frontier group, $G_{front}(x)$ is the group of the gates having fault effect site as input to it. For example, gates $G1$ to $Gm$ are in the $G_{front}$ group of net $w$, i.e. $G_{front}(w) = \{G1, ..Gm\}$. A transition from $w$ is said to propagate to next level in the circuit if at least one of the gates output in $G_{front}(w)$ experience a transition. This condition is formulated in form of boolean algebra as follows. The symbolic variable $w_{prop}$ is set to logic 1 if transition traverse to next level in the circuit.

$$w_{prop} = G1_T \vee G2_T \vee \ldots \vee Gm_T \tag{4}$$

However, propagation has to be progressed to reach to PO or PPO (i.e. last level). Thus, to ensure further propagation of the transition to next levels in the circuit former condition needs to be modified. Thus, the conjunction of successive propagation variables along with transition variables are included. In case of example, propagation should happen further from $G_{front}(w)$ to any of $G_{front}(G1)$ or $G_{front}(G2), ..$ or $G_{front}(Gm)$. This condition if formulated as follows

$$w_{prop} = (G1_T \wedge G1_{prop}) \vee (G2_T \wedge G2_{prop}) \vee \ldots \vee (Gm_T \wedge Gm_{prop}) \tag{5}$$

Finally if $G_{front}$ group is empty or net $x$ is primary output or pseudo-primary output, then propagation is terminated by defining $x_{prop}$ as equal to $x_T$ itself, i.e.

$$x_{prop} = x_T \tag{6}$$

There will be additional one propagation variable defined along with three sensitization variables for each net. SAT clauses defining propagation variable of each net, Eq. 5 for internal nets and Eq. 6 for observation points, will serve as propagation constraints in pseudo-SAT problem.

## 3.3  Test Generation

Delay test for the targeted fault is generated if both, the sensitization and propagation constraints are satisfied. Thus conjunction of above defined constraints are used to produce fault detection condition. In terms of boolean equation, conjunction of symbolic variable representing falling transition (rising transition) and propagation variable at fault site will define the fault detection condition on detection variable, $w_{detectFT}$ ($w_{detectRT}$).

$$w_{detectFF} = w_{FT}.w_{prop}$$

$$w_{detectRF} = w_{RT}.w_{prop}$$

If detection variable $w_{detectFF}$ is set to logic 1 then falling fault at site $w$ is sensitized and propagated hence detected. Otherwise, the fault is still active. All the definitions of fault detection variables are included in optimization problem in form of SAT clauses. Two more variables are included for each net to express detection conditions.

## 4 Power Safety Constraints

The principal focus of this work is to generate delay test which will not consume more power than limit provided by users. In general threshold of functional power is determined based on Monte-Carlo simulations. However, attempts have been made to estimate maximum weighted switching activity in circuit through ATPG based algorithms or using ILP based optimization problem-solving. To constraint power demand of generated test pair under provided limiting value, safety conditions is defined in this section. We considered weighted switching activity (WSA) as the measure of power dissipation of applied test inputs. WSA is defined as the summation of logic transitions occurring at circuit nets weighted by fanout of transition experiencing net.

$$WSA = \sum_{nets} fanout * n_T$$

To get a solution within safe limits, we define a constraint such that WSA is always less than or equal to the defined threshold limit. A region based function power restriction can also be defined in the similar fashion. The region is defined as the group the of gates connected to same VDD and GND power grids in CUT and each region can have different power limits.

$$\sum fanout * G_T <= P_F \tag{7}$$

$$\sum_{Reg} fanout * G_T <= P_{F_{Reg}}$$

Equation 7 defines power safety constraints for full circuit, and equation seven is described for region based power safety. This is the last and third type of constraint added to the optimization problem. Pseudo-SAT solvers can process the conditions expressed in terms of linear inequalities, where variables may or may not be weighted by integer values.

## 5 Optimization Function

The essential part of any optimization problem is the function defined to either minimize or maximize. Here we define optimization function as the summation of faults to be detected under constraints. Initially, function is equal to the summation of all the active faults in the fault list. The solver will solve the problem to generate the solution such that it will maximize the number of fault detected under functional constraints, fault detection constraints and power safety constraints. This helps in generation of the minimal test set possible by targeting maximization of the number of faults detected.

$$F_{opt} = \sum \left( w_{detectFF} + w_{detectRF} \right)$$

Faults detected by the generated solution can be observed by monitoring the detect variable value associated with the particular fault. One of the major advantages of the proposed approach is that fault simulation is not required to identify more detectable faults by test generated, which is one common step in the most algorithm based ATPG approaches. Each time optimization problem is solved all the detected faults under generated test pair are dropped from the fault list ($F_{opt}$), and optimization function is modified accordingly. This step can also be referred as fault dropping process.

We have defined all the definitions of fault detection variables, which are part of optimization function in the form of SAT clauses. If there exist a solution under defined SAT constraints such that fault detect variable of some fault (say $w_{detectFF}$ ) can set to values 1 then the problem will be satisfiable, and optimization function will have non-zero values. Otherwise, if no faults can be detected among active faults in the list, then SAT solver will recognize the problem as UNSAT and optimization function will have a zero value. Thus ATPG process can be terminated after function $F_{opt}$ is set to values 0. This indicates generation of test for all irredundant faults user given power limiting constraints.

# 6    Experimental Result

The proposed optimization has been implemented in C++ language. We have formulated pseudo-SAT based optimization problem. The effectiveness of the method is tested on ISCAS89 benchmark circuits. The optimization problem is solved using open source minisat+ [12] pseudo-SAT solver. Initially, a full test set is generated using commercial ATPG. Based on the threshold value of WSA, test pairs of the set are recognized as power safe or power unsafe pair. All the unsafe tests are eliminated from the set and faults detected only by eliminated tests (unique faults of the test) are marked as undetected faults and added in active fault list to create initial optimization function.

Threshold limit on weighted switching activity for the circuit is defined as 90 set. Consider test pair $(V_x, V_y)$ is a pair in the initial test set such that it stimulates maximum weighted switching activity among all the tests present in the set. If WSA by pair $(V_x, V_y)$ is WSAMax then functional power limit is considered as 90 on analysis of initial set is mentioned in the third column of the table. Values reported as $P_F$ given in percentage total WSA possible in the circuit. Total WSA possible is defined as the summation of WSA possible is all the gates in CUT toggle at the same time.

Fourth and fifth columns of Tables 1 and 2 represent the number of test pairs and fault coverage of initially generated test set of corresponding circuits. As all the vectors violating threshold conditions is eliminated from the initial set, all the unique faults detected by eliminated patterns are now tagged as undetected and added into the optimization function of the problem. Column sixth and column seventh of tables indicates the size of the remaining test set and fault coverage after elimination of power unsafe vectors. Drop in fault coverage number is around 1 to 2% compared to the initial fault coverage. The number listed in the eighth column reports the total number of faults undetected after the screening of unsafe patterns from the initial set.

Table 1. LOC

| Circuit | # PI + PPI | % $P_F$ over total WSA | Initial test set | | Safe test set | | | Final TS $T_{safe}$ | Time [s] |
|---------|------------|------------------------|------------------|------------|---------------|-------------|-------------|---------------------|----------|
| | | | $T_{full}$ | $FC_{full}$ | $\%T_{safe}$ | $\%FC_{drop}$ | $F_{drop}$ | | |
| s298 | 17 | 50.83 | 46 | 86.49 | 38 (8) | 81.89 | 36 | 3 | 0.53 |
| s349 | 26 | 54.94 | 49 | 96.14 | 45 (4) | 90.30 | 55 | 2 | 0.38 |
| s420 | 34 | 48.95 | 47 | 48.58 | 38 (9) | 43.68 | 62 | 1 | 0.328 |
| s820 | 23 | 48.69 | 141 | 85.52 | 133 (8) | 84.26 | 28 | 3 | 4.332 |
| s832 | 23 | 51.29 | 134 | 84.45 | 130 (4) | 83.36 | 24 | 2 | 3.02 |
| s838 | 66 | 54.36 | 88 | 43.48 | 82 (6) | 41.90 | 41 | 1 | 10.408 |
| s1196 | 32 | 46.34 | 191 | 88.10 | 176 (15) | 84.62 | 110 | 7 | 10.864 |
| s1238 | 32 | 46.47 | 187 | 85.65 | 181 (6) | 84.38 | 40 | 4 | 5.748 |
| s1423 | 91 | 54.47 | 112 | 94.76 | 103 (9) | 94.01 | 29 | 3 | 3.876 |
| s5378 | 214 | 47.9 | 212 | 87.69 | 194 (18) | 86.65 | 151 | 4 | 154.244 |
| s9234 | 247 | 43.29 | 430 | 90.32 | 405 (25) | 89.56 | 210 | 5 | 205.076 |
| s13207 | 700 | 36.57 | 523 | 89.50 | 512 (11) | 88.76 | 295 | 7 | 310.32 |
| s15850 | 611 | 28.99 | 362 | 87.14 | 354 (8) | 86.88 | 125 | 4 | 219.196 |
| s35932 | 1763 | 41.51 | 133 | 90.06 | 98 (35) | 88.92 | 1058 | 4 | 715.016 |
| s38417 | 1664 | 47.83 | 291 | 98.87 | 258 (37) | 97.86 | 1130 | 15 | 3176.536 |
| s38584 | 1464 | 40.94 | 456 | 92.35 | 433 (23) | 90.98 | 1464 | 11 | 2964.96 |

The proposed optimization-based test generation is performed for active fault list and number of test patterns required to cover all the targeted faults are shown in column nine. These patterns are sufficient to cover all the active faults. The final length of the test set is smaller than initial test set as formulated problem is to optimize to detect maximum the number of faults that can be detected together under the same solution. As all the faults are detected, final fault coverage is same as the initial value by commercial ATPG. Finally, column eleven represent the time required to generate the final test set in seconds.

Table 2. LOS

| Circuit | # PI + PPI | %$P_F$ over total WSA | Initial test set | | Safe test set | | | Final TS $T_{safe}$ | Time [s] |
|---|---|---|---|---|---|---|---|---|---|
| | | | $T_{full}$ | $FC_{full}$ | %$T_{safe}$ | %$FC_{drop}$ | $F_{drop}$ | | |
| s298 | 17 | 58.10 | 33 | 85.87 | 26 (7) | 79.88 | 46 | 2 | 0.5 |
| s349 | 26 | 53.36 | 48 | 93.74 | 44 (4) | 90.21 | 33 | 2 | 0.388 |
| s420 | 34 | 32.86 | 38 | 50.07 | 30 (8) | 46.06 | 51 | 5 | 0.92 |
| s820 | 23 | 46.67 | 145 | 78.37 | 138 (7) | 77.65 | 17 | 3 | 4.176 |
| s832 | 23 | 44.9 | 132 | 76.58 | 118 (14) | 73.13 | 76 | 3 | 4.432 |
| s838 | 66 | 32.38 | 76 | 47.99 | 65 (11) | 45.88 | 55 | 6 | 10.176 |
| s1196 | 32 | 40.17 | 258 | 85.42 | 229 (8) | 81.90 | 112 | 5 | 104.05 |
| s1238 | 32 | 40.35 | 242 | 84.11 | 223 (20) | 81.85 | 72 | 5 | 11.82 |
| s1423 | 91 | 51.01 | 178 | 96.65 | 167 (11) | 95.73 | 35 | 3 | 4.124 |
| s5378 | 214 | 36.97 | 188 | 83.28 | 180 (8) | 82.75 | 23 | 4 | 34.308 |
| s9234 | 247 | 36.64 | 638 | 93.52 | 623 (15) | 93.14 | 105 | 4 | 145.092 |
| s13207 | 700 | 31.83 | 672 | 93.44 | 666 (8) | 92.93 | 230 | 3 | 98.348 |
| s15850 | 611 | 37.78 | 759 | 93.67 | 750 (9) | 93.38 | 145 | 4 | 246.324 |
| s35932 | 1763 | 48.87 | 298 | 90.21 | 261 (37) | 87.45 | 2544 | 8 | 1335.08 |
| s38417 | 1664 | 30.22 | 686 | 97.74 | 660 (26) | 96.90 | 940 | 18 | 7200 |
| s38584 | 1466 | 34.61 | 677 | 95.44 | 618 (59) | 93.62 | 1945 | 38 | 10686.7 |

# 7    Conclusion and Future Work

A capture power violation issue in the case of delay test the application is targeted in this work to avoid yield loss. We have formulated an optimization based automatic test pattern generation problem to generate transition delay test pair such that user-provided functional power is not exceeded by test generated. Proposed process try to maximize the number of faults detected under given constraints and provide all detected fault by produced solution which in turn helps to create the test set with a small number of patterns without the need for fault simulation. Both LOC and LOS schemes can be incorporated during test generation. This work can be further expanded considering non-zero propagation delays of gates and contemplate switching activity due to glitches and hazards occurring during signal propagation in CUT.

**Acknowledgement.** The authors would like to thank Ministry of Electronics and Information technology, the government of India for supporting research in this field. We also acknowledge all the members of Computer Architecture and Dependable Systems Lab IIT Bombay for the valuable contribution.

# References

1. Devanathan, V.R., Ravikumar, C.P., Kamakoti, V., Glitch-aware pattern generation and optimization framework for power-safe scan test. In: IEEE 25th VLSI Test Symposium, pp. 167–172. IEEE (2007)
2. Eggersglub, S., Schmitz, K., Krenz-Baath, R., Drechsler, R.: Optimization-based multiple target test generation for highly compacted test sets. In: IEEE 19th European Test Symposium (ETS), pp. 1–6. IEEE (2014)
3. Eggersglüß, S., Drechsler, R.: As-robust-as-possible test generation in the presence of small delay defects using Pseudo-Boolean Optimization. In: Design, Automation & Test in Europe Conference & Exhibition (DATE), pp. 1–6. IEEE (2011)
4. Eggersgluss, S., Drechsler, R.: Efficient data structures and methodologies for SAT-based ATPG providing high fault coverage in industrial application. IEEE Trans. Comput. Aided Des. Integr. Circuits Syst. 30(9), 1411–1415 (2011). IEEE
5. Eggersglüß, S., Miyase, K., Wen, X.: SAT-based post-processing for regional capture power reduction in at-speed scan test generation. In: IEEE 21th European Test Symposium (ETS), pp. 1–6. IEEE (2016)
6. Gulve, R., Singh, V.: ILP based don't care bits filling technique for reducing capture power. In: East-West Design & Test Symposium (EWDTS), pp. 1–4. IEEE (2016)
7. Li, Y.-H., Lien, W.-C., Lin, C., Lee, K.-J.: Capture-power-safe test pattern determination for at-speed scan-based testing. IEEE Trans. Comput. Aided Des. Integr. Circuits Syst. 33(1), 127–138 (2014). IEEE
8. Sauer, M., Jiang, J., Reimer, S., Miyase, K., Wen, X., Becker, B., Polian, I.: On optimal power-aware path sensitization. In: IEEE 25th Asian Test Symposium (ATS), pp. 179–184. IEEE (2016)
9. Seo, S., Lee, Y., Lim, H., Lee, J., Yoo, H., Kim, Y., Kang, S.: Scan chain reordering-aware x-filling and stitching for scan shift power reduction. In: IEEE 24th Asian Test Symposium (ATS), pp. 1–6. IEEE (2015)
10. Soeken, M., De Micheli, G., Mishchenko, A.: Busy man's synthesis: combinational delay optimization with SAT. In: 2017 Design, Automation & Test in Europe Conference & Exhibition (DATE), pp. 830–835. IEEE (2017)
11. Yoshimura, M., Takahashi, Y., Yamazaki, H., Hosokawa, T.: A don't care filling method to reduce capture power based on correlation of FF transitions. In: IEEE 24th Asian Test Symposium (ATS), pp. 13–18. IEEE (2015)

# A Configurable and Area Efficient Technique for Implementing Isolation Cells in Low Power SoC

Prokash Ghosh$^{(\boxtimes)}$ and Jyotirmoy Ghosh

NXP India Pvt. Ltd., Noida, U.P., India
{prokash.ghosh, jyotirmoy.ghosh}@nxp.com

**Abstract.** In SoC design, isolation cells are used between different power domains to prevent the floating outputs/inputs of the power gated blocks from affecting the operations of the active circuits. At present, the low power SoCs use millions of isolation cells to implement different power gating modes and the isolation cells occupy considerable silicon area of the SoC. Also, the isolation values in low power designs are pre-determined (either fixed to '0' or '1' in design itself) and are non-configurable in real time operation. Hence, any incorrect isolation value may render the device useless in low power modes. In this paper, we propose a modified clamping circuit design to reduce the area and delay of the isolation cells. We also propose a method to configure the isolation values for certain qualifier signals and the subsequent entry process of the power gated modules into deep-sleep mode. The results show that the proposed technique can improve reliability of the power gating modes and reduce 30% to 50% of isolation cell area compared to that of the conventional isolation technique using logic gates.

**Keywords:** Power gating · Isolation cell · Transmission gate · SoC
Low power · Deep-sleep

## 1 Introduction

Modern SoCs are implemented with several independently switchable power domains with options to keep the domains powered down during inactive periods. This process is popularly known as *power gating* [1, 2]. Outputs/inputs of each of these power gated regions are separated from the active regions by *isolation cells* [1, 3] to prevent spurious behavior of the active blocks due to the floating outputs of the powered down modules. Also, the isolation cells prevent large crowbar currents [1] between the power gated and the powered-on domains. Conventionally, an isolation cell is itself powered by an 'always ON' supply and it clamps its output node to a known logic level: logic '0', or, logic '1'.

To leverage sophisticated low power design, millions of isolation cells are employed in present SoCs [4]. This introduces two major issues in SoC design. Firstly, the area consumed by the conventional isolation cells are considerable compared to the other modules. Secondly, if there is any incorrect isolation value found with any signal, the device may start malfunctioning. For example, we consider the process of pointer

© Springer Nature Singapore Pte Ltd. 2017
B. K. Kaushik et al. (Eds.): VDAT 2017, CCIS 711, pp. 619–627, 2017.
https://doi.org/10.1007/978-981-10-7470-7_59

exchange between two simple state machines in two different power domains P1 and P2, where the read pointer *(rd_ptr[3:0])* is going from P1 to P2 and the write pointer *(wr_ptr[3:0])* is going from P2 to P1. Each state machine triggers a new action when there is a difference between the incoming pointer and its own state. There is a requirement to isolate the pointers with isolation cells as P1 and P2 have independently switchable supplies. Since the state values can change dynamically, any fixed isolation value is invalid as the mismatch with the isolated pointers will trigger some unwanted action. It may even prevent the domain to enter into the power off state.

To address these kinds of challenges and optimize power, we propose two different types of isolation cells and the associated techniques for inserting them on low power SoCs. The first one is a new library cell with *3-T* (transistor) based implementation having pre-defined clamped values similar to conventional approach. The second one is *configurable* isolation cell for which the clamped value can be configured on the fly before entering into power gated mode. The configurable isolation cells are added only for the qualifier signals of the associated interface. The architecture and implementation of the isolation cells have been described in detail in the subsequent sections.

## 2    Review of Previous Works on Isolation Cells

There are two approaches to implement the signal isolation in isolation cells: using Logic Gates (Fig. 1(a) and (b)) and using Clamp Transistors (Fig. 1(c) and (d)).

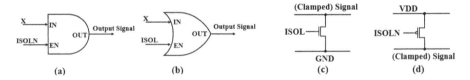

(a)    (b)    (c)    (d)

**Fig. 1.** Conventional isolation cell design

In both of the implantations, the output value is clamped to logic *'0'*, or, logic *'1'* depending on the state of signal *ISOLN* or *ISOL*, respectively. The single transistor implementation is much faster in response; however, it introduces multiple drivers to the power gated nets and requires careful sequencing to avoid contention. Metal migration and reliability issues will be there if a static current flows through them. The logic gate based implementation is most popular as it can reliably isolate the outputs even during power up and keep them isolated until the power is stabilized. Also, since logic gates are devoid of any static current, the sequencing is easy. However, this scheme increases the overall area consumption and adds a full gate delay which may not be allowed in some critical data path (e.g. cache memory interface).

# 3  Proposed Isolation Cells

In view of the drawbacks of the available solutions, three cells have been introduced in this work. The proposed cells can be categorized into two groups: isolation cell with non-configurable value and isolation cell with configurable value *(ISOC)*. The non-configurable cells can be further categorized into clamp to *'0'* cell *(ISON)* and clamp to *'1'* cell *(ISOP)*.

## 3.1  Non-configurable Isolation Cell

The non-configurable isolation cells have been implemented by a *T-gate* (transmission gate) and a clamp transistor. Figure 2(a) shows the clamped to *'1'* isolation cell *ISOP*. When *EN* = *0*, signal $D_{NQi}$ passes to the output. When *EN* = *1*, the T-gate is OFF and the PMOS in ON. Hence, the output is clamped to VDD irrespective of the value of $D_{NQi.}$ As shown in Fig. 2(b), the PMOS is replaced by an NMOS in *ISON*. The T-gate is ON when *EN* = *0*. When *EN* = *1*, the output is clamped to ground by the NMOS

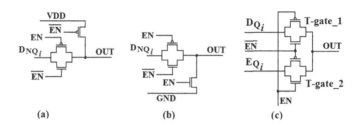

**Fig. 2.** Proposed isolation cells

Since the proposed isolation cells *ISOP* and *ISON* disconnect the input during isolation, there no scope of contention, and consequently, switch on/off sequencing is much easier to implement. Also, there is no output glitch or crowbar current while the supply ramps during power on/off procedure. The solution is area efficient with *50%* reduction in area and provides lesser delay than that of a conventional AND/OR gate.

## 3.2  Configurable Isolation Cell

The circuit of a configurable isolation cell *(ISOC)* has been presented in Fig. 2(c). ISOC is essentially implemented by a simple two-input multiplexer using two T-gates. When *EN* = *0*, *T-gate_1* is enabled and signal $D_{Qi}$ is transmitted to output. When *EN* = *1*, *T-gate_2* is enabled and isolation signal $E_{Qi}$ is transmitted to output. $E_{Qi}$ can be read from a user programmable register and have value either *'0'* or *'1'*. Thus, *ISOC* isolation value can be dynamically changed as per requirement. The cell can be designed with four transistors saving 33% area with respect to that of a standard two-input AND/OR gate which requires six transistors.

For further optimization of SoC area, we propose to use *ISOC* cell only for the *qualifier signals* of a power gated interface. Qualifier signal of a bus can be defined as a signal whose assertion is necessary to pass any transaction. When this signal is de-asserted, no valid transaction will take place even if all other associated signals of the same bus are in asserted condition. For example, *arvalid* and *arready* are qualifier signals for the AXI read address channel [5]. Here the channel cannot pass any transaction if any of the above signals is de-asserted. *ISOC* cell ensures these signals can be configured to correct isolation values before entering low power or power gated mode.

# 4   Implementation of Configurable Isolation Layer in SoC

Fig. 3(a) shows the proposed implementation of isolation cell for a signal bus. Here we have considered that there are $N$ qualifier signals ($D_{Qx0}$ to $D_{Qx(N-1)}$) and they have been isolated using *ISOC* isolation cell. During normal operation, these signal bits pass to the outputs ($O_{Qx0}$ to $O_{Qx(N-1)}$), while in power gated mode the isolation values are retrieved from a register. User can program any spare PMC (Power Management Controller) register of the SoC for this purpose. Among the rest of the non-qualifier signal bits, $I$ bits ($D_{NQxi}$, where $i = 0$ to $I - 1$) are to be clamped at '1' and $J$ bits ($D_{NQxj}$, where $j = 0$ to $J - 1$) are to be clamped at '0' during power gating. Thus, these signals bits are isolated using $I$ *ISOP* cells and $J$ *ISON* cells, respectively.

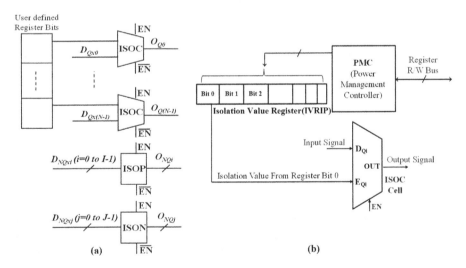

**Fig. 3.**  (a) Implementation of proposed systems with ISOC; (b) ISOC implemented with IVRIP

Implementation of *ISOC* in an SoC has been presented in Fig. 3(b). The *IVRIP* register, which is usually kept inside the PMC block, can store the dynamic isolation values of selected qualifier signals. The values of the register bits are memory mapped and configurable via register read/write bus of SoC design. In the earlier pointer scenario presented in Sect. 1, -bits of the *IVRIP* register can be set by the values of the write pointer. If the value of *wr_ptr* before entering the low power mode is *3'b101*, the associated register bits also become $3'b101$. When $EN = 0$, output of isolation cell is input signal $D_{Qi}$. If $EN = 1$, output of the isolation cell is $E_{Qi}$ which is read from $IVRIP$ register bit to avoid any pointer mismatch.

# 5   Implementation of Configurable Isolation with AXI Interface

The AXI bus [5] is a generic bus which is majorly used in SoC design for connecting different on-chip masters, slaves and interconnects. The signals of a 64-bit AXI bus for different channels along with the qualifier signals have been presented in Table 1. Figure 4(a) shows the configurable isolation cell *(ISOC)* based implementation flow-chart for $X$ number of interface signals *(IFx (x = 0 ... X − 1)* like AXI [5]. The designers need to pick up the first interface *(IF$_0$)* to be power gated and the corresponding qualifier signals *(D$_{Q0n}$)* for that interface. They need to define the register bits for associated qualifier signals in *IVRIP(x)*. The designers will pick up the next interface and continue until all interfaces are covered. The initial values of the *IVRIP* register bits will be the corresponding interface's default isolation values. In case of requirement of dynamic isolation values, designers will implement few logics to bring back the appropriate isolation values from corresponding interface to *IVRIP(x)*.

**Table 1.** 64-bit AXI bus with the qualifier signals

| AXI bus channel | Optimum set of signals required configurable isolation | Signals which does not need configurable isolation | Total configurable isolation cells required | Total non-configurable isolation cells |
|---|---|---|---|---|
| AXI write address | awvalid, awready | awid[0:3]$_r$ awaddrtQ:31], awHen[0:3], awsize[0:3], awbusrt[0:1], awlock[0:1], awcache[0:3]: awprot[0:2], awqos[0:3], awuser[7:0], awregion | 2 | 68 |
| AXI write data | wvalid, wready | wid[0:3], wdata|0:63], wstrb[0:7], wlast, wuser[0:T] | 2 | 83 |

Figure 4(b) shows the basic implementation process for entering into low power *(deep-sleep)* mode. The basic deep-sleep entry/exit process can be found in the SoC design documents [4, 8]. The major change proposed in this work is to configure the isolation values by programming *IVRIP* registers of respective interface/module before entering into low power mode. Here *IVRIP* registers of the respective modules are configured with correct values in case of any qualifier signal or pointer mismatch. If it

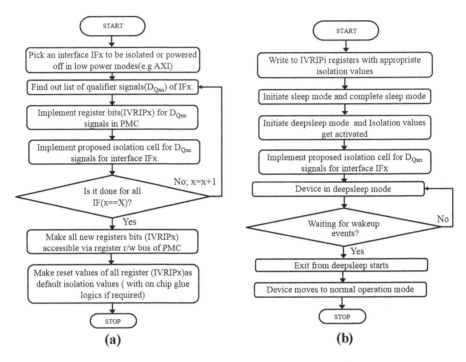

**Fig. 4.** (a) ISOC based implementation flowchart; (b) *deep-sleep* entry/exit process

receives any appropriate event, it starts restoring the power of the switchable supplies. Once the power supplies are restored, device disables the isolations. In the next step, it may restore registers/states if any state retention scheme is implemented. Device moves back to normal mode of operation. The implementation using *ISOP/ISON* will be same as conventional IEEE Unified Power Format [6]/Common Power Format [7] techniques. There is no change for the entry and exit process of *ISOP/ISON* with respect to the conventional steps.

# 6   Results

Table 2 presents a comparison between the area consumption of the conventional isolation cell using logic gates, and the proposed isolation cell in terms of unit transistor (T). Table 1 shows the AXI qualifiers/non-qualifiers signals of write address channel and write data channel. Similarly, qualifiers/non-qualifiers of other channels can be calculated. In total, we get *308* signals. Here qualifiers signals are *10* and non-qualifiers signals are *298*. If all isolation cells are implemented by *ISOP/ISON*, the savings in area are *308 * 3T = 924T*. If qualifier signals *(10)* are isolated with *ISOC*, then the savings in area are *10 * 2T + 298 * 3T = 914T*. In the SoC designs [4] where the isolation signals are in the order of $10^7$, the savings in area will be approximately $3T * 10^7$.

**Table 2.** Area comparison for isolation cells

| Isolation type | Conventional gate | Conventional cell area | Proposed cell | Proposed cell area |
|---|---|---|---|---|
| Clamp to "0" isolation | AND | 6T | ISON | 3 T |
| Clamp to isolation | OR | 6T | ISOP | 3 T |
| Clamp to "0"/"1" isolation | – | – | ISOC | 4 T |

**System Level Simulation Result:** In one of our SoC [4], there is asynchronous pointer exchange based interface between the processor core *(Power PC-e5500)* and Multi-Core Programmable Interrupt Controller *(MPIC)*. In power-gated mode, the interface signals are clamped to *'0'* by conventional isolation cells. This prevents *e5500* to exit powered off mode as the fixed *'0'* isolation values can create a difference with pointer values of *MPIC*. For instance, *Phase-1* of Fig. 5 shows a scenario where the functional value of read pointer *COREINT_RP (1'b0)* and write pointer *COREINT_WP (1'b0)* are same before and after entering the low power mode. As the isolated signals *COREINT_RP_ISO* and *COREINT_WP_ISO* both have clamp to *'0'* isolation. Device exits powered off mode in response to *WAKEUP_EVENT* (at time $T_1$) and asserts *PWR_EN* signal accordingly. On the contrary, in the Phase-2, pointer values changed dynamically with *COREINT_RP (1'b0)* and write pointer *COREINT_WP (1'b1)* not being equal while entering the low power mode. The isolation value for the pointers *(COREINT_RP_ISO and COREINT_WP_ISO)* in the deep-sleep mode are set to *'0'*.

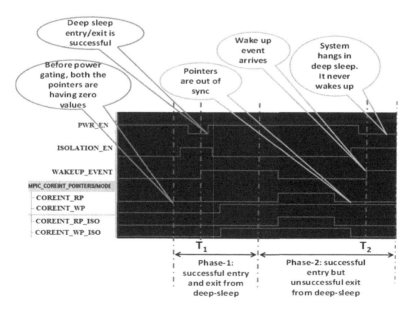

**Fig. 5.** Entry/exit sequence of low power mode with conventional isolation

Thus, the isolation value and pre-deep-sleep actual value of pointers are out of synchronization and creates a deadlock situation on receiving the *WAKEUP_EVENT* (at time $T_2$). Consequently, the device is not able to come out of the deep-sleep mode.

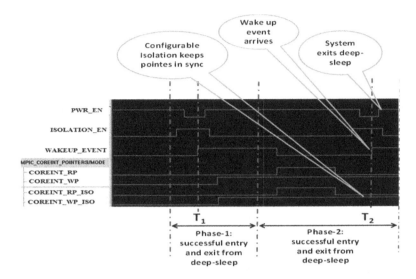

**Fig. 6.** Entry/exit sequence of low power mode with configurable isolation cells

Figure 6 presents the waveform of the similar events cited in the previous example with the isolation scheme for the qualifier signals (*COREINT_RP* and *COREINT_WP*) are being implemented with the proposed configurable isolation technique. Here the isolation values in Phase-2 are same as the present pointer values: $1'b0$ and $1'b1$, respectively. Consequently, at $T_2$, there is no pointer mismatch and the device comes out of deep-sleep mode smoothly in response to *WAKEUP_EVENT*.

## 7   Conclusion and Future Works

Signal isolation is necessary in every power gated module in SoC. The configurable isolation cells provide provision to modify the isolation values on the fly for qualifier signals of any interface and prevent the scope of malfunctioning due to any incorrect isolation value. Also, the proposed design reduces the cell area significantly. The proposed techniques are generic in nature and can be adopted in any SoC design. The future scope of work includes inserting the configurable isolation technique in CPF/UPF.

# References

1. Keating, M., Flynn, D., Aitkens, R., Gibbons, A., Shi, K.: Low-Power Methodology Manual for System-On-Chip Design. Springer, New York (2007). https://doi.org/10.1007/978-0-387-71819-4. www.lpmm-book.org
2. Severson, M.: Low Power SoC Design and Automation. University of California San Diego, Computer Science department, 27 July 2009. https://cseweb.ucsd.edu/classes/wi10/cse241a/slides/Matt.pdf
3. Ali, I., Sharma, P.: System for isolating integrated circuit power domains. US Patent US9407264B1 (2016)
4. Different SoC products description, documentation and reference manual of SoC design 1 (T1040), SoC design 2 (T1024), SoC design 3 (LS1020). www.nxp.com
5. AMBA, AXI3, AXI4 and ACE Bus Specification. https://www.arm.com/products/system-ip/amba-specifications.php
6. IEEE standard 1801-2009 (UPF). www.ieee.org
7. Carver, S., Mathur, A., Sharma, L., Subbarao, P., Urish, S., Wang, Q.: Low-power design using the Si2 common power format. IEEE Des. Test Comput. **29**(2), 62–70 (2012)
8. Ghosh, P., Ghosh, S.: Method to reduce power and wake-up time in low power modes. In: Proceedings of IEEE International Conference Conecct, January 2013, IISc, Bangalore, India (2013)

# RF Circuits

# A 10 MHz, 42 ppm/°C, 69 µW PVT Compensated Latch Based Oscillator in BCD9S Technology for PCM

Vivek Tyagi[1(✉)], M. S. Hashmi[1], Ganesh Raj[2], and Vikas Rana[2]

[1] Indraprastha Institute of Information Technology, New Delhi, India
{vivek15118,mshashmi}@iiitd.ac.in
[2] STMicroelectronics, Greater Noida, India
ganeshraj277@gmail.com, vikas18feb@gmail.com

**Abstract.** In this paper, a PVT compensated, 10 MHz oscillator in 0.11 µm BCD9S (Bipolar CMOS DMOS) technology for embedded phase change memories (PCM) is reported. The proposed oscillator produces a frequency deviation of ±0.4% for typical corner, ±2% for slow corner and ±1.5% for fast corner around 10 MHz across −40 °C to 150 °C at a regulated supply of 1.8 V. It is a significant advancement in the existing state-of-the-art for frequency references.

**Keywords:** PVT compensation · BCD · PCM · PTAT · CTAT · Automotive

## 1 Introduction

It is usual practice to employ MEMS based references for the generation of high accuracy stable frequencies. However, this achieved at the cost of power consumption as well as area. The alternatives, therefore, are non-MEMS based designs utilizing process, voltage and temperature (PVT) compensation techniques. In phase change memories, shown in Fig. 1, it is apparent that a highly stable and accurate frequency reference is a necessity. It is due to the fact that in the 'write' operation of phase change memories (PCM), an oscillator is used to produce high accuracy frequency reference that decides the duration of set and reset pulses. Subsequently, the write pulse decides the duration of current pulse that flows through bit cell during write operation. It is therefore important to generate stable frequency reference across process, voltage, and temperature (PVT) variations to increase the reliability and accuracy of write operation [1].

There have been reports of numerous PVT compensated, non-MEMS based high accuracy frequency references [2–7]. However, majority of them are application specific and often do not cater to the requirements of PCMs for automotive applications. For example, A 7 MHz ring oscillator in 250 nm CMOS technology [2] requires additional on-chip compensation circuit, buffer, and comparator that results in large area as well as increase in power consumption. The 1 MHz relaxation oscillator in 130 nm CMOS technology [3] uses on-chip MIM capacitors and poly resistors, which also needs large on-chip area. A relaxation oscillator [4], controlled by current proportional to mobility is designed in 65 nm CMOS technology and is able to achieve very less frequency variation with low power consumption but generates a frequency reference of only

© Springer Nature Singapore Pte Ltd. 2017
B. K. Kaushik et al. (Eds.): VDAT 2017, CCIS 711, pp. 631–645, 2017.
https://doi.org/10.1007/978-981-10-7470-7_60

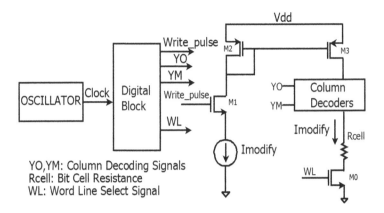

**Fig. 1.** Block diagram for modify operation in PCM

150 kHz. It is therefore suitable only for low frequency applications. The 10 MHz frequency reference in 180 nm CMOS technology [5] although provides compensation for temperature but does not propose any compensation strategy for process variations. Moreover, this technique does not provide frequency variation characteristic for high operating temperature (above 100 °C) and therefore seems less attractive for automotive applications requiring operating temperature range of −40 °C to 150 °C. Other report of 30 MHz frequency reference in 350 nm CMOS technology [6] also is not exciting for automotive applications owing to the fact that it doesn't provide compensation strategy for temperature above 100 °C. Finally, another interesting 14 MHz relaxation oscillator with voltage averaging feedback for temperature compensation in 180 nm CMOS technology [7] although overcomes some of the shortcomings of earlier designs but exhibits more sensitivity on temperature.

In this work, therefore, a new architecture of 10 MHz PVT compensated oscillator is proposed to cater to the needs of automotive applications. The proposed oscillator block is inherently temperature compensated and does not require additional on-chip compensation circuit. The concept of 'digital trimming strategy' is employed to achieve stable frequency of oscillation across different process corners. The oscillator operation is current controlled and this makes the design immune to the supply voltage variations. The design has been simulated for PCM SoC in BCD technology and demonstrates a very good performance across various PVT corners. Furthermore, BCD technology platform provides logic and flash devices, and high performance power devices and therefore the proposed design could also be suitable for embedded memories, aerospace and smart power applications [10].

The Sect. 2 presents the oscillator block operation with incorporated PVT compensation strategies while Sect. 3 discusses about the design issues and simulated results and finally Sect. 4 concludes this paper.

# 2   Oscillator Operation

Figure 2 shows the schematic of proposed PVT compensated latch based oscillator. The architecture of oscillator block consists of cross coupled latch having transistors M1–M4 and equal sized gate capacitors M0 and M5. The reference current ($I_{ref}$) is provided by an on-chip reference current generator, which provides constant current across PVT variations. M16–M25 represents the current mirror transistors that are used to generate '$I_{bias}$', '$I_{curr1}$' and '$I_{curr2}$' from reference current. '$I_{bias}$' is used to charge the cross coupled latch output nodes 'A' and 'B'. '$I_{curr1}$' and '$I_{curr2}$' are equal magnitude currents that are used to charge the gate capacitances present at node 'AN' and 'BN'. M6–M13 transistors acts as a switches used for charging and discharging of gate capacitors. '$V_{dd}$', 'EN' represents the supply voltage and enable signal of oscillator block respectively. Gate capacitances present at the node 'AN' and 'BN' are biased in either strong inversion region or strong accumulation region to get maximum capacitance value.

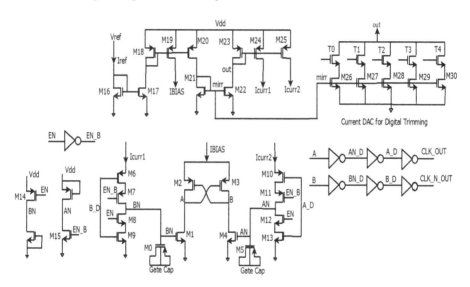

**Fig. 2.**   Schematic of proposed PVT compensated oscillator

## 2.1   Working of Oscillator

Initially enable signal (EN) = 0, M14 and M15 turns on and provides BN = '$V_{dd}$' and AN = 0. Latch stores value of A_D = 0 and B_D = '$V_{dd}$'. These node voltages remains fixed until enable signal goes high. Figure 3 represents charging and discharging path for capacitors when enable signal rises to '$V_{dd}$'. M8 and M9 gets on and discharge the capacitor present at node 'BN' that turns off transistor M1. At same instant, transistors M10 and M11 turns on and '$I_{curr2}$' charges the capacitor present at node 'AN'. Voltage at node 'AN' rises linearly with time, since constant current charges a fixed capacitor value. As the voltage of node 'AN' exceeds the threshold voltage of M4, it turns on and pulls the node B to ground and node A starts rising. The final value stored in latch will be A_D = 'V$_{dd}$' and B_D = 0, which is exactly opposite of initially stored values. This change of state changes the charging and discharging path as shown in Fig. 4.

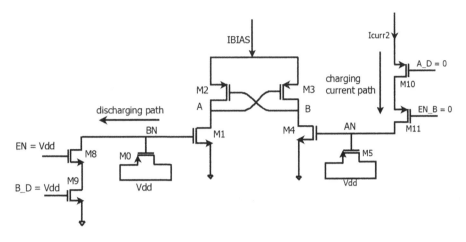

**Fig. 3.** Operation of oscillator when A_D = 0 and B_D = 'V$_{dd}$'

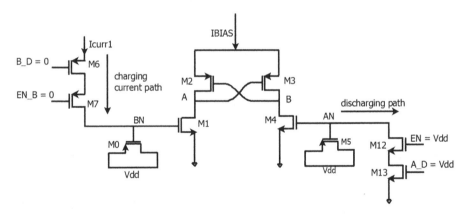

**Fig. 4.** Operation of oscillator when A_D = 'V$_{dd}$' and B _D = 0

At this instant, capacitor at node 'BN' charges by 'I$_{curr1}$' through M6 and M7 and capacitor at node 'AN' discharges by M12 and M13. Charging occurs until voltage at node 'BN' exceeds the threshold voltage of M1, which forces the latch to change its state. This charging and discharging of nodes 'AN' and 'BN' keeps on going till enable signal is high. The charging of capacitor at node 'AN' or 'BN' by constant current (I$_{curr1}$ or I$_{curr2}$) occurs linearly with time with help of M6–M7 or M10–M11 and discharging occurs instantly as the capacitor is connected to ground node directly during discharge path either by M8–M9 or M12–M13.

## 2.2 Temperature Compensation Principle

The principle of temperature compensation employed in this design utilizes the complementary to absolute temperature (CTAT) behavior of threshold voltage and proportional to absolute temperature (PTAT) behavior of overdrive voltage of transistor [9]. Frequency of oscillator is governed by the charging time of the capacitors hence charging time has to remain constant across operating range of temperature. The gate capacitors M0 or M5 will be charged till their voltage level reaches the threshold voltage of either M1 or M4. Charging time ($T_{charging}$) can be written as,

$$T_{charging} = \frac{CV_{gsM1}}{I}$$ (1)

Where I, denotes the charging current either '$I_{curr1}$' or '$I_{curr2}$' and C, denotes the total capacitance at node either 'AN' or 'BN'. In Eq. (1), capacitance (C) and charging current (I) are constant across temperature variations. The term $V_{GSM1}$ can be expressed as:

$$V_{GSM1} = V_{THM1} + \sqrt{\frac{2I_{BIAS}}{\mu_n C_{ox} \left(\frac{W}{L}\right)_{M1}}}$$ (2)

In Eq. (2), threshold voltage exhibits negative temperature coefficient. The aspect ratios of transistor M1 and M4 decides the positive temperature coefficient of overdrive voltage. If negative temperature coefficient of threshold voltage is exactly equal to positive temperature coefficient of overdrive voltage then $V_{GSM1}$ will remain constant across operating range of temperature. The total time period of oscillation is given by:

$$T_{OSC} = 2T_{charging} = \frac{2CV_{gsM1}}{I}$$ (3)

$$f_{osc} = \frac{1}{T_{OSC}} = \frac{I}{2CV_{gsM1}}$$ (4)

## 2.3 Process Variation Compensation

From Eq. (2) it can be inferred that $V_{GSM1}$ is process dependent parameter because of its dependence on threshold voltage and process parameters ($\mu_n C_{ox}$). Hence it can be stated that numerator of Eq. (3) will vary with process variations. The denominator of Eq. (3) can be scaled in same proportion of numerator to keep $T_{OSC}$ constant across different process corners. It means current '$I_{curr1}$' or '$I_{curr2}$' need to be scaled according to the process corners. In order to achieve this trimming bits are introduced in the design to vary the magnitude of current. The different combinations of trimming bits are stored in on-chip digital controller, that helps in achieving the correct oscillation frequency during calibration of the oscillator. As shown in Fig. 5, trimming bits transistors T0–T4 are used to control the overall width of transistor M22.

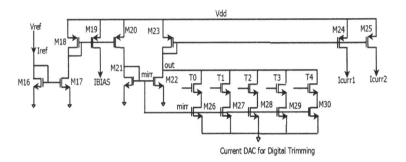

**Fig. 5.** Digital trimming bits T0–T4 used to control the width of transistor M22

This modulation in width changes the amount of current flowing through it, hence decides the magnitude of capacitor's charging current '$I_{curr1}$' and '$I_{curr2}$'. In the proposed oscillator, '5' bit digital trimming is used for obtaining $2^5$ different current levels and used to generate the target frequency of oscillation, according to the different process corner.

### 2.4 Voltage Variation Compensation

It can be observed from Eq. (4), that the frequency of oscillation is independent of supply voltage variations. The parameters present in Eq. (4) I, C and $V_{GSM1}$ all are supply voltage independent terms. However, small frequency variations can be introduced due to supply voltage variations because few inverters are present in the design, whose delay will vary with supply voltage variations. Although proposed design is inherently immune to small voltage variations, but for wide supply voltage variations, on-chip voltage regulator [8] can be integrated in the design to generate stable regulated supply voltage across PVT variations.

## 3    Design and Simulation Results

The proposed oscillator is designed in 0.11 μm BCD9S ST Microelectronics Technology and simulated on post layout extracted netlist in ELDO simulator. The design is simulated for five process corners MAX, MIN, TYP, MAX_MIN (NFPS) and MIN_MAX (NSPF) across –40 °C to 150 °C operating temperature.

### 3.1  Sizing of M1 and M4 for Temperature Compensation

As discussed in previous section, aspect ratio of transistors M1 and M4 decides the accuracy of temperature compensation. Figure 6(a) represents the variation of $V_{GSM1}$ across different values of channel length across −40 °C to 150 °C. At W = 3 µm, L = 6 µm and $I_{bias}$ = 5 µA, $V_{GSM1}$ exhibits better temperature compensated behaviour.

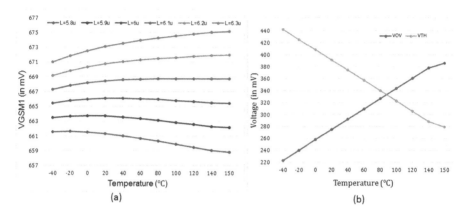

**Fig. 6.** (a) Variation of $V_{GSM1}$ across temperature for different channel length of M1 (b) Variation of threshold voltage ($V_{TH}$) and overdrive voltage ($V_{ov}$) of M1

Figure 6(b) represents the behavior of threshold voltage ($V_{TH}$) and overdrive voltage ($V_{ov}$) for W = 3 µm and L = 6 µm. The threshold voltage exhibits negative temperature coefficient of −0.859 mV/°C and overdrive voltage exhibits positive temperature coefficient of 0.85957 mV/°C.

### 3.2  Effect of Process and Temperature Variations

Figure 7 represents the frequency variation of oscillator in untrimmed case (without digital trimming). Frequency variation of ±16% (8.7 MHz–11.9 MHz) across all process corners from −40 °C to 150 °C is observed in simulation.

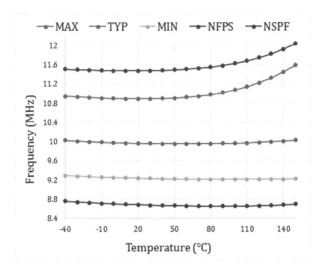

**Fig. 7.** Frequency variation for different process corners across −40 °C to 150 °C in untrimmed case

### 3.3 Variation in Supply Voltage and Reference Current

Figure 8 represents the variation in frequency across ±10% variations in 1.8 V supply voltage for typical process corner. A frequency variation of ±1.65% is observed in simulation, which is due to the variation in delay of inverters used in the design. However, variation due to supply voltage can be compensated by incorporating a voltage regulator in design to generate stable regulated supply voltage, but this will result in increase in chip area as well as power consumption. The accuracy of oscillator is significantly dependent on the accuracy of reference current. The state-of-the-art reference current generator circuits exhibits some dependence on temperature and process variations [11, 12]. For ±5% variation in reference current ($I_{ref}$), frequency variation of ±4.09% is observed as shown in Fig. 9. It is due to the fact that oscillation frequency is directly proportional to reference current (Eq. (4)).

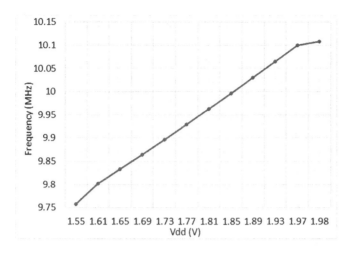

**Fig. 8.** Variation of oscillation frequency across 1.8 ± 10% supply voltage variations

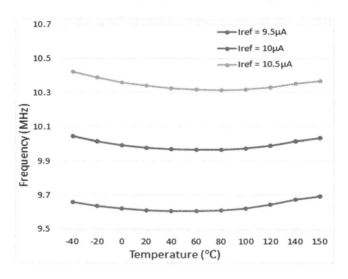

**Fig. 9.** Variation of oscillation frequency across 10 µA ± 5% reference current variations

### 3.4 Monte Carlo Simulations

Predefined corners represents only rare case events hence provides much pessimistic results than actual results. For much better estimate of overall variations (device mismatch and process variability) and yield analysis, Monte Carlo simulation is performed over different operating temperature. There are various parameters (mean, standard deviation, coefficient of variation etc.) obtained from Monte Carlo simulations that are tabulated in Table 1. Figures 10, 11 and 12 show Monte Carlo simulation results for −40 °C, 27 °C and 150 °C respectively in statistical corner.

**Table 1.** Various parameters obtained from Monte Carlo simulation

| Temperature | −40 °C | 27 °C | 150 °C |
|---|---|---|---|
| Mean (μ) (MHz) | 10.04566 | 9.97563 | 10.03540 |
| Standard Deviation (σ) (MHz) | 0.16224 | 0.1426 | 0.12102 |
| Coefficient of Variation (%) | 1.62 | 1.43 | 1.21 |
| μ ± 3 σ Range (MHz) | 9.55–10.53 | 9.54–10.40 | 9.67–10.39 |

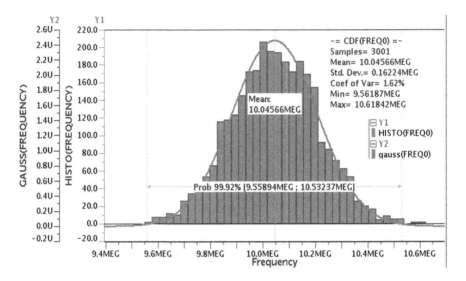

**Fig. 10.** Frequency variation in Monte Carlo simulation over 3001 samples at T = −40 °C

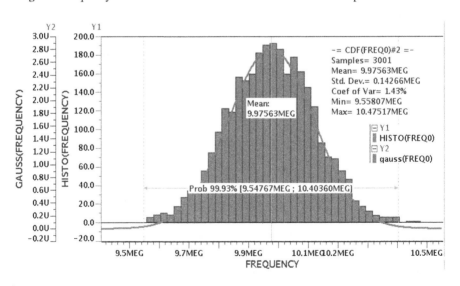

**Fig. 11.** Frequency variation in Monte Carlo simulation over 3001 samples at T = 27 °C

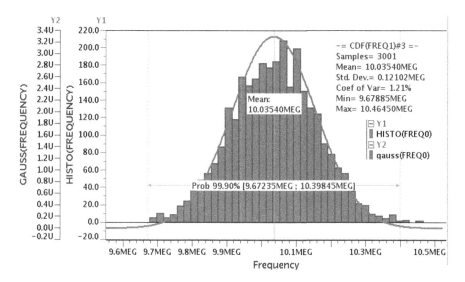

**Fig. 12.** Frequency variation in Monte Carlo simulation over 3001 samples at T = 150 °C

## 3.5   Results with Digital Trimming

Figure 13 shows the frequency variations in different process corners using digital trimming bits combination to achieve correct target frequency of 10 MHz. It is observed that in typical corner, oscillator exhibits frequency variation of ±0.4%, whereas ±2%, ±1.5%, ±1.5% and ±0.65% in MIN, MAX, NFPS and NSPF process corners.

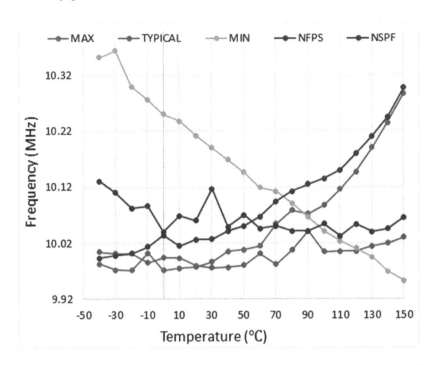

**Fig. 13.**  Variation of frequency across −40 °C to 150 °C for different process corners using digital trimming

Figure 14 represents the transient behavior of internal nodes of oscillator. It is observed from Fig. 15 that the gate capacitance of transistors M0 and M5 exhibits small variations (up to 3–4 fF) during the transient operation. The node 'AN' and 'BN' rises linearly during charging from 0 to 729 mV, this causes variation in capacitance associated at these nodes between (139.5 fF–143 fF). However, this capacitance variation is small up to ±1.2% and does not significantly affect the accuracy of oscillator's frequency.

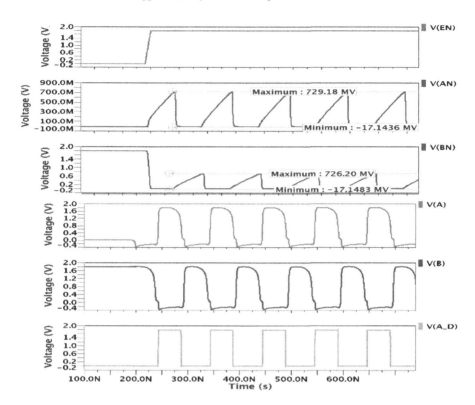

**Fig. 14.** Transient behavior of different internal nodes of latch based oscillator

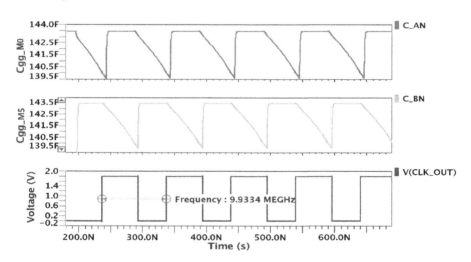

**Fig. 15.** Transient variation of gate capacitance at node 'AN' and 'BN' and final clock output

In literature, there are various figure of merits (FOM's) used in the context of oscillator. Here, the FOM given in Eq. (5) [3] has been used. The term $FOM_1$ relates the frequency to power ratio and is commonly used in low power oscillators.

$$FOM_1 = 10 \log\left(\frac{f}{P}\right) \tag{5}$$

Table 2 compares the frequency variation and power consumption of proposed work in with various state-of-the-art designs. Here TC represents temperature coefficient and defined as:

$$TC \ (ppm/°C) = \frac{\Delta f}{f_0 . T} . 10^6 \tag{6}$$

**Table 2.** Comparison of proposed oscillator with state-of-the-art designs

| Work | Process (nm) | f (MHz) | TC (ppm/°C) | Temp-Range (°C) | Power (μW) | $FOM_1$ (dB) |
|------|-------------|---------|-------------|-----------------|------------|--------------|
| [2], exp | CMOS 250 nm | 7 | 315 | −40 to 125 | 1500 | 96 |
| [3], exp | CMOS 130 nm | 1 | 108 | 25 to 180 | 428 | 93 |
| [4], exp | CMOS 65 nm | 0.15 | 300 | −55 to 125 | 51 | 94 |
| [5], exp | CMOS 180 nm | 10 | 67 | −20 to 100 | 80 | 111 |
| [6], exp | CMOS 350 nm | 30 | 117 | −20 to 100 | 180 | 112 |
| [7], exp | CMOS 180 nm | 14 | 91 | −20 to 100 | 45 | 115 |
| This work, sim | BCD 9S 110 nm | 10 | 42 | −40 to 150 | 69 | 112 |

f: Oscillator Frequency, exp: Experimental Results, sim: Simulated Results

In Eq. (6), $\Delta f$ denotes frequency variation in typical corner, $f_0$ denotes oscillation frequency and T denotes range of operating temperature.

# 4   Conclusions

A PVT compensated oscillator have been presented in 0.11 μm BCD9S Technology for embedded phase change memories, which is inherently temperature compensated and does not require any other on chip analog block or feedback circuit for temperature compensation. It reduces the worst case frequency spread significantly from ±16% (untrimmed) to ±2% (MIN corner) for operating temperature range of −40 °C to +150 °C. The total power consumed by oscillator in worst case is 69 μW, which makes it suitable for low power applications. The oscillator frequency of operation is not significantly dependent on its supply, for ±10% variation in supply, ±1.65% frequency variation is observed in the simulation.

**Acknowledgements.** The authors would like to thanks the Smart-power Technology group at ST Microelectronics, India for providing CAD Tools as well as technical support throughout the work.

# References

1. Bedeschi, F., et al.: 4-Mb MOSFET-selected phase-change memory experimental chip. In: Proceedings of the 30th European Solid-State Circuits Conference, pp. 207–210 (2004)
2. Sundaresan, K., Allen, P., Ayazi, F.: Process and temperature compensation in a 7-MHz CMOS clock oscillator. IEEE J. Solid-State Circuits **41**(2), 433–442 (2006)
3. Sadeghi, N., Bakhtiar, A.S., Mirabbasi, S.: A 0.007 mm2 108-ppm/°C 1-MHz relaxation oscillator for high-temperature applications up to 180 °C in 0.13 µm CMOS. IEEE Trans. Circuits Syst. I, Reg. Papers **60**(7), 1692–1701 (2013)
4. Sebastiano, F., Nauta, B., et al.: A 65-nm CMOS temperature compensated mobility-based frequency reference for wireless sensor networks. In: Proceedings of the ESSCIRCs, pp. 102–105, September 2010
5. Lee, J., Cho, S.: A 10 MHz 80 µW 67 ppm/°C CMOS reference clock oscillator with a temperature compensated feedback loop in 180 nm CMOS. In: Proceedings of the VLSI, pp. 226–227, June 2009
6. Ueno, K., Asai, T., Amemiya, Y.: A 30 MHz, 90-ppm/°C fully integrated clock reference generator with frequency-locked loop. In: Proceedings of the ESSCIRCs, pp. 392–395, September 2009
7. Tokunaga, Y., Saki Yama, S., Matsumoto, A., Dosho, S.: An on-chip CMOS relaxation oscillator with voltage averaging feedback. IEEE J. Solid-State Circuits **45**, 1150–1158 (2010)
8. Milliken, R.J., Silva-Martinez, J., Sanchez-Sinencio, E.: Full on-chip CMOS low-dropout voltage regulator. IEEE Trans. Circuits Syst. I: Regular Papers **54**(9), 1879–1890 (2007)
9. Wolpert, D., Ampadu, P.: Managing Temperature Effects in Nanoscale Adaptive Systems. Springer, New York (2012)
10. Chil, M.N., et al.: Advanced 300 mm 130 nm BCD technology from 5 V to 85 V with Deep-Trench Isolation. In: 2016 28th International Symposium on Power Semiconductor Devices and ICs (ISPSD), Prague, pp. 403–406 (2016)
11. Sengupta, S., Saurabh, K., Allen, P.E.: A process, voltage, and temperature compensated CMOS constant current reference. In: 2004 IEEE International Symposium on Circuits and Systems (IEEE Cat. No. 04CH37512), vol. 1, pp. I-325–I-328 (2004)
12. Wang, D., Tan, X.L., Chan, P.K.: A 65-nm CMOS constant current source with reduced PVT variation. IEEE Trans. Very Large Scale Integr. (VLSI) Syst. **25**(4), 1373–1385 (2017)

# A 1.8 V Gain Enhanced Fully Differential Doubly-Recycled Cascode OTA with 100 dB Gain 200 MHz UGB in CMOS

Antaryami Panigrahi[1](✉) and Abhipsa Parhi[2]

[1] Department of ECE, Central Institute of Technology,
Kokrajhar 783370, Assam, India
a.panigrahi@cit.ac.in
[2] Department of Electrical Engineering, Bineswar Brahma Engineering College,
Kokrajhar 783370, Assam, India

**Abstract.** A fully differential OTA based on modified Doubly Recycling current technique is presented here. The proposed technique uses a Gm boosted Cascode stage at the output, there by enhancing the DC gain of recycling cascode OTA with an improved phase margin. 102 dB of DC gain is achieved, which is almost 20 dB more than the existing architectures designed at 1.8 V supply. Enhancement of gain helps in reducing the input referred noise down to $10\,\mathrm{uV}/\sqrt{\mathrm{Hz}}$. The designed OTA achieves UGB of 200 MHz at a capacitive load of 10 pF which makes it suitable for high speed applications. The OTA is designed in standard 45 nm CMOS Process. The 2 stage OTA uses MCNR approach to emulate first order Phase response before UGB, giving a Phase Margin of more than 69° for typical load of 10 pF. The input referred noise is $10\,\mu\mathrm{V}/\sqrt{\mathrm{Hz}}$ at 10 Hz and Slew Rate 105 V/μS for load of 1 pF.

**Keywords:** Amplifiers · Cascode amplifiers · Folded casacode · OTA

## 1 Introduction

Moving towards high frequency and low voltage applications, circuits based on standard design techniques, such as telescopic cascode demands a higher supply voltage for operation of transistors in strong inversion, also suffers from reduced swing. The regulated cascode and gain boosted cascode suffers from handling large currents and high output impedances at low output voltages. Recently, the folded cascode (FC) amplifier has gained preference over the telescopic owing to the low voltage nature of nanometer CMOS technologies, despite the higher power budget. If we compare telescopic cascode amp [1] and folded cascode amplifier, the former offers better frequency response than the latter but with a limited swing. And gain boosting Cascode amplifier [2], will introduce doublets into the whole system. The phase margin of the boosting amplifier decides the form of the doublets: either real or complex conjugate. A regulated cascode

© Springer Nature Singapore Pte Ltd. 2017
B. K. Kaushik et al. (Eds.): VDAT 2017, CCIS 711, pp. 646–656, 2017.
https://doi.org/10.1007/978-981-10-7470-7_61

provides greater gain, but at the cost more power dissipated by the auxiliary amplifiers [3].

The recycling folded cascode (RFC) [4] amplifier offers double the gain, the bandwidth and the slew rate without increasing the power dissipation, as opposed to conventional folded cascode amplifier depending upon mirroring factor $K$. The optimal value of $K$ is constrained with Slew rate. But the gain is of 60 dB at 1.8 V. Recent literature [4–12] shows many variants of the RFC structure. Li et al. [8] proposed an improved recycling folded cascade (IRFC) OTA shown in Fig. 1, which uses extra shunt current sources $M_{3c}$ and $M_{4c}$ cascoded to the transistors $M_{10,a}$ and $M_{10,b}$. But the gain achieved is still around 70 dB and UGB is 83 MHz at 1.2 V supply.

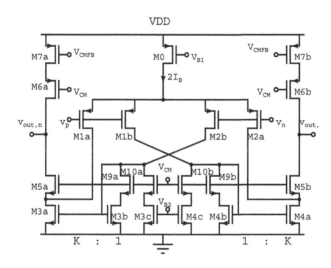

**Fig. 1.** Improved recycling FC OTA [7]

The limited DC gain and Bandwidth offered by IRFC [7] and DRFC [6] is improved in this work by eliminating the folding node and replacing it with another high impedance node and a boosted complimentary output stage [13]. We've tried to enhance the DC gain and UGB of the conventional amplifiers designed at 1.8 V supply without compromising much on the slew rate. To achieve this, we've used the recyclic cascode as input stage of the amplifier and an telescopic output stage. The telescopic amplifier is choosen in the output stage owing to its frequency response and less power consumption, compared with folded-cascode stage [1]. The designed OTA is compared with existing OTAs using recycling structures and other types of OTAs.

## 2    Proposed Gain Enhnced DRFC

The proposed OTA uses the DRFC technique (shown in Fig. 2(a)) to recycle the small signal current generated by $M_{2b}$ with the help of $M_{3d}$ and $M_{10a}$. In this way the equivalent $g_m$ and $r_{out}$ at the node $X$ can be improved as compared to the conventional DRFC [6]. Effectively gain boosting happening at the output stage also improves. This additional signal path connected to the gate of $M_{5a}$ and $M_{6a}$ would enlarge the equivalent output resistance, hence helping in boosting the gain of overall amplifier.

The transconductance at the $X$ node can be written for both the DRFC and the proposed DRC as:

$$G_{mX,DRFC} = g_{m,2b}(1 + M)$$
$$G_{mX,PDRC} = g_{m,2b}(1 + M)$$

(1)

As it can be seen the proposed amplifier shows no improvement on the $G_m$ in comparison to DRFC at $X$ node, but output resistance shows significant improvement due to absence of the additional path from $M_{3b}$ and $M_{8a}$, which would have otherwise come in parallel to the transistors $M_{3c}$ and $M_{9a}$. This fact explains the reduced DC current flowing into the transistor $M_{3a}$, subsequently current flowing into the transistor $M_{11a,b}$ as matter of fact limiting the positive slew rate of the OTA. The quantitative discussion for the slew rate is presented later. The expression for output resistance at the node $X$ can be written by deactivating the input signals coming into the transistors $M_{3c}$ and $M_{1a}$ as;

$$R_{outX,DRFC} = r_{ds1a}||(r_{ds3c}.g_{m9a}r_{ds9a})$$

(2)

$$R_{outX,PDRC} = r_{ds2b}||[r_{ds3c}.g_{m9a}r_{ds9a}||r_{ds3b}.g_{m8a}r_{ds8a}]$$

So the open circuit voltage gain at the $X$ node improves, which is used boost output resistance of the N-MOS cascode formed by the $M_{3a}$ and $M_{5a}$ and PMOS Cascode formed by $M_{6a}$ and $M_{7a}$.

The proposed enhanced DRC amplifier is presented in Fig. 2(b). Note that transistors $M_{9a}$ and $M_{9b}$ conduct a large current value; thus, exhibit large transconductance. Therefore, only the $M_{1c}$ transistor provides the input drive which is mirrored $K$ times through $M_{3a}$ into the output node. $M_{1c}$, $M_{1b}$ transistors of the triplicated driving transistors are used for enhancing the gain at the $X$ node.

### 2.1  Operation

The proposed enhanced DRFC amplifier is presented in Fig. 2(b). The $M_{1c}$ transistor provides the input drive which is mirrored $K$ times through $M_{3a}$ into the output node. This forms amplifier's transconductance (Gm) given by;

$$G_{m,DRFC} \simeq (1 + K.M).g_{m1c}$$
$$G_{m,PDRC} \simeq K.g_{m2b}$$

(3)

$M_{1a}$, $M_{2b}$ transistors of the triplicated driver transistors are used for enhancing the gain at the $X$ node. The input drive of $M_{2b}$ is mirrored through the $M_{3d}$, $M_{10b}$ and $M_{3c}$ transistors into the $X$ node. The output resistance of the node $X$

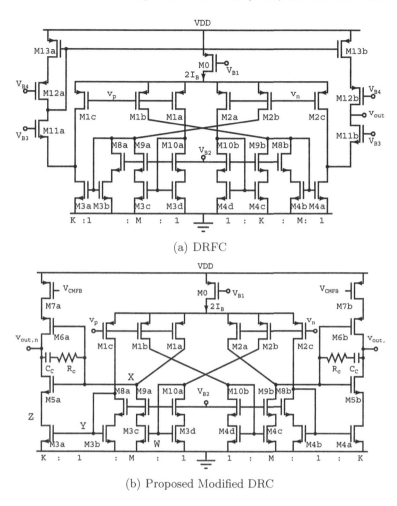

(a) DRFC

(b) Proposed Modified DRC

**Fig. 2.** Modied Recycling Cascodes (a), Doubly Recyling Folded Cascode (DRFC) [6] (b) Proposed DRC

because of cascode structure formed of transistors $M_{3d}$ and $M_{10a}$. As opposed to [6], our approach has a better open circuit voltage gain at this node as inferred from Eqs. 1 and 2. Since the output resistance offered by the cascode pair $M_{3c}$ and $M_{9a}$ are much larger than resistance of the other cascode pair $M_{3b}$ and $M_{8a}$. For the former case the DC current flowing through the cascode pair $M_{3d}$ and $M_{9a}$ is $M\frac{I_b}{3}$, but through $M_{3b}$ and $M_{8a}$ pair it is $(M-1)\frac{I_b}{3}$, so current is flowing through these branches are approximately same, equivalent output resistance at the $X$ node will be $\frac{(r_{ds3c}g_{m9a}r_{ds9a})}{2}$. In the proposed architecture, with the same DC current of $(M-1)\frac{I_b}{3}$ equivalent output resistance at $X$ node is $(r_{ds3c}g_{m9a}r_{ds9a})$. For the same value of $M$, the proposed architecture is able to produce twice the gain i.e. 6 dB improvement at this node which would help enhance the output resistance at the output stage. The value of $K$ is selected equal to 5 and $M = 3$ to keep same power consumption and area. Small signal transconductance for DRFC and Proposed OTA are expressed in Eq. (3).

The complete gain expression is written in Eqs. 5 and 7. The approximated gain of the complete OTA can be written as follows;

$$A_{v_o,DRFC} \simeq (1 + KM).g_{m1c}(r_{ds13b}g_{m12b}r_{ds12b})$$
$$A_{v_o,PDRC} \simeq KM.g_{m2b}(r_{ds7a}g_{m2b}(r_{ds3c}g_{m9a}r_{ds9a})g_{m6a}r_{ds6a}) \tag{4}$$

Note that transistors M3 and M4 conduct a large current value; thus, they have large transconductance. Therefore, beside the input drives (M1 and M2), transistors M3 and M4 can be used as driving transistors [3,5].

$$A_{v_o,DRFC} \simeq (1 + KM).g_{m1c}((r_{ds4a}||r_{ds2c}) \tag{5}$$

$$.g_{m11b}r_{ds11b})||(r_{ds13b}g_{m12b}r_{ds12b}) \tag{6}$$

$$A_{v_o,PDRC} \simeq K.g_{m2b}(r_{ds3a}[Mg_{m2b}(r_{ds3c}g_{m9a} \tag{7}$$

$$r_{ds9a})]g_{m5a}r_{ds5a})||(r_{ds7a}[Mg_{m2b}(r_{ds3c}g_{m9a}r_{ds9a})]g_{m6a}r_{ds6a}) \tag{8}$$

Since $g_{m1c} = g_{m2b}$, as size of the devices as well as the current flowing through the transistors i.e. $M_{1c}$ of DRFC and $M_{2b}$ of the proposed architectures are same, the approximated gain for DRFC is $(1 + KM)g_{m1c}.r_{ds2c}g_{m11b}r_{ds11b}$, whereas for proposed architecture it is $K.g_{m2b}.(r_{ds7a}[Mg_{m2b}(r_{ds3c}g_{m9a}r_{ds9a})]g_{m6a}r_{ds6a}) \simeq KMg_{m2b}.(r_{ds7a}[g_{m2b}(r_{ds3c}g_{m9a}r_{ds9a})]g_{m6a}r_{ds6a})$.

This shows for same value of $K$ and $M$, $g_{m11b}r_{ds11b}$ is much smaller as the DC current flowing through the output branch of the DRFC is $(KM - 1)\frac{I_b}{3}$, whereas $g_{m6a}r_{ds6a}$ is much larger as the DC current through the output stage is only $K\frac{I_b}{3}$. So the gain enhancement is of the order of $A_{v_x}KM^2$ as opposed to $KM$ in DRFC and $K$ times in RFC as shown in Eqs. (5) and (7).

# 3    Non-idealities of the Amplifier

## 3.1    Effect of Internal Parasitics

Each of nodes appearing in the signal path introduces an extra pole in the transfer function i.e. W, X, Y, Z. The first-order roll-off in the low frequency domain is caused due to large resistance at the output node and load capacitance $C_L$, the pole corresponding to this node can be written $p_1$ as;

$$p_1 \simeq \frac{1}{R_{out}.C_L} \tag{9}$$

The first non dominant pole $p_2$ caused at the node $X$ can be written as;

$$p_2 \simeq \frac{1}{R_X(C_{bd9a} + C_{bd1a})} \tag{10}$$

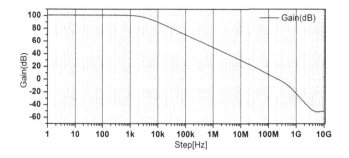

**Fig. 3.** Gain response

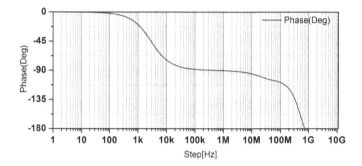

**Fig. 4.** Phase response

this pole is shifted outside the UGB with the help of Miller's compensation using nulling resistor [14] as shown in the Fig. 2.

Although $C_{gd1,a}$, $C_{gd2,b}$, $C_{gd1,c}$, $C_{gd3,a}$, and $C_{gd5,a}$, create zeros at respective nodes i.e. $w$, $x$, $y$, $z$, these zeros occur at very high frequencies, so they are ignored in the analysis.

The existence of compensation capacitor between input and output node of output stage causes the poles associated with them spilt apart, generating dominant and non-dominant pole, moreover feedforward path produces a right-half-plane (RHP) zero.

The absence of the folding node in the output stage in the proposed architecture enhances the band width as compared to the RFC, IRFC, DRFC. But this architecture can have a high impedance node at the $x$, so stability is at stake. For this reason we've used MCNR approach to improve PM [14].

### 3.2   Contribution of Noise

The noise at the output of the OTA in Fig. 7 is contributed mostly by $M_{1a}/M_{2a}$, $M_{1b}/M_{2b}$, $M_{1c}/M_{2c}$, $M_{3a}/M_{4a}$, and $M_{7a}$ $M_{7b}$. Assuming the noise sources in each half of the OTA are uncorrelated their effects on the output can considered individually. Two main sources of noise that can affect the

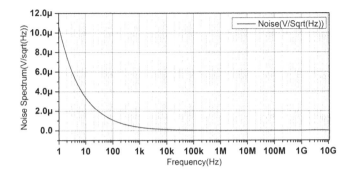

**Fig. 5.** Noise spectrum

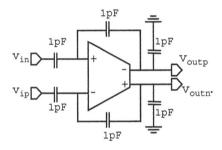

**Fig. 6.** Closed loop test for transient response

performance of the OTA are: flicker Noise and thermal noise. The expression for Flicker Noise can be written as;

$$v^2_{n(1/f)} = \frac{K_f}{g^2_{m1a}C_{ox}f}[\frac{g^2_{m1a}}{(WL)_1}(\frac{1+K^2+M^2}{K^2}) + \frac{g^2_{m3a}}{(WL)_{3a}}$$
$$+\frac{g^2_{m3c}}{(WL)_{3c}}(\frac{1}{K^2}) + \frac{g^2_{m4a}}{(WL)_{4a}}(\frac{1}{K^2})] \qquad (11)$$

Ignoring the thermal noise component due to the Gate resistance and bulk resistance, the approximated thermal noise expression can be written as;

$$v^2_{n(Th)} = \frac{8.K.T.\gamma}{3.g^2_{m1a}}\left[\frac{1+K^2+M^2}{K^2} + \frac{g_{m3a}}{K^2} + \frac{g_{m3c}}{K^2} + \frac{g_{m9a}}{K^2}\right] \qquad (12)$$

The above expression shows that the noise contribution is also lesser owing to the higher value of effective $g_m$, which is also confirmed with the simulation. The proposed OTA has an rms noise of $10\mu V/\sqrt{Hz}$ at $1\,Hz$ and between $1\,kHz$ to $200\,MHz$ it is almost constant at few 10th of $nV/\sqrt{Hz}$.

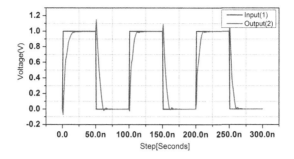

**Fig. 7.** Transient response of amplifier with differential 10 MHz, 1 V$p-p$ input step

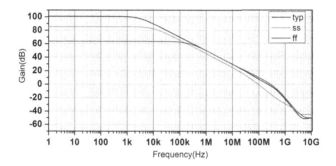

**Fig. 8.** Comparison of Gain responses across corners

## 4    Simulated Results and Discussion

The proposed OTA is simulated using 45 nm CMOS technology is used to simulate the proposed circuit, using BSIM 3v3 model in Mentor TSPICE. The supply voltage used is of 1.8 V. The aspect ratios of the devices are shown in Table 1. In this work, the aspect ratios of all transistors are chosen to maximize both gain and UGB at a reduced input referred noise.

An AC signal of magnitude 1 V, 10 kHz is applied to the circuit with load capacitance of 10 pF. It can be seen that the DC gain is approximately 102 dB, UGB is around 205 MHz and phase margin is around 73° from Figs. 6 and 7. The gain of the proposed OTA is comparable to the other OTAs [1,5,7,15] designed with 1.8 V supply and much higher than the recycling structures [11,12]. The robustness of the OTA across different corners are also simulated. The gain response and phase response for these corners are shown in Figs. 8 and 9. It shows only for the slow-slow (SS), although the PM is degraded, but gain and UGB are still higher in comparison to typical values of FC and RFC amplifiers. The main reason being the improvement of the signal transconductance caused in the output stage i.e. $M_{5a}$ and $M_{6a}$ by the application of boosted current generated at the drain of $M_{3c}$ in Fig. 3 to the gate of $M_{3a}$.

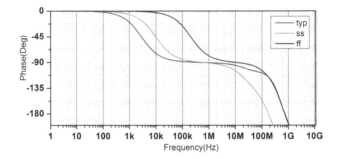

**Fig. 9.** Comparison of Gain responses across corners

**Table 1.** Summary of simulated performances of the OTA

| Parameters | Simulated values |
|---|---|
| Power (mW) | 1.8 |
| DC gain (dB) @ $C_L = 10\,\mathrm{pF}$ | 102 |
| UGB (MHz) @ $C_L = 10\,\mathrm{pF}$ | 203 |
| UGB (MHz) @ $C_L = 1\,\mathrm{pF}$ | 375 |
| Phase Margin (deg) @ $C_L = 10\,\mathrm{pF}$ | 70 |
| Phase Margin (deg) @ $C_L = 1\,\mathrm{pF}$ | 75 |
| Input-Referred Noise ($nV/\sqrt{Hz}$) @ 10 kHz | 80 |
| Slew Rate (V/$\mu$Sec) | 105 |
| Settling time (nSec) | 16.5 |

Noise performance of the OTA is simulated and input referred noise spectral density is shown in Fig. 5, which shows dominance of the flicker noise produced by input stage nMOS-pMOS pair.

To simulate for the slew rate of the OTA, a large pulse of amplitude 1 V, time period 100 nS (having 0.2 nS rise and 0.2 nS fall time) is applied to the OTA in closed loop as shown in Fig. 6, the transient response is shown in Fig. 7. The settling time for 0.1% is 26.8 nS and for 1% time it is 16.5 nS. The slew rate from the response can be found to be 105 V/$uSec$ with same load conditions (10 pF). Total power dissipation by the circuit 1.8 mW. The summaries of simulated results are shown in the Table 2.

Comparison of the results are given in Table 2, which shows the designed OTA has good gain and bandwidth at 1.8 V supply so improving the figure of merit (both $FOM_1$(MHz.pF/mA) and $FOM_2$(dB.MHz/mW)).

**Table 2.** Comparison of different OTAs

| Parameters | This work | FC | RFC [4] | [12] | [11] | [6] | [5] | [15] |
|---|---|---|---|---|---|---|---|---|
| Process used | 45 nm CMOS | 180 nm CMOS | 180 nm CMOS | 180 nm CMOS | 180 nm CMOS | 65 nm CMOS | 65 nm CMOS | 180 nm CMOS |
| Supply Voltage (V) | 1.8 | 1.8 | 1.8 | 1.8 | 1.8 | 1.2 | 2 | 1.8 |
| Power Dissipation ($mW$) | 1.8 | 0.85 | .82 | 0.72 | 1.8 | .8 | 1.37 | 0.72 |
| DC Gain (dB) | 102 | 53 | 60 | 63.4 | 85.3 | 54.5 | 63.4 | 96 |
| Input-referred-Noise @10 kHz ($nV/\sqrt{Hz}$) | 80 | 54 | 49 | NA | 118000 | 8500 | 36000 | NA |
| UGB (MHz) | 265 | 71 | 135 | 136.5 | 987 | 203.2 | 236 | 146 |
| Phase Margin (deg) | 70 | 50 | 57 | 77.2 | 66.7 | 66.2 | 63.6 | 70 |
| Load Cap (pF) | 10 | 5.6 | 5.6 | 2.5 | 1 | 10 | 1 | 15 |
| Settling (1%) | 20.5 | 20.7 | 11.2 | 19.6 | NA | NA | NA | NA |
| Slew Rate (V/uSec) | 105 | 43 | 95 | 89.2 | NA | 87.8 | 19 | 730 |
| $FoM_1$ (MHz.pF/mA) | 2650 | 495 | 940 | 473.3 | 987 | 1161.06 | 344.5 | 730 |
| $FoM_2$ (dB.MHz/mW) | 11334.4 | 2576.3 | 5625 | 12019.5 | 46772.3 | 7256.6 | 15016.7 | 19466.6 |
| $FoM_3$ (V/$\mu$Sec.pF/mW) | 583.34 | 283.3 | 648.7 | 309.72 | NA | 1097.5 | 13.86 | NA |

# 5   Conclusion

A new technique of implementing fully differential OTA using cascode is presented. An excellent management of bias current is shown so as to improve DC gain, UGB and slew rate with the help of recycling structure input stage and current mirror output stage. The proposed OTA not only increases the gain, also shows a good frequency response achieving 100 dB DC gain and 203 MHz UGB at a load of 10 pF. The enhancement of gain, PM and UGB helps in better settling accuracy useful for high speed applications.

# References

1. Mallya, S.M., Nevin, J.H.: Design procedures for a fully differential folded-cascode CMOS operational amplifier. IEEE J. Solid-State Circuits **24**(6), 1737–1740 (1989)
2. Das, M.: Improved design criteria of gain-boosted CMOS OTA with high-speed optimizations. IEEE Trans. Circuits Syst. II **49**(3), 204–207 (2002)
3. Razavi, B.: Design of Analog CMOS Integrated Circuits, 2nd edn. Mc-Graw Hill, New York (2003)
4. Assad, S.M.: The recycling folded cascode: a general enhancement of the folded cascode amplifier. IEEE J. Solid State Circuits **44**(9), 2535–2542 (2009)
5. Liu, M., Mak, P.-I., Yan, Z., Martins, R.P.: High-voltage-enabled recycling folded cascode OpAmp for nanoscale CMOS technologies. In: IEEE ISCAS 2011, pp. 33–36 (2011)
6. Yan, Z., Mak, P.I., Martins, R.P.: Double recycling technique for folded-cascode OTA. Analog Integr. Circuit Signal Process. **71**, 137141 (2012). Springer
7. Assaad, R., Silva-Martinez, J.: Enhancing general performance of folded cascode amplifier by recycling current. Electron. Lett. 43(23), 8th November 2007
8. Sundararajan, A.D., Rezaul Hasan, S.M.: Quadruply split cross-driven doubly recycled gm-doubling recycled folded cascode for microsensor instrumentation amplifiers. IEEE Trans. Circuits Syst. II: Express Briefs 63(6), June 2016
9. Li, Y.L., Han, K.F., Tan, X., Yan, N., Min, H.: Transconductance enhancement method for operational transconductance amplifiers. IET, Electron. Lett. 46(19), 6th September 2010
10. Akbari, M.: Single-stage fully recycling folded cascode OTA for switched-capacitor circuits. IET Electron. Lett. **51**(13), 977–979 (2015)
11. Ahmed, M., Shah, I., Tang, F., Bermak, A.: An improved recycling folded cascode amplifier with gain boosting and phase margin enhancement. In: 2015 IEEE International Symposium on Circuits and Systems, 24–27 May 2015, pp. 2473–2476 (2015)
12. Akbari, M., Hashemipour, O.: Design and analysis of folded cascode OTAs using Gm/Id methodology based on flicker noise reduction. Analog Integr. Circuits Sig. Process. **83**, 343–352 (2015)
13. Bult, K., Gelen, G.J.G.M.: The CMOS Gain-Boosting Technique. Analog Integr. Circ. Sig. Process **1**, 119–135 (1991)
14. Allen, P., Holberg, D.: CMOS Analog Circuit Design, 2nd edn. Oxford University Publications, Oxford (2003)
15. Rezaei, M., Zhian-Tabasy, E., Ashtiani, S.J.: Slew rate enhancement method for folded-cascode amplifiers. IET- Electron. Lett. **44**, 1226–1228 (2008)

# A Low Power, Frequency-to-Digital Converter CMOS Based Temperature Sensor in 65 nm Process

Mudasir Bashir$^{(\boxtimes)}$ (ID), Sreehari Rao Patri, and K. S. R. Krishna Prasad

Department of Electronics and Communication Engineering,
National Institute of Technology, Warangal, India
mudasir.mir7@gmail.com

**Abstract.** A low power all CMOS based smart temperature sensor is introduced without using any bandgap reference or any current/voltage analog-to-digital converter. With the intention of low cost, power and area consumption, the proposed temperature sensor operates in sub-threshold region generating a temperature dependent frequency from the proportional to absolute temperature current. A digital output is obtained from the temperature dependent frequency by using a 12-bit asynchronous counter. A temperature insensitive ring oscillator is designed used a reference clock signal in counter. The temperature sensor is implemented using 65 nm CMOS standard process and its operation is validated through post-layout simulation results, at a power supply of (0.5–1)-V. The sensor has an uncalibrated accuracy of +2.4/–2.1 °C for (–55 to 125) °C and a resolution of 0.28 °C for the same range. The power and area consumed by the sensor is 1.55 μW and 0.024 mm$^2$ respectively.

**Keywords:** Calibration · Counter · Low power · PTAT · Temperature sensor
Temperature insensitive ring oscillator

## 1 Introduction

Due to the progression in pervasive computing, internet of things (IoTs) and the increase in demand of portable and miniature electronic devices, demand of low-cost, high performance temperature sensor is increased. The aggressive scaling techniques and increased transistor integration results in amplified junction temperature gradient. These junction temperature variations affect the lifetime, performance and reliability of the electronic device by increasing the leakage power, timing issues, gate delay, self-heating and the overall cost [1]. Temperature sensors have become an important element in every system on chip (SoC), especially the on-chip temperature sensors, mostly because of their compactness, low cost, high performance and low power consumption. The low power consumption helps in mitigating the self-heating issues of these sensors. The on-chip temperature sensors are mostly used for thermal compensation and power consumption control in SoCs.

Different types of temperature sensors have been realized in CMOS technology. The conventional block diagram of sensor with its interface is shown in Fig. 1.

© Springer Nature Singapore Pte Ltd. 2017
B. K. Kaushik et al. (Eds.): VDAT 2017, CCIS 711, pp. 657–666, 2017.
https://doi.org/10.1007/978-981-10-7470-7_62

A conventional temperature sensor is designed using bipolar junction transistors (BJTs) [2]. The BJT based temperature sensors measure the temperature by comparing the temperature independent voltage with a temperature dependent voltage. These two voltages are created using the characteristics of a vertical PNP voltage [3–6]. The ratio between the proportional to absolute temperature (PTAT) and the reference voltage is fed to an analog to digital converter (ADC) for digital output. The BJT based temperature sensors are able to achieve good resolution with high precision data converters, but result in more sensing errors. In order to mitigate the error, complex calibration techniques involving dynamic element matching (DEM) and chopping techniques are used making the output interface bulky and increasing the overall cost [2]. This resulted in tradeoff between sensing error, power consumption and sensor size. Moreover, the compatibility issue of BJT with CMOS technology increased the overall cost of the sensor. To overcome these issues, metal-oxide-semiconductor (MOS) based temperature sensors are introduced [7–16]. These sensors mostly exploit the thermal dependency of threshold voltage or leakage current of MOS devices. The output of MOS based sensors is usually temperature dependent current, voltage or frequency, with a typical accuracy of $\pm 2$ °C [2].

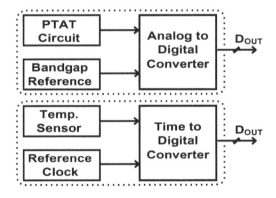

**Fig. 1.** Conventional ADC and TDC based temperature sensor [2].

In this paper, a current-mode MOS based temperature sensor is introduced without using any BJTs. It employs a PTAT frequency generator, operating in sub-threshold region for low power operation, and a low power temperature insensitive ring oscillator (TIRO) used as a reference clock signal for counter. The output of both the temperature sensor and the TIRO is given to a 12-bit asynchronous counter for digital output. The sensor, realized in 65 nm CMOS standard process, results in high resolution, small size and power consumption and is compatible with common CMOS process. The temperature sensor results in an average temperature resolution of 0.28 °C over the military range (–55 °C to 125 °C) and has an uncalibrated inaccuracy of +2.4/–2.1 °C for the same temperature range.

The rest of the paper is organized as follows. Section 2 discusses the block diagram and working principle of the proposed temperature sensor followed by the operation of different sub-blocks. The operation of the sensor is validated through post-layout simulations in Sect. 3. Finally, Sect. 4 presents the conclusion.

## 2 Proposed CMOS Based Temperature Sensor

The block diagram of the proposed temperature sensor is shown in Fig. 2. The different blocks of the temperature senor are: A PTAT current generator, reference current generator, a temperature insensitive ring oscillator and a 12-bit asynchronous counter. The sensor employs the concept of current to frequency translation, where the proportional to absolute temperature current ($I_{PTAT}$) generates a temperature dependent frequency at the capacitor output. The frequency variation due to temperature is given to the counter and a digital output is achieved with respect to the clock frequency of ring oscillator An *Enable* switch is used to reduce the static power consumption.

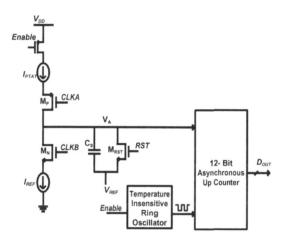

**Fig. 2.** Block diagram of temperature sensor.

### 2.1 Temperature Sensor Core

The schematic of the proposed temperature sensor is shown in Fig. 2. The reference current ($I_{PTAT}$) charges the capacitor ($C_S$) to voltage ($V_A$) with a slope of $I_{PTAT}/C_S$, whereas the PTAT current ($I_{PTAT}$) discharges the $C_S$ with a slope of $I_{REF}/C_S$. The PTAT current generator operating in sub-threshold region is adopted from [10], where the switched capacitor circuit is replaced by a resistor and a startup-circuit is added. The rate of charging and discharging of $C_S$ translates a varying waveform in time corresponding to temperature variations, as given by:

$$V_{A,max} - V_{REF} = (I_{PTAT}/C_S) \times t_r = (I_{REF}/C_S) \times t_f \qquad (1)$$

where $V_{A,max}$ is the maximum value of $V_A$ and $V_{REF}$, $C_S$, $t_r$ and $I_{REF}$ are considered as constants. Therefore, from Eq. (1):

$$t_r \propto I_{PTAT} \propto T \tag{2}$$

where T is the temperature (°C). Moreover, from Eq. (1), the $C_S$ has a negligible effect on the current charging and discharging as $I_{PTAT} \times t_r = I_{REF} \times t_f$. Therefore, the accuracy of the temperature sensor is insensitive to capacitor variation. The clock signals CLKA, CLKB and RST are generated from the CLK signal. The RST is used as $C_S$ reset signal. The timing diagram of all clock signals and the charging and discharging of $C_S$ at different temperatures (T$_1$, T$_2$, T$_3$ and T$_4$) is shown in Fig. 3 and the

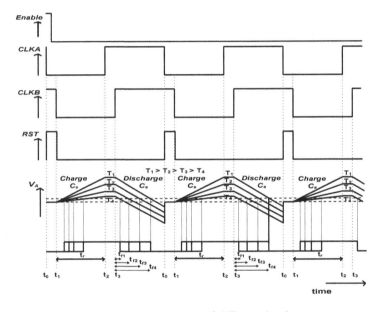

**Fig. 3.** Timing diagram of different signals.

**Table 1.** Operation of temperature sensor at different clock phases.

| Time interinterval | Clock signal | Operation |
|---|---|---|
| During $t_0$-$t_1$ | RST = HIGH | $V_A = V_{REF}$ |
| At $t_1$ | Falling edge of RST | $C_S$ is charged by $I_{PTAT}$ |
| At $t_2$ | Rising edge of CLKA | $M_P$ = OFF;<br>Charging of $C_S$ stops |
| During $t_2$-$t_3$ | CLKA = HIGH | $C_S$ holds on the charge, making $V_A$ constant |
| At $t_3$ | Rising edge of CLKB | $M_N$ = ON;<br>$I_{REF}$ sinks to discharge<br>$C_S$ |
| During<br>$t_3$-$t_0$ | CLKB = HIGH | Conversion is done;<br>Output holds a digital value |

operation is explained in Table 1. As the absolute temperature ($T$) and $t_f$ have linear relationship, the output count-value of counter represents the absolute temperature.

## 2.2  Temperature Insensitive Ring Oscillator

The TIRO, adopted from [17], consists of five stages, where each stage composed of a bootstrap circuit and a driver stage. The schematic of TIRO is shown in Fig. 4. The transistors $M_{P2}$ and $M_{N2}$ are used as switches controlled by the input signal ($V_{IN}$). The capacitors $C_{BP}$ and $C_{BN}$ behave as bootstrap circuit and are pre-charged by transistors MP1 and MN1, respectively. The $INV_N$ and $INV_P$ perform as drivers. To reduce the static power consumption, a NAND gate is employed at the first stage to prevent the unnecessary oscillations. The bootstrapped inverter gives an output swing of $-\beta V_{DD}$ to $2\beta V_{DD}$, where $\beta$ is the boosting efficiency and $V_{DD}$ is the power supply. The increase in the swing improves the driving capability of the transistors $M_{P2}$ and $M_{N2}$ and that of driver stage, so that a high frequency can be attained near the threshold voltage region. Besides the advantages highlighted in [17], this bootstrapped ring oscillator (BTRO) can be used as TIRO, if designed carefully. At a power supply approximately equal to the threshold voltage of MOS transistors, the BTRO operates in sub-threshold or linear

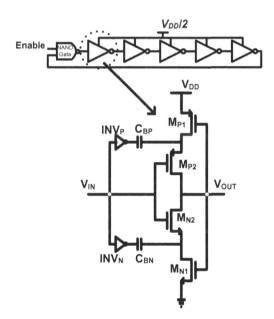

**Fig. 4.** 5-stage TIRO [17].

region during the turned-on transient. Therefore, for one period of oscillations, the BTRO has two operating behaviors during the tuned-on transient operation. The period of BTRO remains invariant with temperature due to the opposite temperature behavior during the tuned-on transients.

The total delay ($\tau_{total}$) of a single stage TIRO is given as:

$$\tau_{total} = \tau_{lin} + \tau_{sub} \tag{3}$$

where $\tau_{lin}$ and $\tau_{sub}$ are the delay in linear and sub-threshold region, respectively. Considering, the current flowing in both the linear and sub-threshold region are equal, therefore the driving capability of both nMOS and pMOS transistors is same. Then, the $\tau_{total}$ is given as:

$$\tau_{total} = \frac{k_f.C_L.(V_{DD} - V_o)}{\mu.C_{dep}.W/L.V_T^2.\exp(\frac{V_{DD}-V_{TH}}{nV_T})} + \frac{C_L(V_o - V_{50\%})}{\mu.C_{ox}.W/L.(\beta 2V_{DD} - V_{TH})} \tag{4}$$

where $C_{dep}$ and $C_{ox}$ are the depletion and oxide capacitors, $\mu$ is the effective mobility, $W/L$ is the aspect ratio of the transistors and $k_f$ is the fitting parameter.

### 2.3   Counter

The frequency signal generated from the temperature sensor converted into digital output through asynchronous counter. The TIRO is used as a reference signal for the counter. The size of the counter is chosen so that it does not overflows the countvalue, mostly at high temperatures. Although more bits can be added to the counter but it increases the static power and will also impact the dynamic power, as the most significant bit (MSB) switching activity is small. A 12-bit asynchronous counter is realized using JK flip-flops, AND gate and buffers, as shown in Fig. 5.

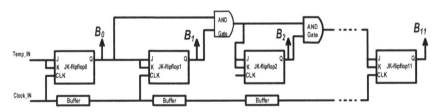

**Fig. 5.**  12-bit asynchronous counter.

## 3   Post-layout Simulation Results

The proposed temperature sensor is realized in 65-nm CMOS process, at (0.5–1) V power supply, and its operation is validated through post-layout simulation results using Cadence IC617 environment. The total area consumed by the sensor (excluding the input/output pads) is 0.024 mm$^2$, as shown in Fig. 6.

The variation of power consumption with respect to temperature (−55 °C to 125 °C) is shown in Fig. 7. The sensor consumes a power of 1.55 µW at room temperature. The variation of VPTAT with temperature is shown in Fig. 8. It is concluded that the slope of the VPTAT varies almost by 50% with rise in temperature.

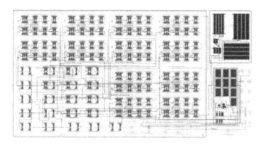

**Fig. 6.** Layout of the proposed temperature sensor.

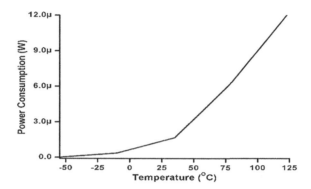

**Fig. 7.** Variation of power consumption with temperature.

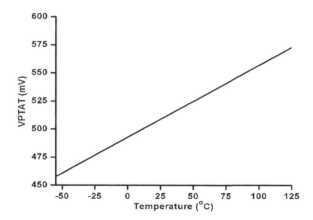

**Fig. 8.** Variation of VPTAT with temperature.

The variation of the reference clock signal used at the counter with temperature is shown in Fig. 9. As can be seen, the TIRO has a frequency of 50 kHz at room temperature and varies within ±10% of the clock frequency over the defined temperature range.

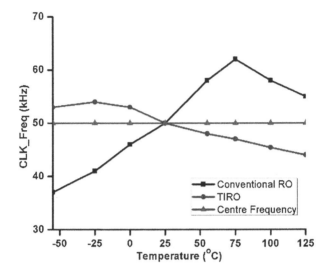

**Fig. 9.** Transient response of TIRO.

The characteristic plot of asynchronous counter is shown in Fig. 10. The count value is taken with respect to a calibration table. As the results are based on post-layout simulation, the actual calibration issues weren't dealt. The sensor has an uncalibrated accuracy of +2.4/–2.1 °C and a resolution of 0.28 °C. Then from the linear fitting curve for a value of $R^2 = 0.9978$, the temperature value is translated from the count value as:

$$Temperature = -0.285 \times count_{value} + 395.3 \tag{5}$$

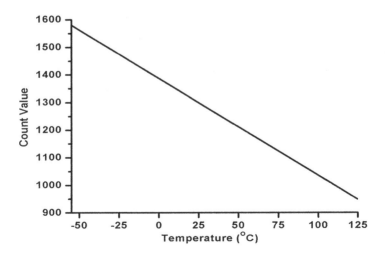

**Fig. 10.** Count characteristics for the temperature sensor.

**Table 2.** Performance comparison with related works.

| This Work[a] | | [11] | [12][a] | [15] | [16] |
|---|---|---|---|---|---|
| Year | 2017 | 2010 | 2014 | 2013 | 2013 |
| Sensor type | Temperature to frequency | Temperature to pulse | Temperature to frequency | Temperature to pulse | Temperature to pulse |
| Temperature range [°C] | −55 to 125 | 0 to 90 | −50 to 125 | 0 to 100 | −40 to 110 |
| CMOS technology [nm] | 65 | 350 | 65 | 350 | 65 |
| VDD [V] | 0.5–1 | 3.3 | 0.3–1 | 2.7–3.3 | 1.2 |
| Resolution [°C] | 0.28 | 0.05 | — | 0.2 | 0.34 |
| Calibration | Two | Two | — | Two | One |
| Accuracy [°C] | +2.4/−2.1[b] | ±0.6 | ±0.8 | +1.0/−0.8 | +2.7/−2.9 |
| Power consumption [μW] | 1.55 | 27.5 | 3.7 | 1.5 | 400 |
| Area [mm²] | 0.024 | 0.25 | — | 0.025 | 0.0013 |

[a]Post-layout simulation results
[b]Uncalibrated accuracy

# 4   Conclusion

In this paper, a low power, frequency to temperature based CMOS smart temperature, operating in sub-threshold region for a temperature range of −55 °C to +125 °C, is introduced in 65-nm CMOS process. The proposed temperature sensor employs two current sources: ideal and proportional to absolute temperature. Based on the charging and discharging of capacitor due to these two current sources with temperature, a varying frequency is generated. A 12-bit asynchronous counter is used for analog-to-digital conversion. The counter uses a slow reference clock of 50 kHz, generated on chip by employing a five stage temperature insensitive ring oscillator. The overall temperature sensor consumes a power and area of 1.55 μW and 0.024 mm2, respectively. The sensor achieves a resolution of 0.28 °C and an uncalibrated accuracy of +2.4/−2.1 °C for a temperature range of −55 °C to +125 °C. To improve the resolution and accuracy of the temperature sensor, vernier time to digital converter or analog-to-digital converter and dynamic element techniques or autozeroing techniques can be employed (Table 2).

# References

1. Bakker, A.: CMOS smart temperature sensors— an overview. In: 2002 Proceedings of the IEEE Sensors, vol. 2, pp. 1423–1427. IEEE (2002)
2. Pertijs, M.A.P., Huijsing, J.H.: Precision Temperature Sensors in CMOS Technology, 1st edn. Springer, Dordrecht (2006). https://doi.org/10.1007/1-4020-5258-8
3. Souri, K., Chae, Y., Makinwa, K.A.A.: A CMOS temperature sensor with a voltage-calibrated inaccuracy of ±0.15 °C (3σ) from −55 °C to 125 °C. IEEE J. Solid-State Circuits 48(1), 292–301 (2013)

4. Aita, L., Pertijs, M.A.P., Makinwa, K.A.A., Huijsing, J.H., Meijer, G.C.M.: Low-power CMOS smart temperature sensor with a batch-calibrated inaccuracy of ±0.25 °C (± 3σ) from −70 °C to 130 °C. IEEE Sens. J. **13**(5), 1840–1848 (2013)

5. Sebastiano, F., Breems, L.J., Makinwa, K.A.A., Drago, S., Leenaerts, D.M.W., Nauta, B.: A 1.2-V 10-μW NPN-based temperature sensor in 65-nm CMOS with an inaccuracy of 0.2 °C (3σ) from −70 °C to 125 °C. IEEE J. Solid-State Circuits **45**(12), 2591–2601 (2010)

6. Souri, K., Makinwa, K.A.A.: A 0.12 mm² 7.4 μW micropower temperature sensor with an inaccuracy of ±0.2 °C (3σ) from −30 °C to +125 °C. IEEE J. Solid-State Circuits **46**(7), 1693–1700 (2011)

7. Hwang, S., Koo, J., Kim, K., Lee, H., Kim, C.: A 0.008 mm² 500 μW 469 kS/s frequency-to-digital converter based CMOS temperature sensor with process variation compensation. IEEE Trans. Circuits Syst. I, Reg. Papers **60**(9), 2241–2248 (2013)

8. Chen, P., Chen, S.C., Shen, Y.S., Peng, Y.J.: All-digital time-domain smart temperature sensor with an inter-batch inaccuracy of −0.7 °C/+ 0.6 °C after one-point calibration. IEEE Trans. Circuits Syst. I, Reg. Papers **58**(5), 913–920 (2011)

9. Bashir, M., Sreehari Roa, P., KrishnaPrasad, K.S.R.: On-chip CMOS temperature sensor with current calibrated accuracy of −1.1 °C to +1.4 (3σ) from −20 °C to 150 °C. In: 19th International Symposium on VLSI Design and Test, pp. 1–5. IEEE, Ahmedabad (2015)

10. Bashir, M., Sreehari Roa, P., KrishnaPrasad, K.S.R.: An ultra-low power, 0.003mm² area, voltage to frequency based smart temperature sensor for −55 °C to +125 °C with one-point calibration. Turkish. J. Electr. Eng. Comput. Sci. **25**(4), 2995–3007 (2017)

11. Chen, C.C., Liu, W.J., Lin, S.H., Lin, C.C.: A CMOS oscillators-based smart temperature sensor for low-power low-cost systems. Procedia Eng. **47**, 92–95 (2012). Elsevier

12. Chen, S.W., Chang, M.H., Hsieh W.C., Hwang, W.: Fully on-chip temperature, process, and voltage sensors. In: Proceedings of 2010 IEEE International Symposium on Circuits and Systems, pp. 897–900. IEEE, Paris (2010)

13. Mohamad, S., Tang, F., Amira, A., Bermak, A., Benammar, M.: A low power oscillator based temperature sensor for RFID applications. In: Proceedings of Fifth Asia Symposium on Quality Electronic Design, ASQED 2013, pp. 50–54. IEEE, Penang (2013)

14. Nebhen, J., Meillère, S., Masmoudi, M., Seguin, J.L., Barthelemy H., Aguir, K.: A temperature compensated CMOS ring oscillator for wireless sensing applications. In: Proceedings of 10th IEEE International NEWCAS Conference, pp. 37–40. IEEE, Montreal (2012)

15. Chen, C.C., Chen, H.W.: A low-cost CMOS smart temperature sensor using a thermal-sensing and pulse-shrinking delay line. IEEE Sens. J. **14**(1), 278–284 (2014)

16. Kim, K., Lee, H., Kim, C.: 366-Ks/s 1.09-nJ 0.0013-mm² frequency-to-digital converter based CMOS temperature sensor utilizing multiphase clock. IEEE Trans. Very Large Scale Integr. (VLSI) Syst. **20**(12), 1–5 (2012)

17. Ho, Y., Yang, Y.S., Su, C.: A 0.2–0.6 V ring oscillator design using bootstrap technique. In: Proceedings of Asian Solid-State Circuits Conference (ASSCC) on Digital Technology Papers, pp. 333–336. IEEE, Jeju (2011)

# Design & Development of High Speed LVDS Receiver with Cold-Spare Feature in SCL's 0.18 μm CMOS Process

Munish Malik$^{(\boxtimes)}$, Ajay Kumar$^{(\boxtimes)}$, and H. S. Jatana$^{(\boxtimes)}$

Semiconductor Laboratory, Mohali, India
{munish,ajay_k,hsj}@scl.gov.in

**Abstract.** This paper presents design and implementation of LVDS Receiver chip in SCL's CMOS 0.18 μm, 3.3 V process. It is compatible with Low Voltage Differential Signaling (LVDS) standard. The receiver is designed for data rate of 1Gbps. This chip consists of four channels of LVDS receiver. The size of the chip is 2130 μm × 1500 μm and is packaged in 16 pin CFP (ceramic flat pack) package. The chip architecture, design, measured results are presented here. The radiation test such as total ionizing dose (TID) upto 300 K rad is performed on chip and single event effects (SEE) test using heavy ions Nickel ($Ni^{58}$) and Silver ($Ag^{107}$) has also been carried out. The performance under radiation environment is also been given.

**Keywords:** CMOS · LVDS · Radiation · Coldspare · SEE · TID

## 1 Introduction

The continuous advances in IC industry have made it possible to achieve high on- chip data rate (1 Gbps) and beyond. The off chip data rate (outside the silicon) has not been increased proportionally. In order to overcome this bottleneck and to cater the required high bandwidth for high end devices, a high speed physical layer interfaces was needed. The power consumption should also be low to extend the battery life at high data rate. The LVDS (Low Voltage Differential Signaling) proposed in [1] fulfils the required objective to reduce the gap between the on chip and off chip data signaling rate and power consumption and hence widely accepted. The other advantages offered by LVDS standard like better noise immunity to common mode noise and Electromagnetic Interference (EMI) immunity are inherent due to its differential nature [2] and it is also compatible with CMOS technology. Low power is due to the use of very small (100 mV to 400 mV) differential swing for logic transmission A typical LVDS link/interface [3] is depicted in Fig. 1.

In Fig. 1, LVDS driver/transmitter circuit at one point converts a digital logic signal into LVDS signal format characterized by a 350 mV differential voltage swing on a common mode of 1.2 V on the two output signal line of LVDS transmitter under typical condition. The receiver circuit placed at the other end point (on receiving IC/board); will convert this differential signal back into a single ended CMOS logic signal format (usually at a lower voltage level, 0 V and core voltage $V_{DD}$). The LVDS receiver must

© Springer Nature Singapore Pte Ltd. 2017
B. K. Kaushik et al. (Eds.): VDAT 2017, CCIS 711, pp. 667–678, 2017.
https://doi.org/10.1007/978-981-10-7470-7_63

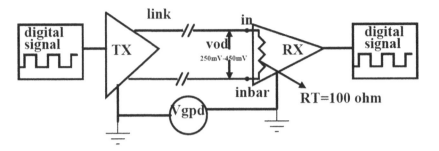

**Fig. 1.** Typical LVDS link

be able to tolerate a 1 V shift between the ground reference of the Transmitter (Tx)/ driver and the Receiver (Rx) ground [1]. Therefore, if an LVDS Transmitter is transmitting a 400 mV signal at 1.2 V common mode, then this signal can be seen at input of Receiver as either of 0 V or 0.4 V (due to −1 V ground potential difference between Tx and Rx) or 2 V or 2.4 V (due to 1 V ground potential difference between Tx and Rx). Hence an LVDS receiver should be able to handle input common mode range from 0 V to 2.4 V. To support this wide common mode voltage (0 V to 2.4 V) requirement for low $V_{DD}$(<3.3 V) and operating at speed of 1 Gb/s or more makes the design of receiver especially the input stage a challenging task. This chip is intended to be part for designing space system. The natural space environment constitutes different type of energetic particle and solar cosmic rays, galactic cosmic rays. The electronics devices when subjected to operate for long term under natural space environment exhibit malfunctioning from their intended operation due to NMOS/PMOS device threshold shifts, increased leakage current and power consumption, timing changes. So, it becomes imperative to test the performance of this chip under radiation environment. The TID and SEE test are required to assure the radiation hardness of electronics devices meant for space applications.

# 2    LVDS Receiver

## 2.1    Block Diagram

The designed LVDS receiver block diagram is shown in Fig. 2. It consists of Pre-driver, Latch and Buffer amplifier block. The Pre-driver block receive the input from data bus. It has the capability to support input common mode (0 V–2.4 V) at very high frequency (≤500 MHz). Output of pre driver is driving a latch circuit which is followed by a buffer to drive capacitive load.

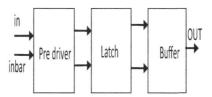

**Fig. 2.** Block diagram of receiver

## 2.2  Pre-driver Stage

The pre driver stage should have the capability to support wide input common mode (0 V–2.4 V). Meeting this specification with 3.3 V supply; is very daunting task keeping in view data speed is in 1 Gb/s. The conventional differential amplifier using PMOS/ NMOS in input differential stage will not meet the objective of supporting required input common mode range (0 V to 2.4 V). The input stage employing only NMOS transistors perform better for high range of input common mode range as the overdrive voltage($V_{GS}$-$V_T$) increases with increase in common mode range and input stage designed with PMOS transistors performs better for lower range of input common mode range as the overdrive voltage($V_{GS}$-$V_T$) decreases with increase in common mode range. The use of both NMOS and PMOS transistors in design of input stage can handle rail to rail common mode range if designed properly. The circuit of Pre-driver stage is shown in Fig. 3. This stage can support common mode range (0 V to 2.4 V). During designing this circuit, there is a choice of using either NMOS source follower followed by PMOS differential pair or PMOS source follower followed by NMOS differential pair. But the first choice (NMOS source follower followed by PMOS differential pair) is preferable because of its low output common mode which makes it feasible to work directly even at lower voltage in the second stage. As NMOS source follower will not work at low common mode voltage. So to support very low input common mode voltages another PMOS differential pair(inner) was added in parallel. Now the circuit can support full rail to rail input common mode voltages. If we analyze this circuit from DC signal point of view, both the PMOS differential pairs will be conducting at very low common mode voltages (even though only inner pair carries ac signals) and hence cause total current of $I_{ss}$ into the load resistor R. But at very high common modes only outer pair will conduct and current through R is only $I_{ss}/2$. Therefore the output common mode of this circuit will vary from $I_{ss} \times R$ to $I_{ss} \times R/2$. To avoid this condition it is better to divert half of the DC current from load resistance at very low common mode voltages so that current flowing through load remains constant.

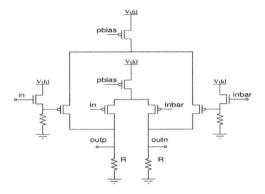

**Fig. 3.** Pre-driver stage

A biasing circuit was added as shown in Fig. 4 to cancel the common mode feed forward. Now the current mirrors will make sure $I_{ss}/2$ current will flow through them and hence only $I_{ss}/2$ current will flow through R for all common mode voltages. In order to handle the high speed data, the bandwidth of circuit should also be high ($\geq$500 MHz).

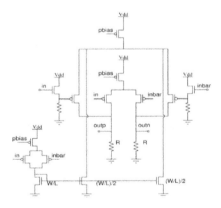

**Fig. 4.** Biasing circuit

### 2.3 Latch

The output common mode in the first stage was kept around 0.5 V in order to work directly with a PMOS latch which is based on comparator [4] and shown in Fig. 5. This is the most widely used component in high speed comparator designs. The hysteresis can be achieved using this structure by choosing the appropriate aspect ratio of transistors m3, m5 and m4, m8.

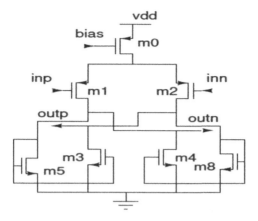

**Fig. 5.** Latch circuit

## 2.4  Buffer

Buffer consist of two stages, first stage is complementary differential amplifier based amplifier as shown in Fig. 6 followed by inverter chain where each inverter is progressively sized up in order to drive the high capacitive load. In this circuit the output swing can be very close to the difference between the two supply rails. This large output swing makes interfacing this circuit to ordinary CMOS logic gates straightforward, since it provides a large margin for variations in the logic threshold of the gates.

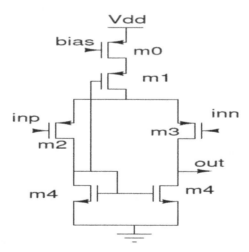

**Fig. 6.** First stage of buffer circuit

### 2.5 Cold-Spare Feature

Many circuit applications (specifically space, military) require the need for redundancy in which a particular function is provided using redundant circuit such that, if one of the circuits fails to provide the desired function, at least one of the other redundant circuits can take over to provide that function. Redundant circuits may operate in either an active mode or a standby mode. In the standby mode, one of the redundant circuits is active to provide the desired function, but the other redundant circuits are on standby. That is, the output of the redundant circuits on standby is not used for any purpose. When the active circuit fails, one of the other redundant is made active. Cold spare circuits are redundant circuits that are not powered up and provide no signal to the output. Here, for Cold-Spare feature, input pads were modified to keep the $I_{off} < 10 \, \mu A$ during cold spare mode. This can be achieved by blocking or eliminating the p-n junction which get forward bias when $V_{DD} = 0$ V and input is active (say at 3 V).

## 3   Layout

The layout of quad LVDS Receiver chip is shown in Fig. 7. The size of the chip is 2130 $\mu$m × 1500 $\mu$m. This chip has been fabricated in SCL's 0.18 $\mu$m CMOS process at SCL, Mohali. The layout technique [5] such as common centroid has been used to improve matching, use of guard rings, digital part and analogue section are spaced apart sufficiently to reduce the interference from digital circuit. The resistors used in the circuits are of poly type due to low process variation. The substrate and n-well contacts are also provided sufficiently as they aid in reducing the substrate resistance and well resistance and improves latch-up immunity of circuit.

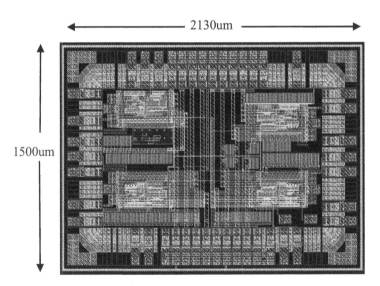

**Fig. 7.** Layout of LVDS receiver

# 4    Test and Measurement

A test setup has been prepared to evaluate the performance of the receiver. The packaged device as shown in Fig. 8 is mounted on a socket on a two layer general purpose PCB. Multiple 0.1 µF decoupling capacitors are placed near to IC power pins. The input (in) signal is fed with 5 cm RG-316 cable. The signals were measured using 16 GHz oscilloscope.

**Fig. 8.** Package device

Oscilloscope measurements are carried out in averaging mode (4096 samples avg.) to improve measurement accuracy. Optimizations are carried out w.r.t. high speed signaling. The measured parameters include supply current, input voltage high/low, output voltage levels, and propagation delay. The measured results (DC electrical parameters) are given in Table 1. All measurement has been performed over temperature range −40 °C and 125 °C to verify the robustness of the LVDS Receiver. The measured results are depicted in Figs. 9, 10 and Table 1. The $I_{CC}$ measurement over the temperature range is done keeping inputs at steady state. The Delay measurement shown in Fig. 10 over a temperature range from −40 °C and 125 °C is performed at 1 MHz. In order to evaluate the performance against common mode variation, the common mode of input signal from 0.05 V to 2.55 V is varied as sinusoidal wave of 100 MHz with differential signal of 200 mV overriding it at data rate of 1 Gb/s. The corresponding output is shown in Fig. 11. The simulation is done at typical corner with 3.3 V power supply. The Fig. 12 shows the dynamic current consumption over range of frequency.

**Table 1.**  Measured results

| Parameters | Value |
| --- | --- |
| Delay (typical) | 4.9 ns |
| Dynamic current at 200 MHz, $C_{load} = 10$ pF | 93 mA |
| Static current (enable) | 32 mA |
| Static current (disable) | 3 mA |
| Power off input current | 10 uA |

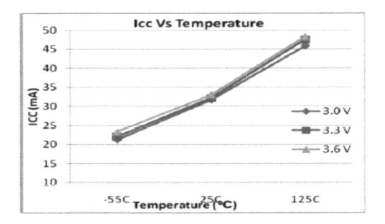

**Fig. 9.** $I_{CC}$ Vs. temperature

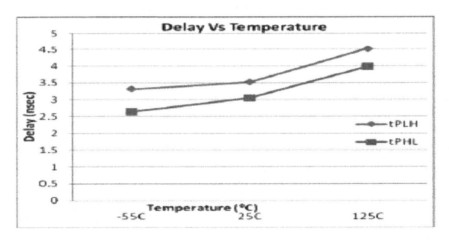

**Fig. 10.** Delay Vs. temperature

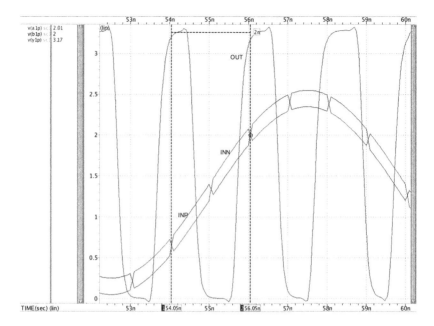

**Fig. 11.** Output with varying common mode signal

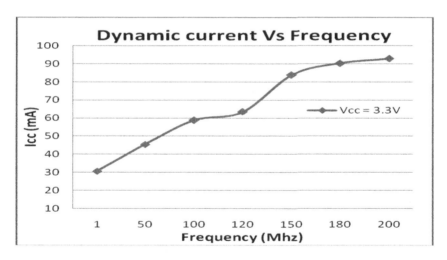

**Fig. 12.** Dynamic current Vs. temperature

## 4.1 Radiation Testing Results

Radiation test to on-board electronics is separated into two categories: Total ionizing dose (TID) and single event effects (SEE) [6]. Total ionizing dose (TID) is accumulative long-term degradation of the device when exposed to ionizing radiation.

The gamma irradiation (TID) was carried out at the Gama chamber, SCL Mohali; using a Co60 (Cobalt 60) radiation source up to the total dose of 300 K rad. The Dose rate of Source was 56.12 rad/s. All the $V_{DD}$ pins of LVDS are supplied by +3.3 V. All $V_{SS}$ pins are grounded. The differential input to all four receivers was 400 mV. The functional tests were performed on non-irradiated and irradiated chips using automated test setup developed in visual basic. During the radiation exposure DUT was in DC biased state as explained above and supply current was monitored. The parameters measured during irradiation measurements are static $I_{DD}$. The $I_{DD}$ measured on pre-radiated device was 31.56 mA. The $I_{DD}$ = 32.05 mA was measured for TID 300 K rad. So, There was no significant change in the device current up to 300 K of radiation dose as shown in Fig. 13.

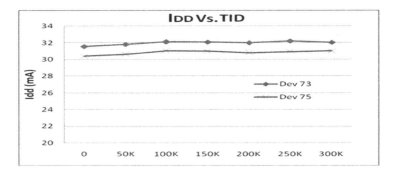

**Fig. 13.** $I_{DD}$ current Vs. TID

Single event effects (SEE) are phenomenon caused by highly energetic particle (such as heavy ion) passing through an integrated circuit. The intense heavy ion environment encountered in space application can cause a variety of transients and destructive effects such as single event upset (SEU), single event latch up (SEL), single event burnout in devices. These phenomenons generate an immediate malfunctioning of one or more transistors which can then influence the entire circuit. The setup consisted of a General Purpose Scattering Chamber (GPSC) beam line of the Pelletron facility at a dedicated centre at Inter University Accelerator Centre (IUAC), New Delhi. The DUT board comprises of the pair of LVDS Transmitter and Receiver is shown in Fig. 14. A custom Automatic program with user friendly interface that communicate with instrument and DUT for running the experiments. The test device is mounted on DUT board kept inside a vacuum chamber that is packaged in 16 pin flat pack is directly soldered on the PCB. During SEE testing, the packaging lid is opened to expose the corresponding die to high energy particle. For SEE test, two heavy ions were considered, Nickel ($Ni^{58}$) and Silver ($Ag^{107}$) because of their high energy. The SEE test results are shown in Table 2. It was observe that the $Ni^{+9}$ ions having energy of 120 meV could penetrate up to 20 μm and could transfer LET of 30 MeV-cm$^2$/mg in 20 min of time during test. While $Ag^{+11}$ ions having energy of 140 meV could penetrate 17 μm and transferred LET of 50 MeV-cm$^2$/mg in 20 min of time during test. During this time no upset or increase in current is seen.

SEU/SEL test was done on LVDS Receiver devices at 50 MeV-cm$^2$/mg of LET and no upsets were reported.

**Fig. 14.** DUT board used for SEE test

**Table 2.** SEE test results

| Ion | Fluence ion/cm$^2$ | LET MeV-cm$^2$/mg | SET count | Cross-section cm$^2$ | Device current $I_{DD}$ |
|---|---|---|---|---|---|
| $^{107}$Ag$^9$ | $10^6$ | 50 0 | 0 | 0 | 0.0447 A |
| $^{58}$Ni$^9$ | $10^6$ | 30 0 | 0 | 0 | 0.0447 A |

**Table 3.** Performance comparison

| Parameter | 3 | 7 | Ours |
|---|---|---|---|
| Technology/VDD | 0.13 µm/3.3 V/1.2 V | 0.35 µm/3.3 V | 0.18 µm/3.3 V |
| Temp range | 0 °C to 125 °C | −40 °C to 150 °C | −40 °C to 125 °C |
| Load (pF) | # | 1 | 10 |
| Delay (ns) | 1.2 | 1.4 | 4.9 |
| Area (mm$^2$) | 0.066 | 0.081 | 3.15* |
| Data rate (Gb/s) | 1.3 | 1.2 | 1 |
| TID (K rad) | NA | NA | 300 |
| SET (counts) | NA | NA | 0 |

*complete chip consist of four channel of LVDS Rx
#load is equivalent to inverter where pmos, nmos sized as 6 µm/0.13 µm, 3 µm/0.13 um

# 5 Conclusion

A Quad LVDS Receiver chip has been designed which meets LVDS standard. This design is suitable for high reliability system design requiring cold-spare functionality for redundant circuit. The performance of the designed chip is compared with other works as specified in Table 3. The simulated data rate is 1 Gbps. The performance of chip has also been evaluated in radiation environment (TID up to 300 K rad & SEE up to 50 Mev-cm$^2$/mg) and no significant change in specifications has been reported.

**Acknowledgement.** The authors also wish to acknowledge the contribution of Gourav Srivastav, Sachin Sharma, Th. Gurmeet Singh, Sunil Bhatnagar from Semi-Conductor Laboratory, Chandigarh (India) during various stages of testing and packaging.

# References

1. Draft standard for Low-Voltage differential signals (LVDS) for Scalable Coherent Interface (SCI) Draft 1.3, 27 November 1985
2. AN-5017 LVDS fundamentals Fairchild Semiconductor application note, December 2000
3. Mandal, G., Mandal, P.: Low-Power LVDS Receiver for 1.3 Gbps Physical Layer interface. In: ISCAS 2005, vol. 3, pp 2180–2183 (2005)
4. Allen, P.E., Holberg, D.R.: CMOS Analog Circuit Design, 2nd edn. Oxford University Press
5. Hasting, A.: The Art of Analog Layout. Prentice Hall, Upper Saddle River (2001)
6. Maurer, R.H., Fraeman, M.E., Martin, M.N., Roth, D.R.: Harsh Environment: space radiation enviornment, effects, mittigation. Johns Hopkins APL Tech. Dig. **28**(1), 17–29 (2008)
7. Boni, A., Pierazzi, A., Vecchi, D.: LVDS I/O interface for Gb/s-per-pin operation in 0.35-μm CMOS. IEEE J. Solid-State Circuits **36**(4), 706–711 (2001)

# Architecture and CAD

# Fast FPGA Placement Using Analytical Optimization

Sameer Pawanekar[⊠] and Gaurav Trivedi

Department of Electronics and Electrical Engineering,
Indian Institute of Technology Guwahati, Guwahati, India
{p.sameer,trivedi}@iitg.ernet.in

**Abstract.** FPGA (Field Programmable Gate Arrays) placement consumes half of the runtime of the design flow. As the number of cells are increasing due to increase in design complexity and size, this problem is gaining importance. Typically placement of blocks in FPGA are based on simulated annealing algorithms. Since the FPGA designs are smaller compared with their ASIC counterparts, simulated annealing algorithms are feasible as the runtime to place them is less. However, as the design size and complexity is increasing, simulated annealing algorithms and genetic programming based algorithms tend to be slower. In this paper, our work is targetted towards improving the runtime of placement in FPGAs. We propose a novel algorithm which is based on nonlinear analytical methods. This method uses density penalty approach, wherein, the spreading of blocks across the die is controlled by the square of penalty for the uneven regions across the die. Our method is fast and, when compared with VPR, we improve the runtime by 750% while providing a reasonably good solution for the placement.

## 1 Introduction

In modern FPGA (Field programmable Gate Array) designs based on nanometer technology, there are millions of transistors on the FPGA. The designs sizes are growing and FPGA tools have to support large scale designs. Large designs have large wirelength which is a bottleneck for speed and performance of the design on FPGA. Placement of blocks on FPGA plays an important role in reducing the wirelength.

The placement procedure identifies the coordinates of all the blocks of the design in such a way that the wirelength of the overall design gets reduced. Typically, wirelength is modeled as HPWL (Half Perimeter Wire Length), also known as bounding box wirelength, is commonly used metric to report wirelength. HPWL is the semi-perimeter of the smallest rectangle that encloses all the cells of a net. Then, sum of semi-perimeters of all the nets are considered to report overall HPWL.

There are several algorithms to perform FPGA placement which can be categorized in three categories: (1) Simulated Annealing (2) Genetic (3) Partition

© Springer Nature Singapore Pte Ltd. 2017
B. K. Kaushik et al. (Eds.): VDAT 2017, CCIS 711, pp. 681–693, 2017.
https://doi.org/10.1007/978-981-10-7470-7_64

Driven. Simulated annealing is the commonly used algorithm for FPGA based placement, example VPR [1]. It optimizes the wirelength efficiently, particularly for smaller designs. However, for large designs, simulated annealing takes a long time. Similarly, algorithms based on genetic methods take a long time to find a solution and work efficiently only for smaller design sizes. Partition driven placement in FPGA relies on the quality of bisection of the netlist. The netlist of design is recursively bisected until there are very few cells in the partitioned netlist. In the end, simulated annealing is performed on the leaf cells of the partitioned output.

Modern FPGA design requires faster algorithm for placement as the design sizes are large. We present an analytical method, which is faster approach to FPGA placement. We approximate the HPWL as log-sum-exponent wirelength and solve differential equations to find a good solution.

The organization of rest of the paper is as follows. In Sect. 2 we present the related work from literature. We define our placement model in Sect. 3. This is followed by the implementation details in Sect. 4. We present the experimental results in Sect. 5 and finally conclude in Sect. 6.

## 2   Related Work

In this section we briefly describe the related works from the literature which will be beneficial to the reader. Jamieson et al. [13], introduced supergenes in a placement method based on genetic algorithm. The introduction of supergenes duplicates genes in the genome and improves the clock speed of the FPGA designs greatly. In their implementation, they controlled the supergene for placement problem via a binary function.

Collier et al. [6] show that traditional recombination operators used in genetic algorithms are not efficient when employed in FPGA placement methods. Thus, they propose new recombination operator which obtain the performance improvement over their traditional counterparts when tested with standard benchmarks.

Legalization is an important step in the placement tools which can cause an increase in wirelength if not implemented efficiently. Wang et al. [20] present a novel window based FPGA legalization method which removes all the overlaps occurring from an analytical placement of blocks.

Huang and Zhang [12] propose a parallel algorithm to reduce the runtime of simulated annealing method. The proposed algorithm moves the blocks concurrently by multiple threads that are run on different processors without affecting the quality of solution significantly.

Gharibian et al. [10] investigated whether system level information can be derived from the input netlist and how this information can be used in performing placement of the blocks. They proposed a reconstruction algorithm which creates meaningful coarse structure of the design.

Fobel et al. [8,9] implemented simulated annealing algorithm on multicore processors. The accelerated the simulated annealing algorithm by means of efficiently generating sets of independent swap operations with the help of GPU programming.

Bostelmann and Sawitzki [2] proposed that instead of randomly initializing the coordinates of the cells, they can be initialized with a self-organizing map. This map is generated from the structural information of the input netlist. This creates training vectors which are used to provide initial solution to the simulated annealing algorithm which decreases runtime.

Pattison et al. [17] proposed analytical engine for FPGA placement. They parallelized the serial analytical algorithm StarPlace and achieved speed up of 13× compared to its serial counterpart.

Our contribution in this paper is a fast method to perform FPGA placement which involves solving differential equations. Our method is fast and produces quality results.

# 3   Analytical Placement Model

In this section we present basic definition of the analytical model used in our work. We use analytical techniques and solve differential equations to solve FPGA placement problem. In the first step, clustering is performed on the input netlist which reduces the problem size. As second step, optimization of the objection function is performed using conjugate gradient method. Legalization of the layout is performed using tetris method as the final step for FPGA placement.

Our method is based on nonlinear analytical placement method proposed in [15]. This approach has also been implemented by [4,5,14]. In this approach, placement problem is regarded as *constrained nonlinear optimization problem*.

The placement problem is physical placement of a hypergraph (netlist) $H = (V, E)$, where $V = \{v_1, v_2, \ldots, v_n\}$ represents the cells and $E = \{e_1, e_2, \ldots, e_n\}$ represents the hyperedges present in $H$. The objective of placement is to find the optimum coordinates of all the cells in $V$, such that the overall HPWL is minimum, there does not exist any overlap among the cells, and all the cells legally occupy the given rows of the layout within the placement region. HPWL is define as Eq. 1.

$$W(x, y) = \sum_{e_k \in e_H} (\max_{\forall i,j \in n_H} |x_i - x_j| + \max_{\forall i,j \in n_H} |y_i - y_j|) \qquad (1)$$

where, $x_i$ and $y_i$ are the $x$ and $y$ coordinates of the movable cell $v_i$.

The die area is divided uniformly into bins and we aim to minimize the overall HPWL with the constraint that cell area present in each of the bins is equalized. This problem can be expressed by the Eq. 2.

$$minW(x, y)s.t.\ \ D_p(x, y) \leq A_g \qquad (2)$$

where, $W(x, y)$ is the wirelength, $D_p(x, y)$ is the potential which is the total area of movable cells in the bin $b$ and $A_g$ is the maximum area of movable cells in bin $b$,

$W(x, y)$ is neither smooth nor differentiable due to which it is not possible to minimize it directly. There are many approximations of HPWL in literature which are smooth and differentiable. Examples of such smooth HPWL functions are quadratic wirelength [7], $L_p$ norm wirelength used in [3] and log-sum-exp wirelength proposed by [15]. We use the log-sum-exp wirelength as it is closer to HPWL and the wirelength parameter is useful to make the wirelength function smoother.

$$W(x, y) = \alpha \sum_{e \in E} (log \sum_{v_k \in e} exp(x_k/\alpha) + log \sum_{v_k \in e} exp(-x_k/\alpha)$$
$$+ log \sum_{y_k \in e} exp(y_k/\alpha) + log \sum_{y_k \in e} exp(-y_k/\alpha)) \tag{3}$$

As the density function $D_p(x, y)$ in Eq. (2) is neither differentiable nor smooth, mPL [3] uses inverse Laplace transformation to smooth the density, whereas APlace [14] uses a bell-shaped function for each cell to cell the density. We use bell-shaped function, $D_b(x, y)$ (from [14]) into our framework which is expressed by Eq. 4.

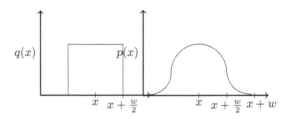

**Fig. 1.** Potential function $q(x)$ is non-smooth whereas $p(x)$ is smooth.

$$D_b(x, y) = \sum_{v \in V} P_x(g, v) P_y(g, v) \tag{4}$$

where, overlap of the cell $v$ and the bin $b$ along the $x$ and $y$ directions is represented by $P_x$ and $P_y$ respectively. A bell-shaped potential function, defined by Eq. (5), is used to smooth $P_x$.

$$p_x(g, v) = \begin{cases} 1 - 2\frac{d_x^2}{w_b^2} & 0 \le d_x \le \frac{w_b}{2} \\ \frac{2}{w_b^2}(d_x - w_b)^2, & w_b/2 \le d_x \le w_b \\ 0, & w_b \le d_x \end{cases} \tag{5}$$

The distance, in the $x$ direction, between the cell $v$ and the bin $b$ is represented by $d_x$ and $w_b$ represents the width of the cell. Similarly, potential $p_y$ is computed along $y$ direction considering the height $h_b$, in place of its width. The non-smooth and smoothed potential functions are shown in Fig. 1. The different variables used in this paper are described in Table 1.

**Table 1.** List of variables used in this work

| | |
|---|---|
| $D_b$ | Density of bin $g_i$ |
| $P_b$ | Potential of bin $g_i$ |
| $A_b$ | Maximum density of bin $g_i$ |
| $w_i, h_i$ | Width and Height of the cell $v_i$ |
| $x_i, y_i$ | Centre coordinates for the cell $v_i$ |
| $w_b, w_h$ | Width and Height of the bin $b$ |
| $\alpha$ | Wirelength parameter |
| $s$ | Step size |
| $\lambda$ | Objective function parameter |

# 4  Details of Implementation of the Proposed FPGA Placer

This section presents the implementation details of our work. The working flow of the proposed method is outlined in the Fig. 2.

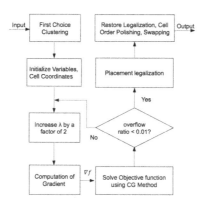

**Fig. 2.** Flow of the proposed FPGA placement algorithm

## 4.1  First Choice Clustering

Placement tools commonly employ clustering to reduce the problem size, thereby improving the runtime of the placement methods. While clustering does degrade the quality of placement solution slightly, it has greater advantage in terms of the reduction of runtime. In the literature, there are two types of clustering that are commonly used. (1) First Choice Clustering and (2) Best Choice Clustering. In first choice clustering, the grouping of cell is based purely on netlist information, whereas, in best choice clustering the grouping is performed based on the physical location of the placed cells.

As a first step of the proposed FPGA placement flow, we perform clustering (first choice clustering) of the input netlist. The clustering is performed recursively till the number of cells/clusters gets reduce to a given number $n_max$. THe clustering algorithm used in our work is derived from the First choice clustering method described in [3]. At first, the cells are sorted in the non-increasing order of their degrees (connectivity index). Then, each cell is considered and affinities for its neighbouring cell (cell with which it shares an hyperedge) is calculated. The affinity between the cells $s$ and $t$ is defined by Eq. 6.

$$r_{st} = \sum_{e \in E|s,t \in e} \frac{w(e)}{(|e| - 1)area(e)} \tag{6}$$

---

**Algorithm 1.** Multilevel FPGA placement Algorithm

**Input:** Netlist $H_0$: FPGA cells placement
**Output:** $(x^*, y^*)$ optimal cell coordinates

1: First Choice Clustering
2: Let FCC be 0 to $L$                                      ▷ $L$ is coarsest
3: Random initialization of cell coordinates
4: **for** $level = L$ to $level = 0$ **do**
5:     Calculate the number of bins.
6:     Compute the potential of each bin
7:     Initialze $\lambda_0$, $iter = 0$
8:     **while** $overflow\_ratio > 0.1$ **do**
9:         Solve min $W(x, y) + \lambda_{iter} \sum (D_b - A_b)^2$
10:        $iter = iter + 1$
11:        $\lambda_{iter} = 2 * \lambda_{iter-1}$
12:        Compute $overflow\_ratio$
13:        **if then**$overflow\_ratio < 0.01$ and $level == 0$
14:            break
15:        **end if**
16:     **end while**
17: **end for**
18: Legalization

---

### 4.2 Quadratic Optimization

In line 3 of our FPGA placement algorithm we perform quadratic optimization. This step is performed for the case when the number of terminal cells placed at the periphery of die area are more than 20. This step is useful to provide an initial solution to the conjugate gradient optimizer discussed later in this section. A similar approach has been used previously in the placement tools [16,19].

Consider a graph $G = (V, E)$ where $V$ and $E$ are the set of vertices and edges, respectively. Further, let $w_{ij} > 0$ be the edge weight of an edge $e_{ij} \in E$.

The *quadratic objective* function, $\phi_G$, is defined as

$$\phi_G(x, y) = \sum_{e_{ij} \in E} w_{ij}[(x_i - x_j)^2 + (y_i - y_j)^2]. \tag{7}$$

Using the matrix representation for $x$ and $y$ components, we have,

$$\phi_G(x, y) = \frac{1}{2}x^T M_x x + c_x^T x + constant. \tag{8}$$

Let $m_{ij}$ be the entries of $i^{th}$ row and $j^{th}$ column of the matrix $M_x$. Further, let $\frac{1}{2}w_{ij}(x_i^2 + x_j^2 - 2x_i x_j)$ be the cost in the $x$ direction between two movable cells $x_i$ and $x_j$. The values in matrix $M_x$ are filled as per to the following rules.

(i) Add $w_{ij}$ to $m_{ii}$ and $m_{jj}$.
(ii) Subtract $w_{ij}$ from $m_{ij}$ and $m_{ji}$. Let $\frac{1}{2}w_{if}(x_i^2 + x_f^2 - 2x_i x_f)$ be the cost in the $x$ direction between a movable cell $x_i$ and a fixed cell $x_f$.
(iii) Add $w_{if}$ to $m_{ii}$.
(iv) Subtract $w_{if}x_f$ from the vector $c_x$ at row $i$.

We solve Eq. (9) to minimize the objective function defined in the Eq. (7). Since the matrix $M_x$ is positive definite, the minimum of $\phi_G(x, y)$ is obtained by solving the Eq. (9),

$$M_x + c_x = 0. \tag{9}$$

## 4.3   Computation of Density and Potential and Their Gradients

An auxilliary grid is formed over the placement area such that uniform rectangular bins are formed. The number of rectangular bins is roughly equal to the square root of the number of blocks in the coarsened hypergraph which is considered for placement. Thus, the number of bins $N_x$ and $N_y$ along $x$ and $y$ direction respectively are $N_x = N_y = \sqrt{n_{max}}$ for the first level. The dimensions of the bins change in the next level as the number of cells in the netlist increase. Once the cells coordinates are initialized, we compute the potential at the bins, gradient of potential at the bins, density at the bins and density gradient at the bins from Eqs. 4 and 5, which are required for solving nonlinear equations.

## 4.4   Solving the Objective Function Using Conjugate Gradient

We solve Eq. 10 at line 9 of our Algorithm 1. This steps is repeated periodically whenever there is an update in the auxilliary grid as shown by Algorithm 1.

$$min(W(x, y) + \lambda \sum_b (D_b(x, y) - A_b)^2) \tag{10}$$

The placement solution depends on the optimization efficiency at this step and thus is critical to the placement solution. Equation 10 consists of two parts.

(1) Wirelength and (2) density penalty. These two parts are added after multiplying the density penalty by a factor of $\lambda$. When the value of $\lambda$ is very small, optimization happens only for wirelength, where cells are brought closer to each other to reduce wirelength. As the value of $\lambda$ increases, density penalty part of the sum increases, and the cells begin to spread around the placement area. Thus, a careful balance of these two parts is crucial to the quality of solution obtained at this step. This balance is obtained by initialization of $\lambda$ with appropriate value which is given by Eq. 11.

$$\lambda = 2\frac{\sum(|\frac{\partial W(x,y)}{\partial x} + \frac{\partial W(x,y)}{\partial y}|)}{\sum_{x_i,y_i}\sum_{bins}|\hat{D}_b - A_b|.(|\frac{\partial \hat{D}_b}{\partial x}| + |\frac{\partial \hat{D}_b}{\partial y}|)} \tag{11}$$

For optimization at subsequent levels, $\lambda$ is calculated as $\lambda_{level-1} = \frac{\lambda_{level}}{4}$. When optimization at a particular level, the value of $\lambda$ is increased by multiplication of 2. As the value of $\lambda$ is increased the cells spread around the placement area and even distribution of the density across the bins is observed. This can be seen from Fig. 3. In order to evaluate the spreading of cells across die area, [5] a parameter called *overflow_ratio*. We use the same parameter *overflow_ratio* in our placement flow which is given in Eq. 12.

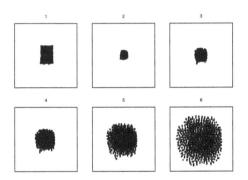

**Fig. 3.** This figure shows how spreading of cells take place for the design alu4. As the value $\lambda$ is increased by multiplication of 2, the cells spread gradually across the placement region.

$$overflow\_ratio = \frac{\sum \max(D_b(x,y) - A_b, 0)}{\sum TotalArea} \tag{12}$$

In order to solve Eq. 10 we use Conjugate Gradient method as described in Algorithm 2.

### 4.5   Legalization of Analytical FPGA Placement

Legalization of FPGA blocks is an important and final step in our flow. During optimization, cells may have overlaps with each other, which is not a legal

---

**Algorithm 2.** Conjugate Gradient Method

---

**Input:** $f(x)$: objective function and $x_0$: initial solution
**Output:** optimal $x^*$

$d_0 = 0;\ g_0 = 0;$
**while** $f(x_k) < f(x_{k-1})$ **do**
  Calculate Directions of gradient $g_k = \nabla f(x_k)$;
  Calculate Polak-Ribiere coefficient $PR$
  $PR = \dfrac{g_k^T (g_k - g_{k-1})}{\|g_{k-1}\|^2};$
  Calculate Conjugate Directions $d_k = -g_k + PRd_{k-1}$;
  Calculate Step Size $\alpha_k = s/\|d_k\|_2$;
  Update the solution $x_k = x_{k-1} + \alpha_k d_k$;
**end while**

---

solution for performing the next steps of FPGA design flow. We use Tetris [11] algorithm for legalization of the solution obtained after Algorithm 1. At first we multiply the x-coordinates of all the cells by a scaling factor (value of scaling factor used in our experiments is 0.99) Secondly, the cells are sorted based on their x-coordinates in increasing order of their values. Then, starting from the cell with the smallest x-coordinate, we aim to find a position for the cell in the layout. Each row is considered for the placement of the cell and the row for which HPWL is least is chosen as the destination of that cell. We perform similar search along the rows for all the ordered cells. With legalization, we observe an increase in HPWL (5%) in the final output. This increase is as per expectation because large number of cells are displaced from their original position from the optimized solution. The legalization method consumes 2% of the overall runtime.

## 5 Experiments and Results

The proposed FPGA placer has been written in C language. The number of lines of our code is approximately 10,000. We have selected gcc as the compiler with "-O3" optimization directive for the compiler. We have conducted our experiments on a 1.6 GHz, 64-bit machine running on OSX operating system.

**Comparison with Other Placers.** We selected VPR [1] as the FPGA placement tool for comparing our work. We chose VPR as it is well known FPGA placement tool is publicly available for research purposes. VPR is based on Simulated Anneling algorithm and produces high quality results for FPGA benchmarks. We obtained VPR from [18].

**Values of Various Parameters.** Table 2 lists down the values of various parameters used in our FPGA placement method. As discussed before in Sect. 4, $\lambda$ is the objective function parameter which has to be updated on every iteration of the

**Table 2.** Parameter values used in our implementation

| Parameter | Value |
|---|---|
| $\lambda_{level}$ | $\lambda_{level-1}/4$ |
| $overflow\_ratio_{min}$ | 0.1 |
| Step_Size | 0.01 |
| $\alpha$ | 1% chip width |
| $Precision$ | $10^{-4}$ |
| $Scaling\_Factor$ | 0.99 |

outer loop of Algorithm 1. It has to be updated according to the values given in the Table 2. The value of $\alpha$, which is the parameter for smoothness of the wirelength function is 1% of the die width. Scaling factor for legalization used in the experiments is 0.99. The overflow ratio at which outer loop of Algorithm 1 is terminated is fixed to be at 0.01. These values are important for obtaining the desired performance and any change in them can affect the performance and quality of solution (Table 3).

**Table 3.** RUNTIME and HPWL comparison for FPGA benchmarks

| Circuits | VPR | | Ours | |
|---|---|---|---|---|
| | HPWL | sec | HPWL | sec |
| alu4 | 11999 | 11.828 | 13549 | 1.628 |
| apex2 | 18477 | 20.015 | 19678 | 2.173 |
| apex4 | 13274 | 10.405 | 14243 | 1.435 |
| des | 13523 | 15.147 | 14077 | 1.827 |
| diffeq | 39333 | 53.479 | 42917 | 11.937 |
| elliptic | 13753 | 8.051 | 15022 | 0.999 |
| ex5p | 37650 | 52.416 | 41603 | 7.619 |
| frisc | 13801 | 12.781 | 14385 | 1.392 |
| misex3 | 9509 | 14.831 | 10851 | 2.457 |
| seq | 18558 | 16.272 | 21194 | 1.936 |
| Average | 0.915 | 7.50 | 1.00 | 1.00 |

**Results of Comparison.** Our FPGA placer performs well compared to state-of-the-art FPGA placement tool VPR. We obtain 750% speed up over VPR, whereas, the wirelength of the designs placed by our tool are marginally (8.5%) longer when compared with VPR. In Fig. 4, we show a break up of runtime of our proposed FPGA placement tool. 21% of the time is spent in computation of gradient of wirelength, which is reasonable, since gradient vector needs to be computed for every iteration of conjugate gradient method. Legalization, greedy cell swapping, cell order polishing and calculation of objective function parameter consumes 11%, 2%, 2% and 2% of the runtime, respectively. We observe that most of the runtime is consumed in evaluating the potential and calculation of the gradient of density. Calculation of density function at each iteration of CG is unavoidable as it is the central idea behind spreading of the FPGA blocks across the placement region. In future, we plan to come up with a look-up table approach to reduce the runtime for evaluation of density gradient.

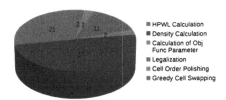

**Fig. 4.** Runtime break-up of the proposed FPGA placement tool

## 6 Conclusion

As the modern FPGA designs are growing rapidly, existing FPGA placement tool algorithms are not efficient in terms of the runtime. Thus, there is room for improvement of the FPGA placement algorithms. This work is targetted to improve the runtime of modern FPGA designs. We propose an analytical framework for placement in FPGAs. Our approach is based on quadratic density penalty method, wherein, we solve differential equations using conjugate gradient method to achieve a fast solution to FPGA placement. The results obtained by our tool are 750% better in terms of runtime over the well known FPGA placement tool VPR. In future we plan to further improve the runtime by performing parallelization of our approach.

## References

1. Betz, V., Rose, J.: VPR: a new packing, placement and routing tool for FPGA research. In: Luk, W., Cheung, P.Y.K., Glesner, M. (eds.) FPL 1997. LNCS, vol. 1304, pp. 213–222. Springer, Heidelberg (1997). https://doi.org/10.1007/3-540-63465-7_226. http://dl.acm.org/citation.cfm?id=647924.738755
2. Bostelmann, T., Sawitzki, S.: Improving FPGA placement with a self-organizing map. In: 2013 International Conference on Reconfigurable Computing and FPGAs (ReConFig), pp. 1–6 (2013). https://doi.org/10.1109/ReConFig.2013.6732302
3. Chan, T., Cong, J., Sze, K.: Multilevel generalized force-directed method for circuit placement. In: Proceedings of the 2005 International Symposium on Physical Design, ISPD 2005, pp. 185–192. ACM, New York (2005). http://doi.acm.org/10.1145/1055137.1055177

4. Chen, J., Zhu, W.: An analytical placer for VLSI standard cell placement. IEEE Trans. Comput. Aid. Des. Integr. Circ. Syst. **31**(8), 1208–1221 (2012). https://doi.org/10.1109/TCAD.2012.2190289
5. Chen, T.C., Jiang, Z.W., Hsu, T.C., Chen, H.C., Chang, Y.W.: NTUplace3: an analytical placer for large-scale mixed-size designs with preplaced blocks and density constraints. IEEE Trans. Comput. Aid. Des. Integr. Circ. Syst. **27**(7), 1228–1240 (2008). https://doi.org/10.1109/TCAD.2008.923063
6. Collier, R., Fobel, C., Richards, L., Grewal, G.: A formal and empirical analysis of recombination for genetic algorithm-based approaches to the FPGA placement problem. In: 2012 25th IEEE Canadian Conference on Electrical and Computer Engineering (CCECE), pp. 1–6 (2012). https://doi.org/10.1109/CCECE.2012.6334856
7. Eisenmann, H., Johannes, F.: Generic global placement and floorplanning. In: Proceedings of Design Automation Conference, pp. 269–274 (1998)
8. Fobel, C., Grewal, G., Stacey, D.: GPU-accelerated wire-length estimation for FPGA placement. In: 2011 Symposium on Application Accelerators in High-Performance Computing, pp. 14–23 (2011). https://doi.org/10.1109/SAAHPC.2011.16
9. Fobel, C., Grwal, G., Collier, R., Stacey, D.: GPU approach to FPGA placement based on star+. In: 10th IEEE International NEWCAS Conference, pp. 229–232 (2012). https://doi.org/10.1109/NEWCAS.2012.6328998
10. Gharibian, F., Shannon, L., Jamieson, P.: Finding system-level information and analyzing its correlation to FPGA placement. In: 2010 International Conference on Field Programmable Logic and Applications, pp. 544–549 (2010). https://doi.org/10.1109/FPL.2010.107
11. Hill, D.: Method and system for high speed detailed placement of cells within an integrated circuit design. US Patent 6370673 (2002). http://www.google.com/patents/US6370673
12. Huang, B., Zhang, H.: Application of multi-core parallel computing in FPGA placement. In: 2013 2nd International Symposium on Instrumentation and Measurement, Sensor Network and Automation (IMSNA), pp. 884–889 (2013). https://doi.org/10.1109/IMSNA.2013.6743419
13. Jamieson, P., Gharibian, F., Shannon, L.: Supergenes in a genetic algorithm for heterogeneous FPGA placement. In: 2013 IEEE Congress on Evolutionary Computation, pp. 253–260 (2013). https://doi.org/10.1109/CEC.2013.6557578
14. Kahng, A.B., Wang, Q.: Implementation and extensibility of an analytic placer. IEEE Trans. Comput. Aid. Des. Integr. Circ. Syst. **24**(5), 734–747 (2005). https://doi.org/10.1109/TCAD.2005.846366
15. Naylor, W.C., Donelly, R., Sha, L.: Non-linear optimization system and method for wire length and delay optimization for an automatic electric circuit placer. U.S. Patent 6301693(12) (2001)
16. Obermeier, B., Ranke, H., Johannes, F.M.: Kraftwerk: a versatile placement approach. In: ISPD 2005, pp. 242–244. ACM, New York (2005). http://doi.acm.org/10.1145/1055137.1055190
17. Pattison, R., Fobel, C., Grewal, G., Areibi, S.: Scalable analytic placement for FPGA on GPGPU. In: 2015 International Conference on ReConFigurable Computing and FPGAs (ReConFig), pp. 1–6 (2015). https://doi.org/10.1109/ReConFig.2015.7393356
18. Versatile Placement Routing Tool: http://www.eecg.toronto.edu/~vaughn/vpr/vpr.html. Accessed 17 Jan 2017

19. Viswanathan, N., Chu, C.: Fastplace: efficient analytical placement using cell shifting, iterative local refinement, and a hybrid net model. IEEE Trans. Comput. Aid. Des. Integr. Circ. Syst. **24**(5), 722–733 (2005). https://doi.org/10.1109/TCAD.2005.846365
20. Wang, Y., Shin, H.: An effective window based legalization algorithm for FPGA placement. In: 2013 International Conference on Reconfigurable Computing and FPGAs (ReConFig), pp. 1–4 (2013). https://doi.org/10.1109/ReConFig.2013.6732270

# A Dependability Preserving Fluid-Level Synthesis for Reconfigurable Droplet-Based Microfluidic Biochips

Arpan Chakraborty, Piyali Datta$^{(\boxtimes)}$, Debasis Dhal,
and Rajat Kumar Pal

Department of Computer Science and Engineering, University of Calcutta,
JD-2, Sector – III, Saltlake, Kolkata 700 106, West Bengal, India
arpanc250506@gmail.com, piyalidatta150888@gmail.com,
debasisdhal06@gmail.com, pal.rajatk@gmail.com

**Abstract.** Due to inherent reconfigurable capability, digital microfluidic bio-chips (Dmfbs) have been a prime platform for critical medical diagnosis, real time bioassays, and lab-on-chip experiments. However, dependability is an urgent need to decide the correct outcome from a bioassay execution. To make a DMFB dependable in high frequency applications, a single electrode must not be frequently used as it may result in over-actuation problem. An over-actuated cell degrades over time and results a failure. Current fluid-level synthesis method only considers in minimizing the total completion time of the assay. Besides, recent technologies use abundant re-execution and perform costly online synthesis whenever such a fault is discovered. Two papers address the dependability issue and propose a placement solution. Here, we present a complete fluid-level synthesis to prepare binding, scheduling, placement, and routing solutions for a given bioassay. The concerned problem is proved to be NP-complete. A dynamic programming formulation is followed to obtain a solution in pseudo-polynomial time. Several benchmarks are used to evaluate the proposed method.

**Keywords:** Dependability · Synthesis · Microfluidics · Graph theory
Dynamic programming

## 1 Introduction

Digital microfluidic biochips (Dmfbs) are the standard lab-on-chip systems for performing various laboratory bioassay protocols with automatic and high precision control [1]. DMFBs are composed of 2D electrode array and peripheral devices (i.e. detector, dispenser). The fundamental fluidic operations (e.g. dispensing, mixing, dilution, and detection) are performed through the external voltage application under a clock control, which manipulates the droplet movements by actuating and de-actuating the underlying electrodes. Through this EWOD principle, the operations are executed throughout the array and in reconfigurable manner [2, 3].

Classically, the design automation is achieved in the Dmfbs with a top down synthesis flow consisting of three phases, namely, *fluid-level*, *chip-level*, and

© Springer Nature Singapore Pte Ltd. 2017
B. K. Kaushik et al. (Eds.): VDAT 2017, CCIS 711, pp. 694–706, 2017.
https://doi.org/10.1007/978-981-10-7470-7_65

*fabrication* [4, 5]. In the fluid-level design (in Fig. 1), a synthesis implementation, i.e. *binding* of the operation-resource pair, *scheduling* time stamp of each operation, *placement* of resources, and deciding droplet *routing* of the given *bioassay graph* is prepared [4, 5]. The main objective at this stage is to minimise the total completion time of the bioassay. After obtaining a synthesis implementation, next a minimal set of pins are decided at the chip-level design to provide the external control signal on the underlying electrodes. Once the pins are assigned to the electrodes, the droplet movements between each *net* becomes defined and restricted. Now, the effective CAD algorithms for the DMFBs carry out the operations in the designed chip with high automation and less human intervention [3].

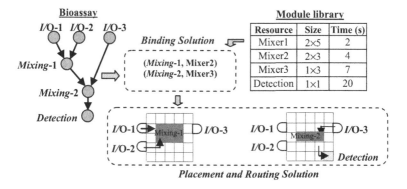

**Fig. 1.** A bioassay graph, module library, and fluid-level tasks.

Deciding correct bioassay outcome in DMFBs is a critical requirement in medical diagnosis [6]. The bioassay run may apparently produce wrong outcome in a faulty environment. In high frequency biochips, the quality of an electrode is degraded with the number of times it is actuated. Usage of this degraded electrode during execution affects the correctness of the bioassay [6, 7]. Besides, uncertainty is inherently involved and at any time during bioassay execution, an overly actuated electrode may either be encountered permanent failure (*type I* fault) or produce erroneous outcome (*type II* fault).

Therefore, to assess the quality of the DMFBs, its dependability must be considered. For the error checking protocols, recently a cyberphysical modelling has been proposed [8]. Most of the methods consider the abundant re-execution capability of DMFBs; e.g., for both *type I* and *type II* faults during an assay run, the predecessors (i.e. operationally dependent operation) of the erroneous operation are to be re-executed. However, at this stage, in a pin-constrained chip, re-allocation of the required resources (i.e. mixers, storage cells, and the module nets) has to be found out. This online synthesis outputs a new synthesis result, e.g. module placement, routing, and storage cells. Evidently, the obtained results may affect the execution of other tasks that are already in run. In the worst case, the bioassay completion time becomes longer violating its deadline. Two papers have addressed the quality degradation problem of electrodes [6, 7]. However, in [6], the researchers have proposed a placement solution and in [7], a chip level design methodology has been developed. A complete fluid-level synthesis considering dependability is left untouched. To handle this, a restriction must be imposed on the number of usage of an electrode. However, at the fluid-level synthesis, we do not have information regarding the faulty electrodes (*type I* or *type II*). These electrodes can only be identified through an error checking protocol applied during the assay run.

Alternately, we may have a limit on the number of actuations on each electrode during the assay run. In doing so, [6] has suggested to partition the electrodes into two groups, say, *overly actuated* (*OA*) and *moderately actuated* (*MA*) electrodes. Now, to decide the placement and routing solution for each operation, the number of electrodes from the *OA* group has to be minimised (or the number of electrodes from the *MA* group is to be maximised) while minimising the overall completion time.

Current synthesis methods deal with the *type I* and *type II* faults separately. Hence, a dependability preserving synthesis avoiding both types of faults is a crucial requisite for ensuring the correctness of the bioassay outcome. Thus, this paper contributes a dependability preserving synthesis method for the efficacy of the DMFBs. Considered problem has been proved to be NP-complete. Our proposed algorithm considers the inherent combinatorial properties of the synthesis tasks. A pseudo polynomial time dynamic programming approach has been made on the proposed graph-theoretic model. For the simulation study, several benchmarks have been considered to validate the obtained results.

## 2   Motivation and Problem Formulation

Let $C$ be a chip of size $x \times y$ and $B$ be a bioassay graph. To execute an operation $O_i$ precisely, the placement of the corresponding working module (say, mixer $M_i$ or storage $S$) must not contain an overly actuated electrode. If a degraded electrode lies within $M_i$, error checking protocol suggests to re-execute $O_i$ into a different location on the chip and taking same or different mixer dimension.

Besides, the probability of an electrode to become malfunctioning due to over-actuation rises with the increase of frequency of the periodic voltage [6, 7]. Hence, a threshold value is imposed on the number of consecutive or periodic actuation of each electrode for its safety. This threshold value has to be taken into consideration for each module placement (or droplet routing) to reduce the chance of re-execution of the task. Thus, it results in greater use of *MA* electrodes and in lesser that of *OA*. The re-execution problem imposes an overhead of finding a new binding, scheduling, placement, and routing solution of a task that has produced erroneous results. Now, an online synthesis procedure in a pin-constrained DMFB needs to find the available (or free) resources on the chip as well as the valid droplet movements through the assigned pins [9]. Moreover, the re-execution should not hinder already running operations. To tackle this problem, off-line top-down synthesis is preferable while avoiding the chances of re-execution by imposing constraints over selection of 'good' electrodes.

Let us consider a bioassay consisting of four operations ($O_1$, $O_2$, $O_3$, and $O_4$). In Fig. 2(a) a feasible binding for the operations is $\langle(O_1, M_1), (O_2, M_2), (O_3, M_3), (O_4, M_4)\rangle$ and a feasible placement for $M_1$, $M_2$, $M_3$, and $M_4$ have been shown.

After completion of $O_1$ and $O_2$, $O_3$ and $O_4$ will start to execute. From the placement solution, it is evident that four electrodes are shared in the two consecutive placements; hence, the probability of being over-actuated for these shared electrodes is increased that in turn increases the chance of re-execution of both $O_3$ and $O_4$. Even if we consider another placement solution for $M_3$ and $M_4$ as shown in Fig. 2(b), the number of shared electrodes in consecutive mixings is four. Here, $M_3$ is not occupying any electrode that was active in the previous mixing. So, only $O_4$ has the probability of re-execution. Taking the placement of $M_1$ and $M_2$ as constraint we cannot find any placement solution for $M_3$ and $M_4$ that is completely free from the chance of over-actuation. Now, if we change the binding for $O_4$, it can be safely placed on the chip avoiding all the electrodes those were used in $M_1$ and $M_2$ as shown in Fig. 2(c).

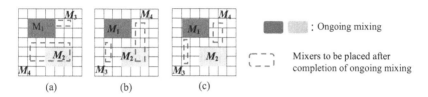

(a)            (b)            (c)

**Fig. 2.** (a) Operations in mixer $M_3$ and $M_4$ start after completion of $M_1$ and $M_2$ and contain some previously used electrodes (b) Mixer $M_3$ does not contain used electrode but $M_4$ does, (c) Both $M_3$ and $M_3$ do not contain used electrodes.

The immediate observations are drawn as follows.

Observation 1: The bioassay execution problem is to solve a series of module placement and droplet routing problems, where a $i$-th placement problem is $P_i$ and that of routing is $R_i$. Each $P_i$ is to place a certain number of independent mixers on the chip, whereas an $R_i$ is to find the inter-mixer routes. Chance of re-execution of any operation can be reduced by deploying only $MA$ electrodes at the time of placement and routing.

Observation 2: To solve a $P_{i+1}$ (or $R_{i+1}$), the electrodes those were not shared in solving $P_i$ (or $R_i$), are preferred to be utilized to reduce the risk of over-actuation. Hence, this set of electrodes is termed as acceptable electrode set ($AEs$) for $P_{i+1}$ (or $R_{i+1}$). However, the remaining electrodes should be avoided to accommodate the operations and termed as forbidden electrode set ($FEs$) during $P_{i+1}$ (or $R_{i+1}$).

Observation 3: Each $P_i$ results a number of feasible placement solutions for a set of independent operations satisfying the area of the chip. Now, $P_i$ and $P_{i+1}$ may contain mutually disjoint electrode sets, i.e. all the electrodes utilized in $P_{i+1}$ belong to $AE$. Also, due to the chip constraints, they may have some common (utilized in $P_i$) electrodes which belong to $FE$. Among these placement solutions, for a successful synthesis implementation preserving dependability, the placements composed of only $AE$ should be selected.

Based on this discussion, the objective of a dependability preserving synthesis is to prepare a fluid-level synthesis implementation for error free bioassay outcome by avoiding electrode faults due to over actuation while minimising the bioassay completion time. The following constraints are to be satisfied.

(a) Chip constraint: Area allocated to all the resources, i.e. mixers, storages, etc. must be less than the total chip area.

(b) Non-overlapping constraint: Any two resources must not overlap at any time.

(c) Non-reconfigurable resource constraint: At any time instant the total number of non-reconfigurable resources including input-output or dispensing port, detection sites, utilized to perform the operations cannot exceed the number of available resources of corresponding type.

(d) Operational dependency constraint: If any two operations are such that $O_i$ is a predecessor of $O_j$ then $O_j$ cannot be started before completion of $O_i$.

(e) Forbidden electrode (*FE*) constraint: Two consecutive resource placement (or droplet routing) must not consider an overly actuated electrode.

## 3  Proposed Strategy

During bioassay execution, we maintain a ready queue that holds a number of operations that are not mutually dependent, and hence they maintain disjunctive property. For high throughput DMFBs, it is essential that the chip performs a high degree of disjunctive operations between any time interval $t_1$ and $t_2$. Evidently, in each $t_1 \leq t \leq t_2$, a number of non-overlapping mixers are placed on the chip satisfying the placement constraints. At this time, if dependability is to be acquired the electrodes from *FE* group must be avoided during the module placement or routing. This imposes a limit on the number of simultaneous operations on a fixed sized chip.

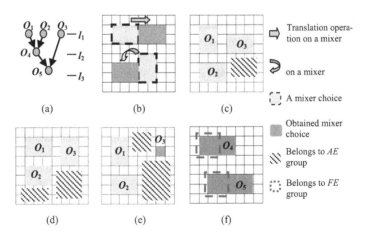

**Fig. 3.** (a) An example bioassay graph, (b) Two mixer choices placed at some position while translation and rotation give two new mixers at different location, (c)-(e) Three placement choices consisting of mixers or storages for level $l_1$ and corresponding acceptable region for the next level, (f) Over-actuation arises between the placement choices of $l_2$ and $l_3$.

Now, for the independent operations $FE$ avoidance constraint between each $P_i$ and $P_{i+1}$ lowers the degree of performing disjunctive operations that in turn reduces the chip-throughput and increases the bioassay completion time. Thus, there is a trade-off between dependability preservation and completion time of a bioassay. To find out feasible placement solutions maintaining the $FE$ avoidance constraint, we propose a data structure called placement library or $Placement_{Lib}$ which finds an association between each successive $P_i$ and $P_{i+1}$ and hence produces a feasible synthesis implementation.

*Example 1:* We consider the bioassay of Fig. 3(a). Each operation of the bioassay graph has a possible mixer choice on the chip defined by the module library of Fig. 1. For $l_1$, three disjunctive operations $O_1$, $O_2$, and $O_3$ have three possible placement choices, as shown in Fig. 3(c), (d) and (e). Notably, for a single placement choice, each operation is either associated with a mixer or with a temporary storage for preserving an intermediate droplet. Thus, for each level, we acquire a set of feasible placement choices through 'translation' and/or 'rotation' of already placed modules on the chip. For an example, the rotation operation on the mixer containing $O_1$ and $O_3$ and a translation on $O_2$ in Fig. 3(c), yields a different choice in Fig. 3(d). In Fig. 3(c), (d) and (e), the acceptable chip region (i.e. $AE$) is identified for $l_2$. However, the choices for $l_2$ and $l_3$ may introduce over-actuation problem due to usage of electrodes from $FE$.

**Definition 1:** Placement Library or $Placement_{Lib}$ is a set of tuples $(Pt_1, Pt_2, ..., Pt_n)$, where a tuple $Pt_i$ contains one or more $(p \geq 1)$ placement choices $h_{pi} \in Pt_i$ of the disjunctive operations for the associated level $l_i$ in the bioassay graph.

Each placement choice $h_{pi} \in Pt_i$ essentially contains the type of resource(s) utilized along with the on-chip placement information of that resource and electrode usage for the execution of an operation. For an example the choice $h_{11} \in Pt_1$ of Fig. 3(c) can be written as $h_{11} = \langle position(mixer\, for\, O_1), position(mixer\, for\, O_2), position(mixer\, for\, O_3), position(electrodes\, from\, AE)\rangle$, whereas $h_{13} \in Pt_1$ of Fig. 3(e) is $h_{13} = \langle position(mixer\, for\, O_1), position(mixer\, for\, O_2), position(storage\, for\, O_3), position (electrodes\, from\, AE)\rangle$

Lemma 1: *Let $(G, l)$ be a bioassay graph with level $l$, $Placement_{Lib} = \{Pt_1, Pt_2, ..., Pt_l\}$ be the placement library, and $h_{pi}$ be a p-th placement choice associated with $Pt_i$. For any two operations $O_m$ and $O_n$ the followings hold true.*

*(i) If $O_m$ and $O_n \in l_i$ and are mutually disjunctive, then a choice $h_{pi} \in Pt_i$ performs the binding and placement tasks.*

*(ii) If $O_m \in l_i$ and $O_n \in l_k$, $i \neq k$, then any two choices $h_{pi} \in Pt_i$ and $h_{qk} \in Pt_k$ maintains conjunctive property implying that to execute $O_n$ the execution of $O_m$ must be completed.*

*Proof:* At any time of bioassay execution, there are two types of on-chip operations; ongoing mixing (or dilution) operation and some operation(s) waiting for the outcome of other operation(s). Now, a choice in $Placement_{Lib}$ is constructed by first selecting an operation (i.e. either mixing or store), forming an operation-resource pair, and placing the resource on a chip position satisfying the non-overlapping and chip constraints.

A resource may be either a mixer from module library or a $1 \times 1$ storage cell. Hence, any choice $h_{pi} \in Pt_i$ contains either a non-overlapping mixer or a storage-cell for the two disjunctive operations $O_m$ and $O_n$ of $l_i$. Evidently, $h_{pi}$ implies a binding and a placement information for the respective operations. The conjunctive property between $O_m \in l_i$ and $O_n \in l_k$, $i \neq k$, implies that the $O_m$ and $O_n$ are operationally dependent. Through $Placement_{Lib}$ we have two choices $h_{pi} \in Pt_i$ and $h_{qk} \in Pt_k$. Let, the resources $m_1$ and $m_2$ are deployed to execute $O_m$ and $O_n$ respectively. Hence, $m_1$ and $m_2$ respectively belong to $h_{pi}$ and $h_{qk}$. Now, the dependency between $O_m$ and $O_n$ suggests to form a droplet path between the modules in the form of a net. From Observation 1, this is indeed a routing problem in between two placement problems. Hence, $h_{pi}$ and $h_{qk-}$ are conjunctively related.    □

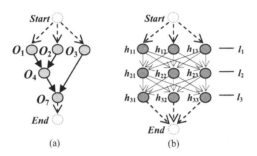

**Fig. 4.** (a) An example bioassay graph with start to end operations, (b) Corresponding choice graph after $Placement_{Lib}$ construction.

Given a bioassay graph $(G, l)$, $Placement_{Lib}$ prepares a number of choices for each of its levels. Following Lemma 1, any two choices belonging to two consecutive levels are operationally dependent implying an existence of a directed edge. Accordingly, a multistage graph, called *choice graph*, is formed. Here, a choice graph $(Gc, l)$ is an $l$-stage multistage graph having a certain number of vertices at each stage and there exists a directed edge only between two vertices of two consecutive stages. Figure 4(b) shows a *choice graph* for the example bioassay of Fig. 4(a).

**Lemma 2:** *A simple path from 'start' to 'end' vertex in the choice graph $(Gc, l)$ represents a fluid-level synthesis implementation for the bioassay graph $(G, l)$.*

Proof: By definition, a simple path from 'start' to 'end' in $(Gc, l)$ is essentially a path with non-repeating vertices and hence accommodates exactly one choice from each level. Following Lemma 1, each choice in $(Gc, l)$ is a candidate binding and placement solution of the disjunctive operations belonging to a certain level of the bioassay graph. Also, we have found that $h_{pi}$ and $h_{q(i+1)}$ are operationally dependent choices. It fundamentally implies that the directed edge from $h_{pi}$ to $h_{q(i+1)}$ is an operational constraint between them and at least one resource module either mixer or storage is there in $h_{q(i+1)}$ which is forming a *net* with at least one resource module in $h_{pi}$ (Fig. 5 gives an explanation). Firstly, each module $m$ in a mixing library has an associated execution time $t(m)$. Secondly, the time for route among the modules can be calculated by observing the Manhattan distance and the required number of stalls on the chip.

Hence, if a choice $h_{pi}$ starts execution at $t$, i.e. $t_{start}(h_{pi}) = t$, its end time stamp $t_{end}(h_{pi})$ is the maximum time taken among its corresponding modules, i.e. $t_{end}(h_{pi}) = t_{start}(h_{pi}) + \max\{t(m)\}$. Also, the successor choice $h_{q(i+1)}$ starts executing at $t_{start}$ $(h_{q(i+1)}) = t_{end}(h_{pi}) + route()$, where $route()$ is the time taken by droplet routing, and its end time stamp is $t_{start}(h_{q(i+1)}) = t_{end}(h_{pi}) + route() + \max\{t(m)\}$. Thus, if a simple path in a $(Gc, l)$ consists of $n$ number of choices, their start and end time stamps can be obtained and hence a scheduling solution can be prepared. As all such $n$ choices together generate placements and produce route paths preserving the operational dependencies of the given bioassay, a fluid-level synthesis implementation of the bioassay is immediately achieved. □

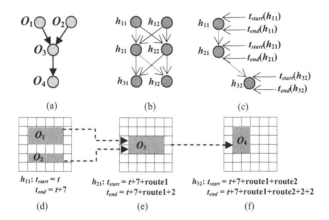

(a)                    (b)                    (c)

$h_{11}: t_{start} = t$          $h_{21}: t_{start} = t+7+route1$          $h_{32}: t_{start} = t+7+route1+route2$
$t_{end} = t+7$          $t_{end} = t+7+route1+2$          $t_{end} = t+7+route1+route2+2+2$

(d)                    (e)                    (f)

**Fig. 5.** (a)-(b) A bioassay graph and its choice graph, where at each level there are exactly two choices, (c) Start and end time of execution of each choice, (d) Dotted lines show the formation of module nets for the operational dependencies. $O_3$ starts after completion of $O_1$ and $O_2$, and $O_4$ starts after that of $O_3$.

If $Placement_{Lib}$ maintains the $FE$ avoidance constraint for enhancement of dependability of the system, obtained simple path from the corresponding choice graph is a dependability-oriented synthesis solution. Categorically, due to the presence of $FE$ group the available space for the mixers on the chip is reduced and thus a choice $h_{pi}$ may contain a greater number of storage cells than that of the concurrent mixing or dilution operation and accordingly the *schedule length* becomes longer. Let, $E1_i$ and $E2_{(i+1)}$ are the set of electrodes required respectively for $h_{pi}$ and $h_{q(i+1)}$. Then, the electrodes only from $E1_i \cap E2_{(i+1)}$ belong to the $FE$ group for an $h_{q(i+1)}$. Evidently, a tradeoff exists between exclusion of electrodes from $E1_i \cap E2_{(i+1)}$ and the *schedule length* of the bioassay. For a practical scenario, we must have a threshold value which allows a limited number of cells to be shared between two consecutive $P_i$ and $P_{i+1}$.

Now, let $E$ is the set of total electrodes of the size restricted chip; we define $a_i = (E1_i \cap E2_{(i+1)})/E$. Then, Dependability Factor $(DF) = (1-a_i)$. $DF = 1$ implies that the chip is 100% dependable during $P_i$ and $P_{i+1}$. Accordingly, it has a longer bioassay time. Thus, for a practical biochip, $DF$ should be less than 1. Hence, to construct an $h_{q(i+1)}$, the usage of electrodes from $E1_i \cap E2_{(i+1)}$ should be minimized such that bioassay completion time lies within a moderate bound.

Problem 1: Simple Path Avoiding Forbidden Electrodes ($SPAFE$).

Instance: A choice graph $(Gc, l)$; a start $(s)$ and end $(t)$ vertices; $i$-th level is denoted as $l_i$; each directed edge $(h_{pi}, h_{q(i+1)})$ is associated with an edge weight $wh_{pqi(i+1)}$; each $wh_{pqi(i+1)}$ defines the amount of over-actuated electrodes from $E1_i \cap E2_{(i+1)}$ among the modules of $h_{pi}$ and $h_{q(i+1)}$; a threshold value $\Delta$ defines an acceptable limit of using the over-actuated electrodes.

Question: Is there a simple path $path(s, t)$ in the choice graph such that the sum of all the edge weights on the path is at most $\Delta$?

Theorem 1: $SPAFE$ is NP-complete.

Proof: Given a choice graph $(Gc, l)$ the certificate for $SPAFE$ is $l$ vertices (or choices) where exactly one vertex is essentially taken from each $l_i$ starting from $s$ and ending to $t$. For each edge $(h_{pi}, h_{q(i+1)})$ on $path(s, t)$, it can be easily checked whether the two choices contain any electrode from $E1_i \cap E2_{(i+1)}$. The sum of all $wh_{pqi(i+1)}$ can easily be checked whether it is within $\Delta$. Evidently, the computation for these $l$ vertices of the simple path takes polynomial time, hence it is in NP.

To prove its NP-hardness, we make a reduction from *Path Avoiding Forbidden Pair* ($PAFP$) problem [10] into $SPAFE$. In $PAFP$, a directed acyclic graph (DAG) $H$ and a set of forbidden edges $\{e_1, e_2, ..., e_{r-1}\}$ are given. A simple path is to be found out in $H$ between 'start' to 'end' vertices, where at most a single vertex from each edge (i.e. avoiding the edge) can be accommodated. Given an instance of $PAFP$ an instance of $SPAFE$ (i.e. a choice graph) is constructed is as follows.

As $H$ is a DAG, using linearization on DAGs $H$ is converted (in polynomial time) into a multistage graph $H'$ having $l$ stages [11]. Let, at $r$-th stage $l_r$ in $(H', l)$ the vertices are denoted as $m_{vr}$. Each forbidden edge has an associated cost $W$. Also, the other edges excluding the forbidden ones have cost $(\Delta/l)$. Then, we perform the following.

Choice graph $(Gc, l)$:

$l_0$ : vertex: $s$

$l_1$ : vertices: $h_{11} = m_{11}, h_{21} = m_{21}, ..., h_{v1} = m_{v1}$

$l_2$ : vertices: $h_{12} = m_{12}, h_{22} = m_{22}, ..., h_{v2} = m_{v2}$

$\quad ... ... ...$

$l_r$ : vertices: $h_{1r} = m_{1r}, h_{2r} = m_{2r}, ..., h_{vr} = m_{vr}$

$\quad ... ... ...$

$l_{l-1}$ : vertex: $t$

$(h_{v1}, h_{v2}) = e_1, (h_{v2}, h_{v3}) = e_2, ..., (h_{v(r-1)}, h_{vr}) = e_{r-1},$

$wh_{jki(i+1)} = W$, if $j, k = v$, and $i = 1$ through $r$

$\quad = (\Delta/l)$, otherwise.

We show that $SPAFE$ has a solution with no $FE$ and of cost at most $\Delta$, if and only if $PAFP$ has a path avoiding forbidden pairs. First we assume that $PAFP$ has a solution.

Evidently, then no $e_i$, $1 \leq i \leq r - 1$, is there on the simple path. By construction, from $(Gc, l)$ only the edges other than $e_i$ is selected to form the path. Also, the total cost of the path becomes $l \times (\Delta/l) = \Delta$, and hence is a solution of *SPAFE*. On the other hand, let *PAFP* has no solution. It signifies that at least one $e_i$ has been included in the path. By construction, the inclusion of this edge increases the cost by $W > (\Delta/l)$. Accordingly, the total cost of the resultant $path(s, t)$ would be at least $W$, and the total cost for the path becomes greater than $\Delta$. Hence, there is no solution in *SPAFE*.    □

### 3.1    A Dynamic Programming Formulation

A feasible solution of *SPAFE* consists of a $path(s, t)$ where every two consecutive choices maintain an overlapping of electrodes within the threshold. However, the usage of lesser forbidden electrodes does not guarantee lesser completion time for the bioassay. Hence, we define two edge costs $\alpha_i$ and $\beta_i$, where $\alpha_i = \left(E1_i \cap E2_{(i+1)}\right)$ and $\beta_i =$ [(total number of electrodes in $E1_i$ if each module in $h_{pi}$ is replaced by the best possible mixer in the module library) – (total number of electrodes in $E1_i$)]. As a smaller mixer takes larger time to complete a mixing [12], lesser $\beta_i$ signifies that better mixers are used in the choice $h_{pi}$. Therefore, in $path(s, t)$, the edges with minimized $(\alpha_i + \beta_i)$ have to be selected.

Here, we present a dynamic programming formulation on multistage graph [13] that finds an exact solution of Problem 1 in a pseudo-polynomial time. Given a multistage choice graph $(Gc, l)$, the dynamic programming approach makes a sequence of $(l–2)$ decisions from start vertex $(s)$ to end vertex $(t)$, where each decision is to select exactly a single choice from each level. As discussed, the cost metric of each edge is defined as $c(h_{pi}, h_{q(i+1)}) = (\alpha_i + \beta_i)$. Now, if $path(i, j)$ is the minimum cost simple path from a $j$-th choice $h_{ji}$ in $l_{i-}$ to the end vertex, then an $i$-th decision is to determine which vertex from $l_{(i+1)}$, $1 \leq i \leq (l–2)$, is to be included in $path(i, j)$. Let, a $k$-th choice is selected from $l_{(i+1)}$. Let, $c(path(i, j))$ is the cost of this path. Then we have the following.

$c(path(i, j)) = \min\{c(j, k) + c(path(i + 1, k))\}$, such that $h_{k(i+1)} \in l_{i+1}$ and $(h_{ji}, h_{k(i+1)}) \in$ edge set of $(Gc, l)$.

## 4    Experimental Results

The proposed methodology for dependability preserving synthesis for the fluid-level of the DMFBs have been implemented in C language on a 1.99 GHz Core i3 machine with 4 GB RAM. Four benchmark bioassay protocols, named In-Vitro Diagnosis (IVD), Polymerase Chain Reaction (PCR), Colorimetric Protein Assay with Exponentiation (CPA_Exp), and Interpolated Colorimetric Protein Assay (CPA_Int) have been chosen for performance evaluation [14]. To demonstrate the efficacy of the proposed method with the minimized bioassay completion time and the corresponding dependability factor of the chip, two different chip-dimensions have been considered. The number of allowable electrodes for successive actuation is also regarded as a constraint. To solve the NP-complete problem, for each step we use logically devised heuristics that mainly follow greedy approach, i.e. after forming a placement library for the concurrent operations a multistage graph is built, and then a dynamic programming formulation finds the shortest simple path based on the cumulative weight sum of the edges.

Table 1 shows the obtained results from our proposed synthesis algorithm. With the increase in the number of allowable electrodes for consecutive operations, the assay completion time is becoming lowered as higher degree of concurrent operations can then be performed on the chip. For an example, on an $8 \times 8$ chip the completion time for CPA_Exp is 78 s if the number of allowable electrodes for consecutive actuation is 10. However, the execution time becomes 75 s when we allow 20 electrodes for consecutive actuation. Now, as previously discussed, if the ratio of allowable sharing of electrodes to that of the total electrodes on the chip is $a_i$, then, dependability Factor $(DF) = (1 - a_i)$. Hence, for an $8 \times 8$ chip, if the chip executing CPA_Exp is 84.37% dependable, the assay completion time becomes 78 s; whereas if the same chip is 68.75% dependable, then the corresponding assay completion time becomes 75 s. In Fig. 6, the graph shows the performance study between $DF$ and bioassay completion time.

**Table 1.** Obtained results through the proposed synthesis method.

| Bioassay | Size of the chip | Dependability factor ($DF$) (%) | # Allowable electrodes for consecutive actuation | Completion time (s) | Execution time (s) |
|---|---|---|---|---|---|
| IVD | $8 \times 8$ | 84.37 | 10 | 15 | 0.504 |
| | | 76.56 | 15 | 15 | 0.517 |
| | $10 \times 10$ | 90 | 10 | 15 | 0.579 |
| | | 85 | 15 | 14 | 0.499 |
| PCR | $8 \times 8$ | 84.37 | 10 | 14 | 0.503 |
| | | 76.56 | 15 | 11 | 0.433 |
| | $10 \times 10$ | 90 | 10 | 18 | 0.395 |
| | | 85 | 15 | 15 | 0.419 |
| CPA_Exp | $8 \times 8$ | 84.37 | 10 | 78 | 0.697 |
| | | 68.75 | 20 | 75 | 0.694 |
| | $10 \times 10$ | 90 | 10 | 64 | 0.842 |
| | | 80 | 20 | 60 | 0.871 |
| CPA_Int | $8 \times 8$ | 84.37 | 10 | 70 | 0.704 |
| | | 68.75 | 20 | 64 | 0.714 |
| | $10 \times 10$ | 90 | 10 | 68 | 0.861 |
| | | 80 | 20 | 66 | 0.851 |

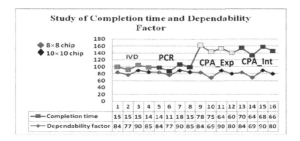

**Fig. 6.** Performance of the benchmarks with respect to bioassay completion time and dependability factor (*DF*) on varying chip dimensions.

# 5 Conclusion

This paper proposes a fluid-level synthesis algorithm considering electrode dependability as an important system attribute. Until now, only a placement solution is there for a reliable biochip platform. However, this paper considers two categorization of fault (*type I* and *type II*) that produces erroneous bioassay outcome. The *type I* fault occurs due to overly actuated cells. Our proposed method makes a chip dependable considering the number of allowable electrodes during execution and hence occurrence of faults is avoided. This is measured by the *DF* value for varying chip-dimensions. Moreover, if on the fly, some electrodes experience permanent failure (i.e. a *type II* fault), they are put into the forbidden electrode set and are never considered and hence avoided during the assay execution. The considered problem is proved as NP-complete and a dynamic programming formulation on a multistage graph is presented that finds the synthesis result in a pseudo polynomial time. Several bioassay protocols have been considered to assess the performance of the proposed method.

# References

1. Ho, T.Y., Chakrabarty, K., Pop, P.: Digital microfluidic biochips: recent research and emerging challenges. In: Proceedings of the Seventh IEEE/ACM/IFIP International Conference on Hardware/Software Co-Design and System Synthesis, pp. 335–344 (2011)
2. Chakrabarty, K., Xu, T.: Digital Microfluidic Biochips: Design automation and Optimization. CRC Press, Boca Raton (2017)
3. Ho, T.Y.: Design automation for digital microfluidic biochips: from fluidic-level toward chip-level. In: IEEE 11th International Conference Solid-State and Integrated Circuit Technology (ICSICT), pp. 1–4 (2012)
4. Ho, T.Y.: Design automation for digital microfluidic biochips. IPSJ Trans. Syst. LSI Des. Methodol. **7**, 16–26 (2014)
5. Chakrabarty, K.: Design automation and test solutions for digital microfluidic biochips. IEEE Trans. Circuits Syst. I Regul. Pap. **57**(1), 4–17 (2010)
6. Chen, Y.H., Hsu, C.L., Tsai, L.C., Huang, T.W., Ho, T.Y.: A reliability-oriented placement algorithm for reconfigurable digital microfluidic biochips using 3-D deferred decision making technique. IEEE Trans. Comput. Aided Des. Integr. Circuits Syst. **32**(8), 1151–1162 (2013)

7. Yu, S.T., Yeh, S.H., Ho, T.Y.: Reliability-driven chip-level design for high-frequency digital microfluidic biochips. IEEE Trans. Comput. Aided Des. Integr. Circuits Syst. **34**(4), 529–539 (2015)

8. Luo, Y., Bhattacharya, B.B., Ho, T.Y., Chakrabarty, K.: Design and optimization of a cyberphysical digital-microfluidic biochip for the polymerase chain reaction. IEEE Trans. Comput. Aided Des. Integr. Circuits Syst. **34**(1), 29–42 (2015)

9. Xu, T., Chakrabarty, K.: Broadcast electrode-addressing for pin-constrained multi-functional digital microfluidic biochips. In: 45th ACM/IEEE Design Automation Conference, pp. 173–178 (2008)

10. Kolman, P., Pangrác, O.: On the complexity of paths avoiding forbidden pairs. Discrete Appl. Math. **157**(13), 2871–2876 (2009)

11. Alwan, N.A., Ibraheem, I.K., Shukr, S.M.: Fast computation of the shortest path problem through simultaneous forward and backward systolic dynamic programming. Int. J. Comput. Appl. **54**(1) (2012)

12. Paik, P., Pamula, V.K., Fair, R.B.: Rapid droplet mixers for digital microfluidic systems. Lab Chip **3**(4), 253–259 (2003)

13. Horowitz, E., Sahni, S.: Fundamentals of Computer Algorithms. Universities Press (2008)

14. Luo, Y., Chakrabarty, K., Ho, T.Y.: Hardware/Software Co-Design and Optimization for Cyberphysical Integration in Digital Microfluidic Biochips. Springer, Cham (2015). https://doi.org/10.1007/978-3-319-09006-1

# Splitting and Transport of a Droplet with No External Actuation Force for Lab on Chip Devices

T. Pravinraj[✉] and Rajendra Patrikar

Centre for VLSI and Nanotechnology, Visvesvaraya National Institute of Technology,
Nagpur 440010, MH, India
pravinraj1711@gmail.com, rajendra@computer.org

**Abstract.** In this work, we have presented a new droplet splitting and transport mechanism using surface wetting phenomenon for lab on chip devices. The proposed methodology can be well utilized to split and transport a droplet without application of any external force or voltage. A 3D multiphase lattice Boltzmann algorithm with partial wetting surface is developed and simulated using D3Q19 model. A superhydrophobic surface is realized experimentally using a selective painting approach. The experimental results validated the predicted result. The surface free energy characteristics are obtained and analyzed with respect to time for droplet transportation.

**Keywords:** Surface wetting · Lattice Boltzmann method (LBM)
Splitting · Superhydrophobic · Lab on a chip (LOC)

## 1 Introduction

With the recent advancements in micro and nano engineering, the control and manipulation of fluids in micro and nano scale have become an interesting research problem. Many useful applications on super hydrophobic surface for droplet splitting and transportation are being contemplated [1]. Microfluidics has already emerged as an useful technology in electronics and it is currently being utilized in micro and nano printing, bio-inspired devices, wearable technologies, DNA chips and medical sensing units [2] combination of rigid electronics with soft microfluidics has a great potential in wearable technologies [3]. The main challenge in micro and nano domains is to handle the difficulty of surface to volume (S/V) ratio [4]. It increases sharply on these problems and hence to achieve precise control over the fluid is difficult. Moreover the multi physics and multi component nature of the domain makes the study even more complex. Lab on a chip (LOC) are miniaturized devices, being developed to perform chemical and biological analysis such as DNA, protein and glucose detection etc. [5]. Lab on a chip devices have principally been developed and utilized in the food, biomedical

© Springer Nature Singapore Pte Ltd. 2017
B. K. Kaushik et al. (Eds.): VDAT 2017, CCIS 711, pp. 707–717, 2017.
https://doi.org/10.1007/978-981-10-7470-7_66

and environmental fields. But recently they have also provided numerous benefits to the biosensor technology. A droplet based LOCs are recently emerged as a cheap, reliable and fast diagnostic tool for many useful bio applications.

A liquid flow in these devices can be actuated either by the pressure sources such as external mechanical pumps or integrated mechanical micropumps or vibration source or by combinations of capillary forces and electrokinetic mechanisms. The pressure driven flow is often not a viable option to force fluid through micro channels as it leads to the breaking and causes the leak in a microchannel. Recently Electrowetting on Dielectrics (EWOD) has emerged as an interesting technology to transport the droplet [6]. However, the main drawback of this technique is, it requires an application of relatively large external voltage typically ranges from 15 V to 300V DC. Moreover, the operating liquid needs to be always maintained as a conductive medium. But in practice, most of the bio fluids and components are much sensitive to such high electric field and hence may kill the interest of the study such as cell components. A typical EWOD device needs a complex on chip electrical pad and ground connection which cannot be tuned with respect to the real time variation of the volume of the fluid. Thus the droplet handling mechanism without external actuation mechanism is the need of the hour in lab on a chip domain [7]. Surface force actuation is considered as a suitable alternative. In the past decade, designing partial wetting platforms such as super hydrophobic surfaces have received much attention with applications in self cleaning, anti icing, heat transport, fuel transfer, nuclear textiles and many more.

Wettability of a liquid on a solid surface is usually identified by its equilibrium contact angle [8]. It is the angle between a solid surface and interface of liquid and air. Based on this, a surface is either considered as non-wettable (hydrophobic, for the liquid is water) if the contact angle is larger than $90°$, or wettable (hydrophilic) if the contact angle is smaller than $90°$. By a suitable hybrid hydrophobic-hydrophilic surface design, one can actuate a surface force variation and move the droplet. Recently, the mesoscopic lattice Boltzmann method (LBM) is effectively proved its tremendous advantages like massive parallelism and easy incorporation of multi physics [9]. It has massively succeeded in simulating complex fluid flows, including multi-phase flow, particle suspension flow, binary mixtures, liquid crystals, blood flow, and microchannel and nanochannel flows [10]. The method solves Boltzmann equation from the scratch and allows the particles to move on discrete lattices. The mass and momentum are locally conserved by streaming and collision among particles.

In this work, we have reported the simulation and experimental study on splitting and transportation of a liquid droplet without external actuation force using surface wetting phenomenon. A 3D Shan-Chen multiphase LBM model is developed and simulated for partial wetting drop dynamics problem of splitting and transportation without external force.

# 2  Methodology

## 2.1  Two Phase Lattice Boltzmann Method

The dynamics of a droplet is usually analyzed with a multiphase lattice Boltzmann method (LBM). The method tracks molecules as each particle then apply the treatment very similar to cellular automata [11–14]. In this study, the D3Q19 (nine-teen velocity on three dimensions) LBM model as shown in Fig. 1 is used. On each lattice point 19 values $f_i(x, t)$ are dumped, each of them assigned to a lattice vector $e_i$. Here we used the common notation that the vectors $e_i$ denoted the $i^{th}$ column vector of the matrix e.

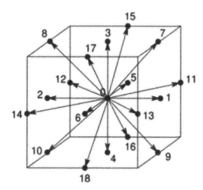

**Fig. 1.** Discrete velocity set of 3 dimension 19-velocity (D3Q19) LBM model.

$$e_i = \begin{bmatrix} 1 & -1 & 0 & 0 & 0 & 0 & 1 & 1 & 1 & 1 & -1 & -1 & -1 & -1 & 0 & 0 & 0 & 0 & 0 \\ 0 & 0 & 1 & -1 & 0 & 0 & 1 & -1 & 0 & 0 & 1 & -1 & 0 & 0 & 1 & 1 & -1 & -1 & 0 \\ 0 & 0 & 0 & 0 & 1 & -1 & 0 & 0 & 1 & -1 & 0 & 0 & 1 & -1 & 1 & -1 & 1 & -1 & 0 \end{bmatrix}$$

The D3Q19 model also has the default weights associated with it which are denoted as $w_i$. The evolution of the particle distribution function ($f_i$) at the point x at time t is given by lattice Boltzmann equation in above predefined 19 direction of the model ($e_i$) as given by Eq. (1)

$$f_i(\overrightarrow{x} + \overrightarrow{e_i}\delta_t, t + \delta_t) - f_i^t(\overrightarrow{x}, t) = -\frac{f_i^t(\overrightarrow{x}, t) - f_i^{eq}(\overrightarrow{x}, t)}{\tau} \qquad (1)$$

where LHS is responsible for streaming and RHS for collision with $i = 0, 1, ..18$ and is the dimensionless single relaxation time in the Bhatnagar-Groos-Krook (BGK) [11–13]collision operator approximation. Here $f_i^{eq}$ is the equilibrium distribution function which will be defined initially as per Eq. (2).

$$f_i^{eq}(\overrightarrow{x}, t) = w_i \rho (1 + \frac{3\overrightarrow{e_i}\,\overrightarrow{u}}{c^2} + \frac{9(\overrightarrow{e_i}\,\overrightarrow{u})^2}{2c^4} - \frac{3(\overrightarrow{u})^2}{2c^2}) \qquad (2)$$

where c is defined as $\frac{1}{\sqrt{3}}$. The lattice weights $w_i$ are defined as

$$w_i = \begin{bmatrix} 1/3 & i = 0 \\ 1/18 & i = 1, 2..5, 6 \\ 1/36 & i = 7, 8..17, 18 \end{bmatrix}$$

The macroscopic density and velocity can be obtained by adding all $f_i$ using Eqs. (3) and (4)

$$\rho(\overrightarrow{x}, t) = \sum_{i=0}^{e_i} f_i^t(\overrightarrow{x}, t) \tag{3}$$

$$\overrightarrow{u}(\overrightarrow{x}, t) = \frac{1}{\rho} \sum_{i=0}^{e_i} f_i \overrightarrow{e_i} \tag{4}$$

For the multiphase simulations, the SC-pseudo potential model incorporates a non-local interaction among particles. The interaction force $F_\alpha$ at each lattice site can be written as

$$F_\alpha = -G_{\alpha\alpha^\sim} \psi^\alpha(x) \sum_i w_i \psi(x + e_i) e_i \tag{5}$$

where $\psi^\alpha(x)$ is the effective mass which is the function of local density and time. The pseudopotential $\psi^\alpha(x) = 1 - exp(-\rho)$ is used to obtain better stability as proposed by Shan-Chen [15]. Here, $G\alpha\alpha^\sim$ is the Green's function. The magnitude of the $G\alpha\alpha^\sim$ determines the strength of interaction and its sign indicates whether the interaction is repulsive (cohesive force) or attractive (adhesive force) [16]. The macroscopic velocity is then updated with respect to force at the lattice point $\alpha$ using Eq. 6

$$\overrightarrow{u}(\overrightarrow{x}, t) = u^{'} + \frac{\tau}{\rho_\alpha} F_\alpha \tag{6}$$

where $u^{'}$ is the velocity obtained earlier. In order to tune the wetting, we used the wetting parameter $\eta_{wet}$ (0 to 1) introduced in the wall. So, the following initial condition must be specified at the wall for desired wetting

$$\rho_{wall} = \eta_{wet} * (\rho_h - \rho_l) + \rho_l \tag{7}$$

where $\rho_h$ and $\rho_l$ are densities of heavier fluid and lighter fluid respectively.

## 2.2    Implementation and Tuning of Contact Angle

The lattice domain $100 \times 100 \times 100$ is first filled with the lighter fluid (air) having density of $\rho_l$. A drop with the density $\rho_h$ of diameter $50\Delta x$ is then positioned at the centre of the domain Lx/2. The simulation parameters are initialized with $\rho_l = 0.0734$, $\rho_h = 2.6429$, and $G = -6.0$. As time evolved, it is evident that the droplet spreads and the equilibrium wetting contact angle with the surface is attained as shown in Fig. 2. This spreading is happened only due to the surface force, because no external force is applied. By varying the introduced tuning parameter $\eta_{wet}$ on walls as described in Eq. (7), the change in static contact angle is observed for corresponding wall density. The obtained contact angle at equilibrium is then measured by curve fitting image processing technique. Fig. 3 shows that for the above fixed density values $\rho_l$ and $\rho_h$, increase in the $\eta_{wet}$ results in decrease of contact angle which yields more surface wetting. From the obtained curve one can choose the desired wetting parameter for realizing hydrophilic surface $(\theta < 90°)$ as $\eta_{wet} > 0.25$ and vice versa for hydrophobic surface.

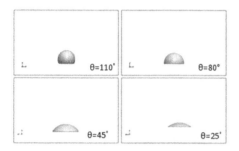

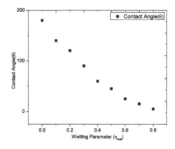

**Fig. 2.** Simulation results of contact angle $(\theta)$ on realized partially wetting surface.

**Fig. 3.** Tuning chart of introduced wetting parameter $(\eta_{wet})$ on contact angle $(\theta)$

# 3   Experimentation

To have a real insight on the study, we have performed wetting experiments using contact angle meter and captured the events using a digital camera. The super hydrophobic surfaces $(\theta = 160°)$ are patterned on a glass substrate using selective painting approach [17]. To obtain chemically homogeneous super hydrophobic surface the substrate was coated uniformly by a never wet spray at approximately 0.5 Mpa. The sample was then allowed to dry at room temperature for 20 mins. Figure 4 shows the scanning electron microscope(SEM) image of the fabricated hydrophobic surface. For hydrophilic substrate the plain Borosil microscope glass slides cleaned by Isopropyl alcohol (IPA) are used.

The experimentally obtained steady state equilibrium contact angles are 160° and 45° for hydrophobic and hydrophilic surfaces respectively as shown in Fig. 5.

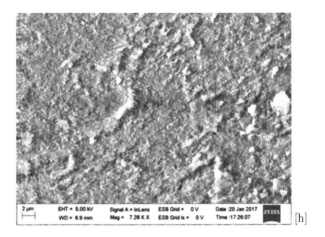

2 μm  EHT = 5.00 kV  Signal A = InLens  ESB Grid = 0 V  Data :20 Jan 2017  ZEISS
WD = 6.9 mm  Mag = 7.28 K X  ESB Grid is = 0 V  Time :17:26:07 [h]

**Fig. 4.** SEM image of fabricated super hydrophobic surface using selective painting.

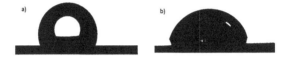

**Fig. 5.** Experimental contact angle of water on (a) hydrophobic surface (b) hydrophilic surface.

# 4   Splitting a Droplet by Surface Gradient Design

The droplet splitting on a partial wetting surface having a finite composite of microscopic patches with two chemical properties distinguished by Young's equilibrium contact angle is considered. The hydrophobic strip is chosen to have a contact angle of $\theta = 160°$ where as the hydrophilic surface is defined as $\theta = 45°$.

The surfaces having these contact angles are chosen so that the results would help to realize the similar surfaces like teflon ($\theta = 160°$) and silicon ($\theta = 45°$). To study the splitting of a droplet due to chemically treated heterogeneous surface, a small hemispherical drop of diameter $30\Delta x$ is placed at the centre. At first, the bottom surface is fully defined as a hydrophilic surface. A narrow hydrophobic strip of width $5\Delta x$ is placed on the centre of the hydrophilic surface. The lattice gradient of surface at normal is defined as zero to ensure no physical slope. Figure 7(a) shows the initial conditions of three cases considered for splitting. For dividing the droplet into two droplets, a plain hydrophobic strip is defined in the middle of domain whereas for dividing the droplet into three and four, the hydrophobic surfaces are designed to be y-shape and cross shape respectively.

It is observed that, as time evolved, the droplet experienced the expansion over the area occupied by hydrophilic surface due to adhesive force. At the same time it also experienced the inward force towards the hydrophobic strip as shown in Fig. 6. Thus, after considerable time, the droplet breaks into two, three and four daughter droplets respectively for corresponding surfaces as shown in Fig. 7(b,c,d). It is also observed that the newly formed daughter droplets continuously experienced the spreading until the equilibrium state is attained. The same phenomenon is also captured experimentally for splitting the drop into two using selective painting approach as shown in Fig. 7(e).

**Fig. 6.** Pressure profile of drop splitting at t = 0.8 ms.

## 5 Droplet Transportation

In order to transport the droplet without applying any external force, the surfaces are tuned to be heterogeneous with four successive chemical bends such as $\theta = 120°$, $\theta = 90°$, $\theta = 60°$ and $\theta = 45°$. The objective is to capture the transport of the droplet from the most hydrophobic bend $\theta = 120°$, to hydrophilic bend $\theta = 45°$. The two cases are studied with this approach. In case (i), the wetting surface is provided only on X plane and in case (ii), the wetting surface is provided on both X and Y plane as shown in Fig. 8(a). In case (i) as expected, the droplet moved from hydrophobic bend to hydrophilic bend (from left to right) with the evolution of time as shown in Fig. 8(b). One can observe that in the movement, the curvature at leading edge A start to elongate first towards the hydrophilic bend followed by pulling of curvature at trailing edge B in the same direction. This happened due to edge A experienced the greater hydrophilicity than edge B. It is also evident from the top view that surface area of liquid-solid interface in hydrophilic region increased only in X plane. This is because of the fact that there exist a strong opposition from hydrophobic surface to spread in Y plane. But in case (ii), due to availability of hydrophilic spreading surface in both the plane, the drop coverd the broader area as time evolved. Similar observation of trailing of edge B over edge A is observed but case (ii) approximately took $10\Delta x$ more time to reach the final bend than case (i). This is due to the fact that in case (ii) the spreading surface in Y direction pulls the drop in its direction against surface in X direction which results in overall speed reduction in X direction. From these result it can be concluded that any directional transport of a droplet for known velocity can be designed by controlling the surface area and location of the hydrophobic bends.

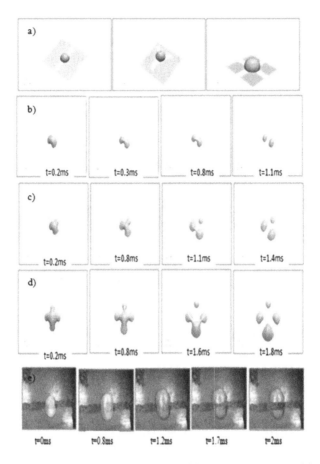

**Fig. 7.** Splitting of droplet (a) initial condition (b) splitting into two (c) splitting into three (d) splitting into four and (e) experimental result of splitting a droplet into two.

In order to understand the transport phenomenon, the surface free energy characteristics, which is similar to the interfacial tension with wetting surface area was studied by our hybrid 2D thermodynamic approach. To obtain the normalized surface free energy (SFE) [1], the gravity can be neglected and chain of 2D images on side view and top view are analyzed. The surface area of the air-liquid interface and liquid-solid interface are then computed for different time steps by curve fitting techniques. Since we considered four chemical bends in a heterogeneous surface, the normalized surface free energy barrier with four chemical bends is realized by the following Eq. (8).

$$\frac{\Delta SFE}{\gamma_{al}} = (A_{al} - A_{al0}) - \sum_{1}^{4} C_{ls} cos\theta_y \qquad (8)$$

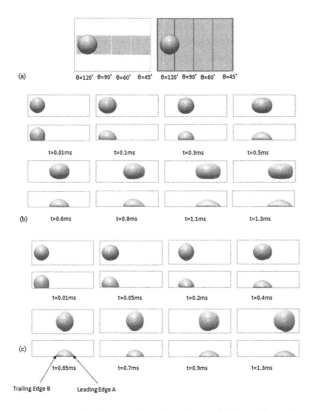

Fig. 8. Transportation of a droplet with surface force (a) initial condition (b) case (i) topview and side view (c) case (ii) top view and side view.

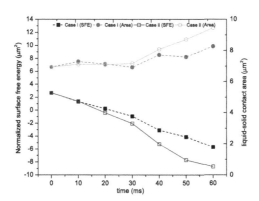

Fig. 9. Surface free energy vs liquid-solid interface area with respect to time.

The change in normalized surface energy and the liquid solid contact area with the evolution of time for case (i) and case (ii) is plotted in Fig. 8. From the results, it is clear that for each case, the liquid solid contact area increases with time along with the corresponding decrease in surface free energy. This shows that the droplet tends to attain the shape to minimize the surface energy which validate the study (Fig. 9).

# 6  Conclusion

In this work, we have briefly demonstrated the splitting and transportation of a droplet purely by means of the surface force. Thus, we have proposed the much easy droplet transport mechanism without applying any external force. A 3D multiphase lattice Boltzmann algorithm was developed and surface wetting was implemented by adapting simple boundary condition of SC model. Experimental results show the prediction to be the same. The droplet transportation is analyzed for two cases and surface free energy characteristics are obtained to prove the validation of the prediction of the droplet transportation.

**Acknowledgement.** The authors would like to acknowledge NPMASS/ADA for the financial support for the establishment of a National MEMS design center at VNIT. We also thanks INUP (Indian Nano User Program) of CEN, IIT Bombay for providing the opportunity to carry out SEM characterization of the fabricated surfaces.

# References

1. Fang, G., et al.: Droplet motion on designed microtextured superhydrophobic surfaces with tunable wettability. Langmuir **24**(20), 11651–11660 (2008)
2. Novak, L., et al.: An integrated fluorescence detection system for lab-on-a-chip applications. Lab Chip **7**(1), 27–29 (2007)
3. Pedersen, C.M., Mortensen, N.A.: Cell sorting using AC dielectrophoresis. Dissertation MS thesis, Department of Micro and Nanotechnology, Technical Univeristy of Denmark. Lyngby, Denmark (2006)
4. Pendharkar, G., Deshmukh, R., Patrikar, R.: Investigation of surface roughness effects on fluid flow in passive micromixer. Microsyst. Technol. **20**(12), 2261–2269 (2014)
5. Luka, G., et al.: Microfluidics integrated biosensors: a leading technology towards lab-on-a-chip and sensing applications. Sensors **15**(12), 30011–30031 (2015)
6. Jain, V., et al.: Design, fabrication and characterization of low cost printed circuit board based EWOD device for digital microfluidics applications. Microsyst. Technol. **23**, 1–9 (2015)
7. Tang, G.H., Xia, H.H., Shi, Y.: Study of wetting and spontaneous motion of droplets on microstructured surfaces with the lattice Boltzmann method. J. Appl. Phys. **117**(24), 244902 (2015)
8. Young, T.: An essay on the cohesion of fluids. Philos. Trans. R. Soc. Lond. **95**, 65–87 (1805)
9. Pravinraj, T., Patrikar, R.: Modelling and investigation of partial wetting surfaces for drop dynamics using lattice Boltzmann method. Appl. Surf. Sci. **409**, 214–222 (2017)

10. Jansen, H.P., et al.: Potential of lattice Boltzmann to model droplets on chemically stripe-patterned substrates. Appl. Surf. Sci. **361**, 122–132 (2016)
11. Yuan, P., Schaefer, L.: Equations of state in a lattice Boltzmann model. Phys. Fluids **18**(4), 042101 (2006)
12. Liu, L., Lee, T.: Wall free energy based polynomial boundary conditions for non-ideal gas lattice Boltzmann equation. Int. J. Mod. Phys. C **20**(11), 1749–1768 (2009)
13. Schmieschek, S., Harting, J.: Contact angle determination in multicomponent lattice Boltzmann simulations. Commun. Comput. Phys. **9**(05), 1165–1178 (2011)
14. Wu, L., et al.: Numerical simulations of droplet formation in a crossjunction microchannel by the lattice Boltzmann method. Int. J. Numer. Meth. Fluids **57**(6), 793–810 (2008)
15. Shan, X., Chen, H.: Lattice Boltzmann model for simulating flows with multiple phases and components. Phys. Rev. E **47**(3), 1815 (1993)
16. Gu, X., Gupta, A., Kumar, R.: Lattice Boltzmann simulation of surface impingement at high-density ratio. J. Thermophys. Heat Transfer **23**(4), 773–785 (2009)
17. Song, D., et al.: Selectively splitting a droplet using superhydrophobic stripes on hydrophilic surfaces. Phys. Chem. Chem. Phys. **17**(21), 13800–13803 (2015)

# Analytical Partitioning: Improvement over FM

Sameer Pawanekar$^{(\boxtimes)}$ and Gaurav Trivedi

Department of Electronics and Electrical Engineering,
Indian Institute of Technology Guwahati, Guwahati, India
{p.sameer,trivedi}@iitg.ernet.in

**Abstract.** Traditionally, VLSI standard cell placement has been driven by hypergraph partitioning tools such as Hmetis and MLPart, which employ FM based partitioning. According to the results seen in recent ISPD placement contests, none of the partition driven placers could produce a good solution. Hence, there is a room for improvement of hypergraph partitioning algorithms. In this paper, we present a novel hypergraph partitioning algorithm, which is based on nonlinear optimization. We solve nonlinear equations to partition the hypergraphs in ISPD98 benchmarks. Our results show an improvement over well-known FM heuristic. Our algorithm outperforms FM in 17 benchmarks out of 18, and an average improvement of 111.5% in the quality the of cuts.

## 1 Introduction

Hypergraph partitioning has been traditionally used in VLSI standard cell placement. Apart from placement, hypergraph partitioning has applications in the field of sparse matrix-vector multiplication [6,8], parallel computing [21,23], data mining [32]. VLSI formal verification [25,28] etc. This problem is known to be NP-complete [14].

A Hypergraph is the general form of a graph where the edges (known as hyperedge in hypergraph) can have more than two vertices as end points. Hypergraph is also called a netlist when dealing with VLSI placement problems. Hypergraph partitioning is the division of the input netlist into two sets of vertices with roughly equal number of vertices in such a way that the number of hyperedges crossing the two sets is reduced.

Hypergraph partitioning has been used in VLSI placement partition driven paradigm. The objective in this approach is to obtain high-quality cuts for the input netlist, which is then continued recursively until the number of cells in the partitioned sub-circuit is less than a given value. If the initial cut obtained from the partitioning tool is poor, it may results in increased wirelength in the recursively partitioned circuit. Hence, a high-quality cut means a good quality solution of the placement objective. Often, netlists have fixed terminals in the layout, which puts a constraint on the partitioner that vertices are initially fixed to a particular partition. A study on the allocation of vertices to a particular region has been conducted and emphasized in [4].

© Springer Nature Singapore Pte Ltd. 2017
B. K. Kaushik et al. (Eds.): VDAT 2017, CCIS 711, pp. 718–730, 2017.
https://doi.org/10.1007/978-981-10-7470-7_67

Hypergraph partitioning methods can be classified into (1) Constructive Methods and (2) Iterative Methods. Methods such as spectral partitioning [31] and network flow based partitioning [10,15] can be categorized as constructive methods. The methods which are based on popular graph partitioning methods Kernighan Lin (KL) [20] and Fiduccia-Mattheyses (FM) [13] come under the second category. There are numerous works on hypergraph partitioning in the literature. Example of these works are Chaco [22], hMetis [18], MLPart [5], PaToH [8], Mondriaan [30] and Parkway [29]. Many of these tools are primarily based on popular graph partitioning methods KL and FM.

Several placement tools [3,7,27] use hypergraph partitioning tools to optimize the wirelength by performing recursive partitioning of the input netlist. From the recent ISPD (International Symposium on Physical Design) contests, it is evident that none of the partition driven placement engines could perform well on the large benchmarks. This indicates that there is room for improvement of the partitioning tools and algorithms in the VLSI placement context.

We organize rest of the paper as follows. In Sect. 2, a survey of existing graph partitioning algorithms is presented. This is followed by Sect. 3 where we present the formulation of the hypergraph partitioning problem used in the proposed partitioner. Then, in Sect. 4 we discuss the implementation details of our method. Results of the experiments conducted for the ISPD98 partitioning benchmarks are analyzed and discussed in Sect. 5.

## 2    Related Work

This section presents a brief survey of the methods of hypergraph partitioning in the literature.

Leland and Hendrickson et al. [22] developed a hypergraph partitioner called Chaco which was based on spectral methods. This was the first approach using multilevel paradigm in hypergraph partitioning. In this method, they considered the geometry of the mesh along with local connectivity information of the hypergraph. The global structure of the netlist was identified by its Eigen values.

The implementation of hMetis by Karypis et al. [17,18] is a high-quality state-of-the-art work which is based on a multilevel implementation of FM. Initially, they cluster the input netlist recursively so that the problem size is reduced. Then, they apply FM method on the clustered netlist. In the last step, the partitioned and coarsened netlist is de-clustered at the original level. Many such cycles of refinement are performed during optimization. Their work is of high-quality and superior in terms of the quality of cuts and runtime compared to many of the partitioning methods proposed later in time.

Another hypergraph partitioning tool popular used in the academia is MLPart. Developed by Alpert et al. [4,5], MLPart is an open source tool and is used by Capo [7] for recursive bisection of the input netlist. Though MLPart is faster than hMetis, it does produce bigger cuts than hMetis for certain benchmarks which is evident from the results in [24]. MLPart is also based on FM method and multilevel clustering.

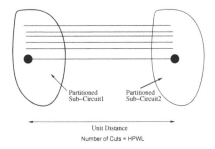

**Fig. 1.** HPWL of bisected hypergraph placed in one-dimensional bin is equal the number of cuts

# 3   Analytical Hypergraph Partitioning Model

In the proposed approach we address the problem of hypergraph partitioning by using analytical technique (by solving nonlinear equations). We perform nonlinear optimization using Conjugate Gradient method.

Analytical placement was proposed in [26], and implemented by [11,16]. The hypergraph partitioning problem can be defined as placement of a hypergraph $H = (V, E)$ in adjacent one-dimensional bins placed adjacent to each other. where $V = \{v_1, \ldots, v_n\}$ represents vertices and $E = \{e_1, \ldots, e_n\}$ represents hyperedges in $H$. Let $x_i$ be the $x$ coordinate of movable vertex $v_i$, the objective of hypergraph partitioning problem is to minimize total Half Perimeter Wire Length (HPWL) by finding optimum coordinates for all the vertices in $V$ and density of vertices in both the bins is equal to the desired distribution. HPWL can be defined using Eq. (1) [19] shown below.

$$W(x,y) = \sum_{e_k \in e_H} \left( \max_{\forall i,j \in n_H} |x_i - x_j| \right) \tag{1}$$

Figure 1 shows the placement of bisected hypergraph into two parts. One of the part of the hypergraph is at the center of a bin, whereas, the other part is placed at the center of another bin.

If the center of the bins are unit distance apart, it can be observed that the HPWL of the bisected hypergraph placement is equal to the number of external hyperedges of the two sub-hypergraphs after bisection. This fact is the motivation behind our approach to analytical hypergraph partitioning. By reducing the HPWL associated with placing one-dimensional hypergraph circuit, we aim to reduce the cut size.

The hypergraph placement area is divided into two uniform bins and total HPWL is minimized in such a way that the total area of vertices in both the bins becomes equal. The problem is expressed using the equations shown below.

$$minW(x,y) \quad suchthat \quad B_b \leq A_b \tag{2}$$

where, $A_b$ is the maximum area of movable vertices in bin-cell $b$, $W(x)$ is the wirelength, $B_b(x)$ is the potential which is the total area of movable vertices in the bin-cell $b$.

Since $W(x)$ is neither differentiable nor smooth, it cannot be directly minimized. Many smooth wirelength approximations have been proposed, such as quadratic wirelength [12], $L_p$ norm wirelength [9] and log-sum-exp wirelength [26]. Among these approximations, log-sum-exp model achieves the best results.

$$W(x,y) = \gamma \sum_{e \in E} (log \sum_{v_k \in e} exp(x_k/\gamma) + log \sum_{v_k \in e} exp(-x_k/\gamma)) \tag{3}$$

For density penalty minimization using nonlinear method, it is desired that the density function should be either differentiable or smooth. Since the density function $B_b(x)$ is also not smooth it cannot be minimized directly. An inverse Laplace Transform based smoothing function is proposed in [9]. A bell shaped density function which is differentiable at all the points is proposed in Aplace [16]. The above density function from [16] is incorporated into our partitioning framework.

$$B_b(x,y) = \sum_{v \in V} Q_x(g,v) \tag{4}$$

where $Q_x$ is the overlap functions of bin-cell $b$ and vertex $v$ along the $x$ directions. Equation (5) states bell-shaped potential for smoothing $Q_x$.

$$q_x(g,v) = \begin{cases} 1 - 2\frac{d_x^2}{w_b^2}, & 0 \leq d_x \leq \frac{w_b}{2} \\ \frac{2}{w_b^2}(d_x - w_b)^2, & w_b/2 \leq d_x \leq w_b \\ 0, & w_b \leq d_x \end{cases} \tag{5}$$

where $d_x$ is the center-to-center distance between the vertex $v$ and the bin-cell $b$ in the $x$-direction and $w_b$ is the bin-cell width. The notation used for different variables in this paper is described in Table 1.

**Table 1.** Variables used in this paper

| | |
|---|---|
| $x_i$ | Center coordinate for the vertex $v_i$ |
| $w_i$ | Width of the vertex $v_i$ |
| $w_b$ | Width of the grid-cell $b$ |
| $Q_b$ | Potential of grid-cell $b_i$ |
| $B_b$ | Density of grid-cell $b_i$ |
| $A_b$ | Maximum density of grid-cell $b_i$ |
| $\gamma$ | Wirelength parameter |
| $\lambda$ | Objective function parameter |
| $\alpha$ | Step size |

# 4  Details of Implementation

In this section we provide the details of implementation of the proposed tool. THe flow of the proposed method is represented by Algorithm 1 which forms the backbone of our approach.

**Algorithm 1.** Analytical Hypergraph Partitioning

**Input:** Hypergraph $H_0$
**Output:** $x^*$ optimal vertex coordinates
1: Randomly initialize vertex coordinates
2: Compute the potential of each bin
3: Initialzation of $\lambda_0$, $m = 0$
4: **while** $overflow\_ratio > 0.1$ **do**
5:    Solve min $W(x) + \lambda_m \sum(B_g - A_g)^2$
6:    $m = m + 1$
7:    $\lambda_m = 2 * \lambda_{m-1}$
8:    Estimate $overflow\_ratio$
9: **end while**

## 4.1   Initial Random Placement of Vertices

Since we consider the physical placement of vertices for HPWL optimization, it is important to initialize the coordinates with pre-defined values. This step is important as it gives a non-zero value to the gradient of wirelength. If random initialization is not performed, the overall wirelength of the netlist is zero and further optimization becomes difficult. As shown in Fig. 2, terminal vertices are placed in the center of the bins, whereas, non-terminal vertices are scattered randomly around the center of one of the bins.

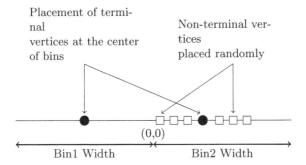

**Fig. 2.** Hypergraph partitioning solution model in the proposed partitioner.

## 4.2   Computation of Potential

Computation of potential of the bins is performed as Algorithm 1 requires the value of density and potential of bins for optimization. Computation of gradient of density and gradient of potential of the bins is carried out at each iteration of Algorithm 1.

## 4.3    Optimization Using Conjugate Gradient Method

At each iteration of **while** loop of the Algorithm 1, we call conjugate gradient method to solve Eq. 6.

$$min(W(x) + \lambda \sum_b (B_b(x) - A_b)^2) \tag{6}$$

The solution of Eq. 6 determines the quality of cut produced and hence it forms the center of this approach of hypergraph partitioning. When conjugate gradient method optimizes Eq. 6 for min-cut, it has to find a careful balance between the spreading of cells and wirelength. Optimizing wirelengh has an effect that brings all the vertices closer to each other, whereas, spreading of the vertices (achieving a balance of vertex count) along the bins has an effect that increases wirelength. To achieve this balance, a parameter $\lambda$ is introduced, which forms the factor for quadratic density penalty. We compute the initial value of $\lambda$ from Eq. 7.

$$\lambda = 2 \frac{\sum(|\frac{\partial W(x)}{\partial x}|)}{\sum_{x_i} \sum_{bin-cells} |\hat{B}_b - A_b|.(|\frac{\partial \hat{B}_b}{\partial x}|)} \tag{7}$$

To measure the even-ness of the distribution of the vertices across the bins, [11] proposed a term called *overflow_ratio* in the context of placement. We use the same quantity for the measurement of even-ness in the hypergraph partitioning context, where the placement is limited to one-dimension. We compute *overflow_ratio* from Eq. 8.

$$Overflow\ Ratio = \frac{\sum \max(B_b(x) - A_b, 0)}{\sum Total\ Area} \tag{8}$$

To solve Eq. (6) we use Conjugate Gradient Method as described in Algorithm 2.

---

**Algorithm 2.** Conjugate Gradient Method

---

**Input:** $f(x)$: objective function and $x_0$: initial solution
**Output:** optimal $x^*$

1: $h_0 = 0$; $d_0 = 0$
2: **while** $f(x_k) < f(x_{k-1})$ **do**
3:    $h_k = \nabla f(x_k)$                                    ▷ Gradient directions
4:    $B_k = \frac{h_k^T(h_k - h_{k-1})}{\|h_{k-1}\|^2}$          ▷ Polak-Ribiere parameter $B_k$
5:    $d_k = -h_k + B_k d_{k-1}$                          ▷ Conjugate directions
6:    $\alpha_k = sw_b/\|d_k\|_2$                          ▷ Step size
7:    $x_k = x_{k-1} + \alpha_k d_k$                        ▷ Solution update
8: **end while**

---

The **while** loop in Algorithm 2 must exit when the conjugate gradient algorithm is not able to optimize wirelength further for a given value of $\lambda$. This exit condition affects the quality of solution and runtime of this algorithm. If the loop exits early, faster runtimes may be observed albeit with a poor solution quality. A large number of iterations of conjugate gradient method not only increase the runtime but also affects the optimization. We obtain this careful balance of exit criteria by setting the condition shown in Eq. 9.

$$f_k(x) < Precision * f_{k-Exit\_iteration}(x) \tag{9}$$

The conjugate gradient method in Algorithm 2, which is used to solve Eq. 6, is dependent on the gradient of the objective function from Eq. 6. The gradients are computed for density, potential and wirelength of the input netlist. Conjugate gradient algorithm requires that step length $\alpha_k$ for the next solution is computed by line search. As line search is time consuming, we compute the step size $\alpha_k$ from Eq. 10.

$$\alpha_k = s \frac{w_b}{\|d_k\|_2} \tag{10}$$

where $s$ is a user-defined constant, $w_b$ is the width of the auxiliary bin and $d_k$ is the conjugate direction. A large value of $s$ facilitates fast convergence of the conjugate gradient algorithm, whereas, a small value of $s$ takes longer runtime and finds a better solution.

Equation 4 is a smooth approximation of HPWL and the value of $\gamma$ in Eq. 4 controls that approximation of HPWL of the input hypergraph. A smaller value of $\gamma$ is a closer approximation of HPWL, whereas, a larger value of $\gamma$ helps in better optimization of wirelength. We need to choose a value that is neither too small (to avoid computer precision problems) nor too big (which may cause deviation of the value from actual HPWL). We choose this value to be equal to 1% of the width of the auxiliary bin.

## 5   Experiments and Results

The proposed partitioner tool has been implemented in C language. We selected gcc compiler with "-O3" optimization option to get lesser runtimes. We performed the experiments on 2.6 GHz, 64-bit, dual core computer running on OSX operating system.

**Benchmarks.** ISPD98 partitioning benchmarks [2] are popular benchmarks used for reporting results in graph partitioning experiments. We use these benchmarks for reporting the results of our graph partitioning experiments. These benchmarks are 18 in number as shown in Table 2.

**Table 2.** Properties of ISPD98 partitioning benchmarks

| Ckt | # Cells | # Pads | # Modules | # Nets | # Pins |
|-----|---------|--------|-----------|--------|--------|
| ibm01 | 12506 | 246 | 12752 | 14111 | 50566 |
| ibm02 | 19342 | 259 | 19601 | 19584 | 81199 |
| ibm03 | 22853 | 283 | 23136 | 27401 | 93573 |
| ibm04 | 27220 | 287 | 27507 | 31970 | 105859 |
| ibm05 | 28146 | 1201 | 29347 | 28446 | 126308 |
| ibm06 | 32332 | 166 | 32498 | 34826 | 128182 |
| ibm07 | 45639 | 287 | 45926 | 48117 | 175639 |
| ibm08 | 51023 | 286 | 51309 | 50513 | 204890 |
| ibm09 | 53110 | 285 | 55395 | 60902 | 222088 |
| ibm10 | 68685 | 744 | 69429 | 75196 | 297567 |
| ibm11 | 70152 | 406 | 70558 | 81454 | 280786 |
| ibm12 | 70439 | 637 | 71706 | 77240 | 317760 |
| ibm13 | 83709 | 490 | 84199 | 99666 | 357075 |
| ibm14 | 147088 | 517 | 147605 | 152772 | 546816 |
| ibm15 | 161187 | 383 | 161570 | 186608 | 715823 |
| ibm16 | 182980 | 504 | 183484 | 190048 | 778823 |
| ibm17 | 184752 | 743 | 185495 | 189581 | 860036 |
| ibm18 | 201341 | 272 | 210613 | 201920 | 819697 |

**Comparison with FM Graph Partitioner.** For comparison of the quality of solution of the proposed partitioner, we selected FM algorithm. FM is a well-known partitioning heuristic employed by many state-of-the-art partitioning tools. The implementation of FM has been taken from [1]. FM algorithm is based on iterative optimization of the partitioning problem, which is a different method from our approach (Table 3).

**Value of Parameters.** The values of various paramters used in our method are listed in Table 4. These values are set when experimenting with ISPD98 benchmarks and are critical to the quality of solution obtained by running the tool. A small change in these values may affect the quality of solution or runtime of the proposed method.

In Fig. 3, we present the variation of objective parameters and functions with the increasing iteration of the conjugate gradient algorithm. In Fig. 3(a), objective function represented by Eq. 6 is shown, which reduces with the increasing iterations of conjugate gradient method. Figure 3(b) presents the cuts obtained during optimization. A Best cut is the best value of cut obtained during the optimization process and the solution for best cut is saved. Figure 3(c) present the variation in the ratio of the area of the two auxiliary bins. Finally, reduction in wirelength is shown in Fig. 3(d).

**Table 3.** Comparison of cuts obtained by our partitioner with existing partitioning tools FM on ISPD98 benchmarks with tolerance of 10%

| Benchmark | FM cut | Runtime (in seconds) | Proposed tool cut | Runtime (in seconds) |
|---|---|---|---|---|
| ibm01 | 630 | 0.151976 | 180 | 5.62 |
| ibm02 | 478 | 0.19297 | 262 | 6.02 |
| ibm03 | 2176 | 0.455931 | 1097 | 5 |
| ibm04 | 1270 | 0.270959 | 703 | 6.99 |
| ibm05 | 3292 | 0.542917 | 2869 | 5.98 |
| ibm06 | 1494 | 0.421936 | 1183 | 10.4 |
| ibm07 | 2349 | 0.703893 | 1241 | 23.4 |
| ibm08 | 3434 | 1.38879 | 1284 | 22.67 |
| ibm09 | 2839 | 1.27481 | 631 | 28.6 |
| ibm10 | 3123 | 1.9947 | 2090 | 35.84 |
| ibm11 | 2992 | 2.71659 | 1141 | 21.25 |
| ibm12 | 2707 | 2.03569 | 4861 | 16.73 |
| ibm13 | 2711 | 1.9937 | 1202 | 29.17 |
| ibm14 | 11806 | 7.01593 | 3767 | 71.49 |
| ibm15 | 10265 | 3.99839 | 8138 | 85.63 |
| ibm16 | 7887 | 5.62014 | 3470 | 65.7 |
| ibm17 | 6513 | 13.251 | 3934 | 67.92 |
| ibm18 | 4510 | 7.79082 | 2093 | 108.06 |
| Average | 2.115 | 0.074 | 1.00 | 1.00 |

**Table 4.** Various Parameters and their values used in the partitioning Flow

| Parameter | Value |
|---|---|
| $\gamma$ | 1% bin width |
| $Exit\_iteration$ | 25 |
| $overflow\_ratio_{min}$ | 0.1 |
| $Precision$ | $10^{-4}$ |

**Runtime of the Proposed Method.** Runtime break-up of the proposed method is shown by a pie-chart in Fig. 4. We observe that computation of ratio of the area of bins, computation of density and its gradient requires less time, whereas, computation of wirelength consumes 51% of time and calculation of cuts consumes 21% of runtime. The runtime of proposed method is more compared to FM heuristic. This is due to the fact that we need to compute gradients in each iteration of the conjugate gradient algorithm, whereas, in FM method, only the gains need to be computed. In future, we plan to reduce the runtime by computing gradient of wirelength and gradient of density by parallel methods.

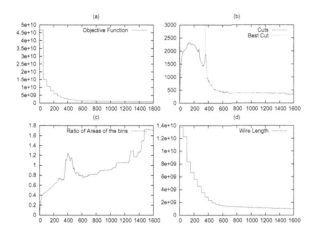

**Fig. 3.** Graphs showing various parameters getting optimized during each iteration of conjugate gradient method

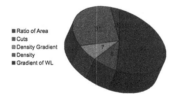

**Fig. 4.** Chart for runtime break up of the proposed partitioner

# 6    Conclusion

Hypergraph partitioning has application in VLSI standard cell placement and is a well-known problem. There are several methods that address this NP-complete problem. In this paper we present a novel approach for solving hypergraph partitioning problem in which the hypergraph is modeled as a circuit to be placed on a one-dimensional auxiliary placement region. At first, we perform random placement of vertices in the two auxiliary bins which are adjacent to each other. As a second step, we perform nonlinear optimization for the log-sum-exponent wirelength while reducing the quadratic density penalty of the bins. The proposed method produces high-quality solution compared to well-known FM heuristic. In future we plan to parallelize the computation of wirelength such that it reduces the runtime of the proposed method.

# References

1. FM hypergraph partitioning code. http://vlsicad.ucsd.edu/UCLAWeb/cheese/codes/code.tar.gz. Accessed 17 Jan 2017
2. Ispd98 hyergraph partitioning benchmarks. http://vlsicad.ucsd.edu/UCLAWeb/cheese/ispd98.html. Accessed 17 Jan 2017
3. Agnihotri, A., Yildiz, M.C., Khatkhate, A., Mathur, A., Ono, S., Madden, P.H.: Fractional cut: improved recursive bisection placement. In: Proceedings of International Conference on Computer Aided Design (ICCAD), pp. 307–310 (2003). https://doi.org/10.1109/ICCAD.2003.1257685
4. Alpert, C., Caldwell, A., Kahng, A., Markov, I.: Hypergraph partitioning with fixed vertices [vlsi cad]. IEEE Trans. Comput. Aided Des. Integr. Circuits Syst. **19**(2), 267–272 (2000). https://doi.org/10.1109/43.828555
5. Alpert, C., Huang, J.H., Kahng, A.: Multilevel circuit partitioning. IEEE Trans. Comput. Aid. Des. Integr. Circ. Syst. **17**(8), 655–667 (1998). https://doi.org/10.1109/43.712098
6. Boman, E., Wolf, M.: A nested dissection partitioning method for parallel sparse matrix-vector multiplication. In: 2013 IEEE High Performance Extreme Computing Conference (HPEC), pp. 1–6 (2013). https://doi.org/10.1109/HPEC.2013.6670333
7. Caldwell, A.E., Kahng, A.B., Markov, I.L.: Can recursive bisection alone produce routable, placements? In: Proceedings of Design Automation Conference, pp. 477–482 (2000). https://doi.org/10.1109/DAC.2000.855358
8. Catalyurek, U., Aykanat, C.: Hypergraph-partitioning-based decomposition for parallel sparse-matrix vector multiplication. IEEE Trans. Parallel Distrib. Syst. **10**(7), 673–693 (1999). https://doi.org/10.1109/71.780863
9. Chan, T., Cong, J., Sze, K.: Multilevel generalized force-directed method for circuit placement. In: Proceedings of the 2005 International Symposium on Physical Design, ISPD 2005, pp. 185–192. ACM, New York (2005). https://doi.org/10.1145/1055137.1055177
10. Alpert, C.J., Yao, S.Z.: Spectral partitioning: the more eigenvectors, the better. In: 32nd Conference on Design Automation, DAC 1995, pp. 195–200 (1995). https://doi.org/10.1109/DAC.1995.250089
11. Chen, T.C., Jiang, Z.W., Hsu, T.C., Chen, H.C., Chang, Y.W.: Ntuplace3: an analytical placer for large-scale mixed-size designs with preplaced blocks and density constraints. IEEE Trans. Comput. Aid. Des. Integr. Circ. Syst. **27**(7), 1228–1240 (2008). https://doi.org/10.1109/TCAD.2008.923063
12. Eisenmann, H., Johannes, F.: Generic global placement and floorplanning. In: Proceedings of Design Automation Conference, pp. 269–274 (1998)
13. Fiduccia, C.M., Mattheyses, R.M.: A linear-time heuristic for improving network partitions. In: Proceedings of the 19th Design Automation Conference, DAC 1982, pp. 175–181. IEEE Press, Piscataway (1982). http://dl.acm.org/citation.cfm?id=800263.809204
14. Garey, M.R., Johnson, D.S.: Computers and Intractability; A Guide to the Theory of NP-Completeness. W. H. Freeman & Co., New York (1990)

15. Hagen, L., Kahng, A.: A new approach to effective circuit clustering. In: 1992 IEEE/ACM International Conference on Computer-Aided Design, ICCAD-92. Digest of Technical Papers, pp. 422–427 (1992). https://doi.org/10.1109/ICCAD.1992.279334
16. Kahng, A.B., Wang, Q.: Implementation and extensibility of an analytic placer. IEEE Trans. Comput. Aid. Des. Integr. Circ. Syst. **24**(5), 734–747 (2005). https://doi.org/10.1109/TCAD.2005.846366
17. Karypis, G., Aggarwal, R., Kumar, V., Shekhar, S.: Multilevel hypergraph partitioning: application in VLSI domain. In: Proceedings of the 34th Design Automation Conference, pp. 526–529 (1997). https://doi.org/10.1109/DAC.1997.597203
18. Karypis, G., Kumar, V.: Multilevel k-way hypergraph partitioning. In: Proceedings of 36th Design Automation Conference, pp. 343–348 (1999). https://doi.org/10.1109/DAC.1999.781339
19. Kennings, A., Markov, I.: Analytical minimization of half-perimeter wirelength. In: Proceedings of the Design Automation Conference, ASP-DAC 2000, Asia and South Pacific, pp. 179–184 (2000). https://doi.org/10.1109/ASPDAC.2000.835093
20. Kernighan, B., Lin, S.: An efficient heuristic procedure for partitioning graphs. Bell Syst. Tech. J. **49**(2), 291–307 (1970)
21. Lee, C., Kim, M., Park, C.: An efficient k-way graph partitioning algorithm for task allocation in parallel computing systems. In: Proceedings of the First International Conference on Systems Integration, Systems Integration 1990, pp. 748–751 (1990). https://doi.org/10.1109/ICSI.1990.138741
22. Leland, R., Hendrickson, B.: An empirical study of static load balancing algorithms. In: Proceedings of the Scalable High-Performance Computing Conference, pp. 682–685 (1994). https://doi.org/10.1109/SHPCC.1994.296707
23. Luo, S., Liu, L., Wang, H., Wu, B., Liu, Y.: Implementation of a parallel graph partition algorithm to speed up BSP computing. In: 2014 11th International Conference on Fuzzy Systems and Knowledge Discovery (FSKD), pp. 740–744 (2014). https://doi.org/10.1109/FSKD.2014.6980928
24. MLPart: Hypergraph partitioning survey. http://web.eecs.umich.edu/~imarkov/pubs/book/part_survey.pdf
25. Narayan, A.: BDD partitioning for formal verification and synthesis of digital systems. Ph.D. thesis, University of California, Berkeley (1998)
26. Naylor, W.C., Donelly, R., Sha, L.: Non-linear optimization system and method for wire length and delay optimization for an automatic electric circuit placer. U.S. Patent 6 301 693(12) (2001)
27. Pawanekar, S., Kapoor, K., Trivedi, G.: Kapees: a new tool for standard cell placement. In: Gaur, M.S., Zwolinski, M., Laxmi, V., Boolchandani, D., Sing, V., Sing, A.D. (eds.) VDAT 2013. CCIS, vol. 382, pp. 66–73. Springer, Heidelberg (2013). https://doi.org/10.1007/978-3-642-42024-5_9
28. Sahoo, D., Iyer, S., Jain, J., Stangier, C., Narayan, A., Dill, D.L., Emerson, E.A.: A partitioning methodology for BDD-based verification. In: Hu, A.J., Martin, A.K. (eds.) FMCAD 2004. LNCS, vol. 3312, pp. 399–413. Springer, Heidelberg (2004). https://doi.org/10.1007/978-3-540-30494-4_28
29. Trifunovic, A., Knottenbelt, W.J.: Parkway 2.0: a parallel multilevel hypergraph partitioning tool. In: Aykanat, C., Dayar, T., Körpeoğlu, İ. (eds.) ISCIS 2004. LNCS, vol. 3280, pp. 789–800. Springer, Heidelberg (2004). https://doi.org/10.1007/978-3-540-30182-0_79
30. Vastenhouw, B., Bisseling, R.: A two-dimensional data distribution method for parallel sparse matrix-vector multiplication. SIAM Rev. **47**(1), 67–95 (2005). https://doi.org/10.1137/S0036144502409019

31. Yang, H., Wong, D.: Efficient network flow based min-cut balanced partitioning. In: IEEE/ACM International Conference on Computer-Aided Design, pp. 50–55 (1994). https://doi.org/10.1109/ICCAD.1994.629743

32. Zha, H., He, X., Ding, C., Simon, H., Gu, M.: Bipartite graph partitioning and data clustering. In: Proceedings of the Tenth International Conference on Information and Knowledge Management, CIKM 2001, pp. 25–32. ACM, New York (2001). https://doi.org/10.1145/502585.502591

# A Lifting Instruction for Performing DWT in LEON3 Processor Based System-on-Chip

Rajul Bansal[1,2(✉)], Mahendra Kumar Jatav[2], and Abhijit Karmakar[1,2]

[1] Academy of Scientific and Innovative Research (AcSIR),
CEERI Campus, Rajasthan 333031, India
rajulbansal@gmail.com
[2] CSIR - Central Electronics Engineering Research Institute (CEERI),
Pilani 333031, Rajasthan, India

**Abstract.** Discrete Wavelet Transform (DWT) calculations form an inherent part of many signal processing applications. Application specific instructions provide a means to increase performance and efficiency of System-on-Chip (SoC) requiring DWT operations. In this paper, lifting scheme based hardware for efficient DWT calculation, is implemented as an instruction to enhance the performance of an SoC. The hardware is integrated using the coprocessor interface of the SPARCv8 ISA based LEON3 processor. This method for attaching lifting hardware is found to be much more efficient than the prevalent system-bus based integration. The performance measure is provided in terms of CPI and MIPS along with FPGA and ASIC implementation results of the SoC.

**Keywords:** Lifting scheme · DWT · LEON3 · SPARCv8 · System-on-Chip
SoC

## 1 Introduction

Application specific instructions of extensible processor as well as coprocessor extensions of any processor, provide significant area and performance improvements by introducing application specific hardware functionality [1]. Custom instructions require architectural modification of processor pipeline that necessitates time consuming reverification of entire processor pipeline. Contrary to this, a coprocessor extension enables addition of application specific hardware as coprocessor instructions, without the need for modifying existing processor pipeline. It is reasoned that custom instructions are suitable for fine grained operations whereas coprocessor extensions are best suited for coarse grained tasks [2]. In this paper, we have proposed an architecture for computation of Discrete Wavelet Transform (DWT), incorporating lifting scheme [3] based custom hardware coprocessor instructions.

DWT is used in modern day audio, video, image and various signal processing applications due to inherent benefits, such as, multiresolution representation, sequential processing [4] and absence of blocking artifacts noticeable in Discrete Cosine Transform (DCT) based image processing. SoCs catering to advanced applications ranging from compressing 3D data such as that of an MRI scan [5] to combustion failure detection of

© Springer Nature Singapore Pte Ltd. 2017
B. K. Kaushik et al. (Eds.): VDAT 2017, CCIS 711, pp. 731–736, 2017.
https://doi.org/10.1007/978-981-10-7470-7_68

IC engines through vibration signal analysis [6], demand higher processing and low power requirement. Thus, making efficient hardware implementation a necessity rather than a requirement.

Most of the lifting-based architectures, including some of the recent ones [7–9], focus on memory reduction, throughput, latency, cycle count, pipeline equalization, frequency of operation, hardware utilization, area and low power. However, the effect of their integration in a modern SoC environment and corresponding results have not been provided. Our paper presents a case where lifting hardware is integrated as an instruction in the open source LEON3 processor pipeline, utilizing the coprocessor interface rather than the standard bus-based approach. The performance analysis is computed and compared both at software as well as hardware implementation level.

## 2   Lifting Hardware

Discrete wavelet transform gained widespread use for various signal processing applications after the proposition of lifting scheme by Sweldens [3] that reduced the hardware requirement for wavelet filter implementation by half. In this paper, we have implemented the lifting hardware for one dimensional, single level DWT and integrated it as an application specific custom coprocessor instruction, in order improve the system level performance.

In our work, a lossless (5, 3) filter is chosen as the wavelet filter for implementation. After breakup of poly-phase matrix and converting it to banded matrices multiplications, the final spatial domain equations formed after all the mathematical steps [3], can be written as (1) and (2) where $j$ represents the DWT level and $i$ represents indexing of input samples. Based on these lifting equations, the designed hardware constituting three lifting steps namely: Split, Predict and Update is as shown in Fig. 1.

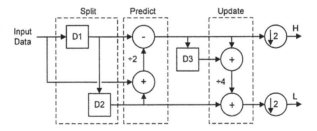

**Fig. 1.**  Lifting hardware

$$odd_{j+1,i} = odd_{j,i} - \left(even_{j,i} + even_{j,i+1}\right)/2 \tag{1}$$

$$even_{j+1,i} = even_{j,i} + \left(odd_{j+1,i-1} + odd_{j+1,i}\right)/4 \tag{2}$$

# 3 Integration with LEON3 Processor

The integration of lifting hardware with SPARCv8 compliant 7-stage pipelined LEON3 processor is accomplished using only the load, store and operate coprocessor instructions. In the detailed integration diagram shown in Fig. 2, FE, DE, RA, EX, MA, XC and WB represent fetch, decode, register access, execute, memory access, exception and write back stages of the LEON3 pipeline. Among the seven stages, control signals only from decode, execute and exception stages are required for lifting coprocessor integration. The signal, *cpo_store* is the only output and carries the store data back to integer unit which is subsequently stored back to data cache and in turn to RAM. The *cpi_lddata* carries data from data cache or RAM, to be loaded in the coprocessor register file.

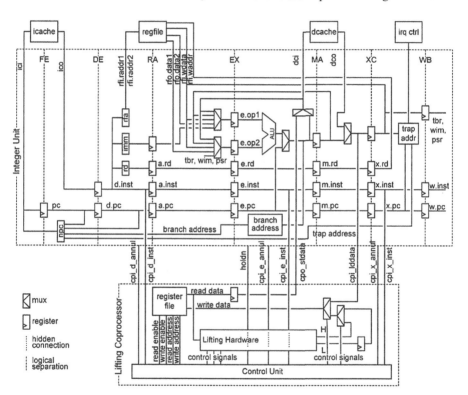

**Fig. 2.** Integration of lifting hardware with LEON3 pipeline

The lifting hardware gets *read data* from register file only when coprocessor operate instruction is issued. The resulting H and L are saved back to register file in alternate cycles. Since DWT in an in-place transform, the input data values can be overwritten and as a result, 32 samples can be operated upon in a single sequence of coprocessor instructions. In case, there is a situation when LEON3 pipeline gets stalled, the stalled status of the processor pipeline is forwarded through *holdn* signal, upon whose arrival the control unit stalls the lifting hardware and prevents loss of synchronization. This is required only when performing coprocessor load and store that must be synchronized with respective stages in the LEON3 pipeline. However, if LEON3 pipeline gets stalled during the coprocessor operate instruction, the lifting hardware operations proceed without any pause and this parallel execution of both the pipelines increases the CPI of the system.

## 4    Performance Analysis and Comparison

System modelling has been done on TSIM2 Instruction Set Simulator (ISS) at higher abstraction level for faster execution of application codes. The application code performs single-level, one-dimensional DWT of an image using coprocessor instructions integrated as assembly code snippets in the embedded C code of the application. To compare the results of our implementation, we have modelled three different SoC configurations. The first configuration (*Config* 1) computes the DWT operation using generic SPARCv8 instructions i.e. without custom lifting instructions. *Config* 2 computes the same using the proposed custom lifting hardware instructions, whereas *Config* 3 computes the same through lifting hardware attached via AHB system bus with requisite bus interface logic.

**Table 1.** Cycles per Instruction (CPI) performance

| Image Size | Parameter | DWT using generic SPARCv8 instructions | DWT using custom instructions | AHB bus coupled hardware based DWT |
|---|---|---|---|---|
| 32 × 32 | Cycles/Instructions | 114992/47456 | 78650/36121 | 94183/42593 |
| | CPI/MIPS | 2.42/41.23 | 2.18/45.93 | 2.21/45.22 |
| 64 × 64 | Cycles/Instructions | 323771/130210 | 178494/85340 | 237035/111012 |
| | CPI/MIPS | 2.49/40.22 | 2.09/47.81 | 2.14/46.83 |
| 128 × 128 | Cycles/Instructions | 1148029/460068 | 570390/283678 | 800963/386150 |
| | CPI/MIPS | 2.49/40.07 | 2.01/49.73 | 2.07/48.21 |
| 256 × 256 | Cycles/Instructions | 4424701/1777188 | 2116118/1073182 | 3034819/1482854 |
| | CPI/MIPS | 2.49/40.16 | 1.97/50.71 | 2.05/48.86 |
| 512 × 512 | Cycles/Instructions | 17490685/7041060 | 8261142/4228126 | 11932355/5866598 |
| | CPI/MIPS | 2.48/40.25 | 1.95/51.18 | 2.03/49.17 |

Based on the results shown in Table 1 for various sizes of an image, *Config* 2 provides an average of 30% reduction in number of cycles from pure software based implementation and 18% reduction in number of cycles from bus-based implementation. The percentage of reduction in number of cycles increases for larger image sizes. Moreover, for DWT using custom instructions, the number of cycles, instructions, CPI and Million Instructions Per Second (MIPS) are found to be better than both *Config* 1 and *Config* 3. It is further seen from Table 1 that the CPI/MIPS benefits grow with increase in the size of the image in case of designs with custom lifting instructions, whereas the CPI/MIPS values remain almost the same for DWT operations done using generic SPARCv8 instructions. It can be reasoned that as the image size is increased, the percentage of coprocessor instructions in the machine code increases, which subsequently causes the decrease of CPI values.

The three design cases are also implemented in HDL targeting Spartan 6 XC6SLX75 FPGA device using Xilinx ISE 13.4. They are further targeted for standard cell based ASIC flow using UMC 180 nm based Faraday standard cell library. Synthesis results presented for both in Table 2 show that there is only a slight increase in resource utilization on integrating additional lifting hardware and this increase can be justified for the amount of performance improvement it provides. Moreover, the increase in the hardware is lesser than the traditional integration approach using system bus. This is because of reduced address decode and control logic within the arbiter unit of AHB bus. The proposed integration achieves lower power consumption than the bus-based design making it power efficient as well.

**Table 2.** FPGA and ASIC synthesis results

| Parameter | Standard design (*Config* 1) | With custom instruction (Config 2) | With bus-based integration (Config 3) |
|---|---|---|---|
| No. of slice registers (93296) | 5666 | 5963 | 6014 |
| No. of slice LUTs (46648) | 20891 | 21210 | 21311 |
| No. of RAM blocks (172) | 42 | 46 | 46 |
| FPGA Power (mW) | 310 | 306 | 314 |
| Total ASIC cell area (um$^2$) | 12758050 | 12879652 | 12884508 |
| ASIC Power (mW) | 549.1 | 554.9 | 555.7 |

# 5   Conclusion

In this paper, we have presented a unique case where lifting hardware is integrated as an instruction in a processor pipeline utilizing the coprocessor interface. Analysis of results suggest that the proposed hardware modification provides significant performance and power benefits. The lifting hardware that is integrated in our design can be used recursively to implement multilevel as well as multidimensional DWT. Moreover, a dual scan architecture can also be integrated to achieve higher hardware utilization and further performance benefits can be attained.

# References

1. O'Melia, S., Elbirt, A.J.: Enhancing the performance of symmetric-key cryptography via instruction set extensions. IEEE Trans. Very Large Scale Integr. (VLSI) Syst. **18**(11), 1505–1518 (2010)
2. Sun, F., Ravi, S., Jha, N.K.: A synthesis methodology for hybrid custom instruction and coprocessor generation for extensible processors. IEEE Trans. Comput. Aided Des. Integr. Circ. Syst. **26**(11), 2035–2045 (2007)

R. Bansal et al.

3. Sweldens, W.: The lifting scheme: a custom-design construction of biorthogonal wavelets. Appl. Comput. Harmonic Anal. 3(2), 186–200 (1996)
4. Potdar, V.M., Han, S., Chang, E.: A survey of digital image watermarking techniques. In: IEEE International Conference on Industrial Informatics (2005)
5. Badawy, W., Weeks, M., Zhang, G., Talley, M., Bayoumi, M.A.: MRI data compression using a 3-D discrete wavelet transform. IEEE Eng. Med. Biol. Mag. 21(4), 95–103 (2002)
6. Shirazi, F.A., Mahjoob, M.J.: Application of discrete wavelet transform (DWT) in combustion failure detection of IC engines. In: International Symposium on Image and Signal Processing and Analysis ISPA (2007)
7. Mohanty, B.K., Mahajan, A., Meher, P.K.: Area- and power-efficient architecture for high-throughput implementation of lifting based 2-D DWT. IEEE Trans. Circ. Syst. II Express Briefs 59(7), 434–438 (2012)
8. Zhang, W., Jiang, Z., Gao, Z., Liu, Y.: An efficient VLSI architecture for lifting-based discrete wavelet transform. IEEE Trans. Circ. Syst. II Express Briefs 59(3), 158–162 (2012)
9. Hu, Y., Jong, C.C.: A memory-efficient high-throughput architecture for lifting-based multi-level 2-D DWT. IEEE Trans. Signal Process. 61(20), 4975–4987 (2013)

# Droplet Position Estimator for Open EWOD System Using Open Source Computer Vision

Vandana Jain$^{(\boxtimes)}$, Vasavi Devarasetty, and Rajendra Patrikar

Centre for VLSI and Nanotechnology, Visvesvaraya National Institute of Technology,
Nagpur 440010, MH, India
vandy087@gmail.com, vasavi.d3@gmail.com, rajendra@computer.org

**Abstract.** Digital microfluidics (DMF) emerged as a popular technology for lab on chip (LOC) application, which allows full and independent control over droplets on an array of electrodes. In this work, we have demonstrated a low-cost open electrowetting on dielectric (EWOD) based system, which is capable of tracking droplet position on the single substrate in real time. Printed circuit board (PCB) technology has been used for fabrication of two dimentional open EWOD device. Bio- compatible polydimethylsiloxane (PDMS) is used as a dielectric as well as a hydrophobic layer. The controlled droplet transport is successfully done on the fabricated device. The detection of droplet position is successfully demonstrated using open source computer vision image processing tool. This work illustrates the promise of open two- dimensional EWOD device for digital microfluidics application.

**Keywords:** Electrowetting on dielectric (EWOD)
Polydimethylsiloxane (PDMS) · Printed circuit board (PCB)
Open source computer vision (OpenCV)

## 1 Introduction

Many microfluidic tools are developed to control fluidics on the microscale level. The first generation is continuous microfluidics and the second generation is digital microfluidics [1]. In continuous microfluidics for liquid flow, we need external components like micropumps and microvalves and also very difficult to manage many operations at a time [2]. Whereas in EWOD based digital microfluidics on a single chip can perform parallel various fluidic operations like dispense, transport, splitting, and merging [3], which offers advantages of portability, automation, higher sensitivity and high throughput in diagnosis applications [4]. EWOD is essentially the phenomenon where the wetting behavior of a conductive droplet placed on a dielectric surface can be modified by application of electric field across the dielectric below the droplet [5]. The contact angle change is predominantly because of accumulation of charge carriers at the solid and liquid interface. We have seen that most reported EWOD chips use a series of electrode pads essentially in a one- dimensional line pattern, designed for a specific task by using highly sophisticated lithography technique [4] and expensive dielectric materials like Teflon-AF or paralene-C [6]. In our previous works, we have demonstrated low-cost one- dimensional EWOD chip using PCB technology [7]. But for desired universal chips allowing reconfigurable user paths would require the electrode pads in a two-dimensional pattern [5,8]. Compared to conventional lithography technique, PCB technology allows high reconfigurability and reusability at lower manufacturing cost [9]. However, the PCB-PDMS based inexpensive approach for two- dimensional EWOD system fabrication is not studied much. Also very less cost effective EWOD systems are available for the continuous monitoring of droplet parameter with accuracy [10], which is essential for precise control and accurate manipulation of droplet for enhancing the system performance. In this work, the development of a PCB-PDMS based two-dimensional open EWOD system with continuous monitoring of droplet position using open source computer vision (OpenCV) is discussed. The rest of the paper is organized as follows; in Sect. 2 experimental aspects of device fabrication is discussed. The measurement setup is discussed in Sect. 3. Results obtained are presented in Sect. 4 followed by conclusions in Sect. 5.

## 2    Device Fabrication

The proposed open EWOD device in this work has dimensions of $3 \times 3$ cm$^2$ PCB, consists of 22 copper electrodes ($2$ mm $\times$ $2$ mm) separated by 150 μm gap. Each electrode pad is connected by eight control signals through a 160 μm wide line. The PCB is designed in such a way that when one electrode is activated it will not affect the adjacent electrode. The pictorial view of eletrode connection is shown in Fig. 1, where the same colour regions are representing electrodes are activated by the same control signal, and black dot is a PTH (Plated through hole) hole which allows the electrode to connect from the bottom side of PCB. The physical design of PCB is shown in Fig. 2(a). Before PDMS coating, we have filled the PTH hole (300 m) of our PCB using soldering paste to avoid leakage. Then coating is done using spin coater. For getting uniform coating, we have coated device two times with different rpm speed. In first time device is coated with 1500rpm and allowed to cure for 45 mins at 100°$C$ and second time device is coated with 2500 rpm and then cured at 100°$C$ for 45 mins. Here PDMS is used as a dielectric as well as a hydrophobic layer. PDMS is a biocompatible and transparent material, which has an average static contact angle of 110°, which

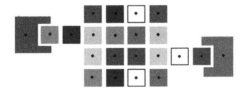

**Fig. 1.** Pictorial representation of electrodes connection.

is capable of easing the droplet operation [11]. The PDMS coatings are removed from contact pads by scraping with a scalpel to facilitate electrical contact. The electrode pad contact is provided through the female connector.

We have used four aluminum wire (catena, diameter $100\,\mu m$) for providing ground connection of droplet. The ground electrode wires are carefully arranged along the centerline of control electrode array on fabricated open EWOD device as shown in Fig. 2.(b).

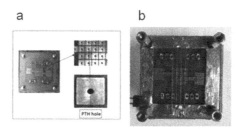

**Fig. 2.** (a) Front view of fabricated device (b) Final device after arranging ground wires.

# 3   System Description

## 3.1   High Voltage Supply Unit

A novel and precise droplet handling system is developed as shown in Fig. 3. A high voltage source is obtained from a DC boost converter. The application of high voltage is programmed by a microcontroller, which actuates a specific electrode through an electromagnetic relay. The complete setup consists of USB digital camera for capturing image/video in real time, XYZ stage for holding the sample, Arm7 based electronic system which has standard circuits for providing actuation of voltage and handling image processing along with HDMI display which is shown in Fig. 4. The system is designed to achieve precise real-time control over the movement of the droplet in real time embedded Linux platform. The C++ and python codes are developed and integrated into Qt GUI interface so that precise control of droplet on the electrode with a positive and negative voltage with respect to ground is achieved. Ground and a positive voltage of power supply are connected respectively to the ground wire and the contact pads of the PCB [7].

## 3.2   Image Processing

The developed system is combined with integrated development environment (IDE) software with OpenCV libraries for continuous mentoring of droplet position. The functionalities of OpenCV library are enhancing the image processing analysis. To characterize the developed DMF device, we have performed droplet transporting with position detection in open EWOD system.

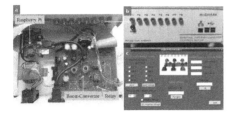

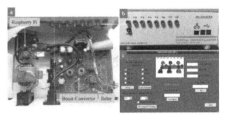

**Fig. 3.** High voltage control unit (a) Top view of boost convertor with raspberry pi (b) Side view (c) Qt based GUI interface.

**Fig. 4.** Test setup.

# 4   Result and Discussion

## 4.1   Droplet Transportation

A 5 µL DI water droplet with 0.1M KCL is placed on electrode pad with the top ground and transport is realized by sequentially energizing the adjacent electrode pad. But high pinning effects and sticky nature of PDMS, transportation of droplet from one pad to another pad is not observed. For getting a proper droplet motion very thin layer of silicone oil (350 mPa.s) is spread on the PDMS coated device. We have noted that with and without oil film there is no change in initial contact angle of the droplet. On the other hand, oil film reduces the minimum electrical field required to move the droplet. Thus all the experiments reported in this paper are performed with PDMS layer covered with silicone oil film. The vertical and horizontal movement of droplet is shown in Fig. 5.

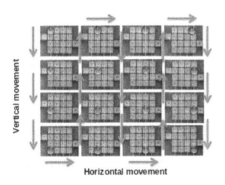

**Fig. 5.** Transportation of droplet.

**Fig. 6.** Droplet position detection (a) Original image (b) Threshold image (c) Terminal image with droplet position.

## 4.2 Droplet Position Detection

The position of a droplet on electrode pads is monitored continuously using OpenCV. Each frame of the live stream is correlated through image processing tools. OpenCV libraries and IDE platform are combined using C++ codes. The written code, along with HSV values of the droplet tincture, plays a vital role in the detection of centroid pixel coordinate of a droplet through colour thresholding as shown in Fig. 6(b). If the droplet centroid pixel coordinates lie within the respective limits of the coordinates of the electrode pads, the position of the droplet is printed on the terminal as shown in Fig. 6(c).

## 5 Conclusion

A low-cost reconfigurable open two-dimensional EWOD device has been demonstrated. User friendly interface electronics is successfully designed and implemented. A droplet transport is performed in both horizontal and vertical directions on the proposed device. The position of the droplet continuously monitored using the open source computer vision (OpenCV) platform. This work shows the potential for low-cost, rapid DMF device for future lab on chip applications.

## References

1. Chung, S.K., et al.: Micro bubble fluidics by EWOD and ultrasonic excitation for micro bubble tweezers. In: IEEE 20th International Conference on Micro Electro Mechanical Systems MEMS 2007. IEEE (2007)
2. Berthier, J.: Micro-Drops and Digital Microfluidics. William Andrew, Norwich (2012)
3. Cho, S.K., Moon, H., Kim, C.J.: Creating, transporting, cutting, and merging liquid droplets by electrowetting-based actuation for digital microfluidic circuits. J. Microelectromech. Syst. **12**(1), 70–80 (2003)
4. Pollack, M.G., Shenderov, A.D., Fair, R.B.: Electrowetting-based actuation of droplets for integrated microfluidics. Lab Chip **2**(2), 96–101 (2002)
5. Mugele, F., Baret, J.-C.: Electrowetting: from basics to applications. J. Phys.: Condens. Matter **17**(28), R705 (2005)
6. Saeki, F., et al.: Electrowetting on dielectrics (EWOD): reducing voltage requirements for microfluidics. Polym. Mater. Sci. Eng. **85**, 12–13 (2001)
7. Jain, V., et al.: Design, fabrication and characterization of low cost printed circuit board based EWOD device for digital microfluidics applications. Microsyst. Technol. **23**, 389–397 (2015)
8. Fair, R.B.: Digital microfluidics: is a true lab-on-a-chip possible? Microfluid. Nanofluid. **3**(3), 245–281 (2007)
9. Gong, J., Kim, C.-J.: Direct-referencing two-dimensional-array digital microfluidics using multilayer printed circuit board. J. Microelectromech. Syst. **17**(2), 257–264 (2008)
10. Li, Y., Li, H., Baker, R.J.: A low-cost and high-resolution droplet position detector for an intelligent electrowetting on dielectric device. J. Lab. Autom. **20**(6), 663–669 (2015)
11. Mata, A., Fleischman, A.J., Roy, S.: Characterization of polydimethylsiloxane (PDMS) properties for biomedical micro/nanosystems. Biomed. Microdevices **7**(4), 281–293 (2005)

# Design and Implementation of Mixed Parallel and Dataflow Architecture for Intra-prediction Hardware in HEVC Decoder

Rituparna Choudhury and P. Rangababu$^{(\boxtimes)}$

Department of Electronics and Communication Engineering,
National Institute of Technology Meghalaya,
Bijni Complex, Laitumkhrah, Shillong 793003, India
rituparnachoudhury.1993@gmail.com, p.rangababu@gmail.com

**Abstract.** The objective of the paper is to implement an area efficient hardware for intra prediction in high efficiency video coding (HEVC) decoder for DC, angular and planar modes of all block sizes. viz., $64 \times 64$, $32 \times 32$, $16 \times 16$, $8 \times 8$ and $4 \times 4$. The proposed hardware is written in Verilog and implemented in field programmable gate array (FPGA) Virtex-7. The clock cycles consumed by the proposed design is the lowest as compared to the existing designs [7] as in the proposed architecture all the three modes ( DC, angular and planar modes) are executed in parallel. The reference pixels are processed and one $4 \times 4$ block is obtained at the output in one clock cycle as the architecture is designed to process 16 pixels (one $4 \times 4$ block) in parallel for all the three modes. Once the prediction for one mode of a block is completed the resources are released and made available to be used by next mode or next block. Thus the resource consumption is less as compared to existing designs where all the modes for each block is executed irrespective of encoder information which results in unnecessary resource usage.

**Keywords:** High efficiency video coding (HEVC) · Intra prediction
Field programmable gate array (FPGA)

## 1 Introduction

High efficiency video coding (HEVC) is the recent standard in video compression. It was developed jointly by Video Coding Experts Group (VCEG) and Moving Picture Experts Group (MPEG) groups [4]. The present work investigates the challenges in intra prediction due to the increased complexity introduced by the newly added modes (i) DC (ii) Planar (iii) 32-Angular modes for different block sizes. In literature, there exists several design of Intra prediction hardware in various platforms. The Intra prediction hardware architecture proposed by Ercan *et al.* [6], reduces the energy consumption by reducing the prediction equations for $4 \times 4$ and $8 \times 8$ blocks. However this design supported only $4 \times 4$ and $8 \times 8$ blocks whereas the proposed hardware supports all the modes and

© Springer Nature Singapore Pte Ltd. 2017
B. K. Kaushik et al. (Eds.): VDAT 2017, CCIS 711, pp. 742–750, 2017.
https://doi.org/10.1007/978-981-10-7470-7_70

prediction sizes. The architecture proposed by Biao *et al.* [8] introduces a fully pipelined architecture by reducing the dependency of data between blocks and thus achieved a throughput of up to four pixels per clock cycle. On the other hand, the optimised architecture proposed by Manel *et al.* [7], exploits the symmetry among the horizontal and vertical modes which decreases the memory overhead. The design proposed by Faraouk *et al.* [2] implements intra prediction using processing elements (PEs). It consists of a pipelined structure with three stages of registers. The design proposed in Jiang*et al.* [5] implements a unified reference sample indexing that avoids wasting cycles on rearrangement or filling-in reference samples to a new buffer. The remainder of the paper is arranged as follows. Section 2 presents the Intra Prediction Algorithm in HEVC decoder. Section 3 describes Proposed Parallel Intra prediction Hardware. Section 4 shows the Results and Discussion followed by Conclusion in Sect. 5.

# 2   Intra Prediction Algorithm

In HEVC, Intra prediction unit (PU) inside a coding unit (CU) is done by exploiting the pixels in the available neighbouring PUs. In DC and planar modes, the predicted pixels are obtained from the reference coefficients of top and left blocks [4].

## 2.1   DC Mode Prediction

If prediction unit size is less than 32, then the prediction is done according to Eqs. (2), (3) and (4)and other values are filled with dc average calculated in Eq. (1). Otherwise all pixels values are filled with dc average value where $x$ and $y$ is the co-ordinates of left and top pixel coefficients respectively [1].

$$dV = \sum_{0}^{pred\_size-1} p[x][0] + \sum_{0}^{pred\_size-1} p[0][y] + pred\_size \qquad (1)$$

$$p[0][0] = (p[0][0] + 2 * dV + p[0][0] + 2) \gg 2 \qquad (2)$$

$$p[x][0] = (p[x][0] + 3 * dV + 2) \gg 2 \qquad (3)$$

*where* $x = 1$ *to* $pred\_size-1$

$$p[0][y] = (p[0][y] + 3 * dV + 2) \gg 2 \qquad (4)$$

*where* $y = 1$ *to* $pred\_size-1$

$$p[x][y] = dV \qquad (5)$$

*where* $x,\ y = 1$ *to* $pred\_size-1$

## 2.2  Planar Prediction

In planar mode, the pixel is calculated according to the Eqs. (6), (7) and (8) where $R_{x,0}$ and $R_{0,y}$ are the left and top pixel coefficients respectively and pred_size is the prediction size [9].

$$P_{x,y}^{V} = (pred\_size - 1 - y) * R_{x,0} + y * R_{0,N+1} \tag{6}$$

$$P_{x,y}^{H} = (pred\_size - 1 - x) * R_{0,y} + x * R_{N+1,0} \tag{7}$$

$$P_{x,y} = (P_{x,y}^{V} + P_{x,y+N}^{H}) \gg (log_2(pred\_size) + 1) \tag{8}$$

## 2.3  Angular Prediction

For angular prediction of pixels according to [4] at various block sizes, there are 33 modes in angular prediction. If prediction angle is positive, then for modes equal to or greater than 18, the first pixels from index number 0 to pred_size of reference buffer is filled with left pixels and for mode less than 18, it is filled with top pixels. Remaining part of reference buffer is filled according to Eq. (10) with left pixels and otherwise for modes less than 18, pixels is obtained by replacing left pixels with top pixels in Eq. (10). But if the prediction angle is negative, then the first pixels from index number 0 to pred_size is filled with top or left pixel according to mode and remaining reference buffer is reconstructed according to Eq. (9) in case of vertical prediction and otherwise top pixel in Eq. (9) is replaced with left pixel.

$$ref[x] = p[0][1 + ((x * invAngle + 128) \gg 8)] \ \ with \ x = \ 0..(pred\_size * intraPredAngle) \gg 5 \tag{9}$$

$$ref[x] = p[x][0] \ \ with \ x = \ pred\_size + 1..2 * pred\_size \tag{10}$$

$$predSamples[x][y] = ((32 - iFact) * ref[x + iIdx + 1] \\ + iFact * ref[x + iIdx + 2] + 16) \gg 5 \tag{11}$$

After choosing the reference buffer, the index to this buffer and weighing factor is evaluated according to Eqs. (12) and (13) respectively for prediction mode less than 18. Otherwise x is replaced with y in Eqs. (12) and (13) for $iIdx$ and $iFact$ respectively. If weighing factor is 0, the pixels are predicted using Eq. (15) for modes less than 18 and y is replaced with x in Eq. (15) for other modes. Otherwise the final pixels are calculated from Eq. (14) for mode less than 18 or from Eq. (11) for other modes [3].

$$iIdx = ((x + 1) * intraPredAngle) \gg 5 \tag{12}$$

$$iFact = ((x + 1) * intraPredAngle)\&31 \tag{13}$$

$$predSamples[x][y] = ((32 - iFact) * ref[y + iIdx + 1]$$
$$+iFact * ref[y + iIdx + 2] + 16) \gg 5 \tag{14}$$

$$predSamples[x][y] = ref[y + iIdx + 1] \tag{15}$$

# 3    Proposed Design

In the proposed work, the calculation of one $4 \times 4$ block of pixel is done in parallel. After processing a $64 \times 64$ block as input, the controller checks what are the modes present in the block. The appropriate inputs are processed into DC mode, planar mode and angular mode modules as shown in Fig. 1 and the three modes are processed in parallel. The advantage of the proposed hardware is that the hardware do not have to wait for one mode to complete which will save the time required to decode whole block.

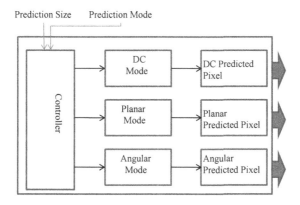

**Fig. 1.** Block diagram of proposed intra-prediction architecture

After getting the inputs state controller checks the mode and prediction size. When mode is asserted as 1, the selected mode is DC mode. The architecture for DC mode is shown in Fig. 3. In DC mode the pixel calculation follow two paths controlled by the master controller. For prediction size more than and equal to 32, the predicted pixels are directly filled with dc values producing 16 pixels per clock cycle. Otherwise, the controller enables the other pixel generator circuit which calculates the pixel value as mentioned in preceding section. For prediction mode less than 32, the pixel calculation starts after the final dc value is calculated. At first the four top and four left pixels are calculated in one clock cycle and this will be continued till all the top and left pixels of the block is predicted as shown in Fig. 3. Once all the top and left pixels are predicted, the filling of dc value in the remaining pixel is done at the rate of 16 pixels per clock cycle till the entire block is predicted. When mode is asserted as 0, the selected

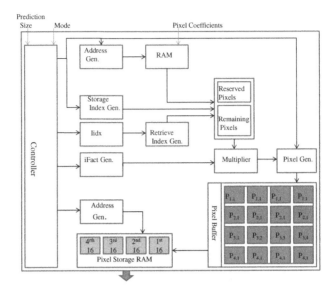

**Fig. 2.** Block diagram of intra-prediction when prediction angle is non-zero

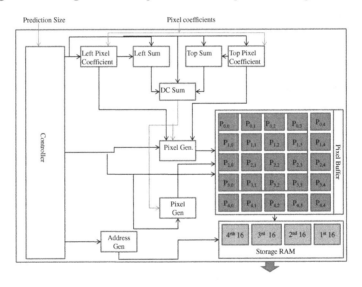

**Fig. 3.** Block diagram of DC mode

mode is planar as shown in Fig. 4. In planar mode to calculate 16 pixels in one clock cycle, 16 sum operations are calculated with respect to the 16 top and 16 left pixel coefficients.

In angular mode prediction of HEVC, there are 35 modes, out of which mode 2 to 34 are angular modes. According to the modes the prediction angle is decided and then the prediction angle is used to choose the architecture to

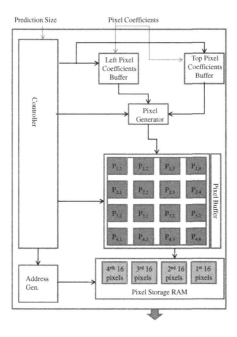

**Fig. 4.** Block diagram of planar mode

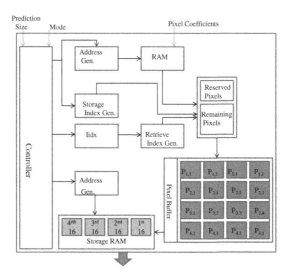

**Fig. 5.** Block diagram of intra-prediction when prediction angle equal to 0

predict the pixel for prediction angle equal to 0 as shown in Fig. 5. Otherwise for nonzero prediction angle the architecture is shown in Fig. 2. Once the required variables ($iFact$ and $iIdx$) for prediction of a pixel has been calculated, the pixel prediction starts. In this manner, 16 pixels are calculated per cycle and it continues till the whole block is predicted.

## 4    Results and Discussions

In this proposed work, we considered FPGA as the target platform (Virtex-7 XC7VX485T) and the design was simulated using Xilinx ISE 14.2 simulator. The synthesized frequency was found to be 119 MHz. As the design calculates 16 pixels in one clock cycle so it completes prediction of a $4 \times 4$ block in 6 clock cycles (including processing cycles) for all the three modes, i.e., angular, DC and planar with minimum resources whereas the design proposed in [7], which is having the lowest number of clock cycles among the existing designs, takes 9 clock cycles to predict all the pixels for one $4 \times 4$ block without planar mode. The $64 \times 64$ block is predicted by breaking one $64 \times 64$ into two $32 \times 32$ blocks. The proposed work takes 23, 85 and 248 clock cycles respectively for $8 \times 8$, $16 \times 16$ and $32 \times 32$ block sizes. The resources used are 112 K LUTs and 12 K registers. The details of the synthesis result and comparison to other related works have been provided in the Table 2. The design proposed in [6] works at 150 MHz but it works for $4 \times 4$ and $8 \times 8$ angular modes only whereas the proposed design works for all prediction sizes and all modes. In [6], it takes 160 clock cycles to predict all the pixels for four $4 \times 4$ blocks without planar mode whereas the proposed design takes only 24($6 \times 4$) clock cycles to predict four $4 \times 4$ blocks with planar mode. The architecture proposed in [2] works at 219 MHZ but needs 25 clock cycles to predict one $4 \times 4$ block and it uses a large number of resources, i.e., 170K slice LUTs and 110 K slice registers resulting in increased cost as it predicts pixel for all the modes and prediction sizes irrespective of the encoder information while proposed design decodes according to encoder information reducing resource usage to only 12 K registers and 112K LUTs and takes only 6 clock cycles for one $4 \times 4$ block and all prediction modes which is less than resources used in [2]. In the design proposed by [5], it uses 64 DSP48Es and 148

**Table 1.** Resource consumption and clock cycles consumed by proposed parallel design for different modes

| Mode | Slice LUTs | Slice registers | BRAM | Maximum frequency (in MHz) | Clock cycles | | | |
|---|---|---|---|---|---|---|---|---|
| | | | | | $4 \times 4$ | $8 \times 8$ | $16 \times 16$ | $32 \times 32$ |
| All | 112 K | 12 K | 2 | 119 | 6 | 23 | 85 | 248 |
| DC | 38 K | 9.5 K | 0 | 167 | 1 | 14 | 32 | 71 |
| Planar | 0.75 K | 8.1 K | 0 | 123 | 3 | 15 | 33 | 93 |
| Angular | 70 K | 2.4 K | 2 | 172 | 2 | 23 | 85 | 248 |

BRAMs and takes 35 clock cycles for DC mode, 28 clock cycles for planar mode and 26 clock cycles for angular mode whereas the proposed design takes only 1 clock cycle for DC mode, 2 clock cycles for angular mode and 3 clock cycles for planar mode for predicting one $4 \times 4$ block as the predicted output for whole $4 \times 4$ block is available in one clock cycle only. Also the proposed design uses 0 DSP48Es and 2 BRAMs. The architecture proposed in [7] takes 9 clock cycles to predict all the pixels which works for $4 \times 4$ block in DC and angular modes only whereas the proposed design takes only 6 clock cycles to predict all the pixels in DC, planar and angular modes and it can be implemented for any mode and all prediction sizes. The design proposed in [8] works for all modes and prediction sizes providing 4 pixels per clock cycle and has a working frequency of 110 MHz whereas the proposed design works at 119 MHz providing 16 pixels per clock cycle thus increasing the frequency and throughput and decreases the clock cycles. Thus this paper achieved a trade-off between area and maximum frequency. The mode and prediction size is obtained from decoder and accordingly the prediction is done which saves the resources (Table 1).

**Table 2.** Comparison and results summary

| Design | Slice LUT | Slice registers | Maximum frequency (in MHz) | Clock cycles | Prediction size and mode | Evaluation platform |
|---|---|---|---|---|---|---|
| Proposed work | 112 K | 12 K | 119 | 6 | All | Virtex7 |
| Ercan et al. [6] | 4 K | - | 150 | 160 | $4 \times 4$ and $8 \times 8$ | Virtex6 |
| Biao et al. [8] | 14 K | 5.5 K | 110 | - | All | FPGA |
| Manel et al. [7] | 1.65 k | - | 234 | 9 | $4 \times 4$ (Angular) | FPGA |
| Farouk et al. [2] | 170 K | 110 K | 219 | 25 | All | Virtex6 |
| Jiang et al. [5] | 690 K | 690 K | 204 | 35 | All | Virtex5 |

# 5    Conclusion

The maximum frequency for proposed design is 119 MHz as tested in Virtex-7 platform and it works for all prediction sizes and modes available in HEVC. These designs predict 16 pixels in one clock cycle and allows decoding of all three modes, i.e., DC, Planar and Angular modes in parallel. Thus the architecture resulted in increased frequency using minimum resources with minimum number of clock cycles.

# References

1. Abramowski, A., Pastuszak, G.: A novel intra prediction architecture for the hardware HEVC encoder. In: Proceedings of 2013 Euromicro Conference on Digital System Design (DSD), pp. 429–436 (2013)
2. Amish, F., Bourennane, E.B.: Fully pipelined real time hardware solution for high efficiency video coding (HEVC) intra prediction. J. Syst. Architect. **64**, 133–147 (2016)
3. Heming, S., Dajiang, Z., Peilin, L.: Fast prediction unit selection and mode selection for HEVC intra prediction. IEICE Trans. Fundam. Electron. Commun. Comput. Sci. **97**(2), 510–519 (2014)
4. ITU-T, ISO/IEC: High efficiency video coding (2013)
5. Jiang, Y., Llamocca, D., Pattichis, M., Esakki, G.: A unified and pipelined hardware architecture for implementing intra prediction in HEVC. In: Proceedings of IEEE Southwest Symposium on Image Analysis and Interpretation (SSIAI), pp. 29–32 (2014)
6. Kalali, E., Adibelli, Y., Hamzaoglu, I.: A high performance and low energy intra prediction hardware for high efficiency video coding. In: Proceedings of 22nd International Conference on Field Programmable Logic and Applications (FPL), pp. 719–722 (2012)
7. Kammoun, M., Atitallah, A.B., Masmoudi, N.: An optimized hardware architecture for intra prediction for HEVC. In: Proceedings of First International Image Processing, Applications and Systems Conference (IPAS), pp. 1–5 (2014)
8. Min, B., Xu, Z., Cheung, R.C.: A fully Pipelined Hardware Architecture for intra prediction of HEVC. IEEE Trans. Circuits Syst. Video Technol. (2016)
9. Sullivan, G.J., Ohm, J., Han, W.J., Wiegand, T.: Overview of the high efficiency video coding (HEVC) standard. IEEE Trans. Circuits Syst. Video Technol. **22**(12), 1649–1668 (2012)

# Design Verification

# A Formal Perspective on Effective Post-silicon Debug and Trace Signal Selection

Binod Kumar[1(✉)], Kanad Basu[2], Ankit Jindal[1], Brajesh Pandey[1],
and Masahiro Fujita[3]

[1] Indian Institute of Technology Bombay, Mumbai, India
{binodkumar,ankitjindal,bp}@ee.iitb.ac.in
[2] Synopsys (India) Pvt. Limited, Bengaluru, India
Kanad.kut@gmail.com
[3] University of Tokyo, Tokyo, Japan
fujita@ee.t.u-tokyo.ac.jp

**Abstract.** In spite of state explosion problem in the present era of complex and large designs, formal methods have been utilized for pre-silicon verification with limited success. This paper critically analyzes some of the reported work on usage of formal principles for effective root-cause finding of bugs during post-silicon validation and debugging. The application of trace buffers assist in mitigating the problem of limited observability of internal states during debug at post-silicon stage. This paper proposes the usage of state restoration principle to increase the efficiency of the formal methods of post-silicon debugging. To solve the problem of trace signal selection, a methodology based on formal principles is presented to increase the effectiveness of trace signals.

**Keywords:** Reachability analysis · Trace signal selection
Restorability · Post-silicon validation · Design bugs
State compaction · Pre-image

## 1 Introduction

During post-silicon validation of first silicon, limited observability of internal states of the design is one of the main challenges [1]. Due to the poor accessibility of internal signals, debug of design/electrical errors in post-silicon environment becomes very difficult. Different techniques attempt to overcome this bottle-neck so that snapshot of the bug can be captured which can assist in isolating its root cause. Scan chains help in increasing the observability and controllability for the purpose of manufacturing testing. However, they are less effective during post-silicon validation and debugging as the chip execution has to be halted to enable read-out of the states of the flip-flops. The use of shadow flip-flops attempts to address this issue at the cost of extremely large area overhead [2] due to the duplication of all flip-flops of the design.

IFRA [1] is a technique proposed for processor based designs, suggesting on-chip recorders which record the states of the critical components of the design as

© Springer Nature Singapore Pte Ltd. 2017
B. K. Kaushik et al. (Eds.): VDAT 2017, CCIS 711, pp. 753–766, 2017.
https://doi.org/10.1007/978-981-10-7470-7_71

instructions get executed. However, these techniques are not easily applicable to any random sequential design. To achieve a non-destructive reading of internal states in these designs, dedicated buffers are incorporated on-chip which store few signals for a limited number of clock cycles as the chip execution progresses. Given the constraint of area overhead, only a small set of signals can be selected for tracing. These signals are decided at the stage of design stage itself. This increases the difficulty of selection of appropriate trace signals. For small designs, design engineers can suggest a few important signals based on the knowledge of circuit behavior. However, there is a need for automated signal selection for large designs [3]. State restoration enables increased visibility as some of the untraced states can be inferred from the traced flip-flop values. This technique has been the guiding principle in most of the proposed solutions for automatic trace signal selection [4], although none of these methods report the efficacy of their selection methods from the point of localizing and detecting the bug. Thus, even if these selection methods achieve a high number of restored signals, the selected signals do not guarantee the detection/localization of errors.

Similar to the idea of placing on-chip trace buffers, synthesis of assertion checkers can be utilized for bug localization. However, an important question here is to decide the set of critical and most important assertions. This can be answered with the help of formal methodologies. The need of the selection of appropriate assertion checkers can be understood from the fact that if all assertions for s35932 circuit are added on-chip, the area overhead is around 20 times of the original circuit [11]. Taatizadeh et al. [11] have proposed a methodology for automatic selection of assertions for bit-flip detection during post-silicon validation. Boule et al. [12] have described an automatic methodology to generate assertion checkers for post-silicon validation from the assertions describing design properties.

BackSpace [5] is a formal method proposed by de Paula et al. for post-silicon validation using reachability analysis and preimage computation. In spite of relying on a formal procedure, this technique achieves appreciable success in finding out the root cause of the bug and can be applied to any digital system. However, there are many issues associated with this formal mechanism for its overall success and wide scale acceptability.

This paper critically analyzes the major formal techniques applicable to the realm of post-silicon validation and debugging. In particular, this paper is aimed at those techniques which are linked with tracing the execution of the chip to isolate root cause of the bug/error. The major contributions of the paper can be briefly stated as follows:

- reported works on formal method based post-silicon debug are investigated with analysis at further improvement for increasing their efficiency,
- state restoration is proposed with respect to the BackSpace framework for enhancing the efficacy of the post-silicon debugging, and
- a formal method to assist trace signal selection is proposed such that selection for observability enhancement is in terms of their effectiveness for their utility in detecting and localizing the error/bug.

The rest of the paper is organized as follows. Related work on BackSpace framework is briefly analyzed in Sects. 2 and 3. The application of state restoration to this framework is discussed in Sect. 4. The formal methodology of signal selection is explained in detail in Sect. 5. Some preliminary results are discussed in Sect. 6. Finally, the paper is concluded in Sect. 7.

# 2 BackSpace: Traversing Back from the Crash State of the Chip to Find Buggy State

## 2.1 Preliminaries of BackSpace

De Paula et al. [6] proposed bug localization using back tracing from a crash state obtained by chip's execution. The methodology involves repetition of four steps. First, the chip is run till its crash point. Second, the states of all the flip-flops in the crash state can be read-out using some on-chip test mechanism (possibly, scan chains). Third, the predecessor of the crash state is to be computed. Fourth, this predecessor state is set as the new breakpoint so that the backtrack process reaches a known initial state. The third step is where the principles of formal methods apply. By using reachability analysis, the predecessor states can be known. However, the main hindrance in this step is that there can be many predecessor states. From these possible states, we have to select the correct predecessor (i.e., which actually lies on the execution path taken by the chip). This is the reason why we require the signature obtained in second step to provide enough information regarding predecessor computation.

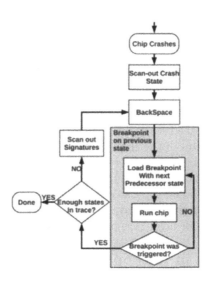

**Fig. 1.** BackSpace Framework [5]

## 2.2  Implementation Issues of BackSpace

We need careful investigation of the components of the Backspace framework so that we can limit the area overhead due to them. For instance- A full breakpoint circuitry when added on-chip needs 61% additional area for the opencore circuit Or1200 (32 bit 5-stage pipeline processor) [5]. Since the on-chip part of the analysis with full states (i.e., states of all flip-flops of design) is virtually impossible, some sort of signature of these states can be collected and scanned-out for off-line processing. Another major component of their debug architecture is the signature collection circuit. This circuit is responsible for collecting history of the most recent signatures for scanning-out. To back trace from this stage, these signature states are to be used by the formal method to calculate the actual states in preimage from the list of candidate predecessor states. To decide as to when stop the dumping of signatures from the circuit, there is breakpoint circuit which is programmed with a breakpoint state. When the current state matches with the loaded breakpoint state, the chip execution is stopped.

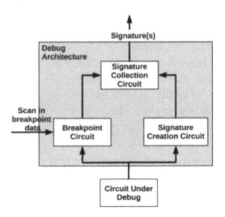

**Fig. 2.** Signature collection in BackSpace Framework [5]

As explained above, the breakpoint matching with full breakpoint state (target state having full states of the chip) leads to excessive overhead for the associated circuitry; hence, only a subset of the total bits of the breakpoint is used. This usage of partial breakpoint leads to false matches [5]. Although the problem of false matches (temporal and spatial) can be solved by using measures like two partial breakpoints, this gives rise to further issues like the hardware overhead (due to the mechanism for arranging partial breakpoints).

## 3  Improvements in BackSpace Framework

### 3.1  Progressive-BackSpace

The primary problem with BackSpace methodology lies in the implementation of its core idea: the explicit enumeration of all previous states and search of the one which is reachable. If this explicit enumeration is avoided, considerable savings in area overhead and run-time can be achieved. Kuan et al. [7] suggested "Progressive BackSpace" methodology which adds only reachable state to the trace eliminating the need of search from a list of predecessor states. Their methodology avoids the cases of false matches (temporal and spatial) using a counting circuit for finding the similarity between the bits in the path already added to the trace and the current execution. This methodology also uses the concept of partial breakpoints to avoid the area overhead issue. The number of required runs is avoided here because of the selective addition of a predecessor state to the error trace.

### 3.2   Utilizing Abstraction: TAB-BackSpace

As an improvement over their original work, De Paula et al. [8] suggested the usage of on-chip trace buffers to extract only a small part of the complete state and using that for breakpoints in "TAB-BackSpace". This is possible mainly because of the concept of abstraction of states belonging to the entire state space. By usage of an abstraction relation, concrete states can be mapped on to the abstract traces. The concept of abstraction can be explained out in 2 steps. First, all the combinational logic that are only in the transitive fan-in of the abstracted state elements are removed. Second, for each removed state element, a primary input is introduced and it is connected to the fanout of the removed state element. Abstraction has a major feature that if a property does not hold in abstracts design, it may/may not hold in concrete design, thus counterexamples generated may be spurious.

### 3.3   The Problems with TAB-BackSpace

In spite of the benefit of reduced state space, there are few caveats with the usage of abstraction within the BackSpace framework as stated above. First, if the abstract preimage includes states that do not correspond to any of the concrete states, this condition results into the addition of a spurious abstract transition to the abstract trace (spurious traces). Second, since breakpoint now depends on the abstract state, we have risk of a false match, when a wrong concrete state and a correct concrete state both map to the same abstract state. The authors in [8] take special measures such as overlap region consideration. The main benefit achieved by usage of trace buffers is the elimination of the need of computation of preimage and the hurdle of finding out the correct predecessor state. The results presented in [8] are for only one design. Hence, it is difficult to predict the benefits from this methodology for generalized circuits as abstraction is useful only for data path circuits.

The BackSpace framework has been utilized for diagnosis of electrical faults which are otherwise very hard to diagnose [9]. Since it is a diagnostic exercise, some fault models are assumed. However, success of the technique still relies on effective signature computation and search of state space for the actual predecessor states.

### 3.4  Efficient Pruning of Candidate Predecessor States

In the preimage computed by reachability analysis of the obtained crash state (or breakpoint), a large number of choices exist for the correct predecessor state. Therefore, it would be highly beneficial if these candidate states $(S)$ are pruned down and we have only a small set of states to try with. Kuan et al. [10] proposed a methodology for pruning of candidate states. Their reasoning lies in the fact that even if we use the signature bits in the BackSpace framework, we are left with large number of states in $S$. They propose to find out correlation among different states of the design. This information is used to get an ordered arrangement of the elements of $S$ so that most likely predecessor state for a given crash state is the first entry. Since the order of the elements of $S$, we can reorder the elements of $S$ so that states in $S$ which are more likely to be the correct predecessor state are tried first and hence run-time for constructing the trace can be reduced.

In the next section, a methodology is proposed which utilizes the information from trace-buffers for choosing correct predecessor states. The method of exploiting correlation in state bits can be used in conjunction with this proposal for more effective pruning of search space.

## 4  Using Restoration Within BackSpace Framework for Candidate Space Pruning

As suggested in [8], on-chip trace buffers help in improving the observability. While the authors in [8] omit the preimage computation step (of the original BackSpace proposal) at the risk of false matches and spurious traces, an alternative technique can be attempted to handle the abstraction of states using the data obtained from trace buffers so as to obtain the execution trace.

**Provided that restored states are correct, the exact predecessor state out of all candidates can be identified with the help of restored states.** This can be justified as below:

State restoration helps to know more state bits in addition to the bits known with the help of traced signals. The total state bits represent the actual execution of the circuit. Due to the presence of some unknowns (which are due to not restored bits), there are many probable choices of the predecessor state. However, if these candidates are fewer in number as compared to the preimages (found out from the exact state while back tracing from the crash state), the efforts in obtaining the true predecessor get reduced.

Let $P_1$ be set of all predecessor states present in preimage and $P_2$ be set of all choices of the restored signal states in the corresponding cycle. Note that $P_2$ can contain one or more states depending on the presence/absence of un restored X bits in the states. In case, theses states contain X bits, corresponding to them restored states are included in $P_2$. Now, there are 2 possible cases: a) $P_2 \subset P_1$ (i.e., $P_1$ is much larger than $P_2$) and b) $P_1 \cap P_2 = P_3$ (i.e., both sets contain common elements). In first case, state restoration is not much useful if there are more than one element in $P_2$. For case (b), the set of actual predecessor states can be given by $P_3$. The diagrams (Figs. 1 and 2) pictorially depict the above cases. First figure shows the first possibility while the second figure depicts the other situation regarding the sizes of set of the preimage and obtained states (restored+traced) from the trace buffer.

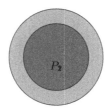

**Fig. 3.** case-(a):Preimage set and restored states set

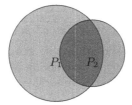

**Fig. 4.** case-(b):Preimage set and restored states set

We illustrate the idea of state restoration and its utility in searching the predecessor states through an example. For a hypothetical design having 8 flip-flops (marked as A,B,C,D,E,F,G and H), two FFs B and G are traced for N cycles where cycle N is assumed to be the crash state. Hence, it is clear that the states of only these two flip-flops are traced (i.e., known) for N cycles. Table 1 shows restored states of other FFs using the traced values of B and G. In the above table, X indicates flip-flop states which could not be restored. If we observe the first two columns, we can deduce that only 4 states are traced and by utilizing restoration, additional 9 states are known. Note that the complete state of the design comprises of states of all these 8 flip-flops. Hence, full execution trace can be obtained if we know other flip-flops too. As per the BackSpace framework, we can get to know the full state bits in the crash state by utilizing already present scan-chains. Thereafter, we have to extend backwards for finding out the correct error trace which can be helpful for bug localization (Figs. 3 and 4).

Due to the un restored flip-flop states in some cycles, the probable ones are all those states obtained by replacing X bits with known bits (1 and 0). For instance- in cycle (N-3), the restored states are included in the set

Table 1. Restored states using debug data obtained from trace buffer

| FF | 1 | 2 | .. | N-4 | N-3 | N-2 | N-1 | N |
|---|---|---|---|---|---|---|---|---|
| A | 1 | 0 | .. | 0 | 0 | 0 | X | 1 |
| B | 0 | 0 | .. | 1 | 0 | 0 | 0 | 1 |
| C | X | X | .. | 0 | X | 1 | 0 | 0 |
| D | 0 | 0 | .. | 0 | X | 0 | 1 | 1 |
| E | 0 | X | .. | 0 | 0 | 1 | 1 | 0 |
| F | 1 | 1 | .. | 0 | 0 | X | X | 0 |
| G | 0 | 1 | .. | 0 | 0 | 1 | 0 | 1 |
| H | 0 | 1 | .. | X | 0 | 0 | X | 0 |

$P_2 =$ 00010000, 00100000, 00110000 and 00000000. *Out of these four states one is the actual predecessor state.* Note that the above proposal relies on the assumption that the restored states are correct and hence act as potential candidates for the predecessor state with in BackSpace framework.

$$reduction = \frac{common\ elements\ in\ restored\ signal\ set}{total\ size\ of\ preimage\ set} \tag{1}$$

The above equation gives the achievable *reduction* in searching the list of states in $P_1$ $(S)$ if we are not using abstraction as suggested in [8]. Note that if we utilize abstraction, we would achieve further reduction in building the error execution trace for the buggy design.

# 5    Formal Perspective for Trace Signal Selection

## 5.1    The Trace Signal Selection Problem

Appropriate trace signal selection becomes a difficult problem as typically only 2–5% of total signals are to be traced. The complexity of this problem can be understood with the help of an example. For s35932 benchmark circuit with 1728 FFs, if we have TB width of 32 (i.e., we need to choose 32 signals out of total 1728), there are $10^{69}$ possible combinations. It is clear that an exhaustive evaluation of all these choices is impossible. Thus, some selection criteria/methodology must be devised to decide the most profitable combination of trace signals out of all possible combinations.

## 5.2    Formal Method of Trace Signal Selection

Signal selection techniques [3,4] utilize the concept of restoration through some heuristics/a mix of techniques employing simulation and heuristics. The goal which these methods attempt to achieve is maximizing state restoration. State restoration is an indicator of increase in the observability of the internal states of the design. These selection techniques are not very effective from the viewpoint of error detection. For the signal selection to be highly beneficial, the traced flip-flops must assist in deriving the execution trace leading to isolation of root cause of the bug. A methodology to select trace signals using formal techniques is proposed which utilizes the time-frame expansion principle. An analysis of the selection of trace signals based on identifying circuit invariants for the purpose of localization of faults was attempted in [13]. They concluded that a trade-off needs to be carried out between trace buffer width and the window-size (in terms of cycles) in which the bug can be localized.

**Tracing of appropriately selected flip-flops assists in determining the unique counterexample for a buggy execution of the chip.** This can be justified as follows:

Let the counterexample $(CE)$ for the buggy execution be given by $PI_i$ and $F_i$. $PI_i$ is known to us as the inputs which lead the chip to the crash state are traced. Hence, $CE$ can be identified uniquely provided $F_i$ is known. $F_i$ consists of $FF_{tr}$ which are traced flip-flops and $FF_{utr}$, the untraced ones. We assume following two conditions for the purpose of selection:

- The trace signal selection is very efficient such that all those flip-flops are traced to which the error propagates.
- We have the golden response available with us (i.e., a correct implementation as per the specifications).

The first assumption basically points to the question as how to obtain the trace signal selection. The second assumption is also not valid always. Therefore, an alternative technique to select trace signals is needed. In the next sub-section, a methodology and formulation for trace signal selection based on formal techniques is explained.

**Preliminaries for the Proposed Methodology:** To establish the relative importance of one signal over other signals, a SAT based formulation is attempted.

- The sequential circuit is unrolled in few time frames (say $n$). The primary inputs, $PI$ and primary outputs, $PO$ are known across all frames i.e., they are traced. As a part of formulation, across each frame input and output values can be applied as constraints to the combinational circuit.
- When a primary output value is wrong, the chip immediately stops. By using scan mechanism, the states of all FF in the last state are obtained $(FF_0)$. This is the crash state and we need to back trace from here to locate the buggy state.
- Regarding FF states for the previous cycles, the states of only the traced ones are obtained i.e., a part of $(FF_1$ to $FF_n)$ where $FF_n$ is the initial state of the circuit-under-debug (Figure 5).

**Formulation of Methodology of Trace Signal Selection:** We make two copies of the circuit (one is bug free and other is buggy). The bug free is used for comparing with the buggy design. In the formulation, the bug is introduced by a method similar to kind of bit-flip model.

- As we assume that primary output values are traced, we know the wrong value $(PO_1)$, while the correct value is given by $PO_1$'.
- Let's assume that no FF is traced. The functions of combinational circuits, at each frame are given by Output function: $f_o(PI, FF)$ and Next state function: $f_n(PI, FF)$.
- We substitute the known variables with their corresponding values. Thus, substitution is performed for $PI_1, PI_2, ...., PI_n, PO_1$', $PO_2, .... PO_n$ and $FF_0$. Note that $FF_0$ is available through scan chain.
- We need to identify states of $FF_1, FF_2, ... FF_n$ which satisfy the above constraints. Since $PI_1, ..... PI_n$ are known as they are traced, knowing $FF_1, FF_2, ... FF_n$ would give us the required counterexample (CE).
- To obtain $FF_1, FF_2, ... FF_n$ duplicate the time frame expanded sequential circuit (Fig. 5). If the circuit has m flip-flops, the variables for all time frames can be expressed as $(ff_i^1, .... ff_i^m)$ for i = 1 to n.
- To introduce error (bug), Inject a bit-flip into each flip-flop at each cycle one by one and find out candidates such that there exists a pattern which satisfies conditions out of bit-flips. For example- in first iteration, we complement the value of first flip-flop in the first predecessor of the crash state $(FF_1)$. Therefore, in the two copies (original and duplicated) of the circuit, the only difference is $(ff_i^1, .... ff_i^m)$ and $(\tilde{}ff_i^1, .... ff_i^m)$. The value of $\tilde{}ff_i^1$ are obtained for which the input and output constraints are satisfied. This process is repeated so as to obtain values for all of $ff_i^1, .... ff_i^m$. Note that since only one CE exists, the states of all the flip-flops are unique (i.e., there is no X bit(s) in them).

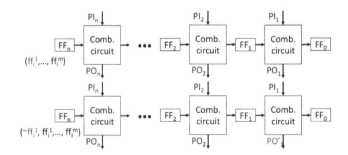

**Fig. 5.** Signal selection formulation illustration

- If $r$ flip-flops are traced, then number of untraced flip-flops is given by $m$-$r$. A SAT formula is created which expresses both the circuits across all frames. Now, for $r$ FFs, we have always same values as they are traced.

– If the SAT formula expressing $m$-$r$ flip-flops for both copies of the design becomes UNSAT, this means there are no two counterexamples. This can be formally stated as– *If across any frame, the problem of finding a flip-flop (among $m$-$r$ FFs) having un identical value in both the copies becomes UNSAT, then there is actually only one counter-example (CE).*
– Therefore, a profitable trace signal selection is such that the above said SAT instance (involving $m$-$r$ FFs) becomes UNSAT resulting into unique CE.
– Suppose, erroneous output is observed at $PO_2$ instead of $PO_1$, the formulation still remains valid with the exception that $FF_1$ assumes role of $FF_0$.

**Possible Caveats and Their Considerations:** It is to be noted that the above trace signal selection formulation is independent of any kind of bug model (i.e., can be applied to both design and electrical errors). However, one of the minor issues is our assumption of unique counterexample leading to the crash state. Although it is quite obvious to expect more than one counter example, in reality, for the kind of bugs which are targeted during post-silicon validation, only very small number of counterexamples exist. This is because of non-exhaustive nature of pre-silicon verification, applied patterns fail to hit the error/bug. However, one additional pattern could have led to the crash state even in the pre-silicon stage and exposed the buggy behavior. Hence, this signal selection formulation with assumption of unique CE is approximately realistic.

**Selecting Appropriate Trace Signals:** As it is clear from the above formulation, selection of trace signals is highly effective if they are able to assist in identifying the unique counterexample. Suppose the assumption that the chip execution followed one unique path holds true, a metric to evaluate different selection of trace signals can be given as the number of counterexamples inferred from the traced signal states. The lesser this metric is, better is the signal selection. Thus, a highly profitable trace signal selection would be one that exactly points to the counterexample leading to the crash state.

# 6    Preliminary Results and Discussion

## 6.1    Experimental Formulation

Some preliminary experiments were performed on few benchmark circuits from the opencore suite [14]. From the two possibilities enumerated in Sect. 4, we calculate the *reduction* metric assuming the best case scenario (in case-(b)). Let's name the metric in this case as $reduction_{res}$ and define it as below:

$$reduction_{res} = \frac{restored\ state\ bits}{total\ state\ bits} \tag{2}$$

Basically, the idea here is to utilize restoration to help in pruning out the search-space which is formed after we perform reachability analysis to obtain a preimage from an *actual state*. Now, this preimage contains more than one states. For instance, design has 10 flip-flops (total no. of states $= 2^{10} = 1024$). Suppose, this preimage has some 60 states (derived by reachability from any particular state, just for the sake of an example). Now, if we trace 3 flip-flops and restore another 3 flip-flops, so some possible estimates, after filling X positions due to non-restored flip-flops, we obtain another state set. Let's assume that we obtain 16 states in this state-set (4 flip-flops are not restored here). Taking the intersection of these states and those 60 states– some common will be there which are now the real candidates of a predecessor state. So, essentially, the reduction boils down to the number of intersecting states which in turn can be achieved with a good restoration–this is quantified by $reduction_{res}$. However, it is different from restoration ratio (RR) in the sense that RR is calculated for certain number of clock cycles, whereas here the analysis (reachability computation) needs to be done for that particular clock cycle only since we are tracing back cycle by cycle and calculating signature for matching with the breakpoint.

To consider the impact of state restoration in knowing about the states of the flip-flops, we consider buggy versions of the opencore benchmark circuits [14]. We injected design bugs in the RTL description of these circuits. Then, we obtained restored values of state bits for these buggy descriptions by utilizing state restoration principle. These bugs are of logical nature and injected in the corresponding designs as depicted below in Table 2. Here, "Change" refers to tampering with the corresponding RTL statement in the design description.

**Table 2.** Description of bugs injected in benchmarks

| Circuit | Bug description |
|---------|-----------------|
| usb | Change in assignment values inside case statement of writeback module |
| nextz80 | Change in assignments of if-else statements of register description module |
| totalcpu | Change in assignment values of variables of Control module |
| mips32r1 | Change in assignment values of variables in MemControl module |
| p16c5x | Change in assignment values of variable of ALU module |

## 6.2  $reduction_{res}$ Computations

For a fixed trace buffer width, we compute the number of restored states and the values computed for the metric considered above in Table 3. We have employed the method of restoration suggested in [4]. We can observe the enhancement in the number of state bits which in turn are capable of assisting the predecessor computation (within BackSpace framework). We obtained the value of this metric as high as 0.33 for the *usb* opencore benchmark circuit. Note that if we can achieve a high value of 0.50, we can reduce the search space of predecessor states by 50% in the best case scenario (in case-(b)). This essentially means we have a smaller sized $P_3$ set.

**Table 3.** *reduction$_{res}$* for benchmark circuits

| Circuit | Total FF | Traced FF | reduction$_{res}$ |
|---------|----------|-----------|-------------------|
| usb | 1719 | 32 | 0.26 |
| nextz80 | 265 | 32 | 0.19 |
| totalcpu | 430 | 32 | 0.27 |
| mips32r1 | 1856 | 32 | 0.33 |
| p16c5x | 739 | 32 | 0.29 |

Since the traced flip-flops are very few in number, we can use the restored states and then obtain the abstraction relation for mapping the abstract states and concrete state. For example- if the abstract state (obtained with usage of trace buffers) is as close to 26% of the concrete state, the dangers associated with abstraction can be easily handled. Moreover, using the on-chip circuitry in the original BackSpace framework [6], the predecessor state computation can be easily carried out as all the states in pre-image need not be utilized for finding out the previous state. With traced and restored states from TB, the set of candidate predecessor states can be easily pruned out to find the correct predecessor state.

# 7   Conclusion

Trace buffers can assist debug engineers in isolating the root cause of buggy behavior of designs at post-fabrication stage. The existing methods of signal selection suffer from an inherent drawback of inability to capture the erroneous behavior. The present work formulated an approach for effective trace signal selection. The idea of tracing back from a crash state to find out the buggy state seems very promising. However, it is marred by the state explosion problem as design size explodes because of prohibitively large number of predecessor states. On-chip trace buffers can store some signal states for few clock cycles, from which unknown signal states can be known by using restoration principle. The proposed approach presented a method for utilizing state restoration for pruning out the search space consisting of potential predecessor states. Experimentation is intended to measure the efficacy of technique and trace signal selection formulation with respect to various designs with different sizes and complexities. The scalability concerns of the proposed technique also need to be addressed.

# References

1. Park, S.B., Mitra, S.: IFRA: instruction footprint recording and analysis for post-silicon bug localization in processors. In: 45th ACM/IEEE Design Automation Conference, DAC 2008, pp. 373–378, June 2008
2. Kuppuswamy, R., DesRosier, P., Feltham, D., Sheikh, R., Thadikaran, P.: Full hold-scan systems in microprocessors: cost/benefit analysis. Intel Technol. J. **8**, 63–71 (2004)
3. Ko, H.F., Nicolici, N.: Algorithms for state restoration and trace-signal selection for data acquisition in silicon debug. IEEE Trans. Comput. Aided Des. Integr. Circuits Syst. **28**(2), 285–297 (2009)
4. Rahmani, K., Mishra, P., Ray, S.: Efficient trace signal selection using augmentation and ILP techniques. In: Fifteenth International Symposium on Quality Electronic Design, pp. 148–155, March 2014
5. Gort, M., Paula, F.M.D., Kuan, J.J.W., Aamodt, T.M., Hu, A.J., Wilton, S.J.E., Yang, J.: Formal-analysis-based trace computation for post-silicon debug. IEEE Trans. Very Large Scale Integr. VLSI Syst. **20**(11), 1997–2010 (2012)
6. Paula, F.M.D., Gort, M., Hu, A.J., Wilton, S.J.E.: Backspace: moving towards reality. In: 2008 Ninth International Workshop on Microprocessor Test and Verification, pp. 49–54, December 2008
7. Kuan, J.J.W., Aamodt, T.M.: Progressive-backspace: efficient predecessor computation for post-silicon debug. In: 2012 13th International Workshop on Microprocessor Test and Verification (MTV), pp. 70–75, December 2012
8. de Paula, F.M., Nahir, A., Nevo, Z., Orni, A., Hu, A.J.: Tab-backspace: unlimited-length trace buffers with zero additional on-chip overhead. In: 2011 48th ACM/EDAC/IEEE Design Automation Conference (DAC), pp. 411–416, June 2011
9. Sengupta, D., de Paula, F.M., Hu, A.J., Veneris, A., Ivanov, A.: Lazy suspect-set computation: fault diagnosis for deep electrical bugs. In: Proceedings of the Great Lakes Symposium on VLSI, GLSVLSI 2012, pp. 189–194. ACM, New York (2012)
10. Kuan, J.J.W., Wilton, S.J.E., Aamodt, T.M.: Accelerating trace computation in post-silicon debug. In: 2010 11th International Symposium on Quality Electronic Design (ISQED), pp. 244–249, March 2010
11. Taatizadeh, P., Nicolici, N.: Automated selection of assertions for bit-flip detection during post-silicon validation. IEEE Trans. Comput.-Aided Des. Integr. Circuits Syst. **35**(12), 2118–2130 (2016)
12. Boule, M., Zilic, Z.: Incorporating efficient assertion checkers into hardware emulation. In: 2005 International Conference on Computer Design, pp. 221–228, October 2005
13. Zhu, C.S., Weissenbacher, G., Malik, S.: Post-silicon fault localisation using maximum satisfiability and backbones. In: International Conference on Formal Methods in Computer-Aided Design, FMCAD 2011, Austin, USA, 30 October–02 November, 2011, pp. 63–66 (2011)
14. http://www.opencores.org/

# Translation Validation of Loop Invariant Code Optimizations Involving False Computations

Ramanuj Chouksey$^{(\boxtimes)}$, Chandan Karfa, and Purandar Bhaduri

Department of Computer Science and Engineering,
Indian Institute of Technology Guwahati, Guwahati 781039, India
{r.chouksey,ckarfa,pbhaduri}@iitg.ernet.in

**Abstract.** Code motion based optimizations are used quite often in electronic design automation (EDA) tools to improve the quality of synthesis results. Ensuring the correctness of such transformation is necessary for reliability of EDA tools. A value propagation (VP) based equivalence checking method of finite state machine with datapaths (FSMD) was proposed in [1] to specifically verify code motion across loops. In this work, we identify some scenarios involving loop invariant code motion where the VP based equivalence checking method fails to establish the equivalence between two actually equivalent FSMDs. We propose an enhancement over the VP based equivalence checking method [1] to overcome this limitation. Experimental results demonstrate that our method can handle the scenario where the VP based equivalence checking method fails.

**Keywords:** Formal verification · Translation validation · Code motion
Equivalence checking · Loop invariant · FSMDs model

## 1 Introduction

Code motion based transformations move operations across the boundaries of basic blocks [6]. They are widely used to improve the quality of synthesis results for designs with complex and nested conditionals and loops. The objectives of code motion are reducing the number of computations at run time and improving register utilization by reducing the lifetime of temporary variables. Code motion techniques [6,10,17] change the data-flow of a program considerably. Therefore, it is necessary to verify the semantic equivalence between the original and the transformed program.

The bisimulation approach presented in [11,12] has been applied successfully to verify structure-preserving code motions. This method fails when the control structure of input behavior is modified by a path based scheduler [2,16]. To overcome this limitation, a path extension based equivalence checking method of FSMDs was first proposed in [9]. This work was later enhanced in [8,13] to handle uniform and non-uniform code motion based optimization techniques. All these methods fail to handle the case of code motion across loops, and loop

© Springer Nature Singapore Pte Ltd. 2017
B. K. Kaushik et al. (Eds.): VDAT 2017, CCIS 711, pp. 767–778, 2017.
https://doi.org/10.1007/978-981-10-7470-7_72

invariant code motion in nested loops, since a path can't be extended beyond a loop by the definition of a path cover. A VP based equivalence checking method was proposed in [1], which can additionally handle code motion across loops.

In this paper, we identify some limitations of the VP based equivalence checking method [1]. Specifically, we show that the VP based equivalence checking method gives *false negative* results when some loop invariant operation op is moved before the loop from inside it, some operation after the loop depends on op and there is a guarantee the loop will execute at least once. As a result of the transformation, a false computation will arise. A computation of an FSMD is called false computation if it never executes. Since the method in [1] cannot identify false computations, it reports a possible non-equivalence of FSMDs (which are actually equivalent). We propose an enhancement to the value propagation based equivalence checking method to handle the above scenario. In particular, at the loop header, we automatically extract a formula that checks whether a loop will always execute at least once under a propagated condition. We check the validity of this formula using the SMT solver Z3 [18] in the theory of linear integer arithmetic. This formula will guide the VP based method during equivalence checking to identify and ignore false computations. More importantly, our method can handle any level of loop nesting. We implement the enhanced VP based equivalence checking method. We identify various test cases where VP based equivalence checking method fails to establish the equivalence, but our method is able to show the equivalence. Experimental results demonstrate the contribution of the paper.

The rest of this paper is organized as follows. A scenario where VP based equivalence checking method presented in [1] gives a false negative result is illustrated in Sect. 2. The FSMD model and the VP based equivalence checking method are briefly explained in Sect. 3. A solution to identify a false computation of an FSMD during equivalence checking is presented in Sect. 4. The enhanced VP based equivalence checking method is presented in Sect. 5. Experimental results are given in Sect. 6. Section 7 concludes the paper.

## 2    Motivational Example

Loop invariant code inside a loop body consists of statements or expressions which produce the same result each time the loop is executed. In other words, these statements are not dependent on loop iterations. This code can be moved outside the loop body without changing the program semantics. Loop invariant code motion improves overall program execution time by reducing the number of times loop invariant expressions are executed by a factor equal to the loop size.

Let us consider the behavior in Fig. 1 and its corresponding FSMDs in Fig. 2. In this example, the operation $x \Leftarrow 5$ is a loop invariant for FSMD $M_0$ in Fig. 2(a). It is placed out of the loop in the transformed FSMD $M_1$ in Fig. 2(b). There are three possible computations, $c_1 = \langle q_{00} \xrightarrow{n \geq 0} q_{01} \xrightarrow{\neg i \leq n} q_{03} \Rightarrow q_{00} \rangle$, $c_2 = \langle q_{00} \xrightarrow{n \geq 0} (q_{01} \xrightarrow{i \leq n} q_{01})^+ \xrightarrow{\neg i \leq n} q_{03} \Rightarrow q_{00} \rangle$ and $c_3 = \langle q_{00} \xrightarrow{\neg n \geq 0} q_{03} \Rightarrow q_{00} \rangle$

```
if(n≥0){
  x=0,y=0;
  for(i=0;i≤n;i++){
    x=5;
    y=y+i;}
  out=x+y;}
else
  out=-1;
```

```
if(n≥0){
  x=5,y=0;
  for(i=0;i≤n;i++){
    y=y+i;}
  out=x+y;}
else
  out=-1;
```

**Fig. 1.** Loop-invariant code motion

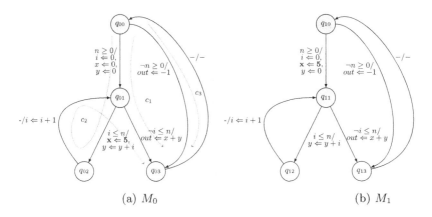

(a) $M_0$                    (b) $M_1$

**Fig. 2.** The FSMDs of the behaviors in Fig. 1

for the FSMD in Fig. 2(a). The computation $c_1$ executes if the loop condition $i \leq n$ is **False** for $n \geq 0$. The computation $c_2$ executes if the loop condition $i \leq n$ is **true** for the input $n \geq 0$. The computation $c_3$ executes for $n < 0$. In this example, when the state $q_{01}$ is reached for the first time, $n$ is always greater than or equal to 0 and $i$ is equal to 0. Therefore, the computation $c_1$ will never execute. In other words, the loop will *execute at least once* for all possible $n \geq 0$ and $i = 0$. The computation $c_1$ is, therefore, a *false computation*. The VP based equivalence method in [1] explores all possible computations of a given FSMD $M_0$. It does not check whether a computation is a false computation or not. During equivalence checking of these two programs, an existing tool will try to prove that these two behaviors are equivalent for all possible computations. Thus, the equivalence checker will try to find the equivalence of computations $c_1$, $c_2$ and $c_3$ in the other FSMD $M_1$. It finds that the computation $c_2$ and $c_3$ of FSMD $M_0$ are equivalent to the computation $\langle q_{10} \xrightarrow{n \geq 0} (q_{11} \xrightarrow{i \leq n} q_{11})^+ \xrightarrow{\neg i \leq n} q_{13} \Rightarrow q_{10} \rangle$, $\langle q_{10} \xrightarrow{\neg n \geq 0} q_{13} \Rightarrow q_{10} \rangle$ of FSMD $M_1$, respectively. However the equivalence checking method finds that the computation $c_1$ of FSMD $M_0$ is not equivalent to the computation $\langle q_{10} \xrightarrow{n \geq 0} q_{11} \xrightarrow{\neg i \leq n} q_{13} \Rightarrow q_{10} \rangle$ of FSMD $M_1$, since they differ in the final value of the variable $x$. It may be noted that the final value of $x$ would be 0 after execution of $c_1$ in $M_0$ and 5 after the execution of $\langle q_{10} \overset{n \geq 0}{\Longrightarrow} q_{11} \overset{\neg i \leq n}{\Longrightarrow} q_{13} \Rightarrow q_{10} \rangle$ in $M_1$. In this example, as described above, the computation $c_1$ will never execute. The non-equivalence of FSMDs reported by this equivalence checking method is due to this false computation. If we can ignore this false computation during equivalence checking, we can establish the equivalence between these two behaviors. Most of the existing state-of-the-art equivalence checking methods fail for such scenario.

In this work, we have enhanced the equivalence checking method reported in [1] to handle the above situation. During equivalence checking, our method will automatically identify the false computation by checking whether a loop always executes or not. If the loop is executed at least once, then our method will ignore the false computation during equivalence checking. Our method is strong enough to handle any nested loops as well.

# 3    Value Propagation Based Equivalence of FSMDs

In this section, the FSMD model and the VP based equivalence checking method presented in [1] are briefly explained. The details can be found in [1].

## 3.1    FSMD Model

FSMDs [5] are an extension of the finite state machine (FSM) model with data/variables used to model behaviors. Unlike FSMs that model the control flow, FSMDs capture the data-flow aspect of the behavior as well. Each transition of an FSMD includes a condition over the data variables and a set of operations transform the variable values.

**Definition 1 (FSMD).** *A FSMD $M$ is defined as a 7 tuple $\langle Q, q_0, I, O, V, f, h \rangle$, where*

- *$Q$ is the finite set of states,*
- *$q_0 \in Q$ is the reset (initial) state,*
- *$I$ is the finite set of input variables,*
- *$O$ is the finite set of output variables,*
- *$V$ is the finite set of storage variables,*
- *$f : Q \times 2^S \to Q$ is the state transition function,*
- *$h : Q \times 2^S \to U$ is the update function.*

*Here $S$ represents the set of relations over arithmetic expression and boolean literals and $U$ represents a set of storage and output assignments. An FSMD is an inherently deterministic model.*

A *walk* from $q_i$ to $q_j$ is a sequence of state transitions of the form $\langle q_i \xrightarrow{c_i} q_{i+1} \xrightarrow{c_{i+1}} \cdots \xrightarrow{c_{i+n-1}} q_{i+n} = q_j \rangle$ where $q_k \in Q$ for all $k$, $i \leq k \leq i+n$, and

$\exists c_k \in 2^S$ such that $f_k(q_k, c_k) = q_{k+1}$ for all $k$, $i \leq k \leq i + n - 1$. A *(finite) path* $\alpha$ is a walk where all the states are different, except the end state $q_j$ may be the same as the start state $q_i$. The *condition of execution* $R_\alpha$ of a path $\alpha$ is a logical expression over $I \cup V$, which must be satisfied by initial data state in order to traverse the path $\alpha$. The *data transformation* $r_\alpha$ of a path $\alpha$ is an ordered pair $\langle s_\alpha, O_\alpha \rangle$, where $s_\alpha$ is an updated variable vector and $O_\alpha$ is an updated output list after executing $\alpha$. Thus $R_\alpha$ and $r_\alpha$ are the weakest precondition of the path $\alpha$ [3]. For a path $\alpha$, $R_\alpha$ and $r_\alpha$ are computed by forward or backward substitution based on symbolic execution.

### 3.2    Equivalence of FSMDs

A computation of an FSMD is a finite walk from the reset state $q_0$ to itself and $q_0$ should not occur in between. For an FSMD $M$, any computation $\mu$ is the concatenation $[\alpha_1 \alpha_2 \cdots \alpha_n]$ of paths of $M$ where for all $k$, $1 \leq k < n$, $\alpha_k$ terminates in the start state of the path $\alpha_{k+1}$, $q_0$ is the start state of $\alpha_1$ and the end state of $\alpha_n$. Two paths $\beta$ and $\alpha$ are equivalent, denoted as $\beta \simeq \alpha$ if $R_\beta \equiv R_\alpha$ and $r_\beta = r_\alpha$. The equivalence of two computations can be defined in a similar fashion. The definition of path cover is as follows.

**Definition 2 (Path cover of an FSMD** [9]**).** *A finite set of paths $P = \{p_0, p_1, \ldots, p_k\}$ is said to be a path cover of an FSMD $M$ if any computation $\mu$ of $M$ can be looked upon as a concatenation of paths from $P$.*

To obtain a path cover, the paper [1] breaks down an FSMD into smaller segments by introducing cut-points so that each loop in an FSMD is cut in at least one cutpoint. This is based on the Flyod–Hoare method of program verification [4,7]. The set of all paths from a cutpoint to another cutpoint without any intermediary occurrences of cutpoint is a path cover of the FSMD. The reset state and all the branching states (state with more than one outgoing transition) are cutpoints of an FSMD.

Let $M_0 = \langle Q_0, q_{00}, I, O, V_0, f_0, h_0 \rangle$ and $M_1 = \langle Q_1, q_{10}, I, O, V_1, f_1, h_1 \rangle$ be two FSMDs having same input(s)/output(s). The correspondence of states and equivalence between $M_0$ and $M_1$ are defined as follow.

**Definition 3 (Corresponding States** [9]**)**

1. *The reset states $q_{00}$ and $q_{10}$ corresponding states.*
2. *The states $q_{0k} \in Q_0$ and $q_{1l} \in Q_1$ are corresponding states if the state $q_{0i} \in Q_0$ and $q_{1j} \in Q_1$ are corresponding states and there exists paths, $\beta$ from $q_{0i}$ to $q_{0k}$ and $\alpha$ from $q_{1j}$ to $q_{1l}$, such that $\beta \simeq \alpha$.*

**Theorem 1** [9]**.** *An FSMD $M_0$ is contained in another FSMD $M_1$ ($M_0 \sqsubseteq M_1$), if there exists a path cover $P_0 = \{p_{00}, p_{01}, \cdots, p_{0k}\}$ of $M_0$ and $P_1 = \{p_{10}, p_{11}, \cdots, p_{1k}\}$ of $M_1$ such that $p_{0i} \simeq p_{1i}$ for all $i$, $0 \leq i \leq k$.*

Two FSMDs $M_0$ and $M_1$ are equivalent, denoted as $M_0 \equiv M_1$, if $M_0 \sqsubseteq M_1$ and $M_1 \sqsubseteq M_0$. Since FSMDs are deterministic. It can be shown that $M_0 \sqsubseteq M_1$ implies $M_1 \sqsubseteq M_0$.

### 3.3  VP Based Equivalence Checking

The VP based equivalence checking method of FSMDs [1] is based on propagating the mismatched values (as a propagated vector) of live variables through all the subsequent path segments until the values match or the final path segment ending in the reset state is reached. In the course of equivalence checking of two FSMDs, two paths, $\beta$ and $\alpha$ say (one from each FSMD), are compared with respect to their corresponding propagated vectors for finding a path equivalence. If the conditions of execution and the data transformations of these paths are equal, then they are declared as unconditionally equivalent (U-equivalent, represented as $\beta \simeq \alpha$). If some mismatch in data transformation is detected then they are declared to be conditionally equivalent (C-equivalent, represented as $\beta \simeq_c \alpha$) provided their final state-pairs eventually lead to some U-equivalent paths; otherwise, these two paths and, therefore, two FSMDs are declared to be not equivalent.

An abstract version of the VP based equivalence checking scheme is given in Algorithm 1. The details can be found in [1]. The function containmentChecker (Algorithm 1) identifies the cutpoints and a path cover in an FSMD. It invokes correspondenceChecker (Algorithm 2) for each corresponding state pairs, one by one. The correspondenceChecker function checks whether for every path emanating from a state in the pair, there is a U- or C-equivalent path from the other member of the pair. Based on the output returned by correspondenceChecker, containmentChecker reports whether the initial FSMD is contained in the transformed FSMD or not.

---

**Algorithm 1.** containmentChecker(FSMD $M_0$, FSMD $M_1$)

---

1  Identify the cutpoints in $M_0$ and $M_1$ and compute their path cover $P_0$ and $P_1$;
   $W_{csp}$ is a set of corresponding state pairs and initially contains $(q_{00}, q_{10})$;
2  **foreach** $(q_{0i}, q_{1j}) \in W_{csp}$ **do**
3      **if** correspondenceChecker$(q_{0i}, q_{1j}, P_0, P_1, W_{csp})$ returns *"Failure"* **then**
4          Report "unable to decide $M_0 \sqsubseteq M_1$" and exit;
5      **end if**
6  **end foreach**
7  Report "$M_0 \sqsubseteq M_1$";

---

## 4  Proposed Enhancement

As described in Sect. 2, we can establish the equivalence between two behaviors shown in Fig. 2 by ignoring the false computation $c_2$ during equivalence checking. In this section, we propose a solution to identify a false computation in an FSMD during equivalence checking. Let us consider the generalized nested loop structure of depth $n$ as shown in Fig. 3 for this purpose. Each iterator $i_x$, $1 \leq x \leq n$, is initialized to $L_x$. Each iterator $i_x$ reaches its upper limit $H_x$ by incrementing

---

**Algorithm 2.** correspondenceChecker($q_{0i}, q_{1j}, P_0, P_1, W_{csp}$)

---

1 **foreach** path $\beta : (q_{0i} \Rightarrow q_{0m})$ in $P_0$ **do**
2     **if** path $\alpha : (q_{1j} \Rightarrow q_{1n})$ can be found in $P_1$ such that $\beta \simeq \alpha$ **then**
3     |   $W_{csp} = W_{csp} \cup \{(q_{0m}, q_{1n})\}$;
4     **else if** path $\alpha : (q_{1j} \Rightarrow q_{1n})$ can be found $P_1$ such that $\beta \simeq_c \alpha$ **then**
5        **if** $q_{0m}$ or $q_{1n}$ is reset state **then**
6        |   **return** *failure*;
7        **else**
8        |   correspondenceChecker($q_{0m}, q_{1n}, P_0, P_1, W_{csp}$);
9        **end if**
10     **else**
11     |   **return** *failure*;
12     **end if**
13 **end foreach**
14 **if** any path of $P_1$ exists which does not pair with a path of $P_0$ **then**
15     |   **return** *failure*;
16 **else**
17     |   **return** *success*;
18 **end if**

---

```
for(i₁=L₁;i₁≤H₁;i₁+=r₁)

    for(i₂=L₂;i₂≤H₂;i₂+=r₂)
        ⋮
        for(iₙ=Lₙ;iₙ≤Hₙ;iₙ+=rₙ)

            Sₙ: ...
```

Fig. 3. Generalized nested loop structure

a step constant $r_x$. The terms $L_x$ and $H_x$, $x = 1, \ldots, n$, are expressions over the input variables, constants or previous loop iterators $i_1 \cdots i_{x-1}$. Let us assume that $C_p$ is a propagated condition at the start of the nested loop structure. Conceptually, the propagated condition in a state $s$ is the condition of a path from the reset state of the behavior to the state $s$. In Fig. 2, for example, the $C_p$ is $n \geq 0$ at state $q_{01}$. We will elaborate on the propagated condition once we discuss the enhanced value propagation method. Under the condition $C_p$, the initial value of the loop iterator ($i_1 = L_1$) must satisfy the initial loop condition (i.e., $L_1 \leq H_1$) to execute a nested loop structure at least once. We can specify this condition by the following formula 1. If formula 1 is valid then a nested loop structure with nesting depth 1 will always execute at least once.

$$C_p \implies L_1 \leq H_1 \tag{1}$$

In other words, if the formula 1 is valid then the outer most loop of the nested loop structure will always execute at least once. The formula 2 is generalized form of the formula 1. If formula 2 is valid then the statement $S_n$ at the generalized loop structure of nesting depth $n$, will always execute at least once.

$$C_p \implies \left( \exists i_1, \exists i_2, \cdots, \exists i_{n-1}, \exists a_1, \exists a_2, \cdots, \exists a_{n-1} \left( (L_n \leq H_n) \wedge \left( \bigwedge_{x=1}^{n-1} f_x \right) \right) \right)$$

$$(2)$$

where $f_x = \left( (L_x \leq i_x \leq H_x) \wedge (i_x = a_x r_x + L_x) \wedge (a_x \geq 0) \right)$. The $C_p$ is the propagated condition before entering the nested loop of depth $n$. We use these formulas to identify the false computation as mentioned in Sect. 2 during equivalence checking. For checking the validity of these formulas, we use the SMT solver Z3 [18] in the theory of linear integer arithmetic. These formulas can be automatically generated in our equivalence checking framework. For example, in Fig. 2 there is a loop $q_{01} \overset{i \leq n}{\Longrightarrow} q_{01}$ of nesting depth 1. At state $q_{01}$ of FSMD $M_0$, the propagation condition $C_p$ is $n \geq 0$. To verify whether the loop $q_{01} \overset{i \leq n}{\Longrightarrow} q_{01}$ will execute at least once, we should check the validity of the formula $n \geq 0 \implies 0 \leq n$. This formula is valid. Thus, the loop will always execute at least once for all possible values of $n \geq 0$. We can say that the computation $\langle q_{00} \overset{n \geq 0}{\Longrightarrow} q_{01} \overset{\neg i \leq n}{\Longrightarrow} q_{03} \Rightarrow q_{00} \rangle$ is a false computation. During equivalence checking, our method will ignore this false computation. By ignoring this false computation, we can show the equivalence between the two behaviors shown in Fig. 2.

# 5    Enhanced Value Propagation (EVP) Based Equivalence of FSMDs

In this section, we present the enhanced VP based equivalence checking method. The existing method gives *false negative* results when some loop invariant operation op is moved before the loop from inside it, some operation after the loop depends on op and there is a guarantee the loop will execute at least once. Let assume that we are at $\langle q_{0i}, q_{1j} \rangle$, a corresponding state pair, during equivalence checking and $q_{0i}$ is a loop header. To handle this type of scenario, we should first check whether a loop starting at state $q_{0i}$ with propagated condition $C_{q_{0i}}$ will execute at least once or not, over all possible inputs in an FSMD. This can be checked by generating the formula 2 at $q_{0i}$, say $f_{q_{0i}}$, as discussed in Sect. 4. If the formula $f_{q_{0i}}$ is valid under the propagated condition $C_{q_{0i}}$, then there is a guarantee that the loop at the state $q_{0i}$ will execute at least once. In this case, any computation till $q_{0i}$ will be always followed by the loop body for some finite number of iterations and then take the exit path of the loop. This is ensured during equivalence checking by:

1. ensuring the path from $q_{0i}$ representing the loop body is considered first for equivalence checking.
2. updating the propagated vector at $q_{0i}$ with the propagated vector after the execution of the loop provided we have already found the U- or C-equivalent path from $q_{1j}$ for the path starting from $q_{0i}$ representing the loop body and propagated vector is loop invariant.

The enhanced version of Algorithm 2 incorporating this idea is presented as Algorithm 3. The point 2 above is reflected by lines 4–6 (for U-equivalence) and by line 12–14 (for C-equivalence). By updating the propagated vectors, we are effectively ensuring that the loop exit path is always preceded by the loop body. This is inherently a guarantee that any computation till $q_{0i}$ is always followed by the loop body and the exit path. Thus, computation $c_1$ as described in Sect. 2 will never be checked during equivalence checking. In Algorithm 3, the `loopTest` function uses the SMT solver Z3 to check the validity of the formula $f_{q_{0i}}$. The `updatePropagatedVector` function updates the propagated vector at the loop header $q_{0i}$ with the propagated vector after the loop.

---

**Algorithm 3.** enhancedCorrespondenceChecker($q_{0i}, q_{1j}, P_0, P_1, W_{csp}$)

```
/* If q0i is a loop header, then the paths from q0i are ordered such
   that the paths corresponding to the loop body are considered
   first                                                            */
```
1  **foreach** path $\beta : (q_{0i} \Rightarrow q_{0m})$ in $P_0$ **do**
2      **if** path $\alpha : (q_{1j} \Rightarrow q_{1n})$ can be found in $P_1$ such that $\beta \simeq \alpha$ **then**
3          $W_{csp} = W_{csp} \cup \{(q_{0m}, q_{1n})\}$
4          **if** $q_{0i}$ is a loop header and `loopTest`($q_{0i}$) returns valid and $R_\beta$ is equivalent to loop condition at $q_{0i}$ **then**
5             | `updatePropagatedVector`($q_{0i}$);
6          **end if**
7      **else if** path $\alpha : (q_{1j} \Rightarrow q_{1n})$ can be found in $P_1$ such that $\beta \simeq_c \alpha$ **then**
8          **if** $q_{1m}$ or $q_{1n}$ is reset state **then**
9             | **return** *failure*;
10         **else**
11            enhancedCorrespondenceChecker($q_{0m}, q_{1n}, P_0, P_1, W_{csp}$);
12            **if** $q_{0i}$ is a loop header and `loopTest`($q_{0i}$) returns valid and $R_\beta$ is equivalent to loop condition at $q_{0i}$ **then**
13               | `updatePropagatedVector`($q_{0i}$);
14            **end if**
15         **end if**
16     **else**
17         | **return** *failure*;
18     **end if**
19 **end foreach**
20 **if** any path of $P_1$ exists which does not pair with a path of $P_0$ **then**
21     | **return** *failure*;
22 **else**
23     | **return** *success*;
24 **end if**

# 6    Experimental Results

In our experimental setup, we replaced the existing `correspondenceChecker` function with the `enhancedCorrespondenceChecker` function. We have tested our implementation on several benchmarks presented in [1,9]. We assume that loop information like nesting depth and loop header are available along with the test cases. This information can easily be obtained during extraction of the FSMD from the input behavior using dominator tree analysis [14,15]. The test cases are run on a laptop with Intel core 2 Duo processor with 2 GHz and 3GB of RAM. The results of the experiments are shown in Tables 1 and 2. The comparison of the execution time required by the VP based equivalence checking method [1] and our EVP method for the benchmarks are tabulated in Table 1. The second column "#loops" represents the number of loops in the behavior. For each benchmark, we have recorded the equivalence result and runtime in milliseconds (ms) obtained by executing these benchmarks in both the tools. Rows 1–6 represent the equivalent scenarios. Both tools are able to establish the equivalence in all these scenarios. We manually introduce some changes in the benchmarks listed in rows 1–6 so that their original and transformed FSMDs become inequivalent. These modified benchmarks are listed in rows 7–12. Again both the tools reported non-equivalence in all these scenarios. If a benchmark has no loop then the execution time obtained by our method is the same as the existing method. When a benchmark has some loop then our method needs a little extra time since at each loop header we invoke the SMT solver Z3 to check whether the loop will execute at least once.

**Table 1.** Experimental results on the benchmarks presented in [1,9]

| Benchmarks | #loops | VP | | EVP | |
|---|---|---|---|---|---|
| | | Equivalent | Time (in ms) | Equivalent | Time (in ms) |
| ASSORT | 2 | Yes | 84 | Yes | 96 |
| DIFFEQ | 1 | Yes | 24 | Yes | 24 |
| MODN | 1 | Yes | 28 | Yes | 28 |
| PERFECT | 1 | Yes | 20 | Yes | 20 |
| QRS | 0 | Yes | 232 | Yes | 232 |
| TLC | 0 | Yes | 60 | Yes | 60 |
| ASSORT-1 | 2 | No | 32 | No | 32 |
| DIFFEQ-1 | 1 | No | 100 | No | 136 |
| MODN-1 | 1 | No | 40 | No | 40 |
| PERFECT-1 | 1 | No | 32 | No | 32 |
| QRS-1 | 0 | No | 220 | No | 220 |
| TLC-1 | 0 | No | 48 | No | 48 |

Table 2 presents some test cases where the VP based method fails to establish the equivalence, but our EVP based method is able to show the equivalence. All the test cases were created manually by us. In all these test cases, some loop invariant operation op is moved before the loop from inside it, some operation after the loop depends on op and there is a guarantee the loop will execute at least once. It is evident from this table that our method outperforms the existing method. The results in Tables 1 and 2 show that our method can handle all the scenarios which can be handled by the VP based equivalence checking method. It can additionally handle the scenarios mentioned in this paper where the existing method gives false negative results.

**Table 2.** Experimental results on test cases with loop invariant code motion

| Benchmarks | #loops | VP | | EVP | |
|---|---|---|---|---|---|
| | | Equivalent | Time (in ms) | Equivalent | Time (in ms) |
| Test 1 | 1 | No | 4 | Yes | 16 |
| Test 2 | 1 | No | 8 | Yes | 16 |
| Test 3 | 2 | No | 16 | Yes | 20 |
| Test 4 | 2 | No | 16 | Yes | 20 |
| Test 5 | 2 | No | 16 | Yes | 16 |

# 7    Conclusion

In this paper we have presented an equivalence checking method to verify loop invariant code transformations. This work is an enhancement to the VP based equivalence checking method presented in [1]. Like the VP based equivalence checking method, our method is also capable of handling control structure modification of input behavior and uniform and non-uniform code motion and code motion across loops. In addition, our method can also handle loop invariant code motions. At a loop header, our method automatically extracts the formula that encodes that a loop executes at least once. It then, invokes SMT solver Z3 to check the validity of the formula. If the formula is valid, our method ignores the false computation during equivalence checking. Thus, our method can prove the equivalence between two FSMDs for cases where the VP based equivalence checking method gives false-negative result. Experimental results demonstrate the advantage of our method over the VP based method.

# References

1. Banerjee, K., Karfa, C., Sarkar, D., Mandal, C.A.: Verification of code motion techniques using value propagation. IEEE Trans. Comput. Aided Des. Integr. Circ. Syst. **33**(8), 1180–1193 (2014)

2. Camposano, R.: Path-based scheduling for synthesis. IEEE Trans. CAD Integr. Circ. Syst. **10**(1), 85–93 (1991)
3. Dijkstra, E.W.: Guarded commands, nondeterminacy and formal derivation of programs. Commun. ACM **18**(8), 453–457 (1975)
4. Floyd, R.W.: Assigning meanings to programs. Math. Aspects Comput. Sci. **19**(1), 19–32 (1967)
5. Gajski, D.D., Dutt, N.D., Wu, A.C.H., Lin, S.Y.L.: High-level Synthesis: Introduction to Chip and System Design. Kluwer Academic Publishers, Norwell (1992)
6. Gupta, S., Savoiu, N., Dutt, N.D., Gupta, R.K., Nicolau, A.: Using global code motions to improve the quality of results for high-level synthesis. IEEE Trans. CAD Integr. Circ. Syst. **23**(2), 302–312 (2004)
7. Hoare, C.A.R.: An axiomatic basis for computer programming. Commun. ACM **12**(10), 576–580 (1969)
8. Karfa, C., Mandal, C.A., Sarkar, D.: Formal verification of code motion techniques using data-flow-driven equivalence checking. ACM Trans. Des. Autom. Electron. Syst. (TODAES) **17**(3), 30 (2012)
9. Karfa, C., Sarkar, D., Mandal, C., Kumar, P.: An equivalence-checking method for scheduling verification in high-level synthesis. IEEE Trans. Comput. Aided Des. Integr. Circ. Syst. **27**(3), 556–569 (2008)
10. Knoop, J., Rüthing, O., Steffen, B.: Lazy code motion. In: Proceedings of the ACM SIGPLAN 1992 Conference on Programming Language Design and Implementation, PLDI 1992, pp. 224–234. ACM, New York (1992)
11. Kundu, S., Lerner, S., Gupta, R.: Validating high-level synthesis. In: Gupta, A., Malik, S. (eds.) CAV 2008. LNCS, vol. 5123, pp. 459–472. Springer, Heidelberg (2008). https://doi.org/10.1007/978-3-540-70545-1_44
12. Kundu, S., Lerner, S., Gupta, R.K.: Translation validation of high-level synthesis. IEEE Trans. CAD Integr. Circ. Syst. **29**(4), 566–579 (2010)
13. Lee, C., Shih, C., Huang, J., Jou, J.: Equivalence checking of scheduling with speculative code transformations in high-level synthesis. In: Proceedings of the 16th Asia South Pacific Design Automation Conference, ASP-DAC 2011, PLDI 1992, pp. 497–502. IEEE, Yokohama (2011)
14. Lengauer, T., Tarjan, R.E.: A fast algorithm for finding dominators in a flowgraph. ACM Trans. Program. Lang. Syst. (TOPLAS) **1**(1), 121–141 (1979)
15. Lowry, E.S., Medlock, C.W.: Object code optimization. Commun. ACM **12**(1), 13–22 (1969)
16. Rahmouni, M., Jerraya, A.A.: Formulation and evaluation of scheduling techniques for control flow graphs. In: Proceedings of EURO-DAC, European Design Automation Conference, EURO-DAC 1995, pp. 386–391. IEEE, England (1995)
17. Rüthing, O., Knoop, J., Steffen, B.: Sparse code motion. In: Proceedings of the 27th ACM SIGPLAN-SIGACT Symposium on Principles of Programming Languages, POPL 2000, pp. 170–183. ACM, New York (2000)
18. Z3. https://github.com/Z3Prover/z3

# A Framework for Automated Feature Based Mixed-Signal Equivalence Checking

Antara Ain[1(✉)], Sayandeep Sanyal[2], and Pallab Dasgupta[2]

[1] Advanced Technology Development Centre,
Indian Institute of Technology Kharagpur, Kharagpur, West Bengal, India
`antara@atdc.iitkgp.ernet.in`
[2] Department of Computer Science and Engineering,
Indian Institute of Technology Kharagpur, Kharagpur, West Bengal, India
`sayandeep.sanyal@gmail.com, pallab@cse.iitkgp.ernet.in`

**Abstract.** The presence of real valued variables that change continuously over dense real time makes it unrealistic to lift the definitions of equivalence used in the digital domain to the analog/mixed-signal domains. Thus the notion of equivalence between infinite state systems such as analog and mixed signal (AMS) circuits have been traditionally expressed in terms of its domain specific *features* or behavioral signatures. This paper formalizes the definition of feature based equivalence and presents a framework for monitoring feature based equivalence using a simulation based approach. The proposed methodology has been illustrated using various AMS circuit families.

**Keywords:** Analog and Mixed-signal · Equivalence checking · Features

## 1 Introduction

Equivalence checking is a common requirement in the AMS circuit domain. In addition to the traditional requirement of monitoring equivalence after a design is tweaked for performance, the recent penetration of AMS behavioral modeling for a wide variety of purposes has necessitated the monitoring of equivalence between AMS circuit netlists and behavioral models at various levels of abstraction.

Formal equivalence checking is a well established step in the design of digital integrated circuits. Formally, two finite state machines, $M_1$ and $M_2$, are said to be equivalent (written as $M_1 \simeq M_2$) if they produce identical outputs for the same input sequence. In the generic form, this problem is called *sequential equivalence checking* between finite state machines (FSMs). There exists several well known algorithms for formally checking sequential equivalence [8,9]. When the mapping between the state variables of the two FSMs is known, sequential equivalence checking can be reduced to the easier problem of combinational equivalence checking. A wide arsenal of tools following this approach are in industrial practice in the digital circuit domain [4,14].

© Springer Nature Singapore Pte Ltd. 2017
B. K. Kaushik et al. (Eds.): VDAT 2017, CCIS 711, pp. 779–791, 2017.
https://doi.org/10.1007/978-981-10-7470-7_73

Lifting the formal definition of equivalence between digital circuits to the AMS domain is not useful in practice for several reasons. AMS models are typically infinite state machines due to the dense domains of the real valued variables and these variables evolve in dense real time (as opposed to discrete clock edges in digital circuits). While the behavior of AMS circuits can be modeled at a high level of abstraction using formal structures such as hybrid automata [2], checking the equivalence between such structures is in general an undecidable problem. Most of the existing literature on equivalence checking between AMS models rely on discrete abstractions of the models [7] and approximate definitions of equivalence (that is, outputs are expected to match within some tolerance). Researchers have started exploring equivalence checking for large AMS circuits [12] given that the methods for analog equivalence checking do not scale to AMS designs of large size.

An important aspect of the notion of equivalence in the AMS domain is that equivalence is often defined in terms of domain specific features of the circuit. Though this notion of equivalence is well understood in the AMS circuit domain, attempts to capture such feature based equivalence definitions formally are absent in the literature. Complex AMS circuits have multiple modes of operation and the definition of equivalence often relates to specific ways in which the circuit is expected to behave in different operating modes. For example, for a Low Dropout regulator (LDO) the *rise time*, which is the time required for the output of the LDO to rise from 10% to 90% of its rated voltage, is a feature of the startup mode of operation for a LDO. The rise time is one of the several features that is typically used in the definition of equivalence between LDOs, that is, we may require that the rise times for two equivalent LDOs must be equal within a tolerance of $0.1\mu s$. We use the term *feature based equivalence* to indicate the equivalence between two designs w.r.t multiple independent feature values (within specified limits of tolerance), or a combination of multiple features.

The focus of this paper is to formalize the notion of *feature based equivalence*. Intuitively, feature based equivalence aims to establish the similarity between the way two AMS circuits/models, of which one is assumed to be the golden model of that circuit family, behave under specific scenarios as defined by the feature. The first step towards automating the task of checking feature based equivalence is in developing a declarative framework for formally specifying the definition of equivalence. The main contributions of this paper are as follows.

1. In a recent work, the Feature Indented Assertion (FIA) Language has been proposed to formally capture features of AMS circuits [1]. This paper extends FIA to formally specify feature based equivalence of AMS circuit families.
2. The paper presents a methodology that uses our language formalism to monitor the equivalence of AMS circuits using a simulation based approach. The tool developed, is compatible with commercial mixed-mode circuit simulators, since we use standard Verilog-AMS interfaces and callback functions.
3. The methodology has been demonstrated on standard AMS circuit families, namely a Linear Dropout (LDO) voltage regulator, and buck regulator.

The rest of the paper is organized as follows. Section 2 presents the existing work on equivalence checking of AMS circuits. Section 3 introduces the notion of feature based equivalence and the language for specifying feature equivalence. The methodology and tool flow for simulation based equivalence checking are explained in Sect. 4. Results are presented in Sect. 5. Section 6 presents the concluding remarks.

## 2  Related Work

There exists some literature on the equivalence checking of analog circuits w.r.t its specification. In [3] the authors propose a methodology to check equivalence of linear analog circuits against its specification. The s-domain transfer function of the linear circuit is discretized to its corresponding z-domain form. The specification of the circuit model and the z-domain representation of the implemented circuit are then represented as finite state machines (FSMs). What follows is the checking of the functional equivalence between these two FSMs. In the frequency domain, the equivalence checking of an analog circuit against its specification is addressed in [11]. Here, equivalence is defined when the magnitude and phase response of the circuit, over a certain range of frequency, is within some tolerance of the specification. Equivalence of linear analog circuits w.r.t its frequency domain specification for all possible parameter values of the circuit is addressed in [6]. Equivalence of two non-linear analog systems was proposed in [5]. In this approach the non-linear state space of the two circuits are compared by forming a nonlinear one-to-one mapping of the state spaces. The author of [10] proposes a methodology for equivalence checking of two AMS designs. The two models of the design may either differ in their implementation or may be modeled at different levels of abstraction. A brief survey of equivalence checking of analog circuits is given in [15].

In contrast with the existing work on equivalence of AMS circuits, the work presented in this paper defines equivalence of AMS circuits in terms of domain-specific features.

## 3  Feature Based Equivalence Checking

In this section we present the notion of feature based equivalence checking of two AMS circuit designs. We first formally define some of the terminologies used throughout the paper.

**Definition 1. Simulation Trace**
*A simulation trace $\tau$ is a mapping $\tau : \mathbb{R}_{\geq 0} \to \mathbb{R}^{|V|}$, where $V = \{v_1, v_2, ..., v_n\}$ is the set of variables (Boolean and Real) representing signals of the system.* □

A feature definition for an AMS circuit and the general syntax for expressing a features in the Feature Indented Assertion (FIA) language is as follows, the details of which is elaborated in [1].

## Definition 2. Feature

*A feature is specified by an assertion (expressed as a sequence-expression S) that specifies the scenarios under which the feature is to be computed, and a signature (a function) $\mathcal{F}$, computed from the match of the assertion. The definition of the signature is overlaid on the definition of the assertion as follows.*

```
feature <feature-name> (<list-of-parameters>);
begin
  var <list-of-local-variables>;
  <sequence-expr> |-> <feature-name> = <feature-expr>;
end
```

□

Over a given simulation trace $\tau$, each time the sequence expression $S$ has a match, the feature value is computed. Since multiple matches of $S$ are possible, a range of feature values is obtained which is explained using Example 1.

*Example 1.* Feature *VoltageRise* computes the rise in output voltage Vout when Vin goes above the rated value of input voltage Vs within 100ms from when it goes above -Vs. The feature, in FIA, is expressed formally as follows:

```
feature VoltageRise(Vs);
begin
  var v1, v2;
  @+(Vin>=-Vs),v1=Vout ##[0:0.1] @+(Vin>=Vs),v2=Vout |-> VoltageRise = v2-v1;
end
```

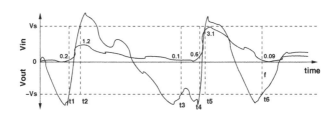

**Fig. 1.** Voltages Vin and Vout vs time.

Let, us denote the sequence expression @+(Vin>=-Vs),v1=Vout ##[0:0.1] @+(Vin>=Vs),v2=Vout as $S$ and the two sub-expressions @+(Vin>=-Vs), v1=Vout and @+(Vin>=Vs),v2=Vout as $s_1$ and $s_2$ respectively. From Fig.1, when $s_1$ is true at the time points t1,t3,t4,t6, the different values of Vout i.e. 0.09,0.1,0.2,0.6 are stored in the local variable v1. Similarly, when $s_2$ is true at the time points t2,t5 the different values of Vout i.e. 1.2,3.1 are stored in the local variable v2. We assume that $S$ has a match at time point t2 and an overlapping match at time point t5 for $s_1$ occurring at the time points t3 and t4. For all these matches of $S$, we compute the feature values and thereby we get a feature range. □

The formal definition for feature based equivalence between a given circuit $M_1$ with the golden model of the circuit $M_0$, can be extended from the FIA language and therefore should have the following components.

1. For each $M_i$, we have a formal feature definition which is syntactically similar to that of FIA.
2. A predicate that defines the equivalence between $M_0$ and $M_1$ in terms of the feature specific signatures computed from the two.

Therefore, equivalence criterion w.r.t each feature, specified in terms of FIA, of a circuit family can be formally expressed as follows.

```
feature <feature-name> (<list-of-parameters>);
begin
  var <list-of-local-variables>;
  <sequence-expr> |-> <feature-name> = <feature-expr>;
end


equivalence ⟨feature-name⟩
begin equiv
  ⟨models-with-feature-instantiations⟩
  goal := ⟨linear-predicate-over-feature⟩
end equiv
```

Broad aspects of the semantics are elaborated as follows:

1. The broad aspect of the *feature* semantics is borrowed from FIA [1] and hence not discussed in this paper.
2. The *equivalence* criterion is specified for each feature, denoted in `feature-name`, for a circuit family.
3. `models-with-feature-instantiations` declares the list of model names (both golden and design under test) along with the respective feature instantiations.
4. The goal, `linear-predicate-over-feature`, is the equivalence predicate of the form:

$$| a_0 \mathcal{F}_0 + a_1 \mathcal{F}_1 | \leq tol$$

where $\mathcal{F}_0$ and $\mathcal{F}_1$ are signature functions computed from $M_0$ and $M_1$ respectively and $a_0$ and $a_1$ are the coefficients of the equation.

Let, us explain the semantics of feature equivalence using Example 2.

*Example 2.* Circuit under test $M_1$, is equivalent to golden model $M_0$ w.r.t feature *risetime*, if their rise time values are within $1ms$ of each other. Now, rise time of a signal is the time taken for a signal (Vout) to rise from 10% to 90% of its rated value (Vs). The equivalence specification for *risetime* is formally expressed as:

```
feature Risetime(Vs);
begin
    var t1, t2;
    @+(Vout>=0.1*Vs),t1=$time ##[0:$] @+(Vout>=0.9*Vs),t2=$time |-> Risetime=t2-t1;
end

equivalence Risetime;
begin equiv
    GM: M₀.Risetime;
    DUT: M₁.Risetime;
    goal:= abs(M₀.Risetime - M₁.Risetime) < 0.001;
end equiv
```

The notable aspects in this specification are the following:

1. First, the feature specification is expressed in FIA, where the feature definition for the circuit family is denoted by @+(Vout>=0.1*Vs),t1=$time ##[0:$] @+(Vout>=0.9*Vs),t2=$time |-> Risetime = t2-t1;.
2. GM: $M_0$ .Risetime; and DUT: $M_1$ .Risetime; denote the models with feature instantiations. It says that $M_0$ is the name of the golden model, denoted as GM, and $M_1$ is the name of the design under test, denoted as DUT.
3. The *equivalence predicate* is abs($M_0$ .Risetime - $M_1$ .Risetime) < 0.001.
□

For the verification of AMS circuits, we have often seen that behavioral models are developed at various levels of abstraction in different levels of design hierarchy. But all these models should be equivalent to the golden model. Therefore, the semantics of equivalence w.r.t a golden model of a circuit family can be defined as follows:

**Definition 3. Feature Equivalence**
*A circuit under test $M_1$ is equivalent to a given golden model of the circuit $M_0$ w.r.t a feature $F$, denoted as $M_0 \simeq_F M_1$, if and only if the goal predicate of $F$ holds for every interpretation of the feature values for $M_0$ and $M_1$.* □

If $[\mathcal{F}_{min_0}, \mathcal{F}_{max_0}]$ and $[\mathcal{F}_{min_1}, \mathcal{F}_{max_1}]$ are the feature ranges obtained for $M_0$ and $M_1$ on the simulation traces $\tau_0$ and $\tau_1$ for the feature $F$, then $M_0 \simeq_F M_1$ iff

$$| a_0 f_{i0} + a_1 f_{j1} | \leq tol$$

$\forall f_{i0} \in [\mathcal{F}_{min_0}, \mathcal{F}_{max_0}]$ and $\forall f_{j1} \in [\mathcal{F}_{min_1}, \mathcal{F}_{max_1}]$. It is an important requirement that the goal predicate is a linear predicate. The equivalence predicate $| a_0 \mathcal{F}_0 + a_1 \mathcal{F}_1 | \leq tol$ can be expanded as

$$-tol \leq min(a_0 \mathcal{F}_0 + a_1 \mathcal{F}_1) \&\& max(a_0 \mathcal{F}_0 + a_1 \mathcal{F}_1) \leq tol$$

Since the equivalence predicate is linear, it suffices to consider only the minimum and maximum values for each $\mathcal{F}_i$. Thus the expression $(a_0 \mathcal{F}_0 + a_1 \mathcal{F}_1)$ can be maximized when we choose $\mathcal{F}_{min_i}$ if $a_i$ is negative and choose $\mathcal{F}_{max_i}$ if $a_i$ is positive. The choices for minimizing $(a_0 \mathcal{F}_0 + a_1 \mathcal{F}_1)$ are therefore opposite.

Thus if $a_0$ is positive, then the equivalence predicate is written as:

$$- tol \leq (a_0 \mathcal{F}_{min_0} + a_1 \mathcal{F}_1) \ \&\& \ (a_0 \mathcal{F}_{max_0} + a_1 \mathcal{F}_1) \leq tol \tag{1}$$

Or, if $a_0$ is negative, then we have:

$$- tol \leq (a_0 \mathcal{F}_{max_1} + a_1 \mathcal{F}_1) \ \&\& \ (a_0 \mathcal{F}_{min_0} + a_1 \mathcal{F}_1) \leq tol \tag{2}$$

The overall behavior of a circuit can be characterized by a set of features, denoted as $\mathbb{F} = \{F_1, F_2, \ldots, F_n\}$. For example, a second-order response of an under-damped system under a step input is generally characterized by the features *rise-time, peak-overshoot, settling time*, etc. Therefore, if we have a set of models for a circuit $\mathbb{M} = \{M_1, M_2, \ldots, M_k\}$, developed at various levels of abstraction for various purposes of the design hierarchy, then we define an equivalence class w.r.t the golden model $M_0$ as follows.

**Definition 4. Equivalence Class**
*Equivalence class w.r.t the golden model $M_0$, denoted as $[M_0]$, is defined to be a set of models $M_i \in \mathbb{M}$ such that for all $F_j \in \mathbb{F}$, $M_0$ is equivalent to $M_i$ w.r.t the feature $F_j$. Therefore, we represent the equivalence class as:*

$$[M_0] = \{M_i \in \mathbb{M} \mid \forall F_j \in \mathbb{F}, M_0 \simeq_{F_j} M_i\}$$

$\square$

## 4   Simulation Based Methodology for Equivalence Checking

This section outlines the methodology and tool flow for evaluating feature based equivalence over simulation output. Verification of AMS circuits is largely dependent on simulation coverage. Therefore, the testbench must drive the circuit

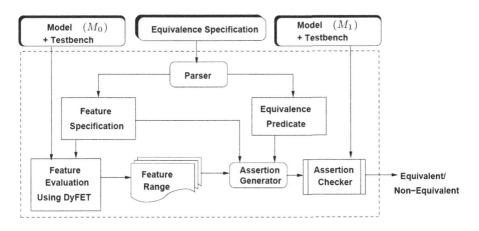

**Fig. 2.** Tool Flow for Simulation Based Feature Equivalence

through its different operating modes such that the behaviors expressed by the features are exhibited. Additionally, the aggregation of the behaviors across multiple matches is an important requirement for feature based equivalence. The overall tool flow for simulation based methodology for checking feature equivalence between two designs, $M_0$ and $M_1$, shown in Fig. 2, is broadly divided into the following parts:

### 4.1   Step-1: Input to the Tool

The inputs to the tool are a golden model of the circuit family and the circuit under test, a testbench, and a formal description of the feature equivalence. Similar testbench is used to drive the circuits through their different modes of operation such that the feature scenarios are exhibited. Circuit models developed at various levels of the design hierarchy can be handled by this tool. The equivalence definitions of the corresponding circuit should be expressed formally in the proposed language as discussed in Sect. 3. This formal specification is used by the tool to automatically find whether the circuit under test is a member of the equivalence class of the golden model.

### 4.2   Step-2: Computing the Feature Ranges of Golden Model $M_0$

From the equivalence specification for a particular feature, we extract out the feature definition. The feature definition, the golden model $M_0$ and its testbench are simulated to evaluate the feature range. We use the DyFET tool, illustrated in [1], for evaluating features. These feature ranges are finally used to generate assertions for $M_1$.

### 4.3   Step-3: Assertion Generation

The assertion generator takes the feature specification, feature ranges computed for $M_0$, and the equivalence predicate to generate assertions for $M_1$. The general syntax of the assertion checking language is as follows.

```
property ⟨property-name⟩(⟨list-of-parameters⟩);
begin
  var ⟨list-of-local-variables⟩;
  ⟨assertion⟩;
endproperty
```

The syntax of **assertion** is
**sequence-expr |-> goal-predicate**
where, **sequence-expr** (denoted as $S$) defines the scenario under which the feature needs to be computed and is specified in the feature specification. The **goal-predicate** (denoted as $P$) is either Eqs. 1 or 2 depending on whether $a_0$ is positive or negative. The assertion generation is explained using Example 2. Let, the feature range for *risetime* computed for the golden model

$M_0$ be [tmin,tmax]. Using the feature range for $M_0$, the feature description, and the equivalence predicate (abs($M_0$.Risetime$-M_1$.Risetime) $<$ 0.001), the assertion generator automatically generates the assertion as follows:

```
property Risetime(Vs2); begin
 var t1, t2;
 @+(Vout > 0.1*Vs2),t1=$time ##[0:$] @+(Vout > 0.9*Vs2),t2=$time
 |-> -0.001<=tmin - (t2-t1) && tmax - (t2-t1)<=0.001
endproperty
```

Therefore, for $M_1$ to be equivalent to $M_0$ with respect to the feature *rise-time*, it is necessary that under all possible valuations of (t2 - t1) of $M_1$ the generated assertion must hold on $M_1$.

## 4.4   Step-4: Evaluating Equivalence by Assertion Checking

The assertion generated in Step-3 is used to check the equivalence of the model $M_1$ w.r.t the golden model $M_0$. We have developed an assertion checker to compute the equivalence. This assertion checker can handle SVA-like AMS properties as shown Sect. 4.3. The inputs to the checker are a circuit model, a testbench (which is same as the one used to compute feature values for $M_0$), and formal description of the set of assertions $\mathcal{A}$ of interest. This assertion checker can handle AMS circuits developed at various levels of design hierarchy. The checker computes the truth intervals of an assertion $A_i \in \mathcal{A}$, where each $A_i$ has a form $A_i : S$ |-> $P$, as follows.

**Definition 5. Time Interval**
*A time interval $I$ is a non-empty convex subset of $\mathbb{R}_{\geq 0}$ expressed as $[a : b]$, $(a : c)$, $(a : c]$, $[a : c)$; where $a, b, c \in \mathbb{R}_{\geq 0}$ and $b \geq a$, $c > a$. $l(I)$ and $r(I)$ are used to denote the left and right ends of interval $I$.*    □

**Definition 6. Truth Interval of an Assertion**
*The truth interval of an assertion, of the form $A_i : S$ |-> $P$, denoted as $I_{A_i}$, is a time interval $I$, iff $\forall t \in I$, $A_i$ is true in its simulation trace $\tau$. The set of truth intervals of $A_i$, denoted as $\mathcal{I}_\tau(A_i)$, is computed from the set of truth intervals of $S$ and $P$ as follows:*

$$\mathcal{I}_\tau(A_i) = \mathcal{I}_\tau(S) \cap \mathcal{I}_\tau(P)$$

□

The set of truth intervals of $S$ and $P$ are computed using interval arithmetic logic as discussed in [1]. The algorithm for evaluating feature equivalence of $M_1$ w.r.t $M_0$ is presented in Algorithm 1. At every sampling point $t$ of the simulator, the algorithm checks for the truth intervals of all $A_i \in \mathcal{A}$. Under various conditions stated in the algorithm, if $\exists A_i \in \mathcal{A}$ which fails at certain time point $t'$ of the total simulation time $T$, then $M_1$ is not equivalent to $M_0$ w.r.t the feature $F_i$ and therefore $M_1$ does not belong to the equivalence class of $M_0$, i.e., $M_1 \notin [M_0]$. Since analog simulations are costly, the users can therefore terminate the simulation as of when they find $M_1 \notin [M_0]$. If the simulation ends

---

**Algorithm 1.** Dynamic Equivalence Evaluation Algorithm

---

**Input**: List of Generated Assertions $\mathcal{A} = \{A_1, \ldots, A_n\}$ corresponding to the list
of features $\mathbb{F} = \{F_1, \ldots, F_n\}$, Model $M_1$ to be simulated.
**Output**: Whether $M_1$ belongs to the equivalence class of $M_0$.
**Initialize**: $currentTime = 0$;
Simulate $M_1$;
**for** *(every sampling point $t$ of the total simulation time $T$)* **do**
   Using Interval Arithmetic compute the truth intervals of $S$ and $P$ $\forall A_i \in \mathcal{A}$;
   $currentTime = \$time$;
   Using Definition 6, compute $\mathbb{T} = \{\mathcal{I}_\tau(A_1), \ldots, \mathcal{I}_\tau(A_n)\}$;
   **foreach** *($A_i \in \mathcal{A}$)* **do**
      **if** *($\mathcal{I}_\tau(A_i) \neq \phi$)* **then**
         $\forall t \in \mathcal{I}_\tau(A_i)$, $A_i$ is true and continue;

      **else**
         **if** *($\mathcal{I}_\tau(S) \neq \phi$)* **then**
            $A_i$ fails i.e. $M_1 \notin [M_0]$;

         **else if** *($\mathcal{I}_\tau(S) == \phi$ && $\mathcal{I}_\tau(P) \neq \phi$)* **then**
            $\forall t \in \mathcal{I}_\tau(P)$, iff $\exists t' \leq currentTime$ where $S$ was true then $A_i$
            fails i.e. $M_1 \notin [M_0]$, else continue;

**if** *(simulation time ends)* **then**
   **if** *($A_i$ is true for $\forall A_i \in \mathcal{A}$)* **then**
      $M_1 \in [M_0]$;

   **else if** *($\exists A_i \in \mathcal{A}$ which is never true/false in $T$ i.e., vacuously true)* **then**
      We cannot establish $M_0 \simeq_{F_i} M_i$ for the given test inputs;

---

and if $\exists A_i \in \mathcal{A}$ for which $A_i$ is vacuously true on the simulation trace, then we cannot establish equivalence of $M_0$ with $M_1$ w.r.t the feature $F_i$ for the given test inputs, else $M_1$ belongs to the equivalence class of $M_0$, i.e., $M_1 \in [M_0]$.

## 5  Experimental Results

Feature ranges are obtained from the golden model of various AMS circuit families using the DyFET tool. These feature ranges are used to generate the assertions that are to be checked on the respective AMS circuit under test for evaluating equivalence with their respective golden models. Tables 2 and 3 present the CPU time and the simulation overhead for evaluating equivalence on different types of implementations of LDO and buck regulator circuit respectively. All the simulations were performed using the Cadence AMS simulator on a 2.33 GHz Intel-Xeon server with 32 GB RAM. We have used industry standard transistor level netlist implementation of LDO and buck regulator circuits, the size of which is presented in Table 1. The behavioral model of LDO is implemented in Verilog-AMS, whereas the buck regulator behavioral model is in Verilog-A. The

**Table 1.** Dimensions of Transistor Level Netlist of Different AMS Circuits

| Testcases | No. of Nodes | No. of Transistors | No. of Capacitors | No. of Resistors | No. of Diodes |
|---|---|---|---|---|---|
| I: LDO | 1434 | 336 | 861 | 1269 | 6 |
| II: Buck | 1787 | 2455 | 350 | 495 | 67 |

**Table 2.** CPU Time for Assertion Checking of Different LDO Models

| Assertions for Feature | Tolerance of Cross Evaluation | | Sampl. Freq. (MHz) | Sim. Time | CPU Simulation Time | |
|---|---|---|---|---|---|---|
| | Time (secs) | Value (V) | | | Only Ckt. | Circuit + Checker |
| **Implementation-I: LDO Behavioral Model in Verilog-AMS** | | | | | | |
| Risetime, | 1e-9 | 1e-6 | 100 | 30ms | 36.29 s | 17 mins 30 s |
| Shrt. Ckt. | 1e-6 | 1e-4 | | | | 16 mins 59 s |
| Current Drop. | 1e-4 | 1e-3 | | | | 16 mins 44 s |
| Volt. | 1e-9 | 1e-6 | 10 | | | 2 mins 24 s |
| | 1e-6 | 1e-4 | | | | 2 mins 21 s |
| | 1e-4 | 1e-3 | | | | 2 mins 20 s |
| **Implementation-II: LDO Transistor Level Netlist** | | | | | | |
| Risetime, | 1e-9 | 1e-6 | 100 | 30 ms | 21 mins 38 s | 59 mins 30 s |
| Shrt. Ckt. | 1e-6 | 1e-4 | | | | 59 mins 10 s |
| Current Drop. | 1e-4 | 1e-3 | | | | 58 mins 56 s |
| Volt. | 1e-9 | 1e-6 | 10 | | | 23 mins 49 s |
| | 1e-6 | 1e-4 | | | | 23 mins 40 s |
| | 1e-4 | 1e-3 | | | | 23 mins 19 s |

tool therefore is capable of handling any types of implementation of the AMS circuit that is compatible with mixed-mode simulator.

In Tables 2 and 3 the first column presents the name of the features w.r.t which the equivalence is checked. We vary the precisions of the cross events to observe the overhead of the checker. Tables 2 and 3 show that increasing the precision (time and value tolerance) for monitoring events leads to marginal increase in simulation overheads. In Tables 2 and 3 we have also presented the results by varying the sampling frequencies of the monitors of the checker. The results show that variation of sampling frequencies has a more profound impact on the simulation overhead of the checker. When a higher sampling clock frequency is used, for each of these sampling points, the algorithm calls the assertion checker to check the truth of the assertion. Thus for higher sampling frequency the number of calls to the checker is much higher leading to increase in the simulation

**Table 3.** CPU Time for Assertion Checking of Different Buck Regulator Models

| Assertions for Feature | Tolerance of Cross Evaluation | | Sampl. Freq. (MHz) | Sim. Time | CPU Simulation Time | |
|---|---|---|---|---|---|---|
| | Time (secs) | Value (V) | | | Only Ckt. | Circuit + Checker |
| **Implementation-I: Buck Regulator Behavioral Model in Verilog-A** | | | | | | |
| Start-up | 1e-9 | 1e-6 | 100 | 250μs | 1 min | 1 min 54 s |
| Curr., Volt. | 1e-6 | 1e-4 | | | 18 s | 1 min 53 s |
| Range in PFM | 1e-4 | 1e-3 | | | | 1 min 53 s |
| mode | 1e-9 | 1e-6 | 10 | | | 1 min 33 s |
| | 1e-6 | 1e-4 | | | | 1 min 30 s |
| | 1e-4 | 1e-3 | | | | 1 min 30 s |
| **Implementation-II: Buck Regulator Transistor Level Netlist** | | | | | | |
| Start-up | 1e-9 | 1e-6 | 100 | 250 μs | 2 hrs | 2 hrs 30 mins |
| Curr., Volt. | 1e-6 | 1e-4 | | | 18 mins | 2 hrs 30 mins |
| Range in PFM | 1e-4 | 1e-3 | | | | 2 hrs 28 mins |
| mode | 1e-9 | 1e-6 | 10 | | | 2 hrs 21 mins |
| | 1e-6 | 1e-4 | | | | 2 hrs 21 mins |
| | 1e-4 | 1e-3 | | | | 2 hrs 19 mins |

overhead. However, a higher sampling clock will capture the assertions more accurately at the cost of an increase in the simulation overhead.

It is interesting to note that the simulation overhead due to variation of cross event accuracy and due to sampling frequency variation are much more in case of light weight behavioral models as compared to the transistor level circuit netlists. It is also the fact that, since a buck regulator netlist is much more complex than the LDO netlist, as apparent from Table 1, the simulation overhead obtained in case of buck regulator netlist is much less than that for the LDO circuit netlist which is clear from the Tables 2 and 3. So we infer that, as the complexity of the circuit increases, the simulation overhead decreases. Therefore, there are no scalability issues for this assertion checker.

# 6    Conclusion

The primary contribution of this paper is to propose a formal declarative specification style for equivalence features in AMS circuit families. As opposed to classical literature on AMS equivalence checking [12,13,15], this paper reports the first attempt to capture equivalence through features. Our observations show that the computational overhead for evaluating the feature based equivalence is nominal as compared to the simulation time for the circuits/models. Therefore, there are no scalability concerns in this approach.

# References

1. Ain, A., da Costa, A.A.B., Dasgupta, P.: Feature indented assertions for analog and mixed-signal validation. IEEE Trans. Comput.-Aided Des. Integr. Circuits Syst. (TCAD) **35**(11), 1928–1941 (2016)
2. Alur, R., et al.: The algorithmic analysis of hybrid systems. Theor. Comp. Sci. **138**, 3–34 (1995)
3. Balivada, A., Hoskote, Y., Abraham, J.: Verification of transient response of linear analog circuits. In: VLSI Test Symposium, pp. 42–47 (1995)
4. Cadence: Conformal Equivalence Checker, https://www.cadence.com/content/cadence-www/global/en_US/home/tools/digital-design-and-signoff/equivalence-checking/conformal-equivalence-checker.html
5. Hedrich, L., Barke, E.: A formal approach to nonlinear analog circuit verification. In: IEEE ICCAD, pp. 123–127 (1995)
6. Hedrich, L., Barke, E.: A formal approach to verification of linear analog circuits with parameter tolerances. In: DATE, pp. 649–655 (1998)
7. Horowitz, M., et. al: Fortifying analog models with equivalence checking and coverage analysis. In: DAC, pp. 425–430, June 2010
8. Kanellakis, P.C., Smolka, S.A.: CCS expressions, finite state processes, and three problems of equivalence. Inf. Comput. **86**(1), 43–68 (1990)
9. Paige, R., Tarjan, R.E.: Three partition refinement algorithms. SIAM J. Comput. **16**(6), 973–989 (1987)
10. Salem, A.: Semi-formal verification of VHDL-AMS descriptions. In: IEEE International Symposium on Circuits and Systems, vol. 5, pp. V-333–V-336 (2002)
11. Seshadri, S., Abraham, J.: Frequency response verification of analog circuits using global optimization techniques. J. Electron. Test. **17**(5), 395–408 (2001)
12. Singh, A., Li, P.: On behavioral model equivalence checking for large analog/mixed signal systems. In: IEEE ICCAD, pp. 55–61, November 2010
13. Steinhorst, S., Hedrich, L.: Equivalence checking of nonlinear analog circuits for hierarchical AMS system verification. In: VLSI-SoC, pp. 135–140 (2012)
14. Synopsys: Formality - User Guide Version, June 2007, http://www.vlsiip.com/formality/ug.pdf
15. Zaki, M.H., Tahar, S., Bois, G.: Formal verification of analog and mixed signal designs: a survey. Microelectron. J. **39**(12), 1395–1404 (2008)

# xMAS Based Accurate Modeling and Progress Verification of NoCs

Surajit Das, Chandan Karfa, and Santosh Biswas[✉]

Department of Computer Science and Engineering,
Indian Institute of Technology Guwahati, Guwahati 781039, India
{d.surajit,ckarfa,santosh_biswas}@iitg.ac.in

**Abstract.** Network on Chip (NoC) plays a significant role in improving computation speed in Tiled Chip Multiprocessor (TCMP) by acting as an efficient interconnection network between the tiles. Designing a NoC satisfying all important functional properties with high efficiency is challenging. Some of the crucial properties to be fulfilled for proper functioning of NoC with efficiency are namely progress, mutual exclusion, starvation freedom, deadlock freedom, congestion freedom and livelock freedom. Exhaustive checking of such system properties in NoC can be done by formal verification method. In existing verification works, NoC are modeled in abstract level. Therefore, the properties verified does not guarantee that they work in real hardware. In our work, we have modeled NoC router using Executable Micro Architectural Specification (xMAS) primitives so that our design becomes near to register transfer level (RTL). In this model, we have verified progress property with help of NuSMV model checker. Experimental results show that our model is scalable for progress verification in Mesh and Ring topologies.

**Keywords:** Network-on-Chip (NoC) · Formal verification · xMAS

## 1 Introduction

Speed of a processor cannot be increased after certain limit, as the generated heat of a very fast processor cannot be dissipated by the state-of-art cooling mechanism. Tiled Chip Multi Processor (TCMP) is therefore, used to achieve the fast computation demand. Performance is limited by their communication or interconnection, but not by processor speed or by memory. In most of the cases, power is primarily used to drive wires and most of the clock cycles are spent on wire delay. In TCMP, an efficient means of communication between tiles is required for better performance. Using dedicated wire for each connection or common bus communication has lot of overhead including area and power. So, there is a requirement of interconnection network in TCMP. Use of an interconnection network and sharing of the bandwidth to route packets among tiles is more efficient rather than dedicated wire connection. This interconnection network in TCMP is called Network-On-Chip (NoC). In simple terms, NoC is a programmable network that transports data between the tiles.

© Springer Nature Singapore Pte Ltd. 2017
B. K. Kaushik et al. (Eds.): VDAT 2017, CCIS 711, pp. 792–804, 2017.
https://doi.org/10.1007/978-981-10-7470-7_74

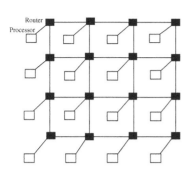

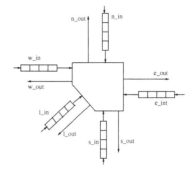

**Fig. 1.** TCMP architecture          **Fig. 2.** A five port NoC router

Figure 1 shows a $4 \times 4$ TCMP which contains processors, routers and communication wires. Routers are present at the intersection of the wires. Block diagram of a five port NoC router is shown in Fig. 2. A router has five input ports and five output ports named as Local (L), East (E), West (W), North (N) and South (S). In NoC communication, a single message can create multiple packets and a single packet can create multiple flits. Flits are the basic unit of communication in NoC network. How a flit will traverse through a NoC network to reach its destination is determined by routing technique. Some of the crucial properties to be fulfilled for proper functioning of NoC with efficiency are namely, mutual exclusion, starvation freedom, deadlock freedom, congestion freedom and livelock freedom. Formal verification plays an important role in ensuring proper functioning of NoC.

There are two primary challenges in formal verification of NoC: (a) building a NoC model which is close to RTL and (b) the model should be scalable. In most of the existing works [2,3,6] on formal verification of NoC, generic NoC model is considered without considering internal details of different NoC components. So, these models do not guarantee that the NoC will function correctly in real hardware. Since these models are not close to register transfer level (RTL) [4], actual properties can not be verified. The objective of this work is to model NoC near to RTL and apply techniques to tackle the scalability issue on RTL implementation. The contributions of the paper are as follows: (i) We have shown that a NoC router can be designed using xMAS [1] primitives. Specifically we have modeled important functional units like switch and arbiter inside a router using xMAS. xMAS is used in our design so that our model becomes close to RTL. (ii) We have shown that progress property is satisfied in this model. Progress means, if there is a flit at a certain state in the network, it will move to other state in the network in subsequent cycles.

This paper is organised as follows. Section 2 describes briefly about the xMAS primitives. In Sect. 3, a NoC router is designed using xMAS. Modeling of different components of NoC router using finite state machine are also represented in this section. Section 4 presents progress verification of NoC using NuSMV. Section 5 shows experimental results for progress verification. Section 6 describes briefly about some existing works on NoC verification. Finally conclusion and future work are presented in Sect. 7.

## 2  xMAS Primitives

Works on xMAS [1] identify a richer set of micro architectural primitives that allow describing complete systems by composition methods. Models designed by xMAS are formal. They can be used for model checking as well as for dynamic validation and for performance modeling. Some of the basic xMAS primitives are queue, function, source, sink, fork, join, switch and merge. These primitives are shown in Fig. 3. The xMAS primitives can be used as basic design units to describe complete system by composition. By designing a micro architecture using xMAS, it becomes closer to hardware design.

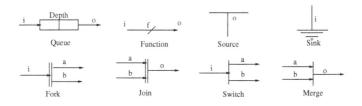

**Fig. 3.** xMAS primitives

(1) *Queue*: It is associated with a parameter called depth, which denotes the number of slots. Data or tokens are read from the head slot and it can be written to a tail slot. If a packet or a token is read from the head slot, all other elements in the queue move forward by one slot towards the head.

(2) *Function*: If there is a need for modification of data, function is applied. It transforms input data to output data using a deterministic function.

(3) *Data or Token Source*: A data source non deterministically injects packets to the network and a token source attempts to send a token on every cycle if there are some empty slots in a queue.

(4) *Data or Token Sink*: A data or token sink consumes packets or tokens from an input channel. Within a specific number of cycles, a data sink non deterministically decides when to consume a waiting data packet. A token sink eagerly consumes tokens from input channel if tokens are available.

(5) *Fork*: It is a synchronization primitive which consumes a data packet or token from an input and produces a packet of the same type as well as a token on the two outputs.

(6) *Join*: It is also a synchronization primitive that consumes a token and data packet from two inputs, and outputs a packet of the same type as that of input type.

(7) *Switch*: It is a routing primitive. Input can be directed to one specific output line from the available output lines.

(8) *Merge*: It is an arbitration primitive that consumes a packet from one of the two inputs and produce it on the output.

# 3   xMAS Based Modeling of NoC

In this section we have modeled router and have shown how a flit traverses. We have also represented switch and arbiter as a finite state machine.

## 3.1   Router Design

We have considered a router with five input ports and five output ports. The five ports are namely, L (Local Port), N (North Port), E (East Port), W (West Port) and S (South Port). There is a switch in each input port and there is an arbiter in each output port. A flit enters a router through one of the input ports. The switching functionality at each input port determines the proper output port through which a flit has to exit the router to reach the next hop. At each switch, XY-routing [13] algorithm is considered. The arbiter present in each output port selects one amongst the competing flits. In this work, we have chosen some basic design unit defined in xMAS [1] to model a five port router. In Fig. 4, we have shown a NoC router which consists of five switches and five arbiters. A switch unit of a router is designed by integrating three Switch primitives of xMAS as shown in Fig. 4. An arbiter unit is designed by integrating Merge primitives of xMAS. For each flit, there is a destination address indicated by $(x_1, y_1)$ in Fig. 4. Current position of a flit is indicated by $(x_0, y_0)$. The switching logic compares X co-ordinate and Y co-ordinate, and determines the output port to which a flit should traverse. For example, let an incoming flit with $(x_1, y_1)$ as its destination address arrive at the router $(x_0, y_0)$ through the switch present in the local port L. If it satisfies $(x_0! = x_1)$ and $(x_0 > x_1)$, according to XY-routing the flit has to move towards the arbiter present in west output port W as shown in Fig. 4. Similarly if it satisfies $(x_0 == x_1)$ and $(y_0 > y_1)$, the flit has to move towards south output port S.

## 3.2   Traversal of a Flit

In Fig. 5, it is diagrammatically shown how a flit has traversed from source $(0, 1)$ to destination $(1, 0)$ via intermediate router in a $2 \times 2$ NoC. A flit has entered the switch at local input port of router $(0, 1)$. As per XY-routing this flit leaves this router via the arbiter at east output port E and enters another router $(1, 1)$ at west input port W. After that it leaves router $(1, 1)$ via south output port S and enters north input port N of router $(1, 0)$. It is the destination for the flit. Finally the flit has entered the local arbiter of the destination router $(1, 0)$.

## 3.3   Finite State Machines for Router Components

In our work, we have converted the different NoC router components into Finite State Machines. Thus the model can be used by model checking tools. Our xMAS design components can be represented by a finite state machine M as

$$M = \{V, S, S_0, S_f, \ \Sigma, \ \Gamma\}$$

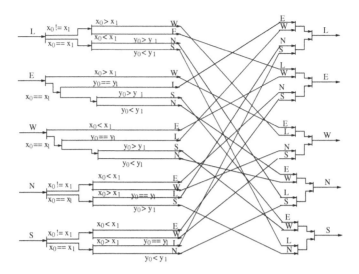

**Fig. 4.** Five input and output ports of a router

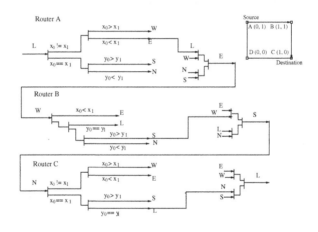

**Fig. 5.** Traversal of a flit

where V is set of input and temporary variables, S is set of states, $S_0$ is set of
initial states, $S_f$ is set of final states, and $S_0, S_f \in S$. $\Sigma$ is a set of arithmetic
predicates of the form, $e \, R \, 0$. Here $e$ is the expression containing arithmetic
and logical operators over the variables $v$, where $v \in V$, and $R$ is the set of
relational operators. Here, $R = \{==, \neq, <, >, \leq, \geq\}$ and $\Gamma$ is a finite set
of transitions of the form $SX2^{\Sigma} \to S$.

**Switch:** Switching in a local port can be represented using automata $M_0$ as
shown in Fig. 6. Here, $M_0 = \{V, S, S_0, S_f, \Sigma, \Gamma\}$. Where, $V = \{x_0, y_0, x_1, y_1\}$,
$S = \{L, E, W, N, S, Y_d\}$, $S_0 = \{L\}$, $S_f = \{L, E, W, N, S\}$ and $\Sigma = \{x_0 - x_1 >$

$0$, $x_0 - x_1 < 0$, $x_0 - x_1 == 0, y_0 - y_1 > 0$, $y_0 - y_1 < 0, y_0 - y_1 == 0\}$. Current position of a flit is $(x_0, y_0)$ and $(x_1, y_1)$ is the destination co-ordinate where the flit wants to travel. All the possible transitions $\Gamma$, are shown in Fig. 6.

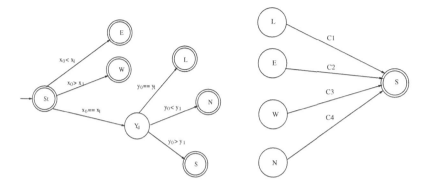

**Fig. 6.** Switching using XY-routing          **Fig. 7.** Round-robin arbiter

**Arbiter:** Arbiter in an output port can be represented using automata $M_1$ as shown in Fig. 7. Here, $M_1 = \{V, S, S_0, S_f, \Sigma, \Gamma\}$, where $V = \{p, L.r, E.r, W.r, N.r\}$, $S = \{L, E, W, N, S\}$, $S_0 = \{L, E, W, N\}$, $S_f = \{S\}$ and $\Sigma = \{(L.r - 1 == 0), (E.r - 1 == 0), (W.r - 1 == 0), (N.r - 1 == 0), (p == 0), (p - 1 == 0), (p - 2 == 0), (p - 3 == 0)\}$. Here, $L.r$ indicates whether a flit is competing to arrive at $S$ from $L$. $L.r == 1$ means a flit is competing for the arbiter from $L$, and $L.r == 0$ means there is no flit to compete from $L$. Other variables like $E.r, W.r, N.r$ also indicate the same. The variable $p$ indicates the preferences. If $p == 0$, flits from $L$ will get preference; if $p == 1$, flits from $E$ will get preference and so on. The value of preference variable $p$ gets updated by following round-robin principle. States of a round-robin arbiter at output port $S$ is shown in Fig. 7. $C1$, $C2$, $C2$ and $C4$ are arithmetic predicates to be satisfied for the transitions between the states are shown in Table 1.

# 4    Progress Verification of NoC

In this section, we have verified progress properties of our xMAS based NoC model with help of NuSMV model checker [12]. xMAS based NoC model is manually converted to NuSMV code for model checking. Progress properties that a NoC component should satisfy are written in LTL and put for verification. We have not considered buffer for verification in our NoC router model.

## 4.1    Progress Verification of a Switch

There are seven possible states in our switch design as shown in Fig. 6. A flit can traverse through these states depending upon its source and destination co-ordinates, and the decisions are taken by XY-routing algorithm. The destination

Table 1. Transitions between states in a round-robin arbiter

| Current State | Arithmetic Predicates | Next State |
|---|---|---|
| L | $\mathbf{C1} = \{[\,(p == 0)\wedge(L.r - 1 == 0)\,]\ V\ [\,(p - 1 == 0)\wedge(E.r == 0)\wedge(W.r == 0)\wedge(N.r == 0)\wedge(L.r - 1 == 0)\,]\ V\ [\,(p - 2 == 0)\wedge(W.r == 0)\wedge(N.r == 0)\wedge(L.r - 1 == 0)\,]\ V\ [\,(p - 3 == 0)\wedge(N.r == 0)\wedge(L.r - 1 == 0)\,]\}$ | S |
| E | $\mathbf{C2} = \{[\,(p - 1 == 0)\wedge(E.r - 1 == 0)\,]\ V\ [\,(p - 2 == 0)\wedge(W.r == 0)\wedge(N.r == 0)\wedge(L.r == 0)\wedge(E.r - 1 == 0)\,]\ V\ [(p - 3 == 0)\wedge(N.r == 0)\wedge(L.r == 0)\wedge(E.r - 1 == 0)\,]\ V\ [\,(p == 0)\wedge(L.r == 0)\wedge(E.r - 1 == 0)\,]\}$ | S |
| W | $\mathbf{C3} = \{[\,(p - 2 == 0)\wedge(W.r - 1 == 0)\,]\ V\ [\,(p - 3 == 0)\wedge(N.r == 0)\wedge(L.r == 0)\wedge(E.r == 0)\wedge(W.r - 1 == 0)\,]\ V\ [\,(p == 0)\wedge(L.r == 0)\wedge(E.r == 0)\wedge(W.r - 1 == 0)\,]\ V\ [\,(p - 1 == 0)\wedge(E.r == 0)\wedge(W.r - 1 == 0)\,]\}$ | S |
| N | $\mathbf{C4} = \{[\,(p - 3 == 0)\wedge(N.r - 1 == 0)\,]\ V\ [\,(p == 0)\wedge(L.r == 0)\wedge(E.r == 0)\wedge(W.r == 0)\wedge(N.r - 1 == 0)\,]\ V\ [\,(p - 1 == 0)\wedge(E.r == 0)\wedge(W.r == 0)\wedge(N.r - 1 == 0)\,]\ V\ [\,(p - 2 == 0)\wedge(W.r == 0)\wedge(N.r - 1 == 0)\,]\}$ | S |

X co-ordinate can be greater, less or equal to its current X co-ordinate. So, there are three possibilities. Similarly there are three possibilities for Y co-ordinate as well. So, there are $7 \times 3 \times 3 = 63$ states in NuSMV representation of a switch design. To satisfy progress in a switch it should satisfy- "if there is a flit at state $S_t$, the flit will move to another state eventually". This property is expressed in LTL as, $G\left(((location == S_t) \wedge (input == 1)) \implies F(location! = S_t)\right)$. Similarly, if there is a flit at $Y_d$, the flit will move to another state eventually (Fig. 6). In LTL, $G\left((location == Y_d) \implies F\ (location! = Y_d)\right)$.

### 4.2 Progress Verification of an Arbiter

In a round-robin arbiter as shown in Fig. 7, preference $(p)$ keeps on changing in round-robin fashion. There are four inputs. A flit can be present or absent in an input. Therefore, there are two possibilities for each input. There are four possible preferences for each input. So for the NuSMV representation there are $2 \times 2 \times 2 \times 2 \times 4 = 64$ possible states. Progress in an arbiter can be expressed as, if there is a request from ArbInput1, the request will be satisfied eventually and preference will set for ArbInput2. Similarly, if there is a request from ArbInput2, the request will be satisfied eventually and preference will set for ArbInput3 and so on. The LTL progress property of an arbiter can be expressed as, $G\,((ArbInput1 == 1) \implies F\,(p == 1))$, $G\,((ArbInput2 == 1) \implies F\,(p == 2))$, $G\,((ArbInput3 == 1) \implies F\,(p == 3))$, and $G\,((ArbInput4 = 1) \implies F\,(p = 0))$.

Similarly, $G\,(((p == 0) \wedge (ArbInput1 == 1)) \implies X\,(p! = 0))$, and $G\,(((p == 0) \wedge (ArbInput1 == 0) \wedge ((ArbInput2 == 1) \vee (ArbInput3 == 1))) \implies X\,(p! = 0))$, should also be satisfied for a round-robin arbiter. All these LTL properties are true in our NuSMV representation of round-robin arbiter.

### 4.3   Progress Verification of a Router

To represent a router in NuSMV we need five switches and five arbiters as shown in Fig. 4. By integrating five switches with five arbiters to represent a router in NuSMV we got approximately $2^{54}$ states. Progress of a flit inside a router from one switch to one arbiter is verified. If a flit travels towards the east output of a switch, present in the local port L, it should be forwarded to the first input of east arbiter E eventually. In LTL it is represented as, $G\,((switchL.location == east) \implies F\,(arbiterE.isArbInput1 == 1))$. Similarly if there is a flit towards the local output L of a switch, present in the north port N, it should be forwarded to the third input of local arbiter L eventually. In LTL it is represented as, $G\,((switchN.location == local) \implies F\,(arbiterL.isArbInput3 == 1))$. These properties are written in NuSMV for all inter connections between switches and arbiters, and they are verified as true.

**Note:** Verification of progress property in a switch, progress in an arbiter, progress from switch to arbiter inside a router, and progress between interconnected routers require detailed modelling (closely related to RTL) of the NoC units. Since the models used in the existing works on NoC verification consider many of these units as black boxes, checking progress properties is not possible. On the other hand, our model is more detailed and close to RTL, which enables verification of the NoC.

## 5   Experimental Results

We have modeled an arbiter, a switch and a router using xMAS primitives as described in Sect. 3. We have also modelled mesh and ring NoCs of different dimension using xMAS based model to show progress in overall network. The experimental results for different models are shown in Table 2. We have used an Intel Core i5 3.20 GHz, 8 GB RAM machine in our experiments. We are able to verify progress properties for a single switch, single arbiter and single router, in less than a hundred milliseconds.

We have integrated switches and arbiters to construct a router and verified progress inside a router successfully. We have represented construction of a $2 \times 2$ NoC mesh network in NuSMV. We need four routers connected to each other. In our $2 \times 2$ NoC mesh representation, it requires approximately $2^{219}$ states. To show overall progress in a NoC, we need to show progress inside

**Table 2.** Progress verification of mesh NoC

| Model | Topology | Execution time (h:m:s:ms) |
|---|---|---|
| Switch | – | 0.0.0.024 |
| Arbiter | – | 0.0.0.018 |
| Router | – | 0.0.0.067 |
| 2 × 2 NoC | Mesh | 0.4.17.024 |
| 3 × 3 NoC | Mesh | 0.14.33.450 |
| 4 × 4 NoC | Mesh | 0.57.32.135 |
| 5 × 5 NoC | Mesh | 1.58.51.821 |
| 6 × 6 NoC | Mesh | 4.33.46.237 |

**Table 3.** Progress verification of ring NoC

| Model | Topology | Execution time (h:m:s:ms) |
|---|---|---|
| 2 × 1 | Ring | 0.0.0.980 |
| 3 × 1 | Ring | 0.0.18.378 |
| 4 × 1 | Ring | 0.01.56.405 |
| 5 × 1 | Ring | 0.4.50.828 |
| 6 × 1 | Ring | 0.13.35.160 |
| 7 × 1 | Ring | 0.23.36.727 |
| 8 × 1 | Ring | 0.56.15.201 |

a router and in all the inter connections between routers in that NoC. To check if interconnections between routers are correct, and to check if a flit can move from one router to another, we have written progress properties in LTL using the interconnections shown in Fig. 8 as, $G$ $((router1.arbiterE.output == 1) \implies F (router2.switchW.input == 1))$. This property indicates "if there is an output at east arbiter E of Router1, this flit traverses to west port W of Router2 eventually" as shown in Fig. 8. Similarly the LTL property, $G$ $((router1.arbiterS.output == 1) \implies F (router4.switchN.input == 1))$, indicates "if there is an output flit at south arbiter of Router1, this flit traverses to north port of Router4 eventually". We have also written progress properties to check if a flit can move from one input port to one output port inside a router. To verify all such progress properties in a NoC, execution time increases due to more number of interconnections. For 2 × 2 NoC, it takes more than four minutes. It is not very difficult to verify progress in a 2 × 2 NoC, as each router are connected with only two other routers. On the other hand, NoCs for 3 × 3, 4 × 4, 5 × 5, 6 × 6 and other bigger mesh topology, routers are connected with two or three or four routers and total number of routers are also high. If we try to represent the whole NoC together, NuSMV can not even calculate the total number of states required for NuSMV representation. Therefore, we have partitioned the NoCs so that each router and its interconnected routers can be verified individually as shown in Fig. 8.

(1) *Active Region for Node 4*: Router4 has three connectivity with neighbouring routers. To verify progress property for Router4, we consider Router1, Router4, Router5 and Router7 as active region, which is shown in Fig. 8 using red color. Approximate number of state is $2^{220}$, while representing model of this region using NuSMV. Verification time required for this region is approximately twenty five seconds.

(2) *Active Region for Node 5*: Router5 has four connectivity with neighbouring routers. To verify progress property for Router5, we consider Router2, Router4, Router5, Router6 and Router8 as active region for Router5, which

is shown in blue color. Approximate number of state is $2^{274}$, to represent them using NuSMV. Verification time required for this region is approximately thirteen minutes. It takes more time as the number of nodes, number of states and number of connections between routers are more in comparison to the previous case.

(3) *Active Region for Node 9*: Router9 has two connectivity with neighbouring routers. To verify progress property for Router2, we consider Router6, Router8 and Router9 as active region. Approximate number of state is $2^{164}$, while representing this region using NuSMV. Verification time required for this region is approximately three seconds.

For mesh NoC of any dimension, we can get only the above three types of active regions with two, three or four connections with neighbouring routers. Any possible path from one source router to one destination router inside a NoC can be obtained by union of paths from one or more active regions. If we can prove progress in all possible active regions, we can conclude that progress property is satisfied for the overall network. Therefore, we have considered all the active regions, and executed them sequentially. Progress properties are satisfied in all the active regions. Verification time for the complete NoC is the addition of verification times for all the active regions. Thus, this method is scalable for mesh NoC of any size. However, if we want to consider the whole NoC at a time, number of states increases exponentially, and the verifier cannot handle such a big state space. Execution time for progress verification of different mesh NoCs using active regions are shown in Table 2.

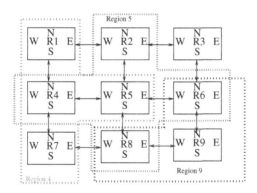

**Fig. 8.** Router interconnection of $2 \times 2$ NoC mesh network

We have also verified some NoCs like $2 \times 1$, $3 \times 1$, $4 \times 1$, $5 \times 1$, $6 \times 1$, $7 \times 1$, $8 \times 1$ of ring topology. As the number of routers and their interconnections are not very high, like mesh topology NoCs, we were able to verify progress properties with out partitioning the network. Progress verification time keeps on increasing as we consider more number of nodes in ring topology, as the number of states increases in NuSMV representation. While representing $8 \times 1$ ring topology in NuSMV, we found that approximately $2^{439}$ states are presents and it takes 56 min. To verify beyond certain limit in ring topology, we have to partition the network and verify each network region separately. Execution time for progress verification of different ring NoCs are shown in Table 3.

# 6   Related Works

Generic NoC [2] mainly efforts on validation of the communication infrastructure without much detail about inside of a node. This model includes topologies, routing algorithms and scheduling policies, without internal details of a node. Generic NoC is based on an abstract view of the communication network of NoC. Works in [3] describe an extension on generic NoC. The scheme demonstrated the transmission of messages on generic communication architecture, with an arbitrary network topology and node interfaces, routing algorithm and switching technique. Movement of packet is simulated in both ACL2 and VHDL. It considers only high-level description while modeling. More refinement is needed for RTL level implementation of this method.

Easy Formal Specification [4] has three main functionalities. There is an injection method which chooses messages amongst pending messages that can go into the network and access network resources. The routing function determines the all possible next hops from the current position and the destination of hop for a message under consideration. The switching policy take decisions if a message can advance to a node. Generic NoC combines these three functionalities to form a network simulator. It presents proof for functional correctness, deadlock, livelock, and starvation freedom in ACL2 for $3 \times 3$ 2D-mesh. Like [2,3], it also considers only high-level descriptions of the NoC.

Bidirectional NoC [5] proposes a Bidirectional channel NoC architecture to enhance the performance of on-chip communication. It allows each communication channel between two routers to be dynamically self configured to transmit flits in either direction. It makes better utilization of on chip hardware resources. This work shows only reduction in packet delivery latency. Formal Modeling of NoC [6] demonstrates verification of Mutual Exclusion and Starvation freedom by considering the proposed Bidirectional NoC design [5]. One drawback is, this work talked about only one router but not about the whole NoC. Further it considers the NoC components in abstract level.

Formal Modeling using xMAS [1] mainly focuses on proposing a modeling framework shown in Fig. 3. By modeling a micro architecture using xMAS, it becomes closer to RTL design. These are some research works [7–11] which use xMAS as modeling framework for verification of communication fabrics and interconnection networks.

Progress verification paper in [8] considers a virtual channel which is designed using xMAS. It focuses on a property called Progress. In this work, end to end progress property is broken down into localized progress properties. Localized progress are more easily provable, and leads to a formal proof of overall progress. ABC verification engine is used for verification.

# 7  Conclusion

Formal verification plays an important role in ensuring the correct functionality of NoCs. In the existing works, many components are treated as black box. So the designs may not be close to RTL. xMAS modeling is closer to hardware level design, so it is gaining popularity. In this work, we present an xMAS based modelling of NoC router. We have implemented switch, arbiter, router, NoCs with ring and mesh topology using xMAS. We have verified the progress in NoC using xMAS model and also propose an active region selection mechanism to make our method scalable. One limitation of this work is that we have not considered buffer in our verification. Our next target is to verify more properties like mutual exclusion, deadlock freedom and starvation freedom by incorporating buffer in our framework.

# References

1. Chatterjee, S., Kishinevsky, M., Ogras, U.: xMAS: quick formal modelling of communication fabrics to enable verification. IEEE Des. Test Comput. **29**(3), 8088 (2012)
2. Borrione, D., Helmy, A., Pierre, L., Schmaltz, J.: A generic model for formally verifying NoC communication architectures: a case study. In: First International Symposium on Networks-on-Chip (NOCS 2007), pp. 127–136 (2007)
3. Borrione, D., Helmy, A., Pierre, L., Schmaltz, J.: Executable formal specification and validation of NoC communication infrastructures. In: Proceedings of the 21st Annual Symposium on Integrated Circuits and System Design, pp. 176–181 (2008)
4. Verbeek, F., Schmaltz, J.: Easy formal specification and validation of unbounded networks-on-chips architectures. ACM Trans. Des. Autom. Electron. Syst. **17**, 1:1–1:28 (2012)
5. Lan, Y.-C., Lo, S.-H., Lin, Y.-C., Hu, Y.-H., Chen, S.-J.: BiNoC: a bidirectional NoC architecture with dynamic self-reconfigurable channel. In: NOCS 2009, pp. 266–275 (2009)
6. Chen, Y.R., Su, W.T., Hsiung, P.A., Lan, Y.C., Hu, Y.H., Chen, S.J.: Formal modeling and verification for network-on-chip. In: The 2010 International Conference on Green Circuits and Systems, pp. 299–304 (2010)
7. Holcomb, D.E., Gotmanov, A., Kishinevsky, M., Seshia, S.A.: Compositional performance verification of NoC designs. In: MEMCODE 2012, pp. 1–10 (2012)
8. Ray, S., Brayton, R.K.: Scalable progress verification in credit-based flow-control systems. In: DATE 2012, pp. 905–910 (2012)
9. Gotmanov, A., Chatterjee, S., Kishinevsky, M.: Verifying deadlock-freedom of communication fabrics. In: Jhala, R., Schmidt, D. (eds.) VMCAI 2011. LNCS, vol. 6538, pp. 214–231. Springer, Heidelberg (2011). https://doi.org/10.1007/978-3-642-18275-4_16
10. Joosten, S.J.C., Schmaltz, J.: Scalable liveness verification for communication fabrics. In: DATE 2014, pp. 1–6 (2014)

11. Burns, F., Sokolov, D., Yakovlev, A.: GALS synthesis and verification for xMAS models. In: DATE 2015, pp. 1419–1424 (2015)

12. Cimatti, A., Clarke, E., Giunchiglia, F., Roveri, M.: NuSMV: a new symbolic model verifier. In: Halbwachs, N., Peled, D. (eds.) CAV 1999. LNCS, vol. 1633, pp. 495–499. Springer, Heidelberg (1999). https://doi.org/10.1007/3-540-48683-6_44

13. Zhang, W., Hou, L., Wang, J., Geng, S., Wu, W.: Comparison research between XY and odd-even routing algorithm of a 2-dimension 3X3 mesh topology network-on-chip. In: 2009 WRI Global Congress on Intelligent Systems, vol. 3, pp. 329–333 (2009)

# Faulty TSVs Identification in 3D IC Using Pre-bond Testing

Dilip Kumar Maity[1($\boxtimes$)], Surajit Kumar Roy[2], and Chandan Giri[2]

[1] Department of Computer Science and Engineering, Academy of Technology,
Hooghly 712121, India
dilip.maity@aot.edu.in
[2] Department of Information Technology, IIEST, Shibpur, Howrah 711103, India
suraroy@gmail.com, chandangiri@gmail.com

**Abstract.** Through-silicon via (TSV) based three-dimensional integrated circuit (3D IC) is gaining remarkable attention in semiconductor industry. The design of 3D IC goes through a complex manufacturing process and testing of TSVs is a critical issue to the researchers. This paper presents an efficient solution for pre-bond TSV testing. The proposed method generates the sequence of test sessions for identifying defective TSVs in a TSV network in reduced test time. Simulation results show the effectiveness of proposed method in terms of test time reduction than the prior works.

**Keywords:** 3D IC · Pre-bond testing · TSV test

## 1 Introduction

The idea of three dimensional integrated circuit (3D IC) is alleviated to overcome the scaling bottleneck of 2D IC. 3D ICs are manufactured by stacking multiple dies vertically and interconnecting the dies using through-silicon vias (TSVs). This promises to achieve performance improvements in terms of reduced interconnection length, reduced power consumption and smaller footprint than conventional 2D IC [1]. But there are several challenges related to testing of 3D IC [2].

TSVs are considered as the path for transporting signal to the upper layer dies of 3D IC. Several types of defects like pinhole or microvoid may arise during manufacturing of 3D ICs and these faults are identified by pre-bond testing [3]. The resistance of a TSV increases due to microvoid whereas the capacitance between TSV and the substrate increases due to pinhole. Capacitance measurement is used for pinhole fault, but resistance measurement is required for microvoid fault [4]. Faults evolved due to alignment, bonding or stress can be identified by post-bond testing. A single faulty TSV can paralyze the whole chip. So, testing of TSVs is necessary for proper functionality of the chip. In this paper, we have considered only pre-bond TSV testing.

It is a challenge to test the TSVs before bonding of different dies due to the small pitch of TSV. A pre-bond TSV probing method is presented in [4] where multiple TSVs are shorted together with a probe needle to form a TSV network. The probing method is modeled by adding an active driver in the probe needle and forming a charge sharing

© Springer Nature Singapore Pte Ltd. 2017
B. K. Kaushik et al. (Eds.): VDAT 2017, CCIS 711, pp. 805–812, 2017.
https://doi.org/10.1007/978-981-10-7470-7_75

circuit between single (multiple) TSV(s) and the probe needle. Capacitor charging time of the charge-sharing circuit is considered as the test time of TSV for resistance measurement of TSV. The charging time with respect to the different parallel active TSVs is detailed in [4].

**Table 1.** Capacitor charging time of parallel TSV test [8]

| Number of TSVs tested in parallel (q) | Charging time t(q) ($\mu$s) |
| --- | --- |
| 1 | 0.80 |
| 2 | 0.53 |
| 3 | 0.42 |
| 4 | 0.38 |

Recently several research works are being undertaken on pre-bond TSV testing. For instance, pre-bond TSV test method is presented in [5] where multiple TSVs can be tested simultaneously. An integer linear programming (ILP) based method to detect faulty TSVs is proposed in [6]. The authors present heuristic methods to identify defective TSVs in reduce the test time in [7, 8]. A session based pre-bond TSV test method is presented in [9]. In this paper we have proposed a fast heuristic method that identifies the defective TSVs efficiently in terms of test set generation and significantly reduces the overall test time.

The rest of this paper is organized as follows: Sect. 2 describes the problem formulation of the proposed methodology. Proposed algorithm for identifying the defective TSVs uniquely is presented in Sect. 3. Proposed methodology is explained using an illustrative example in Sect. 4. Section 5 presents the experimental results and finally Sect. 6 concludes the paper.

## 2    Problem Formulation

Pre-bond TSV testing helps to identify defective dies early i.e. before bonding. Objective of TSV probing is to identify the defective TSVs within a TSV network. The test time can be reduced if the TSVs are tested in parallel. The proposed pre-bond TSV test method generates sequence of test sessions to detect faulty TSVs in reduced test time. A test session is formed by TSVs that are tested simultaneously and number of TSVs within a session indicates the session size (q). The difference in capacitor charging time between faulty and non-faulty TSVs decreases when size of the session increases which affect the resolution [4]. So the size of the session cannot be increased beyond a certain limit. Resolution constraint (number of probe pins) p indicates the upper bound of session size. Now, formally the problem can be stated as follows: *Given n identical TSVs within a n-TSV network, p number of probe pins and the test time t(q), $1 \leq q \leq p$, for the test session containing q number of TSVs, determine the sequence of test sessions to identify faulty TSVs of the n-TSV network such that the test time is minimized as much as possible.*

# 3 Proposed Methodology

We have proposed a heuristic based algorithm to solve the above mentioned problem. The proposed algorithm uses the concept of parallel testing. Parallel TSV testing reduces the test time compared to the sequential TSV testing. Each TSV network has limited number of redundant TSVs ($r$) to repair the network. Finding $r + 1$ number of defective TSVs implies that the network is not repairable; so further test is useless. The proposed algorithm can identify $m$ number of defective TSVs, where $0 \leq m \leq r + 1$. Also the test process can be done without knowing any prior information about the number of faults or number of redundant TSVs. The algorithm starts with the procedure *Test_session_generation()*, which generates a session by picking $p$ number of TSVs from the set of n untested TSVs. Each generated session is tested and the corresponding test time is recorded. If a session is identified as fault-free then all the TSVs of the session are considered as good TSV. But if the session is faulty, then the procedure *Defective_TSV_identification()* is invoked to find the exact position of the first occurrence of the defective TSV within the current session.

---

**Algorithm 1.** Test_session_generation(n, p)

**Input:** number of TSVs (n), number of test pins (p).
**Output:** Set of test sessions, and total test time.
**if** count=r+1**or** n=0 **then return**;
**if** n>0 **then**
    Create a session s by taking all n (if n<p) or p(if n≥p) number of TSVs;
    Modify the session s;                    //by padding non-faulty tested TSVs
    total_test_time:=total_test_time+t(length(s));   //test time accumulation
    **if** session s is tested as being faulty **then**
        j:= Defective_TSV_identification(length(s), p);
        n:=n-length(s)+(j+1); count:=count+1;    //defective TSV is identified at location j
        Test_session_generation (n, p);
    **else**                                    // the session s is fault free
        n= n-length(s); Test_session_generation(n, p);
**end.**

---

---

**Algorithm 2.** Defective_TSV_identification(s, p)

---

**Input:** The faulty session (s), number of probe pins (p).
**Output:** Position of defective TSV.
**if** length(s)=1 **then** return the position of the defective TSV;    //a defective TSV is identified
**else**
    Bi-partition the session s into two new sessions s1 and s2;
    Modify the session s1 and s2;                    //by padding non-faulty tested TSVs
    total_test_time:=total_test_time+t(length($s_1$));    //test time accumulation

    **if** session s1 is tested as being faulty **then** Defective_TSV_identification($s_1$,p);
    **else** Defective_TSV_identification($s_2$,p);    // session $s_1$ is fault free so s2 must be faulty
**end.**

---

The procedure *Defective_TSV_identification( )* divides a faulty session of length *p* into two smaller sessions (as left half and right half). First the left half is tested. If the left half is found to be faulty, subsequent testing is done on this half itself. On the other hand, if the left half is found as fault free, the right half is bi-partitioned and tested. In this fashion a faulty session is bi-partitioned until the length of session is one. Finally the position of the first defective TSV is identified by the algorithm. When the left half is identified as faulty, we have no concrete information about the right half. Therefore, this right half is considered as untested TSVs. During the test process, non-faulty tested TSVs are padded with the smaller sessions to utilize the maximum number of probe pins for reducing the test time.

## 4    Illustrative Example

This section elaborates the proposed method with an example. Consider a problem instance where number of TSVs (n) is16 and number of test pins (p) is 4. TSVs are represented with the numbers 1, 2…16 and initially all are untested. According to the proposed method, procedure *Test_session_generation( )* starts with the formation of a session {1, 2, 3, 4} of length 4 and they can be tested simultaneously. Now the session is tested to check whether there is any faulty TSV or not. If there is no fault, then the next session will be formed from the remaining untested TSVs. Assume that the defective TSVs are 1, 8 and 12. So the session {1, 2, 3, 4} is identified as faulty. Hence, *Defective_TSV_identification( )* procedure is invoked to detect the position of faulty TSV. The procedure *Defective_TSV_identification( )* starts with bi-partitioning the session and generates two new sets {1, 2}, and {3, 4}. The session {1, 2} is tested and detected as faulty. So it is decomposed as {1} and {2}. After testing {1}, it is detected as defective. As the sets {2} and {3,4} are not tested, we cannot make any decision about the TSVs 2, 3,4 that they are faulty or not i.e. they are considered as untested. Now the next session {2, 3, 4, 5} is created from the remaining untested TSVs (2 to 16) and is identified as fault-free.

Similarly, session {6, 7, 8, 9} is identified as faulty and decomposed as {6, 7} and {8, 9}. Now non-faulty tested TSVs can be included randomly with these sets for reducing test time further and the test session {6, 7, 2, 3} is formed. The session {6, 7, 2, 3} is detected as non-faulty and TSVs 6 and 7 are non-faulty. So the fault is within the set {8, 9} which is to be bi-partitioned next. Similarly the session {8, 4, 5, 2} is tested and identified as faulty. Hence, TSV 8 is defective as other TSVs of this session are non-faulty. In a similar fashion, remaining untested TSVs are tested and all the faulty TSVs are detected. At the end of test process following test sessions are generated: {1,2,3,4}, {1,2}, {1}, {2,3,4,5}, {6,7,8,9}, {6,7,2,3}, {8,4,5,2}, {9,10,11,12}, {9,10,3,6}, {11,7,4,5}, {13,14,15,16}.

Here, the underlined numbers indicate that padding is done using these TSVs. The total test time is calculated using Table 1 as $9 \times t(4) + 1 \times t(2) + 1 \times t(1) = 9 \times 0.38 + 0.53 + 0.8 = 4.75$ micro second.

## 5   Experimental Results

The proposed algorithm is coded and compiled in *gcc* compiler and executed on a Intel Core i5 processor with 3 GB RAM. Simulation results are presented for different TSV networks with varying number of probe pins. HSPICE simulations are considered to find the test time for different test sessions. The resistance and capacitance of each TSV are considered as $1\Omega$ and 20 fF respectively as in [4].

Figure 1 shows the variation of reduction in test time with the number of faulty TSVs identified for 20-TSV network. It is seen from the figures that for a given value of test pins the reduction in test time decreases with increasing value of number of faulty TSVs. 13 faults can be identified with reduced test time for 20-TSV network. The reduction of test time will be large for greater number of test pins. Because the number of test sessions will be less for large value of p. There is 15% reduction of test time than serial testing for 20-TSV network such that 12 faulty TSVs can be detected uniquely. From the Fig. 1 it is also observed that, for small m, the differences of reduction in test time with p = 2, p = 3 and p = 4 are significant, but for large value of m, the test time reduction is quite small. This observation also indicates that for large m, sequential testing is better.

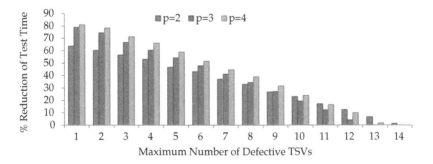

**Fig. 1.** Percentage reduction of test time for 20-TSV network

In Fig. 2, for 20 TSV networks and test pin = 3, our experimental result is compared with [6, 8]. It is seen that the proposed methodology can identify four 4 with reduced test time of 60% & above and 8 faults with reduced test time of 35% & above. Interestingly to detect seven faults our proposed heuristic approach takes slightly more time than [8]. However, this single anomaly can be overlooked when compared with the reduction of time achieved in all other cases. So it can be concluded that the proposed heuristic approach provides an efficient solution for identifying defective TSVs for 3D ICs for larger TSV network.

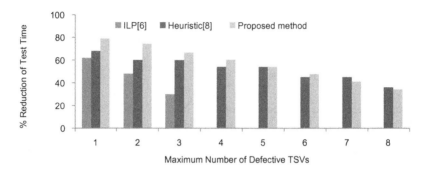

**Fig. 2.** Comparison in test time for 20-TSV network for p = 3

Table 2 shows the comparisons between the dynamically optimized test in [9] and the proposed method for various TSV networks. From Table 2, the following observations can be made. First, it is seen from the table that obtained results are better than [9] in almost all cases. Second, as expected, number tested session increases as number of fault increases. Third, as m increases the average percentage reduction decreases. This is expected as large number of sessions are tested to identify more defective TSVs within a TSV network.

**Table 2.** Comparative study of test sessions and test time constructed by [9] and Heuristic Algorithm

| Number of TSVs, Number of redundant TSVs, Number of probe pin (n, r, p) | Number of defective TSVs identified (m) | Average Case of Dynamically optimized test in [9] (Number of test sessions, time in μs) | Average Case of Heuristic Method (Number of test sessions, time in μs) | Average case reduction by Proposed Heuristic Algorithm over Dynamically optimized test in [9] (sessions, time) |
|---|---|---|---|---|
| (8, 3, 3) | 0 | (5.0, 2.10) | (3.0, 1.26) | (40.00%, 40.00%) |
| | 1 | (5.3, 2.25) | (4.0, 1.72) | (24.53%, 23.78%) |
| | 2 | (6.4, 2.71) | (5.4, 2.55) | (15.63%, 5.90%) |
| | 3 | (7.5, 3.17) | (6.71, 3.09) | (10.53%, 2.52%) |
| (12, 4, 3) | 0 | (7.0, 2.94) | (4.0, 1.68) | (42.86%, 42.86%) |
| | 1 | (7.5, 3.14) | (5.0, 2.12) | (33.33%, 32.52%) |
| | 2 | (8.7, 3.65) | (7.7, 3.38) | (11.49%, 7.51%) |
| | 3 | (10.3, 4.32) | (9.3, 4.19) | (9.71%, 3.01%) |
| | 4 | (11.8, 4.97) | (10.45, 4.75) | (11.44%, 4.43%) |
| (15, 5, 3) | 0 | (8.0, 3.36) | (5.0, 2.10) | (37.50%, 37.50%) |
| | 1 | (9.6, 4.03) | (6.0, 2.55) | (37.50%, 36.77%) |
| | 2 | (11.1, 4.68) | (8.7, 3.67) | (21.62%, 21.52%) |
| | 3 | (12.6, 5.33) | (10.2, 4.53) | (19.05%, 15.08%) |
| | 4 | (14.3, 6.03) | (12.5, 5.53) | (12.59%, 8.29%) |
| | 5 | (15.8, 6.66) | (14.1, 6.32) | (10.70%, 5.11%) |
| (20, 5, 4) | 0 | (9.0, 3.42) | (5.0, 1.90) | (44.44%, 44.44%) |
| | 1 | (10.8, 4.10) | (7.8, 3.02) | (27.78%, 26.34%) |
| | 2 | (12.3, 4.68) | (8.6, 3.37) | (29.92%, 27.93%) |
| | 3 | (13.9, 5.31) | (11.6, 4.64) | (16.55%, 12.67%) |
| | 4 | (15.1, 5.76) | (13.5, 5.52) | (10.60%, 4.17%) |
| | 5 | (18.0, 6.85) | (14.95, 6.11) | (16.94%, 10.80%) |

# 6    Conclusion

3D ICs with TSVs address a major challenge in the semiconductor industry. Defects in TSVs decrease the yield and reliability of 3D ICs. Pre-bond testing ensures the yield of each die before it is stacked. Thus, designing a faster test model is important. In this paper, we have proposed a faster heuristic model to uniquely identify the defective TSVs. As we have seen, the proposed algorithm showed a better result compared to [5, 6, 8, 9] in terms of the percentage of reduction of test time. Besides this, the proposed model was able to identify more than 50% defective TSVs in the reduced test time.

# References

1. Davis, W.R., et al.: Demystifying 3DICs: the pros and cons of going vertical. IEEE Des. Test Comput. **22**(6), 498–510 (2005)
2. Lee, H., Chakrabarty, K.: Test challenges for 3D integrated circuits. IEEE Des. Test Comput. **26**(6), 26–35 (2009)

3. Chen, H., Shih, J., Li, S.W., Lin, H.C., Wang, M., Peng, C.: Electrical tests for Three-Dimensional ICs (3DICs) with TSVs. In: International Test Conference 3D-Test Workshop, pp. 1–6 (2010)
4. Noia, B., Chakrabarty, K.: Pre-bond probing of TSVs in 3D stacked ICs. In: Proceedings of IEEE International Test Conference, pp. 1–10 (2011)
5. Noia, B., Chakrabarty, K.: Identification of defective TSVs in pre-bond testing of 3D ICs. In: Proceedings of IEEE Asian Test Symposium (ATS), pp. 187–194 (2011)
6. Zhang, B., Agrawal, V.D.: Diagnostic tests for pre-bond TSV defects. In: Proceedings of IEEE International Conference on VLSI Design, pp. 387–392 (2014)
7. Roy, S.K., Chatterjee, S., Giri, C.: Identifying faulty TSVs in 3D stacked IC during pre-bond testing. In: Proceedings of IEEE International Symposium on Electronic System Design (ISED), pp. 162–166 (2012)
8. Roy, S.K., Chatterjee, S., Giri, C., Rahaman, H.: Faulty TSVs identification and recovery in 3D stacked ICs during pre-bond testing. In: Proceedings of International 3D Systems Integration Conference (3DIC), pp. 1–6 (2013)
9. Zhang, B., Agrawal, V.D.: An optimal probing method of pre-bond TSV fault identification for 3D stacked ICs. In: IEEE SOI-3D-Subthreshold Microelectronics Technology Unified Conference (S3S) (2014)

# Author Index

Printed in the United States
By Bookmasters